# The Law of International Organizations

# The Law of International Organizations

## Problems and Materials

### THIRD EDITION

Michael P. Scharf

Paul R. Williams

CAROLINA ACADEMIC PRESS

Durham, North Carolina

ISBN: 978-1-59460-907-7
LCCN: 2012950552

Carolina Academic Press
700 Kent Street
Durham, North Carolina 27701
Telephone (919) 489-7486
Fax (919) 493-5668
www.cap-press.com

Printed in the United States of America

*For Eirene and Themis*

# Contents

## Part III
## International Dispute Resolution

## Part V
### Protection of Human Rights and Enforcement of International Criminal Law

## Part VI
## Financial Issues and Institutions

# About the Authors

**Michael P. Scharf** is the John Deaver Drinko-Baker & Hostetler Professor of Law and Associate Dean for Global Legal Studies at Case Western Reserve University School of Law. A graduate of Duke University School of Law, and judicial clerk to Judge Gerald Bard Tjoflat on the Eleventh Circuit Federal Court of Appeals, Scharf is the author of seventy-five scholarly articles and fourteen books, including *Balkan Justice*, which was nominated for the Pulitzer Prize in 1998, *The International Criminal Tribunal for Rwanda*, which was awarded the American Society of International Law's Certificate of Merit for the Outstanding book in International Law in 1999, *Peace with Justice*, which won the International Association of Penal Law Book of the Year Award for 2003, and *Enemy of the State*, which won the International Association of Penal Law Book of the Year Award for 2009. His latest book (with Paul Williams) is *Shaping Foreign Policy in Times of Crisis: The Role of International Law and the State Department Legal Adviser*, published by Cambridge University Press in 2010.

During the first Bush and Clinton Administrations, Scharf served in the Office of the Legal Adviser of the U.S. Department of State, where he held the positions of Counsel to the Counter-Terrorism Bureau, Attorney-Adviser for Law Enforcement and Intelligence, Attorney-Adviser for United Nations Affairs, and delegate to the United Nations General Assembly and to the United Nations Human Rights Commission. In 1993, he was awarded the State Department's Meritorious Honor Award "in recognition of superb performance and exemplary leadership" in relation to his role in the establishment of the International Criminal Tribunal for the former Yugoslavia.

Recipient of the 2005 Case Alumni Association Teacher of the Year Award, Professor Scharf teaches International Law, International Criminal Law, Human Rights Law, the Law of International Organizations, and a War Crimes Research Lab. In 2002, Scharf established the War Crimes Research Office at Case Western Reserve University School of Law, which has provided over 275 research memoranda to the Prosecutors of the International Criminal Tribunal for the former Yugoslavia, the International Criminal Tribunal for Rwanda, the Special Court for Sierra Leone, the Extraordinary Chambers in the Courts of Cambodia, the Special Tribunal for Lebanon, and the International Criminal Court on issues pending before those international tribunals.

From October 2004–March 2005, Professor Scharf served as a member of the elite international team of experts that provided training to the judges and prosecutors of the Iraqi High Tribunal that tried Saddam Hussein, and during a sabbatical from teaching in 2008 he served as Special Assistant to the International Prosecutor of the Cambodian Genocide Tribunal. In 2005, Scharf and the Public International Law and Policy Group, a Non-Governmental Organization he co-founded with Paul Williams, were nominated for the Nobel Peace Prize by six governments and the Prosecutor of an International Criminal Tribunal for the work they have done to help in the prosecution of major war criminals, such as Slobodan Milosevic, Charles Taylor, and Saddam Hussein.

Professor Scharf has testified as an expert before the U.S. Senate Foreign Relations Committee and the House Arms Forces Committee; his Op Eds have been published by the *Washington Post, Los Angeles Times, Boston Globe, Christian Science Monitor*, and *International Herald Tribune*; he has appeared over five hundred times to discuss international legal developments on radio and television news programs, and in 2012 Scharf became host of the Cleveland-based public radio show, "Talking Foreign Policy," available at://www.TalkingForeignPolicy.com.

**Dr. Paul R. Williams** is the Rebecca Grazier Professor of Law and International Relations at American University. Dr. Williams is also the President and co-founder of the Public International Law & Policy Group. Since 1995, PILPG has provided *pro bono* legal assistance to governments involved in peace negotiations, drafting post-conflict constitutions, and prosecuting war criminals. In 2005, Dr. Williams, as Executive Director of PILPG, was nominated for the Nobel Peace Prize by half a dozen of his *pro bono* government clients.

Dr. Williams is regarded as a social entrepreneur for his practical and innovative approach to providing *pro bono* legal assistance to clients. During the course of his legal practice, Dr. Williams has assisted over a dozen clients in major international peace negotiations, including serving as a delegation member in the Dayton negotiations (Bosnia-Herzegovina), Rambouillet/Paris negotiations (Kosovo), Lake Ohrid negotiations (Macedonia), Podgorica/Belgrade negotiations (Serbia/Montenegro), and the Doha negotiations (Darfur). He also advised parties to the Key West negotiations (Nagorno-Karabakh), the Oslo/Geneva negotiations (Sri Lanka), the Georgia/Abkhaz negotiations, and the Somalia peace talks.

He has advised over two dozen parties across Europe, Africa, and Asia on matters of public international law. Dr. Williams has advised the governments of Afghanistan, Bosnia, Iraq, Kosovo, Libya, Montenegro, Nagorno-Karabakh, and Tunisia on the drafting and implementation of post-conflict constitutions. He is has also advised governments on issues of state recognition, self-determination, and state succession including advising the President of Macedonia, the President of South Sudan, and the Foreign Minister of Montenegro. On issues relating to border and sea demarcations and negotiations, Dr. Williams advised the President of Estonia and the Foreign Minister of East Timor.

Previously, Dr. Williams served in the Department of State's Office of the Legal Advisor for European and Canadian Affairs, as a Senior Associate with the Carnegie Endowment for International Peace, and as a Fulbright Research Scholar at the University of Cambridge. He is a member of the Council on Foreign Relations and the American Society of International Law.

Dr. Williams is a leading scholar on peace negotiations and post-conflict constitutions. He has testified on a number of occasions before the U.S. Congress on matters of public international law and peace negotiations. He has authored five books on topics of international human rights, international environmental law, and international norms of justice, and over two dozen articles on a wide variety of public international law topics. Dr. Williams is also a sought-after international law and policy analyst, and has been interviewed more than 500 times by major print and broadcast media. He has published op-eds in the *Washington Post, Los Angeles Times, International Herald Tribune, Chicago Tribune, Wall Street Journal Europe*, and *Le Monde*.

# Preface

Since the creation of the United Nations system almost seventy years ago, much of international law and diplomacy has been developed, shaped, implemented, and enforced through U.N. bodies and related international organizations. But during the decades of the cold war, many of the organizations in the U.N. system too often suffered from paralysis due to East-West and North-South tensions. With the disintegration of the Soviet Bloc in the early 1990s emerged a considerably revitalized United Nations. Bolstered by a new (if only fleeting) era of cooperation, the international organizations associated with the United Nations began to boldly respond to challenges and threats to peace, to human rights, to the environment, and to the world's increasingly interdependent economy.

From 1989–1993, the authors had the good fortune to serve as Attorney-Advisers in the Office of the Legal Adviser of the U.S. Department of State (Scharf as Attorney-Adviser for United Nations Affairs and Williams as Attorney-Adviser for European Affairs), where we participated in and witnessed first-hand what history may consider the modern resurrection of the United Nations and its associated organizations. When we left the State Department to become international law professors, we were surprised to discover that there existed very few teaching texts devoted to the study of international organizations, especially in light of the increasingly prominent role international organizations have begun to play in the formation of international law and resolution of global problems. The rather dated texts that did exist failed to cover what we considered to be some of the most important current issues relating to international organizations. And the issues that were covered were dealt with in a fairly dry fashion that did not appear to be calculated to stimulate student enthusiasm for what should be among the most exciting of subjects.

Consequently, when we were invited to co-teach "The Law of International Organizations" as Visiting Professors of International Law at the University of Paris IX in 1999 and when Michael Scharf taught the same course as a Visiting Professor at the Fletcher School of Law and Diplomacy at Tufts University in 2000 (a position long held by the eminent Leo Gross), we decided to assemble our own teaching materials focusing on the most important current issues relating to international organizations based on our experiences at the State Department, as well as our subsequent work in the field under the auspices of the Public International Law and Policy Group. Rather than gear the materials to the Socratic method or lecture approach, it occurred to us that an effective way to teach this area of law was to approximate the way we learned it at the State Department—by employing simulations, role-play exercises and debates.

In the fall of 2000, at the suggestion of Keith Sipe, Scharf published his Fletcher course materials as a casebook employing this unique active learning approach. The First Edition of "The Law of International Organizations" quickly established itself as a popular casebook, but with the speed in which this unique area of law evolves, the market was soon clamoring for a Second and now a Third, updated, Edition. The Third Edition provides updated information, includes new case studies, and covers an expanded number of international organizations.

Like its predecessor editions, this book is not designed to be a comprehensive text-book on international organizations, but rather a user-friendly casebook that exposes students to the most significant current legal issues relating to international organiza-tions in a stimulating format. In addition to simulations in the form of an introductory problem, the chapters contain excerpts from international treaties, negotiating history, de-cisions by international organizations, international and domestic judicial opinions, diplo-matic correspondence, contemporary news accounts, first-hand narratives, and scholarly articles, as well as a comprehensive Bibliography of Additional Sources. In contrast to the traditional passive reading model of most casebooks in which discussion questions are found at the end of each chapter's readings, the format of this book mirrors the way a legal research assignment would be given in the real world. Here, the questions and problems are presented at the beginning of each chapter, prompting the student to actively read the material with an eye to finding the answer. The book is organized into twenty-three Chapters (corresponding with teaching units) for ease of use in a course that meets twice-a-week. In a once-a-week course, the professor can select the thirteen or fourteen units he or she finds of most interest.

International organizations both make international law and are governed by it. Yet, a distinguished commentator once remarked that the decision-making of international or-ganizations such as the United Nations "is less a question of law than one of political judgment," and that "legal principles and Charter interpretation take a back seat to po-litical and administrative convenience." (L.C. Green, 1967). Throughout, the materials in this book highlight the tension between politics and law in the U.N. System. Given the political context in which international organizations often operate, the reader will find that substantive rules and precedents play a perhaps surprisingly important role in in-fluencing the actions of international organizations. At the same time, it is essential to keep in mind that the decision-making of organizations in the domestic system, including the U.S. Supreme Court, are just as frequently swayed by politics.

Another theme that emerges throughout the book is the important role that process plays in the decision making of international organizations. The international bodies ex-amined in the book include those that make decisions by simple majority vote, by weighted voting, and by unanimous consent. In examining these materials, the reader may consider: why did the framers select the particular voting system for each organization; how strictly do the bodies follow their procedural (as opposed to substantive) rules; and how do the voting rules influence the outcome of the body's decision making.

It is true that very few students will go on to directly participate in any international organization. It is also true that few students will go on to practice Constitutional Law be-fore the Supreme Court, or even the lower courts. Yet "Con Law" is a required law school course and is taught extensively at the undergraduate level in light of the importance the decisions of the Supreme Court play in our daily lives. Given the growing significance of the decisions of international organizations to our well-being and survival, and the promi-nent (if not always decisive) role that law plays in arriving at those decisions, the "Law of International Organizations" may be among the most meaningful courses in the mod-ern curriculum. It is thus our ardent hope that the publication of the Third Edition of this casebook will help foster the growth of courses at the law school and university level de-voted to this important subject.

Michael P. Scharf, Cleveland, Ohio
Paul R. Williams, Washington, D.C.
March 2013

# Acknowledgments and Permissions

We wish to extend a special acknowledgment to Kennan Castel-Fodor, Student General Editor for the Third Edition of *The Law of International Organizations* (2013).

We also wish to gratefully acknowledge all of the hard work from the student contributors to this book: Dhivyaa Boominathan, Allison Bosch, Sara Corradi, Dana Fialova, Effy Folberg, Rachel Gottfried, Morgan Jezierski, David Jims, Emily Zivanov Kaiser, Taylor Karam, Kendall Kozai, Katyln Kraus, Johannes Langer, Katherine Nakazono, Caitlin Potratz, Michael Presas, Carmen Radu, Jesse Ransom, Dina Rezvani, Ben Ristau, Jordan Salberg, Osob Samantar, Brian Soares, Shannon Sweeney, Payne Tatich, Celine Tran, Evan Wilson, and Anthony Yang.

Finally, we wish to gratefully acknowledge permissions from the following authors and/or publishers with respect to use of various materials listed below:

- Jim Anderson, Politics Wins in PLO Office Closure, United Press International, March 11, 1988.
- Leland Goodrich, Edvard Hambro, and Anne Patricia Simons, CHARTER OF THE UNITED NATIONS: COMMENTARY AND DOCUMENTS (3rd ed., Columbia University Press, 1969), 1–4, 10–16.
- Frederic L. Kirgis, Jr., INTERNATIONAL ORGANIZATIONS IN THEIR LEGAL SETTING, West Publishing Co., 2d ed. 1993, pp. 191–193.
- Joy K. Fausey, Does the United Nations' Use of Collective Sanctions to Protect Human Rights Violate Its Own Human Rights Standards? 10 Conn. J. Int't L. 193 (1994).
- Gary C. Hufbauer and Barbara Oegg, Targeted Sanctions: A Policy Alternative?, 32 Law & Policy Int'l Bus. 11 (2000).
- Michael Scharf and Joshua Dorosin, Interpreting U.N. Sanctions: *The Rulings and Role of the Yugoslavia Sanctions Committee*, 19 BROOKLYN J. INT'L L. 771 (1993)
- Hilaire McCoubrey and Nigel White, THE BLUE HELMETS: LEGAL REGULATION OF UNITED NATIONS MILITARY OPERATIONS (1996), pages 11–90.
- Richard A. Falk, FUTURE IMPLICATION OF THE IRAQ CONFLICT: WHAT FUTURE FOR THE U.N. CHARTER SYSTEM OF WAR PREVENTION?, 97 Am. J. Int'l. L. 590, (July 2003).
- Alex J. Bellamy, RESPONSIBILITY TO PROTECT OR TROJAN HORSE? THE CRISIS IN DARFUR AND HUMANITARIAN INTERVENTION AFTER IRAQ, Ethics & Int'l Aff., (October 1, 2005).
- Alia Szopa, Hoarding History: A Survey of Antiquity Looting and Black Market Trade, 13 U. Miami Bus. L. Rev. 55, 64–70 (Fall/Winter 2004).

- Kenneth Hamma, Symposium: V. The New Millennium Finding Cultural Property Online, 19 Cardozo Arts & Ent. L.J. 125, 128–132 (2001).
- Brian Braiker, Art Cops, Newsweek, Jan. 21, 2005.
- Paust, Bassiouni, Williams, Scharf, Gurule, and Zagaris, INTERNATIONAL CRIMINAL LAW: CASES AND MATERIALS (1996), pp. 1175–90.
- Nicholas Rostow, *Before and After: The Changed U.N. Response to Terrorism Since September 11th,* 35 Cornell Int'l L.J. 475.
- Susan Tiefenbrun, *A Semiotic Approach to a Legal Definition of Terrorism,* 9 ILSA J Int'l & Comp L 357 (2003).
- Jennifer Trahan, *Terrorism Conventions: Existing Gaps and Different Approaches,* 8 New Eng. Int'l & Comp. L. Ann. 215 (2002).
- *The ICTR Must Achieve Justice for Rwandans,* 13 American University International Law Review 1469 (1998).
- Rena L. Scott, *Moving From Impunity to Accountability in Post-War Liberia: Possibilities, Cautions, and Challenges,* 33 International Journal of Legal Information 345 (2005).
- Lawrence Weschler, Exceptional Cases in Rome: The United States and the Struggle for an ICC, in THE UNITED STATES AND THE INTERNATIONAL CRIMINAL COURT 85–114 (Sarah Sewall and Carl Kasen, eds., 2000).
- Lee A. Casey, *The Case Against Supporting the International Criminal Court,* Washington University School of Law, Whitney R. Harris Institute for Global Legal Studies, Washington University in St. Louis, International Debate Series, No. 1 (2002).
- Jose Alvarez, Financial Responsibility, THE UNITED NATIONS AND INTERNATIONAL LAW (C. Joyner, ed., 1995).
- Michael Scharf and Tamara Shaw, International Institutions, 33 THE INTERNATIONAL LAWYER 567–570 (1999).
- Richard K. Gordon, Current Developments in Monetary & Financial Law, International Monetary Fund (1999), Chapter 15: ANTI-MONEY-LAUNDERING POLICIES SELECTED LEGAL, POLITICAL, AND ECONOMIC ISSUES.
- Kenneth Abbot & Duncan Snidal, *Why States Act Through Formal International Organizations,* 42 J. CONFLICT RESOL. 1 (1998).
- Jayshree Bajoria, *The China-North Korea Relationship,* Council on Foreign Relations (Oct. 7, 2010).
- Jayshree Bajoria & Carin Zissis, *The Six-Party Talks on North Korea's Nuclear Program: A CFR.org Backgrounder,* Council on Foreign Relations (Jul. 1, 2009).
- Peter Berkowitz, *The Goldstone Report and International Law,* POL'Y REV. (Aug.–Sept. 2010).
- Ronen Bergman, *Letter from Tel Aviv: Netanyahu's Iranian Dilemma,* Foreign Aff. (June 10, 2009). Reprinted by permission of FOREIGN AFFAIRS, (88, 2009) by the Council on Foreign Relations, Inc. www.ForeignAffairs.com.
- Eric Brahm, *Intergovernmental Organizations (IGOs),* beyondintractibility.org (2005).
- Greg Bruno, *CFR.org Interview with Manouchehr Mottaki: What Iran Wants,* Council on Foreign Relations (Sept. 20, 2009).
- Greg Bruno, *Iran's Nuclear Program: A CFR.org Backgrounder,* Council on Foreign Relations (Mar. 10, 2010).
- Center for Arms Control and Non-Proliferation, *Risky Business: Why Attacking Iran Is a Bad Idea,* (Apr. 12, 2007).

- Eric C. Christiansen, *Adjudicating Non-Justiciable Rights: Socio-Economic Rights and the South African Constitutional Court*, 38 COLUM. HUM. RTS. L. REV. 321 (2007).
- John Darby & James Rae, *Peace Processes from 1988–1998: Changing Patterns*, 17 ETHNIC STUD. REP. 46, 53 (1999).
- Erica Downs & Suzanne Maloney, *Getting China to Sanction Iran*, 90.2 Foreign Aff. 15 (Mar.–Apr. 2011). Reprinted by permission of FOREIGN AFFAIRS, (15, 2011) by the Council on Foreign Relations, Inc. www.ForeignAffairs.com.
- Michael W. Doyle & Nicholas Sambanis, *Conclusions, in* MAKING WAR AND BUILDING PEACE 337–342 (2006).
- Trevor Findlay, *The New Peacekeeping and the New Peacekeepers Challenges for the New Peacekeepers, in* CHALLENGES FOR THE NEW PEACEKEEPERS 2, 7–11, 14–15 (Trevor Findlay ed., 1996).
- Thomas M. Franck, Future Implication Of The Iraq Conflict: What Happens Now? The United Nations After Iraq, 97 AM. J. INT'L. L. 590, 607–620 (July 2003).
- Liz Heffernan, *The Nuclear Weapons Opinions: Reflections on the Advisory Procedure of the International Court of Justice*, 28.1 STETSON L. REV. 133 (1998).
- Karen Kenny, *U.N. Accountability for its Human Rights Impact: Implementation Through Participation, in* THE U.N., HUMAN RIGHTS, AND POST-CONFLICT SITUATIONS (Nigel D. White & Dirk Klaasen eds., 2005).
- Josephine K. Mason, *The Role of Ex Aequo Et Bono in International Border Settlement: A Critique of the Sudanese Abyei Arbitration*, 20 AM. REV. INT'L ARB. 519 (Feb. 2011).
- Anna Meijknecht & Byung Sook Patinaje-de Vries, *Is There a Place for Minorities' and Indigenous People's Rights within ASEAN?: Asian Values, ASEAN Values and the Protection of Southeast Asian Minorities and Indigenous Peoples*, 17.1 INT'L J. ON MINORITY & GROUP RTS. 75 (2010).
- Wendy J. Miles & Daisy Mallett, *The Abyei Arbitration and the Use of Arbitration to Resolve Inter-state and Intra-state Conflicts*, 1.2 J. INT'L DISP. SETTLEMENT 313 (2010).
- Sean D. Murphy, *Contemporary Practice of the United States Relating to International Law*, 94 AM. J. INT'L L. 348, 348–54 (2000).
- Makau Mutua, *The Big Idea: are Human Rights Universal? Or Is the West Imposing Its Philosophy on the Rest of the World*, BOSTON GLOBE, Apr. 29, 2001.
- Kiriro Wa Ngugu, *Let's Choose Peace Over Justice in ICC Case*, DAILY NATION (Feb. 2, 2011).
- Tom Parker, Centre for European and Asian Studies, Norwegian School of Management, The Ultimate Intervention: Revitalizing The U.N. Trusteeship Council For The 21st Century (2003).
- Dinah PoKempner, From *Journal of Global Governance: Valuing the Goldstone Report*, Vol. 16 #2. Copyright © 2010 by Lynne Rienner Publishers, Inc. Used with permission by the publisher.
- CESARE ROMANO & THORDIS INGADOTTIR, PROJECT ON INTERNATIONAL COURTS & TRIBUNALS, THE FINANCING OF THE INTERNATIONAL CRIMINAL COURT: A DISCUSSION PAPER 3–6 (2000).
- John Shattuck, *Dignity and Freedom are for Everyone*, BOSTON GLOBE, Apr. 29, 2001.
- Rhona K.M. Smith, *The Fate of Minorities-Sixty Years On*, 1 WEB J. CURRENT L. ISSUES (2009).

- Celine Tran, *Striking a Balance Between Human Rights and Peace and Stability: A Review of the ECtHR's Decision in* Sejdić and Finci v. Bosnia and Herzegovina *and Its Implications*, 18.2 Hum. Rts. Br. 3 (2011).
- Nsongurua J. Udombana, Globalization of Justice and the Special Court for Sierra Leone's War Crimes, 17 Emory Int'l L. Rev. 55, 57–69 (Spring 2003).
- Kevin Jon Heller, "The Sadly Neutered Crime of Aggression", Opiniojuris.org, (June 13, 2010 9:32 PM) http://opiniojuris.org/2010/06/13/the-sadly-neutered-crime-of-aggression/.
- John Currie, Joanna Harrington & Valerie Oosterverld, "Ending War Through Justice — In Time: Amendments to ICC Statute would hold leaders personally responsible for 'aggression'", Canadian Lawyer Magazine, 14 June 2010 (online).

# Part I
# Historic and Legal Background

# Chapter I

# Introduction to the Law of International Organizations

## Introduction

This chapter serves as an introduction to the purposes and structure of the U.N. Charter, the most important instrument in the field of international organizations. The questions and simulation are designed to elicit discussion and debate on the functions of the key provisions of the Charter. Materials on the basic tenets of international law and its application in the United States are provided for students who have not taken another international law course.

## Objectives

- To understand the circumstances surrounding the creation of the United Nations Charter.
- To understand the role and impact of the Charter on the U.N. system.
- To understand the basic structure of the U.N.
- To understand the fundamental relationship between the U.N. and the United States.
- To understand the various sources of international law.
- To examine the role of international law in relation to the United States.

## Problems

Based on the materials in this chapter, come to class prepared to discuss the following questions:

(a) What are the U.S. interests in being a member of the United Nations?

(b) How does the U.N. differ from the League of Nations, and what were the reasons for these differences?

(c) How does the structure of the U.N. especially protect the interests of the major powers?

(d) What is the purpose and implications of the following key provisions of the U.N. Charter?

| | | |
|---|---|---|
| Art. 1(1) | Art. 23(1) | Art. 41 |
| Art. 2(4) | Art. 25 | Art. 42 |
| Art. 2(6) | Art. 33 | Art. 51 |
| Art. 2(7) | Art. 36 | Art. 53 |
| Art. 12(1) | Art. 39 | Art. 92 |
| Art. 13 | Art. 40 | Art. 94 |
| | | Art. 103 |

(e) What functions do the U.N. General Assembly and the U.N. Security Council play in the creation of international law?

(f) Can the U.S. Congress enact domestic legislation contrary to its obligations under the U.N. Charter or imposed by the Security Council? What might be the international ramifications of such Congressional action?

(g) If you were designing an international organization for the purposes of maintaining international peace and security and improving the human rights and economic and social conditions of the people of the world, how would it differ from the U.N. Charter? What countries would likely support and oppose your proposals, and why?

(h) Assume it is the summer of 1945 and you are a member of the drafting Committee working on the Charter of the United Nations. Come to class prepared to debate the following proposed provisions to the Charter.

1. Art. 2(7). The United Nations shall under no circumstances intervene in matters which are essentially within the domestic jurisdiction of any state.

2. Art. 18. (Alternative A) Each Member of the General Assembly shall have a minimum of one vote and an additional vote per one million people in its population.

3. Art. 18. (Alternative B) Each Member of the General Assembly shall have as many votes as the percentage of the U.N. budget that they are assessed under Article 17.

4. Art. 25. The members of the United Nations agree to consider and make their best efforts to carry out the decisions of the Security Council in accordance with the present Charter and their domestic laws.

5. Art. 103. In the event of a conflict between the obligations of the Members of the United Nations under the present Charter and their obligations under any other international agreement, which ever is later in time shall prevail.

6. Art. 110. The present Charter shall be ratified by the signatory states in accordance with their respective constitutional processes. All of its provisions shall be considered self-executing for purposes of domestic law.

# Materials

1. Leland Goodrich, Edvard Hambro, and Anne Patricia Simons, CHARTER OF THE UNITED NATIONS: COMMENTARY AND DOCUMENTS (3rd ed., Columbia University Press, 1969), pp. 1–4, 10–16.

2.  BASIC FACTS ABOUT THE UNITED NATIONS (1992).

3.  U.S. Department of State: Fact Sheet: Advancing U.S. Interests at the United Nations (September 20, 2011) *available at* http://usun.state.gov/documents/organization/ 172984.pdf.

4.  THE RESTATEMENT (THIRD) OF FOREIGN RELATIONS LAW, Introductory Note, §§ 102, 11, 112, 115 (1987).

5.  U.N. CHARTER, available at http://www.un.org/en/documents/charter/.

6.  Bibliography of Additional Sources

---

## 1. Leland Goodrich, Edvard Hambro, and Anne Patricia Simons, Charter of the United Nations: Commentary and Documents

1969
[footnotes omitted by editors]

### Introduction

The Charter of the United Nations, signed at San Francisco on June 26, 1945, was a document with roots in the past and possibilities for the future that could only be imagined. From one point of view, it represented a stage in the historical development of mankind's social organization. Its provisions were based largely on past experience and found substantial if not exact expression in earlier instruments. From another point of view, however, the Charter was a commitment to purposes and principles the realization of which in the light of the changing world conditions might require substantial adaptation of institutional and procedural arrangements.

It is necessary to think of the Charter not only as a treaty embodying the maximum limitations on a state's freedom of action, that nations at that stage of history and in the light of experience were prepared to accept as consistent with their national interests, but also as a constitutional document setting forth guidelines for future development. The exact nature of this development was to be determined not only by the Charter itself but also by the way in which the members of the United Nations interpreted these guidelines and made use of the Organization in dealing with the ever-changing problems of an ever-changing world. The Charter thus provided the constitutional basis for achieving international peace, security, and well being, and pointed the way—but the ultimate verdict was to rest with the actors themselves.

### The Need for a "General International Organization"

The idea of an international organization to keep the peace, worldwide in the scope of its activity, found its first practical expression in the League of Nations. Back of the League, however, was a considerable experience with institutions and procedures of more limited scope which had as their purpose the prevention of war and the promotion of other common purposes by organized international cooperation.

At the end of World War I, the League of Nations was established, largely on the initiative and through the leadership of Woodrow Wilson. Wilson believed that the old system of balance of power had been discredited by the failure of diplomacy to prevent World War I and that the only dependable guarantee of peace was to be found in the willingness of peace-aspiring nations to use their combined forces to restrain aggression. We know that the League failed in its major purpose, but we do not know what would have happened if one of Wilson's major assumptions—that the United States would be an active member — had materialized. Without the United States as a member, the League was congenitally and fatally weak; although it achieved some useful results and demonstrated the need for organized inter-national cooperation, it was not able to survive the holocaust of World War II.

It was a tribute to the validity of the League idea, however, that almost from the beginning of World War II, thought was given in responsible government circles to establishing an international organization to keep the peace once the war ended. In their Declaration of Principles, known as the Atlantic Charter, of August, 1941, President Roosevelt and Prime Minister Churchill expressed their hope "to see established a peace which will afford to all nations the means of dwelling in safety within their own boundaries, and which will afford assurance that all the men in all the lands may live out their lives in freedom from fear and want." By adhering to the Declaration by United Nations of January 1, 1942, the states at war with the Axis Powers, including China, the Soviet Union, the United Kingdom, and the United States, subscribed to the purposes and principles set forth in the Atlantic Charter. Early in 1942, the Advisory Committee on Post-War Foreign Policy was set up in the U.S. State Department to consider international problems that would confront the United States at the conclusion of hostilities. By June, attention was explicitly focused on the problem of a permanent international organization, which soon became a major concern of the committee, as well as of Secretary of State Hull and President Roosevelt.

During 1942 and 1943, official thinking and policy formulation in Washington had so far developed that Secretary Hull was ready to take advantage of the meeting of Allied foreign ministers in Moscow in October, 1943, to secure a firm commitment to the idea of establishing an international organization to keep the peace. By the Moscow Declaration of October 30, 1943, the governments of China, the Soviet Union, the United Kingdom, and the United States declared that they recognize the necessity of establishing at the earliest practicable date a general international organization, based on the principle of the sovereign equality of all peace-loving states, and open to membership by all such states, large and small, for the maintenance of international peace and security.

**Preliminary Negotiation**

The making of a charter to give effect to the Moscow commitment was a complex and lengthy process. In fact, the work of preparation began in the U.S. State Department as early as June, 1942, and continued into the summer of 1944. The Tentative Proposals, the product of this preparatory work, were accepted by the President and by congressional leaders of both parties as the basis for discussion in the Dumbarton Oaks Conversations of August 21–October 7, 1944. The draft which finally emerged reflected the thinking of many minds and had bipartisan support.

It was considered essential to secure the preliminary agreement of the four major powers at the expert level on the proposals to be submitted to a conference of allied nations. The Dumbarton Oaks Conversations took place in two phases: the first, with representatives of the Soviet Union, the United Kingdom, and the United States participating, extended from August 21 to September 28; the second, to which the Republic of China, the United Kingdom, and the United States were parties, lasted from September 29 to October. These negotiations resulted in agreed-upon proposals which, though incomplete, represented substantial acceptance of United States suggestions, modified in some respects by the ideas of other participants. Where unresolvable differences appeared in the course of negotiations, they were left for discussion and resolution at a higher political level.

The Dumbarton Oaks Proposals did not cover such important questions as voting procedure in the Security Council and the role of the proposed international court. They did not deal with other matters of a technical nature — such as privileges and immunities, registration of treaties, and arrangements for non-self-governing territories. The Proposals, however, gave a clear indication of the kind of organization the major powers had in mind and would presumably strongly support at the forthcoming conference. In many respects, it was to be an organization similar to the League of Nations it was to replace.

Following publication of the Dumbarton Oaks Proposals, further negotiations and discussions were necessary to fill some of the gaps left by the Proposals and to prepare the way for subsequent agreements. At the Crimea (Yalta) Conference of February 3, 1945, the heads of government of the Soviet Union, the United Kingdom, and the United States agreed on the formula governing Security Council voting procedure, which was subsequently included in the proposals submitted to the governments invited to the San Francisco Conference. Accord was also reached on the basic principles governing the establishment of a trusteeship system. It was also decided to call a conference of the United Nations in San Francisco on April 25, 1945 "to prepare the Charter of such an organization, along the lines proposed in the informal conversations at Dumbarton Oaks," and that invitations should be extended by the United States on behalf of the Sponsoring Governments to those states that had declared war on Germany or Japan by March 1, 1945, and had signed the Declaration by United Nations.

Two other conferences held before San Francisco helped to lay the groundwork for the 1945 Charter. At the Mexico City Conference of the American Republics, February 2–March 8, 1945, the United States gained support for the Dumbarton Oaks Proposals, and a hemispheric position on the question of regional security was formulated. The meeting of the United Nations Committee of Jurists, April 9–20, 1945, prepared a draft statute of an international court of justice to serve as a basis for discussion at San Francisco.

### The United Nations and the League of Nations Compared

The new organization for which the Charter provided was in many respects like the League of Nations. It was based on the principle of voluntary association of independent sovereign states for the achievement of common purposes. Like the League, it was composed initially of nations victorious in a world war, and while the effort was made to disassociate it to some extent from the peace settlements, there was no avoiding the conclusion that the peace it was expected to keep would, to a large extent, be the peace made by the victorious powers in the war about to end. The structure of the new organization was similar to that of the League: a deliberative organ including all members, quasi-executive organs, a court, and a secretariat. While the Charter provided for three councils instead of the Covenant's one, it must be borne in mind that the League Permanent Mandates Commission had functions similar to those of the Trusteeship Council, and that the Economic and Social Council for which the Charter provided was anticipated in the recommendations of the Bruce Committee in 1939.

There were, however, important differences, at least in emphasis, between the organization provided for by the Charter and that of the Covenant. While both documents emphasized the maintenance of peace as a primary objective, the Charter gave much more recognition to the importance of international cooperation in dealing with economic and social problems, and to the need for safeguarding basic human rights if the world was to be spared another catastrophe. This new emphasis was quite understandable in the light of the role that economic and social dislocations had played in events leading to World

War II, recognition of the increased responsibility of governments in the economic and social fields, and the extent to which the denial of human rights had been associated with aggressive regimes.

An even more striking difference, however, was the approach taken by the Charter to the problem of keeping the peace. Whereas the Covenant had emphasized the legal approach to the prevention of war by placing specific obligations upon members, the Charter approach was essentially political, since in the last analysis the measures to be taken and their effectiveness were made to depend on the readiness of the major military powers to cooperate in defense of common interests. Furthermore, unlike the Covenant, the Charter in effect recognized that the new organization could not be effective in keeping the peace if challenged by a great power. In that event, members would be thrown back on their own resources, supplemented by such cooperative arrangements as might be worked out in the name of collective self-defense.

The Charter also appeared to differ from the Covenant in its more detailed definition and sharper differentiation of functions and powers of the various organs. Whereas the Covenant had defined the functions and powers of the Assembly and Council in the same general terms though according specific duties to each, the Charter—on the assumption that the General Assembly was an organ of deliberation and the Security Council an organ of action—defined in considerable detail the functions and powers of each, emphasizing the primary responsibility of the Council for making specific decisions to maintain or restore peace and security, and the responsibility of the Assembly to develop and recommend general principles of cooperation for strengthening peace and security. To be sure, this differentiation of function appeared to be clearer under the Dumbarton Oaks Proposals than under the Charter as finally adopted. At San Francisco, certain provisions were accepted which blurred the distinction the Dumbarton Oaks conferees had sought to make, and which laid the basis for subsequent extensive development of the responsibilities and powers of the General Assembly in the maintenance of peace and security.

Another important difference between the Charter system and that of the League concerned the role accorded to the international organization in dealing with non-self-governing territories. Apart from a general assurance of just treatment to indigenous populations, the Covenant was concerned with those colonial territories which Germany and the Turkish empire had been forced to relinquish and which the victorious allied powers agreed to place under the League mandates system. In regard to these territories it was almost wholly concerned with eliminating abuses, and only in the case of Class A mandated territories was independence envisaged. The Charter approach is quite different. Members undertake to work for the political, economic, and social development of the inhabitants of all territories under their administration, and, in the case of territories under trusteeship, they assume strong obligations and agree to accept a larger measure of international supervision than under the League mandates system. Furthermore, by making the General Assembly responsible for performing United Nations supervisory functions, the Charter seeks to give assurance that members administering trust territories will not be allowed to escape their obligations. Recognition by members of "the principle of equal rights and self-determination of peoples" (Article 121) is another peg upon which proponents of independence for non-self-governing people have been able to hang their case.

It is a great mistake, however, to attach decisive importance to the differences between the Covenant and the Charter. If the system of the Charter has met with considerable success and still after over two decades is a going concern—in contrast to the failure of the League in a shorter period of time—the principal explanation is not to be found in the technical superiority, or even in the superior validity, of the basic concepts of the Charter. Both the Covenant and the Charter were based on and gave expression to high purposes, and both contained provisions sufficiently general in form and elastic in content to permit members to do what might be necessary to give effect to these purposes. The important difference has been that, from the beginning, the League had to function without the participation and support of the one great power that had the means to make it effective, and never achieved at any one time the degree of universality of the United Nations. Furthermore, the League suffered from the excessive expectations of its friends, and from the failure of many of its leading supporters and members to recognize the price that had to be paid for peace. The United Nations, on the other hand, has functioned in an atmosphere of greater realism and has drawn vitality from the fact that even its most powerful members recognize its value in a world of competing ideas and political systems, and its indispensability to a world capable of instant self-destruction.

### How the United Nations Has Developed

The Charter as signed at San Francisco and subsequently ratified by the original signatories was a treaty, an agreement entered into between states in accordance with customary procedures for so doing. The opening words of the Charter—"We the peoples of the United Nations …"—are misleading, although they convey a meaning that was in the minds of many people at the time. The concluding words of the preamble—"Accordingly, our respective Governments … have agreed to the present Charter of the United Nations and do hereby establish an international organization to be known as the United Nations"—are more accurately descriptive of the process of establishing the Organization and suggestive of the result. Further indication of the treaty-like character of the Charter is to be found in the San Francisco understanding with respect to withdrawal. While the document itself contains no explicit provision regarding withdrawal, the understanding embodied in the declaration accepted by the governments represented at San Francisco was that members might withdraw under certain circumstances. While the declaration attempted to discourage withdrawal by stressing the obligation to cooperate for the purposes set forth in the Charter, it clearly recognized that, legally, the situation was analogous to the case of any multipartite agreement.

But, while the Charter clearly is a treaty, it is also the constitution of an organization. As a constitution it is not an ordinary treaty. The member states commit themselves not only to act in pursuance of its purposes and in conformity with its principles, but also to establish certain organs with defined powers and operating procedures to accomplish these purposes. In addition, they authorize the Organization to ensure that nonmembers as well as members act in accordance with the principles of the Charter, so far as may be necessary for the maintenance of international peace and security.

The Charter as a constitution, and even as a treaty, is not a static thing. It and the Organization that it creates must be adapted to new and changing circumstances and to the desires and expectations of members. One method by which this may be done is formal amendment. The Charter provides for this by a process that reflects to some degree the basic treaty character of the instrument, but it also suggests that this is no ordinary treaty. It provides a method of change which permits a special majority to decide that change shall take place. Nevertheless, the amendment process is difficult. For the major powers, a right of veto does exist. Thus far, the few amendments that have been adopted cannot be considered as affecting the fundamental nature of the Organization or the basic rights and duties of members.

It can generally be said of treaties and of constitutions that substantive changes and adaptations are more commonly achieved by a process of interpretation and application to situations as they arise than by formal amendment. Constitutions of international organizations frequently make explicit provision for a procedure to be used to obtain authoritative interpretations. Such provisions do not substantially affect the responsibility that rests on members and organs to interpret provisions of the constitution in the course of day-to-day operations.

The question of the method of Charter interpretation was considered at some length at San Francisco. It was agreed that no provision of an explicit nature should be made in the Charter itself. Agreement was reached, however, on a statement included in the report of the technical committee dealing with the matter and approved by the Conference.

The statement was as follows:

> In the course of the operations from day to day of the various organs of the Organization, it is inevitable that each organ will interpret such parts of the Charter as are applicable to its particular functions. This process is inherent in the functioning of any body which operates under an instrument defining its functions and powers. It will be manifested in the functioning of such a body as the General Assembly, the Security Council, or the International Court of Justice. Accordingly, it is not necessary to include in the Charter a provision either authorizing or approving the normal operation of this principle.
>
> Difficulties may conceivably arise in the event that there should be a difference of opinion among the organs of the Organization concerning the correct interpretation of a provision of the Charter. Thus, two organs may conceivably hold and may express or even act upon different views. Under unitary forms of national government the final determination of such a question may be vested in the highest court or in some other national authority. However, the nature of the Organization and of its operation would not seem to be such as to invite the inclusion in the Charter of any provision of this nature. If two Member States are at variance concerning the correct interpretation of the Charter, they are of course free to submit the dispute to the International Court of Justice as in the case of any other treaty. Similarly, it would always be open to the General Assembly or the Security Council, in appropriate circumstances, to ask the International Court of Justice for an advisory opinion concerning the meaning of a provision of the Charter. Should the General Assembly or the Security Council prefer another course, an ad hoc committee of jurists might be set up to examine the question and report its views, or recourse might be had to a joint conference. In brief, the Members or the organs of the Organization might have recourse to various expedients in order to obtain an appropriate interpretation. It would appear neither necessary nor desirable to list or to describe in the Charter the various possible expedients.
>
> It is to be understood, of course, that if an interpretation made by any organ of the Organization or by a committee of jurists is not generally acceptable it will be without binding force. In such circumstances, or in cases where it is desired to establish an authoritative interpretation as a precedent for the future, it may be necessary to embody the interpretation in an amendment to the Charter. This may always be accomplished by recourse to the procedure provided for amendment.

Clearly, this statement leaves matters in a rather untidy and uncertain situation for anyone interested in learning what the Charter means at any particular time. Apparently, it can mean different things to different organs and to different members. An interpretation accepted by the General Assembly, for example, may be unacceptable to the Security Council because of its different membership and voting procedure. An interpretation adopted by the Assembly by a two-thirds vote may not be accepted by a substantial minority of members. Can it be said that the Assembly has the power to make a binding decision with respect to its powers when in principle on substantive issues its power is limited under the Charter to making recommendations? The statement quoted above says that an interpretation made by an organ if "not generally acceptable" is without binding force. How many dissents are required to make it possible to say that an interpretation is "not generally acceptable"? In answering this question, is the importance of the dissenters to be considered as well as the number?

The statement envisages the possibility that questions of interpretation will be submitted to the Court. However, such procedure presents problems. If the Court is asked to give an advisory opinion by an organ competent to make such requests, the opinion is presumably not binding on the organ requesting it, although clearly entitled to great respect. For members of the Organization, the same can be said; and for them in particular, the binding force of the interpretation would depend on the extent of its acceptance by the requesting organ and the competence of that organ to impose its conclusions on members. If, however, members submit a dispute involving a question of Charter interpretation to the Court for judgment, that body's decision would be binding on the parties and on members intervening under Article 63 of the Statute. The decision would presumably not be binding on other members, and in any case would not be likely to concern a matter of great political importance.

We are faced then with a situation in which the responsibility for interpreting the Charter and adapting it to specified situations is shared widely and with very limited possibility of an authoritative interpretation. Furthermore, since the responsibility for interpretation is vested in organs and members alike, the process is more likely to be political than judicial. This means that the view taken of the meaning of the Charter in any particular situation is more often than not the result of a bargaining process or an exercise of power than an attempt to apply Charter provisions by a process of reasoning based on accepted principles of interpretation. Decisions tend to reflect the common interests of members in achieving certain results. Considering that the perceived interests of members change and that the voting alignments of members vary according to the issues presented, this politicizing of the interpretation process inevitably produces inconsistencies and confusion in the way the Charter is interpreted and applied.

There has, however, been one thread of continuity in the interpretation and application of the Charter to date. By and large, members, when they rely heavily on the United Nations for the advancement of their national interests and the support of their national policies, tend to take a liberal view with regard to the powers of organs and the capacity of the United Nations to act in furtherance of its purposes. Thus, on the one hand, non-Communist members under the leadership of the United States, during the first decade, took a liberal view of the power and responsibilities of the General Assembly to justify the use of that veto-free organ to support their policies and achieve their purposes in the "Cold War." On the other hand, members, when they do not see the possibility of utilizing the United Nations to serve national interests (possibly because of their being in a minority position on important issues), tend to take a restrictive line in Charter interpretation. They take the view, well stated by Judge Winiarski in his dissenting opinion in the "Certain Expenses" case, that "[t]he Charter, a multilateral treaty which was the result of prolonged and laborious negotiations, carefully created organs and determined their competence and means of action." They do not accept the view that the powers of United Nations organs are to be interpreted liberally in the light of the purposes of the Organization. They would not agree that just because an action is appropriate for the fulfillment of a Charter purpose, the presumption is thereby created that the action is permissible.

For anyone interested in how a particular article of the Charter has been interpreted and applied, the fact that interpretation has been subordinated to such an extent to political considerations creates special difficulties. Quite apart from the inconsistencies and divergences which make generalization difficult, there has been a general tendency to avoid relating a particular decision or course of action to a particular Charter provision. This has been in no small measure the consequence of the bargaining involved in the creation of majorities necessary to the adoption of resolutions. References to specific provisions of the Charter as providing the basis for the proposed action are likely to be among the controversial points that can be sacrificed in the interest of wider agreement. Consequently, the scholar or practitioner interested in relating the development of the United Nations to Charter provisions must often draw inferences from the language used in the decisions of organs and in the statements of United Nations officials and members as to the specific Charter provisions being relied upon.

---

## 2. Basic Facts About the United Nations
### 1992 (updated by the editors)

### Its Structure, Purposes, and Future

The United Nations, which formally came into existence in 1945, is the principal international organization designed to prevent military confrontations among its members and to help resolve international disputes. It has also embarked on numerous other tasks, from simplifying international air travel to the eradication of malaria and smallpox. The following excerpt provides a useful introduction to the U.N.'s structure and activities.

The United Nations is today an organization legally committed to cooperate in supporting the principle and purposes set out in its Charter. These include commitments to eradicate war, promote human rights, maintain respect for justice and international law, and promote social progress and friendly relations among nations.

### Membership

The Charter declares that membership of the United Nations is open to all peace-loving nations which accept its obligations and which, in the judgment of the Organization, are willing and able to carry out these obligations. [As of July 2012, there were 193 Member States in the United Nations. This number includes Bosnia-Herzegovina, Croatia, and Slovenia (all admitted in May 1992), and all of the former Soviet republics with the exception of Georgia.]

The Former Yugoslavia Republic of Macedonia, Eritrea, Monaco, the Czech and Slovak Republics (Czechoslovakia's successor states), and Andorra were admitted in 1993. States are admitted to membership by the General Assembly on the recommendation of the Security Council. The Charter also provides for the suspension or expulsion of Members for violation of the principles of the Charter, but no such action has ever been taken.

### Principal Organs

The Charter established six principal organs of the United Nations:

### The Security Council

The Security Council has primary responsibility, under the Charter, for the maintenance of international peace and security. To be adopted, decisions by the Council require nine affirmative votes out of the fifteen members, with none of the Permanent Members voting no. Decisions taken under the Council's "Chapter VII authority" are binding on all U.N. member states by virtue of Article 25 of the U.N. Charter, and may be imposed on non-U.N. members by virtue of Article 2(6) of the Charter.

**Membership:**

The Council is composed of five permanent members—China, France, Russian Federation, the United Kingdom and the United States—and ten non-permanent members, which are elected to two-year terms by the General Assembly. In [2012], the ten non-permanent members were (with year of term's end):

| | | |
|---|---|---|
| Azerbaijan (2013) | India (2012) | Portugal (2012) |
| Colombia (2012) | Morocco (2013) | South Africa (2012) |
| Germany (2012) | Pakistan (2013) | Togo (2013) |
| Guatemala (2013) | | |

[Chart updated by editors—2012]

**Under the Charter, the functions and powers of the Security Council are:**

- to maintain international peace and security in accordance with the principles and purposes of the United Nations;
- to investigate any dispute or situation which might lead to international friction;
- to recommend methods of adjusting such disputes or the terms of settlement;
- to formulate plans for the establishment of a system to regulate armaments;
- to determine the existence of a threat to the peace or act of aggression and to recommend what action should be taken;
- to call on Members to apply economic sanctions and other measures not involving the use of force to prevent or stop aggression;
- to take military action against an aggressor;
- to recommend the admission of new Members;
- to exercise the trusteeship functions of the United Nations in "strategic areas";
- to recommend to the General Assembly the appointment of the Secretary-General and, together with the Assembly, to elect the Judges of the International Court of Justice.

When a complaint concerning a threat to peace is brought before it, the Council's first action is usually to recommend to the parties to try to reach agreement by peaceful means. In some cases, the Council itself undertakes investigation and mediation. It may appoint special representatives or request the Secretary-General to do so or to use his good offices. It may set forth principles for a peaceful settlement. When a dispute leads to fighting, the Council's first concern is to bring it to an end as soon as possible. On many occasions, the Council has issued cease-fire directives which have been instrumental in

preventing wider hostilities. It also sends United Nations peace-keeping forces to help reduce tensions in troubled areas, keep opposing forces apart and create conditions of calm
in which peaceful settlements may be sought. The Council may decide on enforcement
measures, economic sanctions (such as trade embargoes) or collective military action. A
Member State against which preventive or enforcement action has been taken by the Security Council may be suspended from the exercise of the rights and privileges of membership by the General Assembly on the recommendation of the Security Council. A
Member State which has persistently violated the principles of the Charter may be expelled from the United Nations by the Assembly on the Council's recommendation.

### General Assembly

The General Assembly is the main deliberative organ. It is composed of representatives of all Member States, each of which has one vote. Decisions on important questions, such as those on peace and security, admission of new Members and budgetary
matters, require a two-thirds majority. Decisions on other questions are reached by a
simple majority.

### Functions and Powers

Under the Charter, the functions and powers of the General Assembly include the
following:

- to consider and make recommendations on the principles of cooperation in the
  maintenance of international peace and security, including the principles governing disarmament and the regulation of armaments;

- to discuss any question relating to international peace and security and, except
  where a dispute or situation is currently being discussed by the Security Council,
  to make recommendations on it;

- to discuss and, with the same exception, make recommendations on any question within the scope of the Charter or affecting the powers and functions of any
  organ of the United Nations;

- to consider and approve the United Nations budget and to apportion the contributions among Members;

- to elect the non-permanent members of the Security Council, the members of
  the Economic and Social Council and those members of the Trusteeship Council
  that are elected; to elect jointly with the Security Council the Judges of the International Court of Justice; and, on the recommendation of the Security Council,
  to appoint the Secretary-General.

Under the "Uniting for Peace" resolution adopted by the General Assembly in November 1950, the Assembly may take action if the Security Council, because of a lack of
unanimity of its permanent members, fails to act in a case where there appears to be a
threat to the peace, breach of the peace or act of aggression. The Assembly is empowered
to consider the matter immediately with a view to making recommendations to Members for collective measures, including, in the case of a breach of the peace or act of aggression, the use of armed force when necessary to maintain or restore international peace
and security.

### Sessions

The General Assembly's regular session begins each year on the third Tuesday in September and continues usually until mid-December. At the beginning of each regular session, the Assembly holds a general debate, in which Member States express their views on

a wide range of matters of international concern. Because of the great number of questions which the Assembly is called upon to consider (over 150 agenda items at the 1992 session of the Assembly, for example), the Assembly allocates most questions to its seven Main Committees.

Some questions are considered only in plenary meetings, rather than in one of the Main Committees, and all questions are voted on in plenary meetings, usually towards the end of the regular session, after the committees have completed their consideration of them and submitted draft resolutions to the plenary Assembly. The work of the United Nations year-round derives largely from the decisions of the General Assembly—that is to say, the will of the majority of the Members as expressed in resolutions adopted by the Assembly.

**That work is carried out:**

- by committees and other bodies established by the Assembly to study and report on specific issues, such as disarmament, outer space, peace-keeping, decolonization, human rights and apartheid;

- in international conferences called for by the Assembly; and,

- by the Secretariat of the United Nations—the Secretary-General and his staff of international civil servants.

\* \* \*

### Economic and Social Council

The Economic and Social Council was established by the Charter as the principal organ to coordinate the economic and social work of the United Nations and the specialized agencies and institutions—known as the "United Nations family" of organizations. The Council has 54 members who serve for three years, 18 being elected each year for a three-year term to replace 18 members whose three-year term has expired. Voting in the Economic and Social Council is by simple majority; each member has one vote.

### Relations with Non-Governmental Organizations

Under the Charter, the Economic and Social Council may consult with non-governmental organizations which are concerned with matters within the Council's competence. The Council recognizes that these organizations should have the opportunity to express their views and that they often possess special experience or technical knowledge of value to the Council in its work. Over 900 non-governmental organizations have consultative status with the Council.

### Trusteeship Council

In setting up an International Trusteeship System, the Charter established the Trusteeship Council as one of the main organs of the United Nations and assigned to it the task of supervising the administration of Trust Territories placed under the Trusteeship System. Major goals of the System are to promote the advancement of the inhabitants of Trust Territories and their progressive development towards self-government or independence. The aims of the Trusteeship System have been fulfilled to such an extent that only one of the original 11 Trusteeships remains: Palau, in the Pacific Islands (administered by the United States). The others, mostly in Africa and the Pacific, have attained independence, either as separate States or by joining neighboring independent countries.

### International Court of Justice

The International Court of Justice is the principal judicial organ of the United Nations. Its Statute is an integral part of the United Nations Charter.

## Secretariat

The Secretariat services the other organs of the United Nations and administers the programmes and policies laid down by them. At its head is the Secretary-General, who is appointed by the General Assembly on the recommendation of the Security Council for a term of five years.

## Secretary-General

The Secretary-General is described by the United Nations Charter as the "chief administrative officer" of the Organization. The present Secretary-General of the United Nations, and the sixth occupant of the post, is Boutros-Ghali, of Egypt, who took office on I January 1992. Each Secretary-General also defines the job within the context of his particular day and age.

In 1992, for example, Mr. Boutros-Ghali, at the request of the Security Council, authored "An Agenda for Peace," a far-reaching proposal for effective peace-keeping and peace-building in the post-cold war world. The report first noted the recent changes in the international context, including the shift from a bipolar to a multipolar international system. The Secretary-General also gave four aims for the Security Council to pursue: preventive diplomacy, peacemaking, peacekeeping, and peacebuilding. The report then reaffirmed the basic principle of state sovereignty: "the foundation-stone of this work is and must remain the State" (paragraph 17).

Preventive diplomacy comprises a number of related goals: preventing disputes from arising, preventing existing disputes from escalating into conflicts, and limiting the spread of existing conflicts. Peacemaking consists of mediation by the Secretary-General, referral of disputes to the International Court of Justice, economic assistance, and the use of military force under Article 42 to maintain or restore international peace and security. The Secretary-General called for the establishment of a standing U.N. military force under Article 43 of the Charter, which would exist in addition to peace enforcement units and whose purpose would be to respond to acts of outright aggression.

The report noted that the role of U.N. peacekeeping forces has increased dramatically in the past decade. The Secretary-General asked Member States to establish standby arrangements with the United Nations in order to ensure a supply of personnel and equipment for peacekeeping missions. Other sections of the report included a call for cooperation between the Security Council and regional and sub-regional organizations, as well as proposals for maintaining the financial health of the United Nations as costs rise and funds become scarce. Among the economic proposals were the establishment of a $1 billion U.N. Peace Endowment Fund and a $50 million peacekeeping reserve fund; levies on international travel and arms sales; and authorization for the United Nations to borrow from the World Bank and International Monetary Fund.

The duties carried out by the United Nations Secretariat are as varied as the problems dealt with by the United Nations. These range from administering peace-keeping operations to mediating international disputes. More than 25,000 men and women from more than 150 countries make up the Secretariat staff. As international civil servants, they and the Secretary-General answer to the United Nations alone for their activities and take an oath not to seek or receive instructions from any Government or outside authority. Under Article 100 of the Charter, each Member State undertakes to respect the exclusively international character of the responsibilities of the Secretary-General and the staff and to refrain from seeking to influence them improperly in the discharge of their duties.

* * *

**Intergovernmental Agencies Related to the United Nations**

The intergovernmental agencies related to the United Nations by special agreements are separate, autonomous organizations which work with the United Nations and each other through the coordinating machinery of the Economic and Social Council. Seventeen of the agencies are known as "specialized agencies," a term used in the United Nations Charter. They report annually to the Economic and Social Council. They are the following:

- International Labour Organization (ILO)
- Food and Agriculture Organization of the United Nations (FAO)
- United Nations Educational, Scientific and Cultural Organization (UNESCO)
- World Health Organization (WHO)
- World Bank
- International Bank for Reconstruction and Development (IBRD)
- International Development Association (IDA)
- International Finance Corporation (IFC)
- Multilateral Investment Guarantee Agency (MIGA)
- International Monetary Fund (IMF)
- International Civil Aviation Organization (ICAO)
- Universal Postal Union (UPU)
- International Telecommunication Union (ITU)
- World Meteorological Organization (WMO)
- International Maritime Organization (IMO)
- World Intellectual Property Organization (WIPO)
- International Fund for Agricultural Development (IFAD)
- United Nations Industrial Development Organization (UNIDO)

## *Authors' Note*

As an instrumental member in the formation of the United Nations, the United States has been an integral part of the U.N. system. The role of the U.N. in U.S. politics has garnered much debate. The following material provides an example of the U.S. perspective on the U.N.. This release from the U.S. Department of State details the Obama administration's stance on U.S.-U.N. relations and details the problems and goals the administration wishes to address in the future.

## 3. U.S. Department of State

Fact Sheet: Advancing U.S. Interests at the United Nations (2011)

The Obama Administration has dramatically changed America's course at the United Nations to advance our interests and values and help forge a more secure and prosperous world. We have repaired frayed relations with countries around the world. We have ended needless American isolation on a range of issues. And as a consequence, we have gotten strong cooperation on things that matter most to our national security interest.

What the President calls a "new era of engagement" has led to concrete results at the U.N. that advance U.S. foreign policy objectives and American security. The dividends of U.S. leadership at the U.N. are tangible—the stiffest U.N. sanctions ever against Iran and North Korea, renewed momentum to stop the proliferation of nuclear weapons and materials, strong sanctions and an unprecedented mandate to intervene and save lives in Libya, support for the historic and peaceful independence of Southern Sudan, vital U.N. assistance in Afghanistan and Iraq, vigorous defense of our staunch ally Israel, lifesaving humanitarian assistance to the most vulnerable in the Horn of Africa and initial progress in improving the flawed U.N. Human Rights Council. In a world of 21st-century threats that pay no heed to borders, rebuilding a strong basis for international cooperation has allowed the United States to work together with others to solve common problems at the United Nations, making the American people more secure.

## Nuclear Non-Proliferation

The President's vision for a world without nuclear weapons includes a realistic path to get there. Several significant milestones on this important Administration priority have taken place at the U.N..

- **U.N. Security Council Resolution 1887:** In September 2009, the United States held the presidency of the U.N. Security Council, and President Obama chaired a historic Council Summit on nonproliferation and disarmament, culminating in the unanimous passage of Security Council Resolution 1887. This U.S.-drafted resolution reaffirmed the international community's commitment to the global nonproliferation regime based on the Nuclear Nonproliferation Treaty, supported better security for nuclear weapons materials to prevent terrorists from acquiring materials essential to make a bomb, and made clear that all countries need to comply with their international nuclear obligations.

- **Iran:** In June 2010, the United Nations Security Council voted overwhelmingly to put in place the toughest U.N. sanctions regime ever faced by the Iranian government for its continued failure to live up to its obligations, sending an unmistakable message about the international community's commitment to stopping the spread of nuclear weapons. The new sanctions in Resolution 1929 impose restrictions on Iran's nuclear activities, its ballistic missile program, and its ability to acquire certain conventional weapons. They put a new framework in place to stop Iranian smuggling and crack down on Iran's use of banks and financial transactions to fund proliferation. They also target individuals, entities, and institutions—including those associated with the Islamic Revolutionary Guard Corps— that have supported Iran's nuclear program and prospered from illicit activities at the expense of the Iranian people. The U.S. continues to ensure that these sanctions are vigorously enforced, just as we continue to refine and enforce our own sanctions on Iran alongside those of our friends and allies.

- **North Korea:** In response to North Korea's announced 2009 nuclear test, the United States secured the unanimous adoption of Security Council Resolution 1874, which put in place a tough array of sanctions, including asset freezes, financial sanctions, a broad-based embargo on arms exports and imports, and an unprecedented framework for the inspection of suspect vessels. Since the adoption of Resolution 1874, countries have intercepted and seized tons of contraband cargo. These interdictions show that countries are taking seriously their obligations to enforce these tough new measures. The United States will continue to press on sanctions implementation until there is concrete, verifiable progress on denuclearization.

- **NPT Review Conference:** In May 2010, NPT parties adopted by consensus a Final Document that advances a realistic path towards a world without nuclear weapons. This document includes calls for strengthened verification and compliance, recognizes the New START agreement and the need for deeper reductions of nuclear weapons, and calls for the entry into force of the Comprehensive Test Ban Treaty and the immediate start of talks on a Fissile Material Cutoff Treaty. It also supports efforts to pursue international fuel banks and related mechanisms to broaden access to peaceful nuclear energy without creating new proliferation risks. This major achievement is a vindication of the broad thrust of U.S. efforts to inject new energy and renewed effort into stopping the spread of nuclear weapons.

- **U.N. Security Council Resolution 1977:** In April 2011, the Security Council unanimously adopted Resolution 1977, underscoring the vital importance of the Committee established pursuant to U.N. Security Council Resolution 1540 by extending its mandate for an additional ten years. The 1540 Committee is charged with assisting U.N. Member States in the implementation of UNSCR 1540's obligations to take and enforce effective measures against the proliferation of weapons of mass destruction (WMD), their means of delivery, and related materials, important elements in achieving U.S. nonproliferation objectives. The United States is making a $3 million donation to the United Nations trust fund for global and regional disarmament to help the Committee in its implementation efforts.

### Bolstering Progress in Afghanistan and Iraq

- Afghanistan: Since 2009, the United States has pursued a strategy in Afghanistan that places much greater emphasis on the role of international civilian assistance, while our troops work to secure the country and transition to a mission in support of Afghan security forces taking responsibility for their own security. To support this goal, the United States has worked to ensure that the U.N. Assistance Mission in Afghanistan (UNAMA) has the resources and political support to carry out its vital mission to lay the foundation for a sustainable peace and a prosperous future, including providing assistance with security, elections, governance, economic development, and humanitarian assistance. The United States will continue to work to strengthen all aspects of the U.N. presence in the country so that UNAMA can best complement efforts to support the Government of Afghanistan by the United States and the International Security Assistance Force and better coordinate donor support.

- Iraq: The United States and the international community are keeping their commitments to the Government and the people of Iraq, and as the United States is completing the withdrawal of U.S. forces, the United Nations Assistance Mission in Iraq (UNAMI) continues to play a critical role. The United States strongly supports the work of the UNAMI as it continues to provide important technical assistance to the Government of Iraq, assists displaced persons in Iraq and provides humanitarian assistance. Additionally, the United States played a key role in the passage of three resolutions that mark an important milestone in normalizing Iraqi ties to the international community that were significantly limited when Iraq was ruled by Saddam Hussein. The Security Council, in a special session chaired by Vice President Biden, passed Resolutions 1956, 1957 and 1958 to help return Iraq to the legal and international standing it held prior to the 1990 invasion of Kuwait.

<u>Promoting American Values</u>

- Protecting Civilians in Libya: In March, the United Nations took unprecedented quick and strong action to protect civilians in Libya. Resolution 1973 provided legal authority for the international community to intervene to save lives in Libya. The resolution authorized states to take all necessary measures to protect civilians and enforce a no-fly zone, saving countless lives. The Security Council also imposed on the Qadhafi regime and on Libya's major financial institutions a sweeping regime of financial sanctions and other measures to pressure the Qadhafi regime to end its brutal crackdown on demonstrators. Among other things, Resolutions 1970 and 1973 provided for an arms embargo, a ban on flights by Libyan-operated aircraft and asset freezes and travel bans on Qadhafi and his inner circle. These measures helped to isolate the Qadhafi regime from the international financial system, restricting its ability to fund military operations and to maintain support in Tripoli.

  The people of Libya are now taking the initial steps to rebuild their country and transition to an inclusive democracy. There are still many issues to be resolved in the coming days, but the United States is very encouraged by early the steps the TNC has taken. The United States, the United Nations, and our international partners are helping the TNC build a government that reflects the aspirations of the Libyan people. The United States and our partners have worked through the United Nations to unfreeze billions of dollars in order for Libya to get access to their state assets to meet critical humanitarian needs. The United States will continue to work with the TNC to ensure that these funds are disbursed in a transparent, accountable manner. The United States is also providing over $90 million to U.N. agencies, international organizations and NGOs to address humanitarian needs generated by the crisis in Libya.

  Moreover, the Security Council has adopted a new resolution to promote Libya's recovery from its recent conflict and support its transition to a free society. This resolution mandates a new, three-month U.N. mission that will assist Libyan efforts to restore security and the rule of law, protect human rights, and undertake an inclusive political dialogue towards establishing a democratic government. It also begins the process of unwinding the U.N. sanctions that were imposed last spring. Although some measures will remain in place, ensuring that funds previously frozen are released in a transparent and responsible way, the Libyan authorities are now able to pursue a reenergized Libyan economy.

- **Promoting a Peaceful Transition to South Sudan Independence:** On July 9, the Republic of South Sudan celebrated its independence. This action took place following months of intensified diplomatic efforts in the lead up to the historic, peaceful referendum on independence in January. Much of this work was accomplished working within or alongside the United Nations, including last year's high-level meeting at which President Obama delivered remarks to galvanize international action to ensure a credible and timely referendum.

  The United States continues to work closely with the U.N. and other international partners to support full implementation of the Comprehensive Peace Agreement and improve the humanitarian situation on the ground. In June, the Security Council created UNISFA, a U.N. peacekeeping force that will monitor the redeployment of armed forces from the Abyei area and that is authorized to use force to protect civilians and humanitarian workers. In July, the Security Council created UNMISS, a new U.N. peacekeeping force in the Republic of South Sudan, to consolidate peace and security and to help establish conditions for economic and political development.

The United States continues to work to end genocide and conflict in Darfur, including by supporting the joint U.N. and African Union peacekeeping mission (UNAMID), and calling for the Government of Sudan to end aerial bombardments, improve conditions and freedoms on the ground, and allow humanitarian access.

- **Horn of Africa Famine:** With more than 13.3 million people—primarily in Ethiopia, Kenya, and Somalia—in need of emergency assistance in the Horn of Africa, the United Nations is at the forefront of a large-scale international response, and the United States is the largest donor of humanitarian assistance to the region, providing over $600 million in life-saving humanitarian assistance to those in need. Much of this funding is funneled through various U.N. agencies and supports humanitarian assistance to refugees, internally displaced persons (IDPs), and other drought affected populations.

Additionally, the United States helped garner international support for the Transitional Federal Government and the African Union Mission in Somalia (AMISOM), including by supporting U.N. funding to keep international peacekeepers in the country. The United States has been a strong supporter of recent efforts to augment the number of troops deployed in AMISOM, which now has a force of nearly 9,600. Since AMISOM's deployment in 2007, the United States has obligated more than $258 million in assistance to AMISOM and over $85 million to the Somali transitional government's National Security Force.

## Defending Israel

- **Standing up for Israel at the U.N.:** The Obama Administration has consistently and forcefully opposed unbalanced and biased actions against Israel in the Security Council, the U.N. General Assembly, and across the U.N. system. President Obama has pledged that we will continue U.S. efforts to combat all international attempts to challenge the legitimacy of Israel—including and especially at the United Nations.

When an effort was made to insert the Security Council into matters that should be resolved through direct negotiations between Israelis and Palestinians, we vetoed it. When the 2009 Durban Review Conference advanced anti-Israel sentiment, we withdrew. When the U.N. General Assembly voted for a commemoration in September 2011 of the original 2001 Durban conference, we voted against it and announced we would not participate. When the Goldstone Report was released, we stood up strongly for Israel's right to defend itself. When anti-Israel resolutions come up at the U.N. Human Rights Council, the General Assembly, UNESCO, and elsewhere, we consistently oppose them.

## Strengthening U.N. Peacekeeping and Conflict Prevention Efforts

- **Improving Peacekeeping Effectiveness:** In his first visit as President to the United Nations, President Obama hosted the first-ever meeting with the leaders of the top troop-contributing nations to U.N. peacekeeping operations, underscoring America's commitment to this vital tool, which allows countries around the world to share the burden for protecting civilians and supporting fragile peace processes in societies emerging from war. The U.S. continues to advance initiatives to strengthen U.N. peacekeeping capabilities, including by seeking to expand the

number, capacity, and effectiveness of troop and police contributors, helping secure General Assembly approval for vital peacekeeping reforms, and working with
fellow Security Council members to craft more credible and achievable mandates
for operations in Haiti, Sudan, the Democratic Republic of the Congo, Liberia
and several other current operations.

- **Haiti:** After the devastating earthquake of January 2010, which claimed the lives
of over 100 U.N. personnel and the U.N. Mission's leadership, the United States
worked extremely closely with the U.N. to help the Government of Haiti ensure
security and deliver vital humanitarian relief to the people of Haiti. Tens of thousands of U.S. forces were able to withdraw from Haiti within a few months, as
countries from Latin America and around the world moved quickly to share the
burden and augment the U.N. peacekeeping presence. In addition, the total U.S.
2010 and 2011 humanitarian assistance funding provided is $1.2 billion for the
earthquake and $75 million for cholera.

- **Liberia:** The United States built an international consensus to maintain a robust
U.N. Mission in Liberia (UNMIL) peacekeeping operation for an additional 12
months, ensuring continued support for the 2011 elections. Security Council resolution 2008, which was adopted unanimously on September 17, also calls for a
technical assessment mission in spring of 2012 to evaluate potential reductions in
UNMIL's authorized strength.

- **Democratic Republic of the Congo (DRC):** The United States continues to cham-
pion improved protection of civilians, especially by demanding an end to the epidemic of rape and gender-based violence. The United States has worked successfully
to secure new Security Council sanctions against key leaders of armed groups operating in the DRC, including one individual linked to crimes involving sexual
and gender based violence and child soldier recruiting. Additionally, the United
States led the adoption of a U.N. Security Council resolution that supported, for
the first time, due diligence guidelines for individuals and companies operating in
the mineral trade in Eastern Congo and agreed to practice due diligence when
considering targeted sanctions.

- **Ivory Coast:** In April, the United States welcomed the end of former President
Laurent Gbabgo's illegitimate claim to power in Ivory Coast, following robust implementation of Security Council Resolution 1975, which demanded that Gbagbo
step down as President, imposed sanctions on him and his close associates, reaffirmed the international recognition given to Alassane Ouattara as President of
Ivory Coast, and reiterated that the U.N. Operation in Ivory Coast (UNOCI) could
use "all necessary means" in its mandate to protect civilians under imminent threat
of attack. Early in the conflict, the United States worked with partners to renew
UNOCI's mandate and increase its ranks by 2,000 troops, further bolstering the
mission's ability to protect civilians.

    The United States supports accountability on all sides for atrocities committed
during the electoral crisis, and we will continue to support U.N. efforts in Ivory
Coast as the nation recovers from this crisis. The Ivory Coast has accepted the jurisdiction of the International Criminal Court, and President Ouattara requested
that the Prosecutor open an investigation into the most serious crimes committed in during the post-electoral crisis.

- **Eritrea:** In 2009, the United States supported the African Union's call to sanction
Eritrea for that country's role in destabilizing Somalia and the region and its fail-

ure to comply with Security Council Resolution 1862 concerning Eritrea's border dispute with Djibouti. As a direct result of U.S. and African leadership, the Security Council adopted Resolution 1907 to impose an arms embargo and targeted financial and travel sanctions on Eritrean officials. Eritrea is paying a price for its sponsorship of foreign extremist groups. The Security Council, with the support of the U.N.'s Somalia and Eritrea Monitoring Group, continue to review additional measures to respond to Eritrea's acts to destabilize its neighbors.

### Protecting and Empowering Women and Girls

**Women, Peace and Security:** The United States continues to lead efforts across the U.N. focused on women's important roles in preventing, managing, and resolving conflict, as well as ending conflict-related sexual violence. In 2009, with Secretary of State Hillary Clinton presiding, the United States led the Security Council in unanimously adopting Resolution 1888, which strengthens the international response to sexual violence in conflict by establishing a dedicated U.N. Special Representative and creating of a team of experts to assist individual governments in strengthening their capacities to address sexual violence in conflicts within their borders.

Building upon this success, during the 2010 U.S. presidency of the Security Council, the United States supported the adoption of Resolution 1960, which expressed deep concern that violence against women and children in situations of armed conflict continues to occur. The resolution also improved reporting mechanisms on gender-based violence in conflict. On the margins of this year's General Assembly, Secretary of State Clinton will join other women leaders from across the world in spotlighting the importance of women's political participation in times of peace, conflict, and transition. And in the year to come, the United States will continue to lead efforts to support women's decision-making in matters of conflict prevention and international security by releasing its National Action Plan on Women, Peace, and Security.

- **U.N. Women:** The United States was also instrumental in the establishment of a new U.N. agency called U.N. Women. This vital new organization combines four separate U.N. offices into one stronger, streamlined and more efficient entity working in support of women around the world. U.N. Women will work to elevate women's issues within the U.N. system, on the ground in member states, and on the international stage. The United States is working very closely with Michelle Bachelet, the former President of Chile, as the first head of U.N. Women. In addition, when elections were held for the 41-member Executive Board, the United States secured a seat and supported other countries with strong records on women's rights, while successfully leading efforts to block Iran's bid for membership.

### Promoting Human Rights

- **Human Rights Council:** At the beginning of the Obama Administration, the United States made the decision to join the Human Rights Council, and that decision has paid real dividends for oppressed people around the world. Though the Council remains flawed, the United States has worked tirelessly to create the political will necessary for the Council to realize its full potential. While much work remains, in particular ending the Council's excessive focus on Israel, the Council has taken great strides in speaking up for those suffering under the world's cruelest regimes and focusing on the major human rights abuses worldwide.

In the past two years, the United States has spoken out on serious human rights abuses in Iran, Burma, Sudan, China, Zimbabwe, Venezuela, Syria, Yemen, Russia, Sri Lanka and elsewhere. With active U.S. leadership, the Council authorized international mandates to closely monitor and address the human rights situations in Iran, Libya, Syria, Ivory Coast, Burma, North Korea, Cambodia and Sudan. With U.S. engagement, Council members also voted to keep Iran and Syria from gaining seats on the Council.

We have also worked cooperatively with governments such as those of Haiti, Somalia, Kyrgyzstan, Guinea and Tunisia, as they experienced crises and sought help from the Council to strengthen their human rights capabilities and help their countries rebuild. For example, last year the United States partnered with the government of Afghanistan to build international support for efforts to prevent attacks on Afghan school children, especially girls, who seek to be educated.

In 2011, the United States has shown leadership that has led to additional concrete results. On Iran, the Council took assertive action to highlight Iran's deteriorating human rights situation by establishing a Special Rapporteur on the Human Rights Situation in Iran. In June, the Human Right's Council appointed Ahmed Shaheed to serve as Special Rapporteur. He will serve as a voice for all those Iranians who have suffered egregious human rights violations. This is the first new country mandate established since the Human Rights Council was formed in 2006.

U.S. leadership has led to two Special Sessions on the situation in Syria, sending President Assad a clear message that the world is watching what he does and that atrocities and human rights violations would not go unnoticed. At the most recent special session, the Council established a Commission of Inquiry to investigate all violations of international human rights law by Syrian Authorities and help the international community address the serious human rights abuses in Syria and ensure that those responsible are held to account.

The United States also played a pivotal role in convening the Council's Special Session in February 2011 during which the Council condemned the human rights violations and other acts of violence committed by the Government of Libya, and created an independent Commission of Inquiry to investigate those violations. Additionally on March 1, 2011 the General Assembly unanimously suspended Libya from the Human Rights Council because of the atrocities the Libyan authorities are committing against its own people. This was the first time that either the Human Rights Council or its predecessor, the Human Rights Commission, suspended any member state for gross violations of human rights.

In March 2011, the Council took an important step away from the deeply problematic concept of defamation of religion by adopting a constructive new resolution that promotes tolerance for all religious beliefs, promotes education and dialogue and is consistent with U.S. laws and universal values. Previous resolutions adopted under the concept of defamation of religion have been used to rationalize laws criminalizing blasphemy, and challenging widely held freedoms of expression and the press, rather than protecting religious freedom and human rights.

In June, the Human Rights Council took historic, bold and assertive action to highlight violence and human rights abuses faced by lesbian, gay, bisexual, and transgender (LGBT) persons around the world by passing the first U.N. resolution solely focused on LGBT persons. The United States co-sponsored, strengthened, and gained support for a South African initiative, which was ultimately joined by countries from every U.N. geographic region and paves the way for the first U.N. report on the challenges faced by LGBT people and sustained Council attention to LGBT issues.

Along with our international partners and the NGO community, the United States has made important initial steps toward improving the work of the Council. The United States will run for re-election next year so that we can continue the progress the Council has made over the last two years.

- **LGBT Rights:** In a reversal of the previous Administration's policy, the United States supported a landmark General Assembly declaration condemning human rights violations based on sexual orientation. The United States also spearheaded an effort that led to a decisive victory in the United Nations Economic and Social Council, which voted to grant consultative status to the International Lesbian and Gay Human Rights Commission (ILGHRC), a U.S.-based non-governmental organization that does invaluable work around the globe to protect basic human rights, combat discrimination, and fight against the scourge of HIV/AIDS. When a committee vote removed a reference in a resolution condemning extrajudicial killings based on sexual orientation, the United States led a successful campaign to reinstate that reference in the final General Assembly resolution. And the United States joined the LGBT core group in New York for the first time.

- **Convention on the Rights of Persons with Disabilities:** On behalf of the President, Ambassador Rice signed the Convention on the Rights of Persons with Disabilities, the first new human rights treaty of the 21st century.

- **DRIP:** In another important reversal of the previous Administration's policy, President Obama announced U.S. support for the United Nations Declaration on the Rights of Indigenous Peoples (DRIP).

- **Health Security:** The United States has taken a multi-faceted approach to dealing with infectious diseases, whatever their cause, through fora such as the U.N. Security Resolution 1540, the Biological Weapons Convention (BWC), and World Health Organization (WHO). The BWC Review Conference in December offers an important opportunity to revitalize international efforts against these threats, helping to build global capacity to combat infectious disease, and prevent biological weapons proliferation and bioterrorism. This week the United States is signing an agreement with the WHO on Global Health Security, affirming their shared commitment to strengthen cooperation on common health security priorities. Improving global capacities to detect, report and respond to infectious diseases quickly and accurately lies at the heart of the WHO's International Health Regulations. The U.S. is committed to have in place these vital IHR core capacities as soon as 2012.

## Reforming the United Nations

- **U.N. Arrears:** Working with the U.S. Congress, the Administration cleared hundreds of millions in arrears to the United Nations, which accumulated between 2005 and 2008, and is now working to stay current with payments to the Organization.

- **Budget Discipline:** As the largest financial contributor to the U.N., ensuring that U.S. funds are spent wisely and not wasted is vital. The United States has worked to contain the growth of the U.N. budget and consistently pressed the issue of efficiency and accountability in our discussions with the U.N., pushing for a focus on results. In 2009, the Administration successfully negotiated an agreement that held constant the share of U.S. assessed contributions to the United Nations.

- **U.N. Peacekeeping:** In 2011, the United States rallied major financial contributors to thwart an effort by troop-contributing countries to impose a 57% increase in the reimbursement rate for troops in peacekeeping missions, which would have cost the organization well over $700 million annually. The United States was able to insert a new provision to prevent reimbursement for troops who have been repatriated for disciplinary reasons, including violation of the U.N. zero tolerance policy on sexual exploitation and abuse.

U.S. leadership was instrumental in ensuring adoption of the Global Field Support Strategy, a sweeping reform of how the U.N. undertakes administrative and logistics support for U.N. field operations. This initiative will improve the quality, consistency, and efficiency of service delivery by capturing inefficiencies within peacekeeping operations and improving the U.N.'s capacity to support complex field missions.

- **Oversight and Accountability:** The United States advocated and supported adoption of key elements of an accountability framework for the U.N.. The United States has also blocked attempts to curb the authority and operational independence of the Office of Internal Oversight Services (OIOS) and succeeded in March 2010 in preserving OIOS' existing mandate and authority, allowing OIOS to fill many long-vacant positions.

The United States has consistently and aggressively supported OIOS to be a strong and independent watchdog so that U.S. taxpayers' money is spent wisely and U.N. programs are managed effectively. And, while OIOS has provided valuable recommendations to improve the U.N.'s effectiveness and served as a deterrent in the area of waste, fraud, and sexual exploitation and abuse, it has fallen short, especially in the area of investigations. The United States has pushed hard for improvements in that function so that OIOS can more vigorously pursue fraud and misconduct. The United States was pleased to see quick action by Carman LaPointe, the Head of OIOS, in filling several leadership positions in that critical office. The United States was successful in ensuring that the position of Director of Investigations, vacant for almost two years, was filled by a qualified candidate who is tasked, among other things, with reigniting the former financial crimes unit of OIOS.

- **Transparency:** The United States has promoted transparency throughout the United Nations system for many years. We have pushed for the Office of Internal Oversight Services and the Funds and Programs to take a number of important steps toward public disclosure of all internal audit, oversight and financial reports, and have seen significant progress. For example, Carman LaPointe has announced that she will post internal audits of the U.N. Secretariat on her website for public viewing starting in January 2012. Additionally, the United Nations Children's Fund (UNICEF), Development Program (UNDP), the United Nations Office of Project Services (UNOPS), and the United Nations Population Fund (UNFPA) gave access to internal audit reports to the Global Fund and other intergovernmental donors. All of these organizations also voted to let governments who fund their programs — like the United States — read audit reports remotely from all over the world, instead of keeping audits under lock and key in New York. This

September, leaders at all of these New York based funds and programs announced their support for full public disclosure of internal audits on the internet. Every agency in the U.N. system is a public institution and should open its doors to public scrutiny.

- **Human Resources Reform:** In December 2010, the United States pushed through reforms that led to harmonization of conditions of service for staff serving in the most difficult locations in the world, eliminating disparities in practices between organizations—including reducing the unreasonably high levels of allowances paid by some organizations—to ensure a balance between fiscal responsibility and ensuring that the organization is able to attract and retain the most qualified staff for service in hardship locations.

  The United States also demanded a review of the recent action by the International Civil Service Commission (ICSC) to increase the post (cost of living) adjustment for staff in New York, in light of the ongoing pay freeze in the U.S. federal civil service—whose salaries and benefits serve as the basis for those of professional staff at the U.N.—and the difficult international economic climate.

*No Claim to Original U.S. Government Works.*

## Authors' Note

The following material provides a basic understanding of the role of international law, explaining the purpose of customary international law and law by convention. The Restatement provides an introduction to the various sources of international law. The material then focuses on the impact of international law on the law of the United States. These sections analyze the relationship between international agreements and the supreme law of the United States.

## 4. Third Restatement of the Foreign Relations Law, Introductory Note, Sections 102, 111, 114, 115
### 1987

**Introductory Note**

International law is the law of the international community of states. It deals with the conduct of nation-states and their relations with other states, and to some extent also with their relations with individuals, business organizations, and other legal entities.

*The international community of states.* The principal entities of the international political system are states. The system includes also international (intergovernmental) organizations with independent status and character, for example, the United Nations, the International Monetary Fund, the Organization of American States. Nongovernmental organizations, juridical persons (e.g., national and "multinational" companies), and individuals are not primary actors in the system but may influence it and are affected by it.

The international political system is loose and decentralized. Its principal components—"sovereign" states—retain their essential autonomy. There is no "world government" as the term "government" is commonly understood. There is no central legislature with general law-making authority; the General Assembly and other organs of the United Nations influence the development of international law but only when their product is accepted by states. There is no executive institution to enforce law; the United Nations Security Council has limited executive power to enforce the provisions of the Charter and to maintain international peace and security, but it has no authority to enforce international law generally; within its jurisdiction, moreover, the Council is subject to the veto power of its five permanent members, viz. People's Republic of China, France, the U.S.S.R., the United Kingdom, and the United States. There is no international judiciary with general, comprehensive and compulsory jurisdiction; the International Court of Justice decides cases submitted to it and renders advisory opinions but has only limited compulsory jurisdiction.

Law, however, is essential to the system. International law has the character and qualities of law, and serves the functions and purposes of law, providing restraints against arbitrary state action and guidance in international relations.

*International law as law.* The absence of central legislative and executive institutions had led to skepticism about the legal quality of international law. Many observers consider international law to be only a series of precepts of morality or etiquette, of cautions and admonitions lacking in both specificity and binding quality. Governments, it is sometimes assumed, commonly disregard international law and observe it only when they deem it to be in their interest to do so.

These impressions are mistaken. International law is law like other law, promoting order[and] guiding, restraining, and regulating behavior. States, the principal addressees of international law, treat it as law, consider themselves bound by it, [and] attend to it with a sense of legal obligation and with concern for the consequences of violation. Some states refer to international law in their constitutions; many incorporate it into their domestic legal systems; all take account of it in their governmental institutional arrangements and in their international relations. There is reference to the "Law of Nations" in the Constitution of the United States (Article I, Section 8). It is part of the law of the United States, respected by Presidents and Congresses, and by the States, and given effect by the courts.

*International law based on acceptance.* While there have been relations between "states" since early human history, and some law governing those relations, modern international law is commonly dated from the Peace of Westphalia (1648) and the rise of the secular state. There have been major changes in that law, but its basic concepts and general outlines have remained essentially intact, even in our times when ideological conflict has polarized the international political system, and when many states—newly independent, non-Western, less-developed—were disposed to reexamine the international system into which they came.

Modern international law is rooted in acceptance by states which constitute the system. Specific rules of law also depend on state acceptance. Particular agreements create binding obligations for the particular parties, but general law depends on general acceptance. Law cannot be made by the majority for all, although states may be bound by a rule of customary law that they did not participate in making if they did not clearly dissociate themselves from it during the process of its development. There has been a growing practice in international organizations and at law-making conferences of seeking agreement by "consensus" (rather than by vote), a practice that also discourages dissent and puts pressure on dissidents to acquiesce. In principle, law that has been generally accepted cannot be later modified unilaterally by any state, but particular states and groups of states can contribute to the process of developing (and modifying) law by their actions as well as by organized attempts to achieve formal change.

*Custom and international agreement.* International law is made in two principal ways—by the practice of states ("customary law") and by purposeful agreement among states (sometimes called "conventional law," i.e., law by convention, by agreement). Until recently, international law was essentially customary law: agreements made particular arrangements between particular parties, but were not ordinarily used for general lawmaking for states. In our day, treaties have become the principal vehicle for making law for the international system; more and more of established customary law is being codified by general agreements. To this day, however, many rules about status, property, and international delicts are still customary law, not yet codified. The law of international agreements itself has recently been codified (in the Vienna Convention on the Law of Treaties), but the basic principle that makes international agreements (including the Vienna Convention itself) binding is the principle of customary law that agreements must be observed. Indeed, codification itself assumes the essential validity of the customary law that is being codified and the authenticity of its substantive content. Even after codification, moreover, custom maintains its authority, particularly as regards states that do not adhere to the codifying treaty. Customary law, then, remains an important element of international law and its rules and principles are included in this Restatement.

Customary international law has developed slowly and unevenly, out of action and reaction in practice, rather than systematically or by major leaps. National courts required to determine questions of international law must do so by imprecise methods out of uncertain materials, and they must look at a process that is worldwide and includes the actions and determinations of foreign actors (including foreign courts). Determinations by United States courts are also part of the process. A determination of international law by the Supreme Court of the United States resolves the matter for purposes of the law of the United States; it is not conclusive as to what international law is for other states, and perhaps not even as to what it is for the United States in its relations with other countries.

*Observance of international law.* A principal weakness perceived in international law is the lack of effective police authority to enforce it. That is indeed a weakness, but the criticism reflects misplaced emphasis. Effective police authority deters violations of law, but there are other inducements to compliance. In the international system, law is observed because of a combination of forces, including the unarticulated recognition by states generally of the need for order, and of their common interest in maintaining particular norms and standards, as well as every state's desire to avoid the consequences of violation, including damage to its "credit" and the particular reactions by the victim of a violation. There are occasional, sometimes flagrant, violations, but all nations generally observe their obligations under international law, and an international legal system exists and functions as a working reality. That states (governments) make law, interpret law for their own guidance, and respond to interpretations and actions by others, makes for a complex legal-political-diplomatic process, but it is no less "legal" even if it is less structured than domestic law in developed national societies.

*Content of international law.* International law is made by states, but the law so created deals not only with the conduct of states and international organizations and with relations among them, but increasingly also with relations of states with juridical and natural persons, including those in the state's own territory. International law includes norms, standards and principles, not different in character (and sometimes in complexity) from those in developed national law. Much international law is specific, for example the rules of diplomatic intercourse and immunity. Some international law mandates essentially a rule of reason, which leaves much room for disagreement, but such rules are not much more uncertain than, say, principles such as "unreasonable" search and seizure, "cruel and unusual" punishments, or "due process of law," in United States constitutional law. That in the international system there is no mandatory, authoritative process for deciding what the law is and where lines shall be drawn makes an important difference, but, in general, even broadly stated rules and principles of international law are respected and observed.

International law includes the basic, classic concepts of law in national legal systems— status and property, obligation and delict. It includes substantive law, process and procedure, remedies. International law is still often described as "primitive" but increasing complexity in international relations has brought increasingly complex international law. A law that not long ago was almost wholly customary is now overlaid by an elaborate network of treaties. At one time, international law dealt largely with rules of "abstention" by states inter se; now it includes a growing law of cooperation through a web of international organizations and other multilateral arrangements, law addressing the activities of giant "juridical persons" (multinational companies), and the human rights of individuals in their own national societies.

International law does not address all conduct of states or international organizations, or all of their relations. International law does not address some matters because they are not of sufficient international concern, and it is accepted that they are and should remain essentially "domestic." Some matters clearly of international concern are not regulated because the international community has not addressed them or has not been able to agree on how to deal with them.

*Consequences of violation.* States are responsible for violations of their obligations under international law. Comment e. In general, the obligation and the remedy run to a particular state. The victim of a violation can make claim for one or more forms of relief, e.g., cessation of the violation, compensation, specific performance, repair or other restoration of the situation, apology. See § 902. In some circumstances the victim may resort to reasonable forms of self-help. See § 905. By special agreement, the victim may have special remedies, or resort to special "machinery," e.g., judicial or arbitral proceedings, mediation or conciliation by international bodies. See Part IX.

*International adjudication.* Impartial adjudication of disputes is a common feature of the international legal system, mostly by arbitration or by special commissions established by agreement of the parties. See §§ 903–904.

A permanent tribunal, the International Court of Justice, was established under the auspices of the United Nations and is declared to be its principal judicial organ. United Nations Charter, Article 92. (It succeeded the Permanent Court of International Justice created under the League of Nations.) The Court functions in accordance with its Statute, which is annexed to the United Nations Charter. See 59 Stat. 1055 (1945), T.S. No. 933. The Court decides cases that the states parties refer to it, whether ad hoc or pursuant to earlier agreement. Statute of the Court, Articles 34–36. By declaration in advance, states may accept the compulsory jurisdiction of the Court in relation to any other state doing so, on a reciprocal basis. Id. Article 36(2). The Court's docket tends to be light, but judgments of the Court are generally accepted and carried out by the parties. The Security Council has authority to enforce such judgments (United Nations Charter, Article 94(2)) but as of 1986 had never done so. The Court also renders advisory opinions at the request of the Security Council, the General Assembly, or other United Nations organs or Specialized Agencies. United Nations Charter, Article 96. See generally this Restatement § 903.

\* \* \*

## 102. Sources of International Law

(1) A rule of international law is one that has been accepted as such by the international community of states

(a) in the form of customary law;

(b) by international agreement; or

(c) by derivation from general principles common to the major legal systems of the world.

(2) Customary international law results from a general and consistent practice of states followed by them from a sense of legal obligation.

(3) International agreements create law for the states parties thereto and may lead to the creation of customary international law when such agreements are intended for adherence by states generally and are in fact widely accepted.

(4) General principles common to the major legal systems, even if not incorporated or reflected in customary law or international agreement, may be invoked as supplementary rules of international law where appropriate.

\* \* \*

### Reporters' Notes

*1. Statute of International Court of Justice and sources of law.*

This section draws on Article 38(1) of the Statute of the International Court of Justice, a provision commonly treated as an authoritative statement of the "sources" of international law. Article 38(1) provides:

The Court, whose function is to decide in accordance with international law such disputes as are submitted to it, shall apply:

(a) international conventions, whether general or particular, establishing rules expressly recognized by the contesting states;

(b) international custom, as evidence of a general practice accepted as law;

(c) the general principles of law recognized by civilized nations;

(d) ... judicial decisions and the teachings of the most highly qualified publicists of the various nations, as subsidiary means for the determination of rules of law.

The Statute of the International Court of Justice does not use the term "sources," but this Restatement follows common usage in characterizing customary law, international agreements, and general principles of law as "sources" of international law, in the sense that they are the ways in which rules become, or become accepted as, international law. International lawyers sometimes also describe as "sources" the "judicial decisions and the teachings of the most highly qualified publicists of the various nations," mentioned in Article 38(1)(d) of the Statute of the Court, *supra*. Those, however, are not sources in the same sense since they are not ways in which law is made or accepted, but opinion-evidence as to whether some rule has in fact become or been accepted as international law. See § 103.

*2. Customary law.*

No definition of customary law has received universal agreement, but the essence of Subsection (2) has wide acceptance. See generally Parry, The Sources and Evidences of International Law (1965). Each element in attempted definitions has raised difficulties. There have been philosophical debates about the very basis of the definition: how can practice build law? Most troublesome conceptually has been the circularity in the suggestion that law is built by practice based on a sense of legal obligation: how, it is asked, can there be a sense of legal obligation before the law from which the legal obligation derives has matured? Such conceptual difficulties, however, have not prevented acceptance of customary law essentially as here defined. Perhaps the sense of legal obligation came originally from principles of natural law or common morality, often already reflected in principles of law common to national legal systems (see Comment 1); practice built on that sense of obligation then matured into customary law. Compare Article 38(1)(b) of the Statute of the International Court of Justice (Reporters' Note 1), which refers to "international custom, as evidence of a general practice accepted as law." Perhaps the definition reflects a later stage in the history of international law when governments found practice and sense of obligation already in evidence, and accepted them without inquiring as to the original basis of that sense of legal obligation.

Earlier definitions implied that establishment of custom required that the practice of states continue over an extended period of time. That requirement began to lose its force after the Second World War, perhaps because improved communication made the practice of states widely and quickly known, at least where there is broad acceptance and no or little objection. In North Sea Continental Shelf Cases, the International Court of Justice agreed that "the passage of only a short period of time is not necessarily, or of itself, a bar to the formation of a new rule of customary international law." [1969] I.C.J. Rep. 3, 44. The doctrine of the continental shelf, § 515, is sometimes cited as an example of "instant customary law." The Truman Proclamation of 1945 was not challenged by governments and was followed by similar claims by other states. The International Law Commission, engaged in codifying and developing the law of the sea during the years 1950–56, avoided a clear position as to whether the continental shelf provisions in its draft convention were codifying customary law or proposing a new development. The provisions were included in the 1958 Convention on the Continental Shelf. It was soon assumed that the doctrine they reflected was part of international law even for states that did not adhere to the Convention. See the opinion of the International Court of Justice in North Sea Continental Shelf Cases, *supra*, at 43. The doctrine of the continental shelf became accepted as customary law on the basis of assertions of exclusive jurisdiction by coastal states and general acquiescence by other states, although for some years actual mining on the continental shelf (outside a state's territorial sea) was not technologically feasible. The "practice" may be said to have consisted of acts by governments claiming exclusive rights and denying access to others.

The practice of states that builds customary law takes many forms and includes what states do in or through international organizations. The United Nations General Assembly in particular has adopted resolutions, declarations, and other statements of principles that in some circumstances contribute to the process of making customary law, insofar as statements and votes of governments are kinds of state practice, and may be expressions of opinio juris. The contributions of such resolutions and of the statements and votes supporting them to the lawmaking process will differ widely, depending on factors such as the subject of the resolution, whether it purports to reflect legal principles, how large a majority it commands and how numerous and important are the dissenting states, whether it is widely supported (including in particular the states principally affected), and whether it is later confirmed by other practice. "Declarations of principles" may have greater significance than ordinary resolutions. A memorandum of the Office of Legal Affairs of the United Nations Secretariat suggests that: in view of the greater solemnity and significance of a "declaration," it may be considered to impart, on behalf of the organ adopting it, a strong expectation that Members of the international community will abide by it. Consequently, insofar as the expectation is gradually justified by State practice, a declaration may by custom become recognized as laying down rules binding upon States. [E/CN.4/L. 610, quoted in 34 U.N. ESCOR, Supp. No. 8, p. 15, U.N. Doc. E/3616/Rev. 1 (1962)]. The Outer Space

Declaration, for example, might have become law even if a formal treaty had not followed, since it was approved by all, including the principal "space powers." See Declaration of Legal Principles Governing the Activities of States in the Exploration and Uses of Outer Space, G.A. Res. 1962, 18 U.N. GAOR, Supp. No. 15, at 15. A spokesman for the United States stated that his Government considered that the Declaration "reflected international law as accepted by the members of the United Nations," and both the United States and the U.S.S.R. indicated that they intended to abide by the Declaration. See 18 U.N. GAOR, 1st Committee, 1342d meeting, 2 Dec. 1963, pp. 159, 161.

For the effect of General Assembly resolutions on the development of the principle of self-determination, see Western Sahara (advisory opinion), [1975] I.C.J. Rep. 4, 31. The contribution of a resolution of a multilateral conference (on the law of the sea) to customary law is cited in Fisheries Jurisdiction Case (*United Kingdom v. Iceland*), [1974] I.C.J. Rep. 3, 24–26, 32.

Resolutions that may contribute to customary law are to be distinguished from resolutions that are legally binding on members. The latter, too, may reflect state practice or opinio juris, but they derive their authority from the charter of the organization, an international agreement in which states parties agreed to be bound by some of its acts.

International conferences, especially those engaged in codifying customary law, provide occasions for expressions by states as to the law on particular questions. General consensus as to the law at such a conference confirms customary law or contributes to its creation.

The development of customary law has been described as part of a "process of continuous interaction, of continuous demand and response," among decision-makers of different states. These "create expectations that effective power will be restrained and exercised in certain uniformities of pattern.... The reciprocal tolerances ... create the expectations of patterns and uniformity in decision, of practice in accord with rule, commonly regarded as law." McDougal, "The Hydrogen Bomb Tests and the International Law of the Sea," 49 Am.J. Int'l L. 357–58 (1955).

That a rule of customary law is not binding on any state indicating its dissent during the development of the rule is an accepted application of the traditional principle that international law essentially depends on the consent of states. Refusal of states to adopt or acquiesce in a practice has often prevented its development into a principle of customary law, but instances of dissent and exemption from practice that developed into principles of general customary law have been few. Scandinavian states successfully maintained a four-mile territorial sea although a three-mile zone was generally accepted, and Norway successfully maintained a different system of delimitation of its territorial zone. See Fisheries Case (*United Kingdom v. Norway*), [1951] I.C.J. Rep. 116.

An entity that achieves statehood becomes subject to international law, notably customary law as it had developed. After the Second World War, many new states came into existence within a brief period. Their spokesmen rhetorically asked why they should be bound by preexisting law created by European, Christian, imperialistic powers. In fact, however, the basic principles of customary law were accepted, with new states joining in the process of law-making, and seeking desired changes in the law through accepted procedures, notably by international agreements codifying, developing, and sometimes modifying the law.

*3. Binding resolutions of international organizations.*

The United States has recognized the binding character of such resolutions, for example, the resolution imposing an embargo on products of Southern Rhodesia. See 22

U.S.C. § 287c. Many other organs of international organizations have limited authority to impose some binding obligations, for example to determine the budget and the "dues" of each member. See, for example, the authority of the United Nations General Assembly under Article 17 of the Charter. A number of international organizations have authority to recommend rules but states are not compelled to adopt them.

*4. Conflict between customary law and international agreement.*

A subsequent agreement will prevail over prior custom, except where the principle of customary law has the character of jus cogens, but an agreement is ordinarily presumed to supplement rather than to replace a customary rule. Provisions in international agreements are superseded by principles of customary law that develop subsequently, where the parties to the agreement so intend, in which case the earlier provision in the agreement is deemed to have expired by mutual agreement or by desuetude. If an international agreement provides for denunciation, it will ordinarily be assumed that the agreement was not intended to be replaced by subsequent custom unless the parties denounce the earlier agreement. See Akehurst, "The Hierarchy of the Sources of International Law," 47 Brit. Y.B. Int'l L. 273 (1974–75). Modification of customary law by agreement is not uncommon, sometimes through bilateral agreements, notably in the various multilateral codifications of recent decades, such as the Vienna Convention on the Law of Treaties, the conventions on diplomatic and consular immunities, and the conventions on the law of the sea. There have been few instances of rules of customary law developing in conflict with earlier agreements, but that may happen more frequently as state practice responds to widespread political demands, for example, when states adopted 200-mile exclusive resource zones in the sea, in effect superseding the 1958 Law of the Sea Conventions. Compare Arbitration between the United Kingdom and France on the Delimitation of the Continental Shelf (Decision of June 30, 1977), 18 Int'l Leg. Mat. 397 (1979), 18 R. Int'l Arb. Awards 3 (1983).

*5. Agreements codifying customary law.*

An international agreement may declare that it merely codifies preexisting rules of customary international law. Such a declaration is evidence to that effect but is not conclusive on parties to the agreement. The recent "codification treaties" adopted under United Nations auspices declare that their aim is both codification and progressive development, thus leaving open whether a particular provision is declaratory of old law or a formulation of new law. See, for example, the Vienna Convention on the Law of Treaties. Even such a declaration is evidence that the agreement reflects existing law in some respects, and as to these the declaration may itself be viewed as a form of state practice confirming the customary international law. Of course, states may disagree as to whether the agreement as a whole or a particular provision reflects existing law. See generally Baxter, "Treaties and Custom," 129 Recueil des Cours 25 (1970).

International agreements that do not purport to codify customary international law may in fact do so. International agreements may also help create customary law of general applicability. In North Sea Continental Shelf Cases, the Court held that the Convention on the Continental Shelf codified the doctrine of the continental shelf as well as its basic principles, but not provisions as to which reservations were permitted. The Court suggested that a treaty rule might become "a general rule of international law" if there were "a very widespread and representative participation in the convention ... provided it includes that of States whose interests were particularly affected." Id. at 42. Article 38 of the Vienna Convention on the Law of Treaties declares: "Nothing in Articles 34 to 37 precludes a rule set forth in a treaty from becoming binding upon a third state as a customary rule of international law, recognized as such."

*6. Peremptory norms (jus cogens).*

The concept of *jus cogens* is of relatively recent origin. See Schwelb, "Some Aspects of International *Jus Cogens* as Formulated by the International Law Commission," 61 Am.J.Int'l L. 946 (1967). It is now widely accepted, however, as a principle of customary law (albeit of higher status). It is incorporated in the Vienna Convention on the Law of Treaties, Articles 53 and 64. See § 331(2) and Comment e to that section. The Vienna Convention requires that the norm (and its peremptory character) must be "accepted and recognized by the international community of States as a whole" (Art. 53). Apparently that means by "a very large majority" of states, even if over dissent by "a very small number" of states. See Report of the Proceedings of the Committee of the Whole, May 21, 1968, U.N. Doc. A/Conf. 39/11 at 471–72.

Although the concept of *jus cogens* is now accepted, its content is not agreed. There is general agreement that the principles of the United Nations Charter prohibiting the use of force are *jus cogens*. See Comment k; Verdross and Simma, Universelles Volkerrecht 83–87 (1976). It has been suggested that norms that create "international crimes" and obligate all states to proceed against violations are also peremptory. Compare Report of the International Law Commission on the work of its twenty-eighth session, draft Art. 19, [1976] 2 Y.B. Int'l L. Comm'n 95, 121. Such norms might include rules prohibiting genocide, slave trade and slavery, apartheid and other gross violations of human rights, and perhaps attacks on diplomats.

*7. General principles.*

Article 38(1)(c) of the Statute of the International Court of Justice, speaks of "general principles of law recognized by civilized nations." It has become clear that this phrase refers to general principles of law common to the major legal systems of the world. The general principles are those common to national legal systems; the view of Soviet scholars that the reference is to principles of international law that have been accepted by states generally has not gained acceptance. Compare Tunkin, Theory of International Law 190 (1974). See, generally, Virally, "The Sources of International Law," in Manual of Public International Law 143–48 (Sorensen, ed. 1968). In contrast, references to "general principles of international law" ordinarily mean principles accepted as customary international law whether or not they derive from principles common to national legal systems.

Whether a general principle common to national legal systems is appropriate for absorption by international law may depend on the development of international law. For example, there is now substantial international law on human rights, and it is plausible to conclude that a rule against torture is part of international law, since such a principle is common to all major legal systems.

In addition to being an independent, though secondary source of law, general principles are also supportive of other sources. That a principle is common to the major legal systems may be persuasive in determining whether it has become a rule of customary law or is implied in an international agreement. See Opinion of Judge Dillard in Appeal Relating to the Jurisdiction of the ICAO Council (*India v. Pakistan*), [1972] I.C.J. Rep. 46, 109. For example, "good faith," a principle "universally recognized" (preamble, Vienna Convention on the Law of Treaties, § 321, Reporters' Note 1) was perhaps originally a principle common to the major legal systems, but is now accepted as a principle of customary law. Compare Case Relating to the Arbitral Award Made by the King of Spain (*Honduras v. Nicaragua*), [1960] I.C.J. Rep. 192, 219, 220, 222, 228, 236 (state cannot in good faith contest long-accepted arbitral award), and Case of the Temple of Preah Vihear (*Cambodia v. Thailand*), [1962] id. 6, 23, 42 (state cannot in good faith challenge long-accepted boundary). See Lachs, "Some Thoughts on the Role of Good Faith in International Law," in Declarations on Principles: A Quest for Universal Peace 47 (Akkerman, van Krieker & Pannenberg eds., 1977); Virally, "Good Faith In Public International Law," 77 Am.J.Int'l L. 130 (1983).

*8. Equity.*

The principle of equity is frequently invoked in discourse between states but there are few references to equity as a legal principle in international judicial decisions. One such reference was in the Fisheries Jurisdiction Case (*United Kingdom v. Iceland*), [1974] I.C.J. Rep. 3. "Equitable principles" have been explicitly accepted as applicable in the delimitation of boundaries between the continental shelves and between the exclusive economic zones of states, and the concept has been considered by international tribunals in that context. [ ... ]

\* \* \*

## § 111. International Law and Agreements as Law of the United States

(1) International law and international agreements of the United States are law of the United States and supreme over the law of the several States.

(2) Cases arising under international law or international agreements of the United States are within the Judicial Power of the United States and, subject to Constitutional and statutory limitations and requirements of justiciability, are within the jurisdiction of the federal courts.

(3) Courts in the United States are bound to give effect to international law and to international agreements of the United States, except that a "non-self-executing" agreement will not be given effect as law in the absence of necessary implementation.

(4) An international agreement of the United States is "non-self-executing"

(a) if the agreement manifests an intention that it shall not become effective as domestic law without the enactment of implementing legislation,

(b) if the Senate in giving consent to a treaty, or Congress by resolution, requires implementing legislation, or

(c) if implementing legislation is constitutionally required.

\* \* \*

### Reporters' Notes

*1. International law applied where United States law applicable.*

International law will be applied as United States law by United States courts in circumstances in which United States law is applicable. However, when in the circumstances of a case before it, under applicable conflict of laws principles, a United States court would not apply United States substantive law but the law of another state, the court would apply international law if it is part of the law of the other state. Cf. *Banco Nacional de Cuba v. Sabbatino*, 376 U.S. 398, 84 S.Ct. 923, 11 L.Ed.2d 804 (1964); see Henkin, "Act of State Today: Recollections in Tranquility," 6 Colum.J. Transnat'l L. 175, 181 (1976).

The non-formal character of customary law, and the uncertainties in determining whether and when it has come into effect and what is its content, affect its application in the constitutional system. The President's authority and duty to take care that a principle of customary law be faithfully executed, Comment c, and the doctrine that a new customary law becomes United States law automatically and supersedes at least State law, § 115, Comment e, depend on an authoritative determination that the particular principle has in fact become part of customary law.

*2. International law and agreements as supreme federal law.*

In *United States v. Belmont*, 301 U.S. 324, 331, 57 S.Ct. 758, 761, 81 L.Ed. 1134 (1937), Justice Sutherland said:

Plainly, the external powers of the United States are to be exercised without regard to state laws or policies.... And while this rule in respect of treaties is established by the express language of cl. 2, Art. VI, of the Constitution, the same rule would result in the case of all international compacts and agreements from the very fact that complete power over international affairs is in the national government and is not and cannot be subject to any curtailment or interference on the part of the several states.... In respect of all international negotiations and compacts, and in respect of our foreign relations generally, state lines disappear....

Justice Sutherland apparently found such supremacy not by interpretation of the words of Article VI but by inference from the paramount and exclusive authority of the United States in international relations. Compare *United States v. Curtiss-Wright Export Corp.*, 299 U.S. 304, 57 S.Ct. 216, 81 L.Ed. 255 (1936). The same result might be reached under the Supremacy Clause by giving the same broad interpretation to the words "treaties" and "laws" that has been adopted for purposes of judicial power and jurisdiction. See Comment e and Reporters' Note 4.

As to customary international law (§ 102(2)), Justice Gray stated in The Paquete Habana, 175 U.S. 677, 700, 20 S.Ct. 290, 299, 44 L.Ed. 320 (1900):

International law is part of our law, and must be ascertained and administered by the courts of justice of appropriate jurisdiction, as often as questions of right depending upon it are duly presented for their determination.

The Supreme Court did not there address the question of the supremacy of customary international law over State law, but Justice Sutherland's reasoning in Belmont would apply. See also Reporters' Note 3.

*3. Customary international law as federal law.*

State determinations of international law were originally not thought to be subject to review by the United States Supreme Court. See Introductory Note, this chapter. See *York Life Insurance Co. v. Hendren*, 92 U.S. (2 Otto) 286, 23 L.Ed. 709 (1875); *Oliver American Trading Co. v. Mexico*, 264 U.S. 440, 44 S.Ct. 390, 68 L.Ed. 778 (1924); *Wulfsohn v. Russian Socialist Federated Republic*, 266 U.S. 580, 45 S.Ct. 89, 69 L.Ed. 451 (1924), per curiam dismissing a writ of error for want of jurisdiction, 234 N.Y. 372, 138 N.E. 24 (1923).

In *Bergman v. De Sieyes*, 170 F.2d 360, 361 (2d Cir.1948), upholding the immunity from jurisdiction of a diplomat in transit in the United States, Judge Learned Hand said:

Moreover, since the defendant was served while the cause was in the state court, the law of New York determines its validity, and although the courts of that state look to international law as a source of New York law, their interpretation of international law is controlling upon us, and we are to follow them so far as they have declared themselves. Whether an avowed refusal to accept a well-established doctrine of international law, or a plain misapprehension of it, would present a federal question we need not consider, for neither is present here.

Earlier, however, Professor Jessup had expressed the view that "It would be unsound as it would be unwise to make our state courts our ultimate authority for pronouncing the rules of international law." Jessup, "The Doctrine of *Erie Railroad v. Tompkins* Applied to International Law," 33 Am.J.Int'l L. 740 (1939). In *Banco Nacional de Cuba v. Sabbatino*, 376 U.S. 398, 425, 84 S.Ct. 923, 939, 11 L.Ed.2d 804 (1964), in discussing the "act of state" doctrine, the Supreme Court said:

[W]e are constrained to make it clear that an issue concerned with a basic choice regarding the competence and function of the Judiciary and the National Executive in ordering our relationships with other members of the international community must be treated exclusively as an aspect of federal law. It seems fair to assume that the Court did not have rules like the act of state doctrine in mind when it decided *Erie R. Co. v. Tompkins*. Soon thereafter, Professor Philip C. Jessup, now a judge of the International Court of Justice, recognized the potential dangers were Erie extended to legal problems affecting international relations. He cautioned that rules of international law should not be left to divergent and perhaps parochial state interpretations.

Based on the implications of Sabbatino, the modern view is that customary international law in the United States is federal law and its determination by the federal courts is binding on the State courts. That conclusion was anticipated long ago. In *Chisholm v. Georgia*, 2 U.S. (2 Dall.) 419, 474, 1 L.Ed. 440 (1793), Chief Justice Jay said that, even before the Constitution, as the "United States were responsible to foreign nations for the conduct of each State, relative to the laws of nations, and the performance of treaties ... the inexpedience of referring all such questions to State Courts, and particularly to the Courts of delinquent States became apparent."

For the view that *Erie v. Tompkins* did not preclude and indeed ushered in a new federal common law, see Friendly, "In Praise of Erie—and of the New Federal Common Law," 39 N.Y.U.L.Rev. 383 (1964).

*4. Cases "arising under" international law and agreements.*

Under Article III, Section 2, of the Constitution: "The judicial Power shall extend to all Cases, in Law and Equity, arising under this Constitution, the Laws of the United States, and Treaties made, or which shall be made, under their authority...."

The statutory provision in 28 U.S.C. § 1331 gives the district courts original jurisdiction (but not exclusive of State courts) "of all civil actions arising under the Constitution, laws, or treaties of the United States.

"Removal by defendant of such a case, brought in a State court, to a federal district court is provided for in 28 U.S.C. § 1441. Supreme Court review of such federal questions, generally on writ of certiorari, is provided in 28 U.S.C. § 1254 for cases coming from the federal courts of appeals, and in 28 U.S.C. § 1257 for those coming from State courts.

Cases arising under treaties are explicitly included both in Article III of the Constitution and in 28 U.S.C. § 1331. The Judicial Power, however, extends also to cases arising under international agreements other than treaties, or under customary international law. In construing § 5 of the Judiciary Act of 1891, providing for direct appeal of a judgment of a lower federal court to the Supreme Court in "any case in which the constitutionality of any law of the United States or the validity or construction of any treaty made under its authority is drawn in question," the Supreme Court said:

We think that the purpose of Congress was manifestly to permit rights and obligations of that character to be passed upon in the Federal court of final resort, and that matters of such vital importance arising out of opposing constructions of international compacts, sometimes involving the peace of nations, should be subject to direct and prompt review by the highest court of the Nation. While it may be true that this commercial agreement, made under authority of the Tariff Act of 1897, § 3, was not a treaty possessing the dignity of one requiring ratification by the Senate of the United States, it was an international compact, negotiated between the representatives of two sovereign nations and made in the name and on behalf of the contracting countries, and dealing with important commercial relations between the two countries, and was proclaimed by the President. If not technically a treaty requiring ratification, nevertheless it was a compact authorized by the Congress of the United States, negotiated and proclaimed under the authority of its President. We think such a compact is a treaty under the Circuit Court of Appeals Act, and, where its construction is directly involved, as it is here, there is a right of review by direct appeal to this court.

B. *Altman & Co. v. United States*, 224 U.S. 583, 601, 32 S.Ct. 593, 597, 56 L.Ed. 894 (1912). While in Altman the matter arose under a Congressional-Executive agreement (s 303(2)), the Court's statement would seem to apply as well to any international agreement made under the authority of the United States, even sole executive agreements based on the President's own constitutional authority. See *Weinberger v. Rossi*, 456 U.S. 25, 102 S.Ct. 1510, 71 L.Ed.2d 715 (1982) (in statute prohibiting discrimination against United States citizens in employment on military bases overseas unless permitted by treaty, "treaty" includes executive agreement); see also the Belmont case, quoted in Reporters' Note 2.

Matters arising under customary international law also arise under "the laws of the United States," since international law is "part of our law" (The Paquete Habana, Reporters' Note 2) and is federal law. That federal common law is within "the laws of the United States" for purposes of both the "judicial Power of the United States" (Article III) and the jurisdiction of the federal district courts (28 U.S.C. § 1331) is now established. In *Illinois v. Milwaukee*, 406 U.S. 91, 92 S.Ct. 1385, 31 L.Ed.2d 712 (1972), the Supreme Court concluded that "§ 1331 jurisdiction will support claims founded upon federal common law as well as those of statutory origin." 406 U.S. at 100, 92 S.Ct. at 139. The Court quoted with approval an earlier opinion by Justice Brennan:

The contention cannot be accepted that since petitioner's rights are judicially defined, they are not created by "the laws ... of the United States" within the meaning of § 1331.... In another context, that of state law, this Court has recognized that the statutory word "laws" includes court decisions. The converse situation is presented here in that federal courts have an extensive responsibility of fashioning rules of substantive law.... These rules are as fully "laws" of the United States as if they had been enacted by Congress.

*Romero v. International Terminal Operating Co.*, 358 U.S. 354, 393, 79 S.Ct. 468, 491, 3 L.Ed.2d 368 (1959) (Brennan, J., dissenting and concurring). The Court also invoked an opinion by Judge Lumbard in *Ivy Broadcasting Co. v. American Tel. & Tel. Co.*, 391 F.2d 486, 492 (2d Cir. 1968):

We believe that a cause of action similarly "arises under" federal law if the dispositive issues stated in the complaint require the application of federal common law.... The word "laws" in § 1331 should be construed to include laws created by federal judicial decisions as well as by congressional legislation. The rationale of the 1875 grant of federal question jurisdiction—to insure the availability of a forum designed to minimize the danger of hostility toward, and specially suited to the vindication of, federally created rights— is as applicable to judicially created rights as to rights created by statute.

For these purposes, there is no reason to treat claims arising under international law any differently from those arising under other federal law. In determining international law, judges are less free in their "sources" and are subject to international constraints (see Introductory Note to Chapter 1 of this Part), but the law they find is "part of our law" like other nonstatutory law and is properly treated like federal common law. See Comment d. However, a case "arises under" international law or an international agreement only if the law or agreement confers legal rights on the plaintiff. See §§ 703, 713, 906–907.

Customary law does not ordinarily confer legal rights on individuals or companies, even rights that might be enforced by a defensive suit such as one to enjoin or to terminate a violation by the United States (or a State) of customary law. Foreign governments or diplomats might sue to enjoin or to undo violations, for example, of sovereign or diplomatic immunity, but foreign governments and officials are generally reluctant to resort to national courts of other states to vindicate rights under international law. Moreover, foreign governments and officials, and aliens generally, can invoke the jurisdiction of the federal courts on bases of jurisdiction other than 28 U.S.C. § 1331, including in some cases the original jurisdiction of the Supreme Court. See Comment f. For a suit by an alien in tort for a violation of customary law, see the Filartiga case, § 703, Reporters' Note 7.

Treaties and other international agreements sometimes confer rights that would support a cause of action by private parties (see §§ 703, 713, 906–907), but many agreements that may ultimately benefit individual interests do not give them justiciable legal rights. See, e.g., *Dreyfus v. Von Finck*, 534 F.2d 24 (2d Cir. 1976), certiorari denied, 429 U.S. 835, 97 S.Ct. 102, 50 L.Ed.2d 101 (1977). In a number of cases a defendant alien was able to invoke a treaty in his defense, e.g. *Asakura v. Seattle*, 265 U.S. 332, 44 S.Ct. 515, 68 L.Ed. 1041 (1924), and other cases cited in Reporters' Note 5. In such circumstances, he might have been able to sue to enjoin the United States or the State from acting against him in violation of his rights under the treaty and perhaps to undo or repair the violation.

In Republic of the *Philippines v. Marcos*, 806 F.2d 344 (2d Cir.1986), the Court of Appeals held that an action brought by a foreign state seeking to recover assets alleged to have been unlawfully acquired by its former president while in office "necessarily require[s] determinations that will directly and significantly affect American foreign relations" (806 F.2d at 352), and therefore came within federal question jurisdiction under 28 U.S.C. § 1331.

*5. Self-executing and non-self-executing agreements.*

The distinction between self-executing and non-self-executing treaties was formulated early by Chief Justice Marshall. He said:

Our constitution declares a treaty to be the law of the land. It is, consequently, to be regarded in courts of justice as equivalent to an act of the legislature, wherever it operates of itself, without the aid of any legislative provision. But when the terms of the stipulation import a contract, when either of the parties engages to perform a particular act, the treaty addresses itself to the political, not the judicial department; and the legislature must execute the contract, before it can become a rule for the court.

*Foster v. Neilson*, 27 U.S. (2 Pet.) 253, 314, 7 L.Ed. 415 (1828). In that case, Marshall decided that the treaty was not self-executing, relying in part on the fact that Congress had apparently so assumed. Later, the Court held that treaty to be self-executing in another case, after the Spanish text was called to the Court's attention. *United States v. Percheman*, 32 U.S. (7 Pet.) 51, 8 L.Ed. 604 (1833).

Since generally the United States is obligated to comply with a treaty as soon as it comes into force for the United States, compliance is facilitated and expedited if the treaty is self-executing. Moreover, when Congressional action is required but is delayed, the United States may be in default on its international obligation. Therefore, if the Executive Branch has not requested implementing legislation and Congress has not enacted such legislation, there is a strong presumption that the treaty has been considered self-executing by the political branches, and should be considered self-executing by the courts. (This is especially so if some time has elapsed since the treaty has come into force.) In that event, a finding that a treaty is not self-executing is a finding that the United States has been and continues to be in default, and should be avoided.

In general, agreements that can be readily given effect by executive or judicial bodies, federal or State, without further legislation, are deemed self-executing, unless a contrary intention is manifest. Obligations not to act, or to act only subject to limitations, are generally self-executing. In an opinion characterized by the Supreme Court as "very able" (see *United States v. Rauscher*, 119 U.S. 407, 427–28, 7 S.Ct. 234, 244–45, 30 L.Ed. 425 (1886)), the Court of Appeals of Kentucky said:

When it is provided by treaty that certain acts shall not be done, or that certain limitations or restrictions shall not be disregarded or exceeded by the contracting parties, the compact does not need to be supplemented by legislative or executive action, to authorize the courts of justice to decline to override those limitations or to exceed the prescribed restrictions, for the palpable and all-sufficient reason, that to do so would be not only to violate the public faith, but to transgress the "supreme law of the land." *Commonwealth v. Hawes*, 76 Ky. (13 Bush) 697, 702–03 (1878).

Provisions in treaties of friendship, commerce, and navigation, or other agreements conferring rights on foreign nationals, especially in matters ordinarily governed by State law, have been given effect without any implementing legislation, their self-executing character assumed without discussion. This has been true from early in United States history, e.g., *Ware v. Hylton*, 3 U.S. (3 Dall.) 199, 1 L.Ed. 568 (1796) (treaty protected British creditors against cancellation of their debts by Virginia); *Fairfax's Devisee v. Hunter's Lessee*, 11 U.S. (7 Cranch) 603, 3 L.Ed. 453 (1813) (treaty protected British property owners against Virginia forfeiture). See the numerous treaties assuring aliens the right to inherit property in the United States, e.g., those considered in *Hauenstein v. Lynham*, 100 U.S. (10 Otto) 483, 25 L.Ed. 628 (1880); *Nielsen v. Johnson*, 279 U.S. 47, 49 S.Ct. 223, 73 L.Ed. 607 (1929); *Clark v. Allen*, 331 U.S. 503, 67 S.Ct. 1431, 91 L.Ed. 1633 (1947); *Kolovrat v. Oregon*, 366 U.S. 187, 81 S.Ct. 922, 6 L.Ed.2d 218 (1961). See also *Asakura v. Seattle*, Reporters' Note 4 (treaty granting alien equal right to engage in trade); *United States v. Rauscher, supra*, 119 U.S. at 418, 7 S.Ct. at 240, (1886) (alien extradited to United States invoked treaty limitations); *Chew Heong v. United States*, 112 U.S. 536, 5 S.Ct. 255, 28 L.Ed. 770 (1884) (treaty assuring alien right to leave country and return). Other cases holding treaties to be self-executing include *Bacardi Corp. v. Domenech*, 311 U.S. 150, 61 S.Ct. 219, 85 L.Ed. 98 (1940) (Inter-American Trade-Mark Convention); *Cook v. United States*, 288 U.S. 102, 119, 53 S.Ct. 305, 311, 77 L.Ed. 641 (1933) (liquor treaties with Great Britain). Compare *United States v. Forty-three Gallons of Whiskey*, 93 U.S. (3 Otto) 188, 196, 23 L.Ed. 846 (1876) (provision in Indian treaty applying United States laws on sale of liquor in Indian country).

In *Asakura v. Seattle*, Reporters' Note 4, a Japanese alien, who was engaged in the business of pawnbroking, contested the validity of a city ordinance limiting the issuance of pawnbroker licenses to citizens of the United States and making it unlawful to conduct such a business without a license. He invoked a provision of a treaty between the United States and Japan which provided that nationals of the two states should have the right "to carry on trade," and "to own or lease and occupy houses or shops" in the other state. The Supreme Court decided that the treaty authorized the Japanese national to engage in pawnbroking. The Court said:

The treaty is binding within the State of Washington.... The rule of equality estab-lished by it cannot be rendered nugatory in any part of the United States by municipal ordinances or state laws. It stands on the same footing of supremacy as do the provisions of the Constitution and laws of the United States. It operates of itself without the aid of any legislation, state or national; and it will be applied and given authoritative effect by the courts. 265 U.S. at 341, 44 S.Ct. at 515.

Treaties were held non-self-executing in *Cameron Septic Tank Co. v. Knoxville*, 227 U.S. 39, 33 S.Ct. 209, 57 L.Ed. 407 (1913) (giving effect to Congressional view that industrial property treaty was non-self-executing). Compare *Holden v. Joy*, 84 U.S. (17 Wall.) 211, 246, 21 L.Ed. 523 (1872) (treaty undertaking to convey land to Indian nation). Treaties on subjects that Congress has regulated extensively are more likely to be interpreted as non-self-executing. See, e.g., *Robertson v. General Electric Co.*, 32 F.2d 495 (4th Cir.1929), cer-tiorari denied, 280 U.S. 571, 50 S.Ct. 28, 74 L.Ed. 624 (1929) (peace treaty undertaking regarding patents on industrial property). The human rights provisions of the United Nations Charter were held to be non-self-executing in Sei *Fujii v. California*, 217 P.2d 481 (Cal.App.1950), rehearing denied, 218 P.2d 595 (Cal.Dist.Ct.App. 1950), reversed on this question but affirmed on other grounds, 38 Cal.2d 718, 242 P.2d 617 (1952). See § 703, Reporters' Note 7. See generally 14 Whiteman, Digest of International Law 302 (1970).

In *United States v. Postal*, 589 F.2d 862 (5th Cir.1979), certiorari denied, 444 U.S. 832, 100 S.Ct. 61, 62 L.Ed.2d 40 (1979), the court found that the 1958 Convention on the High Seas was not self-executing. It suggested that in the absence of a clear intention to that effect, a multilateral treaty should not readily be held self-executing in the United States in view of the "lack of mutuality between the United States and countries that do not recognize treaties as self-executing." 589 F.2d at 878. That suggestion seems miscon-ceived. A treaty is generally binding on states parties from the time it comes into force for them, whether or not it is self-executing. If a treaty is not self-executing for a state party, that state is obliged to implement it promptly, and failure to do so would render it in de-fault on its treaty obligations. The purpose of having a treaty self-executing is to make it easier for the United States to carry out its international undertakings. It is not clear why the fact that some other states do not consider treaties as self-executing should govern United States practice. In fact, few other states distinguish between self-executing and non-self-executing treaties; and whether or not a treaty or provision will be self-executing for a particular state party, and any lack of mutuality in this respect, have generally not been considerations when states enter into treaty obligations, whether multilateral or bi-lateral. If, in some instance, a state party fails to take any necessary steps to implement a treaty, and as a result comes into material default in its obligations to the United States, the United States may suspend or terminate its obligation under the treaty, whether or not the treaty is self-executing in the United States. See §§ 335, 337, 339 and Reporters' Note 1 to § 339.

Self-executing treaties were contemplated by the Constitution and have been common. They avoid delay in carrying out the obligations of the United States. They eliminate the need for participation by the House of Representatives (which the Framers of the Con-stitution had excluded from the treaty process), and for going to the Senate a second time for implementing legislation after the Senate had already consented to the treaty by two-thirds vote. Nevertheless, United States representatives negotiating agreements are often sensitive to claims, particularly by members of the House of Representatives, that some matters cannot be self-executing under the Constitution (Subsection (4) and Comment i), and to political or administrative considerations making it preferable that a treaty not become law in the United States until it is implemented by Congress. The Senate also, when consenting to a treaty, has sometimes insisted that it should not go into effect until implementing legislation had been enacted. See Subsection (4)(b), and § 314, Comment d. A proposal to amend the Constitution to render all treaties non-self-executing was not adopted. See the Bricker Amendment, Reporters' Note 8.

*6. Constitutional restraints on self-executing character.*

There is no definitive authority for the rule set forth in Comment i that agreements on some subjects cannot be self-executing. That a subject is within the legislative power of Congress does not preclude a treaty on the same subject. See § 303, Comment c. No particular clause of the Constitution conferring power on Congress states or clearly implies that the power can be exercised only by Congress and not by treaty. (Contrast the provision that Congress shall have the power to "exercise exclusive legislation in all Cases whatsoever" over the District of Columbia and other places acquired for "needful Buildings," U.S. Constitution, Article I, Section 8, clause 17.) But see the dissenting opinion in *Edwards v. Carter,* 580 F.2d 1055 (D.C.Cir.1978), certiorari denied, 436 U.S. 907, 98 S.Ct. 2240, 56 L.Ed.2d 406 (1978), § 303, Reporters' Note 2. The power of Congress to declare war is not characterized or designated in any way that would distinguish it from, say, the power to regulate commerce with foreign nations, yet regulation of such commerce is surely a proper subject for a self-executing treaty. The provision that "No money shall be drawn from the Treasury, but in Consequence of Appropriations made by Law," lends itself better to the suggestion that an international agreement cannot itself "appropriate" money. Even here, it might have been possible to conclude that since treaties are declared to be "law" (Art. VI) and are treated as equal to an act of Congress for other purposes, an appropriation of funds through an international agreement is an appropriation "made by law." Compare § 115.

The principle declared in Comment i is nevertheless generally assumed for the cases given. For an important instance of its recognition, see the North Atlantic Treaty, signed April 4, 1949, 63 Stat. 2241, T.I.A.S. No. 1964, 34 U.N.T.S. 243, which provides that "This Treaty shall be ratified and its provisions carried out by the parties in accordance with their respective constitutional processes" (Art. 11). Under Congressional rules and practice, however, a treaty may serve as "authorization" for the appropriation of funds, requiring only appropriation legislation. Criminal law to implement the foreign relations of the United States is wholly statutory. See U.S. Constitution, Article I, Section 8, giving Congress power "to define and punish Piracies and Felonies committed on the high Seas, and Offences against the Law of Nations"; cf. *United States v. Hudson,* 11 U.S. (7 Cranch) 32, 3 L.Ed. 259 (1812) (no federal common law crimes); *United States v. Smith,* 18 U.S. (5 Wheat.) 153, 5 L.Ed. 57 (1820) (upholding statute to punish "piracy, as defined by law of nations").

*7. Obligation of Congress to implement international agreement.*

Although there may be no way to enforce the obligation, it has long been urged that Congress is "constitutionally and morally obligated" to appropriate money or enact legislation necessary to implement obligations assumed by the United States by international agreement. The House of Representatives, in particular, has asserted a right to consider anew whether to appropriate such money or to enact such legislation, but these assertions were rejected early in our history, and repeatedly thereafter, as an improper attempt to give the House of Representatives an effective part in the Treaty Power contrary to the clear intention of the Framers. In fact, Congress has rarely refused to implement an admittedly valid international agreement. Congress may, of course, question the validity of an international agreement, especially if not made as a treaty in accordance with constitutional procedures, and refuse to implement the agreement on that ground. See § 303(1). Congress has sometimes passed legislation inconsistent with an earlier international agreement (see § 115), and such legislation has been given effect. Such action by Congress raises different issues, however. It implies a later change of policy by both houses of Congress (and perhaps the President, unless the law is adopted over his veto), not an effort by the House alone, contemporaneously with the treaty, to prevent a treaty from coming into effect. See Henkin, Foreign Affairs and the Constitution 161–62 (1972).

*8. International agreement as basis for act of Congress.*

Under Article 1, Section 8, of the United States Constitution, Congress has the power "to make all laws which shall be necessary and proper for carrying into Execution ... all other Powers vested by this Constitution in the Government of the United States, or in any Department or Officer thereof." Congress therefore has the power to enact legislation necessary and proper for carrying into execution a treaty properly made by the President with the consent of the Senate, or an executive agreement within the President's authority under the Constitution.

In *Missouri v. Holland*, 252 U.S. 416 (1920), the Court upheld the constitutionality of the Migratory Bird Treaty Act, enacted by Congress to implement a treaty with Great Britain to protect birds flying between Canada and the United States, legislation which, it was assumed, Congress had no power to enact in the absence of treaty. Justice Holmes said: "It is obvious that there may be matters of the sharpest exigency for the national well being that an act of Congress could not deal with but that a treaty followed by such an act could." 252 U.S. at 433. During 1953–55 there was an extended but unsuccessful effort led by Senator Bricker of Ohio to amend the Constitution, so as, inter alia, to deny power to Congress to enact law pursuant to treaty which it could not enact in the absence of treaty. See S.J.Res. 130, 82d Cong.; S.J.Res. 1 and 43, 83d Cong.; S.J.Res. 1, 84th Cong. Articles discussing the Amendment are cited in Bishop, International Law 112, n. 39 (3d ed. 1971).

\* \* \*

## § 114. Interpretation of Federal Statute in Light of International Law or Agreement

Where fairly possible, a United States statute is to be construed so as not to conflict with international law or with an international agreement of the United States.

\* \* \*

**Reporters' Notes**

*1. Interpretation to avoid violation of international obligation.*

Chief Justice Marshall stated that "an Act of Congress ought never to be construed to violate the law of nations if any other possible construction remains...." *Murray v. Schooner Charming Betsy*, 6 U.S. (2 Cranch) 64, 118, 2 L.Ed. 208 (1804). See also *Lauritzen v. Larsen*, 345 U.S. 571, 578, 73 S.Ct. 921, 926, 97 L.Ed. 1254 (1958). On several occasions the Supreme Court has interpreted acts of Congress so as to avoid conflict with earlier treaty provisions. *Chew Heong v. United States*, 112 U.S. 536, 539–40, 5 S.Ct. 255, 255–56, 28 L.Ed. 770 (1884) (later immigration law did not affect treaty right of resident Chinese alien to reenter); *Weinberger v. Rossi*, 456 U.S. 25, 33, 102 S.Ct. 1510, 1516, 71 L.Ed.2d 715 (1982); cf. *Clark v. Allen*, 331 U.S. 503, 67 S.Ct. 1431, 91 L.Ed. 1633 (1947) (Trading with the Enemy Act not incompatible with treaty rights of German aliens to inherit realty which were succeeded to by the United States). See also *Cook v. United States*, 288 U.S. 102, 53 S.Ct. 305, 77 L.Ed. 641 (1933), in which the Supreme Court found that reenactment, after a series of "liquor treaties" with Great Britain, of prior statutory provisions for boarding vessels did not reflect a purpose of Congress to supersede the effect of the treaties as domestic law. Construing an international agreement to avoid conflict with a statute is more difficult since the proper interpretation of a treaty is an international question as to which courts of the United States have less leeway. The disposition to seek to construe a treaty to avoid conflict with a State statute is less clear. Compare *Nielsen v. Johnson*, 279 U.S. 47, 52, 49 U.S. 223, 224, 73 L.Ed. 607 (1929), with *Guaranty Trust Co. v. United States*, 304 U.S. 126, 143, 58 S.Ct. 785, 794, 82 L.Ed. 1224 (1938).

*2. "Where fairly possible."*

The phrase "where fairly possible" derives from one of the principles of interpretation to avoid serious doubts as to the constitutionality of a federal statute, set forth by Justice Brandeis in *Ashwander v. TVA*, 297 U.S. 288, 346–48, 56 S.Ct. 466, 482–483, 80 L.Ed. 688 (1936) (concurring opinion).

\* \* \*

## § 115. Inconsistency Between International Law or Agreement and Domestic Law

### Law of the United States

(1) (a) An act of Congress supersedes an earlier rule of international law or a provision of an international agreement as law of the United States if the purpose of the act to supersede the earlier rule or provision is clear or if the act and the earlier rule or provision cannot be fairly reconciled.

(b) That a rule of international law or a provision of an international agreement is superseded as domestic law does not relieve the United States of its international obligation or of the consequences of a violation of that obligation.

(2) A provision of a treaty of the United States that becomes effective as law of the United States supersedes as domestic law any inconsistent preexisting provision of a law or treaty of the United States.

(3) A rule of international law or a provision of an international agreement of the United States will not be given effect as law in the United States if it is inconsistent with the United States Constitution.

\* \* \*

### Reporters' Notes

*1. Equality of international agreements and statutes.*

The principle that United States treaties and federal statutes are of equal authority, so that in case of inconsistency the later in time should prevail, was derived early from the Supremacy Clause, Article VI of the Constitution. That article declares the Constitution, the laws of the United States, and treaties to be "the supreme Law of the Land"; the courts inferred that treaties are law equal in authority to United States statutes. Head Money Cases, 112 U.S. 580, 5 S.Ct. 247, 28 L.Ed. 798 (1884); *Whitney v. Robertson*, 124 U.S. 190, 8 S.Ct. 456, 31 L.Ed. 386 (1888); The Chinese Exclusion Case, 130 U.S. 581, 599, 9 S.Ct. 623, 627, 32 L.Ed. 1068 (1889). Some have questioned that inference as unwarranted. Moreover, the cases that declared that doctrine dealt with conflict between a statute and a bilateral agreement; it has been urged that the doctrine should not apply to inconsistency between a statute and general international law established by a general multilateral treaty. For that case at least, there have been suggestions that the United States might better adopt the jurisprudence of some European countries, which gives effect to an international agreement even in the face of subsequent legislation. Compare Article 55 of the Constitution of France (1958) and Article 94 of the Constitution of the Netherlands (1983). The doctrine expressed in this section, however, is established, and a distinction between bilateral and multilateral agreements has not taken root. See Henkin, Foreign Affairs and the Constitution 163–64 (1972).

The doctrine that laws and treaties are equal in authority and the later prevails in case of conflict has been applied in several cases giving effect to a later act of Congress. E.g., The Chinese Exclusion Case, *supra*; *Whitney v. Robertson, supra*; Head Money Cases, *supra*; The Cherokee Tobacco, 78 U.S. (11 Wall.) 616, 20 L.Ed. 227 (1871); *Diggs v. Shultz*, 470 F.2d 461 (D.C. Cir. 1972), certiorari denied, 411 U.S. 931, 93 S.Ct. 1897, 36 L.Ed.2d 390 (1973) (upholding statute permitting imports contrary to United Nations Security Council embargo on Rhodesian products). A later treaty was given effect in the face of an earlier statute in *Cook v. United States*, 288 U.S. 102, 53 S.Ct. 305, 77 L.Ed. 641 (1933).

*2. Federal statute does not "repeal" international law or agreement.*

It is inexact to say that Congress has the power to "repeal a treaty." Congress has no authority to act on the treaty itself. But acting within its legislative authority under the Constitution, Congress may enact laws that are inconsistent with the law as previously represented by a self-executing international agreement. The courts, and the President, being unable to give effect to both the agreement and the statute as domestic law, will give effect to the later in time. See Henkin, Foreign Affairs and the Constitution 164, 413–14 (1972).

*3. President's power to supersede international law or agreement.*

There is authority for the view that the President has the power, when acting within his constitutional authority, to disregard a rule of international law or an agreement of the United States, notwithstanding that international law and agreements are law of the United States and that it is the President's duty under the Constitution to "take care that the Laws be faithfully executed." Article II, Section 3. Compare the authority of the President to terminate international agreements on behalf of the United States, § 339. That the courts will not compel the President to honor international law may be implied in Supreme Court statements that courts will give effect to international law "where there is no treaty, and no controlling executive or legislative act or judicial decision," and "in the absence of any treaty or other public act of their own government in relation to the matter." The Paquete Habana, 175 U.S. 677, 700, 708, 20 S.Ct. 290, 299, 302, 44 L.Ed. 320 (1900); compare *Brown v. United States*, 12 U.S. (8 Cranch) 110, 128, 3 L.Ed. 504 (1814). *Tag v. Rogers*, 267 F.2d 664 (D.C. Cir.1959), certiorari denied, 362 U.S. 904, 80 S.Ct. 615, 4 L.Ed.2d 555 (1960); and The Over the Top, 5 F.2d 838 (D.Conn.1925) are sometimes cited, but those cases addressed the power of Congress to act contrary to international law, not the powers of the President.

In 1986, in *Garcia-Mir v. Meese*, 788 F.2d 1446 (11th Cir. 1986), certiorari denied, U.S. 107 S.Ct. 289, 93 L.Ed.2d 263 (1986), the court, relying on The Paquete Habana, gave effect to an action of the Attorney General authorizing detention of aliens although it accepted that such detention was in violation of international law. Citing this Reporters' Note (as it appeared in Tentative Draft No. 6 of this Restatement, § 135, Reporters' Note 3), the court concluded that "the power of the President to disregard international law in service of domestic needs is reaffirmed." However, the President may have power to act in disregard of international law "when acting within his constitutional authority," but the Court of Appeals failed to find any constitutional authority in the President to detain the aliens in question. See Henkin, "The Constitution and United States Sovereignty: A Century of Chinese Exclusion and its Progeny," 100 Harv.L.Rev. 853, 878–86 (1987).

Some courts may be disposed to treat a claim that the President was violating international law as raising a "political question" and not justiciable. See, e.g., *United States v. Berrigan*, 283 F.Supp. 336, 342 (D.Md.1968) affirmed, 417 F.2d 1009 (4th Cir.1969), certiorari denied, 397 U.S. 909, 90 S.Ct. 907, 25 L.Ed.2d 90 (1970). See § 1, Reporters' Note 4.

*4. Rule of international law inconsistent with pre-existing United States law or agreement.*

There seem to have been no cases in which a court was required to determine whether to give effect to a principle of customary law in the face of an inconsistent earlier statute or international agreement of the United States. Since international customary law and an international agreement have equal authority in international law (s 102, Comment j), and both are law of the United States (s 111), arguably later customary law should be given effect as law of the United States, even in the face of an earlier law or agreement, just as a later international agreement of the United States is given effect in the face of an earlier law or agreement. *Cook v. United States*, Reporters' Note 1. But customary law is made by practice, consent, or acquiescence of the United States, often acting through the President, and it has been argued that the sole act of the President ought not to prevail over a law of the United States. See Reporters' Note 5. The Executive Branch is unlikely to engage or acquiesce in a practice that is inconsistent with an earlier act of Congress, especially if the statute is recent. But see the President's action in regard to the law of the sea, Comment d. Courts in the United States will hesitate to conclude that a principle has become a rule of customary international law if they are required to give it effect in the face of an earlier inconsistent statute.

*5. Sole executive agreement inconsistent with State or federal law.*

A sole executive agreement made by the President on his own constitutional authority is the law of the land and supreme to State law. *United States v. Belmont*, 301 U.S. 324, 57 S.Ct. 758, 81 L.Ed. 1134 (1937); *United States v. Pink*, 315 U.S. 203, 62 S.Ct. 552, 86 L.Ed. 796 (1942). It has been held, however, that an executive agreement made by the President on a matter expressly within the constitutional authority of Congress, such as the regulation of commerce with foreign nations, is subject to the controlling authority of Congress and will not be given effect in the face of an inconsistent Congressional act. *United States v. Guy W. Capps, Inc.*, 204 F.2d 655 (4th Cir. 1953), affirmed on other grounds, 348 U.S. 296, 75 S.Ct. 326, 99 L.Ed. 329 (1955) (executive agreement bypassing procedures prescribed by Congress for limiting imports); *Swearingen v. United States*, 565 F.Supp. 1019 (D.Colo.1983) (executive agreement inconsistent with Internal Revenue Code); cf. *American Cetacean Society v. Baldrige*, 768 F.2d 426 (D.C.Cir.1985), reversed on other grounds, U.S., 106 S.Ct. 2860, 92 L.Ed.2d 166 (1986) (Supreme Court interpreted statute so as to render subsequent executive agreement not in conflict with statute.) See also § 803, Comment c and Reporters' Note 4. A different principle might govern an executive agreement on a matter within the President's primary constitutional authority such as the recognition of governments (e.g., an agreement like that involved in Belmont and Pink, *supra*). Even in such cases, it has been argued, the act of a single person, even the President, cannot repeal an act of Congress. On the other hand, it has been argued that a sole executive agreement within the President's constitutional authority is federal law, and United States jurisprudence has not known federal law of different constitutional status. "All Constitutional acts of power, whether in the executive or in the judicial department, have as much legal validity and obligation as if they proceeded from the legislature." The Federalist No. 64 (Jay), cited in *United States v. Pink, supra*, 315 U.S. at 230, 62 S.Ct. at 565. See Henkin, Foreign Affairs and the Constitution 186, 432–33

(1972). Of course, even if a sole executive agreement were held to supersede a statute, Congress could reenact the statute and thereby supersede the intervening executive agreement as domestic law.

In *Dames & Moore v. Regan*, 453 U.S. 654, 101 S.Ct. 2972, 69 L.Ed.2d 918 (1981), the Supreme Court upheld Presidential action pursuant to a sole executive agreement in the face of a claim that, by the Foreign Sovereign Immunities Act (see Part IV, Chapter 5, Subchapter A), Congress had divested the President of authority to conclude such an agreement. The Court upheld the President's authority to conclude the agreement, in large part because Congress had long accepted and had repeatedly acquiesced in the power of the President to make such agreements. It also found that the Foreign Sovereign Immunities Act did not purport to prohibit the President.

## 5. U.N. Charter
see http://www.un.org/en/documents/charter/

## 6. Bibliography of Additional Sources

- Lyonette Louis-Jacques and Jeanne S. Korman, INTRODUCTION TO INTERNATIONAL ORGANIZATIONS (1996).

- Guide to the United States and the United Nations, United States. Dept. of State (1999).

- Benedetto Conforti, THE LAW AND PRACTICE OF THE UNITED NATIONS (2000).

- Anne-Marie Slaughter Burley, International Law and International Relations Theory: A Dual Agenda, 87 THE AMERICAN JOURNAL INTERNATIONAL LAW 205 (1993).

- Richard A. Falk & Wolfram F. Hanrieder (eds.), INTRODUCTION TO INTERNATIONAL LAW AND ORGANIZATIONS (1968).

- Richard A. Falk, THE RELEVANCE OF POLITICAL CONTEXT TO THE NATURE AND FUNCTIONING OF INTERNATIONAL LAW: AN INTERMEDIATE VIEW IN THE RELEVANCE OF INTERNATIONAL LAW (Karl W. Deutsch & Stanley Hoffmann, eds., 1968).

- Peter Hajnal, Academic Council on the United Nations System, Directory of United Nations Documentary and Archival Sources (1991) (introduction to the documentation system of the United Nations and basic bibliographic tools. Extensive annotated bibliography of major publications within the United Nations system of organizations).

- Edward C. Luck, MIXED MESSAGES: AMERICAN POLITICS AND INTERNATIONAL ORGANIZATIONS, 1919–1999 (1999).

- Kumiko Matsuura (ed.), CHRONOLOGY AND FACT BOOK OF THE UNITED NATIONS (8th ed., 1992).

- Stanley Meisler, UNITED NATIONS: THE FIRST FIFTY YEARS (1995).

- Daniel Patrick Moynihan, INTERNATIONAL LAW, FOREIGN POLICY, AND THE REAGAN YEARS: A REVIEW OF THE LAW OF NATIONS (1991).

- M.J. Peterson, THE GENERAL ASSEMBLY IN WORLD POLITICS (1988).

- Ellen G. Schaffer and Randall J. Snyder, CONTEMPORARY PRACTICE OF PUBLIC INTERNATIONAL LAW (1997).

- U.N. Department of Public Information, Basic Facts About the United Nations (1947).
- U.N., A Guide to Information at the United Nations (1995) (guide to the activities and publications of each of the principal organizations and bodies within the United Nations system. Each organizational entry describes the following: mandates; major programs; recent expenditures; publications and information contacts).
- Wellington, Ministry of External Relations and Trade, United Nations Handbook (1976) (list of U.N. organs, agencies, specialized agencies, regional development banks. Descriptions include functions, structure, current membership and activities).
- American Society of International Law, Reports and other Documents, United Nations: United Nations Decade of International Law (Report of the Secretary-General), 39 INT'L LEGAL MATERIALS 966 n.4 (2000).
- American Society of International Law, Reports and other Documents, United Nations: Group of High Level Intergovernmental Experts to Review the Efficiency of The Administrative and Financial Functioning of the U.N. — Report, 26 INT'L LEGAL MATERIALS 145 n.1 (1987).
- American Society of International Law, Reports and other Documents, United Nations: General Assembly Resolution on Restructuring the Economic and Social Sectors of the U.N. System, 17 INT'L LEGAL MATERIALS 235 n.1 (1978).
- Lori F. Damrosch, "Sovereignty" and International Organizations, 3 U.C. DAVIS J. INT'L L. & POL'Y 159 (1997).
- David P. Fidler, A Symposium on Reenvisioning the Security Council, Caught Between Traditions: The Security Council in Philosophical Conundrum, 17 MICH. J. INT'L L. 411 (1996).
- James E. Hickey, Jr., The Source of International Legal Personality in the 21st Century, 2 Hofstra L. & Pol'y Symp. 1 (1997).
- Erwin C. Surrency, Is a Universal Collection of Treaties Feasible? 90 LAW LIBR. J. 77 (1998).
- Mala Tabory, Recent Developments in United Nations Treaty Registration and Publication Practices, 76 AM. J. INT'L L. 350 (1982).
- Charles Tiefer, Adjusting Sovereignty: Contemporary Congressional-Executive Controversies About International Organizations, 35 TEX. INT'L L.J. 239 (2000).

# Part II
# Membership and Legal Status

# Chapter II

# U.N. Membership: Admission and Credentials Challenge

## Introduction

This chapter investigates the requirements for membership in the United Nations and the substantive and procedural law governing the seating of representatives of a member state. It introduces the reader to the role and functions of the Credentials Committee and explores some of the more controversial credential challenges that have arisen in the United Nations system. As a prerequisite to this discussion, this chapter will begin by examining the concept of statehood for the purposes of international legal recognition and for U.N. membership.

## Objectives

- To understand the criteria for United Nations membership.
- To understand the four main criteria of statehood and how they relate to each other.
- To understand the complex relationship between U.N. membership and recognition of states under international law.
- To understand the process for challenging the credentials of a member state.
- To evaluate the U.S. position with respect to credentials challenges.
- To debate whether one member state may challenge the credentials of another member state.

## Problems

Students should come to class prepared to discuss the following questions:

1. What is a "state" for purposes of membership in the United Nations?
2. Must states have a minimum population or territory?
3. Can states such as Liechtenstein, Monaco, and the Marshall Islands, which have given other States control over their foreign policy, be members?

4.  Is Palestine a state?

5.  Why is China represented by the People's Republic of China and not Taiwan in the United Nations? Is Taiwan a state?

6.  By what means was South Africa barred from participating in the United Nations from 1974–1994?

7.  Why do member states generally discourage credentials challenges?

# Case Studies and Negotiation Simulations

Drawing from the materials in this chapter, students should come to class prepared to participate in the following case studies:

**Negotiation Simulation: U.N. Credentials Committee**

**Cyprus:** The 1960 Constitution of Cyprus, adopted upon gaining independence from the United Kingdom, apportioned power in the national government between the Greek Cypriot and Turkish Cypriot communities, according to their relative populations (70% Greek, 30% Turkish). In 1964, however, the Turkish Cypriots withdrew from the government, and civil war erupted. Subsequently, the island of Cyprus was divided into two semi-independent states. After Cyprus was recently given membership in the European Union (EU), the Turkish Cypriots relinquished their claims to independence and sought proportionate representation in the institutions and bodies of the national government pursuant to the 1960 Constitution. When the Greek Cypriots insisted on a majority take-all approach in violation of the power-sharing provisions of the 1960 Constitution, the Turkish Cypriots sent a note to the U.N. Secretary-General, challenging the credentials of the all-Greek U.N. delegation of Cyprus.

**Burma:** Burma has been under military rule almost exclusively since it gained independence from Britain in 1948. In 1988, a military junta deposed self-appointed President Ne Win, and held general parliamentary elections in 1990. In the election, the junta's main political opposition, the National League for Democracy (NLD) won a landslide victory with eighty percent of the seats in Parliament. The junta refused to hand over power, however, and many of the NLD members elected to Parliament were either arrested or went into exile. A number of those (from both the NLD and other parties opposed to the junta) elected in the 1990 elections then formed the Members of Parliament Union (MPU) in 1996. The MPU meets outside of Burma and holds no territory, although it has some support from Burmese rebel groups who hold substantial amounts of territory in Burma's border regions. On September 8, 2008, the Vice President of the MPU, Daw San San, sent a letter to the Secretary-General of the United Nations, effectively challenging the credentials of the delegation representing the ruling military junta.

# Materials

1.  U.N. Charter, Arts. 3–5.

2.  Montevideo Convention on the Rights and Duties of States, Dec. 26, 1933, 165 I.N.T.S. 19.

3. Restatement (Third) of Foreign Relations Law §§ 201–2, 222 (1987).

4. Letter from Burmese Members of Parliament Union to Ban Ki-Moon (Sept. 8, 2008).

5. U.N. Gen. Assembly, Rules of Procedure of the General Assembly ch. IV, §§ 27–9, U.N. Doc. A/520/Rev.17, (2008).

6. U.N. General Assembly, *Credentials Committee.*

7. Senate Committee on Foreign Relations Report: Credentials Considerations in the United Nations General Assembly (1983).

8. S.C. Res. 919, U.N. Doc. S/RES/919 (May 25, 1994).

9. Bibliography of Additional Sources

# 1. U.N. Charter, Articles 3, 4, 5

## Chapter 2: Membership

### Article 3

The original Members of the United Nations shall be the states which, having participated in the United Nations Conference on International Organization at San Francisco, or having previously signed the Declaration by United Nations of 1 January 1942, sign the present Charter and ratify it in accordance with Article 110.

### Article 4

1. Membership in the United Nations is open to all other peace-loving states which accept the obligations contained in the present Charter and, in the judgment of the Organization, are able and willing to carry out these obligations.

2. The admission of any such state to membership in the United Nations will be effected by a decision of the General Assembly upon the recommendation of the Security Council.

### Article 5

A Member of the United Nations against which preventive or enforcement action has been taken by the Security Council may be suspended from the exercise of the rights and privileges of membership by the General Assembly upon the recommendation of the Security Council. The exercise of these rights and privileges may be restored by the Security Council.

## *Authors' Note*

Chapter 2 of the U.N. Charter establishes the basic requirements for membership in the U.N., but does not define the term "state." It does not address whether statehood is achieved for the purposes of U.N. membership when other states recognize an entity as a state or when an entity meets a set of predetermined criteria. Under the declaratory theory of statehood, an entity achieves legal statehood when it meets a set of predetermined criteria, regardless of whether it has been recognized by other states as such. This theory is known as the "declaratory" theory of statehood because the recognition of other states is merely a declaration, and does not, in itself, confer legal statehood. Under the constitutive theory, however, the recognition of an entity's statehood is itself the source of the state's legal status. Both theories ultimately rely on a determination of the international community—whether the entity meets the criteria of statehood or whether the community wishes recognize the state—and most states tend to rely on the generally accepted criteria of statehood.

The materials that follow discuss this concept of legal "statehood" under international law as a prerequisite to being a U.N. Member State. The Montevideo Convention on the Rights and Duties is one of the earliest clear statements of consensus on the criteria for statehood. The Restatement discusses more in depth the declaratory versus constitutive theories of statehood.

# 2. Montevideo Convention on the Rights and Duties of States
## 1933

**Convention on Rights and Duties of States**

The Governments represented in the Seventh International Conference of American States:

Wishing to conclude a Convention on Rights and Duties of States, have appointed the following Plenipotentiaries:

\* \* \*

Who, after having exhibited their Full Powers, which were found to be in good and due order, have agreed upon the following:

### Article 1

The state as a person of international law should possess the following qualifications: (a) a permanent population; (b) a defined territory; (c) government; and (d) capacity to enter into relations with the other states.

### Article 2

The federal state shall constitute a sole person in the eyes of international law.

### Article 3

The political existence of the state is independent of recognition by the other states. Even before recognition the state has the right to defend its integrity and independence, to provide for its conservation and prosperity, and consequently to organize itself as it sees fit, to legislate upon its interests, administer its services, and to define the jurisdiction and competence of its courts.

The exercise of these rights has no other limitation than the exercise of the rights of other states according to international law.

### Article 4

States are juridically equal, enjoy the same rights, and have equal capacity in their exercise. The rights of each one do not depend upon the power which it possesses to assure its exercise, but upon the simple fact of its existence as a person under international law.

### Article 5

The fundamental rights of states are not susceptible of being affected in any manner whatsoever.

### Article 6

The recognition of a state merely signifies that the state which recognizes it accepts the personality of the other with all the rights and duties determined by international law. Recognition is unconditional and irrevocable.

## Article 7

The recognition of a state may be express or tacit. The latter results from any act which implies the intention of recognizing the new state.

## Article 8

No state has the right to intervene in the internal or external affairs of another.

## Article 9

The jurisdiction of states within the limits of national territory applies to all the inhabitants.

Nationals and foreigners are under the same protection of the law and the national authorities and the foreigners may not claim rights other or more extensive than those of the nationals.

## Article 10

The primary interest of states is the conservation of peace. Differences of any nature which arise between them should be settled by recognized pacific methods.

## Article 11

The contracting states definitely establish as the rule of their conduct the precise obligation not to recognize territorial acquisitions or special advantages which have been obtained by force whether this consists in the employment of arms, in threatening diplomatic representations, or in any other effective coercive measure. The territory of a state is inviolable and may not be the object of military occupation nor of other measures of force imposed by another state directly or indirectly or for any motive whatever even temporarily.

## Article 12

The present Convention shall not affect obligations previously entered into by the High Contracting Parties by virtue of international agreements.

## Article 13

The present Convention shall be ratified by the High Contracting Parties in conformity with their respective constitutional procedures. The Minister of Foreign Affairs of the Republic of Uruguay shall transmit authentic certified copies to the governments for the aforementioned purpose of ratification. The instrument of ratification shall be deposited in the archives of the Pan American Union in Washington, which shall notify the signatory governments of said deposit. Such notification shall be considered as an exchange of ratifications.

## Article 14

The present Convention will enter into force between the High Contracting Parties in the order in which they deposit their respective ratifications.

## Article 15

The present Convention shall remain in force indefinitely but may be denounced by means of one year's notice given to the Pan American Union, which shall transmit it to the other signatory governments. After the expiration of this period the Convention shall cease in its effects as regards the party which denounces but shall remain in effect for the remaining High Contracting Parties.

## Article 16

The present Convention shall be open for the adherence and accession of the States which are not signatories. The corresponding instruments shall be deposited in the archives of the Pan American Union which shall communicate them to the other High Contracting Parties.

In witness whereof, the following Plenipotentiaries have signed this Convention in Spanish, English, Portuguese and French and hereunto affix their respective seals in the city of Montevideo, Republic of Uruguay, this 26th day of December, 1933.

**Reservations**

\* \* \*

The Delegation of the United States, in voting "yes" on the final vote on this committee recommendation and proposal, makes the same reservation to the eleven articles of the project or proposal that the United States Delegation made to the first ten articles during the final vote in the full Commission, which reservation is in words as follows:

> "The policy and attitude of the United States Government toward every important phase of international relationships in this hemisphere could scarcely be made more clear and definite than they have been made by both word and action especially since March 4. I [Secretary of State Cordell Hull, chairman of U.S. delegation] have no disposition therefore to indulge in any repetition or rehearsal of these acts and utterances and shall not do so. Every observing person must by this time thoroughly understand that under the Roosevelt Administration the United States Government is as much opposed as any other government to interference with the freedom, the sovereignty, or other internal affairs or processes of the governments of other nations.

> "In addition to numerous acts and utterances in connection with the carrying out of these doctrines and policies, President Roosevelt, during recent weeks, gave out a public statement expressing his disposition to open negotiations with the Cuban Government for the purpose of dealing with the treaty which has existed since 1903. I feel safe in undertaking to say that under our support of the general principle of non-intervention as has been suggested, no government need fear any intervention on the part of the United States under the Roosevelt Administration. I think it unfortunate that during the brief period of this Conference there is apparently not time within which to prepare interpretations and definitions of these fundamental terms that are embraced in the report. Such definitions and interpretations would enable every government to proceed in a uniform way without any difference of opinion or of interpretations. I hope that at the earliest possible date such very important work will be done. In the meantime in case of differences of interpretations and also until they (the proposed doctrines and principles) can be worked out and codified for the common use of every government, I desire to say that the United States Government in all of its international associations and relationships and conduct will follow scrupulously the doctrines and policies which it has pursued since March 4 which are embodied in the different addresses of President Roosevelt since that time and in the recent peace address of myself on the 15th day of December before this Conference and in the law of nations as generally recognized and accepted".

The delegates of Brazil and Peru recorded the following private vote with regard to article 11: "That they accept the doctrine in principle but that they do not consider it codifiable because there are some countries which have not yet signed the Anti-War Pact of Rio de Janeiro 4 of which this doctrine is a part and therefore it does not yet constitute positive international law suitable for codification".

# 3. Third Restatement of the Foreign Relations Law, Sections 201, 202, 222

### 1987
### [internal citations omitted by editors]

## 201. State Defined

Under international law, a state is an entity that has a defined territory and a permanent population, under the control of its own government, and that engages in, or has the capacity to engage in, formal relations with other such entities.

### Comments & Illustrations

*a. Definition of state.*

While the definition in this section is generally accepted, each of its elements may present significant problems in unusual situations. In the absence of judicial or other means for authoritative and consistent determination, issues of statehood have been resolved by the practice of states reflecting political expediency as much as logical consistency. The definition in this section is well-established in international law; it is nearly identical to that in Article 1 of the Montevideo Convention on the Rights and Duties of States.

*b. Defined territory.*

An entity may satisfy the territorial requirement for statehood even if its boundaries have not been finally settled, if one or more of its boundaries are disputed, or if some of its territory is claimed by another state. An entity does not necessarily cease to be a state even if all of its territory has been occupied by a foreign power or if it has otherwise lost control of its territory temporarily.

*c. Permanent population.*

To be a state an entity must have a population that is significant and permanent. Antarctica, for example, would not now qualify as a state even if it satisfied the other requirements of this section. An entity that has a significant number of permanent inhabitants in its territory satisfies the requirement even if large numbers of nomads move in and out of the territory.

*d. Government.*

A state need not have any particular form of government, but there must be some authority exercising governmental functions and able to represent the entity in international relations.

*e. Capacity to conduct international relations.*

An entity is not a state unless it has competence, within its own constitutional system, to conduct international relations with other states, as well as the political, technical, and financial capabilities to do so. An entity that has the capacity to conduct foreign relations does not cease to be a state because it voluntarily turns over to another state control of its foreign relations, as in the "protectorates" of the period of colonialism, the case of Liechtenstein, or the "associated states" of today. States do not cease to be states because they have agreed not to engage in certain international activities or have delegated authority to do so to a "*supra*national" entity, e.g., the European Communities. Clearly, a state does not cease to be a state if it joins a common market.

*f. Claiming statehood.*

While the traditional definition does not formally require it, an entity is not a state if it does not claim to be a state. For example, Taiwan might satisfy the elements of the definition in this section, but its authorities have not claimed it to be a state, but rather part of the state of China.

*g. States of the United States.*

A State of the United States is not a state under international law since under the Constitution of the United States foreign relations are the exclusive responsibility of the Federal Government. A State may not make treaties (Article I, section 10) or otherwise engage in or intrude upon foreign relations to any substantial extent.

*h. Determination of statehood.*

Whether an entity satisfies the requirements for statehood is ordinarily determined by other states when they decide whether to treat that entity as a state. Ordinarily, a new state is formally recognized by other states, but a decision to treat an entity as a state may be manifested in other ways. Since membership in the principal international organizations is constitutionally open only to states, admission to membership in an international organization such as the United Nations is an acknowledgment by the organization, and by those members who vote for admission, that the entity has satisfied the requirements of statehood.

**Reporters' Notes**

*1. Defined territory.*

The requirement of a defined territory does not deny statehood to entities that at their creation were involved in substantial controversies about their boundaries—e.g., Israel in 1948; Kuwait in 1963; Estonia, Latvia, and Albania, in 1919.

*2. Government.*

Some entities have been assumed to be states when they could satisfy only a very loose standard for having an effective government, e.g., the Congo (Zaire) in 1960. A state may continue to be regarded as such even though, due to insurrection or other difficulties, its internal affairs become anarchic for an extended period of time.

*3. Military occupation.*

Military occupation, whether during war or after an armistice, does not terminate statehood, e.g., Germany's occupation of European states during World War II, or the allies' occupation of Germany and Japan after that war. An entity's statehood would be terminated if all of its territory were lawfully annexed, but not where annexation is in violation of the United Nations Charter. Compare the policy of the United States in the case of Estonia, Latvia, and Lithuania, occupied and annexed before the United Nations Charter was adopted.

*4. Assignment of control over foreign relations.*

In the past, one state sometimes turned over to another some or all control of its foreign relations, retaining the right to reassert such control. Some such arrangements persist, largely for reasons of convenience and economy, e.g., Liechtenstein. Liechtenstein was admitted as a party to the Statute of the International Court of Justice for which only states are eligible, and its capacity to participate in the Nottebohm Case was not contested.

Relationships characterized as "protectorate," "suzerainty," etc., were characteristic of the French and British empires. Most such arrangements were terminated during the period of decolonization after World War II.

Since World War II there have been United Nations trusteeships and "associated territories" that have not had full control over their foreign relations.

*5. Independence.*

Some writers add independence to the criteria required for statehood. Compare the Austro-German Customs Union case, in which the court advised that a proposed customs union violated Austria's obligation under the Treaty of St. Germain to retain its independence.

*6. The European Community.*

"The European Community," or "The European Communities," are sometimes used to refer collectively to the European Economic Community (EEC), the European Coal and Steel Community (ECSC), and the European Atomic Energy Community (EURATOM). The creation of the European Community did not terminate the statehood of its constituent members, although the Community assumed international responsibility for a number of matters previously in the control of the individual states. The Community is not a state, but it has become party to some international agreements in its own right, e.g., the EEC is a party to the Wheat Trade Convention of 1971.

*7. The Vatican and the Holy See.*

The Vatican (an entity whose territory is surrounded by Italy) is generally accepted as a state, and the Holy See (the central administration of the Catholic Church) as its government. Nearly 90 states maintain diplomatic relations with the Vatican, and the Vatican (or the Holy See) is a party to many international agreements on subjects ranging from arbitration to nuclear nonproliferation. The Vatican is a member of several international organizations open only to states. On the other hand, it has the smallest population (less than 1000) of any entity claiming to be a state, and Italy performs for it many of the functions normally assumed by states.

*8. Taiwan.*

After the Second World War Japan renounced claims to Taiwan (Formosa). Both the regime governing Taiwan and the regime governing the mainland of China have claimed Taiwan as part of China, and other states have either confirmed or acquiesced in that claim. The Nationalist authorities on Taiwan continued to claim Taiwan was part of China (and that they were the government of China), even after the regime in Peking was generally recognized as the government of China. As of 1986, since the authorities on Taiwan do not claim that Taiwan is a state of which they are the government, the issue of its statehood has not arisen. If Taiwan should claim statehood, it would in effect be purporting to secede from China.

*9. States of the United States.*

Under the United States Constitution, a State of the United States may make compacts or agreements with a foreign power with the consent of Congress (Article I, Section 10, clause 2), but such agreements are limited in scope and subject matter. In international terms, a State makes such agreements by permission of the United States. A State may make some agreements with foreign governments without the consent of Congress so long as they do not impinge upon the authority or the foreign relations of the United States. A State cannot exchange ambassadors and engage generally in relations with a foreign government, but States send commercial representatives to other countries.

Foreign compacts or agreements made by States with the consent of Congress might be international agreements under Part III of this Restatement.

*10. United States territories.*

The United States conducts foreign relations for various territories linked to it by special arrangements which allow these entities substantially more authority in international matters than States have under the Constitution. Puerto Rico has been permitted by Act of Congress to become a member of regional institutions such as the Caribbean Development Bank.

## 202. Recognition or Acceptance of States

(1) A state is not required to accord formal recognition to any other state but is required to treat as a state an entity meeting the requirements of § 201, except as provided in Subsection (2).

(2) A state has an obligation not to recognize or treat as a state an entity that has attained the qualifications for statehood as a result of a threat or use of armed force in violation of the United Nations Charter.

### Comments & Illustrations

*a. Recognition or treatment as state.*

Recognition of statehood is a formal acknowledgment by another state that an entity possesses the qualifications for statehood as set forth in § 201, and implies a commitment to treat that entity as a state. States may recognize an entity's statehood by formal declaration or by recognizing its government, but states often treat a qualified entity as a state without any formal act of recognition.

*b. Statehood not dependent on recognition.*

An entity that satisfies the requirements of § 201 is a state whether or not its statehood is formally recognized by other states. As a practical matter, however, an entity will fully enjoy the status and benefits of statehood only if a significant number of other states consider it to be a state and treat it as such, in bilateral relations or by admitting it to major international organizations.

*c. Treating an entity as a state.*

The requirement that other states accept a qualified entity and treat it as a state implies that they have duties under international law toward that entity like those owed to states formally recognized. These include the duty to respect its territorial sovereignty and its property; to accept its right to grant nationality to persons and vessels and to assume the responsibility flowing there from under international law; and to fulfill other obligations that states owe to other states generally under international law. However, states need not accord to such an entity the prerogatives commonly accorded to a recognized state, such as the right to own property and carry on activities in their territory and to sue in their courts, or to have full effect given to its laws, decrees, and judgments.

The obligation not to treat an entity as a state under Subsection (2) includes a duty not to exchange diplomatic representatives with its government or to vote for that entity's membership in international organizations, and perhaps a duty not to recognize its claims to state property abroad. It does not prevent states from recognizing the validity of some of that entity's actions affecting private rights.

*d. Withholding recognition because of doubt as to viability.*

Even when an entity appears to satisfy the requirements of § 201, other states may refuse to treat it as a state when circumstances warrant doubt that it will continue to satisfy the requirements of statehood — for example, where the new entity is attempting to secede from another state which continues to resist the secession. In such circumstances, refusing to treat it as a state may be not only justified but required, since premature acceptance is a violation of the territorial integrity of the state theretofore in control of that territory.

*e. Establishing or eliminating a state in violation of international law.*

International law forbids treating as a state an entity that was created by threat or use of force by one state upon another in violation of the United Nations Charter. The United Nations Security Council, acting within its mandatory authority, may impose upon member states an obligation not to treat an entity as a state, as it did in respect of Rhodesia under the Smith regime (1965–1980) before the establishment of the state of Zimbabwe. Similarly, states are obligated not to recognize or accept the incorporation of a state into another state as a result of conquest in violation of the Charter.

A determination by the Security Council that there had been a threat or use of force in violation of the Charter is binding on all members of the United Nations. In the absence of such an authoritative determination by the Security Council, states are guided by their own determinations as to whether the Charter has been violated and, in time, are more likely to accept a fait accompli. A mandatory decision by the Security Council under Chapter VII that an entity shall not be recognized as a state, as was taken in the case of Rhodesia, is binding on all United Nations members under Article 25 of the Charter.

*f. Unlawful recognition or acceptance.*

Treating an unqualified entity as a state will ordinarily affect the interests of another state. For example, accepting as a state an entity that seeks to secede from another state, but has not yet succeeded in achieving complete control of its territory, is an improper interference in the internal affairs of the parent state, and if the seceding entity is given military support, may constitute the threat or use of force against the territorial integrity of the parent state in violation of Article 2(4) of the United Nations Charter. Treating as a state an entity that has achieved the qualifications for statehood as a result of the use of force in violation of the United Nations Charter affects adversely the interests of the state that was the victim of that use of force. In some circumstances such an action may itself be a violation of the Charter, for example, if accepting the entity as a state is inconsistent with measures adopted by the United Nations Security Council.

*g. Derecognition of a state.*

The duty to treat a qualified entity as a state also implies that so long as the entity continues to meet those qualifications its statehood may not be "derecognized." If the entity ceases to meet those requirements, it ceases to be a state and derecognition is not necessary. Ordinarily, that occurs when a state is incorporated into another state, as when Montenegro in 1919 became a part of the Kingdom of Serbs, Croats, and Slovenes (later Yugoslavia).

**Reporters' Notes**

*1. Statehood and recognition.*

The literature of international law reflects disagreement as to the significance of the recognition of statehood. Under the "declaratory" theory, an entity that satisfies the requirements of §201 is a state with all the corresponding capacities, rights, and duties, and other states have the duty to treat it as such. Recognition by other states is merely "declaratory," confirming that the entity is a state, and expressing the intent to treat it as a state. Another view has been that recognition by other states is "constitutive," i.e., that an entity is not a state in international law unless it is generally recognized as such by other states. Some writers, such as Lauterpacht, Recognition in International Law (1947), while adopting the "constitutive" theory, argued that states had an obligation to recognize an entity that met the qualifications set forth in § 201.

This section tends towards the declaratory view, but the practical differences between the two theories have grown smaller. Even for the declaratory theory, whether an entity satisfies the requirements for statehood is, as a practical matter, determined by other states. On the other hand, the constitutive theory lost much of its significance when it was accepted that states had the obligation to treat as a state any entity having the characteristics set forth in § 201. Delays in recognizing or accepting statehood have generally reflected uncertainty as to the viability of the new state or the view that it was created in violation of international law, in which case there is a duty not to recognize or accept the entity's statehood.

That an entity meeting the requirements for statehood must be treated as a state "independent of recognition" by other states, is affirmed by such agreements as the Inter-American Convention on Rights and Duties of States, and the Charter of the Organization of American States, as amended by the Protocol of Amendment in 1967.

In the past, when a state treated an entity as a state without formal recognition it was sometimes said to be extending *de facto* as opposed to *de jure* recognition. Those terms, used with varying and uncertain meaning, are avoided in this Restatement.

*2. Determining qualifications for statehood.*

While the grant or denial of formal recognition is a political act within the discretion of governments (and usually of their executive branches), whether an entity meets the qualifications of § 201 and is entitled to be treated as a state is an objective question, though it is often difficult to determine the relevant facts. In theory, those questions might be subject to judicial determination by international or national tribunals. National courts generally defer to the executive as to whether an entity is a state. An international tribunal might be called upon to decide whether a foreign entity was entitled to treatment as a state, as where the entity had purported to become a party to an international agreement containing a submission to international adjudication or arbitration and other parties refused to concede its statehood. However, no such decision has been found.

*3. Treating an entity as a state.*

For the implications of the obligation to treat an entity as a state see Mugerwa, "Subjects of International Law" in Sorensen ed., Manuel of Public International Law 269 (1968). Compare, for example, the history of relations between the United States and North Korea. The Korean War was terminated in 1953 by an armistice agreement signed by representatives of the United States, which held the unified command of the United Nations forces, and by the communist regimes in China and North Korea, although the United States did not recognize or accept a state of North Korea, and did not recognize or accept either communist regime as the government of any state. In 1968, without having recognized North Korea, the United States asserted that North Korea had violated international law in attacking a United States vessel, The Pueblo, [ ... ].

*4. Withholding recognition because of doubt as to viability as state.*

Especially in circumstances of secession followed by civil war, a long time may elapse before it becomes clear whether a new state has been established. Premature recognition or acceptance of statehood is itself a violation of the rights of the "parent" state, and, if accompanied by armed support for the rebels, would constitute the use of force against the territorial integrity of the parent state contrary to Article 2(4) of the United Nations Charter. Most states refrained from recognizing the secession of Biafra from Nigeria in

1967–70. During the years of decolonization, however, there were numerous instances in which many states recognized the independence of a territory as a new state, such as Algeria or Guinea Bissau, while the troops of the colonial power still seemed in firm control of the territory.

*5. Acquiring characteristics of statehood through violation of United Nations Charter.*

An entity might acquire the characteristics of statehood (§ 201) unlawfully, if its territory is detached from that of another state and its independence is achieved as a result of the use of force by other states in violation of Article 2(4) of the United Nations Charter.

Whether there has been an unlawful threat or use of force, however, may be disputed. The number of entities acquiring the characteristics of statehood allegedly through violation of law has not been large. Some states, particularly after a lapse of time, have been willing to accept a fait accompli. On a few occasions, the United Nations Security Council, or perhaps the General Assembly, might resolve the question. Compare the resolutions declaring North Korea and China aggressors against the Republic of Korea. In most instances, the issue is not subject to authoritative determination. For example, many governments judged India's intervention in Bangladesh to be a violation of the Charter, but contrary arguments were made, justifying India's use of force as in support of self-determination or as humanitarian intervention. States generally recognized or treated Bangladesh as a state, and Bangladesh was admitted to the United Nations. In principle, an entity that has acquired statehood unlawfully is ineligible for admission to an organization open only to states.

"The unilateral declaration of independence by the racist minority in Southern Rhodesia" was condemned by Security Council Resolutions Nos. 216 and 217 of November 12 and 20, 1965, which called upon "all states not to recognize this illegal authority." Compare the Security Council resolutions that forbade recognition of the legitimacy of continued occupation of Namibia by the Republic of South Africa, which were accepted as binding on the United States.

Issues implicating statehood sometimes arise when a state has lost all or a large part of its territory to conquest by another state. International law requires states not to recognize or accept a "territorial acquisition resulting from the threat or use of force." Declaration on Principles of International Law Concerning Friendly Relations and Co-operation among States in Accordance with the Charter of the United Nations. That principle has been universally accepted as regards territory conquered by use of force in violation of the United Nations Charter. It is disputed, however, as to territory acquired by force which was not unlawful, for example, if a victim of aggression, acting in self-defense in accordance with Article 51 of the Charter, conquers territory of the aggressor and proceeds to annex it. That exception might weaken the principle, especially since often neither the facts of an international dispute, nor the lawfulness of a use of force in the circumstances, are subject to reliable and authoritative international determination. It remains to be seen, moreover, whether states will persist in refusing to recognize or to accept territorial conquest after many years elapse.

*6. Contemporary issues of statehood for the United States.*

As of January 1, 1987, the United States faced only a few situations raising questions of statehood, most of the post-World War II issues having been resolved.

*Transkei.*

Like most other states, the United States does not recognize or accept the Transkei as a state, in accordance with a General Assembly resolution denouncing the creation of that entity as a "sham" and a device furthering apartheid in South Africa.

*Zimbabwe-Rhodesia.*

After a long period during which the Smith regime was not recognized, Reporters' Note 5, the state of Zimbabwe was established in 1979–80 and is now generally accepted.

*Namibia (Southwest Africa).*

In accordance with United Nations resolutions and with the advisory opinion in Legal Consequences for States of the Continued Presence of South Africa in Namibia, the United States does not recognize the legitimacy of South African control over this former mandate territory. See the United States statement in connection with G.A. Res. 34/92, which requested the admission of Namibia (as represented by the United Nations Council for Namibia) to specialized agencies and international conferences.

*Estonia, Latvia, and Lithuania.*

The Baltic States were conquered before World War II, but "[t]he United States has not recognized the incorporation of Estonia, Latvia and Lithuania into the Union of Soviet Socialist Republics. The Department of State regards treaties between the United States and those countries as continuing in force." The United States still treats the consul general or charge d'affaires of these states as duly accredited; otherwise, this policy has had limited practical consequences.

*Ukraine and Byelorussia.*

These two entities were given separate memberships in the United Nations and are parties to certain other treaties, but they are not active in international relations separately from the Soviet Union and few other states treat them as states generally.

*Democratic People's Republic of Korea.*

North Korea increasingly maintains relations with other countries and is a party to international agreements and a member of some United Nations Specialized Agencies. The United States has not formally recognized the statehood of North Korea, but it has indicated that it "is prepared to move towards improved relations with North Korea." The United States has also indicated that it was "prepared to see North Korea enter the United Nations along with the Republic of Korea."

*Vietnam.*

It has been accepted that the separate Republic of Vietnam (South Vietnam) ceased to exist. The 1986 edition of Treaties in Force states that the status of agreements that were in force with the Republic of Vietnam (South Vietnam) was "under review." The United States had "begun discussions to explore the possibility of normalizing relations" with the People's Republic of Vietnam.

*The Palestinians.*

In the 1970's governments began to assert the right of the Palestinian people to self determination. Some governments have accepted the Palestine Liberation Organization (PLO) as the representative of the Palestinian people, and the PLO has been given observer status by the United Nations and some other organizations. The United States has not recognized or accepted any formal status for the PLO. There have been international calls for a "homeland" for the Palestinians, but it has not been claimed that a state of Palestine exists.

### 222. Membership in International Organizations

(1) The membership of an international organization consists of the states that are parties to its constitutive agreements, other states that become members in accordance with its provisions, and such other entities as may be provided for in the agreement.

(2) Questions as to succession to a state's membership or to its representation are determined by decision of the organization.

**Reporters' Notes**

*1. Membership in the United Nations.*

Article 4 of the Charter provides:

> 1. Membership in the United Nations is open to all other peace loving states which accept the obligations contained in the present Charter and, in the judgment of the Organization, are able and willing to carry out these obligations.

> 2. The admission of any such state to membership in the United Nations will be effected by a decision of the General Assembly upon the recommendation of the Security Council.

In an advisory opinion, the International Court of Justice said that a member could not make its consent to the admission of a state depend on conditions not provided in Article 4(1).

A Security Council recommendation of a state to the General Assembly for membership in the United Nations is subject to veto by a permanent member of the Council. At various times permanent members have exercised the veto against the applications of Italy, Finland, Mongolia, the Republic of Korea, the Democratic Republic of Vietnam, the Provisional Revolutionary Government of South Vietnam, the Socialist Republic of Vietnam, Bangladesh, and Angola. The United States exercised its first veto in such a case in 1975 in the case of Vietnam.

The United Nations has admitted to membership "micro" or "ministates," with populations as small as 60,000 and budgets as small as $20,000,000 without questioning whether they are "able [ ... ] to carry out" the obligations of the Charter. Proposals to lighten the burden for mini-states through limited associate membership have not been adopted. Some specialized agencies, such as UNESCO and WHO, do have associate members. Liechtenstein was denied membership in the League of Nations on the ground that it was too small. It has not sought membership in the United Nations but is a party to the statute of the International Court of Justice.

*2. Admission of successor states as members.*

In recent practice, former colonies that became independent applied for admission to the United Nations and other organizations as new members. If a member state is absorbed by another state or enters into a federal union, its membership ordinarily lapses. Upon the breakup of a federal union, as in the case of the United Arab Republic in 1961, or when a state separates from a unitary state, as in the case of Pakistan and India in 1947, or Singapore and Malaysia in 1965, questions as to the membership of the successor states are decided by the organization. The difference between joining an organization as a new member and succeeding to the membership of an existing state can be significant. For example, a successor government assumes the obligations of its predecessor for expenses, and may inherit amounts standing to the predecessor's credit. A new member of the International Monetary Fund is assigned a quota, measuring its obligation to contribute to the Fund's resources and its right to draw on those resources.

*3. Withdrawal from membership.*

It is generally accepted that, unless otherwise provided in the charter of the organization, a state may withdraw at any time. Withdrawal from the United Nations is not dealt with in its Charter, but explicit provisions permitting withdrawal appear in the Convention on International Civil Aviation, and in the charters of the International Labour Organization and UNESCO. In 1965 Indonesia purported to withdraw from the United Nations but in 1966 "decided" to "resume full cooperation with the United Nations." The United Nations Office of Legal Affairs took the position that Indonesia had not withdrawn and hence did not have to be readmitted.

Article 5 of the United Nations Charter provides for suspension "from the exercise of the rights and privileges of membership," and Article 6 deals with expulsion. That authority has not been exercised, although the expulsion of South Africa has been discussed.

The United States withdrew from the International Labour Organization in 1978 and rejoined in 1980. Although the United States became a member pursuant to authorization by a joint resolution of Congress, and accepted an amendment to the ILO Charter by treaty, both the withdrawal and the rejoining were effected by Presidential action alone. Compare § 339, comment a.

The United States and the United Kingdom withdrew from UNESCO in 1985.

*4. Representation and credentials.*

The seating of representatives of a state in an international organization may be subject to provisions different from those applicable to admission of members. In the United Nations it has been accepted that the General Assembly decides which of two claimant delegations is the proper representative of a member. Thus, between 1949 and 1971 the Assembly seated the delegation of the regime on Taiwan (the Republic of China) as the representatives of China. However, in 1971, the Assembly decided that the representatives of the Beijing regime (the People's Republic of China) were the only lawful representatives of China and voted to "expel the representatives of Chiang Kai Shek." Other issues of representation arose from the Hungarian crisis of 1956, the troubles in the Congo in 1960, the Dominican crisis of 1965, and the fighting in Cambodia in 1973 and afterward. The practice seems difficult to reconcile with Articles 5 and 6 of the Charter, which require that the suspension or expulsion of a member be by the General Assembly on the recommendation of the Security Council, but the General Assembly has rejected credentials of representatives and refused to permit them to be seated, as a means of imposing a sanction on, or expressing disapproval of, that state. In 1970, the Assembly rejected the credentials of the representatives of South Africa because of its apartheid policy and its illegal occupation of Namibia. In 1974, the President of the General Assembly ruled that the rejection of their credentials meant that the representatives of South Africa could not participate in the General Assembly. The United States voted against these actions on the ground that they were illegal. With United States support, the Organization of American States in 1962 denied the privilege of participation to the representatives of the Cuban government.

## Authors' Note

The practice of the Credentials Committee has generally been to accept credentials that are submitted in accordance with the technical requirements of the Rules of Procedure. However, during the 1990s, the U.N. General Assembly approved the credentials of the delegations of five governments that did not have actual control over the state they represented, denying the credentials submitted by the delegations representing the governments in physical control of the states. The states involved were Haiti, Sierra Leone, Cambodia, Liberia, and Afghanistan.

A number of scholars have noted that these decisions departed markedly from the Credentials Committee's practice during the Cold War of playing a strictly technical role. The decision to accredit the delegations from the governments perceived as more democratic in these states signified increased consensus among Member States on the promotion of democracy and less concern with the technical credentialing practice of previous decades. Subsequent challenges testing political influence on the Credentials Committee, including the challenges by the Burmese MPU and Palestinian authorities, have been denied since 2000, leaving room for debate as to whether the pro-democracy decisions of the Credentials Committee in the 1990s will continue. As you read the following materials regarding the procedure and function of the Credentials Committee, consider the arguments for both the "technical" and the "political" role of the Credentials Committee.

## 4. Letter from Burmese Members of Parliament Union
### 2008

H.E Mr. Ban Ki-Moon
Secretary-General of the United Nations
Office of the Secretary-General
885 Second Avenue
New York, N.Y. 10017
U.S.A.

H.E. Mr. Ban Ki-Moon

Whereas the legitimate, democratically elected leaders of the Burmese people, organized in the Members of Parliament Union, have set up at the seat of the United Nations a permanent mission to maintain necessary contact with the Secretariat of the Organization,

Now therefore I, Daw San San, Vice President, Members of Parliament Union, have appointed and by these presents do confirm as Permanent Representative to the United Nations His Excellency U Thein Oo, elected representative of Mandalay Constituent, Southwest Constituency 2.

His Excellency U Thein Oo is instructed to represent the people of Burma and the legitimate, democratically elected Members of Parliament in all organs of the United Nations. He is also authorized to designated a substitute to act temporarily on his behalf after due notice to Secretary-General.

In faith whereof I have signed these presents on 8 September 2008.

Daw San San
Vice President
Signing on Behalf of the President
Members of Parliament Union

## 5. Rules of Procedure, Rules 27–29
### United Nations General Assembly, 2008

**IV. Credentials**

**Submission of Credentials**

**Rule 27**

The credentials of representatives and the names of the member of a delegation shall be submitted to the Secretary-General if possible not less than one week before the opening of the session. The credentials shall be issued either by the Head of the State or Government or by the Minister for Foreign Affairs.

### Credentials Committee

### Rule 28

A Credentials Committee shall be appointed at the beginning of each session. It shall consist of nine members, who shall be appointed by the General Assembly on the proposal of the President. The Committee shall elect its own officers. It shall examine the credentials of representatives and report without delay.

### Provisional Admission to a Session

### Rule 29

Any representative to whose admission a Member has made objection shall be seated provisionally with the same rights as the other representatives until the Credentials Committee has reported and the General Assembly has given its decision.

## 6. Credentials Committee Structure and Functions
### United Nations General Assembly

The credentials of representatives and the names of members of the delegation of each Member State are submitted to the Secretary-General and are issued either by the Head of the State or Government or by the Minister for Foreign Affairs (Rule 27 of the Rules of Procedure of the General Assembly).

A Credentials Committee is appointed at the beginning of each regular session of the General Assembly. It consists of nine members, who are appointed by the General Assembly on the proposal of the President.

The Committee is mandated to examine the credentials of representatives of Member States and to report to the General Assembly thereon (Rule 28 of the Rules of Procedure of the General Assembly). Special and emergency special sessions of the General Assembly as well as conferences convened under its auspices also appoint a Credentials Committee having the same composition as that of the Credentials Committee at its most recent regular session.

## 7. Senate Committee on Foreign Relations Report: Credentials Considerations in the United Nations General Assembly
### 1983

### I. Introduction

Efforts in 1982 to affect the participation of a United Nations member by rejecting the credentials of the General Assembly delegation of that member raised questions for some about the role of the Assembly's credentials process.

The Credentials Committee is supposed to examine and accept the credentials of delegations to the Assembly, assuring that they have been signed either by the Head of State or Government or by the Minister for Foreign Affairs of the member nation. The Assembly then considers and approves the report of the Committee. In this way, credentials of the majority of U.N. members have been routinely accepted for participation in each session of the General Assembly since it first convened in early 1946. However, some credentials have been challenged, usually to change the political status of the country or government involved or to promote the foreign policies of the challenging country.

This paper discusses the role of the credentials process in the U.N. General Assembly and provides information on the way these issues have been raised and resolved in the past. The eight cases presented are illustrative rather than exhaustive and are those normally cited by U.N. officials during U.N. debate and in the journal literature on U.N. General Assembly credentials matters.

Information on these cases might be set forth in a chart as shown below.

| SUMMARY OF DATA ON THE CASES | | | | |
|---|---|---|---|---|
| | Rival Claimants | Two Sets of Credentials | Change in Government | Committee/ Assembly Action on Challenge |
| China | Yes | Only in 1950 | Yes | Ruled out-of-order |
| Hungary | No | No | Yes | Took no decision, thereby accepting challenge |
| Congo | Yes | No | Yes/No | Rejected challenge |
| Yemen | No | No | Yes | No challenge; approved latest credentials received |
| Cambodia/ Khmer | Yes | No | No | Accepted challenge |
| South Africa | Yes | No | Yes | Rejected challenge |
| Israel | No | No | No | Rejected challenge in Assembly |

## II. The Credentials Process in the General Assembly

As each new session of the Assembly convenes, the 157 member nations submit to the U.N. Secretary-General credentials identifying the representatives and names of members of their delegations to that session of the Assembly. A nine-member Credentials Committee examines these credentials and reports its findings to the General Assembly which then adopts a resolution accepting the report of the Committee.

Rules 27, 28, and 29 of the General Assembly's Rules of Procedure govern the submission and consideration of credentials for delegations to the Assembly. No later than a week before a session convenes, the credentials are to be submitted to the Secretary-General. They should be issued either by the Head of State or Government or by the Minister for Foreign Affairs (Rule 27).

The Credentials Committee, appointed by the Assembly on recommendation of its President at the start of each session, "shall examine the credentials of representatives and report without delay." (Rule 28) While the membership of the Committee changes each year, since 1952 the United States and the Soviet Union have always been members of the

Credentials Committee. Since 1972, after the People's Republic of China took the seat of China in the United Nations, China has also always been a member of the Committee.

During the early history of the Assembly, the Committee met at two separate times during the session, considering credentials received in mid-fall initially and the rest of the credentials near the end of the session. During the 1960's and until 1974, the normal procedure of the Committee was to meet only once, during the last month before adjournment of the Assembly session, to review all credentials and report to the Assembly. Thus, challenges to credentials would be considered near the end of the Assembly session, giving a challenged delegation the opportunity to participate provisionally through most of the session (see Rule 29). In 1974, the Committee met a few days after being appointed at the start of the session and submitted its first report by the end of September. Since that time, the Committee has returned to its pre-1960s practice of meeting on two separate occasions during an Assembly session.

The Committee meets to receive and consider the Secretary-General's memorandum identifying credentials received in accordance with Rule 27 and to approve its report to the Assembly accepting those credentials. Members discuss specific cases and on occasion consider challenges to a delegation's credentials by the delegation of another state or in the form of credentials from a rival delegation from the same state. The Committee then almost always "accepts the credentials of the representatives of the Member States concerned" and recommends to the Assembly that it approve the report of the Credentials Committee. Between the years of 1946 and 1950, these reports were not published but presented orally by the chairman of the Committee to the Assembly. From the sixth session in 1951 through the present, the reports have been issued as documents of the Assembly.

Further challenges may be made during the Assembly's consideration of the Committee's report. After it votes on any proposed amendments to the report, the Assembly takes final action by approving the report of the Committee. This decision may be taken by a recorded vote (requested by any representative), a non-recorded vote (only the final tally, not the way each member votes, appears in official records of the vote), or by consensus. Throughout its history, the Assembly has normally approved the recommendations of the Credentials Committee.

### III. The Proper Role of the Credentials Process

On a number of occasions throughout the 37-year history of the Assembly, U.N. member states have discussed the role of the credentials process. Sometimes the debate found its way into the deliberations of the Credentials Committee but often the scene was the plenary meetings of the Assembly. The Committee's findings usually reflected the technical and legal process of approving the credentials received without comment on the nature of the governments issuing the credentials. The challenges on the basis of the latter factor would be made in the Assembly as amendments to the report of the Committee. In a few instances, the Committee's findings reflected the influence of discussions involving the substance of governments presenting credentials.

### Background

The first credentials challenge in the General Assembly came about in 1950 as a result of the takeover of the government of China by the People's Republic of China and the move of the Nationalist government to Taiwan. Each government presented credentials and the Nationalist delegation was challenged during the first meeting of the Assembly session in September 1950. At that time, the Assembly seated the delegation from the Nationalist Government (Assembly resolution 490 (V)), pending completion of the work of a special committee established by the same resolution to "consider the question of Chinese representation and to report back, with recommendations to the present session." The special committee did not present any recommendations to the Assembly during the session and the Nationalist Government remained in the seat of China.

Simultaneously, the 1950 session of the Assembly considered a separate agenda item on the "question of recognition by the United Nations of the representation of a Member State." This item referred not only to the question of credentials of delegations but also to the legality of the Assembly deciding which government should represent a member state. During the debate on this item, three standards were often cited as appropriate criteria for determining representation questions. They were:

(a) The extent to which the new authority exercises effective control over the territory of the member state concerned and is generally accepted by the population;

(b) The willingness of that authority to accept responsibility for the carrying out by the member state of its obligations under the Charter;

(c) The extent to which that authority has been established through internal processes in the member state.

The resolution adopted by the Assembly on December 14, 1950 (resolution 396 (V)) did not include these criteria but did recommend that:

Whenever more than one authority claims to be the government entitled to represent a Member State, in the United Nations and this question becomes the subject of controversy in the United Nations, the question should be considered in the light of the Purposes and Principles of the Charter and the circumstances of each case.

The resolution also recommended that the General Assembly consider any such question when it arises, and that the position adopted by the Assembly should be taken into account in other organs of the United Nations and in the specialized agencies.

From 1950 through 1971, when the Assembly finally decided the Chinese question in favor of the People's Republic of China, efforts to resolve it on the basis of credentials challenges were rebuffed on point of order in the Credentials Committee and the Assembly, following the recommendation of Resolution 396 (V), considered the question as a separate agenda item.

The next watershed for credentials questions came in the 1970's as steps were taken to affect the participation of South Africa in the U.N. General Assembly. In 1970, the U.N. Legal Council stated that participation in meetings of the General Assembly was one of the important rights and privileges of U.N. membership and that suspension of this right through rejection of credentials would be contrary to the Charter. However, the Assembly excluded South Africa from further participation in the Assembly in 1974 and has since then supported its decision on three occasions.

### A Technical or Political Process?

Since 1950, the Credentials Committee and, to a greater extent, the General Assembly, have debated the role of the credentials process as controversial credentials questions have arisen. Some countries maintain that the role of the committee and of the Assembly in this matter is purely legal and technical. They argue that neither body, and certainly not the committee, is authorized to judge the nature of the governments involved. "The validity of credentials must be objectively and impartially ascertained on technical and legal grounds alone, without consideration of a Government's political orientation or policies." Another nation argued that:

[r]ejecting the credentials of a delegation because the Government that issues them is illegitimate would be equivalent to affirming that all those whose credentials have been accepted are legitimate, and that is something which my delegation does not and would not wish to affirm.

Still another country pointed out that "It was not for the Committee to judge the 'morality of regimes." If it did, "many representatives would not be sitting among us."

On the other hand, some countries oppose this view of the credentials process as purely technical, arguing that the decision must address political problems. According to one nation:

Credentials bestow legitimacy on the representative and on the work that is being attended to. But who or what is the source of that legitimacy? It is the Government of the country being represented. And which is the Government that taking upon itself the issuing of credentials to its representatives? It is the Government that is in power in the country, that functions as its executive authority, that works as its legislative body.

Another nations' representative observed that "every past case has been a special case, that the solutions adopted by the General Assembly varied from case to case and that there are no common rules of universal applicability. That is why we say that this is a political problem going beyond the narrow framework of a technical issue...." He continued "... the technical validity of credentials is but one aspect of the question, and it is regrettable that the practice of the Committee does not allow it to submit information to the General Assembly that would enable it to take informed political decisions. If that were done it would remove the ambiguity that might lead to the belief that it is sufficient to submit credentials in the proper form to the Committee for them to be approved subsequently by the Assembly."

## U.S. Response

The U.S. response to most credentials issues has been to support the technical interpretation of the General Assembly Rules of Procedure. In addition, it has viewed as illegal any efforts to circumvent the provisions of the U.N. Charter requiring Security Council recommendation for suspension or expulsion from membership. As it became clear during the first quarter of 1982 that Arab States might try to affect Israel's participation in the U.N. system, the House and the Senate each passed a resolution expressing its concerns and outlining a response to any denial of Israel's right to participate in the General Assembly or in any U.N. agency. In addition, after the IAEA General Conference rejected Israel's credentials, Secretary of State George Shultz issued a strong statement of the U.S. position and the probable U.S. response if the ITU or the U.N. General Assembly took action affecting Israel's participation.

However, from 1956 through 1962, the United States took the position that the Credentials Committee should take no action on the credentials presented by the representatives of Hungary because that government had been established through military intervention by a foreign power whose forces remained in Hungary despite the Assembly's request that they withdraw. Since 1980, however, the United States has not taken the same position with respect to the credentials of the Afghanistan Government imposed and maintained by the Soviet Union although U.S. representatives have stated for the record during credentials debates that U.S. acceptance of the Afghan credentials in no way implies approval of that country's government.

## IV. Key Cases of Credentials Controversies

Eight cases are commonly cited in U.N. debates or journal articles as examples of instances when credentials of General Assembly delegations were not handled routinely.

While most credentials are accepted by the Committee and the Committee's report is generally approved by the Assembly, without debate, these eight cases are considered representative of the instances in which delegations' credentials have been challenged. These cases illustrate the primary reasons that lead to challenges, the ways in which these challenges have been resolved, and the factors that have influenced these decisions.

Of the eight selected cases, seven (Hungary, China, Congo, Cambodia, Kampuchea, South Africa, and Israel) involved challenges to credentials. The credentials of the Yemen delegation were not challenged. The Committee rejected challenges to credentials in five of these seven cases (China, Congo, Cambodia, Kampuchea, and Israel [consideration by the Assembly only]). Most of the five were rejected because acceptance of the challenge would "politicize" the credentials process; the result of the decisions in these cases was to support a technical/legal role for the credentials process. Only in the case of Kampuchea was the challenge rejected for political reasons — that is, because of the nature of the new government. In two cases, challenges to credentials were accepted; in both (Hungary and South Africa), political considerations about the nature of the government challenged overruled the technical/legal role of the credentials process. Overall, the credentials process was upheld as having only a technical/legal role in five of the eight selected cases.

A review of the cases discussed below illustrates that political considerations often initiate the situation; that is, credentials are challenged on the basis of a political disagreement or with a view toward changing the political status of a situation. If there is not enough political support for that challenge, then the credentials process is allowed to proceed as a technical one. However, if sufficient support can be gathered, decisions in Committee and in plenary can be based primarily on political, rather than on legal/technical, considerations.

One of the major factors leading to a credentials challenge is a change in government in a U.N. member nation. Six of the eight cases involved changes in government. These included changes brought about by external forces, by creation of a second government, or by internal revolution. In three cases (Hungary, Congo, and Cambodia), credentials submitted by the new government were challenged, and two of these challenges were rejected (Congo and Cambodia). The Committee decided to accept the challenge to Hungary's credentials, not by rejecting the credentials but by taking "no decision." The delegation participated in the Assembly on a provisional basis. Credentials from old (ousted) governments were challenged in two instances (China and Kampuchea) but the Committee repeatedly rejected challenges to the Kampuchean credentials. The Committee refused to consider Soviet challenges to the credentials of the Republic of China from 1950 through 1960.

The challenges to the credentials issued by South Africa and Israel were not based on changes in government but on the policies of the two governments. In the case of South Africa, the challenges were based on the government's continued adherence to the policy of apartheid that denied full participation of the entire population of the country in its government. Thus, the government signing the credentials was viewed as not representing all its people. Challenges to the Israeli credentials were based on the government's alleged violation of U.N. Security Council and General Assembly resolutions.

Among the factors likely to have an impact on Committee and Assembly decisions on these cases are the following — existence of a rival government; whether credentials of the challenged delegation had been accepted previously; whether credentials of the rival claimant had been submitted to the United Nations; the extent or depth of support for or against the challenge by the Group of 77, the United States, and/or the Soviet Union; and role of the President of the General Assembly.

## China

The question of Chinese representation in the United Nations, and more specifically in the U.N. General Assembly, arose in 1950 when the Secretary-General received two sets of credentials—one from the Nationalist Government that had moved to Taiwan in 1949 and one from the People's Republic of China. In 1950, the Assembly decided to seat the delegation of the Nationalist Government (ROC) provisionally while a special Assembly committee met to consider recommendations on the question of Chinese representation. This committee was not able to make a recommendation.

From 1951 through 1960, the Assembly's General Committee rejected Soviet efforts, required by the recommendation in Assembly resolution 396 (V), to place the question of Chinese representation on the Assembly's agenda as a separate item. Subsequent Soviet requests in the Credentials Committee to challenge the ROC credentials were ruled out of order, in view of Resolution 396 (V) and of the decision by each session of the Assembly to reject the question of Chinese representation as an agenda item. Thus, any consideration of proposals to exclude the Nationalist delegation and to seat representatives of the People's Republic of China was postponed.

In 1961, the Assembly included the representation question on its agenda for discussion for the first time. Ten years later, on October 25, 1971, the Assembly adopted a resolution recognizing the representatives of the People's Republic of China as the only lawful representatives of China to the United Nations and unseating the delegation of the Nationalist Government as the representative of China in the United Nations.

Throughout this 20-year period, the United States supported Nationalist Government participation in the United Nations, as it was brought up by the Soviet Union in the General Committee as a separate agenda item and in the Credentials Committee. The United States maintained that the PRC was not entitled to participate in the United Nations because it did not meet the criterion of being "peace-loving." The United States also opposed the expulsion of the Republic of China, arguing that that part of the resolution changing the representation of China would deny U.N. participation to a country of 13 million people, thus working against the principle of universality of membership for the United Nations. One of the options supported by United States officials in 1971 but not accepted by the U.N. General Assembly was dual representation; that is, a seat and a vote for each government.

## Hungary

As a result of the 1956 revolt in Hungary and the subsequent takeover by Soviet troops, the U.N. General Assembly met in two emergency special sessions. The U.N. Secretary-General was informed that members of the Hungarian mission to the United Nations had not yet been authorized to take part in the sessions. As the government changed hands (a Soviet-imposed government took over), doubts were expressed in the Assembly as to the validity of the credentials issued by the new government. The Credentials Committee agreed not to take any decision regarding the credentials of the representatives of Hungary at this time pending further clarification. The Assembly approved the report of the Credentials Committee on November 9, 1956.

In February 1957, during Credentials Committee consideration of credentials for the 11th regular session of the Assembly, the U.S. representative suggested that the "Committee take no decision regarding the credentials submitted on behalf of the representatives of Hungary," pointing out that the credentials had been issued by authorities established through military intervention by a foreign power whose forces remained in Hungary despite requests by the Assembly for their withdrawal. His motion was adopted and the Committee report was approved by the Assembly. This position was maintained by the United States and upheld in the Credentials Committee and by the Assembly from 1957 through 1962. However, during this time the Hungarian delegation was never excluded from participation in the Assembly. In 1963, the United States dropped its objection to the credentials of the Hungarian delegation.

## Congo

After the 15th session of the U.N. General Assembly admitted the Republic of the Congo (Leopoldville) to membership on September 20, 1960, it referred the matter of its delegation to the Credentials Committee. The controversy over the Congo delegation arose when the Chief of State President Kasavubu dismissed Prime Minister Lumumba and appointed a new government. Mr. Lumumba requested Parliament to dismiss Kasavubu but it refused. Then, Mr. Mobutu, appointed by President Kasavubu as Chief of the Army, announced formation of a third government which was accepted by Mr. Kasavubu. Proponents of Mr. Lumumba, including the Soviet Union which had provided assistance to him, challenged credentials submitted by Mr. Kasavubu but did not submit competing credentials.

On November 9, the Credentials Committee began consideration of the Congo credentials submitted the day before by Chief of State Kasavubu on behalf of the third government. It adopted a U.S. draft resolution recommending that the Assembly accept these credentials. The General Assembly adopted the report of the Credentials Committee the following week after a lengthy debate.

## Yemen

When the Credentials Committee met on December 20, 1962, the last day of the Assembly's 17th session, it found that more than one set of credentials for the delegation of Yemen had been received. On September 27, the Secretary-General received credentials signed by the Imam of Yemen and dated September 9; on December 10, the Secretary-General received credentials for the delegation of the Kingdom of Yemen dated December 7 and signed by the Minister for Foreign Affairs; and on December 17, the Secretary-General received credentials for the delegation of the Yemen Arab Republic signed by the President of the Republic and dated December 8.

The first two sets of credentials were submitted by the same government, the first from the Imam who died in September and the second from his son who replaced him. The last set of credentials was submitted by a "republican" government that had been established by revolutionary coup. Although Egypt aided the republican government with troops and other kinds of military assistance, many experts did not view the "republican" government as having been installed by troops of a foreign power or as the puppet of a foreign government. At the time of the considerations by the Credentials Committee and the Assembly, the ousted Imam had begun a counter-revolutionary drive to retake towns captured by republican government forces. However, the Committee judged at that time that the republican government was in effective control of the country and voted, 6 to 0, with 3 abstentions, to accept the credentials signed by the President of the Republic. The U.S. Government recognized the republican government on the same day that the Assembly adopted the Credentials Committee report accepting the credentials of the Yemen Arab Republic.

## Cambodia/ Khmer Republic (1973–1974)

The question of conflicting claims to Cambodian representation arose during the 1973 and 1974 regular Assembly sessions both as a separate agenda item and as a matter before the Credentials Committee. These considerations, however, were not successful. The government then representing Cambodia (renamed the Khmer Republic) was headed by Ion Nol, who took over the position of Head of State from Prince Norodom Sihanouk on March 18, 1970, while Sihanouk was out of the country. During the General Assembly session in 1970, the credentials of the Ion Nol government were accepted without objection.

In early September 1973, the Fourth Summit Conference of Non-Aligned Countries requested support for formal recognition of the Royal Government of National Union on Cambodia (GRUNK), under Prince Sihanouk, and its representation in the United Nations as Cambodia. A month later, 31 U.N. member states requested the inclusion on the Assembly agenda of an item, "Restoration of the lawful rights of the Royal Government of National Union of Cambodia in the United Nations." The General Committee and the Assembly approved inclusion of that item which was discussed in plenary meetings of the Assembly in December. A draft resolution under consideration would have recognized the representatives of GRUNK "as the sole legal representatives of Cambodia" in the United Nations and expelled the "representatives of the Ion Nol group." On December 5, the Assembly voted to adjourn debate and defer further discussion until its 1974 session.

On November 26, 1974, the General Assembly resumed consideration of the question of Khmer representation. In addition to the 1973 draft resolution, which had been re-submitted to the 1974 Assembly session, a resolution was submitted urging a peaceful settlement between the conflicting parties and providing that no other action take place until talks between the parties had occurred. By implication, this draft resolution supported occupation of the Assembly seat by the Khmer Republic representatives. The Assembly amended, then adopted, this second draft resolution without considering the first draft resolution. The adopted resolution included a preambular paragraph noting the authority of Prince Norodom Sihanouk over a segment of Cambodia but recognizing that the Government of the Khmer Republic "still has control over a preponderant number of Cambodian people."

The other forum for consideration of this issue was the Credentials Committee. When it met on December 11, 1973, the Committee did not accept a proposal that the credentials of the Khmer Republic be rejected on the grounds that GRUNK was the real representative of the Cambodian people. The U.S. representative argued that the credentials submitted y the Khmer Republic met the requirements of Rule 27 and that the role of the Committee was not to debate the political questions of representation. The Assembly rejected an amendment to the Credentials Committee report that would have allowed GRUNK to replace the Khmer Republic delegation.

Prince Sihanouk's supporters continued their efforts to unseat the Khmer Republic during a December 12, 1974 meeting of the Credentials Committee. The representative of Senegal proposed that the Committee take no action on the credentials of the Khmer Republic, arguing that the Assembly resolution of November 1974 urged that no further action be taken until the next session of the Assembly and that that resolution did not accord legitimacy to the Khmer Republic. The Senegalese representative proposed that the Committee not accept the credentials of either of the contending parties. The United States opposed that proposal, arguing that acceptance of the credentials of the Khmer

Republic would be in accordance with Rule 27 and that the November 1974 resolution should not be interpreted as extending to credentials matters. The Senegalese proposal was rejected by the Committee, which recommended acceptance of all the credentials then before it. On December 16, the Assembly defeated a proposal, submitted as an amendment to the Committee report, to reject the credentials of the Khmer Republic. The Khmer Republic delegation thus remained in the Assembly seat.

## South Africa

The November 12, 1974 action by the General Assembly in upholding a ruling of its President to exclude the delegation of South Africa from further participation in that session of the Assembly marked a dramatic departure from previous General Assembly actions on credentials. It was the first time the Assembly excluded a member from Assembly participation solely on the basis of improper credentials. In addition, this issue caused the Credentials Committee to meet within days after being appointed at the start of the session rather than waiting until the last month of the session, as had been its recent practice, to review credentials.

Background: Since the early years of the organization, members of the United Nations had expressed concern over the practice of apartheid by the Republic of South Africa and the extent to which this practice violated the human rights of the great majority of the population of the country. After the substantial increase in U.N. membership in 1960, especially of African states, statements of concern and demands for a change in conditions increased markedly. Members particularly expressed concern for the lack of political participation in the government by the black majority.

Pre-1974 Credentials Considerations: In 1965, the General Assembly adopted a resolution that, for the first time, took "no decision on the credentials submitted on behalf of the representatives of South Africa" (Assembly Resolution 2113 B (XX), December 21, 1965). This was similar to the language on Hungary in the Credentials Committee reports between 1956 and 1962. No efforts were made in the Credentials Committee during the 1966, 1967, and 1969 regular Assembly sessions to affect the credentials of South Africa.

However, in 1968, the Credentials Committee, by a vote of 5 to 3, with 1 abstention, rejected a Tanzanian proposal to declare "invalid the credentials of the representatives of the Government of South Africa." The U.S. delegation remained opposed to rejection of South Africa's credentials arguing that the credentials appeared to be valid under Rule 27 of the rules of procedure and that it was more helpful to have the "South African delegation ... present in the debate of the United Nations organs so that it could experience directly the intensity of feelings of the Member States against its policies." This language was not proposed as an amendment to the Committee report during Assembly consideration of the report.

The next credentials action on South Africa was taken in 1970 when an amendment (introduced on November 11) was adopted that resulted in Assembly approval of the report of the Credentials Committee, "except with regard to the credentials of the representatives of the Government of South Africa" (Assembly Resolution 2636 (XXV), November 13, 1970).

This action raised the broader issue of whether non-approval of credentials should also mean exclusion from participation in the General Assembly. The Assembly President requested and received from the United Nations Legal Counsel a statement on the scope of credentials issues in Rule 27 of the Assembly Rules of Procedure. After exploring the general practice relative to treatment of credentials for the General Assembly, the Legal Counsel offered the following opinion:

Should the General Assembly, satisfying the requirements of rule 27 for the purpose of excluding a Member State from participation in its meetings, this would have the effect of suspending a Member State from the exercise of rights and privilege of membership in a manner not foreseen by the Charter. Article 5 of the Charter lays down the following requirements for the suspension of a Member State from the rights and privileges of membership:

(a)  Preventive or enforcement action has to be taken by the Security Council against the Member State concerned;

(b)  The Security Council has to recommend to the General Assembly that the Member State concerned be suspended from the exercise of the rights and privileges of membership;

(c)  The General Assembly has to act affirmatively on the foregoing recommendation by a two-thirds vote, in accordance with Article 18, paragraph 2. of the Charter, which lists "the suspension of the rights and privileges of membership" as an "important question".

The participation in meetings of the General Assembly is quite clearly one of the important rights and privileges of membership. Suspension of this right through the rejection of credentials would not satisfy the foregoing requirements and would therefore be contrary to the Charter.

The President of the 25th session of the Assembly, Edvard Hambro (Norway), then issued the following statement, thereafter known as the Hambro ruling on this issue, to the Assembly:

I reach the conclusion that a vote in favor of the amendment would mean, on the part of this Assembly, a very strong condemnation of the policies pursued by the Government of South Africa. It would also constitute a warning to that Government as solemn as any such warning could be. But that, apart from that, the amendment as it is worded at present would not seem to me to mean that the South African delegation is unseated or cannot continue to sit in this Assembly; if adopted it will not affect the rights and privileges of membership of South Africa. That is my understanding.

On November 13, 1970, the Assembly voted in favor of the amendment 60 to 42 (including the United States), with 12 abstentions, and then approved the Credentials Committee report, as amended. In keeping with the Hambro ruling, the delegation from South Africa continued to participate in the Assembly, which in its sessions between 1971 through 1973, adopted the same kind of resolution, with similar results.

South Africa Credentials in 1974: The Credentials Committee, after being appointed on September 17, began its considerations on September 27 with a proposal to reject South Africa's credentials. Debate included discussion of whether the Committee should recommend action that would in effect suspend or expel a member state. Opponents of such action argued that it would go beyond a strict interpretation of Assembly Rules 27 and 28 and that it would constitute action which under the Charter could only be taken upon recommendation of the Security Council. The Committee, by a vote of 5 to 3 (including the United States), with 2 abstentions, adopted a resolution to accept credentials already received, "with the exception of the credentials of the representatives of South Africa" (language nearly identical to that adopted in previous years). On September 30, this resolution was upheld by the General Assembly when it approved the report of the Credentials Committee by a vote of 98 to 23 (United States), with 14 abstentions.

On the same day, the General Assembly called on the Security Council to review the relationship between South Africa and the United Nations in "the light of the constant violation by South Africa of the principles of the Charter and the Universal Declaration of Human Rights." Efforts in the Security Council to recommend the "immediate expulsion of South Africa from the United Nations in compliance with Article 6 of the Charter" were vetoed on October 30 by France, United Kingdom, and the United States.

On November 12, the General Assembly considered the report of the Council on the relationship of South Africa to the United Nations. After hearing a number of speakers, the President of the Assembly ruled that: on the basis of the consistency with which the General Assembly has regularly refused to accept the credentials of the delegation of South Africa, one may legitimately infer that the General Assembly would in the same way reject the credentials of any other delegation authorized by the Government of the Republic of South Africa to represent it, which is tantamount to saying in explicit terms that the General Assembly refuses to allow the delegation of South Africa to participate in its work.

The U.S. representative challenged this ruling on the grounds that in effect it constituted a suspension from membership of South Africa in contravention of the U.N. Charter provisions for suspension and expulsion. The Assembly, however, by a vote of 91 to 22 (United States), with 19 abstentions, upheld the President's ruling. The delegation from South Africa did not participate any further in that session of the Assembly.

Post-1974 Actions: Since 1974, South Africa has attempted to participate in sessions of the Assembly on three occasions. In each instance, the Assembly met to discuss only the Question of Namibia. During the resumed 33rd session, in May 1979, the presence of a representative in the South African seat in the Assembly hail was challenged and the Assembly referred the matter to the Credentials Committee. The Committee had before it only a 1977 letter from the South African Government on participation by its permanent representative in the organs of the United Nations (a standard communication on this issue) and a verbal notification that South Africa intended to participate in the resumed session. The Committee voted, 7 to 2, that these credentials were not in the proper form and therefore not acceptable. The Assembly, by a vote of 96 in favor to 19 against (including the United States), with 9 abstentions, accepted the report of the Credentials Committee.

At the start of the resumed 35th session of the Assembly, on March 2, 1981, the presence of the South African delegation was again challenged. South Africa had submitted credentials to the Secretary-General for participation in the resumed session that was to consider the Question of Namibia. The Credentials Committee met the same day and voted, 6 to 1, with 2 abstentions, to reject the credentials of the South African delegation. That afternoon, the Committee chairman made an oral report on this meeting to the Assembly which then decided, 112 in favor, 22 against (United States), with 6 abstentions, to approve the report of the Committee.

Again, in September 1981, South Africa submitted credentials for participation in the Eighth Emergency Session of the Assembly, on Namibia. The Credentials Committee, on September 3, by a vote of 6 to 1, with 2 abstentions, rejected the credentials of South Africa. The next day, the Assembly, by a vote of 117 in favor, 22 against (United States), with 6 abstentions, approved the report of the Credentials Committee.

## Kampuchea (1979–1982)

On September 18, 1979, the General Assembly referred to the Credentials Committee for its urgent consideration, the credentials of the delegation of Democratic Kampuchea, the regime which, under Pol Pot, had ruled Kampuchea since 1975. The People's Republic of Kampuchea, the Vietnam-sponsored regime under Heng Samrin, challenged these credentials in a letter informing the Secretary-General that it would send a delegation to the 1979 session of the Assembly. The rival government situation had been created when, in late 1978, the Vietnamese Government formed a puppet Khmer authority, invaded and occupied much of Kampuchean territory, including the capital, Phnom Penh, and established the People's Republic of Kampuchea.

Some members of the Credentials Committee argued that the role of the Committee was restricted to ascertaining whether the credentials from Democratic Kampuchea were or were not in order. Those who supported a more extensive role for the Committee, however, argued the Committee should determine which, if either, of the two regimes was presenting legitimate credentials, taking into account whether the People's Republic had or had not been established by force and whether the previous government of Democratic Kampuchea had or had not been "tyrannical." Some Committee members argued in support of leaving the seat vacant, until such time as the Assembly resolved the political problem, in keeping with Assembly resolution 396 (V). The Committee decided, by a vote of 6–3, to accept the credentials of the delegation of Democratic Kampuchea on technical grounds, and, on September 21, 1979, the Assembly approved the report of the Committee on this matter, by a vote of 71 (United States) to 35, with 34 abstentions.

The Assembly considered this question during each succeeding regular session, in 1980, 1981, and 1982. In each instance, the Credentials Committee accepted the credentials of

| VOTE IN PLENARY MEETING OF ASSEMBLY ON THE AMENDMENT | | | |
|---|---|---|---|
| | 1980 | 1981 | 1982 |
| In favor of amendment | 35 | 31 | 29 |
| Against amendment (United States) | 14 | 11 | 90 |
| Abstentions | 32 | 31 | 29 |

Democratic Kampuchea and the Assembly rejected a challenge to those credentials, in the form of an amendment to add the words, "except with regard to the credentials of the representatives of Democratic Kampuchea," to the draft resolution approving the report of the Committee. Each year, the Assembly then approved the report of the Committee without a vote. If the Assembly had adopted the amendment and approved the report, as amended, the result might have been a vacant seat for Kampuchea, pending acceptance of credentials from the Vietnamese-sponsored regime.

The increase in nations voting against the amendment in 1982 was possibly due to the composition of the Coalition Government of Democratic Kampuchea, formed in July 1982, which included Prince Norodom Sihanouk as President and non-Communists, such as Son Sann, as well as Communists. The Coalition, the product of consultations among the ASEAN (Association of Southeast Asian Nations) governments, was opposed to the Vietnamese occupation and broadly representative of the Khmer people.

**Israel (1982)**

The only time before 1982 that Israel's credentials in the U.N. General Assembly were seriously threatened was in 1975. During that year, there were a number of calls for expulsion or suspension of Israel from membership in the United Nations and its specialized agencies. However, widespread opposition to this action led Libya's U.N. representative, on September 29, 1975, to register only "strongest reservations on the credentials of the Zionist delegation to the thirtieth session of the General Assembly" to the Credentials Committee. Libya did not challenge Israel's credentials either in Committee or in the Assembly on October 1, when the Committee's report was brought up for approval.

During the spring of 1982, some Arab nations initiated a campaign to challenge Israel's General Assembly credentials. They argued that Israel had persistently violated the United Nations Charter and resolutions of the U.N. Security Council and was no longer a "peace-loving" nation. By September 1982, the campaign for action in the General Assembly had diminished while attention turned to the International Atomic Energy Agency (IAEA).

**International Atomic Energy Agency (IAEA)**

The concern in IAEA over Israeli participation originated in June 1981 when the IAEA Board of Governors recommended consideration of a suspension of the privileges and rights of membership by Israel in response to Israel's June 7, 1981 attack on an Iraqi nuclear facility. A September 1981 IAEA General Conference resolution condemned the attack and suspended assistance to Israel under IAEA technical assistance programs. The General Conference also decided to consider at its next session the suspension of Israel, if Israel had not complied with a U.N. Security Council resolution to place its nuclear facilities under IAEA safeguards.

Thus, it was expected that the 1982 IAEA General Conference, meeting in Vienna between September 20 and 24, would consider the matter of Israel's suspension from the privileges and rights of IAEA membership. On the morning of the last day of the session, the General Conference rejected a resolution to suspend Israel from the privileges and rights of membership. The vote, 43 in favor of suspending Israel to 27 against, with 17 abstentions, did not have the two/thirds majority required for passage.

That afternoon, Iraq challenged Israel's credentials in the form of an amendment to include the words, "except Israel," in the report of the Credentials Committee which had accepted Israel's credentials. The initial vote of 40 in favor to 40 against defeated the amendment (and thus supported Israel) since it did not receive a majority. However, one delegate, who had not been in the room during the vote, returned after the voting was over and indicated he would have voted in favor of the amendment (i.e. to reject Israel's credentials). The President of the General Conference, after receiving advice from the legal counsel that the vote could be counted, ruled that the vote would be counted. This ruling was appealed and the vote on the appeal—37 in favor of the appeal and 40 against the appeal—upheld the ruling, thus changing the vote on the amendment to 41 in favor to 40 against and reversing the result of the General Conference decision.

The final vote on the report of the Credentials Committee, as amended to reject the credentials of Israel, was 41 in favor to 39 against, with 5 abstentions. Israel was not able to participate any further in that session of the IAEA General Conference. But, since the Credentials Committee report had been moved to the end of the substantive issues on the Conference agenda, the session had, for all practical purposes, ended and the decision of the Conference not to accept the credentials of Israel for that session of the Conference had only symbolic effect.

The United States argued against the injection of political issues into a technical agency such as the IAEA and protested the illegality of the ruling and of the rejection of Israel's credentials. The U.S. delegation walked out of the General Conference and the State Department announced that the United States was reassessing further participation in IAEA.

### International Telecommunication Union (ITU)

The focus of actions to challenge Israel's participation moved to the International Telecommunication Union (ITU) the following week (September 28, 1982) when its Plenipotentiary Conference convened in Nairobi, Kenya. Algeria proposed preventing Israel from further participation in that or any future meeting or conference of the ITU, in effect removing Israel from an essential element of ITU membership. British compromise proposals included language condemning Israel for its invasion of Lebanon but called for the deletion of language expelling Israel from participation in future ITU meetings and conferences.

On October 16, Secretary of State George Shultz announced that if Israel were excluded, the United States would withdraw its delegation from the ITU Plenipotentiary Conference and suspend further payments to ITU.

On October 22, the Plenipotentiary Conference took three votes that resulted in a defeat of the Algerian attempt to expel Israel from participation. The Conference accepted the British compromise proposals as a package amendment by a vote of 62 in favor to 58 against, with 9 abstentions (there were 4 invalid votes). The British amendment was then adopted, 61 in favor to 57 against, with 9 abstentions (there were 5 invalid votes). The resolution, as amended, was adopted 85 in favor to 31 against, with 13 abstentions (there were 2 invalid votes). While the United States voted yes on the first two votes, it was one of the 31 states voting against the resolution as amended, primarily because of the language condemning Israel. After these efforts to remove Israel from participation in ITU conferences and meetings failed, there was no attempt, as occurred in the IAEA General Conference, to carry the fight to the report of the Credentials Committee. The Plenipotentiary Conference ended on November 5, 1982.

### United Nations General Assembly

On October 6, 1982, the Credentials Committee met and accepted all the credentials received by the Secretary-General thus far, including credentials for the delegation from Israel. On October 8, the U.N. representatives of the Arab League States met and decided to challenge the credentials of Israel when the report of the Credentials Committee came to the Assembly for approval. The basis for this action was to be the failure of Israel to abide by resolutions of the U.N. Security Council and General Assembly and to adhere to the principles of the Charter. In addition, they declared that Israel was not a "peace-loving" state. On October 12, members of the Organization of the Islamic Conference offered a compromise alternative to challenging Israel's credentials. Under this proposal, the Arabs would sign a letter expressing reservations over Israel's credentials in view of its flagrant violations of international law and United Nations resolutions. On October 19, members of the Arab League accepted this proposal and on October 25, Libya introduced such a letter that was signed by 48 countries, including most Arab States and the Soviet Union and its allies.

The letter, however, did not end consideration of this issue because during the October 25 meeting of the Assembly, Iran insisted on challenging Israel's credentials in spite of the compromise that had been worked out. When the Assembly convened the next day, Finland, on a point of order, moved to adjourn debate on the amendment to the Credentials Committee report, under Rule 74 of the Assembly's Rules of Procedure. The

Assembly adopted that motion, 74 in favor to 9 against, with 31 abstentions. Most of the 42 absent nations attended a meeting of the Arab caucus group, scheduled for that afternoon so that the Arab nations would not have to participate in the vote of the Assembly. The Committee report was then approved by consensus.

## The United States Response

As it became evident early in 1982 that efforts to affect Israel's participation in U.N. agencies might be made, concurrent resolutions were introduced in both the House and Senate. As passed by the Senate on April 14, 1982, S. Con. Roe. 68 expresses the sense of Congress that if Israel or any other democratic state were illegally expelled, suspended, denied its credentials, or in any other manner denied its right to participate in the General Assembly of the United Nations or any specialized agency of the United Nations, the United States should suspend its participation in the General Assembly or other U.N. agency involved and that the United States should withhold its assessed contribution to the United Nations or to the specialized agency involved until the action is reversed. In addition, the Secretary of State was requested to communicate this resolution to the member states of the United Nations.

On May 10, 1982, the House considered and on May 12, by a vote of 401 yeas to 3 nays, agreed to H. Con. Roe. 322. This resolution was identical to S. Con. Roe. 68 except for the deletion of any reference to "any other democratic state." This was done in order to avoid problems in defining "democratic state." On December 1, Senators Percy and Pell, chairman and ranking member of the Foreign Relations Committee, in order to expedite the passage of the resolution agreed to the discharging of the committee. The Senate passed H. Con. Roe. 322. Even so, the resolutions both expressed the sense of Congress rather than stipulating a legal requirement. However, executive branch spokesmen referred to the resolutions during the fall as they sought to stop actions against Israel.

The major policy statement by the United States was issued by Secretary of State George P. Shultz on October 16 and widely distributed to all U.N. and ITU members. To ensure that all nations recognized the seriousness of U.S. intentions if Israel were removed from U.N. Assembly or ITU participation, the statement not only identified U.S. policy, it also identified the concrete measures the United States would take. The statement set forth the position of the United States that it viewed these threats with "grave concern." Exclusion of Israel from the U.N. General Assembly would be "a clear-cut violation of the United Nations Charter." Exclusion of Israel from U.N. bodies would also be "a serious setback for progress toward peace in the Middle East."

The statement then identified the steps the United States had taken with respect to the IAEA and the steps the United States would take as evidence of its "determination to oppose such actions." The U.S. delegation had already been withdrawn from the IAEA General Conference on September 24, along with an announcement of a reassessment of U.S. participation in the IAEA. In addition, the United States suspended participation in a broad range of IAEA activities and, pending the outcome of the reassessment, the United States made no further payments on our contributions to the IAEA. If similar moves were made in other U.N. bodies, Secretary Shultz stated that the United States would take similar action in those bodies, as well.

If Israel were excluded from the General Assembly or from ITU conferences, Shultz pledged that the United States would withdraw from participation in the Assembly and withhold payments to the United Nations or withdraw our delegation from the ITU Conference and suspend further payments to the ITU, pending reversal of those decisions.

In mid-December 1982, Congress stipulated that U.S. contributions to IAEA included in the continuing resolution (section 159, H.J. Roe. 631, Public Law 97-377, approved December 21, 1982) would be provided only after Congress received from the Secretary of State a certification by the IAEA Board of Governors that Israel was "allowed to participate fully as a member nation in the activities of that Agency."

On February 22, 1983, the State Department announced the President's decision to renew U.S. participation in the IAEA and to send a U.S. delegation to the IAEA Board of Governors meeting February 22–25. At that time the Board approved a letter by Director General Hans Blix certifying that Israel is allowed to participate fully as a member nation in the activities of IAEA. This letter was transmitted to the Congress on March 1, 1983, thereby allowing funds that had been appropriated in the continuing resolution to be made available for payment to the IAEA.

## Appendices

* * *

## B. Memorandum on the Legal Aspects of the Problem of Representation in the United Nations, 1950

Letter dated 8 March 1950 from the Secretary-General to the President of the Security Council transmitting a memorandum on the legal aspects of the problem of representation in the United Nations:

> During the month of February 1950 I had a number of informal conversations with members of the Security Council in connection with the question of representation of States in the United Nations. In view of the proposal made by the representative of India for certain changes in the rules of procedure of the Security Council on this subject, I requested the preparation of a confidential memorandum on the legal aspects of the problem for my information. Some of the representatives on the Security Council to whom I mentioned this memorandum asked to see it, and I therefore gave copies to those representatives who were at that time present in New York.

> References to this memorandum have now appeared in the Press and I feel it appropriate that the full text now be made available to all members of the Council. I am therefore circulating copies of this letter and of the memorandum unofficially to all members and am also releasing the text of the memorandum to the Press.

> (Signed) Trygve Lie,
> Secretary-General,
> February 1950.

### Legal Aspects of Problems of Representation in the United Nations

The primary difficulty in the current question of the representation of Member States in the United Nations is that this question of representation has been linked up with the question of recognition by Member Governments.

It will be shown here that this linkage is unfortunate from the practical standpoint, and wrong from the stand in legal theory.

From a practical standpoint, the present position in that representation depends entirely on a numerical count of the number of Members in a particular organ which recognize one government or the other, it is quite possible [for the majority of the Members in one organ to recognize one government, and] for the majority of Members in another organ to recognize the rival government. If the principle of individual recognition is adhered to, then the representatives of different governments could sit in different organs. Moreover in organs like the Security Council, of limited membership, the question of representation may be determined by the purely arbitrary fact of the particular governments which happen to have been elected to serve at a given time.

From the standpoint of legal theory, the linkage of representation in an international organization and recognition of a government is a confusion of two institutions which have superficial similarities but are essentially different.

The recognition of a new State, or of a new government of an existing State, is a unilateral act which the recognizing government can grant or withhold. It is true that some legal writers have argued forcibly that when a new government, which comes into power through revolutionary means, enjoys, with a reasonable prospect of permanency, the habitual obedience of the bulk of the population, other States are under a legal duty to recognize it. However, while States may regard it as desirable to follow certain legal principles in according or withholding recognition, the practice of States shows that the act of recognition is still regarded as essentially a political decision, which each State decides in accordance with its own free appreciation of the situation.

A recent expression of this doctrine occurred during the consideration of the Palestine question in the Security Council, when the representative of Syria questioned the United States recognition of the Provisional Government of Israel. The representative of the United States (Mr. Austin) replied:

> I should regard it as highly improper for me to admit that any country on earth can question the sovereignty of the United States of America in the exercise of that high political act of recognition of the de facto status of a State.
>
> Moreover, I would not admit here, by implication or by direct answer, that there exists a tribunal of justice or of any other kind, anywhere, that can pass judgment upon the legality or the validity of that act of my country.
>
> There were certain powers and certain rights of a sovereign State which were not yielded by any of the Members who signed the United Nations Charter and in particular this power to recognize the de facto authority of a provisional Government was not yielded. When it was exercised by my Government, it was done as a practical step, in recognition of realities: the existence, of things, and the recognition of a change that had actually taken place. I am certain that no nation on earth has any right to question that, or to lay down a proposition that a certain length of time of the exercise of de facto authority must elapse before that authority can be recognized.

Various legal scholars have argued that thin rule of individual recognition through the free choice of States should be replaced by collective recognition through an international organization such as the United Nations (e.g. Lauterpacht, Recognition in International Law). If this were now the rule then the present impasse would not exist, since there would be no individual recognition of the new Chinese Government, but only action by the appropriate United Nations organ. The fact remains, however, that the States have refused to accept any such rule and the United Nations does not possess any authority to recognize either a new State or a new government of an existing State. To establish the rule of collective recognition by the United Nations would require either an amendment of the Charter or a treaty to which all Members would adhere.

On the other hand membership of a State in the United Nations and representation of a State in the organs is clearly determined by a collective act of the appropriate organs; in the case of membership, by vote of the General Assembly on recommendation of the Security Council, in the case of representation, by vote of each competent organ on the credentials of the purported representatives. Since, therefore, recognition of either State or government is an individual act, and either admission to membership or acceptance of representation in the Organization are collective acts, it would appear to be legally inadmissible to condition the latter acts by a requirement that they be preceded by individual recognition.

This conclusion is clearly born out by the practice in the case of admission to membership in both the League of Nations and in the United Nations.

In the practice of the League of Nations, there were a number of cases in which Members of the League stated expressly that the admission of another State to membership did not mean that they recognized such new Member as a State (e.g. Great Britain in the case of Lithuania; Belgium and Switzerland in the case of the Soviet Union; Colombia in the case of Panama).

In the practice of the United Nations there are, of course, several instances of admission to membership of States which had not been recognized by all other Members, and other instances of States for whose admission votes were cast by Members which had not recognized the candidates as State. For example, Yemen and Burma were admitted by a unanimous vote of the General Assembly at a time when they had been recognized by only a minority of Members. A number of the Members who, in the Security Council, voted for the admission of Transjordan [Jordan] and Nepal, had not recognized these candidates as States. Indeed, the declarations made by the delegation of the Soviet Union and its neighbors that they would not vote for the admission of certain States, (e.g. Ireland, Portugal and Transjordan [Jordan]), because they were not in diplomatic relations with these applicants, were vigorously disputed by most other Members, and led to the request for an advisory opinion of the International Court of Justice by the General Assembly.

The Court was requested to answer the question whether a Member, in its vote on the admission to membership of another State, was "juridically entitled to make its consent to the admission dependent on conditions not expressly provided" by paragraph 1 of Article 4 of the Charter. One of the conditions which had been stated by Members had been the lack of diplomatic relations with the applicant State. The Court answered the question in the negative. At its fourth session the General Assembly recommended that each Member act in accordance with the opinion of the Court.

The practice as regards representation of Member States in the United Nations organs has, until the Chinese question arose, been uniformly to the effect that representation is distinctly separate from the issue of recognition of a government. It is a remarkable fact that, despite the fairly large number of revolutionary changes of government and the larger number of instances of breach of diplomatic relations among Members, there was not one single instance of a challenge of credential of a representative in the many thousands of meetings which were held during four years. On the contrary, whenever the reports of credentials committees were voted on (as in the sessions of the General Assembly), they were always adopted unanimously and without reservation by any Members.

The Members have therefore made clear by an unbroken practice that:

(1) a Member could properly vote to accept a representative of a Government which it did not recognize, or with which it had no diplomatic relations, and

(2) that such a vote did not imply recognition or a readiness to assume diplomatic relations.

In two instances involving non-members, the question was explicitly raised—the cases of granting the Republic of Indonesia and Israel the right to participate in the deliberations of the Security Council. In both cases, objections were raised on the grounds that these entities were not States; in both cases the Security Council voted to permit representation after explicit statements were made by members of the Council that the vote did not imply recognition of the State or government concerned.

The practice which has been thus followed in the United Nations is not only legally correct but conforms to the basic character of the Organization. The United Nations is not an association limited to like-minded States and governments of similar ideological persuasion (as in the case in certain regional associations). As an Organization which aspires to universality, it must of necessity include States of varying and even conflicting ideologies.

The Chinese case is unique in the history of the United Nations, not because it involves a revolutionary change of government, but because it is the first in which two rival governments exist. It is quite possible that such a situation will occur again in the future and it is highly desirable to see what principle can be followed in choosing between the rivals. It has been demonstrated that the principle of numerical preponderance of recognition is inappropriate and legally incorrect. Is any other principle possible?

It is submitted that the proper principle can be derived by analogy from Article 4 of the Charter. This Article requires that an applicant for membership must be able and willing to carry out the obligations of membership. The obligations of membership can be carried out only by governments which in fact possess the power to do so. Where a revolutionary government presents itself as representing a State, in rivalry to an existing government, the question at issue should be which of these two governments in fact is in a position to employ the resources and direct the people of the State in fulfillment of the obligations of membership. In essence, this means an inquiry as to whether the new government exercises effective authority within the territory of the State and is habitually obeyed by the bulk of the population.

If so, it would seem to be appropriate for the United Nations organs, through their collective action, to accord it the right to represent the State in the Organization, even though individual Members of the Organization refute, and may continue to refuse, to accord it recognition as the lawful government for reasons which are valid under their national policies.

## C. Scope of "Credentials" in Rule 27 of the Rules of Procedure of the General Assembly, Statement by the Legal Counsel, 1970

1. The rules of procedure of the General Assembly do not contain a definition of 'credentials.' Rule 27, however, provides, "the credentials of representatives and the names of members of a delegation shall be submitted to the Secretary-General if possible not less than one week before the date fixed for the opening of the session. The credentials shall be issued either by the Head of the State or Government or by the Minister for Foreign Affairs."

2. From this rule one may derive three essential elements with respect to credentials to the General Assembly:

   (a) "Credentials" designate the representatives of the Member State to the General Assembly;

   (b) They are to be submitted to the Secretary-General; and

(c) They are to be issued by the Head of the State or Government or by the Minister for Foreign Affairs.

3. Thus, credentials for the General Assembly may be defined as a document issued by the Head of State or Government or by the Minister for Foreign Affairs of a State Member of the United Nations submitted to the Secretary-General designating the persons entitled to represent that Member at a given session of the General Assembly. Unlike the acceptance of credentials in bilateral relations, the question of recognition of a Government of a Member State is not involved, and substantive issues concerning the status of Governments do not arise except as examined in the following paragraph.

4. While normally the examination of credentials, both in the Credentials Committee and in the General Assembly, is a procedural matter limited to ascertaining that the requirements of rule 27 have been satisfied, there have nevertheless been a few instances involving rival claimants where the question of which claimant represents the true government of the State has arisen as a substantive issue. This issue of representation may, as in the case of the Republic of the Congo (Leopoldville) at the fifteenth session and Yemen at the sixteenth session, be considered in connection with the examination of credential, or it may, as in the case of China, be dealt with both in connection with credentials and as a separate agenda item.

5. Questions have also been raised in the Credentials Committee with respect to the representatives of certain Members, notably South Africa and Hungary, where there was no rival claimant. There has, however, been no case where the representatives were precluded from participation in the meetings of the General Assembly. The General Assembly, in the case of Hungary from the eleventh to the seventeenth session and in the case of South Africa at the twentieth session, decided to take no action on the credentials submitted on behalf of the representatives of Hungary and South Africa. Under rule 29 any representative to whose admission as a Member has made objection is seated provisionally with the same rights as other representatives until the Credentials Committee has reported and the General Assembly has given its decision.

6. Should the General Assembly, where there is no question of rival claimants, reject credentials satisfying the requirements of rule 27 for the purpose of excluding a Member State from participation in its meeting, this would have the effect of suspending a Member State from the exercise of right, and privileges of membership in a manner not foreseen by the Charter. Article 5 of the Charter lays down the following requirements for the suspension of a Member State from the rights and privileges of membership:

(a) Preventive or enforcement action has to be taken by the Security Council against the Member State concerned;

(b) The Security Council has to recommend to the General Assembly that the Member State concerned be suspended from the exercise of the rights and privileges of membership;

(c) The General Assembly has to act affirmatively on the foregoing recommendation by a two-thirds vote, in accordance with Article 18, paragraph 2, of the Charter, which lists "the suspension of the rights and privileges of membership" as an "important question"

The participation in meetings of the General Assembly is quite clearly one of the important rights and privileges of membership. Suspension of this right through the rejection of credentials would not satisfy the foregoing requirements and would therefore be contrary to the Charter.

**D. Statement on Israel's Participation in the United Nations by George P. Schultz, Secretary of State, October 16, 1982**

Recently there have been proposals at the U.N. General Assembly in New York and at the plenipotentiary conference of the International Telecommunication Union Nairobi against the continued participation of Israel in those organizations. The United States views these threats with grave concern.

The exclusion of Israel from the General Assembly or the ITU in these circumstances would be contrary to the principles of the United Nations. In the case of the General Assembly, it would be a clear-cut violation of the U.N. Charter. Such action defeats the very purpose of the United Nations—to resolve disputes among nations—by creating further conflict and division. It would do grave damage to the entire U.N. system, and it would hurt us all.

The exclusion of Israel from U.N. bodies would also be a serious setback for progress toward peace in the Middle East, to which the United States and virtually all members of the United Nations are committed. It would be a tragic irony if such moves against Israel in the U.N. system were to succeed just at the time when there is renewed hope for progress in the Middle East.

The United States has always made clear that any attack on Israel's right to participate in any U.N. organization, if successful, would have grave consequences for our own continued participation and support. As evidence of our determination to oppose such actions, we withdrew our delegation from the conference of the International Atomic Energy Agency (IAEA) following the wrongful rejection of Israel's credentials on September 24, announced that we would reassess our participation in the IAEA, and suspended participation in a broad range of agency activities. Pending the outcome of our reassessment, we are making no further payments to the IAEA. We will take such action in other U.N. organizations if there are similar moves.

If Israel were excluded from the General Assembly, the United States would withdraw from participation in the Assembly and would withhold payments to the United Nations until Israel's right to participate was restored.

We would also withdraw our delegation from the 1W plenipotentiary conference in Nairobi if Israel were excluded and suspend further payments to that organization. The ITU, the IAEA, and other technical agencies must not be undermined or destroyed by such political attacks on the rights of member states.

We trust that the majority of nation members of the United Nations and all its agencies recognize the grave dangers of any further attacks on Israel's right to participate in U.N. bodies and will work to turn aside such initiatives.

# 8. Resolution 919

## United Nations Security Council, 1994

Adopted by the Security Council at its 3379th meeting, on 25 May 1994

*The Security Council,*

*Recalling* its resolutions on the question of South Africa, in particular resolutions 282 (1970), 418 (1977), 421 (1977), 558 (1984) and 591 (1986),

*Welcoming* the first all-race multiparty election and the establishment of a united, democratic, non-racial government of South Africa, which was inaugurated on 10 May 1994,

*Taking note of* the letter of 18 May 1994 from President Nelson R. Mandela of the Republic of South Africa (S/1994/606, annex),

*Stressing* the urgent need to facilitate the process of reintegration of South Africa in the international community, including the United Nations system,

1. *Decides*, acting under Chapter VII of the Charter of the United Nations, to terminate forthwith the mandatory arms embargo and other restrictions related to South Africa imposed by resolution 418 (1977) of 4 November 1977;

2. *Decides also* to end forthwith all other measures against South Africa contained in resolutions of the Security Council, in particular those referred to in resolutions 282 (1970) of 23 July 1970, 558 (1984) of 13 December 1984 and 591 (1986) of 28 November 1986;

3. *Decides further* to dissolve the Committee of the Security Council established by resolution 421 (1977) concerning the question of South Africa, in accordance with rule 28 of the provisional rules of procedure of the Security Council, effective from the date of the adoption of the present resolution;

4. *Invites* all States to consider reflecting the provisions of this resolution as appropriate in their legislation.

## 9. Bibliography of Additional Sources

- Gambhir Bhatta, Reforms at the United Nations: Contextualizing the Annan Agenda (2000).

- Omar Burleson, Views on United States Membership in the United Nations (1962).

- Benjamin V. Cohen, Voting and Membership in the United Nations, U.S. Department of State (1949).

- Ellen C. Collier & Bradford Westerfield, The Problem of Membership in the United Nations (1954).

- Conditions of Admission of a State to Membership in the United Nations (Article 4 of Charter), Advisory Opinion, 1948 I.C.J. 57 (May 28).

- G. Shabbir Cheema, *Corruption and How it Affects the Political Legitimacy of the State*, 35 U.N. Chronicle (1998).

- Chester A. Crocker, *The Lessons of Somalia: Not Everything Went Wrong*, 74 Foreign Affairs (May/June 1995).

- L. Gberia, *Fighting for Peace: The United Nations, Sierra Leone and Human Security*, 37 U.N. Chronicle (2000).

- Matthew Griffin, *Accrediting Democracies: Does the Credentials Committee of the United Nations Promote Democracy Through Its Accreditation Process, and Should It?*, 32 N.Y.U. J. Int'l L. & Pol. 725 (2000).

- The New Interventionism, 1991–1994: United Nations Experience in Cambodia, Former Yugoslavia, and Somalia (James Mayall Cambridge ed., 1996).

- NGO's, The U.N. and Global Governance (Thomas G. Weiss & Leon Gardenker eds., 1996).

- Suellen Ratliff, *U.N. Representation Disputes: A Case Study of Cambodia and a New Accreditation Proposal for the Twenty-First Century*, 87 CALIF. L. REV. 1207 (Oct. 1999).

- Report of the Credentials Comm., U.N. GAOR, 52d Sess., Agenda Item 3, ¶ 4, at 1, ¶ 9, at 3, U.N. Doc. A/52/719 (1997).

- Robert D. Sloane, *The Changing Face of Recognition in International Law: A Case Study of Tibet*, 16 EMORY INT'L L. REV. 107 (2002).

- Eric Stein, SOME IMPLICATIONS OF EXPANDING UNITED NATIONS MEMBERSHIP (1956).

- Harvey Thomas, *Somaliland Seeks Special Status from U.N.*, THE FINANCIAL TIMES (Aug. 15, 2000).

- Sebla Uludag, *U.N. Resolution No.186 Must Be Discussed Instead of Annan Plan for Cyprus*, JTW (May 26, 2006).

- U.N. Dep't of Legal Affairs, Repertory of Practice of United Nations Organs, suppl. 9, art. 9, U.N. Sales No. E.01.V.6 (2011).

- Davis J. Whittaker, UNITED NATIONS IN THE CONTEMPORARY WORLD (1977).

- *Will There Be Justice?*, 128 U.S. NEWS & WORLD REPORT (May 29, 2000).

# Chapter III

# International Organizations and State Succession

## Introduction

Over the past few decades a number of states have dissolved into smaller states or have had large sections of territory break away and become independent states themselves. These instances of state secession inevitably lead to complicated legal questions regarding which successor state is entitled to assume the membership in international organizations of the predecessor state, how the debts and assets are divided, and what becomes of the international treaty rights and obligations of the predecessor state, among others.

This chapter will provide a basis for examining the legal issues associated with state succession though a review of the succession to the U.N. membership of the successor states of the former Soviet Union, Yugoslavia, and Czechoslovakia, as well as the succession of membership and the allocation of the debts and assets of Yugoslavia and Czechoslovakia in the World Bank and IMF. The chapter will also provide a basis for examining the rather unique event of the creation of the EU Arbitration Commission to provide guidance to the EU on the legal questions arising from the dissolution of Yugoslavia.

## Objectives

- To understand the fundamental principles and the legal framework applicable to state succession.

- To understand the role played by international organizations in facilitating the resolution of legal questions arising from the break-up of states.

- To understand the relationship between international law and political considerations in the context of state succession.

- To understand the role played by *ad hoc* arbitration commissions in resolving legal questions relating to state succession.

- To evaluate the degree to which the traditional law of state succession has evolved as a result of state practice over the past three decades.

# Problems

Students should come to class prepared to discuss the following questions:

1. What are the alternative approaches that the U.N. could have adopted for determining the question of succession to membership? What are the pros and cons of the alternative approaches?

2. What are the "rules" the U.N. has adopted for deciding when a new State can automatically assume the membership of a U.N. Member State that has broken apart or dissolved? What interests do these rules serve?

3. Applying the rules for succession to membership, why was Russia permitted to inherit the Soviet Union seat, but Serbia-Montenegro not permitted to inherit the Yugoslavia seat? What political factors might have been important to the outcome of the two cases?

4. Did S.C. Res. 777 (1992) constitute a legal rejection of Serbia-Montenegro's claim to the Yugoslavia seat, a suspension of Yugoslavia from the U.N., or something entirely new?

5. What were the politics/interests behind the particular wording of S.C. Res. 777?

6. What are the ramifications of S.C. Res. 777 for Serbia's claim to continue Yugoslavia's membership in other international organizations, both within and outside the U.N. system?

7. What are the possible ramifications of S.C. Res. 777 for Serbia's claim to the foreign assets and embassies of the former Yugoslavia?

8. What factors should international organizations use to resolve the distribution of assets?

9. How should international financial institutions determine national debt, territorial debt, and local debt?

10. What are the implications of considering the continuation of states in determining obligations debts and assumption of assets?

# Case Studies and Negotiation Simulations

Drawing from the materials in this chapter, students should come to class prepared to participate in the following simulations:

**Negotiation Simulation: Yemen**

Drawing from the materials in this chapter, students should come to class prepared to discuss and resolve the U.N. membership status of the two Yemeni states and any financial liabilities to international organizations like the World Bank and IMF. Students should be able to discuss any relevant claims of continuity or dissolution.

Roles to be assigned:

1. Representative of the Republic of Yemen (North Yemen)

2. Representative of the People's Democratic Republic of Yemen (South Yemen)

3. The U.N. Legal Counsel

### 4.   The World Bank Legal Counsel

In 1990, the former independent nations of the Yemen Arab Republic (North Yemen) and the People's Democratic Republic of Yemen (South Yemen) merged to form the Republic of Yemen. Both had been members of the United Nations before the merger, and the newly unified country continued the membership of North Yemen in the United Nations and other international organizations including the International Monetary Fund (IMF) and World Bank.

Though the two parts of Yemen are roughly equal in size and population, they have very different histories and were adversaries in numerous wars before uniting. North Yemen gained its independence from the former Ottoman Empire in 1918 and was one of the first countries to join the United Nations after the original fifty in 1947. It was ruled by an Inman, or religious king, until a military coup established a republic in 1962. South Yemen only gained independence from Great Britain in 1967. Shortly afterwards, a communist regime came to power, and the country was admitted to the U.N.. Agreements for the unification of North and South Yemen were signed in 1971 and 1981 but were never implemented because of reccurring warfare between the two countries. In 1989, the eventual unifying agreement was made and came into fruition the following year. This merger has been a tenuous one. In 1993, a nine-week civil war broke out between secessionist former South Yemen army units who were ultimately defeated by pro-unionist North Yemen army units.

For the purpose of this simulation, assume that another Yemeni civil war has recently ended, but this time the secessionist South Yemen movement has won. North Yemen claims to be the continuation of the Republic of Yemen and argues that it need not reapply for United Nations membership and is entitled to all the rights and benefits of the former united Yemen in the U.N. and other organizations including the IMF and World Bank. North Yemen has stated that it recognizes international treaties such as the ICCPR and the Genocide Convention, but has not ratified or signed the treaties as North Yemen. Currently there is a pending case before the ICJ, *North Yemen v. South Yemen*, for possible violations of international human rights obligations and border disputes. Additionally, there are a substantial number of persons living within North Yemen who sympathize with the dominant political party in South Yemen. North Yemen has refused to grant North Yemeni citizenship to these individuals and their children born in North Yemen.

South Yemen has taken its old title of the People's Democratic Republic of Yemen and claims the right to resume South Yemen's previous membership in the U.N. and other international organizations without submitting a formal application for membership. Continued membership is seen as important to South Yemen because the General Assembly has condemned the South Yemen government for failing to prosecute its military commanders who committed war crimes during the recent war for secession, so the General Assembly is unlikely to approve a South Yemen application for membership at this time.

North Yemen takes no position on whether South Yemen should be automatically admitted into the United Nations but it maintains that South Yemen should be held accountable for one-half of the unified country's former liabilities to international organizations. In particular, North Yemen argues that South Yemen should be responsible for fifty percent of the $10 million in dues that Yemen owes the United Nations for the year, and for repaying half of a $200 million World Bank loan that had been issued to the unified country before secession. South Yemen argues that it should only be responsible for 25 percent of the dues and loan since the South Yemen Gross Domestic Product is only one quarter the size of that of North Yemen and most of the development projects undertaken with the loan money occurred in North Yemen.

**Negotiation Simulation: South Sudan**

Drawing from the materials in this chapter, students should come to class prepared to discuss and resolve the financial liabilities to the IMF, World Bank, Paris Club, and London Club. Should these organizations allow an equitable allocation or zero option? Students should be prepared to discuss the rules that govern the allocation of national debt, territorial debt, and local debt.

Roles to be assigned:

1. IMF Representative
2. World Bank Representative
3. South Sudan Representative
4. Sudan Representative
5. International Actor(s)

After 20 years of civil war between the north and the south, South Sudan voted in a referendum in January 2011 to become a fully independent country. Because of this decision, the government in Khartoum is faced with difficult decisions — defining new national borders, sharing oil wealth, and dividing national assets. An additional question is the allocation of the debt. What should come of the debt accumulated by both north and south?

Beginning in 1958, the World Bank provided loan assistance to Sudan totaling $1.52 billion. The majority of the funding was concentrated on infrastructure projects, such as railways and port facilities, and agriculture. Only eleven percent of the funding for these projects was provided by the World Bank's hard-loan facility, the International Bank for Reconstruction and Development (IBRD). The remaining eighty-nine percent, or $1.35 billion, was provided by the World Bank's concessional financing facility, the International Development Association.

In 1993, after the Sudanese government went arrears on loan repayments, the World Bank suspended its lending program. However, in the mid-2000s as a part of the international community's efforts to promote recovery and reconstruction after the destructive decades-long civil war the World Bank restarted its engagement. Currently, the World Bank administers two multi-donor trust funds (MDTF) in Sudan and as of mid-2010 the two MDTFs had approved 36 projects totaling roughly $770 million.

Historically, this debt has evolved. Throughout the 1970s, Sudan generally maintained low and stable levels of external debt ($385 million in 1970 and $1.6 billion in 1975). However, its debt burden grew substantially over the ensuing ten-year period with obligations reaching over $9 billion by 1985. Roughly twenty percent of this debt was owed to bilateral Paris Club creditors; thirty percent to multilateral institutions; and thirty percent to non-Paris Club bilateral creditors. In addition to new loans, debt service and interest arrears caused debt stocks to compound rapidly. As debt servicing became more costly, Sudan's terms of trade declined and left the country with even greater external financing needs. According to the IMF and World Bank, Sudan currently is in "debt distress." By the end of 2009, Sudan's public and publicly guaranteed external debt stood at roughly $34.7 billion in net present value.

# Materials

1. U.N. Charter, arts. 3, 4, 5, 93.

2. Michael P. Scharf, *Musical Chairs: The Dissolution of States and Membership in the United Nations*, 28 CORNELL INT'L L.J. 29 (1995).

3. S.C. Res. 1326, U.N. Doc. S/RES/1326 (Oct. 31, 2000).

4. United Nations Conference on Succession of States in Respect of State Property, Archives and Debts, Vienna, Austria, Mar. 1–Apr. 8, 1983, *Vienna Convention on Succession of States in Respect of State Property, Archives and Debts*, U.N. Doc. A/CONF.117/14 (Apr. 8. 1983).

5. Paul R. Williams & Jennifer Harris, *State Succession to Debts and Assets: The Modern Law and Policy*, 42 HARVARD INT'L L.J. 355 (2001).

6. Conference on Yugoslavia Arbitration Commission, *Opinions on Questions Arising From the Dissolution of Yugoslavia*, 31 I.L.M. 1488 (1992).

7. *Report of the Committee of Legal Advisors on Public International Law for the Council of Europe, 4th Meeting* (Sept. 14–15, 1992).

8. Paul R. Williams, *State Succession and the International Financial Institutions: Political Criteria v. Protection of Outstanding Financial Obligations*, 43 INT'L & COMP. L.Q. 776 (1994).

9. Bibliography of Additional Sources

---

## 1. U.N. Charter Articles 3, 4, 5, 93

### Article 3

The original Members of the United Nations shall be the states which, having participated in the United Nations Conference on International Organization at San Francisco, or having previously signed the Declaration by United Nations of 1 January 1942, sign the present Charter and ratify it in accordance with Article 110.

### Article 4

1. Membership in the United Nations is open to all other peace-loving states which accept the obligations contained in the present Charter and, in the judgment of the Organization, are able and willing to carry out these obligations.

2. The admission of any such state to membership in the United Nations will be effected by a decision of the General Assembly upon the recommendation of the Security Council.

### Article 5

A Member of the United Nations against which preventive or enforcement action has been taken by the Security Council may be suspended from the exercise of the rights and privileges of membership by the General Assembly upon the recommendation of the Security Council. The exercise of these rights and privileges may be restored by the Security Council.

### Article 93

All Members of the United Nations are ipso facto parties to the Statute of the International Court of Justice.

A state which is not a Member of the United Nations may become a party to the Statute of the International Court of Justice on conditions to be determined in each case by the General Assembly upon the recommendation of the Security Council.

## 2. Michael P. Scharf, Musical Chairs: The Dissolution of States and Membership in the United Nations
### Cornell International Law Journal, 1995
[footnotes omitted by editors]

### Introduction

In the waning days of 1991, a national headline proclaimed: "The Soviet Union, as We Long Knew It, Is Dead. What's Next?" For the United Nations, faced with the sudden disintegration of one of the five permanent members of the Security Council, that question raised novel issues of international law and Charter interpretation. Ultimately, without public debate or fanfare, the Russian Federation—the largest of the former Soviet Republics—was permitted to take over the Soviet seat as the "continuation" of the Soviet Union, and the other former Republics were invited to apply for their own U.N. membership.

Less than a year later, when four of the six republics that made up the Socialist Federal Republic of Yugoslavia (SFRY) declared their independence and applied for membership in the United Nations, the rump Federal Republic of Yugoslavia (FRY) sought to follow in Russia's footsteps and quietly inherit the Yugoslav seat at the U.N.. Instead, the FRY's claim to automatic membership encountered stiff resistance by not only the Security Council, but also by the General Assembly, which ultimately adopted a somewhat bizarre resolution barring the FRY from participating in the General Assembly but permitting it to continue to operate a U.N. mission, to circulate documents, and to participate in other U.N. bodies.

Before the dust had even begun to settle on the contentious issue of Yugoslav membership, a third U.N. member-State—Czechoslovakia—announced that it too was splitting apart. In an effort to avoid controversy within the United Nations, the two resulting States agreed that they would each apply for U.N. membership as a new member of that organization. At the same time, however, they sought to divide between themselves the seats that had been assigned to the former Czechoslovakia in a variety of U.N. subsidiary organs and Specialized Agencies. The United Nations rejected this attempt, and instead required formal elections to fill the vacancies.

As Attorney-Adviser for United Nations Affairs at the U.S. Department of State when these three cases arose, the author of this Article was involved in the legal analysis, policy formulation, negotiations, and compromises that shaped the results described above. From the contrary ways that the United Nations handled these cases, one might conclude, as one commentator long ago suggested, that the question of succession to membership in the United Nations is less a question of law than one of political judgment, and that in such matters legal principles and Charter interpretation take a back seat to political and administrative convenience. Yet, careful analysis of these cases indicates that such a conclusion would mistakenly undervalue the important role played by legal theory and precedent in the context of succession to membership in the United Nations.

To provide a backdrop for this analysis, the Article begins with a discussion of the relevant provisions of the U.N. Charter and a detailed examination of the United Nations' first case of succession to membership, which came about in 1947 when British India split into India and Pakistan. From the positions taken by the members of the Security Council and General Assembly in that case, the Article distills the principles that strongly influenced the results reached in the Russia, Yugoslavia, and Czechoslovakia cases and which are likely to guide the organization's response to questions of succession to membership in the future. In so doing, the Article explores the broader question of the role of law versus politics in the internal functioning of the United Nations.

## Background

### A. The U.N. Charter

Membership in the United Nations by new States is equivalent to affirmation of their full personality as international entities and is essential to the complete enjoyment of their newly acquired status in an increasingly interdependent world. Until a new state attains U.N. membership, it is excluded from participating in several hundred multilateral conventions that provide networks of international co-operation in a variety of fields. Moreover, upon admission to the United Nations, a new State is entitled to automatic membership in virtually every functional organization within the U.N. system simply by informing the Secretariat that it accepts the obligations of the constituent instruments of these organizations. It is small wonder, then, that the newly emerging states of the former Soviet Union, Yugoslavia, and Czechoslovakia immediately applied for U.N. membership upon declaring their independence.

Article 4(1) of the U.N. Charter sets out the criteria for eligibility for new members. It reads: "Membership in the United Nations is open to all other peace-loving states which accept the obligations contained in the present Charter and, in the judgment of the Organization, are able and willing to carry out these obligations." Article 4(2), which sets out the process for admission of new members, provides that they "will be elected by a decision of the General Assembly upon the recommendation of the Security Council."

While the Charter provisions described above governed new membership for the former republics of the Soviet Union, Yugoslavia, and Czechoslovakia, the Soviet situation also raised difficult issues related to the disposition of the Soviet Union's seat on the Security Council. Based on its status as a major power at the conclusion of the Second World War, the Soviet Union—along with the Republic of China, France, the United Kingdom of Great Britain and Northern Ireland, and the United States of America—was assigned permanent Security Council membership under article 23 of the U.N. Charter. With permanent membership on the Council comes the right to veto substantive decisions—a right that would-be successors to the Soviet Union obviously desired dearly.

Surprisingly, the U.N. Charter contains no provision for succession to membership. Nor are the traditional rules on treaty succession controlling in the context of international organizations. Instead, such questions are governed by principles and precedents that have developed over time. In addition, even within the U.N. system, various organizations have developed different approaches to membership succession.

### B. Historical Precedent

The breakup of the Soviet Union is not the first time the United Nations has witnessed the division of a member-State. Whenever a member-State breaks apart, there are several possible ways the United Nations could respond. First, drawing upon the traditional rules of treaty succession, it could permit all of the resulting States to succeed to the former State's membership, that is, to become automatically U.N. members. Second, it could require that all of the resulting States apply for membership as new members before they are allowed to participate in the United Nations. Finally, it could allow one of the resulting States to continue the former State's membership while requiring the others to apply for new membership. For a variety of reasons detailed below, the U.N. has rejected the first option and opts to follow either the second or third options depending on the circumstances.

The United Nations first faced such a situation just two years after its founding, on August 15, 1947, when Great Britain granted independence to British India, an original member of the United Nations, and divided its territory into the separate Dominions of India and Pakistan. On that day, the Ministry of Foreign Affairs of Pakistan sent a cable to the United Nations Secretary-General expressing the opinion that "both the Dominions of India and Pakistan should become Members of the United Nations, automatically, with effect from 15 August." Because Pakistan desired to participate in the upcoming session of the General Assembly without delay, the cable indicated that if the Secretary-General were not willing to accept Pakistan's claim to automatic membership, he should construe the cable as a formal application for admission by Pakistan.

The Secretary-General promptly transmitted the cable as an application for admission to the Security Council, which considered the question on August 18, 1947. During the Security Council's debate, France supported Pakistan's argument for automatic membership, but most members took the position that Pakistan should be formally admitted to membership. Consistent with the conclusions of a legal opinion drafted ten days earlier in anticipation of this situation by Dr. Ivan Kerno, the Assistant Secretary-General for Legal Affairs, there was no challenge to India's continued membership. The Polish delegate remarked, however, that "this precedent cannot be cited in the future as a justification in the event another State should split up into several States and all of those should ask for automatic admission, thereby depriving the Security Council of the privilege of making recommendations with regard to new Members." Notwithstanding this statement, the India/Pakistan case became the primary precedent against which the cases of the Soviet Union, Yugoslavia, and Czechoslovakia would be gauged nearly fifty years later.

When the Security Council transmitted the resolution to admit Pakistan to the General Assembly, it was referred to the First Committee, where the representative of Argentina expressed the opinion that both India and Pakistan were either members by inheritance or they both had to be formally admitted. Although there was substantial support for Argentina's position, it was agreed that Pakistan's participation should not be delayed. Accordingly, the First Committee voted to recommend to the General Assembly that it admit Pakistan while simultaneously referring the legal question of succession to the Sixth (Legal) Committee. The question addressed to the Sixth Committee was framed as follows: "What are the legal rules to which, in the future, a State or States entering into international life through the division of a Member State of the United Nations should be subject?"

In response to this question, the Sixth Committee adopted and transmitted the following principles to the First Committee as general guidance for future cases:

> 1. That, as a general rule, it is in conformity with legal principles to presume that a State which is a Member of the Organization of the United Nations does not cease to be a Member simply because its Constitution or its frontier have been subjected to changes, and that the extinction of the State as a legal personality recognized in the international order must be shown before its rights and obligations can be considered thereby to have ceased to exist.

> 2. That when a new State is created, whatever may be the territory and the populations which it comprises and whether or not they formed part of a State Mem-

ber of the United Nations, it cannot under the system of the Charter claim the status of a Member of the United Nations unless it has been formally admitted as such in conformity with the provisions of the Charter.

3. Beyond that, each case must be judged according to its merits.

In the context of the India/Pakistan case, the first of these principles suggests that there is a presumption against treating a State's U.N. membership as extinguished despite the division or dismemberment of that State. The second principle, analogous to the rule of primogeniture, suggests that no more than one State can claim to be the continuation of a U.N. member-State that has undergone such changes; all other States formed in the division or dismemberment must formally apply for new membership. The third principle seeks to limit the importance of precedent and to preserve the political flexibility of the United Nations in responding to future membership questions.

Before describing how the India/Pakistan precedent and the principles propounded by the Sixth Committee influenced the disposition of the Soviet, Yugoslav, and Czech seats in the United Nations, it is worthwhile first to examine the validity of the legal position taken by the Assistant Secretary-General for Legal Affairs, the Security Council, and the General Assembly on the question of Pakistan's membership. As described below, there are three troubling aspects of the case that undermine its value as precedent.

The primary problem with the U.N.'s handling of the India/Pakistan case was that it treated Pakistan as having broken away from India rather than treating both India and Pakistan as simultaneously emerging as independent States from the United Kingdom. According to the records of the Parliamentary debate on the partition of British India, the United Kingdom intended to set up in British India two co-successor States as stipulated in the Indian Independence Act of 1947. In this regard, Dr. Kerno's analogy between the separation of Pakistan from India and the Irish Free State from the United Kingdom and Belgium from the Netherlands is of doubtful historical accuracy. As one commentator noted, "all these were cases of secession, separation, or defection rather than division, partition or dismemberment." If the United Kingdom rather than British India is viewed as the predecessor State, there is no legal reason why the two Dominions should not have been dealt with as co-successors, in which case they should have either both been given automatic membership or both been required to apply for membership.

Second, the devolution agreement between India and Pakistan, which provided that membership in all international organizations would devolve solely upon the Dominion of India, should have been discounted by the United Nations for a variety of reasons. Due to the coercive circumstances surrounding the negotiations in the Partition Council, Pakistan had little choice but to accept the provision. In addition, the provision runs counter to the intention and contents of the Indian Independence Act of 1947. Moreover, since the only parties to the devolution agreement were India and Pakistan, it could not have any automatic effect on the United Nations without the consent and acceptance of the members of that organization. Finally, Pakistan itself treated the agreement as a nullity when it claimed to have the same right as India to membership in the United Nations.

A third problem is that the precedent was not initially applied uniformly throughout the U.N. system. The International Telecommunications Union (ITU), for example, consciously departed from the General Assembly's approach to the question of Pakistan's membership. At the International Telecommunications Conference on September 4, 1947, the Argentine Delegation made the following Statement:

The fact we must face is this: a member of the International Telecommunications Union, British India, has been divided into two neighboring States which today form part of the "Commonwealth" of British nations under conditions of absolute legal equality. One of these dominions, India, retains its old constitutional and political name; the other acquires a new designation: Pakistan. But the two States, are, in reality, the legitimate successors to the rights and commitments acquired by British India within the International Telecommunication Union when it signed the Madrid Convention. Therefore, it is not fitting to bring up the question of an "admission".... On the contrary, what is fitting, purely and simply, is to "recognize" that both these new States are equally the lawful successors of the old Member of the Union which was called British India, and nothing more.

Accordingly, Argentina proposed that the ITU "recognize" India and Pakistan as members "in their capacity as successors of the British India, without subjecting them to any process of admission." The chairman of the conference observed that the opinion expressed by the Argentine delegation had given rise to no objection, and that Pakistan should be considered admitted to the ITU. Pakistan participated in the balance of the conference and signed the International Telecommunications Convention of Atlantic City in 1947.

Moreover, in 1961, the United Nations appeared to depart without reason from the precedent and the principles adopted by the Sixth Committee in handling the dissolution of the United Arab Republic. Just three years after uniting with Egypt to form the United Arab Republic, Syria broke away from the nascent Union by revolution on September 28, 1961, and claimed its independence under a new name—the Syrian Arab Republic. A week after achieving independence, Syria sent the following note to the President of the General Assembly:

> It may be recalled that the Syrian Republic was an original member of the United Nations under Article Three of the Charter and continued its membership in the form of joint association with Egypt under the name of United Arab Republic. In resuming her formal status as an independent State the Government of the Syrian Arab Republic has the honour to request that the United Nations take note of the resumed membership in the United Nations of the Syrian Arab Republic.

Syria's request appears to contravene the India/Pakistan precedent and the Sixth Committee's second principle, which states that:

> When a new State is created, whatever may be the territory and the population which it comprises and whether or not they formed part of a State Member of the United Nations, it cannot under the system of the Charter claim the status of a Member of the United Nations unless it has been formally admitted as such in conformity with the provisions of the Charter.

The situation of a State, which has surrendered its independence and its U.N. seat to join a Union and then breaks away from that Union and asserts its independence, is little different than that of a territory like Pakistan becoming independent as an entirely new State by secession.

The President of the General Assembly consulted a number of delegations and announced that "the consensus seemed to be that, in view of the special circumstances of this matter, Syria, an original member of the United Nations, may be authorized to be represented in the General Assembly as it has specifically requested." No objection was made and Syria resumed its U.N. membership without having to go through the application process. Egypt, for its part, continued its membership in the U.N. under the name UAR until it notified the Secretary-General on September 2, 1971, that it had changed its name to the Arab Republic of Egypt. The Syria/UAR case can perhaps be distinguished from the India/Pakistan case in that the old Syria had been an original member of the United Nations, and the new Syria was, in effect, reasserting a temporarily suspended personality, the emphasis being on continuity rather than disruption.

The U.N. decision to follow the third of the possible options listed above for dealing with succession to the British India seat was likely motivated by practical concerns. If Pakistan had been treated as the co-successor to the British India seat, the United Nations would have had to accept an automatic increase in the number of its original members. This would not, however, have been the case with Syria's secession from the UAR, since Syria had been one of the original members in its own right. As the above quoted statement by the Polish delegate to the Security Council indicates, the members of the Council jealously guarded their right to approve new members. This was particularly true during the early years of the United Nations, when membership was not viewed as "universal" and admission decisions were often held hostage to Cold War politics. Technical organizations like the ITU, on the other hand, were less encumbered by such political strife. Moreover, given the Soviet Union's demand when the United Nations was founded to include all fifteen of its republics as original members of the United Nations, there may have been legitimate concerns that member-States might attempt to reconfigure themselves into smaller units in an effort to increase their voting strength in the General Assembly. Finally, if India had been required to apply for membership as was Pakistan, this would have meant the disappearance of an original member at a time when, due to East-West tensions, there was no guarantee that new membership for India would be swiftly forthcoming.

### C. Legal Doctrine

While it may have been motivated by political factors, the U.N. decision on the issue of India's membership can also be justified on legal grounds. It is said that membership in an international organization like the United Nations creates "a multiplicity of obligations, all of which are strictly personal in character," and therefore "the contractual relationship of the member to the organization is dependent on the former's continued personality." Under this "continuity theory," membership may still pass to States that have lost extensive portions of their territories and/or have undergone radical changes in government as long as they are considered to have inherited the essential "legal identity" of the former member. In this regard, a distinction must be made between the concepts of "continuity" and "state succession." In the former, the same State is deemed to continue to exist, while in the latter, one or more successor States are deemed to have replaced the former State.

Under the continuity theory, there can be only two ways to view the division of a U.N. member-State: (1) as a "breakaway," in which one of the divisions represents the continuing existence of the State while the others represent States that have seceded from it; or (2) as a complete "dissolution," in which the State has been dissolved and none of the resulting States represent its continuity. Thus, the determination of whether the changes in a State constitute an extinction of its legal personality is critical to the disposition of its U.N. membership. The legal identity of a State might be destroyed if, for example, through division, it lost certain essential portions of its territory such as its seat of government, its original territorial nucleus, or areas from which it obtained extensive revenues necessary for the carrying out of its obligations of membership in international organizations.

Moreover, the case for continuity might vary from organization to organization depending on the nature and functions of the organization and the obligations of its members.

While most commentators accept the continuity-succession dichotomy, there is little practical basis for the distinction with respect to membership in the United Nations. The distinction is said to be justified because "membership of any international organization has as its essence a willingness to co-operate in the furtherance of schemes of international solidarity. Such a willingness cannot be assumed on the part of a new State whose territory falls within the ambit of these schemes." This rationale for not allowing a successor State to inherit its predecessor's U.N. membership, however, would seem to be equally applicable to situations in which a continuing State has undergone a radical change of government. The schemes of the organization may well be just as inimical to a new government as to a new State. Yet, unlike a new State, a continuing State in which a democratic government is replaced by a totalitarian or communist regime retains its U.N. membership under the continuity theory. Furthermore, there is little practical difference between the obligation of a U.N. member-State and the obligation of a non-member-State to comply with the binding decisions of the Security Council—sanctions can be imposed on either for non-compliance. Therefore, willingness to co-operate in furthering U.N. schemes would not provide a legitimate basis for treating successor States differently than continuing States. Indeed, the rationale for the distinction actually turns logic on its head, since it is not a question of the United Nations imposing obligations on the successor State; rather, it is the successor State which desires to inherit its predecessor's U.N. membership with all the attendant obligations. Yet, despite the dubious origins of the India/Pakistan precedent and the questionable nature of the legal doctrine supporting it, there is no doubt it greatly influenced the U.N.'s response to the breakups of the Soviet Union, Yugoslavia, and Czechoslovakia.

## When Russia Came Knocking: Succession to the Soviet Seat

### A. History: The Empire Crumbles

During the seventy years since its birth in 1917, the Soviet state, comprised of fifteen republics in a federal union, gradually expanded to occupy one-sixth of the earth's land surface. By 1991, its population had swelled to over 290 million, its armed forces numbered over 3.7 million members, it possessed some 27,000 nuclear weapons, its gross national product was over $ 2.5 trillion, and it had concluded over 15,000 international agreements. The precise moment of this superpower's collapse may be subject to debate, but there is little doubt that the failed coup by hardline Communists on August 19–21, 1991 provided the fatal blow to the central government's struggle to maintain its eroding power.

Following the attempted coup, the central government immediately allowed the former republics of Estonia, Latvia, and Lithuania to secede from the Union, while Soviet President Mikhail Gorbachev labored unsuccessfully for three months to convince other independence-minded republics to remain in some form of modified union. Gorbachev's proposed "Union of Sovereign States" envisaged a hybrid half-federation, half-confederation in which the Union would act in international relations in the capacity of a sovereign State and an entity in international law, while each republic party to the Union would also be a sovereign State and a full member of the international community. Consequently, the "center" would retain the Soviet seat at the United Nations and would "support applications of the union republics to the United Nations to recognize them as subjects of international law."

Notwithstanding apparent progress in Gorbachev's efforts to preserve the Union, on December 1, 1991, ninety percent of Ukranian voters voted for independence. The surprising outcome of the Ukrainian vote persuaded the other republics that Gorbachev's attempts to negotiate a new Union treaty were doomed. Summing up the resulting situation, then C.I.A. Director Robert M. Gates stated that "the center is evaporating before our eyes." A week after the Ukrainian vote, the leaders of Russia, Ukraine, and Byelorussia formally announced the dissolution of the Soviet Union and said they had agreed to establish a "Commonwealth of Independent States" in its place. Shortly after this announcement, eleven of the twelve remaining former republics signed a Commonwealth Accord.

The Commonwealth Accord contemplates a conference of heads of state and government based in the Byelorussian capital of Minsk as the main political institution of the Commonwealth, with the chairmanship rotating among the member-States. Although the Commonwealth would coordinate foreign affairs, defense, economics, and transportation, Russian President Boris Yeltsin made clear that, in contrast to the approach embodied in the Union Treaty proposed by Gorbachev, "the Commonwealth is not a State." With respect to the Soviet seat in the United Nations, in a display of George Orwell's maxim that "all animals are equal, but some animals are more equal than others," the Commonwealth leaders underscored the preeminence of Russia in the new grouping by voting unanimously for Russia to assume the seat. Under the Commonwealth Accord, the other members of the Commonwealth (except Byelorussia and Ukraine, which were already U.N. members) would insist on their rights as independent States to apply for their own membership in the United Nations.

A sweeping series of decrees by Russian President Boris Yeltsin and action by the Russian parliament followed, transferring to Russia many of the central government's agencies and institutions, including the Soviet parliament, the Soviet Central Bank, the Soviet Foreign Ministry, and all Soviet embassies abroad. As one commentator noted, "Yeltsin's decree assuming direct control over the Kremlin, a walled city of palaces and cathedrals adjoining Red Square, is the equivalent of a takeover of the White House and Capitol Hill rolled into one." In the end, President Gorbachev, left ruling nothing but "a kingdom of air," agreed to step down and end the Soviet Union on December 31, 1991.

### B. Russia Assumes the Soviet Seat

Russia's quest to inherit the U.S.S.R.'s U.N. seat took some U.S. officials by surprise. Yeltsin's suggestion to Secretary of State James Baker during their meeting in Moscow on December 16, 1991, that Russia would seek the Soviet seat drew a noncommittal response. Baker said only that the question would have to be taken to the United Nations, at which point the United States would offer a view. As late as December 22, U.S. officials were still publicly stating that for Russia to replace the Soviet Union on the Security Council, it must "first apply for the seat, after which the matter would be debated by the General Assembly and Security Council." Meanwhile, Russian President Yeltsin sent a letter to the U.N. Secretary-General suggesting a far less cumbersome process. His letter proposed that Russia would simply "continue" the membership of the Soviet Union in the United Nations and requested that the United Nations use the name "The Russian Federation" in place of the name "The Union of Soviet Socialist Republics."

Finally, during a Christmas Eve televised speech to the American people, President Bush announced that the United States would "support Russia's [automatic] assumption of the U.S.S.R.'s seat as a permanent member of the United Nations' Security Council." A week later, the former Soviet representative, sitting behind a shiny new nameplate emblazoned with the words "The Russian Federation," took part in the first Security Council meeting of the new year without challenge. Within twelve months, the United Nations approved the applications for membership of the other former Soviet republics without dissent.

## C. Political Backdrop

In retrospect, given the swiftness and apparent ease with which the Soviet seat was passed to Russia, this result might seem the only sensible solution. During the period of transition, however, the United States and other members of the Security Council seriously considered a variety of other proposals. One option was to treat the Soviet seat as having expired. This would have been consistent with the declaration made by the leaders of the former Soviet republics in December that "the U.S.S.R. is ceasing its existence as a subject of international law and a geopolitical reality." Another proposal would have allowed the Commonwealth of Independent States to take the Soviet U.N. seat. To understand the choice ultimately made, one must begin by examining the motivations of the members of the Security Council.

The question of the disposition of the Soviet Union's seat came against a backdrop of efforts to seek amendment of the U.N. Charter to provide for greater representation on the Security Council and to abolish or modify the veto. As mentioned above, the U.N. Charter specifically names the Soviet Union as one of the five permanent members of the Security Council with veto power (the "Perm Five"). The other members of the Perm Five worried that any change to the Soviet seat would set off a scramble by other countries for Security Council reform.

Since 1966, when the members of the United Nations amended the U.N. Charter to enlarge the Security Council from eleven to fifteen members, proposals have been made to make other States permanent members of the Security Council (with or without the veto) in addition to or instead of some of the Perm Five. In recognition of their role as economic superpowers paying a rising share of U.N. bills, Japan and Germany have been pressing for permanent Security Council seats, and India, Brazil, and Nigeria have been mentioned as possible candidates for permanent membership without a veto. A proposal gaining increasing support among many countries would merge the British and French permanent seats and give this new single seat to the European Community, with the leftover seat going to Japan.

The permanent members of the Security Council thus had an interest in ensuring that changes to Soviet membership in the United Nations would not produce challenges to other features of the Security Council, such as the permanent five/rotating ten number and composition, the inseparability of the veto from a permanent seat, and the non-rotation of permanent members. Although amendments cannot be made to the U.N. Charter without the consent of the permanent members of the Security Council, other members of the United Nations are free to propose such changes and have ample opportunities to pressure the Security Council and the General Assembly to adopt such proposals. As one commentator noted, "The one thing the United States, Britain and France want to avoid at all costs is anything that would open up the Pandora's box of a Charter amendment altering the present membership of the Security Council and possibly ending the right of veto."

In particular, the permanent members reportedly feared that leaving the Soviet seat vacant would be seen as an open invitation to other members to push their proposals for expanding or altering the composition of the Perm Five. Similarly, they were said to have been worried that allowing the Commonwealth of Independent States to replace the Soviet Union would further fuel proposals to replace Britain and France with the European Community on the Council. According to press reports, they were also concerned that giving the seat to the Commonwealth would bestow permanent member status upon an entity with little real authority which, because it must constantly seek consensus among the republics, would at best produce delays in Security Council action and at worst paralyze the Council altogether on particular questions such as those relating to Middle East issues.

The permanent members therefore desired the disposition to be undertaken smoothly without requiring or inviting Charter amendment and in a manner that would not undermine the effectiveness of the Council. In light of the precedent discussed in the next section of this article, allowing Russia to take the seat in place of the Soviet Union seemed the most orderly way to accomplish this goal.

### D. Fitting Within U.N. Precedent

During the month of December 1991, Russia's characterization of the breakup of the Soviet Union underwent a radical change. At the beginning of the month, Russia, along with the leaders of Ukraine and Byelorussia, declared that the Soviet Union had "ceased to exist as a subject of international law and a geopolitical reality." The Commonwealth Accord signed later in the month by eleven of the former republics similarly states that "with the formation of the Commonwealth of Independent States, the Union of Soviet Socialist Republics ceases to exist." A letter from Boris Yeltsin to President Bush stated, "the end of existence of the USSR as a subject of international law require that … the question of the Security Council permanent member's seat be urgently addressed.… Russia would be a State-successor to the USSR with respect to its seat in the U.N. and the Security council [sic]."

In contrast, Yeltsin's December 26 letter to the Secretary-General made no such references to the extinction of the Soviet Union and did not use the term "State-successor." Rather, Yeltsin asserted that the Soviet Union's U.N. membership "is continued" by the Russian Federation. The change in the way Yeltsin described the Soviet situation was not mere happenstance. Instead, it clearly reflects the Russian leadership's growing understanding of the U.N. precedent regarding succession to membership. To better reflect the legal strength of its claim to the Soviet seat, Russia recast the Soviet situation in terms that would more closely follow that precedent. To be consistent with that precedent, Russia would have to argue that it would occupy the Soviet seat not as an entirely new State succeeding to the rights of the Soviet Union (a "Successor State") after the Soviet Union had ceased to exist, but as that part of the Soviet Union that has survived the breakaway of the other republics.

In many ways, the India/Pakistan precedent and Russia's succession to the Soviet seat present factually similar cases. India could easily be characterized as the continuation of British India because it retained seventy-five percent of the territory and eighty percent of the population of British India, it kept the name India, and it kept the seat of the government and virtually the same governmental machinery. Moreover, on its face, the devolution agreement between India and Pakistan seemed to clarify that the two States regarded India as solely entitled to succeed to the British India seat.

Similarly, Russia—which had three-fourths of the former Soviet Union's land area, more than half of the Soviet Union's population of 280 million, most of the Soviet Union's resources, nuclear weapons, nuclear assembly plants, and its army, whose territory contained the seat of the former Soviet Government, which had taken over most of the former Soviet Government institutions and agencies, and which had obtained the formal agreement of the other republics that it should take over the Soviet seat in the United Nations—could make a compelling case that it should be treated as the continuation of the Soviet Union just as India was treated as the continuation of British India. More-over, Russia could argue that, because two of the larger republics—Byelorussia and Ukraine—had been independent members of the United Nations since its inception, the residual Soviet Union, for purposes of U.N. membership, has always consisted over-whelmingly of Russia. Even history could be used to bolster Russia's position: when Czarist Russia became the Soviet Union after the revolution of October 1917, the inter-national community insisted that the Soviet Union was not a new State, but simply a new regime.

Obviously, the case would have been different if there had been no dominant entity re-maining which could be considered to possess the political, economic, and military power of the entity to which it sought to succeed, especially with respect to a State that had per-manent Security Council membership. Indeed, despite Soviet Foreign Minister Alexan-der Bessmertnykh's protestations that "Russia will remain a great power," if not for the political concerns described earlier, proposals may well have been made to allow the So-viet Security Council seat simply to expire on the ground that this special status was ac-corded the Soviet Union based upon unique historical circumstances and its superpower status. After all, a superpower is more than "a central Eurasian arsenal that used to be a country."

Assertions by the leaders of Russia and the other former republics that the Soviet Union ceased to exist initially placed the logic and legal basis of Russian succession to the Soviet seat in serious doubt. Clearly, the India/Pakistan precedent turned on this point. As characterized by the United Nations, while India's sovereignty had changed, at no time did it become legally extinct as a State. By the same logic, the Russian letter to the Secretary-General asserting that Russia was the continuation of the Soviet Union fortified Russia's case.

The timing of Russia's effort to inherit the Soviet seat may have also been important. Russia made its bid at a time when only the Security Council was in session and when the next session of the General Assembly was months away. Having participated in the Security Council for several months without objection, Russia minimized the possibility that mem-bers of the General Assembly would be able to challenge its assumption of the Soviet seat. As one involved diplomat remarked, "Frankly, we were lucky the General Assembly wasn't in session ... Otherwise we might have had howls of fury to contend with."

## The Exclusion of the "New Yugoslavia"

### A. The Dissolution of Yugoslavia and the Question of FRY Continuity

Prior to its fragmentation, the Socialist Federal Republic of Yugoslavia had an overall population of 23.7 million people and the third largest army in Europe. Yugoslavia con-sisted of six republics: Serbia (with a population of 9.8 million people), Croatia (4.7 mil-lion), Bosnia-Herzegovina (4.1 million), Macedonia (2.1 million), Slovenia (1.9 million), and Montenegro (0.5 million). The death of the great Yugoslav leader Joseph Broz Tito and the collapse of the Soviet Union unleashed the centrifugal forces which led to the country's disintegration beginning in June 1991. Over the course of the next ten months, four of the six Yugoslav republics—Slovenia, Croatia, Macedonia, and Bosnia-Herze-govina—declared their independence and were formally recognized as sovereign States by the international community. In response, Serbia sent the former Yugoslavia National Army (JNA) into Slovenia, Croatia, and Bosnia, setting off a conflict which by 1993 had claimed over 200,000 lives. Together with local insurgent forces, the JNA quickly seized control of one-third of the territory of Croatia and two-thirds of Bosnia.

On April 27, 1992, a joint session of the Parliamentary Assembly of the former Socialist Federal Republic of Yugoslavia, the National Assembly of the Republic of Serbia, and the Assembly of the Republic of Montenegro adopted a declaration expressing the will of the citizens of Serbia and Montenegro to "stay in the common State of Yugoslavia...." At the time of this declaration, the U.N. Security Council was considering imposing economic sanctions against Serbia for its involvement in the hostilities in Croatia, Slovenia, and Bosnia. In this context, the Security Council was unlikely to approve an application by Serbia-Montenegro for new membership in the United Nations. Consequently, it was critically important to Serbia-Montenegro that it be viewed as the continuation of the former Yugoslavia so that it could circumvent the application process. Thus, the April 27 declaration proclaimed that the "Federal Republic of Yugoslavia (FRY) continues the State, international legal and political personality of the Socialist Federal Republic of Yugoslavia." To justify the treatment of the FRY as the continuation of the former Yugoslavia, Serb officials asserted that the FRY had "all the physical and material as well as legal conditions for Yugoslavia's uninterrupted identity and existence." A comparison between the Yugoslavian situation and the Russian and Indian precedents provides a framework for assessing that claim.

Several factors support the FRY's claim to be the continuation of the former Yugoslavia. First, the other former Yugoslav republics split off from Yugoslavia at different times. Second, the FRY never claimed to be a new State but rather maintained that it continued the legal personality of the former Yugoslavia after the breakaway of the other republics. Third, the FRY, like Russia, has the most land mass and largest population of all the Yugoslav republics. Serbia and Montenegro's combined territory of 102,000 square kilometers comprises forty percent of the territory of the former Yugoslavia, and its population of 10.3 million is forty-five percent of that of the former Yugoslavia. Just as Russia formed the historic hub of the Soviet Union, Serbia and Montenegro formed the historic nucleus of Yugoslavia, including the federal capital of Belgrade. The FRY retained most of the former Yugoslavia's central government institutions and control of a majority of the former Yugoslavia's federal armed forces.

The Yugoslavia situation and the earlier precedents, however, proved far from a perfect match. In contrast to Russia and India, Serbia and Montenegro together do not comprise a majority, let alone a substantial majority, of Yugoslavia's land, population, or resources. Moreover, unlike Russia and India, no devolution agreement existed between the republics of the former Yugoslavia providing that the FRY shall continue the former Yugoslavia's membership in the United Nations. Indeed, the other former republics were quick to assert that Yugoslavia had dissolved and that the FRY should not be entitled to the former Yugoslavia's seat at the United Nations. Finally, by undertaking and supporting aggressive actions in Croatia, Slovenia, and Bosnia, the FRY provided the members of the United Nations with a strong political reason to block the FRY's effort to assume the Yugoslavia seat.

### B. The Initial Reaction of the International Community

The United States, Canada, Japan, and most of the members of the European Community (EC) boycotted the April 27 ceremony inaugurating the FRY, and an EC spokesman declared that the disposition of the former Yugoslavia's seat at the United Nations was a matter that all the former members of the Yugoslav Federation had to decide together. Later that week, when the FRY circulated a copy of the April 27 Declaration to the members of the Security Council, Australia, Canada, the EC, and the United States responded by sending communications to the Presidents of the Security Council and the General Assembly expressly reserving their position as to whether the FRY should be treated as the continuation of the former Yugoslavia for purposes of membership in the United Nations. Austria went even farther in its communication, stating that "there is no legal basis for an automatic continuation of the legal existence of the former Socialist Federal Republic of Yugoslavia by the Federal Republic of Yugoslavia, which therefore cannot be considered to continue the Yugoslav membership in the United Nations."

The issue next arose on May 22, 1992, when the Security Council and General Assembly voted to admit three of the other former Yugoslav republics as new members of the United Nations. The FRY circulated a document in the General Assembly, which stated:

> The fact that the Republic of Slovenia, the Republic of Croatia, and the Republic of Bosnia and Herzegovina have become Member States of the United Nations in no way challenges the international legal personality and continuity of membership of the Federal Republic of Yugoslavia in the United Nations and its specialized agencies.

The United States responded in a statement to the General Assembly that "if Serbia and Montenegro desire to sit in the U.N., they should be required to apply for membership and be held to the same standards as all other applicants." According to the then Legal Adviser of the U.S. Department of State, "the U.S. position was very simple in this regard: because the SFRY no longer exists, and Serbia-Montenegro is not the continuation of, or the sole successor to, the former Yugoslavia, Serbia-Montenegro is not entitled to assume the seat of the former Yugoslavia in international organizations."

Despite these statements, no immediate action was taken to prevent the FRY from participating in U.N. meetings. During the next several months, the United States consulted with foreign ministries around the world to enlist their support for the American strategy to oust the FRY from the United Nations. There were several possible ways to accomplish the task consistent with the U.S. view that the FRY was not the continuation of the former Yugoslavia. One possibility was to mount a credentials challenge, as against South Africa in 1974. Another option was for the General Assembly to pass a resolution rejecting the FRY's claim to be the continuation of the former Yugoslavia, much as the General Assembly had unseated the delegation of the Nationalist Government as the representative of China in the United Nations in 1971. A third option was for the General Assembly to act upon the recommendation of the Security Council, following the Charter's formula for other membership questions by analogy.

The permanent members of the Security Council found the last of these options the most attractive because, by requiring the approval of the Security Council as a prerequisite for General Assembly action, their ability to unilaterally block this type of action against other members in the future was preserved. During the last week of May 1992, the United States sought to implement its proposal as part of Resolution 757, which imposed economic sanctions on the FRY. The other permanent members of the Council, however, were not ready to take such action, and the language ultimately adopted in the resolution merely noted that the FRY's claim to the U.N. seat "has not been generally accepted."

One month later, a decision by the Arbitration Commission of the International Conference on the Former Yugoslavia breathed new life into the U.S. proposal. On July 4, 1992, the Commission issued three opinions stating that the former Yugoslavia has been dissolved and that it "no longer exists"; that the FRY "is a new State"; and that none of the successor States, including the FRY, can claim sole entitlement to "the membership rights previously enjoyed by the Socialist Federal Republic of Yugoslavia." While the FRY responded that the Commission's opinions went beyond the scope of the Arbitration

Agreement and were therefore "null and void and non-binding," the EC decided that it would support proposals to bar the FRY from participating as the continuation of the former Yugoslavia in international bodies.

## C. Security Council Resolution 777 and General Assembly Resolution 47/1

With the EC finally on board and the opening session of the General Assembly approaching, the United States felt the time was right to press the issue in the Security Council. The United States circulated a draft resolution that would have:

> [R]ecommend[ed] to the General Assembly that it deny the claim by the Federal Republic of Yugoslavia (Serbia and Montenegro) to continue automatically the membership of the former Socialist Federal Republic of Yugoslavia in the United Nations and that it confirm that Yugoslavia's membership in the United Nations has been extinguished.

In order to obtain Russian support, however, the resolution, as finally adopted, was substantially weakened to read:

> *Considering* that the State formerly known as the Socialist Federal Republic of Yugoslavia has ceased to exist,

> *Recalling* in particular resolution 757 (1992) which notes that "the claim by the Federal Republic of Yugoslavia (Serbia and Montenegro) to continue automatically the membership of the former Socialist Federal Republic of Yugoslavia in the United Nations has not been generally accepted",

> 1. *Considers* that the Federal Republic of Yugoslavia (Serbia and Montenegro) cannot continue automatically the membership of the former Socialist Federal Republic of Yugoslavia in the United Nations; and therefore recommends to the General Assembly that it decide that the Federal Republic of Yugoslavia (Serbia and Montenegro) should apply for membership in the United Nations and that it shall not participate in the work of the General Assembly;

> 2. *Decides* to consider the matter again before the end of the main part of the forty-seventh session of the General Assembly.

As adopted, Resolution 777 contains language that is ambiguous and internally inconsistent. On the one hand, the resolution appears to reflect the U.S. view that Yugoslavia has ceased to exist and that the FRY must apply for membership in the United Nations. On the other, the only consequence that the resolution draws is that the FRY shall not participate in the work of the General Assembly. Normally, one would turn to the Security Council's record of debate to illuminate an ambiguously worded text. In this case, however, the statements made by the members of the Council at the time of voting on the resolution were as inconsistent as the language of the resolution itself.

To enable the reader to appreciate these contradictions fully, the statements of Russia and the United States are quoted at some length below. Before voting on the resolution, Russia stated:

> The delegation of the Russian Federation is ready to support the draft resolution agreed upon by members of the Security Council in the course of their consultations, on the basis of the fact that the prevailing view in the international community is that none of the republics that have emerged in the place of the former Socialist Federal Republic of Yugoslavia can claim automatic continued membership in the United Nations. We agree that the Federal Republic of Yugoslavia, like other former Yugoslav republics, will have to apply for membership in the United Nations, and we will support such an application.

At the same time, we were unable to agree with the proposal, put forward by some States, that the Federal Republic of Yugoslavia should be excluded formally or de facto from membership in the United Nations....

The compromise that has been reached — that the Federal Republic of Yugoslavia should not participate in the work of the General Assembly — may seem unsatisfactory to some.... At the same time, the decision to suspend the participation of the Federal Republic of Yugoslavia in the work of the General Assembly will in no way affect the possibility of participation by the Federal Republic of Yugoslavia in the work of other organs of the United Nations, in particular the Security Council, nor will it affect the issuance of documents to it, the functioning of the Permanent Mission of the Federal Republic of Yugoslavia to the United Nations or the keeping of the nameplate with the name Yugoslavia in the General Assembly Hall and the rooms in which the Assembly's organs meet.

The United States, on the other hand, made the following statement:

For the first time, the United Nations is facing the dissolution of one of its Members without agreement by the successor States on the status of the original United Nations seat. Moreover, none of the former republics of the former Yugoslavia is so clearly a predominant portion of the original State as to be entitled to be treated as the continuation of that State. For these reasons, and in the absence of agreement among the former republics on this issue, my Government has made it clear all along that we cannot accept Serbia and Montenegro's claim to the former Yugoslavia's United Nations seat.

We are gratified that the current resolution endorses this view and recommends that the General Assembly take action to confirm that the membership of the Socialist Federal Republic of Yugoslavia has expired and because Serbia and Montenegro is not the continuation of the Socialist Federal Republic of Yugoslavia it must apply for membership if it wishes to participate in the United Nations.

I would like to comment on the provision of the resolution that Serbia and Montenegro shall not participate in the work of the General Assembly. This provision flows inevitably from the determination by the Council and the General Assembly that Serbia and Montenegro is not the continuation of the former Yugoslavia and must apply for membership in the United Nations. To state the obvious, a country which is not a member of the United Nations cannot participate in the work of the General Assembly.

Russia thus maintained that the resolution merely "suspended" the FRY from the work of the General Assembly and permitted the FRY to continue to participate in all other respects as a member of the United Nations. The United States, on the other hand, asserted that the action confirmed that Yugoslavia's membership had "expired" and that the FRY could not participate in the work of the General Assembly because it was not a member of the United Nations. The United Kingdom attempted to clarify the matter when it introduced General Assembly Resolution 47/1, implementing the Security Council's recommendation:

The text before us does two things. First, the Assembly would decide that the Federal Republic of Yugoslavia (Serbia and Montenegro) shall not participate in the work of the General Assembly: this means in particular that no representative of the Federal Republic of Yugoslavia will sit in the seat of Yugoslavia in any organ of the Assembly. Second, the Assembly would decide that the Federal Republic of Yugoslavia (Serbia and Montenegro) would apply for membership in the United Nations. In other words, as regards the need to submit an application for membership, the Federal Republic of Yugoslavia (Serbia and Montenegro) is in precisely the same position as other components of the former Socialist Federal Republic of Yugoslavia....

In no sense is this draft resolution a punitive measure, nor one designed to undermine the peace process. Quite the contrary. It is a measure that we have been forced to take by the completely unjustified claim by the Federal Republic of Yugoslavia (Serbia and Montenegro) to represent the continuity of the Socialist Federal Republic of Yugoslavia.

Yet, the United Kingdom's statement served only to muddle the issue further. By stating that the resolution was not designed as a "punitive measure" but was necessary because of the FRY's "completely unjustified claim" to be the continuity of the former Yugoslavia, it seemed to support the U.S. view as opposed to Russia's characterization of the measure as a "suspension." On the other hand, by stating that the FRY representatives "may not sit in the seat of Yugoslavia in any organ of the Assembly," it gave support to the position that the action was not intended to limit the FRY's continuing participation in other U.N. bodies.

Understandably, some members of the U.N. Secretariat were initially confused about the meaning of this resolution. The morning after Resolution 47/1 was adopted, the flag of Yugoslavia was not raised with those of the other members of the United Nations. When asked at a press briefing if that meant Yugoslavia's membership in the organization had expired as the United States had asserted, the spokesman for the President of the General Assembly responded that "a misunderstanding of a technical nature had occurred and that the flag would be hoisted within the next 30 minutes." He added "that there were still 179 Member States of the United Nations." In an attempt to settle the matter, Croatia and Bosnia transmitted a letter to the Secretary-General requesting a legal opinion as to the FRY's status in the United Nations. The FRY, in turn, sent a letter to the Secretary-General arguing for a narrow interpretation of Security Council Resolution 777 and General Assembly Resolution 47/1.

On September 29, then Under-Secretary-General for Legal Affairs of the United Nations, Carl-August Fleischhauer, circulated a legal opinion on the meaning of the resolutions, which stated as follows:

The following sets forth the understanding of the United Nations Secretariat regarding the practical consequences of the resolution.

1. While the General Assembly has stated unequivocally that the Federal Republic of Yugoslavia (Serbia and Montenegro) cannot automatically continue the membership of the former Socialist Federal Republic of Yugoslavia in the United Nations and that the Federal Republic of Yugoslavia (Serbia and Montenegro) should apply for membership in the United Nations, the only practical consequence that the resolution draws is that the Federal Republic of Yugoslavia (Serbia and Montenegro) shall not *participate* in the work of the General Assembly.

2. Representatives of the Federal Republic of Yugoslavia can no longer *participate* in the work of the General Assembly, its subsidiary organs, nor conferences and meetings convened by it.

3. The resolution neither terminates nor suspends Yugoslavia's membership in the Organization. Consequently,

a) The seat and nameplate remain as before, but in Assembly bodies representatives of the Federal Republic of Yugoslavia (Serbia and Montenegro) cannot sit behind the sign "Yugoslavia." In addition, Yugoslav missions at United Nations Headquarters and offices may continue to function and may receive and circulate documents. At Headquarters, the Secretariat continues to fly the flag of the old Yugoslavia as it is the last flag of Yugoslavia used by the Secretariat.

b) The resolution does not take away the right of Yugoslavia to participate in the work of organs other than Assembly bodies.

c) The admission to the United Nations of a new Yugoslavia under Article 4 of the Charter will terminate this situation.

4. Resolution 47/1 applies directly only to the United Nations and is not legally binding on the specialized and related agencies.

The members of the United Nations were generally taken aback by the spin the U.N. Legal Counsel had given the resolutions. By a vote of 109 in favor and 57 opposed, the General Assembly adopted a resolution "urging Member States and the Secretariat in fulfilling the spirit of resolution 47/1, to end the de facto working status of Serbia and Montenegro." Under pressure from the Islamic countries in particular, the Security Council adopted Resolution 821, which "*recommended* to the General Assembly that, further to the decisions taken in resolution 47/1, it decide that the Federal Republic of Yugoslavia (Serbia and Montenegro) shall not participate in the work of the Economic and Social Council," the other major organ of the United Nations. At the same time, efforts were launched to exclude the FRY from participating in U.N. specialized and related agencies. While the U.N. Legal Counsel's opinion had said that the resolutions were not legally binding on the specialized and related agencies, this was not viewed as precluding action on their part to exclude the FRY through their own resolutions. During the next few months, the International Civil Aviation Organization, the International Fund for Agricultural Development, the International Maritime Organization, the United Nations Industrial Development Organization, the World Health Organization, and several other organizations adopted resolutions modeled after General Assembly Resolution 47/1.

### D. Making Sense of the FRY Precedent

Commentators have argued over the meaning of Security Council Resolution 777 and General Assembly Resolution 47/1, and even the International Court of Justice has stated that the solution adopted through those resolutions "is not free from legal difficulty." Clearly, the resolutions did not achieve the specific result the United States had sought, namely the complete exclusion of the FRY from the United Nations until such time as it is formally admitted on the legal ground that it was not the continuation of the former Yugoslavia. At the same time, the U.N. action cannot be viewed as merely a disguised suspension as the Russian delegation characterized it. First, the primary sponsor of Resolution 47/1 explicitly stated when introducing the resolution that this was not a punitive measure but was the legally compelled result of the FRY's unjustified claim to be the continuation of the former Yugoslavia. Second, the relevant resolutions all make clear that the only way the FRY can participate again in the General Assembly, Economic and Social Council, and various specialized agencies is to apply and be admitted as a new member. The resolutions, in effect, placed the FRY's membership in a sort of twilight zone pending its admission into the organization as a new member. This interim arrangement allowed the FRY to operate a U.N. mission and circulate documents but excluded the FRY from participating as a member in the vast majority of bodies within the U.N. system.

The solution crafted by the Security Council was obviously motivated by political factors, most importantly (1) the desire to preserve the Council's control over this type of membership question rather than allow the General Assembly to act unilaterally on the issue, and (2) the desire to maintain continuing contacts with FRY authorities at the United Nations to facilitate a peace settlement. In reaching this decision, however, the United Nations did not simply disregard the U.N. Charter and U.N. precedent. Rather, the decision was guided by the principles adopted by the Sixth Committee in 1947, which suggested that a State would cease to be a member of the United Nations if "the extinction of the State as a legal personality" could be shown. Nor were the India and Russia precedents overlooked in deciding to exclude the FRY from participation. Rather, the distinctions between the FRY situation and those precedents formed the basis of the decision. Thus, the U.N. Legal Counsel's opinion stresses that Resolution 47/1:

> Deals with a membership issue which is not foreseen in the Charter of the United Nations, namely, the consequences for purposes of membership in the United Nations of the disintegration of a Member State on which there is no agreement among the immediate successors of that State or among the membership of the Organization at large.

### E. Rebirth of the Forgotten Alternative

For nearly fifty years, the United Nations has approached succession to membership as a question of continuity. Since deciding in 1947 that both India and Pakistan could not succeed to the British India seat, it has never looked back. One U.N. specialized agency, however, has recently departed from the continuity theory and the India/Pakistan precedent. While the United Nations was wrestling with the question of whether the FRY could be deemed the continuity of Yugoslavia, the International Monetary Fund (IMF) decided to allow Bosnia, Croatia, Slovenia, Macedonia, and the FRY all to succeed to the membership of the former Yugoslavia. Under this approach, "the successor will be considered to have been a member without interruption since the dissolution of the SFRY and to have continued, for its share, the membership of the SFRY in the IMF."

The IMF's solution to the problem stands in stark contrast to the conventional view that, because of the personal nature of membership in an organization, the only way membership can be retained after the breakup of a member-State is through a finding of continuity. The IMF plainly selected the one alternative that the United Nations decided to forego in determining succession to membership. The United Nations would soon be presented with a case—the breakup of Czechoslovakia—in which the IMF's approach would better serve its political interests than strict adherence to the continuity theory. The U.N. response to the Czechoslovakia case would therefore test the value placed on precedent in deciding membership issues.

### The Czechoslovakia Split

#### A. The Velvet Divorce

On January 1, 1993, in what has become known as the "velvet divorce," the country of Czechoslovakia divided into the newly independent Czech Republic and Slovak Republic. Following the India and Russia precedents, the Czech Republic—which made up a substantial majority of the territory, population, and resources of the former Czechoslovakia—had a strong case for continuing Czechoslovakia's U.N. membership. Two weeks before the division, however, Czechoslovakia's Ministry of Foreign Affairs informed the United Nations that "the Czech and Slovak Federal Republic [CSFR] as well as the CSFR membership of the United Nations will cease to exist on December 31, 1992. Both successor States—the Czech Republic and the Slovak Republic—are determined to apply for the U.N. membership in the very first days of 1993."

Like India and Russia, the Czech and Slovak republics had entered into a devolution agreement. Their agreement, however, did not provide for Czechoslovakia's membership in the United Nations and related bodies to devolve on one of the two new States. Rather, it purported to divide up Czechoslovakia's membership between the two.

### B. The United Nations Response

The U.N. Legal Counsel circulated an opinion stating that "Czechoslovakia has ceased to exist as of 1 January 1993; there was no continuity by an entity under the same or different name. The membership of the United Nations was reduced to 178 as of that date." As a consequence, the United Nations took the position that the seats that had been occupied by the former Czechoslovakia in U.N. subsidiary organs became vacant as of January 1, 1993.

On January 19, 1993, the General Assembly, acting on the recommendation of the Security Council, approved the admission of the Slovak Republic and the Czech Republic as new members of the United Nations. The United Nations did not, however, allow the Czech Republic and Slovak Republic automatically to fill the vacancies created by the extinction of Czechoslovakia's membership. Instead, it required that the vacancies be filled through the method appropriate to each body, namely by appointment of the President of the General Assembly, by nomination of the President of the General Assembly and agreement of the members of the General Assembly, or by formal elections. Similarly, the U.N. Specialized Agencies took the position "that neither one nor both of the newly formed republics can automatically continue the membership of Czechoslovakia in the agency concerned. Consequently the new republics will be admitted as new members according to the procedures established in the constitution of the respective agencies."

The Czechoslovakia case confirmed a number of points concerning succession to membership in the United Nations. First, only one State can be the continuation of a former member. The Czech and Slovak republics' effort to divide the former Czechoslovakia's seat in U.N. subsidiary bodies and specialized agencies was viewed as incompatible with this principle. Second, the case indicates that, notwithstanding the strength of the factors counseling for a finding of continuity, a would-be successor forgoes the continuity option if it applies for and is admitted into the United Nations as a new member. In other words, a State cannot simultaneously be a new member and a continuing member of the United Nations.

### Conclusion

In the aftermath of the Cold War, the State system has become increasingly fluid, with the centrifugal forces of nationalism perpetually eroding the glue that binds federal States. Across the globe, the recent spate of secessions and dissolutions shows no sign of abating. For example, Canada may soon lose the province of Quebec to secession, North and South Yemen may soon (again) split into two countries, Iraq, Somalia, and Ethiopia totter toward disintegration, and a recent U.S. Defense Department report concluded that "China fares a 50–50 chance of breaking up Soviet-style after the death of leader Deng Xiaoping." As Professor Oscar Schachter recently observed, "these events are not only the stuff of history; they foreshadow the future."

Before 1991, U.N. decisions on membership succession were largely governed by a single precedent, the India/Pakistan split, and the general principles propounded by the U.N. Legal Committee in 1947 in response to that case. With the recent breakup of the U.S.S.R.,

Yugoslavia, and Czechoslovakia, there now exists a sufficient range of precedent to map with some precision the contours of U.N. law of succession to membership.

Under the generally accepted legal theory of succession to membership in international organizations, succession is possible only if the successor can establish sufficient legal identity with the former member. The India, U.S.S.R., Yugoslavia, and Czechoslovakia cases suggest that in determining whether a potential successor is the continuation of the member or whether the member's international personality has been extinguished, the relevant factors include whether the potential successor has: (a) a substantial majority of the former member's territory (including the historic territorial hub), (b) a majority of its population, (c) a majority of its resources, (d) a majority of its armed forces, (e) the seat of the government and control of most central government institutions, and (f) entered into a devolution agreement on U.N. membership with the other components of the former State.

There were two main reasons why India and Russia were treated as continuation cases and Yugoslavia and Czechoslovakia were treated as dissolutions. First, the United Nations placed great emphasis on the existence of devolution agreements which provided that Russia would be entitled to the Soviet Union's membership in international organizations and that India would be entitled to British India's membership in international organizations. No such agreement existed between the components of the former Yugoslavia, and the agreement between the Czech and Slovak Republics purported to divide up seats within U.N. subsidiary bodies and specialized agencies—something which is not compatible with the all-or-nothing nature of continuity. Second, both Russia and India constituted a substantial majority of the former State's territory and had a majority of its population and resources. The FRY, in contrast, occupied only forty percent of the former Yugoslavia's territory and possessed only forty-five percent of the former Yugoslavia's population and significantly less of its resources. The Czech Republic, on the other hand, could have made a compelling case for continuity based on its size, population, and resources, but it forfeited the option when it applied for U.N. membership as a new State.

Given the political nature of the United Nations, it would have come as no real surprise if it handled the question of succession to membership in a completely ad hoc basis without any passing reference to precedent or legal doctrine. While one might still be able to explain the disposition of the U.S.S.R., Yugoslavia, and Czechoslovakia seats as a function of politics, the results were in fact enunciated in the context of previously established principles and precedent. There are a variety of reasons why this should be so. First, the development of, and adherence to, generally applicable rules of succession to membership has the practical benefit of predictability and fairness in future cases. Second, the appeal to the authority of law in deciding membership questions reflects an acknowledgment that the U.N. Charter is ultimately a multinational treaty whose interpretation and application should be based on legal principles. Third, in light of the biting criticism the United Nations endured during the twelve years it refused without legal justification to allow the government of the People's Republic of China to represent China in the Security Council and General Assembly, U.N. members are now especially sensitive to the public perception of the United Nations as an organization whose membership questions are governed by the rule of law. Even today's most powerful countries desire to avoid what may appear to be acts of arbitrary discretion in deciding such questions, especially in the very public forum of the U.N. General Assembly. This is not to suggest that the rules governing succession to membership have not been, or cannot be, manipulated for political reasons; what is significant is that the members of the United Nations have found it in their interests to act (or at least to depict their actions) concerning membership succession in conformity with legal principles and precedent.

On the other hand, it makes little sense for the United Nations to continue to follow a rule simply because it was promulgated in the early years of its existence. It makes still less sense "if the grounds upon which it was laid down have vanished long since, and the rule simply persists from blind imitation of the past." While the continuity approach may have made sense during the Cold War, in an era in which U.N membership is said to be "universal," there is no compelling reason why all of the successor States should not be permitted to inherit the predecessor State's membership in the same way new States succeed to multilateral treaties. To the extent a successor State, such as the FRY, persists in violating the principles contained in the U.N. Charter, rather than reject its claim to membership based on a theory of discontinuity, the better approach might be to expel or suspend the member under articles 5 and 6 of the Charter. Now that the International Monetary Fund has departed from the continuity approach in dealing with succession to Yugoslavia's and Czechoslovakia's membership, the time seems ripe for the United Nations to revisit the continuing logic of the India/Pakistan precedent in a manner that does not disrupt its commitment to the rule of law, perhaps by requesting the International Law Commission to undertake a thorough study of the question of succession to membership in the United Nations.

## Authors' Note

In the midst of a popular revolt, Slobodan Milosevic resigned as President of the Federal Republic of Yugoslavia on October 6, 2000. One of the first acts of the new Yugoslav government was to submit an application for membership in the U.N., which was quickly approved.

## 3. Resolution 1326
### United Nations Security Council, 2000

Adopted by the Security Council at its 4215th meeting, on 31 October 2000.

*The Security Council,*

*Having examined* the application of the Federal Republic of Yugoslavia for admission to the United Nations (S/2000/1043),

*Recommends* to the General Assembly that the Federal Republic of Yugoslavia be admitted to membership in the United Nations.

## 4. Vienna Convention on Succession of States in Respect of State Property, Archives and Debts
*opened for signature* 1983

\* \* \*

### Article 28: Newly Independent State

1. When the successor State is a newly independent State:

(a) archives having belonged to the territory to which the succession of States relates and having become State archives of the predecessor State during the period of dependence shall pass to the newly independent State;

(b) the part of State archives of the predecessor State, which for normal administration of the territory to which the succession of States relates should be in that territory, shall pass to the newly independent State;

(c) the part of State archives of the predecessor State, other than the parts mentioned in subparagraphs *(a)* and *(b)*, that relates exclusively or principally to the territory to which the succession of States relates, shall pass to the newly independent State.

2. The passing or the appropriate reproduction of parts of the State archives of the predecessor State, other than those mentioned in paragraph 1, of interest to the territory to which the succession of States relates, shall be determined by agreement between the predecessor State and the newly independent State in such a manner that each of those States can benefit as widely and equitably as possible from those parts of the State archives of the predecessor State.

3. The predecessor State shall provide the newly independent State with the best available evidence from its State archives which bears upon title to the territory of the newly independent State or its boundaries, or which is necessary to clarify the meaning of documents of States archives of the predecessor State which pass to the newly independent State pursuant to other provisions of the present article.

4. The predecessor State shall cooperate with the successor State in efforts to recover any archives which, having belonged to the territory to which the succession of States relates, were dispersed during the period of dependence.

5. Paragraphs 1 to 4 apply when a newly independent State is formed from two or more dependent territories.

6. Paragraphs 1 to 4 apply when a dependent territory becomes part of the territory of a State other than the State which was responsible for its international relations.

7. Agreements concluded between the predecessor State and the newly independent State in regard to State archives of the predecessor State shall not infringe the right of the peoples of those States to development, to information about their history, and to their cultural heritage.

### Article 29: Uniting of States

When two or more States unite and so form one successor State, the State archives of the predecessor States shall pass to the successor State.

### Article 30: Separation of Part or Parts of the Territory of a State

1. When part or parts of the territory of a State separate from that State and form a State, and unless the predecessor State and the successor State otherwise agree:

(a) the part of State archives of the predecessor State, which for normal administration of the territory to which the succession of States relates should be in that territory, shall pass to the successor State;

(b) the part of State archives of the predecessor State, other than the part mentioned in subparagraph (a), that relates directly to the territory to which the succession of States relates, shall pass to the successor State.

2. The predecessor State shall provide the successor State with the best available evidence from its State archives which bears upon title to the territory of the successor State or its boundaries, or which is necessary to clarify the meaning of documents of State archives of the predecessor State which pass to the successor State pursuant to other provisions of the present article.

3. Agreements concluded between the predecessor State and the successor State in regard to State archives of the predecessor State shall not infringe the right of the peoples of those States to development, to information about their history and to their cultural heritage.

4. The predecessor and successor States shall, at the request and at the expense of one of them or on an exchange basis, make available appropriate reproductions of their State archives connected with the interests of their respective territories.

5. The provisions of paragraphs 1 to 4 apply when part of the territory of a State separates from that State and unites with another State.

**Article 31: Dissolution of a State**

1. When a State dissolves and ceases to exist and the parts of the territory of the predecessor State form two or more successor States, and unless the successor States concerned otherwise agree:

(a) the part of the State archives of the predecessor State which should be in the territory of a successor State for normal administration of its territory shall pass to that successor State;

(b) the part of the State archives of the predecessor State, other than the part mentioned in subparagraph (a), that relates directly to the territory of a successor State shall pass to that successor State.

2. The State archives of the predecessor State other than those mentioned in paragraph 1 shall pass to the successor States in an equitable manner, taking into account all relevant circumstances.

3. Each successor State shall provide the other successor State or States with the best available evidence from its part of the State archives of the predecessor State which bears upon title to the territories or boundaries of that other successor State or States, or which is necessary to clarify the meaning of documents of State archives of the predecessor State which pass to that State or States pursuant to other provisions of the present article.

4. Agreements concluded between the successor States concerned in regard to State archives of the predecessor State shall not infringe the right of the peoples of those States to development, to information about their history and to their cultural heritage.

5. Each successor State shall make available to any other successor State, at the request and at the expense of that State or on an exchange basis, appropriate reproductions of its part of the State archives of the predecessor State connected with the interests of the territory of that other successor State.

## Article 32: Scope of the Present Part

The articles in the present Part apply to the effects of a succession of States in respect of State debts.

## Article 33: State Debt

For the purposes of the articles in the present Part, "State debt" means any financial obligation of a predecessor State arising in conformity with international law towards another State, an international organization or any other subject of international law.

## Article 34: Effects of the Passing of State Debts

The passing of State debts entails the extinction of the obligations of the predecessor State and the arising of the obligations of the successor State in respect of the State debts which pass to the successor State, subject to the provisions of the articles in the present Part.

## Article 35: Date of the Passing of State Debts

Unless otherwise agreed by the States concerned or decided by an appropriate international body, the date of the passing of State debts of the predecessor State is that of the succession of States.

## Article 36: Absence of Effect of a Succession of States on Creditors

A succession of States does not as such affect the rights and obligations of creditors.

\* \* \*

## Article 38: Newly Independent State

1. When the successor State is a newly independent State, no State debt of the predecessor State shall pass to the newly independent State, unless an agreement between them provides otherwise in view of the link between the State debt of the predecessor State connected with its activity in the territory to which the succession of States relates and the property, rights and interests which pass to the newly independent State.

2. The agreement referred to in paragraph 1 shall not infringe the principle of the permanent sovereignty of every people over its wealth and natural resources, nor shall its implementation endanger the fundamental economic equilibria of the newly independent State.

## Article 39: Uniting of States

When two or more States unite and so form one successor State, the State debt of the predecessor States shall pass to the successor State.

## Article 40: Separation of Part or Parts of the Territory of a State

1. When part or parts of the territory of a State separate from that State and form a State, and unless the predecessor State and the successor State otherwise agree, the State debt of the predecessor State shall pass to the successor State in an equitable proportion, taking into account, in particular, the property, rights and interests which pass to the successor State in relation to that State debt.

2. Paragraph 1 applies when part of the territory of a State separates from that State and unites with another State.

## Article 41: Dissolution of a State

When a State dissolves and ceases to exist and the parts of the territory of the predecessor State form two or more successor States, and unless the successor States otherwise agree, the State debt of the predecessor State shall pass to the successor States in equitable proportions, taking into account, in particular, the property, rights and interests which pass to the successor States in relation to that State debt.

* * *

## 5. Paul Williams and Jennifer Harris, State Succession to Debts and Assets: The Modern Law and Policy
Harvard International Law Journal, 2001
[footnotes omitted by editors]

* * *

### Assessment of Liability, and Allocation and Rescheduling of the Paris Club Debts

In June 1992, Slovenia, which was making payments to the Paris Club members, requested that the Paris Club assess individual liability, allocate the debt of the former Yugoslavia, and change its accounting procedures to provide Slovenia credit for the debt it had already paid. Because the Paris Club neither assessed individual liability nor allocated the debt, and the commercial banks applied standard accounting procedures, it credited payments, regardless of their source, to the oldest outstanding claims. As a result, payments made by Slovenia were being applied against Serbian debt, creating a disincentive for Slovenia to continue payments.

As in the case of the former Soviet Union, Germany, which was owed the greatest share of outstanding obligations, took the lead in proposing an allocation of the debt. As a result of Slovenia's request, Germany proposed at the July 1992 Paris Club meeting that the Paris Club recognize the EC Arbitration Commission ruling that the former Yugoslavia no longer existed and that Serbia/Montenegro could not be considered its continuation. Germany also noted that most of the external debt of the former Yugoslavia could be allocated among the successor states.

Germany therefore proposed that the creditors agree to allocate payments received on the basis of which successor states made the payment rather than crediting the payment to the oldest claim. Each creditor would then conclude new bilateral agreements with Slovenia and Croatia on their identifiable share of the debt, including a share of the non-identifiable debt. The non-identifiable debt would be allocated in the same proportion as the respective successor state's share of the identifiable debt. If the successor states subsequently reached an agreement on a different allocation of the debt, that agreement could be substituted for the interim allocation. Germany further proposed that successor states currently at war or not recognized would still be expected to make the payments when they fell pursuant to the original contracts. This latter determination was consistent with the declarative view of recognition since the successor states have an international legal personality and are liable for the debt obligations of the predecessor state regardless of recognition. By 1993, the Paris Club creditor countries had reached tentative agreements in principle with Slovenia, which were finalized in 1996, and they concluded similar agreements with Croatia in March 1995.

### Assessment of Liability and Allocation of the London Club Debts

At Slovenia's initiative, in June 1993 the London Club of private foreign creditors began the process of bilateral negotiations with each of the successor states of the former Yugoslavia, except Serbia/Montenegro. The primary issues with respect to the London Club debt related to: (1) a determination of whether the newly reconstituted National Bank of Yugoslavia, which operated under the jurisdiction of Serbia/Montenegro, continued the legal personality of the National Bank of Yugoslavia, which operated under the jurisdiction of the SFRY, and was therefore authorized to negotiate with the London Club on behalf of all the successor states; (2) the proper allocation of responsibility for identifiable and unidentifiable debt; and (3) the proper means for adjusting the joint and several liability provisions of the original New Financing Agreement concluded with the SFRY and the members of the London Club for U.S.$7.3 billion.

To resolve the question of whether the new National Bank of Yugoslavia continued the legal personality of the former National Bank of Yugoslavia, Slovenia and Croatia persuaded the co-chairs of the Peace Conference to request a ruling from the Arbitration Commission. In Opinion No. 15, the Commission found that the new National Bank of Yugoslavia did not continue the legal personality of the former National Bank of Yugoslavia and that the successor states were not required to resolve the question of debt allocation to private lenders within the confines of the Working Group. However, they could properly engage in bilateral negotiations with representatives of the London Club.

As with the Paris Club debt, a significant percentage of the debt obligations could be allocated on the basis of the identifiable projects which were financed by the debt. However, the question of how to allocate the unidentifiable debt obligations remained. The London Club decided that an initial allocation of unidentifiable debt could be determined on the basis of the percentage of identifiable debt held by the successor states, but that the allocation could be adjusted to compensate for the fact that the successor states, as republics of the former Yugoslavia, had consented to be jointly and severally liable with the other republics and with the central government of the SFRY at the time of the initial loan. The London Club thus increased Slovenia's and Croatia's allocation to account for the fact that they were in a better position than the other successor states to service the debt obligations.

### Allocation of Assets

Due to the unwillingness of the third-party states to freeze or preserve the assets of the former Yugoslavia located abroad, and the location of almost all of the former Yugoslavia's national assets in Belgrade, Serbia/Montenegro was effectively able to seize most of the national assets of the former Yugoslavia, a significant percentage of which were used to finance Serbia's efforts to destabilize Croatia and Bosnia. The other four successor states will thus inherit at most a negligible fraction of the national assets of the former Yugoslavia.

As a result of the economic sanctions on Serbia/Montenegro, the assets of the former Yugoslavia located in foreign banks were eventually frozen, including the gold and foreign currency reserves held by the Bank of International Settlements in Basle. Unfortunately, this action occurred after most of the accounts were substantially depleted by Serbia/Montenegro. Although the other successor states were not subject to sanctions, they were denied access to the frozen accounts.

Negotiations regarding the remaining assets of the former Yugoslavia remained stagnant until December 18, 2000, when official negotiations resumed in Brussels. The resumption of negotiations occurred following the defeat of Slobodan Milosevic by President Vojislav Kostunica and the change in position that arose due to the transition in leadership. Leaders of Serbia/Montenegro no longer claimed that it was solely entitled to the assets of the former Yugoslavia, thereby allowing for a resumption of talks. The continuing Brussels round is the first step forward toward a final distribution of assets.

The above examination of the former Yugoslavia, which involved the adversarial breakup of a state, helped clarify the significant evolution of the norms and regimes relating to the identification of national, territorial, and identifiable debt, as well as the further evolution of the principle of *pacta sunt servanda*, in particular how the creditor states sought to ensure compliance with this principle when the successor states failed to agree on an assumption or allocation of debts and assets. With regard to the principle of equitable allocation, the Yugoslav case provides an opportunity to further explore the contrast between the intense role of creditor states in the allocation of debts with their negligible role in the allocation of assets. It also shows how creditor states sought to allocate responsibility for the predecessor state's debt absent an agreement among the successor states, and how the allocation of assets was then linked to the allocation of debts.

Given that the break-up of Yugoslavia was the first modern instance of a dissolution where no successor state clearly continued the international legal personality of the predecessor state—despite Serbia-Montenegro's claim—this case provides an opportunity to compare and contrast the actual significance of the distinction between continuity and dissolution on important questions of state succession to debts and assets. Moreover, the Yugoslav case study provides insight into the role international law may play in enabling creditor states to structure a resolution of the many questions of state succession to debts and assets in a situation where the successor states are unable to reach agreement among themselves.

* * *

### Distinction Between National and Territorial Debts and Assets

Recent state practice confirms the past state practice of drawing a distinction between national and territorial debts, notwithstanding the contrary position of the 1983 Vienna Convention. Recent practice also affirms the distinction between national and territorial assets articulated in both past state practice and the 1983 Vienna Convention.

In comparing the three cases, the confirmation of the distinction between territorial and national debts was the weakest in the case of the break-up of the Soviet Union, where the entire debt was treated as national debt. The basis of this treatment partly resulted from (1) an inability to identify the territorial application of the debt, (2) the nature of the debt in terms of general assistance, and (3) the centralized nature of the Soviet system, with all debt payments and servicing passing through Moscow. In this case, however, the identification of territorial assets did occur, with the successor states being entitled to the assets located on their territory. In fact, territorial assets were the only assets over which the successor states ever achieved control.

The cases of Yugoslavia and Czechoslovakia both strongly supported the distinction between national and territorial debts and assets. In both cases the creditor and successor states determined that the successor states would be liable for territorial debts and entitled to territorial assets. In the case of Yugoslavia, this allocation occurred by default and at the initiative of the creditor states, but in the case of Czechoslovakia it was initiated by the successor states and confirmed by the creditor states.

The break-ups of Yugoslavia and Czechoslovakia also served to modify the definition of territorial debt and broaden it to that of identifiable debt. Identifiable debt included traditional territorial debt, recognized as debts contracted by the state's national government for projects in a specific region, and also debt identifiable to a particular bank or financial institution located on the territory of a particular successor state. The creditor states assumed that if the funds were loaned to or serviced by a bank located on the territory of a successor state, then the debt must have benefited that state.

The reconfirmed distinction between territorial and national debt is a useful development for future break-ups of states, as it appears to be quite functional in allocating substantial portions of the debts and assets of predecessor states, particularly in cases of non-consensual break-up. The expansion of the territorial principle to include identifiable debt is welcomed by the creditor states since it enlarges the portion of debt which can be identified and secured as territorial debt. However, it should be received by successor states with caution as it can be used to ascribe debt obligations from which successor states might not actually have benefited. In rare cases, the identifiable debt ascribed to the successor states might even belong to the category of odious debt, for which the successor state should not be liable.

* * *

## The Determination of an Equitable Allocation

### The Assessment of Liability and the Allocation of Debts and Assets

Recent state practice provides an elaboration on the definition of an "equitable proportion" of debts and assets. In the case of the former Soviet Union, the creditor states determined that it was "equitable" to hold all of the successor states jointly and severally liable for the debt of the predecessor state. The creditor states justified this approach in part on the basis that the debt of the former Soviet Union was national in character, and it was not possible to establish an equitable allocation among the successor states. The primary rationale was that the creditor states were highly exposed to the former Soviet Union and were concerned that if they attempted to allocate the debt or permitted the successor states to assume individual responsibility for the debt, some of the debt would go unassessed or unallocated, the successor states might never agree on an allocation, and some of the successor states would inevitably default on their debt obligations. The creditor states did not participate in any efforts to allocate the assets of the former Soviet Union equitably, and in fact when called upon by Ukraine to preserve those assets for future allocation, they declined to do so.

While committing to the joint and several liability provision, the successor states endeavored to allocate their responsibility to contribute to the servicing of that debt equitably. The specific criteria used by the successor states are unclear, apart from their reliance upon "economic indicators" to allocate the debt. As the creditor states had feared, however, some of the successor states failed to participate in this allocation meaningfully, while other states actively opposed their allocated share. Successor states sought to allocate the assets of the Soviet Union equitably by adopting the territorial principle for non-moveable assets located within the territory of the former Soviet Union and the principle that successor states would be entitled to a share in the moveable assets and assets located abroad commensurate with their share of liability for the debt of the former Soviet Union. Although Russia's assumption of the national assets violated this agreement, the eventual conclusion of zero-option agreements with all of the successor states except Ukraine brought Russia back into compliance with this agreement and in effect created an equitable allocation of the debts and assets, with Russia held liable for all the debts and entitled to all the national assets.

In the case of the former Yugoslavia, the creditor states assessed liability and allocated most of the debt among the successor states based upon an expanded definition of territorial debt. In order to allocate the remaining national debt, the creditor states calculated the proportionate share of each successor state's territorial debt and then held the respective successor states liable for that share of the remaining national debt. Thus, the creditor states assumed that it was equitable to hold the successor states liable for national debts in the same proportion that they were liable for territorial debts. The creditor states were willing to make this logical leap, as most of the debt of the former Yugoslavia could be allocated as territorial debt. The creditor states did not seek to allocate or preserve the assets of the former Yugoslavia, despite calls from four of the six successor states to do so.

The successor states of the former Yugoslavia did not participate in an agreement on an equitable allocation of its debts and assets. They reluctantly agreed to accept the shares of debt assigned to them by the creditor states in exchange for the ability to participate in the international financial community. The successor states, however, expressed discontent at being held liable for a share of the debt of the former Yugoslavia without being able to access any of its assets. The assets of the former Yugoslavia have not been subject to any equitable allocation, but rather have been wholly assumed by Serbia/Montenegro.

In the case of the former Czechoslovakia, the successor states equitably apportioned the debts and assets on the basis of both a territorial principle and a population principle. The territorial debts and assets became the responsibility of the successor state with whose territory those debts and assets were associated, and the remaining national debts and assets were divided on a two-to-one basis consistent with the proportion of the population of Czechoslovakia retained by the respective successor states. The allocation effected by these two principles was circumscribed by the application of the principle of efficiency and the principle of relevance. The essential aim of these two additional principles was to ensure an efficient as well as equitable allocation. The creditor states did not participate in the allocation of the debts and assets, but did accept the allocations agreed upon by the successor states.

The developments of international law relating to the use and definition of the concept of equitable proportion, if adopted with the necessary caution, can play a useful role in structuring the allocation of the debts and assets in future break-ups. The principle of joint and several liability, as noted above, is unsuitable for most successor states, but might appropriately be used as a principle of liability for continuing states. In the case of continuity, creditor states can seek to hold the individual successor states liable for a proportionate share of the predecessor state's debt, but can then safeguard the repayment of that debt by holding the continuing state jointly and severally liable in the event of a default on that debt by the other successor states. This would in a sense make the continuing state the guarantor of the debt allocated to the other successor states. Holding the continuing state jointly and severally liable would be considered appropriate as the state would retain the rights and privileges of the predecessor state in other matters of state succession and would be more capable of meeting the debt obligations of the predecessor state.

The use of the proportion of territorial debt as a basis for the allocation of national debt should also be greeted with cautious optimism. This method of allocation provides a pragmatic tool for allocating national debt in non-consensual break-ups; however, there is not necessarily a rational connection between each successor state's actual benefit from national debts and its proportionate share of territorial debts. Similarly, there is a problem with identifying the territorial debts of the successor state on whose territory the national bank of the predecessor state was located. The state containing the predecessor state's national bank is likely to receive too large a share of identifiable debt, as much of the national debt would be processed through banks on its territory, and thus it would also be assigned a disproportionate share of the truly national debt. But, absent the promulgation of a better principle in the case of non-consensual break-up, this formula will necessarily be used.

The use of population and economic indicators to determine the share of national debt, as noted above, should also be cautiously relied upon when used by the creditor states to dictate an allocation of debts. However, where the break-up is consensual, these factors appear quite reasonable and might be expanded to include factors such as contribution to gross national product, proportion of territory, and proportion of natural resources. The use of population and economic indicators for allocating national debt in non-consensual cases should not readily be adopted in cases of the dissolution of states with centrally controlled economies, since third-party states are unlikely to have ready access to such data, and the veracity of such data is subject to question. Although successor states are more likely to have access to such data and might be more willing to accept its veracity, the objections of Uzbekistan to the determination of its share of debt based on "economic indicators" is testimony to the caution which should be exercised when utilizing such criteria to allocate national debt.

*Linking the Allocation of Debts to the Allocation of Assets*

Recent creditor state practice rejects, while recent successor state practice confirms, the principle put forth in the 1983 Vienna Convention that a determination of an equitable allocation should take into account the extent of assets passing to the successor states. The assignment of joint and several liability to the successor states of the former Soviet Union by its very nature cannot take into account the share of the assets received by each successor state. In fact, when specifically called upon by Ukraine to preserve the assets of the former Soviet Union for equitable allocation or to modify its responsibility for the debts of the former Soviet Union in relation to its actual share of assets, the creditor states declined. In allocating the territorial and national debt to the successor states of the former Yugoslavia, the creditor states took no account of the fact that none of the successor states except Serbia/Montenegro had access to the assets of the former Yugoslavia, and they did not even attempt to preserve those assets for a future equitable allocation. In the case of the former Czechoslovakia, the creditor states did accept the allocation of debts by the successor states, which corresponded to the allocation of assets. There is no evidence, however, that if the successor states had themselves failed to take into consideration the allocation of assets when assigning liability for debts, the creditor states would have intervened to require such considerations.

Despite the unwillingness of the creditor states to balance liability for debts with access to assets, the successor states generally pursued such a balance. As noted above, the successor states of the former Soviet Union agreed that states would be entitled to access to assets in the same amount as they were liable for debts and that they would eventually sign zero-option agreements providing that they would not be liable for contribution to the debt payments and in return not entitled to access to any national assets. The four successor states of Yugoslavia that did not achieve access to its assets strongly protested against the assumption of the assets by Serbia/Montenegro and continue to seek some compensation. The successor states of Czechoslovakia provided that the allocation of assets would be carried out under the same principles as those applied to the allocation of debts and thus acted consistently with the 1983 Vienna Convention.

The creditor states' reluctance to become involved in the allocation of assets is subject to criticism. Creditor states have substantial power with respect to the allocation of debts and assets, and they have been unwilling to exercise that power regarding the allocation of assets. In addition to improving the chances of having the allocated debt adequately serviced, as noted below, involvement of creditor states in cases of non-consensual breakups is likely the only way in which an equitable allocation of assets might occur.

\* \* \*

**The Role of International Law**

\* \* \*

International law has played an effective role in further preserving the rights of creditor states and in countenancing reasonable agreements reached by the successor states. In all of the recent cases of state succession, the creditor states relied upon the international law of *pacta sunt servanda* and the 1983 Vienna Convention to require that the successor states were bound by the debt of the predecessor state and to dictate or consent to an allocation of that debt. This reliance on international law naturally was coupled with a clear warning that if the successor states wished to participate in the financial community, they would have to agree to service their allocation of debt. In the case of the former Czechoslovakia, the creditor states also successfully relied upon international law to sanction the agreement of the successor states to allocate the debt on a two-to-one basis.

Although international law provided for the link between the allocation of the debts and assets of the predecessor state, this link was only established in the cases of the former Soviet Union and Czechoslovakia upon the initiative and for the benefit of the successor states. With respect to the former Soviet Union, the creditor states ignored this link and pursued their own interest in joint and several liability. In the case of the former Yugoslavia, the successor states were unable to establish a link between the allocation of debts and assets among themselves, and the creditor states showed no interest in establishing such a link. The lack of interest on the part of creditor states in establishing a link between the allocation of debts and assets was short-sighted. If such a link were created, successor states would be more willing and able to service their share of the debt. Not only would the successor states see the allocation as just and fair, but they would be able to use or convert their assets in order to generate income to pay the debt.

Similarly, although international law provides for an equitable allocation of debts and assets, it has not been able to force or dictate an allocation by the successor states in nonconsensual break-ups, nor has it been able to persuade third-party states to become involved in allocating or preserving the assets for future allocation. Creditor states, in fact, have relied upon the lack of an obligation in international law to preserve or allocate the assets of the predecessor state as justification for their inaction. In the absence of an effective utilization of international law to preserve or allocate the assets of a predecessor state, it appears that the old axiom that possession is nine-tenths of the law takes precedence. Although international law has not been effectively used to ensure that those states seizing the assets of the predecessor state are entitled to retain those assets, caution should be exercised in future dissolutions such that international law is not used for such purpose.

International law has been useful in consensual break-ups for providing guidance as to how to allocate debts and assets. With respect to debts, it does appear that whether or not the break-up is consensual, the creditor states will invoke the principles of equitable allocation and consent of creditors to ensure that the debt is fully allocated in a manner likely to ensure that it is properly serviced. Interestingly, the expansion of international law with respect to the definition of an equitable allocation occurred at the initiative of the successor states themselves and absent any meaningful assistance from the legal experts of CAHDI or the EC Arbitration Commission.

The enhanced application of the role of international law with respect to succession to the debts and assets of predecessor states would benefit from: (1) a requirement to consider the allocation of assets when assigning liability for debts; (2) a detailed definition of an equitable allocation, with criteria such as proportion of population and economic indicators as employed in the cases of the former Soviet Union and former Czechoslovakia; (3) a greater willingness and ability of international legal bodies to articulate and apply the principles of international law and to reject expedited and vague conclusions; and (4) the rejection of inequitable principles such as joint and several liability for all successor states regardless of their share of the assets or actual ability to repay the entire debt of the predecessor state.

The reasonable and relatively fair application of the principles of international law, as well as their significant evolution and refinement, in the breakups of the Soviet Union, Yugoslavia, and Czechoslovakia demonstrates the utility of relying on international law to structure a resolution of the many questions relating to state succession to debts and assets. With the modifications suggested above, the modern law and policy of state succession to debts and assets may be relied on to aid in the resolution of highly contentious disputes arising from the future break-ups of states, and may thus enable successor states, international mediators, and other interested third parties to resolve more readily many of the other political and legal issues that arise when a state breaks up.

## Authors' Note

The Arbitration Commission of the Conference on Yugoslavia, popularly known as the Badinter Committee, was a commission set up by the Council of Ministers of the European Economic Community (EEC) on August 27, 1991. In a number of opinions handed down between late 1991 and the middle of 1993, the Badinter Commission made rulings on various legal issues regarding the fragmentation of Yugoslavia. Robert Badinter, a French judge, was appointed president of the five-member Commission consisting of presidents of constitutional courts in the EEC. The Committee's mandate was somewhat vague. At the outset it was envisaged that the Committee would rule by means of binding decisions upon request from "valid Yugoslavian authorities." The Arbitration Commission handed down 15 opinions on major legal questions that arose during the breakup of the former Yugoslavia.

## 6. Conference on Yugoslavia Arbitration Commission: Opinions on Questions Arising From the Dissolution of Yugoslavia
### International Law Materials, 1992

Paris, 4 July 1992
   CONFERENCE FOR PEACE IN YUGOSLAVIA
   ARBITRATION COMMISSION
   OPINION No. 8

On 18 May the Chairman of the Arbitration Commission received a letter from Lord Carrington, Chairman of the Conference for Peace in Yugoslavia, putting three questions to the Commission, the text of which is reproduced in the interlocutory decision delivered this day by the Arbitration Commission.

In the opinion of the Commission, the answers to the first and third questions depend on the answer given to the second. The Commission will therefore start by giving its opinion on Question No 2. Questions Nos 1 and 3 will be dealt with in Opinions Nos 10 and 9 respectively.

Question No 2 runs as follows:

Question No 2

"In its Opinion No 1 of 29 November 1991 the Arbitration Commission was of the opinion "that the SFRY (was) in the process of dissolution". Can this dissolution now be regarded as complete?

The Commission has taken note of the memos, observations and papers sent by the Republics of Bosnia-Herzegovina, Croatia, Macedonia, Montenegro, Serbia and Slovenia.

In an interlocutory decision today, the Commission found that this matter was within its competence.

1. In its Opinion No 1 of 29 November, the Arbitration Commission found that:

– A state's existence or non-existence had to be established on the basis of universally acknowledged principles of international law concerning the constituent elements of a state;

– The SFRY was at that time still a legal international entity but the desire for independence had been expressed through referendums in the Republics of Slovenia, Croatia and Macedonia, and through a resolution on sovereignty in Bosnia-Herzegovina;

– The composition and functioning of essential bodies of the Federation no longer satisfied the intrinsic requirements of a federal state regarding participation and representativeness;

– Recourse to force in different parts of the Federation had demonstrated the Federation's impotence;

– The SFRY was in the process of dissolution but it was nevertheless up to the Republics which so wished to constitute, if appropriate, a new association with democratic institutions of their choice;

– The existence or disappearance of a state is, in any case, a matter of fact.

2. The dissolution of a state means that it no longer has legal personality, something which has major repercussions in international law. It therefore calls for the greatest caution.

The Commission finds that the existence of a federal state, which is made up of a number of separate entities, is seriously compromised when a majority of these entities, embracing a greater part of the territory and population, constitute themselves as sovereign states with the result that federal authority may no longer be effectively exercised.

By the same token, while recognition of a state by other states has only declarative value, such recognition, along with membership of international organizations, bears witness to these states' conviction that the political entity so recognized is a reality and confers on it certain rights and obligations under international law.

3. The Arbitration Commission notes that since adopting Opinion No 1:

– The referendum proposed in Opinion No 4 was held in Bosnia-Herzegovina on 29 February and 1 March: a large majority of the population voted in favour of the Republic's independence;

– Serbia and Montenegro, as Republics with equal standing in law, have constituted a new state, the "Federal Republic of Yugoslavia", and on 27 April adopted a new constitution;

– Most of the new states formed from the former Yugoslav Republics have recognized each other's independence, thus demonstrating that the authority of the federal state no longer held sway on the territory of the newly constituted states;

– The common federal bodies on which all the Yugoslav republics were represented no longer exist: no body of that type has functioned since;

– The former national territory and population of the SFRY are now entirely under the sovereign authority of the new states;

– Bosnia-Herzegovina, Croatia and Slovenia have been recognized by all the Member States of the European Community and by numerous other states, and were admitted to membership of the United Nations on 22 May 1992

– U.N. Security Council Resolutions Nos 752 and 757 (1992) contain a number of references to "the former SFRY";

– What is more, Resolution No 757 (1992) notes that "the claim by the Federal Republic of Yugoslavia (Serbia and Montenegro) to continue automatically (the membership) of the former Socialist Federal Republic of Yugoslavia (in the United Nations) has not been generally accepted";

– The declaration adopted by the Lisbon European Council on 27 June makes express reference to "the former Yugoslavia".

4. The Arbitration Commission is therefore of the opinion:

– That the process of dissolution of the SFRY referred to in Opinion No 1 of 29 November 1991 is now complete and that the SFRY no longer exists.

Paris, 4 July 1992
CONFERENCE FOR PEACE IN YUGOSLAVIA
ARBITRATION COMMISSION
OPINION No. 9

On 18 May 1992 the Chairman of the Arbitration Commission received a letter from Lord Carrington, Chairman of the Conference for Peace in Yugoslavia, asking for the Commission's opinion on the following question:

"If this is the case, (is the dissolution of the SFRY now complete?) on what basis and by what means should the problems of the succession of states arising between the different states emerging from the SFRY be settled?"

The Commission has taken note of memos, observations and papers sent by the Republics of Bosnia-Herzegovina, Croatia, Macedonia, Montenegro, Serbia and Slovenia.

In an interlocutory decision today, the Commission found that this matter was within its competence.

1. As the Arbitration Commission found in Opinion No 8, the answer to this question very much depends on that to Question No 2 from the Chairman of the Conference.

In Opinion No 8, the Arbitration Commission concluded that the dissolution of the Socialist Federal Republic of Yugoslavia (SFRY) had been completed and that the state no longer existed.

New states have been created on the territory of the former SFRY and replaced it. All are successor states to the former SFRY.

2. As the Arbitration Commission pointed out in its first Opinion, the succession of states is governed by the principles of international law embodied in the Vienna Conventions of 23 August 1978 and 8 April 1983, which all Republics have agreed should be the foundation for discussions between them on the succession of states at the Conference for Peace in Yugoslavia.

The chief concern is that the solution adopted should lead to an equitable outcome, with the states concerned agreeing procedures subject to compliance with the imperatives of general international law and, more particularly, the fundamental rights of the individual and of peoples and minorities.

3. In the declaration on former Yugoslavia adopted in Lisbon on 27 June 1992, the European Council stated that:

"The Community will not recognize the new federal entity comprising Serbia and Montenegro as the successor State of the former Yugoslavia until the moment that decision has been taken by the qualified international institutions. They have decided to demand the suspension of the delegation of Yugoslavia at the CSCE and other international fora and organizations."

The Council thereby demonstrated its conviction that the Federal Republic of Yugoslavia (Serbia and Montenegro) has no right to consider itself the SFRY's sole successor.

4. The Arbitration Commission is therefore of the opinion that:

– The successor states to the SFRY must together settle all aspects of the succession by agreement;

– In the resulting negotiations, the successor states must try to achieve an equitable solution by drawing on the principles embodied in the 1978 and 1983 Vienna Conventions and, where appropriate, general international law;

– Furthermore full account must be taken of the principle of equality of rights and duties between states in respect of international law;

– The SFRY's membership of international organizations must be terminated according to their statutes and that none of the successor states may thereupon claim for itself alone the membership rights previously enjoyed by the former SFRY;

– Property or the SFRY located in third countries must be divided equitably between the successor states;

– The SFRY's assets and debts must likewise be shared equitably between the successor states;

– The states concerned must peacefully settle all disputes relating to succession to the SFRY which could not be resolved by agreement in line with the principle laid down in the United Nations Charter;

– They must moreover seek a solution by means of inquiry, mediation, conciliation, arbitration or judicial settlement;

– Since, however, no specific question has been put to it, the Commission cannot at this stage venture an opinion on the difficulties that could arise from the very real problems associated with the succession to the former Yugoslavia.

* * *

## Authors' Note

The Council of Europe formed the Committee of Legal Advisors on Public International Law (CAHDI) as a mechanism to organize inter-state relations. CAHDI met for the first time in 1991 as a response to the on-going debates on the legal status of the Baltic States. Made up of international legal advisers, CAHDI included representatives of ministries of foreign affairs of the member States of the Council of Europe as well as observer states and organizations. CAHDI serves as the only body of pan-European legal advisors that meet biannually to discuss issues on public international law. CAHDI has addressed issues such as state succession, state recognition, state immunity, international tribunals, and the ICC. The relevant meeting highlighted in this chapter was intended to create a consensus on key issues of state succession arising from the dissolution of Yugoslavia and the Soviet Union.

# 7. Report on Public International Law for the Council of Europe
## Committee of Legal Advisors Meeting, 1992

* * *

## STATE SUCCESSION IN EUROPE RELATING TO TREATIES, STATE PROPERTY, ARCHIVES AND DEBTS

4. The committee decided to examine this question in the light of the latest developments in Europe. The following aspects were discussed:

### State continuation and state succession

5. Several delegations agreed that, in this connection, the situation of the former Soviet Union was very different from that of former Yugoslavia, as the continuation of the Soviet Union by Russia had a historical basis which was absent in Yugoslavia's case. Moreover, the agreement of Alma-Ata had shown that the other republics accepted Russia as principle successor in the United Nations; no such agreements had been reached between the republics of former Yugoslavia.

6. The great majority of delegations were in agreement that all the states of former Yugoslavia had to be treated in an equal manner.

7. One delegation considered, however, that in international law, there was nothing against the former state continuing to exist, providing that it did so within the corresponding territorial boundaries.

8. One observer pointed out that the Badinter Commission had concluded that Serbia and Montenegro were not a continuation of former Yugoslavia. They had become an entity that was not recognized. The observer wondered whether the entity ought not to be given international recognition.

9. The observers from Croatia and Slovenia explained that the process of disintegration now extended to the whole territory of former Yugoslavia. All the new states are equal. The fact that Serbia and Montenegro were together did not give them more rights that the other states. The observer from Slovenia made it clear that his country was not against Serbia Montenegro using the name "Yugoslavia," but that the use of this name could not serve as a pretext for giving them more rights than other states.

* * *

### Property and debts

22. The observer from Russia said that the agreements between the states had defined each country's share (agreement of 4 December 1991 on the foreign debt). Each state could claim its portion of property if it shouldered its share of the debt. So far only Russia was in the process of paying. Russia was currently negotiating with one republic with a view to reaching an agreement whereby Russia might possibly take over the republic's share of debt and its portion of property.

23. The question of the ownership of ships and aircraft was raised. The authorities of third countries, including their judicial authorities, might have to make a decision in this connection. In the opinion of one delegation, the port of registration supplied the answer as far as ships were concerned.

24. Most participants pointed out that the question of ownership of property was a matter to be settled on a fair basis through agreement among the successor states without the intervention of States. However the agreement should not be detrimental to other states.

25. The observer from Slovenia stated that the property of former Yugoslavia was being used exclusively by Serbia-Montenegro, to the detriment of other States. He therefore requested the freezing of all assets.

**Vienna Conventions**

26. Many participants thought that the Vienna Conventions on Succession of States in respect of Treaties (1978) and on Succession of States in respect of State Property, Archives and Debt (1983) did not reflect the current international law on the subject. On the other hand, other delegations felt that these texts were useful and worth consulting as a reference.

**Chairman's summing up**

27. The Chairman summed up the discussion as follows:

i. The discussion showed that State succession was an important topic in which everybody was engaged. The *Vienna Conventions* from 1978 and 1983 do not always reflect the current international law on the subject and must therefore be used with diligence.

\* \* \*

iv. *Membership of international organizations and conferences*: Normally, a new State should apply for membership. In some cases this is necessary in order that other States parties can be informed of national points of contact foreseen by the treaty establishing the organisation etc.

v. *Property and debts*: this is a matter to be settled on a fair basis through agreement among the successor States;

vi. *Former Yugoslavia*: this is a delicate matter but all the States of former Yugoslavia should be treated in an equal manner;

vii. It would be advisable to stay in contact with all *former Soviet Republics* with respect to the recent meeting in Moscow on State succession, in order to keep them informed about the development in this field.

\* \* \*

# 8. Paul R. Williams, State Succession and the International Financial Institutions: Political Criteria v. Protection of Outstanding Financial Obligations

International and Comparative Law Quarterly, 1994
[footnotes omitted by editors]

\* \* \*

## II. The International Law of State Succession Pertaining to International Organizations, and the Past Practice of the IMF and World Bank

The primary questions faced by an international organisation upon the break-up of one of its member States are: what becomes of the membership of the predecessor State, and what becomes of the assets and debts of the predecessor State? As this article will discuss later, the IMF and World Bank were faced with additional questions that arose out of the political circumstances surrounding the break-up of Yugoslavia and Czechoslovakia.

* * *

## Public International Law

Although issues of State succession have a long history in public international law, there is scant precedent regarding the specific issues of succession to membership in international organisations, and the allocation of the assets and debts of a predecessor State.

### Membership of international organisations

Under the general rules of public international law, it is generally assumed that upon the break-up of a State, the continuing State, if it exists, will assume the membership of the predecessor State in international organisations, and the newly independent State or States must seek new membership. In the case of a dissolution it is at best unclear as to which States may inherit the membership of the predecessor State. The uncertainty over whether which successor States, if any, may inherit the membership of the predecessor State upon break-up of that State is further complicated by the fact that, until recently, no clear precedent existed, outside the arena of decolonisation, as to how to determine whether the break-up of a State is a continuation or dissolution.

The break-up of British India into the States of India and Pakistan was generally considered as a case of continuation, with India being treated as the continuity of British India. In the case of the break-up of the Union of Soviet Socialist Republics, Russia was generally considered to be the continuation of the Soviet Union. Although the case of the former Yugoslavia is still outstanding in many international organisations, it is generally considered that no successor State is the continuation but, rather, that the former Yugoslavia dissolved and all successor States are treated equally. And although the case of the dissolution of Czechoslovakia is also outstanding in many international organisations, neither the Czech Republic nor Slovakia is considered to be the continuing State.

One consistency that can be found among these precedents is that the continuing State, if one exists, retains a substantial portion of the predecessor State's population, territory and resources. The determination of continuity has also been affected by the existence of a devolution agreement between the successor States indicating that a particular successor State should assume the predecessor State's membership in international organisations.

### The assumption of assets and debts

*(a) Debts.* Under international law State debt obligations are generally divided into the categories of "debts contracted in the general interest by the national government of the state" (national debt), "debts contracted by the national government of the state for identifiable projects in a specific region" (territorial debt), and "debts of local government entities". The debts of Yugoslavia and Czechoslovakia to the IMF and World Bank are both national debt and territorial debt.

The international law governing State succession to international debt is governed both by State practice and the 1983 Vienna Convention on Succession of States in Respect of State Property and Debts (1983 Vienna Convention). The State practice with regard to national debt in the circumstances of a continuation of a State is that the continuing State is obligated to the full amount of the predecessor State's national debt, unless there is agreement between the continuing State and the breakaway State as to the allocation of the national debt, or unless the breakaway State agrees with the creditors to be obligated to a certain portion of the debt.

Although there is virtually no clear State practice with regard to the assumption of debts by successor States in the case of a dissolution, international law would be likely to apply the same doctrine of *pacta sunt servanda,* which holds a continuing State liable in the case of continuation, to hold the individual successor States liable where a State has dissolved and there is no continuing State.

With regard to territorial debt, State practice is for successor States to assume liability for any debt associated with the acquisition of specific property or benefits within a particular successor State's territory. The obligation of the successor States arises from the doctrines of unjust enrichment and acquired rights. In this instance, State practice does not draw a distinction between cases of continuation or dissolution. Finally, State practice provides that the creditor must consent to any agreement between the successor States allocating the debt. This practice exists to prevent the successor States from allocating the debt in such a manner that it is unlikely to be repaid.

The 1983 Vienna Convention does not draw a distinction between the cases of continuation or dissolution. Neither does the Convention draw a distinction between national and territorial debt. The primary principle underlying the Convention is that the rights of the creditor States or entities should not be prejudiced by the dissolution of the debtor State.

The 1983 Vienna Convention therefore provides that in the case of the break-up of a State, unless the successor States otherwise agree, "the State debt of the predecessor State shall pass to the successor States in an equitable proportion, taking into account, in particular, the property, rights and interests which pass to the successor States in relation to that State debt". Although the Convention provides for the equitable allocation of debt, it does not establish any criteria for determining what is an equitable amount, nor does it permit creditor States to dictate to successor States a determination of an equitable amount. As with State practice, the Convention does not, however, require creditor States to accept an allocation of debt decided upon by the debtor States which might prejudice the rights of the creditor States.

The discussion above generates the general conclusion that successor States are obligated in some manner to accept an equitable share of the national and territorial debt of the predecessor State. This obligation is subject, however, to the consent of the successor States. The precise allocation of the debt is determined by the successor States, subject to the final consent of the creditor States.

*(b) Assets.* The 1983 Vienna Convention addresses the allocation of State property among successor States. Although more specifically orientated towards physical property, the Convention defines State property as "property, rights and interests which, at the date of the succession of States, were, according to the internal law of the predecessor State, owned by that State". Unlike the case of debts, the Convention draws a distinction between the treatment of national assets and territorial assets. The Convention provides that, unless the successor States agree otherwise, movable State property connected with the territory of a particular successor State passes to that State, while movable State property not connected with the territory of a particular successor State passes to the successor States in equitable proportions.

\* \* \*

**III. The Practice of the IMF and World Bank in the Case of the Dissolution of Yugoslavia**

\* \* \*

## Claims of the Successor States and Interests of Member States

As noted above, Serbia/Montenegro claimed to be the continuation of the former Yugoslavia and thereby entitled to its rights and obligations. In the case of the IMF and World Bank such a claim included a claim to continue the membership of Yugoslavia, be entitled to its assets, and be obligated by its liabilities. Serbia/Montenegro's claim of continuity would naturally preclude Slovenia, Croatia, Bosnia-Herzegovina, and Macedonia from succession to membership and any share of Yugoslavia's assets. These successor States of course asserted that Yugoslavia had dissolved and that they were equally entitled to succeed to the membership of Yugoslavia and share in the allocation of its assets.

The United States, and most of the members of the European Community, took the position that Yugoslavia had dissolved for purposes of the IMF and World Bank, and that Serbia/Montenegro should be temporarily excluded from membership, as part of the multilateral effort to punish Serbia/Montenegro for its territorial oppression against Bosnia-Herzegovina.

* * *

## Consideration of the Consequences of Continuation v. Dissolution

As a first step to addressing the questions of State succession, the IMF and World Bank made the following determinations regarding the effect of characterising the break-up of Yugoslavia as either a continuation or a dissolution.

### Continuation

Consistent with State practice and the past practice of the financial institutions, the IMF and World Bank determined that, in the case of continuation, the former Yugoslavia would continue to exist in the form of Serbia/Montenegro. Serbia/Montenegro would be obliged to fulfill the liabilities of Yugoslavia to the IMF and World Bank, but would also retain all Yugoslavia's assets. The breakaway republics would retain no liability for the debt of Yugoslavia, and not be entitled to any share of its assets. Serbia/Montenegro would also be entitled to continue the membership of Yugoslavia, with the breakaway republics being required to apply for new membership.

### Dissolution

The IMF and World Bank determined that, in the case of dissolution, the former Yugoslavia would no longer exist and therefore cease to be a member of the IMF and World Bank. The assets and liabilities of Yugoslavia would be divided among the successor States, with membership of the successor States being determined either through admission or by succession.

### Options for Succession

Taking into consideration the consequences associated with the two theories of State succession, the IMF and World Bank developed and considered two possible options for dealing with the question of membership of the Yugoslav successor States and the allocation of assets and debts: admission to membership, and succession to membership. Considering that the international community had rejected Serbia/Montenegro's claim to be the continuation, the proposals considered by the financial institutions under the admission and succession options, except one, were premised on the dissolution of Yugoslavia.

Because the issue of membership first arose in the IMF, the IMF developed the options for addressing the question of successor State membership. The World Bank, although not obliged to follow the lead of the IMF on questions of succession, provided substantial comment since, as discussed above, a State may not be a member of the World Bank unless it is a member of the IMF.

### Admission to membership

The admission to membership option entailed a determination by the IMF and World Bank that Yugoslavia had dissolved, and that none of the successor States would be entitled to assume the seat of the former Yugoslavia. Each of the successor States would be required to apply to the IMF and World Bank as new members in accordance with their standard membership procedures and conditions.

Because under this option Yugoslavia's membership would terminate, the IMF and World Bank would be required to settle accounts with the successor States. Since the Articles of Agreement do not provide for the settlement of accounts with dissolved member States, the IMF reasoned by analogy that the Fund's rules on settlement of accounts with withdrawing members would apply. Under this procedure, the successor States would be required to redeem the shares of Yugoslavia in the SDR department, minus Yugoslavia's SDR shares still held by the department. The successor States would also lose Yugoslavia's entitlement to share in any potential capital gains that would result from the disposal of the Fund's gold reserve through a sale of that gold, or liquidation of the Fund. And, since the SDRs allocated to Yugoslavia would be cancelled, when the successor States became members they would be entitled to SDRs only in proportion to their quotas.

The World Bank suggested a modified version of this membership approach which would have permitted the continuation of the membership of Yugoslavia with individual successor States applying for membership at will. This approach would have permitted Serbia/Montenegro to retain the membership of Yugoslavia, complete with Yugoslavia's assets, while requiring the other successor States to apply anew and forgo any access to those assets.

### Succession to membership

The alternative option to new membership for the successor States was to permit the successor States to succeed to the membership of Yugoslavia. Succession to the membership of Yugoslavia would entail a finding that Yugoslavia had dissolved and that each successor State was entitled to succeed to its membership. The succeeding States would be assigned a share of Yugoslavia's quota equal to each State's share of Yugoslavia's assets and liabilities. The succeeding States would therefore be permitted to retain a share of Yugoslavia's SDRs in proportion to their quota, and would retain the right to any capital gains that might result from the future disposal of the Fund's gold.

The IMF and World Bank developed three alternative scenarios for succession: complete, partial and conditional. The primary variables motivating the IMF and World Bank to create these options were twofold. First, there was the concern whether the IMF and World Bank would be exposed to outstanding liabilities if the successor States did not unanimously agree upon the allocation of debt owed to the IMF and World Bank. Second, was the political desire to exclude Serbia/Montenegro from participation in the IMF and World Bank.

*(a) Complete succession.* The option of complete succession provided that the IMF and World Bank would make a determination of the allocation of quotas, assets and liabilities and present this determination with an offer of automatic succession of membership to the successor States. When all the successor States had agreed to their respective allocations, they would be entitled as a group to succeed to membership. If any one successor State refused to agree to the allocation, none of the successor States would be entitled

to membership. After succession to membership, the IMF and World Bank could suspend the membership of any successor State that did not meet its obligations under the financial institutions' respective Articles of Agreement.

The benefit of this approach was that the debt obligations of the predecessor State would be fully obligated prior to any of the successor States assuming membership. The disadvantages were that it permitted one State to frustrate, intentionally or unintentionally, the membership of the other successor States. And it provided for the membership of Serbia/Montenegro.

*(b) Partial succession.* The partial succession approach provided that each individual successor State could succeed to the membership of Yugoslavia as soon as it agreed to its allocation of the quota, assets and liabilities, and met the necessary prerequisites.

The advantage of this approach was that the membership of an individual successor State could not be frustrated by one of its fellow successor States. The primary disadvantages were that it permitted successor States to assume membership without the full amount of debt to the IMF and World Bank being accounted for, and without all the successor States agreeing among themselves on the allocation of the quota, assets and liabilities. And, like the complete succession approach, permitted Serbia/Montenegro to attain membership.

*(c) Conditional succession.* The conditional succession approach developed by the IMF and opposed by the World Bank provided that the successor States would be entitled to succeed to the membership of Yugoslavia if they were able to meet specific conditions of succession set by the IMF. The intent of the conditional succession approach was specifically both to develop a succession model whereby all the successor States with the exclusion of Serbia/Montenegro could succeed to membership and to condition the succession to membership on an agreement of each particular State's allocation of Yugoslavia's debt and assets. The two proposals for conditions developed by the IMF were as follows.

*(c)(i) Succession as deemed appropriate.* The first proposal made succession to membership conditional upon a finding by the IMF that an offer of succession would be appropriate at a particular time, with an offer of succession being deemed inappropriate if there were strong opposition among the members of the IMF to the membership of a particular State. The IMF suggested this condition derived from Article II, section 2 of the IMF Articles of Agreement, which provides that membership shall be open to States at such times and in accordance with such terms as may be stipulated by the IMF. Although disguised as a timing condition, this condition basically sets forth the requirement that a State may be denied an offer of succession if such an offer would be opposed by a significant number of the IMF member States.

Two separate cases of precedent within the IMF constrained its ability to pursue this condition of appropriateness. The first arose from previous findings by the IMF, in the context of admission of small States, that although it could delay membership applications for a period of time until the criteria for membership had been met, it could not delay applications indefinitely with the purpose of frustrating membership. Although delays frequently occurred between submission of a membership application and admission, these delays were directly related to the applicant's ability to meet the criteria for membership, and did not occur after the State had met those criteria.

The second restraining precedent also occurred in the context of the admission of small States. Relying on the International Court of Justice's *Advisory Opinion on the Conditions of Admission of a State to Membership in the United Nations,* the IMF had previously determined that it could impose only criteria for membership that were directly derived from the IMF Articles of Agreement. And that, once an applicant had met the criteria for membership, it was entitled to membership.

The IMF also reasoned that the discretionary condition of "appropriateness" would have the effect of negating the offer of succession, as "an offer that remains subject to the entire discretion of the offeror is not a conditional offer, it is not an offer at all". From this premise, the IMF reasoned that a conditional offer based on "appropriateness" would not constitute a valid offer, and the absence of a valid offer at the time of dissolution would result in the requirement that all successor States apply for membership anew.

*(c) (ii) Succession based on ability to meet the obligations of the Articles of Agreement.* The second proposal made succession to membership conditional upon the ability and willingness of the successor States to fulfill the obligations of membership as set forth in the Articles of Agreement. This condition derives from the IMF's implicit authority to require that a State is capable of carrying out its obligations to the IMF before membership is granted.

In order to transform this implicit requirement into an explicit requirement capable of excluding Serbia/Montenegro, the IMF developed the additional condition that the IMF affirmatively determine that the successor State is "able to meet its obligations under the Articles". Relieving any doubt that this criterion was intended to exclude Serbia/Montenegro from membership, the IMF noted in proposing the condition that the finding of ability would include "an assessment of the probability that the successor state is, and will remain in the foreseeable future, able to fulfill its obligations, including its financial obligations to the Fund. In this respect, the expected effect on the country of international sanctions would be relevant."

In addition to the "willing and able" condition, the IMF also proposed that succession be conditional on the requirement that the successor State "be current with the Fund at the time of succession". And, in order to disguise the subjectivity of the first condition, the IMF proposed that succession also be conditional on the successor State adopting "any necessary legislation to accept the offer and to carry out its membership obligations".

The World Bank's General Counsel voiced criticism with this conditional succession approach and characterised it as "at best legally questionable" on the grounds that it was inconsistent with past practice and would expose the financial institutions to the possibility of non-assumption of a significant portion of Yugoslavia's outstanding obligations.

The General Counsel first objected to the conditional approach on the ground that it blurs the line between admission and succession by making the succession of member States conditional on discretionary case-by-case determinations to be made by the financial institutions. The World Bank views membership questions as subject to criteria, while succession is an automatic occurrence. Thus, conditions might be appropriate in the case of new membership, but in the case of succession a State is either a successor State or it is not. If the World Bank therefore treats a succession issue as a membership issue, an excluded State might successfully claim before a board of arbitration that the World Bank's inappropriate exclusion of that State provides cause for the excluded State to be relieved of the obligation to pay its share of the predecessor State's liabilities.

The General Counsel also objected to the specific condition that the IMF make a determination that the individual successor States are willing and able to carry out the obligations of membership. Recognising that this condition was politically motivated and would provide the tool to exclude Serbia/Montenegro, the General Counsel considered that an arbitral tribunal might find the question to be fraught with subjectivity and that the executive directors of the Bank might act inappropriately as representatives of the political will of their sponsoring countries, and not as unbiased determiners of ability and willingness.

Finally, the General Counsel objected to the IMF's conditional approach on the ground that it did not make the succession of the member States conditional on their unanimous agreement on the apportionment of Yugoslavia's assets in and obligations to the financial institutions. The General Counsel contended that lack of agreement might subject the Bank to arbitration by a successor State not agreeing to its allocation of responsibility. The concerns of the General Counsel here are inconsistent with his argument that succession may not be conditional, and that either succession of membership occurs as a matter of law or the States must seek new membership.

As a result of these criticisms, the World Bank's General Counsel found that only three approaches to succession would be legally defensible:

(1) assume the dissolution of Yugoslavia and require the successor States to seek membership anew;

(2) delay action on the membership of Yugoslavia and permit the individual successor States to apply for membership anew; and

(3) permit the automatic succession of all the successor States simultaneously.

Despite the reservations of the World Bank, the IMF pursued the conditional succession approach.

### Decision of the IMF and World Bank

#### IMF

On 15 December 1992 the IMF announced that it "found that [Yugoslavia] has ceased to exist and has therefore ceased to be a member of the IMF". The IMF considered the States of Slovenia, Croatia, Bosnia-Herzegovina, Macedonia, and Serbia/Montenegro to be the successors to the assets and liabilities of Yugoslavia in the IMF, and had allocated those assets and liabilities among the successor States, as well as the quota of the former Yugoslavia.

The successor States were permitted to notify the IMF within one month whether they agreed to their allocations of assets and liabilities. The IMF provided that if a particular successor successfully challenged its allocation of assets and liabilities, the shares of the other successor States would be adjusted on a pro rata basis.

Formal succession to membership of Yugoslavia in the IMF would be open to all successor States at such time as they met the following conditions:

(1) notification to the IMF that the State agrees to the allocation of its share in the assets and liabilities of Yugoslavia;

(2) notification to the IMF that the State agrees "in accordance with its law, to succeed to the membership in accordance with the terms and conditions specified by the IMF and has taken all the necessary steps to enable it to succeed to such membership and carry out all of its obligations under the Articles of Agreement";

(3) it has been determined by the IMF that the State is "able to meet its obligations under the Articles"; and

(4) the State has no overdue financial obligations to the IMF.

The IMF provided that the successor States would have a period of up to six months within which to meet these conditions.

Subsequent to this decision of the IMF, Slovenia, Croatia, Bosnia-Herzegovina, and Macedonia have succeeded to membership of the IMF. Serbia/Montenegro's request for succession has been denied, and the six-month period has expired.

### World Bank

On 25 February 1993 the executive directors of the World Bank determined that Yugoslavia had ceased to exist and that the shares of Yugoslavia's assets and liabilities in the
Bank would pass to the successor States, with those States being permitted to succeed to
the membership of Yugoslavia upon the satisfaction of certain conditions.

The World Bank's determination of dissolution and opportunity for succession differed from the IMF's in two important respects. First, the World Bank secured agreement
among all the successor States regarding their allocations of assets prior to announcing
the dissolution of Yugoslavia. And, although attaching conditions to the succession of
membership, the World Bank did not require a specific finding that a particular successor State would be able to carry out the obligations required under the Articles of Agreement. The World Bank was able to forgo the requirement of a finding of ability in order
to exclude Serbia/Montenegro as Serbia/Montenegro could not succeed to membership
in the World Bank until it had succeeded to membership in the IMF.

Subsequent to the decision of the World Bank, Slovenia, Croatia, Bosnia-Herzegovina,
and Macedonia have succeeded to membership in the World Bank, with Serbia/Montene-
gro being prohibited from seeking succession until it has attained membership in the IMF.

\* \* \*

### V. Conclusion

As a result of the break-up of Yugoslavia and Czechoslovakia, the IMF and World Bank
have for the first time developed a conditional succession approach to address the questions posed by the break-up of a member State. The succession aspect of the approach was
born out of the desire to preserve the assets of successor States, while the conditional aspect was born out of the political desire to exclude the participation of Serbia/Montene-
gro, and the financial desire to provide for complete assumption of the debt obligations
of the predecessor States. This approach adopted by the IMF and opposed by the World
Bank derived its basis from the international law of succession, and the past practice of
the IMF and World Bank, but quickly moved beyond the basic principles established
therein.

The desire to provide the successor States with a mechanism to succeed to the membership of the predecessor State, and to assume the assets and debts of the predecessor
State, is well founded in international law and past practice. However, the addition of
political criteria, no matter how disguised, finds no basis in either international law or the
past practice of the financial institutions.

Nonetheless, the mere fact that making succession conditional on political criteria has
no basis in international law or past practice does not invalidate such conditions. What
does, however, weaken the authority to impose political conditions is the arbitrary and
inconsistent approach taken by the IMF and World Bank with regard to the imposition
of those conditions. The condition that a State must be found by the IMF to be capable
of carrying out its rights and obligations, although established for political reasons, has
some basis in the IMF's Articles of Agreement. Yet, if the true motive for the financial institutions was to ensure succession consistent with the Articles of Agreement, then the
World Bank should also have imposed that condition on the Yugoslav successor States, and

both the IMF and World Bank should have made the succession of the Czech Republic and Slovakia conditional on a similar finding.

Similarly, despite the World Bank's view that the imposition of conditions was legally questionable, it imposed the condition that the successor States must unanimously agree to the allocation of the predecessor's assets and debts. The IMF and World Bank also imposed the condition of simultaneous succession of the Czech Republic and Slovakia, which has no basis in international law or past practice.

Once the reservations against conditional succession had been overcome or disregarded, the IMF and World Bank proceeded to attach conditions on a case-by-case basis, with little concern for consistency. The dangers involved in this approach are that Serbia/Montenegro, or any future successor State faced with similarly inconsistent conditions, might successfully contend before an arbitration tribunal that it has been unjustly precluded from the right to succeed to the membership and assets of the predecessor State, and therefore should not be deemed liable for any portion of the debts of the predecessor State.

In adjudicating such a claim, the arbitral tribunal would look to the rational basis for the imposition of the specific conditions. Although the tribunal might be able to determine a rational basis for the particular condition imposed on Serbia/Montenegro, the immediate practice of the IMF and World Bank would threaten such a determination by casting doubt on the entire practice of conditional succession, and the true motivation of the financial institutions for the imposition of particular conditions, regardless of their apparently rational basis.

## 9. Bibliography of Additional Sources

- Alfred R. Cowger, Jr., *Rights and Obligations of Successor States: An Alternative Theory*, 17 Case W. Res. J. Int'l L. 285 (1985).

- *Digest of Decisions of National Courts Relating to Succession of States and Governments* [1963] 2 Y.B. Int'l L. Comm'n 131, U.N. Doc. A/CN.4/151.

- Lawrence M. Frankel, *International Law of Succession: New Rules for a New Era*, 14 Hous. J. Int'l L. 521 (1992).

- Institut de Droit International, *State Succession in Matters of Property and Debts* (2001).

- Ronald J. Klein, *Consensual Merger as a Means of State Succession and Its Relation to Treaty Obligations*, 13 Case W. Res. J. Int'l L. 413 (Spring 1981).

- Yilma Makannen, International Law and the New States of Africa: A Study of the International Legal Problems of State Succession in the Newly Independent States of Eastern Africa (1983).

- Krystina Marek, Identity and Continuity of States in Public International Law (1968).

- Edward McWhinney, The United Nations and a New World Order for a New Millennium: Self-Determination, State Succession, and Humanitarian Intervention (2000).

- Holly A. Osterland, *National Self-Determination and Secession: The Slovak Model*, 25 Case W. Res. J. Int'l L. 655 (1993).

- Alain Pellet, *The Opinions of the Badinter Arbitration Committee; A Second breath for the Self-Determination of Peoples*, 3 Eur. J. Int'l L. 178 (1992).

# Chapter IV

# Privileges and Immunities

## Introduction

This chapter examines the special legal rights that U.N. Missions, Members of Delegations to the U.N., and U.N. officials possess by virtue of the various international agreements between the United Nations and the United States as host country. The materials focus on the case study of the United States' attempt to shut down the Mission of the PLO, which was the subject of a World Court case and domestic litigation. In addition, this chapter focuses on two important developments related to the interpretation of the privileges and immunities of U.N. Missions and Representatives. The first involved the U.S. attempt to prevent Yasser Arafat from entering the country in 1986 to speak to the U.N. General Assembly. The second involved a commercial landlord's attempt to evict the Zaire U.N. Mission from its premises for failure to pay rent.

## Objectives

- To understand the agreement for the establishment of the U.N. headquarters in the U.S.
- To understand the privileges and immunities afforded under convention agreements.
- To understand the privileges that are afforded to international organizations.
- To understand the limitations on U.S. actions related to diplomatic missions to the U.N.
- To examine the scope of the U.N. privileges and immunities within the U.S.

## Problems

1. Come to class prepared to discuss the following questions:
   (a) Why would an international organization, its staff, and the delegates of its member states need privileges and immunities?
   (b) If writing on a blank slate, what key privileges and immunities would be desirable from the point of view of the organization and its members?

(c) From the point of view of the host country, what limitations or exceptions to these privileges and immunities would you seek?

2. Applying the U.N. Charter, the U.N. Headquarters Agreement, the U.N. Headquarters Agreement Act, and the Convention on Privileges and Immunities of the U.N., come to class prepared to discuss the following fictional situation involving a U.N. Delegate.

Assume that a local New York ordinance permits the NYPD to search and conduct an arrest in any building upon the issuance of a warrant by a magistrate, or in the absence of a warrant, when there is a showing of probable cause. Now assume that local police observed Juan Gonzales, the Deputy Head of the Mexican Delegation, purchase a bag of cocaine on the public sidewalk outside the U.N. Headquarters Building. With the police running after him, Gonzales ducked into the U.N. Building. Unfortunately for Gonzales, there was a long line at the security check point in the lobby. The police followed Gonzales into the U.N. Building, arrested him while he was waiting in line in the lobby, and took him and the drugs into custody. In a pretrial motion, Gonzales argues that the charges against him for possession of a narcotic must be dropped because he is a Delegate to the U.N. and because he was arrested inside the U.N. Building without the consent of the Secretary-General.

(a) What result? Why?

(b) Would the case come out differently if the U.N. Secretary-General expressly consented to the prosecution of Mr. Gonzales?

(c) Would the case come out differently if Mr. Gonzales was a security guard to the Mexican Delegation rather than a diplomat?

(d) Would the case come out differently if Mr. Gonzales was a member of an official Observer Mission, rather than a Member State's Delegation?

3. Applying the U.N. Charter, the U.N. Headquarters Agreement, the U.N. Headquarters Agreement Act, and the Convention on Privileges and Immunities of the U.N., come to class prepared to discuss the following fictional situation involving a U.N. Delegate.

Assume that the Chief of Mission of Canada, Pierre Prospect, signs a form contract with the local Toyota dealer to purchase a Toyota Camry. Mr. Prospect fails to make the first payment, and after several warnings the Toyota dealer brings legal action in a local court for return of the vehicle and damages. Mr. Prospect files a motion to dismiss on the grounds that as an official U.N. diplomat he can't be sued.

(a) What result? Why?

(b) Would it make a difference if Mr. Prospect purchased the Toyota Camry for exclusive use for official Mission business?

(c) Would it make a difference if Mr. Prospect was the Mission chauffeur, rather than the Chief of Mission? What if he was a U.S. citizen who happened to work for the Canadian Mission as its chauffeur?

4. Come prepared to discuss the following questions about the PLO Mission Case:

(a) Why did the U.S. government go to court seeking an injunction to expel the PLO from its Mission rather than just sending the U.S. Marshals in and requiring the PLO to seek an injunction to prevent its expulsion?

(b) What was the U.S. argument before the District Court? What was the PLO argument? How did the Court decide the case?

(c) Do you agree with the Court's interpretation of the legislative history of the Anti-Terrorism Act of 1987?

(d) Could the Court have instead reconciled the apparent conflict between the Anti-Terrorism Act and the Headquarters Agreement by relying on the "national security reservation" contained in Section 6 of the Headquarters Agreement Act?

(e) Why do you think the U.S. government decided not to appeal the District Court's decision to the Federal Court of Appeals?

(f) How far does the inviolability of an Observer Mission extend? Does it include the Mission's bank account?

5. Come prepared to discuss the following questions about the right of entry:

(a) The U.S. denied a Visa to Yasser Arafat to speak at the U.N. in 1986. What are the legal arguments for and against this action?

(b) The U.S. has denied Visas to members of the Iranian delegation to the U.N., who as students had participated in the seizure of the U.S. embassy in 1979. What are the legal arguments for and against this action?

(c) Assume the Foreign Minister of Libya has requested a Visa to speak at the U.N. He had served as the head of the Libyan Intelligence Agency at the time of the Pan Am 103 bombing in 1988. The indictment in the Lockerbie case alleges that the two Libyans that planted the bomb worked for the Libyan Intelligence Agency, which had ordered them to blow up the aircraft. What are the legal arguments for and against denying the Libyan foreign minister permission to enter the country to speak at the U.N.?

6. Come prepared to discuss the following questions about the Zaire Mission Case:

(a) The U.S. has expelled members of the Zaire mission in order to get Zaire to pay rent to its New York landlord. What are the legal arguments for and against this action?

(b) What was the basis of the Second Circuit Court of Appeals holding that the Zaire mission could not be evicted from its Mission premises for failure to pay rent?

(c) What other options do a U.S. landlord have when a U.N. Member fails to pay its rent on its Mission premises?

# Materials

1. The U.N. HEADQUARTERS AGREEMENT, especially Sections 1, 8, 11, 12, 15 (4), 21, see http://daccess-ods.un.org/TMP/9118182.06310272.html.

2. The U.N. HEADQUARTERS AGREEMENT ACT of 1947, especially Section 6.

3. THE CONVENTION ON THE PRIVILEGES AND IMMUNITIES OF THE UNITED NATIONS, especially Section 11 (g), 16, 22, and the U.S. reservation reprinted at footnote 2, see http://daccess-ods.un.org/TMP/6115843.65367889.html.

4. VIENNA CONVENTION ON DIPLOMATIC RELATIONS, Articles 22 and 25, see http://untreaty.un.org/ilc/texts/instruments/english/conventions/9_1_1961.pdf.

5. THE INTERNATIONAL ORGANIZATIONS IMMUNITIES ACT OF 1945, Sections 1, 7, and 8(b)–22 U.S.C. § 288 (2000).

6. International organizations entitled to enjoy the privileges, exemptions, and immunities conferred by 22 USCS §§ 288 et seq.

7. Jim Anderson, Politics Wins in PLO Office Closure, UPI, March 11, 1988.

8. World Court Rules Against U.S. in PLO Mission Closure, CHICAGO TRIBUNE, April 27, 1988.

9. U.S. Court Rules PLO Mission Cannot be Closed, INTER PRESS SERVICE, June 29, 1988

10. *U.S. v. PLO*, 695 F. Supp. 1456 (S.D. N.Y. 1988).

11. Don Oberdorfer, U.S. Denies Entry Visa to Arafat, THE WASHINGTON POST, November 27, 1988.

12. What the Host Must Not Do, THE NEW YORK TIMES, November 29, 1988.

13. Josh Friedman, U.N. Going to Geneva for Arafat, NEWSDAY, December 3, 1988.

14. Ronald Sullivan, Judge, No Diplomat, Orders Zaire to Pay U.N. Office Rent, NEW YORK TIMES, March 26, 1992.

15. Deborah Pines, Eviction of Mission Prohibited Based on International Law, NEW YORK LAW JOURNAL, March 8, 1993.

16. *767 Third Avenue Associates v. Permanent Mission of the Republic of Zaire to the U.N.*, 988 F. 2d 295 (2nd Cir. 1993).

17. Obama Gives Interpol Free Hand in U.S., WASHINGTON EXAMINER, December 30, 2009.

18. Jake Tapper, Just What Did President Obama's Executive Order Regarding INTERPOL Do?, ABC NEWS BLOG, December 30, 2009.

19. Executive Order — Amending Executive Order 12425, Office of the Press Secretary, December 17, 2009.

20. *Brzak v. The United Nations*, 597 F.3d 107 (2nd Cir. 2010).

21. Bibliography of Additional Sources

---

## *Authors' Note*

The following two excerpts provide an understanding of the basis for the special relationship between the United States and the United Nations concerning the placement of the U.N. headquarters in New York. Material 1 is selected provisions from the international agreement for the establishment of the headquarters including discussion of the privileges and immunities afforded to resident representatives to the U.N. Material 2 is U.S. Congressional resolution authorizing the President to bring the U.N. Headquarters Agreement into effect.

# 1. The U.N. Headquarters Agreement
## Sections 1, 8, 11, 12, 15 (4), 21

see http://daccess-ods.un.org/TMP/2051644.32525635.html

### Article I — Definitions

### SECTION 1

In this agreement:

(a) the expression 'headquarters district' means (1) the area defined as such in Annex 1, (2) any other lands or buildings which from time to time may be included therein by supplemental agreement with the appropriate American authorities;

(b) the expression 'appropriate American authorities' means such federal, state, or local authorities in the United States as may be appropriate in the context and in accordance with the laws and customs of the United States, including the laws and customs of the state and local government involved;

(c) the expression 'General Convention' means the Convention on the Privileges and Immunities of the United Nations approved by the General Assembly of the United Nations 13 February 1946, as acceded to by the United States;

(d) the expression 'United Nations' means the international organization established by the Charter of the United Nations, hereinafter referred to as the 'Charter';

(e) the expression 'Secretary-General' means the Secretary-General of the United Nations.

\* \* \*

### SECTION 8

The United Nations shall have the power to make regulations, operative within the headquarters district, for the purpose of establishing therein conditions in all respects necessary for the full execution of this functions. No federal, state or local law or regulation of the United States which is inconsistent with a regulation of the United Nations authorized by this section shall, to the extent of such inconsistency, be applicable within the headquarters district. Any dispute, between the United Nations and the United States, as to whether a regulation of the United Nations is authorized by this section or as to whether a federal, state or local law or regulation is inconsistent with any regulation of the United Nations authorized by this section, shall be promptly settled as provided in Section 21. Pending such settlement, the regulation of the United Nations shall apply, and the federal, state or local law or regulation shall be inapplicable in the headquarters district to the extent that the United Nations claims it to be inconsistent with the regulation of the United Nations. This section shall not prevent the reasonable application of fire protection regulations of the appropriate American authorities.

\* \* \*

### Article IV — Communications and Transit

### SECTION 11

The federal, state or local authorities of the United States shall not impose any impediments to transit to or from the headquarters district of (1) representatives of Members or officials of the United Nations, or of specialized agencies as defined in Article 57, paragraph 2, of the Charter, or the families of such representatives or officials, (2) experts performing missions for the United Nations or for such specialized agencies, (3) representatives of the press, or of radio, film or other information agencies, who have been accredited by the United Nations (or by such a specialized agency) in its discretion after consultation with the United States, (4) representatives of non-governmental organizations recognized by the United Nations for the purpose of consultation under Article 71 of the Charter, or (5) other persons invited to the headquarters district by the United Nations or by such specialized agency on official business. The appropriate American authorities shall afford any necessary protection to such persons while in transit to or from the headquarters district. This section does not apply to general interruptions of transportation which are to be dealt with as provided in Section 17, and does not impair the effectiveness of generally applicable laws and regulations as to the operation of means of transportation.

## SECTION 12

The provisions of Section 11 shall be applicable irrespective of the relations existing between the Governments of the persons referred to in that section and the Government of the United States.

* * *

## Article V — Resident Representatives to the United Nations

## SECTION 15

(1) Every person designated by a Member as the principal resident representative to the United Nations of such Member or as a resident representative with the rank of ambassador or minister plenipotentiary,

(2) such resident members of their staffs as may be agreed upon between the Secretary-General, the Government of the United States and the Government of the Member concerned,

(3) every person designated by a Member of a specialized agency, as defined in Article 57, paragraph 2, of the Charter, as its principal resident representative, with the rank of ambassador or minister plenipotentiary, at the headquarters of such agency in the United States, and

(4) such other principal resident representatives of members to a specialized agency and such resident members of the staffs of representatives to a specialized agency as may be agreed upon between the principal executive officer of the specialized agency, the Government of the United States and the Government of the Member concerned, shall, whether residing inside or outside the headquarters district, be entitled in the territory of the United States to the same privileges and immunities, subject to corresponding conditions and obligations, as it accords to diplomatic envoys accredited to it. In the case of Members whose governments are not recognized by the United States, such privileges and immunities need be extended to such representatives, or persons on the staffs of such representatives, only within the headquarters district, at their residences and offices outside the district, in transit between the district and such residences and offices, and in transit on official business to or from foreign countries.

* * *

## SECTION 21

(a) Any dispute between the United Nations and the United States concerning the interpretation or application of this agreement or of any supplemental agreement, which is not settled by negotiation or other agreed mode of settlement, shall be referred for final decision to a tribunal of three arbitrators, one to be named by the Secretary-General, one to be named by the Secretary of State of the United States, and the third to be chosen by the two, or, if they should fail to agree upon a third, then by the President of the International Court of Justice.

(b) The Secretary-General or the United States may ask the General Assembly to request of the International Court of Justice an advisory opinion on any legal question arising in the course of such proceedings. Pending the receipt of the opinion of the Court, an interim decision of the arbitral tribunal shall be observed on both parties. Thereafter, the arbitral tribunal shall render a final decision, having regard to the opinion of the Court.

## 2. The U.N. Headquarters Agreement Act of 1947

Partial text of Public Law 80-357 [S.J. Res. 144], 61 Stat. 756, approved August 4, 1947

JOINT RESOLUTION Authorizing the President to bring into effect an agreement between the United States and the United Nations for the purpose of establishing the permanent headquarters of the United Nations in the United States and authorizing the taking of measures necessary to facilitate compliance with the provisions of such agreement, and for other purposes.

Whereas the Charter of the United Nations was signed on behalf of the United States on June 26, 1945, and was ratified on August 8, 1945, by the President of the United States, by and with the advice and consent of the Senate, and the instrument of ratification of said Charter was deposited on August 8, 1945; and

Whereas the said Charter of the United Nations came into force with respect to the United States on October 24, 1945; and

Whereas article 104 of the Charter provides that "The Organization shall enjoy in the territory of each of its Members such legal capacity as may be necessary for the exercise of its functions and the fulfillment of its purposes"; and

Whereas article 105 of the Charter provides that:

"1. The Organization shall enjoy in the territory of each of its Members such privileges and immunities as are necessary for the fulfillment of its purposes.

"2. Representatives of the Members of the United Nations and officials of the Organization shall similarly enjoy such privileges and immunities as are necessary for the independent exercise of their functions in connection with the Organization.

"3. The General Assembly may make recommendations with a view to determining the details of the application of paragraphs 1 and 2 of this article or may propose conventions to the Members of the United Nations for this purpose."; and

Whereas article 28 and other articles of the Charter of the United Nations contemplate the establishment of a seat for the permanent headquarters of the Organization; and

Whereas the interim arrangements concluded on June 26, 1945, by the governments represented at the United Nations Conference on International Organization instructed the Preparatory Commission established in pursuance of the arrangements to "make studies and prepare recommendations concerning the location of the permanent headquarters of the Organization"; and

Whereas during the labors of the said Preparatory Commission, the Congress of the United States in H. Con. Res. 75, passed unanimously by the House of Representatives December 10, 1945, and agreed to unanimously by the Senate December 11, 1945, invited the United Nations "to locate the seat of the United Nations Organization within the United States"; and whereas the General Assembly on December 14, 1946, resolved "that the permanent headquarters of the United Nations shall be established in New York City in the area bounded by First Avenue, East Forty-eighth Street, the East River, and East Forty-second Street' ; and

Whereas the General Assembly resolved on December 14, 1946, "That the Secretary-General be authorized to negotiate and conclude with the appropriate authorities of the United States of America an agreement concerning the arrangements required as a result of the establishment of the permanent headquarters of the United Nations in the city of New York" and to be guided in these negotiations by the provisions of a preliminary draft agreement which had been negotiated by the Secretary-General and the Secretary of State of the United States; and

Whereas the General Assembly resolved on December 14, 1946, that pending the coming into force of the agreement referred to above "the Secretary-General be authorized to negotiate and conclude arrangements with the appropriate authorities of the United States of America to determine on a provisional basis the privileges, immunities, and facilities needed in connection with the temporary headquarters of the United Nations"—and

Whereas the Secretary of State of the United States, after consultation with the appropriate authorities of the State and city of New York, signed at Lake Success, New York, on June 26, 1947, on behalf of the United States an agreement with the United Nations regarding the headquarters of the United Nations, which agreement is incorporated herein; and

Whereas the aforesaid agreement provides that it shall be brought into effect by an exchange of notes between the United States and the Secretary-General of the United Nations: Therefore, be it

Resolved by the Senate and House of Representatives of the United States of America in Congress assembled. That the President is hereby authorized to bring into effect on the part of the United States the agreement between the United States of America and the United Nations regarding the headquarters of the United Nations, signed at Lake Success, New York, on June 26, 1947 (hereinafter referred to as the "agreement"), with such changes therein not contrary to the general tenor thereof and not imposing any additional obligations on the United States as the President may deem necessary and appropriate, and at his discretion, after consultation with the appropriate State and local authorities, to enter into such supplemental agreements with the United Nations as may be necessary to fulfill the purposes of the said agreement: That any supplemental agreement entered into pursuant to Section 5 of the agreement incorporated herein shall be submitted to the Congress for approval. The agreement follows:

Sec. 2. For the purpose of carrying out the obligations of the United States under said agreement and supplemental agreements with respect to United States assurances that the United Nations shall not be dispossessed of its property in the headquarters district, and with respect to the establishment of radio facilities and the possible establishment of an airport:

(a) The President of the United States, or any official or governmental agency authorized by the President, may acquire in the name of the United States any property or interest therein by purchase, donation, or other means of transfer, or may cause proceedings to be instituted for the acquisition of the same by condemnation.

(b) Upon the request of the President, or such officer as the President may designate, the Attorney General of the United States shall cause such condemnation or other proceedings to be instituted in the name of the United States in the district court of the United States for the district in which the property is situated and such court shall have full jurisdiction of such proceedings, and any condemnation proceedings shall be conducted in accordance with the Act of August 1, 1888 (25 Stat. 357), as amended, and the Act of February 26, 1931 (46 Stat. 1421), as amended.

(c) After the institution of any such condemnation proceedings, possession of the property may be taken at any time the President, or such officer as he may designate, determines is necessary, and the court shall enter such orders as may be necessary to effect entry and occupancy of the property.

(d) The President of the United States, or any officer or governmental agency duly authorized by the President, may, in the name of the United States, transfer or convey possession of and title to any interest in any property acquired or held by the United States, pursuant to paragraph (a) above, to the United Nations on the terms provided in the agreement or in any supplemental agreement, and shall execute and deliver such conveyances and other instruments and perform such other acts in connection therewith as may be necessary to carry out the provisions of the agreement.

(e) There are authorized to be appropriated, out of any money in the Treasury not otherwise appropriated, such sums as may be required to enable the United States to carry out the undertakings hereby authorized: Provided, That any money appropriated under this authorization shall be spent only on a basis of reimbursement by the United Nations in accordance with section 3 of the agreement, and that the money thus reimbursed shall be deposited and covered into the Treasury of the United States as miscellaneous receipts.

Sec. 3. The President, or the Secretary of State under his direction, is authorized to enter into agreements with the State of New York or any other State of the United States and to the extent not inconsistent with State law, with any one or more of the political subdivisions thereof in aid of effectuating the provisions of the agreement.

Sec. 4. Any States, or, to the extent not inconsistent with State law, any political subdivisions thereof, affected by the establishment of the headquarters of the United Nations in the United States are authorized to enter into agreements with the United Nations or with each other consistent with the agreement and for the purpose of facilitating compliance with the same: Provided, That, except in cases of emergency and agreements of a routine contractual character, a representative of the United States, to be appointed by the Secretary of State, may, at the discretion of the Secretary of State, participate in the negotiations, and that any such agreement entered into by such State or States or political subdivisions thereof shall be subject to approval by the Secretary of State.

Sec. 5. The President is authorized to make effective with respect to the temporary headquarters of the United Nations in the State of New York, on a provisional basis, such of the provisions of the agreement as he may deem appropriate, having due regard for the needs of the United Nations at its temporary headquarters.

Sec. 6. Nothing in the agreement shall be construed as in any way diminishing, abridging, or weakening the right of the United States to safeguard its own security and completely to control the entrance of aliens into any territory of the United States other than the headquarters district and its immediate vicinity, as to be defined and fixed in a supplementary agreement between the Government of the United States and the United Nations in pursuance of section 13(3)(e) of the agreement, and such areas as it is reasonably necessary to traverse in transit between the same and foreign countries. Moreover, nothing in section 14 of the agreement with respect to facilitating entrance into the United States by persons who wish to visit the headquarters district and do not enjoy the right of entry provided in section 11 of the agreement shall be construed to amend or suspend in any way the immigration laws of the United States or to commit the United States in any way to effect any amendment or suspension of such law.

## 3. The Convention on the Privileges and Immunities of the United Nations, Especially Sections 11(g), 16, 22, and the U.S. Reservation Reprinted at Footnote 2
1946, see http://daccess-ods.un.org/TMP/6855749.48787689.html

## 4. Vienna Convention on Diplomatic Relations, Articles 22 and 25
1961, see http://untreaty.un.org/ilc/texts/instruments/
english/conventions/9_1_1961.pdf

## Authors' Note

The next two materials discuss the extension of immunities to other international organizations within the United States. Material 5, an act of the U.S. Congress, details the specific privileges, exceptions, and immunities that extend to international organizations within the U.S. Material 6 presents a list of international organizations that enjoy the privileges, exemptions, and immunities conferred by 22 USC § 288.

## 5. The International Organizations Immunities Act of 1945, Sections 1, 7, and 8(b)
22 U.S.C. § 288, 2000

TITLE 22. FOREIGN RELATIONS AND INTERCOURSE

CHAPTER 7. INTERNATIONAL BUREAUS, CONGRESSES, ETC.

PRIVILEGES AND IMMUNITIES OF INTERNATIONAL ORGANIZATIONS

Former International Organizations Immunities Act of 1945 Public Law 79-291 (H.R. 4489)

§ 288. Definition of "international organization"; authority of President

For the purposes of this title, the term "international organization" means a public international organization in which the United States participates pursuant to any treaty or under the authority of any Act of Congress authorizing such participation or making an appropriation for such participation, and which shall have been designated by the President through appropriate Executive order as being entitled to enjoy the privileges, exemptions, and immunities herein provided. The President shall be authorized, in the light of the functions performed by any such international organization, by appropriate Executive order to withhold or withdraw from any such organization or its officers or employees any of the privileges, exemptions, and immunities provided for in this title (including the amendments made by this title) or to condition or limit the enjoyment by any such organization or its officers or employees of any such privilege, exemption, or immunity. The President shall be authorized, if in his judgment such action should be justified by reason of the abuse by an international organization or its officers and employees of the privileges, exemptions, and immunities herein provided or for any other reason, at any time to revoke the designation of any international organization under this section, whereupon the international organization in question shall cease to be classed as an international organization for the purposes of this title.

## § 288a. Privileges, exemptions, and immunities of international organizations

International organizations shall enjoy the status, immunities, exemptions, and privileges set forth in this section, as follows:

(a) International organizations shall, to the extent consistent with the instrument creating them, possess the capacity

(i) to contract;

(ii) to acquire and dispose of real and personal property;

(iii) to institute legal proceedings.

(b) International organizations, their property and their assets, wherever located, and by whomsoever held, shall enjoy the same immunity from suit and every form of judicial process as is enjoyed by foreign governments, except to the extent that such organizations may expressly waive their immunity for the purpose of any proceedings or by the terms of any contract.

(c) Property and assets of international organizations, wherever located and by whomsoever held, shall be immune from search, unless such immunity be expressly waived, and from confiscation. The archives of international organizations shall be inviolable.

(d) Insofar as concerns customs duties and internal-revenue taxes imposed upon or by reason of importation, and the procedures in connection therewith; the registration of foreign agents; and the treatment of official communications, the privileges, exemptions, and immunities to which international organizations shall be entitled shall be those accorded under similar circumstances to foreign governments.

## § 288b. Baggage and effects of officers and employees exempted from customs duties and internal revenue taxes

Pursuant to regulations prescribed by the Commissioner of Customs with the approval of the Secretary of the Treasury, the baggage and effects of alien officers and employees of international organizations, or of aliens designated by foreign governments to serve as their representatives in or to such organizations, or of the families, suites, and servants of such officers, employees, or representatives shall be admitted (when imported in connection with the arrival of the owner) free of customs duties and free of internal-revenue taxes imposed upon or by reason of importation.

## § 288c. Exemption from property taxes

International organizations shall be exempt from all property taxes imposed by, or under the authority of, any Act of Congress, including such Acts as are applicable solely to the District of Columbia or the Territories.

## § 288d. Privileges, exemptions, and immunities of officers, employees, and their families; waiver

(a) Persons designated by foreign governments to serve as their representatives in or to international organizations and the officers and employees of such organizations, and members of the immediate families of such representatives, officers, and employees residing with them, other than nationals of the United States, shall, insofar as concerns laws regulating entry into and departure from the United States, alien registration and fingerprinting, and the registration of foreign agents, be entitled to the same privileges, exemptions, and immunities as are accorded under similar circumstances to officers and employees, respectively, of foreign governments, and members of their families.

(b) Representatives of foreign governments in or to international organizations and officers and employees of such organizations shall be immune from suit and legal process relating to acts performed by them in their official capacity and falling within their functions as such representatives, officers, or employees except insofar as such immunity may be waived by the foreign government or international organization concerned.

### § 288e. Personnel entitled to benefits

(a) Notification to and acceptance by Secretary of State of personnel. No person shall be entitled to the benefits of this title unless he (1) shall have been duly notified to and accepted by the Secretary of State as a representative, officer, or employee; or (2) shall have been designated by the Secretary of State, prior to formal notification and acceptance, as a prospective representative, officer, or employee; or (3) is a member of the family or suite, or servant, of one of the foregoing accepted or designated representatives, officers, or employees.

(b) Deportation of undesirables. Should the Secretary of State determine that the continued presence in the United States of any person entitled to the benefits of this title is not desirable, he shall so inform the foreign government or international organization concerned, as the case may be, and after such person shall have had a reasonable length of time, to be determined by the Secretary of State, to depart from the United States, he shall cease to be entitled to such benefits.

(c) Extent of diplomatic status. No person shall, by reason of the provisions of this title, be considered as receiving diplomatic status or as receiving any of the privileges incident thereto other than such as are specifically set forth herein.

### § 288f. Applicability of reciprocity laws

The privileges, exemptions, and immunities of international organizations and of their officers and employees, and members of their families, suites, and servants, provided for in this subchapter, shall be granted notwithstanding the fact that the similar privileges, exemptions, and immunities granted to a foreign government, its officers, or employees, may be conditioned upon the existence of reciprocity by that foreign government: Provided, That nothing contained in this subchapter shall be construed as precluding the Secretary of State from withdrawing the privileges, exemptions, and immunities provided in this subchapter from persons who are nationals of any foreign country on the ground that such country is failing to accord corresponding privileges, exemptions, and immunities to citizens of the United States.

## 6. International Organizations Entitled to Enjoy the Privileges, Exemptions, and Immunities Conferred by 22 USC § 288 et seq.

The following international organizations have been designated as public international organizations entitled to enjoy the privileges, exemptions, and immunities conferred by 22 USCS §§ 288 et seq.:

- The African Development Bank, designated by Ex. Or. No. 12403 of Feb. 8, 1983, 48 Fed. Reg. 6087.

- The African Development Fund, designated by Ex. Or. No. 11977 of March 14, 1977, 42 Fed. Reg. 14671.

- The Asian Development Bank, designated by Ex. Or. No. 11334 of March 7, 1967, 32 Fed. Reg. 3933.

- African Union, Ex. Ord. No. 13377, Apr. 13, 2005, 70 F.R. 20263.

- The Border Environment Cooperation Commission, designated by Ex. Or. No. 12904 of March 16, 1994, 59 Fed. Reg. 13179.
- The Caribbean Organization, designated by Ex. Or. No. 10983 of Dec. 30, 1961, 27 Fed. Reg. 32.
- The Commission for Environmental Cooperation, designated by Ex. Or. No. 12904 of March 16, 1994, 59 Fed. Reg. 13179.
- The Commission for Labor Cooperation, designated by Ex. Or. No. 12904 of March 16, 1994, 59 Fed. Reg. 13179.
- The Commission for the Study of Alternatives to the Panama Canal, designated by Ex. Or. No. 12567 of Oct. 2, 1986, 51 Fed. Reg. 35495.
- Council of Europe in Respect of the Group of States Against Corruption (GRECO), Ex. Ord. No. 13240, Dec. 18, 2001, 66 F.R. 66257.
- The Customs Cooperation Council, designated by Ex. Or. No. 11596 of June 5, 1971, 36 Fed Reg 11079.
- The European Bank for Reconstruction and Development, designated by Ex. Or. No. 12766 of June 18, 1991, 56 Fed. Reg. 28463.
- The European Space Agency, designated by Ex. Or. No. 11318 of Dec. 5, 1966, 31 Fed. Reg. 15307; Ex. Or. No. 11351 of May 22, 1967, 32 Fed. Reg. 7561; Ex. Or. No. 11760 of Jan. 17, 1974, 39 Fed. Reg. 2343; Ex. Or. No. 12766 of June 18, 1991, 56 Fed. Reg. 28463.
- The Food and Agriculture Organization, designated by Ex. Or. No. 9698 of Feb. 19, 1946, 11 Fed. Reg. 1809.
- The Great Lakes Fishery Commission, designated by Ex. Or. No. 11059 of Oct. 23, 1962, 27 Fed. Reg. 1040
- Global Fund to Fight AIDS, Tuberculosis and Malaria, Ex. Ord. No. 13395, Jan. 13, 2006, 71 F.R. 3203
- The Hong Kong Economic and Trade Offices, designated by Ex. Or. No. 13052 of June 30, 1997, 62 Fed. Reg. 35659.
- The Inter-American Defense Board, designated by Ex. Or. No. 10228 of March 26, 1951, 16 Fed. Reg. 2676.
- The Inter-American Development Bank, designated by Ex. Or. No. 10873 of April 8, 1960, 25 Fed. Reg. 3097, as amended Ex. Or. No. 11019 of April 30, 1962, 27 Fed. Reg. 4145.
- The Inter-American Institute of Agricultural Sciences, designated by Ex. Or. No. 9751 of July 12, 1946, 11 Fed. Reg. 7713.
- The Inter-American Investment Corporation, designated by Ex. Or. No. 12567 of Oct. 2, 1986, 51 Fed. Reg. 35495.
- The Inter-American Statistical Institute, designated by Ex. Or. No. 9751 of July 12, 1946, 11 Fed. Reg. 7713.
- The Inter-American Tropical Tuna Commission, designated by Ex. Or. No. 11059 of Oct. 23, 1962, 27 Fed. Reg. 10405.
- The Intergovernmental Maritime Consultative Organization, designated by Ex. Or. No. 10795 of Dec. 16, 1958, 23 Fed. Reg. 9709.
- The International Atomic Energy Agency, designated by Ex. Or. No. 10727 of Aug. 31, 1957, 22 Fed. Reg. 7099.

- The International Bank for Reconstruction and Development, designated by Ex. Or. No. 9751 of July 12, 1946, 11 Fed. Reg. 7713.

- The International Boundary and Water Commission, United States and Mexico, designated by Ex. Or. No. 12467 of March 2, 1984, 49 Fed. Reg. 8229.

- The International Centre for Settlement of Investment Disputes, designated by Ex. Or. No. 11966 of Jan. 19, 1977, 42 Fed. Reg. 4331.

- The International Civil Aviation Organization, designated by Ex. Or. No. 9863 of June 2, 1947, 12 Fed. Reg. 3559.

- The International Coffee Organization, designated by Ex. Or. No. 11225 of May 22, 1965, 30 Fed. Reg. 7093.

- The International Committee of the Red Cross, designated by Ex. Or. No. 12643 of June 23, 1988, 53 Fed. Reg. 24247.

- The International Cotton Advisory Committee, designated by Ex. Or. No. 9911 of Dec. 22, 1947, 12 Fed. Reg. 8719.

- The International Cotton Institute, designated by Ex. Or. No. 11283 of May 27, 1966, 31 Fed. Reg. 7667.

- The International Criminal Police Organization (INTERPOL) (limited privileges), designated by Ex. Or. No. 12425 of June 16, 1983, 48 Fed. Reg. 28069; Ex. Or. No. 12971 of Sept. 15, 1995, 60 Fed. Reg. 48617.

- The International Development Association, designated by Ex. Or. No. 11966 of Jan. 19, 1977, 42 Fed. Reg. 4331.

- The International Development Law Institute, designated by Ex. Or. No. 12842 of March 29, 1993, 58 Fed. Reg. 17081.

- The International Fertilizer Development Center, designated by Ex. Or. No. 11977 of March 14, 1977, 42 Fed. Reg. 14671.

- The International Finance Corporation, designated by Ex. Or. No. 10680 of Oct. 4, 1956, 21 Fed. Reg. 7647.

- The International Food Policy Research Institute, designated by Ex. Or. No. 12359 of April 22, 1982, 47 Fed. Reg. 17791.

- The International Fund for Agricultural Development, designated by Ex. Or. No. 12732 of Oct. 31, 1990, 55 Fed. Reg. 46489.

- The International Hydrographic Bureau, designated by Ex. Or. No. 10769 of May 29, 1958, 23 Fed. Reg. 3801.

- The International Joint Commission—United States and Canada, designated by Ex. Or. No. 9972 of June 28, 1948, 13 Fed. Reg. 4920.

- The International Labor Organization, designated by Ex. Or. No. 9698 of Feb. 19, 1946, 11 Fed. Reg. 1809.

- The International Maritime Satellite Organization, designated by Ex. Or. No. 12238 of Sept. 12, 1980, 45 Fed. Reg. 60877.

- The International Monetary Fund, designated by Ex. Or. No. 9751 of July 12, 1946, 11 Fed. Reg. 7713.

- The International Pacific Halibut Commission, designated by Ex. Or. No. 11059 of Oct. 23, 1962, 27 Fed. Reg. 10405.

- The International Secretariat for Volunteer Service, designated by Ex. Or. No. 11363 of July 20, 1967, 32 Fed. Reg. 10779.

- The International Telecommunication Union, designated by Ex. Or. No. 9863 of June 2, 1947, 12 Fed. Reg. 3559.

- The International Telecommunications Satellite Organization (INTELSAT), designated by Ex. Or. No. 11718 of May 14, 1973, 38 Fed. Reg. 12797; Ex. Or. No. 11966 of Jan. 19, 1977, 42 Fed. Reg. 4331.

- The International Union for Conservation of Nature and Natural Resources (limited privileges), designated by Ex. Or. No. 12986 of Jan. 18, 1996, 61 Fed. Reg. 1693.

- The International Wheat Advisory Committee (International Wheat Council), designated by Ex. Or. No. 9823 of Jan. 24, 1947, 12 Fed. Reg. 551.

- The Interparliamentary Union, designated by Ex. Or. No. 13097 of Aug. 7, 1998, 63 Fed. Reg. 43065.

- The Israel-United States Binational Industrial Research and Development Foundation, designated by Ex. Or. 12956 of March 13, 1995, 60 Fed. Reg. 14199.

- The Korean Peninsula Energy Development Organization, designated by Ex. Or. No. 12997 of April 1, 1996, 61 Fed. Reg. 14949.

- The Multilateral Investment Guarantee Agency, designated by Ex. Or. No. 12647 of Aug. 2, 1988, 53 Fed. Reg. 29323.

- The Multinational Force and Observers, designated by Ex. Or. No. 12359 of April 22, 1982, 47 Fed. Reg. 17791.

- The North American Development Bank, designated by Ex. Or. No. 12904 of March 16, 1994, 59 Fed. Reg. 13179.

- The North Pacific Anadromus Fish Commission, designated by E. Or. No. 12895 of Jan. 26, 1994, 59 Fed. Reg. 4239.

- The North Pacific Marine Science Organization, designated by Ex. Or. 12894 of Jan. 26, 1994, 59 Fed. Reg. 4237.

- The Organization for European Economic Cooperation (Organization for Economic Cooperation and Development), designated by Ex. Or. No. 10133 of June 27, 1950, 15 Fed. Reg. 4159.

- The Organization for the Prohibition of Chemical Weapons, designated by Ex. Or. No. 13049 of June 11, 1997, 62 Fed. Reg. 32471.

- The Organization of American States (including Pan American Union), designated by Ex. Or. No. 10533 of June 3, 1954, 19 Fed. Reg. 3289.

- The Organization of Eastern Caribbean States, designated by Ex. Or. No. 12669 of Feb. 20, 1989, 54 Fed. Reg. 7753.

- The Pacific Salmon Commission, designated by Ex. Or. No. 12567 of Oct. 2, 1986, 51 Fed. Reg. 35495.

- The Pan American Health Organization (includes the Pan American Sanitary Bureau), designated by Ex. Or. No. 10864 of Feb. 19, 1960, 25 Fed. Reg. 1507.

- The Preparatory Commission of the International Atomic Energy Agency, designated by Ex. Or. No. 10727 of Aug. 31, 1957, 22 Fed. Reg. 7099.

- The Provisional Intergovernmental Committee for the Movement of Migrants from Europe (Intergovernmental Committee for European Migration), designated by Ex. Or. No. 10335 of March 28, 1952, 17 Fed. Reg. 2741.

- The South Pacific Commission, designated by Ex. Or. No. 10086 of Nov. 25, 1949, 14 Fed. Reg. 7147.

- The United International Bureau for the Protection of Intellectual Property, designated by Ex. Or. No. 11484 of Sept. 29, 1969, 34 Fed. Reg. 15337.

- The United Nations, designated by Ex. Or. No. 9698 of Feb. 19, 1946, 11 Fed. Reg. 1809.

- The United Nations Educational, Scientific, and Cultural Organization, designated by Ex. Or. No. 9863 of June 2, 1947, 12 Fed. Reg. 3559.

- The United Nations Industrial Development Organization, designated by Ex. Or. No. 12628 of March 8, 1988, 53 Fed. Reg. 7725.

- United States-Mexico Border Health Commission, Ex. Ord. No. 13367, Dec. 21, 2004, 69 F.R. 77605.

- The Universal Postal Union, designated by Ex. Or. No. 10727 of Aug. 31, 1957, 22 Fed. Reg. 7099.

- The World Health Organization, designated by Ex. Or. No. 10025 of Dec. 30, 1948, 13 Fed. Reg. 9361.

- The World Intellectual Property Organization (WIPO), designated by Ex. Or. No. 11866 of June 18, 1975, 40 Fed. Reg. 26015.

- The World Meteorological Organization, designated by Ex. Or. No. 10676 of Sept. 4, 1956, 21 Fed. Reg. 6625.

- The World Tourism Organization, designated by Ex. Or. No. 12508 of March 22, 1985, 50 Fed. Reg. 11837.

- The World Trade Organization, designated by Ex. Or. No. 13042 of April 9, 1997, 62 Fed. Reg. 18017.

## *Authors' Note*

### *Notes for Chart*

1. The following table presents the general privileges and exemptions as conferred by 22 USC § 288. The employees of certain foreign countries may enjoy higher level of privileges and immunities on the basis of special agreements.

2. Reasonable constrains may, however, be applied in emergency situations involving self-defense, public safety, or the prevention of serious criminal acts.

3. A small number of senior officers are entitled to be treated identical to "diplomatic agents."

4. Note that consular residents are sometimes located within the official consular premises. In such cases, only the official office space is protected from police entry.

| UN OBSERVER MISSIONS | | | | | |
|---|---|---|---|---|---|
| | Embassy? | Nature | Functional Immunity under IOIA | Diplomatic P+I? | License Plates (Plan) |
| Switzerland | Yes | State | Yes | Head only | Head — D Other — S |
| N. Korea S. Korea | No Yes | State State | Yes Yes | No Deputy only | Everyone — S Deputy — D (13 of 16 are consuls or vice-consul) Others — S |
| Monaco | No | State | Yes | No | Others — S |
| Holy See | Yes | State | Yes | Head and Deputy | Everyone — S |
| Euro Communities | Yes 22 USC 28(h) | *Supra*national Organization | No | Everyone (Kissinger Directive) | Head & Deputy — D |
| Asian-African Legal Consultative Committee | No | | No | No | Everyone — D |
| Latin America Economic System | No | | No | No | Nothing |
| Organization of African Unity | No | | Yes 28 USC 288 (f)(2) | No | Everyone — S |
| Organization of Islamic Conference | No | | No | No | Nothing |
| Palestine Liberation Organization | No | | No | No | Nothing |
| South West African Peoples Organization | No | | No | No | Nothing |

| DIPLOMATIC AND CONSULAR IMMUNITIES CHART | | | | | | |
|---|---|---|---|---|---|---|
| Category | May Be Arrested or Detained | Residents May Be Entered Subject to Ordinary Procedures | May Be Issued Traffic Citations | May Be Subpoenaed As a Witness | May Be Prosecuted | Recognized Family Members |
| Diplomatic Agent | NO | NO | YES | NO | NO | Same as sponsor (full immunity & inviolability) |
| Member of Admin. Tech Staff | NO | NO | YES | NO | NO | Same as sponsor (full immunity & inviolability) |
| Service Staff | YES | YES | YES | YES | NO for Official acts Otherwise, YES | No immunity or inviolability |
| Career Consular Officer | YES, if for a felony and pursuant to a warrant | YES | YES | NO for official acts. Testimony may not be compelled in any case | No for Official acts Otherwise, YES | No immunity or inviolability |
| Honorary Consular Office | YES | YES | YES | No for official acts. YES in all other cases | No for Official acts. Otherwise, YES | No immunity or inviolability |
| Consular Employees | YES | YES | YES | No for Official acts. Otherwise YES | No for Official acts. Otherwise, YES | No immunity or inviolability |
| Int'l Org. Staff[3] | YES | YES | YES | YES | No for Official acts. Otherwise, YES | No immunity or inviolability |
| Diplomatic Level Staff of Missions to Int'l Org. | NO | NO | YES | NO | NO | Same as sponsor (full immunity & inviolability) |
| Support Staff of Missions to Int'l Org. | YES | YES | YES | YES | NO, for Official acts. Otherwise, YES | No immunity or inviolability |

## Authors' Note

The following four materials discuss the legality of the United States government's attempt to close the office of the Palestine Liberation Organization. Material 7, an article from the United Press International, provides a background view of the political incident. Material 8, an article from the *Chicago Tribune*, discusses the World Court's ruling that the U.S. could not close the PLO office. Materials 9 and 10 discuss the U.S. court ruling similarly rules that the PLO office cannot be closed under international agreement and law. These materials provide a glimpse into the limitations on U.S. actions with respect to the privileges and immunities afford to international missions to the U.N.

## 7. Jim Anderson, Politics Wins in PLO Office Closure
### UPI, 1988

The administration decision to order the closure of the PLO mission at the United Nations was fought on the battleground of the law, foreign policy and politics. Politics won. As a result, Secretary of State George Shultz, in the midst of a long-shot attempt to revive the Arab-Israeli peace process, saw his chances of talking to Arabs—and particularly the Palestinian Arabs—diminish.

Clovis Maksoud, representative of the Arab League—of which the PLO is a member—described the timing of the decision as "a gift for (Israeli Prime Minister Yitzhak) Shamir." Shamir, due to arrive in Washington Monday to give his answer to Shultz's peace proposals, has said Israel would never negotiate with the Palestine Liberation Organization.

Assistant Attorney General Charles Cooper, at a news conference announcing the closure, was asked why the decision could not have been delayed or why it was not made earlier when the announcement had been scheduled and then abruptly postponed. He said the timing was dictated by the need to give the PLO reasonable notice before its expulsion date of March 21.

The Anti-Terrorism Act of 1987, which ordered the expulsion, has been fought by the American Civil Liberties Union and other civil rights organizations on the ground that it is an infringement of First Amendment rights.

Shultz called the law "one of the dumber things Congress has done" and opposed it energetically on several grounds:

> The law was a direct infringement on his—and the president's—exclusive right to carry out foreign policy.

> The expulsion of an accepted delegation to the United Nations would cast doubt on the U.S. ability to carry out its host-country obligations to the United Nations and its ability to carry out other existing treaty agreements.

Cooper said the constitutional issue was considered and rejected on the narrow ground that the United States does not have diplomatic relations with the PLO. He said it would be "clearly unconstitutional, if Congress were to pass a similar law ordering the expulsion of the Soviet mission since the United States diplomatically recognizes the Soviet Union.

Cooper said the Supreme Court has established that any law passed by Congress abrogates a treaty, if the law is inconsistent with that treaty.

Maksoud said neither the PLO nor the Arab League would fight the order in the U.S. courts because "this is a matter between the United States and the United Nations."

But Congress, in the heat of an presidential election campaign, listened instead to several powerful pro-Israeli organizations, including the American Jewish Congress.

The bill was co-sponsored by Jack Kemp, R.-N.Y., and Robert Dole, R-Kan., both presidential contenders at the time of the bill's passage.

Ironically, in the ensuing debate, some of the pro-Israeli groups, including the AJC, have reconsidered their position and have withdrawn their support for the PLO expulsion.

## 8. World Court Rules against U.S. in PLO Mission Closure
### *Chicago Tribune*, 1988

The World Court ruled Tuesday against the U.S. attempt to close the Palestine Liberation Organization's mission to the United Nations in New York. The ruling supported the U.N. position that the dispute must be submitted to independent arbitration. The court has no enforcement powers and depends on voluntary adherence to its rulings. The PLO office dispute emanates from anti-terrorist legislation signed into law by President Reagan last December. The U.N. contends the order violates a 1947 pact under which member and observer nations and diplomats are guaranteed the right to operate at the world body.

## 9. U.S. Court Rules PLO Mission Cannot Be Closed
### Inter Press Service, 1988

The U.S. government today suffered a major legal setback when a New York District Court ruled that the Palestine Liberation Organization's (PLO) Observer Mission to the United Nations cannot be ordered closed under a 1987 "Anti-Terrorism Act."

In a 90-page ruling, U.S. District Court Judge Edmund Palmieri held that the Anti-Terrorism Act did not require the closure of the PLO mission "nor do the act's provisions impair the continued exercise of its appropriate functions."

The court's decision was immediately welcomed by U.N. Secretary-General Javier Perez de Cuellar, who said he was gratified by the judgement "which demonstrates the respect of the United States courts for the international obligations of the country."

PLO permanent representative to the United Nations Zuhdi Terzi also hailed the court's decision, as did the League of Arab States.

Palmieri ruled that the headquarters agreement between the United States and the United Nations, as well as past practice and interpretation "leaves no doubt that it places an obligation upon the U.S. to refrain from impairing the function" of the PLO mission.

He said that the legislative history of the Anti-Terrorism Act did not manifest the U.S. Congress' intent "to abrogate this obligation."

The judge further noted in his ruling that the act did not supersede the headquarters agreement and therefore could not be applied to the PLO mission.

Palmieri, nevertheless, said the statute "remains a valid enactment of general application." He further stated that the act's restrictions on PLO activity within the United States "were appropriate aside from application to the U.N. mission."

The court's ruling ends seven months of uncertainty for the PLO, which had been ordered by the U.S. attorney general to close its mission to the United Nations within 90 days, following passage of the anti-terrorism legislation by Congress.

The PLO has maintained offices in New York since 1974, when it was granted observer status by the U.N. General Assembly.

In response to the attorney generals order, the Secretary-General tried to get the issue arbitrated as called for under the headquarters agreement between the United States and the United Nations. The U.S. government refused to proceed to arbitration.

The 43rd General Assembly was then called back into session and a decision was made to ask the International Court of Justice for a ruling on the dispute.

On April 26, the World Court ruled that the United States had to enter into arbitration on the issue.

Instead, the United States took the issue to its domestic courts, the end result being today's ruling.

Terzi noted "if there is a victory, it is for the U.N. And respect for obligations under international agreements."

## 10. *United States of America v. The Palestine Liberation Organization, et al.*

Southern District of New York, 1988
[citations omitted by editors]

EDMUND L. PALMIERI, United States District Judge

The Anti-terrorism Act of 1987 (the "ATA"), is the focal point of this lawsuit. At the center of controversy is the right of the Palestine Liberation Organization (the "PLO") to maintain its office in conjunction with its work as a Permanent Observer to the United Nations. The case comes before the court on the government's motion for an injunction closing this office and on the defendants' motions to dismiss.

### I. Background

The United Nations' Headquarters in New York were established as an international enclave by the Agreement Between the United States and the United Nations Regarding the Headquarters of the United Nations (the "Headquarters Agreement"). This agreement followed an invitation extended to the United Nations by the United States, one of its principal founders, to establish its seat within the United States ...

Today, 159 of the United Nations' members maintain missions to the U.N. in New York. U.N. Protocol and Liaison Service, Permanent Missions to the United Nations No. 262 3–4 (1988) (hereinafter "Permanent Missions No. 262"). In addition, the United Nations has, from its incipiency, welcomed various non-member observers to participate in its proceedings. Of these, several non-member nations, intergovernmental organizations, and other organizations currently maintain "Permanent Observer Missions" in New York.

The PLO falls into the last of these categories and is present at the United Nations as its invitee. The PLO has none of the usual attributes of sovereignty. It is not accredited to the United States and does not have the benefits of diplomatic immunity. There is no recognized state it claims to govern. It purports to serve as the sole political representative of the Palestinian people. The PLO nevertheless considers itself to be the representative of a state, entitled to recognition in its relations with other governments, and is said to have diplomatic relations with approximately one hundred countries throughout the world.

In 1974, the United Nations invited the PLO to become an observer at the U.N., to "participate in the sessions and the work of the General Assembly in the capacity of observer." The right of its representatives to admission to the United States as well as access to the U.N. was immediately challenged under American law. Judge Costantino rejected that challenge in *Anti-Defamation League of B'nai B'rith v. Kissinger*, Civil Action No. 74 C 1545. The court upheld the presence of a PLO representative in New York with access to the United Nations, albeit under certain entrance visa restrictions which limited PLO personnel movements to a radius of 25 miles from Columbus Circle in Manhattan. It stated from the bench:

> This problem must be viewed in the context of the special responsibility which the United States has to provide access to the United Nations under the Headquarters Agreement. It is important to note for the purposes of this case that a primary goal of the United Nations is to provide a forum where peaceful discussions may displace violence as a means of resolving disputed issues. At times our responsibility to the United Nations may require us to issue visas to persons who are objectionable to certain segments of our society.

Since 1974, the PLO has continued to function without interruption as a permanent observer and has maintained its Mission to the United Nations without trammel, largely because of the Headquarters Agreement, which we discuss below.

## II. The Anti-Terrorism Act

In October 1986, members of Congress requested the United States Department of State to close the PLO offices located in the United States. That request proved unsuccessful, and proponents of the request introduced legislation with the explicit purpose of doing so.

The result was the ATA. It is of a unique nature. We have been unable to find any comparable statute in the long history of Congressional enactments. The PLO is stated to be "a terrorist organization and a threat to the interests of the United States, its allies, and to international law and should not benefit from operating in the United States." The ATA was added, without committee hearings, as a rider to the Foreign Relations Authorization Act for Fiscal Years 1988–89, which provided funds for the operation of the State Department, including the operation of the United States Mission to the United Nations. The bill also authorized payments to the United Nations for maintenance and operation.

The House version of the spending bill contained no equivalent provision, and the ATA was only briefly discussed during a joint conference which covered the entire spending bill. The House conferees rejected, 8–11, an exemption for the Mission, after which they acceded to the Senate's version.

The ATA, which became effective on March 21, 1988, forbids the establishment or maintenance of "an office, headquarters, premises, or other facilities or establishments within the jurisdiction of the United States at the behest or direction of, or with funds provided by" the PLO, if the purpose is to further the PLO's interests. The ATA also forbids spending the PLO's funds or receiving anything of value except informational material from the PLO, with the same mens rea requirement.

Ten days before the effective date, the Attorney General wrote the Chief of the PLO Observer Mission to the United Nations that "maintaining a PLO Observer Mission to the United Nations will be unlawful," and advised him that upon failure of compliance, the Department of Justice would take action in federal court.

The United States commenced this lawsuit the day the ATA took effect, seeking injunctive relief to accomplish the closure of the Mission. The United States Attorney for this District has personally represented that no action would be taken to enforce the ATA pending resolution of the litigation in this court.

There are now four individual defendants in addition to the PLO itself. Defendant Zuhdi Labib Terzi, who possesses an Algerian passport but whose citizenship is not divulged, has served as the Permanent Observer of the PLO to the United Nations since 1975. Defendant Riyad H. Mansour, a citizen of the United States, has been the Deputy Permanent Observer of the PLO to the United Nations since 1983. Defendant Nasser Al-Kidwa, a citizen of Iraq, is the Alternate Permanent Observer of the PLO to the United Nations. And defendant Veronica Kanaan Pugh, a citizen of Great Britain, is charged with administrative duties at the Observer Mission. These defendants contend that this court may not adjudicate the ATA's applicability to the Mission because such an adjudication would violate the United States' obligation under Section 21 of the Headquarters Agreement to arbitrate any dispute with the United Nations. Apart from that, they argue, application of the ATA to the PLO Mission would violate the United States' commitments under the Headquarters Agreement. They assert that the court lacks subject matter and personal jurisdiction over them and that they lack the capacity to be sued. Defendant Riyad H. Mansour additionally moves to dismiss for failure to state a claim upon which relief can be granted.

### III. Personal Jurisdiction over the Defendants

[Here, the court finds no difficulty in establishing personal jurisdiction over the PLO and the individual defendants]

### IV. The Duty to Arbitrate

Counsel for the PLO and for the United Nations and the Association of the Bar of the City of New York, as amici curiae, have suggested that the court defer to an advisory opinion of the International Court of Justice. That decision (Applicability of the Obligation to Arbitrate Under Section 21 of the U.N. Headquarters Agreement of 26 June 1947) holds that the United States is bound by Section 21 of the Headquarters Agreement to submit to binding arbitration of a dispute precipitated by the passage of the ATA. Indeed, it is the PLO's position that this alleged duty to arbitrate deprives the court of subject matter jurisdiction over this litigation.

In June 1947, the United States subscribed to the Headquarters Agreement, defining the privileges and immunities of the United Nations' Headquarters in New York City, thereby becoming the "Host Country"—a descriptive title that has followed it through many United Nations proceedings. The Headquarters Agreement was brought into effect under United States law, with an annex, by a Joint Resolution of Congress approved by the President on August 4, 1947. The PLO rests its argument, as do the amici, on Section 21(a) of the Headquarters Agreement, which provides for arbitration in the case of any dispute between the United Nations and the United States concerning the interpretation or application of the Headquarters Agreement. Because interpretation of the ATA requires an interpretation of the Headquarters Agreement, they argue, this court must await the decision of an arbitral tribunal yet to be appointed before making its decision.

Section 21(a) of the Headquarters Agreement provides, in part:

> "Any dispute between the United Nations and the United States concerning the interpretation or application of this agreement or of any supplemental agreement, which is not settled by negotiation or other agreed mode of settlement, shall be referred for final decision to a tribunal of three arbitrators...."

Because these proceedings are not in any way directed to settling any dispute, ripe or not, between the United Nations and the United States, Section 21, is, by its terms, inapplicable. The fact that the Headquarters Agreement was adopted by a majority of both Houses of Congress and approved by the President might lead to the conclusion that it provides a rule of decision requiring arbitration any time the interpretation of the Headquarters Agreement is at issue in the United States Courts. That conclusion would be wrong for two reasons.

First, this court cannot direct the United States to submit to arbitration without exceeding the scope of its Article III powers. What sets this case apart from the usual situation in which two parties have agreed to binding arbitration for the settlement of any future disputes, requiring the court to stay its proceedings is that we are here involved with matters of international policy. This is an area in which the courts are generally unable to participate. These questions do not lend themselves to resolution by adjudication under our jurisprudence. The restrictions imposed upon the courts forbidding them to resolve such questions (often termed "political questions") derive not only from the limitations which inhere in the judicial process but also from those imposed by Article III of the Constitution.

The conduct of the foreign relations of our Government is committed by the Constitution to the executive and legislative — the "political" — departments of the government. As the Supreme Court noted in *Baker v. Carr*, not all questions touching upon international relations are automatically political questions. Nonetheless, were the court to order the United States to submit to arbitration, it would violate several of the tenets to which the Supreme Court gave voice in *Baker v. Carr*. Resolution of the question whether the United States will arbitrate requires "an initial policy determination of a kind clearly for nonjudicial discretion;" deciding whether the United States will or ought to submit to arbitration, in the face of a determination not to do so by the executive, would be impossible without the court "expressing lack of the respect due coordinate branches of government;" and such a decision would raise not only the "potentiality" but the reality of "embarrassment from multifarious pronouncements by various departments on one question." It is for these reasons that the ultimate decision as to how the United States should honor its treaty obligations with the international community is one which has, for at least one hundred years, been left to the executive to decide. Consequently the question whether the United States should submit to the jurisdiction of an international tribunal is a question of policy not for the courts but for the political branches to decide.

Section 21 of the Headquarters Agreement cannot provide a rule of decision regarding the interpretation of that agreement for another reason: treating it as doing so would require the courts to refrain from undertaking their constitutionally mandated function. The task of the court in this case is to interpret the ATA in resolving this dispute between numerous parties and the United States. Interpretation of the ATA, as a matter of domestic law, falls to the United States courts. In interpreting the ATA, the effect of the United States' international obligations — the United Nations Charter and the Headquarters Agreement in particular — must be considered. As a matter of domestic law, the interpretation of these international obligations and their reconciliation, if possible, with the ATA is for the courts. It is, as Chief Justice Marshall said, "emphatically the province and duty of the judicial department to say what the law is." That duty will not be resolved without independent adjudication of the effect of the ATA on the Headquarters Agreement. Awaiting the decision of an arbitral tribunal would be a repudiation of that duty.

Interpreting Section 21 as a rule of decision would, at a minimum, raise serious constitutional questions. We do not interpret it in that manner. It would not be consonant with the court's duties for it to await the interpretation of the Headquarters Agreement by an arbitral tribunal, not yet constituted, before undertaking the limited task of interpreting the ATA with a view to resolving the actual dispute before it.

In view of the foregoing, the court finds that it is not deprived of subject matter jurisdiction by Section 21 of the Headquarters Agreement and that any interpretation of the Headquarters Agreement incident to an interpretation of the ATA must be done by the court.

## V. The Anti-Terrorism Act and the Headquarters Agreement

If the ATA were construed as the government suggests, it would be tantamount to a direction to the PLO Observer Mission at the United Nations that it close its doors and cease its operations *instanter*. Such an interpretation would fly in the face of the Headquarters Agreement, a prior treaty between the United Nations and the United States, and would abruptly terminate the functions the Mission has performed for many years. This conflict requires the court to seek out a reconciliation between the two.

Under our constitutional system, statutes and treaties are both the supreme law of the land, and the Constitution sets forth no order of precedence to differentiate between them. Wherever possible, both are to be given effect. Only where a treaty is irreconcilable with a later enacted statute and Congress has clearly evinced an intent to supersede a treaty by enacting a statute does the later enacted statute take precedence.

The long standing and well-established position of the Mission at the United Nations, sustained by international agreement, when considered along with the text of the ATA and its legislative history, fails to disclose any clear legislative intent that Congress was directing the Attorney General, the State Department or this Court to act in contravention of the Headquarters Agreement. This court acknowledges the validity of the government's position that Congress has the power to enact statutes abrogating prior treaties or international obligations entered into by the United States. However, unless this power is clearly and unequivocally exercised, this court is under a duty to interpret statutes in a manner consonant with existing treaty obligations. This is a rule of statutory construction sustained by an unbroken line of authority for over a century and a half. Recently, the Supreme Court articulated it in *Weinberger v. Rossi*.

It has been maxim of statutory construction since the decision in *Murray v. The Charming Betsy*, that "an act of Congress ought never to be construed to violate the law of nations, if any other possible construction remains...."

The American Law Institute's recently revised Restatement (Third) Foreign Relations Law of the United States (1988) reflects this unbroken line of authority:

> § 115. Inconsistency Between International Law or Agreement and Domestic Law: Law of the United States.
>
> (1)(a) An Act of Congress supersedes an earlier rule of international law or a provision of an international agreement as law of the United States if the purpose of the act to supersede the earlier rule or provision is clear and if the act and the earlier rule or provision cannot be fairly reconciled.

We believe the ATA and the Headquarters Agreement cannot be reconciled except by finding the ATA inapplicable to the PLO Observer Mission.

## A. The Obligations of the United States under the Headquarters Agreement.

The obligation of the United States to allow transit, entry and access stems not only from the language of the Headquarters Agreement but also from forty years of practice under it. Section 11 of the Headquarters Agreement reads, in part,

The federal, state or local authorities of the United States shall not impose any impediments to transit to or from the headquarters district of: (1) representatives of Members..., (5) other persons invited to the headquarters district by the United Nations ... on official business.

These rights could not be effectively exercised without the use of offices. The ability to effectively organize and carry out one's work, especially as a liaison to an international organization, would not be possible otherwise. It is particularly significant that Section 13 limits the application of United States law not only with respect to the entry of aliens, but also their residence. The Headquarters Agreement thus contemplates a continuity limited to official United Nations functions and is entirely consistent with the maintenance of missions to the United Nations. The exemptions of Section 13 are not limited to members, but extend to invitees as well.

In addition, there can be no dispute that over the forty years since the United States entered into the Headquarters Agreement it has taken a number of actions consistent with its recognition of a duty to refrain from impeding the functions of observer missions to the United Nations. It has, since the early days of the U.N.'s presence in New York, acquiesced in the presence of observer missions to the U.N. in New York.

After the United Nations invited the PLO to participate as a permanent observer, the Department of State took the position that it was required to provide access to the U.N. for the PLO. The State Department at no time disputed the notion that the rights of entry, access and residence guaranteed to invitees include the right to maintain offices.

The view that under the Headquarters Agreement the United States must allow PLO representatives access to and presence in the vicinity of the United Nations was adopted by the court in *Anti-Defamation League of B'nai B'rith v. Kissinger*. The United States has, for fourteen years, acted in a manner consistent with a recognition of the PLO's rights in the Headquarters Agreement. This course of conduct under the Headquarters Agreement is important evidence of its meaning.

Throughout 1987, when Congress was considering the ATA, the Department of State elaborated its view that the Headquarters Agreement contained such a requirement. Perhaps the most unequivocal elaboration of the State Department's interpretation was the letter of J. Edward Fox, Assistant Secretary for Legislative Affairs, to Dante Fascell, Chairman of the House Committee on Foreign Affairs (November 5, 1987):

The United States has acknowledged that [the invitations to the PLO to become a permanent observer] give rise to United States obligations to accord PLO observers the rights set forth in sections 11–13 of the Headquarters Agreement. See, e.g., 1976 Digest of United States Practice in International Law 74–75. The proposed legislation would effectively require the United States to deny PLO observers the entry, transit, and residence rights required by sections 11–13 and, as a later enacted statute, would supersede the Headquarters Agreement in this regard as a matter of domestic law.

The proposed legislation would also ... break a 40-year practice regarding observer missions by nations hosting U.N. bodies and could legitimately be viewed as inconsistent with our responsibilities under sections 11–13 of the United Nations Headquarters Agreement.

\* \* \*

Shortly before the adoption of the ATA, during consideration of a report of the Committee on Relations with the Host Country by the General Assembly of the United Nations, the United States' representative noted "that the United States Secretary of State had stated that the closing of the mission would constitute a violation of United States obligation under the Headquarters Agreement." He had previously stated that "closing the mission, in our view, and I emphasize this is the executive branch, is not consistent with our international legal obligations under the Headquarters Agreement." And the day after the ATA was passed, State Department spokeswoman Phyllis Oakley told reporters that the ATA, "if implemented, would be contrary to our international legal obligations under the Headquarters Agreement, [so the administration intends] … to engage in consultations with the Congress in an effort to resolve this matter."

It seemed clear to those in the executive branch that closing the PLO mission would be a departure from the United States' practice in regard to observer missions, and they made their views known to members of Congress who were instrumental in the passage of the ATA. In addition, United States representatives to the United Nations made repeated efforts to allay the concerns of the U.N. Secretariat by reiterating and reaffirming the obligations of the United States under the Headquarters Agreement. A chronological record of their efforts is set forth in the advisory opinion of the International Court of Justice. The U.N. Secretariat considered it necessary to request that opinion in order to protect what it considered to be the U.N.'s rights under the Headquarters Agreement. The United Nations' position that the Headquarters Agreement applies to the PLO Mission is not new.

"Although not conclusive, the meaning attributed to treaty provisions by the Government agencies charged with their negotiation and enforcement is entitled to great weight." The interpretive statements of the United Nations also carry some weight, especially because they are in harmony with the interpretation given to the Headquarters Agreement by the Department of State.

Thus the language, application and interpretation of the Headquarters Agreement lead us to the conclusion that it requires the United States to refrain from interference with the PLO Observer Mission in the discharge of its functions at the United Nations.

## B. Reconciliation of the ATA and the Headquarters Agreement.

The lengths to which our courts have sometimes gone in construing domestic statutes so as to avoid conflict with international agreements are suggested by a passage from Justice Field's dissent in Chew Heong:

> I am unable to agree with my associates in their construction of the act … restricting the immigration into this country of Chinese laborers. That construction appears to me to be in conflict with the language of that act, and to require the elimination of entire clauses and the interpolation of new ones. It renders nugatory whole provisions which were inserted with sedulous care. The change thus produced in the operation of the act is justified on the theory that to give it any other construction would bring it into conflict with the treaty; and that we are not at liberty to suppose that Congress intended by its legislation to disregard any treaty stipulations.

Chew Heong concerned the interplay of legislation regarding Chinese laborers with treaties on the same subject. During the passage of the statute at issue in Chew Heong, "it was objected to the legislation sought that the treaty of 1868 stood in the way, and that

while it remained unmodified, such legislation would be a breach of faith to China...."
In spite of that, and over Justice Field's dissent, the Court, in Justice Field's words, "narrow[ed] the meaning of the act so as measurably to frustrate its intended operation." Four years after the decision in *Chew Heong*, Congress amended the act in question to nullify that decision. With the amended statute, there could be no question as to Congress' intent to supersede the treaties, and it was the later enacted statute which took precedence.

The principles enunciated and applied in Chew Heong and its progeny require the clearest of expressions on the part of Congress. We are constrained by these decisions to stress the lack of clarity in Congress' action in this instance. Congress' failure to speak with one clear voice on this subject requires us to interpret the ATA as inapplicable to the Headquarters Agreement. This is so, in short, for the reasons which follow.

First, neither the Mission nor the Headquarters Agreement is mentioned in the ATA itself. Such an inclusion would have left no doubt as to Congress' intent on a matter which had been raised repeatedly with respect to this act, and its absence here reflects equivocation and avoidance, leaving the court without clear interpretive guidance in the language of the act. Second, while the section of the ATA prohibiting the maintenance of an office applies "notwithstanding any provision of law to the contrary," it does not purport to apply notwithstanding any treaty. The absence of that interpretive instruction is especially relevant because elsewhere in the same legislation Congress expressly referred to "United States law (including any treaty)." Thus Congress failed, in the text of the ATA, to provide guidance for the interpretation of the act, where it became repeatedly apparent before its passage that the prospect of an interpretive problem was inevitable. Third, no member of Congress expressed a clear and unequivocal intent to supersede the Headquarters Agreement by passage of the ATA. In contrast, most who addressed the subject of conflict denied that there would be a conflict: in their view, the Headquarters Agreement did not provide the PLO with any right to maintain an office. Here again, Congress provided no guidance for the interpretation of the ATA in the event of a conflict which was clearly foreseeable. And Senator Claiborne Pell, Chairman of the Senate Foreign Relations Committee, who voted for the bill, raised the possibility that the Headquarters Agreement would take precedence over the ATA in the event of a conflict between the two. His suggestion was neither opposed nor debated, even though it came in the final minutes before passage of the ATA.

A more complete explanation begins, of course, with the statute's language. The ATA reads, in part:

> It shall be unlawful, if the purpose be to further the interests of the PLO [...] —
>
> * * *
>
> (3) notwithstanding any provision of law to the contrary, to establish or maintain an office, headquarters, premises, or other facilities or establishments within the jurisdiction of the United States at the behest or direction of, or with funds provided by the PLO [ ... ].

22 U.S.C. § 5202(3).

The Permanent Observer Mission to the United Nations is nowhere mentioned in haec verba in this act, as we have already observed. It is nevertheless contended by the United States that the foregoing provision requires the closing of the Mission, and this in spite of possibly inconsistent international obligations. According to the government, the act is so clear that this possibility is nonexistent. The government argues that its position is supported by the provision that the ATA would take effect "notwithstanding any provision of law to the contrary," suggesting that Congress thereby swept away any inconsistent international obligations of the United States. In effect, the government urges literal application of the maxim that in the event of conflict between two laws, the one of later date will prevail: leges posteriores priores contrarias abrogant.

We cannot agree. The proponents of the ATA were, at an early stage and throughout its consideration, forewarned that the ATA would present a potential conflict with the Headquarters Agreement. It was especially important in those circumstances for Congress to give clear, indeed unequivocal guidance, as to how an interpreter of the ATA was to resolve the conflict. Yet there was no reference to the Mission in the text of the ATA, despite extensive discussion of the Mission in the floor debates. Nor was there reference to the Headquarters Agreement, or to any treaty, in the ATA or in its "notwithstanding" clause, despite the textual expression of intent to supersede treaty obligations in other sections of the Foreign Relations Authorization Act, of which the ATA formed a part. Thus Congress failed to provide unequivocal interpretive guidance in the text of the ATA, leaving open the possibility that the ATA could be viewed as a law of general application and enforced as such, without encroaching on the position of the Mission at the United Nations.

That interpretation would present no inconsistency with what little legislative history exists. There were conflicting voices both in Congress and in the executive branch before the enactment of the ATA. Indeed, there is only one matter with respect to which there was unanimity — the condemnation of terrorism. This, however, is extraneous to the legal issues involved here. At oral argument, the United States Attorney conceded that there was no evidence before the court that the Mission had misused its position at the United Nations or engaged in any covert actions in furtherance of terrorism. If the PLO is benefiting from operating in the United States, as the ATA implies, the enforcement of its provisions outside the context of the United Nations can effectively curtail that benefit.

The record contains voices of congressmen and senators forceful in their condemnation of terrorism and of the PLO and supporting the notion that the legislation would close the mission. There are other voices, less certain of the validity of the proposed congressional action and preoccupied by problems of constitutional dimension. And there are voices of Congressmen uncertain of the legal issues presented but desirous nonetheless of making a "political statement." During the discussions which preceded and followed the passage of the ATA, the Secretary of State and the Legal Adviser to the Department of State, a former member of this Court, voiced their opinions to the effect that the ATA presented a conflict with the Headquarters Agreement.

Yet no member of Congress, at any point, explicitly stated that the ATA was intended to override any international obligation of the United States.

The only debate on this issue focused not on whether the ATA would do so, but on whether the United States in fact had an obligation to provide access to the PLO. Indeed, every proponent of the ATA who spoke to the matter argued that the United States did not have such an obligation. For instance, Senator Grassley, after arguing that the United States had no obligation relating to the PLO Mission under the Headquarters Agreement, noted in passing that Congress had the power to modify treaty obligations. But even there, Senator Grassley did not argue that the ATA would supersede the Headquarters Agreement in the event of a conflict. This disinclination to face the prospect of an actual conflict was again manifest two weeks later, when Senator Grassley explained, "as I detailed earlier...., the United States has no international legal obligation that would preclude it from closing the PLO Observer Mission." As the Congressional Record reveals, at the time of the ATA's passage (on December 15 in the House and December 16 in the Senate), its proponents were operating under a misapprehension of what the United States' treaty obligation entailed.

In sum, the language of the Headquarters Agreement, the long-standing practice under it, and the interpretation given it by the parties to it leave no doubt that it places an obligation upon the United States to refrain from impairing the function of the PLO Observer Mission to the United Nations. The ATA and its legislative history do not manifest Congress' intent to abrogate this obligation. We are therefore constrained to interpret the ATA as failing to supersede the Headquarters Agreement and inapplicable to the Mission.

## C. The Continued Viability of the ATA.

We have interpreted the ATA as inapplicable to the PLO Mission to the United Nations. The statute remains a valid enactment of general application. It is a wide gauged restriction of PLO activity within the United States and, depending on the nature of its enforcement, could effectively curtail any PLO activities in the United States, aside from the Mission to the United Nations. We do not accept the suggestion of counsel that the ATA be struck down. The federal courts are constrained to avoid a decision regarding unconstitutionality except where strictly necessary. In view of our construction of the statute, this can be fairly avoided in this instance. The extent to which the First Amendment to the Constitution and the Bill of Attainder Clause, Art. I, §9, cl. 3, guide our interpretation of the ATA is addressed in *Mendelsohn v. Meese*, post.

## VI. Conclusions.

The Anti-Terrorism Act does not require the closure of the PLO Permanent Observer Mission to the United Nations nor do the act's provisions impair the continued exercise of its appropriate functions as a Permanent Observer at the United Nations. The PLO Mission to the United Nations is an invitee of the United Nations under the Headquarters Agreement and its status is protected by that agreement. The Headquarters Agreement remains a valid and outstanding treaty obligation of the United States. It has not been superseded by the Anti-Terrorism Act, which is a valid enactment of general application ...

The motion of the United States for summary judgment is denied, and summary judgment is entered for the defendants, dismissing this action with prejudice.

SO ORDERED.

---

## *Authors' Note*

In 1988, the United States decided to deny Yasser Arafat, chairman of the PLO, an entry visa to address the U.N. General Assembly under the reasoning that he was a terrorist or had supported terrorism. Material 11, an article from *The Washington Post*, provides background information on the situation and the implications of the denial on U.S. obligations to U.N. The next article, Material 12, details specifically why the denial of an entry visa to Arafat was a violation of long-standing obligations to the U.N. Material 13, an article from *Newsday*, describes the U.N. response to move the General Assembly gathering to Geneva in order for Arafat to address Assembly.

## 11. Don Oberdorfer, U.S. Denies Entry Visa to Arafat
### *The Washington Post*, 1988

Secretary of State George P. Shultz, citing "associations with terrorism," yesterday barred PLO Chairman Yasser Arafat from flying to New York this week to address the United Nations General Assembly.

Shultz's surprise decision to reject Arafat's application for a U.S. visa, which is likely to be among the most controversial of his stewardship of U.S. diplomacy, was described by State Department officials as an unusually personal act arising from his abhorrence of terrorism. Sources said Shultz went against the advice of the department's Middle East experts and of Undersecretary of State Michael H. Armacost. The White House said President Reagan was not involved in the decision.

Arafat declined to comment on the U.S. action on his arrival last night in Amman, Jordan, for meetings with King Hussein, but was expected to speak with reporters today, United Press International reported.

PLO political adviser Bassam Abu Sharif, who was traveling with Arafat, said, "the American administration committed a big mistake.... If Arafat is a terrorist, he is as much a terrorist as George Washington."

Earlier, a PLO spokesman in Tunis told UPI that the visa denial violates U.S. obligations to the United Nations and means "the Americans have rejected any chance for peace in the Middle East."

Under a 1947 headquarters agreement with the United Nations, the United States is committed to facilitating business travel to the world body. In approving the agreement, however, Congress retained authority to bar the travel of aliens on national security grounds.

This authority was cited by Shultz in a written statement released at 2 p.m. yesterday. Aides said he made the decision overnight after hearing arguments on all sides from State Department officials Friday.

"The PLO through certain of its elements has employed terrorism against Americans," said the State Department, which cited the killing of a wheelchair-bound American, Leon Klinghoffer, during the October 1985 hijacking of the Italian cruise ship, the Achille Lauro.

"Mr. Arafat, as chairman of the PLO, knows of, condones and lends support to such acts; he, therefore, is an accessory to such terrorism," the statement said.

Aides said Shultz was particularly indignant that Abu Abbas, a PLO executive committee member who was convicted in absentia in Italy of the murder of Klinghoffer, was present at the Algiers meeting this month of the Palestine National Council, the PLO's legislative arm. Abbas was quoted by a New York Times correspondent in Algiers as saying with a half-smile of Klinghoffer, who was shot and dumped overboard, "maybe he was trying to swim for it."

Shultz, who unsuccessfully sought to restart the stalled Arab-Israeli peace process in a burst of personal diplomacy last spring and summer, acknowledged that the recent PLO legislative session in Algiers "produced signs that there are Palestinians who are trying to move the PLO in a constructive way."

"This is encouraging and should continue," the statement said. But it added that "the blight of terrorism still afflicts the Palestinian cause and leaves no alternative to decisions such as the secretary has taken today."

Arab and Western European governments in recent days sought to persuade the United States to take a more positive view of the PLO shifts at the Algiers meeting on grounds this would encourage further movement. The meeting for the first time voted to accept U.N. Resolution 242, a basic underpinning of Arab-Israeli diplomacy. It also proclaimed an independent Palestinian state in the West Bank and Gaza Strip.

Ambassador Clovis Maksoud, permanent representative of the Arab League to the United Nations, said at least 12 Arab foreign ministers, including those of Egypt and Saudi Arabia, had planned to come to the United Nations later this week for the debate on Palestine that Arafat had hoped to address.

Maksoud, who said Shultz's decision "signals that moderation is costly and appears to be inconsequential to the U.S. administration," reported that Arab diplomats will probably ask that the Palestine debate be postponed and, in an extraordinary gesture, moved from New York to Geneva.

In an interview with the Kuwaiti news agency before the State Department announcement, Arafat said he would urge the transfer of the debate to Geneva if he were denied a visa. "This is our right and the right of our friends, so that we can work freely and without blackmail from Israel and others at U.N. headquarters," he said.

A senior Arab diplomat here, who asked not to be identified, called Shultz's decision "a tragedy" and said it will bring "a great letdown for Arab leaders who stuck their necks out based on Shultz's urging." The diplomat said Shultz in his last trip to the region spoke to Arab leaders of the need to urge the Palestinians "to be flexible and cooperative" to restart the peace process.

The Israeli Embassy through spokesman Yossi Gal called Shultz's decision "very encouraging as an expression of the determination of the United States to fight against terrorism."

The immediate reactions of U.S. groups was as expected, with Arab-American spokesmen decrying the decision and Jewish-American spokesmen hailing it. Former senator James Abourezk, chairman of the American-Arab Anti-Discrimination Committee, called the decision "both embarrassing and against American interests." He said, "it is shameful that Secretary of State Shultz would allow Israel to dictate whom the American people can or cannot hear."

Ira Silverman, executive vice president of the American Jewish Committee, said he was "gratified" by Shultz's action. "The whole civilized world was shocked when Arafat wore a gun on last addressing the United Nations. We have no reason to think he is any less a supporter of terrorism and an enemy of Israel than he was then."

Abraham H. Foxman, national director of the Anti-Defamation League of Blnai Blrith, called the decision "a welcome and courageous blow by the secretary of state against international terrorism."

Arafat was given a U.S. visa to address the United Nations in November 1974, when Henry A. Kissinger was secretary of state. A State Department official said the major change since then was the rise of terrorism as a national and international issue.

Policy-making about his appearance began Nov. 8, shortly before the Algiers conference was convened, when the PLO notified the United Nations it wanted a visa for Arafat to address the General Assembly in early December. The United Nations notified the State Department and asked that the visa be expedited but State, in an unusual move, required that the PLO chairman apply in person for the travel document. Arafat and three aides did so Friday through the U.S. Embassy in Tunis.

Meanwhile, 51 members of the Senate sent a letter to Shultz urging that the visa application be denied. The letter was sponsored by Sen. Dennis DeConcini (D-Ariz.).

Because the law governing visa applications gives decision-making responsibility to the secretary of state, Shultz took unusual latitude in deciding the Arafat issue himself. A White House spokesman in Santa Barbara, Calif., where Reagan is spending Thanksgiving vacation at his mountain-top ranch, said Reagan "had no role in the decision" but was aware of it.

A State Department official said Reagan had been briefed on the decision and "was comfortable with it." The official said he did not believe Shultz had consulted either President-elect George Bush or Secretary of State-designate James A. Baker III, who will have to deal with the consequences of the decision. Bush told reporters, in a shouted exchange as he jogged in Kennebunkport, Maine, that he had no comment.

State's Bureau of International Organization Affairs and office of Counter-Terrorism are reported to have urged Shultz to deny the visa to Arafat. State Department legal adviser Abraham Sofaer is said to have cited arguments on both sides.

The Bureau of Near Eastern and South Asian Affairs is said to have favored approval of the visa on grounds it would facilitate Mideast diplomacy. Undersecretary Armacost, State's third-ranking official, reportedly took the same view.

In contrast to the decision against Arafat, the PLO's "foreign minister" Farouk Kaddoumi was granted a visa last week and is expected to arrive in New York shortly. A State Department official said Kaddoumi had filed his request in early November.

Staff writer John Goshko contributed to this report.

---

## 12. What the Host Must Not Do

*The New York Times*, 1988

Secretary-General Javier Perez de Cuellar and officials of many member nations have challenged the legality of the American decision to deny a visa to Yasser Arafat, the P.L.O. chairman, who had been invited to address the General Assembly. Here are the relevant sections of Article IV of the 1947 Headquarters Agreement between the United States and the United Nations concerning the obligation of the United States as host country not to impede the travel of people on United Nations business.

### Section 11

The federal, state or local authorities of the United States shall not impose any impediments to transit to or from the headquarters district of representatives of members or officials of the United Nations, or of specialized agencies or representatives of nongovernmental organizations recognized by the United Nations for the purpose of consultation.

### Section 12

The provisions of Section 11 shall be applicable irrespective of the relations existing between the governments of the persons referred to in that section and the Government of the United States.

### Section 13

a) Laws and regulations in force in the United States regarding the entry of aliens shall not be applied in such manner as to interfere with the privileges referred to in Section 11. When visas are required for persons referred to in that section, they shall be granted without charge and as promptly as possible.

b)   Laws and regulations in force in the United States regarding the residence of aliens shall not be applied in such manner as to interfere with the privileges referred to in Section 11.

---

## 13. Josh Friedman, U.N. Going to Geneva for Arafat
### *Newsday*, 1988

By a lopsided 154 to 2, the U.N. General Assembly yesterday rebuked the United States for barring Palestinian leader Yasser Arafat and decided to meet in Geneva for three days to hear a speech by Arafat.

The Geneva meeting, Dec. 13–15, will be the first General Assembly meeting outside the United States since 1951 when it met in Paris because the U.N.'s headquarters on the East River were still under construction.

"This is happening only because of the intransigence of the host country and its lack of respect for international law and international obligations," Palestine Liberation Organization U.N. representative Zuhdi Terzi told the Assembly.

"The PLO specializes in hijacking airplanes and ships," said Israel U.N. Ambassador Johanan Bein."Now it seems they have expanded their activities and are trying to hijack the Assembly.

Only Israel and the United States voted against the resolution, which was sponsored by several Arab countries. Only Britain abstained.

Virtually all of the United States' traditional allies had abandoned it on the grounds that barring Arafat violated the obligations of the United States as the U.N.'s host country.

The vote ended a week of reaction to Secretary of State George Shultz' decision last Saturday to withhold a visa from Arafat on the grounds that he is "an accessory" to terrorism committed by the Palestinian Liberation organization.

After the vote, the highest-ranking U.S. official at the United Nations, Undersecretary-General Joseph Verner Reed, sent a personal letter to President Ronald Reagan, appealing to him to let Arafat speak.

The letter was widely but not officially circulated, and Reed said he was not responsible for leaking it to the press.

"The bottom line, Mr. President, is that the action to deny a visa to an invited guest of the United Nations has done incalculable damage to United States credibility in the world arena.

Reed said the United States is a "proponent of free speech all over the world, yet it will not permit Chairman Arafat to enter the United States to speak in a public forum on international territory …

"Does this spell the end of the United Nations in the United States and the United States in the United Nations …?

The meeting will cost the U.N. about $ 650,000, U.N. officials said yesterday. They said they will ask member countries to put up $ 440,700 for the meeting.

## *Authors' Note*

The next three materials address the question of whether a permanent mission to the U.N. can be evicted for failure to pay its rent. These materials present an analysis of the attempted eviction of the Zaire Mission. Material 14, an article from *The New York Times*, discusses the federal district court ruling that held that the Zaire Mission could be evicted under the reasoning that immunity does not cover nonpayment of rent. Material 15 assesses the legality of the incident through the lens of international law and U.N. obligations. Material 16 is the opinion from the U.S. Court of Appeals for the Second Circuit, which overturned the district court's ruling that the Zaire Mission was not immune from eviction. This incident demonstrates the tension that can exist between the local authorities within the U.S. as the host country and the respect of privileges and immunities under U.N. obligations.

## 14. Ronald Sullivan, Judge, No Diplomat, Orders Zaire to Pay U.N. Office Rent

*The New York Times*, 1992

While diplomatic immunity may cover crimes from mischief to murder, a Federal District judge in Manhattan has ruled that it does not extend to nonpayment of rent.

Judge Leonard B. Sand, in a ruling issued Tuesday, ordered the Zaire Mission to the United Nations evicted from its midtown offices by United States marshals if it does not pay more than $400,000 in back rent by April 20.

Moreover, the State Department has warned Zaire that if the $400,000 is not paid two days before the deadline set by the judge, two of its diplomats at the United Nations will be expelled.

While the lawyer for Zaire, Jeffrey M. Rubin, said he would appeal the ruling, he conceded there was no way to prevent the State Department from carrying out its threat.

He also said Zaire intended to pay the rent. Asked when, Mr. Rubin replied, "They didn't give me a time frame."

Philip Arnold, a spokesman for the United States Mission to the United Nations, said Zaire was the first member to face having its diplomats expelled for failure to pay rent. "We are making a strong effort to have them understand the seriousness of the situation," Mr. Arnold said. A State Department official said at least four other missions owed at least six months of back rent.

An official at the Zaire Mission who declined to identify herself said she had no comment on the ruling.

The thorny issues of United Nations missions, failing to pay their bills or flouting city parking regulations has long troubled the Office of Host Country Affairs at the United States Mission and the New York City Commission for the United Nations, which handle most such complaints.

The State Department must defend the immunity of diplomats to avoid any incident that might discredit the United States abroad. But the department also feels compelled to exert pressure on diplomats to be responsible guests by paying their debts.

The issue became more pressing on Tuesday when Judge Sand ruled on a suit brought over a year ago by the owners of the building at 767 Third Avenue, at 47th Street, where Zaire's Mission occupies the 25th floor.

An Assistant United States Attorney, M. Chinta Gaston, appearing on Zaire's behalf, argued that Zaire's 10-year occupancy was protected by diplomatic immunity and that the mission could not be evicted. But in a brief filed with the court last week, the State Department disclosed that the African nation had been warned that two diplomats at the United Nations would be expelled for "abuse of the privilege of residence" unless the back rent is paid.

In his ruling, Judge Sand said that because Zaire had no lease on the offices and had not paid any rent for 18 months, it had no legal right to remain in the building, which is owned by 767 Third Avenue Associates and the Sage Realty Corporation.

---

## 15. Deborah Pines, Eviction of Mission Prohibited Based on International Law
### *New York Law Journal*, 1993

The Inviolability of a United Nations mission under international and U.S. law precludes forcibly evicting the mission even for owing thousands of dollars in back rent, a federal appeals panel has ruled, reversing a lower court.

The district court erred in carving out an exception for the non-payment of more than $ 400,000 in rent for an East Side apartment by the Permanent United Nations Mission of the Republic of Zaire, Judge Richard J. Cardamone wrote for the U.S. Court of Appeals for the Second Circuit. His ruling, in *767 Third Avenue Associates v. Permanent Mission of the Republic of Zaire*, 92–7184, was filed on March 4.

The reason for no exceptions "is not blind adherence to a rule of law in an international treaty, uncaring of justice at home, but that by upsetting existing treaty relationships American diplomats abroad may well be denied lawful protection of their lives and property to which they would otherwise be entitled," Judge Cardamone wrote.

"That possibility weighs so heavily on the scales of justice that it militates against enforcement of the landlord's right to obtain possession of its property for rental arrears."

Judge Cardamone's opinion reversed, in part, a Jan. 15, 1992 ruling by Southern District Judge Leonard Sand stemming from a long-standing dispute between the mission and its landlords at 767 Third Avenue. Since 1982, the mission had been erratic in paying rent on its $19,350-a-month apartment encompassing the 25th floor.

Against tradition, Judge Cardamone affirmed Judge Sand's order that the mission pay damages of $387,154.72 for rent owed through Oct. 31, 1991 and $832.19 for each day after Nov. 1, 1991 the mission occupied the premises. The payments were owed to 767 Third Avenue Associates, a partnership which owns the building, and Sage Realty, its managing agent.

Judge Cardamone noted that damages had been paid following intervention by the U.S. State Department, although the mission recently has lagged in its rent payments again.

But he reversed Judge Sand's eviction order which required the U.S. Marshal to remove the mission if it refused to vacate by Jan. 31, 1992. That order was contrary to common-law tradition and all relevant governing treaties, especially the 1961 Vienna Convention, Judge Cardamone wrote.

He found the lower court erred in relying on an interpretation of the Foreign Sovereign Immunities Act which was not intended to alter either diplomatic or consular immunity from earlier treaties like the Vienna Convention.

Article 22 of that Convention declares a mission premises "shall be inviolable" and that agents of a receiving state "may not enter them, except with the consent of the head of the mission," Judge Cardamone wrote.

He noted that even more extreme circumstances than non-payment of rent, such as the 1979 bombing of the Soviet mission to the U.N., were found insufficient to warrant entry by law enforcement officers to the mission without the mission's consent.

While saying his ruling has "negative policy implications" in the burden it places on private landlords, Judge Cardamone said Congress, not the courts, should provide remedies such as limiting mission inviolability.

Meanwhile, Judge Cardamone wrote that landlords may use diplomatic efforts to pressure deadbeat tenants for back rent, as was done in this case, or seek in advance a waiver of inviolability or additional security.

Judge Cardamone's opinion was joined by Second Circuit Judges Wilfred Feinberg and Jon O. Newman.

Joseph Ferraro, Robert J. Ward, and Jean-Marie L. Atamian of Shea & Gould represented the landlords.

Jeffrey M. Rubin of Rubin & Shang represented the Zaire mission. M. Chinta Gaston and James L. Cott, Assistant U.S. Attorneys in the Southern District of New York, Edwin D. Williamson, Bruce Rashkow and Richard K. Lahn, of the State Department, represented the government, which filed an amicus brief on behalf of the mission.

## 16. *767 Third Avenue Associates v. Permanent Mission of the Republic of Zaire to the U.N.*

The U.S. Court of Appeals for the Second Circuit, 1993

CARDAMONE, Circuit Judge:

This appeal emerges out of a landlord-tenant dispute. When the Zaire mission to the United Nations occupying leased space on the east side of midtown Manhattan repeatedly fell into arrears on its rent, it was sued by its landlord. The tenant's defense against being evicted was diplomatic immunity. A district court refused to credit this defense and instead granted summary judgment to the landlord for back rent and also awarded it possession of the premises, ordering United States Marshals to remove the Mission physically if it failed to vacate in a timely manner.

Enforcement of an owner's common law right to obtain possession of its premises upon the tenant's non-payment of rent may not override an established rule of international law. Nor under the guise of local concepts of fairness may a court upset international treaty provisions to which the United States is a party. The reason for this is not a blind adherence to a rule of law in an international treaty, uncaring of justice at home, but that by upsetting existing treaty relationships American diplomats abroad may well be denied lawful protection of their lives and property to which they would otherwise be entitled. That possibility weighs so heavily on the scales of justice that it militates against enforcement of the landlord's right to obtain possession of its property for rental arrears.

## BACKGROUND

Plaintiffs, 767 Third Avenue Associates, are a partnership owning a building at 767 Third Avenue in Manhattan, and its managing agent, Sage Realty (collectively plaintiffs, landlord or Sage Realty). The defendant is the Permanent United Nations Mission of the Republic of Zaire (Mission, Zaire, tenant or appellant), a tenant in the building. The landlord-tenant relationship began on May 19, 1982 when Sage Realty and Zaire entered into a ten-year lease for all of the 25th floor at 767 Third Avenue. The building is conveniently located near the United Nations Headquarters in New York City. In 1987 a dispute arose when Zaire failed to make its rental payments. Sage Realty sued and obtained a default judgment in August 1989 terminating Zaire's lease. Under the judgment plaintiffs were awarded possession and $244,157.49 in damages. After Zaire paid the damage award, plaintiffs allowed it to continue in the premises on a month-to-month basis at a rental of $19,350 per month.

When in 1991 the Mission again defaulted in its rental payments, plaintiffs notified it on April 26 that they were terminating the mission's month-to-month tenancy. On July 22 the landlord sued Zaire in the Southern District seeking unpaid rent, attorneys' fees and possession. On November 14, 1991 the district court granted plaintiffs summary judgment, directed the Mission to vacate the premises, and awarded plaintiffs damages of $387,154.72 through October 31 and $832.19 for each day after November 1, 1991 that the Mission occupied the premises. In addition the district court directed the U.S. Marshal to remove the Mission if it refused to vacate the 767 Third Avenue space. Because the order did not specify the date by which Zaire was to vacate, the district court issued a supplemental order on January 15, 1992, identical to its earlier November 14, 1991 judgment, but now adding a direction for the U.S. Marshal to remove the Mission and its belongings from the premises physically if Zaire did not leave by January 31, 1992.

The Zairian Mission subsequently sought a stay of this order, and in a March 24, 1992 opinion the trial court granted a limited stay until April 20, 1992 — in order to avoid a "hasty eviction" and to permit the Mission to protect the confidentiality of its papers — but refused a more extended stay pending appeal on the grounds that none of the treaties invoked by the Mission or the Foreign Sovereign Immunities Act of 1976 (Act) provided support for appellant's position or demonstrated the likelihood of its success on the merits.

The parties have stipulated that enforcement of the district court's eviction order is stayed pending resolution of this appeal. Due to the United States State Department's intervention — including numerous meetings between U.S. officials, the United Nations Legal Counsel, and Zaire's Charge d'Affaires Lukabu Khabouji N'Zaji, and a March 13, 1992 ultimatum to the Mission that two Zairian officials and their families would be expelled from the United States if Zaire did not pay the damages due — Zaire paid its rental arrears in full by three checks sent to Sage Realty on April 9, 23, and 27, 1992. Since that time, Zaire has again lagged in its payments because of the continuing financial crisis in that country. Sage Realty insists that it wants the Mission evicted from its building, even though it appears the parties are continuing to negotiate a new lease.

Zaire appeals from the district court's final judgment of January 15, 1992 granting the landlord summary judgment that awarded damages and directed its physical removal from its leased premises by U.S. Marshals. The United States has filed an amicus brief and appeared in support of the Mission.

## DISCUSSION

### I. Inapplicability of Foreign Sovereign Immunities Act

The inviolability of a United Nations mission under international and U.S. law precludes the forcible eviction of the Mission. Applicable treaties, binding upon federal courts to the same extent as domestic statutes establish that Zaire's Permanent Mission is inviolable. The district court erred in misinterpreting the applicable treaties and in carving out a judicial exception to the broad principle of mission inviolability incorporated in those agreements.

Although the United States' support for appellant is based solely on a number of relevant treaties, the district court rested its decision in part on an interpretation of the Foreign Sovereign Immunities Act. That Act deserves brief discussion since the landlord continues to raise its provisions. While Sage Realty correctly asserts that Congress aimed to permit courts to make sovereign immunity determinations plaintiffs give short shrift to the Act's explicit provision that it operates "[s]ubject to existing international agreements to which the United States is a party." Because of this provision the diplomatic and consular immunities of foreign states recognized under various treaties remain unaltered by the Act.

### II. International Agreements

### A. Generally

The international agreements presented [to] us and relied upon by the United States all pre-date the Foreign Sovereign Immunities Act. They include the United Nations Charter the Agreement Between the United Nations and the United States of America Regarding the Headquarters of the United Nations, the Convention on the Privileges and Immunities of the United Nations, adopted Feb. 13, 1946, and the Vienna Convention on Diplomatic Relations.

The first three of those treaties provide for various diplomatic protections and immunities without specific reference to mission premises. The U.N. Charter, for example, provides "[r]epresentatives of the Members of the United Nations and officials of the Organization shall similarly enjoy such privileges and immunities as are necessary for the independent exercise of their functions in connection with the Organization." The U.N. Headquarters Agreement states that representatives of member states "shall, whether residing inside or outside the headquarters district, be entitled in the territory of the United States to the same privileges and immunities … as it accords to diplomatic envoys accredited to it." The Convention on Privileges and Immunities of the United Nations recites in somewhat more detail that representatives of member states shall "enjoy the following privileges and immunities: (a) immunity from personal arrest or detention … ; (b) inviolability for all papers and documents; … (g) such other privileges, immunities and facilities not inconsistent [with] the foregoing as diplomatic envoys enjoy.…" U.N. Convention on Privileges and Immunities.

### B. Vienna Convention

While these Treaty provisions standing alone shed little light on the immunities granted a permanent mission, the 1961 Vienna Convention speaks directly to the issue of mission premises. Article 22 of that Convention declares:

1. The premises of the mission shall be inviolable. The agents of the receiving State may not enter them, except with the consent of the head of the mission

Article 22, section 2 of the Vienna Convention goes on to note a host state's "special duty" to protect "the premises of the mission" from "any intrusion or damage" and "prevent any disturbance of the peace of the mission or impairment of its dignity"; Article 22, section 3 further states that the premises of a mission shall be immune from "search, requisition, attachment or execution." Mission premises covered by the Convention include both owned and leased property.

The other treaties referred to above are consistent with the Vienna Convention's broad interpretation of inviolability, and support the notion that the United States and the United Nations recognize extensive immunity and independence for diplomats, consulates and missions abroad. But because the Vienna Convention remains the most applicable of the treaties cited, our discussion centers on it.

With that connection as a starting predicate, we observe that the district court's judgment — and Sage's arguments supporting it — fail to take into full account the plain language of Article 22. That language contains the advisedly categorical, strong word "inviolable" and makes no provision for exceptions other than those set forth in Article 31, which are irrelevant to our discussion because they relate to personal activities not carried out on behalf of the sending state. Instead of interpreting the deliberately spare text of the Vienna Convention, the district court read into it an exception of its own making. It first observed that "the notion of protection from eviction from privately owned leased premises was not specifically addressed by any of the treaties." This statement is correct so far as it goes. But we part company with the district court when — using that statement as a foundation — it improperly concluded that this case must therefore fall under an unspecified exception to the rule safeguarding a mission's inviolability.

As the United States correctly points out, the drafters of the Vienna Convention considered and rejected exceptions, opting instead for broad mission inviolability. For instance, one proposal in an early Convention draft offered an exception to the prohibition on any non-consensual entry by the receiving state. The exception posed was one to be strictly limited to emergencies presenting "grave and imminent risks" to life, property or national security. This proposed exception that would have altered the rule of mission inviolability then existing under customary international law, id. at 16, was not adopted. The 1957 draft of the article covering the subject of mission inviolability rejected the proposed exception, and this exception never resurfaced in later drafts. The commentary to the draft article that was ultimately adopted explicitly emphasized the lack of exceptions to inviolability, stating "the receiving State is obliged to prevent its agents from entering the premises for any official act whatsoever." Nothing could be stated more plainly.

## C. History Leading to Vienna Convention

History supports the concept of inviolability expressed in Article 22. Among the laws of nations is the notion that ambassadors must be received and that they must suffer no harm. Beginning 1000 years ago when merchants went to foreign lands seeking trade, they sought to have their disputes settled by judges of their choice administering their own national laws. In 1060, for example, Venice was granted the right to send magistrates to Constantinople to try Venetians charged in civil and criminal cases. A similar process occurred in the western part of the Mediterranean basin where special magistrates called "consul judges" were appointed to settle disputes between foreign traders and local merchants. Because of the growth of international trade the use of consuls spread. By 1251 Genoa had a consul in Seville and in 1402 there were consuls of the Italian republics in London and the Netherlands. Before the end of the fifteenth century England had consuls in Italy and Scandinavia.

In the 16th and 17th centuries individual states took over from traders the task of sending consuls, and the function of the consul was dramatically altered. Judicial duties were eliminated and replaced by the diplomatic functions of looking after the state's interests in trade, industry and shipping. As official state representatives, consuls enjoyed corresponding privileges and immunities. By the 18th century all the major trading states had exchanged consuls. The United States set up its first consulate in France in 1780.

Because of the extraordinary growth of consulates during the 19th century, attempts to codify the rules of international law on that subject began in the 20th century. A forerunner of these attempts was the Congress of Vienna in 1815. In 1927 the Inter-American Commission of Jurists prepared a draft of 26 articles on consuls, which served as the basis for the Convention regarding Consular Agents signed at Havana, Cuba on February 28, 1928. In 1932 Harvard Law School prepared drafts of conventions for the codification of international law on diplomatic privileges and immunities. The International Law Commission added the subject "consular intercourse and immunities" to those selected for codification at the first session of the United Nations Secretariat in 1949, which the General Assembly approved, and began by the usual appointment of a Special Rapporteur on this question. The study continued from 1956 to 1959 and his commentary provided the foundation work leading to the 1961 Vienna Convention at which 81 nations participated.

The Vienna Convention entered into force April 24, 1964. One hundred and thirteen member states have ratified it, including the United States on December 13, 1972. History establishes beyond question therefore that the Vienna Convention on Diplomatic Relations was intended to and did provide for the inviolability of mission premises, archives documents, and official correspondence.

## III. Inviolability Recognized Without Exception

### A. Under International Law

The fact that the Vienna Convention codified longstanding principles of customary international law with respect to diplomatic relations further supports the view that the Convention recognized no exceptions to mission inviolability.

Under such law the inviolability of mission premises had become by the 18th century an established international practice and represented an integral part of the diplomatic privileges accorded envoys abroad. The United States and other nations had abided by the inviolability of mission premises long before the Vienna Convention entered into force.

Although diplomatic privilege and mission inviolability arose under various now-outdated theories, including Grotius' notion of the "sacredness of Ambassadors" and the conception of the diplomat as personifying the foreign state's sovereign modern international law has adopted diplomatic immunity under a theory of functional necessity. Under that doctrine, the United States recognizes the privileges of foreign diplomats in the U.S. with the understanding that American diplomats abroad will be afforded the same protections from intrusions by the host state. The most secure way to guarantee this protection, the United States tells us, is through blanket immunities and privileges without exception.

The risk in creating an exception to mission inviolability in this country is of course that American missions abroad would be exposed to incursions that are legal under a foreign state's law. Foreign law might be vastly different from our own, and might provide few, if any, substantive or procedural protections for American diplomatic personnel. Were the United States to adopt exceptions to the inviolability of foreign missions here, it would be stripped of its most powerful defense, that is, that international law precludes the nonconsensual entry of its missions abroad. Another related consideration is the frequent existence of a small band of American nationals residing in foreign countries, often business personnel. Recent history is unfortunately replete with examples demonstrating how fragile is the security for American diplomats and personnel in foreign countries; their safety is a matter of real and continuing concern. Potential exposure of American diplomats to harm while serving abroad and to American nationals living abroad is not "pure conjecture," as plaintiffs blithely assert.

The narrow reading of the Vienna Convention urged by Sage Realty and adopted by the district court is inadequately supported. Citing only selective examples of the protection accorded by the Convention and other international agreements, Sage Realty fails to account for the functional necessity of mission inviolability. In a weak attempt to demonstrate that only extreme behavior is covered by Article 22, plaintiffs refer to a 1986 meeting of the U.N. General Assembly urging the suppression of terrorist action against missions and a 1967 U.N. study noting that the U.S. is under an obligation to protect the U.N. headquarters district from "hostile demonstrations" outside mission premises. Similarly, the district court relied upon selected search and seizure type of protections afforded to missions and their documents to insist that only sudden unexpected intrusions are governed by the Convention. However, as explained below, the circumstance of a sudden intrusion is largely beside the point and results in a restricted view of the Vienna Convention at odds with its purport and practice.

### B. Purpose and Practice Under Article 22

To begin with, the examples used by the district court do not conflict with the broad language of "inviolability" appearing in the Convention's text, nor do they confute the longstanding international support for mission inviolability. Instead, upon proper analysis, sudden intrusion and protection against search and seizure further support the sanctity of mission premises. Nothing in the commentary to the draft articles suggests that fears about "mob violence" and "unannounced seizures" were ever the main concerns underlying diplomatic immunities, as the district court mistakenly believed. Perhaps most telling, no support may be found for an interpretation of limited inviolability in either the commentary to the Vienna Convention or the scholarly literature concerning the convention and the customary international law principles it codified.

Plaintiffs' position is also refuted by what has occurred in practice. The United States has consistently respected the complete inviolability of missions and consulates. Even in extreme cases U.S. authorities will not enter protected premises without permission following, for example, bomb threats. Nor have local authorities been permitted to enter to conduct health and building safety inspections without the consent of the mission involved. An affidavit from the counselor for Host Country Affairs for the United States Mission to the United Nations attests that after the Soviet mission to the U.N. was bombed in 1979, the FBI and local police officers were all refused entry to the mission until the Soviets consented to allow certain law enforcement officers to enter. Absent such consent, the United States tells us, government officials would not have attempted to enter the Soviet mission's premises.

Additional support for the position we take here is found in decisional law. The Supreme Court has made clear: "When the parties to a treaty both agree to the meaning of a treaty provision, and that interpretation follows from the clear treaty language[, the court] must, absent extraordinarily strong contradictory evidence, defer to that interpretation." This case presents such a situation. Treaty language uses the term "inviolability" and the Convention contains no exceptions relevant to this case. Because the United States agrees to an accepted interpretation of the Vienna Convention, and because no evidence appears of a contrary interpretation advanced by any of the United Nation members, all of whom are parties to the Convention.

Hence, that portion of the district court's order awarding Sage Realty immediate possession of the premises and directing U.S. Marshals to remove the mission, its effects, and its personnel physically from the premises must be reversed.

## IV. Contrary Holding Foreclosed

We recognize that there are negative policy implications from the ruling we propose. The undisputed economic burden of inviolability, for example, falls most heavily upon the private landlord, not on the government that urges inviolability of mission premises. Yet, an interest in fairness to the landlord does not justify creating a judicial gloss on the concept of mission inviolability

Particularly in recent years, attention has focused on an array of abuses of diplomatic privilege, see, e.g., Higgins, Abuse of Diplomatic Privileges (noting diplomats and their families committing wide range of petty and more serious offenses in England), and a number of reforms to various diplomatic immunities have been suggested. See Shapiro, Developments. Nevertheless, reform of mission inviolability has not been undertaken, and the doctrine continues without exception to be the rule. Cf. Higgins, Abuse of Diplomatic Privileges ("[N]otwithstanding popular and ill-informed views to the contrary, the inviolability of premises is not lost by the perpetration from them of unlawful acts."). Reforming the Vienna Convention may well be a valid objective. But federal courts are an inappropriate forum to accomplish the amendment of a multilateral treaty to which the United States is a party. See Shapiro, Developments (judicial reform "would threaten a loss of consistency in the application of the Vienna Convention from country to country and could have dangerous international repercussions in the form of reciprocal action by other states").

Congress is of course the branch of government best suited to address the full array of concerns involved in altering the Vienna Convention. Already, the legislature has enacted the Diplomatic Relations Act of 1978 to counter some of the more flagrant abuses of diplomatic privilege observed in this country. That Act gives the President the power "on the basis of reciprocity" to establish privileges and immunities for missions and their members "which result in more favorable or less favorable treatment than is provided under the Vienna Convention." Although the act requires liability insurance coverage for diplomatic missions and their representatives and families to insure against negligence arising from the operation of motor vehicles, vessels or aircraft it contains no restrictions on mission inviolability. While Congress and the President—via the Diplomatic Relations Act—possess the power to limit mission inviolability, neither has chosen to exercise that power. Our sister branches of government may more appropriately initiate whatever revision, if any, of the Vienna Convention is deemed necessary. Cf. Palestine Liberation Org. ("Congress has the power to enact statutes abrogating prior treaties or international obligations entered into by the United States").

This is not to say that Sage Realty is left wholly without a remedy for the mission's egregious, albeit explicable, shortcoming in rent payments. The Zairian Mission has not raised any challenge to the district court's authority to award monetary damages in favor of the landlord. Such judgment—even absent forcible eviction—is not without weight: to date, diplomatic efforts and pressure have proven extraordinarily successful at getting Zaire to pay the judgment for its back rent. The State Department has diligently pursued the matter on behalf of plaintiffs and went so far as to demand the expulsion of several Zairian diplomats if the judgment was not paid by a certain deadline.

A landlord in Sage Realty's position that desires to rent to a foreign mission may also be able to protect itself by requesting a waiver of inviolability in advance or by demanding additional security. The market rate for rent to such tenants might itself rise to incorporate risks posed by mission inviolability. In any event, the district court's worry that landlords in New York's rental market might shut out foreign missions because of their untouchable status appears overblown, especially since Sage Realty apparently continues negotiating for a new lease with the Zairian mission. If a sophisticated landlord like Sage Realty bears some risk in renting to a U.N. mission, it is not without notice of the diplomatic immunities with which it may later become entangled.

## CONCLUSION

Accordingly, the portion of the district court's order granting the landlord possession of the premises and ordering the U.S. Marshals forcibly to seize the premises, if necessary, is reversed. That portion of the district court's order awarding plaintiffs monetary damages is affirmed.

Affirmed, in part, reversed, in part.

---

## *Authors' Note*

The following three materials detail President Obama's addition of Interpol to the list of international organizations that enjoy immunities and privileges. Material 17, an article from *The Washington Examiner*, outlines the potential harms that would result from the President's actions. Material 18 provides a comprehensive look at Obama's decision including a background analysis of Obama's actions with respect to similar acts by past presidents. Material 19 is the Executive Order issued to place Interpol on the list of international organizations.

---

## 17. Obama Gives Interpol Free Hand in U.S.
### *The Washington Examiner*, 2009

No presidential statement or White House press briefing was held on it. In fact, all that can be found about it on the official White House Web site is the Dec. 17 announcement and one-paragraph text of President Obama's Executive Order 12425, with this innocuous headline: "Amending Executive Order 12425 Designating Interpol as a public international organization entitled to enjoy certain privileges, exemptions, and immunities." In fact, this new directive from Obama may be the most destructive blow ever struck against American constitutional civil liberties. No wonder the White House said as little as possible about it.

There are multiple reasons why this Obama decision is so deeply disturbing. First, the Obama order reverses a 1983 Reagan administration decision in order to grant Interpol, the International Criminal Police Organization, two key privileges. First, Obama has granted Interpol the ability to operate within the territorial limits of the United States without being subject to the same constitutional restraints that apply to all domestic law enforcement agencies such as the FBI. Second, Obama has exempted Interpol's domestic facilities—including its office within the U.S. Department of Justice—from search and seizure by U.S. authorities and from disclosure of archived documents in response to Freedom of Information Act requests filed by U.S. citizens. Think very carefully about what you just read: Obama has given an international law enforcement organization that is accountable to no other national authority the ability to operate as it pleases within our own borders, and he has freed it from the most basic measure of official transparency and accountability, the FOIA.

*The Examiner* has asked for but not yet received from the White House press office an explanation of why the president signed this executive order and who among his advisers was involved in the process leading to his doing so. Unless the White House can provide credible reasons to think otherwise, it seems clear that Executive Order 12425's consequences could be far-reaching and disastrous. To cite only the most obvious example, giving Interpol free rein to act within this country could subject U.S. military, diplomatic, and intelligence personnel to the prospect of being taken into custody and hauled before the International Criminal Court as "war criminals."

As National Review Online's Andy McCarthy put it, the White House must answer these questions: Why should we elevate an international police force above American law? Why would we immunize an international police force from the limitations that constrain the FBI and other American law-enforcement agencies? Why is it suddenly necessary to have, within the Justice Department, a repository for stashing government files that will be beyond the scrutiny of Congress, American law enforcement, the media, and the American people?

## 18. Jake Tapper, Just What Did President Obama's Executive Order Regarding INTERPOL Do?
### ABC News Blog, 2009

Some viewers/readers have asked me about an executive order President Obama signed earlier this month regarding INTERPOL, an issue that has exploded on the conservative blogosphere with all sorts of nefarious insinuations and accusations.

Here are some background and the facts:

On June 16, 1983, President Reagan signed Executive Order 12425, which designated the International Criminal Police Organization (INTERPOL) as a public international organization entitled to enjoy the privileges, exemptions and immunities conferred by the International Organizations Immunities Act.

The International Organizations Immunities Act, signed into law in 1945, established a special group of foreign or international organizations whose members could work in the U.S. and enjoy certain exemptions from U.S. taxes and search and seizure laws.

Experts say there are about 75 organizations in the U.S. covered by the International Organizations Immunities Act—including the United Nations, the International Atomic Energy Agency, the International Monetary Fund, the International Committee of the Red Cross, even the International Pacific Halibut Commission and Inter-American Tropical Tuna Commission. (These privileges are not the same as the rights afforded under "diplomatic immunity," they are considerably less. "Diplomatic immunity" comes from the Vienna Convention on Diplomatic Relations, which states that a "diplomatic agent shall enjoy immunity from the criminal jurisdiction of the receiving State." That is NOT what the International Organizations Immunities Act is.)

Basically, recognizing a group under the International Organizations Immunities Act means officials from those organizations are exempt from some taxes and customs fees, and that their records cannot be seized.

This, I'm told, is so these organizations can work throughout the world without different countries spying on each other by accessing the records of these groups.

Each president has designated some organizations covered by the International Organizations Immunities Act.

President Nixon did it for the United International Bureau for the Protection of Intellectual Property.

President Reagan bestowed these privileges to the African Development Bank, the International Boundary and Water Commission, United States and Mexico, and the World Tourism Organization, among others.

President Bush through Executive Orders covered the European Central Bank, the African Union and the Global Fund to Fight AIDS Tuberculosis and Malaria.

INTERPOL is course a different type of organization—it's an investigative law enforcement body. In fact, it's the world's largest international police organization.

Created in 1923, INTERPOL has 188 member countries including the U.S.. Its purpose is to facilitate cross-border police co-operation and to work with other legitimate law enforcement organizations worldwide to prevent and combat international crime, with a focus on: drugs and criminal organizations; financial and high-tech crime; fugitives; public safety and terrorism; trafficking in human beings; and corruption.

The U.S. historically has participated whole-heartedly in INTERPOL; the current Secretary General of INTERPOL is Ronald Noble, a former Undersecretary of Enforcement of the Department of the Treasury during the Clinton administration.

"The FBI and other law enforcement agencies have closely coordinated with INTERPOL for many, many years," a former counterterrorism official who served during the Bush administration says approvingly.

In Lyon, France, 2003, then-Attorney General John Ashcroft spoke to INTERPOL and said to Noble, "INTERPOL was already a top-flight law enforcement organization, but your dynamic leadership has brought new dimensions to this global crime-fighting resource."

Reagan's 1983 executive order, however, did not provide blanket exemptions for INTERPOL officials, who at the time did not have a permanent office in the U.S.. The provisions of the International Organizations Immunities Act that INTERPOL officials were not exempt from included:

- Section 2(c), which provided officials immunity from their property and assets being searched and confiscated; including their archives;
- the portions of Section 2(d) and Section 3 relating to customs duties and federal internal-revenue importation taxes;
- Section 4, dealing with federal taxes;
- Section 5, dealing with Social Security; and
- Section 6, dealing with property taxes.

I'm told INTERPOL didn't have a permanent office in the U.S. until 2004, which is why it wasn't until this month afforded the same full privileges given, say, the Inter-American Tropical Tuna Commission by President Kennedy in 1962.

In September 1995, President Clinton updated Reagan's executive order with Executive Order No. 12971, giving INTERPOL officials exemption from some of the customs duties and federal internal-revenue importation taxes'.

Then in his December 17, 2009, executive order President Obama exempted INTERPOL from the rest of the exceptions Reagan listed — Section 2(c), Section 3, Section 4, Section 5, and Section 6.

So what does the counterterrorism official from the Bush years think of this?

He can't believe it's taken this long.

"To the extent that granting these immunities to INTERPOL furthers the efficacy or ease of information-sharing or joint action on an expedited basis to act on warrants seems like a no brainer to me," the official says.

"Conservatives can't have it both ways," the official says. "You can't be complaining about the hypothetical abdication of U.S. jurisdiction at the same time you're complaining the Obama administration is not being tough enough on national security."

Obama administration officials say this new executive order doesn't allow INTERPOL to do any more than they were allowed to do once Reagan recognized them as a public international organization. Though clearly the Executive Order does prohibit U.S. law enforcement from searching and seizing INTERPOL records, officials say, those provisions can be waived by the president if need be.

## 19. Executive Order — Amending Executive Order 12425

Office of the Press Secretary, 2009

EXECUTIVE ORDER

AMENDING EXECUTIVE ORDER 12425 DESIGNATING INTERPOL
AS A PUBLIC INTERNATIONAL ORGANIZATION ENTITLED TO
ENJOY CERTAIN PRIVILEGES, EXEMPTIONS, AND IMMUNITIES

By the authority vested in me as President by the Constitution and the laws of the United States of America, including section 1 of the International Organizations Immunities Act (22 U.S.C. 288), and in order to extend the appropriate privileges, exemptions, and immunities to the International Criminal Police Organization (INTERPOL), it is hereby ordered that Executive Order 12425 of June 16, 1983, as amended, is further amended by deleting from the first sentence the words "except those provided by Section 2(c), Section 3, Section 4, Section 5, and Section 6 of that Act" and the semicolon that immediately precedes them.

BARACK OBAMA

THE WHITE HOUSE,
December 16, 2009.

## *Authors' Note*

The following case before the U.S. Court of Appeals for the Second Circuit details the jurisprudence relevant to the scope of the immunities within the U.S. In particular, the case addresses questions of domestic litigation and whether the immunity is absolute. The holding also presents and answers the question of the constitutionality of extending such immunities when the affected party is a U.S. citizen.

## 20. *Brzak v. The United Nations, et al.*
### The U.S. Court of Appeals for the Second Circuit, 2010

### BACKGROUND

Except as noted, the facts are not contested. Brzak is an American citizen who worked in Geneva, Switzerland, for the United Nations High Commissioner for Refugees ("UNHCR"). Ishak is a French and Egyptian national who also worked in Geneva for the UNHCR. Defendant Kofi Annan was formerly the Secretary-General for the United Nations, and worked in New York City. Defendant Lubbers was the United Nations High Commissioner for Refugees, and defendant Wendy Chamberlin was a deputy to the Commissioner. Both worked in Geneva. Brzak contends that during the course of a meeting of UNHCR staff members in Geneva in 2003, Lubbers improperly touched her. On the advice of Ishak, Brzak filed a complaint against Lubbers with the United Nations' Office of Internal Oversight Services ("OIOS"). The OIOS issued a report confirming Brzak's complaint and recommending that the United Nations discipline Lubbers. Brzak alleges that Annan disregarded the finding and eventually exonerated Lubbers. Brzak then appealed through the United Nations' internal complaint adjustment process. The plaintiffs allege that, as a consequence of Brzak's complaint, and Ishak's assistance pursuing it, United Nations officials and employees retaliated against them by taking steps such as manipulating Brzak's work assignments and denying Ishak merited promotions.

The plaintiffs sued the United Nations and the individual defendants in the United States District Court for the Southern District of New York, alleging sex discrimination and retaliation in violation of Title VII of the Civil Rights Act of 1964, violations of the Racketeer Influenced and Corrupt Organizations Act ("RICO"), and various state common law torts (brought in federal court through supplemental jurisdiction). The United Nations formally returned the complaint to the American ambassador to the United Nations and moved to dismiss on the grounds of immunity, a motion supported by the United States Attorney's office for the Southern District of New York. The district court granted the motion. Judge Sweet concluded that the Convention on Privileges and Immunities of the United Nations, Feb. 13, 1946, *entered into force with respect to the United States* in Apr. 29, 1970, 21 U.S.T. 1418, (the "CPIUN"), granted the United Nations absolute immunity, which it had not waived, and dismissed the complaint. With regard to the individual defendants, Judge Sweet concluded that the CPIUN granted them the same form of functional immunity former diplomats enjoy under international law. This functional immunity, Judge Sweet held, applied to employment-related suits. This appeal followed. We review *de novo* a district court's dismissal of a claim for lack of subject-matter jurisdiction. We also review *de novo* legal conclusions which grant or deny immunity.

## DISCUSSION

As the District Court correctly concluded, the United States has ratified the CPIUN which extends absolute immunity to the United Nations. Specifically, the CPIUN provides that "[t]he United Nations ... shall enjoy immunity from every form of legal process except insofar as in any particular case it has expressly waived its immunity." If the CPIUN applies, then appellants' claims fail. The answer to this question turns on whether the CPIUN is self-executing.

The parties do not dispute that the CPIUN is binding on the United States as a matter of international law. However, they disagree about whether American courts must recognize the immunity it adopts in domestic litigation.

Brzak and Ishak contend that the CPIUN should not be enforced by American courts because it is not self-executing, and consequently cannot be enforced absent additional legislation which was never passed. Whether a treaty is self-executing depends on whether "the treaty contains stipulations which ... require no legislation to make them operative;" if so, "they have the force and effect of a legislative enactment."

In determining whether a treaty is self-executing, we look to the text, the negotiation and drafting history, and the postratification understanding of the signatory nations. Additionally, the executive branch's interpretation of a treaty "is entitled to great weight." Based on these criteria, we have little difficulty concluding that the CPIUN is self-executing.

CPIUN Section 34 states "[i]t is understood that, when an instrument of accession is deposited on behalf of any Member, the Member will be in a position under its own law to give effect to the terms of this convention." When the United States acceded to the CPIUN in 1970 (by the President's ratification, with the advice and consent of the Senate), it was affirming that it was "in a position under its own law to give effect" to the CPIUN's terms at that time. This means that the treaty became effective at ratification, and therefore, is self-executing. "[T]he label 'self-executing' usually is applied to any treaty that according to its terms takes effect upon ratification."

The ratification history of the CPIUN reinforces this conclusion. During testimony before the Senate Foreign Relations Committee as it considered whether to recommend that the Senate ratify the CPIUN, the Legal Advisor to the State Department stated that: "It is clear from the language of the convention ... that the convention is self-executing and no implementing legislation is necessary." The Foreign Relations Committee's report on the CPIUN also expressed the view that "the convention is self-executing and will require no implementing legislation."

Finally, the executive branch continues to assert that the CPIUN is self-executing. These views, as we have seen, are entitled to "great weight." Consequently, we hold that the CPIUN is self-executing and applies in American courts without implementing legislation.

As the CPIUN makes clear, the United Nations enjoys absolute immunity from suit unless "it has expressly waived its immunity." Although the plaintiffs argue that purported inadequacies with the United Nations' internal dispute resolution mechanism indicate a waiver of immunity, crediting this argument would read the word "expressly" out of the CPIUN. The United Nations has not waived its immunity. Consequently, the United Nations enjoys absolute immunity and the district court's decision to dismiss the claims against the United Nations was correct.

Our conclusion is further confirmed by the International Organizations Immunities Act of 1945, 22 U.S.C. §288a(b) (the "IOIA"), which provides that international organizations designated by the President should receive the "same immunity from suit and every form of judicial process as is enjoyed by foreign governments." The United Nations has been so designated. The plaintiffs argue that designated international organizations no longer have absolute immunity in all cases, because, since that act was passed, Congress has passed the Foreign Sovereign Immunities Act, 28 U.S.C. which strips foreign sovereigns of their immunity in certain circumstances. Plaintiffs argue that it is this narrower definition of sovereign immunity that now defines what sort of immunity the IOIA applies to international organizations. Although this argument has been rejected by at least one other Court of Appeals, we need not resolve whether plaintiffs' argument is correct for at least two reasons. The first is that, whatever immunities are possessed by other international organizations, the CPIUN unequivocally grants the United Nations absolute immunity without exception. The second is that the plaintiffs have not presented any argument, either at the district level or to us, which would suggest that one of FSIA's exceptions to immunity would apply. Therefore, even under the plaintiffs' interpretation of the IOIA, the United Nations would still be immune from suit.

The plaintiffs also sued three former United Nations officials. The CPIUN also addresses their immunity: "The Secretary-General and all Assistant Secretaries-General shall be accorded ... the privileges and immunities ... accorded to diplomatic envoys, in accordance with international law." *Id.* art. v, sect. 19. As we have determined above that the CPIUN is a self-executing treaty, this provision is binding on American courts. International law provides extensive protection for diplomatic envoys. *See* The Vienna Convention on Diplomatic Relations, Apr. 18, 1961, *entered into force with respect to the United States Dec.* 13 (the "VCDR"). Although current diplomatic envoys enjoy absolute immunity from civil and criminal process, former diplomatic envoys retain immunity only "with respect to acts performed by such a person in the exercise of his functions" as a diplomatic envoy. As the plaintiffs have sued former United Nations officials, each of whom held a rank of Assistant Secretary-General or higher, it is this functional immunity, which the CPIUN incorporates by reference, that is relevant. The Diplomatic Relations Act of 1978, 22 U.S.C. makes pellucid that American courts must dismiss a suit against anyone who is entitled to immunity under either the VCDR or other laws "extending diplomatic privileges and immunities." As CPIUN section 19 is such a law, the remaining question is whether the plaintiffs' allegations against the individual defendants involve acts that the defendants performed in the exercise of their United Nations functions.

When a court attempts to determine whether a defendant is seeking immunity "with respect to acts performed by such a person in the exercise of his functions," VCDR art. 39, para. 2, the court must do so without judging whether the underlying conduct actually occurred, or whether it was wrongful.[...] Of the plaintiffs' seven claims, all except the fourth make allegations with respect to acts that the defendants performed in exercise of their official functions, namely, their management of the office in which the plaintiffs worked. The first two claims allege that defendants discriminated against Brzak in the conditions of her employment and retaliated against her, both in violation of Title VII. The fifth claim alleges that the defendants retaliated against Ishak in violation of Title VII as well. These allegations involve personnel management decisions falling within the ambit of the defendants' professional responsibilities. Brzak's third claim, for intentional infliction of emotional distress, also relates to the management of the office, because it challenges the defendants' conduct in investigating Brzak's claims, and charges retaliation through changes of her work assignments. The sixth and seventh claims, which allege violations of RICO, also relate to Annan's and Lubbers' roles as United Nations officials.

The only remaining claim is the fourth, in which Brzak alleges Lubbers committed the state law tort of battery. We have said that if a plaintiff's federal claims are dismissed before trial, "the state claims should be dismissed as well." Because Brzak's federal claims were dismissed on jurisdictional grounds at the very beginning of the case, there was no colorable basis for the district court to exercise supplemental jurisdiction over her state law claim. We thus affirm the district court's dismissal without reaching Brzak's argument that the claim involves conduct outside the scope of the defendant's immunity. Brzak is free to refile her battery claim in the state courts. If she does so, the state court would need to adjudicate in the first instance the defendant's claim of immunity.

The appellants raise several constitutional objections to the proposition that the United Nations and its former officials enjoy immunity. Specifically, they contend that such a grant of immunity would violate their procedural due process right to litigate the merits of their case, their substantive due process right to access the courts, their First Amendment right to petition the government for redress of grievances, and their Seventh Amendment right to a jury trial on their common law claims. Each of these arguments fails, as each does no more than question why immunities in general should exist.

The short—and conclusive—answer is that legislatively and judicially crafted immunities of one sort or another have existed since well before the framing of the Constitution, have been extended and modified over time, and are firmly embedded in American law. *See, e.g.,* Act for the Punishment of Certain Crimes Against the United States, 25, 1 Stat. 112, 117–18 (1790) (diplomatic immunity). If appellants' constitutional argument were correct, judicial immunity, prosecutorial immunity, and legislative immunity, for example, could not exist. Suffice it to say, they offer no principled arguments as to why the continuing existence of immunities violates the Constitution.

## CONCLUSION

The judgment of the district court is affirmed.

---

## 21. Bibliography of Additional Sources

- PERMANENT MISSIONS TO THE UNITED NATIONS, UNITED STATES MISSION TO THE UNITED NATIONS (1963).

- UNITED NATIONS CONFERENCE ON DIPLOMATIC INTERCOURSE AND IMMUNITIES, VIENNA (1961).

- Susan M. Akram, Scheherezade Meets Kafka: Two Dozen Sordid Tales of Ideological Exclusion, 14 GEO. IMMIGR. L.J. 51 (1999).

- David Foster Bartlett, *767 Third Avenue Associates v. Permanent Mission of the Republic of Zaire*: An Uncompensated Governmental Taking, 45 DEPAUL L. REV. 165 (1995).

- Charles H. Brower II, International Immunities: Some Dissident Views in the Role of Municipal Courts, 41 VA. J. INT'L L. 1 (2000).

- James Englert, (Comment) Congress, The PLO, The World Order and The Constitution: What's a Court To Do? 57 U. CIN. L. REV. 1393 (1989).

- Thomas M. Franck & Faiza Patel, The Gulf Crisis in International and Foreign Relations Law: U.N. Police Action in Lieu of War: The Old Order Changeth, 85 A.J.I.L. 63 (1991).

- Michael Gerber (Note) The Anti-Terrorism Act of 1987: Sabotaging the United Nations and Holding the Constitution Hostage, 65 N.Y.U.L. Rev. 364 (1990).

- Lance A. Harke, The Anti-Terrorism Act of 1987 and American Freedoms: A Critical Review, 43 U. Miami L. Rev. 667 (1989).

- James E. Hickey & Annette Fisch, The Case to Preserve Criminal Jurisdiction Immunity Accorded Foreign Diplomatic and Consular Personnel in the United States, 41 Hastings L.J. 351 (1990).

- Douglas Hollowell, Practitioner's Survey: 1991–2 Survey of International Law in the Second Circuit, 19 Syracuse J. Int'l L. & Com. 98 (1993).

- Jesse A. Lynn, (Case Comment) Caveat Lessor? The Takings Clause and The Doctrine of Mission Inviolability: *767 Third Avenue Associates v. Permanent Mission of the Republic of Zaire to the United Nations,* 76 B.U.L. Rev. 399 (1996).

- W. Michael Reisman, (Comment) The Arafat Visa Affair: Exceeding the Bounds of Host State Discretion, 83 A.J.I.L. 519 (1989).

- John M. Rodgers, (Symposium) "Intensional Contexts" and the Rule that Statutes Should be Interpreted as Consistent with International Law, 73 Notre Dame L. Rev. 637 (1998).

- John Quigley, The New World Order and the Rule of Law, 18 Syracuse J. Int'l L. & Com. 75 (1992).

- Roberta Smith, (Note) America Tries to Come to Terms with Terrorism: The United States Anti-Terrorism and Effective Death Penalty Act of 1996 v. British Anti-Terrorism Law and International Response, 5 Cardozo J. Int'l & Comp. L. 249 (1997).

- Peter D. Trooboff, (Decision) Treaties—Agreement Between the United States and the United Nations Regarding U.N. Headquarters, 82 A.J.I.L. 833 (1988).

- M.A. Thomas, (Comment) When the Guests Move In: Permanent Observers to the United Nations Gain the Right to Establish Permanent Missions in the United States, 78 Calif. L. Rev. 197 (1990).

- Sydney D. Bailey, The General Assembly of the United Nations: A Study of Procedure and Practice (1964).

- Robert W. Gregg, About Face? The United States and the United Nations (1993).

- H.G. Nichols, The U.N. As a Political Institution (1975).

- Kumiko Matsuura et al., Chronology and Fact Book of the United Nations: 1941–1991 (1992).

- Musa E. Mazzaut, Palestine and the Law: Guidelines for the Resolution of the Arab-Israel Conflict (1997).
- Veronica L. Maginnis, Limiting Diplomatic Immunity: Lessons Learned from the 1946 Convention on the Privileges and Immunities of the United Nations, 28 Brook. J. Int'l L. 989 (2002–2003).

- Anthony J. Miller, United Nations Experts on Mission and their Privileges and Immunities, 4 Int'l Organizations L. Rev. 11 (2007).

# Part III
# International Dispute Resolution

# Chapter V

# The Role of International Organizations in the Peace Process

## Introduction

This chapter examines the three major roles that international organizations play in peace processes. The first, and most common, role of established international organizations in peace negotiations is their function as an arbitrator or mediator in conflict and post-conflict environments. Second, international organizations often play a pivotal role in implementing peace agreements after agreements have been negotiated and signed. This role often includes international organization involvement or leadership during transition periods. Third, international organizations often find their genesis during the peace process through the creation of ad hoc international organizations. These unique organizations develop as a result of the peace negotiations and the implementation of peace agreements, and often their sole function relates to a specific conflict and outcome. Ad hoc international organizations are often created to aid in governing during the transition period as well as monitor the implementation of peace agreements. In this chapter, students will study the conflict in Sri Lanka and examine the role of international organizations in the peace process, as well as the fundamental difficulty of involving international organizations in a domestic conflict.

## Objectives

- To understand the role of international organizations in peace negotiations by analyzing conflicts in Angola, Bosnia, El Salvador, Nagorno-Karabkh, Kosovo, Darfur, and Sri Lanka.
- To understand the role of international organizations as mediators during peace negotiations.
- To understand the role of international organizations in the implementation of peace agreements after they have been negotiated and accepted.
- To understand how ad hoc international organizations are created and their roles as *sui generis* entities in the peace process.

201

- To be able to recognize other incidental roles that international organizations might play in the peace process.
- To understand the potential consequences of involving international organizations in the peace process.
- To examine whether international organizations play an effective role in the peace process.

# Problems

Students should come to class prepared to discuss the following questions:

1. What roles might an international organization play in the peace process, in addition to mediation and implementation?

2. What are some potential negative impacts that international organizations could have in the process or outcome of a peace negotiation?

3. How do religious, cultural, and ethnic divisions affect the peace process? How might an international organization help or hinder the tensions that these divisions create? How should an international organization approach these types of tensions?

4. How does state sovereignty affect the participation of international organizations in the peace process?

5. What effect do third-party political agendas have in the peace process? How do international organizations deal with this type of outside pressure?

# Case Studies and Negotiation Simulations

Drawing from the materials in this chapter, students should come to class prepared to participate in the following case studies:

**Angola:** The conflict in Angola lasted over forty years, beginning as an anti-colonial struggle against Portugal and continuing with the fight for independence. Two separate nationalist movements emerged, the Marxist Popular Movement for the Liberation of Angola (MPLA), backed by USSR and Cuba, which became the government, and the National Union for the Total Independence of Angola (UNITA), backed by the U.S. and South Africa. At the end of the Cold War, various third-party actors became involved in Angola and tried to put an end to this violent conflict. Students should come to class prepared to discuss potential problems international organizations face during the mediation process and options to overcome these problems.

**Bosnia:** In 1992, Muslim and Croatian people of Bosnia and Herzegovina overwhelmingly voted for independence from Yugoslavia. Though the European Community and U.S. recognized the new state of Bosnia-Herzegovina, the new 'Republika Srpska' launched attacks on Muslim and Croatian populations in the region. In 1995, the two sides signed a peace treaty, the Dayton Accord. The office of the High Representative played a central role in negotiations and implementation of the peace agreement. Students should come to class prepared to discuss the effectiveness of international organizations in dealing with long standing local cultural and ethnic conflicts.

**El Salvador:** In 1980s, El Salvador struggled through a brutal civil war. The conflict occurred between the government and the Frente Farabundo Martí para la Liberación Nacional (FMLN), which was not content with the social, economic and political conditions in the country. Although the Salvadoran government adopted its first peace agreement in 1990, the lack of the government's political will to comply with the peace agreement created a stumbling block. Moreover, the lack of progress in disarmament and the destruction of weapons caused a significant obstacle to sustainable peace. With the creation of the U.N. Mission in El Salvador, ONUSAL, El Salvador was able to successfully and peacefully end the conflict. Students should come to class prepared to discuss other groups created by the United Nations, their roles, and effectiveness.

**Nagorno-Karabakh:** The conflict in Nagorno-Karabakh dates back to 1988 and is the main dispute between Armenia and Azerbaijan. During the Soviet era, the contested region belonged to Azerbaijan with an Armenian minority. Around 20,000 people died and more than a million were displaced throughout the long conflict. A ceasefire agreement was signed in 1994, but Nagorno-Karabakh was not internationally recognized as a sovereign state. Armenia is trying to normalize the territory and maintain the status quo, while Azerbaijan continues to try to isolate Nagorno-Karabakh and lobby for international support for control over the territory. The Minsk Group at the OSCE remains the principal mediator. Students should come to class prepared to discuss the effect of national and international agendas and their effect in the role of an international organization during the peace process.

**Negotiation Simulation: Sri Lanka**

Students should come to class prepared to participate in a role-play exercise concerning negotiation and mediation of a peace agreement to end the Sri Lanka dispute, as well as the subsequent implementation of that peace agreement.

Roles to be assigned:

1.  Sri Lankan Negotiator

2.  Tamil Tigers Negotiator

3.  Norwegian International Mediator

Assume that the Sri Lankan government is skeptical about the involvement of the international community. Discuss the grounds for challenging or supporting the third-party involvement of the Norwegian mediators.

Assume that the Sri Lankan government refuses to sign the 2002 ceasefire agreement. Discuss the options available to international organizations in supporting a ceasefire or peace agreement.

Assume the parties involved reach a peace agreement. Discuss which international actors might be involved, and what mechanisms the parties and organizations would use to implement the peace agreement. Discuss the structure, function, and role an *ad hoc* international organization would play if created during the peace process.

# Materials

1.  Jacob Bercovitch & Allison Houston, *The Study of International Mediation: Theoretical Issues and Empirical Evidence, in* Resolving International Conflicts: The Theory and Practice of Mediation 11 (Jacob Bercovitch ed., 1996).

2.  Eric Brahm, *Intergovernmental Organizations (IGOs)*, beyondintractibility.org (2005).

3. Kenneth Abbot & Duncan Snidal, *Why States Act Through Formal International Organizations*, 42 J. CONFLICT RESOL. 1 (1998).

4. John Darby & James Rae, *Peace Processes from 1988–1998: Changing Patterns*, 17 ETHNIC STUD. REP. 46, 53 (1999).

5. Background Note, European Parliament, The Role of the EU in Conflict Prevention, European Parliamentary Meeting: The Future of Europe: From Reflection to Action (Dec. 4–5, 2006).

6. Background Note, United States Department of State, Angola.

7. S.C. Res. 804, U.N. Doc. S/RES/804 (Jan. 29, 1993).

8. S.C. Res. 952, U.N. Doc. S/RES/952 (Oct. 27, 1994).

9. Lusaka Protocol, Gov. Rep. Ang.—Union Total Indep. Ang., Nov. 15, 1994.

10. Dayton Peace Accords, Bosn. & Herz.-Croat.-F.R.Y., Annex 1A, Annex 3, Annex 7, Dec. 16, 1995.

11. Dayton Peace Accords, Bosn. & Herz.-Croat.-F.R.Y., Annex 10, Dec. 16, 1995.

12. Conclusions, Peace Implementation Council, Bonn Conference (1998).

13. Geneva Agreement, El Sal.—Frente Farabundo Martí para la Liberación Nacional, Apr. 4, 1990, *in The United Nations and El Salvador 1990–1995*, 4 UNITED NATIONS BLUE BOOKS SERIES 164–65 (1995).

14. Chapultepec Peace Agreement, El Sal.—Frente Farabundo Martí para la Liberación Nacional, Jan. 16, 1992, *in The United Nations and El Salvador 1990–1995*, 4 UNITED NATIONS BLUE BOOKS SERIES 193–230 (1995).

15. Background Note, Nagorno-Karabakh, United States Department of State.

16. Conference on Security and Cooperation in Europe Parliamentary Assembly, Budapest Declaration: Towards A Genuine Partnership in a New Era, DOC.RC/1/95 (July 5, 1992).

17. Organization for Security and Cooperation in Europe Minsk Group, Comprehensive Agreement on the Nagorno-Karabakh Conflict ("The Package Deal") (July 1997).

18. Organization for Security and Cooperation in Europe Minsk Group, Agreement on the End of the Nagorno-Karabakh Conflict ("The Step-by-Step Deal") (Dec. 1997).

19. Organization for Security and Cooperation in Europe Minsk Group, On the Principles for a Comprehensive Settlement of the Armed Conflict over Nagorno-Karabakh ("The Common State Deal") (Nov. 1998).

20. Eur. Parl. Ass. Res. 1416 (Jan. 25, 2005).

21. Press Release, U.N. News Centre News Focus: Sudan & South Sudan, Joint A.U.-U.N. Road-map for Darfur Political Process, U.N. Doc. (June 8, 2007).

22. Rambouillet Agreement, F.R.Y.—Kos. (Feb. 23, 1999).

23. S.C. Res. 1244, U.N. Doc. S/RES/1244 (June 10, 1999).

24. Ceasefire Agreement, Sri Lanka—Liberation Tigers of Tamil Eelam (Feb. 22, 2002).

25. Jan Petersen, Foreign Minister of Norway, Announcement of Sri Lanka Ceasefire (Feb. 22, 2002).

26. Bibliography of Additional Sources

## Authors' Note

The roles of international organizations in the peace process are varied and complex. This chapter begins with excerpts of articles that discuss the role international organizations in the peace process and is followed by sections on Angola, Bosnia, El Salvador, Nagorno-Karabakh, Darfur, Kosovo, and Sri Lanka. Each section contains documents relating to the conflict and peace process in their respective countries. With the background information provided by the articles in this first section and the documents from each state, look for the roles that international organizations play. Search for instances when international organizations had to adapt and try to analyze how they might have changed their approach.

The first five materials in this section (1–5) provide background and insight on the roles that international organizations play in the peace process.

---

## 1. Jacob Bercovitch and Allison Houston, The Study of International Mediation: Theoretical Issues and Empirical Evidence

*Resolving International Conflicts: The Theory and Practice of Mediation*, 1996

Conflict is one of the most pervasive—and inevitable—features of all social systems, however simple or complex they may be and irrespective of their location in time and space. This is true of personal, group, and organizational, as well as international systems.

\* \* \*

There are a number of ways of dealing with or managing conflict. These may range from avoidance and withdrawal, through bilateral negotiation, to various forms of third-party intervention. Third-party intervention in conflict, particularly of the non-binding, non-coercive kind, is in many ways as old as conflict itself. It has played an important role in industrial and preindustrial societies. Its popularity as a way of dealing with conflict grows each year, as does its applicability to different realms. Unresolved problems and conflicts create the conditions for third-party intervention in one form or another.

\* \* \*

As a form of international conflict management, mediation is likely to occur when (1) a conflict has gone on for some time, (2) the efforts of the individuals or actors involved have reached an impasse, (3) neither actor is prepared to countenance further costs or escalation of the dispute, and (4) both parties welcome some form of mediation and are ready to engage in direct or indirect dialogue.

Whatever its specific characteristics, mediation must in essence be seen as an extension of the negotiation process whereby an acceptable third party intervenes to change the course or outcome of a particular conflict. The third party, with no authoritative decision making power, is there to assist the disputants in their search for a mutually acceptable agreement. As a form of conflict management, mediation is distinguishable from more binding forms of third-party intervention, such as arbitration and adjudication, in that it is initiated upon request and it leaves the ultimate decision making power with the disputants.

\* \* \*

## 2. Eric Brahm, Intergovernmental Organizations (IGOs)
BeyondIntractability.org, 2005

Intergovernmental organizations (IGOs) have become increasingly prominent both in facilitating conflict resolution between states, but also in dealing with intractable conflicts within states. They serve a number of basic functions that enhance the possibility of cooperation. Created after World War I, the League of Nations was an early attempt to systematize third party mediation in international conflict. However, it proved too weak because important states did not join, which limited its ability to function. After World War II, the United Nations was created and, although it worked better than the League of Nations, the Cold War impeded its effectiveness for many years. Following the end of the Cold War, the U.N. has taken on new roles, and regional organizations around the world have also become more active. Growing activism from these organizations, however, does not mean that they operate flawlessly. This essay will briefly review the general purpose of IGOs in minimizing interstate conflict and then proceed to discuss their expanded roles in dealing with the internal conflicts of sovereign states.

### General Issues

Intergovernmental organizations are constructed by states to facilitate cooperation. The primary utility of IGOs lies in providing states with a forum which they can use to negotiate conflicts. IGOs are also useful to states in a number of additional ways.

- First, by providing a forum for discussion, they make it less costly for states to discuss issues with one another.

- Second, IGOs often serve as information providers. The enhanced transparency helps to minimize misperceptions.

- Third, IGOs help to facilitate issue linkages, which may facilitate cooperation.

- Fourth, IGOs help allow states to take a long-term perspective, which makes them less concerned about immediate payoffs.

- Fifth, the multilateral nature of IGOs lends an air of impartiality that enhances their effectiveness.

\* \* \*

### The Role of Regional Organizations

Recognizing that the U.N. lacked resources and local expertise to fully deal with new types of missions, Boutros-Ghali led an effort to give primacy to regional organizations in dealing with many conflicts. During the Cold War, regional organizations served as a substitute for the U.N. when superpower conflict hampered the functioning of the Security Council. The current trend appears to be that the U.N. seems willing to hand over responsibility for peace and security to any form of "coalition of the willing." The U.N. itself reached this conclusion in a recent report, saying:

> The United Nations does not have, at this point in its history, the institutional capacity to conduct military enforcement measures under Chapter VII (of the U.N. Charter). Under present conditions, ad hoc Member States coalitions of the willing offer the most effective deterrent to aggression or to the escalation or spread of an ongoing conflict ... The Organization still lacks the capacity to implement rapidly and effectively decisions of the Security Council calling for the dispatch

of peacekeeping operations in crisis situations. Troops for peacekeeping missions are in some cases not made available by Member States or made available under conditions that constrain effective response. Peacemaking and human rights operations, as well as peacekeeping operations, also lack a secure financial footing, which has a serious impact on the viability of such operations.

\* \* \*

Regional organizations have both expanded in number and, because many often overlap in a given territory, have increasingly begun to coordinate their activities. And, since the end of the Cold War, examples abound of regional organizations expanding their capacity to take on a mediation role:

- The Organization of African Unity (OAU) — now the African Union (A.U.) — added a section to its Secretariat to aid in conflict resolution,
- The Association of South East Asian Nations (ASEAN) has established a new mediation role.
- Within Africa, the Inter-Governmental Agency on Drought and Development (IGADD) in the Horn of Africa,
- The Southern African Development Community (SADC),
- The Economic Community of West African States (ECOWAS), and
- The West African Economic Community (CEAO) has all mediated disputes within their respective regions.
- NATO and ECOMOG (ECOWAS Peace Monitoring Group) are two groups that have engaged in peace enforcement.

\* \* \*

## 3. Kenneth Abbot and Duncan Snidal, Why States Act through Formal International Organizations

Journal of Conflict Resolution, 1998
[footnotes omitted by editors]

\* \* \*

Formal international organizations (IOs) are prominent (if not always successful) participants in many critical episodes in international politics. [ ... ] On an ongoing basis, formal organizations help manage many significant areas of interstate relations, from global health policy (the WHO) to European security (OSCE and NATO) to international monetary policy (IMF). What is more, participation in such organizations appears to reduce the likelihood of violent conflict among member states.

IOs range from simple entities like the APEC secretariat with an initial budget of $2 million, to formidable organizations like the European Union (EU) and the World Bank, which have thousands of employees and multiple affiliates and lends billions of dollars each year. Specialized agencies like the ILO, ICAO, and FAO play key roles in technical issue areas. New organizations like UNEP, the EBRD, and the International Tribunal for the former Yugoslavia are regularly created. Older IOs like NATO and the Security Council are rethought and sometimes restructured to meet new circumstances.

\* \* \*

## *Authors' Note*

**World Bank:** The World Bank has been heavily involved in post-conflict reconstruction in many different states. Its involvement occurred mostly through grants or loans to post-conflict countries, such as Bosnia, Sri Lanka, El Salvador, Rwanda, and others. Moreover, the World Bank has been involved at various stages of the post-conflict process, offering findings and recommendations to the failed country. After 1997, the Board of the World Bank created Post-Conflict Unit, which deals with policy development, development of expertise, and cross-country learning.

## 4. John Darby and James Rae, Peace Processes from 1988–1998: Changing Patterns

### Ethnic Studies Report, 1999
[footnotes omitted by editors]

\* \* \*

Over the eleven years, the number of U.N.-brokered agreements has declined in relation to other approaches to peace accords. The processes in Namibia, Cambodia, El Salvador, Mozambique, Somalia, and Angola may be regarded as test cases for the U.N. in realizing a new post Cold War world order. These were attempts to reconstruct and rehabilitate national institutions, identity, and government in a comprehensive manner. To varying degrees, U.N. missions were expanded to include political, administrative, security, and sometimes economic affairs. The U.N. was thrust into the most difficult of situations, and the record is mixed. The most notable failure was Rwanda where the U.N.'s limited initial role and the international reluctance to intervene saw the worst genocide in decades.

In contrast to the enforcement limitations so sharply revealed by its interventions in Bosnia and Somalia, where armed militias resented external involvement and were prepared to demonstrate their feelings, the U.N. employed multidimensional approaches to peacekeeping in Cambodia and El Salvador which may yet provide a model for future U.N. activities. This was based on a stronger attempt to secure consensus rather than impose force, and it required co-operation between the state and the international community, and between U.N. peacekeepers and a host of other actors including civilian police and non-governmental organizations (NGOs). It involved the U.N. in peacemaking, peacekeeping, and peace-building sometimes simultaneously. The U.N. mission was "not merely to create conditions for negotiations between the parties, but to develop strategies and support structures that would bring about a lasting peace."

\* \* \*

## 5. European Parliamentary Meeting, The Role of the EU in Conflict Prevention

### Background Note, December 2006

#### Executive Summary

European integration and EU enlargement have been a contribution to conflict prevention in Europe over the past half century. The Union has successfully contributed to spreading democracy, prosperity, security and stability across most of the European continent. During the 1990s this peace project was transformed into the core of the EU's external policy under the Common Foreign and Security Policy (CFSP). A decision to develop a distinct conflict prevention policy emerged from the 2000 Nice European Council, when the Secretary General/High Representative (SG/HR) for CFSP and the Commission submitted a joint report with concrete recommendations for developing the role of the Union on Conflict Prevention.

Initial progress in developing CFSP for conflict prevention was far from successful as highlighted by the absence of a coherent EU approach towards the Balkan Wars. The result was a distinct EU approach to adjust the treaties (1992 Maastricht, 1997 Amsterdam and 2000 Nice) and create new structures (such as the SG/HR for CFSP and the Political and Security Committee) and the development of a comprehensive policy framework based upon Conflict Prevention and Crisis Management.

The EU's present conflict prevention activities are linked to strengthened coordination with other international agencies acting to prevent conflicts, *in primis* the U.N.. Such coordination is evident in the field (DR of Congo, Lebanon etc) as well as at headquarters levels (with liaison officers and support to the U.N. Peace building Commission). The EU depends on strong partnerships with other actors in conflict prevention — including the Council of Europe, OSCE and NATO.

* * *

## Authors' Note

**Angola:** The conflict in Angola spans several decades and includes numerous attempts at reaching a viable peace agreement. International organizations played key roles at various stages in mediating and implementing the various peace agreements.

## 6. United States Department of State, Angola

### Background Note

As decolonization progressed [in Angola], three independence movements emerged: the Popular Movement for the Liberation of Angola (MPLA), with a base among Kimbundu and the mixed-race intelligentsia of Luanda and links to communist parties in Portugal and the East Bloc; the National Front for the Liberation of Angola (FNLA), with an ethnic base in the Bakongo region of the north and links to the United States and the Mobutu regime in Kinshasa; and the National Union for the Total Independence of Angola (UNITA), with an ethnic and regional base in the Ovimbundu heartland in the center of the country and ethnic and regional base in the Ovimbundu heartland in the center of the country and links to the People's Republic of China (P.R.C.) and apartheid South Africa.

From the early 1960s, elements of these movements fought against the Portuguese. A 1974 coup d'etat in Portugal established a military government that promptly ceased the war and agreed ... to hand over power in Angola to a coalition of the three movements. The ideological differences between the three movements eventually led to armed conflict. The intervention of [international] troops ... that year effectively internationalized the conflict. Retaining control of Luanda, the coastal strip, and increasingly lucrative oil fields in Cabinda, the MPLA declared independence on November 11, 1975, the day the Portuguese abandoned the capital. UNITA and the FNLA formed a rival coalition government based in the interior city of Huambo. [T]he MPLA was recognized by the United Nations in 1976.

The FNLA's military failures led to its increasing marginalization, internal divisions, and abandonment by international supporters. An internationalized conventional civil war between UNITA and the MPLA continued until 1989. For much of this time, UNITA controlled vast swaths of the interior and was backed by U.S. resources and South African troops. Similarly, tens of thousands of Cuban troops remained in support of the MPLA, often fighting South Africans on the front lines. A U.S.-brokered agreement resulted in withdrawal of foreign troops in 1989 and led to the Bicesse Accord in 1991, which spelled out an electoral process for a democratic Angola under the supervision of the United Nations. Another peace accord, known as the Lusaka Protocol, was brokered in Lusaka, Zambia, and signed in 1994. This agreement, too, collapsed into renewed conflict. The Angolan military launched a massive offensive in 1999, which destroyed UNITA's conventional capacity and recaptured all major cities previously held.... On April 4, 2002, the Angolan Government and UNITA signed the Luena Memorandum of Understanding (MOU), which formalized the de facto cease-fire. In accordance with the MOU, UNITA recommitted to the peace framework in the 1994 Lusaka Protocol.

# 7. Resolution 804
## United States Security Council, 1993

The Security Council,

\* \* \*

*Gravely disturbed* by the recent outbreak of heavy fighting in parts of Angola and the further deterioration of the already dangerous political and military situation in the country,

\* \* \*

*Reaffirming* its commitment to preserve the unity and territorial integrity of Angola,

*Recognizing* that the Angolans themselves bear ultimate responsibility for the restoration of peace and national reconciliation of their country,

\* \* \*

*Strongly condemns* the persistent violations of the main provisions of the "Acordos de Paz", in particular the initial rejection by UNITA of the election results, its withdrawal from the new Angolan armed forces, its seizure by force of provincial capitals and municipalities and the resumption of hostilities;

*Demands* that the two parties cease fire immediately, restore at their meeting in Addis Ababa continued and meaningful dialogue, and agree on a clear timetable for the full implementation of the "Acordos de Paz", in particular with regard to confinement of their troops and collection of their weapons, demobilization and formation of the unified national armed forces, effective restoration of the Government administration throughout the country, the completion of the electoral process and the free circulation of people and goods;

*Supports* fully the Secretary-General and his Special Representative in their continuing efforts to restore the peace process and to carry out the mandate of UNAVEM II under extremely difficult conditions;

\* \* \*

*Approves* the recommendation of the Secretary-General to maintain a Special Representative for Angola based in Luanda, with the necessary civilian, military and police staff with the mandate as described in paragraph 29 of the report of the Secretary-General;

*Decides* to extend the mandate of UNAVEM II for a period of three months until 30 April 1993, with the proviso that, as a provisional measure based on security considerations, the Secretary-General is authorized to concentrate UNAVEM II deployment in Luanda, and at his discretion in other provincial locations, with the levels of equipment and personnel he deems appropriate to be retained in order to allow the subsequent expeditious redeployment of UNAVEM II as soon as this become feasible, with a view to the resumption of its functions in accordance with the "Acordos de Paz" and previous resolutions on this matter;

*Requests* the Secretary-General to submit to it as soon as the situation warrants, and in any case before 30 April 1993, a report on the situation in Angola together with his recommendations for the further role of the United Nations in the peace process, and in the meantime to keep the Council regularly informed;

* * *

## 8. Resolution 952
### United Nations Security Council, 1994

The Security Council,

* * *

*Commending* the efforts of the Secretary-General, his Special Representative and the Force Commander and personnel of the United Nations Angola Verification Mission (UNAVEM II), the three observer States to the Angolan Peace Process, the Organization of African Unity (OAU) and some neighbouring States in particular Zambia, and *encouraging* them to continue their efforts aimed at the earliest resolution of the Angolan crisis through negotiations within the framework of the "Acordos de Paz" and relevant Security Council resolutions,

* * *

*Authorizes*, with the aim of consolidating the implementation of the peace agreement in its initial and most critical stages, the restoration of the strength of UNAVEM II to its previous level of 350 military observers and 126 police observers with an appropriate number of international and local staff, the deployment of such additional personnel to take place upon receipt of a report from the Secretary-General to the Council that the parties have initialed a peace agreement and that an effective cease-fire is in place;

* * *

## 9. Lusaka Protocol
### 1994

15 November 1994

The Government of the Republic of Angola (GRA) and the Union for the Total Independence of Angola (UNITA);

With the mediation of the United Nations organization, represented by the Special Representative of the Secretary-General of the United Nations in Angola, Mr. Alioune Blondin Beye;

In the presence of the Representatives of the Observer States of the Angolan peace process:

- Government of the United States of America
- Government of the Russian Federation
- Government of Portugal;

\* \* \*

Accept as binding the documents listed below, which constitute the Lusaka Protocol:

\* \* \*

### The United Nations Mandate

### I. General Principles

\* \* \*

3. The Government and UNITA invite the United Nations to perform, in addition to its missions of good offices and mediation, the tasks defined in the present mandate with a view to the full implementation of the Peace Accords for Angola (Bicesse) and the Lusaka Protocol. The Observers of the peace process (the United States of America, Portugal and the Russian Federation) give their full support to this invitation.

4. The Government and UNITA reaffirm their clear wish that the United Nations, within the framework of its new mandate, should play an enlarged and reinforced role in the implementation of the Peace Accords for Angola (Bicesse) and the Lusaka Protocol, as agreed in the areas of military issues, National Police, National Reconciliation and the completion of the electoral process. Both parties reiterate their determination to respect and protect the Mission of the United Nations in Angola, its operations, all its staff, its facilities and property.

5. The Government and UNITA invite the United Nations, within the framework of its new mandate, to assume the chairmanship of the Joint Commission and of all relevant meetings between the Government and UNITA, in the presence of the representatives of the Observers.

6. As soon as the United Nations Security Council authorizes the establishment of the new United Nations mission in Angola, an agreement regulating the status of the mission and its members shall be concluded, without delay, between the United Nations and the Government on the basis of the relevant United Nations model agreement, the content of which shall be communicated by the Government to UNITA in advance.

\* \* \*

9. The United Nations will perform the tasks entrusted to it within the framework of its new mandate, in strict respect for the sovereignty of the Angolan State and the relevant provisions of the Peace Accords for Angola (Bisesse) and the Lusaka Protocol.

\* \* \*

### II. Specific Principles

The Government and UNITA invite the United Nations, within the framework of its new mandate, to undertake the following tasks:

1) Military Issues (Agenda Item II.1)

1.1 Overall supervision, control and verification of the reestablished ceasefire, with the participation of the Government and UNITA (General principle no. 4).

\* \* \*

1.9 Reinforcement of existing United Nations personnel, both military observers and armed peacekeeping forces (Modalities no. 6; Timetable of modalities, phase two, step one).

\* \* \*

1.14 Creation and putting in place of U.N. teams to monitor and verify the cessation of hostilities throughout the country and to investigate alleged ceasefire violations (Timetable of modalities, phase one, step two).

\* \* \*

2) Police Activities (Agenda Item II.2)

2.1 Verification and monitoring of the activities of the Angolan National Police, placed under the legitimate authority, in order to guarantee its neutrality (Specific principle no. 1).

\* \* \*

4) Completion of the Electoral Process (Agenda Item II.5)

\* \* \*

4.2 Appropriate support, verification and monitoring of the organization by the competent Angolan State institutions, namely the National Electoral Council, of the second round of the presidential elections (General principles no. 4).

\* \* \*

**The Role of Observers in the Implementation of the Peace Accords and the Lusaka Protocol**

1. The Governments of the United States of America, Russian Federation and Portugal are the observers of the peace process in Angola. In this capacity, they shall sit on the Joint Commission.

2. The functions of the Representatives of the observers are:

\* \* \*

2.3 Monitor the implementation of all the political, administrative and military provisions not yet implemented of the Peace Accords for Angola (Bicesse) and of all the political, administrative and military provisions of the Lusaka Protocol.

**The Joint Commission**

The Joint Commission shall have the composition, functions and rules of operation specified hereunder:

1. COMPOSITION

The Joint Commission shall be composed of:

1.1 attending in their capacity as members:

- the Government of the Republic of Angola;
- UNITA;

1.2 attending in the capacity of chairman:

- the United Nations organization. The Special Representative of the Secretary-General in Angola shall assume the functions of good offices and of mediation.

1.3 attending in their capacity as observers:

- the Government of the United States of America;
- the Government of Portugal;
- the Government of the Russian Federation.

## 2. FUNCTIONS

2.1 To watch over the implementation of all the political, administrative and military provisions not yet implemented of the Peace Accords for Angola (Bicesse), and all the provisions of the Lusaka Protocol, in accordance with the understandings in the areas related to the military, national police, national reconciliation and completion of the electoral process.

2.2 To monitor the implementation of the relevant resolutions of the United Nations Security Council.

\* \* \*

## Authors' Note

Bosnia: The conflict in Bosnia followed the dissolution of Yugoslavia and resulting political, ethnic, and cultural chaos. The Socialist Republic of Bosnia and Herzegovina declared independence in early 1992 in the wake of the collapse of Yugoslavia. With its diverse ethnic and religious population, the new state was soon embroiled in a complex conflict between ethnic Serbs, Bosniaks, and Croats all vying for independence. Ethnic Serbs in Bosnia, with the support of the Socialist Republic of Serbia, begin a campaign of ethnic cleansing of Muslim Bosniaks in order to secure territory. Bosnian Croats, who switched allegiances from Bosnia to Serbia, were also pushing for an independent Croat state. The conflict was devastating, resulting in mass violations of human rights, gang rapes, ethnic cleansing, and genocide. NATO intervened and effectively stopped the Serbian advance. After a number of failed negotiations, the parties signed a peace agreement in December of 1995. The peace agreement called the General Framework Agreement for Peace in Bosnia and Herzegovina is often referred to as the Dayton Accord, or Dayton Peace Accord.

The following three excerpts (10, 11 and 12) are from documents produced during, or as a result of, the peace process in Bosnia. Excerpts 10 and 11 are from the Dayton Peace Accord, and excerpt 12 is from the Peace Implementation Council's Bonn Conclusions. Note the numerous roles that international organizations play in the process.

## 10. Dayton Peace Accords
General Framework Agreement for Peace in
Bosnia and Herzegovina, 1995

\* \* \*

Annex 1A

**Agreement on the Military Aspects of the Peace Settlement**

\* \* \*

**Article I: General Obligations**

1. The Parties undertake to recreate as quickly as possible normal conditions of life in Bosnia and Herzegovina. They understand that this requires a major contribution on their part in which they will make strenuous efforts to cooperate with each other and with the international organizations and agencies which are assisting them on the ground. They welcome the willingness of the international community to send to the region, for

a period of approximately one year, a force to assist in implementation of the territorial and other militarily related provisions of the agreement as described herein.

a. The United Nations Security Council is invited to adopt a resolution by which it will authorize Member States or regional organizations and arrangements to establish a multi-national military Implementation Force (hereinafter "IFOR"). The Parties understand and agree that this Implementation Force may be composed of ground, air and maritime units from NATO and non-NATO nations, deployed to Bosnia and Herzegovina to help ensure compliance with the provisions of this Agreement (hereinafter "Annex"). The Parties understand and agree that the IFOR will begin the implementation of the military aspects of this Annex upon the transfer of authority from the UNPROFOR Commander to the IFOR Commander (hereinafter "Transfer of Authority"), and that until the Transfer of Authority, UNPROFOR will continue to exercise its mandate.

b. It is understood and agreed that NATO may establish such a force, which will operate under the authority and subject to the direction and political control of the North Atlantic Council ("NAC") through the NATO chain of command. They undertake to facilitate its operations. The Parties, therefore, hereby agree and freely undertake to fully comply with all obligations set forth in this Annex.

\* \* \*

## Annex 3

## Agreement on Elections

\* \* \*

### Article II: The OSCE Role

1. **OSCE.** The Parties request the OSCE to adopt and put in place an elections program for Bosnia and Herzegovina as set forth in this Agreement.

2. **Elections.** The Parties request the OSCE to supervise, in a manner to be determined by the OSCE and in cooperation with other international organizations the OSCE deems necessary, the preparation and conduct of elections for the House of Representatives of Bosnia and Herzegovina; for the Presidency of Bosnia and Herzegovina; for the House of Representatives of the Federation of Bosnia and Herzegovina; for the National Assembly of the Republika Srpska; for the Presidency of the Republika Srpska; and, if feasible, for cantonal legislatures and municipal governing authorities.

3. **The Commission.** To this end, the Parties request the OSCE to establish a Provisional Election Commission ("the Commission").

4. **Timing.** Elections shall take place on a date ("Election Day") six months after entry into force of this Agreement or, if the OSCE determines a delay necessary, no later than nine months after entry into force.

\* \* \*

## Annex 7

## Agreement on Refugees and Displaced Persons

\* \* \*

### Article III: Cooperation with International Organizations and International Monitoring

1. The Parties note with satisfaction the leading humanitarian role of UNHCR, which has been entrusted by the Secretary-General of the United Nations with the role of co-

ordinating among all agencies assisting with the repatriation and relief of refugees and displaced persons.

2. The Parties shall give full and unrestricted access by UNHCR, the International Committee of the Red Cross ("ICRC"), the United Nations Development Programme ("UNDP"), and other relevant international, domestic and nongovernmental organizations to all refugees and displaced persons, with a view to facilitating the work of those organizations in tracing persons, the provision of medical assistance, food distribution, reintegration assistance, the provision of temporary and permanent housing, and other activities vital to the discharge of their mandates and operational responsibilities without administrative impediments. These activities shall include traditional protection functions and the monitoring of basic human rights and humanitarian conditions, as well as the implementation of the provisions of this Chapter.

* * *

## *Authors' Note*

**Office of High Representative and EU Special Representative — Bosnia:** Through the peace process in Bosnia, the Dayton Peace Accord created the Office of the High Representative. The following is information on the OHR taken from the OHR website. (The Office of the High Representative and EU Special Representative, OHR Introduction).

"The Office of the High Representative (OHR) is an *ad hoc* international institution responsible for overseeing implementation of civilian aspects of the accord ending the war in Bosnia and Herzegovina. The position of High Representative was created under the General Framework Agreement for Peace in Bosnia and Herzegovina, usually referred to as the Dayton Peace Agreement, that was negotiated in Dayton, Ohio, and signed in Paris on 14 December 1995. The High Representative, who is also EU Special Representative (EUSR) in Bosnia and Herzegovina, is working with the people and institutions of Bosnia and Herzegovina and the international community to ensure that Bosnia and Herzegovina evolves into a peaceful and viable democracy on course for integration into Euro-Atlantic institutions. [T]he OHR is working towards transition — the point when Bosnia and Herzegovina is able to take full responsibility for its own affairs."

## 11. Dayton Peace Accords

General Framework Agreement for Peace in Bosnia and Herzegovina, 1995

**Annex 10**

**Agreement on Civilian Implementation**

The Republic of Bosnia and Herzegovina, the Republic of Croatia, the Federal Republic of Yugoslavia, the Federation of Bosnia and Herzegovina, and the Republika Srpska (the "Parties") have agreed as follows:

**Article I: High Representative**

1. The Parties agree that the implementation of the civilian aspects of the peace settlement will entail a wide range of activities including continuation of the humanitarian aid effort for as long as necessary; rehabilitation of infrastructure and economic reconstruction; the establishment of political and constitutional institutions in Bosnia and Herzegovina; promotion of respect for human rights and the return of displaced persons and refugees; and the holding of free and fair elections according to the timetable in Annex 3 to the

General Framework Agreement. A considerable number of international organizations and agencies will be called upon to assist.

2. In view of the complexities facing them, the Parties request the designation of a High Representative, to be appointed consistent with relevant United Nations Security Council resolutions, to facilitate the Parties' own efforts and to mobilize and, as appropriate, coordinate the activities of the organizations and agencies involved in the civilian aspects of the peace settlement by carrying out, as entrusted by a U.N. Security Council resolution, the tasks set out below.

### Article II: Mandate and Methods of Coordination and Liaison

1. The High Representative shall:

   a. Monitor the implementation of the peace settlement;

   b. Maintain close contact with the Parties to promote their full compliance with all civilian aspects of the peace settlement and a high level of cooperation between them and the organizations and agencies participating in those aspects;

   c. Coordinate the activities of the civilian organizations and agencies in Bosnia and Herzegovina to ensure the efficient implementation of the civilian aspects of the peace settlement. The High Representative shall respect their autonomy within their spheres of operation while as necessary giving general guidance to them about the impact of their activities on the implementation of the peace settlement. The civilian organizations and agencies are requested to assist the High Representative in the execution of his or her responsibilities by providing all information relevant to their operations in Bosnia-Herzegovina;

   d. Facilitate, as the High Representative judges necessary, the resolution of any difficulties arising in connection with civilian implementation;

   e. Participate in meetings of donor organizations, particularly on issues of rehabilitation and reconstruction;

   f. Report periodically on progress in implementation of the peace agreement concerning the tasks set forth in this Agreement to the United Nations, European Union, United States, Russian Federation, and other interested governments, parties, and organizations;

   g. Provide guidance to, and receive reports from, the Commissioner of the International Police Task Force established in Annex 11 to the General Framework Agreement.

2. In pursuit of his or her mandate, the High Representative shall convene and chair a commission (the "Joint Civilian Commission") in Bosnia and Herzegovina. It will comprise senior political representatives of the Parties, the IFOR Commander or his representative, and representatives of those civilian organizations and agencies the High Representative deems necessary.

3. The High Representative shall, as necessary, establish subordinate Joint Civilian Commissions at local levels in Bosnia and Herzegovina.

4. A Joint Consultative Committee will meet from time to time or as agreed between the High Representative and the IFOR Commander.

5. The High Representative or his designated representative shall remain in close contact with the IFOR Commander or his designated representatives and establish appropriate liaison arrangements with the IFOR Commander to facilitate the discharge of their respective responsibilities.

6. The High Representative shall exchange information and maintain liaison on a regular basis with IFOR, as agreed with the IFOR Commander, and through the commissions described in this Article.

7. The High Representative shall attend or be represented at meetings of the Joint Military Commission and offer advice particularly on matters of a political-military nature. Representatives of the High Representative will also attend subordinate commissions of the Joint Military Commission as set out in Article VIII(8) of Annex 1A to the General Framework Agreement.

8. The High Representative may also establish other civilian commissions within or outside Bosnia and Herzegovina to facilitate the execution of his or her mandate.

9. The High Representative shall have no authority over the IFOR and shall not in any way interfere in the conduct of military operations or the IFOR chain of command.

### Article III: Staffing

1. The High Representative shall appoint staff, as he or she deems necessary, to provide assistance in carrying out the tasks herein.

2. The Parties shall facilitate the operations of the High Representative in Bosnia and Herzegovina, including by the provision of appropriate assistance as requested with regard to transportation, subsistence, accommodations, communications, and other facilities at rates equivalent to those provided for the IFOR under applicable agreements.

3. The High Representative shall enjoy, under the laws of Bosnia and Herzegovina, such legal capacity as may be necessary for the exercise of his or her functions, including the capacity to contract and to acquire and dispose of real and personal property.

4. Privileges and immunities shall be accorded as follows:

a. The Parties shall accord the office of the High Representative and its premises, archives, and other property the same privileges and immunities as are enjoyed by a diplomatic mission and its premises, archives, and other property under the Vienna Convention on Diplomatic Relations.

b. The Parties shall accord the High Representative and professional members of his or her staff and their families the same privileges and immunities as are enjoyed by diplomatic agents and their families under the Vienna Convention on Diplomatic Relations.

c. The Parties shall accord other members of the High Representative staff and their families the same privileges and immunities as are enjoyed by members of the administrative and technical staff and their families under the Vienna Convention on Diplomatic Relations.

### Article IV: Cooperation

The Parties shall fully cooperate with the High Representative and his or her staff, as well as with the international organizations and agencies as provided for in Article IX of the General Framework Agreement.

### Article V: Final Authority to Interpret

The High Representative is the final authority in theater regarding interpretation of this Agreement on the civilian implementation of the peace settlement.

* * *

## Authors' Note

**Peace Implementation Council — Bosnia:** Following the Dayton Peace Accords, the international community formed an organization to monitor and implement the peace agreement in Bosnia. The Peace Implementation Council ("PIC") regularly released reports and conclusions on the progress in Bosnia. The following information is from the Office of the High Representative's website. (The Office of the High Representative and EU Special Representative, *The Peace Implementation Council and its Steering Board*).

"Following the successful negotiation of the Dayton Peace Agreement in November 1995, a Peace Implementation Conference was held in London on December 8–9, 1995, to mobilise international support for the Agreement. The meeting resulted in the establishment of the Peace Implementation Council (PIC). The PIC comprises 55 countries and agencies that support the peace process in many different ways — by assisting it financially, providing troops for SFOR, or directly running operations in Bosnia and Herzegovina. There is also a fluctuating number of observers."

# 12. Peace Implementation Council's Bonn Conclusions, Bosnia and Herzegovina: Self-Sustaining Structures
## 1998

\* \* \*

### XI. High Representative

d. The Council commends the efforts of the High Representative and his staff in pursuing the implementation of the Peace Agreement. It emphasises the important role of the High Representative in ensuring the creation of conditions for a self-sustaining peace in Bosnia and Herzegovina and his responsibility for co-ordination of the activities of the civilian organisations and agencies in Bosnia and Herzegovina.

\* \* \*

e. The Council welcomes the High Representative's intention to use his final authority in theatre regarding interpretation of the Agreement on the Civilian Implementation of the Peace Settlement in order to facilitate the resolution of difficulties by making binding decisions, as he judges necessary, on the following issues:

a. timing, location and chairmanship of meetings of the common institutions;

b. interim measures to take effect when parties are unable to reach agreement, which will remain in force until the Presidency or Council of Ministers has adopted a decision consistent with the Peace Agreement on the issue concerned;

c. other measures to ensure implementation of the Peace Agreement throughout Bosnia and Herzegovina and its Entities, as well as the smooth running of the common institutions. Such measures may include actions against persons holding public office or officials who are absent from meetings without good cause or who are found by the High Representative to be in violation of legal commitments made under the Peace Agreement or the terms for its implementation.

\* \* \*

## Authors' Note

**El Salvador:** In 1980, after years of political and economic strife, El Salvador erupted in civil war. A communist group called the Frente Farabundo Martí para la Liberación Nacional (FMLN) engaged government troops in an effort to control the country. The conflict lasted until early 1992. Hundreds of thousands of people died. In January 1992, the FMLN and the government of El Salvador signed a peace accord, the Chapultepec Agreement that ended the civil war. International organizations played a significant role in the negotiations, which lasted for several years. The following two agreements (13 and 14) cover the peace process in El Salvador.

## 13. Geneva Agreement, El Salvador

### 1991

At the request of the Central American Presidents and within the framework of the mandate of good offices conferred on me by the Security Council under resolution 637 of 27 July 1989, I have held consultations with the Government of El Salvador and the Frente Farabundo Martí para la Liberación Nacional (FMLN) in order to agree on the format, mechanism and pace of a process aimed at bringing about as speedily as possible, under my auspices, a definitive end to the armed conflict in that country. I have agreed to carry out this effort at the request of the Government and FMLN and because I have received assurances from both parties that there is a serious and good faith intention to seek to bring about such an end through negotiations. As a result of my consultations, the Government and FMLN have agreed on the points set forth below, which are designed to ensure that the process is conducted in an efficient and serious manner and promotes mutual trust through appropriate guarantees.

I believe that in addition to their intrinsic importance, the scrupulous maintenance of these guarantees will demonstrate the desire and ability of the parties to carry out any commitments they make during the negotiations. On this understanding, the Government and FMLN have pledged not to abandon the negotiating process.

1. The purpose of the process shall be to end the armed conflict by political means as speedily as possible, promote the democratization of the country, guarantee unrestricted respect for human rights and reunify Salvadorian society.

The initial objective shall be to reach political agreements which lay the basis for a cessation of the armed conflict and of any acts that infringe the rights of the civilian population, which will have to be verified by the United Nations, subject to the approval of the Security Council. Once that has been achieved, the process shall lead to the establishment of the necessary guarantees and conditions for reintegrating the members of FMLN, within a framework of full legality, into the civil, institutional and political life of the country.

2. The process shall be conducted under the auspices of the Secretary-General, on a continuous and uninterrupted basis.

3. In order to ensure the success of the negotiating process, the Government and FMLN agree to an approach which shall involve two types of complementary activities: direct dialogue between the negotiating commissions with the active participation of the Secretary-General or his Representative, and an intermediary role by the Secretary-General or his

Representative between the parties to ensure that both the Government and FMLN are committed at the highest level. The Secretary-General shall seek to ensure that these activities are conducted in a manner that genuinely contributes to the success of the process. The Government and FMLN shall ensure that their negotiating commissions have full powers to discuss and conclude agreements.

4. The Government and FMLN agree that the process shall be conducted in the strictest secrecy. The only public information on its progress shall be that provided by the Secretary-General or his authorized Representative.

5. The Secretary-General, at his discretion, may maintain confidential contacts with Governments of States Members of the United Nations or groups thereof that can contribute to the success of the process through their advice and support.

6. The Government of El Salvador and FMLN agree that the political parties and other representative social organizations existing in El Salvador have an important role to play in the attainment of peace. They also recognize the need for both the Government and FMLN to maintain appropriate, ongoing information and consultation mechanisms with such parties and social organizations in the country, and that the latter must undertake to preserve the secrecy necessary to the success of the dialogue process. When it is deemed appropriate and on the basis of mutual consent, the commissions may call upon representatives of these parties and organizations in order to receive their inputs.

7. The Government and FMLN likewise recognize that it is useful for the Secretary-General to maintain contacts with Salvadorian individuals and groups whose input may benefit his efforts.

\* \* \*

*In the capacity assigned to me by the United Nations Security Council in resolution 637 (1989)*

(*Signed*) Javier PÉREZ DE CUÉLLAR

Secretary-General of the United Nations

---

## 14. Chapultepec Peace Agreement, El Salvador
### 1992

The Government of El Salvador and the Frente Farabundo Martí para la Liberación Nacional (hereinafter referred to as "the Parties"),

*Reaffirming* that their purpose, as set forth in the Geneva Agreement of 4 April 1990, is "to end the armed conflict by political means as speedily as possible, promote the democratization of the country, guarantee unrestricted respect for human rights and reunify Salvadorian society",

*Bearing in mind* the San José, Mexico and New York Agreements of 26 July 1990, 27 April 1991 and 25 September 1991 respectively, arrived at by them in the course of the negotiating process conducted with the active participation of the Secretary-General of the United Nations and of his Representative, which Agreements form a whole with the Agreement signed today,

\* \* \*

**Chapter VII — Cessation of the Armed Conflict**

\* \* \*

3. The CAC [Cessation of Armed Conflict] consists of four elements, as defined herein:

    a. The cease-fire;

    b. The separation of forces;

    c. The end of the military structure of FMLN and the reintegration of its members, within a framework of full legality, into the civil, political and institutional life of the country;

    d. United Nations verification of all the abovementioned activities.

* * *

### The cease-fire

4. The cease-fire shall enter into force officially on D-Day.

5. As of that date, each of the parties shall, as appropriate, refrain from carrying out any hostile act or operation by means of forces or individuals under its control, meaning that neither party shall carry out any kind of attack by land, sea or air, organize patrols or offensive manoeuvres, occupy new positions, lay mines, interfere with military communications or carry out any kind of reconnaissance operations, acts of sabotage or any other military activity which, in the opinion of ONUSAL, might violate the cease-fire, or any act that infringes the rights of the civilian population.

* * *

### United Nations verification

30. The numbers of ONUSAL military and civilian personnel shall be increased to enable it to fulfill its tasks related to the agreed processes, as described in this Agreement.

31. The Secretary-General shall request the Security Council to approve this increase in the mandate and personnel of ONUSAL. He shall also request the General Assembly to provide the necessary funding from the budget. The composition by country of the military component of ONUSAL and the appointment of the commander of its military division shall be decided by the Security Council on the recommendation of the Secretary-General, who shall first consult with the two parties. In order to fulfill its new tasks effectively, ONUSAL will require, as in the other aspects of its mandate, complete freedom of movement throughout the territory of El Salvador.

32. To facilitate the application of this Agreement, a joint working group shall be set up immediately after the Agreement has been signed. The working group shall consist of the ONUSAL Chief Military Observer, as Chairman, and one representative from each of the parties. The members of the working group may be accompanied by the necessary advisers. The Chairman of the working group shall convene its meetings on his own initiative or at the request of either or both of the parties.

### Chapter VIII — United Nations Verification

1. The United Nations shall verify compliance with this Agreement and with the San José, Mexico City and New York Agreements of 26 July 1990, 27 April 1991 and 25 September 1991, respectively, with the cooperation of the Parties and of the authorities whose duty it is to enforce them.

2. The international cooperation referred to in this Agreement shall be coordinated by the United Nations and shall be subject to a formal application by the Government, compliance with official formalities and the appropriate consultations.

* * *

## *Authors' Note*

**Nagorno-Karabakh:** The conflict in Nagorno-Karabakh has been ongoing for over twenty-five years. The dispute, between ethnic Armenians in Azerbaijan and Armenia, began before the fall of the Soviet Union in 1988. Intense international pressure, along with heavy involvement of various international organizations, has failed to fully end the conflict. The following six materials (15, 16, 17, 18, 19, and 20) deal with the conflict in Nagorno-Karabakh. Note that the parties to the conflict neither accepted nor signed the proposals contained in materials 17, 18, and 19.

## 15. United States Department of State, Nagorno-Karabakh
### Background Note

The current conflict over Nagorno-Karabakh began in 1988 when ethnic Armenian demonstrations against Azerbaijani rule broke out in both Nagorno-Karabakh and Armenia, and the Nagorno-Karabakh Supreme Soviet voted to secede from Azerbaijan. In 1990, after violent episodes ... the Soviet Union's Government in Moscow declared a state of emergency in Nagorno-Karabakh, sent troops to the region, and forcibly occupied Baku. Azerbaijan declared its independence from the U.S.S.R. on August 30, 1991. In September 1991, Moscow declared it would no longer support Azerbaijani military action in Nagorno-Karabakh. Armenian militants then stepped up the violence. In October 1991, a referendum in Nagorno-Karabakh approved independence.

More than 30,000 people were killed in the fighting from 1992 to 1994. In May 1992, Armenian and Karabakhi forces seized Shusha (the historical Azerbaijani-populated capital of Nagorno-Karabakh) and Lachin (thereby linking Nagorno-Karabakh to Armenia). By October 1993, Armenian and Karabakhi forces controlled almost all of Nagorno-Karabakh, Lachin, and large adjacent areas in southwestern Azerbaijan. As Armenian and Karabakhi forces advanced, hundreds of thousands of Azerbaijani refugees fled to other parts of Azerbaijan. In 1993, the U.N. Security Council adopted resolutions calling for the cessation of hostilities, unimpeded access for international humanitarian relief efforts, and the eventual deployment of a peacekeeping force in the region. The U.N. also called for immediate withdrawal of all occupying forces from the occupied areas of Azerbaijan. Fighting continued, however, until May 1994 when Russia brokered a cease-fire.

Negotiations to resolve the conflict peacefully have been ongoing since 1992 under the aegis of the Minsk Group of the OSCE. The Minsk Group is currently co-chaired by Russia, France, and the U.S. and has representation from several European nations, Armenia, and Azerbaijan. Despite the 1994 cease-fire, sporadic violation, sniper fire, and landmine incidents [have claimed] many lives.

Since 1997, the Minsk Group Co-Chairs have presented a number of proposals to serve as a framework for resolving the conflict. One side or the other rejected each of those proposals, but negotiations have continued at an intensified pace since 2004. In November 2007 ... representatives of the three Co-Chair countries presented the sides with a proposal on the "Basic Principles for the peaceful settlement of the Nagorno-Karabakh conflict." In 2008, Azerbaijani President Aliyev and Armenian President Serzh Sargsian met twice, in June in St. Petersburg and in November in Moscow. After the Moscow talks, the two Presidents signed a declaration expressing their intent to seek a political settlement to the conflict, to resume confidence-building measures, and to intensify negotiations within the Minsk Group framework on the basis of the Madrid proposal. The Co-Chairs have continued their intensive consultations with the sides to narrow differences on the revised Basic Principles, including through three meetings between the Presidents of Armenia and Azerbaijan in 2010. In December 2010, the Armenian and Azerbaijani Presidents, along with the heads of delegation of the Minsk Group Co-Chair countries, issued a joint statement during the OSCE Summit in Astana, acknowledging the need for more decisive efforts to resolve the Nagorno-Karabakh conflict and reaffirming their commitment to seek a final settlement based on the principles and norms of international law; the United Nations Charter; the Helsinki Final Act; and previous joint statements by the Presidents of the Minsk Group Co-Chair countries.

## 16. Office for Security and Cooperation in Europe, Budapest Declaration: Toward a Genuine Partnership in a New Era
### Parliamentary Assembly, 1994

* * *

**Intensification of CSCE action in relation to the Nagorno-Karabakh conflict**

1. Deploring the continuation of the conflict and the human tragedy involved, the participating States welcomed the confirmation by the parties to the conflict of the ceasefire agreed on 12 May 1994 through the mediation of the Russian Federation in cooperation with the CSCE Minsk Group. They confirmed their commitment to the relevant resolutions of the United Nations Security Council and welcomed the political support given by the Security Council to the CSCE's efforts towards a peaceful settlement of the conflict. To this end they called on the parties to the conflict to enter into intensified substantive talks, including direct contacts. In this context, they pledged to redouble the efforts and assistance by the CSCE. They strongly endorsed the mediation efforts of the CSCE Minsk Group and expressed appreciation for the crucial contribution of the Russian Federation and the efforts by other individual members of the Minsk Group. They agreed to harmonize these into a single co-coordinated effort within the framework of the CSCE.

2. To this end, they have directed the Chairman-in-Office, in consultation with the participating States and acting as soon as possible, to name co-chairmen of the Minsk Conference to ensure a common and agreed basis for negotiations and to realize full co-ordination in all mediation and negotiation activities. The co-chairmen, guided in all of their negotiating efforts by CSCE principles and an agreed mandate, will jointly chair meetings of the Minsk Group and jointly report to the Chairman-in-Office. They will regularly brief the Permanent Council on the progress of their work.

3. As a first step in this effort, they directed the co-chairmen of the Minsk Conference to take immediate steps to promote, with the support and cooperation of the Russian Federation and other individual members of the Minsk Group, the continuation of the existing ceasefire and, drawing upon the progress already achieved in previous mediation activities, to conduct speedy negotiations for the conclusion of a political agreement on the cessation of the armed conflict, the implementation of which will eliminate major consequences of the conflict for all parties and permit the convening of the Minsk Conference. They further requested the co-chairmen of the Minsk Conference to continue working with the parties towards further implementation of confidence-building measures, particularly in the humanitarian field. They underlined the need for participating States to take action, both individually and within relevant international organizations, to pro-

vide humanitarian assistance to the people of the region with special emphasis on alleviating the plight of refugees.

4. They agreed that, in line with the view of the parties to the conflict, the conclusion of the agreement mentioned above would also make it possible to deploy multinational peacekeeping forces as an essential element for the implementation of the agreement itself. They declared their political will to provide, with an appropriate resolution from the United Nations Security Council, a multinational CSCE peacekeeping force following agreement among the parties for cessation of the armed conflict. They requested the Chairman-in-Office to develop as soon as possible a plan for the establishment, composition and operations of such a force, organized on the basis of Chapter III of the Helsinki Document 1992 and in a manner fully consistent with the Charter of the United Nations. To this end the Chairman-in-Office will be assisted by the co-chairmen of the Minsk Conference and by the Minsk Group, and be supported by the Secretary General; after appropriate consultations he will also establish a high-level planning group in Vienna to make recommendations on, *inter alia*, the size and characteristics of the force, command and control, logistics, allocation of units and resources, rules of engagement and arrangements with contributing States. He will seek the support of the United Nations on the basis of the stated United Nations readiness to provide technical advice and expertise. He will also seek continuing political support from the United Nations Security Council for the possible deployment of a CSCE peacekeeping force.

5. On the basis of such preparatory work and the relevant provisions of Chapter III of the Helsinki Document 1992, and following agreement and a formal request by the parties to the Chairman-in-Office through the co-chairmen of the Minsk Conference, the Permanent Council will take a decision on the establishment of the CSCE peacekeeping operation.

\* \* \*

# 17. Conference on Security and Cooperation in Europe Parliamentary Assembly, Comprehensive Agreement to Resolve the Nagorno-Karabakh Conflict, Package Deal

### Minsk Group Proposal, 1997

**Comprehensive agreement on the resolution of the Nagorno-Karabakh conflict**

**Co-Chairs of the Minsk Group of the OSCE**

**Preamble:**

The Sides, recognizing fully the advantages of peace and cooperation in the region for the flourishing and wellbeing of their peoples, express their determination to achieve a peaceful resolution of the prolonged Nagorno Karabakh conflict. The resolution laid out below will create a basis for the joint economic development of the Caucasus, giving the peoples of this region the possibility of living a normal and productive life under democratic institutions, promoting wellbeing and a promising future. Cooperation in accordance with the present Agreement will lead to normal relations in the field of trade, transport and communications throughout the region, giving people the opportunity to restore, with the assistance of international organizations, their towns and villages, to create the stability necessary for a substantial increase in external capital investment in the region, and to open the way to mutually beneficial trade, leading to the achievement of natural development for all peoples, the basis for which exists in the Caucasus region.

Conciliation and cooperation between peoples will release their enormous potential to the benefit of their neighbours and other peoples of the world.

In accordance with these wishes, the Sides, being subject to the provisions of the U.N. Charter, the basic principles and decisions of the OSCE and universally recognized norms of international law, and expressing their determination to support the full implementation of U.N. Security Council Resolutions 822, 853, 874 and 884, agree herewith to implement the measures laid out in Agreement I in order to put an end to armed hostilities and re-establish normal relations, and to reach an agreement on the final status of Nagorno Karabakh, as laid out in Agreement II.

**Agreement I — The end of armed hostilities**

The Sides agree:

\* \* \*

IV. To cooperate with the deployment of international OSCE peacekeeping forces in the buffer zone in order to guarantee security in conjunction with the Permanent Joint Commission. OSCE peacekeeping forces will consist of forces appointed by the OSCE, whose mandate will be defined by U.N. Security Council resolution and renewed on the recommendation of the OSCE Chairman-in-Office.

\* \* \*

VI. That simultaneously with the withdrawal of armed forces measures will be implemented aimed at the restoration of roads, railways, electricity transmission lines and connections, trade and other relations, including any other actions implied in the achievement of these goals. The Sides guarantee the free use of these connections for all, including ethnic minorities, and guarantee the latter access to their ethnic groups located in other parts of the region. Each Side pledges to remove all blockades and to allow the passage of goods and people to all other Sides. Armenia and Azerbaijan guarantee the free and safe rail connection between their territories, including the Baku-Horadiz-Meghri-Ordubad-Nakhichevan-Yerevan route.

VII. To cooperate with the International Committee of the Red Cross and the United Nations High Commission for Refugees and other international humanitarian organizations to secure the return of all persons detained as a result of the conflict, ascertainment of the fate of those disappeared without trace and the repatriation of all remains.

\* \* \*

X. To establish a Permanent Joint Commission (PJC) to observe the implementation of measures foreseen in the present Agreement addressing the problems of Azerbaijan and Nagorno Karabakh. The PJC has three co-chairs: one Azerbaijani, one from Nagorno Karabakh and one representative of the Chairman-in-Office of the OSCE. The implementation of the Agreement forms the principal responsibility of the Azerbaijani and Nagorno Karabakh co-chairs; mediation and arbitration in case of dispute forms the main responsibility of the OSCE co-Chair. The PJC has the following sub-commissions: military, economic, humanitarian and cultural. The functions of the PJC and its sub-commissions are laid out in Appendix II.

\* \* \*

XII. To establish a Bilateral Armenian-Azerbaijani Commission (BAAC), with one co-chair from the Republic of Armenia and one from the Republic of Azerbaijan. The Chairman-in-Office of the OSCE will be represented in this commission. The BAAC will work to prevent border incidents and will maintain links between the border forces and other corresponding security forces of both countries, and will observe the implementation of measures to open roads, railways, communications, pipelines, trade and other relations.

XIII. The United Nations Security Council is the guarantor of the present Agreement.

XIV. The present Agreement will remain in force until the conclusion at the OSCE Minsk Conference of a comprehensive peace agreement, which will, in part, establish permanent security and peacekeeping mechanisms replacing those foreseen in the present Agreement.

\* \* \*

### Agreement II — Status

\* \* \*

### Confidence building measures for the Nagorno Karabakh Conflict

As a demonstration of their will to achieve a peaceful settlement of the conflict the Sides may implement, without expectation of any further agreement, any or all of the following measures for the enhancement of trust and security:

\* \* \*

B. The Sides may agree on an increase in the OSCE Chairman-in-Office's observer mission, in order to implement additional monitoring in connection with Nagorno Karabakh, for example along the Armenian-Azerbaijani border in the Ijevan-Kazakh sector;

C. Dialogue with the assistance of the U.N. High Commissioner on Refugees and the International Committee of the Red Cross (ICRC) in order to assess humanitarian needs (for both displaced Azerbaijani populations and within Nagorno Karabakh itself). This could be implemented in agreement with either the U.N. High Commissioner or the ICRC;

\* \* \*

# 18. Organization for Security and Cooperation in Europe, Agreement on the End of the Nagorno-Karabakh Conflict, Step-by-Step Deal
## Minsk Group Proposal, 1997

### Agreement on the end of the Nagorno Karabakh armed conflict

\* \* \*

I. The Sides reject the use of force or the threat of the use of force as a means of settling disputes between them. They will resolve disputes, including such disputes as may arise in connection with the implementation of the present Agreement, by peaceful means, in the first instance by means of negotiations, including negotiations within the framework of the Minsk Process of the OSCE.

II. The Sides withdraw their armed forces in accordance with the following provisions and the detailed discussion in Appendix 1:

A. In the first phase armed forces currently situated along the line of contact to the east and south of Nagorno Karabakh will be withdrawn to the line shown in Appendix 1 and in accordance with the timetable indicated in it, taking into due consideration the recommendations of the High Level Planning Group (HLPG), with the aim of making possible an initial deployment of multinational OSCE divisions in a militarily secure buffer zone, the separation of the Sides along this line and to guarantee security conditions for the second phase of withdrawal.

\* \* \*

IV. In accordance with the decisions of the OSCE Budapest summit of 1994 the Sides invite and will assist with the deployment of multinational OSCE peacekeeping forces (PKF), which will work together with the Permanent Joint Commission (PJC) and the Armenian-Azerbaijani intergovernmental commission (AAIC) stipulated in Article 7. The PKF observes the withdrawal of armed forces and heavy weaponry, the prohibition of military flights, support of the demilitarization regime and the situation on the Armenian-Azerbaijani border, as laid out in Appendix 2. The Sides call upon the U.N. Security Council to adopt a resolution appropriate to these objectives for an initial period of not more than one year and to renew the status of this resolution according to necessity as determined by the recommendations of the OSCE Chairman-in-Office. The Sides agree that the overall duration of the peacekeeping mission will be the minimum necessary relative to the situation in the region and the pace of the wider resolution of the conflict. The Sides fully cooperate with the PKF, in order to guarantee the implementation of the present Agreement and to avoid any disruption or interruption of peacekeeping operations.

\* \* \*

IX. The Sides without delay establish a Permanent Joint Commission (PJC) to observe the implementation of the provisions envisaged in the present Agreement relating to the problems affecting Azerbaijan and Nagorno Karabakh. The chair of the PJC is a representative of the Chairman-in-Office of the OSCE, working with one vice-president from Azerbaijan and one vice-president from Nagorno Karabakh. The principal obligation of the PJC is to observe the implementation of the Agreement; the obligations of the OSCE Chair likewise include mediation in cases of disagreement and the sanctioning of measures taken to deal with emergency situations, such as natural disasters. The PJC has sub-commissions for military, economic, humanitarian, cultural and communications affairs. The structure, functions and other details concerning the PJC are laid out in Appendix 4.

The Sides establish without delay an Armenian-Azerbaijani Intergovernmental Commission (AAIC) in order to avoid border incidents between Armenia and Azerbaijan, the conduct of communications between border forces and other security forces of both countries and the monitoring and assistance of measures to open roads, railways, communications, pipelines, trade and other relations. The AAIC has two co-chairs, one from Armenia and one from Azerbaijan. A representative appointed by the Chairman-in-Office of the OSCE forms part of the Commission. The structure, functions and other details concerning the AAIC are laid out in Appendix 5. The Azerbaijan Republic and the Republic of Armenia establish communications offices in each other's capital cities.

\* \* \*

XI. The three Sides in the present Agreement, having thus put an end to the military aspects of the conflict, agree to continue the conduct of negotiations in good faith and with the assistance of the Minsk Conference co-Chairs and other Sides invited as appropriate by the Chairman-in-Office of the OSCE, aimed at the urgent achievement of a comprehensive settlement for other aspects of the conflict, including political aspects such as the determination of the status of Nagorno Karabakh and the resolution of the problems posed in Lachin, Shusha and Shaumian; following the attainment of an agreement at

these negotiations and its signing by the three above-mentioned Sides, it would be subject to recognition by the international community at the Minsk Conference, to be convened as soon as possible.

* * *

XIII. In addition to the concrete provisions concerning peacekeeping and the monitoring of military withdrawal laid out above, and recalling the corresponding principles and
obligations of the OSCE, including those expressed in the Helsinki document of 1992
and the Budapest document of 1994, using the appropriate mechanisms the OSCE observes the complete implementation of all aspects of the current Agreement and takes
appropriate steps in accordance with these principles and decisions to avoid the violation of the conditions laid down in the present Agreement and opposition to it. Witnesses
of the present Agreement, acting through the offices of the Permanent Council of the
OSCE and the United Nations Security Council, assist in its complete implementation.
In case of serious violation of the present Agreement they consult among themselves regarding necessary measures to be taken, inform without delay the Chairman-in-Office
of the OSCE, the Chair of the United Nations Security Council and the Secretary-General
of the United Nations, and request that the OSCE Permanent Council or the U.N. Security Council consider appropriate measures in this regard.

* * *

## 19. Organization for Security and Cooperation in Europe, On the Principles for a Comprehensive Agreement to Settlement of the Armed Conflict over Nagorno-Karabakh, Common State Deal

### Minsk Group Proposal, 1998

**On the principles for a comprehensive settlement of the armed conflict over Nagorno
Karabakh**

Firmly resolved to realize the peaceful settlement of the Nagorno Karabakh conflict in
accordance with the norms and principles of international law, including the principles
of the territorial integrity of states and the self-determination of peoples, Armenia, Azerbaijan and Nagorno Karabakh agree the following:

* * *

In case of disputes or disagreements not overcome within the framework of the Joint
Committee, the Sides may call for the consultative opinion of the OSCE Chairman-in-
Office, which will be taken into consideration before the adoption of a final decision.

The status of Nagorno Karabakh will also include the rights and privileges listed below
in the formulations used in the Agreement on the Status of Nagorno Karabakh, approved
by the Minsk Conference.

* * *

### III. Concerning the towns of Shusha and Shaumian

The Sides agree that all Azerbaijani refugees may return to their former places of permanent residence in the town of Shusha. The appropriate authorities of Nagorno Karabakh
will guarantee their security. They will enjoy equal rights with all other citizens of Nagorno
Karabakh, including the right to form political parties, to participate in elections at all lev-

els, to be elected to state legislative bodies and institutions of local government, and to work in official posts including those in law enforcement agencies.

Armenian refugees returning to the town of Shaumian will enjoy the same rights.

Inhabitants of the towns of Shusha and Shaumian will have guaranteed access by roads, communications and other means with other parts of Azerbaijan and Nagorno Karabakh.

The authorities in Nagorno Karabakh and Azerbaijan will cooperate with the deployment and activities in the towns of Shusha and Shaumian respectively of representative offices of the Office for Democratic Institutions and Human Rights of the OSCE.

The agreement on the status of Nagorno Karabakh will be signed by the three Sides and come into force after its approval by the Minsk Conference.

## IV. Agreement on Ending the Armed Conflict

The Sides agree that the Agreement on Ending the Armed Conflict will include the following provisions:

I. The Sides agree to reject the use of force or the threat of the use of force to resolve disputes between them. They resolve all such conflicts, including those that may arise in connection with the implementation of the Agreement on Ending the Armed Conflict by peaceful means, in the first instance through direct negotiations or within the framework of the OSCE Minsk Process.

\* \* \*

IV. In accordance with the decisions of the OSCE Budapest summit of 1994 the Sides invite and assist in the deployment of multinational OSCE peacekeeping forces (PKF), which will work in conjunction with the Permanent Joint Commission (PJC) and the Armenian-Azerbaijani Intergovernmental Commission (AAIC). The PKF observes the withdrawal of armed forces and heavy weaponry, the prohibition of military flights, support of the demilitarization regime and the situation on the Armenian-Azerbaijani border, as set out in Appendix 2.

The peacekeeping mission is established in accordance with an appropriate resolution of the U.N. Security Council for an initial period of not more than one year and is renewed as required on the recommendation of the Chairman-in-Office of the OSCE. The Sides agree that the overall duration of the peacekeeping mission will be the minimum necessary relative to the situation in the region and the pace of the wider resolution of the conflict. The Sides fully cooperate with the PKF, in order to guarantee the implementation of the present Agreement and to avoid any disruption or interruption of peacekeeping operations.

\* \* \*

XII. In addition to the concrete provisions concerning peacekeeping and the monitoring of military withdrawal laid out above, and recalling the corresponding principles and obligations of the OSCE, including those expressed in the Helsinki document of 1992 and the Budapest document of 1994, using the appropriate mechanisms the OSCE observes the complete implementation of all aspects of the current Agreement and takes appropriate steps in accordance with these principles and decisions to avoid the violation of the conditions laid down in the present Agreement and opposition to it.

XIII. The Agreement on Ending the Armed Conflict will be signed by the three Sides and will come into effect after its approval by the Minsk Conference and ratification by the Parliaments of the three Sides.

\* \* \*

## V. On Guarantees

* * *

2. The U.N. Security Council will follow closely the implementation of the comprehensive agreement.

3. The Agreement on the Status of Nagorno Karabakh and the Agreement on Ending the Armed Conflict may be signed by the Minsk Conference co-Chairs as witnesses. The presidents of Russia, the United States and France affirm the intention of their three countries to act together to ensure the thorough monitoring of progress in the implementation of agreements and the adoption of the appropriate measures for the fulfilment of this Agreement. In case of need, the OSCE or the U.N. Security Council may take diplomatic, economic or, in the last instance, military measures in accordance with the U.N. Charter.

---

# 20. Resolution 1416

## Council of Europe, 2005

**The conflict over the Nagorno-Karabakh region dealt with by the OSCE Minsk Conference**

1. The Parliamentary Assembly regrets that, more than a decade after the armed hostilities started, the conflict over the Nagorno-Karabakh region remains unsolved. Hundreds of thousands of people are still displaced and live in miserable conditions. Considerable parts of the territory of Azerbaijan are still occupied by Armenian forces, and separatist forces are still in control of the Nagorno-Karabakh region.

2. The Assembly expresses its concern that the military action, and the widespread ethnic hostilities which preceded it, led to large-scale ethnic expulsion and the creation of mono-ethnic areas which resemble the terrible concept of ethnic cleansing. The Assembly reaffirms that independence and secession of a regional territory from a state may only be achieved through a lawful and peaceful process based on the democratic support of the inhabitants of such territory and not in the wake of an armed conflict leading to ethnic expulsion and the de facto annexation of such territory to another state. The Assembly reiterates that the occupation of foreign territory by a member state constitutes a grave violation of that state's obligations as a member of the Council of Europe and reaffirms the right of displaced persons from the area of conflict to return to their homes safely and with dignity.

3. The Assembly recalls Resolutions 822 (1993), 853 (1993), 874 (1993) and 884 (1993) of the United Nations Security Council and urges the parties concerned to comply with them, in particular by refraining from any armed hostilities and by withdrawing military forces from any occupied territories. The Assembly also aligns itself with the demand expressed in Resolution 853 of the United Nations Security Council and thus urges all member states to refrain from the supply of any weapons and munitions which might lead to an intensification of the conflict or the continued occupation of territory.

4. The Assembly recalls that both Armenia and Azerbaijan committed themselves upon their accession to the Council of Europe in January 2001 to use only peaceful means for settling the conflict, by refraining from any threat of using force against their neighbours. At the same time, Armenia committed itself to use its considerable influence over Nagorno-Karabakh to foster a solution to the conflict. The Assembly urges both governments to comply with these commitments and refrain from using armed forces against each other and from propagating military action.

5. The Assembly recalls that the Council of Ministers of the Conference on Security and Cooperation in Europe (CSCE) agreed in Helsinki in March 1992 to hold a conference in Minsk in order to provide a forum for negotiations for a peaceful settlement of the conflict. Armenia, Azerbaijan, Belarus, the former Czech and Slovak Federal Republic, France, Germany, Italy, the Russian Federation, Sweden, Turkey and the United States of America agreed at that time to participate in this conference. The Assembly calls on these states to step up their efforts to achieve the peaceful resolution of the conflict and invites their national delegations to the Assembly to report annually to the Assembly on the action of their government in this respect. For this purpose, the Assembly asks its Bureau to create an ad hoc committee comprising, *inter alia*, the heads of these national delegations.

6. The Assembly pays tribute to the tireless efforts of the co-chairs of the Minsk Group and the Personal Representative of the OSCE Chairman-in-Office, in particular for having achieved a ceasefire in May 1994 and having constantly monitored the observance of this ceasefire since then. The Assembly calls on the OSCE Minsk Group co-chairs to take immediate steps to conduct speedy negotiations for the conclusion of a political agreement on the cessation of the armed conflict. The implementation of this agreement will eliminate major consequences of the conflict for all parties and permit the convening of the Minsk Conference. The Assembly calls on Armenia and Azerbaijan to make use of the OSCE Minsk Process and to put forward to each other, via the Minsk Group, their constructive proposals for the peaceful settlement of the conflict in accordance with the relevant norms and principles of international law.

7. The Assembly recalls that Armenia and Azerbaijan are signatory parties to the Charter of the United Nations and, in accordance with Article 93, paragraph 1 of the Charter, ipso facto parties to the statute of the International Court of Justice. Therefore, the Assembly suggests that if the negotiations under the auspices of the co-chairs of the Minsk Group fail, Armenia and Azerbaijan should consider using the International Court of Justice in accordance with Article 36, paragraph 1 of its statute.

* * *

12. The Assembly calls on the Secretary General of the Council of Europe to draw up an action plan for support to Armenia and Azerbaijan targeted at mutual reconciliation processes, and to take this resolution into account in deciding on action concerning Armenia and Azerbaijan.

13. The Assembly calls on the Congress of Local and Regional Authorities of the Council of Europe to assist locally elected representatives of Armenia and Azerbaijan in establishing mutual contacts and interregional co-operation.

14. The Assembly resolves to analyse the conflict-settlement mechanisms existing within the Council of Europe, in particular the European Convention for the Peaceful Settlement of Disputes, in order to provide its member states with better mechanisms for the peaceful settlement of bilateral conflicts as well as internal disputes involving local or regional territorial communities or authorities which may endanger human rights, stability and peace.

* * *

## Authors' Note

**Darfur:** The conflict in Darfur, Sudan has caused over 300,000 deaths and displaced at least 2.5 million people. The conflict dates back to 2003, when the war broke out between the government of Sudan's militia, called the Janjaweed, and other rebel forces. Many atrocities, including genocide and rape as a tool of warfare, have called the world's attention to the region. With increasing global attention focused on the conflict in Darfur, many international organizations have become involved. First among them, the U.N. and the A.U. decided to unite their efforts by creating a joint/hybrid A.U./U.N. peace-keeping operation in Darfur and creating a joint A.U./U.N. Chief Mediator for Darfur.

**Joint A.U./U.N. Chief Mediator for Darfur:** The A.U./U.N. Chief Mediator position is a unique post created out of the conflict in Darfur. Beyond the peace-keeping operations of the United Nations in Darfur, the A.U. and the U.N. joined together to create a hybrid peace-keeping force. As a separate development, but still with the major goal of ending the conflict, the United Nations and the African Union created a hybrid mediation force. As is often the case, international organizations are forced to adapt, reorganize, and re-focus depending on the unique situation on the ground. Here two organizations, the U.N. and A.U., with unique interests in ending the conflict in Darfur, came together to create a hybrid mediation team to focus their efforts on a successful peace process in addition to having forces on the ground to keep the peace.

From A.U./U.N. negotiations and their mutual effort to stop the violence in the region, an A.U./U.N. mediation team was created. After cooperation on the creation of a Joint Mediation Support Team, the United Nations Security Council Resolution 1769 authorized the creation UNAMID, an A.U./U.N. Hybrid operation to act as a peace keeping force in Darfur. This gave teeth to the A.U./U.N. efforts.

The following document is a road-map for peace in Darfur created by the A.U. Special Envoy Salim Ahmed Salim and the U.N. Special Envoy Jan Eliasson. This statement was issued a little over a month before the Security Council created the A.U./U.N. Hybrid operation through Resolution 1769.

---

## 21. Joint A.U.-U.N. Road-Map for Darfur Political Process
### 2007

On the basis of the Addis Ababa conclusions of 16 November 2007, A.U. and U.N. Special Envoys, Salim Ahmed and Jan Eliasson, have been working closely together and consulted with the parties and a wide range of stakeholders on how to end the Darfur conflict.

The Tripoli Consensus on the political process for Darfur adopted on 29 April 2007 underlined the urgency of finding a comprehensive and sustainable solution to the crisis. Recognizing the value of regional initiatives, the meeting agreed on the need for coordination and convergence of all initiatives under the A.U.-U.N. lead.

There is consensus that priority must be given to an all-inclusive political process, under A.U. and U.N. leadership. Progress on the political track must be accompanied by an end to widespread violence and insecurity, a strengthened ceasefire supported by an effective peacekeeping force, as well as an improvement in the humanitarian situation and serious prospects for socio-economic recovery in Darfur.

**This roadmap for the political process consists of three phases: Convergence of Initiatives and Consultations; Pre-Negotiations; and Negotiations.**

As a point of departure for the implementation of the road-map, the A.U. and U.N. expect all parties to declare their serious commitment to:

   – achieve a political solution to the Darfur crisis;

   – create a security environment in Darfur conducive to negotiations;

   – participate in and commit to the outcome of the negotiation effort;

– cease all hostilities immediately.

It is expected that the A.U. Peace and Security Council and the U.N. Security Council hold all parties accountable to these commitments, with the understanding that obstruction to the peace process will have consequences.

The A.U. and U.N. will consult closely with regional actors to ensure exchange of information, coordination and collaboration. The Special Envoys will also utilize the Tripoli format, to ensure maximum coherence and convergence of national, regional and international efforts. The international community's support to the implementation of this road-map will be coordinated through the A.U. and U.N..

The A.U.-U.N. Joint Mediation Support Team (JMST) will support the Special Envoys in the implementation of this roadmap and provide technical and professional backstopping to the process. The team is being strengthened and JMST staff is being deployed in Khartoum and Darfur to ensure access to all parties to the conflict and be able to undertake extensive contacts with the non-signatories, regional actors and other stakeholders. Mediation and thematic experts on key issues and on logistics will be recruited to support the ongoing efforts.

The JMST will design and implement an effective communication strategy utilizing local, regional and international media and stakeholders to broaden information-sharing on the political process and to build a constituency of support for its outcome.

## I. Convergence of Initiatives and Consultations Phase (May–June 2007)

The A.U. and U.N. will work with all national, regional and international actors to ensure that all initiatives currently underway converge and are integrated within the broader A.U.-U.N. framework by the end of June. Simultaneously, the A.U. and U.N. will continue extensive consultations on the political process and parties' positions with all stakeholders inside and outside Sudan. To this end, the A.U. and U.N. will:

* * *

iii. Work closely together with non-government organizations which have expertise and capacity to contribute to the political process.

* * *

vi. Develop a Negotiation Strategy, incorporating lessons learned from the Abuja talks. This strategy will take into consideration the parties' positions and devise a methodology to include also concerns/views of those who were not represented in the Abuja negotiations.

* * *

## II. Pre-Negotiation Phase (June–July 2007)

* * *

Simultaneously, the A.U.-U.N. will continue and finalize consultations with the Government of Sudan, signatories and non-signatories, civil society, tribal leaders and representatives of IDPs, refugees and women's groups. This process will further refine the Negotiation Strategy including the development of a mechanism to channel views and positions into the final talks. The following actions will be pursued:

i. Enhance cohesion among the parties and broaden the base of support for a political solution to the crisis;

ii. Determine the basic parameters of parties' positions vis-à-vis existing agreements, and ascertain the parties' core grievances and positions on key issues, including power-sharing, wealth-sharing and security arrangements.

iii. Intensify engagement between the signatories, non-signatories and the Government of Sudan on the substance of the renewed talks, with the aim of narrowing gaps on divergent positions.

\* \* \*

vi. Engage key regional actors to reinforce the complementarity of efforts, collaborate and ensure all support to the political process in Darfur is coordinated within the broader A.U.-U.N. framework.

**III. Negotiation Phase (August 2007)**

\* \* \*

The political process and any ensuing agreement will be supported by the envisaged A.U.-U.N. hybrid peacekeeping operation which will be mandated to verify compliance and the implementation of all agreed commitments, as well as to and contribute to the restoration of security and protection of the population of Darfur.

\* \* \*

## Authors' Note

**Kosovo:** The Kosovo Conflict occurred between the forces from the Former Yugoslavia and Kosovo Liberation Army ("KLA"). Ethnic Albanians from Kosovo began an armed military campaign against Yugoslavian and Serbian forces. In March 1999, after Serbia refused to sign the peace treaty at the Rambouillet Conference and the talks fell apart, NATO forces undertook a humanitarian intervention in Yugoslavia. On June 10, 1999, the United Nations Security Council passed resolution 1244, which created a U.N. mission, The United Nations Interim Administration Mission in Kosovo (UNMIK). UNMIK was given the broad authority to govern Kosovo.

The peace process in Rambouillet was mediated by an eclectic collection of people and organizations. Although it was never signed or adopted, the Rambouillet Agreement is an example of the roles that various organizations play as mediators. Additionally, resolution 1244 resulted in the creation of a special mission supported by numerous international organizations. The documents below, 22 and 23, are excerpts of the unsigned Rambouillet Agreement and of Security Council Resolution 1244. Note the numerous international organizations involved and their various roles.

## 22. Rambouillet Agreement, Interim Agreement for Peace and Self-Government in Kosovo

### 1999

**Interim Agreement for Peace and Self-Government in Kosovo**

The Parties to the present Agreement,

<u>Convinced</u> of the need for a peaceful and political solution in Kosovo as a prerequisite for stability and democracy,

\* \* \*

<u>Recognizing</u> the need for democratic self-government in Kosovo, including full participation of the members of all national communities in political decision-making,

\* \* \*

Have agreed as follows:

**Framework**

## Article I: Principles

\* \* \*

7. The Parties agree to cooperate fully with all international organizations working in Kosovo on the implementation of this Agreement.

## Article II: Confidence-Building Measures

*End of Use of Force*

1. Use of force in Kosovo shall cease immediately. In accordance with this Agreement, alleged violations of the cease-fire shall be reported to international observers and shall not be used to justify use of force in response.

\* \* \*

4. The Parties shall cooperate fully with all efforts by the United Nations High Commissioner for Refugees (UNHCR) and other international and non-governmental organizations concerning the repatriation and return of persons, including those organizations monitoring of the treatment of persons following their return.

*Access for International Assistance*

5. There shall be no impediments to the normal flow of goods into Kosovo, including materials for the reconstruction of homes and structures. The Federal Republic of Yugoslavia shall not require visas, customs, or licensing for persons or things for the Implementation Mission (IM), the UNHCR, and other international organizations, as well as for non-governmental organizations working in Kosovo as determined by the Chief of the Implementation Mission (CIM).

\* \* \*

## Chapter 4 A
## Humanitarian Assistance, Reconstruction and Economic Development

\* \* \*

3. The international community will provide immediate and unconditional humanitarian assistance, focusing primarily on refugees and internally displaced persons returning to their former homes. The Parties welcome and endorse the UNHCR's lead role in co-ordination of this effort, and endorse its intention, in close co-operation with the Implementation Mission, to plan an early, peaceful, orderly and phased return of refugees and displaced persons in conditions of safety and dignity.

\* \* \*

## Chapter 5
## Implementation I

## Article I: Institutions

*Implementation Mission*

1. The Parties invite the OSCE, in cooperation with the European Union, to constitute an Implementation Mission in Kosovo. All responsibilities and powers previously vested in the Kosovo Verification Mission and its Head by prior agreements shall be continued in the Implementation Mission and its Chief.

*Joint Commission*

2. A Joint Commission shall serve as the central mechanism for monitoring and coordinating the civilian implementation of this Agreement. It shall consist of the Chief of the Implementation Mission (CIM), one Federal and one Republic representative, one representative of each national community in Kosovo, the President of the Assembly, and a representative of the President of Kosovo. Meetings of the Joint Commission may be attended by other representatives of organizations specified in this Agreement or needed for its implementation.

3. The CIM shall serve as the Chair of the Joint Commission. The Chair shall coordinate and organize the work of the Joint Commission and decide the time and place of its meetings. The Parties shall abide by and fully implement the decisions of the Joint Commission. The Joint Commission shall operate on the basis of consensus, but in the event consensus cannot be reached, the Chair's decision shall be final.

4. The Chair shall have full and unimpeded access to all places, persons, and information (including documents and other records) within Kosovo that in his judgment are necessary to his responsibilities with regard to the civilian aspects of this Agreement.

*Joint Council and Local Councils*

5. The CIM may, as necessary, establish a Kosovo Joint Council and Local Councils, for informal dispute resolution and cooperation. The Kosovo Joint Council would consist of one member from each of the national communities in Kosovo. Local Councils would consist of representatives of each national community living in the locality where the Local Council is established.

## Article II: Responsibilities and Powers

1. The CIM shall:

(a) supervise and direct the implementation of the civilian aspects of this Agreement pursuant to a schedule that he shall specify;

(b) maintain close contact with the Parties to promote full compliance with those aspects of this Agreement;

(c) facilitate, as he deems necessary, the resolution of difficulties arising in connection with such implementation;

\* \* \*

2. The CIM shall also carry out other responsibilities set forth in this Agreement or as may be later agreed.

## Article III: Status of Implementation Mission

1. Implementation Mission personnel shall be allowed unrestricted movement and access into and throughout Kosovo at any time.

2. The Parties shall facilitate the operations of the Implementation Mission, including by the provision of assistance as requested with regard to transportation, subsistence, accommodation, communication, and other facilities.

3. The Implementation Mission shall enjoy such legal capacity as may be necessary for the exercise of its functions under the laws and regulations of Kosovo, the Federal Republic of Yugoslavia, and the Republic of Serbia. Such legal capacity shall include the capacity to contract, and to acquire and dispose of real and personal property.

\* \* \*

### Article V: Authority to Interpret

The CIM shall be the final authority in theater regarding interpretation of the civilian aspects of this Agreement, and the Parties agree to abide by his determinations as binding on all Parties and persons.

* * *

### Chapter 7
### Implementation II

### Article I: General Obligations

1. The Parties undertake to recreate, as quickly as possible, normal conditions of life in Kosovo and to co-operate fully with each other and with all international organizations, agencies, and non-governmental organizations involved in the implementation of this Agreement. They welcome the willingness of the international community to send to the region a force to assist in the implementation of this Agreement.

a. The United Nations Security Council is invited to pass a resolution under Chapter VII of the Charter endorsing and adopting the arrangements set forth in this Chapter, including the establishment of a multinational military implementation force in Kosovo. The Parties invite NATO to constitute and lead a military force to help ensure compliance with the provisions of this Chapter. They also reaffirm the sovereignty and territorial integrity of the Federal Republic of Yugoslavia (FRY).

b. The Parties agree that NATO will establish and deploy a force (hereinafter "KFOR") which may be composed of ground, air, and maritime units from NATO and non-NATO nations, operating under the authority and subject to the direction and the political control of the North Atlantic Council (NAC) through the NATO chain of command. The Parties agree to facilitate the deployment and operations of this force and agree also to comply fully with all the obligations of this Chapter.

c. It is agreed that other States may assist in implementing this Chapter. The Parties agree that the modalities of those States' participation will be the subject of agreement between such participating States and NATO.

2. The purposes of these obligations are as follows:

* * *

b. to provide for the support and authorization of the KFOR and in particular to authorize the KFOR to take such actions as are required, including the use of necessary force, to ensure compliance with this Chapter and the protection of the KFOR, Implementation Mission (IM), and other international organizations, agencies, and non-governmental organizations involved in the implementation of this Agreement, and to contribute to a secure environment.

* * *

## Authors' Note

The United Nations Interim Administration Mission in Kosovo: After the failure at Rambouillet and the subsequent NATO intervention, the United Nations created a special mission for Kosovo under Security Council Resolution 1244. The special mission, UNMIK, was given a broad mandate, including power to govern the territory. The following background information is from the UNMIK website.

"The mandate of the United Nations Interim Administration Mission in Kosovo (UNMIK) was established by the Security Council in its resolution 1244 (1999).

The Mission is mandated to help ensure conditions for a peaceful and normal life for all inhabitants of Kosovo and advance regional stability in the western Balkans.

The Mission is headed by the Special Representative of the Secretary-General, who enjoys civilian executive power as vested in him by the Security Council in resolution 1244 (1999).

The Special Representative ensures a coordinated approach by the international civil presence operating under UNSC resolution 1244, including the Organization for Security and Cooperation in Europe (OSCE), which retains the status of UNMIK's pillar for institution building.

The Special Representative also ensures coordination with the head of the European Union Rule of Law Mission in Kosovo (EULEX), which has operational responsibility in the area of rule of law. EULEX is deployed under Security Council resolution 1244 (1999), and operates under the overall authority of the United Nations."

---

## 23. Resolution 1244
### United Nations Security Council, 1999

*The Security Council,*

*Bearing* in mind the purposes and principles of the Charter of the United Nations, and the primary responsibility of the Security Council for the maintenance of international peace and security,

\* \* \*

*Determined* to resolve the grave humanitarian situation in Kosovo, Federal Republic of Yugoslavia, and to provide for the safe and free return of all refugees and displaced persons to their homes,

\* \* \*

*Determining* that the situation in the region continues to constitute a threat to international peace and security,

*Determined* to ensure the safety and security of international personnel and the implementation by all concerned of their responsibilities under the present resolution, and *acting* for these purposes under Chapter VII of the Charter of the United Nations,

1. *Decides* that a political solution to the Kosovo crisis shall be based on the general principles in annex 1 and as further elaborated in the principles and other required elements in annex 2;

\* \* \*

3. *Demands* in particular that the Federal Republic of Yugoslavia put an immediate and verifiable end to violence and repression in Kosovo, and begin and complete verifiable phased withdrawal from Kosovo of all military, police and paramilitary forces according to a rapid timetable, with which the deployment of the international security presence in Kosovo will be synchronized;

\* \* \*

5. *Decides* on the deployment in Kosovo, under United Nations auspices, of international civil and security presences, with appropriate equipment and personnel as required, and welcomes the agreement of the Federal Republic of Yugoslavia to such presences;

6. *Requests* the Secretary-General to appoint, in consultation with the Security Council, a Special Representative to control the implementation of the international civil presence, and further requests the Secretary-General to instruct his Special Representative to coordinate closely with the international security presence to ensure that both presences operate towards the same goals and in a mutually supportive manner;

* * *

9. *Decides* that the responsibilities of the international security presence to be deployed and acting in Kosovo will include:

* * *

(c) Establishing a secure environment in which refugees and displaced persons can return home in safety, the international civil presence can operate, a transitional administration can be established, and humanitarian aid can be delivered;
(d) Ensuring public safety and order until the international civil presence can take responsibility for this task;

* * *

(f) Supporting, as appropriate, and coordinating closely with the work of the international civil presence;

* * *

10. *Authorizes* the Secretary-General, with the assistance of relevant international organizations, to establish an international civil presence in Kosovo in order to provide an interim administration for Kosovo under which the people of Kosovo can enjoy substantial autonomy within the Federal Republic of Yugoslavia, and which will provide transitional administration while establishing and overseeing the development of provisional democratic self-governing institutions to ensure conditions for a peaceful and normal life for all inhabitants of Kosovo;

11. *Decides* that the main responsibilities of the international civil presence will include:

(a) Promoting the establishment, pending a final settlement, of substantial autonomy and self-government in Kosovo, taking full account of annex 2 and of the Rambouillet accords (S/1999/648);

(b) Performing basic civilian administrative functions where and as long as required;

(c) Organizing and overseeing the development of provisional institutions for democratic and autonomous self-government pending a political settlement, including the holding of elections;

(d) Transferring, as these institutions are established, its administrative responsibilities while overseeing and supporting the consolidation of Kosovo's local provisional institutions and other peacebuilding activities;

(e) Facilitating a political process designed to determine Kosovo's future status, taking into account the Rambouillet accords (S/1999/648);

(f) In a final stage, overseeing the transfer of authority from Kosovo's provisional institutions to institutions established under a political settlement;

(g) Supporting the reconstruction of key infrastructure and other economic reconstruction;

(h) Supporting, in coordination with international humanitarian organizations, humanitarian and disaster relief aid;

(i) Maintaining civil law and order, including establishing local police forces and meanwhile through the deployment of international police personnel to serve in Kosovo;

(j) Protecting and promoting human rights;

(k) Assuring the safe and unimpeded return of all refugees and displaced persons to their homes in Kosovo;

\* \* \*

18. *Demands* that all States in the region cooperate fully in the implementation of all aspects of this resolution;

19. *Decides* that the international civil and security presences are established for an initial period of 12 months, to continue thereafter unless the Security Council decides otherwise;

\* \* \*

### Annex 1

**Statement by the Chairman on the conclusion of the meeting of the G-8 Foreign Ministers held at the Petersberg Centre on 6 May 1999**

The G-8 Foreign Ministers adopted the following general principles on the political solution to the Kosovo crisis:

– Immediate and verifiable end of violence and repression in Kosovo;

– Withdrawal from Kosovo of military, police and paramilitary forces;

– Deployment in Kosovo of effective international civil and security presences, endorsed and adopted by the United Nations, capable of guaranteeing the achievement of the common objectives;

– Establishment of an interim administration for Kosovo to be decided by the Security Council of the United Nations to ensure conditions for a peaceful and normal life for all inhabitants in Kosovo;

– The safe and free return of all refugees and displaced persons and unimpeded access to Kosovo by humanitarian aid organizations;

– A political process towards the establishment of an interim political framework agreement providing for a substantial self-government for Kosovo, taking full account of the Rambouillet accords and the principles of sovereignty and territorial integrity of the Federal Republic of Yugoslavia and the other countries of the region, and the demilitarization of the KLA;

– Comprehensive approach to the economic development and stabilization of the crisis region.

### Annex 2

Agreement should be reached on the following principles to move towards a resolution of the Kosovo crisis:

\* \* \*

3. Deployment in Kosovo under United Nations auspices of effective international civil and security presences, acting as may be decided under Chapter VII of the Charter, capable of guaranteeing the achievement of common objectives.

4. The international security presence with substantial North Atlantic Treaty Organization participation must be deployed under unified command and control and authorized to establish a safe environment for all people in Kosovo and to facilitate the safe return to their homes of all displaced persons and refugees.

5. Establishment of an interim administration for Kosovo as a part of the international civil presence under which the people of Kosovo can enjoy substantial autonomy within the Federal Republic of Yugoslavia, to be decided by the Security Council of the United Nations. The interim administration to provide transitional administration while establishing and overseeing the development of provisional democratic self-governing institutions to ensure conditions for a peaceful and normal life for all inhabitants in Kosovo.

\* \* \*

## Authors' Note

Sri Lanka: For over twenty-five years, the government of Sri Lanka and the separatist group, the Liberation Tigers of Tamil Eelam ("LTTE"), also called the Tamil Tigers, engaged in a costly civil war. Thousands of lives were claimed in the conflict. In 2002 the government of Sri Lanka and the LTTE signed a ceasefire. Although a significant event, the ceasefire did not last and the conflict re-erupted. It finally ended in 2009 after the Sri Lankan military defeated the LTTE and assumed control of Tamil territory. The following two materials deal with the 2002 ceasefire. For historical and cultural background on the conflict see Dagmar Hellman-Rajanayagam, *Drawing in Treacle: Mediation Efforts in Sri Lanka, 1983 to 2007,* INTERNATIONALES ASIENFORUM, Vol. 40 (2009).

## 24. Ceasefire between the Government of the Democratic Socialist Republic of Sri Lanka and the Liberation Tigers of Tamil Eelam

### 2002

Preamble

The overall objective of the Government of the Democratic Socialist Republic of Sri Lanka (hereinafter referred to as the GOSL) and the Liberation Tigers of Tamil Eelam (hereinafter referred to as the LTTE) is to find a negotiated solution to the ongoing ethnic conflict in Sri Lanka.

\* \* \*

[... T]he Parties have agreed to enter into a ceasefire, refrain from conduct that could undermine the good intentions or violate the spirit of this Agreement and implement confidence-building measures as indicated in the articles below.

Article 1: Modalities of a ceasefire

The Parties have agreed to implement a ceasefire between their armed forces as follows:

1.1 A jointly agreed ceasefire between the GOSL and the LTTE shall enter into force on such date as is notified by the Norwegian Minister of Foreign Affairs in accordance with Article 4.2, hereinafter referred to as D-day.

Military operations

1.2 Neither Party shall engage in any offensive military operation. This requires the total cessation of all military action and includes, but is not limited to, such acts as:

a. The firing of direct and indirect weapons, armed raids, ambushes, assassinations, abductions, destruction of civilian or military property, sabotage, suicide missions and activities by deep penetration units;

b. Aerial bombardment;

c. Offensive naval operations.

1.3 The Sri Lankan armed forces shall continue to perform their legitimate task of safe-guarding the sovereignty and territorial integrity of Sri Lanka without engaging in offensive operations against the LTTE.

Separation of forces

\* \* \*

1.6 The Parties shall provide information to the Sri Lanka Monitoring Mission (SLMM) regarding defense localities in all areas of contention, cf. Article 3. The monitoring mission shall assist the Parties in drawing up demarcation lines at the latest by D-day + 30.

\* \* \*

1.8 Tamil paramilitary groups shall be disarmed by the GOSL by D-day + 30 at the latest. The GOSL shall offer to integrate individuals in these units under the command and disciplinary structure of the GOSL armed forces for service away from the Northern and Eastern Province.

Freedom of movement

\* \* \*

1.10 Unarmed GOSL troops shall, as of D-day + 60, be permitted unlimited passage between Jaffna and Vavunyia using the Jaffna-Kandy road (A9). The modalities are to be worked out by the Parties with the assistance of the SLMM.

1.11 The Parties agree that as of D-day individual combatants shall, on the recommendation of their area commander, be permitted, unarmed and in plain clothes, to visit family and friends residing in areas under the control of the other Party. Such visits shall be limited to six days every second month, not including the time of travel by the shortest applicable route. The LTTE shall facilitate the use of the Jaffna-Kandy road for this purpose. The Parties reserve the right to deny entry to specified military areas.

1.12 The Parties agree that as of D-day individual combatants shall, notwithstanding the two-month restriction, be permitted, unarmed and in plain clothes, to visit immediate family (i.e. spouses, children, grandparents, parents and siblings) in connection with weddings or funerals. The right to deny entry to specified military areas applies.

1.13 Fifty (50) unarmed LTTE members shall as of D-day + 30, for the purpose of political work, be permitted freedom of movement in the areas of the North and the East dominated by the GOSL. Additional 100 unarmed LTTE members shall be permitted freedom of movement as of D-day + 60. As of D-day + 90, all unarmed LTTE members shall be permitted freedom of movement in the North and the East. The LTTE members shall carry identity papers. The right of the GOSL to deny entry to specified military areas applies.

### Article 2: Measures to restore normalcy

The Parties shall undertake the following confidence-building measures with the aim of restoring normalcy for *all* inhabitants of Sri Lanka:

2.1 The Parties shall in accordance with international law abstain from hostile acts against the civilian population, including such acts as torture, intimidation, abduction, extortion and harassment.

2.2 The Parties shall refrain from engaging in activities or propagating ideas that could offend cultural or religious sensitivities. Places of worship (temples, churches, mosques and other holy sites, etc.) currently held by the forces of either of the Parties shall be vacated by D-day + 30 and made accessible to the public. Places of worship which are situated in "high security zones" shall be vacated by all armed personnel and maintained in good order by civilian workers, even when they are not made accessible to the public.

\* \* \*

2.5 The Parties shall review the security measures and the set-up of checkpoints, particularly in densely populated cities and towns, in order to introduce systems that will prevent harassment of the civilian population. Such systems shall be in place from D-day + 60.

2.6 The Parties agree to ensure the unimpeded flow of non-military goods to and from the LTTE-dominated areas with the exception of certain items as shown in Annex A. Quantities shall be determined by market demand. The GOSL shall regularly review the matter with the aim of gradually removing any remaining restrictions on non-military goods.

\* \* \*

### Article 3: The Sri Lanka Monitoring Mission

The Parties have agreed to set up an international monitoring mission to enquire into any instance of violation of the terms and conditions of this Agreement. Both Parties shall fully cooperate to rectify any matter of conflict caused by their respective sides. The mission shall conduct international verification through on-site monitoring of the fulfilment of the commitments entered into in this Agreement as follows:

3.1 The name of the monitoring mission shall be the Sri Lanka Monitoring Mission (hereinafter referred to as the SLMM).

3.2 Subject to acceptance by the Parties, the Royal Norwegian Government (hereinafter referred to as the RNG) shall appoint the Head of the SLMM (hereinafter referred to as the HoM), who shall be the final authority regarding interpretation of this Agreement.

3.3 The SLMM shall liaise with the Parties and report to the RNG.

3.4 The HoM shall decide the date for the commencement of the SLMM's operations.

3.5 The SLMM shall be composed of representatives from Nordic countries.

3.6 The SLMM shall establish a headquarters in such place as the HoM finds appropriate. An office shall be established in Colombo and in Vanni in order to liaise with the GOSL and the LTTE, respectively. The SLMM will maintain a presence in the districts of Jaffna, Mannar, Vavuniya, Trincomalee, Batticaloa and Amparai.

3.7 A local monitoring committee shall be established in Jaffna, Mannar, Vavuniya, Trincomalee, Batticaloa and Amparai. Each committee shall consist of five members, two appointed by the GOSL, two by the LTTE and one international monitor appointed by the HoM. The international monitor shall chair the committee. The GOSL and the LTTE appointees may be selected from among retired judges, public servants, religious leaders or similar leading citizens.

3.8 The committees shall serve the SLMM in an advisory capacity and discuss issues relating to the implementation of this Agreement in their respective districts, with a view to establishing a common understanding of such issues. In particular, they will seek to resolve any dispute concerning the implementation of this Agreement at the lowest possible level.

3.9 The Parties shall be responsible for the appropriate protection of and security arrangements for all SLMM members.

3.10 The Parties agree to ensure the freedom of movement of the SLMM members in performing their tasks. The members of the SLMM shall be given immediate access to areas where violations of the Agreement are alleged to have taken place. The Parties also agree to facilitate the widest possible access to such areas for the local members of the six above-mentioned committees, cf. Article 3.7.

3.11 It shall be the responsibility of the SLMM to take immediate action on any complaints made by either Party to the Agreement, and to enquire into and assist the Parties in the settlement of any dispute that might arise in connection with such complaints.

3.12 With the aim of resolving disputes at the lowest possible level, communication shall be established between commanders of the GOSL armed forces and the LTTE area leaders to enable them to resolve problems in the conflict zones.

3.13 Guidelines for the operations of the SLMM shall be established in a separate document.

**Article 4: Entry into force, amendments and termination of the Agreement**

4.1 Each Party shall notify its consent to be bound by this Agreement through a letter to the Norwegian Minister of Foreign Affairs signed by Prime Minister Ranil Wickremesinghe on behalf of the GOSL and by leader Velupillai Pirabaharan on behalf of the LTTE, respectively. The Agreement shall be initialled by each Party and enclosed in the above-mentioned letter.

4.2 The Agreement shall enter into force on such date as is notified by the Norwegian Minister of Foreign Affairs.

4.3 This Agreement may be amended and modified by mutual agreement of both Parties. Such amendments shall be notified in writing to the RNG.

4.4 This Agreement shall remain in force until notice of termination is given by either Party to the RNG. Such notice shall be given fourteen (14) days in advance of the effective date of termination.

* * *

# 25. Statement by Mr. Jan Petersen, Foreign Minister of Norway, Announcement of Sri Lanka Ceasefire

## 2002

As from 00:00 hours on 23 February 2002, a ceasefire agreement enters into force between the Government of Sri Lanka and the Liberation Tamil Tigers of Eelam (LTTE). The ceasefire document, signed by Sri Lankan Prime Minister Ranil Wickremesinghe and LTTE leader Vellipulai Prabhakaran, has been deposited with the Norwegian Government, and we have been asked to make the agreement public.

The overall objective of the parties is to find a negotiated solution to the ethnic conflict in Sri Lanka, which has cost 60,000 lives and caused widespread human suffering. The ceasefire will pave the way for further steps towards negotiations.

Through this formalized ceasefire the parties commit themselves to putting an end to the hostilities. They commit themselves to restoring normalcy for all the inhabitants of Sri Lanka, whether they are Sinhalese, Tamils, Muslims or others. And they commit themselves to accepting an international monitoring mission, led by Norway, which will conduct on-site monitoring.

Both sides have taken bold steps to conclude the ceasefire, and this agreement is a message that they are prepared to continue taking bold steps to achieve peace. They are embarking on a long road towards a political solution. It will not be easy. It will require determination and courage. The parties will face risks and uncertainties, and they will have to make hard choices. But no hardships are worse than those of conflict and bloodshed. No gains are greater than those of peace and prosperity.

On the journey to peace and prosperity, the inhabitants of Sri Lanka, and their leaders, will need the solidarity of the international community. It must mobilize political and financial support for peace and reconciliation. Norway will continue to accompany the parties in this demanding process.

I shall now provide some more detail about the ceasefire agreement.

First, it outlines the modalities of the ceasefire, including the total cessation of all offensive military operations, the separation of forces, and increased freedom of movement for unarmed troops on both sides.

Second, measures to restore normalcy for all the inhabitants of Sri Lanka—Sinhalese, Tamils, Muslims and others—putting an end to hostile acts against civilians, allowing the unimpeded flow of non-military goods, opening roads and railway lines, and a gradual easing of fishing restrictions.

Third, a small international monitoring mission, led by Norway. The mission will conduct international on-site monitoring of the fulfilment of the commitments made by the Parties. Let me underline, however, that it is up to the parties to respect the agreement and to impose sanctions on those individuals on either side who act contrary to the agreement.

\* \* \*

## 26. Bibliography of Additional Sources

- Ademola Abass, *The United Nations, The African Union and the Darfur Crisis: of Apology and Utopia*, 54 Neth. Int'l L. Rev. 415 (2007).

- Dame Margaret J. Anstee, *The Role of International Mediators in Conflicts: Lessons Learned from Angola*, 14 Cambridge Rev. Int'l Aff. 70 (2001).

- Jacob Bercovitch & Gerald Schneider, *Who Mediates? The Political Economy of International Conflict Management*, 37 J. Peace Res. 145 (2000).

- Carl Bildt, Peace Journey: The Struggle for Peace in Bosnia (1998).

- Bidisha Biswas, *Can't We Just Talk? Reputational Concerns and International Intervention in Sri Lanka and Indonesia (Aceh)*, Int'l Negotiation 14 (2009).

- Thobias Bohmelt, *The Effectiveness of Tracks of Diplomacy Strategies in Third-Party Interventions,* 47 J. Peace Res. 167 (2010).

- Terhi Hakala, *The OSCE Minsk Process: A Balance After Five Years,* 9 Helsinki Monitor 5 (1998).

- Herding Cats: Multiparty Mediation in a Complex World (Chester Crocker et. al. eds., 1999).

- Kristine Hoglund & Isak Svensson, *Damned if You Do, and Damned if You Don't: Nordic Involvement and Images of Third-Party Neutrality in Sri Lanka,* Int'l Negotiation (2008).

- Kristine Hoglund & Isak Svensson, *Should I Stay or Should I Go? Termination as a Tactic and Norwegian Mediation in Sri Lanka,* 4 Int'l Ass'n for Conflict Mgmt. & Wiley Periodicals 12 (2011).

- Kristine Hoglund & Isak Svensson, *"Sticking One's Neck Out": Reducing Mistrust in Sri Lanka's Peace Negotiations,* Negotiation J., 22 (Oct. 2006).

- David Holiday & William Stanley, *Building the Peace: Preliminary Lessons from El Salvador,* 46 J. Int'l Aff. 415 (1993).

- International State-Building After Violent Conflict: Bosnia Ten Years After Dayton (Mark Weller & Stefan Wolf eds., 2008).

- Louis Kriesberg, *Varieties of Mediating Activities and Mediators in* International Relations, Resolving International Conflicts: The Theory and Practice of Mediation (Jacob Bercovitch ed., 1996).

- Arthur S. Lall, Multilateral Negotiation and Mediation (1985).
- Tommie Sue Montgomery, *Getting to Peace in El Salvador: The Role of the U.N. Secretariat and ONUSAL,* 37 J. Interamerican Stud. & World Aff. 139 (1995).

- Resolving International Conflicts: the Theory and Practice of Mediation (Jacob Bercovitch ed., 1996).

- Alvaro de Soto and Graciana del Castillo, *Obstacles to Peacebuilding,* 94 Foreign Pol'y 69 (Spring 1994).

- U.N. Secretary-General, *The Deployment of the African Union-United Nations Hybrid Operation in Darfur: Rep. of the Secretary-General,* U.N. Doc. S/2008/304 (May 9, 2008).

- U.N. Secretary-General, *The African Union-United Nations Hybrid Operation in Darfur (UNAMID): Rep. of the Secretary-General,* U.N. Doc. S/2010/538 (Oct. 18, 2010).

- Thomas de Wall, *Remaking the Nagorno-Karabakh Peace Process,* Survival (Aug. 2010).

- Marc Weller, Contested Statehood: Kosovo's Struggle for Independence (2009).

- Marc Weller, The Crisis in Kosovo 1989–1999: From the Dissolution of Yugoslavia to Rambouillet and the Outbreak of Hostilities (1999).

- Teresa Whitfield, *The Role of the United Nations in El Salvador and Guatemala: A Preliminary Comparison, in* Comparative Peace Processes in Latin America (Cynthia Arnson ed., 1999).

# Chapter VI

# International Dispute Resolution: Arbitration

## Introduction

The purpose of this chapter is to provide a foundation for understanding the role of arbitration within the peace negotiation process. International organizations often play an important role in resolving conflicts through associated standing or ad hoc arbitral bodies. The chapter reviews the legal authority for establishing arbitral bodies and for implementing their decisions.

The use of arbitration in the peace process is a rather narrow, but expanding field. Given that peace process arbitration often involves non-state actors, this chapter will pay particular attention to the rules and procedures designed to bring non-state actors into the process of arbitration. A key question for discussion will be the utility of arbitration in the peace process—whether a formalistic legal process has a role in what is primarily a political process. The chapter will also emphasize the degree to which arbitral decisions are enforceable in the context of a peace process.

## Objectives

- To understand the basic rules and procedures applicable to the arbitration of disputes.
- To understand the potential role of arbitration in the peace process.
- To understand the political complications associated with utilizing arbitration as a part of the peace process.
- To understand the difficulty with enforcing arbitral awards given the highly politicized nature of a peace process.
- To generate ideas for improving the role of arbitral bodies in the peace process and for enhancing the enforceability of their decisions.

# Problems

Students should come to class prepared to discuss the following questions:

1.  How effective is international arbitration in ending conflict?

2.  What challenges do states face in opting for international arbitration as a means for promoting the resolution of inter-state or intra-state disputes?

3.  What are the advantages and disadvantages of engaging in arbitration during the peace process?

4.  What are the legal and political implications of arbitrating discrete issues within the context of more far reaching peace negotiations?

5.  How should an international tribunal define and execute its role when the resolution of legal issues may have political consequences?

6.  To what extent should tribunals seek to make awards politically acceptable, both to the parties to the conflict and to the international community?

7.  Should tribunals be concerned with the enforcement of politically sensitive awards or should they adhere strictly to the law?

# Simulation

Drawing from the materials in this chapter, students should come to class prepared to participate in the following simulation:

**Negotiation Simulation: Bosnia and Herzegovina:**

Roles to be assigned:

1.  Serbian Representative

2.  Croatian/Muslim Representative

3.  International Arbitrator

On February 29, 1992, the Muslim and Croatian people of Bosnia-Herzegovina voted overwhelmingly for independence from Yugoslavia. At the time of the vote, Bosnia was composed of three main ethnic groups: Slavic Muslims (forty-three percent of the population), Serbs (thirty-one percent) and Croats (seventeen percent). Although the majority of Bosnian Serbs boycotted the poll, sixty-three percent of the electorate voted in favor of independence. Upon international recognition of Bosnia-Herzegovina, the Bosnian Serbs, under the leadership of their self-styled president Radovan Karadzic proclaimed the formation of an independent "Republika Srpska" (Serbian Republic of Bosnia and Herzegovina), whose government was located in the city of Pale in south-east Bosnia. After launching attacks against the Croatian and Muslim populations, the Yugoslav National Army (JNA) and Serb insurgent forces seized control of seventy percent of Bosnia's territory. By 1995, the Muslim and Croat forces had gained back nearly fifty percent of Bosnian territory. In November of that year, both sides agreed to a peace treaty, the Dayton Accord, to end the conflict. Article V of Annex 2 of the Dayton Accords provides for binding arbitration to determine where the boundary should be drawn between the Muslim-Croat federation and the Serb Republic within the town of Brcko. Differing versions of events in Brcko have made arbitration difficult, as the Muslim and Croat population claims persecution, forced removal, and mass rape by Serbian occupiers, and the Serbs deny any claims of violence or abuse towards the Muslims and Croats.

From the Serbian perspective, argue for the division of Brcko, allowing 15,000 Muslims to move to the region and requiring 10,000 Serbians to vacate their homes. From the Muslim and Croatian perspective, argue for the return of Brcko to pre-war composition, and request compensation for the alleged murder and torture of their people. From the perspective of the arbitrators, identify possible award scenarios that would allow this zone to remain neutral. Additionally, you may consider the following potential scenario's in discussion:

    a.    The Arbitrators award $100 million to the Bosnian Muslims to compensate them for their homes, but the Bosnian Serbs refuse to pay. The Bosnian Serbs have $100 million in a bank account in Cyprus, which is a party to the New York Convention. Can the Bosnian Muslims access those funds to enforce their arbitral award. On what grounds can the Bosnian Serbs challenge enforcement of the award or access to funds in the Cyprus account?

    b.    One of the Arbitrators accepted a bribe from the Bosnian Muslims. Would this be grounds for challenging the validity of the arbitral award?

    c.    The Counsel to the Bosnian Muslims is present for the arbitration, but Counsel to the Bosnian Serbs is not, and the Arbitral Panel issues a default judgment. Would this be grounds for challenging the validity of the arbitral award. Are there any circumstances that would forgive the Counsel's absence?

    d.    One of the selected Arbitrators came down with the flu and sent a handpicked replacement to judge the Arbitration proceedings. Would this be grounds for challenging the validity of the arbitral award?

    e.    Despite overwhelming evidence for the Bosnian Serb position, the arbitration panel sides with the Bosnian Muslims. Would this be grounds for challenging the validity of the arbitral award?

    f.    The Arbitral Panel's written decision indicates a clearly erroneous interpretation of the Geneva Conventions. Would this be grounds for challenging the validity of the arbitral award?

# Materials

1. RESTATEMENT (THIRD) OF THE FOREIGN RELATIONS LAW §§ 902, 904 (1987).

2. Convention on the Recognition and Enforcement of Foreign Arbitral Awards, June 10, 1958, 330 U.N.T.S. 38.

3. General Framework Agreement for Peace in Bosnia and Herzegovina, Annex 2, art. V, Dec. 14, 1995, 35 I.L.M. 75.

4. Convention (IV) Relative to the Protection of Civilian Persons in Time of War, arts. 4, 49, Aug. 12, 1949, 75 U.N.T.S. 287.

5. Michael P. Scharf, *History of the Yugoslav Crisis, in* BALKAN JUSTICE: THE STORY BEHIND THE FIRST INTERNATIONAL WAR CRIMES TRIAL SINCE NUREMBURG, 21–30 (1997).

6. Dunja Tadic, *Brcko — Still No Closer to a Solution*, AGENCE FRANCE-PRESSE, Nov. 20, 1996.

7. Norman Cigar & Paul Williams, *Reward Serbs with Town of Brcko? Don't Do It*, CHRISTIAN SCIENCE MONITOR, Mar. 11, 1998.

8. "Final Award of the Tribunal," *Permanent Court of Arbitration*, July 22, 2009.

9. Josephine K. Mason, *The Role of Ex Aequo Et Bono in International Border Settlement: A Critique of the Sudanese Abyei Arbitration*, 20 AM. REV. INT'L ARB. 519 (Feb. 2011).

10. Wendy J. Miles & Daisy Mallett, *The Abyei Arbitration and the Use of Arbitration to Resolve Inter-state and Intra-state Conflicts*, 1.2 J. INT'L DISP. SETTLEMENT 313 (2010).

11. Bibliography of Additional Sources

## Authors' Note

The first four materials in this chapter are persuasive and/or binding documents in international arbitration law. Material 1, the Third Restatement of the Foreign Relations Law, includes an extensive compilation of case law and general principles of common law in regard to foreign relations. In particular, sections 902 and 904 discuss relevant common law materials on dispute resolution between states, peace negotiations, and arbitration. Although not binding authority, the Restatement serves as a highly persuasive secondary authority on the law, which judges and practitioners often rely upon. Material 2, the New York Convention on the Recognition and Enforcement of Foreign Arbital Awards is the most important mechanism for international enforcement of arbitration awards. The Convention requires signatory states to enforce private arbitration agreements and arbitration awards made in other signatory states. Material 3, the Dayton Peace Accords' article on the Arbitration for the Brcko Area, is essentially an arbitration clause establishing that the boundaries of the Bosnian Brcko District would be determined by arbitration between the Bosnian Federation and the Republika Srpska. Material 4, the Fourth Geneva Convention, concerning the Protection of Civilian Persons in Time of War, is binding on all states that are signatories to the Geneva Conventions. The Fourth Convention protects civilians during a time of armed hostilities, providing that the enemy or occupying power must guarantee civilians' fundamental human rights.

# 1. Third Restatement of the Foreign Relations Law, Sections 902, 904

1987

[internal citations omitted by editors]

### 902. Interstate Claims and Remedies

(1) A state may bring a claim against another state for a violation of an international obligation owed to the claimant state or to states generally, either through diplomatic channels or through any procedure to which the two states have agreed.

(2) Under Subsection (1), a state may bring claims, *inter alia*, for violations of international obligations resulting in injury to its nationals or to other persons on whose behalf it is entitled to make a claim under international law.

\* \* \*

## Reporters' Notes

### 1. *Standing to claim*

In South West Africa Cases (Second Phase) (*Ethiopia and Liberia v. South Africa*), the International Court of Justice rejected the contention that international law recognizes "the equivalent of an '*actio popularis*,' or right resident in any member of a community to take legal action in vindication of a public interest." [1966] I.C.J. Rep. 6, 47. A few years later, however, the Court declared that:

> An essential distinction should be drawn between the obligations of a State towards the international community as a whole, and those arising vis-a-vis another State in the field of diplomatic protection. By their very nature the former are the concern of all States. In view of the importance of the rights involved, all States can be held to have a legal interest in their protection; they are obligations *erga omnes*.

> Such obligations derive, for example, in contemporary international law, from the outlawing of acts of aggression, and of genocide, as also from the principles and rules concerning the basic rights of the human person, including protection from slavery and racial discrimination. Some of the corresponding rights of protection have entered into the body of general international law [Reservations to the Convention on the Prevention and Punishment of the Crime of Genocide (Advisory Opinion), [1951] I.C.J. Rep. 15, 23]; others are conferred by international instruments of a universal or quasi-universal character.

Some universal and some regional human rights conventions allow any party to the convention to bring before an international commission or court any breach of the convention by another party, provided both parties have accepted an optional clause on the subject. [ ... ]

### 2. *Lapse of time*

In the George W. Cook case, 1927, the General Claims Commission between United States and Mexico stated that there is "no rule of international law putting a limitation of time on diplomatic action or upon the presentation of an international claim to an international tribunal." On the other hand, in the Walter H. Faulkner case before the same Commission, it was noted that international "tribunals have in some instances declared that one government should not call upon another government to respond in damages when such action, after a long lapse of time, clearly puts the respondent government in an unfair position in making its defense, particularly in the matter of collecting evidence."

In the *Ambatielos* case, the arbitral tribunal did not accept the British contention that the Greek claim ought to be rejected because of undue delay in its presentation. The tribunal endorsed the principle stated by the Institute of International Law in 1925 that it is "left to the unfettered discretion of the international tribunal" to determine the existence of an "undue delay." In Lighthouses Case, Greece invoked a delay of more than 40 years as barring the French claims, but the tribunal rejected the defense in the circumstances, especially in view of the troubled conditions caused by successive wars between 1912 and 1923.

### 3. *Consent to third-party settlement*

"It is well established in international law that no State can, without its consent, be compelled to submit its disputes with other States either to mediation or to arbitration, or to any other kind of pacific settlement." International claims "cannot, in the present state of the law as to international jurisdiction, be submitted to a tribunal, except with the consent of the States concerned."

The Permanent Court of International Justice held that "the consent of a State to the submission of a dispute to the Court may not only result from an express declaration, but may also be inferred from acts conclusively establishing it," such as "the submission of arguments on the merits, without making reservations in regard to the question of jurisdiction."

### 4. Forms of third-party settlement

The most common means for the settlement of international disputes are good offices, mediation, commissions of inquiry, and conciliation commissions. See United Nations Charter, Art. 33. While some international agreements draw clear distinctions among these procedures, in practice they are often combined. International organizations also use these procedures, but their mandates to commissions, committees, or individuals often confuse the various functions, especially good offices and mediation.

If relations between parties are severed or strained, they may ask for, or accept, *the good offices* of a third party. The third party may bring them to the negotiating table, induce them to resort to arbitration, or help them to reach a solution on the merits.

A *mediator* tries to reconcile the views and claims of the parties and in appropriate cases makes confidential suggestions for this purpose. Such suggestions have no binding force.

An offer of good offices or mediation "can never be regarded by either of the parties in dispute as an unfriendly act."

The main function of a *commission of inquiry* is to elucidate the facts by means of an impartial and conscientious investigation, which may involve hearing witnesses or a visit to the area where the breach of international obligation is said to have occurred. Such a commission often includes representatives of both parties and sometimes consists solely of such representatives.

A *conciliation commission* examines the claims of the parties and the evidence submitted by them, and makes proposals to them for an amicable settlement. If an agreement is not reached, the commission prepares a report stating its conclusions on all questions of fact or law relevant to the matter in dispute, together with such recommendations as the commission may deem appropriate for an amicable settlement. Neither its conclusions nor its recommendations are binding upon the parties.

### 5. Dispute settlement in or by international organization

An agreement establishing an international organization may empower the organization to deal with disputes between its members and sometimes also with those involving non-members. The United Nations, its specialized agencies, regional organizations, such as the Organization of American States, the Organization of African Unity, and the Council of Europe, and organizations such as the General Agreement on Tariff and Trade (GATT) and the organizations established by various commodity agreements, frequently deal with international disputes by arranging for good offices, mediation, or commissions of inquiry or conciliation. The European Commission of Human Rights considers disputes between states involving human rights violations within the framework of the European Human Rights Convention, and presents reports on them, which are then considered by the Committee of Ministers of the Council of Europe. For a discussion of an interstate proceeding, see e.g., Becket, "The Greek Case Before the European Human Rights Commission."

Under some agreements, the parties are obligated to refer some categories of disputes to a bilateral commission, such as the joint boundary waters commissions between the United States and Canada and between the United States and Mexico.

The Charter of the United Nations authorizes any member state to bring any dispute (even one to which the member state is not a party), or any situation which is likely to endanger the maintenance of international peace and security, to the attention of the Security Council or of the General Assembly. Even a non-member state may bring to the attention of these organs any dispute to which it is a party. The Security Council may recommend appropriate procedures or methods of adjustment, or may recommend such terms of settlement as it considers appropriate. The General Assembly "may recommend measures for the peaceful adjustment of any situation, regardless of origin which it deems likely to impair the general welfare or friendly relations among nations." Many disputes have been submitted to the Security Council and the General Assembly under these provisions, and a solution acceptable to the parties was found in a number of them. For a comprehensive list of measures taken by the Security Council in the 41 disputes submitted to it between January 1970 and December 1978, see Repertory of Practice of United Nations Organs, Supp. No. 5, Vol. II.

Under some regional agreements, there is an obligation to resort to regional bodies or procedures prior to bringing the matter before the United Nations. For instance, the Charter of the Organization of American States provides that "[a]ll international disputes that may arise between American States shall be submitted to the peaceful procedures set forth in the Charter, before being referred to the Security Council of the United Nations." Members of the United Nations that are parties to regional arrangements are obligated to make every effort to achieve pacific settlement of local disputes through such regional arrangements before referring them to the Security Council, but any dispute likely to endanger the maintenance of peace and security may be referred directly to the United Nations.

Some international agreements empower an organization to render binding decisions, e.g., United Nations Charter, Arts. 25, 39, 41, 42 (Security Council decisions may not, however, impose a settlement of a dispute).

* * *

### 6. Negotiation as condition to third-party settlement

According to the Permanent Court of International Justice, the obligation to negotiate is "not only to enter into negotiations, but also to pursue them as far as possible, with a view to concluding agreements," although it is not necessarily an obligation to reach an agreement. Railway Traffic between Lithuania and Poland. The International Court of Justice also pointed out that "the parties are under an obligation to enter into negotiations with a view to arriving at an agreement ...; they are under an obligation so to conduct themselves that the negotiations are meaningful, which will not be the case when either of them insists upon its own position without contemplating any modification of it."

Many international agreements require negotiation or consultation prior to resort to more institutionalized procedures for the settlement of disputes. In particular, many international agreements relating to the pacific settlement of disputes provide that other means of settlement can be resorted to only with respect to disputes "which it has not been possible to settle by diplomacy." See, e.g., the Geneva General Act for the Pacific Settlement of International Disputes, 1928, Art. 1, 93 L.N.T.S. 345, which provides for conciliation, arbitration, and judicial settlement of all disputes (as of 1986, it had been acceded to by 22 states, but some of these had denounced it; the United States was not a party); and the Revised General Act for the Pacific Settlement of International Disputes, 1949, Art. 1, 71 U.N.T.S. 101, which adapted the 1928 Act to the United Nations system (as of 1986 it had been acceded to by seven states, but the United States was not a party). For a list of other such treaties containing this requirement, see United Nations, Systematic Survey of Treaties for the Pacific Settlement of International Disputes, 1928–1948, at 13–23 (1949); for a list of 20 pre-World War II United States conciliation treaties, resort to which is conditional on failure of "ordinary diplomatic proceedings."

Whether a negotiation has become futile or whether all means have been exhausted is not easy to determine. The Permanent Court of International Justice said that "the question of the importance and chances of diplomatic negotiations is essentially a relative one." Negotiations "do not of necessity always presuppose a more or less lengthy series of notes and dispatches; it may suffice that a discussion has been commenced, and ... a deadlock is reached, or if finally a point is reached at which one of the Parties definitely declares himself unable, or refuses, to give way."

### 7. Dispute as prerequisite to resort to settlement procedures

Before resorting to some settlement procedures, the claimant state must prove the existence of an "international dispute," but ordinarily such proof is not difficult. The Permanent Court of International Justice defined a dispute broadly as "a disagreement on a point of law or fact, a conflict of legal views or of interests between two persons" or states.

### 8. International claims practice of the United States

The United States has a long tradition of settling international claims by negotiation or international arbitration. Some claims implicated national interests directly, such as boundary disputes; some claims by the United States were for injury to private interests of its nationals. Sometimes a single dispute was settled or arbitrated, sometimes several disputes were combined; sometimes a dispute involved large numbers of claims, usually private claims. Thus, in 1794, the United States and Great Britain referred to a mixed commission more than 500 claims relating to maritime seizures. The United States-Mexican Commission established in 1868 disposed of some 2,000 claims. Two United States-Mexico claims commissions were established in 1923 to deal with more than 6,000 claims, mostly by the United States against Mexico, and a few by Mexico against the United States. Under the Algiers Declaration of 1981, more than 3,000 claims were submitted to an Iran-United States Claims Tribunal, most of them by United States nationals against Iran, some by Iranians against the United States, and some claims were between the two governments.

Matters affecting the national interest directly are generally resolved or submitted to international arbitration by treaty made with the consent of the United States Senate; most agreements settling claims of nationals have been made by executive agreement. [ ... ]As the Supreme Court noted in *Dames and Moore*, Congress has generally acquiesced in this exercise of presidential power. In 1974, however, Congress found a proposed agreement with Czechoslovakia unacceptable and adopted the Gravel Amendment to the Trade Act of 1974, requesting that the agreement be renegotiated and submitted to Congress as part of any agreement entered under that Act; gold belonging to Czechoslovakia was not to be released to that country.

The Department of State is authorized to pay any small (less than $15,000) "meritorious claim" against the United States presented by a foreign government.

* * *

### 904. Interstate Arbitration

(1) States parties to a dispute may submit it to arbitration by special agreement (compromis).

(2) A state party to a dispute with another state may submit the dispute to an arbitral tribunal pursuant to a bilateral or multilateral agreement providing for the submission to arbitration of a category of disputes that includes the claim in question.

(3) An award by an arbitral tribunal is binding on the parties unless they have agreed otherwise.

* * *

**Reporters' Notes**

*1. Consent requirement*

In Ambatielos Case (Obligation to Arbitrate) (*Greece v. United Kingdom*), the International Court of Justice identified two issues involved in determining whether the parties had consented to submit a particular claim to an arbitral tribunal. First, whether there has been consent to arbitrate, for a state "may not be compelled to submit its disputes to arbitration without its consent." Second, whether the consent of the parties extends to the claim submitted to the tribunal.

*2. Compromis*

Most arbitrations are based on a special agreement (*compromis*) concluded after a dispute has arisen. Such an agreement may relate to a single dispute or to a group of disputes; it may involve a claim or claims by one state against the other, or by each state against the other. The main purpose of the agreement is to define the subject of the dispute, and it often specifies the exact questions to be answered by the tribunal. It usually specifies, in addition, the method of constituting the tribunal; the number of arbitrators; a third party authorized to appoint the arbitrators, if not designated in due time by one or both of the parties; the rules of law to be applied by the tribunal, including sometimes the exact principles to be applied, or an authorization to the tribunal to decide *ex aequo et bono;* the procedure to be followed by the tribunal; the majority vote required for an award; the time within which the award is to be rendered; whether the members of the tribunal may attach dissenting or individual opinions to the award; how the costs of the arbitration are to be apportioned. [ ... ]

*3. Failure to agree on terms of compromis*

Many states, including the United States, are parties to treaties that provide for compulsory arbitration, *i.e.*, arbitration that may be initiated by unilateral application of one party if the two states cannot agree on a *compromis*. Such treaties often specify that if the compromis is not concluded within a certain time, usually three to six months, either party may initiate a special procedure for supplying the terms of reference for the arbitration. Some treaties provide for third-party appointment of members of an arbitral tribunal who then draw up the *compromis*; a few treaties provide for the appointment of a special commission for the sole purpose of preparing the *compromis*. The Model Rules on Arbitral Procedure, prepared by the International Law Commission (see Reporters' Note 4), envisage the possibility of the tribunal proceeding to hear and decide the case on the application of either party even without a *compromis*.

*4. Arbitration procedure*

Most agreements to arbitrate do not specify the details of the arbitration procedure but refer to some generally accepted treaty on the subject (though the parties to the *compromis* may not be parties to that treaty), or to model rules prepared by an international institution. Such rules were first codified in the 1899 Hague Convention for the Pacific Settlement of International Disputes and considerably revised by the 1907 Hague Convention. (As of 1986, this convention was in force for the United States and 74 other states.) These conventions established the Permanent Court of Arbitration, which is not a court but a panel of available arbitrators consisting of four persons appointed by each state party for six-year terms.

Many arbitration agreements follow the General Act for the Pacific Settlement of International Disputes, adopted under the auspices of the League of Nations in 1928 and revised by the United Nations in 1949. Similar provisions, with some variations, are contained in the 1957 European Convention for the Peaceful Settlement of Disputes. Different patterns have been followed by the 1948 American Treaty on Pacific Settlement ("Pact of Bogota") and by the 1964 Protocol to the Charter of the Organization of African Unity, which established the Commission of Mediation, Conciliation and Arbitration, from whose 21 members an arbitral tribunal may be chosen by the parties.

The International Law Commission submitted to the General Assembly in 1958 "Model Rules on Arbitral Procedure," which the General Assembly approved for possible use by member states in drawing up treaties of arbitration or *compromis*. [ ... ]

### 5. Provisional measures

An agreement to arbitrate may expressly authorize the arbitral tribunal to adopt provisional measures necessary to safeguard the rights of the parties, but such jurisdiction may also be implied; in some cases it has been exercised without any basis in the agreement. See, e.g., Case Concerning the Air Service Agreement between the United States and France, 1978, (tribunal has power to decide on interim measures of protection, "regardless of whether this power is expressly mentioned or implied in its statute"). [ ... ]

### 6. Binding force of arbitral awards

Most arbitral awards are intended to be binding, but some are intended to be advisory only. A *compromis* may provide expressly that the award will be final and binding. See, *e.g.*, the Declaration Concerning the Settlement of Claims by the United States and Iran, Reporters' Note 2, Art. 4(1), (providing also that any "award which the Tribunal may render against either government shall be enforceable against such government in the courts of any nation in accordance with its laws,"). Some international agreements, however, provide that the dispute should be submitted to a tribunal for "an advisory report"; they sometimes provide also that the parties "will use their best efforts under the powers available to them to put into effect the opinion expressed in any such advisory report."

### 7. Compliance with arbitral awards

A study of the execution of some 300 arbitral awards between 1794 and 1936 uncovered only 20 cases of noncompliance. A few instances of noncompliance have occurred since 1936, *e.g.*, with respect to an award concerning the dispute over the Beagle Channel islands between Argentina and Chile. This dispute was finally settled by mediation in 1985.

Article 35 of the Model Rules on Arbitral Procedure, prepared by the International Law Commission (Reporters' Note 4), allows a party to challenge the validity of an arbitral award only on the following grounds:

(a) that the tribunal exceeded its powers;

(b) that there was corruption on the part of a member of the tribunal;

(c) that there was a failure to state the reasons for the award or a serious departure from a fundamental rule of procedure;

(d) that the undertaking to arbitrate or the *compromis* is a nullity.

This Article does not include among the grounds for invalidity either errors of law or erroneous findings of fact. Article 38, however, envisages the possibility of revising an award if a fact is discovered "of such nature as to constitute a decisive factor, provided that when the award was rendered that fact was unknown to the tribunal and to the party requesting revision."

\* \* \*

## 2. Conference on International Commercial Arbitration, "Convention on the Recognition and Enforcement of Foreign Arbitral Awards"
### United Nations, 1958

### Article I

1. This Convention shall apply to the recognition and enforcement of arbitral awards made in the territory of a State other than the State where the recognition and enforcement of such awards are sought, and arising out of differences between persons, whether physical or legal. It shall also apply to arbitral awards not considered as domestic awards in the State where their recognition and enforcement are sought.

2. The term "arbitral awards" shall include not only awards made by arbitrators appointed for each case but also those made by permanent arbitral bodies to which the parties have submitted.

3. When signing, ratifying or acceding to this Convention, or notifying extension under article X hereof, any State may on the basis of reciprocity declare that it will apply the Convention to the recognition and enforcement of awards made only in the territory of another Contracting State. It may also declare that it will apply the Convention only to differences arising out of legal relationships, whether contractual or not, which are considered as commercial under the national law of the State making such declaration.

### Article II

1. Each contracting State shall recognize an agreement in writing under which the parties undertake to submit to arbitration all or any differences which have arisen or which may arise between them in respect of a defined legal relationship, whether contractual or not, concerning a subject matter capable of settlement by arbitration.

2. The term "agreement in writing" shall include an arbitral clause in a contract or an arbitration agreement, signed by the parties or contained in an exchange of letters or telegrams.

3. The court of a Contracting State, when seized of an action in a matter in respect of which the parties have made an agreement within the meaning of this article, shall, at the request of one of the parties, refer the parties to arbitration, unless it finds that the said agreement is null and void, inoperative or incapable of being performed.

### Article III

Each Contracting State shall recognize arbitral awards as binding and enforce them in accordance with the rules of procedure of the territory where the award is relied upon, under the conditions laid down in the following articles. There shall not be imposed substantially more onerous conditions or higher fees or charges on the recognition or enforcement of arbitral awards to which this Convention applies than are imposed on the recognition or enforcement of domestic arbitral awards.

### Article IV

1. To obtain the recognition and enforcement mentioned in the preceding article, the party applying for recognition and enforcement shall, at the time of the application, supply:

(a) The duly authenticated original award or a duly certified copy thereof;

(b) The original agreement referred to in article II or a duly certified copy thereof.

2. If the said award or agreement is not made in an official language of the country in which the award is relied upon, the party applying for recognition and enforcement of the award shall produce a translation of these documents into such language. The translation shall be certified by an official or sworn translator or by a diplomatic or consular agent.

## Article V

1. Recognition and enforcement of the award may be refused, at the request of the party against whom it is invoked, only if that party furnishes to the competent authority where the recognition and enforcement is sought, proof that:

(a) The parties to the agreement referred to in article II were, under the law applicable to them, under some incapacity, or the said agreement is not valid under the law to which the parties have subjected it or, failing any indication thereon, under the law of the country where the award was made; or

(b) The party against whom the award is invoked was not given proper notice of the appointment of the arbitrator or of the arbitration proceedings or was otherwise unable to present his case; or

(c) The award deals with a difference not contemplated by or not falling within the terms of the submission to arbitration, or it contains decisions on matters beyond the scope of the submission to arbitration, provided that, if the decisions on matters submitted to arbitration can be separated from those not so submitted, that part of the award which contain decisions on matters submitted to arbitration may be recognized and enforced; or

(d) The composition of the arbitral authority or the arbitral procedure was not in accordance with the agreement of the parties, or, failing such agreement, was not in accordance with the law of the country where the arbitration took place; or

(e) The award has not yet become binding on the parties, or has been set aside or suspended by a competent authority of the country in which, or under the law of which, that award was made.

2. Recognition and enforcement of an arbitral award may also be refused if the competent authority in the country where recognition and enforcement is sought finds that:

(a) The subject matter of the difference is not capable of settlement by arbitration under the law of that county; or

(b) The recognition or enforcement of the award would be contrary to the public policy of that country.

## Article VI

If an application for the setting aside or suspension of the award has been made to a competent authority referred to in article V(1)(e), the authority before which the award is sought to be relied upon may, if it considers it proper, adjourn the decision on the enforcement of the award and may also, on the application of the party claiming enforcement of the award, order the other party to give suitable security.

## Article VII

1. The provisions of the present Convention shall not affect the validity of multilateral or bilateral agreements concerning the recognition and enforcement of arbitral awards entered into by the Contracting States nor deprive any interested party of any right he may have to avail himself of an arbitral award in the manner and to the extent allowed by the law or the treaties of the country where such award is sought to be relied upon.

\* \* \*

## Article XI

In the case of a federal or non-unitary State, the following provisions shall apply:

(a) With respect to those articles of this Convention that come within the legislative jurisdiction of the federal authority, the obligations of the Federal Government shall to this extent be the same as those of Contracting States which are not federal States;

(b) With respect to those articles of this Convention that come within the legislative jurisdiction of constituent states or provinces which are not, under the constitutional system of the federation, bound to take legislative action, the federal Government shall bring such articles with a favourable recommendation to the notice of the appropriate authorities of constituent states or provinces at the earliest possible moment;

(c) A federal State Party to this Convention shall, at the request of any other Contracting State transmitted through the Secretary-General of the United Nations, supply a statement of the law and practice of the federation and its constituent units in regard to any particular provision of this Convention, showing the extent to which effect has been given to that provision by legislative or other action.

\* \* \*

## Article XIII

1. Any Contracting State may denounce this Convention by a written notification to the Secretary-General of the United Nations. Denunciation shall take effect one year after the date of receipt of the notification by the Secretary-General.

2. Any State which has made a declaration or notification under article X may, at any time thereafter, by notification to the Secretary-General of the United Nations, declare that this Convention shall cease to extend to the territory concerned one year after the date of the receipt of the notification by the Secretary-General.

3. This Convention shall continue to be applicable to arbitral awards in respect of which recognition or enforcement proceedings have been instituted before the denunciation takes effect.

## Article XIV

A Contracting State shall not be entitled to avail itself of the present Convention against other Contracting States except to the extent that it is itself bound to apply the Convention.

\* \* \*

# 3. Dayton Peace Agreement,
# Arbitration for the Brcko Area Article V
## 1995

(1) The Parties agree to binding arbitration of the disputed portion of the Inter-Entity Boundary Line in the Brcko area indicated on the map attached at the Appendix.

(2) No later than six months after the entry into force of this Agreement, the Federation shall appoint one arbitrator, and the Republika Srpska shall appoint one arbitrator. A third arbitrator shall be selected by agreement of the Parties' appointees within thirty days thereafter. If they do not agree, the third arbitrator shall be appointed by the President of the International Court of Justice. The third arbitrator shall serve as presiding officer of the arbitral tribunal.

(3) Unless otherwise agreed by the Parties, the proceedings shall be conducted in accordance with the UNCITRAL rules. The arbitrators shall apply [the Geneva convention (IV)—reproduced below].

(4) Unless otherwise agreed, the area indicated in paragraph 1 above shall continue to be administered as currently.

(5) The arbitrators shall issue their decision no later than one year from the entry into force of this Agreement. The decision shall be final and binding, and the Parties shall implement it without delay.

---

# 4. Convention (IV) Relative to the Protection of Civilian Persons in Time of War Articles 4, 49
## 1949

\* \* \*

### Article 4

Persons protected by the Convention are those who, at a given moment and in any manner whatsoever, find themselves, in case of a conflict or occupation, in the hands of a Party to the conflict or Occupying Power of which they are not nationals.

\* \* \*

### Article 49

Individual or mass forcible transfers, as well as deportations of protected persons from occupied territory to the territory of the Occupying Power or to that of any other country, occupied or not, are prohibited, regardless of their motive.

Nevertheless, the Occupying Power may undertake total or partial evacuation of a given area if the security of the population or imperative military reasons demand. Such evacuations may not involve the displacement of protected persons outside the bounds of the occupied territory except when for material reasons it is impossible to avoid such displacement. Persons thus evacuated shall be transferred back to their homes as soon as hostilities in the area in question have ceased.

The Occupying Power undertaking such transfers or evacuations shall ensure, to the greatest practicable extent, that proper accommodation is provided to receive the protected persons, that the removals are effected in satisfactory conditions of hygiene, health, safety and nutrition, and that members of the same family are not separated.

The Protecting Power shall be informed of any transfers and evacuations as soon as they have taken place.

The Occupying Power shall not detain protected persons in an area particularly exposed to the danger of war unless the security of the population or imperative military reasons so demand.

The Occupying Power shall not deport or transfer parts of its own civilian population into the territory it occupies.

---

## *Authors' Note*

The following three materials discuss several issues relevant to the Brcko arbitration. Material 5, an interview with former British Foreign Secretary Lord David Owen, explores the Yugoslavian history that led to the conflict and colored the subsequent Brcko arbitration. Material 6, written following the Dayton Accords, discusses acute challenges that impeded the successful resolution of the Brcko situation. Material 7 argues against ceding control of Brcko to Bosnian Serbs, as doing so would undermine Bosnian unification and promote the secession of a Bosnian Serb state.

## 5. Michael P. Scharf, History of the Yugoslav Crisis

### Balkan Justice: The Story Behind the First International War Crimes Trial Since Nuremburg, 1997

Prior to its dissolution in 1991, Yugoslavia was not so much an ethnic melting pot as a boiling cauldron of ethnic tension with deep historic roots. Although the people of the different regions of the former Yugoslavia shared a common language (Serbo-Croatian) and physical characteristics (Slavic), differences among their religions and historical experiences led to the growth of strong separate ethnic identities. The region's strategic position at the southern crossroads of Europe and Asia has been the source of its historic turmoil. Since recorded time, the region has been invaded, contested, and ruled successively or concurrently by the Macedonian, Roman, Byzantine, Slav, Bulgar, Venetian, Austro-Hungarian, Ottoman, and the Nazi German empires.

By the ninth century, Christianity had become the predominant faith throughout the region, with the western portion (what is now Croatia and Slovenia) largely Roman Catholic, and the eastern section (Bosnia-Herzegovina, Serbia, Montenegro, and Macedonia) mostly Eastern Orthodox. The defining moment in the early history of the region occurred on St. Vitus Day (June 28) in 1389, when the Ottoman Turks defeated Serbian forces at the battle of Kosovo Polje (Field of the Blackbirds). Thereafter, the eastern portions of the Balkans were plunged into a period of Ottoman occupation from which they did not emerge until the early twentieth century. During the Ottoman subjugation, many of the Balkan people were able to preserve their culture by accepting second-class status within the Ottoman Empire. Others (predominantly in the cities of what is now Bosnia) converted to Islam to avoid persecution and the oppressive taxes required of non-Muslims. Current-day Serbian hostility toward Bosnian Muslims stems in large part from what they believe was betrayal of the true faith by their ancestors over six hundred years ago. While Serbia and Bosnia existed under five centuries of Ottoman domination, the Catholic Slovenes and Croats were absorbed by the Hapsburg Empire and were influenced by centuries of close contact with Austria, Hungary, and Italy.

Two Balkan wars were fought in 1912 and 1913, which resulted in the liberation of the Balkan Peninsula from Ottoman control. During these conflicts, Serbian nationalists resorted to ethnic violence on a massive scale. As the International Commission to Inquire into the Causes and Conduct of the Balkan Wars reported in 1914, "houses and whole villages [were] reduced to ashes, unarmed and innocent populations [were] massacred en masse, incredible acts of violence, pillage and brutality of every kind such were the means which were employed by the Serbo-Montenegrin soldiery, with a view to the entire transformation of the ethnic character of these regions."

Having expelled the Turks, Serb nationalists turned their attention to the Hapsburg Empire, which had annexed Bosnia-Herzegovina in 1908. World War I began when Gavrilo Princip, a Bosnian Serbian nationalist, assassinated Austrian Archduke Ferdinand in Sarajevo on June 28, 1914. It was no coincidence that the archduke, who was heir to the Hapsburg throne, was killed on the anniversary of the Battle of Kosovo. Independence from foreign domination was finally realized after the First World War when King Alexander of Serbia proclaimed the Kingdom of Serbs, Croats, and Slovenes, which became known as Yugoslavia, meaning "Land of the South Slavs."

The unity achieved under King Alexander was fragile, with the Croats pushing for ever greater self-government within a looser confederation. In 1929, with the support of Italian dictator Benito Mussolini, the Ustasha (meaning "uprising") movement was born with the goal of Croatian independence—if necessary through violence. In 1934, a member of the Ustasha assassinated King Alexander, and a weak regency was appointed to rule in place of Alexander's ten-year-old son. This set the stage for the invasion of Yugoslavia by the Axis powers in 1941.

During World War II, the Axis powers occupied Yugoslavia and partitioned the country into German and Italian spheres of influence. Croatia became a puppet state (comprised of today's Croatia and Bosnia-Herzegovina) of Hitler's Nazi Germany, with the Ustasha leader, Ante Pavelic, placed in charge. The Ustasha regarded Croatia's two million Serbs as a threat and set about to eliminate them through mass extermination. To that end, Pavelic stated "the Slavoserbs are the rubbish of a nation, the type of people who will sell themselves to anyone and at any price, and to every buyer." Mile Budak, one of Pavelic's chief deputies, declared the Ustasha plan for the Croatian and Bosnian Serbs on July 22, 1941: "We shall slay one-third of the Serbian population, drive away another third, and the rest we shall convert to the Roman Catholic faith and thus assimilate into Croats. Thus we will destroy every trace of theirs and all that which will be left will be an evil memory of them." Echoing this policy, the governor of western Bosnia, Victor Gutisch, urged that the territory under his control be "thoroughly cleansed of Serbian dirt." Hence, the term "ethnic cleansing" was first coined, not by the Serbs, but by the Croats and Bosnians during World War II.

To accomplish its goal, the Ustasha established an extermination camp at Jasenovac which rivaled the infamous Nazi death camp at Auschwitz in its brutal efficiency. In all, a million and a half Serbs were "ethnically cleansed" by the Ustasha during the Second World War. Over five hundred thousand were killed and a million were driven from the territory to seek refuge in other countries. At one point, the German authorities were reportedly forced to close the Danube to swimming because of the large number of Serb corpses being thrown into the river by the Croatian Ustasha.

Resistance to the Axis occupation of Yugoslavia came from the communist Partisan forces, led by the Croatian-born Josip Broz Tito. With the support of the Allies, Tito's partisans eventually secured control over the entire Yugoslav territory. In revenge for the Croat atrocities, the partisans murdered over one hundred thousand Croatian prisoners when the Ustasha surrendered in May 1946.

After the war, Tito established a federal system in Yugoslavia consisting of six republics: Serbia, Croatia, Slovenia, Bosnia-Herzegovina, Macedonia, and Montenegro and two autonomous provinces (Kosovo and Vojvodina) within the Republic of Serbia. The reordered internal boundaries were aimed at containing Serbian nationalism by stranding Serb minorities in each of the republics outside Serbia itself. In addition, Tito successfully dealt with ethnic tensions within and among the republics through stern repression at the hands of the secret police known as the GZNA.

In 1948, the Soviet Premier, Joseph Stalin, expelled Yugoslavia from the Cominform, an organization of eastern Communist nations, for "pursuing an unfriendly policy towards the Soviet Union." This action led to fears of a Soviet attack, fears which intensified after the Soviet invasion of Czechoslovakia in 1968. As much as anything else, the Soviet threat provided the glue which held Tito's Yugoslavia together. To counter this threat, Tito initiated a doctrine known as "Total National Defense" which required universal military service and coordinated training in guerrilla warfare. Training facilities, weapons caches, and supply stores were placed throughout the country and the military organized reserve units around work places to provide the wide distribution of forces and weapons. The Yugoslav National Army became the third-largest in all of Europe.

Tito's death on May 4, 1980, and the collapse of the Soviet threat in the late 1980s, unleashed the long-festering centrifugal forces which would soon lead to Yugoslavia's disintegration. After the break up of Yugoslavia, the Total National Defense system would be used not against a foreign invader, but against Yugoslavia's own republics. An emphasis on guerrilla warfare, a decentralized command system, and the enlistment of civilian volunteers would reappear in the tactics of each of the warring factions.

History of the region might suggest that the war in 1991 was little more than a continuation of the endemic ethnic strife in the area. Yet to attribute the tragedy of Yugoslavia solely to stoppable historic forces is to turn a blind eye to the critical role played by the rise of Serb nationalism among Belgrade intellectuals in mid-1980s and the subsequent harnessing of nationalist rhetoric by Slobodan Milosevic. As Warren Zimmermann, then U.S. ambassador to Belgrade, put it, "The breakup of Yugoslavia was a classic example of nationalism from the top down."

In 1986, members of the Serbian Academy of Arts and Sciences prepared a Manifesto attacking the Yugoslavia Constitution. The document, known as the SAAS Memorandum, argued that Tito had consistently discriminated against the Serbs and that Serbia had been subject to economic domination by Croatia and Slovenia. It spoke of the "physical, political, legal and cultural genocide against the Serb population in Kosovo" as well as discrimination against Serbs who resided in other Republics.

Later that year, Slobodan Milošević, riding a wave of Serbian nationalism, became Serbian Communist Party chief. Milošević solidified his position by provoking and then using federal troops to ruthlessly crush successive crises in the region of Serbia known as Kosovo, where Albanians outnumbered Serbs ten to one. Kosovo became Milošević's launching pad in his quest to extend his power to the rest of Yugoslavia. If, as one commentator put it, "the hatred that astounded the world in Yugoslavia was engineered, not innate," it was Milošević who was the chief engineer. According to Ambassador Zimmermann, "Those who argue that ancient Balkan hostilities account for the violence that overtook and destroyed Yugoslavia ignore the power of television in the service of officially provoked racism." Through a barrage of propaganda via the state-owned media, Milošević played on Serb fears and feelings of victimization, going back to their defeat by the Ottomans at Kosovo in 1389 and emphasizing their treatment at the hands of the Ustasha during World War II. "The virus of television," Ambassador Zimmermann recounts, "spread ethnic hatred like an epidemic."

The ascent of a hardline Serbian nationalist government in Serbia fanned anti-Serb nationalism in the republics of Croatia and Slovenia. At the same time, Milošević's efforts to create a more centralized Yugoslavia under Serbian dominance engendered strident resistance from the leaders of Croatia and Slovenia, Franjo Tudjman and Milan Kučan, who desired to convert Yugoslavia into a loose confederation that would dilute Serbian influence. Flexing his political muscle in the spring of 1991, Milošević blocked Stipe Mesić, a Croat, from assuming the federal presidency, despite the fact that the constitution provided that the presidency rotate annually among the republics and it was Croatia's turn.

After a series of negotiations with Milošević over a new Yugoslav constitution proved futile, Croatia and Slovenia declared their independence on June 25, 1991, without offering concrete guarantees for the security of the five hundred thousand Serbs living within their borders. While visiting Belgrade a week earlier, U.S. Secretary of State James Baker had warned of the "dangers of disintegration." He urged that Yugoslavia maintain "territorial integrity" and said that the United States "would not recognize unilateral declarations of independence." Milošević took this as a green light to use force to halt secession and to protect the Serbs living in Croatia and Slovenia. "What they read between the lines of the Baker visit," writes Ambassador Zimmermann, "was that the United States had no intention of stopping them by force." Milošević began by sending the Serb-dominated Yugoslav National Army (JNA) into Slovenia to crush that republic's nascent militia. After the Slovenes withstood repeated attacks and actually defeated the JNA in several engagements, Milošević agreed to a European Community-brokered cease-fire, while he turned his attention to Croatia.

The JNA, aided by local Serbian insurgents, inflicted heavy casualties on the inexperienced and outgunned Croatian forces and quickly took control of one-third of Croatia's territory. On November 20, 1991, one of the Yugoslav conflict's most egregious acts was committed when Serb forces captured the Croatian town of Vukovar. Upon entering the city, Serb forces massacred some two hundred Croatian patients (mostly wounded soldiers) in the Vukovar hospital and disposed of their bodies in a mass grave that was later discovered by U.N. forensic investigators.

For six months, repeated efforts by the European community and the Conference on Security and Cooperation in Europe to broker a durable cease-fire in Croatia failed to yield tangible success. Finally, in January of 1992, after thousands had been killed in the fighting, Croatia and Serbia agreed to the deployment of a United Nations peace-keeping force (known as UNPROFOR) to oversee the withdrawal of the JNA and the disarming of local forces in the areas of conflict inside Croatia. Later that month, the European Community formally recognized the new independent state of Croatia. During the next four years, Croatia, under cover of the United Nations and backed by Germany, would arm and make preparations for a successful campaign to retake its lost territory.

In the meantime, the Bosnians were forced to choose between remaining in what had become a Serbian ethnic dictatorship or seeking a hazardous independence. The leader of the Bosnian Serb political party, a psychiatrist named Radovan Karadžić, warned that pursuing independence would "make the Muslim people disappear, because the Muslims cannot defend themselves if there is war." But his warning (or threat) was not heeded. On February 29 and March 1, 1992, the Muslim and Croatian people of Bosnia-Herzegovina voted overwhelmingly for independence. At the time of the vote, Bosnia consisted of three main ethnic groups: Slavic Muslims (43 percent of the population), Serbs (31 percent), and Croats (17 percent). While these groups are defined on the basis of religion, Bosnia was largely a secular society; a 1985 survey found that only 17 percent of its people considered themselves believers and interfaith marriage was extremely common.

Although the majority of Bosnian Serbs boycotted the poll, independence was the choice of 63 percent of the total electorate. On April 6, the European Community recognized the new independent nation of Bosnia-Herzegovina, with the United States following suit the next day. That same day, the Bosnian Serbs, under the leadership of their self-styled president, Radovan Karadžić, proclaimed the formation of an independent "Republic Srpska" (Serbian Republic of Bosnia and Herzegovina), whose government was located in the city of Pale in southeast Bosnia. The Serbs immediately launched attacks against the Croatian and Muslim populations in northeast and southern Bosnia with the goal of connecting Serb populated regions in north and west Bosnia to Serbia in the east. According to one observer, "The Bosnian Serbs, with JNA help, seized TV Sarajevo reporters around Bosnia and reprogrammed them to carry TV-Belgrade, a key factor in the incitement of ethnic hatred." Assisted by some forty-five thousand JNA troops, the Serb insurgent forces seized control of 70 percent of Bosnia's territory municipality by municipality. By the middle of April, the Muslims were left with control over only a few islands of territory within Bosnia-Sarajevo, Mostar, Bihac, Tuzla, Srebrenica, and Gorazde, and these were shelled relentlessly by JNA and Serb insurgent forces.

The Serbs had planned their attack well in advance. Milošević had begun to arm and finance local Serb militias more than six months before Bosnia declared its independence. Moreover, according to Borisav Jović, who had been commander of the JNA, in January 1992, Milošević issued a secret order to start transferring all Serbian JNA officers who had been born in Bosnia back to their native republic. On May 19, 1992, in an unsuccessful attempt to head off the threat of United Nations sanctions for its involvement in the hostilities in Bosnia, Serbia announced the withdrawal of the JNA from Bosnia-Herzegovina. When the JNA pulled out, however, it demobilized 85 percent of the officers and men and left behind most of the army's equipment. The demobilized troops, under the command of former JNA 9th Army Corps Chief of Staff Ratko Mladić, together with local insurgents and Serbia based-militias, became a new army known as the VRS, which continued to receive assistance and instructions from Serbia. Not deceived by this tactic, on May 30 the Security Council adopted Resolution 757, which imposed a sweeping trade embargo on Serbia-Montenegro.

Throughout this period, recurrent efforts by European Community and United Nations mediators to broker a lasting cease-fire and a framework for peace met with little success. The United Nations did manage to obtain permission from the warring sides to send in an UNPROFOR contingent to secure the Sarajevo airport in order to open a humanitarian aid pipeline into the besieged city. However, UNPROFOR proved unable to keep the pipeline open on a sustained basis due to frequent attacks on the aircraft bringing in humanitarian aid.

At the same time, international observers, including information-gathering missions under the auspices of the United Nations Human Rights Commission, the European Community, the Conference on Security and Cooperation in Europe, the International Committee of Red Cross, Amnesty International, and Helsinki Watch began to document widespread abuses occurring in Bosnia. Through these releases the world learned of mass forced-population transfers of Muslims, organized massacres, the physical destruction of whole towns, systematic and repeated rape of thousands of Muslim women and girls, and the existence of over four hundred Serb-run detentions. Based on the observations of his own special envoy, Secretary-General of the United Nations Boutros Boutros-Ghali reported to the Security Council that the Serbs of Bosnia-Herzegovina, with support from the JNA, were "making a concerted effort ... to create ethnically pure regions" in the republic, and that the "techniques used the seizure of territory by military force and intimidation of the non-Serb population." These methods were as effective as they were brutal. By the end of 1994, the Serbs had expelled, killed or imprisoned 90 percent of the 1.7 million non-Serbs who once lived in Serbian held areas of Bosnia.

Among the most abhorrent cases of "ethnic cleansing" involved the town of Kozarac, a predominantly Muslim community in the Prijedor region of Bosnia. It was the town which Duško Tadić had called home. As described by BBC correspondent Misha Glenny, "The Muslims of Kozarac surrendered without a struggle, but the Serb forces destroyed the village completely, perpetrating a massacre of hundreds of civilians in the process.... Muslims were thrown out of their houses and forced to sign papers handing all their property and worldly goods over to the Serbs."

Muslim women were herded into schools and warehouses and raped repeatedly. Those Muslim men who were not executed on the spot were taken to Serb-run concentration camps, which served as central locations to terrorize individuals and intimidate the entire target population. As a reporter for the New York Times recounted: "The men were taken from the village at gunpoint and forced into freight cars. As many as 180 were jammed, standing, into boxcars measuring 39 by 6 feet. They were kept that way for three days, without water or food, as the train moved slowly across the countryside. Nazis transporting Jews in 1942? No, Serbs transporting Muslim Bosnians in 1992." Roy Gutman of Newsday, the first journalist to visit the Bosnian Serb concentration camps, wrote on August 2: "The Serb conquerors of northern Bosnia have established two concentration camps in which more than a thousand civilians have been executed or starved and thousands more are being held until they die." Four days later, on August 6, Penny Marshall of International Television News (ITN) filmed conditions at the Omarska concentration camp in Northern Bosnia. She captured startling footage of "men at various stages of human decay and affliction; the bones of their elbows and wrists protrude like pieces of jagged stone from the pencil thin stalks to which their arms have been reduced." The ITN footage resulted in an international outcry to stop the atrocities.

---

## 6. C. Dunja Tadic, Brcko—Still No Closer to a Solution
### Agence France-Presse, 1996

A year after the Dayton peace negotiations, the one territorial issue left unresolved in the accords—the future of the northern town of Brcko—is still no closer to a solution.

Brcko, a key strategic town claimed by both sides, has been described by the architect of the accords, Richard Holbrooke, as "the most explosive place in the country."

Under Dayton, its fate was due to be decided by an arbitration committee comprising a Serb, a Moslem and an international mediator by December 14 this year.

However, Bosnian President Alija Izetbegović said Friday that the arbitration deadline might have to be put off for two months.

In an interview with the Bosnian media, Izetbegović said that U.S. mediator Roberts Owen had suggested the postponement as he was unable to come to the right decision.

"I think we will accept his suggestion," the president added.

For now, the committee has yet to agree even on the terms of the negotiations.

Brcko, which had a non-Serb majority before the war, lies in a narrow corridor of Serb-held land linking the two halves of Bosnian Serb entity, the Republika Srpska.

The Serbs—who have not turned up at arbitration committee meetings—only want to discuss a widening of this corridor while the Moslems and Croats want the town returned, which the Serbs say would cut their territory in two.

Brcko, now badly damaged and filled with Serb refugees from other parts of the country, is an important road and rail junction, an industrial centre and a port on the Sava river.

In Bosnia's September elections, the Serbs tried to get Serb refugees from the Federal Republic of Yugoslavia to come to vote in Brcko in a bid to swing the results of the arbitration commission their way.

In campaigning for the polls, Izetbegović used the town as a symbol for the Moslems' frustration at their inability to return to homes from which they were driven or fled during almost four bloody years of war.

He told a crowd of cheering refugees in Moslem-Croat federation territory that there would be "serious trouble" if they were not allowed to return.

"It's not just a problem of returning people to Brcko—the problem is for all places in Bosnia-Herzegovina," he said.

"We will not give up. There are hundreds of villages and tens of towns from which we were forced out. We will come back to Brcko very soon, God willing, and other places later, but first Brcko."

---

# 7. Norman Cigar and Paul Williams, Reward Serbs with Town of Brcko? Don't Do It

*Christian Science Monitor*, 1998

On March 15, a decision is due by the international community's representative on the future of the disputed Bosnian town of Brcko. It could be a turning point for that country's future and could make the difference between a united Bosnia and a dismembered one.

Brcko sits strategically astride what has become known as the "corridor" linking the two parts of the Bosnian Serb entity. Before the war, Serbs comprised 20 percent of the town's 87,000 inhabitants. But Serb militias and the Yugoslav Army seized control in 1992, conducting an ethnic cleansing drive in which the Department of State estimates 3,000 non-Serbs were murdered.

The Bosnian Serbs have held the ethnically cleansed town ever since. The 1995 Dayton accords, which ended the fighting in Bosnia, postponed the decision on who would control Brcko by requiring the parties to submit to binding arbitration. Pending a final disposition, a temporary Bosnian Serb administration has governed the city.

The Bosnian government seeks the return of Brcko, arguing that the town is vital because, as a port on the Sava River, it provides badly needed access to the outside world. It further argues that failure to reverse the town's seizure by force would mean rewarding ethnic cleansing.

The Bosnian Serbs claim that Brcko should be theirs, because they are entitled to a secure, Serb-only link between the two parts of Bosnia over which they exert territorial control: Banja Luka and eastern Bosnia.

Yet, if the Bosnian Serbs are committed to living in a united Bosnia, as they agreed in writing, then control of Brcko shouldn't matter. The Bosnian Serbs need the Brcko link only if they plan to break away from Bosnia.

Tellingly, some foreign policymakers have hinted that the more pragmatic, albeit still nationalistic, Bosnian Serb officials installed recently—led by Biljana Plavšić and Milorad Dodik—should be encouraged and rewarded by concessions such as the disputed town of Brcko. As a way to exert pressure on the pending decision, Mr. Dodik and Mr. Plavšić have taken the cue, warning that failure to grant Brcko to the Serbs could undermine their credibility in favor of more radical rivals.

Yet, even apart from the moral aspect, it makes little sense to relinquish such a crucial lever over the Serbs' good behavior. Even if Plavšić and Dodik were to fall (and that's unlikely), whoever replaced them would not be immune to geography. Without Brcko, the Bosnian Serbs would not control a continuous area, and therefore would be compelled by geography to cooperate with the rest of Bosnia and the international community in implementing the Dayton Accords and promoting stability and security in order to keep their road and air communications open.

With Brcko in their sole possession, on the other hand, the Bosnian Serb authorities can be expected to flout the rest of Bosnia and the international community and work toward partition.

In short, if the Bosnian Serbs are awarded Brcko, a united Bosnia becomes highly unlikely; if not, a united Bosnia is at least possible. If the goal of the United States is still a united and stable Bosnia, there is little that would undercut that objective as completely as allotting Brcko to the Serbs.

The international community should, instead, establish a transitional NATO-led Stabilization Force (SFOR) mandate over the city as an interim solution. The SFOR authority would work to reestablish the city's original ethnic balance by securing the return of refugees and freedom of movement. And once there is a functioning and unified Bosnian government, control over Brcko could be formally relinquished to the joint central government authorities.

This not only would pave the way for a smooth transition, but it also would make meaningless protests by more radical Serb elements. Most important, it would give Bosnia the chance for peace it deserves.

## Authors' Note

In July 2008, under the guidance of the Permanent Court of Arbitration (PCA), the government of Sudan and the Sudan's People's Liberation Movement/Army (SPLM/A), established a five-member arbitrational tribunal to decide the boundaries of the Abyei region. The parties agreed to abide by the PCA Optional Rules for Arbitrating Disputes between Two Parties of Which Only One is a State. The arbitrational tribunal's final award map is the second attempt to settle the boundaries between the Sudanese government in the north and the SPLM/A in the south, the first being during the Comprehensive Peace Agreement following the Second Sudanese Civil War.

In 2004, after intense deadlock on Abyei boundaries, a mandate was created by the Protocol on the Resolution in Abyei Area under the 2004 Comprehensive Peace Agreement (CPA) to create the Abyei Boundary Commission (ABC). Under the mandate prescribed by the Abyei protocol, the ABC was composed of fifteen members from the government of Sudan, SPLM/A, Intergovernmental Authority on Development, United States, and the United Kingdom. The ABC's report settled with a boundary at approximately 10°22'30"N., 87 kilometers (54 miles) north of the town of Abyei.

Complicating the situation is the significant amount of crude oil located in Abyei, and the fact the Greater Nile Oil Pipeline travels through Abyei, which is crucial to Sudan's oil output. Additionally, the arbitration was conducted while the Government of Sudan (more precisely the ruling National Congress Party, or NCP), and the SPLM/A were conducting ongoing peace negotiations with an eye towards referendums on self-determination in Abyei and Southern Sudan, as provided in the CPA. The Tribunal was thus tasked with rendering a legal decision in a case with highly politically sensitive overtones.

The mandate of the Tribunal was designed to resolve the boundaries of Abyei. At the outset, the Tribunal asserted that it would limit its inquiry based on the parameters of the

Arbitration Agreement and affirmed that its role was essentially legal. The Tribunal concluded that the parties intended for international law to apply to the proceedings. However, the final award settled the boundary in such a way that was politically suitable. Under this legal framework, the Tribunal defined its limited role as assessing, under a reasonableness test, whether the Abyei Boundary Commission (ABC) Experts had exceeded their mandate, which was to "define and demarcate the area of the nine Ngok Dinka chiefdoms transferred to Kordofan in 1905." The Tribunal examined both the ABC Experts' interpretation and implementation of their mandate.

On July 22, 2009 the five-member arbitral tribunal rendered a final award. The Tribunal concluded that the ABC Experts' interpretation of their mandate was reasonable, even when viewed in the context of the peace process in Sudan. The Tribunal determined, however, that the ABC Experts had exceeded their mandate in its implementation by failing to provide sufficient reasoning for its conclusions. Rather than nullify the entire ABC Commission Report, the Tribunal offered its own determinations on the boundaries of Abyei. In the final award, the Tribunal settled the eastern and western boundaries at 29°E and 27°50'E.

One member of the Tribunal, Judge Awn Al-Khasawneh, dissented from the award. Judge Al-Khasawneh argued that in trying to find a compromise position for its award, the Tribunal exceeded its own legal authority. Judge Al-Khasawneh condemned the Tribunal for basing its award largely on only one source for the 29°E and 27°50'E, which Judge Al-Khasawneh describes as misinterpreted quotes and "non-contemporaneous remarks made in 1951 by Howell." Judge Al-Khasawneh argued that the Tribunal's award did not follow the specific mandate that commissioned their task. Judge Al-Khasawneh criticized the Tribunal for choosing to award a compromise rather than using reason and the documents furnished to settle the boundaries. Judge Al-Khasawneh noted that the Tribunal's job was to validate the boundary set by the ABC, not to redraw the boundaries. Instead Judge Al-Khasawneh claimed that the Tribunal drew boundaries that never before existed and which historically belonged to the Misseriya tribes. Moreover, although the Tribunal wanted to contribute to the peace process, delimiting the area only increased the dispute and tensions in the area.

The materials below discuss the Abyei decision in further detail. Material 8 includes excerpts from the final award decreed by the Tribunal and excerpts from the dissenting opinion by Judge Al-Khasawneh. The additional materials in this chapter analyze the implications of the award and arguments made by both parties. The readings discuss a central theme of policy determinations that the Tribunal either made or policy determinations that impacted the Tribunal's decision. The readings also review and examine whether the mandate prescribed a task that was purely legal, or whether it is also appropriate to view the Tribunal's decision as an effort to influence the parties' political and social actions.

---

## 8. Final Award of the Tribunal

### Permanent Court of Arbitration, 2009

IN THE MATTER OF AN ARBITRATION BEFORE A TRIBUNAL
CONSTITUTED IN ACCORDANCE WITH ARTICLE 5 OF THE ARBITRATION
AGREEMENT BETWEEN THE GOVERNMENT OF SUDAN AND THE SUDAN
PEOPLE'S LIBERATION MOVEMENT/ARMY ON DELIMITING ABYEI AREA

– and –

THE PERMANENT COURT OF ARBITRATION OPTIONAL RULES
FOR ARBITRATING DISPUTES BETWEEN TWO PARTIES OF
WHICH ONLY ONE IS A STATE

– between –

THE GOVERNMENT OF SUDAN

– and –

THE SUDAN PEOPLE'S LIBERATION MOVEMENT/ARMY

\* \* \*

**The Tribunal's Task Pursuant to the Arbitration Agreement**

**1. The Two Stages of Review Under the Arbitration Agreement**

395. At the outset, a few preliminary observations regarding the Tribunal's own mandate are in order. The tasks and competence of the Tribunal are based on the Parties' consent, as expressed in the Arbitration Agreement. The critical passage is Article 2, which, as will be recalled, defines the "Scope of Dispute" in the following manner:

> The issues that shall be determined by the Tribunal are the following:
>
> a. Whether or not the ABC Experts had, on the basis of the agreement of the Parties as per the CPA, exceeded their mandate which is "to define (i.e. delimit) and demarcate the area of the nine Ngok Dinka chiefdoms transferred to Kordofan in 1905" as stated in the Abyei Protocol, and reiterated in the Abyei Appendix and the ABC Terms of Reference and Rules of Procedure.
>
> b. If the Tribunal determines, pursuant to Sub-article (a) herein, that the ABC Experts did not exceed their mandate, it shall make a declaration to that effect and issue an award for the full and immediate implementation of the ABC Report.
>
> c. If the Tribunal determines, pursuant to Sub-article (a) herein, that the ABC Experts exceeded their mandate, it shall make a declaration to that effect, and shall proceed to define (i.e. delimit) on map the boundaries of the area of the nine Ngok Dinka chiefdoms transferred to Kordofan in 1905, based on the submissions of the Parties.

396. In addition, the preamble of the Arbitration Agreement explains, in its penultimate recital, that "the Parties differed over whether or not the ABC Experts exceeded their mandate as per the provisions of the CPA, the Abyei Protocol, the Abyei Appendix, and the ABC Terms of Reference and Rules of Procedure." It is this dispute that the Parties have "agreed to refer … to final and binding arbitration." Given these provisions, the Tribunal's initial function is to determine whether, in light of its *lex specialis* (Article 3 of the Arbitration Agreement, which, among others, refers to the CPA, the Abyei Protocol and the Abyei Appendix), the ABC Experts' conduct and findings "exceeded their mandate."

397. In accordance with Article 2 of the Arbitration Agreement, the Tribunal is to proceed in two distinct and contingent stages, comprising two distinct juridical tasks. The first enterprise under Article 2(a) is for the Tribunal to determine whether the ABC Experts exceeded their mandate. The second task, which is to be undertaken under Article 2(c) only if it determines "that the ABC Experts exceeded their mandate," requires the Tribunal to reach its own findings on the specific question that had been submitted to the ABC. The contingent nature of Article 2(c) is somewhat obscured by the consolidated nature of these proceedings, such that the Parties have adduced evidence and presented arguments with respect to an Article 2(c) determination before the Tribunal had made its

Article 2(a) determination. Nevertheless, the Tribunal is mindful of the need to maintain the separation between the distinct modes of inquiry called for with respect to Article 2(a) and Article 2(c). It will now turn, as it must, to an examination of the scope and limitations of its Article 2(a) mandate.

## 2. The Tribunal's Task pursuant to Article 2(a) of the Arbitration Agreement is Limited

### (a) The Sequence of Article 2 Prohibits a *de novo* Review of the ABC's Findings under Article 2(a)

398. The contingent sequence and distinct inquiries required by Article 2's partition of the Tribunal's jurisdiction provide an important indication of the levels of scrutiny that the Parties intended the Tribunal to undertake with respect to subparagraphs (a) and (c) of Article 2. A *de novo* review of all relevant evidence is sought by the Parties only under Article 2(c), that is, in the event that the Tribunal has found that the ABC Experts exceeded their mandate. Conversely, it appears that the Parties did not expect or authorize the Tribunal to make any definitive substantive determination — for the purpose of its analysis under Article 2(a) of the Arbitration Agreement — as to the ABC Experts' correctness of fact or law with respect to its delimitation of the Abyei Area in 1905.

399. Had the Parties, when drafting the Arbitration Agreement, inverted the sequence of Article 2, thereby charging the Tribunal with first determining the "correct" extension of the Abyei Area and necessarily confirming or correcting the ABC Experts' decision as appropriate, the Tribunal may well have arrived at a different determination from that of the ABC Experts' Report (not least because the Tribunal's composition and fields of expertise are so different from those of the ABC Experts as to virtually ensure a different result). Yet the Parties did not invert the sequence. As Article 2 of the Arbitration Agreement stands, the Tribunal must conclude that the Parties contemplated the possibility that the Tribunal (or some of its Members) might incline to the view that one or more of the ABC Experts' findings were erroneous as a matter of law or fact, without however concluding that the ABC Experts had for that reason exceeded their mandate.

400. The sequence of Article 2 of the Arbitration Agreement therefore indicates that the extent of permissible "excess of mandate" analysis pursuant to Article 2(a) is limited: regardless of whether the Tribunal, in 2009 and with the benefit of the Parties' submissions (including factual evidence and expert opinion not submitted to the ABC in 2005), would have reached similar conclusions, the Tribunal must limit itself to considering whether the ABC Experts' definition of the Abyei Area in their 2005 Experts' Report can be understood as a reasonable, or at least a not unreasonable, discharge of their mandate. By contrast, the question of the correct location of the boundaries of the Abyei Area as the Tribunal sees it is outside the scope of permissible Article 2(a) review and will only be addressed should the Tribunal conclude that the ABC committed an excess of mandate.

* * *

407. The Tribunal's task under the Arbitration Agreement is essentially a legal one. This is made clear in the "applicable law" clause of Article 3 of the Arbitration Agreement (see discussion *infra*), which requires the Tribunal to apply a variety of legal instruments as well as "general principles of law." The Tribunal's proceedings were to be conducted within the framework of the Permanent Court of Arbitration (PCA), using a set of Rules prepared for "Arbitrating Disputes Between Two Parties of Which Only One Is a State." While the Arbitration Agreement does not specify, in terms, that the arbitrators were to be international lawyers, it was agreed that only persons on the PCA's list of arbitrators or persons who had served as arbitrators in PCA proceedings would be eligible for nomination to the Tribunal. Moreover, in the appointment of the Presiding Arbitrator, Article 5(8) of

the Arbitration Agreement provides that "he/she shall be a renowned lawyer of high professional qualifications, personal integrity and moral reputation." Consistent with these provisions, the Parties selected jurists and scholars of international law as arbitrators. The clear implication was that a Tribunal composed of international lawyers will adjudge, using legal standards, whether the ABC Experts exceeded their mandate and, if this is found to be the case, delimit "on map" the Abyei Area by applying the Parties' *lex specialis*.

\* \* \*

### 3. The Scope of the Tribunal's Authority under Article 2 to Declare an Excess of Mandate Respecting Certain Parts of the ABC Experts' Report, while Retaining the ABC Experts' Core Conclusions

\* \* \*

424. ... [T]he Tribunal will comply with its duty under general principles of law to keep to a minimum the scope of nullity, subjecting only those parts of the ABC Experts' findings which are discrete and severable to an independent and separate analysis. In accordance with Judge Weeramantry's opinion (quoted above) that "boundary disputes, where different segments of the total matter in dispute can be decided as separate and distinct problems, the answers to which can stand independently of each other," if an excess of mandate is found to have occurred with respect to a particular finding or conclusion of the ABC Experts, "the segments of the dispute that have been properly determined can maintain their integrity though the findings on other segments are assailed or do not exist." If the Tribunal should find that certain discrete and severable findings or conclusions of the ABC Experts are rendered in excess of mandate but which are not fundamentally related to other findings or conclusions, it will set aside only those conclusions, while confirming those parts of the ABC Experts' Report which prove to have been within their mandate.

### 4. The Applicable Law Governing these Proceedings

425. Article 3 of the Arbitration Agreement prescribes the law and instruments that must be applied by the Tribunal in the exercise of its mandate:

1.  The Tribunal shall apply and resolve the disputes before it in accordance with the provisions of the CPA, particularly the Abyei Protocol and the Abyei Appendix, the Interim National Constitution of the Republic of Sudan, 2005, and general principles of law and practices as the Tribunal may determine to be relevant.

2.  This Agreement, which consolidates the Abyei Road Map signed on June 8th 2008 and the Memorandum of Understanding signed on June 21st 2008 by the Parties with the view of referring their dispute to arbitration, shall also be applied by the Tribunal as binding on the Parties.

426. In contrast with the ABC Experts (who were required to arrive at their decision "based on scientific analysis and research"), Article 3 makes clear that the Tribunal shall decide, by applying legal methods, whether the ABC Experts exceeded their mandate under Article 2(a) of the Arbitration Agreement and, if and to the extent that it finds that there were such excesses, the delimitation of the boundary of the Abyei Area under Article 2(c).

427. In addition to the provisions of the CPA (particularly the Abyei Protocol and the Abyei Appendix) and the Interim National Constitution, the Tribunal must also apply "general principles of law and practices" which it determines to be relevant. Neither the CPA nor the Arbitration Agreement is a treaty. They are, rather, agreements between the government of a sovereign state, on the one hand, and, on the other, a political party/movement, albeit one which those agreements recognize may—or may not—govern over a

sovereign state in the near future. But, in addition to the reference to "general principles of law and practice," there are a number of other indications that the Parties intended that international law play a crucial role in the resolution of this dispute.

\* \* \*

429. Second, the Parties' chosen method and forum for settling the dispute also manifests their intention to have international law apply. The Parties opted for arbitration administered under the auspices of the PCA, an international dispute resolution organization, and in accordance with the PCA Rules.

\* \* \*

434. But international law is only one part of the applicable law. The Tribunal is mindful of the entire *lex specialis* prescribed by the Parties and the interrelations between its component parts. Article 3(1) prescribes a functional hierarchy among the applicable sources of law that reflects the specific concerns of the Parties: the CPA (particularly those components of the CPA that directly bear upon Abyei within the North-South peace process) takes precedence in application, followed by the Interim National Constitution, followed by "general principles of law and practices." It should also be emphasized that Article 3(2) explicitly calls for the Tribunal to apply the Arbitration Agreement, and Article 2 of the Arbitration Agreement plays a central role in clarifying the scope and limits of the Tribunal's juridical inquiry.

435. The Tribunal is sensitive to the extent to which principles and practices of international law, insofar as they prove applicable, must be adapted to the specific context of this dispute. As the following sections will demonstrate, the special character of the ABC Experts and the specific object and purpose of the ABC's constitutive instruments within the broader Sudan peace process, and a particular source's place in the hierarchy of applicable law sources, will affect the role which legal principles and precedent from other areas of law are to play. Although it is permissible to apply relevant international law where appropriate, the Tribunal will be particularly attentive to the wording, context, object and purpose of the Abyei Protocol, the Abyei Appendix, the Interim National Constitution and the Arbitration Agreement.

\* \* \*

## Failure to State Reasons in the Implementation of the Mandate

\* \* \*

### 3. The Eastern and Western Boundaries of the Abyei Area

702. The ABC Experts' Report and the Parties' pleadings both present arguments and evidence relating to the northern and southern boundary lines of the Abyei Area. In stark contrast, the Tribunal observes that the eastern and western boundaries of the "area of the nine Ngok Dinka chiefdoms transferred to Kordofan in 1905" were barely discussed. This is surprising, given the fact that the delimitation of these western and eastern lines were just as integral to the ABC's mandate as other components of the Abyei Area. Having carefully considered the evidence presented relating to these boundaries, the Tribunal finds that the ABC Experts' decision regarding the eastern and western boundary lines is insufficiently motivated; this absence of sufficient reasoning constitutes, in turn, an excess of mandate concerning those parts of the ABC Experts' findings. This insufficiency on the part of the ABC Experts may be traced, to an extent, to the scarcity of the evidence, but that of itself does not suffice to validate the findings of the ABC Experts in respect of the eastern and western boundaries.

703. Proposition 9 of the ABC Experts' Report states:

> The Abyei Area is defined as the territory of Kordofan encompassed by latitude
> 10°35'N in the north to longitude 29°32'E in the east, and the Upper Nile, Bahr
> el-Ghazal and Darfur provincial boundaries as they were at the time of inde-
> pendence in 1956. (SPLM/A Presentation, Appendix 3.2)

704. The ABC Experts attempted to explain the eastern boundary line by indicating that
it was reasonable to adopt longitude 29°32'E since neither "the Ngok nor the SPLM/A
had presented claims to the territory east of longitude 29°32'15." This terse statement
does not constitute a sufficiently reasoned justification of the eastern boundary; rather,
it is a mere summary of one of the Parties' positions (the SPLM/A's). The Report remains silent on the GoS's arguments concerning this point, and the ABC Experts do not
indicate any independent conclusions that they would have drawn as a result of their
analysis.

705. The only other possible justification of the eastern boundary that the Tribunal can
discern from the Report stems from the ABC Experts' analysis of a sketch map produced
by the SPLM/A. The ABC Experts briefly refer to the sketch map produced by the SPLM/
A during their final presentation to the ABC before proceeding to state that this evidence
is "inconclusive" (given the absence of a copy of a 1974 presidential decree). However,
although the ABC Experts themselves do not ascribe much probative value to the sketch
map, they nevertheless seem to rely on this very map to determine that the villages presented by the SPLM/A as Ngok villages were mostly "contained within the area of latitude
10°35'N and longitude 29°32'15"E ..." While the appreciation of evidence by the ABC
Experts is beyond the Tribunal's review mandate under Article 2(a), it is contradictory (not
to mention inappropriate in its failure to articulate reasons based on the best available
evidence) for the ABC Experts to base their decision exclusively on evidence which they
themselves have qualified as inconclusive. Beyond these contradictory reasons, the Tribunal
finds no further explanation from the ABC Experts relating to the eastern boundary.

706. With respect to the determination of the western boundary line, this Tribunal notes
that the selection of the 1956 Kordofan-Darfur boundary is entirely unreasoned. Indeed,
it is noteworthy that the ABC Experts did not make any specific pronouncement as to
the location of the western boundary line of the Abyei Area; instead, the ABC Experts
stated that: "[a]ll other boundaries of the area that coincide with the provincial boundaries as they were at independence on 1 January 1956 shall remain as they are." No supporting evidence is presented, and no analysis is provided which would expose the line
of reasoning adopted by the ABC Experts to reach the conclusion that the 1956 boundary between the provinces of Kordofan and Darfur also represents the westernmost limits of the area of the nine Ngok Dinka chiefdoms transferred to Kordofan in 1905. While
the Tribunal understands the importance of the 1956 boundaries in the broader context
of the peace process and the possible secession of South Sudan (should it choose to do
so in the exercise of self-determination), as indicated by Sections 1 and 8 of the Abyei
Protocol, reliance on the Darfur-Kordofan boundary without any supporting analysis
does not allow the Tribunal and the readers of the Report to understand how the Experts
arrived at this conclusion.

707. The Tribunal takes note of the ABC Experts' reference in Proposition 9 to the SPLM/
A Presentation before the ABC (Appendix 3 of ABC Experts' Report, Part 2). However,
Appendix 3 sheds no light on how the ABC Experts arrived at their conclusions regarding the eastern and western longitudes up to 10°10'N. Rather, the SPLM/A Presentation
as reproduced in the Report exposes the SPLM/A's claims regarding the presence of the
Ngok Dinka north of the river Kir, and makes no attempt at identifying the 1905 location of the nine Ngok Dinka chiefdoms on the east and the west.

708. Thus, the ABC Experts did not provide sufficient reasoning with respect to essential elements of the decision, namely the determination of the eastern and western boundary lines of the Abyei Area. As indicated above in Section D 2.(b)(ii), a failure to state reasons constitutes an excess of mandate when it relates to a point "necessary to the tribunal's decision." The ABC was expressly tasked with the responsibility of delimiting the Abyei area and the requirement to provide sufficient reasoning with respect to the delimitation of its eastern and western components was an integral part of that responsibility. This Tribunal recalls that the "target audience" of the ABC Experts' Report were the multiple stakeholders of the Sudanese peace process, ranging from the Presidency to the local residents of Abyei. As such, the failure to state sufficient reasons or indeed, to state any reasons at all, as in the case of the western boundary, does not allow the reader to understand the basis on which the ABC Experts decided on the western and eastern boundaries of the Abyei Area.

* * *

### The Tribunal's Determination of the Abyei Area's Eastern and Western Boundaries Pursuant to Article 2(C) of the Arbitration Agreement

710. Having upheld the reasonableness of the ABC Experts' predominantly tribal interpretation of the Formula, this Tribunal considers itself obliged to proceed with the delimitation phase of the mandate without departing from the same predominately tribal approach. This conclusion applies *a fortiori* given the Tribunal's determination that the northern limit of the area of permanent habitation of the nine Ngok Chiefdoms transferred in 1905 (i.e., the ABC Experts' findings and delimitation at latitude 10°10'N) was reasoned and within the ABC Experts' mandate. As discussed above, the retained northern boundary of the Abyei Area was drawn by the ABC Experts on the basis of a predominantly tribal interpretation as opposed to a predominantly territorial interpretation.

* * *

*Dissenting Opinion by Judge Awn Al-Khasawneh*

* * *

### 1. The Experts went on a Frolic of their Own

1. The ABC Experts were tasked with a straightforward and specific mandate. It was not to ascertain where the Ngok people lived in 1905 nor to pronounce on land uses in southern Kordofan. Their mandate was simply to ascertain the spatial implications with reference to a single defining date (1905) and a single defining event (the transfer to Kordofan of [the area of] [the nine Ngok Dinka Chiefdoms]). To be sure, the provincial boundary between Kordofan and Bahr el Ghazal was not as clear as the provincial boundaries of a late 20th-century, highly centralised State would be, but they were, by the standards of their time and place, clear enough to effect a delimitation, and the mandate itself assumed the existence of such a boundary. At any rate it was the job of the Experts to clarify any confusion or doubts—an achievable task by reference to, and close reading of, Condominium documents and other available evidence. Ironically it was this very confusion that caused the Experts to abandon their mandate and to embark on a frolic of their own with no apparent justification.

* * *

5. The Tribunal has now, for reasons that have more to do with compromise than principle, impugned the northern line which stood at 10° 22'N where the Experts had bisected the Goz area on the basis of one of their theories relating to the "equal division of shared natural resources", a concept with which I am not familiar. The Tribunal replaced

that line with a shortened line at 10° 10'N, which was not the Experts' northern boundary line of the area, but only where the Experts concluded that the Ngok Dinka "dominant rights" stopped. In addition to impugning the northern line, the Tribunal has also impugned the eastern and western lines. But at this point, the Tribunal has not drawn what is the only possible conclusion, namely, that nothing is now left of the Experts' Report except sociological theories and clues from human geography, and that therefore the Report must be set aside. Only after drawing that conclusion should the Tribunal have embarked on its own delimitation on the basis of the submissions of the Parties and the benefit it derived from guidance by learned counsel. Instead, it has opted, without sanction from its own mandate permitting partial nullity, (for this reason it is in excess of mandate), to effect new straight lines. These are unsupported by any "conclusive evidence", the standard the Tribunal has applied in impugning the northern line, or by "adequate reasoning", the standard it has applied to the impugning of the eastern and western boundaries. This is another reason why by drawing boundary lines without the reasoning it required of the Experts, the Tribunal is by the same standards in excess of mandate. To substantiate these assertions, this Dissenting Opinion will begin by examining the evidence for the new boundary lines.

## 2. The Supporting Evidence and Reasoning for the Eastern and Western Boundaries and their Intersection with the Northern Boundary at 10° 10' N

6. "The house of hope is built on sand," as Hafiz of Shiraz once wrote, and indeed if we are to look in the Award for a "*fondation solide*" on which to delimit the tribal boundaries of the Ngok Chiefdoms we will seek in vain. The Tribunal cannot, with all the hopes that the hearts of my learned colleagues may contain, erect its reasoning for allotting such a vast area on such meagre factual evidence. The only source for the 29°E and 27° 50'E lines are the imprecise, non-contemporaneous remarks made in 1951 by Howell which the majority quoted out of context and misinterpreted. The ABC Experts were aware of Howell's writings and quoted them at length in their own Report, however they did not base their delimitations of the boundary on those remarks—whether out of recognition of their generality or because they would not have included enough territory especially to the east is a matter of speculation.

7. The relevant extract from Howell's "Notes on the Ngork Dinka of Western Kordofan" reads:

"The Ngok Dinka occupy the area between approximately long 27° 50' and long 29° on the Bahr el Arab, extending northwards along the main watercourse of which the largest is the Ragaba Um Biero."

8. First, Howell's use of the word "approximately" suggests that he was trying to give a general and approximate appreciation of the area. Surely—for the meticulous at least—that is no basis on which to draw a vertical line stretching due north some 50 kilometres from the Bahr el Arab where it meets the Upper Nile border at around 9° 40'N to the 10° 10'N line, and to allot the enclosed area to the Ngok. This is simply an affront to the science of delimitation.

9. Secondly, the Ngok do extend northwards, but not *ad infinitum* and Howell, who reminded the reader that the longitudes are approximate (as befits a tribe and not a regimented army) indicated that the area of occupation was "along the middle reaches of the Bahr el Arab" and its tributaries.

Neither the Bahr el Arab nor its Ragabas in their middle reaches are anywhere near 10° 10'N. Moreover, neither the Bahr el Arab nor the Ragabas are horizontal or latitudinal, let alone forming straight lines: they follow a north-westerly direction from 9° 20'5

N at the eastern border of Kordofan to approximately 9° 50'5 N at the Kordofan/Darfur border. The Ragaba Um Biero meets the Bahr el Arab and is filled by it at Chweng approximately at 9° 30'3 N; it reaches beyond the 10° N line near the Darfur border (although no one is sure as to where its upper reaches end). The Ragaba ez Zarga, the most northerly of the Ragabas, enters Kordofan at approximately 9° 40'5" N, goes up in a north-westerly direction, meanders at a more or less straight line around 9° 50'N and then starts to climb at about 28°30 E to somewhere on or above latitude 10° N (although, again, no one knows whether it reaches the 10° 10 N line or above). Thus "along their middle reaches", where Howell placed the Ngok, is nowhere near the 10° 10'N line. It would follow, by necessary implication, that in 1951 when the Ngok may have reached, in their northward expansion, the Ragaba ez Zarga/Ngol, there is no evidence, even by then, that the vast area north and north-east of the Ragaba ez Zarga, ascribed to the Ngok by the Experts, ever had any collective Ngok Dinka presence in it, and the same applies to the reduced area ascribed by the Award without a shred of evidence let alone "conclusive evidence" to the Ngok, that is, the area north of the Ragaba ez Zarga and to the east of it until the 10° 10'N line meets, arbitrarily, longitude 29° E and the areas bordering Darfur which have always been traditional Homr lands.

10. Howell, an anthropologist and a British official — who was by all accounts a distinguished civil servant in an exceptionally meticulous civil service — would have been appalled at how his words were twisted by my learned colleagues. He would have been equally appalled by how he was quoted out of context by a Tribunal that has, elsewhere in the Award, stressed the importance of context, such as for example the fact that the Experts were social scientists, if only in that other instance, to prove doubtful propositions or to infuse doubt into clear ones — something to which I shall return later in my Dissenting Opinion — but I shall revert first to Howell and try to put his opinion in context.

11. In his 1951 publication, Howell says about the Ngok:

"Permanent villages, and cultivations are set along the higher ground north of Bahr el Arab, while dry season grazing grounds are for the most part in the open grassland (*toich*) south of the river. Villages are usually built close to the river or to one of the main watercourses, since water is more easily available during the early part of the dry season, either in pools or in shallow wells dug in the river bed. Clusters of homesteads each consisting of several living-huts (*ghot*) and one or more cattle byres (*luak*) are built in an almost continuous line along these rivers."

12. And still if any doubt remains as to where the Ngok were located when Howell wrote his Notes, he supplies a general answer at the outset, by way of introduction:

"The Ngork Dinka ... occupy an area along the middle reaches of the Bahr el Arab. They border the Rueng Alor Dinka in the south-east and the Twij Dinka to the south, and with both of these peoples have close cultural affinities. To the south-west are the Malwal Dinka. North of the Ngok are the Baggara Arabs of the Messeria Humr, with whom they have direct and seasonal contact ..."

13. Yet again Howell makes the observation that the Ngok were along "the middle reaches of the Bahr el Arab". As already noted, Howell had observed in 1948 that the area of occupation of the Ngok lies "along the middle reaches of the Bahr el Arab and its tributaries" and that "[d]uring the dry season the Homr Messiria mingle freely with them in pastures". A simple exercise in logic would show that the Ngok were in the "middle reaches", not the upper reaches, of the Bahr el Arab, the Ragaba Zarga and the Ragaba Um Biero, and this tallies completely with all contemporaneous cartographic and written evidence and with the evidence of Cunnison on whom the Award rightly heaps justified praise.

The idea that they had moved even further north and east beyond the Ragaba ez Zarga, where the Award wishes to place them is, to put it mildly, quite remarkable.

\* \* \*

## Conclusion

192. From the beginning the Tribunal faced a dilemma. Its reasoning was deployed with the avid aim of shielding the ABC Experts' Report from criticism and annulment. Thus, the Tribunal was too generous, at the expense of Sudan, in ascribing to the Experts prescriptive powers that went beyond a strictly fact-finding mission. Such a presumption, totally unsupported, should not have been made too lightly, given that the Sudan never gave the Experts a carte blanche to dispose of its territories as they pleased. The Tribunal then went on to endow the Experts with a power of discretion to interpret their mandate that they did not have, all allowance being made for *Kompetenz-Kompetenz*. This so-called reasonableness standard could not have been the expectation of the two Parties when they conferred on the Tribunal its mandate. We should not assume that the SPLM/A expected that the delimitation of Abyei, which could become an international boundary, would be located not based on a correct interpretation but only on a reasonable one.

193. The Experts knew how vital to breaking the deadlock over Abyei was the territorial interpretation by the Government of their mandate. If they were not sure what their mandate was they should have gone back to the Parties or rendered a factual *non liquet*. To say that they had to proceed on a different interpretation because they were expected to delimit the area as part of the peace process is totally unconvincing. By proceeding as they did, they in fact derailed that peace process and caused a conflict in which Abyei itself was destroyed.

194. Moreover, the Tribunal started by defining its mandate in a rigid manner, then clouded that self-imposed distinction, which could not, in logic, admit of an intermediate solution, by partially invalidating the Experts' decision. It contradicted itself by doing so with regard to the very distinction between Sub-articles 2 *(a)* and 2 *(c)* of its mandate. Equally importantly, by proceeding to a partial annulment without express or implied sanction from its own mandate, the Tribunal committed an excess of mandate. An assertion that highly skilled jurists have committed an excess of mandate, the very accusation they were mandated to investigate and to redress if found to be true, is not an assertion to be made lightly and it is not being made lightly but this is the truth of the matter and it is an inescapable conclusion that neither the Tribunal's reasoning nor its skill and status can hide. The Tribunal, still deploying its intellectual resources to shield the Experts' Report, bestowed upon the Experts the status of "preferred arbiters of fact", a status contextually wholly inappropriate given the area of their expertise and the accusations of procedural improprieties which are not disputed on the facts. These devices and other techniques reveal a low standard of review which excluded fundamental error (a standard that the Tribunal could and indeed should have applied even *proprio motu* if only to account for the fantastic difference between contemporaneous evidence and the results achieved by the Experts). In short all these assumptions devices and techniques should have seen the Experts' Report safely to shore i.e., intact but of course as removed from reality as it is possible to be.

195. However, and this is where a simple mistake metamorphosed into a dilemma, the Tribunal decided to dabble in compromise, always a hazardous and ill-advised venture for tribunals, but especially so in the present case. This compromise took cartographic shape by the impugning, i.e., invalidating, of the eastern and western lines of the Abyei area as delimited by the Experts for lack of reasoning, and this is where the Tribunal committed

its second excess of mandate. It redrew the eastern and western boundaries at 29°E and 27°50'E respectively with no "reasoning" or no "adequate reasoning", the very standards it used to invalidate the Experts' eastern and western boundaries, except that its own excess of mandate was more inexcusable than that of the Experts. For it had the benefit of hindsight, of learned and extensive legal arguments, and of being composed of prominent jurists. Considerable efforts were devoted to support the new lines but any close reading of the evidence will reveal it to be disparate in sources and desperate in tone. [ ... ]

196. Here, what started as a dilemma, namely, how to shield the Experts whilst effecting a compromise that would impugn all their lines, at the same time becomes a fully-fledged trilemma: how to shield the Experts, impugn all their lines, and, acting in its own delimitation, how to draw these lines not only with no evidence, but in spite of contrary evidence as to where the Ngok and the Homr actually were. And this is why I felt that it would be useful, if only in defence of realism and credulity, to review all the evidence I could find on where the Ngok and Homr were located circa 1905. The picture that emerges and which is reflected in the Map appended to this Dissenting Opinion is totally different from both the Experts' and the Tribunal's lines.

197. In doing this I am assuming, for the sake of exploring all the logical possibilities, that the transfer of 1905 to Kordofan is a tribal one. For me this is only one assumption; for my learned colleagues they consider themselves obliged, by their earlier finding that a predominantly tribal transfer was a reasonable interpretation of the "formula", to adopt the same interpretation for the Tribunal's own delimitation. But no reason is given for this conclusion. Under Sub-article *(c)* of the Arbitration Agreement, the mandate of this Tribunal requires it, in the event of a finding of excess of mandate, "to proceed to define (i.e. delimit) on map the boundaries of the area ... based on the submissions of the Parties", not to adopt and recycle those parts of the Experts' Report that it considers "reasonable". The moment the majority had freed themselves from their self-imposed shackles, they could follow any delimitation i.e., what was more accurate on the basis of the submissions of the Parties and not what was just reasonable.

198. The Tribunal also failed in inquiring into the two key concepts of the Experts' thought process: the assumption of "dominant" (Ngok) rights versus "secondary" (Misseriya) rights. Presumably the reason for this reticence was that the Tribunal would classify such a concept as part of the assessment of facts left to the Experts as "preferred arbiters of fact". But this is not the case, this concept is a crucial step in the Experts' reasoning that was neither reasoned nor supported as to its existence and applicability to Kordofan. The second crucial concept in the reasoning of the Experts, which the Tribunal failed to review, is the assumption of Ngok continuity of occupation which is more than an appreciation of facts. It is a wholesale abandonment of the temporal limitation on the Experts' mandate by turning it on its own head, and it should have been reviewed by the Tribunal, such review on the basis of lack of reasoning being within our mandate. Here the Tribunal may have been acting *infra petita* with regard to not answering questions about two crucial steps in the Tribunal's reasoning.

199. Moreover, having impugned so much, the Tribunal, by any standard of separability, should have set aside the remainder of the Report for, apart from the southern line drawn by Condominium officials, nothing was left. The Report was so thin and truncated that it could not stand on its own. The Tribunal contradicted itself in a fundamental way. It cornered itself by making a sharp distinction between Sub-articles 2 *(a)* and 2 *(c)* of its mandate and then clouded that distinction. The fact that inseparability was the obvious consequence not only of the wording of Sub-article 2 *(b)* but also of the distinction

between Sub-articles 2 *(a)* and 2 *(c)* was overlooked by my learned colleagues. The dichotomous distinction between the Tribunal's "enquiry" under Sub-articles 2 *(a)* and 2 *(c)* cannot accommodate the power of partial annulment that it has assumed. Formalism and teleology are words that do not sit together well.

200. Lastly, the Tribunal used "lack of reasoning" to impugn parts of the Experts' reasoning, but did so inconsistently. Thus, with regard to the area north of 10° 10'N, it used "lack of conclusive evidence", but it did not use the same lack of conclusive evidence south of 10° 10'N and north of Ragaba ez Zarga, although there is no shred of evidence, let alone conclusive evidence, that the Ngok were there in 1905 or indeed at any time after that, not even in 1965, the year of maximum Ngok Dinka expansion. The majority was inconsistent in demolishing the western and eastern lines for lack of reasoning or adequate reasoning and then replacing them with new lines, which it did on the basis of frivolous reasoning and hastily assembled evidence, without thinking twice about using evidence prepared after the dispute had arisen and tainted by accusations of intimidation. To use evidence tainted by accusations of duress that were not properly answered is not—to put it mildly—the zenith in maintaining evidentiary standards and no court should engage in such practice. To construct straight lines on the basis of <u>approximate</u> evidence and <u>rough areas</u> is an affront to the science of delimitation and no country should accept such a delimitation. The authors of the Award may congratulate themselves on their Herculean efforts, but the result is, not for lack of cleverness on their part, a feeble and modest construct with much to be modest about.

201. In the introduction to this Dissenting Opinion, I described the considerations that prompted me to explain comprehensively the reasons for my dissent. I believe that I have now substantiated my criticisms of the Award's conclusions and the reasoning deployed by the Majority to reach them. I need therefore say no more regarding the Award but leave it instead to the sand on which it has been built. I do however need to say a few words regarding another aspect of this unusual arbitration. I have already mentioned the likelihood that the Award may have a profound impact on the future of Sudan as a State and the peace and well being of all its citizens regardless of ethnicity or creed.

202. I am saddened that in this arbitration, which provided a perfect and rare chance for the Tribunal to contribute to the process of peace and reconciliation in Abyei and in the Sudan, that chance has been missed because of a wish to marry an ill-advised, misconceived compromise to a self-imposed restrictive interpretation of its mandate, the Tribunal neither maintained the integrity of its reasoning nor contributed to a durable peace. International law and indeed law in general sometimes provide only simple recipes for complex situations where populations and tribes intermingle and where the livelihood of certain groups transcends borders. In such cases, defensible compromises may sometimes bring more acceptable, more durable and indeed fairer solutions. After all Kipling, who knew a few things about the Sudan, and more about human nature, once wrote:

> "Man, a bear in most relations—
> worm and savage otherwise,—
> Man propounds negotiations,
> Man accepts the compromise."

203. This Tribunal could have been a peace-maker had it realised the obvious fact that peace-making is more difficult than law-making and judgment drafting. To be successful a compromise does not have to be a non-principled solution. On the contrary its chances of success increase if it is perceived by those the Award called the "stakeholders" as a fair and workable scheme. The stakeholders in this case are not only the Government and the SPLM/A, they are also the Ngok and the Misseriya. Today, we are more remote from achieving

a durable peace than before the rendering of this Award, because of the very simple fact that the Award failed utterly to take the rights of the Misseriya into consideration and could have the effect of denying them access to the waters of the Bahr, except for a small piece of land on the border of Darfur (and nothing in the Award on traditional rights changes this fact). Therefore the question that will never go away is who, in the process of delimiting the area of the nine Ngok Dinka Chiefdoms transferred to Kordofan in 1905, gave the Experts or this Tribunal the right to reduce the Misseriya to second class citizens in their own land and to create conditions which may deny them access to water. This would disrupt the very livelihood of the Misseriya that has depended for as long as they have been in Kordofan on access to the Abyei area. I can only hope that both Misseriya and Ngok Dinka will reach into their traditions and common history to find solutions better suited to their community of existence that should transcend all boundaries.

---

## 9. Josephine K. Mason, The Role of Ex Aequo et Bono in International Border Settlement: A Critique of the Sudanese Abyei Arbitration

American Review of International Arbitration, 2011
[footnotes omitted by editors]

\* \* \*

### III. The Meaning Of *Ex Aequo Et Bono*

Although the *Abyei* Tribunal was not obligated to address each of the questions presented by the parties, the arbitrators missed a valuable opportunity by failing to address the *ex aequo et bono* issue. Both of the parties raised legitimate arguments regarding the role of *ex aequo* adjudication in the case—but both parties also demonstrated a fundamental misunderstanding of what is meant by ex aequo et bono. This Section will summarize how *ex aequo et bono* has been defined in international law, and will assess the parties' arguments with regard to the *ex aequo et bono* issue.

Nearly all arbitral bodies require arbitral tribunals to adjudicate disputes according to positive law, except where the parties expressly permit them to decide them *ex aequo et bono*. In general, adjudication *ex aequo et bono* is characterized as a decision that takes into account issues of fairness and subjective justice. Many conflate a decision taken *ex aequo et bono* with one that is decided in equity because they are both based in fairness and a high level of discretion in applying legal principles. However, mainstream international jurisprudence draws a distinction between a decision taken *ex aequo et bono* and one decided on equitable principles.

The distinction most commonly drawn is that an equitable decision is rooted in legal principles, and that principles of fairness are used only for specific purposes within the legal framework. In formalist terms, equity may be used to perform three functions: to fill the gaps in the law (*equity praeter legem*); to justify a refusal to apply unjust laws (*equity contra legem*); and to adapt the law to the facts of individual cases (*equity infra legem*). As one modern scholar described it, "[e]quity is a part of international law, serving to temper the application of strict rules, to prevent injustice in particular cases, and to furnish a basis for extension where lines have been forged by experience." Thus, an equitable decision is one that is consistent with legal principles.

In contrast, a decision taken *ex aequo et bono* is most commonly defined as one that is decided in terms of fairness, equitability, or conscience, irrespective of the applicable law; that is, decided without deference to the strictures of positive law. Note that a choice of law clause referring to "general principles of law" means it must stay within the bounds of existing positive law; such a clause does not amount to permitting a decision *ex aequo et bono*. Moreover, an *ex aequo* decision is not necessarily contrary to the law—it is merely an "extra-legal" decision that takes into account more than a legal decision would normally permit. For example, an *ex aequo* adjudication might take into account more pragmatic or political factors than a legally based decision would, or take into account interests that do not normally rise to the level of a legal right. Thus, while an equitable decision is founded in the law, a decision *ex aequo et bono* is founded on extra-legal considerations and is made regardless of the applicable law.

One scholar described *ex aequo et bono* adjudication as creating a "new adjustment of interests." Such interests might include traditional duties, such as the duties of landowners to those who depend on their land for sustenance; other examples might include the sharing of natural resources where it is not required by positive law. Where these duties and interests are not delineated by positive law, but rather arise from traditional relationships or resource-sharing arrangements, an arbitral decision relating to such interests or duties cannot be said to be grounded in law.

In light of the foregoing definition of *ex aequo et bono*, it appears that both the Government and the SPLM/A were in part correct and in part incorrect in different aspects of their arguments. The Government was incorrect in arguing that equitable and *ex aequo et bono* adjudications are one and the same. On the other hand, the SPLM/A was incorrect in arguing that an *ex aequo et bono* decision is necessarily contrary to the law. The SPLM/A was also incorrect in its contention that adjudication *ex aequo et bono* does not generally require the express consent of both parties—although they made a plausible argument that only the Tribunal, and not the Experts, were beholden to this rule.

The SPLM/A's argument that the Goz had been delimited according to equitable principles also lacked merit, because the Experts had not employed the legal tactics that characterize an equitable decision: they were not applying a legal principle, so they were not applying equity *contra legem* or equity *infra legem*. Furthermore, the Experts were not merely compensating for lacunae in the applicable law, since they did not identify a framework of principle of positive law in which they found "gaps" in need of filling. Therefore, the analysis was not based on equity *praeter legem*, either. Indeed, the SPLM/A did not contend that this was the case—they instead argued that the delimitation of the Goz was "in no way *ex aequo et bono*; [rather,] it was a wise resolution of a problem." However, contrary to what the SPLM/A implied with this statement, a decision *ex aequo et bono* is often defined as just that: a wise resolution to a problem.

In the end, the Tribunal did not find it necessary to respond to either party's contention, nor to explicate any reliance on *ex aequo et bono* jurisprudence. The Tribunal merely inquired whether the Experts had made a reasoned decision, and did not investigate the reasons themselves.

Nevertheless, it would appear that the Experts did in fact delimit the Goz on an *ex aequo et bono* basis, but not for the precise reasons set out by the parties. The Experts decided that the Goz would be bisected and shared between the North and South because "[t]he two parties lay equal claim to the shared areas and accordingly it is reasonable and equitable to divide the Goz between them." This is a decision *ex aequo et bono* because it is not based in positive law but in general fairness and on "splitting the difference." The overlapping traditional rights of the Ngok Dinka and the Misseriya may be fairly characterized as interests not rising to the level of legal rights, but interests that are nonetheless crucial for peace and stability in the area. Therefore, the Experts' sensitivity to the overlapping seasonal usage by the two tribes further indicates a reliance on *ex aequo*-like considerations.

Finally, Professor Johnson's public statement regarding the location of the oil strongly indicates that the arbitrators were attempting to reach a solution that would distribute oil in a way that was politically expedient, rather than letting the oil be distributed among the parties "as it lays." Although the parties did not mention it, the Experts' consideration of the oil wells also indicates that large portions of the Abyei border were drawn up *ex aequo et bono*. Professor Johnson's reasoning ("if the boundary is defined one way, it puts quite a lot of oil in the Abyei area, and therefore more of that oil revenue has to be shared") reveals that pragmatic and political factors did play a considerable role in the Abyei delimitation. This is especially true because neither party could claim a legal right to the oil in the area—it was a natural resource, the title to which would be determined by the arbitration. Thus, each party's stake in future oil revenues was an important interest, but one which did not rise to the level of a legally recognized right. In order to promote wealth-sharing and prevent future violence over the allocation of oil, the Experts delimited the area in such a way that they believed would be fair to both parties and which would avoid future conflict, regardless of the applicable law. In this sense, it was a textbook example of a decision taken *ex aequo et bono*.

## IV. A Place For *Ex Aequo Et Bono* In International Border Arbitration?

The Tribunal did not inquire into whether the Experts decided any sections of the border on an *ex aequo* basis; instead, it exhibited a high degree of deference for the Experts' decisions. However, if the Experts did decide on an *ex aequo et bono* basis, thereby exceeding their mandate, it is surprising that the arbitrators did not scrutinize the Experts' methods more thoroughly. Decisions *ex aequo et bono* are often regarded as illegitimate, the product of nearly unfettered discretion. If the Tribunal had acknowledged that the Experts had engaged in *ex aequo et bono* border delimitation, such an approach might have undermined the legitimacy of the peace process in the estimation of the international community. At the same time, the Tribunal was reluctant to interfere too much with the Experts' determinations and thus substitute their own judgment *in toto*. This Section will explore the reasons the Tribunal exhibited such deference and adhered assiduously to formal principles of law, and why the arbitrators were reluctant to address the *ex aequo et bono* issue. Ultimately, I will argue that, contrary to popular opinion within the arbitration community, *ex aequo et bono* adjudication could prove an expedient method of international border arbitration.

Although the International Court has not to date engaged in *ex aequo et bono* adjudication, is by no means unknown in international border settlement. Indeed, nearly a dozen disputes have included an *ex aequo et bono* clause in their arbitration agreement, even if the tribunal did not ultimately choose that route as the basis for its decision.

Nevertheless, the parties to the Abyei arbitration seemed intent upon settling their differences according to positive law and historical fact. This desire for formalism likely arose from the need for international legitimacy and the appearance of impartiality. Procedural regularity is often conceptually tied to the appearance of fairness and legitimacy: so long as the right process is followed, the outcome will appear to be fair. As Professor Franck explained,

> Legitimacy ... expresses the preference for order, which may or may not be conducive to change. Nevertheless, it is a key factor in fairness, for it accommodates a deeply felt popular belief that for a system of rules to be fair, it must be firmly

rooted in a framework of formal requirements about how rules are made, interpreted, and applied.

As the Experts discovered while seeking to determine the appropriate boundaries of the Abyei area, the traditional boundaries of the area were all but unfathomable from the available data, and the legal principles apposite to the dispute were murky at best. The English colonial borders had apparently long been abandoned, and resorting to the colonial borders, or those established fifty years later would have been an arbitrary and altogether unreasoned designation.

Moreover, the Experts found they could hardly carry out their task without considering the political consequences, as Professor Johnson noted in his interview with the Sudan Tribune. The distribution of the oil was a practical consideration that the Experts recognized was an important factor in the success of the peace process, and one that would have been foolish to ignore.

The question, then, is whether the Experts and the Tribunal should have remained committed to following positive law, or whether they should have taken into account political and equitable considerations and attempted to reach a decision that would be fair to all involved even if not based on the strictures of established law. In short, would a decision taken overtly *ex aequo et bono* have been appropriate in this international border arbitration?

The *Abyei* Tribunal, however, declined to address the issue and declined to adopt a legislative and political function, instead justifying its decision on highly formalized reasoning. The Tribunal's decision to approach the Experts' findings with a highly deferential standard of review was inspired by formal sources of law. For instance, the Tribunal undertook a strict textual interpretation of the Arbitration Agreement, borrowed concepts of limited review from American and German administrative law, extended the principle of *Kompetenz-Kompetenz* to apply to the Experts' interpretation of its own mandate, and cited case law regarding the standard of review for *excès de pouvoir* of arbitral tribunals. But by approaching the *Abyei* case with a highly deferential standard of review and applying the rigid standards of positive law, did the parties and the Tribunal miss an opportunity to forge a true compromise and a lasting peace?

This case illustrates the difficulties inherent in a one-size-fits-all approach to applying formal legal principles. Some scholars have criticized the use of formalized procedures and the "rule of law" to make important policy choices such as resource allocation and the relative fate of residents. They have argued that assiduous adherence to the "rule of law" too often interferes with well-reasoned policy decisions. As Professor Kennedy observed, the mechanical application of formal legal principles may undermine the very goals sought to be achieved:

> The puzzle is how easily one loses sight of these traditional issues of political and economic theory when the words "rule of law" come into play. There is something mesmerizing about the idea that a formal rule of law could somehow substitute for struggle over these issues and choices—could replace contestable arguments about the consequences of different distributions with the apparent neutrality of legal best practice.

This observation about the "dark sides" of formalism is particularly salient in this case. The goal of the *Abyei* arbitration was the pacific settlement of a political conflict. The Experts and the arbitrators were asked to make an essentially political determination—where the border between two warring states should be. Yet in cases such as this the arbitral body responsible for the case is often seen as a purely legal instrument, and not as a vehicle for deciding legislative or political disputes. I argue that even if this is true for ordinary arbitrations, for peace-process arbitration such as the Abyei case, such political determinations are desirable and even necessary. This is why I advocate an *ex aequo* approach to peace-process border arbitrations.

Because *ex aequo et bono* adjudication may take into account extra-legal interests, it necessarily requires reliance on pragmatic and often politically-charged factors. For this reason, some scholars posit that it is "legislative" in nature. Many scholars hold that international tribunals should not engage in this type of quasi-legislation. This constraint is perhaps comparable to the concept of a "political question" of American constitutional law—and indeed, many international law scholars are of the opinion that *ex aequo et bono* adjudication does not have a place in international tribunals and courts, much as cases deemed political questions are not properly heard in American federal court. Indeed, international courts have reiterated the position that legislative tasks have no place in international courts and tribunals.

In the *Free Zones of Savoy* case, for example, the International Court of Justice declared that legislative and political functions "lie outside the function of a court of law." However, this position has been criticized by some scholars, who argue that international courts and tribunals should not be prevented from carrying out purely political or legislative tasks, so long as that is what the parties have requested.

Indeed, the parties in this case did request such a legislative undertaking. The delimitation of international borders is a necessarily political determination, since it involves resource allocation and the balancing of various interests, including sovereignty and self-determination. Rather than relying on legal principles such as *uti possidetis*, I contend that arbitrators in peace-process border delimitation cases should forthrightly consider approaching the task *ex aequo et bono*.

The parties in this case did not expressly agree to a decision *ex aequo et bono*. While the Experts apparently did decide on a partial *ex aequo* basis, the Experts' approach was inconsistent and haphazard—precisely the result the parties sought to avoid when they expressed a desire for procedural regularity. An all-or-nothing approach to an *ex aequo et bono* adjudication would have been preferable to the piecemeal application of *ex aequo et bono* principles. While this relative chaos is in part due to the Tribunal's approach, it is equally attributable to ambiguity in the Arbitration Agreement—as well as the unsuitability of formal law for the task of border delimitation.

A forthright *ex aequo et bono* decision might have been more effective in stemming violence than a decision based on formalistic legal principles because it would have taken into account the myriad interests at stake. International border delimitation is a task that inherently involves resource allocation because it divvies up land and the natural assets on the land. Such a determination also may have a profound impact on the residents of disputed areas where their citizenship status depends on a tribunal's decision, as it did in this case. And because border arbitrations are designed to resolve current conflict and prevent future conflict, arbitrators in such cases must make political and pragmatic determinations and arrive at an outcome that will be viewed as fair to all parties involved.

In contrast to litigation-style arbitration, where the parties have allegedly violated one another's rights or breached a legal duty, arbitration of international borders should by design be conciliatory, workable and fair. Thus, peace-process border settlement is particularly well-suited to *ex aequo et bono* adjudication.

What is normally appealing about an Award decided on the basis of positive legal principles is that it will be seen as legitimate. The theory is that the legitimacy of the process is important in settling disputes because the losing party in the dispute will be satisfied that justice was done, even if the losing party is disappointed in the outcome. The theory is that justice lies in the fairness and regularity of the process of adjudicating legal rights, not in whether a particular party wins or loses. However, I submit that this logic does not apply with as much force in the context of border settlement that is part of a larger peace process.

For one thing, there are not only legal rights at stake, but political and economic interests not necessarily tied to legal rights. After all, the legal title to resources at stake in the dispute will be determined by the outcome of the border settlement. This becomes clear in the *Abyei* arbitration. The dispute was not over one party using the other's oil resources without permission, and seeking to collect damages or royalties; rather, the dispute (or one salient factor of the dispute) was over which party would be entitled to use those resources. The *Abyei* arbitration involved the creation of legal rights, not the adjudication of pre-existing legal rights. In this context, border adjudication is uniquely suited to non-legal, or *ex aequo et bono*, adjudication.

Secondly, peace-process border settlement is unique because the parties are less likely than in commercial or legal arbitrations to accept the result if it is not in their favor. Even if the adjudication is procedurally regular and embodies the "rule of law" ideal, the legitimacy of the process is less likely to appease an embattled party than is a compromise that distributes resources and draws borders in a fair and workable manner. As I have argued, this is the other key reason that *ex aequo et bono* adjudication may prove to be a superior model in peace-process border arbitrations than strictly legal models.

As Michael Harbottle of the Centre for International Peacebuilding observed, there is no easy solution to creating a workable peace:

> Peacebuilding focuses on the removal of the structural causes of conflict—the social, economic, humanitarian, ethnic, sectarian and even the environmental influences which create the situation in which open, or manifest, violence erupts. Until these conflict elements are satisfactorily resolved no amount of peace-making and peacekeeping can have a lasting effect.

### Conclusion

Although the initial reaction to the Abyei Award was positive, time will tell whether the approach taken in this arbitration will ultimately contribute to peace in the Sudan, or whether it will ultimately make matters worse. In light of the goals of this particular arbitration, perhaps a more pragmatic, fair-minded approach of the type advocated by Judge Al-Khasawneh, the dissenting arbitrator in this case, would have been better advised. The *Abyei* arbitration was meant to bring peace and stability to a region that has for decades been ravaged by war and unable to settle its differences peacefully. The delimitation of the Abyei area was crucial for a workable peace between the North and the South. At stake is the sovereignty of Abyei and the South, the peaceful coexistence among those who are culturally Arabic and culturally sub-Saharan, and the fair allocation of water, grazing land, and oil revenues among the diverse peoples of the Sudan.

A lasting peace will require a sophisticated balancing of the competing interests of those involved, not a mechanical application of formal rules. In future peace-process border arbitrations, perhaps the parties will be less hesitant to request *ex aequo et bono* adjudication, so that disputes may truly be settled fairly, pragmatically, and "in good conscience."

## 10. Wendy J. Miles and Daisy Mallett, The Abyei Arbitration and the Use of Arbitration to Resolve Inter-State and Intra-State Conflicts

Journal of International Dispute Settlement, 2010
[footnotes omitted by editors]

\* \* \*

### 4. The Use of Arbitration Clauses to Resolve Intra-state and Inter-state Conflicts

### A. Introduction

The Abyei Arbitration, in its use of arbitration to settle a politically volatile intra-state dispute, between the state and a people or group within its borders, was not unprecedented. There are other scenarios where groups of peoples and/or states have used arbitration as a method of resolving conflict. In some instances arbitration clauses are included as dispute resolution mechanisms in peace agreements, leading to the arbitration of disputes arising in the implementation and interpretation of peace agreements. In other cases arbitration is selected as a method of dispute resolution only after the dispute has arisen, for example to resolve a conflict between two parties regarding the determination of a territorial boundary or, in the case of the Abyei Arbitration Agreement, to determine whether an independent body had exceeded its mandate in the definition of a territorial region.

While negotiation and mediation are powerful dispute resolution tools, in deeply entrenched disputes regarding sovereignty over land and valuable natural resources or disputes relating to the implementation of peace agreements, political leaders are often unable to enter into a negotiated settlement, or accept a mediated settlement, because of the demands of the constituents or interest groups they represent. By way of example, it may be simply impossible for a political leader to agree voluntarily to forsake even the smallest area of land claimed by his or her constituents, yet that same leader may be able to agree to respect a binding determination of an independent body being imposed on both parties to the conflict. Matters which are politically controversial between parties can therefore benefit significantly from determination by an arbitral tribunal, which is an independent body quite removed from the issues in dispute.

Disputes in the context of political conflicts, by their very nature, rarely lend themselves to being resolved by national courts. Almost invariably, one party will not have confidence in the independence or neutrality of the decision-making process of state courts. Arbitration, on the other hand, is an attractive form of dispute resolution in such circumstances because it enables the parties to choose a panel of independent decision-makers with relevant expertise and experience. Where appropriate, the parties can agree to nominate decision-makers with specific technical, cultural, legal, political and social backgrounds. Moreover, arbitration generally leads to a binding award, with limited avenues for appeal, so the parties are provided with certainty with respect to their legal rights and obligations.

Arbitration is also an appealing method of resolving conflicts because of its inherent flexibility. As arbitration is founded on the parties' mutual consent to have their dispute resolved through the arbitral process, and the parties draft the arbitration agreement themselves, parties can mold the procedures of the arbitration to reflect the specific circumstances and nature of their dispute. Not only are the parties able to determine the characteristics and number of decision-makers, but they can also establish the procedure for the process and dictate the timeframe in order to ensure that the arbitral process meets their specific, and often unique, needs.

Less flexible, however, is the arbitral process itself. There now exists an established body of jurisprudence that governs the arbitral process. Even in arbitration proceedings concerning fundamentally political and/or constitutional issues, parties who choose to arbitrate are choosing a flexible but still relatively formal, and clearly established process. Tribunals are almost certainly lawyers or judges and parties expect them to make their decisions in accordance with due process and principles of law. It is the role and the responsibility of arbitral tribunals to uphold the rule of law. In the event that parties require a less formalistic legal approach, they may opt for a less formalistic dispute resolution mechanism, such as mediation or negotiation. At the very least, parties may expressly consent to the tribunal's power to make a decision ex aequo et bono. If the parties do not do so, it is incumbent on the tribunal to render a decision that upholds the rule of law.

## B. A Survey of the Use of Arbitration to Resolve Inter-state and Intra-state Conflicts

It is instructive to consider, compare and contrast other instances where arbitration has been used to resolve intra-state and inter-state conflicts.

### (ii) Eritrea-Yemen Arbitration Agreement

In 1995, Eritrea and Yemen entered into armed conflict in respect of the territorial sovereignty of the Red Sea Islands and the location of the international maritime boundary in the highly sensitive, frequently traversed waters to the south of the Suez Canal. Although the violence ceased, the parties were unsuccessful in negotiating an agreement. In October 1996, the two states entered into an Arbitration Agreement to provide a final and binding determination of the issues in dispute.

The Arbitration Agreement set out in detail the procedures which the parties had agreed would govern the arbitration. Specifically, it established that the tribunal would be composed of five impartial arbitrators. Each party was required to appoint two arbitrators, and failing the agreement of the party-appointed arbitrators, the chairman would be appointed by the President of the International Court of Justice. All the decisions of the tribunal were to be made unanimously, and where this was not possible, by majority (and if the tribunal was divided, the chairman's vote would be determinative). The Arbitration Agreement established a provisional timeline for the procedural elements of the arbitration, including two distinct phases. The first phase was to resolve the issues of territorial sovereignty and the scope of the dispute, with the second stage addressing the delimitation of the maritime boundaries. A tight timetable was imposed for each stage of the arbitration, with maximum periods of permissible extensions and a three-month deadline from the conclusion of the merits hearing in each phase to the delivery of the award in respect of that phase. The Arbitration Agreement also specifically established that the parties were to bear the costs of the arbitration equally, including the administrative, tribunal and legal costs.

The Arbitration Agreement empowered the tribunal to order provisional measures. Specifically, it provided that the tribunal could make orders 'which it considers appropriate under the circumstances and to prevent irreparable harm or damage to the natural resources of the area or to preserve the status quo as of 21 May 1996'. This provision was intended to enable the tribunal to address any actions by the parties following the entry into force of the Arbitration Agreement which impacted upon either party's case in the arbitration, such as the movement of military or civilians.

The Arbitration Agreement also established that the tribunal's decisions would be final and binding, setting out as follows:

> The awards of the Tribunal shall be final and binding. The Parties commit themselves to abide by those awards ... They shall consequently apply in good faith and immediately the awards of the Tribunal, at any rate within the time periods as provided by the Tribunal pursuant to Article 12, paragraph 1(b) of this Arbitration Agreement.

Provisions for the publication of the tribunal's final award and its reasons were included in the Arbitration Agreement. In order for the final award to gain recognition within the international community, it was established that the Final Award would be deposited with the United Nations, the Organization of African Unity and the Arab League.

The arbitral tribunal duly issued awards in each phase of the arbitration, in 1998 and 1999 respectively, with each award unanimously consented to by all members of the tribunal. The awards granted sovereignty of the islands to Yemen, and Eritrea has acted in accordance with the tribunal's findings, removing its military presence from the islands designated as belonging to Yemen. Extending beyond a strict interpretation of its mandate, the tribunal also included in its awards provisions recognized the traditional fishing rights of both Yemeni and Eritrean peoples in the disputed territory.

### (iii) Eritrea-Ethiopia Boundary Commission Agreement

In December 2000, Eritrea and Ethiopia entered into a peace agreement terminating hostilities between the two states. As part of this agreement, the parties agreed to establish a Boundary Commission to delimit and demarcate the territorial border between the two states. This agreement, and the peace process generally, had the public support of the United Nations and the African Union.

Article 4 of the peace agreement established the mechanisms governing the Boundary Commission. While the entire article is too lengthy to set out in full, interesting provisions include the following:

> 2. The parties agree that a neutral Boundary Commission composed of five members shall be established with a mandate to delimit and demarcate the colonial treaty border based on pertinent colonial treaties (1900, 1902 and 1908) and applicable international law. The Commission shall not have the power to make decisions ex aequo et bono.
>
> 3. The Commission shall be located in The Hague.

* * *

> 11. The Commission shall adopt its own rules of procedure based upon the 1992 Permanent Court of Arbitration Optional Rules for Arbitrating Disputes Between Two States. Filing deadlines for the parties' written submissions shall be simultaneous rather than consecutive. All decisions of the Commission shall be made by a majority of the commissioners.
>
> 12. The Commission shall commence its work not more than 15 days after it is constituted and shall recognize to make its decision concerning delimitation of the border within six months of its first meeting. The Commission shall take this objective into consideration when establishing its schedule. At its discretion, the Commission may extend this deadline.

* * *

15. The parties agree that the delimitation and demarcation determinations of the Commission shall be final and binding. Each party shall respect the border so determined, as well as territorial integrity and sovereignty of the other party.

In addition to the provisions set out above, the agreement also provided that none of the Boundary Commission's five members were permitted to be a national or resident of the two state parties. Each party was to appoint two members and, failing agreement of the party-appointed members of the Boundary Commission on the President, the President was to be appointed by the Secretary-General of the United Nations, following consultation with the parties. Taking into account the highly volatile political context in which the Commission was to operate, the agreement specifically provided the members of the Boundary Commission and its staff with the same privileges and immunities as diplomatic agents under the Vienna Convention on Diplomatic Relations.

Due to the centrality of this dispute to peace and stability between Ethiopia and Eritrea and to the region more generally, the parties wanted a border determination as quickly as possible. The Boundary Commission was therefore given the objective of providing a final delimitation of the border within six months of its first meeting. The parties agreed the Boundary Commission's determination would be final and binding. In the event that the determination required the transfer of control of certain territory from one state party to the other, the parties were to request the United Nations to facilitate resolution of any associated issues. The United Nations committed to providing technical support to the Boundary Commission in the delimitation and demarcation process and established a trust fund for this purpose.

In April 2002, the Boundary Commission delivered its final and binding determination. The delimitation allocated certain tracts of the disputed territory to each state, with Badme, which had been the centre point of the conflict, located on the Eritrean side. Initially both states agreed to adhere to the Boundary Commission's determination and permit the physical demarcation of the border to be carried out in accordance with the terms of the Arbitration Agreement. Ethiopia subsequently issued qualifications to its acceptance of the decision and refused to permit physical demarcation of the central and western sections of the border. In response, Eritrea stated its unwillingness to cooperate with the Boundary Commission's demarcation in the eastern section of the border unless physical demarcation simultaneously took place in the central and western sections of the border.

The international community has provided strong support for the decision of the Boundary Commission and, in recognition of this, the United Nations Security Council attempted to exert pressure on the parties to comply with the award through issuing a series of resolutions demanding that both states abide by the award. Indeed, the Security Council issued 18 resolutions urging the parties to co-operate fully with the Boundary Commission.

The parties' refusal to co-operate fully with the Boundary Commission prevented it from demarcating a boundary by fixing boundary pillars to the land. As a result, in November 2006, the Boundary Commission issued a further decision, providing the parties with a maximum of 12 months to reach an agreement in relation to the physical placement of the boundary pillars. To the extent the parties were unable to reach consensus, the tribunal ordered that an alternative interpretation of their mandate was to demarcate the boundary by reference to points at specified grid and geographical coordinates, rather than physically demarcating the boundary on the land itself. In making this determination, the tribunal emphasized that it remained in existence and continued to be ready and willing to demarcate the boundary physically for a further 12-month period. However, the

parties failed to reach agreement over the following year and consequently the border between the two states was not physically demarcated by the Boundary Commission.

The November 2006 solution proposed by the Boundary Commission, to demarcate
the boundary in the Award by reference to grid co-ordinates, was an attempt to establish
an identifiable boundary for the parties and the international community to rely upon,
even in the absence of a physically demarcated boundary. The Boundary Commission
sought to achieve final determination of the parties' dispute, even in the face of the parties' failure to co-operate with the physical demarcation of the boundary. This flexibility
is an attractive feature of international arbitration, provided that the tribunal does not step
outside of its jurisdiction as conferred by the parties in agreeing its mandate.

(iv) Tamil Tigers' Peace Agreement Proposal In October 2003, a proposal was put forward by the Tamil Tigers of Tamil Eelam to the government of Sri Lanka for a peace agreement, proposing the establishment of an interim self-governing authority for the Tigers
of Tamil Eelam in the northeast of Sri Lanka. This peace agreement proposal included an
arbitration clause as follows:

> Where a dispute arises between the Parties to this Agreement as to its interpreta-
> tion or implementation, and it cannot be resolved by any other means accept-
> able to the Parties including conciliation by the Royal Norwegian Government,
> there shall be an arbitration before a tribunal consisting of three members, two
> of whom shall be appointed by each Party. The third member, who shall be the
> Chairperson of the tribunal, shall be appointed jointly by the Parties concerned.
> In the event of any disagreement over the appointment of the Chairperson, the
> Parties shall ask the President of the International Court of Justice to appoint the
> Chairperson. In the determination of any dispute the arbitrators shall ensure the
> parity of status of the LTTE and the GOSL and shall resolve disputes by reference
> only to the provisions of this Agreement. The decision of the arbitrators shall be
> final and conclusive and it shall be binding on the Parties to the dispute.

This proposed dispute resolution clause would be triggered in the event of disputes between the parties as to the interpretation or the implementation of the peace agreement.
Therefore, should disputes arise following the entry into force of the peace agreement, the
parties would have a framework for the peaceful resolution of their concerns.

The proposal provided for the first step in the dispute resolution process to be formal
conciliation meetings, with a conciliator representing the Norwegian government. This
would enable the parties to meet together to discuss their differences, and encourage a consensual agreement through the input of an independent third party conciliator. In the
event conciliation was unsuccessful, the dispute resolution clause provided for arbitration
of the dispute before a three-member tribunal. Each party would have the opportunity
to choose one arbitrator and together the party appointed arbitrators would seek to agree
upon a chairman. To the extent the parties were unable to agree upon the chairman of
the tribunal, they were to request the President of the International Court of Justice to
make the appointment. The involvement of the International Court of Justice arguably
added credibility to the arbitral process and authority to the chairman's determination.
The decision of the arbitral tribunal was to be 'final', 'conclusive' and 'binding' upon the
parties to provide finality and closure to the dispute.

This proposal was not accepted by the Sri Lankan government, and the peace agreement was never entered into. Nonetheless, this proposed arbitration agreement provides
an interesting template for consideration when drafting arbitration clauses in peace treaties
in the future.

### 5. The Future for Arbitration Clauses in Resolving Intra-state and Inter-state Conflicts

### A. Is there a Future for the Use of Arbitration in Resolving Intra-state and Inter-state Conflicts?

There is an important role for arbitration in resolving intra-state and inter-state conflicts. Arbitration can be a useful mechanism for resolving disputes both in respect of the originating conflict itself (for example by referring a conflict regarding the delimitation of a territorial boundary to arbitration), or as a default mechanism for resolving disputes arising in the implementation or interpretation of a peace agreement. Where the parties to a conflict genuinely desire a final and peaceful resolution to their dispute, arbitration can offer an attractive solution politically, because it results in the imposition of a binding decision by a third party (usually not associated with the dispute).

Unlike a negotiated settlement, arbitration involves a decision being imposed upon the parties, and as such the party representatives are not required to agree to the determination. In deeply rooted and emotive disputes, where parties' positions are based on fear, resentment, grief and/or ambition, this can make a dispute in which the parties are simply unable to compromise, politic-ally possible. Indeed, it is common commercial practice for many business executives who choose to refer their disputes to commercial arbitration, rather than negotiation and mediation, in order to transfer responsibility for the decision to an arbitral tribunal. Arbitration distances the resolution of the dispute from the emotional or entrenched positions of the disputing entities to an independent tribunal selected by the parties to resolve the dispute.

Where arbitration is used to resolve an existing conflict, the parties will need to agree to arbitrate whilst the dispute is live, when parties frequently find it difficult to agree on anything at all. Yet as the above examples of the Abyei Arbitration Agreement, the Eritrea and Ethiopia Boundary Commission Agreement, the Eritrea—Yemen Arbitration Agreement and the Dayton Peace Agreement all demonstrate, parties are from time to time able to agree to have an existing dispute resolved by means of arbitration, usually in circumstances where the subject matter of the dispute makes any compromise by the parties almost impossible and continuation of the status quo unacceptable.

By including in peace agreements an arbitration clause that permits disputes regarding the interpretation or implementation of the peace agreement to be referred to arbitration (such as in the Tamil Tigers Peace Agreement Proposal), the peaceful resolution of future disputes between the parties is promoted. Disputes regularly arise out of the interpretation or implementation of peace agreements. Absent prior agreement on a mechanism to deal with such disputes, the parties often return to violent conflict. Continued political compromise between parties can be extremely difficult due to the differing interests of each party's stakeholders, particularly if the unique combination of factors that existed at the time of the peace agreement (often involving the international community) have moved on.

### B. Risks of Arbitration as a Method of Dispute Resolution in the Context of Intra-state and Inter-state Conflicts

As with any method of dispute resolution, the use of arbitration to resolve disputes entails some shortcomings which it is important to consider in assessing whether arbitration is a suitable dispute resolution mechanism for the particular conflict in question.

First, only the parties to the arbitration agreement (or the peace agreement in which the arbitration clause is included) will be entitled to initiate the arbitration. Moreover, it is likely that only the rights and obligations of those parties will be capable of being determined in the arbitration. Great care should be taken at the time of drafting the arbitration agreement to examine which entities should be parties to the agreement.

Second, there may be difficulties in enforcing the parties' agreement to resolve their dispute through arbitration. While an arbitration agreement will impose a legal obligation on the parties to resolve their dispute by way of arbitration, a party cannot be required to engage in an arbitral process. Just as a state or non-state entity may choose to flaunt a peace agreement, such an entity may also choose to act in disregard of an agreement to arbitrate. To address this concern, arbitration agreements can be drafted to include rules which enable one party to pursue arbitration, and have an awarded rendered, even in the face of the other party's refusal to participate in proceedings.

Third, there may be practical concerns regarding the enforcement of an arbitral award rendered in an intra-state or inter-state dispute. One of the most often-cited attributes of international arbitration is the ability to enforce arbitral awards in a vast number of jurisdictions across the globe. The international enforcement of arbitration awards is addressed in the Convention on the Recognition and Enforcement of Foreign Arbitral Awards of 1958 (the New York Convention), wherein signatory countries agree to enforce foreign arbitral awards made in the territory of a foreign state (although many countries have exercised their right to limit enforcement to only those awards made in the territory of another member state). At the time of writing, the New York Convention had 144 state signatories, resulting in arbitral awards being widely enforceable.

However, in the context of intra-state and inter-state conflicts, there are a number of important limitations to the ability of parties to enforce arbitral awards. Most crucially, numerous member states have exercised their right to reserve the applicability of the New York Convention to commercial arbitral awards. The New York Convention entitles parties to declare 'that it will apply the Convention only to differences arising out of legal relationships, whether contractual or not, which are considered as commercial under the national law of the State making such declaration'. It is unlikely that an arbitral award resulting from an intra-state or inter-state conflict would be characterized as an award arising out of commercial legal relationships, unless perhaps the ownership of significant and valuable natural resources is at stake.

In addition, the New York Convention applies only to 'foreign' arbitral awards. Foreign awards are defined in the New York Convention as awards 'made in the territory of another (Contracting) State'. An arbitral award relating to a dispute between two intra-state parties, rendered in the same state, would not be enforceable in that state's national courts pursuant to the New York Convention, even if the state were a member of the New York Convention. It may be possible to overcome this by having the arbitral award rendered in a third state. An award made in the territory of a foreign state in respect of a domestic matter in the state in which it is to be enforced may therefore be enforceable pursuant to the New York Convention. This does, however, presuppose that the content of the award is capable of enforcement by domestic courts.

The subject matter of an award resulting from an intra-state or inter-state conflict is by its very nature likely to be difficult to enforce. Unlike a monetary award which is capable of enforcement through national courts and the attachment of assets, an award specifying rights and obligations of a state or intra-state party is likely to be difficult to impose upon a recalcitrant party. Such awards generally require the good faith of the parties to implement. Indeed, the enforcement of arbitral awards against a state can be difficult in any context, as the state against whom the award is sought to be enforced can simply refuse to comply. This has been a recurring issue in the context of investment arbitration awards, as some states simply refuse to act in accordance with awards rendered against them. However, the vast majority of states do respect arbitral awards and comply with their determinations.

The prospects of implementation of arbitral awards resolving inter-state or intra-state conflict can be enhanced by involving the international community in the arbitral process from the outset through to enforcement. Publicizing the dispute and the arbitral process frequently leads to political pressure being placed upon the parties at the international level to comply with the award. The involvement of international institutions in the arbitral process, such as the PCA, the International Court of Justice and the United Nations in administering or appointing tribunal members also has the effect of raising the profile of the parties' dispute and adding legitimacy to the award. Similarly, measures such as agreeing that the arbitral award be deposited with international institutions such as the United Nations, African Union, Arab League and European Union adds authority and legitimacy to the arbitral award.

Perhaps surprisingly, practice to date demonstrates that there is a high level of adherence by state and intra-state parties to arbitral awards rendered in the context of such conflicts. It may be that the parties' willingness to enter into an arbitration agreement in the first place is indicative of their willingness to settle their dispute by peaceful means and recognize the authority of the eventual decision. It also appears that the involvement of the international community in the arbitral process encourages parties to respect arbitral awards. Of course, there are cases, such as the Ethiopia-Eritrea arbitration, where the parties have refused to implement an arbitral award despite significant pressure from the international community to do so.

Fourth, the arbitration process is a judicial process governed by procedural rules (agreed by parties and/or imposed by institutional rules), governed by procedural arbitration laws (imposed by national statute in the seat) and governed by the substantive law or laws chosen by the parties. It is not a political or mediated process and nor should it be made into one. The uniformity of practice and procedure in international arbitration gives the parties certainty and contributes vastly to the success of arbitration. The continued consistent application of an established body of procedural law, and proper application of the parties' chosen substantive law, is essential to the integrity of the process. Commercial parties would not expect the same purely commercial factors that might have led to a recommended outcome in mediation to inform or determine a legal and binding award in arbitration proceedings. To the contrary, the parties would expect the latter to be in accordance with legal principles as identified by the parties as applying to their relationship and disputes. So too should parties to political conflict be entitled to legal and binding awards, based on legal principles rather than political compromise. The only exception to this might be where the parties expressly consent to giving the tribunal power to decide ex aequo et bono.

## 6. Conclusions

Arbitration can be a powerful mechanism in the resolution of seemingly intractable conflicts, and is well suited to the resolution of intra-state and inter-state conflicts. In short, arbitration provides parties with a flexible process which can be tailored to suit the parties' particular requirements, the dispute is determined by a panel of independent persons selected by the parties, and the award rendered is likely to have the support of the international community. Thus, where parties are unable to compromise and negotiate a peaceful and final resolution to their dispute, arbitration is an attractive method of dispute resolution.

\* \* \*

One of the primary reasons why a properly rendered arbitral award, as opposed to outcomes generated by other less formal forms of dispute resolution, is capable of achieving some finality to conflict disputes, is that there is an established and internationally recognized system of arbitration law. The jurisprudence in international arbitration is vast, established and, to a significant degree, uniform. There is a body of law — procedural and substantive. Parties who agree to arbitrate non-commercial, political disputes need to recognize that a political outcome is not, or at least should not be, the objective of this process. Other dispute resolution mechanisms permit a politically-motivated, compromise result. Arbitration only permits, or ought only to permit, an outcome that upholds the rule of law.

As the above discussion highlights, arbitration is from time to time agreed to by parties when other forms of dispute resolution have failed. Where the arbitration process is agreed to by the parties, they tend to recognize the final arbitral award, if not resulting in full implementation and a final resolution of their dispute, at least moving forward towards that ultimate goal. There is significant opportunity for arbitration to be invoked more frequently in the context of intra-state and inter-state conflicts, and in particular it is hoped that where parties are able to resolve their disputes in settlement agreements, they will more regularly include dispute resolution clauses which trigger arbitration in the event of a dispute in the implementation or interpretation of their agreement. In sum, arbitration should weigh heavily in the minds of those educating parties on their options for peaceful dispute resolution in conflict situations and in drafting peace agreements.

## 11. Bibliography of Additional Sources

* Babak Barin, CARSWELL'S HANDBOOK OF INTERNATIONAL DISPUTE RESOLUTION RULES (1999).

* Jacob Bercovitch & Allison Houston, *Why Do They Do It Like This? An Analysis of the Factors Influencing Mediation Behavior in International Conflicts*, 44 J. CONFLICT RESOL. 170 (2000).

* Richard B. Bilder, *International Third Party Dispute Settlement*, 17 DENV. J. INT'L L. & POL'Y 471 (1989).

* KENNETH S. CARLSTON, THE PROCESS OF INTERNATIONAL ARBITRATION (Greenwood Press, 1972) (1946).

* David D. Caron, *The Nature of the Iran-United States Claims Tribunal and the Evolving Structure of International Dispute Resolution*, 84 AM. J. INT'L L. 104 (1990).

* Jonathan I. Charney, *The Implications of Expanding International Dispute Settlement Systems: The 1982 Convention on the Law of the Sea*, 90 AM. J. INT'L L. 69 (1996).

* Convention on the Settlement of Investment Disputes Between States and Nationals of Other States, Mar. 18, 1965, 575 U.N.T.S. 160.

* John R. Crook, *Applicable Law in International Arbitration: The Iran-U.S. Claims Tribunal Experience*, 83 A.J.I.L. 278 (1989).

* Arthur Eyefinger, THE INTERNATIONAL COURT OF JUSTICE (1996).

* Richard Happ & Noah Rubins, DIGEST OF ICSID AWARDS AND DECISIONS (2009).

* William E. Huth, *Iraq Claims Tribunal: A New Approach to Settlement of International Commercial Disputes*, 23 INT'L. BUS. L. 430 (1995).

- Albert Jan van den Berg, INTERNATIONAL DISPUTE RESOLUTION: TOWARDS AN IN-TERNATIONAL ARBITRATION CULTURE (1998).

- A.T. Mahan, ARMAMENTS AND ARBITRATION: OR, THE PLACE OF FORCE IN THE INTERNATIONAL RELATIONS OF STATES (2nd ed. 2000).

- THE PERMANENT COURT OF ARBITRATION: INTERNATIONAL ARBITRATION AND DISPUTE RESOLUTION: SUMMARIES OF AWARDS, SETTLEMENT AGREEMENTS, AND REPORTS (P. Hamilton et al. eds., 1999).

- Permanent Court of Arbitration, *Optional Rules for Arbitrating Disputes Between Two Parties of Which Only One is a State*, *available at* http://www.pca-cpa.org/upload/files/1STATENG.pdf.

- Patrick M. Regan & Allan C. Stam, *In the Nick of Time: Conflict Management, Mediation Timing, and the Duration of Interstate Disputes* (Statistical Data Included), 44 INT'L STUD. Q. 239 (June 2000).

# Chapter VII

# Peace versus Justice

## Introduction

International organizations and their member states involved in the arena of conflict resolution are often faced with the age-old dilemma of peace versus justice. On one hand are those who argue that there can be no lasting peace without justice, while on the other there are those who argue that their duty is to save lives by negotiating with all parties and bringing an end to the conflict, and that justice is a moral luxury that should not interfere with their efforts to end the conflict.

The creation of numerous ad hoc international tribunals such as the Yugoslav and Rwanda tribunals, as well as the hybrid Sierra Leone and Cambodia tribunals, has led to a resurgence in the role of justice in the process of conflict resolution. Domestic efforts to prosecute those responsible for atrocities, such as the Iraqi High Tribunal and the Uganda War Crimes Tribunal have contributed to the ability of certain individual states to pursue justice. The formation of the permanent International Criminal Court may have permanently changed the dynamic relationship between peace and justice. This chapter provides the foundation for a discussion as to role of justice in the process of conflict resolution and for an evaluation of the extent to which the ICC may impact future of peace processes.

## Objectives

- To understand the complex relationship between accountability and peace.
- To analyze the advantages and disadvantages of the respective roles of accountability and immunity in the peace process.
- To understand whether there is an international duty to prosecute those responsible for crimes against humanity.
- To debate conflicting viewpoints posed by scholars, the human rights community, and international organizations in prioritizing securing peace and achieving justice.
- To develop ideas for reconciling the perceived stark dichotomy between the need for accountability and the need to end conflict.
- To evaluate the significance of the creation of the ICC in promoting accountability and its impact on the peace process.

- To understand the risks associated with the distinct conflict resolution approaches of "coercive appeasement" and "justice first."

# Problems

Students should come to class prepared to discuss the following questions:

1.  What would have been the benefits of offering amnesty and asylum to individuals such as Charles Taylor or Saddam Hussein?

2.  What would have been the negative consequences of offering amnesty and asylum to such persons?

3.  Would amnesty or asylum violate an international duty to prosecute in the following situations:

    a.  Adolf Hitler of Nazi Germany in 1943.

    b.  Pol Pot of Cambodia in 1977.

    c.  Slobodan Milosevic of Serbia in 1999.

    d.  The Hutu leaders of Rwanda in July 1994.

4.  What would have been the implications of providing head of state immunity to:

    a.  Saddam Hussein of Iraq in March 2003.

    b.  Charles Taylor of Liberia in August 2003.

    c.  Omar al-Bashir of Sudan in 2011.

    d.  Muammar Gaddafi of Libya in 2011.

5.  What might be the broader, long-term consequences arising from the fact that justice mechanisms are now woven into the peace process?

6.  How should international organizations deal with contrasting responsibilities to balance accountability and lasting peace?

7.  Is it possible for negotiations to achieve peace through amnesty without sacrificing accountability or redress? Is exile a trade-off between peace and justice?

8.  How do you conduct a peace process in the shadow of the ICC and the new environment of global justice?

# Materials

1.  Nsongurua J. Udombana, Globalization of Justice and the Special Court for Sierra Leone's War Crimes, 17 Emory Int'l L. Rev. 55, 57–69 (Spring 2003).

2.  United States Holocaust Memorial Museum, Speaker Series: Negotiating with Killers: Expert Insights on Resolving Deadly Conflict (September 2005).

3.  Michael P. Scharf, *From the eXile Files: An Essay on Trading Justice for Peace*, 63.1 Wash. & Lee L. Rev. 339 (Winter 2006).

4.  Paul R. Williams & Michael P. Scharf, Peace with Justice?: War Crimes and Accountability in the Former Yugoslavia 29–35, 79–85 (2002).

5.  Michael P. Scharf, Swapping Amnesty for Peace: Was There a Duty to Prosecute International Crimes in Haiti?, 31.1 Texas Int'l L. J. 39–41 (Winter 1996).

6.  Human Rights Watch, ICC: Prosecutor to Open an Investigation in Libya: Q&A on Libya and the International Criminal Court, Mar. 3, 2011.

7.  Kiriro Wa Ngugu, *Let's Choose Peace Over Justice in ICC Case*, Daily Nation (Feb. 2, 2011).

8.  Kofi Annan, U.N. Secretary-General, Address at the Time Warner Center: Urging End to Impunity, Annan Sets Forth Ideas to Bolster U.N. Efforts to Protect Human Rights (Dec. 8, 2006).

9.  Bibliography of Additional Sources

## 1. Nsongurua J. Udombana, Globalization of Justice and the Special Court for Sierra Leone's War Crimes

*Emory International Law Review*, 2003
[footnotes omitted by editors]

\* \* \*

### GLOBALIZATION OF JUSTICE

#### A Globalized World

One of the major developments in international law in contemporary times has been the gradual "withering away" of state sovereignty. This trend is due to the integration of states in international or supranational regimes or organizations and through the expansion of human rights and the international instruments to enforce them. Globalization, with its emphasis on interdependence, has limited the exclusivity of statehood. Human rights law, in turn, has torn the veil of reserve domain and emancipated individuals from the regime of the states with all the consequences of becoming an independent player in international relations.

Globalization refers to the compression of the world and the intensification of consciousness of the world as a whole. It is the catchword for a shrinking world in which interactions and linkages between peoples, economies, environmental conditions, and cultures increasingly permeate the borders of the nation-state. It is common to identify globalization with cultural uniformity and to contrast it with cultural diversity. Others, however, link it to the proliferation of intergovernmental organizations and transnational interest groups concerned with human rights, the environment, or economic issues, and to the emergence of a new normative framework, distinct from classical international law, for "global civil society" and "cosmopolitan democracy." What is important is that globalization is not just an esoteric phenomenon: "it refers not only to the emergence of large-scale world systems, but also to transformations in the very texture of everyday life." It is a real world phenomenon, "affecting even intimacies of personal identity." "To live in a world where the image of Nelson Mandela is more familiar than the face of one's next door neighbour is to move in quite different contexts of social action from those that prevailed previously."

#### Expanding International Criminal Norms

As with economics, culture, and the environment, crime and justice is also affected by globalization. Former President Bill Clinton succinctly stated the problem: "In our global village, progress can spread quickly, but trouble can too. Trouble on the far end of town soon becomes a plague on everybody's house." Such examples include:

[T]he Iraqi assault against its own Kurdish and Shiite populations and against
Kuwait; ethnic cleansing in Bosnia and Croatia; genocide in Burundi and Rwanda;
widespread terror and murder in Angola, Chechnya, Ethiopia, Haiti, Liberia, Somalia, and Sri Lanka; the human depravity of recent decades echoed in the courtrooms and public arenas of Argentina, Chile, Ethiopia, Guatemala, and Honduras;
and the unforgettable genocide in Cambodia. Together they have sparked global
indignation and prompted calls for national and international remedies.

Consequently, justice is no longer only local; it has gone global, spurred by the development of the concept of state, and in particular, individual responsibility for crimes against
international humanitarian and human rights norms. Globalization of justice simply means
international justice for local crimes of global dimensions. When domestic transgressions
have regional and international consequences and involve significant violations of international humanitarian law, there is a growing trend to explore international remedies. At
any rate, the concepts of guilt and responsibility can easily be carried over from one type
of crime to another. Besides, "modern international law increasingly recognizes that crimes
against humanity can be committed within a single country and without any nexus to war,
and that certain crimes can be committed in civil as well as international wars."

Whereas state responsibility has always been part of classical international law, the concept of individual criminal responsibility in international law is of recent development,
though there were some minimal instances of such recognition before the nineteenth century. Piracy and slavery, for example, have always been considered crimes against the international
society, permitting any state to prosecute pirates or slave dealers, no matter where their acts
were committed. But beyond those specific crimes, as the Roman maps would state: "hic
sunt leones." However, international law and the international community no longer accept such hackneyed defense of State sovereignty, recognizing there are certain crimes against
humanity that transcend the narrow requirements of sovereign jurisdiction. Over the years,
the list of these crimes has grown gradually taking in such crimes as "offenses against the
peace and security of mankind" and, indeed, the whole corpus of what is now regarded as
international criminal law, encompassing international humanitarian law applicable to international and internal armed conflicts. More significantly, such crimes may now be prosecuted at any time, as there is no statute of limitations.

The foundational principles and interests underlying this emerging system of justice do
not exist in a normative vacuum; rather, they echo, in the arena of international affairs, the
loftiest aspirations of an ever-advancing civilization. Throughout history, women and men,
with roots in different cultures and societies, have, individually and jointly, lived and acted
in the belief that the forces of evil and destruction should not be allowed to prevail; in short,
they believe that evil should not have victory over virtue. They believe that respect for human
rights, in particular human dignity, and the desire for a just society should be the standard
of conduct and achievement. International cooperation, therefore, is needed as a means of
creating conditions that foster the progressive development and the acceptance and enforcement of standards of elementary justice. International justice, in particular, is necessary in situations where a country in which mass crimes occur is not able or is unwilling to
render justice, for lack either of strong judicial institutions or of political will.

International accountability has even gone further to tear the veil of sovereign immunity, as the British House of Lords' decision in *Regina v. Bartle, Ex Parte Pinochet* demonstrated. As Lord Nicholls stated:

International law has made plain that certain types of conduct, including torture
and hostage-taking, are not acceptable conduct on the part of anyone. This ap-

plies as much to heads of states, or even more so, as it does to everyone else; the contrary conclusion would make a mockery of international law.

The Pinochet case has clearly set new precedents against the impunity of dictators and war criminals, and human rights non-governmental organizations (NGOs) are cashing in on it. Thus, on February 4, 2000, a Senegalese court indicted the exiled former dictator of Chad, Hissene Habre, on charges that he committed egregious and systematic abuses of human rights during his rule. Unfortunately, the case became enmeshed in Senegalese political waters, despite the enviable record the country had as the first to ratify the ICC Statute. The Pinochet principle was also invoked in the request for extradition of Miguel Cavallo from Mexico to Spain for alleged torture in Argentina. Cavallo was an Argentine official during the reign of the military junta in that country from 1976 to 1983. He was arrested in Mexico under a warrant and extradition request from the same judge in Spain who, in 1998, requested the U.K. to extradite Augusto Pinochet. Cavallo allegedly participated in the torture of Spanish citizens in Argentina while the junta was in power.

## Engaging International Criminal Institutions

Clearly, it has been shown that individuals can be punished for violations, not only under municipal law, but also under international law. Indeed,

> [s]ince the latter half of the nineteenth century it has been generally recognized that there are acts or omissions for which international law imposes criminal responsibility on individuals and for which punishment may be imposed, either by properly empowered international tribunals or by national courts and military tribunals. These tribunals exercise an international jurisdiction by reason of the law applied and the constitution of the tribunal, or, in the case of national courts, by reason of the law applied and the nature of jurisdiction (the exercise of which is justified by international law).

The emergence of international criminal institutions to punish breaches of international criminal law is, thus, one of the achievements of the modern age, even if the norms themselves are not new. The breakdown of the bipolar world since 1989 has enabled major powers to find common, rather than opposed, interest in punishing violations of international law. However, this move began in the 1940s, when the horrible crimes committed by the Nazis and Japanese during World War II led to a quick conclusion of agreements among the Allied Powers — Britain, France, the United States, and the USSR. The agreement led to the establishment of the Nuremberg and Tokyo International Military Tribunals "for the trial of war criminals whose offences have no particular geographical location whether they be accused individually or in their capacity as members of organizations or groups or in both capacities." These special jurisdictions also took into account new categories of crimes against humanity and crimes against peace.

In several of its decisions, the Nuremberg Tribunal, for example, held the principle of individual criminal responsibility "has long been recognized," reasoning that, "[c]rimes against international law are committed by men, not by abstract entities, and only by punishing individuals who commit such crimes can the provisions of international law be enforced." In fact, the prosecution and the judgment of the Tribunals "were based on concepts and norms, some of which had deep roots in international law and some of which represented a significant development of that law that opened the path toward the later formulation of fundamental human rights norms." It may be said, therefore, that "whatever the state of the law in 1945, Article 6 of the Nuremberg Charter has since come to represent general international law."

The emergence of these international criminal tribunals, from Nuremberg to The Hague, Rwanda, and Rome illustrates that the mode of implementing humanitarian law has shifted from state-to-state diplomacy to individual criminal responsibility. Each of these tribunals, in particular the ICTY and ICTR, is regarded as a means of rendering justice and enhancing the peace by identifying, from within the larger population, those specific individuals responsible for war crimes. The jurisprudence of these tribunals on individual criminal responsibility has also grown over the years. The Rome Statute, in particular, has firmly entrenched the principle of individual criminal responsibility.

Overall, it may be said that the establishment of these tribunals has contributed significantly to the development of international humanitarian law and its extension to non-international armed conflicts. "Employing the Nuremberg concept of crimes against humanity in Rwanda [and, a fortiori, Yugoslavia] constitutes an important legal development, as it implies the extension of international humanitarian law to internal conflicts." The work of the tribunals has served, and will continue to serve, both as a "procedural laboratory for the enforcement of the law of war and, much more importantly, as a test of the true will of the international community to allow the criminal process to unfold."

* * *

## 2. Negotiating with Killers: Expert Insights on Resolving Deadly Conflict

United States Holocaust Memorial Museum Speaker Series, 2005

* * *

### Section 5: Balancing the Demands of Peace and Justice

One of the most troubling dilemmas involved in negotiating with killers is whether to place the highest priority on securing peace or achieving justice. Perpetrators of war crimes and atrocities often demand amnesty from prosecution for these crimes as a condition for laying down arms. If an amnesty from war crimes prosecution helps speed an end to violence, can such a concession be justified? Or are there some crimes so heinous that they should never be forgiven? By allowing the perpetrators of atrocities to escape judicial accountability for their crimes, do we reinforce the "culture of impunity," thereby signaling our silent acceptance of the cycle of violence in conflict-torn regions?

John Roth is Director of the Center for the Study of the Holocaust, Genocide, and Human Rights at Claremont McKenna College. He reflects on the moral complexities that confront diplomats who deal with the perpetrators of atrocities:

Where, if at all, is the place for straightforward moral discourse in negotiation, naming it what it is, where mass murder is taking place or where killing has taken place and destroys lives of defenseless people?

Ambassador Donald Steinberg argues that the quest for justice is a moral imperative, whether or not it supports a lasting settlement of violent conflict. Negotiators who neglect the mandate to seek justice inevitably undermine future prospects for peace and the rule of law:

I am one of those people who firmly believes that "amnesty" means that men with guns forgive other men with guns for violence committed mostly against civilians and particularly women.

Professor Paul Williams at American University Law School is director of the Public International Law and Policy Group, which provides legal advice to countries in peace negotiations. He served on the Bosnian delegation at the Dayton peace talks of 1995 and on the Kosovar delegation at the Rambouillet talks in 1999. Williams believes that justice is also a pragmatic requirement for a lasting peace:

> I tend to argue justice first for practical reasons, that you will actually get a better peace agreement, you will get a better deal, if you are guided by justice or norms of justice as opposed to a purely pragmatic saving lives, getting the deal done, "getting to yes" type of approach.

Williams says that instead of taking effective coercive action against the aggressor, third-party states often pressure the victims of the aggression to accept agreements that enable the aggressors to achieve their primary objectives. He calls this diplomatic approach "coercive appeasement":

> [C]oercive appeasement begins when politically and militarily powerful third parties or states, such as the United States and the European Union, seek to resolve a conflict by accommodating the primary interests of a rogue regime despite the regime's use of force and the commission of atrocities to achieve its objectives. This is something that is very common among peacebuilders and peacemakers is, "Let's engage in an approach of accommodation. It's a legitimate approach." It often slips into coercive appeasement.

Now, peacebuilders seldom intentionally set out to implement a strategic approach of coercive appeasement. Rather, it is frequently the case that tactical decisions along the way, taken in an ad hoc fashion, which are designed to achieve very short-term objectives, cumulatively come to frame and perpetuate this approach of coercive appeasement.

Williams recalls his experience as a State Department lawyer in the early 1990s, when he worked on policy toward the former Yugoslavia:

> Now, by most professional and historical accounts, this approach was a failed one with the consequences that over 200,000 to 250,000 individuals were killed, thousands were raped, and millions were displaced.

The reluctance of the international community, in my view, to invoke a norm of justice as a viable alternative to this approach of coercive appeasement facilitated the ability of the Serbian regime to carry out the genocide in Bosnia and the attempted genocide in Kosovo.

Yet some observers argue that there can be no "one-size-fits-all" solution to balancing the demands of peace and justice. Nor can the perpetrators of atrocities always be sidelined from negotiations. Donald Steinberg says that:

> [T]hey assume that because they put a low value on human life that others do the same. In movements that are dominated by a killer there tends to be a centralized power structure. It is almost impossible to negotiate with anyone else other than the leader involved. No one else in the movement will stick out his neck because it can literally be chopped off.

But negotiators in these situations also have opportunities to shift the focus from the killers and diminish their influence. Prudence Bushnell:

> We should no longer put our emphasis on preventing conflict.[...] We should be putting our emphasis on promoting peace. And what happens if you do that, if you start looking through the prism of promoting peace versus preventing

conflict? One of the things I think that happens, is that you take these killers out of the spotlight. As long as you are trying to prevent conflict, they are the main actors, because they're the ones who are performing the conflict. If you then say, well, forget that, what we want to do is promote peace, you end up putting the spotlight on an entirely new group of people, and you end up taking those people to five-star hotels and feeding them good meals, and giving them resources and high-level attention.

As the U.S. Ambassador-at-Large for War Crimes Issues from 1997 to 2001, David Scheffer confronted a cold logic in his dealings with perpetrators ranging from Slobodan Milosevic of Serbia to Foday Sankoh of Sierra Leone:

> Even in the presence of evil one may still make a pragmatic cost-benefit analysis as a negotiator about "how far can I proceed with this individual for the benefit of other objectives?"

We can deal with the issue of evil as long as we don't let the benefit of negotiating with a war criminal overcome our recognition that he still embodies evil and we have to confront that evil at some point and achieve accountability.

---

## 3. Michael P. Scharf, From the eXile Files: An Essay on Trading Justice for Peace
### *Washington and Lee Law Review*, 2006
### [footnotes omitted by editors]

### I. Introduction

Since 1990, three different U.S. Presidents have accused Iraqi leader Saddam Hussein of committing grave breaches of the 1949 Geneva Conventions and acts of genocide. Although the Geneva Conventions and the Genocide Convention require state parties to bring offenders to justice, on the eve of the 2003 invasion of Iraq, President George W. Bush offered to call off the attack if Saddam Hussein and his top lieutenants would agree to relinquish power and go into exile. This was no publicity stunt, as some have characterized it. Working through President Hosni Mubarak of Egypt, the United States actively pursued the matter with several Mideast countries, ultimately persuading Bahrain to agree to provide sanctuary to Hussein if he accepted the deal. When Hussein rejected the proposal, Bush promised that the Iraqi leader would be forced from power and prosecuted as a war criminal.

Admittedly, thousands of lives could have been spared if Hussein had accepted the deal. But at the risk of being accused of blindly embracing Kant's prescription that "justice must be done even should the heavens fall," this Article argues that it was inappropriate for the Bush Administration even to make the offer, and that if implemented the exile-for-peace deal would have seriously undermined the Geneva Conventions and the Genocide Convention, which require prosecution of alleged offenders without exception.

A few months after the invasion of Iraq, U.S. officials helped broker a deal whereby Liberian President Charles Taylor, who had been indicted for crimes against humanity by the Special Court for Sierra Leone, agreed to give up power and was allowed to flee to Nigeria, where he received asylum. At the time, forces opposed to Taylor, which had taken over most of the country, were on the verge of attacking the capital city Monrovia, and tens of thousands of civilian casualties were forecast. The exile deal averted the crisis and set the stage for insertion of a U.N. peacekeeping mission that stabilized the country and set it on a path to peace and democracy. In contrast to the Hussein case, the Taylor arrangement did not in any way violate international law. This Article explains why international law should treat the two situations differently, prohibiting exile and asylum for Saddam Hussein while permitting such a justice-for-peace exchange in the case of Charles Taylor.

This is the first scholarly article in recent years to focus on the significant issue of exile. Scholarship on the analogous issue of amnesty has been written largely from the point of view of aggressive advocates of international justice, whose writing is based on the assumption that the widespread state practice favoring amnesties constitutes a violation of, rather than a reflection of, international law in this area. Before analyzing the relevant legal principles, the Article begins with an examination of the practical considerations that counsel for and against the practice of "trading justice for peace." Next, using the Saddam Hussein and Charles Taylor cases as a focal point, the Article analyzes the relevant international instruments which require prosecution under limited circumstances. This is followed by a critique of the popular view that customary international law and the principle of *jus cogens* broadly prohibit actions that prevent prosecution of crimes under international law. The Article establishes that there does not yet exist a customary international law rule requiring prosecution of war crimes in internal armed conflict or crimes against humanity, but that there is a duty to prosecute in the case of grave breaches of the Geneva Conventions, the crime of genocide, and torture. Where the duty to prosecute does apply, it is important that states and international organizations honor it, lest they signal disrespect for the important treaties from which the duty arises, potentially putting their own citizens at risk and generally undermining the rule of law.

## II. Practical Considerations

### A. Interests Favoring Exile, Asylum, and Amnesty

Notwithstanding the popular catch phrase of the 1990s, "no peace without justice," achieving peace and obtaining justice are sometimes incompatible goals, at least in the short term. In order to end an international or internal conflict, negotiations often must be held with the very leaders who are responsible for war crimes and crimes against humanity. When this is the case, insisting on criminal prosecutions can prolong the conflict, resulting in more deaths, destruction, and human suffering.

Reflecting this reality, during the past thirty years, Angola, Argentina, Brazil, Cambodia, Chile, El Salvador, Guatemala, Haiti, Honduras, Ivory Coast, Nicaragua, Peru, Sierra Leone, South Africa, Togo, and Uruguay have each, as part of a peace arrangement, granted amnesty to members of the former regime that committed international crimes within their respective borders. With respect to five of these countries—Cambodia, El Salvador, Haiti, Sierra Leone, and South Africa—"the United Nations itself pushed for, helped negotiate, or endorsed the granting of amnesty as a means of restoring peace and democratic government."

In addition to amnesty (which immunizes the perpetrator from domestic prosecution), exile and asylum in a foreign country (which puts the perpetrator out of the jurisdictional reach of domestic prosecution) is often used to induce regime change, with the blessing and involvement of significant states and the United Nations. Peace negotiators call this the "Napoleonic Option," in reference to the treatment of French emperor Napoleon Bonaparte who, after his defeat at Waterloo in 1815, was exiled to St. Helena rather than face trial or execution. More recently, a number of dictators have been granted sanctuary abroad in return for relinquishing power. Thus, for example, Ferdinand Marcos fled the Philippines for Hawaii; Baby Doc Duvalier fled Haiti for France; Mengisthu Haile Miriam fled Ethiopia for Zimbabwe; Idi Amin fled Uganda for Saudi Arabia; General Raoul Cedras fled Haiti for Panama; and Charles Taylor fled Liberia for exile in Nigeria—a deal negotiated by the United States and U.N. envoy Jacques Klein.

As Payam Akhavan, then Legal Adviser to the Office of the Prosecutor of the International Criminal Tribunal for the Former Yugoslavia, observed a decade ago: "[I]t is not unusual in the political stage to see the metamorphosis of yesterday's war monger into today's peace broker." This is because, unless the international community is willing to use force to topple a rogue regime, cooperation of the leaders is needed to bring about peaceful regime change and put an end to violations of international humanitarian law. Yet, it is not realistic to expect them to agree to a peace settlement if, directly following the agreement, they would find themselves or their close associates facing potential life imprisonment.

This conclusion finds support in the observations of the 2004 Report of the International Truth and Reconciliation Commission for Sierra Leone:

> The Commission is unable to condemn the resort to amnesty by those who negotiated the Lomé Peace Agreement [which provides amnesty to persons who committed crimes against humanity in Sierra Leone]. The explanations given by the Government negotiators, including in their testimonies before the Truth and Reconciliation Commission, are compelling in this respect. In all good faith, they believed that the RUF [insurgents] would not agree to end hostilities if the Agreement were not accompanied by a form of pardon or amnesty.
>
> * * *
>
> The Commission is unable to declare that it considers amnesty too high a price to pay for the delivery of peace to Sierra Leone, under the circumstances that prevailed in July 1999. It is true that the Lomé Agreement did not immediately return the country to peacetime. Yet it provided the framework for a process that pacified the combatants and, five years later, has returned Sierra Leoneans to a context in which they need not fear daily violence and atrocity.

In brokering the Charles Taylor exile deal, the United States and United Nations were particularly encouraged by the success of similar amnesty/exile for peace arrangements relating to Haiti and South Africa in the 1990s. From 1990–1994, Haiti was ruled by a military regime headed by General Raol Cedras and Brigadier General Philippe Biamby, which executed over 3000 civilian political opponents and tortured scores of others. The United Nations mediated negotiations at Governors Island in New York Harbor, in which the military leaders agreed to relinquish power and permit the return of the democratically elected President (Jean-Bertrand Aristide) in return for a full amnesty for the members of the regime and a lifting of the economic sanctions imposed by the U.N. Security Council. Under pressure from the United Nations mediators, Aristide agreed to the amnesty clause of the Governors Island Agreement. The Security Council immediately "declared [its] readiness to give the fullest possible support to the Agreement signed on Governors Island," which it later said constitutes "the only valid framework for the resolution of the crisis in Haiti." When the military leaders initially failed to comply with the Governors Island Agreement, on July 31, 1994, the Security Council took the extreme step of authorizing an invasion of Haiti by a multinational force. On the eve of the invasion on September 18, 1994, a deal was struck, whereby General Cedras agreed to retire his command and accept exile in response to a general amnesty voted into law by the Haitian parliament and an offer by Panama to provide him asylum.

The amnesty deal had its desired effect: The democratically elected Aristide was permitted to return to Haiti and reinstate a civilian government, the military leaders left the country for sanctuary in Panama, much of the military surrendered their arms, and most of the human rights abuses promptly ended—all with practically no bloodshed or resistance. Although the situation in Haiti has once again deteriorated, with a wave of violent protests and strikes erupting in 2004, the more recent problems were due largely to President Aristide's mismanagement and corruption, not the fact that the military leaders escaped punishment ten years earlier.

South Africa stands as another success story, indicating the potential value of trading justice for peace. From 1960 to 1994, thousands of black South Africans were persecuted and mistreated under that country's apartheid system. With the prospect of a bloody civil war looming over negotiations, "[t]he outgoing leaders made some form of amnesty for those responsible for the regime a condition for the peaceful transfer to a fully democratic society." The leaders of the majority black population decided that the commitment to afford amnesty was a fair price for a relatively peaceful transition to full democracy. In accordance with the negotiated settlement between the major parties, on July 19, 1995, the South African Parliament created a Truth and Reconciliation Commission, consisting of a Committee on Human Rights Violations, a Committee on Amnesty, and a Committee on Reparation and Rehabilitation. Under this process, amnesty would be available only to individuals who personally applied for it and who disclosed fully the facts of their apartheid crimes. After conducting 140 public hearings and considering 20,000 written and oral submissions, the South African Truth Commission published a 2739-page report of its findings on October 29, 1998. Most observers believe the amnesty in South Africa headed off increasing tensions and a potential civil war.

It is a common misconception that trading amnesty or exile for peace is equivalent to the absence of accountability and redress. As in the Haitian and South African situations described above, amnesties can be tied to accountability mechanisms that are less invasive than domestic or international prosecution. Ever more frequently in the aftermath of an amnesty- or exile-for-peace deal, the concerned governments have made monetary reparations to the victims and their families, established truth commissions to document the abuses (and sometimes identify perpetrators by name), and have instituted employment bans and purges (referred to as "lustration") that keep such perpetrators from positions of public trust. While not the same as criminal prosecution, these mechanisms do encompass much of what justice is intended to accomplish: prevention, deterrence, punishment, and rehabilitation. Indeed, some experts believe that these mechanisms do not just constitute "a second best approach" when prosecution is impracticable, but that in many situations they may be better suited to achieving the aims of justice.

B. Factors Favoring Prosecution

Although providing amnesty and exile to perpetrators may be an effective way to induce regime change without having to resort to force, there are several important countervailing considerations favoring prosecution that suggest amnesty/exile should be a bargaining tool of last resort reserved only for extreme situations. In particular, prosecuting leaders responsible for violations of international humanitarian law is necessary to discourage future human rights abuses, deter vigilante justice, and reinforce respect for law and the new democratic government.

While prosecutions might initially provoke resistance, many analysts believe that national reconciliation cannot take place as long as justice is foreclosed. As Professor Cherif Bassiouni, then Chairman of the U.N. Investigative Commission for Yugoslavia, stated in 1996, "[i]f peace is not intended to be a brief interlude between conflicts," then it must be accompanied by justice.

Failure to prosecute leaders responsible for human rights abuses breeds contempt for the law and encourages future violations. The U.N. Commission on Human Rights and its Sub-Commission on Prevention of Discrimination and Protection of Minorities have concluded that impunity is one of the main reasons for the continuation of grave violations of human rights throughout the world. Fact finding reports on Chile and El Salvador indicate that the granting of amnesty or de facto impunity has led to an increase in abuses in those countries.

Further, history teaches that former leaders given amnesty or exile are prone to recidivism, resorting to corruption and violence and becoming a disruptive influence on the peace process. From his seaside villa in Calabar, Nigeria, for example, Charles Taylor orchestrated a failed assassination plot in 2005 against President Lansana Conte of Guinea, a neighboring country that had backed the rebel movement that forced Taylor from power.

What a new or reinstated democracy needs most is legitimacy, which requires a fair, credible, and transparent account of what took place and who was responsible. Criminal trials (especially those involving proof of widespread and systematic abuses) can generate a comprehensive record of the nature and extent of violations, how they were planned and executed, the fate of individual victims, who gave the orders, and who carried them out. While there are various means to develop the historic record of such abuses, the most authoritative rendering of the truth is possible only through the crucible of a trial that accords full due process. Supreme Court Justice Robert Jackson, the Chief Prosecutor at Nuremberg, underscored the logic of this proposition when he reported that the most important legacy of the Nuremberg trials was the documentation of Nazi atrocities "with such authenticity and in such detail that there can be no responsible denial of these crimes in the future." According to Jackson, the establishment of an authoritative record of abuses that would endure the test of time and withstand the challenge of revisionism required proof of "incredible events by credible evidence."

In addition to truth, there is a responsibility to provide justice. While a state may appropriately forgive crimes against itself, such as treason or sedition, serious crimes against persons, such as rape and murder, are an altogether different matter. Holding the violators accountable for their acts is a moral duty owed to the victims and their families. Prosecuting and punishing the violators would give significance to the victims' suffering and serve as a partial remedy for their injuries. Moreover, prosecutions help restore victims' dignity and prevent private acts of revenge by those who, in the absence of justice, would take it into their own hands.

While prosecution and punishment can reinforce the value of law by displacing personal revenge, failure to punish former leaders responsible for widespread human rights abuses encourages cynicism about the rule of law and distrust toward the political system. To the victims of human rights crimes, amnesty or exile represents the ultimate in hypocrisy: While they struggle to put their suffering behind them, those responsible are allowed to enjoy a comfortable retirement. When those with power are seen to be above the law, the ordinary citizen will never come to believe in the principle of the rule of law as a fundamental necessity in a society transitioning to democracy.

Finally, where the United Nations or major countries give their imprimatur to an amnesty or exile deal, there is a risk that leaders in other parts of the world will be encouraged to engage in gross abuses. For example, history records that the international amnesty given to the Turkish officials responsible for the massacre of over one million Armenians during World War I encouraged Adolf Hitler some twenty years later to conclude that Germany could pursue his genocidal policies with impunity. In a 1939 speech to his reluctant General Staff, Hitler remarked, "Who after all is today speaking about the destruction of the Armenians?" Richard Goldstone, the former Prosecutor of the International Criminal Tribunal for the former Yugoslavia, has concluded that "the failure of the international community to prosecute Pol Pot, Idi Amin, Saddam Hussein and Mohammed Aidid, among others, encouraged the Serbs to launch their policy of ethnic cleansing in the former Yugoslavia with the expectation that they would not be held accountable for their international crimes." When the international community encourages or endorses an amnesty or exile deal, it sends a signal to other rogue regimes that they have nothing to lose by instituting repressive measures; if things start going badly, they can always bargain away their responsibility for crimes by agreeing to peace.

### III. The Limited International Legal Obligation to Prosecute

In a few narrowly defined situations (described below) there is an international legal obligation to prosecute regardless of the underlying practical considerations. Where this is the case, failure to prosecute can amount to an international breach. An amnesty or asylum given to the members of the former regime could be invalidated in a proceeding before either the state's domestic courts or an international forum. International support for such an amnesty or asylum deal would undermine international respect for and adherence to the treaties that require prosecution. Finally, it would be inappropriate for an international criminal court to defer to a national amnesty or asylum in a situation where the amnesty or asylum violates obligations contained in the very international conventions that make up the court's subject matter jurisdiction.

* * *

### C. Amnesty/Exile and the International Criminal Court

The above discussion indicates that there are frequently no international legal constraints on the negotiation of an amnesty/exile-for-peace deal, and that in certain circumstances swapping amnesty/exile for peace can serve the interests of both peace and justice. However, an international criminal tribunal is not bound to defer to a domestic amnesty/exile arrangement. During the negotiations for the Rome Statute creating the International Criminal Court (ICC), the United States and a few other delegations expressed concern that the ICC would hamper efforts to halt human rights violations and restore peace and democracy in places like Haiti and South Africa.

According to the Chairman of the Rome Diplomatic Conference, Philippe Kirsch of Canada, the issue was not definitively resolved during the Diplomatic Conference. Rather, the provisions that were adopted reflect "creative ambiguity" that could potentially allow the prosecutor and judges of the ICC to interpret the Rome Statute as permitting recognition of an amnesty or asylum exception to the jurisdiction of the court.

#### 1. The Preamble

The preamble to the Rome Statute suggests that deferring a prosecution because of the existence of a national amnesty or asylum deal would be incompatible with the purpose of the court, namely to ensure criminal prosecution of persons who commit serious international crimes. In particular, the Preamble:

> Affirm[s] that the most serious crimes of concern to the international community as a whole must not go unpunished and that their effective prosecution must be ensured ...
> Recall[s] that it is the duty of every State to exercise its criminal jurisdiction over those responsible for international crimes ...

[And] Emphasiz[es] that the International Criminal Court established under this Statute shall be complementary to national criminal jurisdictions.

Preambular language is important because international law provides that "[a] treaty shall be interpreted in good faith in accordance with the ordinary meaning to be given to the terms of the treaty in their context and in the light of its object and purpose." Thus, the Rome Statute's preamble constitutes a critical source of interpretation because it indicates both the treaty's context and its object and purpose. Yet, notwithstanding this preambular language, there are several articles of the Rome Statute (discussed below) that might be read as permitting the court under certain circumstances to recognize an amnesty exception to its jurisdiction. The apparent conflict between these articles and the preamble reflects the schizophrenic nature of the negotiations at Rome: The preambular language and the procedural provisions were negotiated by entirely different drafting groups, and in the rush of the closing days of the Rome Conference, the drafting committee never fully integrated and reconciled the separate portions of the Statute.

2. Article 16: Action by the Security Council

With respect to a potential amnesty/asylum exception, the most important provision of the Rome Statute is Article 16. Under that article, the ICC would be required to defer to a national amnesty if the Security Council adopts a resolution under Chapter VII of the United Nations Charter requesting the court not to commence an investigation or prosecution, or to defer any proceedings already in progress. The Security Council recently invoked its right under Article 16 of the Rome Statute in adopting Resolution 1593, referring the Darfur atrocities to the ICC for prosecution but at the same time providing that the ICC could not exercise jurisdiction over foreign military personnel in Darfur who are from states (other than Sudan) that are not parties to the Rome Statute.

The Security Council has the legal authority to require the court to respect an amnesty or asylum if two requirements are met, namely: (1) the Security Council has determined the existence of a threat to the peace, a breach of the peace, or an act of aggression under Article 39 of the U.N. Charter; and (2) the resolution requesting the court's deferral is consistent with the purposes and principles of the United Nations with respect to maintaining international peace and security, resolving threatening situations in conformity with principles of justice and international law, and promoting respect for human rights and fundamental freedoms under Article 24 of the U.N. Charter.

The decision of the Appeals Chamber of the Yugoslavia Tribunal in the *Tadic* case suggests that the ICC could assert that it has the authority to independently assess whether these two requirements were met as part of its incidental power to determine the propriety of its own jurisdiction (competence de la competence). One commentator has characterized this aspect of the Appeals Chamber decision as "strongly support[ing] those who see the U.N. Charter not as unblinkered license for police action but as an emerging constitution of enumerated, limited powers subject to the rule of law." It is possible, then, that the ICC would not necessarily be compelled by the existence of a Security Council resolution to terminate an investigation or prosecution were it to find that an amnesty contravenes international law.

While an amnesty or exile arrangement accompanied by the establishment of a truth commission, victim compensation, and lustration might be in the interests of justice in the broad sense, it would nonetheless be in contravention of international law where the grave breaches provisions of the 1949 Geneva Conventions, the Genocide Convention, or the Torture Convention are applicable. It is especially noteworthy that the Geneva Conventions require parties "to provide effective penal sanctions for persons committing, or ordering to be committed, any of the grave breaches of the present Convention," that the Genocide Convention requires parties "to provide effective penalties for persons guilty of genocide," and that the Torture Convention requires parties to make torture "punishable by appropriate penalties which take into account their grave nature."

This would suggest that the ICC might not defer to the Security Council under Article 16 of the Rome Statute where the accused is charged with grave breaches of the 1949 Geneva Conventions, the crime of genocide, or torture. Yet, a strong counterargument can be made that the Rome Statute codifies only the substantive provisions of the 1949 Geneva Conventions, the Genocide Convention, and the Torture Convention, and does not incorporate those procedural aspects of the Conventions that require prosecution (which apply to the state parties but not to the ICC, which has its own international legal personality). Accordingly, the nature of the charges might constitute a factor to be considered but would not necessarily be a bar to deferring to an amnesty or exile arrangement.

### 3. Article 53: Prosecutorial Discretion

Where the Security Council has not requested the ICC to respect an amnesty or exile-for-peace deal and thereby to terminate a prosecution, the court's prosecutor may choose to do so under Article 53 of the Rome Statute. That article permits the prosecutor to decline to initiate an investigation (even when a state party has filed a complaint) where the prosecutor concludes there are "substantial reasons to believe that an investigation would not serve the interests of justice." However, the decision of the prosecutor under Article 53 is subject to review by the pretrial chamber of the court. In reviewing whether respecting an amnesty or exile deal and not prosecuting would better serve "the interests of justice," the pretrial chamber would have to evaluate the benefits of a particular amnesty or exile arrangement and consider whether there is an international legal obligation to prosecute the offense (as discussed above).

### 4. Article 17: Complementarity

Where neither the Security Council nor the prosecutor has requested the ICC to defer to a national amnesty, the concerned state can attempt to raise the issue under Article 17(1)(a) of the Rome Statute. That article requires the court to dismiss a case where "[t]he case is being investigated or prosecuted by a State which has jurisdiction over it, unless the State is unwilling or unable genuinely to carry out the investigation or prosecution." It is significant that the article requires an investigation but does not specify that it be a criminal investigation. The concerned state could argue that a truth commission (especially one modeled on that of South Africa) constitutes a genuine investigation. On the other hand, subsection (2) of Article 17 suggests that the standard for determining that an investigation is not genuine is whether the proceedings are "inconsistent with an intent to bring the person concerned to justice"—a phrase that might be interpreted as requiring criminal proceedings.

In sum, the Rome Statute is purposely ambiguous on the question of whether the ICC should defer to an amnesty/exile-for-peace arrangement in deciding whether to exercise its jurisdiction. While amnesties and exiles are sometimes a necessary bargaining chip in negotiations for the peaceful transfer of political power, it must be recognized that such arrangements can vary greatly. Some, as in South Africa and Haiti, are closely linked to mechanisms for providing accountability and redress; others, as in the case of the exile of Charles Taylor, are simply a mindful forgetting. The ICC should take only the former types of amnesties/exiles into account in prosecutorial decisions. Moreover, the ICC should be particularly reluctant to defer to an amnesty/exile in situations involving violations of international conventions that create obligations to prosecute, such as the Genocide Convention and the grave breaches provisions of the Geneva Conventions. The other international agreements and customary international law crimes that make up the ICC's subject matter jurisdiction make prosecution for related crimes possible, but not mandatory, and should be treated as such by the court in the broader interests of peace and international security.

## IV. Conclusion

This Article has described how, under the present state of international law, the international procedural law imposing a duty to prosecute is far more limited than the substantive law establishing international offenses. The reason for this is historical: With respect to all but the most notorious of international crimes, it was easier for states to agree to recognize permissive jurisdiction than to undertake a duty to prosecute. But where the duty to prosecute does apply, it is critical that states and international organizations honor it, lest they express contempt for the important treaties from which the duty arises, potentially putting their own citizens at risk pursuant to the international law principle of reciprocity.

This is not to suggest, however, that states must rush to prosecute all persons involved in offenses under these treaties. Selective prosecution and use of "exemplary trials" is acceptable as long as the criteria used reflect appropriate distinctions based upon degrees of culpability and sufficiency of evidence. Moreover, while the provisions of the treaties requiring prosecution are nonderogable even in time of public emergency that threatens the life of the nation, the doctrine of *force majeure* can warrant temporary postponement of prosecutions for a reasonable amount of time until a new government is secure enough to take such action against members of the former regime or until a new government has the judicial resources to undertake fair and effective prosecutions.

In the case of Saddam Hussein, the United States had accused the Iraqi leader of grave breaches of the Geneva Conventions and violations of the Genocide Convention. Both the United States and Iraq were parties to these treaties, which contain an absolute obligation to prosecute offenders. By offering to permit exile and perpetual sanctuary in Bahrain in lieu of invasion and prosecution, the Bush administration signaled that the provisions of these treaties are inconsequential, thereby undermining the rule of law in a critical area of global affairs. This must be viewed also in light of other U.S. actions involving application of the Geneva Conventions to the conflict in Iraq, most notably the infamous White House memos authored by now Attorney General Alberto Gonzales. The memos refer to the Geneva Conventions as "obsolete" and "quaint," and wrongly opine that the Torture Convention permits mild forms of torture, thereby creating a climate of disdain toward international humanitarian law and opening the door to the abuses committed at Abu Ghraib prison in Iraq. In a statement before the Senate Judiciary Committee, Admiral John Hutson, Judge Advocate General of the U.S. Navy from 1997–2000, urged the Bush administration to officially and unequivocally repudiate Gonzales's erroneous position. In doing so, Hutson stressed that:

> Since World War II and looking into the foreseeable future, United States armed forces are more forward-deployed both in terms of numbers of deployments and numbers of troops than all other nations combined. What this means in practical terms is that adherence to the Geneva Conventions is more important to us than to any other nation. We should be the nation demanding adherence under any and all circumstances because we will benefit the most.

Because Hussein did not accept the exile-for-peace offer, the damage to the rule of law in this instance was negligible. Would greater damage to the rule of law have nevertheless been acceptable if it succeeded in averting a war which has resulted in tens of thousands of casualties on both sides since 2003? This Article has described the policy reasons generally favoring prosecution, including the fact that former leaders who have resorted to war crimes and crimes against humanity tend to be recidivists. Saddam Hussein himself launched a coup and initiated his policy of terror after he was released from prison through a domestic amnesty in 1968. It is not hard to imagine the dangers Hussein could present to the Iraqi democratic transition from exile in nearby Bahrain. Moreover, the people of Iraq have insisted on Hussein's trial before the Iraqi Special Tribunal. Morally, what right would American negotiators have to trade away the ability of thousands of Hussein's victims to see the dictator brought to justice? Finally, it is worth stressing that the duty to prosecute Hussein arising from these treaties did not require or even justify the invasion of Iraq. Rather, it merely prohibited actions that are manifestly incompatible with the prosecution of Hussein, such as arranging for exile and sanctuary in Bahrain.

The situation involving Charles Taylor is distinguishable. Taylor has been charged by the Special Court for Sierra Leone with complicity in crimes against humanity and war crimes in an internal armed conflict. As the Special Court itself has recognized, since there is no treaty-based nor customary international law duty to prosecute crimes against humanity or war crimes in an internal conflict, an amnesty or exile-for-peace deal would not constitute a violation of international law.

The distinction reflects the fact that, notwithstanding the natural law rhetoric of *jus cogens* employed by proponents of a broad duty to prosecute, the international legal order is still governed by principles of positive law under the 357-year-old Westphalian concept of sovereignty. State practice belies the existence of a customary international law duty (based on the positive law notion of state acquiescence to rules over time) to prosecute outside of the treaty framework. Consequently, the obligation to prosecute and the corresponding duty to refrain from frustrating prosecution through amnesty or exile applies only to certain treaty-based crimes where the treaty sets forth such an obligation and the affected states are party to the treaty at the time of the acts in question. This conclusion is analogous to that of the House of Lords in the *Pinochet* case, in which the British High Court held that the head of state immunity doctrine prevented the United Kingdom from extraditing to Spain former Chilean President Augusto Pinochet for crimes against humanity, with the exception of crimes of torture committed after the U.K., Chile, and Spain had all ratified the Torture Convention. Thus, while there was a treaty-based duty to prosecute Saddam Hussein under the Geneva Conventions and Genocide Convention, no such duty existed in the case of Charles Taylor, who was accused of crimes against humanity.

This does not mean that the Special Court for Sierra Leone has to honor the Charles Taylor exile-for-peace deal. The Special Court made clear that amnesty and exile arrangements are only binding within the state(s) granting them. They do not apply to other states or to international tribunals such as the Special Court. Moreover, it is important to recognize that amnesty, exile, and sanctuary arrangements are often temporary in nature. They are not a permanent right of the recipient, but a privilege bestowed by the territorial state, which can be revoked by a subsequent government or administration. The trend in recent years is to use amnesty and exile as a transitional step toward eventual justice, not as an enduring bar to justice. As a U.S. Department of State official explained with respect to Charles Taylor, "First we'll get him out of Liberia, then we'll get him to the Court."

## 4. Paul R. Williams and Michael P. Scharf, *Peace with Justice?:*
## *War Crimes and Accountability in the Former Yugoslavia*
### 2002
### [footnotes omitted by editors]

\* \* \*

### The Tradition of Conflict between Justice and Accommodation

Traditionally, many foreign policy practitioners and scholars have perceived of justice and peace in conflicting terms. The choices are often cast in terms of either working toward peace and ignoring justice or seeking justice at the price of jeopardizing any chance for peace. Proponents of peace are typically characterized as "more aware, more worldly," while those in favor of justice are characterized as "living in an unreal world, shall we say, a metaphysical or idealistic realm."

While this distinction is overly artificial, historically, amnesty or de facto immunity from prosecution has often been the price for peace. The Turks, who many considered responsible for the genocidal massacre of over one million Armenians during World War I were given amnesty in the 1923 Treaty of Lausanne; the French and Algerians responsible for the slaughter of thousands of civilians during the Algerian war were given amnesty in the Evian Agreement of 1962; and Bangladesh gave amnesty in 1973 to Pakistanis charged with genocide in exchange for political recognition by Pakistan.

During the 1980s, in order to facilitate a transition to democracy the governments of Argentina, Chile, El Salvador, Guatemala, and Uruguay each granted amnesty to members of the former regime who commanded death squads that tortured and killed thousands of civilians within their respective countries. To this list must be added the modern practice of the United Nations, which in the early 1990s worked to block inclusion of provisions in the Cambodia peace accords providing for the prosecution of former Khmer Rouge leaders for their atrocities, pushed the Mandela government to accept an amnesty for crimes committed by the apartheid regime in South Africa, and helped negotiate, and later endorsed, a broad amnesty for the leaders of the Haitian military regime in order to induce them to relinquish power.

Even the Nuremberg experience eventually involved the bartering away of accountability as the cost for German support of the Western alliance during the beginning of the Cold War. Within ten years of the conclusion of the Nuremberg Tribunals, all 150 of the convicted German war criminals (including several who were serving life sentences and a few who were sentenced to death) were released from Landsberg prison pursuant to a controversial clemency program. While this program removed a "diplomatic pebble from the State Department's shoes," it had the effect of undermining the purpose of the Nuremberg trials. In a nationwide survey conducted by the U.S. State Department, West Germans overwhelmingly indicated their belief that the reason for American leniency was that "they realize the injustice of the trials."

As explained by an anonymous U.N. official, the quest for justice and retribution is traditionally believed to hamper the search for peace, which in turn prolongs the conflict, enables the continuation of atrocities, and increases human suffering. The U.N. official also asserts that the intrusion of fact-finding missions seeking to investigate crimes committed by one side may complicate the task of peace negotiations to the point where they become prolonged or impossible.

Efforts to build peace in the former Yugoslavia were not exempt from the conflict between justice and accommodation. According to Payam Akhvan of the Office of the Prosecutor of the Tribunal, "from it very inception in 1993, the International Criminal Tribunal for the former Yugoslavia was surrounded by the so-called 'peace versus accountability' controversy." According to Akhvan, "it was argued indicting political and military leaders such as Radovan Karadzic and Ratko Mladic would undermine the prospects of a peace settlement because they were indispensable to on-going negotiations, and because they would have no incentive to put an end to the fighting without assurances of immunity or amnesty." In fact, during his tenure as co-chairman of the Yugoslav Peace Conference, David Owen expressly opposed the prosecution of Serbian officials engaged in the peace negotiations on the basis that this would undermine his efforts to craft a settlement.

Even after the massacre in Srebrenica and the clear pattern of genocide, policymakers doubted the compatibility of justice and accommodation. As noted by Richard Goldstone, "particularly at the time of the negotiations at Dayton, Ohio, in September 1995, there were many astute politicians and political commentators who suggested that, in fact, peace and justice were in opposition, and that the work of the Yugoslav Tribunal was retarding the peace process in the Balkans." Some commentators even noted that with Radovan Karadzic's alleged approval rating among Bosnian Serbs of 79 percent, any NATO efforts to capture him would undermine the implementation of the Dayton Peace Accord and foster the Serbian people's belief that they were subject to perpetual injustice and persecution. Goldstone rightly expressed surprise at this view, especially in light of the atrocities which had been committed over four years.

In some cases, the existence of a mechanism of justice, such as a tribunal, may be used to further the efforts of those pursuing an approach of accommodation by indicating that the norm of justice plays a role outside the peace process and that questions of culpability belong solely with that mechanism. For instance, in February 1994, when Secretary of State Warren Christopher was under pressure by the media to identify those responsible for the commission of war crimes in Bosnia, which would have limited his ability to accommodate the interests of those individuals, his standard press guidance was: "I would like to emphasize that no conclusion can or should be drawn at this stage as to the culpability of particular individuals. This is a question that should be reserved for the War Crimes Tribunal or other court, where the question of culpability will be considered on a case-by-case basis."

Still others, like Richard Holbrooke, asserted that in order to achieve the aims of justice, it was necessary to negotiate with and if necessary accommodate/appease those who were responsible for the commission of atrocities. As such, the insistence on a role for justice was characterized as something which undermined the effectiveness of the negotiator. When asked by Senator Smith during his confirmation hearing why he had systematically declined to ever indicate Milosevic's guilt for the war and atrocities in the former Yugoslavia, Holbrooke responded, "This is tough slogging, and my job was not to make moral judgments. I leave that to moralists anyway.... I was well aware of the fact that I might have to continue to be engaged on other issues. And the highest goal here was to avoid war, bring peace."

Many peace builders also assert that the conflict between accommodation and justice reflects the perspectives of those on the ground trying to save lives versus those more distant from the conflict. For instance, during his confirmation testimony, Ambassador Holbrooke responded to criticisms of his persistent failure to acknowledge Milosevic's culpability as made "by people who haven't been there, who haven't tried to end wars and prevent wars." Similar statements were made by numerous general serving in UNPROFOR, who also invoked the mantra of "saving lives" over pursuing justice." In fact, as reported by Cambridge historian Brendan Simms, many of the actual troops on the ground in the safe areas, and particularly SAS troops were keenly aware of the failings of accommodation and urged for a stronger use of force in the pursuit of justice.

The "saving lives" rationale while encapsulated in only two words, is a powerful tool used by the negotiators to undermine the influence of the norm of justice. By characterizing accommodation/appeasement of war criminals in the cloak of "saving lives," it automatically infers that those interested in justice are not interested in saving lives, or at least are willing to permit more killing in order to accomplish an idealistic objective. This view is succinctly stated by an anonymous U.N. official who criticized the then Yugoslav Tribunal prosecutor and president at the time for their public pressure on the Dayton negotiators. The U.N. official argues that "their 'ill-considered statements' could have led to a breakdown of delicate negotiations in Dayton.... Everyone who was at the Dayton proximity talks knew that if this issue [mandatory cooperation with the Tribunal] were pressed it could have ruined the talks." He declared that they were acting "irresponsibly" and asked, "in the name of what moral principle would one be able to defend those [further] deaths?" As evidenced by the subsequent conflict in Kosovo, it was in fact the act of accommodation at Dayton that resulted in further deaths, and that only the use of force, coupled with the indictment of Milosevic, brought an end to ethnic cleansing perpetrated by Serbian forces.

Some scholarly commentators assert that the tension between justice and accommodation is inherent in that "the need to establish power sharing structures that accommodate rival factions and interests may well clash with the desire to punish perpetrators of human rights abuses [and] the need to reform the police and the military may be at odds with the practical need to bring those powerful groups into the peace process." In their eyes, the inherent tension "prompt[s] the question of which model works best in a given situation, the power-sharing conflict manager's model, or the democratizer's political justice model? Empirical evidence suggests that a concern for justice must be tempered by the realities of negotiation and by the parties' interests in reaching a political settlement."

In response, defenders of the justice norm have argued, "in short, there is a grudging but emerging widespread acceptance—even among the so-called 'realists'—that regional peace and stability, democratization and multiethnic coexistence in Bosnia-Herzegovina are at best precarious without the arrest and prosecution of indicted persons," and that "the [Yugoslav Tribunal] demonstrates that far from being irreconcilable, peace and accountability, realities and ideals, are inextricably interlinked." According to Richard Goldstone, "if one is talking about short term cease-fires, short term cessation of hostilities, it could be that the investigation of war crimes is a nuisance. But if one is concerned with real peace, enduring and effective peace, if one is talking about proper reconciliation, the, in my respectful opinion, there is and can be no contradiction between peace and justice."

Despite the tradition of an apparent overwhelming preference for accommodation over justice, there is no clear evidence that this approach promotes lasting peace. In fact, the opposite may be the case. For example, history records that the international amnesty given to the Turkish officials responsible for the massacre of the Armenians during World War I encouraged Adolf Hitler some twenty years later to conclude that Germany could pursue his genocidal policies with impunity. In 1939, in relation to the acts of genocide and aggression committed by German forces, Hitler remarked, "Who after all is today speaking about the destruction of the Armenians?" As David Matas, a Canadian expert on international law, observed, "nothing emboldens a criminal so much as the knowledge he can get away with a crime. That was the message the failure to prosecute for the Armenian massacre gave to the Nazis. We ignore the lesson of the Holocaust at our peril."

Richard Goldstone declared that in the case of the former Yugoslavia the failure of the of the international community to prosecute Pol Pot (Cambodia), Idi Amin (Uganda), Saddam Hussein (Iraq), and Mohammed Aidid (Somalia), among others, encouraged the Serbs to launch their policy of ethnic cleansing with the expectation that they would not be held accountable for their international crimes. When the international community encourages or endorses an amnesty for human rights abuses, it sends a signal to other rogue regimes that they have nothing to lose by instituting repressive measures; if things start going badly, they can always bargain away their crimes by agreeing to peace. The apprehension of Slobodan Milosevic in the spring of 2001 may be the first step in the reversal of this long history of accommodation and de facto immunity.

Given the poor track record for accommodation, there has been increasing demand for an inclusion of the norm of justice in peace-building since the end of the Cold War. For example, since 1989, some level of justice, in the form of international tribunals and truth commissions, has been pursued in Argentina, Cambodia, Chile, East Timor, El Salvador, Ethiopia, Guatemala, Honduras, Rwanda, Sierra Leone, and South Africa, as well as the former Yugoslavia. As discussed in the next section, there is a role for each of the approaches of accountability, accommodation, economic inducement, and use of force in the peace-building process. And as noted in the subsequent chapters, it appears that the international community, while eventually acknowledging the need to employ a mix of approaches, continued to disproportionately favor accommodation and as such weakened the foundations for a lasting peace.

## Getting the Right Mix of Approaches

* * *

Individual peace-building approaches generally are not capable of building a lasting peace in isolation from other peace-building approaches. Moreover, when peace-building approaches operate, they generally do so in relation to other approaches. The task of foreign policy practitioners is to ascertain the proper role for each approach and to apply an appropriate mix. As noted by General Nash, "the reality is, that all the world is a compromise of many, many issues and as you try to go towards an objective state and objective goal, you've got to work things in stages and you have to balance things."

Although some diplomats contend that the approach of accommodation may be sufficient in and of itself, most commentators would agree with the assessment that "the military and security components of peace-building are a critical part of the peacemaking process," and that "peacekeeping remains essential to international efforts to prevent the renewed outbreak of violence or military hostilities in a country." Furthermore, the prompt deployment of competent and capable peacemakers may promote confidence in the peace-building process.

In the case of Bosnia for instance, most observers would acknowledge that "the final factor smoothing the path to Dayton was the international community's new willingness to use force, especially air power, as a partner to diplomacy." Observers would also readily acknowledge that the application of economic sanctions on the FRY were insufficient in and of themselves to deter Serbia's aggression against neighboring states. As will be discussed below, however, the employment of economic inducements against Croatia and later Serbia to turn over indicted war criminals to The Hague for trial, and thus neutralize their ability to inhibit the peace-building process, and the use of economic inducements to prompt the handover of Slobodan Milosevic, were highly effective.

Unfortunately, foreign policymakers frequently underestimate the need to adequately employ all relative approaches, and thus in the Bosnia case, they were slow to utilize the approach of the use of force. According to Elizabeth Cousens, despite the fact that very clear legal justification existed for the use of force, "various explanations account for the under-use of armed force to respond to the Yugoslav wars, from the nationally parochial through the bureaucratically predisposed and militarily arcane, to the ontologically confused." This failure to grasp the utility of the use of force is all the more difficult to understand as key foreign policymakers often set forth compelling rationales for the use of force to protect human rights. For instance, in a now declassified memorandum from Assistant Secretary of State John Shattuck to Secretary Christopher on 19 July 1995, Mr. Shattuck argues:

> We know from these recent and past events what will happen if the Bosnian Serbs' "ethnic cleansing" campaign is not stopped. And, we know that the ever growing refugee problem poses both a humanitarian catastrophe and a security problem as population flows disrupt the delicate balance in the Bosnian Federation and neigh-boring countries. On human rights and humanitarian grounds alone, the disaster of Srebrenica demands that the international community use the authority it has to protect the remaining safe areas, including through the use of military force.

Regrettably, on frequent occasion, foreign policymakers may inartfully mix the em-ployment of most or all of the approaches, resulting in the creation of a set of circum-stances where the approaches work at cross-purposes and are inconclusive to the establishment of peace. For instance, in the Bosnia conflict the U.N. deployed lightly armed peacekeepers which provided some protection to civilians, but did not act decisively when confronted with large-scale ethnic cleansing and genocide against Bosnian Mus-lims. During the same period, policymakers enacted, but initially failed to enforce a no-fly zone over Bosnia; established safe areas without protecting them; and authorized, but never employed, force to deliver humanitarian aid.

When EU policymakers sought to address the initial conditions of conflict in Bosnia, and the Serbs and Croats escalated their behavior, the prevailing guide to action for the EU lay in accommodation and tightly calibrated displays of force, rather than the mean-ingful use of force. The contradictory employment of the various approaches came to a head when in the summer of 1995 NATO forces were prohibited from using force to pro-tect the U.N. designated safe areas of Srebrenica and Zepa because of the risk of Serb re-taliation against lightly armed peacekeepers stationed in those safe areas.

In large part because of the failure of the international peace builders to settle on a proper and effective mix of approaches, Yugoslavia slid into a decade of war marked by crimes against humanity and acts of genocide.

* * *

## Self-Identity and Self-Interest: The Institutional Response

* * *

In addition to the states mentioned above, a number of international institutions played a key role in the development of a response to the Balkan conflict. The most im-portant institutions were the European Union and the United Nations.

### The European Union

The approach of the European Union was characterized by its desire to further cement cohesion within the union by demonstrating its ability to adeptly deal with foreign pol-icy crises on the European continent. The approach of the EU was also characterized by deep internal rivalries, a general lack of competence necessary to handle the Yugoslav cri-sis, and a pull toward moral equivalence. On the whole, the policy that emerged from this set of circumstances was a policy of supporting a unified Yugoslavian state.

At the time of the Yugoslav crisis, the European Union was in the process of deepening the political and economic commitments of its members and expanding the authority of the European Commission. In particular, the European Union had recently adopted an initiative to establish a common foreign and security policy, and the Yugoslav conflict was seen as the first test of that initiative. With the now infamous words of Luxembourg foreign minister Jacques Poos on 28 June 1991, "this is the hour of Europe. It is not the hour of the Americans," the European Union signaled its desire to replace the United States as the primary agent of political stability on the European continent. The EU was also seized with a touch of Euro-nationalism, which expressed itself in the following declaration by Jacques Delors, president of the European Community in 1991, "we do not interfere in American affairs, we trust America will not interfere in European affairs." The United States easily embraced this Euro-nationalism, with Secretary of State James Baker noting in his memoir, "It was time to make the Europeans step up to the plate and show that they could act as a unified power. Yugoslavia was as good a first test as any."

As further explained by Mark Almond, in 1991 the European Union member states were preparing to sign the Maastricht Treaty, which set the foundation for a fully integrated Europe. The prospect of the dissolution of a state occurring while the Europeans were on the brink of the further integration of independent states caused serious cognitive dissonance and prevented them from adequately grasping the nature of the Yugoslav conflict. Moreover, the member states of the EU feared that a crisis in Yugoslavia could derail their own efforts toward further integration. As a result, the president of the EC Council of Ministers, Jacques Santer, declared "we have to try all means to save the Yugoslav Federation at this moment," with John Major adding that "the great prize is to hold the federation together."

After the outbreak of hostilities, the European Union generally supported plans for partition of Croatia and Bosnia, while rejecting calls for the use of force beyond traditional peacekeeping. The European Union representatives also sought to draw on the European Union's prestige and relative financial wealth to offer the parties to the conflict closer political relations with the European Union and economic incentives for parties willing to cooperate, such as access to the European Union market and financial assistance.

The approach of the EU was thus heavily criticized by accommodation and economic inducement. For example, in 1991 the EU extended the hope of EU "association and possible membership to a *united* Yugoslavia, hoping that this 'carrot' would induce the presidents of the six Yugoslav republics to reach a peaceful agreement." At the time, the EU also offered an aid package of nearly $1 billion. When these efforts failed, the EU adopted economic sanctions.

The ability of the European Union to cope with the Yugoslav crisis and to adequately embrace the norm of justice was handicapped by the fact, that despite the goals and hopes of a common foreign and security policy, Europe was rife with national divisions. As explained by the European historian Mark Almond, "The European Community remain[ed] bedeviled by national rivalries despite all the talk of common policies and a new united identity," and by a reliance on outdated political and historical perspectives. As a result, "the breakdown of Yugoslavia brought out deep-seated Anglo-French suspicions of Germany which were partly shared and partly played on by the Serbian regime. Just as British and French politicians revealed that in their heart of hearts they could not see Germany as anything other than in essence a domineering and aggressive nation, so they remained trapped with an inherited vision of 'plucky little Serbia,' the ancient ally against the *Boche*."

As observed by former Secretary of State James Baker the ability of the EU to grapple with the crisis was hampered by the approach of unanimity, which required "rigid adherence to acting only when every EC member state was in agreement," and resulted in an approach that "caused both delays (as all members had to be polled for even the smallest decision) and lowest-common-denominator policies." The EU approach was further hampered by their "tendency to become prisoners of their own history, falling back on alliances that had been developed decades or even centuries before," and as such, "the parties in the region quickly learned to play the Europeans off against one another, effectively neutralizing the EC."

The efforts of the European Union were further undermined by the unilateral behavior of some of its members, in particular Greece. For instance, on 9 February 1994, in response to the Sarajevo marketplace massacre, NATO indicated it was prepared to use air strikes if the civilian massacres did not cease. On 15 February, Greek foreign minister Carlos Papoulias traveled to Serbia to meet with Slobodan Milosevic, where he expressed Greece's significant reservations regarding any NATO action. At this time, Greece held the rotating presidency of the EU. According to a now declassified State Department cable, the Greek foreign minister and Milosevic publicly agreed that threats of air strikes were "damaging to the negotiating process because they encouraged the forces that advocate the military option."

## The United Nations

Given the failure of the EU to adequately address the Yugoslav crisis, and France and the United Kingdom's desire to minimize Germany's influence, the United Nations became the international institution most involved in seeking a resolution of the conflict. While the Security Council created the Tribunal, and voted for the deployment of U.N. peacekeepers, and the eventual use of force in Bosnia, the overall approach of the Security Council was one of accommodation and economic inducement, with the approach of the Secretary-General and his designates being one of appeasement as determined by a subsequent U.N. report, and one of anti-justice characterized by moral equivalence.

While the United Nations is generally presumed to represent the views of its constituent members, in the case of the Yugoslav conflict, the U.N. Secretariat, under the leadership of the Secretary-General Boutros Boutros-Ghali, possessed its own agenda, which differed from those of many of its members, and in particular from the Security Council. This situation was augmented by the fact that Secretary-General Boutros Boutros-Ghali maintained a particularly acrimonious relationship with the U.S. Ambassador to the United Nations, and he held the U.S. role in the United Nations in low esteem.

The Secretariat of the United Nations perceived itself to be the custodians of the New World Order, which was not to be dominated by the only remaining superpower, as the United States believed, and balanced by the European Union, as the Western European states believed, but rather was to be guided and shaped by the United Nations. The Secretariat also eschewed the use of force, preferring a continuation of the United Nation's traditional peacekeeping mandate, with no extension into peace making of peace-enforcing. Finally, it generally resented the focus on crises in Europe over Africa. Notably, while visiting besieged Sarajevo, the Secretary-General proclaimed that he could name at least ten places in Africa where the conditions were worse.

The Secretary-General's approach was also deeply influenced by his preference for accommodation over all other approaches to peace-building. In June 1995, one month prior to the Srebrenica massacre, he confided to *Washington Times* columnist Georgie Anne Geyer, "the result of the negotiations may not be equity, but it may be peace. Then you have a problem: what is more important, peace or peace at the expense of certain principles of equity? My theory is that what happens in a war is so terrible that peace is better, even if it is not a just peace." He also predicted, "in six months, nobody would talk about Yugoslavia and they would continue killing themselves for years." Thus, even when the Security Council adopted the statute for the Yugoslav Tribunal, the Secretariat supported its creation, but threw up unnecessary administrative obstacles to its quick establishment and its effective operation, so that it would not interfere with the conduct of negotiations.

As a result of these perceptions, the Secretary-General persistently sought to limit the mandate of the UNPROFOR units serving in Bosnia and Croatia to use force, even after the Security Council had explicitly authorized the use of force. The Secretary-General also sought to prevent states from using force outside of the UNPROFOR framework after such force was approved by the Security Council. In close cooperation with Boutros-Ghali, the Secretary-General's representative for Bosnia, Yasushi Akashi, consistently denied permission for NATO to use air strikes in response to gross violations of the U.N. protected safe areas, and Akashi sought to undermine the ability of NATO to effectively deter acts of violence by limiting which targets could be struck when NATO air strikes were employed. As recounted by Georgie Anne Geyer "the U.N. representative in Bosnia, Yasushi Akashi, was stoically intent on not using force even in the face of European genocide." According to Akashi, use of force was not possible, because "we would be perceived as the enemy and that would endanger our carefully constructed relations with the parties. We are impartial; we are in a war, but we are not at war. Once we became a party to the war, we would have to liquidate our efforts—withdraw or cut down."

The result of this approach was, according to Geyer, that the U.N. acted "with a rigid moral neutralism, a non-use of force, and a utopian idea that fanatics like the Serbs can be won over by rationality. With this mentality, the approach soon became devoid of any sense of justice or any element of truth." According to former Japanese U.N. ambassador Yoshio Hatano, as recounted by Geyer, "as a Japanese, Akashi may still retain some of the Japanese character, which places peace above justice." The ambassador noted that "in Japan, peace tends to equal justice. Because of Japan's experience in the last war, justice tends to be sacrificed." Mr. Akashi may also have been influenced by his desire to engage Japanese forces in U.N. peacekeeping operations and the recognition that this hope would be dashed if U.N. forces became involved in the direct use of force in Bosnia.

As a consequence, when NATO did finally employ air strikes, in the spring of 1995, the U.N. did not redeploy its peacekeepers. In fact a number of UNPROFOR troops remained in Serb headquarters during the air campaign, as according to Akashi, "they had to be there," as "they were [the] liaison with the Serbs, ..." and "for reassurance to the Serbs and for keeping channels of communication." They, of course, became hostages. In the end, according to Michael Sells, "by focusing the U.N. mission on the supply of humanitarian aid while refusing to stop the campaign of genocide, the U.N. Security Council created a system that put U.N. peacekeepers as suppliers of humanitarian aid to Bosnia—as hostages." In his view, "whether or not they were actually detained by radical Serb militias was not important. They could be detained at will and thus served as hostages whether or not they were confined." Serbian forces were thus able to "violate with impunity dozens of U.N. resolutions demanding free flow of humanitarian aid, liberation of concentration camps, access to camps by war crimes investigators, and protection of civilians."

The meaningful use of force was further undermined by the efforts of the U.N. and EU negotiators as well as the early UNPROFOR commanders to create and maintain a perception of moral equivalence between the victims and the aggressors. As recounted by Peter Maass, in his memoir, the first Canadian commander of UNPROFOR, General

MacKenzie told French president Francois Mitterrand, 'there is strong but circumstantial evidence that some really horrifying acts of cruelty attributed to the Serbs were actually orchestrated by the Muslims against their own people, for the benefit of an international audience." According to Maass, MacKenzie has since softened this assertion, but he continues to claim "there is more than enough blame to go around for all sides, with some left over." After the conflict, General MacKenzie is reported to have been retained by Serb-Net, a Serbian lobby, and paid $10,000 per public speech.

As a consequence of this approach, as noted by one Scandinavian UNPROFOR soldier, "this is a ridiculous war, none of us can figure our why in God's name we're here. In our area, we hear shooting all the time, but we are forbidden—get that, forbidden!—to know who is shooting. U.N. rules!" The coercive appeasement employed by UNPROFOR led to deadly consequences. As recounted by Michael Sells, on 8 January 1993, "a French contingent of U.N. peacekeepers was escorting the Bosnian Deputy Prime Minister, Dr. Hakija Turajlic, into Sarajevo. They were stopped at a Serb army checkpoint. When the Serb soldiers asked the French peacekeepers to open up the armored car—against their orders and with the certain knowledge of what would follow—they complied, then stood aside and watched as a Serb soldier shot the unarmed Dr. Turajlic dead. When the same French peacekeepers came home to France, they were decorated for heroism."

Such action led to the convoluted attempts of UNPROFOR forces to justify their action. For instance when the U.N. commander General Rose refused to protect the U.N. safe area of Gorazde in the spring of 1994 from Serbian attacks, he declared that he had not been authorized to "protect" the safe area, only to "deter" attacks on it. Yet it was Rose who had refused to use a credible threat of NATO air strikes to deter the Serb army from violating the enclave in the first place. Earlier, in the autumn of 1993 General Rose and French General Bertrand de Lapresle responded to the Serbian aerial bombardment of the Bihac safe zone by limiting NATO air strikes to the runway from which the planes were being launched, despite the presence of place in nearby hangars. Moreover, it has been reported that, during the same period of time, the SAS forces "were supposed to give NATO coordinates for the air strikes against Serb artillery an anti-aircraft batteries, but they deliberately held back the coordinates or gave false coordinates to thwart the effectiveness of any NATO strikes."

It is important to note that not all UNPROFOR commanders fit this mold, and that in particular, British lieutenant general Rupert Smith "and many U.N. officials in besieged Sarajevo believed that the Bosnian Serbs needed to be confronted by force. As long as they were allowed to block U.N. supply convoys, shell U.N. safe areas and storm U.N. observation posts, the Bosnian Serbs would only be emboldened and their behavior worsen." Unfortunately, such officers were often perceived as tainted in their views by more senior U.N. officials and were referred to as "in 'le milieux Bosnjak' or in the Bosnian Muslim world in Sarajevo and therefore couldn't see the war from the proper perspective." According to David Rohde, "the difference was that Smith saw the Serbs as abusing their advantage in firepower and had to be challenged. Janvier, on the other hand, viewed the Muslims as abusing the safe areas to draw the U.N. into fighting the war for them."

The approach of the U.N. eventually culminated in a passive UNPROFOR response in the face of the Srebrenica massacre. In fact, according to David Rohde, "later that day [12 July 1995, the commencement of the fall of Srebrenica], Akashi would send a cable and a sample letter to the U.N. in New York criticizing the French Security Council resolution calling for the U.N. to use force to retake the safe area [Srebrenica]. Akashisaid the resolution raised 'unrealistic expectations' and it 'blurs the lines between neutral 'peacekeeping' and taking sides or 'peace enforcement.'" As a result, the U.N. was replaced by NATO and the United States as the primary institutions responsible for bringing an end to the conflict.

## *Authors' Note*

The impact of justice on the peace process is heightened by the willingness and ability of international tribunals to indict heads of state, heads of government, and major rebel leaders, all of whom are naturally key players in the peace process.

**In the International Criminal Court (ICC):**

**Muammar Gaddafi**—Leader of Libya; indicted by the ICC upon referral from the United Nations Security Council on February 26, 2011.

**Omar al-Bashir**—President of Sudan; indicted by the ICC for crimes of genocide, war crimes, and crimes against humanity on July 12, 2010; the first ever sitting head of state indicted by the ICC.

**Joseph Kony**—Head of the Lord's Resistance Army which operated in Uganda, Sudan, and the Democratic Republic of Congo; indicted by the ICC on October 6, 2005, for war crimes and crimes against humanity.

**Thomas Lubanga**—Founder and leader of the Union of Congolese Patriots (UPC) within the Democratic Republic of Congo; indicted by the ICC for war crimes on March 17, 2006; the first person ever arrested under a warrant issued by the ICC.

**Jean-Pierre Bemba**—Leader of the Movement for the Liberation of Congo (MLC); indicted by the ICC for crimes against humanity and war crimes on May 23, 2008, for crimes committed in the Central African Republic.

**In the International Criminal Tribunal for the Former Yugoslavia (ICTY):**

**Slobodan Milošević**—President of Serbia and Yugoslavia; indicted by the ICTY for crimes against humanity, genocide, and war crimes for actions in Kosovo (indicted May 24, 1999), Croatia (indicted October 8, 2001), and Bosnia and Herzegovina (indicted November 22, 2001).

**Ratko Mladić**—Former Chief of Staff of the Army of the Republika Srpska; fugitive from the ICTY accused of genocide, war crimes, and crimes against humanity; indicted July 25, 1995, by the ICTY.

**Radovan Karadžić**—First President of Republika Srpska; initially indicted by the ICTY on July 25, 1995, for war crimes, genocide, and crimes against humanity; also accused of the Srebrenica massacre by the ICTY; currently detained by the United Nations.

**Ramush Haradinaj**—Prime Minister of Kosovo; indicted by the ICC for crimes against humanity and violations of the laws or customs of war on March 4, 2005, for actions while regional commander of the Kosovo Liberation Army. Haradinaj was acquitted on April 3, 2008, but a retrial was ordered on July 21, 2010.

**In the Special Court for Sierra Leone (SCSL):**

**Charles Taylor**—Former warlord and former President of Liberia; indicted by the Special Court for Sierra Leone (SCSL) on March 3, 2003, for war crimes and crimes against humanity.

**Foday Sankoh**—Leader and founder of the Revolutionary United Front (RUF) in Sierra Leone; indicted by the SCSL on March 7, 2003, for war crimes, crimes against humanity, recruitment of child soldiers, and extermination.

**Issa Sesay**—Senior military officer and commander in the RUF and Armed Forces Revolutionary Council (AFRC); indicted by the SCSL on March 7, 2003, for crimes against humanity and war crimes.

**In the Extraordinary Chambers in the Courts of Cambodia (ECCC):**

**Kang Kek Iew**—Former leader in the Khmer Rouge communist movement; indicted by the ECCC on July 31, 2007, for crimes against humanity; the first Khmer Rouge leader to be tried by the ECCC.

**Ieng Sary**—Former Minister of Foreign Affairs of Democratic Kampuchea; indicted by the ECCC on September 15, 2010, for crimes against humanity committed under the Democratic Kampuchea regime.

**Ieng Thirith**—Wife of Ieng Sary and former Minister of Social Welfare; indicted by the ECCC on September 15, 2010, for crimes against humanity committed under the Democratic Kampuchea regime.

**Khieu Samphan**—Former head of state; indicted by the ECCC on September 15, 2010, for crimes against humanity committed under the Democratic Kampuchea regime.

**Nuon Chea**—Former Deputy to Khmer Rouge founder Pol Pot; indicted by the ECCC on September 15, 2010, for crimes against humanity committed under the Democratic Kampuchea regime.

---

## 5. Michael P. Scharf, Swapping Amnesty for Peace: Was There a Duty to Prosecute International Crimes in Haiti?

*Texas International Law Journal*, 1996
[footnotes omitted by editors]

\* \* \*

[D]id the Haitian amnesty achieve a proper mix between law and political reality? On the political side, we have seen that the decision to provide amnesty to members of the former military regime was largely imposed upon the Aristide government by the United States and United Nations, whose overriding concern was to restore the democratic government to power without having to introduce troops into a combat situation in Haiti. Haitian interests in discouraging future atrocities, deterring vigilante justice, and reinforcing respect for law and the new democratic government through prosecutions were never given serious attention.

What makes the Haitian situation so unique is that the United States and United Nations actually participated in the negotiation of the amnesty-for-peace deal with the Haitian military leaders, pressured the Aristide Government to accept the deal, and then endorsed the deal as the only acceptable way to resolve the Haitian situation. While the amnesty achieved the desired short-term benefit (i.e., the democratic government was restored with almost no bloodshed and the human rights abuses came to an end), the long-term implications were perhaps not fully appreciated at the time. For, like a genie that has been let out of a bottle, this precedent cannot be undone. Nor will it be ignored. Instead, as Justice Goldstone and Graham Blewitt feared, the Haitian amnesty is likely to serve as a beacon of hope for those accused of some of history's most shocking atrocities in Bosnia, Iraq, and Cambodia. In other parts of the globe, future dictators will be encouraged by the Haitian amnesty to commit new atrocities with impunity.

Before supporting or endorsing such amnesties and thereby condoning acts of international barbarism, the United Nations, as an organization committed to furthering human rights, and the United States, as the twentieth century's last remaining superpower, should more fully consider whether peace achieved in this manner is worth the long-term price. Perhaps a more appropriate response would parallel U.S. policy with respect to terrorism, which prohibits the government from "making concessions of any kind to terrorists" on the ground that "such actions would only lead to more terrorism." If the United States and the United Nations cannot prevent atrocities from occurring, they should at least seek to punish the perpetrators. This policy was the rationale behind the recent establishment of the International Criminal Tribunals for the Former Yugoslavia and Rwanda—a rationale that has been undermined by the participation of the United Nations and United States in the Haitian amnesty deal.

And what of international law? Professor Anthony D'Amato recently wrote that he knew of no "international lawyer who has objected" to the Haitian amnesty-for-peace deal. The reason public international law generalists have (until now) been silent is not that international law has nothing to say on the issue of amnesty for perpetrators of atrocities, but rather that it did not apply to the situation in Haiti. Had the atrocities in Haiti occurred during an international conflict, the Geneva Conventions would have required prosecution; had the violence been directed at ethnic, national, racial, or religious groups, the Genocide Convention would have required prosecution; and had Haiti been a party to the Torture Convention, it would have required prosecution. Any amnesty conferred would have constituted a violation of treaty law and would be subject to challenge in a variety of domestic and international fora. Unfortunately, none of these conventions applied to the Haitian situation, and, therefore, they played no role in the decision to swap amnesty for peace. Nor would these conventions apply to most of the other countries now wrestling with their repressive pasts that have concluded, or are considering, similar amnesty-for-peace deals. Like Haiti, few of these countries are party to the Torture Convention, abuses are most often targeted at political groups, and the situation rarely constitutes an international armed conflict.

While the international criminal conventions are unlikely to apply to such situations, there is growing recognition of a duty for states to do something to give meaning to the human rights enumerated in the Covenant on Civil and Political Rights and the American Convention on Human Rights, which are much more likely to be applicable. Yet, the "something" required is not necessarily prosecution of former leaders responsible for violations of these general human rights treaties. Given the precedent discussed earlier, it is likely that both the Human Rights Committee and the Inter-American Court of Human Rights would agree that the Aristide Government—which has established a truth commission, instituted purges of officers from the military, conducted limited prosecutions, and has put into place a program of victim compensation and civil redress—adequately discharged its duty to ensure human rights, notwithstanding its failure to prosecute the military leaders responsible for violations of those rights.

On the other hand, the analysis contained in this Article demonstrates that the Haitian atrocities almost certainly constituted crimes against humanity under customary international law. Customary international law recognizes permissive jurisdiction to prosecute leaders responsible for such crimes either nationally or before an international tribunal. From a legal standpoint, it would be perfectly appropriate, for example, to extend the Yugoslavia and Rwanda Tribunal's jurisdiction to cover the crimes against humanity committed by the Haitian military leaders, although the politics of the Security Council suggest such a course of action is highly unlikely.

In addition, there are a host of compelling policy and jurisprudential reasons in favor of an international duty to prosecute crimes against humanity, which would preclude the granting of amnesties for perpetrators. Yet, despite a large collection of General Assembly resolutions calling for prosecutions of crimes against humanity, and notwithstanding the wishful thinking of a number of international legal scholars, state practice plainly does not support the existence of an obligation under international law to refrain from conferring amnesty for crimes against humanity. That the United Nations, itself, felt free of legal constraints in endorsing the Haitian amnesty deal underscores this conclusion.

In this regard, our inquiry into the permissibility of the Haitian amnesty has placed us in the midst of one of the most enduring of international legal questions—namely, what is the nature of customary international law? There are those, especially in the field of human rights, who would focus entirely on the words, texts, votes, and excuses themselves and disregard inconsistent practice as either unimportant or as the exception that proves the rule. The trouble with such an approach that focuses so heavily on words is "that it is grown like a flower in a hot-house and that it is anything but sure that such creatures will survive in the much rougher climate of actual state practice." A "rule" that is so divorced from the realities of state practice is unlikely to achieve substantial compliance in the real world and, therefore, cannot be said to be a binding rule at all, but rather an aspiration.

On the other side of the debate are those, including the author of this Article, who acknowledge that such proclamations may constitute a starting point in the formation of customary international law, but look beyond the rhetoric emanating from the halls of the United Nations for evidence of actual state practice. If there exists widespread practice in conformity with these proclamations, then it can be said that a rule has ripened into binding customary international law. In such cases, a few instances of departure from the rule will not disprove the existence of customary international law, but when the departures are the norm and compliance is the exception as is the case of prosecuting crimes against humanity of a prior regime, a customary international law duty cannot be deemed to exist.

Yet, given the compelling justifications for an international duty to prosecute crimes against humanity, waiting for state practice to catch up with the views expressed in General Assembly resolutions does seem an unsatisfactory approach. As opposed to brokering amnesty-for-peace deals, the better approach would be for the U.N. Security Council to play a preemptive role by deciding in specific situations, such as Haiti, which constitute threats to international peace and security, that no amnesty for the perpetrators of atrocities shall be permitted or internationally respected. At the very least, the United Nations, having taken the lead in attempting to fashion an emerging rule of customary international law that would require prosecutions of crimes against humanity, should oppose amnesty in countries where it has become deeply involved.

---

## 6. ICC: Prosecutor to Open an Investigation in Libya Q&A on Libya and the International Criminal Court

### Human Rights Watch, 2011

On March 3, 2011, the prosecutor of the International Criminal Court (ICC) announced he would open an investigation into the situation in Libya. This follows the referral on February 26, 2011 by the United Nations (U.N.) Security Council—by a vote of 15-0—of the situation in the Libya since February 15, 2011 to the ICC prosecutor.

The ICC is a permanent international court with jurisdiction over crimes of genocide, war crimes, and crimes against humanity. Currently, 114 states are parties to the ICC. Anti-government protests began in Libya on February 17, 2011, following widespread protests in Tunisia and Egypt. Security forces that day attacked peaceful demonstrators in cities across the country.

The U.N. Security Council resolution followed the establishment by the U.N. Human Rights Council of an international commission of inquiry to investigate alleged human rights violations in the face of reports of escalating violence in Libya. The Arab League, African Union, and the Secretary General of the Organization of the Islamic Conference condemned the violence. The U.N. General Assembly suspended Libya's membership in the U.N. Human Rights Council as of March 1.

**1. What does it mean that the situation in Libya was referred by the Security Council to the ICC prosecutor?**

Under the Rome Statute, the ICC's founding treaty, the U.N. Security Council can refer a situation in any country to the ICC prosecutor under its Chapter VII mandate if it determines that a situation constitutes a threat to the maintenance of international peace and security. Security Council referrals are one of three so-called "triggers" for the ICC's jurisdiction and are an important avenue through which serious crimes occurring in states, such as Libya, that are not party to the Rome Statute can be prosecuted by the court.

The other two triggers are ICC state party referrals and the ICC prosecutor's initiation of an investigation on his own initiative (known as "proprio motu" investigations). These triggers are however limited to situations occurring within the jurisdiction of ICC states parties or for alleged crimes committed by nationals of ICC states parties. In addition, under article 12(3) of the Rome Statute, a non-state party may accept the court's jurisdiction in relation to a particular situation.

The Security Council passed a resolution on February 26 under its Chapter VII powers to refer the situation in Libya to the ICC prosecutor. Security Council Resolution 1970 referred the situation as of February 15, 2011. The resolution also requires the Libyan authorities to cooperate with the ICC and its prosecutor and imposed travel bans on key Libyan leaders and froze their assets.

**2. Is this the first time the Security Council has referred a situation to the ICC prosecutor?**

This is the second time. In March 2005, the Security Council passed Resolution 1593 to refer the situation in the Darfur region of Sudan. The ICC prosecutor opened an investigation in June 2005. To date, as a result of investigations in Darfur, the ICC has issued four arrest warrants, including two for President Omar al-Bashir of Sudan on charges of genocide, crimes against humanity, and war crimes. The ICC has also issued summonses to appear for three rebel leaders on charges related to attacks on an African Union peacekeeping mission in Darfur. All three rebel leaders have voluntarily appeared in The Hague, although one case was subsequently dropped for lack of evidence. The targets of the warrants, Al-Bashir, Ahmed Haroun, then the country's minister for humanitarian affairs and now governor of Southern Kordofan state, and Ali Kosheib, a "Janjaweed" militia leader, remain fugitives.

The Libya referral is notable, however, for the speed with which the Security Council acted. It was only after months of discussions and years after the massive human rights violations in Darfur were brought to the attention of the international community that the Security Council referred the situation to the ICC. In the Libya case, the referral came within weeks after the first reports of unlawful attacks by state security forces on anti-government protesters. The situation was also unique in that Libya's representatives to the U.N. had sought Security Council action. The unanimous resolution reflects a growing recognition that there will be accountability for those associated with widespread atrocities and the important potential role of the ICC in delivering justice. It is the first time the United States or China, neither of which are states parties to the ICC, have voted affirmatively to send a case to the ICC.

\* \* \*

**4. What should the prosecutor consider in deciding whether to open an investigation?**

The ICC prosecutor's decision to initiate an investigation following a Security Council referral is guided by requirements set out in the Rome Statute.

First, there must be a reasonable basis to believe that a crime within the jurisdiction of the court has been or is being committed. ICC crimes include genocide, crimes against humanity, and war crimes.

Currently, crimes against humanity may be relevant to the situation in Libya. Under article 7 of the Rome Statute, a crime against humanity encompasses any of a number of acts, including murder, torture, or rape when committed as part of a widespread or systematic attack directed against any civilian population, with knowledge of the attack.

Second, even where an ICC crime or crimes have been committed, the ICC prosecutor must determine whether possible cases arising out of an investigation would be admissible. For a case to be admissible, it must be of a certain gravity—assessed according to the scale, nature, and manner of commission of the crimes, as well as their impact. In addition, since the ICC is a court of last resort, which steps in only where national authorities are unwilling or unable to act, there must be no credible investigations or prosecutions of the case at the national level. This latter requirement is known as "complementarity" and makes the ICC's international jurisdiction secondary to that of national authorities.

**5. What happens now? How long will it take for cases to come to trial?**

There are many steps between the opening of an investigation and the eventual trial of a case.

It is important to understand that investigations by the ICC prosecutor may not necessarily lead to prosecutions. While the initial decision to open an investigation is based on information available to the prosecutor at that time, the prosecutor must then conduct an independent investigation. On the basis of this investigation, the prosecutor may determine that there is insufficient evidence that crimes committed within the court's jurisdiction have taken place. Or the prosecutor may determine that there are proceedings at the national level that would make any case before the ICC inadmissible or that a prosecution is not in the interests of justice. If the prosecutor decides not to proceed with prosecutions following investigations, this decision can be reviewed by ICC judges sitting in a pre-trial chamber.

If, based on the investigation, the prosecutor wishes to pursue prosecutions, he will need to ask ICC judges to issue arrest warrants for individuals on the basis of specific charges. The prosecutor must establish to the satisfaction of the pre-trial chamber that there are reasonable grounds to believe that the individual named in the request has committed a crime within the jurisdiction of the court and that an arrest is necessary to ensure that the person will appear at trial or that the person will not obstruct or endanger the investigation or the court proceedings, or that a warrant is needed to prevent ongoing crimes. The prosecutor can also request a voluntary summons to appear if he considers that a summons is sufficient to ensure the individual's appearance before the court.

It is difficult to predict how long it might be between the beginning of an investigation and the issuance of arrest warrants or summonses. To date, the court's investigations have lasted between 10 and 20 months before the first arrest warrants have been issued. Most recently, the ICC prosecutor conducted an investigation in the situation in Kenya for eight months before asking the pre-trial chamber to issue summonses for six people on charges of crimes against humanity. A decision on those requests is pending.

In addition, because the ICC does not have its own police force and must rely on governments and the United Nations to enforce the warrants and effect arrests, some of its warrants have been outstanding for more than five years.

When an individual appears before the Court, following either an arrest or a summons, retrial proceedings known as the "confirmation of charges" take place to determine whether the available evidence establishes substantial grounds to believe that the person committed each of the crimes charged in the indictment. When and if a charge or charges are confirmed, a trial date is set.

The ICC's first trial—of Thomas Lubanga—began in January 2009, nearly five years after the situation in the Democratic Republic of Congo was referred by its government to the ICC prosecutor and three years after Lubanga was transferred to ICC custody. The trial has yet to reach completion. While the start of Lubanga's trial was delayed for reasons that are unlikely to recur and the two other trials ongoing at the ICC have moved more quickly, the ICC's unique pre-trial proceedings and the complicated nature of cases tried by the court mean that proceedings are likely to last two to three years from arrest to verdict.

* * *

## 7. Will the ICC have jurisdiction over forces participating in the current U.N.-authorized military operations in Libya?

Security Council Resolution 1970, adopted on February 15, 2011, says that nationals from a state outside Libya that is not a party to the ICC Statute shall not be subject to ICC jurisdiction for all alleged acts arising out of operations in Libya established or authorized by the Security Council. On March 17, the Security Council adopted Resolution 1973, which authorizes member states "to take all necessary measures to protect civilians and civilian populated areas under threat of attack" in Libya. Of the 12 countries that have provided notice to the U.N. secretary-general as of March 24 about their participation in military operations under Resolution 1973, all are parties to the ICC Statute except the United States, the United Arab Emirates, Qatar and the Ukraine. All states, including these four, remain obligated under international law, however, to investigate and prosecute any members of their armed forces implicated in war crimes.

The ICC prosecutor has indicated that the focus of his current investigation in Libya relates only to the 15-day period following the adoption of Resolution 1970. The prosecutor has suggested that he may open a second investigation later, relating to the subsequent armed conflict. ICC jurisdiction for alleged acts arising out of Security Council-authorized operations in Libya could therefore be the subject of this potential second investigation, though it appears not to be an issue for the prosecutor's current investigation.

Human Rights Watch opposes the exemption from ICC jurisdiction under Resolution 1970 as running counter to core international legal principles of jurisdiction, including territoriality. In addition, the exemption—by limiting jurisdiction over nationals of non-ICC states accused of war crimes in Libya to the "exclusive jurisdiction" of their own country—undercuts the ability of domestic courts in third countries to prosecute such nationals under the principle of universal jurisdiction. Similar language had been included in the Security Council's referral of the situation in Darfur in 2005 to the ICC and risks obstructing justice for the most serious crimes.

**8. Will the ICC have jurisdiction over non-Libyan nationals recruited by the Libyan leader, Col. Muammar Gaddafi, into his armed forces?**

The ICC will have jurisdiction over foreign nationals in the Libyan armed forces. Resolution 1970 excludes from ICC jurisdiction only foreign nationals participating in operations in Libya established or authorized by the Security Council. Those fighting in the Libyan armed forces are not participating in U.N.-authorized operations.

**9. Even if the prosecutor seeks to bring charges against individuals, will there ever be arrests?**

Securing arrests is one of the most difficult challenges faced by the ICC. Without its own police force, the court must rely on states and the international community to assist in arrests. To date, only five of the 14 individuals sought by ICC arrest warrants have been apprehended. But while arrests may take time—particularly where those sought are high-ranking government officials—with sufficient international support they are possible. Charles Taylor, the former Liberian president, was apprehended in Nigeria following a three-year request to arrest him. He is on trial before the Special Court of Sierra Leone.

**10. Where else is the ICC investigating? Is it true that the ICC is targeting only African leaders for prosecution?**

The ICC is currently investigating in five countries—Democratic Republic of Congo, Uganda, Central African Republic, the Darfur region of Sudan, and Kenya. While this means that the ICC's investigations are all in Africa, three out of these investigations (DRC, Uganda, and CAR) were referred voluntarily by the governments where the crimes were committed, and Darfur was referred by the U.N. Security Council. In addition, the ICC prosecutor is analyzing a number of situations in countries or territories around the world, including Afghanistan, Colombia, Cote d'Ivoire, Gaza, Georgia, Guinea, Honduras, the Republic of Korea, and Nigeria.

The ICC makes decisions about its investigations based on a variety of factors, including whether it has jurisdiction over the crimes. Some of the worst crimes in violation of international law since the court's authority began in 2002 have been committed in states that are not parties to the ICC and are thus outside the court's jurisdiction. In such instances, the court can only obtain jurisdiction if the Security Council refers the matter to the ICC or a non-state party voluntarily gives the court the authority to address crimes committed on its territory. African states played an active role at the negotiations on the ICC statute in Rome, and African countries were among the founding states to ratify the Rome Treaty. Of the ICC's 114 states parties, 31 are in Africa. Africans are among the highest-level officials and staff at the ICC, including judges who have been nominated by African governments. African states—Tanzania and Benin—were among the Security Council members that referred Darfur to the ICC, while South Africa, Nigeria, and Gabon voted along with all other Security Council members to refer Libya to the ICC.

At the same time, the landscape in which international justice is applied has been uneven, with leaders from or supported by powerful states less likely to be prosecuted by international courts if they are associated with war crimes, crimes against humanity and genocide. Nevertheless, justice should not be denied because there are political obstacles to ensuring justice for all. Rather, governments should work to extend the reach of accountability to wherever serious international crimes occur. This can be achieved by working to increase the number of states that are parties to the ICC and insisting on justice for such crimes committed in states that are not parties to the court, such as Sri Lanka and Israel.

## 7. Kiriro Wa Ngugu, Let's Choose Peace over Justice in ICC Case
### *Daily Nation*, 2011

The U.N. Security Council will soon decide on an application by Kenya to have the prosecution of six Kenyans named by International Criminal Court (ICC) chief prosecutor Luis Moreno-Ocampo deferred for 12 months.

Both Britain and the U.S. have given little hope that they will support Kenya's application, which is backed by the African Union and China.

Who is the ICC? The court established under the Rome Statute is not, in fact, a global international entity, such as the United Nations, for example. The U.S., Russia, China, India, Japan, Malaysia, and most south Asian countries are not members. Less than 25 per cent of the world's population are members.

The Rome Statute is a creation of European states who are essentially the former colonisers of Africa—Britain, France, Germany, Italy, Spain and Portugal—and its agenda is imperial. It is a tool for legal interventions and regime change, where deemed necessary in Africa.

Military interventions, monetary structural adjustment programmes of the 1980s and 1990s, the aid and hand-outs, as well as strategic support to dictators like Mobutu Sese Seko of the former Zaire, or more recently Hosni Mubarak of Egypt, have all become unsustainable, hence the latest new idea; legal interventions in the guise of criminal law enforcement by the "international" community.

But before we were colonised, we in Africa knew how to live. Even now, we should be free to choose how we want to live. In our current predicament about the post-election violence, we can choose peace ahead of justice.

We have made this choice before—at independence when Jomo Kenyatta preached a doctrine of "forgive but do not forget" what the colonisers and their loyalists had done to us.

South Africa chose peace ahead of justice for the victims of apartheid. In Northern Ireland, after 30 years of religious-based violence, the people chose peace ahead of justice.

Those who had been convicted and jailed for murder and bombings were given amnesty and released. Those suspected to have panned, financed, and perpetrated criminal activities were also pardoned. All charges against known criminals were dropped and peace has prevailed.

Kenya can make a similar choice. The ICC should not make that choice for us, nor stop us from choosing that route.

It is our right to debate loudly, so long as we can tolerate the noise, even from the NGO types who shout loudest for and on behalf of the ICC.

We know where they get their funding from, so we understand and sympathise with our NGO brothers and sisters when they sometimes fail to see the bigger picture.

It is our right to choose how we go forward following the historic passing of a new Constitution. We owe it to ourselves to try a fresh new start. We can and should prioritise peace ahead of justice.

In the street fight of Kenya versus the Rome Statute, I root for Kenya!

---

## 8. Kofi Annan, Urging End to Impunity

Keynote Speech By U.N. Secretary-General, 2006

My dear friends,

Thank you all for being here. I could not ask for better company, on the last International Human Rights Day of my time in office, than this group of courageous human rights leaders from around the world.

I don't need to tell you, of all people, that the United Nations has a special stake, and a special responsibility, in promoting respect for human rights worldwide. But equally — and less happily — I don't need to tell you that the U.N. has often failed to live up to that responsibility. I know that ten years ago many of you were close to giving up on any hope that an organization of governments, many of which are themselves gross violators of human rights, could ever function as an effective human rights defender.

One of my priorities as Secretary-General has been to try and restore that hope, by making human rights central to all the U.N.'s work. But I'm not sure how far I have succeeded, or how much nearer we are to bringing the reality of the U.N. in line with my vision of human rights as its "third pillar", on a par with development and peace and security.

Development, security and human rights go hand in hand; no one of them can advance very far without the other two. Indeed, anyone who speaks forcefully for human rights but does nothing about security and development — including the desperate need to fight extreme poverty — undermines both his credibility and his cause. Poverty in particular remains both a source and consequence of rights violations. Yet if we are serious about human deprivation, we must also demonstrate that we are serious about human dignity, and vice versa.

Are you any more confident today than you were ten years ago that an intergovernmental organization can really do this job? I fear the answer may be No, and that the first steps of the Human Rights Council, which we all fought so hard to establish, may not have given you much encouragement. So this morning I suggest that we try and think through, together, what is really needed.

**First,** we must give real meaning to the principle of "Responsibility to Protect".

As you know, last year's World Summit formally endorsed that momentous doctrine — which means, in essence, that respect for national sovereignty can no longer be used as an excuse for inaction in the face of genocide, war crimes, ethnic cleansing and crimes against humanity. Yet one year later, to judge by what is happening in Darfur, our performance has not improved much since the disasters of Bosnia and Rwanda. Sixty years after the liberation of the Nazi death camps, and 30 years after the Cambodian killing fields, the promise of "never again" is ringing hollow.

The tragedy of Darfur has raged for over three years now, and still reports pour in of villages being destroyed by the hundred, and of the brutal treatment of civilians spreading into neighbouring countries. How can an international community which claims to uphold human rights allow this horror to continue?

There is more than enough blame to go around. It can be shared among those who value abstract notions of sovereignty more than the lives of real families, those whose reflex of solidarity puts them on the side of governments and not of peoples, and those who fear that action to stop the slaughter would jeopardize their commercial interests.

The truth is, none of these arguments amount even to excuses, let alone justifications, for the shameful passivity of most governments. We have still not summoned up the collective sense of urgency that this issue requires.

Some governments have tried to win support in the global South by caricaturing responsibility to protect, as a conspiracy by imperialist powers to take back the hard-won national sovereignty of formerly colonized peoples. This is utterly false.

We must do better. We must develop the responsibility to protect into a powerful international norm that is not only quoted but put into practice, whenever and wherever it is needed.

Above all we must not wait to take action until genocide is actually happening, by which time it is often to late to do anything effective about it. Two years ago I announced an action plan for the prevention of genocide, and appointed a Special Adviser to help me implement it. While his work has been extremely valuable, much more needs to be done. I hope my successor will take up this banner, and that member states will support him.

**Second,** we must put an end to impunity.

We have made progress in holding people accountable for the world's worst crimes. The establishment of the International Criminal Court, the work of the U.N. tribunals for Yugoslavia and Rwanda, the hybrid ones in Sierra Leone and Cambodia, and the various Commissions of Experts and Inquiry, have proclaimed the will of the international community that such crimes should no longer go unpunished.

And yet they still do. Mladic and Karadzic, and the leaders of the Lord's Resistance Army—to name but a few—are still at large. Unless these indicted war criminals are brought to court, others tempted to emulate them will not be deterred.

Some say that justice must sometimes be sacrificed in the interests of peace. I question that. We have seen in Sierra Leone and in the Balkans that, on the contrary, justice is a fundamental component of peace. Indeed, justice has often bolstered lasting peace, by de-legitimizing and driving underground those individuals who pose the gravest threat to it. That is why there should never be amnesty for genocide, crimes against humanity and massive violations of human rights. That would only encourage today's mass murderers—and tomorrow's would-be mass murderers—to continue their vicious work.

*  *  *

**Fourth,** let's not content ourselves with grand statements of principle. We must work to make human rights a reality in each country.

Of course, protecting and promoting human rights is first and foremost a national responsibility. Every member state of the U.N. can draw on its own history to develop its own ways of upholding universal rights. But many states need help in doing this, and the U.N. system has a vital role to play.

Over the past decade, the U.N. has rapidly expanded its operational capacity for peacekeeping, and for development and humanitarian aid. Our capacity to protect and promote human rights now needs to catch up.

*  *  *

The truth is, it's not enough just to have the right principles and say what we think should happen. We also have to ask who is going to make it happen. **Who can we look to for support? Who is going to insist that these principles are acted on?**

First, I look to Africa to take the lead.

Africa's many conflicts are, almost invariably, accompanied by massive human rights violations. Unless Africa wholeheartedly embraces the inviolability of human rights, its struggle for security and development will not succeed.

As I said when I first addressed African heads of state, at Harare in 1997, to treat human rights as an imposition by the industrialized West, or a luxury of the rich countries for which Africa is not ready, demeans the yearning for human dignity that resides in every African heart. Human rights are, by definition, also African rights. It should be every African government's first priority to ensure that Africans can enjoy them.

South African heroes, like Nelson Mandela and Desmond Tutu, have shown the way. The African Union led the way among international organizations on the responsibility to protect, by proclaiming in its Constitutive Act "the right of the Union to intervene in a Member State ... in respect of grave circumstances, namely war crimes, genocide and crimes against humanity". It has also tried harder than anyone else to act on that doctrine in Darfur, and to bring the former Chadian dictator Hissène Habré to justice.

This is encouraging, but much more needs to be done. In practice, many African governments are still resisting the responsibility to protect. Many, even among the most democratic, are still reluctant to play their role in the Human Rights Council by speaking out impartially against all abuses. They can, and must, do more.

Secondly, I look to the growing power of women—which means we must give priority to women's rights.

The "equal rights of men and women" promised by the U.N. Charter 61 years ago, are still far from being a reality. The U.N. can and must play a greater role in empowering women, and to do so, will require a strengthening of the U.N.'s gender architecture. I strongly encourage member states to make this a real priority.

And thirdly, I look to civil society—which means you!

We need dedicated individuals and dynamic human rights defenders to hold governments to account. States' performance must be judged against their commitments, and they must be accountable both to their own people and to their peers in the international community.

\* \* \*

## 9. Bibliography of Additional Sources

- Kate Allan, *Prosecution and Peace: A Role for Amnesty Before the ICC?*, 39 DENV. J. INT'L L. & POL'Y 239 (2011).

- Amnesty International, 2007–2008 Fact Sheets: The Globalization of Justice.

- Andrew T. Cayley, *The Prosecutor's Strategy in Seeking the Arrest of Sudanese President al Bashir on Charges of Genocide*, 6 J. INT'L CRIM. JUST. 829 (2008).

- Mahnoush H. Arsanjani, Zeid Ra'ad Zeid Al Hussein & Marieke Wierda, *Peace v. Justice: Contradictory or Complementary*, 100 AM. SOC. INT'L L. 361 (2006).

- Jonathan I. Charney, *The Impact on the International Legal System of the Growth of International Courts and Tribunals*, 31 N.Y.U. J. INT'L L. & POL. 697 (1998).

- Anthony D'Amato, *Peace vs. Accountability in Bosnia*, 88 AM. J. INT'L L. 500 (July 1994).

- Sam Dealey, *Omar al-Bashir Q&A: "In Any War, Mistakes Happen on the Ground,"* TIME, Aug. 14, 2009.

- Michael Drexler, *Whither Justice? Uganda and Five Years of the International Criminal Court*, 5 INTERDISC. J. HUM. RTS. L. 97 (2011).

- Jacqueline Geis & Alex Mundt, *When to Indict? The Impact of Timing of International Criminal Indictments on Peace Processes and Humanitarian Action*, Feb. 2009.

- *ICC Justice: The Debate Continues*, NEW AFRICAN 487 (Aug.–Sept. 2009).

- International Criminal Court Office of the Prosecutor, *ICC Prosecutor to Open an Investigation in Libya*, Mar. 2, 2011.

- Jean-Marie Kamatali, *From the ICTR to ICC: Learning from the ICTR Experience in Bringing Justice to Rwandans*, 12 NEW ENG. J. INT'L & COMP. L. 89 (2005).

- Jacob Kushner, *"Baby Doc" Duvalier Back in Haiti After Long Exile Return Poses a Quandary to Struggling Nation*, ASSOCIATED PRESS, Jan. 16, 2011.

- Jude Lal Fernando & Claire de Jong, *People's Tribunal on Sri Lanka: Why a Tribunal on Sri Lanka?*, IRISH FORUM FOR PEACE IN SRI LANKA (Dec. 7, 2009).

- Wendy Lambourne, Transitional Justice and Peacebuilding after Mass Violence, 3 INT'L J. TRANSITIONAL JUST. 28 (2009).

- Lisa J. Laplante, *Outlawing Amnesty: The Return of Criminal Justice in Transitional Justice Schemes*, 49 VA. J. INT'L L. 915 (2009).

- Frédéric Mégret, *Justice in Times of Violence*, 14 EUR. J. INT'L L. 327 (2003).

- Vasuki Nesiah, *Truth vs. Justice? Commissions and Courts*, in HUMAN RIGHTS & CONFLICT 375 (Julie A. Mertus & Jeffrey W. Helsing eds., 2006).

- MARGARET POPKIN, PEACE WITHOUT JUSTICE: OBSTACLES TO BUILDING THE RULE OF LAW IN EL SALVADOR (2000).

- Eric A. Posner & Jon C. Yoo, *Judicial Independence in International Tribunals*, 93.1 CALIF. L. REV. 1 (Jan. 2005).

- Michael P. Scharf, *The Case for a Permanent International Truth Commission*, 7 DUKE J. COMP. & INT'L L. 375–410 (1996–1997).

- Michael P. Scharf & Paul R. Williams, *The Functions of Justice and Anti-Justice in the Peace-Building Process*, 35 CASE W. RES. J. INT'L L. 161 (2003).

- Paul R. Williams, *The Norm of Justice and the Negotiation of the Rambouillet/Paris Peace Accords*, 13.1 LEIDEN J. INT'L L. 207 (2000).

# Chapter VIII

# The International Court of Justice: Jurisdiction, Admissibility & U.S. Withdrawal

## Introduction

The International Court of Justice (ICJ) is the primary judicial body within the U.N. system. Within the context of a fictional Law of the Sea dispute (based loosely on the recent Spanish-Canadian dispute), this chapter introduces the reader to the functions of the World Court and the limits to its jurisdictional reach.

Following the adverse judgment in the Nicaragua Case in 1986, the United States decided to withdraw from the compulsory jurisdiction of the International Court of Justice. This chapter examines the rationales for and the consequences of the U.S. decision to withdraw from the Court's compulsory jurisdiction.

## Objectives

- To understand the establishment of the ICJ and the role of the ICJ in the U.N. system.
- To understand the functions and structure of the ICJ.
- To understand the jurisdiction granted to the ICJ and the requirements for admissibility of cases before the Court.
- To understand the circumstances surrounding the U.S. decision to terminate its acceptance of the ICJ's compulsory jurisdiction.
- To examine the implications of the U.S. withdrawal from the ICJ.

# Problems

1.  Come to class prepared to participate in the following simulation of a case before the ICJ between the Spain (Applicant) and Canada (Respondent).

    Members of Group A will represent Spain.

    Members of Group B will represent Canada.

    Members of Group C will role play the ICJ Panel.

2.  Come to class prepared to participate in a debate about whether the U.S. should re-submit to the compulsory jurisdiction of the World Court, and if so, under what circumstances.

# Simulation

Come to class prepared to participate in a simulated argument of the (fictional) Fish Conflict Case (*Spain v. Canada*) before the International Court of Justice.

For purposes of the simulation, assume the following facts:

(a) Since 1945, Canada and Spain have both been parties to the compulsory juris-diction of the International Court of Justice under Article 36(2) (the optional clause) of the ICJ Statute. Spain's acceptance of jurisdiction contained the fol-lowing reservation: "Spain's acceptance of the jurisdiction of the International Court of Justice shall not apply to disputes arising under a multilateral treaty un-less all parties to the treaty affected by the decision are also parties to the case be-fore the Court." Canada's acceptance of compulsory jurisdiction contained no reservations.

(b) On September 1, 2012, Canada enacted emergency legislation prohibiting its na-tionals from fishing turbot in order to allow stocks of the depleted species to re-build. (The turbot is a slime-coated bottom-feeding flatfish that dwells in the Grand Banks area off the coast of Newfoundland, Canada.) The legislation also extends Canada's regulatory and enforcement power over foreign vessels that en-gage in fishing of turbot in the Grand Banks within 300 nautical miles from Canada's coast.

(c) Upon signing the new law, the Prime Minister of Canada declared: "This is about conservation and protecting endangered stocks of fish. Although the enforce-ment area includes parts of the ocean that were traditionally defined as The High Seas, the legislation is warranted to prevent extinction of the turbot species which is rapidly being depleted by predatory fishing practices engaged in by European fisherman."

(d) The next day, the Spanish Foreign Minister sent a letter of protest to the Govern-ment of Canada, stating that "as many as 100,000 Spanish fishermen face the loss of their livelihoods if they are prevented from fishing turbot in these international waters."

(e) On September 7, 2012, Spain sent several naval gunboats to protect Spanish and other European fishing vessels operating in the Grand Banks. On September 14, a Spanish gunboat fired warning shots at a Canadian Coast Guard cutter attempting to seize a Portuguese-flagged trawler, which had been fishing turbot 280 nautical miles off the coast of Canada (thus well outside of Canada's territorial sea and exclusive economic zone). The Canadian Coast Guard cutter returned fire, but missed the Spanish gunboat and instead killed a French sailor aboard the Portuguese trawler. Afterward, the Canadian Coast Guard cutter, the Portuguese trawler, and the Spanish gunboat retreated from the area without further confrontation.

(f) In response to this incident, Spain has filed suit against Canada in the International Court of Justice in order to prove "that Canada's new law is an unacceptable violation of the international law of the sea, that Spain was justified in firing upon the Canadian Coast Guard Cutter which was engaged in an armed attack against a Portuguese trawler, and that Canada is liable for the death of the French sailor." In a communication addressed to the World Court, Canada stated that it "would appear before the Court to contest the Court's jurisdiction over this dispute."

# Materials

1. The Court at a Glance at http://www.icj-cij.org/icjwww/igeneralinformation/inotice.pdf.

2. THIRD RESTATEMENT OF FOREIGN RELATIONS LAW, Section 903.

3. STATUTE OF THE INTERNATIONAL COURT OF JUSTICE, especially Articles 36, 38, and 59.

4. The Norwegian Loans Case (*France v. Norway*) (1957).

5. Articles 2 (4) and 51 of the U.N. CHARTER, see http://www.un.org/en/documents/charter/.

6. THIRD RESTATEMENT OF FOREIGN RELATIONS LAW:

   A.  Section 521: (Freedom of the High Seas).

   B.  Section 522: (Enforcement Jurisdiction over Foreign Ships in the High Seas).

   C.  Section 211: (Nationality of Individuals).

7. Case Concerning Military and Paramilitary Activities (*Nicaragua v. United States*) (1984) (jurisdiction).

8. Text of U.S. Statement on Withdrawal from the Case Before the World Court, THE NEW YORK TIMES, January 19, 1985.

9. U.S. Terminates Acceptance of ICJ Compulsory Jurisdiction, DEPARTMENT OF STATE BULLETIN, January 1986.

10. Justinian, U.S. Withdrawal Another Blow to World Court, FINANCIAL TIMES, October 15, 1985.

11. ABA International Law Section, Recommendation Adopted by the House of Delegates in 1994, 29 INT'L LAW 295 (1995).

12. Bibliography of Additional Sources

## Authors' Note

The following three materials provide an introduction to the ICJ as an organ with the U.N. system. Material 1 provides an overview of the purpose, function, and structure of the Court. This selection includes a discussion of the Court's jurisdiction and the ability to render an advisory opinion. Material 2, an excerpt from the Third Restatement of Foreign Relations Law, provides a more comprehensive look at the operation and role of the ICJ. Material 3 provides selected articles from the Statute of the International Court of Justice. This selection provides the legal framework that forms the ICJ's jurisdiction, the applicable legal precedents, and its relationship with Member States.

---

# 1. The Court at a Glance

### The International Court of Justice

The International Court of Justice is the principal judicial organ of the United Nations. Its seat is at the Peace Palace in The Hague (Netherlands). It began work in 1946, when it replaced the Permanent Court of International Justice which had functioned in the Peace Palace since 1922. It operates under a Statute largely similar to that of its predecessor, which is an integral part of the Charter of the United Nations.

### Functions of the Court

The Court has a dual role: to settle in accordance with international law the legal disputes submitted to it by States, and to give advisory opinions on legal questions referred to it by duly authorized international organs and agencies.

### Composition

The Court is composed of 15 judges elected to nine-year terms of office by the United Nations General Assembly and Security Council sitting independently of each other. It may not include more than one judge of any nationality. Elections are held every three years for one-third of the seats, and retiring judges may be re-elected. The Members of the Court do not represent their governments but are independent magistrates. The judges must possess the qualifications required in their respective countries for appointment to the highest judicial offices, or be jurists of recognized competence in international law. The composition of the Court has also to reflect the main forms of civilization and the principal legal systems of the world. When the Court does not include a judge possessing the nationality of a State party to a case, that State may appoint a person to sit as a judge *ad hoc* for the purpose of the case.

### Contentious Cases between States

### The Parties

Only States may apply to and appear before the Court. The Member States of the United Nations [ ... ] are so entitled.

### Jurisdiction

The Court is competent to entertain a dispute only if the States concerned have accepted its jurisdiction in one or more of the following ways:

(1) by the conclusion between them of a special agreement to submit the dispute to the Court;

(2) by virtue of a jurisdictional clause, i.e., typically, when they are parties to a treaty containing a provision whereby, in the event of a disagreement over its interpretation or application, one of them may refer the dispute to the Court. Several hundred treaties or conventions contain a clause to such effect;

(3) through the reciprocal effect of declarations made by them under the Statute whereby each has accepted the jurisdiction of the Court as compulsory in the

event of a dispute with another State having made a similar declaration. The declarations of 67 States are at present in force, a number of them having been made subject to the exclusion of certain categories of dispute.

In cases of doubt as to whether the Court has jurisdiction, it is the Court itself which decides.

## Procedure

The procedure followed by the Court in contentious cases is defined in its Statute, and in the Rules of Court adopted by it under the Statute. The latest version of the Rules dates from 5 December 2000. The proceedings include a written phase, in which the parties file and exchange pleadings, and an oral phase consisting of public hearings at which agents and counsel address the Court. As the Court has two official languages (English and French) everything written or said in one language is translated into the other.

After the oral proceedings the Court deliberates in camera and then delivers its judgment at a public sitting. The judgment is final and without appeal. Should one of the States involved fail to comply with it, the other party may have recourse to the Security Council of the United Nations.

The Court discharges its duties as a full court but, at the request of the parties, it may also establish a special chamber. The Court constituted such a chamber in 1982 for the first time, formed a second one in 1985, constituted two in 1987 and two more in 2002. A Chamber of Summary Procedure is elected every year by the Court in accordance with its Statute. In July 1993 the Court also established a seven-member Chamber to deal with any environmental cases falling within its jurisdiction.

Since 1946 the Court has delivered 92 Judgments on disputes concerning inter alia land frontiers and maritime boundaries, territorial sovereignty, the non-use of force, non-interference in the internal affairs of States, diplomatic relations, hostage-taking, the right of asylum, nationality, guardianship, rights of passage and economic rights.

## Sources of Applicable Law

The Court decides in accordance with international treaties and conventions in force, international custom, the general principles of law and, as subsidiary means, judicial decisions and the teachings of the most highly qualified publicists.

## Advisory Opinions

The advisory procedure of the Court is open solely to international organizations. The only bodies at present authorized to request advisory opinions of the Court are five organs of the United Nations and 16 specialized agencies of the United Nations family.

On receiving a request, the Court decides which States and organizations might provide useful information and gives them an opportunity of presenting written or oral statements. The Court's advisory procedure is otherwise modeled on that for contentious proceedings, and the sources of applicable law are the same. In principle the Court's advisory opinions are consultative in character and are therefore not binding as such on the requesting bodies. Certain instruments or regulations can, however, provide in advance that the advisory opinion shall be binding.

Since 1946 the Court has given 25 Advisory Opinions, concerning inter alia the legal consequences of the construction of a wall in the occupied Palestinian territory, admission to United Nations membership, reparation for injuries suffered in the service of the United Nations, territorial status of South-West Africa (Namibia) and Western Sahara, judgments rendered by international administrative tribunals, expenses of certain United

Nations operations, applicability of the United Nations Headquarters Agreement, the status of human rights rapporteurs, and the legality of the threat or use of nuclear weapons.

\* \* \*

## 2. Third Restatement of the Foreign Relations Law, Section 903

### 1987

### § 903 International Court of Justice

(1) A state party to a dispute with another state may submit that dispute to the International Court of Justice for adjudication, and the Court has jurisdiction over that dispute, if the parties:

(a) have, by a special agreement (compromis) or otherwise, agreed to bring that dispute before the Court; or

(b) are bound by an agreement providing for the submission to the Court of a category of disputes that includes the dispute in question; or

(c) have made declarations under Article 36(2) of the Statute of the Court accepting the jurisdiction of the Court generally or in respect of a category of legal disputes that includes the dispute in question.

(2) The Court may render an advisory opinion at the request of:

(a) the General Assembly or the Security Council on any legal question; or

(b) other organs and specialized agencies of the United Nations, authorized by the General Assembly to request such an opinion, on legal questions arising within the scope of their activities.

(3) The Court has authority to determine whether it has jurisdiction to decide a dispute submitted to it, or whether to issue an advisory opinion requested of it.

### Reporters' Notes:

*1. Statute of International Court of Justice.*

The Statute of the Court is annexed to the Charter of the United Nations and forms an integral part of it. United Nations Charter, Art. 92. The Statute of the Court is based on the statute of its predecessor, the Permanent Court of International Justice (id.) and differs from it only slightly. The Court has frequently followed the precedents established by its predecessor. (The United States was not a party to the Permanent Court. See Hudson, The World Court, 1921–1938, pp. 237–321 (1938).)

The Court consists of 15 independent judges, no two of whom may be nationals of the same state. I.C.J. Statute, Art. 3(1). Judges are elected, at separate meetings held simultaneously, by the General Assembly and the Security Council of the United Nations by an absolute majority of votes of each body. The voting in the Security Council is not subject to the veto that applies with respect to other substantive issues. Id. Arts. 4, 8, and 10. The members of the Court are elected for nine years and may be re-elected. The elections are held in rotation, with five judges elected every three years. Id. Art. 13. A member elected to fill a vacancy holds office only for the remainder of his predecessor's term. Id. Art. 15.

The Court decides cases either by a full bench or in a chamber of three or more judges established to deal with a particular case or category of cases. There is also a chamber of summary procedure, composed of five judges, designed for speedy dispatch of business. Id. Arts. 25–29.

All questions are decided by a majority of the judges present. In case of a tie vote, the President of the Court has a casting vote, id. Art. 55. This happened in South West Africa Cases (Second Phase) (*Ethiopia and Liberia v. South Africa*), [1966] I.C.J. Rep. 6, 51.

*2. Access to and jurisdiction of the International Court.*

States members of the United Nations are automatically parties to the Court's Statute. States not members of the United Nations may become parties to the Statute of the Court by accepting both the Statute and the obligations of a member state under Article 94 of the Charter of the United Nations concerning compliance with, and enforcement of, the judgments of the Court. Art. 93(2) of the Statute of the Court, as implemented by G.A. Res. 91(I), U.N.Doc. A/64/Add 1, at 182 (1947). Switzerland, Liechtenstein, and San Marino have deposited such instruments of acceptance. [1985–86] I.C.J. Y.B. 45–46. Without becoming a party to the Statute, a state may by special declaration accept the obligations of the Statute and of Article 94 of the Charter, either in respect of a particular dispute or with respect to all or some future disputes. Art. 35(2) of the Statute of the Court, as implemented by S.C.Res. 9 (1946). Several states did so prior to becoming members of the United Nations, but their declarations expired upon their admission to membership. [1985–86] I.C.J. Y.B. 46–48.

International organizations may not bring a contentious case before the Court, but the Court may ask them to present information to the Court relevant to cases before it, or they may present such information to the Court on their own initiative (an international version of an amicus brief). This may be done, in particular, whenever the construction of the constituent instrument of an international organization, or of an international convention adopted pursuant to that instrument, is in question before the Court. I.C.J. Statute, Art. 34(2) and (3). As to requests, by international organizations for advisory opinions, see Reporters' Note 12.

Article 36(1) of the Statute of the Court confers jurisdiction on the Court with respect to "all cases which the parties refer to it."

The consent of the parties to the jurisdiction of the Court need not be expressed in advance or in any particular form. See Corfu Channel Case (*United Kingdom v. Albania*), [1948] I.C.J. Rep. 15, 27. When a party to a dispute submits a case to the Court, the other party, though it had not previously accepted the Court's jurisdiction, may accept it for that proceeding, either explicitly or by responding on the merits without raising a jurisdictional objection. Jurisdiction as forum prorogatum requires some conduct or statement by the respondent state "which involves an element of consent regarding the jurisdiction of the Court." Anglo-Iranian Oil Co. Case (*United Kingdom v. Iran*), [1952] I.C.J. Rep. 93, 114. In that case, the Court held that it had no jurisdiction since the government of Iran had consistently denied the Court's jurisdiction. In the Corfu Channel Case, the Albanian Government, while denying the right of the United Kingdom to bring the case to the Court by unilateral application, sent a letter to the Court announcing that, notwithstanding the irregularity of the United Kingdom action, Albania was prepared to appear before the Court, but that "its acceptance of the Court's jurisdiction for this case cannot constitute a precedent for the future." *Supra*, at 18–19. The Court held that this letter constituted "a voluntary and indisputable acceptance of the Court's jurisdiction." Id. at 27. In another case, the Court held that, as all "the questions submitted to it have been argued by them on the merits, and no objection has been made to a decision on the merits," the parties' conduct was sufficient to confer jurisdiction on the Court. Haya de la Torre Case (*Colombia v. Peru*), [1951] I.C.J. Rep. 71, 78. For a discussion of the Court's jurisprudence on forum prorogatum, see H. Lauterpacht, The Development of International Law by the International Court 103–107 (1958).

Many states have consented to the jurisdiction of the Court by becoming parties (i) to bilateral or multilateral agreements for the peaceful settlement of disputes that provide for the submission to the Court of any legal disputes arising between them, or (ii) to agreements on particular subjects containing a provision for reference to the Court of any dispute between the parties relating to the interpretation of application of the agreement. There are some 250 such agreements. See [1985–86] I.C.J. Y.B. 54–59, 93–109. In addition, many agreements which originally conferred jurisdiction on the Permanent Court of International Justice are still in force, and any dispute arising under them may, pursuant to Article 37 of the Statute of the International Court of Justice, be referred to that Court. While parties sometimes refer cases to the Court by ad hoc agreement, most cases are brought before the Court under bilateral and multilateral agreements, either those transferred from the predecessor Court or those concluded since 1945.

As of 1986, 57 states had made declarations under Article 36(2) of the Statute of the Court accepting compulsory jurisdiction of the Court; 11 of these declarations have expired or have been terminated. Forty-six declarations are in force; 44 by members of the United Nations, and two by non-members (Liechtenstein and Switzerland). Declarations in effect are by states of Western Europe, the Americas, Africa, Asia, and the Pacific; there are no declarations by states of Eastern Europe. Several of the declarations antedate the International Court of Justice and originally conferred jurisdiction on the Permanent Court of International Justice, but under Article 36(5) of the Statute of the International Court of Justice such declarations are deemed to be acceptances of the jurisdiction of the successor Court.

Some of the declarations are without limit of time; others are for a specific period (usually five or ten years), in many instances with an automatic renewal clause. Many declarations reserve the right to terminate by a notice of withdrawal effective upon receipt by the Secretary-General of the United Nations. Some declarations specify that they apply only to disputes arising after the declaration was made or concerning situations or facts subsequent to a specified date. Seventeen declarations are without any reservation; the remaining declarations are accompanied by a variety of reservations. Many states have modified their reservations, some of them several times.

The most common reservation excludes disputes committed by the parties to other tribunals or which the parties have agreed to settle by other means of settlement. Another common reservation excludes disputes relating to matters that are "exclusively" or "essentially" within the domestic jurisdiction of the declarant state; some of these reservations provide in addition that the question whether a dispute is essentially within the domestic jurisdiction is to be determined by the declaring state (a so-called "self-judging" clause). Several declarations exclude disputes arising under a multilateral treaty "unless all parties to the treaty affected by the decision are also parties to the case before the Court" or, more broadly, "unless all parties to the treaty are also parties to the case before the Court." Some reservations exclude disputes as to a particular subject, such as territorial or maritime boundaries or other law of the sea issues.

A few declarations, using various formulas, exclude disputes arising out of hostilities to which the declarant state is a party; the most comprehensive of these reservations is that of India which excludes "disputes relating to or connected with facts or situations of hostilities, armed conflicts, individual or collective actions taken in self-defense, resistance to aggression, fulfillment of obligations imposed by international bodies, and other similar or related acts, measures or situations in which India is, has been or may in future be involved." A reservation of the United Kingdom made in 1957 excluded disputes "relating to any question which, in the opinion of the Government of the United Kingdom, affects the national security of the United Kingdom or of any of its dependent territories"; this clause was restricted in the United Kingdom's 1958 declaration to certain past disputes and was omitted in its 1963 declaration.

An increasing number of states have added to their declarations clauses designed to avoid surprise suits by states that accept the Court's jurisdiction and immediately bring a case against another state. For instance, some states have excluded any dispute that was brought before the Court by a party to a dispute less than 12 months after the party had accepted the jurisdiction of the Court with respect to that category of disputes. Many states have reserved the right to modify or terminate a declaration peremptorily by means of a notification to the Secretary-General of the United Nations, with effect from the moment of that notification.

In 27 contentious cases (as of 1986), objections were raised as to the Court's jurisdiction or the admissibility of an application; the Court dismissed almost half of these cases. A few cases were terminated by the Court when it was informed that the defendant had not previously accepted the Court's jurisdiction and was not willing to accept it ad hoc for the particular case. Several cases were discontinued by agreement between the parties. See [1985–86] I.C.J. Y.B. 48, 50, 123, 124.

### 3. The United States and the International Court of Justice.

In 1946, the United States made a declaration under Article 36(2) of the Statute of the Court, accepting the Court's jurisdiction but excluding:

(a) disputes the solution of which the parties shall entrust to other tribunals by virtue of agreements already in existence or which may be concluded in the future;

(b) disputes with regard to matters which are essentially within the domestic jurisdiction of the United States of America as determined by the United States of America; and

(c) disputes arising under a multilateral treaty, unless (1) all parties to the treaty affected by the decision are also parties to the case before the Court, or

(2) the United States of America specially agrees to jurisdiction.

These reservations applied only to the Court's jurisdiction pursuant to Article 36(2). They did not apply to a suit that was within the Court's jurisdiction under Article 36(1) of the Court's Statute and was brought pursuant to an international agreement in which the United States agreed to the jurisdiction of the Court with respect to any dispute relating to the interpretation or application of that agreement (See Comment c). According to a report of the Senate Committee on Foreign Relations regarding the 1958 Law of the Sea Convention, 86th Cong., 2d sess., Exec. Rep. No. 5, at 9, the acceptance of such a provision "means that with respect to subjects covered by these conventions the United States would not attempt to reserve to itself the right to determine whether or not a matter lay within the domestic jurisdiction of the United States." Such a provision is common in United States treaties of friendship, commerce, and navigation, and in several constitutions of international organizations of which the United States is a member, as well as in various multilateral treaties accepted by the United States. For instance, by the 1961 Protocol to the Vienna Convention on Diplomatic Relations, the United States and about 50 other states agreed to the jurisdiction of the Court for all disputes arising out of the interpretation or application of that Convention. 23 U.S.T. 3374, T.I.A.S. No. 7502, 500 U.N.T.S. 241. That Protocol provided jurisdiction for the Court in the case brought by the United States relating to the U.S. Diplomatic and Consular Staff in Tehran (*United States v. Iran*), [1980] I.C.J. Rep. 3. For a list of multipartite treaties containing such provisions to which the United States is party, see Sen. Comm. on Foreign Relations, International Convention on the Prevention of the Crime of Genocide, S. Exec. Rep. No. 98–50, 98th Cong. 2d sess., at 37–41 (1984); see also 106 Cong. Rec. 11194 (1960). In consenting to the ratification of the Genocide Convention the United States Senate required a reservation to the clause accepting the jurisdiction of the Court for disputes under the Convention. 132 Cong. Rec. S1377 (1986).

—Domestic jurisdiction reservation. Paragraph (b) of the United States declaration (including the self-judging clause, the so-called Connally Amendment) did not reflect reluctance to submit to the jurisdiction of the Court generally, but fear that the Court might be persuaded to assert jurisdiction over certain questions that were essentially within the domestic jurisdiction of the United States, such as the issues that might arise under United States immigration or tariff laws or with respect to the Panama Canal. See the statement by Senator Connally, 92 Cong.Rec. 10624 (1946); see also a series of articles in 40 Am.J.Int'l L. 699–736, 778–81 (1946). In a report to the Senate Foreign Relations Committee in 1959, the Department of State declared that it was the understanding of the Senate when the automatic proviso was adopted that this reservation would never be improperly invoked and that the United States would be bound in good faith to accept the Court's jurisdiction in every case involving matters not essentially within the domestic jurisdiction of the United States. Thus, the United States as a matter of policy would expect to invoke the reservation only in those cases in which the Court itself would probably uphold a plea of domestic jurisdiction if interposed by the United States on the basis of the domestic jurisdiction reservation without the automatic proviso. 12 Whiteman, Digest of International Law 1309 (1971).

The United States did not interpret paragraph (b) as reserving an absolute right to refuse to submit to the jurisdiction of the Court. It was the United States policy, therefore, that the determination whether a matter is essentially within its domestic jurisdiction will be made in good faith. For example, a question of treaty interpretation is not a question "essentially within the domestic jurisdiction of the United States." However, the Department of State interpreted paragraph (b) to mean that, while the reservation should be exercised in good faith, any determination by the United States that a matter was essentially within the domestic jurisdiction of the United States was not reviewable by the Court. Since the declaration was subject to reciprocity, that interpretation applied also when the United States brought a claim against another state and the latter invoked the United States reservation.

In Certain Norwegian Loans Case, the Court allowed Norway to invoke, on the basis of reciprocity, a Connally-type reservation in the French declaration; the French claim was dismissed for want of jurisdiction. [1957] I.C.J. Rep. 9, 27. The United States invoked the reservation in the Interhandel case brought against it by Switzerland, but the Court dismissed the case on other grounds. [1959] I.C.J. Rep. 6, 25–26. When the United States brought a claim against Bulgaria arising from the shooting down of an Israeli aircraft carrying several United States nationals, Bulgaria invoked the United States reservation by reciprocity. After first contending that the reservation could not be invoked for matters that were clearly international, and that the Bulgarian objection to the Court's jurisdiction should be rejected as not being bona fide, the United States changed its position; it agreed that, while to apply the reservation to such matters was an abuse of the reservation, its invocation by a party was final and binding on the Court. Consequently, the United States withdrew the case. Case Concerning the Aerial Incident of 27 July 1955, [1960] I.C.J. Rep. 146; see Gross, "Bulgaria Invokes the Connally Amendment," 56 Am.J.Int'l L. 357 (1962).

Since a declaration under Article 36 is optional, the declaring state can, subject to the Court's Statute, determine the scope and limits of its acceptance of the Court's jurisdiction. After a declaration is deposited, however, its proper interpretation is a question of international law; later interpretations by the declaring state are entitled to some weight but are not conclusive. Anglo-Iranian Oil Co. Case (*United Kingdom v. Iran*), [1952] I.C.J. Rep. 93, 106–07. Compare § 325. Since the Court has authority to determine whether it has jurisdiction over a dispute submitted to it (Subsection (3)), it would have to decide whether a particular invocation of the declaration to support or defeat the Court's jurisdiction was in accordance with the proper meaning of the declaration. The Court has not had occasion to consider the State Department's interpretation of "the Connally Amendment," paragraph (b) in the United States Declaration. In Case Concerning Military and Paramilitary Activities in and Against Nicaragua (*Nicaragua v. United States*), the United States informed the Court that it had decided not to invoke the Connally Amendment at this time, but "without prejudice to the rights of the United States under the proviso in relation to any subsequent pleadings, proceedings, or cases before this Court." [1984] I.C.J. Rep. 392, 422. Nevertheless, in later stages of the case, the United States refrained from invoking this reservation.

Multilateral treaty reservation. This reservation was originally suggested by Senator Vandenberg, and was sometimes called the "Vandenberg Amendment." It excluded disputes "arising under a multilateral treaty," and required that "all parties to the treaty affected by the decision" be parties to the case before the Court. In *Nicaragua v. United States*, *supra*, as Nicaragua relied in its application on the Charter of the United Nations, the Charter of the Organization of American States, and two other inter-American treaties, the United States contended that the Court had no jurisdiction unless all states parties to these treaties that would be affected by a decision were parties before the Court, and that Nicaragua's three neighbors—Honduras, Costa Rica, and El Salvador—would clearly be affected, "in a legal and practical sense," by adjudication of the claims submitted by Nicaragua. [1984] I.C.J. Rep. 392, 422. The Court pointed out that these three states had made declarations accepting the compulsory jurisdiction of the Court, that once Nicaragua was also bound by that jurisdiction, these states were free to institute proceedings against Nicaragua, or to resort to the incidental procedure for intervention under Articles 62 and 63 of the Court's Statute. Id. at 425. The Court held that "the question of what States may be 'affected' by the decision on the merits is not in itself a jurisdictional problem," and that, consequently, the United States objection based on the multilateral treaty reservation "does not possess, in the circumstances of the case, an exclusively preliminary character" and does not constitute an obstacle to further proceedings. Id. at 425–26. The Court also noted that in any event the multilateral treaty reservation would not warrant the Court in dismissing the claims of Nicaragua under principles of customary international law, such as those relating to non-use of force, non-intervention, or respect for the independence and territorial integrity of states. Although these principles have been enshrined in multilateral conventions, they continue to be binding as part of customary international law, "even as regards countries that are parties to such conventions." Id. at 424. In its decision on the merits, the Court decided that it could not apply the multilateral treaties invoked by Nicaragua, since El Salvador would be "affected" by the decision of the Court on the lawfulness of resort by the United States to collective self-defense under those treaties; but the Court held that the United States reservation does not bar the application of identical rules of customary international law. [1986] I.C.J. Rep. 14, 36, 38, 95.

—Modification of United States declaration. The United States declaration of 1946 provided that it "shall remain in force for a period of five years and thereafter until the expiration of six months after notice may be given to terminate this declaration." In 1984 the United States, having learned that Nicaragua was about to bring a claim against the United States before the International Court of Justice, deposited with the Secretary-General of the United Nations a declaration stating that:

… the aforesaid declaration shall not apply to disputes with any Central American State or arising out of or related to events in Central America, any of which disputes shall be settled in such manner as the parties to them may agree.

Notwithstanding the terms of the aforesaid declaration, this provision shall take effect immediately and shall remain in force for two years....

[1984–85] I.C.J. Y.B. 100.

The United States argued that since its new declaration did not terminate but only modified its 1946 declaration, it was not subject to the six-month notice clause; and that the new declaration, therefore, was effective immediately and the Court did not have jurisdiction over the case brought by Nicaragua against the United States. The Court rejected the United States distinction between a modification and a termination of a declaration, and held that the United States notification was intended "to secure a partial and temporary termination" of the United States obligation "to subject itself to the Court's jurisdiction with regard to any application concerning disputes with Central American States." [1984] I.C.J. Rep. 392, 417–18. Even if a state perhaps has the right to terminate a declaration of indefinite duration, the principle of good faith requires a reasonable period of notice, and a period of a few days (in this case from April 6 to 9) would not amount to a "reasonable time." Id. at 420.

— Termination of United States declaration. The 1984 modification was to expire in April 1986, but on October 7, 1985, the United States delivered to the Secretary-General of the United Nations a note terminating the 1946 declaration, effective six months from the date of delivery. 85 Dep't State Bull. 82 (1985). This termination of the United States declaration under Article 36(2) of the Court's Statute did not affect the jurisdiction of the Court under Article 36(1) over cases as to which the United States accepted jurisdiction by an international agreement. See Comment c and Reporters' Note 2.

See generally Damrosch, ed., The International Court of Justice at a Crossroads (1987).

4. *Appellate jurisdiction of the Court.*

In addition to its original jurisdiction, the Court also has a limited appellate jurisdiction. For instance, the Convention on International Civil Aviation (1944) provides for appeals to the Court from the decisions of the Council of the International Civil Aviation Organization (ICAO). Art. 84, 3 Bevans 944, 15 U.N.T.S. 295. The International Air Services Transit Agreement (1944) utilizes the same procedure for disputes arising thereunder. See Art. 2(2), 3 Bevans 916, 84 U.N.T.S. 389. When India appealed to the Court from a decision of the ICAO Council in favor of Pakistan, Pakistan contended that the Court had no jurisdiction because India's appeal related to the Council's decision concerning its jurisdiction, not to a final decision on the merits. The Court held that a jurisdictional decision was a "substantive" decision and the appeal could be heard. Appeal Relating to the Jurisdiction of the ICAO Council (*India v. Pakistan*). [1972] I.C.J. Rep. 46, 52–57.

The Court has also reviewed several judgments of administrative tribunals of international organizations in the exercise of its advisory jurisdiction (Reporters' Note 12). See Judgments of the Administrative Tribunal of the International Labour Organization upon Complaints Made Against UNESCO, [1956] I.C.J. Rep. 77 (Advisory Opinion); Application for Review of Judgment No. 158 of the United Nations Administrative Tribunal, [1973] id. 166 (Advisory Opinion); Application for Review of Judgment No. 273 of the United Nations Administrative Tribunal, [1982] id. 325 (Advisory Opinion); and Application for Review of Judgment No. 333 of the United Nations Administrative Tribunal, [1987] id. 18 (Advisory Opinion). The last three cases were submitted to the Court by the Committee on Applications for Review of Administrative Tribunal Judgments established especially for that purpose by the General Assembly in 1955. G.A. Res. 957, 10 U.N. GAOR Supp. No. 19, at 30–31; the 1982 case was sent to the Court on request of the United States [1982] I.C.J. Rep. 325, 330.

*5. Requirement of legal dispute.*

The jurisdiction of the Court is limited to "disputes," Comment d. In Nuclear Tests Cases (*Australia and New Zealand v. France*), the International Court of Justice stated that "the Court can exercise its jurisdiction in contentious proceedings only when a dispute genuinely exists between the parties." [1974] I.C.J. Rep. 253, 271; 457, 476. The term "dispute" is defined loosely. See §902, Reporters' Note 7. The Permanent Court of International Justice said that "the manifestation of the existence of the dispute in a specific manner, as for instance by diplomatic negotiations, is not required." The Court added, however, that it "would no doubt be desirable that a State should not proceed to take as serious a step as summoning another State to appear before the Court without having previously, within reasonable limits, endeavoured to make it quite clear that a difference of views is in question which has not been capable of being otherwise overcome." Interpretation of Judgments Nos. 7 and 8 (Factory at Chorzow Case (*Germany v. Poland*)), P.C.I.J., ser. A, No. 13, at 10–11 (1927). In some cases the Court has rejected a claim on the ground that the claimant did not establish the existence of a dispute. See, e.g., Electricity Company of Sofia and Bulgaria Case (*Belgium v. Bulgaria*), P.C.I.J., ser. A/B, No. 77, at 64, 83 (1939). While the jurisdiction of the Court over cases brought pursuant to declarations under Article 36(2) of the Courts Statute (Subsection 1(c)) is limited to "legal disputes," the framers of the Statute rejected a proposal to impose that limitation also on cases submitted by the parties ad hoc pursuant to Article 36(1). "[W]hen parties agreed to go before the Court, the Court's jurisdiction should not be limited with respect to the nature of the dispute" 14 Docs.U.N.Conf. on Int'l Org. 204–205, 221–29, 288, 318 (1945).

Except where parties agree to submit a political dispute for decision ex aequo et bono (see Reporters' Note 9), the Court may hear only disputes that are essentially legal. This is implied in Article 38(1) of the Statute, which specifies that the function of the Court is "to decide in accordance with international law such disputes as are submitted to it." In Northern Cameroons Case, the Court noted:

> There are inherent limitations on the exercise of the judicial function which the Court, as a court of justice, can never ignore. There may thus be an incompatibility between the desires of an applicant, or, indeed, of both parties to a case, on the one hand, and on the other the duty of the Court to maintain its judicial character. The Court itself, and not the parties, must be the guardian of the Court's judicial integrity.

Northern Cameroons Case (*Cameroon v. United Kingdom*), [1963] I.C.J. Rep. 15, 29. In that case the Court refused to consider the plaintiff's claims since its judgment would have no practical effect on the existing situation and an examination of the merits of the claim would serve no purpose. The Court has not rejected any case on the ground that it involved nonlegal issues. Judges Dillard, Jimenez de Arechaga, Onyeama and Sir Humphrey Waldock, in their dissenting opinion in Nuclear Tests Cases (*Australia and New Zealand v. France*), stated that "[n]either in contentious cases nor in requests for advisory opinions has the Permanent Court [of International Justice] or [the International Court of Justice] ever at any time admitted the idea that an intrinsically legal issue could lose its legal character by reasons of political considerations surrounding it." [1974] I.C.J. Rep. 312, 366–67.

In Case Concerning United States Diplomatic and Consular Staff in Tehran, Reporters' Note 3, Iran contended that the conflict between the United States and Iran was not one relating to interpretation and application of treaties but arose from a political "situation containing much more fundamental and more complex elements." The Court pointed out that "legal disputes between sovereign States by their very nature are likely to occur in political contexts, and often form only one element in a wider and long standing political dispute." The Court found unacceptable the view that, "because a legal dispute submitted to the Court is only one aspect of a political dispute, the Court should decline to resolve for the parties the legal questions at issue between them"; it refused to impose such "a far reaching and unwarranted restriction upon the role of the Court in the peaceful solution of international disputes." [1980] I.C.J. Rep. 3, 19–20. The Court rejected a similar objection in the *Nicaragua v. United States* case. [1984] I.C.J. Rep. 392, 439–40.

### 6. Provisional measures.

The Court treats a request for provisional measures of interim protection under Article 41 of its Statute as a matter of urgency. I.C.J., Rules of Court, Article 61. Consequently, the Court has not been willing to postpone ordering such measures until it definitely resolved objections to its jurisdiction; it has indicated interim measures as soon as it has ascertained that plaintiff's claims appear prima facie to fall within the Court's jurisdiction. See Nuclear Tests Cases (*Australia and New Zealand v. France*) (Interim Protection), [1973] I.C.J. Rep. 99, 103; 135, 139–40. In *Nicaragua v. United States* (Reporters' Note 3), when Nicaragua requested provisional measures, the Court held that in order to "indicate" such measures it did not have to satisfy itself finally that it had jurisdiction on the merits of the case, but only that there appeared to be a prima facie basis for the Court's jurisdiction. The Court proceeded to indicate provisional measures but reserved the question of its jurisdiction on the merits for future determination. [1984] I.C.J. Rep. 169, 179, 186.

As of 1986, the Court had considered requests for interim measures of protection in 11 cases; the request was granted, inter alia, in Nuclear Tests Cases, *supra*; *Nicaragua v. United States*, Reporters' Note 3; and Frontier Dispute (Burkina Faso/Mali) (Provisional Measures), [1986] I.C.J. Rep. 3; it was denied, inter alia, in Interhandel Case (*Switzerland v. United States*) (Interim Protection), [1957] I.C.J. Rep. 105. In most cases the respondents refused to comply with an interim order, usually on the ground that the Court had no jurisdiction over the case. See, e.g., Anglo-Iranian Oil Co. Case (*United Kingdom v. Iran*) (Interim Protection), [1951] I.C.J. Rep. 89. In that case, the United Kingdom asked the Security Council to call upon Iran to act in conformity with the Court's order, but in view of doubts about the authority of the Council to enforce non-final decisions, the Council decided to postpone the matter until the Court had ruled on its own jurisdiction. United Nations, [1946–51] Repertoire of Practice of the Security Council 235–38 (1951).

The Court usually includes in its interim orders a request that the parties avoid any action that may aggravate the tension between the parties or render the dispute more difficult of solution. See, e.g., Case Concerning United States Diplomatic and Consular Staff in Tehran (*United States v. Iran*) (Provisional Measures), [1979] I.C.J. Rep. 7, 21. In its later judgment in that case, the Court noted that the attempt by the United States to rescue the hostages through an incursion into the territory of Iran while the Court was deliberating on the judgment was "of a kind calculated to undermine respect for the judicial process in international relations." [1980] I.C.J. Rep. 3, 43.

Another purpose of the provisional measures is to prevent irreparable prejudice to the rights that are the subject of dispute. In Nuclear Tests Cases, *supra*, the Court concluded that possible radioactive fallout from the French tests might cause damage to Australia that would be irreparable. [1973] I.C.J. Rep. 99, 105; 135, 141.

In Case Concerning the Frontier Dispute (Burkina Faso/Mali), when grave incidents took place between the armed forces in the border region between the two countries, each party requested the Chamber of the Court (to which the case was submitted by agreement) to indicate differing provisional measures. The Chamber indicated that both Governments "should withdraw their armed forces" to agreed positions and that failing an agreement on the terms of the troop withdrawal "the Chamber will itself indicate them." [1986] I.C.J. Rep. 3, at 11–12. The parties complied with the request. Report of the I.C.J., 41 U.N. GAOR Supp. No. 4, at 18 (1986).

As the Statute of the Court uses the ambiguous word "indicate" rather than "order" or "determine," there has been uncertainty as to whether the Court's orders indicating provisional measures are binding. The General Acts for the Settlement of International Disputes of 1928 and 1949 (see § 904, Reporters' Note 4) expressly provide that the "parties to the dispute shall be bound to accept" the provisional measures adopted in the Court (or by an arbitral tribunal). Art. 33(1). Opinions of scholars are divided on the subject. The binding character of provisional measures is supported by Fitzmaurice, "The Law and Procedure of the International Court of Justice, 1951–4," 34 Brit. Y.B. Int'l L. 1, 122 (1958) (the "whole logic of the jurisdiction to indicate interim measures entails that, when indicated, they are binding"); Hudson, The Permanent Court of International Justice, 1920–1942, at 426 (1943) ("a State is under an obligation to respect the Court's indication of provisional measures"); Stone, Legal Controls of International Conflict 132 (1959) (Article 41 "represents the only respect in which by mere acceptance of the Statute a State renders itself liable to the imposition of obligations by Court action"). See also Elkind, Interim Protection: A Functional Approach 153–66 (1981), supporting this view, and Dumbauld, Interim Measures of Protection in International Controversies 168–69 (1932), supporting an intermediate view that the Court merely declares "what action is required by international law to safeguard legal rights of the parties"; the parties have the duty "to fulfill their obligations under international law," and it is the law, not the order of the Court, that is binding on them. But see Rosenne, Procedure in the International Court 149–57 (1983) ("these indications are of an advisory character, imposing upon the States to which they are directed no more than an obligation to examine them in good faith"); Schwarzenberger and Brown, A Manual of International Law 204 (6th ed. 1976) ("the effect of such interlocutory order is moral rather than legal"); Sztucki, Interim Measures in the Hague Court 283–84 (1983) (citing a number of authors adhering to the view that interim measures are not binding). See also Reichert, "Provisional Measures in International Litigation: A Comprehensive Bibliography," 19 Int'l Law. 1429 (1985).

### 7. Intervention.

The Statute of the Court provides for intervention by a state in a case between other states in two circumstances: a state that considers that "it has an interest of a legal nature which may be affected by the decision in the case" may be permitted by the Court to intervene, Art. 62; a state that is a party to a convention the construction of which is before the Court has the right to intervene in the proceedings, Art. 63. In both circumstances the decision of the Court is binding on the intervening party. In the Permanent Court of International Justice, there was only one case of intervention, by the Government of Poland in the Wimbledon Case, which involved the interpretation of the Peace Treaty of Versailles of 1919. P.C.I.J., ser. A, No. 1 at 11–13 (1923). In 1951, the International Court of Justice allowed Cuba to intervene in the Haya de la Torre Case between Colombia and Peru, which involved the interpretation of the 1928 Havana Convention on Asylum, to which Cuba was a party. [1951] I.C.J. Rep. 71, 76–77. In later cases involving permissive interventions under Article 62, the Court took a more restrictive attitude and refused to grant permission to intervene. See Nuclear Tests Cases, Reporters' Note 3, [1974] I.C.J. Rep. 530, 535 (Fiji's application to intervene lapsed when the proceedings were termi-

nated because the main case "no longer has any object"); Case Concerning the Continental Shelf (Tunisia/Libyan Arab Jamahiriya) (Application of Malta for Permission to
Intervene), [1981] I.C.J. Rep. 3, 19 (Malta's interests were no greater than those of other
Mediterranean states, and her application was so restricted by various reservations that
the decision in the case could not affect any of her legal interests); Case Concerning the
Continental Shelf (Libyan Arab Jamahiriya/Malta) (Application of Italy for Permission
to Intervene), [1984] I.C.J. Rep. 3, 18–28 (to permit Italy to intervene would introduce
a fresh dispute; Article 62 was not intended as an alternative means of bringing an additional dispute as a case before the Court); Case Concerning Military and Paramilitary
Activities in and Against Nicaragua (*Nicaragua v. United States*) (Declaration of Intervention of the Republic of El Salvador), [1984] I.C.J. Rep. 215, 216 (although El Salvador's declaration invoked Article 63, this declaration addressed the substance of the
dispute and was inadmissible at the stage of proceedings relating only to the Court's jurisdiction). Later, in a decision concluding that it had jurisdiction of the case, the Court
noted that if Costa Rica, El Salvador, and Honduras should find that "they might be affected by the future decision of the Court" in the case, they would be free to institute proceedings against Nicaragua or resort to the incidental procedures for intervention under
Articles 62 and 63 of the Statute. [1984] I.C.J. Rep. 392, 425. No further action was taken
by Costa Rica or Honduras, but proceedings against them were instituted by Nicaragua
in 1986. 25 Int'l Leg.Mat. 1290, 1293 (1986) (applications by Nicaragua); [1986] I.C.J. Rep.
548, 551 (procedural orders); [1987] id. 182 (order recording the discontinuance by
Nicaragua of the proceedings against Costa Rica).

### 8. Sources of law and Court decisions.

The sources of law to be applied by the Court are specified in Article 38 of the Statute
(quoted in § 102, Reporters' Note 1). While Article 59 provides that a "decision of the Court
has no binding force except between the parties and in respect of that particular case," the
Court's decisions are generally considered authoritative statements of international law.
See § 103, Comment b; see also § 102, Reporters' Note 1. The Court seldom cites decisions
of other tribunals, but it frequently relies on its own prior decisions and advisory opinions
and on those of its predecessor, the Permanent Court of International Justice.

### 9. Equity and ex aequo et bono.

Under Article 38(2) of the Statute of the Court, the parties may authorize the Court
to decide a case ex aequo et bono, i.e., according to what is equitable and good, departing if necessary from existing legal principles. This should be distinguished from application by the Court of the basic principles of equity that are part of customary international
law. See § 102, Comment m; Sohn, "The Role of Equity in the Jurisprudence of the International Court of Justice," in Melanges Georges Perrin 303 (1984). As of 1987, there
had been no case in which the parties authorized the Court to decide ex aequo et bono.

The 1982 Convention on the Law of the Sea provides that the delimitation of maritime boundaries in the exclusive economic zone or on the continental shelf shall be by
agreement "in order to achieve an equitable solution." Arts. 74 and 83; see § 517(2) and
Comment c. In two cases relating to maritime boundaries, the Court was authorized by
the parties to apply, and did apply, equitable principles. Continental Shelf Case (Tunisia/
Libyan Arab Jamahiriya) [1982] I.C.J. Rep. 18, 21, 58–60 (the Court should "take account of equitable principles and the relevant circumstances which characterize the area");
Continental Shelf Case (Libyan Arab Jamahiriya/Malta) [1985] I.C.J. Rep. 13, 31, 38–40,
57 ("the delimitation is to be effected in accordance with equitable principles and taking
account of all relevant circumstances, so as to arrive at an equitable result").

*10. Declaratory judgments.*

In the Corfu Channel Case (*United Kingdom v. Albania*); the International Court of Justice declared that the action of the British Navy had constituted a violation of Albanian sovereignty. It added that this declaration "is in itself appropriate satisfaction." [1949] I.C.J. Rep. 4, 35. In the Eastern Greenland Case, the Permanent Court of International Justice declared that the 1931 proclamation placing Eastern Greenland under Norwegian sovereignty and later steps taken by the Norwegian Government "constitute a violation of the existing legal situation and are accordingly unlawful and invalid." P.C.I.J. ser. A/B No. 53, at 75 (1933). Two days later Norway revoked the 1931 proclamation. 3 Hudson, World Court Reports 148 (1938). In the North Sea Continental Shelf Cases (Fed. Rep. of Germany/Denmark and the Netherlands), the International Court of Justice was asked to decide what "principles and rules of international law are applicable to the delimitation" of the continental shelf areas in the North Sea. The parties had agreed that they would delimit the shelf as between them pursuant to the decision of the Court, and after the Court established the basic principles, the parties delimited their boundary accordingly. [1969] I.C.J. Rep. 3, 6, 53–54; for the 1971 agreements, see 10 Int'l Leg.Mat. 600–12 (1971). A similar procedure was followed in Continental Shelf Case (Tunisia/Libyan Arab Jamahiriya) [1982] I.C.J. Rep. 18, 21, 92–94.

*11. Compliance with judgments of the Court.*

The judgments of the Court have been generally complied with, but there have been exceptions. For instance, Albania did not comply with the Court's judgment in the Corfu Channel Case (Reporters' Note 10) awarding compensation to the United Kingdom for damage to its warships and the loss of life caused thereby; and Iran failed to comply with the Court's judgment in the United States Diplomatic and Consular Staff in Tehran Case (Reporters' Note 5). In 10 cases submitted to the Court by application of a party to a dispute, the other party failed to appear; when judgment was rendered against it, it refused to comply. For a list of these cases, see [1985–86] I.C.J. Y.B. 124, n. 1.

In the *Nicaragua v. United States* case, after the Court rejected the arguments of the United States and decided that it had jurisdiction, the United States refused to participate further in the proceedings and reserved "its rights in respect of any decision by the Court regarding Nicaragua's claims." [1986] I.C.J. Rep. 14, 23. The Court declared that this reservation has "no effect on the validity" of its judgment. Id. at 23–24. In July 1986, the United States vetoed a resolution of the Security Council calling for compliance with the Court's 1986 judgment in this case. U.N. Docs. S/18250 (1986) and S/PV. 2704 (1986), reprinted in 25 Int. Leg.Mat. 1352–65 (1986). The General Assembly adopted a resolution calling for "full and immediate compliance" with the Court's Judgment. U.N. Doc. A/RES/41/31 (1986).

*12. Advisory opinions.*

Under the Court's Statute, some international organizations may request advisory opinions; states have no right to request an advisory opinion or to demand that an international organization do so.

Some international agreements between an international organization and a state provide that disputes relating to the interpretation or application of the agreement shall be submitted to the Court for an advisory opinion, which "shall be accepted as decisive by the parties," See, e.g., Convention on the Privileges and Immunities of the United Nations, 1946, sec. 30, 21 U.S.T. 1418, T.I.A.S. No. 6900, 1 U.N.T.S. 16.

In addition to the General Assembly and the Security Council, four other organs of the United Nations have been authorized by the General Assembly to request advisory opinions: the Economic and Social Council, the Trusteeship Council, the Interim Committee of the General Assembly (which stopped functioning in 1952), and the Committee on Applications for Review of Administrative Tribunal Judgments (which has requested three opinions). Fifteen specialized agencies have also been authorized to request advisory opinions, and three of these (UNESCO, WHO, and IMCO) have made one request each. As to the development of the advisory jurisdiction of the Court, see 2 Rosenne, The Law and Practice of the International Court 651–757 (1965). As of 1986, the Court had rendered 18 advisory opinions. For a list, see [1985–86] I.C.J. Y.B. 51, nn. 3–4, and 52, nn. 1–4.

*13. Jurisprudence of the Court and its predecessor.*

The International Court of Justice frequently follows the jurisprudence of its predecessor, the Permanent Court of International Justice. See Reporters' Note 1. In the 65 disputes that came before it, the Permanent Court rendered 32 judgments, 27 advisory opinions, and more than 200 orders. It effected settlement of numerous disputes, each of which was important to the parties and some of which were of wider significance. The matters considered by the Court included several disputes between Poland and Germany and between Poland and Danzig; a number of disputes between other Eastern European countries relating to the interpretation and application of treaties for the protection of minorities; a claim of domestic jurisdiction in the Anglo-French dispute concerning nationality decrees in Tunis and Morocco; boundary disputes between Czechoslovakia and Poland, Iraq and Turkey, and France and Switzerland (concerning the Free Zones); sovereignty over Eastern Greenland (*Denmark v. Norway*); the attempted customs union between Germany and Austria; jurisdiction of states in cases of collisions at sea; competence of the International Labour Organization with respect to regulation of agricultural labor, women in supervisory positions, and incidental work of employers; restoration of railway traffic between Poland and Lithuania; navigation on the Danube and Oder Rivers and through the Kiel Canal; diversion of water from the River Meuse by Belgium (the first Court decision on the basis of equity); validity of the gold clause in international loans; and various claims involving violations of international law with respect to private persons and the right of states to present claims on their behalf.

The cases that have come before the International Court of Justice are also impressive. Since the first application was submitted to the Court in 1947, 73 cases had been presented to it by 1986, and by that date the Court had rendered 48 judgments, 18 advisory opinions, and 213 orders (mostly procedural). [1985–86] I.C.J. Y.B. 3. It has rendered several decisions relating to the law of the sea — Norway's maritime boundary, transit of warships through the Corfu Channel, the delimitation of the North Sea continental shelf, fisheries jurisdiction of Iceland, the continental shelf boundaries between Tunisia and Libya and between Libya and Malta, the maritime boundary between Canada and the United States in the Gulf of Maine area, the last a decision by a panel of the Court; it dealt with several territorial disputes — between France and the United Kingdom concerning the Minquiers and Ecrehos islands, the boundary between Honduras and Nicaragua, sovereignty over certain Belgian enclaves in the Netherlands, the ownership of the Temple of Preah Vihear on the Cambodia-Thailand boundary; right of asylum (Colombia-Peru); claims on behalf of stockholders in a foreign company (Barcelona Traction Case); and safety of diplomatic and consular personnel (United States-Iran). The Court's advisory opinions dealt with: the right of the United Nations to present claims on behalf of its injured officials; several issues relating to South West Africa (Namibia); the admission of members to the United Nations; decisions of the United Nations Administrative Tribunal; the effect of reservations to general international agreements; the authority of the

United Nations to engage in peacekeeping activities and the obligation of member states to pay for those activities; the interpretation of an agreement relating to a regional office of an international organization; and the status of Western Sahara.

*14. Other international courts.*

There are several specialized international courts. The Court of Justice of the European Communities has broad jurisdiction and is open not only to states but also to the organs of the Community and to private persons. The European Court of Human Rights and the Inter-American Court of Human Rights have jurisdiction relating to human rights questions. These courts can render binding decisions, and there are special provisions for the execution of their judgments. Treaty Establishing the European Community, Arts. 187, 192 (decisions of the Court of Justice of the European Communities that impose a pecuniary obligation on persons other than states are to be enforced pursuant to rules of civil procedure in force in the state in whose territory the execution takes place); European Convention for the Protection of Human Rights and Fundamental Freedoms, Art. 54 (§ 906, Reporters' Note 1) (the Committee of Ministers of the Council of Europe shall supervise the execution of the judgments of the European Court of Human Rights); American Convention on Human Rights, Art. 68 (a judgment of the Inter-American Court of Human Rights that stipulates compensatory damages may be executed in the country concerned in accordance with domestic procedure governing the execution of judgment against the state). The Inter-American Court has broad jurisdiction to render advisory opinions. On the scope of that jurisdiction, see Advisory Opinion of Sept. 24, 1982, Inter-Am. Court Hum.Rt., ser. A, No. 1, 22 Int'l Leg.Mat. 51 (1983). The International Tribunal of the Law of the Sea to be established under Annex VI of the Convention on the Law of the Sea (see Part V of this Restatement) will have jurisdiction not only over disputes between states but also over disputes involving international organizations, state enterprises, or natural or juridical persons. LOS Convention, Art. 187, and Annex VI, Art. 20.

# 3. Statute of the International Court of Justice, Articles 36, 38, and 59

## Article 36

1. The jurisdiction of the Court comprises all cases which the parties refer to it and all matters specially provided for in the Charter of the United Nations or in treaties and conventions in force.

2. The states parties to the present Statute may at any time declare that they recognize as compulsory ipso facto and without special agreement, in relation to any other state accepting the same obligation, the jurisdiction of the Court in all legal disputes concerning:

   a. the interpretation of a treaty;

   b. any question of international law;

   c. the existence of any fact which, if established, would constitute a breach of an international obligation;

   d. the nature or extent of the reparation to be made for the breach of an international obligation.

3. The declarations referred to above may be made unconditionally or on condition of reciprocity on the part of several or certain states, or for a certain time.

4. Such declarations shall be deposited with the Secretary-General of the United Nations, who shall transmit copies thereof to the parties to the Statute and to the Registrar of the Court.

5. Declarations made under Article 36 of the Statute of the Permanent Court of International Justice and which are still in force shall be deemed, as between the parties to the present Statute, to be acceptances of the compulsory jurisdiction of the International Court of Justice for the period which they still have to run and in accordance with their terms.

6. In the event of a dispute as to whether the Court has jurisdiction, the matter shall be settled by the decision of the Court.

* * *

### Article 38

1. The Court, whose function is to decide in accordance with international law such disputes as are submitted to it, shall apply:

    a. international conventions, whether general or particular, establishing rules expressly recognized by the contesting states;

    b. international custom, as evidence of a general practice accepted as law;

    c. the general principles of law recognized by civilized nations;

    d. subject to the provisions of Article 59, judicial decisions and the teachings of the most highly qualified publicists of the various nations, as subsidiary means for the determination of rules of law.

2. This provision shall not prejudice the power of the Court to decide a case ex aequo et bono, if the parties agree thereto.

* * *

### Article 59

The decision of the Court has no binding force except between the parties and in respect of that particular case.

## Authors' Note

The following case before the ICJ represents a dispute between two countries concerning compulsory jurisdiction. The case discusses the principle of reciprocity and the application of reservations to the compulsory jurisdiction of the ICJ.

## 4. The Norwegian Loans Case (*France v. Norway*)
### International Court of Justice, 1957

French nationals owned bonds issued before World War I by the Kingdom of Norway and two Norwegian banks. These bonds initially contained varying clauses that France claimed expressly promised and guaranteed payment in gold. Norway later passed legislation allowing payment of the bonds with Bank of Norway notes, which were not convertible into gold.

The French government espoused the claims of its nationals. During diplomatic negotiations, it proposed that the problem be submitted to a commission of economic and financial experts, to arbitration, or to the ICJ. The Norwegian government maintained that the bondholders' claims were within the jurisdiction of the Norwegian courts and that these claims were solely matters of domestic law.

The French government then brought the case to the ICJ, where it argued that the bonds were international loans that "cannot be unilaterally modified by [Norway] without negotiation with the holders, with the French State which has adopted the cause of its nationals, or without arbitration." The French asked that the Court stipulate the amount of the lender's obligation in gold, and that the lender then pay off this amount.]

The Application [of France] expressly refers to Article 36, paragraph 2, of the Statute of the Court and to the acceptance of the compulsory jurisdiction of the Court by Norway on November 16th, 1946 and by France on March 1st, 1949. The Norwegian Declaration reads:

> I declare on behalf of the Norwegian Government that Norway recognizes as compulsory ipso facto and without special agreement, in relation to any other State accepting the same obligation, that is to say, on condition of reciprocity, the jurisdiction of the International Court of justice in conformity with Article 36, paragraph 2, of the Statute of the Court, for a period of ten years as from 3rd October 1946.

The French Declaration reads:

> On behalf of the Government of the French Republic, and subject to ratification, I declare that I recognize as compulsory ipso facto and without special agreement, in relation to any other State accepting the same obligation, that is on condition of reciprocity, the jurisdiction of the International Court of justice, in conformity with Article 36, paragraph 2, of the Statute of the said Court, for all disputes which may arise in respect of facts or situations subsequent to the ratification of the present declaration, with the exception of those with regard to which the parties may have agreed or may agree to have recourse to another method of peaceful settlement.

This declaration does not apply to differences relating to matters which are essentially within the national jurisdiction as understood by the Government of the French Republic....

After presenting the first ground of its first Preliminary Objection on the basis that the loan contracts are governed by municipal law, the Norwegian Government continues in its Preliminary Objections:

> There can be no possible doubt on this point. If, however, there should still be some doubt, the Norwegian Government would rely upon the reservations made by the French Government in its Declaration of March 1st, 1949. By virtue of the principle of reciprocity, which is embodied in Article 36, paragraph 2, of the Statute of the Court and which has been clearly expressed in the Norwegian Declaration of November 16th, 1946, the Norwegian Government cannot be bound, vis-a-vis the French Government, by undertakings which are either broader or stricter than those given by the latter Government....

It will be recalled that the French Declaration accepting the compulsory jurisdiction of the Court contains the following reservation:

> This declaration does not apply to differences relating to matters which are essentially within the national jurisdiction as understood by the Government of the French Republic.

In the Preliminary Objections filed by the Norwegian Government it is stated:

> The Norwegian Government did not insert any such reservation in its own Declaration. But it has the right to rely upon the restrictions placed by France upon her own undertakings.

Convinced that the dispute which has been brought before the Court by the Application of July 6th, 1955, is within the domestic jurisdiction, the Norwegian Government considers itself fully entitled to rely on this right. Accordingly, it requests the Court to decline, on grounds that it lacks jurisdiction, the function which the French Government would have it assume.

In considering this ground of the Objection the Court notes in the first place that the present case has been brought before it on the basis of Article 36, paragraph 2, of the Statute and of the corresponding Declarations of acceptance of compulsory jurisdiction; that in the present case the jurisdiction of the Court depends upon the Declarations made by the Parties in accordance with Article 36, paragraph 2, of the Statute on condition of reciprocity; and that, since two unilateral declarations are involved, such jurisdiction is conferred upon the Court only to the extent to which the Declarations coincide in conferring it. A comparison between the two Declarations shows that the French Declaration accepts the Court's jurisdiction within narrower limits than the Norwegian Declaration; consequently, the common will of the Parties, which is the basis of the Court's jurisdiction, exists within these narrower limits indicated by the French reservation.

France has limited her acceptance of the compulsory jurisdiction of the Court by excluding beforehand disputes "relating to matters which are essentially within the national jurisdiction as understood by the Government of the French Republic." In accordance with the condition of reciprocity to which acceptance of the compulsory jurisdiction is made subject in both Declarations and which is provided for in Article 36, paragraph 31 of the Statute, Norway, equally with France, is entitled to except from the compulsory jurisdiction of the Court disputes understood by Norway to be essentially within its national jurisdiction.

The Court does not consider that it should examine whether the French reservation is consistent with the undertaking of a legal obligation and is compatible with Article 36, paragraph 6, of the Statute, which provides:

> In the event of a dispute as to whether the Court has jurisdiction, the matter shall be settled by the decision of the Court.

The validity of the reservation has not been questioned by the Parties. It is clear that France fully maintains its Declaration, including the reservation, and that Norway relies upon the reservation.

For these reasons, the Court, by twelve votes to three, finds that it is without jurisdiction to adjudicate upon the dispute which has been brought before it by the Application of the Government of the French Republic of July 6th, 1955.

# 5. U.N. Charter, Articles 2(4) and 51

**Article 2**

The Organization and its Members, in pursuit of the Purposes stated in Article 1, shall act in accordance with the following Principles.

The Organization is based on the principle of the sovereign equality of all its Members.

All Members, in order to ensure to all of them the rights and benefits resulting from membership, shall fulfill in good faith the obligations assumed by them in accordance with the present Charter.

All Members shall settle their international disputes by peaceful means in such a manner that international peace and security, and justice, are not endangered.

All Members shall refrain in their international relations from the threat or use of force against the territorial integrity or political independence of any state, or in any other manner inconsistent with the Purposes of the United Nations.

All Members shall give the United Nations every assistance in any action it takes in accordance with the present Charter, and shall refrain from giving assistance to any state against which the United Nations is taking preventive or enforcement action.

The Organization shall ensure that states which are not Members of the United Nations act in accordance with these Principles so far as may be necessary for the maintenance of international peace and security.

Nothing contained in the present Charter shall authorize the United Nations to intervene in matters which are essentially within the domestic jurisdiction of any state or shall require the Members to submit such matters to settlement under the present Charter; but this principle shall not prejudice the application of enforcement measures under Chapter VII.

### Article 51

Nothing in the present Charter shall impair the inherent right of individual or collective self-defense if an armed attack occurs against a Member of the United Nations, until the Security Council has taken measures necessary to maintain international peace and security. Measures taken by Members in the exercise of this right of self-defense shall be immediately reported to the Security Council and shall not in any way affect the authority and responsibility of the Security Council under the present Charter to take at any time such action as it deems necessary in order to maintain or restore international peace and security.

## Authors' Note

Material 6 provides guidance for this chapter's simulation between Spain and Canada before the ICJ. The Restatement excepts provide relevant international law on the law of the sea and other legal principles that would affect arguments for and against jurisdiction in the simulation.

## 6. Third Restatement of the Foreign Relations Law, Sections 521, 522, and 211

### § 521 Freedom of High Seas

(1) The high seas are open and free to all states, whether coastal or land-locked.

(2) Freedom of the high seas comprises, inter alia:

(a) freedom of navigation;

(b) freedom of overflight;

(c) freedom of fishing;

(d) freedom to lay submarine cables and pipelines;

(e) freedom to construct artificial islands, installations, and structures; and

(f) freedom of scientific research.

(3) These freedoms must be exercised by all states with reasonable regard to the interests of other states in their exercise of the freedom of the high seas.

**Source Note:**

This section is based on Article 2 of the 1958 Convention on the High Seas, and Articles 87 and 89 of the LOS Convention.

**Reporters' Notes:**

*1. Interference with navigation on high seas.*

The use of the high seas by ships is normally subject to regulation and control only by the flag state; for centuries, the freedom of ships from control or interference by ships of other states has been jealously safeguarded. Small deviations from that rule have been made in order to protect all states against common enemies such as pirates, slave traders, and, more recently, "pirate" broadcasters. See § 404 and Reporters' Note 1 thereto. The increasing concern over illicit traffic in narcotic drugs may lead to a recognition of the right to stop and search foreign vessels suspected of such traffic, and even to confiscate the drugs or arrest the ship and its crew.

The movement of ships in certain areas of the high seas is frequently hampered by naval exercises and the testing of conventional weapons, missiles, and nuclear weapons. As to various attempts to restrict such testing, see 4 Whiteman, Digest of International Law 710–26 (1965). See also McDougal and Schlei, "The Hydrogen Bomb Tests in Perspective: Lawful Measures for Security," 64 Yale L.J. 648 (1955); Margolis, "The Hydrogen Bomb Experiments and International Law," 64 Yale L.J. 629 (1955); Taubenfeld, "Nuclear Testing and International Law," 16 Sw.L.J. 365 (1962). See also Nuclear Tests Cases (*Australia and New Zealand v. France*), [1974] I.C.J.Rep. 253, 457.

\* \* \*

*3. Fishing.*

Both the 1958 Convention on Fishing and Conservation of the Living Resources of the High Seas and the LOS Convention recognize the freedom of fishing on the high seas; both impose the obligation on states to regulate such fishing in order to conserve the living resources of the oceans. See Comment e. In particular, where the nationals of several states are engaged in exploiting identical living resources, or different living resources in the same area of the high seas, states are obligated to cooperate, and to take the necessary joint or parallel measures, either directly or through a regional or subregional fisheries organization with a view to protecting the resources against over-exploitation. 1958 Convention on Fishing and Conservation of the Living Resources of the High Seas, Art. 3; LOS Convention, Art. 118. As the International Court of Justice noted in the Fisheries Jurisdiction Case (*United Kingdom v. Iceland*), one of the advances in maritime international law is that "the former laissez-faire treatment of the living resources of the sea in the high seas has been replaced by a recognition of a duty to have due regard to the rights of other States and the needs of conservation for the benefit of all." [1974] I.C.J.Rep. 3, at 31.

Special problems have arisen with respect to "straddling stocks," where the same fish stock is to be found within both an exclusive economic zone of a state and a neighboring high seas area. The complex provisions on the subject in the 1958 Convention have not been applied in practice, and the LOS Convention has only a general provision about seeking an agreement on the subject. 1958 Convention on Fishing, *supra*, Arts. 6–12; LOS Convention, Arts. 63, 116(b). For the conservation of highly migratory species and marine mammals, see id. Arts. 64–65, 116(b), 120; § 514, Comment f.

\* \* \*

*7. Previous Restatement.*

The principal reference to high seas in the previous Restatement was contained in §21, Comment b. That Comment is consistent with Subsection (1) of this section and Comment a.

## §522. Enforcement Jurisdiction Over Foreign Ships on High Seas

(1) A warship, or other ship owned or operated by a state and used only on government noncommercial service, enjoys complete immunity on the high seas from interference by any other state.

(2) Ships other than those specified in Subsection (1) are not subject to interference on the high seas, but a warship or clearly-marked law enforcement ship of any state may board such a ship if authorized by the flag state, or if there is reason to suspect that the ship

(a) is engaged in piracy, slave trade, or unauthorized broadcasting;

(b) is without nationality; or

(c) though flying a foreign flag or refusing to show its flag, is in fact of the same nationality as the warship or law enforcement ship.

**Reporters' Notes:**

*1. Warships and other government ships.*

A United States Coast Guard ship is considered a warship. *United States v. Conroy*, 589 F.2d 1258, 1267 (5th Cir.1979), certiorari denied, 444 U.S. 831, 100 S.Ct. 60, 62 L.Ed.2d 40 (1979). Some convention provisions grant immunity to "government ships operated for non-commercial purpose" (e.g., 1958 Convention on the Territorial Sea and the Contiguous Zone, Art. 22; LOS Convention, Arts. 31–32); others provide immunity to "ships owned or operated by a State and used only on government non-commercial service" (e.g., 1958 Convention on the High Seas, Art. 9; LOS Convention, Art. 96). It is not clear that any difference was intended. As long as a ship is operated for noncommercial purposes, it is entitled to immunity if it is either owned or operated by the government, for instance, a government-owned ship operated by an oceanographic institute, and engaged on a government-sponsored hydrographic survey, or a private-owned ship chartered by the government for a meteorological service.

*2. Piracy and hijacking.*

Acts indicated in Comment c are piracy only if they are by private ships and for private ends. Seizure of a ship for political purposes is not considered piracy. See the Santa Maria incident in 1961, 4 Whiteman, Digest of International Law 665 (1965). Crew members forced to assist the pirates are not, under the above definition, considered pirates. Wrongful acts by governmental ships are not included in the definition of piracy, but are addressed by general principles of international law governing state responsibility for violations of international obligations. See §§ 207 and 901.

The definition of piracy, Comment c, includes acts by a private ship or aircraft against "another ship or aircraft on the high seas" (para. (1)(a)). That clause was designed to cover acts against a ship or a sea plane floating on the sea; acts committed in the air by one aircraft against another were not included in the definition of piracy but left for regulation outside the framework of the law of the sea. The definition includes also acts committed in "a place outside the jurisdiction of any state" (para. (1)(b)). That reference is to "acts committed by a ship or aircraft on an island constituting terra nullius or on the shores of an unoccupied territory," so as to ensure that such acts would not escape all penal jurisdiction. Report of the International Law Commission, [1956] 2 Y.B. Int'l L. Comm'n 282, 11 U.N. GAOR Supp. No. 9 at 28.

As to piracy, see also 1958 Convention on the High Seas, Arts. 14–21; LOS Convention, Arts. 100–107; 18 U.S.C. § 1651 et seq., and 33 U.S.C. § 381 et seq.; United States-Thailand Agreement for the Protection of Refugees Against Pirates, 1980, T.I.A.S. No. 9886; In re Piracy Jure Gentium, [1934] A.C. 586 (P.C.); Johnson, "Piracy in Modern International Law," 43 Trans. Grotius Soc'y 63 (1957). For special international agreements relating to the unlawful seizure of aircraft, see § 404, Reporters' Note 1; § 475, Reporters' Note 5; Lowenfeld, Aviation Law: Cases and Materials, ch. 8 (2d ed. 1981).

* * *

*6. Other situations justifying inspection or seizure.*

It may be suggested that the right to inspect and to seize foreign ships be extended to ships carrying stolen nuclear materials or escaping terrorists, but the present international law on the subject is unclear.

*7. Stateless ships.*

A stateless vessel is not entitled to the protection of this section against boarding and search. *United States v. Cortes*, 588 F.2d 106, 109–10 (5th Cir. 1979) (applying the 1958 Convention on the High Seas). See also *Molvan v. Attorney General for Palestine*, [1948] A.C. 351, 369 (P.C.). A ship displaying two flags, or displaying a flag other than that of the state of registry, may be assimilated to a stateless ship. See 1958 Convention on the High Seas, Art. 6(2); LOS Convention, Arts. 92(2), 110(1)(d); Legal Opinion of the Chief Counsel of the U.S. Coast Guard, September 1976, [1976] Digest of U.S. Practice in Int'l L. 304; *United States v. Martinez*, 700 F.2d 1358 (11th Cir. 1983). A ship attempting to change a flag while on the high seas is also assimilated to a stateless ship. *United States v. Dominguez*, 604 F.2d 304, 307–09 (4th Cir.1979), certiorari denied, 444 U.S. 1014, 100 S.Ct. 664, 62 L.Ed.2d 644 (1980).

*8. Consent of flag state to seizure of ships.*

Except in cases of privacy, slave trade, or unauthorized broadcasting, Subsection (2), a state may interfere with the ships of another state on the high seas only when expressly authorized by international agreement. 1958 Convention on the High Seas, Art. 22; LOS Convention, Art. 110. States have been reluctant to accord such authority, but a few states have done so in special circumstances.

For instance, by agreement in 1981, the United Kingdom gave permission to United States authorities to board, search, and seize ships under the British flag in an area comprising the Gulf of Mexico, the Caribbean Sea, and a portion of the Atlantic Ocean, in any case in which United States authorities reasonably believe that a ship "has on board a cargo of drugs for importation into the United States in violation of the laws of the United States"; but the United States agreed to release the ship or any United Kingdom national found on board the ship, if the United Kingdom should, within a specified period, "object to the continued exercise of United States jurisdiction" over the ship or person. 1981 Agreement to Facilitate the Interdiction by the United States of Vessels of the United Kingdom Suspected of Trafficking in Drugs, T.I.A.S. No. 10296. This agreement was applied in *United States v. Layne*, 599 F.Supp. 689 (S.D. Fla.1984); *United States v. Reeh*, 780 F.2d 1541 (11th Cir.1986); and *United States v. Quemener*, 789 F.2d 145 (2d Cir. 1986), certiorari denied, ___ U.S. ___, 107 S.Ct. 110, 93 L.Ed.2d 58 (1986). In several other instances involving illicit maritime traffic in narcotic drugs, the Coast Guard has relied on informal arrangements with flag state officials providing for consent by radiotelephone. A challenge to this practice was rejected in *United States v. Romero-Galue*, 757 F.2d 1147 (11th Cir. 1985), and *United States v. Gonzalez*, 776 F.2d 931 (11th Cir.1985).

See also [1976] Digest of U.S. Practice in Int'l L. 302–304; *United States v. Hensel*, 699 F.2d 18 (1st Cir.1983), certiorari denied, 461 U.S. 958, 103 S.Ct. 2431, 77 L.Ed.2d 1317 (1983); *United States v. Loalza-Vasquez*, 735 F.2d 153 (5th Cir.1984). Congress confirmed the practice in the Maritime Drug Law Enforcement Act, embodied in § 3202 of the Anti-Drug Abuse Act of 1986, Pub. L. 99-570. That statute defines a "vessel of the United States" as including any "vessel registered in a foreign nation where the flag nation has consented or waived objection to the enforcement of United States law by the United States," and provides that such consent "may be obtained by radio, telephone, or similar oral or electronic means, and may be proved by certification of the Secretary of State or the Secretary's designee." Id. § 3(b).

In 1981, Haiti authorized United States authorities to board Haitian flag vessels on the high seas for the purpose of ascertaining whether there were any Haitians on board intending to commit an offense against United States immigration laws. The agreement authorized United States authorities to detain any vessel with such migrants aboard, and to return the vessel and persons aboard the vessel to a Haitian port or to release them on the high seas to a representative of Haiti. T.I.A.S. No. 10241. See § 433, Reporters' Note 4; § 513, Reporters' Note 5.

* * *

### § 211 Nationality of Individuals

For purposes of international law, an individual has the nationality of a state that confers it, but other states need not accept that nationality when it is not based on a genuine link between the state and the individual.

**Reporters' Notes:**

*1. "Genuine link."*

The Nottebohm Case (*Liechtenstein v. Guatemala*), [1955] I.C.J. Rep. 4, ruled that because there was no genuine link between Nottebohm and Liechtenstein, Guatemala did not have to recognize his Liechtenstein nationality and Liechtenstein could not bring proceedings before the International Court of Justice on his behalf against Guatemala. Nottebohm, originally of German nationality, was a long-time resident of Guatemala. He had taken a brief trip to Liechtenstein during which he complied with its requirements for naturalization and then returned to Guatemala. Although Liechtenstein's naturalization law required a showing of loss of prior nationality, and German law provided for loss of German nationality upon acquisition of another nationality, Guatemala, at war with Germany, treated Nottebohm as an alien enemy. Liechtenstein objected and brought a proceeding before the International Court of Justice. The Court referred to international arbitral decisions holding that the state to which a dual national has stronger ties is the one entitled to extend protection against third states. See Comment f. It is not clear from the opinion whether a third country would have been entitled to ignore Liechtenstein's naturalization of Nottebohm, since the court stressed the comparative ties of Nottebohm to Liechtenstein and to Guatemala. Nothing in the case suggests that a state may refuse to give effect to a nationality acquired at birth, regardless of how few other links the individual had at birth or maintained later.

Formal diplomatic protection is an "extraordinary legal remedy" generally limited to nationals. See Borchard, The Diplomatic Protection of Citizens Abroad § 134a (1922); 9 Whiteman, Digest of International Law 1216 (1967).

*2. Involuntary nationality.*

The United States has taken the position that it is a violation of international law for a state to impose its nationality upon a person after birth without that person's consent.

The United States and other states have protested legislation of other countries providing that aliens who reside in the country for specified periods, acquire land there, or have children born in the country, automatically become nationals even if they object. However, legislation that operates only prospectively and gives the alien a reasonable opportunity to avoid the imposition of nationality would probably not violate international law. Laws that provide that a woman automatically acquires her husband's nationality upon marriage are questionable if the woman objects, under the principle of gender equality now internationally recognized, e.g., in the Convention on the Nationality of Women, 49 Stat. 2957, T.S. No. 875 (1934), and in the Universal Declaration of Human Rights and the principal human rights covenants. See Introductory Note to Part VII; § 702, Comment l. Where nationality is imposed upon a stateless person, there is no encroachment upon the authority of a state with a preexisting link of nationality, and no state is available to provide such person diplomatic protection. See Reporters' Note 5; Weis, Nationality and Statelessness in International Law 102-15 (2d ed. 1979). But imposing nationality in such circumstances may violate international human rights law. Compare § 701, Reporters' Note 6. Nationality may be imposed on persons without their consent in circumstances of state succession. See § 208, Comment c.

*3. Dual nationality.*

Dual nationality problems arise in a variety of situations ranging from liability to military service or taxation to the availability of diplomatic protection. Attempts have been made by treaty to limit the incidence of dual nationality or its effects. The United States was a party to the Convention Establishing the Status of Naturalized Persons who again Take Up Residence in the Country of their Origin, 37 Stat. 1653, T.S. No. 575 (1908), which provides a presumption of surrender of a nationality acquired by naturalization after two years' residence in the country of origin. However, the United States terminated its adherence to the Convention after the Supreme Court ruled that the presumption of surrender of nationality is subject to constitutional limitations. See § 212, Reporters' Note 4. Compare the Convention on the Nationality of Women, Reporters' Note 2. The United States is a party to the 1930 Hague Protocol relating to Military Obligations in Certain Cases of Double Nationality, 50 Stat. 1317, T.S. No. 913, 178 L.N.T.S. 227. It is not a party to the 1930 Hague Convention on Certain Questions relating to the Conflict of Nationality Laws, 179 L.N.T.S. 89, 24 Am.J.Int'l L. 192 (Supp.1930).

*4. Renunciation and involuntary loss of nationality.*

The United States has long taken the position that the "right of expatriation is a natural and inherent right of all people...." Rev.Stat. § 1999. Not all countries have agreed with that view.

As concerns involuntary loss of nationality, international law is moving toward limits on state discretion. Article 15 of the Universal Declaration of Human Rights says that no person should be "arbitrarily deprived of his nationality." The term "arbitrarily" should encompass racial, sexual, and other forms of discrimination. Compare the Convention on the Nationality of Women, Reporters' Note 2. The deprivation of nationality is most serious in its impact when it renders a person stateless.

*5. Statelessness.*

A stateless individual has no state to afford him diplomatic protection. If the country in which he resides expels him, there is no country that is required to accept him. The United States is a party to the Protocol to the Convention Relating to the Status of Refugees, 19 U.S.T. 6223, T.I.A.S. No. 6577, 606 U.N.T.S. 267, 1968, which gives considerable protection to stateless refugees. However, it is not a party to the United Nations Convention relating to the Status of Stateless Persons, 360 U.N.T.S. 117 (1954), or to the United Nations Convention on the Reduction of Statelessness (U.N. Doc. A/Conf. 9/15). The Convention on the Reduction of Statelessness bars denationalization except for serious acts of disloyalty, if the result would be to render persons stateless. It specifically forbids states to deprive a person of nationality upon marriage to a foreign national where that would result in the person being stateless.

*6. Nationality and citizenship distinguished.*

Citizenship is an ancient concept, but its implications differ from state to state. Today, it generally entails full political rights, including the right to vote and hold office, and many states accord important rights and benefits to citizens only. Nationality has international consequences, notably for diplomatic protection and jurisdiction, Comment a. United States law distinguishes between nationality and citizenship. See §212, Comment a.

*7. Residence under international law.*

Under the International Covenant on Civil and Political Rights, states recognize the right of a person lawfully resident in a state to choose his place of residence within the state. The resident alien is not subject to arbitrary expulsion. Arts. 12 and 13, International Covenant on Civil and Political Rights, 21 G.A.O.R. Supp. No. 16 at 52 (1966), 61 Am.J.Int'l L. 870 (1967). The United States has signed but not yet ratified the Covenant. Resident aliens are given special treatment in numerous articles of tax treaties, e.g., the Convention between the United States and the Federal Republic of Germany for the Avoidance of Double Taxation with respect to Taxes on Income of 1954, 5 U.S.T. 2768, T.I.A.S. No. 3133, 239 U.N.T.S. 3. See §413.

---

## Authors' Note

The remaining materials in this chapter address the withdrawal of the U.S. from acceptance of the compulsory jurisdiction before the ICJ. Material 7 is the case before the ICJ which was the catalyst for the U.S. withdrawal. Materials 8 and 9 provide the rationale and perspective of the U.S. for terminating its submission to compulsory jurisdiction. These selections portray the American standpoint by addressing concerns of sovereignty, national security, and misuse of the ICJ for political purposes. Material 10, an article from the Financial Times, discusses the ramifications of the American withdrawal. Material 11 represents the recommendation by the ABA International Law Section for the U.S. to once again accept ICJ compulsory jurisdiction.

---

## 7. Case Concerning Military and Paramilitary Activities, *Nicaragua v. United States*
### International Court of Justice, 1984

**Background:**

The Court faced a major challenge to its jurisdiction when Nicaragua sued the United States in 1984 over U.S. support of the Contras. (It was also a challenge, as we shall see, to respect for its judgments.) Nicaragua alleged in its Application that started the proceeding that the United States "is using military force against Nicaragua and intervening in Nicaragua's internal affairs.... The United States has created an "army" of more than 10,000 mercenaries ... installed them in more than ten base camps in Honduras along the border with Nicaragua, trained them, paid them, supplied them with arms, ammunition, food and medical supplies, and directed their attacks against human and economic targets inside Nicaragua."

1. On April 9, 1984, the Ambassador of the Republic of Nicaragua to the Netherlands filed in the Registry of the Court an Application instituting proceedings against the United States of America in respect of a dispute concerning responsibility for military and paramilitary activities in and against Nicaragua. In order to found the jurisdiction of the Court the Application relied on declarations made by the Parties accepting the compulsory jurisdiction of the Court under Article 36 of its Statute.

* * *

5. In the Memorial, the Republic of Nicaragua contended that, in addition to the basis of jurisdiction relied on in the Application, a Treaty of Friendship, Commerce and Navigation signed by the Parties in 1956 provides an independent basis for jurisdiction under Article 36, paragraph 1, of the Statute of the Court.

* * *

11. The present case concerns a dispute between the Government of the Republic of Nicaragua and the Government of the United States of America occasioned, Nicaragua contends, by certain military and paramilitary activities conducted in Nicaragua and in the waters off its coasts, responsibility for which is attributed by Nicaragua to the United States. In the present phase the case concerns the jurisdiction of the Court to entertain and pronounce upon this dispute, and the admissibility of the Application by which it was brought before the Court. The issue being thus limited, the Court will avoid not only all expressions of opinion on matters of substance, but also any pronouncement which might prejudge or appear to prejudge any eventual decision on the merits.

* * *

13. Article 36, paragraph 2, of the Statute of the Court provides. The United States made a declaration, pursuant to this provision, on August 14, 1946, containing certain reservations, to be examined below, and expressed to remain in force for a period of five years and thereafter until the expiration of six months after notice may be given to terminate this declaration.

On 6 April 1984 the Government of the United States of America deposited with the Secretary-General of the United Nations a notification, signed by the United States Secretary of State, Mr. George Shultz, referring to the Declaration deposited on 26 August 1946. This notification will be referred to, for convenience, as the "1984 notification."

14. In order to be able to rely upon the United States Declaration of 1946 to found jurisdiction in the present case, Nicaragua has to show that it is a "State accepting the same obligation" within the meaning of Article 36, paragraph 2, of the Statute. For this purpose, Nicaragua relies on a Declaration made by it on 24 September 1929 pursuant to Article 36, paragraph 2, of the Statute of the Permanent Court of International justice. [ ... ] Nicaragua relies further on paragraph 5 of Article 36 of the Statute of the present Court, which provides that:

> Declarations made under Article 36 of the Statute of the Permanent Court of international justice and which are still in force shall be deemed, as between the parties to the present Statute, to be acceptances of the compulsory jurisdiction of the International Court of justice for the period which they still have to run and in accordance with their terms.

15. The circumstances of Nicaragua's Declaration of 1929 were as follows.

* * *

[The United States challenged whether Nicaragua had ever become a party to the Statute of the Permanent Court of International justice (PCIJ). If Nicaragua had not, then Nicaragua could not have accepted the compulsory jurisdiction of the PCIJ, and consequently its 1929 acceptance was not still in force within the meaning of Article 36(5) of the Statute of the present ICJ.

The facts were that Nicaragua had formally decided to ratify the PCIJ Statute in 1934–1935. In 1939 Nicaragua sent a telegram to the Secretary-General of the League of Nations saying that that PCIJ Statute and a protocol "have already been ratified. Will send you in due course Instrument Ratification." The League of Nations informed Nicaragua in 1942 that no instrument had been received. The files of the League of Nations, moreover, contained no record of actually receiving the instrument of ratification. There was, of course, a world war going on during this period, and the instrument probably would have been sent by sea, which would possibly have made it subject to the attacks then on commercial shipping.

The Court found that, even though the instrument of ratification apparently never reached the League of Nations, the absence of the formality did not exclude the operation of Article 36(5) transferring the Declaration from the PCIJ to the ICJ. The Court noted that Nicaragua had signed and ratified the U.N. Charter and thereby accepted the ICJ Statute. The Court also found that the "constant acquiescence of Nicaragua in affirmations, to be found in United Nations and other publications, of its position as bound by the optional clause constitutes a valid manifestation of its intent to recognize the compulsory jurisdiction of the Court."

(¶ 109 of ICJ opinion.)

The Court then turned to the question of the 1984 notification by the United States that disputes with Central American states were excluded from the coverage of the 1946 U.S. declaration, effective immediately.]

* * *

59. Declarations of acceptance of the compulsory jurisdiction of the Court are facultative, unilateral engagements that States are absolutely free to make or not to make. In making the declaration a State is equally free either to do so unconditionally and without limit of time for its duration, or to qualify it with conditions or reservations. In particular, it may limit its effect to disputes arising after a certain date; or it may specify how long the declaration itself shall remain in force, or what notice (if any) will be required to terminate it. However, the unilateral nature of declarations does not signify that the State making the declaration is free to amend the scope and the contents of its solemn commitments as it pleases. In the Nuclear Tests cases the Court expressed its position on this point very clearly:

> It is well recognized that declarations made by way of unilateral acts, concerning legal or factual situations, may have the effect of creating legal obligations. Declarations of this kind may be, and often are, very specific. When it is the intention of the State making the declaration that it should become bound according to its terms, that intention confers on the declaration the character of a legal undertaking, the State being thenceforth legally required to follow a course of conduct consistent with the declaration. (I.Cj. Reports 1974, p.267, para. 43; p.472, para. 46.)

60. In fact, the declarations, even though they are unilateral acts, establish a series of bilateral engagements with other States accepting the same obligation of compulsory ju-

risdiction, in which the conditions, reservations and time-limit clauses are taken into consideration. [ ... ]

61. The most important question relating to the effect of the 1984 notification is whether the United States was free to disregard the clause of six months' notice which, freely and by its own choice, it had appended to its 1946 Declaration. In so doing the United States entered into an obligation which is binding upon it vis-a-vis other States parties to the Optional-Clause system. Although the United States retained the right to modify the contents of the 1946 Declaration or to terminate it, a power which is inherent in any unilateral act of a State, it has, nevertheless assumed an inescapable obligation towards other States accepting the Optional Clause, by stating formally and solemnly that any such change should take effect only after six months have elapsed as from the date of notice.

62. The United States has argued that the Nicaraguan 1929 Declaration, being of undefined duration, is liable to immediate termination, without previous notice, and that therefore Nicaragua has not accepted "the same obligation" as itself for the purposes of Article 36, paragraph 2, and consequently may not rely on the six months' notice proviso against the United States. The Court does not however consider that this argument entitles the United States validly to act in non-application of the time-limit proviso included in the 1946 Declaration. The notion of reciprocity is concerned with the scope and substance of the commitments entered into, including reservations, and not with the formal conditions of their creation, duration or extinction. It appears clearly that reciprocity cannot be invoked in order to excuse departure from the terms of a State's own declaration, whatever its scope, limitations or conditions. As the Court observed in the Interhandel case:

> Reciprocity enables the State which has made the wider acceptance of the jurisdiction of the Court to rely upon the reservations to the acceptance laid down by the other party. There the effect of reciprocity ends. It cannot justify a State, in this instance, the United States, in relying upon a restriction which the other party, Switzerland, has not included in its own Declaration. (I.C.J. Reports 1959, p. 23.)

> The maintenance in force of the United States Declaration for six months after notice of termination is a positive undertaking, flowing from the time-limit clause, but the Nicaraguan Declaration contains no express restriction at all. It is therefore clear that the United States is not in a position to invoke reciprocity as a basis for its action in making the 1984 notification which purported to modify the content of the 1946 Declaration.

\* \* \*

63. Moreover, since the United States purported to act on 6 April 1984 in such a way as to modify its 1946 Declaration with sufficiently immediate effect to bar an Application filed on 9 April 1984, it would be necessary, if reciprocity is to be relied on, for the Nicaraguan Declaration to be terminable with immediate effect. But the right of immediate termination of declarations with indefinite duration is far from established. It appears from the requirements of good faith that they should be treated, by analogy, according to the law of treaties, which requires a reasonable time for withdrawal from or termination of treaties that contain no provision regarding the duration of their validity. Since Nicaragua has in fact not manifested any intention to withdraw its own declaration, the question of what reasonable period of notice would legally be required does not need to be further examined: it need only be observed that from 6 to 9 April would not amount to a "reasonable time."

\* \* \*

65. In sum, the six months' notice clause forms an important integral part of the United States Declaration and it is a condition that must be complied with in case of either termination or modification.

Consequently, the 1984 notification, in the present case, cannot override the obligation of the United States to submit to the compulsory jurisdiction of the Court vis-a-vis Nicaragua, a State accepting the same obligation.

\* \* \*

67. The question remains to be resolved whether the United States Declaration of 1946, though not suspended in its effects vis-a-vis Nicaragua by the 1984 notification, constitutes the necessary consent of the United States to the jurisdiction of the Court in the present case, taking into account the reservations which were attached to the declaration. Specifically, the United States has invoked proviso (c) to that declaration, which provides that the United States acceptance of the Court's compulsory jurisdiction shall not extend to disputes arising under a multilateral treaty, unless (1) all parties to the treaty affected by the decision are also parties to the case before the Court, or (2) the United States of America specially agrees to jurisdiction.

This reservation will be referred to for convenience as the "multilateral treaty reservation." Of the two remaining provisos to the declaration, it has not been suggested that proviso (a), referring to disputes the solution of which is entrusted to other tribunals, has any relevance to the present case. As for proviso (b), excluding jurisdiction over "disputes with regard to matters which are essentially within the domestic jurisdiction of the United States of America as determined by the United States of America," the United States has informed the Court that it has determined not to invoke this proviso, but "without prejudice to the rights of the United States under that proviso in relation to any subsequent pleadings, proceedings, or cases before this Court."

68. The United States points out that Nicaragua relies in its Application on four multilateral treaties, namely the Charter of the United Nations, the Charter of the Organization of American States, the Montevideo Convention on Rights and Duties of States of 26 December 1933, and the Havana Convention on the Rights and Duties of States in the Event of Civil Strife of 20 February 1928. In so far as the dispute brought before the Court is thus one "arising under" those multilateral treaties, since the United States has not specially agreed to jurisdiction here, the Court may, it is claimed, exercise jurisdiction only if all treaty parties affected by a prospective decision of the Court are also parties to the case. The United States explains the rationale of its multilateral treaty reservation as being that it protects the United States and third States from the inherently prejudicial effects of partial adjudication of complex multiparty disputes. Emphasizing that the reservation speaks only of States "affected by" a decision, and not of States having a legal right or interest in the proceedings, the United States identifies, as States parties to the four multilateral treaties above mentioned which would be "affected," in a legal and practical sense, by adjudication of the claims submitted to the Court, Nicaragua's three Central American neighbors, Honduras, Costa Rica and El Salvador.

69. The United States recognizes that the multilateral treaty reservation applies in terms only to "disputes arising under a multilateral treaty," and notes that Nicaragua in its Application asserts also that the United States has "violated fundamental rules of general and customary international law." However, it is nonetheless the submission of the United States that all the claims set forth in Nicaragua's Application are outside the jurisdiction of the Court. According to the argument of the United States, Nicaragua's claims styled as violations of general and customary international law merely restate or paraphrase its

claims and allegations based expressly on the multilateral treaties mentioned above, and Nicaragua in its Memorial itself states that its "fundamental contention" is that the conduct of the United States is a violation of the United Nations Charter and the Charter of the Organization of American States. The evidence of customary law offered by Nicaragua consists of General Assembly resolutions that merely reiterate or elucidate the United Nations Charter; nor can the Court determine the merits of Nicaragua's claims formulated under customary and general international law without interpreting and applying the United Nations Charter and the Organization of American States Charter, and since the multilateral treaty reservation bars adjudication of claims based on those treaties, it bars all Nicaragua's claims.

\* \* \*

73. [ ... ] The Court cannot dismiss the claims of Nicaragua under principles of customary and general international law, simply because such principles have been enshrined in the texts of the conventions relied upon by Nicaragua. The fact that the above-mentioned principles, recognized as such, have been codified or embodied in multilateral conventions does not mean that they cease to exist and to apply as principles of customary law, even as regards countries that are parties to such conventions. Principles such as those of the non-use of force, non-intervention, respect for the independence and territorial integrity of States, and the freedom of navigation, continue to be binding as part of customary international law, despite the operation of provisions of conventional law in which they have been incorporated. Therefore, since the claim before the Court in this case is not confined to violation of the multilateral conventional provisions invoked, it would not in any event be barred by the multilateral treaty reservation in the United States 1946 Declaration.

74. The Court would observe, further, that all three States have made declarations of acceptance of the compulsory jurisdiction of the Court, and are free, at any time, to come before the Court, on the basis of Article 36, paragraph 2, with an application instituting proceedings against Nicaragua — a State which is also bound by the compulsory jurisdiction of the Court by an unconditional declaration without limit of duration — if they should find that they might be affected by the future decision of the Court. Moreover, these States are also free to resort to the incidental procedures of intervention under Articles 62 and 63 of the Statute, to the second of which El Salvador has already unsuccessfully resorted in the jurisdictional phase of the proceedings, but to which it may revert in the merits phase of the case. There is therefore no question of these States being defenseless against any consequences that may arise out of adjudication by the Court, or of their needing the protection of the multilateral treaty reservation of the United States.

\* \* \*

76. At any rate, this is a question concerning matters of substance relating to the merits of the case: obviously the question of what States may be "affected" by the decision on the merits is not in itself a jurisdictional problem.... [The Court has no choice but to avail itself of Article 79, paragraph 7, of the present Rules of Court, and declare that the objection based on the multilateral treaty reservation of the United States Declaration of Acceptance does not possess ... an exclusively preliminary character, and that consequently it does not constitute an obstacle for the Court to entertain the proceedings instituted by Nicaragua under the Application of 9 April 1984.

[FCN TREATY]

77. [ ... I]n its Memorial [Nicaragua] invokes also a 1956 Treaty of Friendship, Commerce and Navigation between Nicaragua and the United States as a complementary foundation for the Court's jurisdiction.

\* \* \*

81. Article XXIV, paragraph 2, of the Treaty [ ... ], signed at Managua on 21 January 1956, reads as follows:

> Any dispute between the Parties as to the interpretation or application of the present Treaty, not satisfactorily adjusted by diplomacy, shall be submitted to the International Court of justice, unless the Parties agree to settlement by some other pacific means.

The treaty entered into force on 24 May 1958 on exchange of ratifications. [ ... ] The provisions of Article XXIV, paragraph 2, are in terms which are very common in bilateral treaties of amity or of establishment, and the intention of the parties in accepting such clauses is clearly to provide for such a right of unilateral recourse to the Court in the absence of agreement to employ some other pacific means of settlement (cf. United States Diplomatic and Consular Staff in Tehran, I.C.J. Reports 1980, p.27, para. 52). [ ... ]

82. Nicaragua in its Memorial submits that the 1956 Treaty has been and was being violated by the military and paramilitary activities of the United States in and against Nicaragua, as described in the Application; specifically, it is submitted that these activities directly violate the following Articles:

> Article XIX. — providing for freedom of commerce and navigation, and for vessels of either party to have liberty "to come with their cargoes to all ports, places and waters of such other party open to foreign commerce and navigation," and to be accorded national treatment and most favored-nation treatment within those ports, places and waters.

> Article XIV. — forbidding the imposition of restrictions or prohibitions on the importation of any product of the other party, or on the exportation of any product to the territories of the other party. [ ... ]

> Article XX. — providing for freedom of transit through the territories of each party. [ ... ]

83. Taking into account these Articles of the Treaty of 1956, particularly the provision in, inter alia, Article XIX, for the freedom of commerce and navigation, and the references in the Preamble to peace and friendship, there can be no doubt that [ ... ] there is a dispute between the Parties, inter alia, as to the "interpretation or application" of the Treaty. That dispute is also clearly one which is not "satisfactorily adjusted by diplomacy" within the meaning of Article XXIV of the 1956 Treaty. [ ... ] Accordingly, the Court finds that [ ... ] the Court has jurisdiction under that Treaty to entertain such claims. [ ... ]

[ADMISSIBILITY]

84. The Court now turns to the question of the admissibility of the Application of Nicaragua. The United States of America contended in its Counter-Memorial that Nicaragua's Application is inadmissible on five separate grounds, each of which, it is said, is sufficient to establish such inadmissibility, whether considered as a legal bar to adjudication or as "a matter requiring the exercise of prudential discretion in the interest of the integrity of the judicial function." Some of these grounds have in fact been presented in terms suggesting that they are matters of competence or jurisdiction rather than admissibility, but it does not appear to be of critical importance how they are classified in this respect. These grounds will now be examined. [ ... ]

86. The first ground of inadmissibility relied on by the United States is that Nicaragua has failed to bring before the Court parties whose presence and participation is neces-

sary for the rights of those parties to be protected and for the adjudication of the issues raised in the Application. The United States first asserts that adjudication of Nicaragua's claim would necessarily implicate the rights and obligations of other States, in particular those of Honduras, since it is alleged that Honduras has allowed its territory to be used as a staging ground for unlawful uses of force against Nicaragua. [ … ]

88. There is no doubt that in appropriate circumstances the Court will decline [ … ] to exercise the jurisdiction conferred upon it where the legal interests of a State not party to the proceedings "would not only be affected by a decision, but would form the very subject-matter of the decision" (I.C.J. Reports 1954, p.32). Where however claims of a legal nature are made by an Applicant against a Respondent in proceedings before the Court, and made the subject of submissions, the Court has in principle merely to decide upon those submissions, with binding force for the parties only, and no other State, in accordance with Article 59 of the Statute. As the Court has already indicated (paragraph 74, above) other States which consider that they may be affected are free to institute separate proceedings, or to employ the procedure of intervention. There is no trace, either in the Statute or in the practice of international tribunals, of an "indispensable parties" rule of the kind argued for by the United States. [ … ]

89. Secondly, the United States regards the Application as inadmissible because each of Nicaragua's allegations constitutes no more than a reformulation and restatement of a single fundamental claim, that the United States is engaged in an unlawful use of armed force, or breach of the peace, or acts of aggression against Nicaragua, a matter which is committed by the Charter and by practice to the competence of other organs, in particular the United Nations Security Council. All allegations of this kind are confided to the political organs of the Organization for consideration and determination; the United States quotes Article 24 of the Charter, which confers. upon the Security Council "primary responsibility for the maintenance of international peace and security." [ … ]

\* \* \*

91. It will be convenient to deal with this alleged ground of inadmissibility together with the third ground advanced by the United States namely that the Court should hold the Application of Nicaragua to be inadmissible in view of the subject-matter of the Application and the position of the Court within the United Nations system, including the impact of proceedings before the Court on the ongoing exercise of the "inherent right of individual or collective self-defence" under Article 51 of the Charter. This is, it is argued, a reason why the Court may not properly exercise "subject-matter jurisdiction" over Nicaragua's claims. Under this head, the United States repeats its contention that the Nicaraguan Application requires the Court to determine that the activities complained of constitute a threat to the peace, a breach of the peace, or an act of aggression, and proceeds to demonstrate that the political organs of the United Nations, to which such matters are entrusted by the Charter, have acted, and are acting, in respect of virtually identical claims placed before them by Nicaragua. [ … ]

\* \* \*

93. The United States is thus arguing that the matter was essentially one for the Security Council since it concerned a complaint by Nicaragua involving the use of force. However, having regard to the United States [ … ]

\* \* \*

108. In the light of the foregoing, the Court is unable to accept either that there is any requirement of prior exhaustion of regional negotiating processes as a precondition to seiz-

ing the Court; or that the existence of the Contadora process constitutes in this case an obstacle to the examination by the Court of the Nicaraguan Application and judicial determination in due course of the submissions of the Parties in the case. The Court is therefore unable to declare the Application inadmissible, as requested by the United States, on any of the grounds it has advanced as requiring such a finding. [ ... ]

\* \* \*

113. For these reasons, the Court,

(1)(a) finds, by eleven votes to five, that it has jurisdiction to entertain the Application filed by the Republic of Nicaragua on 9 April 1984, on the basis of Article 36, paragraphs 2 and 5, of the Statute of the Court;

\* \* \*

(b) finds, by fourteen votes to two, that it has jurisdiction to entertain the Application filed by the Republic of Nicaragua on 9 April 1984, in so far as that Application relates to a dispute concerning the interpretation or application of the Treaty of Friendship, Commerce and Navigation between the United States of America and the Republic of Nicaragua signed at Managua on 21 January 1956, on the basis of Article XXIV of that Treaty;

\* \* \*

(c) finds, by fifteen votes to one, that it has jurisdiction to entertain the case:

\* \* \*

(2) finds, unanimously, that the said Application is admissible.

---

# 8. Text of U.S. Statement on Withdrawal from Case before the World Court
## 1985

The United States has consistently taken the position that the proceedings initiated by Nicaragua in the International Court of Justice are a misuse of the Court for political purposes and that the Court lacks jurisdiction and competence over such a case. The Court's decision of Nov. 26, 1984, finding that it has jurisdiction, is contrary to law and fact. With great reluctance, the United States has decided not to participate in further proceedings in this case.

### U.S. Policy In Central America

United States policy in Central America has been to promote democracy, reform and freedom; to support economic development; to help provide a security shield against those—like Nicaragua, Cuba and the U.S.S.R—who seek to spread tyranny by force, and to support dialogue and negotiation both within and among the countries of the region. In providing a security shield, we have acted in the exercise of the inherent right of collective self-defense, enshrined in the United Nations Charter and the Rio Treaty. We have done so in defense of the vital national security interests of the United States and in support of the peace and security of the hemisphere.

Nicaragua's efforts to portray the conflict in Central America as a bilateral issue between itself and the United States cannot hide the obvious fact that the scope of the problem is far broader. In the security dimension, it involves a wide range of issues: Nicaragua's huge buildup of Soviet arms and Cuban advisers, its cross-border attacks and promotion of insurgency within various nations of the region, and the activities of indigenous opposition groups within Nicaragua. It is also clear that any effort to stop the fighting in the region would be fruitless unless it were part of a comprehensive approach to political settlement, regional security, economic reform and development, and the spread of democracy and human rights.

## Role of the International Court of Justice

The conflict in Central America, therefore, is not a narrow legal dispute; it is an inherently political problem that is not appropriate for judicial resolution. The conflict will be solved only by political and diplomatic means—not through a judicial tribunal. The International Court of Justice was never intended to resolve issues of collective security and self-defense and is patently unsuited for such a role. Unlike domestic courts, the World Court has jurisdiction only to the extent that nation-states have consented to it. When the United States accepted the Court's compulsory jurisdiction in 1946, it certainly never conceived of such a role for the Court in such controversies. Nicaragua's suit against the United States—which includes an absurd demand for hundreds of millions of dollars in reparations—is a blatant misuse of the Court for political and propaganda purposes.

As one of the foremost supporters of the International Court of Justice, the United States is one of only 44 of 159 member states of the United Nations that have accepted the Court's compulsory jurisdiction at all. Furthermore, the vast majority of these 44 states have attached to their acceptance reservations that substantially limit its scope. Along with the United Kingdom, the United States is one of only two permanent members of the U.N. Security Council that have accepted that jurisdiction. And of the 16 judges now claiming to sit in judgment on the United States in this case, 11 are from countries that do not accept the Court's compulsory jurisdiction.

Few if any other countries in the world would have appeared at all in a case such as this which they considered to be improperly brought. Nevertheless, out of its traditional respect for the rule of law, the United States has participated fully in the Court's proceedings thus far, to present its view that the Court does not have jurisdiction or competence in this case.

## The Decision of Nov. 26

On Nov. 26, 1984, the Court decided—in spite of the overwhelming evidence before it—that it does have jurisdiction over Nicaragua's claims and that it will proceed to a full hearing on the merits of these claims.

This decision is erroneous as a matter of law and is based on a misreading and distortion of the evidence and precedent:

The Court chose to ignore the irrefutable evidence that Nicaragua itself never accepted the Court's compulsory jurisdiction. Allowing Nicaragua to sue where it could not be sued was a violation of the Court's basic principle of reciprocity, which necessarily underlies our own consent to the Court's compulsory jurisdiction. On this pivotal issue in the Nov. 26 decision—decided by a vote of 11–5—dissenting judges called the Court's judgment "untenable" and "astonishing" and described the U.S. position as "beyond doubt." We agree.

El Salvador sought to participate in the suit to argue that the Court was not the appropriate forum to address the Central American conflict. El Salvador declared that it was under armed attack by Nicaragua and, in exercise of its inherent right of self-defense, had requested assistance from the United States. The Court rejected El Salvador's application summarily—without giving reasons and without even granting El Salvador a hearing, in violation of El Salvador's right and in disregard of the Court's own rules.

The Court's decision is a marked departure from its past, cautious approach to jurisdictional questions. The haste with which the Court proceeded to a judgment on these issues—noted in several of the separate and dissenting opinions—only adds to the impression that the Court is determined to find in favor of Nicaragua in this case.

For these reasons, we are forced to conclude that our continued participation in this case could not be justified.

In addition, much of the evidence that would establish Nicaragua's aggression against its neighbors is of a highly sensitive intelligence character. We will not risk U.S. national security by presenting such sensitive material in public or before a Court that includes two judges from Warsaw Pact nations. This problem only confirms the reality that such issues are not suited for the International Court of Justice.

### Longer-Term Implications of the Court's Decision

The Court's decision raises a basic issue of sovereignty. The right of a state to defend itself or to participate in collective self-defense against aggression is an inherent sovereign right that cannot be compromised by an inappropriate proceeding before the World Court.

We are profoundly concerned also about the long-term implications for the Court itself. The decision of Nov. 26 represents an overreaching of the Court's limits, a departure from its tradition of judicial restraint and a risky venture into treacherous political waters. We have seen in the United Nations, in the last decade or more, how international organizations have become more and more politicized against the interests of the Western democracies. It would be a tragedy if these trends were to infect the International Court of Justice. We hope this will not happen, because a politicized Court would mean the end of the Court as a serious, respected institution. Such a result would do grievous harm to the goal of the rule of law.

These implications compel us to clarify our 1946 acceptance of the Court's compulsory jurisdiction. Important premises on which our initial acceptance was based now appear to be in doubt in this type of case. We are therefore taking steps to clarify our acceptance of the Court's compulsory jurisdiction in order to make explicit what we have understood from the beginning, namely that cases of this nature are not proper for adjudication by the Court.

We will continue to support the International Court of Justice where it acts within its competence—as, for example, where specific disputes are brought before it by special agreement of the parties. One such example is the recent case between the United States and Canada before a special five-member Chamber of the Court to delimit the maritime boundary in the Gulf of Maine area. Nonetheless, because of our commitment to the rule of law, we must declare our firm conviction that the course on which the Court may now be embarked could do enormous harm to it as an institution and to the cause of international law.

---

## 9. U.S. Terminates Acceptance of ICJ Compulsory Jurisdiction
### Department of State Bulletin, 1986

SECRETARY'S LETTER TO U.N. SECRETARY-GENERAL, OCT. 7, 1985

Dear Mr. Secretary-General:

I have the honor on behalf of the Government of the United States of America to refer to the declaration of my Government of 26 August 1946, as modified by my note of 6

April 1984, concerning the acceptance by the United States of America of the compulsory jurisdiction of the International Court of Justice, and to state that the aforesaid declaration is hereby terminated, with effect six months from the date hereof.

Sincerely yours, GEORGE P. SHULTZ

## DEPARTMENT STATEMENT, OCT. 7, 1985[1]

In accordance with the instructions of the President, on October 7, 1985, the Secretary of State deposited with the Secretary-General of the United Nations formal notice of termination of the U.S. declaration, deposited on August 26, 1946, accepting the optional compulsory jurisdiction of the International Court of Justice (ICJ). This action will become effective 6 months after the deposit of that notice.

This decision is fully compatible with the Statute of the ICJ, which leaves it to the discretion of each state to determine its relationship with the World Court. That Statute also explicitly refers to the right to condition acceptance of the Court's compulsory jurisdiction on the principle of reciprocity.

When President Truman signed the U.S. declaration accepting the World Court's optional compulsory jurisdiction on August 1, 1946, this country expected that other states would soon act similarly. The essential underpinning of the U.N. system, of which the World Court is a part, is the principle of universality. Unfortunately, few other states have followed our example. Fewer than one-third of the world's states have accepted the Court's compulsory jurisdiction, and the Soviet Union and its allies have never been among them. Nor, in our judgment, has Nicaragua. Of the five permanent members of the U.N. Security Council, only the United States and the United Kingdom have submitted to the Court's compulsory jurisdiction.

Our experience with compulsory jurisdiction has been deeply disappointing. We have never been able to use our acceptance of compulsory jurisdiction to bring other states before the Court but have ourselves been sued three times. In 1946 we accepted the risks of our submitting to the Court's compulsory jurisdiction because we believed that the respect owed to the Court by other states and the Court's own appreciation of the need to adhere scrupulously to its proper judicial role would prevent the Court's process from being abused for political ends. Those assumptions have now been proved wrong. As a result, the President has concluded that continuation of our acceptance of the Court's compulsory jurisdiction would be contrary to our commitment to the principle of the equal application of the law and would endanger our vital national interests.

On January 18, 1985, we announced that the United States would no longer participate in the proceedings instituted against it by Nicaragua in the International Court of Justice. Neither the rule of law nor the search for peace in Central America would have been served by further U.S. participation. The objectives of the ICJ to which we subscribe — the peaceful adjudication of international disputes — were being subverted by the effort of Nicaragua and its Cuban and Soviet sponsors to use the Court as a political weapon. Indeed, the Court itself has never seen fit to accept jurisdiction over any other political conflict involving ongoing hostilities.

This action does not signify any diminution of our traditional commitment to international law and to the International Court of Justice in performing its proper functions. U.S. acceptance of the World Court's jurisdiction under Article 36(1) of its Statute re-

---

1. Made available to news correspondents by State Department deputy spokesman Charles Redman.

mains strong. We are committed to the proposition that the jurisdiction of the Court comprises all cases which the parties refer to it and all matters that are appropriate for the Court to handle pursuant to the U.N. Charter or treaties and conventions in force. We will continue to make use of the Court to resolve disputes whenever appropriate and will encourage others to do likewise. Indeed, as we have announced today, we have reached agreement in principle with Italy to take a longstanding dispute to the Court.

## LEGAL ADVISER SOFAER STATEMENT, DEC. 4, 1985[2]

I welcome this opportunity to discuss the background to the President's decision of October 7 terminating our acceptance of the compulsory jurisdiction of the International Court of Justice (ICJ). This decision will take effect 6 months from that date. I will discuss what the President's decision means in practical terms before turning to some of the reasons for it.

### Jurisdiction of the Court

The ICJ has limited jurisdiction, based on its Statute and on the consent of states. Under Article 36(1) of the Court's Statute, the ICJ has jurisdiction when states sign a special agreement referring a dispute to it or are parties to a treaty providing for ICJ dispute resolution. The President's action does not affect this basis for jurisdiction. Indeed, we have just agreed with Italy to submit an important dispute, involving millions of dollars, to the Court for adjudication. We also are party to some 60 treaties providing for adjudication of disputes by the ICJ.

The second basis for ICJ jurisdiction exists when a state accepts the Court's compulsory jurisdiction under Article 36(2) of the Statute—the so-called optional clause. Historically, acceptance of compulsory jurisdiction has been less important as a basis for the Court's work than specific agreement between the parties to a dispute.

A state accepts compulsory jurisdiction by depositing with the Secretary-General of the United Nations a declaration to the effect that it agrees to be sued by any state depositing a similar declaration. In return, the filing state may bring suit under compulsory jurisdiction against any other state filing such a declaration. Generally, a state has no way of knowing in advance by whom or on what issue a suit may be filed. A declaration covers any issue of international law, except to the extent that the state excludes specific disputes or categories of disputes. A state faced with a suit under compulsory jurisdiction may invoke any exclusion in its declaration and, on the basis of reciprocity, any exclusion in its opponent's declaration to seek to defeat jurisdiction. It also may raise nonjurisdictional objections to the Court's taking the case. If the parties disagree over the scope of a declaration or its exclusions, the Court itself decides the issue.

Under the Court's Statute, a state is free to accept or to decline the Court's compulsory jurisdiction. A state accepting the Court's compulsory jurisdiction likewise is free to terminate or modify its acceptance whenever the state concerned believes that doing so would serve its interests. The President's action terminating our 1946 declaration, thus, is entirely consistent with our international legal obligations.

The President's action also is consistent with his domestic legal authority. Declarations under Article 36(2) of the Statute are not treaties under either international law or the Constitution. Nevertheless, in 1946 the executive branch considered that congressional approval of the declaration was necessary for several reasons. Any such a declaration necessarily entails an open-ended exposure to suit, including potential financial

---

2. Made before the Senate Foreign Relations Committee by Abraham D. Sofaer.

liability. In addition, Congress traditionally had been reluctant to allow the President to enter into compulsory third-party dispute settlement arrangements, as the fate of repeated executive efforts to have the United States accept the jurisdiction of the predecessor Court, the Permanent Court of International Justice, showed.

The termination of the 1946 declaration, on the other hand, does not expose the United States to new commitments or obligations. On the contrary, it reduces or eliminates that exposure. Furthermore, by its terms, the declaration authorizes termination on 6 months' notice, and our October 7 note is consistent with that condition. Finally, the Constitution allows the President unilaterally to terminate treaties consistent with their terms; and his authority is even clearer with respect to lesser instruments such as the 1946 declaration.

### Reasons for U.S. Review

Our experience in the case instituted against the United States by Nicaragua in April 1984 provided the chief motivation for the Administration's review of our acceptance of the Court's compulsory jurisdiction. The principal basis of jurisdiction cited by Nicaragua in bringing that case was the 1946 U.S. declaration accepting compulsory jurisdiction. We believed at the time, and still believe, that Nicaragua itself never had validly accepted the Court's compulsory jurisdiction. More important, Nicaragua sought to bring before the Court political and security disputes that were never previously considered part of the Court's mandate to resolve. In our view, the Court's decision last November that Nicaragua had, indeed, accepted compulsory jurisdiction and that Nicaragua's claims were justifiable could not be supported as a matter of law. These considerations led the President to decide last January that we would no longer participate in the case.

The Court's decision also caused us to undertake a thorough evaluation of our 1946 declaration and its place in the system of compulsory jurisdiction established by Article 36(2) of the Court's Statute. That we were evaluating these questions was well known. The issues at stake were considered and debated in government and private groups interested in this question. All the relevant points were carefully considered.

We recognized, first of all, that the hopes originally placed in compulsory jurisdiction by the architects of the Court's Statute have never been realized and will not be realized in the foreseeable future. We had hoped that wide-spread acceptance of compulsory jurisdiction and its successful employment in actual cases would increase confidence in judicial settlement of international disputes and, thus, eventually lead to its universal acceptance.

Experience has dashed these hopes only 47 of the 162 states entitled to accept the Court's compulsory jurisdiction now do so. This number represents a proportion of states that is substantially lower than in the late 1940s. The United Kingdom is the only other permanent member of the U.N. Security Council that accepts compulsory jurisdiction in any form. Neither the Soviet Union nor any other Soviet-bloc state has ever accepted compulsory jurisdiction. Many of our closet friends and allies—such as France, Italy, and the Federal Republic of Germany—do not accept compulsory jurisdiction. Moreover, a substantial number of the states accepting compulsory jurisdiction have attached reservations to their acceptances that deprive them of much of their meaning. The United Kingdom, for example, retains the power to decline to accept the Court's jurisdiction in any dispute at any time before a case is actually filed.

Compulsory jurisdiction cases have not been the principal part of the Court's overall jurisprudence. Of some 50 contentious cases between 1946 and the end of 1983, 22 were based on the Court's compulsory jurisdiction, of which only five resulted in final judgment on the merits. The last case decided under the Court's compulsory jurisdiction, the

Temple of Preah Vihear, was completed in 1962. In the remaining 17 cases, objections to the Court's jurisdiction were sustained in 13; four were dismissed on other grounds.

Another consideration we weighed is the fact that, although we have tried seven times, we have never been able successfully to bring a state before the Court. We have been barred from achieving this result not only by the fact that few other states accept compulsory jurisdiction but also by the principle of reciprocity as applied to our 1946 declaration. That principle allows a respondent state to invoke any reservation in the applicant state's declaration to seek to defeat the Court's jurisdiction. Thus, respondent states may invoke reservations in our 1946 declaration against us. The so-called Connally reservation in our 1946 declaration provides that the United States does not accept compulsory jurisdiction over any dispute involving matters essentially within the domestic jurisdiction of the United States, as determined by the United States. In other words, we reserve to ourselves the power to determine whether the Court has jurisdiction over us in a particular case. Any state we sue may avail itself of that power on a reciprocal basis to defeat jurisdiction.

This is, in fact, precisely what happened when we tried to sue Bulgaria in 1957 on claims arising out of the loss of American lives and property when Bulgaria shot down an unarmed civilian airliner that had strayed into its airspace. Bulgaria claimed that the Court had no jurisdiction because the matter in dispute was within Bulgarian domestic jurisdiction as determined by Bulgaria. Even though we had pledged never to invoke our Connally reservation in bad faith to cover a manifestly international dispute, we were compelled to acknowledge that its invocation in any case would be binding as a matter of law. Hence, Bulgaria's reciprocal invocation of the Connally reservation forced us to discontinue the case.

On a more general level, other countries, the international legal community, and, indeed, the executive branch have severely criticized the "self-judging" nature of the Connally reservation. Some commentators even argue that the Connally reservation made the 1946 declaration a legal nullity because of its wholly unilateral and potentially limitless character. Certainly, that reservation has undercut the example the United States tried to set for other countries by its acceptance of compulsory jurisdiction.

For these reasons we have never been able successfully to bring another state before the Court on the basis of our acceptance of compulsory jurisdiction. On the other hand, we have been sued under it three times: by France in the Rights of Nationals of the United States in Morocco case in 1950–1952; by Switzerland in the Interhandel case in 1957–1959; and, finally, by Nicaragua last year.

The terms of our acceptance of compulsory jurisdiction contain an additional weakness. Nothing in it prevents another state from depositing an acceptance of compulsory jurisdiction solely for the purpose of bringing suit against the United States and, thereafter, withdrawing its acceptance to avoid being sued by anyone in any other matter. Students of the Court long have recognized that this "sitting duck" or "hit-and-run" problem is one of the principal disadvantages to the system of compulsory jurisdiction under Article 36(2). It places the minority of states that have accepted compulsory jurisdiction at the mercy of the majority that have not.

The Court's composition also is a source of institutional weakness. At present, 9 of 15 judges come from states that do not accept compulsory jurisdiction; most of these states have never used the Court at all. Judges are elected by the General Assembly and Security Council, frequently after intense electioneering. One reasonably may expect at least some judges to be sensitive to the impact of their decisions on their standing with the

U.N. majority. Whereas in 1945 the United Nations had some 50 members, most which were aligned with the United States and shared its views regarding world order, there are now 160 members. A great many of these cannot be counted on to share our view of the original constitutional conception of the U.N. Charter, particularly with regard to the special position of the permanent members of the Security Council in the maintenance of international place and security. This same majority often opposes the United States on important international questions.

## The Nicaragua Case

None of the weaknesses deriving from the Court's composition and our 1946 declaration is new. We have hitherto endured them on the assumption that the respect states owed to the Court and the Court's own scrupulous adherence to its judicial role would insulate us from abuses of the Court's process for political or propaganda ends. The Nicaragua case showed that it would be unrealistic to continue to rely on that assumption.

Several aspects of the Court's decisions in the Nicaragua case were disturbing. First, the Court departed from its traditionally cautious approach to finding jurisdiction. It disregarded fundamental defects in Nicaragua's claim to have accepted compulsory jurisdiction. This question involves more than a legal technicality. It goes to the heart of the Court's jurisdiction, which is the consent of states. International law—in particular, the Court's own Statute—establishes precise rules that states must follow in order to manifest that consent. The purpose of such technical rules is to ensure that a state's consent is genuine and that all other states are given objective notice of it. Nicaragua never complied with those rules, and the historical evidence makes clear that its failure to do so was deliberate and designed to ensure that Nicaragua could never be sued successfully under Article 36(2). A majority of the Court, on the other hand, was prepared to discover an exception to those rules that allowed Nicaragua to bring suit, an exception that is inconsistent with the Court's prior jurisprudence on the subject. The result-oriented illogic of the majority's position was vigorously exposed in the opinions of the dissenting judges.

Furthermore, the Court engaged in unprecedented procedural actions—such as rejecting without even a hearing El Salvador's application to intervene as of right—that betrayed a predisposition to find that it had jurisdiction and that Nicaragua's claims were justiciable, regardless of the overwhelming legal case to the contrary. In the particular case of the Salvadoran intervention, the Court ignored Article 63 of the Statute, which deprives the Court of discretion to reject such interventions. The Court sought to cover itself by holding out the possibility of accepting the Salvadoran intervention at the merits stage—at which point Salvadoran objections to the Court's jurisdiction and the justiciability of Nicaragua's claims would have been too late.

Even more disturbing, for the first time in its history, the Court has sought to assert jurisdiction over a controversy concerning claims related to an ongoing use of armed force. This action concerns every state. It is inconsistent with the structure of the U.N. system. The only prior case involving use-of-force issues—the Corfu Channel case—went to the Court after the disputed actions had ceased and the Security Council had determined that the matter was suitable for judicial consideration. In the Nicaragua case, the Court rejected without a soundly reasoned explanation our arguments that claims of the sort made by Nicaragua were intended by the U.N. Charter exclusively for resolution by political mechanisms—in particular, the Security Council and the Contadora process—and that claims to the exercise of the inherent right of individual and collective self-defense were excluded by Article 51 of the Charter from review by the Court.

I cannot predict whether the Court's approach to these fundamental Charter issues in the jurisdictional phase of the Nicaragua case will be followed in the Court's judgment on the merits. Nevertheless, the record gives us little reason for confidence. It shows a Court majority apparently prepared to act in ways profoundly inconsistent with the structure of the Charter and the Court's place in that structure. The Charter gives to the Security Council—not the Court—the responsibility for evaluating and resolving claims concerning the use of armed force and claims of self-defense under Article 51. With regard to the situation in Central America, the Security Council exercised its responsibility by endorsing the Contadora process as the appropriate mechanism for resolving the interlocking political, security, economic, and other concerns of the region.

## Implications for U.S. National Security

The fact that the ICJ indicated it would hear and decide claims about the ongoing use of force made acceptance of the Court's compulsory jurisdiction an issue of strategic significance. Despite our deep reluctance to do so and the many domestic constraints that apply, we must be able to use force in our self-defense and in the defense of our friends and allies. We are a law-abiding nation, and when we submit ourselves to adjudication of a subject, we regard ourselves as obliged to abide by the result. For the United States to recognize that the ICJ has authority to define and adjudicate with respect to our right of self-defense, therefore, is effectively to surrender to that body the power to pass on our efforts to guarantee the safety and security of this nation and of its allies.

This development particularly concerned us as a matter of principle and for reasons bearing directly on the capacity of the ICJ to reach sound, correct decisions on use-of-force issues and to enforce principles it eventually may articulate on our communist adversaries. The Court has no expertise in finding facts about ongoing hostilities or any other activities occurring in areas such as Central America. Based on my years as a trial judge and considerable experience with complicated cases, I doubt that the 16 judges sitting on the Nicaragua case may reliably resolve the evidentiary problems presented. The ICJ is similar to an appellate court, more at home with abstract legal questions than with competing factual claims. Moreover, the Court's rejection of El Salvador's application to intervene deprived it of that nation's indispensable contribution to a true picture of the situation in Central America, a contribution that goes to the heart of our legal position.

Even if the Court were inclined to allow participation by all necessary parties, it has no power to compel that participation. We have, for example, no doubt that Cuba, and quite probably the Soviet Union, help Nicaragua's efforts to subvert the democratic regime in El Salvador as well as to undertake unlawful acts against Costa Rica and Honduras. But, in view of their consistent refusal to submit to the Court's jurisdiction in any other matter, neither Cuba nor the Soviet Union can be expected to join in the proceedings, and the Court cannot force them to do so. These facts render even more questionable the capacity of the Court to determine the facts concerning Nicaragua's aggressive acts.

The Court's lack of jurisdiction over Soviet-bloc nations, especially the Soviet Union, also has long-term significance for the strategic acceptability of ICJ review of self-defense issues. The Soviets have long advanced the view—by the Brezhnev doctrine and otherwise, and by their actions in places like Czechoslovakia and Afghanistan—that force is acceptable in order to keep a nation in the socialist orbit or to promote a socialist revolution but have not hesitated to condemn responsive uses of force as violating the U.N. Charter.

We reject this view. We believe that, when a nation asserts a right to use force illegally and acts on that assertion, other affected nations have the right to counter such illegal activities. The United States cannot rely on the ICJ properly and fairly to decide such questions. Indeed, no state can do so. If we acquiesce in this claimed authority, we would be bound by the Court's decisions that limited our ability to confront Soviet expansionism, even though the Soviets could and would do as they pleased. That most of the Court's judges come from nations that do not submit to its jurisdiction, including Soviet-bloc nations and other states that routinely support that bloc, is of special concern on these fundamental issues.

Mr. Chairman [Sen. Richard Lugar], in considering this complex and important subject, I hope that you and the other members of this distinguished committee weigh carefully the national security implications of accepting the Court as a forum for resolving use-of-force questions. For example, would the Court be the proper forum for resolving the disputes that gave rise to such actions as the Berlin airlift, the Cuban missile crisis, and, most recently, our diversion of the Achille Lauro terrorists? Each event involved questions of international law.

At the same time, however, at stake on each occasion were interests of a fundamentally political nature, going to our nation's security. Such matters cannot be left for resolution by judicial means, let alone by a court such as the ICJ; rather, they are the ultimate responsibilities assigned by our Constitution to the President and Congress. We did not consider such issues to be subject to review by the ICJ at the time we accepted the Court's compulsory jurisdiction, and we do not consider them to be encompassed by that acceptance now. The Court's apparent willingness to construe our declaration otherwise left us with no prudent alternative but to terminate that aspect of our use of its facilities.

We carefully considered modifying our 1946 declaration as an alternative to its termination, but we concluded that modification would not meet our concerns. No limiting language that we could draft would prevent the Court from asserting jurisdiction if it wanted to take a particular case, as the Court's treatment of our multilateral treaty reservation in the Nicaragua case demonstrates. That reservation excludes disputes arising under a multilateral treaty unless all treaty partners affected by the Court's decision are before the Court. Despite Nicaragua's own written and oral pleadings before the Court — which expressly implicated El Salvador, Honduras, and Costa Rica in the alleged violations of the U.N. and OAS [Organization of American States] Charters and prayed for a termination of U.S. assistance to them — and statements received directly from those countries, a majority of the Court refused to recognize that those countries would be affected by its decision and refused to give effect to the reservation. Furthermore, merely having filed a declaration is enough for the Court to indicate provisional measures against the filing party, whether or not the Court later found it had jurisdiction under the declaration. Finally, the 1946 declaration expressly provides only for its termination, and we would not wish to have the legality or effectiveness of any lesser step open to question.

### Conclusion

Looked at from the standpoint of the reality of compulsory jurisdiction today, the decision to terminate our 1946 acceptance was a regrettable but necessary measure taken in order to safeguard U.S. interests. It does not signify a lessening of our traditionally strong support for the Court in the exercise of its proper functions, much less a diminution of our commitment to international law. We remain prepared to use the Court for the resolution of international disputes whenever possible and appropriate.

We recognize that this nation has a special obligation to support the ICJ and all other institutions that advance the rule of law in a world full of terror and disorder. Our belief in this obligation is what led us to set an example by accepting the Court's compulsory jurisdiction in 1946 and by continuing that acceptance long after it became clear that the world would not follow suit and that our acceptance failed to advance our interests in any tangible manner.

Yet, the President also is responsible to the American people and to Congress to avoid potential threats to our national security. The ICJ's decisions in the Nicaragua case created real and important additional considerations that made the continued acceptance of compulsory jurisdiction unacceptable, despite its symbolic significance. We hope that, in the long run, this action, coupled with our submission of disputes under Article 36(1), will strengthen the Court in the performance of its proper role in the international system established by the U.N. Charter and the Court's own Statute.

---

## 10. Justinian, U.S. Withdrawal Another Blow to "World Court"

*Financial Times* (London), 1985

THE ANNOUNCEMENT from Washington last week that the U.S. would no longer accept the jurisdiction of the International Court of Justice, except in those cases brought to the court voluntarily by both parties, is a blow to the development of an international legal order.

It also confirms the waning respect for, and authority of, the court by the great powers, and reflects the lessening in the applications from all members of the United Nations to the court over the last 10 years.

It is doubly regrettable because withdrawal comes in the wake of an adverse ruling in the case brought by Nicaragua in April 1984 over the alleged military and paramilitary activities in and against Nicaragua.

Last October the court heard representatives of Nicaragua and of the U.S. in public sittings, and a month later it delivered a judgment in which it found that it had jurisdiction to entertain the case and that Nicaragua's application was admissible.

In January of this year the U.S. wrote to the court saying that the court was wrong and that the U.S. did not intend to participate further in the proceedings.

On September 12 the court began its oral proceedings on the merits of the case, in the absence of the U.S. representatives. The blanket withdrawal of the U.S. is blamed directly on the court's ruling in favour of jurisdiction to hear the Nicaraguan complaint, because the "objectives of the court were being subverted by the efforts of Nicaragua and its Cuban and Soviet sponsors to use the court as a political weapon."

This is not a new cry in the international law field, but it is the first time that a major power has reacted directly against an adverse finding in so radical a manner.

The acceptance of the court as an instrument of international justice has never been strong. In 1920 the Committee of Jurists which prepared the statute of the Permanent Court of International Justice (the forerunner of the International Court of Justice) had proposed a system of true compulsory jurisdiction based upon the unilateral application to the court by the complaining state.

This idea, however, encountered strong opposition, particularly from the great powers of that epoch. In the end a proposal was adopted whereby the compulsory jurisdiction arose only by means of a unilateral declaration of a state indicating its acceptance of the jurisdiction of the court, and was not to be implied directly in the statute of the court.

When the architects of the United Nations considered the court's role, it affirmed the compromise solution under the League of Nations, known as the optional clause.

There were some drafting changes, but the article of the court's statute remained intact. When accepting the compulsory jurisdiction of the court, states tended, nevertheless, to append reservations to their acceptance of compulsory jurisdiction, mostly unobjectionable.

For example, the condition of reciprocity was often inserted, although in law it was unnecessary to say that a state would only submit to the court's jurisdiction if an applicant state, by its declaration, would likewise submit if brought before the court.

Frequently, states excluded disputes where there were other methods of resolving them. Commonwealth countries excluded disputes between themselves because they could be resolved within the institutions of the Commonwealth.

Another example has been in relation to disputes within the state's domestic jurisdiction. From time to time, however, states have taken it upon themselves to say whether the dispute is or is not within their domestic jurisdiction.

The late Judge Lauterpacht, who was the British judge on the court in the 1950s, expressed the view that declarations of acceptance with such reservations were "incapable of giving rise to a legal obligation, in that they effectively secured the right of unilateral determination of the extent and existence of the obligation of settling disputes before the International Court."

"These reservations," Judge Lauterpacht said, "tended to impair the legal and moral authority of the optional clause."

If that is true of the self-determining reservation, how much more so is it true of the almost total withdrawal by the U.S. from the court's jurisdiction?

Throughout two thirds of a century it has failed to attract the status of an ordinary court, to which all the constituent parties adhere. Those who have favoured the compulsory jurisdiction of the court have been chiefly the small powers, and its chief opponents the great powers.

The composition of the two groups has changed to some extent, but generally the two antagonistic points of view have on the whole been clearly marked. The U.S. declaration is the latest.

The court has not been blameless in its declining authority. In the case brought in the 1950s by Ethiopia and Liberia against South Africa to enforce the mandate conferred after the First World War by the League of Nations in respect of South-West Africa (Namibia), the court accepted that it had jurisdiction to hear the question of the legal enforcement by the U.N. of the mandatory powers. When the case came before the court a few years later to determine the merits, the court did a volte face.

Under the presidency of an Australian, Judge Spender, the court by the casting vote of the president reversed its decision to accept jurisdiction. Not only did that ruling set back the solution to the problem of Namibia (which is still unresolved) it also disheartened the smaller states which had been the loudest proponents of the court. Since then no issue of major political importance has come before the court.

The long-term effect of the U.S. disavowal of the court in matters that touch the U.S. Government's interests will be that cases involving international legal, commercial or border problems alone will be the staple diet of the court.

The International Court of Justice never was properly the "World Court." It is even less so today.

## 11. ABA International Law Section, Recommendations Adopted by the House of Delegates in 1994

The International Lawyer, 1995
[footnotes omitted by editors]

American Bar Association Section of International Law and Practice and the Standing Committee on World Order under Law Reports to the House of Delegates*

* These Recommendations and Reports were adopted by the House of Delegates in August 1994.

### I. International Court of Justice

### RECOMMENDATION

BE IT RESOLVED, that the American Bar Association recommends that the United States Government present a declaration recognizing as compulsory the jurisdiction of the International Court of Justice that should read as follows:

I, President of the United States of America, declare on behalf of the United States of America, under Article 36, paragraph 2, of the Statute of the International Court of Justice, and in accordance with the Resolution of the Senate of the United States of America (two-thirds of the senators present concurring therein), that the United States of America recognizes as compulsory ipso facto and without special agreement, in relation to any other State accepting the same obligation, that is to say on the condition of reciprocity, the jurisdiction of the International Court of Justice in all legal disputes hereafter arising concerning

(a) the interpretation of a treaty;

(b) any question of international law;

(c) the existence of any fact which, if established, would constitute a breach of an international obligation;

(d) the nature or extent of the reparation to be made for the breach of an international obligation;

Provided, that this Declaration shall not apply to

(a) disputes the solution of which the parties shall entrust to other tribunals by virtue of agreements already in existence or which may be concluded in the future; or

(b) disputes in respect of which any other party to the dispute has accepted the compulsory jurisdiction of the International Court of Justice only in relation to or for the purpose of the dispute; or where the acceptance of the Court's compulsory jurisdiction on behalf of any other party to the dispute was deposited or ratified less than twelve months prior to the filing of the application bringing the dispute before the Court; or

(c) disputes relating to action taken pursuant to decisions of the Security Council of the United Nations or of a regional arrangement or agency fulfilling the requirements of Article 52 of the Charter of the United Nations.

Provided further, that this Declaration may be modified or terminated with effect as from the moment of expiration of six months after notice has been given to the Secretary-General of the United Nations, except that in relation to any State with a shorter period of notification of modification or termination, the notification by the United States of America shall take effect at the end of such shorter period, and in relation to any State which may modify or terminate its declaration as from the moment of notification, the notification by the United States of America shall take effect as from the moment of notification.

## REPORT

This recommendation is the first in a series of five recommendations which deal with important issues of international law that are crucial to the maintenance of international peace and security and justice. They have been developed by the Section of International Law and Practice, through its Working Group on Improving the Effectiveness of the United Nations, as a contribution of the American Bar Association to the 50th Anniversary of the United Nations, in fulfillment of the American Bar Association's Goal VIII—to advance the rule of law in the world. This recommendation addresses the issue of the settlement of international disputes, with emphasis on the preparation by the United States of a draft declaration accepting the jurisdiction of the International Court of Justice.

The United States is a party to the Statute of the International Court of Justice ("World Court" or I.C.J.). In this capacity the United States may sue and be sued in that Court, but only where consent to suit is founded on mutual agreement or on acceptance of the Court's compulsory jurisdiction by declarations filed pursuant to Article 36(2) of the Statute of the Court. The United States filed such a declaration in 1946, but withdrew it in 1986 owing to the Court's willingness to accept jurisdiction of Nicaragua's complaint that the United States had violated international law through its actions in support of the Contras in Nicaragua. The Working Group examined the question whether the United States should restore its acceptance of the Court's compulsory jurisdiction.

In reaching its decision to recommend that the United States file a new declaration accepting the Court's compulsory jurisdiction pursuant to Article 36(2), the Working Group considered four major issues:

1. Whether acceptance of the Court's compulsory jurisdiction is in the national interest;

2. Whether a new United States declaration should include the "Connally reservation," that is, whether to include a reservation that excludes from the Court's jurisdiction matters that are "essentially within [U.S.] domestic jurisdiction ... as determined by the United States;"

3. Whether the declaration should exclude issues of national security from the Court's jurisdiction, that is, whether the declaration should extend to uses of force, actions in self-defense, or matters connected with ongoing armed conflicts; and

4. What other conditions or reservations should be attached to the new U.S. declaration.

Apart from the proviso that introduces reciprocity into the termination clause, the Working Group's draft Declaration contains only three reservations: proviso (a) concerning alternative methods of dispute resolution; proviso (b) concerning declarations made in relation to particular disputes; and proviso (c) concerning collective measures. The Working Group agreed that there should be no domestic jurisdiction reservation and that there should be no national security, use of force, or self-defense reservation.

The Working Group's support for renewing U.S. acceptance of the Court's compulsory jurisdiction is rooted in support for the rule of law. As it is within nations, adjudication is a necessary feature of the rule of law among nations. Although no nation can be certain of winning every International Court case in which it is a party, dispute settlement by law and not by force is in the long-range interest of all. Moreover, as a world leader having many and varied interests throughout the world, dispute settlement by law is especially in the interest of the United States. Acceptance of the Court's compulsory jurisdiction serves that interest.

The domestic jurisdiction reservation contained in proviso (b) of the U.S. 1946 Declaration was both unnecessary and destroyed the effectiveness of that declaration. The proviso was not needed because under the U.N. Charter the Court has no authority to "intervene in matters which are essentially within the domestic jurisdiction of any State." The proviso rendered the U.S. declaration ineffective because, owing to the Court's requirement of reciprocity in the acceptance of compulsory jurisdiction, any state that the United States might seek to bring before the Court could avoid the Court's jurisdiction by invoking the U.S. domestic jurisdiction reservation. What is more, the self-judging feature of the U.S. domestic jurisdiction reservation ("as determined by the United States") conflicts with Article 36(6) of the I.C.J. Statute. Under that provision, the Court has jurisdiction to determine its own jurisdiction: When there is a dispute as to whether the Court has jurisdiction, as is the case when a party claims that a matter falls within its domestic jurisdiction, the dispute is to be settled by the decision of the Court, not by the self-determination of one of the parties. For all these reasons, the Working Group considered it inappropriate to include a domestic jurisdiction reservation in the new declaration.

A national security, use of force, or self-defense reservation presents two major issues. First, there is the question of principle. Should matters relating to national security be excluded from the Court's compulsory jurisdiction? Second, there is a technical or practical problem in conducting litigation subject to such a proviso. Is it technically feasible to achieve the presumed objective of the proviso's proponents—that is, to preclude judicial scrutiny of the merits of sensitive issues—without engaging in prolonged litigation over related issues at the jurisdictional phase?

With regard to the issue of principle, the reasons that led the Working Group to support renewal of U.S. acceptance of the Court's compulsory jurisdiction cut against the exclusion of national security, self-defense, and use of force issues. Extraterritorial action taken in the name of national security or self-defense is governed by international law; such action does not fall within national discretion or domestic jurisdiction. The United States would be ill-served by an international law system that did not seek to subject the use of force to the discipline of law. Here, as elsewhere, effectiveness in the rule of law requires access to adjudication. In the long-run the interests of all states are furthered by bringing the use of force within the domain of law.

As to practical problems of litigation, the objective of a national security, use of force, or self-defense reservation would be to secure the dismissal of the case at the outset, that is, at a preliminary hearing on jurisdiction. In many cases this would not be possible, because the Court would have to examine certain merit issues at the jurisdictional phase in order to satisfy itself that the conditions for invoking the reservation were met. For example, a reservation that excludes Court review of acts of self-defense would require a showing that the challenged act was indeed an act of self-defense. This would require both a presentation of the facts and legal argument to show that the action is properly characterized as self-defense. Unless the reservation is self-judging ("self-defense as determined by the United States"), the Court would need to hear the merits of the claim and would dismiss the case only if it concluded that the U.S. action was indeed justified as an act of self-defense. A "national security" reservation could probably not satisfy its own proponents unless the determination concerning U.S. security interests were made self-judging; but for the reasons discussed above concerning the Connally Amendment, the Working

Group concluded that self-judging reservations of any kind should be avoided. While some other proposals might avoid the self-judging problem—for example, by leaving it to the Court to determine from the pleadings or from ascertainable facts whether the dispute concerned "force" or "hostilities"—we concluded that the effort to formulate an "objective" test that could be readily applied at the threshold of the case was elusive. More importantly, such an exercise seemed unwarranted in view of our unanimous agreement that, because of the reciprocal character of reservations, it is in the interest of the United States to draw all reservations to the Court's jurisdiction as narrowly as possible.

With regard to other possible reservations, the Working Group decided to recommend three reservations.

First, in proviso (a) the Working Group decided to retain the 1946 Declaration's alternative dispute settlement proviso. Under this proviso the Declaration does not apply to "disputes the solution of which the parties shall entrust to other tribunals by virtue of agreements already in existence or which may be concluded in the future."

Second, in proviso (b) the Working Group decided to exclude disputes that are brought to the Court pursuant to a declaration that was made only for the purpose of bringing the dispute to the Court. Such an exclusion in effect requires other states to accept the Court's compulsory jurisdiction on a broader basis before they may utilize the U.S. Declaration to bring the United States before the Court.

Third, in proviso (c) the Working Group decided to exclude disputes relating to collective action. In the judgment of the Working Group, legal challenges to collective actions should require a broader jurisdictional basis than the acceptance by the United States of the compulsory jurisdiction of the Court. Judicial review of collective actions would advance the rule of law, but the Court's review would be effective only if both the responsible institution and all affected states participate in the process. Such a process would require both rethinking of the basis for collective action and amendment of the Statute of the Court.

Finally, the Working Group decided to retain the six months' notice provision of the 1946 Declaration, but to insert into that provision a requirement of reciprocity.

Respectfully submitted,
James H. Carter
Chair
August 1994

## 12. Bibliography of Additional Sources

- INTERNATIONAL COURT OF JUSTICE, Yearbook (1946).

- Vaughan Lowe and Malgosia Fitzmaurice, FIFTY YEARS OF THE INTERNATIONAL COURT OF JUSTICE (1996).

- Leo Gross, THE FUTURE OF THE INTERNATIONAL COURT OF JUSTICE (1976).

- A.S. Muller, D. Raic, and J.M. Thuránszky, THE INTERNATIONAL COURT OF JUSTICE: ITS FUTURE ROLE AFTER FIFTY YEARS (1997).

- Bowett, THE INTERNATIONAL COURT OF JUSTICE: PROCESS, PRACTICE AND PROCEDURE (1997).

- Ram Prakash Anand, COMPULSORY JURISDICTION OF THE INTERNATIONAL COURT OF JUSTICE (1962).

- American Society of International Law, Official Document: Case Concerning Military and Paramilitary Activities in and Against Nicaragua (*Nicaragua v. United States of America*): International Court of Justice, 78 A.J.I.L. 750 (1984).

- Herbert W. Briggs, Comment: *Nicaragua v. United States*: Jurisdiction and Admissibility, 79 A.J.I.L. 373 (1985).

- Maura A. Bleichert, Comments: The Effectiveness of Voluntary Jurisdiction in the ICJ: *El Salvador v. Honduras*, A Case in Point, 16 FORDHAM INT'L L.J. 799 (1993).

- Jonathan I. Charney, Article: Compromissory Clauses and the Jurisdiction of the International Court of Justice, 81 A.J.I.L. 855 (1987).

- Abram Chayes, Article: Nicaragua, The United States, and The World Court, 85 COLUM. L. REV. 1445 (1985).

- Ilene R. Cohn, Comment: *Nicaragua v. United States*: Pre-Seisin Reciprocity and the Race to The Hague, 46 OHIO ST. L.J. 699 (1985).

- Anthony D'Amato, Comment: Modifying U.S. Acceptance of the Compulsory Jurisdiction of the World Court, 79 A.J.I.L. 385 (1985).

- Anthony D'Amato, Comment, The United States Should Accept, By a New Declaration, the General Compulsory Jurisdiction of The World Court, 80 A.J.I.L. 331 (1986).

- Ernest S. Easterly III, The Rule of Law and the New World Order, 22 S.U. L. REV. 161 (1995).

- Douglas J. Ende, Comment: Reaccepting the Compulsory Jurisdiction of the International Court of Justice: A Proposal for a New United States Declaration, 61 WASH. L. REV. 1145 (1986).

- Michael J. Glennon, Note: *Nicaragua v. United States*: Constitutionality of U.S. Modification of ICJ Jurisdiction, 79 A.J.I.L. 682 (1985).

- William B.T. Mock, Game Theory, Signaling and International Legal Relations, 26 GW J. INT'L L. & ECON. 34 (1992).

- John Norton Moore, Article: The Secret War in Central America and the Future of World Order, 80 A.J.I.L. 43 (1986).

- Fred L. Morrison, Essay: The Future of International Adjudication, 75 MINN. L. REV. 827 (1991).

- R.L. O'M., Note: Applying the Critical Jurisprudence of International Law to the Case Concerning Military and Paramilitary Activities in and Against Nicaragua, 71 VA. L. REV. 1183 (1985).

- Ernst-Ulrich Petersmann, Article: Constitutionalism and International Adjudication: How to Constitutionalize the U.N. Dispute Settlement System?, 31 N.Y.U. J. INT'L L. & POL. 753 (1999).

- Patrick Reilly, Comment: While the United Nations Slept: Missed Opportunities in the New World Order, 17 LOY. L.A. INT'L & COMP. L.J. 951 (1995).

- Gary L. Scott & Craig L. Carr, Article: The ICJ and Compulsory Jurisdiction: The Case For Closing the Clause, 81 A.J.I.L. 57 (1987).

- Gary L. Scott et al., Articles and Essays: Recent Activity Before the International Court of Justice: Trend or Cycle?, 3 ISLA J INT'L & COMP L 1 (1996).

- Susan W, Tiefenbrun, Article: The Role of the World Court in Settling International Disputes: A recent Assessment, 20 Loy. L.A. Int'l & Comp. L.J. 1 (1997).

- The United States and the Compulsory Jurisdiction of the International Court of Justice (Anthony Clark Arend ed., University Press of America 1986).

- The International Court of Justice at a Crossroads (Lori Fisler Damrosch ed., Transnational Publishers, Inc. 1987).

- Michael Dunne, The United States and the World Court, 1920–1935 (1988).

- Arthur Eyefinger, The International Court of Justice 126–48 (1996).

- Richard Falk, Reviving the World Court XV–XVII (1986).

- Fifty Years of the International Court of Justice 154–62 (Vaughan & Malgosia Fitzmaurice eds., Cambridge University Press 1996).

- Edward McWhinney, The International Court of Justice and the Western Tradition of International Law 55–132 (1987).

- Shabtai Rosenne, The World Court: What it is and How it Works (1995).

# Part IV
# Peace and Security

# Chapter IX

# The Security Council:
# Powers & Reform

## Introduction

This chapter introduces the reader to the process and functions of the U.N. Security Council, the most powerful body within the U.N. system. It explores the efficacy of the enforcement measures available to the Council, including condemnation, imposition of economic and diplomatic sanctions, creation of No Fly Zones and Safe Areas, establishment of investigative commissions and ad hoc international criminal tribunals, and authorization for use of force.

While the Security Council is potentially the most powerful body within the U.N. system, its effectiveness is often undermined by the threat or use of the veto by the Permanent Members. In addition, the fifteen-member Council is increasingly seen as non-representative of the membership of the United Nations as a whole, and U.N. members who do not have a seat on the Council are showing an increasing proclivity to disregard the Council's decisions. It is in this context that the United Nations is currently considering a variety of proposals for Security Council reform. This chapter examines the case for reform and the pros and cons of the current reform proposals.

## Objectives

- To understand the powers available to the U.N. Security Council.
- To encourage debate on the usage of Security Council powers when applied to specific situations.
- To form a basic understanding of the complexities of Security Council decision making.
- To evaluate the pros and cons of Security Council reform: the veto power structure and permanent member status.
- To understand the various positions of Member States in efforts to institute reform.

# Problems

1.  You will be assigned to represent one of the countries participating in the simulation described in the readings. You should come to class prepared to represent your country in a simulated Security Council crisis session concerning the fictional Venezuela-Guyana conflict described in the readings.

    (a) Prepare a short (1 minute) speech, identifying your country's position and recommended steps for resolving the conflict.

    (b) Which provisions of the above Security Council Resolutions would your country support?

    (c) Which would it oppose?

    (d) How should the provisions be modified to make them more effective?

2.  At the end of the session, the class will break into two groups.

    (a) Group 1 will consist of those countries whose statements indicate they favor relatively more aggressive Security Council action.

    (b) Group 2 will consist of those that favor less aggressive action.

    (c) Each group will meet between class sessions to draft a Security Council Resolution, drawing upon the model provisions contained in the readings.

    (d) Come to the following class prepared to debate and vote on the draft Security Council Resolutions, and then discuss lessons learned from the simulation.

3.  What are the pros and cons of the possible Security Council reforms identified in the readings for this week? What would be the pros and cons from the point of view of your assigned country?

4.  What are the political and procedural obstacles to the various Security Council reform proposals? How might these be overcome or circumvented?

# Materials

1.  List of Security Council Countries for the Simulation.

2.  (Fictional) Report of the Secretary-General Concerning the Situation in the Essequibo Region, Guyana, for use in the Simulation.

3.  U.N. CHARTER, Articles 39–41.

4.  Frederic L. Kirgis, Jr., INTERNATIONAL ORGANIZATIONS IN THEIR LEGAL SETTING, West Publishing Co., 2d ed. 1993, pp. 191–193.

5.  Michael P. Scharf, History of the Yugoslav Crisis, BALKAN JUSTICE, pp. 21–36.

6.  Model Security Council Actions:

    A.  S.C. Res. 667: Condemnation (Iraq).

    B.  S.C. Res. 757: Economic Sanctions (Serbia).

    C.  S.C. Res. 816: No Fly Zone (Bosnia).

D. S.C. Res. 824: Safe Areas (Bosnia).

E. S.C. Res. 780: Investigative Commission (Bosnia).

F. S.C. Res. 678: Use of Force (Iraq).

7. U.N. Charter, Articles 108 and 109, see http://www.un.org/en/documents/charter/.

8. Timothy Penny and Mark Mullenbach, U.N.'s Chosen Few—A Tricky Feat, THE CHRISTIAN SCIENCE MONITOR, September 24, 1997.

9. Richard Butler, United Nations: The Security Council Isn't Performing, INTERNATIONAL HERALD TRIBUNE, August 5, 1999.

10. Amb. Gerhard Benze, Creating a New U.N. Security Council, YALE DAILY NEWS, March 29, 1999.

11. U.N. Reforms Could Limit Security Council's Power of Veto, AGENCE FRANCE PRESSE, July 8, 1999.

12. Imron Cotan, U.N. Council Needs Urgent Reform, THE JAKARTA POST, October 20, 1997.

13. Tsutomu Wada, Japan Fails in Effort to Secure Permanent Seat of Power at U.N., THE NIKKEI WEEKLY, December 8, 1997.

14. Bibliography of Additional Sources

# 1. List of Security Council Countries for the Simulation

PARTICIPATING COUNTRIES

Below is a list of the different countries that will be represented in the simulation. If there are not enough students to represent all of the countries, choose representatives for the countries that play the most important roles in the conflict.

COUNTRIES INVOLVED IN SIMULATION

Permanent Members
China
France
Russia
United Kingdom
United States

Non-Permanent Members
Chile
Colombia
Costa Rica
Czech Republic
Japan
Laos
Norway
Rwanda
South Africa
Uganda

Parties in Dispute:
  Guyana
  Venezuela

---

# 2. (Fictional) Report of the Secretary-General Concerning the Situation in the Essequibo Region, Guyana, for Use in the Simulation

UNITED NATIONS
Security Council
Distr. GENERAL

## REPORT OF THE SECRETARY-GENERAL CONCERNING THE SITUATION IN THE ESSEQUIBO REGION, GUYANA

### I. INTRODUCTION

1. It is my duty under Article 99 of the United Nations Charter to bring to the attention of the Security Council the emerging conflict between Venezuela and Guyana, which may threaten international peace and security. Five days ago, Venezuelan forces invaded the Essequibo region of Guyana, and negotiations between the concerned parties have broken down. An emergency meeting of the Security Council has been called to try to resolve the conflict.

2. This is a report of the background of the conflict and a summary of recent events for your consideration.

3. I am sure that the Council will wish to consider this matter at the earliest possible moment in exercise of its primary responsibility in the maintenance of international peace and security.

### II. POLITICAL ASPECTS

Background of the Guyana-Venezuela Crisis

The following true facts form the basis for our simulated crisis

4. Guyana and Venezuela are two countries next to each other on the northeastern coast of South America. For a long time Venezuela has said that it owns the Essequibo region, an area that covers two thirds of Guyana. The Essequibo region extends from the Orinoco River to the Essequibo River. The Essequibo region has a large amount of natural resources such as timber, gold, copper, iron ore, nickel, chromium, tungsten, graphite, uranium and oil, which both Guyana and Venezuela would like to have.

5. The history of the dispute over the Essequibo Valley goes back to 1814, when, by the Treaty of Paris, England acquired the Essequibo region. Venezuela has questioned whether both banks were Dutch possessions at the time of the English acquisition. The British have said that the boundaries of the territory are marked by the extreme limit of the watershed of all the rivers flowing into the Essequibo. In 1899 an arbitration panel awarded the region to Guyana which, at that time, was still a British colony. Although Venezuela accepted the panel's decision, it has recently stated that the United States and Britain forced Venezuela to agree to this.

6. In 1966, when Guyana became an independent country, Guyana and Venezuela signed an agreement in Geneva which created a group that would try to settle the dispute. Although the group met sixteen times between 1966 and 1970, the group was unable to

reach a solution agreeable to both countries. Then in 1970, Guyana and Venezuela signed a treaty called "The Protocol of the Port-of-Spain." This treaty stated that neither Venezuela nor Guyana would try to take control of the Essequibo Region as long as the group's discussions continued. "The Protocol of the Port-of-Spain" was good for twelve years. In 1982 the treaty expired and the two countries were still unable to reach an agreement. Since then the relationship between the two countries has worsened.

7. Today Venezuela has a population of 20 million people and a territory of 347,000 square miles. Venezuela has close ties with the OPEC countries, Italy and Colombia being members.

8. Guyana, on the other hand, has a population of only 800,000 people and has a territory of just 83,000 square miles (about 1/4 the size of Venezuela). Guyana, although independent, still has close ties with Britain and is a member of the British Commonwealth. Guyana also has close ties with China and the English-speaking Caribbean countries. Guyana has become a leader among Third World countries.

## III. RECENT EVENTS

The following facts are not true but are to be taken as true for the purpose of our Security Council simulation.

9. In the past six months, Guyana has begun to develop the Essequibo region by setting up large oil and mineral projects in the area. It has attracted outside investment in these projects on an enormous scale especially from France, South Africa and China. Venezuela protested that such development was a violation of the spirit of the Geneva agreement and "The Protocol of the Port-of-Spain." Therefore, Venezuela argued that Guyana's development of the Essequibo region gave Venezuela the right to take over the region using force.

10. Five days ago, a force of 50,000 Venezuelan troops entered the Essequibo territory and announced that it was taking over the region. Although Guyana is being aided by over 1,000 mercenaries from Costa Rica, Guyana's small army is no match for Venezuela's well-armed forces. The first reports about the invasion say that the Venezuelan forces have set out to brutalize the Guyanese people living in the region in order to drive them out. Human Rights NGOs have reported widespread massacres of civilians and systematic rape of as many as 10,000 Guyanese women. Guyana, in turn, has asked for help from Chile and the United Kingdom. The United Kingdom has moved an aircraft carrier into position off the coast of Venezuela to launch air strikes in the Essequibo region if such action becomes necessary. Colombia has deployed 10,000 troops to its eastern border as a preventive measure.

11. Two days ago, Guyana requested an emergency meeting of the Organization of American States (OAS). Yesterday, the OAS passed a resolution noting that the OAS Charter is against wars of aggression and that victory by force does not confer rights on a country. Most importantly, the OAS requested that the U.N. Security Council take immediate action to compel Venezuela to withdraw its forces from the Essequibo region. Under the U.N. Charter, no country can use force in a conflict unless the Security Council authorizes it, or unless it is in self-defense.

12. Note: The Organization of American States (OAS) is a regional organization founded in 1960. Its 35 members are located in North America, South America and the Caribbean. The OAS was set up as a place where the member countries can solve problems, discuss policies, economies and education. The OAS can be thought of as a regional version of the United Nations. The current members of the Security Council that are also members of the OAS are Chile, Colombia, Costa Rica, and the United States.

## IV. SECRETARIAT RECOMMENDATIONS

13. These are my recommendations to the Security Council:

    1.  Stop the bloodshed;
    2.  Force Venezuela to withdraw its forces;
    3.  Convince Venezuela and Guyana to agree to a lasting peace which would finally settle their long-standing dispute over the Essequibo territory;
    4.  Help enact a peace plan.

14. To achieve these goals, the Security Council must try to pass a resolution(s) which will bring an end to the fighting and make Venezuela and Guyana agree to a lasting peace agreement. Also consider the importance of the Organization of American States (OAS) and the Organization of Petroleum Exporting Countries (OPEC). There are often one or more organizations or groups involved in a conflict, and they can have a strong influence over decisions that are made.

15. In conclusion, I should like to express my faith in the Security Council's ability to bring about a lasting peace in the Essequibo region.

# 3. U.N. Charter, Articles 39–41

## CHAPTER VII

ACTION WITH RESPECT TO THREATS TO THE PEACE, BREACHES OF THE PEACE, AND ACTS OF AGGRESSION

### Article 39

The Security Council shall determine the existence of any threat to the peace, breach of the peace, or act of aggression and shall make recommendations, or decide what measures shall be taken in accordance with Articles 41 and 42, to maintain or restore international peace and security.

### Article 40

In order to prevent an aggravation of the situation, the Security Council may, before making the recommendations or deciding upon the measures provided for in Article 39, call upon the parties concerned to comply with such provisional measures as it deems necessary or desirable. Such provisional measures shall be without prejudice to the rights, claims, or position of the parties concerned. The Security Council shall duly take account of failure to comply with such provisional measures.

### Article 41

The Security Council may decide what measures not involving the use of armed force are to be employed to give effect to its decisions, and it may call upon the Members of the United Nations to apply such measures. These may include complete or partial inter-ruption of economic relations and of rail, sea, air, postal, telegraphic, radio, and other means of communication, and the severance of diplomatic relations.

## *Authors' Note*

The following two materials explore the Security Council's exercise of its Charter-au-thorized powers. Material 4 discusses the usage of veto powers from the five permanent members of the Security Council. In particular, this article discusses the interpretative issues that limit, as well as complicate, the exercise of veto power. Material 5 examines the internal debate that affects the determination of which Security Council powers to authorize through the lens of the Security Council's struggle with the crisis in Bosnia. These materials depict the constraints that exist when the Security Council uses its various powers.

---

## 4. Frederic L. Kirgis, Jr., International Organizations in Their Legal Setting
### 1993, pp. 191–193
### [footnotes omitted by editors]

\* \* \*

### Procedural Issues

Voting in the Security Council is governed by article 27 of the Charter. Its most striking feature, of course, is the grant of veto power to the five permanent members. As one would expect, problems of interpretation involving article 27 have centered on the authority of the permanent members. There have been three major issues:

(1) Under article 27(2), procedural matters are not subject to the veto. But what if there is a controversy over whether a particular matter is procedural or substantive? If a permanent member could veto a ruling or resolution stating that the matter is procedural, there would be a double veto — first a veto to prevent a matter from being treated as procedural, and then a veto on the merits.

The "San Francisco Statement" of four of the permanent members (the U.S., U.K., Soviet Union and Republic of China), which is part of the preparatory work for the Charter, tends to support the double veto except for a few enumerated matters that would unquestionably be procedural. On three occasions in early Security Council practice, such a double veto was exercised. In 1949 the General Assembly intervened in G.A. Resolution 267 (III), setting forth a list of categories it regarded as procedural. On the few occasions thereafter when questions within those categories have arisen in the Security Council and a permanent member has attempted to prevent them from being considered procedural, the Security Council has disregarded the attempted veto.

(2) From time to time, some members have questioned whether Security Council decisions on substantive matters could be made if any permanent member abstained from voting. Note that article 27(3) calls for the concurring votes of the permanent members," with a proviso that seems to distinguish abstention from a concurring vote." The proviso might be thought to set forth a narrow, exclusive class of cases in which the abstention of a permanent member would not preclude a substantive decision. There is some preparatory work to support that interpretation.

The Security Council has nevertheless consistently adopted substantive resolutions on a wide variety of matters (not limited to those mentioned in the article 27(3) proviso) despite permanent member abstention, and those resolutions have been accepted as valid within the Organization. Would you consider the Security Council's practice in this regard to have any legal significance?

In November 1975, the Legal Adviser of the U.S. Department of State characterized this practice as "a positive contribution to the work of the Council, and hence to members of the United Nations in general, and as an excellent example of how the language of the charter permits important evolutionary changes without requiring textual changes."

What criteria could be used to determine whether, or to what extent, evolutionary change of any given provision without Charter revision is permissible? Would the latitude for evolutionary change be different for provisions setting forth substantive standards (such as article 4(1)) than for purely procedural rules such as the "concurring vote" rule in article 27(3)?

(3) Article 27(3) says that in decisions under Chapter VI of the Charter, "a party to a dispute shall abstain from voting." The principle, of course, is that a state should not be both judge and party in its own cause. Chapter VI, though, refers not only to "disputes," but to "any situation which might lead to international friction or give rise to a dispute." See article 34. Consequently it is arguable that there is a juridical distinction between a "dispute" and a "situation" under Chapter VI, and that an interested Security Council member must abstain from voting only if the case at hand is a "dispute" and that member is a party to it. Although the preparatory work for the Charter suggests that no such fine distinction was intended for article 27(3), the distinction has been observed in practice.

The World Court has had some occasions to consider whether a matter is a within the meaning of a compromissory or arbitration clause in an international agreement. In the Mavrommatis Palestine Concessions involving a compromissory clause in a League of Nations mandate, the Court said that a dispute is "a disagreement on a point of law or fact, a conflict of legal views or of interests between two persons." In the Interpretation of Peace Treaties Case, an advisory opinion interpreting arbitration clauses in World War II peace treaties with Bulgaria, Hungary and Romania, the Court said:

> Whether there exists an international dispute is a matter for objective determination. The mere denial of the existence of a dispute does not prove its non-existence. In the diplomatic correspondence submitted to the Court, the United Kingdom [and four other states] charged Bulgaria, Hungary and Romania with having violated, in various ways, the provisions of the articles dealing with human rights and fundamental freedoms in the Peace Treaties and called upon the three Governments to take remedial measures to carry out their obligations under the Treaties. The three Governments, on the other hand, denied the charges. There has thus arisen a situation in which the two sides hold clearly opposite views concerning the question of the performance or non-performance of certain treaty obligations. Confronted with such a situation, the Court must conclude that international disputes have arisen.

* * *

## 5. Michael P. Scharf, History of the Yugoslav Crisis

Balkan Justice, pp. 31–36
[footnotes omitted by editors]

Most experts agree that the Security Council could have acted to stop the atrocities in Bosnia. When Bosnia's president Alija Izetbegovic visited Washington at the end of 1991, he asked for the deployment of preventive peacekeepers in Bosnia. A year later, the United States would employ this very tactic with great success in Macedonia, but the opportunity to prevent the Bosnian war with a trip-wire force was squandered. After the fighting began in 1992, the Bosnian president pleaded for preventive air strikes by NATO, but the United States responded that "no military resolution from outside was possible." Such

NATO air strikes could have been used to disrupt the Bosnian Serb Army's command and control, as well as its crucial supply lines from Serbia. In addition, the main prison camps and associated installations were located in western and northern Bosnia, not in the mountains that covered most of the country, and thus would have made easy targets for surgical air strikes. Finally, NATO aircraft could have lifted the siege of Sarajevo and maintained the safety and integrity of the other "safe areas." But this was not to be. "Had NATO met [the Serb] aggression with airstrikes in the summer of 1992," wrote Warren Zimmermann, the last U.S. ambassador to Yugoslavia, "I believe that a negotiated result would soon have followed. The NATO air campaign [in 1995] came three years and more than a hundred thousand deaths after America's first real opportunity to help war." In his memoir on the Balkan conflict, Zimmermann concludes that "the refusal of the Bush administration to commit [air] power early in the Bosnian war was our greatest mistake of the entire Yugoslav crisis."

After the collapse of the Soviet Union, Yugoslavia had lost its importance to Washington. Preoccupied with the Persian War and the future of the disintegrating Soviet Union, the United States was satisfied to leave the handling of the Yugoslav con to the European Community. In 1989, when Milosevic was coming to power, an interagency review by the Bush Administration concluded that Yugoslavia held no strategic interests for the United States. When the fighting began in 1991, Secretary of State James Baker bluntly explained the United States' lack of interest by saying, don't have a dog in that fight."

Even after receiving reports of Serb-run death camps in Bosnia, Washington was hesitant to act. According to George Kenny, the U.S. State Department official who resigned in protest, the State Department policy at the time amounted to "Let's pretend this is not happening." The day after the ITN footage of Omarska aired worldwide, President Bush told a news conference: "We know there is horror in these detention camps. But in all honesty, I can't confirm to you some of the claims that there is indeed a genocidal process going on there." Thereafter, U.S. officials were instructed to avoid using the "genocide" label with respect to Bosnia so as not to trigger obligations under the Genocide Convention, which obliges parties to prevent and punish acts of genocide.

That policy did not change when the Clinton team took over in 1993. Testifying before Congress in May 1993, Secretary of State Christopher refused to acknowledge that Serbs were committing genocide in Bosnia, asserting instead that "all sides" were responsible for the atrocities there, thus removing the imperative for action. Notwithstanding clear evidence to the contrary, this would remain the party line until two years later, in March 1995, when Clinton Administration officials would leak the finding of a classified CIA study that 90 percent of ethnic cleansing had been carried out by Serbs pursuant to a policy designed to destroy and disperse the non-Serb population.

Britain and France, for their part, insisted on limiting international action in Bosnia to a relief effort assisted by the United Nations Protection Force (UNPROFOR). The British and French governments then argued that the presence of their troops in UNPROFOR made assertive military action, such as airstrikes against the Serbs, impossible because the Serbs would retaliate against the U.N. forces. The United States found it hard to disagree because it was opposed to any deployment of U.S. ground troops in Bosnia. As one political analyst concluded at the time, "Risk avoidance appears to have acquired the force of doctrine at the Pentagon. In the Clinton administration, the concern borders on an obsession with both military and civilian leaders whose view on the use of force was molded by the war in Vietnam."

Britain, moreover, had taken the lead in trying to relaunch the stalled peace process by hosting the International Conference on the Former Yugoslavia in August 1992. The conference participants, with the subsequent endorsement of the Security Council, decided to unify European and United Nations mediation efforts in Bosnia under the cochairmanship of U.N. envoy Cyrus Vance and Lord David Owen of Britain. The Vance Owen venture came under intense criticism for delinking Serbian abuses from the peace negotiations. "It's fine to argue that human rights and negotiations should be kept separated," said one critic, "but the negotiations should not give the appearance of condoning genocide." In addition, the negotiations were seen as legitimizing the ethnic division of Bosnia and allowing the Serbs to buy time while continuing to push ahead with ethnic cleansing. Asbjorn Eide, the United Nations' Special Rapporteur on the Human Rights of Minorities, said that "the effect of the Vance-Owen plan was to accelerate ethnic purity in the regions controlled by the three ethnic groups, instead of trying to protect minorities or arrange for their harmonious coexistence within the boundaries of Bosnia." "This," he concluded, "had set a dangerous precedent for handling minorities elsewhere in Europe." Despite these criticisms, the British government was firmly committed to the success of the Vance-Owen venture. In its view, the best way to stop the atrocities was to stop the war. Britain was, therefore, reluctant to embrace any actions against the Bosnian Serbs that could potentially disrupt the peace negotiations which limped on without a major breakthrough for four years.

Russia, for its own very different reasons, was also strongly opposed to aggressive actions by the United Nations against the Bosnian Serbs. Russia is linked to Serbia by religion, alphabet, and history, and when the war began in 1991, scores of sympathetic Russians went to the Serb side. Russian hard-liners exploited these links and pressured the Yeltsin government to exercise a de facto veto at the Security Council whenever forceful measures were being considered. Moreover, the Yeltsin government had its own interest in precluding setting of an interventionist precedent by the international community— a precedent that could be used against Moscow in its deal with its own minorities. With its human rights record under constant attack in recent years, the fifth permanent member of the Security Council, China, had a similar motivation for opposing forceful by the U.N. in Bosnia. But, unlike Russia, China had rarely exercised its veto in the Security Council, preferring instead to express satisfaction through abstention.

Thus, despite growing public pressure to respond to the Bosnian atrocities, the permanent members of the Security Council—the United States, Britain, France, Russia, and China—remained unwilling institute vigorous actions to halt the bloodshed and abuses. Instead, they imposed a one-sided arms embargo; they adopted a resolution authorizing the use of military force which was never implemented; they imposed toothless economic sanctions that were so riddled with loopholes as to be completely ineffective; they established a "no-fly zone" which was violated over four hundred times with impunity; and they created "safe areas" which became the sites of the conflict's worst massacres.

After fighting broke out in Slovenia and Croatia in 1991, Belgrade requested that the Security Council impose an arms embargo on Yugoslavia to prevent an escalation of the conflict. Later, the Security Council reaffirmed that its arms embargo would continue to apply to all parts of the former Yugoslavia, "any decisions on the question of the recognition of the independence of certain republics notwithstanding." The only state truly effected by the arms embargo was Bosnia, which was left with no means to defend itself, while Serbia and Croatia had all they needed in terms of military equipment and Supplies. President Clinton had campaigned on a pledge to lift the arms embargo on Bosnia, but when he came to office, Russia, Britain, and France made clear that they "would not tolerate a lifting of the arms embargo under any circumstances." Meanwhile, Bosnia was literally pushed to the brink of extinction.

The main thrust of early Security Council action in Bosnia was to provide humanitarian aid. This led to a gradual expansion of the size and mandate of UNPROFOR, which had originally been created to monitor the cease-fire between Serbia and Croatia. In response to frequent Serb attacks on U.N. humanitarian aid convoys, on August 13, 1992, the Security Council adopted Resolution 770 authorizing governments to take "all measures necessary" to ensure the safe delivery of relief aid in Bosnia. This was the same formula that in Resolution 678 authorized the use of massive military force to expel Iraq from Kuwait. International expectations were high for a corresponding response in Bosnia. But, unlike Resolution 678, Resolution 770 led to no military intervention. There was no attempt to launch airstrikes and no plan to send in coalition forces. As U.S. Secretary of State Lawrence Eagleburger explained two weeks after the adoption of the resolution, such action would "not be stomached on either side of the Atlantic." For three years the resolution would remain a dead letter and a monument to the Security Council's lack of will to stop the killing in Bosnia.

Yet the Security Council was not willing to let Serb ethnic cleansing go completely unpunished. The Council decided to impose an economic embargo on Serbia in order to disrupt its economy and thereby "apply pressure on Serbia-Montenegro to meet U.N. demands to cease outside aggression and interference in Bosnia." However, the initial sanctions resolution (Resolution 757) was substantially watered down to satisfy Russian objections. For example, an exception was inserted into the resolution allowing for the transshipment of goods across the territory of Serbia, which were readily diverted to destinations within Serbia itself. Another exception allowed for the shipment of humanitarian items to Serbia, including cigarettes, vodka, clothing, and heating oil, which were freely diverted to the Serb army and paramilitary forces. The embargo, moreover, did not cover shipments to Serb-controlled territories in Bosnia.

In addition, the resolution provided for no enforcement such as maritime interdiction of vessels trading with Serbia-Montenegro or the placement of monitors at Serbia's borders. These loopholes and the lack of enforcement enabled Serbia to successfully circumvent the sanctions. Even after the sanctions were incrementally strengthened through the adoption of Resolution 787 in November 1992 and Resolution 820 in April 1993, they had no perceptible impact on the willingness or ability of the Bosnian Serbs to continue to wage war and commit atrocities.

Another type of sanction pursued was the suspension of Serbia from the General Assembly. When Yugoslavia broke apart in 1992, Croatia, Slovenia, Bosnia, and Macedonia each applied and was accepted as a new member of the United Nations. Serbia knew that the Security Council was unlikely to approve its application any time soon, so Serbia and Montenegro announced that they were the continuation of the old Yugoslavia and were thus entitled to continue its membership at the United Nations. This was, after all, what Russia had been allowed to do after the breakup of the Soviet Union in 1991. The United States, however, did not see that precedent as applicable. In contrast to Russia, Serbia-Montenegro did not comprise a majority of the former Yugoslavia's land, population, or resources, and there had been no agreement between the former Yugoslav republics providing that Serbia-Montenegro should continue Yugoslavia's membership in the United Nations. The United States circulated a draft Security Council resolution that would have denied Serbia-Montenegro's claim and confirm that Yugoslavia's membership in the United Nations had been extinguished with the dissolution of that country. In order to obtain Russian support, however, the resolution was substantially weakened and the U.N. legal counsel interpreted the text as precluding Serbia-Montenegro from participating in the General Assembly, but permitting it to continue to maintain its mission at New York and participate in other U.N. bodies. What was intended to be a legal rejection of Serbia-Montenegro's claim to the Yugoslav seat at the United Nations became, in effect, a new kind of suspension which the International Court of Justice later said was "not free from legal difficulty."

While waiting for the sanctions to take effect, the Security Council found itself faced with a new challenge when Bosnian Serb aircraft began to attack civilian targets from their air base in the Bosnian Serb-controlled city of Banja Luka. The Muslims, who had no airforce, were extremely vulnerable to such "ethnic cleansing by air" and the casualties quickly mounted. In response, on October 9, 1992, the Security Council adopted Resolution 781 imposing a "no-fly zone" over Bosnia. At the urging of the British and French, the clause providing for enforcement of the no-fly zone was omitted from the resolution.

Instead, the resolution called only for monitors to report violations. They had plenty to report. During the next six months there were over 465 documented violations of the no-fly zone. Yet it was not until March 31, 1993, that the Security Council adopted Resolution 816 authorizing NATO to enforce the no-fly zone, and it was not until February 8,1994, that NATO would finally take action to shoot down Serb aircraft violating the ban. This year-and-a-half delay was not a logistical one; it was purely political.

By far the most controversial of all of the (non)actions taken by the Security Council was the creation of so-called "safe areas" in response to the sustained Serb attacks on the Muslim population centers at the beginning of 1993. In the spring of 1993, the attacks on Srebrenica in eastern Bosnia were particularly ruthless, and by the beginning of April, the city was on the brink of collapse. On April 16, the Security Council adopted Resolution 819 which demanded that all parties treat the city as a "safe area" free from armed attack. A week later, the Council adopted Resolution 824 designating the predominantly Muslim cities of Sarajevo, Tuzla, Zepa, Gorazde, and Bihac as additional safe areas. As a quid pro quo for the withdrawal of Serb forces, UNPROFOR was assigned the task of overseeing the demilitarization of the safe areas. Yet the Council provided no real enforcement component to the safe area concept. While the UNPROFOR commander indicated that it would take 35,000 troops to protect the safe areas, "the Council irresponsibly chose a 'light option' of a 7,500 troop reinforcement to carry out the mandate." When the Serbs attacked the safe areas, the blue helmets retreated, and tens of thousands of defenseless civilians were massacred and carted off to mass graves in the nearby countryside. "Historians will show," wrote the editors of The New Republic shortly after the fall of Srebrenica, "that the most important allies of the Bosnian Serbs have been the peacekeeping forces of the United Nations."

## Authors' Note

The following six Security Council resolutions demonstrate the implementation of the Security Council's Chapter VII powers granted by the U.N. Charter. The powers include condemnation (Iraq, 1990), economic sanctions (Serbia, 1992), no-fly zone (Bosnia, 1992), safe areas (Bosnia, 1993), investigative commission (Bosnia, 1992), and the use of force (Iraq, 1990). These resolutions show the spectrum of powers that are available to the Security Council, depicting the different level of severity.

# 6. Model Security Council Actions

## A. S.C. Res. 667: Condemnation (Iraq)

Adopted by the Security Council at its 2940th meeting, on 16 September 1990.

*The Security Council,*

*Reaffirming* its resolutions 660 (1990), 661 (1990), 662 (1990), 664 (1990), 665 (1990) and 666 (1990),

*Recalling* the Vienna Conventions of 18 April 1961 on diplomatic relations and of 24 April 1963 on consular relations, to both of which Iraq is a party,

*Considering* that the decision of Iraq to order the closure of diplomatic and consular missions in Kuwait and to withdraw the immunity and privileges of these missions and their personnel is contrary to the decisions of the Security Council, the international Conventions mentioned above and international law,

*Deeply concerned* that Iraq, notwithstanding the decisions of the Security Council and the provisions of the Conventions mentioned above, has committed acts of violence against diplomatic missions and their personnel in Kuwait,

*Outraged* at recent violations by Iraq of diplomatic premises in Kuwait and at the abduction of personnel enjoying diplomatic immunity and foreign nationals who were present in these premises,

*Considering also* that the above actions by Iraq constitute aggressive acts and a flagrant violation of its international obligations which strike at the root of the conduct of international relations in accordance with the Charter of the United Nations,

*Recalling* that Iraq is fully responsible for any use of violence against foreign nationals or against any diplomatic or consular mission in Kuwait or its personnel,

*Determined* to ensure respect for its decisions and for Article 25 of the Charter of the United Nations,

*Considering further* that the grave nature of Iraq's actions, which constitute a new escalation of its violations of international law, obliges the Council not only to express its immediate reaction but also to consult urgently to take further concrete measures to ensure Iraq's compliance with the Council's resolutions,

*Acting* under Chapter VII of the Charter of the United Nations,

1. *Strongly condemns* aggressive acts perpetrated by Iraq against diplomatic premises and personnel in Kuwait, including the abduction of foreign nationals who were present in those premises;

2. *Demands* the immediate release of those foreign nationals as well as all nationals mentioned in resolution 664 (1990);

3. *Also demands* that Iraq immediately and fully comply with its international obligations under resolutions 660 (1990), 662 (1990) and 664 (1990) of the Security Council, the Vienna Conventions on diplomatic and consular relations and international law;

4. *Further demands* that Iraq immediately protect the safety and well-being of diplomatic and consular personnel and premises in Kuwait and in Iraq and take no action to hinder the diplomatic and consular missions in the performance of their functions, including access to their nationals and the protection of their person and interests;

5. *Reminds* all States that they are obliged to observe strictly resolutions 661 (1990), 662 (1990), 664 (1990), 665 (1990) and 666 (1990);

6. *Decides* to consult urgently to take further concrete measures as soon as possible, under Chapter VII of the Charter in response to Iraq's continued violation of the Charter, of resolutions of the Council and of International law.

Adopted unanimously.

---

### B. S.C. Res. 757: Economic Sanctions (Serbia)

*The Security Council,*

*Reaffirming* its resolutions 713 (1991) of 25 September 1991, 721 (1991) of 27 November 1991, 724 (1991) of 15 December 1991, 727 (1992) of 8 January 1992, 740(1992) of 7 February 1992, 743 (1992) of 21 February 1992. 749 (1992) of 7 April 1992 and 752 (1992) of 15 May 1992,

*Noting* that in the very complex context of events in the former Socialist Federal Republic of Yugoslavia all parties bear some responsibility for the situation,

*Reaffirming* its support for the Conference on Yugoslavia, including the efforts undertaken by the European Community in the framework of the discussions on constitutional arrangements for Bosnia and Herzegovina, and recalling that no territorial gains or changes brought about by violence are acceptable and that the borders of Bosnia and Herzegovina are inviolable.

*Deploring* the fact that the demands in resolution 752 (1992) have not been complied with, including its demands that:

- All panics and others concerned in Bosnia and Herzegovina stop the fighting immediately,
- All forms of interference from outside Bosnia and Herzegovina cease immediately,
- Bosnia and Herzegovina's neighbors take swift action to end all interference and respect the territorial integrity of Bosnia and Herzegovina,
- Action be taken as regards units of the Yugoslav People's Army in Bosnia and Herzegovina, including the disbanding and disarming with weapons placed under effective international monitoring of any units that are neither withdrawn nor placed under the authority of the Government of Bosnia and Herzegovina,
- All irregular forces in Bosnia and Herzegovina be disbanded and disarmed,

*Deploring also* that its call for the immediate cessation of forcible expulsions and attempts to change the ethnic composition of the population has not been heeded, and reaffirming in this context the need for the effective protection of human rights and fundamental freedoms, including those of ethnic minorities,

*Dismayed* that conditions have not yet been established for the effective arid unhindered delivery of humanitarian assistance, inducting safe and secure access to and from Sarajevo and other airports in Bosnia and Herzegovina,

*Deeply concerned* that those United Nations Protection Force personnel remaining in Sarajevo have been subjected to deliberate mortar and small-arms fire, and that the United Nations Military Observers deployed in the Mostar region have had to be withdrawn,

*Deeply concerned also* at developments in Croatia, including persistent cease-fire violations and the continued expulsion of non-Serb civilians, and at the obstruction of and lack of cooperation with the Force in other parts of Croatia,

*Deploring* the tragic incident on 18 May 1992 which caused the death of a member of the International Committee of the Red Cross team in Bosnia and Herzegovina,

*Noting* that the claim by the Federal Republic of Yugoslavia (Serbia and Montenegro) to continue automatically the membership of the former Socialist Federal Republic of Yugoslavia in the United Nations has not been generally accepted,

*Expressing its appreciation* for the report of the Secretary-General of 26 May 1992 submitted pursuant to Security Council resolution 752 (1992),

*Recalling* its primary responsibility under the Charter of the United Nations for the maintenance of international peace and security,

*Recalling also* the provisions of Chapter VIII of the Charter, and the continuing role that the European Community is playing in working for a peaceful solution in Bosnia and Herzegovina, as well as in other republics of the former Socialist Federal Republic of Yugoslavia,

*Recalling further* its decision in resolution 752 (1992) to consider further steps to achieve a peaceful solution in conformity with its relevant resolutions, and affirming its determination to take measures against any party or parties which fail to fulfill the requirements of resolution 752 (1992) and its other relevant resolutions,

*Determined* in this context to adopt certain measures with the sole objective of achieving a peaceful solution and encouraging the efforts undertaken by the European Community and its member States,

*Recalling* the right of States, under Article 50 of the Charter, to consult the Council where they find themselves confronted with special economic problems arising from the carrying out of preventive or enforcement measures,

*Determining* that the situation in Bosnia and Herzegovina and in other parts of the former Socialist Federal Republic of Yugoslavia constitutes a threat to international peace and security,

*Acting* under Chapter VII of the Charter,

1. *Condemns* the failure of the authorities in the Federal Republic of Yugoslavia (Serbia and Montenegro), including the Yugoslav People's Army, to take effective measures to fulfill the requirements of resolution 752 (1992);

2. *Demands* that any elements of the Croatian Army still present in Bosnia and Herzegovina act in accordance with paragraph 4 of resolution 752 (1992) without further delay

3. *Decides* that all States shall adopt the measures set out below, which shall apply until the Council decides that the authorities in the Federal Republic of Yugoslavia (Serbia and Montenegro), including the Yugoslav People's Army, have taken effective measures to fulfill the requirements of resolution 752 (1992);

4. *Decides also* that all States shall prevent:

   (a) The import into their territories of all commodities and products originating in the Federal Republic of Yugoslavia (Serbia and Montenegro) exported therefrom after the date of the present resolution;

   (b) Any activities by their nationals or in their territories which would promote or are calculated to promote the export or transshipment of any commodities or products originating in the Federal Republic of Yugoslavia (Serbia and Montenegro); and any dealings by their nationals or their flag vessels or aircraft or in their territories in any commodities or products originating in the Federal Republic of Yugoslavia (Serbia and Montenegro) and exported therefrom after the date of the present resolution, including in particular any transfer of funds to the Federal Republic of Yugoslavia (Serbia and Montenegro) for the purposes of such activities or dealings;

(c) The sale or supply by their nationals or from their territories or using their flag vessels or aircraft of any commodities or products, whether or not originating in their territories—but not including supplies intended strictly for medical purposes and foodstuffs notified to the Security Council Committee established pursuant to resolution 724 (1991) on Yugoslavia—to any person or body in the Federal Republic of Yugoslavia (Serbia and Montenegro) or to any person or body for the purposes of any business carried on in or operated from the Federal Republic of Yugoslavia (Serbia and Montenegro), and any activities by their nationals or in their territories which promote or are calculated to promote such sale or supply of such commodities or products;

5. *Decide further* that no State shall make available to the authorities in the Federal Republic of Yugoslavia (Serbia and Montenegro) or to any commercial, industrial or public utility undertaking in the Federal Republic of Yugoslavia (Serbia and Montenegro), any funds or any other financial or economic resources and shall prevent their nationals and any persons within their territories from removing from their territories or otherwise making available to those authorities or to any such undertaking any such funds or resources and from remitting any other funds to persons or bodies within the Federal Republic of Yugoslavia (Serbia and Montenegro), except payments exclusively for strictly medical or humanitarian purposes and foodstuffs;

6. *Decides* that the prohibitions in paragraphs 4 and 5 shall not apply to the transshipment through the Federal Republic of Yugoslavia (Serbia and Montenegro) of commodities and products originating outside the Federal Republic of Yugoslavia (Serbia and Montenegro) and temporarily present in the territory of the Federal Republic of Yugoslavia (Serbia and Montenegro) only for the purpose of such transshipment, in accordance with guidelines approved by the Security Council Committee established by resolution 724 (1991);

7. *Decides* that all States shall:

(a) Deny permission to any aircraft to take off from, land in or overfly their territory if it is destined to land in or has taken off from the territory of the Federal Republic of Yugoslavia (Serbia and Montenegro), unless the particular flight has been approved, for humanitarian or other purposes consistent with the relevant resolutions of the Council, by the Security Council Committee established by resolution 724 (1991);

(b) Prohibit, by their nationals or from their territory, the provision of engineering and maintenance servicing of aircraft registered in the Federal Republic of Yugoslavia (Serbia and Montenegro) or operated by or on behalf of entities in the Federal Republic of Yugoslavia (Serbia and Montenegro) or components for such aircraft, the certification of airworthiness for such aircraft, and the payment of new claims against existing insurance contracts and the provision of new direct insurance for such aircraft

8. *Decides also* that all States shall:

(a) Reduce the level of the staff at diplomatic missions and consular posts of the Federal Republic of Yugoslavia (Serbia and Montenegro);

(b) Take the necessary steps to prevent the participation in sporting events on their territory of persons or groups representing the Federal Republic of Yugoslavia (Serbia and Montenegro);

(c) Suspend scientific and technical cooperation and cultural exchanges and visits involving persons or groups officially sponsored by or representing the Federal Republic of Yugoslavia (Serbia and Montenegro);

9. *Decides further* that all States, and the authorities in the Federal Republic of Yugoslavia (Serbia and Montenegro), shall take the necessary measures to ensure that no claim shall lie at the instance of the authorities in the Federal Republic of Yugoslavia (Serbia and Montenegro), or of any person or body in the Federal Republic of Yugoslavia (Serbia and Montenegro) or of any person claiming through or for the benefit of any such person or body, in connection with any contract or other transaction where its performance was affected by reason of the measures imposed by the present resolution and related resolutions;

10. *Decide* that the measures imposed by the present resolution shall not apply to activities related to the United Nations Protection Force, to the Conference on Yugoslavia or to the European Community Monitoring Mission, and that States, parties and others concerned shall cooperate fully with the Force, the Conference and the Mission and respect fully their freedom of movement and the safety of their personnel;

11. *Calls upon* all States, including States not members of the United Nations, and all international organizations, to act strictly in accordance with the provisions of the present resolution, notwithstanding the existence of any rights or obligations conferred or imposed by any international agreement or any contract entered into or any license or permit granted prior to the date of the present resolution;

12. *Request* all States to report to the Secretary-General by 22 June 1992 on the measures they have instituted for meeting the obligations set out in paragraphs 4 to 9;

13. *Decides* that the Security Council Committee established by resolution 724 (1991) shall undertake the following tasks additional to those in respect of the arms embargo established by resolutions 713 (1991) and 727 (1992):

(a) To examine the reports submitted pursuant to paragraph 12 above;

(b) To seek from all States further information regarding the action taken by them concerning the effective implementation of the measures imposed by paragraphs 4 to 9;

(c) To consider any information brought to its attention by States concerning violations of the measures imposed by paragraphs 4 to 9 and, in that context, to make recommendations to the Council on ways to increase their effectiveness;

(d) To recommend appropriate measures in response to violations of the measures imposed by paragraphs 4 to 9 and to provide information on a regular basis to the Secretary-General for general distribution to Member States;

(e) To consider and approve the guidelines referred to in paragraph 6 above;

(f) To consider and decide upon expeditiously any applications for the approval of flights for humanitarian or other purposes consistent with the relevant resolutions of the Council in accordance with paragraph 7 above;

14. *Calls upon* all States to cooperate fully with the Security Council Committee established by Security Council resolution 724 (1991) in the fulfillment of its tasks, including supplying such information as may be sought by the Committee in pursuance of the present resolution;

15. *Requests* the Secretary-General to report to the Security Council, not later than 15 June 1992 and earlier if he considers it appropriate, on the implementation of resolution 752 (1992) by all parties and others concerned;

16. *Decides* to keep under continuous review the measures imposed by paragraphs 4 to 9 with a view to considering whether such measures might be suspended or terminated following compliance with the requirements of resolution 752 (1992);

17. *Demands* that all parties and others concerned create immediately the necessary conditions for unimpeded delivery of humanitarian supplies to Sarajevo and other destinations in Bosnia and Herzegovina, including the establishment of a security zone encompassing Sarajevo and its airport and respecting the agreements signed at Geneva on 22 May 1992;

18. *Requests* the Secretary-General to continue to use his good offices in order to achieve the objectives contained in paragraph 17 above, and invites him to keep under continuous review any further measures that may become necessary to ensure unimpeded delivery of humanitarian supplies;

19. *Urges* all States to respond to the Revised Joint Appeal for humanitarian assistance of early May 1992 issued by the United Nations High Commissioner for Refugees, the United Nations Children's Fund and the World Health Organization;

20. *Reiterates* the call in paragraph 2 of resolution 752 (1992) that all parties continue their efforts in the framework of the Conference on Yugoslavia arid that the three communities in Bosnia and Herzegovina resume their discussions on constitutional arrangements for Bosnia and Herzegovina;

21. *Decides* to remain actively seized of the matter and to consider immediately, whenever necessary, further steps to achieve a peaceful solution in conformity with its relevant resolutions.

Adopted at the 3082nd meeting by 13 votes to none, with 2 abstentions (China, Zimbabwe).

---

### C. S.C. Res. 816: No-Fly Zone (Bosnia)

*The Security Council,*

*Recalling* its resolutions 781 (1992) of 9 October 1992 and 786 (1992) of 10 November 1992,

*Recalling* also paragraph 6 of resolution 781 (1992) and paragraph 6 of resolution 786 (1992) in which the Council undertook to consider urgently, in the case of violations of the ban on military flights in the airspace of the Republic of Bosnia and Herzegovina, the further measures necessary to enforce the ban,

*Deploring* the failure of some parties concerned to cooperate fully with airfield monitors of the United Nations Protection Force in the implementation of resolutions 781 (1992) and 786 (1992),

*Deeply concerned* by the various reports of the Secretary-General concerning violations of the ban on military flights in the airspace of Bosnia and Herzegovina,"

*Deeply concerned* in particular by the letters dated 12 and 16 March 1993 from the Secretary-General to the President of the Security Council concerning new blatant violations of the ban on military flights in the airspace of Bosnia and Herzegovina, and recalling in this regard the statement by the President of the Security Council of 17 March 1993, and in particular the reference to the bombing of villages in Bosnia and Herzegovina,

*Recalling* the provisions of Chapter VIII of the Charter of the United Nations,

Determining that the grave situation in Bosnia and Herzegovina continues to be a threat to international peace and security,

*Acting* under Chapter VII of the Charter,

1. *Decides* to extend the ban established by resolution 781 (1992) to cover flights by all fixed-wing and rotary-wing aircraft in the airspace of the Republic of Bosnia and Herzegovina, this ban not to apply to flights authorized by the United Nations Protection Force in accordance with paragraph 2 below,

2. *Requests* the Force to modify the mechanism referred to in paragraph 3 of Resolution 781 (1992) so as to provide for the authorization, in the airspace of Bosnia and Herzegovina, of humanitarian fights and other flights consistent with relevant resolutions of the Council;

3. *Also requests* the Force to continue to monitor compliance with the ban on flights in the airspace of Bosnia and Herzegovina, and calls on all parties urgently to cooperate with the Force in making practical arrangements for the close monitoring of authorized flights and improving the notification procedures;

4. *Authorizes* Member States, seven days after the adoption of the present resolution, acting nationally or through regional organizations or arrangements, to take, under the authority of the Security Council and subject to close coordination with the Secretary-General and the Force, all necessary measures in the airspace of Bosnia and Herzegovina, in the event of further violations, to ensure compliance with the ban on fights referred to in paragraph 1 above, and proportionate to the specific circumstances and the nature of the flights;

5. *Requests* the Member States, the Secretary-General and the Force to coordinate closely on the measures they are taking to implement paragraph 4 above, including the rules of engagement, and on the starting date of its implementation, which should be no later than seven days from the date when the authority conferred by paragraph 4 above takes effect, and to report the starting date to the Council through the Secretary-General.

6. *Decides* that, in the event of the Co-Chairmen of the Steering Committee of the International Conference on the Former Yugoslavia notifying the Council that all the Bosnian parties have accepted their proposals on a settlement before the starting date referred to in paragraph 5 above, the measures set forth in the present resolution will be subsumed into the measures for implementing that settlement;

7. *Also requests* the Member States to inform the Secretary-General immediately of any action they take in exercise of the authority conferred by paragraph 4 above.

8. *Requests* the Secretary-General to report regularly to the Council on the matter and to inform it immediately of any action taken by the Member States concerned in exercise of the authority conferred by paragraph 4 above;

9. *Decides* to remain actively seized of the matter.

Adopted at the 3191st meeting by 14 votes to none, with 1 abstention (China).

---

### D. S.C. Res. 824: Safe Areas (Bosnia)

Adopted by the Security Council at its 3208th meeting, on 6 May 1993.

*The Security Council,*

   *Reaffirming* all its earlier relevant resolutions,

*Reaffirming* also the sovereignty, territorial integrity and political independence of the Republic of Bosnia and Herzegovina,

*Having considered* the report of the Mission of the Security Council to the Republic of Bosnia and Herzegovina (S/25700) authorized by resolution 819 (1993), and in particular, its recommendations that the concept of safe areas be extended to other towns in need of safety,

*Reaffirming again* its condemnation of all violations of international humanitarian law, in particular, ethnic cleansing and all practices conducive thereto, as well as the denial or the obstruction of access of civilians to humanitarian aid and services such as medical assistance and basic utilities,

*Taking into consideration* the urgent security and humanitarian needs faced by several towns in the Republic of Bosnia and Herzegovina as exacerbated by the constant influx of large numbers of displaced persons including, in particular, the sick and wounded,

*Taking also into consideration* the formal request submitted by the Republic of Bosnia and Herzegovina (S/25718),

*Deeply concerned* at the continuing armed hostilities by Bosnian Serb paramilitary units against several towns in the Republic of Bosnia and Herzegovina and determined to ensure peace and stability throughout the country, most immediately in the towns of Sarajevo, Tuzla, Zepa, Gorazde, Bihac, as well as Srebrenica,

*Convinced* that the threatened towns and their surroundings should be treated as safe areas, free from armed attacks and from any other hostile acts which endanger the well-being and the safety of their inhabitants,

*Aware* in this context of the unique character of the city of Sarajevo, as a multicultural, multiethnic and plurireligious centre which exemplifies the viability of coexistence and interrelations between all the communities of the Republic of Bosnia and Herzegovina, and of the need to preserve it and avoid its further destruction,

*Affirming* that nothing in the present resolution should be construed as contradicting or in any way departing from the spirit or the letter of the peace plan for the Republic of Bosnia and Herzegovina,

*Convinced* that treating the towns referred to above as safe areas will contribute to the early implementation of the peace plan,

*Convinced also* that further steps must be taken as necessary to achieve the security of all such safe areas,

*Recalling* the provisions of resolution 815 (1993) on the mandate of UNPROFOR and in that context acting under Chapter VII of the Charter,

1. *Welcomes* the report of the Mission of the Security Council established pursuant to resolution 819 (1993), and in particular its recommendations concerning safe areas;

2. *Demands* that any taking of territory by force cease immediately;

3. *Declares* that the capital city of the Republic of Bosnia and Herzegovina, Sarajevo, and other such threatened areas, in particular the towns of Tuzla, Zepa, Gorazde, Bihac, as well as Srebrenica, and their surroundings should be treated as safe areas by all the parties concerned and should be free from armed attacks and from any other hostile act;

4. *Further declares* that in these safe areas the following should be observed:

(a) The immediate cessation of armed attacks or any hostile act against these safe areas, and the withdrawal of all Bosnian Serb military or paramilitary units from these towns to a distance where from they cease to constitute a menace to their security and that of their inhabitants to be monitored by United Nations military observers;

(b) Full respect by all parties of the rights of the United Nations Protection Force (UNPROFOR) and the international humanitarian agencies to free and unimpeded access to all sate—areas in the Republic of Bosnia and Herzegovina and full respect for the safety of the personnel engaged in these operations;

5. *Demands* to that end that all parties and others concerned cooperate fully with UNPROFOR and take any necessary measures to respect these safe areas;

6. *Requests* the Secretary—General to take appropriate measures with a view to monitoring the humanitarian situation in the safe areas and to that end, authorizes the strengthening of UNPROFOR by an additional 50 United Nations military observers, together with related equipment and logistical support; and in this connection, also demands that all parties and all others concerned cooperate fully and promptly with UNPROFOR;

7. *Declares* its readiness, in the event of the failure by any party to comply with the present resolution, to consider immediately the adoption of any additional measures necessary with a view to its full implementation, including to ensure respect for the safety of United Nations personnel;

8. *Declares also* that arrangements pursuant to the present resolution shall remain in force up until the provisions for the cessation of hostilities, separation of forces and supervision of heavy weaponry as envisaged in the peace plan for the Republic of Bosnia and Herzegovina, are implemented;

9. *Decides* to remain seized of the matter.

---

### E. S.C. Res. 780: Investigative Commission (Bosnia)

Adopted by the Security Council at its 3119th meeting, on 6 October 1992.

*The Security Council,*

*Reaffirming* its resolution 713 (1991) of 25 September 1991 and all subsequent relevant resolutions,

*Recalling* paragraph 10 of its resolution 764 (1992) of 13 July 1992. in which it reaffirmed that all parties are bound to comply with the obligations under international humanitarian law and in particular the Geneva Conventions of 12 August 1949. 1/ and that persons who commit or order the commission of grave breaches of the Conventions are individually responsible in respect of such breaches,

*Recalling also* its resolution 771 (1992) of 13 August 1992, in which, *inter alia*, it demanded that all parties and others concerned in the former Yugoslavia, and all military forces in Bosnia and Herzegovina, immediately cease and desist from all breaches of international humanitarian law,

*Expressing* once again its grave alarm at continuing reports of widespread violations of international humanitarian law occurring within the territory of the former Yugoslavia and especially in Bosnia and Herzegovina, including reports of mass killings and the continuance of the practice of ethnic cleansing,

1. *Reaffirms* its call, in paragraph 5 of resolution 77]. (1992), upon States and, as appropriate, international humanitarian organizations to collate substantiated information in their possession or submitted to them relating to the violations of humanitarian law, including grave breaches of the Geneva Conventions being committed in the territory of the former Yugoslavia, and requests States, relevant United Nations bodies, and relevant organizations to make this information available within thirty days of the adoption of the present resolution and as appropriate thereafter, and to provide other appropriate assistance to the Commission of Experts referred to in paragraph 2 below;

2. *Requests* the Secretary-General to establish, as a matter of urgency, an impartial Commission of Experts to examine and analyse the information submitted pursuant to resolution 771 (1992) and the present resolution, together with such further information as the Commission of Experts may obtain through its own investigations or efforts, of other persons or bodies pursuant to resolution 771 (1992), with a view to providing the Secretary—General with its conclusions on the evidence of grave breaches of the Geneva Conventions and other violations of international humanitarian law committed in the territory of the former Yugoslavia;

3. *Also requests* the Secretary-General to report to the Council on the establishment of the Commission of Experts;

4. *Further requests* the Secretary-General to report to the Council on the conclusions of the Commission of Experts and to take account of these conclusions in any recommendations for further appropriate steps called for by resolution 771 (1992);

5. *Decides* to remain actively seized of the matter.

---

### F. S.C. Res. 678: Use of Force (Iraq)

Adopted by the Security Council at its 2963rd meeting, on 29 November 1990.

*The Security Council,*

*Recalling and reaffirming* its resolutions 660 (1990) of 2 August 1990, 661 (1990) of 6 August 1990, 662 (1990) of 9 August 1990, 664 (1990) of 18 August 1990, 665 (1990) of 25 August 1990, 666 (1990) of 13 September 1990, 667 (1990) of 16 September 1990, 669 (1990) of 24 September 1990, 670 (1990) of 25 September 1990, 674 (1990) of 29 October 1990 and 677 (1990) of 28 November 1990,

*Noting* that, despite all efforts by the United Nations, Iraq refuses to comply with its obligation to implement resolution 660 (1990) and the above-mentioned subsequent relevant resolutions, in flagrant contempt of the Security Council,

*Mindful* of its duties and responsibilities under the Charter of the United Nations for the maintenance and preservation of international peace and security,

*Determined* to secure full compliance with its decisions,

*Acting* under Chapter VII of the Charter,

1. *Demands* that Iraq comply fully with resolution 660 (1990) and all subsequent relevant resolutions, and decides, while maintaining all its decisions, to allow Iraq one final opportunity, as a pause of goodwill, to do so;

2. *Authorizes* Member States co-operating with the Government of Kuwait, unless Iraq on or before 15 January 1991 fully implements, as set forth in paragraph 1 above, the foregoing resolutions, to use all necessary means to uphold and implement resolution 660

(1990) and all subsequent relevant resolutions and to restore international peace and security in the area;

3. *Requests* all States to provide appropriate support for the actions undertaken in pursuance of paragraph 2 of the present resolution;

4. *Requests* the States concerned to keep the Security Council regularly informed on the progress of actions undertaken pursuant to paragraphs 2 and 3 of the present resolution;

5. *Decides* to remain seized of the matter.

Adopted by 12 votes to 2 (Cuba and Yemen), with 1 abstention (China).

## *Authors' Note*

The rest of this chapter will focus on the efforts to reform the structure and operation of the Security Council. Material 7 provides the relevant U.N. Charter articles that are necessary to amend the Charter. Materials 8, 9, 10, and 11 provide a glimpse into the frustration that motivated the calls for reform of the Security Council. These materials also provide suggestions for remedying the problems of the veto power structure and the number of countries represented in both a permanent and non-permanent status in the Council. As there has been no reform in the veto power structure and permanent membership status, these arguments and suggestions are just as salient now as they were during the close of the 20th century.

## 7. U.N. Charter, Articles 108 and 109

see http://www.un.org/en/documents/charter/

### Article 108

Amendments to the present Charter shall come into force for all Members of the United Nations when they have been adopted by a vote of two thirds of the members of the General Assembly and ratified in accordance with their respective constitutional processes by two thirds of the Members of the United Nations, including all the permanent members of the Security Council.

### Article 109

A General Conference of the Members of the United Nations for the purpose of reviewing the present Charter may be held at a date and place to be fixed by a two-thirds vote of the members of the General Assembly and by a vote of any nine members of the Security Council. Each Member of the United Nations shall have one vote in the conference.

Any alteration of the present Charter recommended by a two-thirds vote of the conference shall take effect when ratified in accordance with their respective constitutional processes by two thirds of the Members of the United Nations including all the permanent members of the Security Council.

If such a conference has not been held before the tenth annual session of the General Assembly following the coming into force of the present Charter, the proposal to call such a conference shall be placed on the agenda of that session of the General Assembly, and the conference shall be held if so decided by a majority vote of the members of the General Assembly and by a vote of any seven members of the Security Council.

## 8. Timothy Penny and Mark Mullenbach, U.N.'s Chosen Few — A Tricky Feat

*The Christian Science Monitor*, 1997

Last week, the United Nations General Assembly opened its 52nd annual session with the issue of Security Council reform on the minds of many diplomats.

The United States caused a stir over the summer when the State Department announced its support for expanding the permanent membership of the Security Council by five countries, including seats for Japan, Germany, and three developing countries. This announcement was a cause for concern for some countries, such as Italy, which were left out of the restructuring formula.

Italy, which has the world's fifth-largest economy and ranks fifth in overall contributions to the U.N., has participated in several multinational peacekeeping and peace-enforcement operations in recent decades, including Lebanon, the Persian Gulf, Somalia, Mozambique, and Bosnia. Earlier this year, Italy led a multinational protection force in Albania following weeks of chaos in that country.

In response to the State Department's announcement, the Italian Foreign Ministry issued a statement suggesting the U.S. proposal "privileged certain countries to the damage of Italy."

U.S. ambassador to the U.N. Bill Richardson was unable to calm Italy's anger during a summer trip to Rome, and he later said the matter "should not become a litmus test of our enormous friendship" with Italy.

But Italy is only one of several countries that view the issue as one of national prestige and have been mentioned as possible candidates for permanent seats. Besides Germany, Japan, and Italy, other candidates include India, Pakistan, Indonesia, Brazil, Argentina, Mexico, Nigeria, Egypt, and South Africa.

One of the most challenging problems facing the U.N. is choosing just five countries from the list of potential candidates. There is little consensus as to which of these countries and others ought to be added to an expanded Security Council.

For example, India is the world's second most populous country, but it faces serious opposition from its adversary, Pakistan, which has the potential support of other Islamic countries. India also suffers from the perception that while it is a major regional power in South Asia and a frequent contributor to U.N. peacekeeping operations, it hasn't proven itself a global military, economic, or political power.

While Germany and Japan have proven to be major economic powers, they've contributed less to international peace and security expected of a permanent member of the Security Council, although both countries have begun to participate in more peacekeeping operations in recent years.

None of the other candidates have anywhere close to the level of economic, military, or political capabilities that would make them a sure bet for a permanent seat.

Beyond the lack of consensus on which countries to add to the Security Council, there is some question as to whether any additional permanent members of the Security Council should be given the veto power now wielded by the U.S., Russia, China, France, and Great Britain.

Would an expansion in the veto power limit the ability of the council to reach consensus on security-related matters? Since the end of the cold war, the Security Council has functioned reasonably well. The five current permanent members have cooperated on most major security issues. Although they rarely did so during the cold war, Russia and China have begun to participate in some U.N. peacekeeping operations, and Russia agreed last year to participate in the NATO-led mission in Bosnia.

The U.N. working group is expected to make a formal recommendation regarding Security Council expansion this session. Given the controversies linked to the issue, expansion of membership on the Security Council might best be achieved by this formula:

- Permanent membership with veto power for the U.S., Russia, China, France, Great Britain.

- Semipermanent membership without veto power — five rotating seats for two-year terms from among Japan, Germany, Italy, India, Pakistan, Indonesia, Republic of Korea, Brazil, Argentina, Mexico, Canada, Egypt, Nigeria, South Africa, and Ukraine.

- Non-permanent membership without veto power — 10 rotating seats for two year-terms from the rest of the members.

Absent considerable international consensus, there is little chance of meaningful change in the current structure of the Security Council. We would argue that this issue needs to be settled at least in the short term, so that the U.N. can begin to deal with the many problems facing the international community in the next century.

---

## 9. Richard Butler, United Nations: The Security Council Isn't Performing

*International Herald Tribune*, 1999

For the first half of the decade since the Cold War's end, the atmosphere in the United Nations Security Council was decidedly improved. With less East-West divisiveness, the council met more frequently and did more business.

Only seven vetoes were cast in the post-Cold War period, versus 240 in the first 45 years of U.N. life. Twenty peacekeeping operations were mandated, more than the total for all the preceding years.

But then the initial optimism about the council's ability to get its job done in a veto-less world turned sour. During the past 12 months it has been particularly dismaying to watch as the council has been bypassed, defied and abused.

The council was bypassed when NATO began military action against Slobodan Milosevic's Yugoslavia without first seeking Security Council approval. The NATO countries knew that their action would be vetoed by Russia and China.

The significance of NATO's slight was not diminished by its agreement, after the conflict, with Russia to seek Security Council endorsement and U.N. participation in the policing and administration of Kosovo.

In another example, Saddam Hussein defied the Security Council. He assessed correctly that he could get away with disobeying its disarmament resolutions thanks to a combination of influential friends there, a general loss of will within the body and a sympathetic secretary-general.

During the past eight years, many but not all of Iraq's weapons of mass destruction have been eliminated. Disarmament tasks remain to be completed, however, and monitoring and verification systems need to be secured to ensure that Saddam does not reconstitute his illegal weapons.

Yet the Security Council has been unable to reach a decision that would restore, even in a modified way, the implementation of its own law. Indeed, some members — including, incredibly, Canada, a non-permanent council member — have sought to lower the standard of Iraqi compliance.

There has also been abuse of council procedures. China recently prevented minor peacekeeping operations from proceeding in Guatemala and Macedonia because those countries had dealt with Taiwan.

Vetoes driven by national interest more than by any sense of collective responsibility were common during the Cold War. They had been less so since, and there was nothing comparable to these Chinese vetoes and threats of veto.

The Security Council's ability to function as the guardian of international peace and security has been thrown into question by such incidents. In all these cases, permanent members have weighted their narrow national interests over collective responsibility. Clearly, the Security Council is not working adequately. To fix it, two key areas must be addressed urgently.

First is the veto, which has been abused by permanent members in defense of their interests, client states and ideological concerns — subjects which very often had nothing to do with maintaining international peace and security.

Even if it is accepted, for argument's sake, that the profligate use of the veto during the bitter contest of the Cold War might have forestalled its worst consequence, nuclear holocaust, still, in the current context, the raw exercise of veto power is no longer appropriate, much less necessary. Today's world is more interdependent and, if it is threatened, it is by weapons proliferation, not by superpower rivalry.

The veto issue is a vexed one. Clearly the major powers will not give up their veto power voluntarily, and the U.N. Charter allows them to block any proposal that would remove the power to exercise a veto.

The question thus becomes whether the major powers can voluntarily agree to a more constructive interpretation of the nature of the veto and of the uses to which it may legitimately be put. If the United States, the undisputed lone superpower, indicated a willingness to discipline its own use of the veto, it could then ask other permanent members to do the same.

Certainly, in the absence of an American concession, nothing will change. If others will not agree, then neither should the United States.

Only if there is success in reforming the use of veto power can the Security Council be rescued from its present breakdown. An American initiative, however, would also have another advantage: It would temper the growing anxiety in the international community about the policies of its one superpower and America's position in the unipolar world. A move by the United States to effectively share authority would speak volumes. —

Arms control is the second area that requires urgent attention.

Thirty years ago, the international community began a process of drawing up treaties on the nonproliferation of weapons of mass destruction, starting with nuclear and then working through biological, chemical and missile technologies. One of the key questions that inevitably arose was who would enforce such treaties, especially in the event of a detected breach.

Typically, the answer given — sometimes in writing within a particular treaty, but certainly in political terms — was the U.N. Security Council.

The council is the custodian of nonproliferation. It has the task of providing confidence to the international community that the tapestry of treaties designed to ensure that weapons of mass destruction do not spread is enforced and kept whole. There is simply no other body that can do this job, and this is widely understood.

How does the council's decision-making process, including the use of the veto, square with its obligation to enforce the nonproliferation treaties?

A case in point is North Korea, which clandestinely continues to develop nuclear weapons in contravention of its obligations under the Nuclear Nonproliferation Treaty. Because of Chinese, and to some extent Russian, interests, the Security Council has responded inadequately.

The attempted solution to the problem was agreed on largely outside the council, and is not proving viable.

Iraq represents an even more profound failure. Saddam Hussein has broken all its nonproliferation undertakings. He has lied to the United Nations' weapons inspectors. Data indicate that he continues to conceal illegal weapons of mass destruction. Unquestionably, he retains the capacity to make them.

These facts are known in the Security Council, in particular by those permanent members who have given Saddam strong support.

Russia, Iraq's strongest backer in the council, is fully aware of Iraq's weapon status, not least because the Soviet Union was Saddam's major supplier of arms and the means to manufacture them.

The authority of the council is deeply challenged when objective cases of treaty violation such as these end up being judged on a narrow, subjective political basis by veto-wielding permanent members.

Were this to become the council's standard way of dealing with weapons proliferation, it would amount to a profound and, I suspect, mortal failure.

If the permanent members could make reforms in the areas of arms control and veto power, it might help the Security Council get over its "annus horribilis" — as well as serve the interests of the international community in the 21st century. —

The writer is diplomat in residence at the Council on Foreign Relations. He was formerly executive chairman of the United Nations Special Commission, the body charged with disarming Iraq; before that he served for five years as Australia's permanent representative to the United Nations. This article, distributed by New York Times Special Features, was adapted from a longer version in Foreign Affairs.

---

## 10. Amb. Gerhard Benze, Creating a New U.N. Security Council
### Yale Daily News, 1999

Most of the 185 United Nations Member States have been actively involved during the last five years in the work regarding a reform of the Security Council. The key questions relate to additional permanent members and to the future use of the veto power, questions that are again being discussed this year by a Working Group of the General Assembly in New York. Germany, next to Japan the country most frequently considered as a candidate for a new permanent seat, has in this context presented future-oriented proposals for the core issues which are at the center of a particularly heated discussion.

The starting point of the discussion about the reform which is generally considered as being necessary is the structure of the Security Council. It was designed at the Founding Conference in 1945 in San Francisco and has essentially remained unchanged. It consists of five permanent and (after an increase of four in 1965) ten non permanent members, with the non-permanent members changing every two years. This structure is a reflection of the immediate post-war world which was characterized by the outstanding position of the victorious powers and the fact that at that time many countries still were colonies depending on the former colonial powers. After the bitter experience of the failure of the League of Nations and the disastrous Second World War, the U.S., the USSR, Great Britain, France and China wanted to ensure, above all, the maintenance of international peace and security.

The Charter entrusted the Security Council with this task. Since they believed that this was the most effective way to maintain peace in the world the U.S. and others made the right of veto in all essential questions relate to the Security Council a recondition for their membership.

The five above mentioned permanent members thus obtained the right of veto which enable every on of them to unilaterally block all "non-procedural" decisions of the Security Council including those regarding Chapter VII of the Charter (actions with respect to threats to or breaches of international peace), but also other substantial decisions such as the admission or exclusion of U.N. members, the election of the Secretary-General and, in particular, the reform of the Charter.

Since then, the original U.N. Membership of 51 states has grown to 185 Member States and almost all former colonies have achieved their independence. After the Cold War, the nuclear capabilities which for so long were exclusively in the hands of the five permanent members no longer play the same role. Most importantly, there are new political and economic power centers. It is the goal of the reform to take account of these developments by adding additional permanent and non-permanent seats and thus to make the Security Council more democratic and more efficient. In this context, a broad majority of Member States has been emerging since early 1997 which favors an expansion to a total of 24 members including five new permanent and four new non-permanent members.

The question of limiting the existing permanent members' right to veto and of extending it to potential new members remains a highly controversial issue.

Indeed, during the Cold War, the right to veto caused the Security Council to be completely hamstrung. The USSR, for example, use the veto 81 times between early 1946 and late 1955, often to prevent new countries which they considered to be "in the other camp" from becoming members of the U.N.. Even in the era following the East-West conflict, the Security Council has often remained inactive. Considerable affinities (example: Russia-Serb) or antagonism (example: U.S.-Cuba, China-Taiwan) between permanent Member States and third parties often have an excessive influence over Security Council decisions. The effect of the right to veto is increased even more by the fact that the scope of action is often decided in non-public "informal consultations" before the official meetings of the Security Council take place.

In that way it becomes unnecessary to use the veto formally, since it is enough to announce its use during the informal consultations. On the other hand, one should not forget that, without the assent of the most powerful countries, Security Council decisions could never really be carried out. In the end the threat to international peace must be countered frequently with the credible threat of military force in order to preserve the peace.

Therefore the at times ardent criticism that many states express of the right to veto seems to be justified not so much in principle but rather due to its ambiguously defined scope of application, which invites arbitrariness. Above all, the majority of permanent Security Council members continues to be little inclined to abandon the right to veto or to allow any restrictions. Therefore it is unrealistic to expect the agreement of all permanent members on a reform of the veto—the prerequisite for any reform of the U.N. Charter.

At the same time, the question arises whether the right to veto should be transferred onto the new permanent members. The most popular candidates, be their legitimization particularly on the fact that, due to their economic strength (and their corresponding share in the U.N. budget), due to their population size and their democratic and cultural achievements, they have an outstanding position within the international community as the existing permanent members.

It seems to make sense to provide them with the same rights and obligations as the existing permanent members. On the other hand many countries, whose agreement is needed to achieve the necessary two thirds majority of all Member States (i.e., 124) for a reform, view the transferal of U.N. restricted veto power to additional Security Council members with considerable skepticism. They fear that mis-uses would multiply. The existing permanent members, likewise, believe that the efficiency of the Council would be jeopardized in that way. These concerns are directed particularly against candidates from the Southern hemisphere.

In view of all this, the reform of the Security Council may at times seems like an attempt to square the circle. Nevertheless the situation is not hopeless. On the threshold of the third millennium, states should be motivated less by ideas derived from the past about colonial politics and by areas of interests assigned to individual states, but rather by a future that will be characterized by interest becoming more and more linked at a global level.

It is such a future-oriented concept that Germany has introduced into the discussion on Security Council reform. This concept is based on a realistic approach which at this time suggest not a restriction of the right of veto in the U.N. Charter but instead a unilateral commitment by individual states to limiting its use. The permanent members would thus commit themselves, according to resolution 267 (III) of 1949, not to use the veto in cases of solely procedural matters as defined by that resolution. In addition they would commit themselves to present a written explanation every time they use their veto. Great Britain and France have already expressed their willingness to do so.

As to new permanent members, Germany suggested reviewing their performance after a certain period (between ten and twenty years). This idea would allow for a democratic control through the U.N. General Assembly and has since met with the broadest approval. The most difficult issue is the question of veto power for new permanent members. The German proposal envisages to extend a limited right of veto to the new members until a yet to be formed working group will agree on a final modus. Such a "probation phase" would help overcome the reservations of the permanent members.

A limited right of veto could, for example, refer only to military enforcement actions pursuant to Chapter VII of the U.N. Charter (use of military force to re-establish peace, sanctions against states which breach the peace), or it could be used only jointly with at least one other new permanent member.

By implementing this proposal, the international community would create an instrument that could help shape the 21st century, which without question will be the century of globalization. The existing permanent members could thus share the burden that corresponds to their privileges. The Member States as a whole would enjoy a more equal and effective representation of their varied interests.

In the long run there is even reason to hope that a more balanced and future-oriented voting system in the Security Council would favor greater willingness to compromise and improve cooperation between all states.

The reform of the Security Council would also bestow greater legitimacy to its decisions, which, more and more often, is being question with the result that decisions are not always fully implemented. No one can have an interest in questioning the effectiveness of the Security Council.

In the decade following the fall of the Berlin Wall and the end of the East-West conflict, it has become the only body which can authorize the use of military and other enforcement actions. That is a great achievement which should not be put at risk.

*Dr. Gerhard Henze is the German Ambassador to the United Nations.*

---

## 11. U.N. Reforms Could Limit Security Council's Power of Veto
### Agence France-Presse, 1999

Reforms which could include limiting the United Nations Security Council's power of veto and giving more muscle to the organisation's General Assembly were discussed here on Thursday.

Senior U.N. officials, including High Commissioner for Refugees Mary Robinson, and non-governmental organisations are meeting at the U.N.'s European headquarters to discuss subjects for the General Assembly's first meeting of the new millennium, which is scheduled for the final quarter of next year.

The two-day meeting is chaired by Maltese President Guido de Marco, who proposed changes to the power of veto held by the Security Council's five permanent members, the United States, China, France, Russia and Britain.

He proposed that a veto could only be tabled if at least two countries voted against a decision, a change which would limit the possibilities of blocking a vote.

At present only one negative vote from a permanent member is required for power of veto.

De Marco also suggested that the General Assembly — the U.N.'s main deliberative body — meet three times a year instead of once, adding sessions in the first half of the year to the traditional meeting from September to December.

Thursday's meeting agreed on the need to link non-political questions with U.N. decisions. The participants also wanted to see an approach integrating economic development, human rights and peace and security.

The executive secretary of the U.N.'s European economic commission, Yves Berthelot, put forward a proposal to hold a forum of non-political participants early next year in an bid to push the U.N.'s 185 member states towards reform.

The proposals will be forwarded to U.N. Secretary-General Kofi Annan for consideration ahead of the General Assembly.

## Authors' Note

The final two materials provide insight into the reform of the Security Council from the viewpoint of specific Member States. Material 12 illustrates the problems and suggestions for reform from the perspective of Indonesia. This article demonstrates the divisive effects of particular proposed plans for reform. The article emphasizes the effects such plans would have on Indonesia and other States; noting the strong case for Indonesia to be awarded a permanent status on the Council. Material 13 depicts Japan's attempt to garner a spot on the Security Council as a permanent member. This article shows some of the impediments to reform as well as Japan's exasperation at not attaining what it feels to be its well-deserved spot on the Council.

## 12. Imron Cotan, U.N. Council Needs Urgent Reform
### *The Jakarta Post*, 1997

JAKARTA (JP): The United Nations General Assembly is undergoing its 52nd session in New York and as has been previously predicted, the reform of some of its institutions, especially that of the Security Council, is indeed high on the agenda.

Notwithstanding the fact that it has recently resumed its pivotal role in maintaining international peace and security—as stipulated in Chapter V, Article 24, of the U.N. Charter—many attempts have been made to reform the Security Council.

There have been at least two underlining reasons upon which the international community's call for the reform of this powerful organ of the United Nations is based.

First, it is now being considered as nonrepresentative since the members of the United Nations have drastically increased to 185 states.

Second, and of no less importance, the Security Council created undemocratic rules to cater to the cold-war era, allowing a selected few of its members holding permanent seats—namely the United States, Russia (formerly the U.S.S.R.), the United Kingdom, France and China—to exercise individual veto powers over any decisions the Security Council might take.

The need to reform the Security Council has furthermore gained ground, especially among developing countries, due to an increasingly common perception that the Security Council seems to be more of a political tool for the most powerful countries to multilaterally legalize goals relating to their national interests.

The stern and continuous actions taken against Iraq are indeed a striking example and seem to have been blown out of proportion. Ironically, in the meantime, the Security Council is incomprehensibly speechless regarding tragedies of similar magnitude in Bosnia-Herzegovina, Burundi, Israel and Zaire to name but a few cases which it has long been confronted with.

Unfortunately, the attempts to reform the Security Council have so far failed to achieve the looked-for results. It is against this backdrop that the president of the 51st session of the U.N. General Assembly, Ambassador Razali Ismail of Malaysia has taken the initiative to try to reform the Security Council.

His proposals contain the following basic ideas:

First, the permanent members should be increased to ten countries compared to the current five.

Second, two out those five additional seats should be given to Germany and Japan, as they represent the strongest economic powerhouses in our recent history, while the remaining three should be openly contested among the members of the regional groupings of Asia, Africa and Latin America (including the Caribbean), each having one seat respectively.

According to the devised plan, candidates from developing countries could only be elected if they manage to secure the vote of two-thirds of the members of the General Assembly. The initiative furthermore highlighted that all five of the additional permanent members should enjoy no veto rights.

Third, four countries should be elected to function as additional non-permanent members of the Security Council representing respectively, African states, Asian states, Eastern European states and Latin American and Caribbean states.

Fourth, the veto rights of the current permanent members should be subject to scrutiny in the future for eventual abolishment—for the maintenance of such power is being perceived as legitimizing undemocratic values, originating from the cold-war era, which all developing nations object to.

The proposals put forward by Razali seem to be very attractive. They, however, contain elements which demand a closer look. Of cardinal importance is the selection process of the permanent members originating from the developing world.

Unlike Germany and Japan, the three representatives of the developing countries are obligated to freely compete in the General Assembly.

Hence, these countries would not actually represent the aspirations of the region concerned, while at the same time opening the possibility of non-regional countries in the General Assembly to determine the representative of a particular region which they do not belong to.

The best way to circumvent this delicate situation is to select the regional representatives based on a consensus. This, of course, is no easy task either.

The political realities in the regions of Asia, Africa, and Latin America and the Caribbean certainly pose formidable hurdles to consensus-building efforts which would determine the representative country best-suited for each region.

In Asia, India would be questioned by Pakistan and Indonesia. In Africa, Egypt would be challenged by Nigeria or South Africa and vice-versa. While in Latin America and the Caribbean, Brazil would be antagonized by either Argentina or Mexico and the other way around.

Another innovative solution has to be invented. The proposal put forward by Indonesia's Foreign Minister Ali Alatas before the 52nd session of the General Assembly recently is indeed praiseworthy. Alatas proposed that, instead of one, Asia should be given two additional permanent seats in the Security Council.

If this would be applied as well to the two remaining regions, it would greatly help the regions pave the way for achieving a consensus decision.

Without a modification such as Alatas' suggestion, the proposals offered by Razali would not address the nonrepresentative nature of the Security Council. As one might recall in its early inception, the Security Council consisted of 11 countries with the United Nations having 51 members (21.5 percent of the U.N. membership was therefore also part of the Security Council).

Should Razali's formulas be acceptable, the Security Council would merely have 24 members with the United Nations having 185 members. That means the membership of the Security Council would only constitute 15 percent of the total United Nations membership—far less than it was in its early establishment.

While this idea is indeed totally unacceptable, it may lead as well to the question of validity or invalidity of the decisions taken in this would-be nonrepresentative body.

What is most striking is that, for the case of Germany and Japan, the election of these two countries would be based on economic parameters—disregarding the fact that they were the predominant Axis Powers during World War II, inflicting horrendous and unmeasurable damages to mankind and its civilization.

Furthermore, these economic criteria are doomed to be short-lived, for in the not-so-distant future many countries will also be able to claim that they are eligible as well for permanent seats on the Security Council based on their tremendous progress in economic fields and their huge contribution to the United Nations budget.

These might, for example, include the Republic of Korea and Singapore, while politically and demographically they do not adequately represent any constituencies.

In an attempt to thwart this totally unacceptable formula, the potential candidates from Asia, especially Indonesia, have to campaign openly and assertively.

Establishing beforehand a set of criteria for suitable candidates is indeed the right thing to do. As one might recall, Alatas has on many occasions stated that those candidates should be chosen not only by geography but also from their political, economic and demographic weight and their track record of contributing to world peace (The Jakarta Post, Oct. 2, 1997).

One additional important factor that should be included in this set of criteria is that the candidates have to represent the existing powerhouses of the real world.

Indeed, the current Security Council does not have any representative from the Moslem world. Albeit Indonesia does not claim itself as an Islamic state, it is still a member of the Organization of Islamic Conferences. No single country can contest that Indonesia is a suitable candidate to serve as a representative of this important and yet developing constituency of the world.

Not until after all countries unanimously agree to specific criteria can Indonesia entertain the idea of reforming the Security Council. If not, we should stand in the way of reforms not supported by all members, for Indonesia is too big a country to fall to any pressures. We should stand firm for a right and just course for the world and for Indonesia.

*The writer is a former United Nations Disarmament Fellow and an expert on international peace and security affairs, residing in Jakarta.*

## 13. Tsutomu Wada, Japan Fails in Effort to Secure Permanent Seat of Power at U.N.

*The Nikkei Weekly, 1997*

Once again this year, Japan has failed to realize its longtime hope of attaining a permanent seat on the United Nations Security Council.

The U.N. General Assembly discussed Security Council reform last week but reached no decision. The Japanese government is now reconsidering its strategy, but the situation will unlikely improve in the next year.

"When some countries like the U.S. championed Japan's participation as a permanent member, there was some hesitancy among members of the Japanese cabinet. Now

Hashimoto's cabinet is fully supportive, but international politics interrupt us. It is very difficult to get a permanent seat on the U.N. Security Council," said a top official of the Ministry of Foreign Affairs.

Early this year, Japanese government officials thought that if things went well, Japan could be on track to gain a permanent seat on the Security Council before the end of the year.

Ismail Razali, a Malaysian diplomat and president of the U.N. General Assembly in 1996, proposed reorganizing the Security Council and increasing the permanent seats by five—two for developed countries and three for one representative each of Asia, Latin America and Africa, but the new members would have no veto. The two developed countries were expected to be Japan and Germany. Razali's proposal also called for adding five or six non-permanent seats on the Security Council.

At the General Assembly in September, Foreign Minister Keizo Obuchi expressed Japan's eagerness for a permanent seat. "Japan, with the endorsement of many countries, is prepared to discharge its responsibilities as a permanent member of the Security Council in accordance with its basic philosophy of not resorting to the use of force as prohibited by its constitution," Obuchi said.

### Italian resolution

But a resolution by Italy, announced in October, dashed Japan's hopes. Italy insisted that sufficient time be taken to discuss Security Council reorganization, particularly the selection of permanent members. Italy has opposed Germany becoming the third Western European country, after the U.K. and France, to gain a permanent seat.

Japan and other countries fought Italy's proposal but failed to realize any sort of reorganization this year. Moreover, a breakthrough in the debate about Security Council reorganization is not expected to come in the near future, analysts said.

Other proposals have been made since Lazali's. In April, the nonaligned countries called for expanding the Security Council to at least 26 seats, which implied 10 permanent seats and 16 non-permanent ones. In June, the Organization of African Unity said that two permanent seats should be given to representatives of Africa, which would have meant 10 permanent seats.

In July, the U.S. said the Security Council should be expanded to no more than 21 seats to ensure effective discussions. Under the U.S. position, five new permanent seats and only one non-permanent one would be added.

The main point of contention is how many seats an expanded Security Council would have, a Foreign Ministry official said, with the proposals ranging from 21 to 26. Japan, balancing the goals of enhancing representativeness and maintaining efficient deliberations, called for a number in the low 20s.

Besides the number of Security Council seats, member countries are also divided on which countries would be entitled to represent each region. For instance, India and Pakistan both offered themselves for the Asia representative permanent seat. Even more candidates are vying to represent Latin America and Africa.

### Seeking more influence

The Japanese government, especially the Foreign Ministry, was disappointed by the failure to become a permanent member of the Security Council. Foreign Ministry officials contend that Japan should assume a position in international politics commensurate with its economic clout. Japan's share of the U.N. budget, determined by the economic capacity of its member countries, is 15.65% for 1997, second only to the U.S. at 25.0%.

However, the cabinets before Hashimoto's had maintained prudent stances because some lawmakers from the coalition parties did not support ardently seeking a permanent seat.

"The situation has changed in the last few years," said Yoshio Hatano, who was Japan's ambassador to the U.N. from 1990 to 1994 and worked aggressively to gain Japan a permanent seat. "In 1994, the situations in international society afforded ample scope for Japan's activities, but Japan did not make the most of it. Now what Japan can do is persuade developing countries to unify their opinion."

The key to achieving a successful reorganization plan is concerted action at an early stage by developing countries that can overcome minority opinions like Italy's, Hatano said. To gain such cooperation, some package of reforms, including not only changes in the Security Council but also in the U.N.'s fiscal and development functions may be needed, he said.

But some observers have been cool about Security Council reorganization and Japan's ambition for a permanent seat.

"This year, there has been no coordination. U.N. members should start again discussing for what purpose they would reform the Security Council," said Toshiki Mogami, a professor of international law at International Christian University in Tokyo.

"It is not realistic to think that Japan can join the permanent members automatically if the council is enlarged. The government also should rethink how Japan will contribute to the international community," Mogami said.

## 14. Bibliography of Additional Sources

- UNITED NATIONS SECURITY COUNCIL SUMMIT CONFERENCE (1992).
- Sydney D. Bailey, THE PROCEDURE OF THE U.N. SECURITY COUNCIL (1975).
- Benjamin B Ferencz, NEW LEGAL FOUNDATIONS FOR GLOBAL SURVIVAL: SECURITY THROUGH THE SECURITY COUNCIL (1994).
- AFRICAN YEAR BOOK OF INTERNATIONAL LAW (1994), vol. 2, pp. 157–171.
- Juan Somavia, The Humanitarian Responsibilities of the Security Council, The Gilbert Murray Lecture at Oxfam, Oxford UK, June 1996.
- John J. Kim and Gregory Gerdes, International Institutions, 32 INT'L LAW 575 (1998).
- Thomas Yoxall, Iraq and Article 51: A Correct Use of Limited Authority, 25 INT'L LAW 967 (1991).
- Alissa Pyrich, United Nations: Authorizations of Use of Force-Security Council Resolution 665, August 25, 1990, reprinted in 29 I.L.M. 1329 (1990), and Security Council Resolution 678, November 29, 1990, reprinted in 29 I.L.M. 1565 (1990), 32 HARV. INT'L L.J. 265 (1991).

# Chapter X

# U.N. Sanctions

## Introduction

The Security Council's most often employed tool for responding to international conflicts is the economic sanction, sometimes referred to as the "money bomb." One of the least known but most important bodies within the U.N. system is the Sanctions Committee. Its function is to issue interpretations of the Security Council's sanctions resolutions on a case-by-case basis. Its decisions, therefore, affect thousands of businesses and billions of dollars in world trade. Using actual Sanctions Committee cases involving Yugoslavia as a backdrop, this chapter provides an in-depth examination of this U.N. body. Sanctioning terrorist organizations poses special challenges. This chapter also examines some of the issues with sanctions targeted against individuals and non-state groups.

## Objectives

- To understand the role of sanctions in the U.N. system and the foundation for such Security Council power in the U.N. Charter.
- To understand the origination and role of the Sanctions Committee.
- To understand the types and roles of the various sanctions available to the Security Council.
- To debate the appropriateness of collective sanctions versus targeted sanctions.
- To understand the usage of targeted sanctions against individuals.

## Problems

1. How can sanctions be made "smarter"?
2. Come prepared to discuss the following questions relating to interpretation of Sanctions Resolutions:
   (a) Under what provisions of the U.N. Charter did the Security Council impose sanctions on the Former Yugoslavia?
   (b) Under S.C. Res. 713, what constitutes "military equipment"?

(c)  Did the arms embargo on Yugoslavia continue to apply to Bosnia after it had attained its independence?

(d)  Under S.C. Res. 757(4), what are "commodities and products"?

(e)  Under S.C. Res. 757(5), what are "financial or economic resources"?

(f)  What are the potential problems with having a trans-shipment exception, as contained in S.C. Res. 757(6)?

(g)  Does S.C. Res. 757(8)(a) override the Vienna Convention on Diplomatic Relations?

(h)  What is a "group representing the Federal Republic of Yugoslavia," for purposes of S.C. Res. 757(8)(c)?

(i)  What means of enforcement are envisioned for S.C. Res. 757?

(j)  What are "medical supplies," "foodstuffs," and "commodities and products for essential humanitarian need" for purposes of S.C. Res. 760?

3.  Assume Syria, with the help of North Korea and Iran, has constructed a "breeder reactor," whose enriched uranium and plutonium by-products can be used to make nuclear weapons. Although it insists the reactor is used only for peaceful electric power generation, Syria has refused to allow officials from the International Atomic Energy Agency to inspect the reactor to ensure that it is not being used to develop nuclear weapons in violation of the Nuclear Non-Proliferation Treaty. In order to induce Syria to permit inspection of the facility, the U.N. Security Council is contemplating imposing sweeping economic sanctions. If you were a member of the Security Council, which of the following commodities and services would you exempt from the sanctions for humanitarian or other reasons?

(a)  Foodstuffs.

(b)  Medicines and medical equipment.

(c)  Clothing fabric.

(d)  Legal services.

(e)  Mail and parcel post.

(f)  Air transport for religious travel (Hajj).

(g)  Commodities intended solely for transshipment through Syria to a third State.

(h)  Equipment for the independent news media.

(i)  Student exchange programs.

(j)  Payments for retirement pensions,

Come to class prepared to provide justifications for your choices.

4.  Come prepared to participate in a simulated session of the Yugoslavia Sanctions Committee, which will be considering the cases described *infra*. You will represent the same country that you role-played for the earlier Security Council simulation.

5.  Come prepared to discuss the following questions:

(a)  What purposes and functions does the U.N. Sanctions Committee serve?

(b)  How does the U.N. Sanctions Committee differ from a traditional judicial body? Are those differences benefits or drawbacks?

(c) What roles do law and politics play in Sanctions Committee decisions? How do the Sanctions Committee's procedures affect its decision making?

(d) What are some of the potential ways the Sanctions Committee could be reformed, and what are the pros and cons of each?

6. What are some of the issues posed by sanctions targeting individuals?

# Materials

1. U. N. Charter, Articles 39–42.

2. SECURITY COUNCIL SANCTIONS COMMITTEES: AN OVERVIEW at http://www.un.org/sc/committees/.

3. Security Council Sanctions Resolutions Concerning the Former Yugoslavia:

   A. S.C. Res. 713 (para. 6): Arms Embargo

   B. S.C. Res. 727 (para. 6): Extending Arms Embargo

   C. S.C. Res. 757

      (para. 4a): Prohibiting imports

      (para. 4c): Prohibiting exports

      (para. 8a): Diplomatic ties

      (para. 8b): Sporting events

      (para. 8c): Official visits

      (paras. 5, 6, & 10): Exceptions

4. Summary of Sanctions Committee Cases (1992–1993)

5. Michael Scharf and Joshua Dorosin, Interpreting U.N. Sanctions: The Rulings and Role of the Yugoslavia Sanctions Committee, 19 BROOKLYN J. INT'L L. 771 (1993).

6. Joy K. Fausey, Does the United Nations' Use of Collective Sanctions to Protect Human Rights Violate Its Own Human Rights Standards? 10 Conn. J. Int't L. 193 (1994).

7. Gary C. Hufbauer and Barbara Oegg, Targeted Sanctions: A Policy Alternative?, 32 LAW & POLICY INT'L BUS. 11 (2000).

8. MAKING TARGETED SANCTIONS EFFECTIVE GUIDELINES FOR THE IMPLEMENTATION OF U.N. POLICY OPTIONS at http://www.un.org/Docs/sc/committees/sanctions/initiatives.htm.

9. Anti-Terrorism Sanctions: Targeting Individuals

   A. S.C. Res. 1267

   B. Council Regulation (EC) No 881/2002 (Article 2)

   C. The *Kadi* Case

10. Bibliography of Additional Sources

# 1. U.N. Charter, Articles 39–42

CHAPTER VII

ACTION WITH RESPECT TO THREATS TO THE PEACE, BREACHES OF THE PEACE, AND ACTS OF AGGRESSION

### Article 39

The Security Council shall determine the existence of any threat to the peace, breach of the peace, or act of aggression and shall make recommendations, or decide what measures shall be taken in accordance with Articles 41 and 42, to maintain or restore international peace and security.

### Article 40

In order to prevent an aggravation of the situation, the Security Council may, before making the recommendations or deciding upon the measures provided for in Article 39, call upon the parties concerned to comply with such provisional measures as it deems necessary or desirable. Such provisional measures shall be without prejudice to the rights, claims, or position of the parties concerned. The Security Council shall duly take account of failure to comply with such provisional measures.

### Article 41

The Security Council may decide what measures not involving the use of armed force are to be employed to give effect to its decisions, and it may call upon the Members of the United Nations to apply such measures. These may include complete or partial interruption of economic relations and of rail, sea, air, postal, telegraphic, radio, and other means of communication, and the severance of diplomatic relations.

### Article 42

Should the Security Council consider that measures provided for in Article 41 would be inadequate or have proved to be inadequate, it may take such action by air, sea, or land forces as may be necessary to maintain or restore international peace and security. Such action may include demonstrations, blockade, and other operations by air, sea, or land forces of Members of the United Nations.

# 2. Security Council Sanctions Committees: An Overview

Under Chapter VII of the Charter, the Security Council can take enforcement measures to maintain or restore international peace and security. Such measures range from economic and/or other sanctions not involving the use of armed force to international military action.

The use of mandatory sanctions is intended to apply pressure on a State or entity to comply with the objectives set by the Security Council without resorting to the use of force. Sanctions thus offer the Security Council an important instrument to enforce its decisions. The universal character of the United Nations makes it an especially appropriate body to establish and monitor such measures.

The Council has resorted to mandatory sanctions as an enforcement tool when peace has been threatened and diplomatic efforts have failed (see below). The range of sanctions has included comprehensive economic and trade sanctions and/or more targeted measures such as arms embargoes, travel bans, financial or diplomatic restrictions.

At the same time, a great number of States and humanitarian organizations have expressed concerns at the possible adverse impact of sanctions on the most vulnerable segments of the population, such as women and children. Concerns have also been expressed at the negative impact sanctions can have on the economy of third countries.

In response to these concerns, relevant Security Council decisions have reflected a more refined approach to the design, application and implementation of mandatory sanctions. These refinements have included measures targeted at specific actors, as well as humanitarian exceptions embodied in Security Council resolutions. Targeted sanctions, for instance, can involve the freezing of assets and blocking the financial transactions of political elites or entities whose behavior triggered sanctions in the first place. Recently, smart sanctions have been applied to conflict diamonds in African countries, where wars are funded in part by the trade of illicit diamonds for arms and related materiel.

As part of its commitment to ensure that fair and clear procedures exist for placing individuals and entities on sanctions lists and for removing them, as well as for granting humanitarian exemptions, the Security Council, on 19 December 2006, adopted resolution 1730 (2006) by which the Council requested the Secretary-General to establish within the Secretariat (Security Council Subsidiary Organs Branch), a focal point to receive delisting requests and perform the tasks described in the annex to that resolution. The Security Council took another significant step in this regard by establishing, by its resolution 1904 (2009) the Office of the Ombudsperson.

On 17 April 2000, the members of the Security Council established, on a temporary basis, the Informal Working Group on General Issues of Sanctions to develop general recommendations on how to improve the effectiveness of United Nations sanctions. In 2006 the Working Group submitted its report to the Security Council (S/2006/997), which contained recommendations and best practices on how to improve sanctions.

## Authors' Note

The next three materials demonstrate the role of the U.N. Security Council Sanctions Committee through an analysis of the Security Council sanctions that were rendered against the Former Yugoslavia. Material 3 presents the various sanctions that were used by the Security Council under Chapter VII powers. Material 4 illustrates the actions of the Sanctions Committee in relation to the implementation of the Security Council sanctions. Material 5, a journal article from *Brooklyn Journal of International Law*, provides a comprehensive look at the role of the Sanctions Committee in interpreting the resolutions passed by the Security Council. This article analyzes the impact of the Sanctions Committee's rulings and the implications for other sanctions regimes.

## 3. Security Council Sanctions Resolutions
### Concerning the Former Yugoslavia

**A. S.C. Res. 713: Arms Embargo**

The Security Council,

* * *

6. *Decides*, under Chapter VII of the Chatter of the United Nations, that all States shall, for the purposes of establishing peace and stability in Yugoslavia, immediately implement a general and complete embargo on all deliveries of weapons and military equipment to

Yugoslavia until the Council decides otherwise following consultation between the Secretary-General and the Government of Yugoslavia;

7. *Calls upon* all States to refrain from any action which might contribute to increasing tension and to impeding or delaying a peaceful and negotiated outcome to the, conflict in Yugoslavia, which would permit all Yugoslavs to decide upon and to construct their future in peace;

8. *Decides* to remain seized of the matter until a peaceful solution is achieved.

Adopted unanimously at the 3009th meeting.

---

### B. S.C. Res. 727: Extending Arms Embargo

The Security Council,

\* \* \*

6. *Reaffirms* the embargo applied in paragraph 6 of resolution 713 (1991) and in paragraph 5 of resolution 724 (1991), and decides that the embargo applies in accordance with paragraph 33 of the report of the Secretary-General;[1]

7. *Encourages* the Secretary-General to pursue his humanitarian efforts in Yugoslavia;

8. *Decides* to remain actively seized of the matter until a peaceful solution is achieved.

Adopted unanimously at the 3028th meeting.

---

### C. S.C. Res. 757: Economic Sanctions

The Security Council,

\* \* \*

4. *Decides also* that all States shall prevent:

(a) The import into their territories of all commodities and products originating in the Federal Republic of Yugoslavia (Serbia and Montenegro) exported therefrom after the date of the present resolution;

(b) Any activities by their nationals or in their territories which would promote or are calculated to promote the export or transshipment of any commodities or products originating in the Federal Republic of Yugoslavia (Serbia and Montenegro); and any dealings by their nationals or their flag vessels or aircraft or in their territories in any commodities or products originating in the Federal Republic of Yugoslavia (Serbia and Montenegro) and exported therefrom after the date of the present resolution, including in particular any transfer of funds to the Federal Republic of Yugoslavia (Serbia and Montenegro) for the purposes of such activities or dealings;

(c) The sale or supply by their nationals or from their territories or using their flag vessels or aircraft of any commodities or products, whether or not originating in their territories — but not including supplies intended strictly for medical purposes and foodstuffs notified to the Security Council Committee established pursuant to

---

1. Para 33 of the referenced report provided: "indeed, Mr. Vance added that the arms embargo would continue to apply to all areas that have been part of Yugoslavia, any decisions on the question of the recognition of the independence of certain republics notwithstanding." U.N. Doc. 5/23363 (1992).

resolution 724 (1991) on Yugoslavia—to any person or body in the Federal Republic of Yugoslavia (Serbia and Montenegro) or to any person or body for the purposes of any business carried on in or operated from the Federal Republic of Yugoslavia (Serbia and Montenegro), and any activities by their nationals or in their territories which promote or are calculated to promote such sale or supply of such commodities or products;

5. *Decide further* that no State shall make available to the authorities in the Federal Republic of Yugoslavia (Serbia and Montenegro) or to any commercial, industrial or public utility undertaking in the Federal Republic of Yugoslavia (Serbia and Montenegro), any funds or any other financial or economic resources and shall prevent their nationals and any persons within their territories from removing from their territories or otherwise making available to those authorities or to any such undertaking any such funds or resources and from remitting any other funds to persons or bodies within the Federal Republic of Yugoslavia (Serbia and Montenegro), except payments exclusively for strictly medical or humanitarian purposes and foodstuffs;

6. *Decides* that the prohibitions in paragraphs 4 and 5 shall not apply to the transshipment through the Federal Republic of Yugoslavia (Serbia and Montenegro) of commodities and products originating outside the Federal Republic of Yugoslavia (Serbia and Montenegro) and temporarily present in the territory of the Federal Republic of Yugoslavia (Serbia and Montenegro) only for the purpose of such transshipment, in accordance with guidelines approved by the Security Council Committee established by resolution 724 (1991);

\* \* \*

8. *Decides also* that all States shall:

(a) Reduce the level of the staff at diplomatic missions and consular posts of the Federal Republic of Yugoslavia (Serbia and Montenegro);

(b) Take the necessary steps to prevent the participation in sporting events on their territory of persons or groups representing the Federal Republic of Yugoslavia (Serbia and Montenegro);

(c) Suspend scientific and technical cooperation and cultural exchanges and visits involving persons or groups officially sponsored by or representing the Federal Republic of Yugoslavia (Serbia and Montenegro);

\* \* \*

10. *Decide* that the measures imposed by the present resolution shall not apply to activities related to the United Nations Protection Force, to the Conference on Yugoslavia or to the European Community Monitoring Mission, and that States, parties and others concerned shall cooperate fully with the Force, the Conference and the Mission and respectfully their freedom of movement and the safety of their personnel;

\* \* \*

21. *Decides* to remain actively seized of the matter and to consider immediately, whenever necessary, further steps to achieve a peaceful solution in conformity with its relevant resolutions.

Adopted at the 3082nd meeting by 13 votes to none, with 2 abstentions (China, Zimbabwe).

———————————————————

### D. S.C. Res. 760: Humanitarian Exception

The Security Council,

* * *

*Acting* under Chapter VII of the Charter of the United Nations,

*Decides* that the prohibitions in paragraph 4 (c) of resolution 757 (1992) concerning the sale or supply to the Federal Republic of Yugoslavia (Serbia and Montenegro) of commodities or products, other than medical supplies and foodstuffs, and the prohibitions against financial transactions related thereto contained in resolution 757 (1992) shall not apply, with the approval of the Security Council Committee established by resolution 724 (1991) on Yugoslavia under the simplified and accelerated "no objection" procedure, to commodities and products for essential humanitarian need.

Adopted unanimously at the 3086th meeting.

---

## 4. Summary of Sanctions Committee Cases (1992–1993)

### I. Arms Embargo

(1)  German request regarding application of arms embargo to police helicopters for Croatia, Slovenia, and the Federal Republic of Yugoslavia ("FRY").

(2)  Canadian request regarding application of arms embargo to ambulance helicopter for Bosnia.

(3)  German request to ship nitroglycerin to FRY for mining coal.

(4)  Hungarian request to ship mine detection devices to Croatia.

### II. Exports to FRY

#### A. Humanitarian Exception

(5)  Requests for food, medicines, emergency shelters, and clothing to FRY.

(6)  Requests by U.K. to ship Land Rover Station wagon to FRY for use by charity OXFAM in food distribution.

(7)  Request by Germany to ship 3 million boxes of matches to FRY.

(8)  Request by Bulgaria to ship heating oil to FRY.

(9)  Request by Bulgaria to ship cigarettes to FRY.

(10)  Request by Netherlands to ship wine and vodka to FRY.

#### Pharmaceuticals

(11)  Request by Ethiopia to import penicillin from FRY.

(12)  Request by Nigeria to ship pharmaceutical precursors to FRY.

#### Humanitarian Remittances

(13)  Request by Netherlands to pay $3,840/month to several hundred orphaned children in FRY.

(14)  Request by Greece to pay tuition, room and board to Greek students studying in FRY.

(15)  Request by Australia to make pension payments to Australians living in FRY.

### Diplomatic Exception

(16) Greek inquiry about application of sanctions to shipments of oil and car for operation of Greek embassy in FRY.

(17) Bulgaria inquiry about application of sanctions to shipments of equipment and money from FRY to FRY embassy in Bulgaria.

### Information Materials

(18) Request by Belgium to allow DHL to operate parcel post delivery in the FRY.

(19) U.S. Request to ship equipment to independent media (Studio B TV and Radio Pancevac) in FRY.

(20) France Request to ship newsprint paper to independent press organizations in FRY.

### Trans-shipment

(21) Greek inquiry about application of sanctions to payment of tolls on FRY roads.

(22) Hungary inquiry about application of sanctions to payment of tolls on the Danube in violation of Danube Convention.

## III. Imports from the FRY

(23) U.S. Request to import a religious sculpture from FRY.

(24) Turkish request for return of Turkish aircraft that were serviced in FRY prior to imposition of sanctions.

(25) U.S. Request for return of fabrics belonging to Liz Claiborne, Inc, that had not yet been processed into finished garments in FRY.

(26) Mongolian request for hotel furniture it had bought and paid for prior to imposition of sanctions.

## IV. Maritime sanctions

(27) U.S. inquiry regarding application of sanctions to FRY-owned, Maltese-flagged, vessels calling on U.S. ports.

(28) Denmark request to provide food, water, and other humanitarian services to the crew of FRY vessels.

(29) Netherlands request to unload from FRY-owned vessel 63,000 tons of hot coal in danger of spontaneous ignition.

(30) Request by U.S. to release impounded coal that originated from FRY-owned vessel to Exxon on grounds it was an "innocent owner."

(31) Romania inquiry regarding application of sanctions to FRY vessels on the Danube river in light of Danube Convention's guarantee of freedom of navigation.

(32) Romania inquiry regarding application of sanctions to FRY vessels seeking to use Romanian locks.

## V. Sporting Events

(33) Sweden inquiry regarding application of sanctions to participation of Yugoslav soccer team in Sweden for European Cup finals.

(34) FRY inquiry regarding application of sanctions to FRY participation in Olympic Games in Barcelona.

## 5. Michael Scharf and Joshua Dorosin, Interpreting U.N. Sanctions: The Rulings and Role of the Yugoslavia Sanctions Committee

*Brooklyn Journal of International Law*, 1993

In response to the evolving crisis in Yugoslavia, the United Nations Security Council adopted several resolutions imposing first an arms embargo on the territory of the former Yugoslavia and later sweeping economic sanctions against the Federal Republic of Yugoslavia (Serbia-Montenegro) (FRY), which was viewed as primarily responsible for the continuing hostilities. As in the five other sanctions regimes imposed by U.N. Security Council resolutions (against South Africa, Iraq, Somalia, Libya, and Haiti), enforcement of the Yugoslavia sanctions was left to individual states. Thus, the legal interpretation of the meaning of the sanctions provisions—and consequently the way in which the sanctions would be implemented—was in the first instance left to individual states. Inevitably, questions about the meaning of the provisions arose, both as states themselves grappled with often arcane and ambiguous language and as disputes ensued between states interpreting the language of the sanctions resolutions differently.

Questions concerning the interpretation of the sanctions resolutions are brought before the U.N. Sanctions Committee, a quasi-judicial body created by the Security Council to facilitate the implementation of the sanctions. The Sanctions Committee issues interpretations of the sanctions resolutions on a case-by-case basis in the form of U.N. press releases or communications from the Chairman of the Committee to the particular states involved. These communications, much like opinions of the U.N. Legal Counsel, serve as the authoritative pronouncement of the United Nations on the questions involved. Although the Yugoslavia Sanctions Committee has already issued over 2,000 communications interpreting the Yugoslavia sanctions, its operation has until now received scant public attention.

Part I of this article provides, for the first time, a systematic analysis of over one hundred key rulings of the U.N. Yugoslavia Sanctions Committee, grouping them into categories for easy reference. It is hoped that this digest of important Sanctions Committee rulings will aid the members of the Sanctions Committee in identifying and following precedent, aid governments in implementing the sanctions, and assist businesses (and their lawyers) in operating under them. This Article does not, however, purport to be a comprehensive survey of all of the Sanctions Committee's cases, or even all of its important cases. Indeed, one of the main purposes of this piece is to demonstrate the need for such a comprehensive undertaking by the U.N. Secretariat. Rather, this Article focuses on those Sanctions Committee cases that establish important precedent, significantly expand or contract the reach of the sanctions, or tell us something useful about the nature and operation of the Sanctions Committee. Drawing from this material, Part II of the Article seeks to provide broader insights into the process of U.N. Security Council resolution implementation and suggests several possible changes to improve the way in which the Sanctions Committee operates.

### I. THE RULINGS OF THE SANCTIONS COMMITTEE

The Yugoslavia Sanctions Committee was originally established by Security Council Resolution 724 to recommend appropriate measures to the Security Council in response to violations of the arms embargo. The Committee's mandate was later expanded by Security Council Resolutions 757 and 760, which authorized the Sanctions Committee to recommend appropriate measures to the Council in response to violations of the economic sanctions, to promulgate guidelines for sanctions implementation, and (under a no-objection procedure) to decide upon applications for the approval of humanitarian shipments. Although the Security Council has never expressly given the Sanctions Committee a general mandate to issue interpretations of the sanctions resolutions, as will be seen below, the Committee has taken on this function in responding to communications received from states seeking clarification of the sanctions resolutions' reach.

The Sanctions Committee is composed of representatives of the fifteen states that are members of the Security Council. While unanimous decision of the Committee is technically required only for those questions that are governed by the Committee's "no-objection" procedure (such as approval of humanitarian shipments into the FRY), in practice the Committee makes all of its decisions by consensus. Cases come before the Committee through communications by states seeking the Committee's views on, or its authorization for, proposed action. In the United States, the State Department will transmit a request for a Sanctions Committee ruling usually in response to an application submitted to the Department of Treasury's Office of Foreign Assets Control for a license to export an otherwise prohibited item. The Sanctions Committee's Secretariat then circulates a draft response, which the members of the Committee send to their capitols for approval or comment. When there is objection to the proposed communication, members of the Committee may table substitute (or revised) drafts for circulation. Routine cases are handled as a paper exercise. The full Committee normally meets on a weekly basis to discuss and take action on the more complex or controversial cases on its agenda.

Drawing from the record of these meetings as well as the Sanctions Committee's formal communications, this section of the Article analyzes the Sanctions Committee's rulings within the context of the following five broad categories: (1) the arms embargo; (2) restrictions on exports to the FRY; (3) restrictions on imports from the FRY; (4) restrictions on FRY shipping; and (5) restrictions on FRY participation in sporting events.

## A. The Arms Embargo

The Security Council sanctions resolutions impose "a general and complete embargo on all deliveries of weapons and military equipment to Yugoslavia." The initial resolution imposing the arms embargo, resolution 713, was adopted in September 1991 — several months before Croatia, Slovenia, and Bosnia-Herzegovina were recognized by the international community as independent states separate from Yugoslavia. Through indirect action that escaped the notice of most commentators as well as many governments, the Security Council later reaffirmed that the arms embargo continued to apply to each of the states that emerged from the territory of the former Yugoslavia.

In light of armed attacks by forces under the direction of the FRY against Bosnia-Herzegovina, the application of the arms embargo to Bosnia became a matter of controversy. On March 20, 1993, the government of Bosnia-Herzegovina submitted a request for provisional measures (the equivalent of a preliminary injunction) to the International Court of Justice, arguing that resolution 713 and other relevant Security Council resolutions must be construed to allow states to provide Bosnia-Herzegovina with military equipment in accordance with its inherent right of individual and collective self-defense under Article 51 of the U.N. Charter. While the International Court of Justice declined to rule on the issue on jurisdictional grounds, the United States Department of State has taken the position that "[i]f the United States were to act in a manner inconsistent with the Security Council's Chapter VII arms embargo on Bosnia on the theory that Bosnia's right of self-defense supersedes the actions of the Council, the authority of the Security Council would be severely undermined." As indicated below, notwithstanding Bosnia's arguments concerning its right of self-defense, the Sanctions Committee has continued to apply the arms embargo to all of the states of the former Yugoslavia including Bosnia.

Several of the first cases brought before the Sanctions Committee concerned "dual-use" items—that is, items that could be used either for military or civilian purposes. The first such case, considered by the Committee on March 16, 1992, concerned Germany's refusal to return several Yugoslav helicopters to the FRY, Croatia, Macedonia, and Slovenia after the completion of routine servicing. The FRY sought assistance from the Committee in its efforts to secure the return of one of the aircraft, which it described as a civilian helicopter not subject to the arms embargo. Germany informed the Committee that, although not armed, the helicopters had nevertheless been classified as dual-purpose aircraft under the relevant German regulations. Germany felt that, since the deployment of the helicopters in connection with armed conflicts in the former Yugoslavia could not be ruled out, it could not approve the re-export of the helicopters in view of the arms embargo unless it was authorized to do so by the Sanctions Committee. Although the Chairman of the Committee initially expressed doubts regarding whether the Committee had the competence to address the question of dual-use items, after discussion by the Committee he ruled that the question of dual use was germane to the Committee's work. The Committee then decided that the position of the German authorities in this case was well-founded and decided not to authorize the re-export of the helicopter to the FRY.

The March 16, 1992 ruling on the dual-use helicopter case can be viewed as the *Marbury v. Madison* of Yugoslavia Sanctions Committee jurisprudence. Finding that the Security Council resolution establishing its mandate "did not have to be interpreted restrictively," the Committee in effect asserted its authority to issue interpretations of the sanctions resolutions as incidental to its mandate.

The Committee soon had occasion to refine its position on dual-use helicopters when it approved a request from Canada to authorize the sale of a medevac helicopter to Bosnia-Herzegovina. The Committee distinguished the Canadian request, involving a specifically equipped ambulance helicopter which would have to be dismantled before it could be converted to military use, from the German-held police helicopters, which the Committee believed were relatively easy to modify for military use.

In a different dual-use context, the Committee declined to authorize a request by Germany to ship DM 24,100 worth of nitroglycerin to be used by the FRY in mining coal to meet the country's humanitarian electric needs, pending adequate assurances that the end use would not be military. Similarly, the Committee refused to authorize a request from Hungary to export one hundred mine-detection devices to Croatia, despite assurances that the end-user of the devices would be the special mine-sweeping unit of the Croatian police which is not involved in any military activity, and that the devices would be used solely to secure the safe return of the civilian population to the territories evacuated by the Serbian Army.

An important factor in such cases is that the "humanitarian exception" applicable to other aspects of the sanctions does not apply to the arms embargo. The only organization authorized to receive and use military equipment in the former Yugoslavia is UNPROFOR, the U.N. Peacekeeping force. Therefore, the only relevant issue in these cases is whether there were sufficient assurances that the items would not be put to a military use.

The resolutions imposing the arms embargo do not contain any provisions concerning the disposition of items seized in violation of the embargo. When Croatia reported that it seized a cargo of military weapons unloaded from an Iranian airliner at Zagreb airport, the Committee authorized the Croatian authorities to destroy immediately all the military equipment in question under the supervision of UNPROFOR. This is to be contrasted with the Committee's position on embargoed items seized outside the country upon which sanctions have been imposed. In such cases the Committee has authorized the seizing state to dispose of the items as it sees fit so long as "no funds or benefits related to the [seized items] should be made available to entities in or operating from the [embargoed country]."

## B. Exports to the FRY

The main purpose of the Security Council imposed sanctions on the FRY was to disrupt the FRY economy, and thereby "apply pressure on Serbia-Montenegro to meet U.N. demands to cease outside aggression and interference in Bosnia and Herzegovina." The key to this was a comprehensive embargo imposed on exports to the FRY. This was not to be a complete embargo, however. As discussed in the following section of this Article, the Security Council expressly created certain exceptions, which the Sanctions Committee interpreted broadly, and the Sanctions Committee itself created a host of other exceptions to the embargo.

### 1. The Humanitarian Exception

The meaning and scope of the "humanitarian exception"—those provisions in the sanctions regime which carved exceptions to restrictions on exports to the FRY for foodstuffs, medicines, and other humanitarian items as well as financial transactions related to such humanitarian shipments—have been the source of continuous debate both within the United Nations and among states seeking to implement the sanctions regime. With the possible exception of the problems encountered in the interpretation of the provisions regarding shipping on the high seas, in territorial waters, and on the Danube River, the humanitarian provision has provided the Sanctions Committee with a greater amount of case work than any other category of the sanctions.

When first established, the Yugoslavia sanctions regime's humanitarian exception was limited to the supply of commodities or products intended strictly for medical purposes and foodstuffs, which could be shipped to the FRY after the state of origin notified the Sanctions Committee of the shipment. During the Sanctions Committee's meeting on June 10, 1992, the Chairman of the Committee tabled a draft communication stating that the exemption to the sanctions set forth in paragraph 10 of resolution 757 (for activities related to UNPROFOR, to the Conference on Yugoslavia, and to the European Community Monitor Mission) applied as well to the emergency relief assistance being provided by the U.N. High Commissioner for Refugees, the World Health Organization, the International Committee of the Red Cross, the United Nations Development Programme, and UNICEF.

The United Kingdom's Sanctions Committee representative believed that the proposed interpretation was unfounded. Instead, he took the position that a new Security Council resolution containing language similar to paragraph 20 of resolution 687 concerning Iraq was needed. The representatives of the United States, Belgium, Austria, Japan, and France, on the other hand, expressed the view that the Committee could include such a provision in its guidelines without waiting for Security Council action. Their position on this matter gave an early indication of the willingness of the Sanctions Committee to interpret Security Council sanctions resolutions liberally. Ultimately, a compromise was reached whereby the Committee decided to promulgate the proposed guideline without delay, but also simultaneously to suggest that the Security Council meet to adopt a new resolution on the matter.

The resulting Security Council resolution, resolution 760, went beyond the need identified by the Committee for authorization for the relief activities of certain international humanitarian organizations. Instead, with Sanctions Committee approval under the "no-objection" procedure, any state or organization could now ship commodities and products "for essential humanitarian need" to the FRY.

In contrast to resolution 687 on Iraq, which provided a list of specific articles presumed to be "materials and supplies for essential civilian needs," the Sanctions Committee decided not to attempt to formulate a guiding list of exempted humanitarian items for Yugoslavia. Rather, the Committee stated that it preferred to "consider specific questions" concerning proposed humanitarian exports to the FRY "on a case by case basis, as they arise."

As interpreted by the Committee, the scope of the humanitarian exception was held to encompass a wide variety of goods and services, most of which were of no surprise to the international community. Such commodities as medicines, foodstuffs, emergency shelters, and clothing were consistently approved by the Sanctions Committee on a routine basis. Despite an inherent risk of diversion, the Committee also routinely approved the shipment of items that were not themselves of a humanitarian nature, but were related to the transport and distribution of food and medicine.

There were, however, several cases that the Committee rejected which seemed at first blush to serve a clear humanitarian purpose. In one such case, the Committee "could find no justification based on humanitarian need" for the shipment to Serbia of boxes of matches. Though the record of the Committee's discussion of the case sheds little light on its motives, it is likely that the Committee's rejection was related to the time of the year (summer), the large number of matches requested (3 million boxes), and, in particular, the fact that Serbians were reported to have engaged in widespread burning of Bosnian towns and villages. In a similar vein, the Committee denied the FRY's request for heating oil "for the operation of purely humanitarian institutions ... during the approaching winter season," in the absence of "a system to monitor the final use of the oil" in light of its potential military applications.

On the other hand, the Committee has approved many items that would seem to be dubious candidates for the humanitarian exception, including cigarettes, chocolate bars, potato chips, wine, and vodka. While it is true that enumerating legitimate items of essential humanitarian need might indeed be impractical, there seems to be no reason why the Sanctions Committee could not develop a short list of items, including cigarettes and vodka, deemed to fall outside the humanitarian exception. The denial of such items would likely have a strong psychological impact on the Serb population. To date, however, such suggestions have not been well received within the Sanctions Committee.

### 2. Pharmaceutical Precursors

The United States member of the Sanctions Committee initially took the position that pharmaceutical precursors (chemicals used in the production of finished pharmaceutical products) should not be permitted under the humanitarian exception of resolution 757 as "supplies intended strictly for medical purposes." Here, as distinct from dual-use military items, the risk was not that the chemicals would be used for non-humanitarian purposes. Rather, in the view of the United States, the danger was that the pharmaceutical precursors would be used to keep the FRY's sizeable pharmaceutical industry in operation (and thereby prop up the FRY's economy) rather than for immediate domestic consumption. The United Kingdom, France, Belgium, and Russia, on the other hand, argued that opposing the import of components for the FRY pharmaceutical industry would prevent the FRY from producing necessary drugs and might create additional needs for humanitarian assistance.

Since it was isolated on the issue, the United States reluctantly withdrew is objection, but subsequently urged the Committee to revisit its decision to allow shipments of pharmaceutical precursors when the Committee received reports that companies in the FRY were exporting finished pharmaceuticals in contravention of the ban on exports established by the sanctions regime. The Sanctions Committee responded by restricting imports of pharmaceutical precursors to companies which had been identified as exporting finished pharmaceuticals. Thus, upon notification by a firm of its intention to export precursors to specified FRY pharmaceutical companies, the Sanctions Committee would place a "hold" on the transaction pending an examination of the probable end use of the product.

Repeated requests by the Sanctions Committee for investigations of illegal exports of finished pharmaceuticals by several FRY firms were ignored or deflected by FRY officials with denials that such transactions had occurred. Finally, in February of 1993, the Sanctions Committee decided to prohibit all exports to the eight FRY firms identified as having engaged in illegal exports until FRY authorities provided the Committee with the complete report on the exportation of pharmaceuticals from Serbian firms to Slovenia. The information was never provided. Consequently, pharmaceutical precursors cannot be exported to the FRY under the exception for "supplies intended strictly for medical purposes" when there is reason to believe that the precursors will be used for export purposes rather than for domestic medical consumption.

### 3. The Exception for Humanitarian Remittances/Pensions

Paragraph five of resolution 757 proscribes the remittance of "any funds" to persons or bodies within the FRY, "except payments exclusively for strictly medical or humanitarian purposes and foodstuffs." While the Committee routinely approved requests by international humanitarian organizations such as UNICEF, the U.N. High Commissioner for Refugees, and the World Food Programme to transfer funds into the FRY for their activities, it struggled with a range of cases involving direct "humanitarian" payments to persons in the FRY.

On one end of the spectrum were the cases of obvious humanitarian need, such as the Committee's approval of a request for a Netherlands-based organization to make monthly remittances amounting to $3,840 to several hundred Yugoslav children orphaned in the hostilities. Falling in the middle of this range of cases was a request by Greece for authorization to make remittances to Greek students studying in the FRY. Rather than give a blanket authorization for all students studying in the FRY, the Committee confined its authorization to exceptional cases and to students who were about to complete their studies.

At the other end of the spectrum was the tricky issue of pension payments to individuals in the FRY. The Sanctions Committee initially took a restrictive view of the authority of states to transfer pension payments to individuals in the FRY under the remittance clause of resolution 757. While the members of the Committee recognized the general humanitarian nature of pensions, some members were concerned by the amount of hard currency which these payments could make available to FRY authorities. According to one estimate, payment of such benefits would make available to the FRY some $1.5 billion per year in foreign exchange.

The Sanctions Committee first considered the question of allowing pension payments to be made when the government of Australia requested the Committee's view "on the possibility of continuing to pay out pension funds to eligible Australian recipients in Serbia and Montenegro." The Committee rejected the request for a blanket authorization for pension payments as over-broad, but stated that this decision would not prejudice the Committee's position in considering more specific requests in the future. During the next several months, in response to similar requests for blanket authorization for pension payments, the Committee consistently reconfirmed that it would only approve individual requests on a case-by-case demonstration of humanitarian need.

This position, however, gradually changed as it became apparent that some states continued to transfer pensions without consulting with the Sanctions Committee, since paragraph 5 of resolution 757 did not require notification to or authorization by the Sanctions Committee before making humanitarian payments. Since it lacked a mechanism by which to control such payments, the Committee, by the fall of 1992, decided to turn the matter completely over to the individual states, determining that in appropriate circumstances such remittances would not violate resolution 757, and that it was for individual states to determine whether such payments were warranted in each case.

### 4. The Diplomatic Exception

Although the sanctions resolutions do not contain an express exception for the operation of diplomatic missions, the Sanctions Committee has interpreted the sanctions resolutions as containing such an exception "to maintain the normal functioning of diplomatic missions in accordance with the norms of international law." Citing the precedent of allowing diplomatic missions to continue functioning despite the imposition of the Iraqi sanctions regime, the Committee determined that "the embargo did not apply to imports and exports for the sole needs of embassies and consular missions or the import and export of personal household effects of diplomats and non-diplomats."

The Committee later clarified that its reference to the "norms of international law" was to the Vienna Convention on Diplomatic Relations of 1961. The Vienna Convention provides for entry into the receiving state of "articles for the official use of the Mission" and "articles for the personal use of a diplomatic agent or members of his family forming part of his household, including articles intended for his establishment." The Convention also provides that "the receiving State shall accord full facilities for the performance of the functions of the mission," that "the diplomatic bag shall not be opened or detained," and that the diplomatic agent's papers, correspondence, and property "shall enjoy inviolability." The Vienna Convention does not, however, address the continuing shipment of goods to diplomatic missions during a U.N. imposed economic embargo.

As the Sanctions Committee has pointed out in another context, "under the Charter of the United Nations and the relevant resolutions of the Security Council [states have the] obligation to implement the sanctions regime notwithstanding the existence of any rights or obligations under any other international agreement." In the absence of an express provision creating a diplomatic exception, or any references in the record to the Security Council's intention that such a residual exception should be read into the sanctions resolutions, the Sanctions Committee could have ruled that the sanctions override the above provisions of the Vienna Convention. Indeed, this would seem to have been the intention of the Security Council as evidenced by paragraph 8 of resolution 757, which requires states to reduce the number of staff at FRY diplomatic missions within their territory. Instead, based on its Iraqi precedent and perhaps a desire to facilitate diplomatic pressure on the FRY through continuing diplomatic contact in Belgrade, the Sanctions Committee took the position that the sanctions were not intended to prohibit shipments to or from diplomatic missions and their personnel in the FRY in accordance with the Vienna Convention. While "diplomatic shipments," therefore, do not require specific Sanctions Committee approval, states frequently notify the Sanctions Committee of such shipments in advance to obtain from the Committee a document confirming that the sanctions are not applicable to the shipment.

Consistent with the international law principle of reciprocity, the Sanctions Committee has also opined that the sanctions "should not impede the normal functioning" of FRY diplomatic and consular missions abroad. Consequently, the Committee has ruled that bank accounts for the sole purpose of FRY diplomatic and consular missions are exempt from the sanctions. However, the Committee has narrowly construed this exception. For example, when the FRY requested the Committee's authorization for the release of its embassy's funds on deposit with Jugobanka, New York, which the United States government had frozen, the Committee responded "that several banks in the United States are licensed to carry accounts of the FRY, and that the Government is free to deposit fresh funds into those accounts for the use of its embassies and consulates abroad."

### 5. Informational Materials Exception

Yet another exception to the sanctions created by the Sanctions Committee pertains to informational materials such as mail, newsprint for nongovernmental newspaper operations, and broadcasting equipment for the independent media in the FRY. The Committee has justified this exception on the ground that the particular informational material was not a commodity or product, or that it fell within the essential humanitarian need exception.

On August 12, 1992, the Sanctions Committee had occasion to rule on the application of the sanctions to parcel post delivery in response to a request by Belgium for advice on the transport operations of the company DHL International, based in Belgrade, which is a subsidiary of DHL Worldwide Express, Brussels. On the ground that there were no specific provisions within Security Council Resolution 757 limiting or prohibiting the delivery of mail to or from the FRY, the Committee stated that it had no objection to the continued transport operations by the subsidiary of the Belgium company. This ruling created a gaping loophole in the embargo. Under this ruling, many otherwise prohibited items can be shipped into the FRY via the mails and DHL without limitation on size, weight, or value.

In the fall of 1992, the United States requested the Sanctions Committee's approval to grant licenses to several nonprofit, philanthropic organizations to supply independent, democratic media organizations in Serbia-Montenegro with essential technical equipment which would enable them to continue their independent and democratic reporting of events in Yugoslavia. The United States argued that the supplies should be allowed under the humanitarian exception to the sanctions because the continued operation of independent, democratic media in Serbia-Montenegro was essential for the fulfillment of the Yugoslav people's fundamental right to freedom of information as recognized in Article 19 of the 1948 Universal Declaration of Human Rights, Article 19 of the International Covenant on Civil and Political Rights, and Article 10 of the European Convention on Human Rights. On November 19, the Sanctions Committee approved the request, along with a similar request by the United Kingdom, on condition that the proper use of the equipment would be monitored by the International Media Fund, a United States nongovernmental organization, and that any suspected misuse or diversion of the equipment would be reported promptly to the Committee.

Once it had been established that television and radio equipment could be supplied to independent media under the "humanitarian exception" to the sanctions, France quickly submitted a request to supply newsprint, magazine paper, and other supplies to four independent press organizations in Serbia. The Committee approved the request without any special conditions. While an exception to support the continued operation of the independent (anti-government) media promotes the goals of the sanctions, the rationale for the exception (i.e., freedom of information) leaves the Sanctions Committee with no principled basis to deny similar exports for government controlled media.

## 6. The Transshipment Exception

Perhaps the single largest flaw in the sanctions regime was the initial decision by the Security Council to permit the transshipment of goods across the territory of the FRY as a general exception to the sanctions. While the Sanctions Committee worked for several months following the adoption of resolution 757 to standardize approval procedures, ultimately conveyances carrying "transshipped" goods provided the single largest source of illegal commodities imported into the FRY.

The regime as established by resolution 757, under whose terms commodities were allowed to cross FRY borders without the approval of the Sanctions Committee, was fraught with problems. First, use of the term "transshipment" initially caused confusion among those charged with implementing the sanctions on the borders of the FRY. "Transshipment" is generally understood as describing the process whereby goods being shipped are transferred from one form of conveyance to another—such as from a ship to a truck—en route to a final destination. As used in resolution 757, however, the term embraced a different meaning: namely, the routing, either in one form of conveyance or by any number of conveyances, of goods from one country to another country through the territory of the FRY. As the Sanctions Committee made clear, the purpose of the resolution was to limit the transfer of goods into the FRY, not across its territory to other countries. Thus, the Sanctions Committee issued an interpretation stating clearly that the term "transshipment" as used in the sanctions resolutions "is to be construed as including 'transit' as well."

A second problem concerning the interpretation of the transshipment clause was raised when the FRY demanded that tolls be paid for the use of roads, creating a tension between paragraph 5's prohibition on making available to the FRY "funds and economic resources" and operative paragraph 6's statement that such prohibitions "shall not apply" to transshipment. The Sanctions Committee approved a Greek payment of tolls to authorities of the FRY "since it is a basic requirement of such transshipment, which is permitted under the terms of resolution 757." The FRY took advantage of this ruling to require the payment of exorbitant transit charges from vessels passing through the FRY portion of the Danube River, which became a major source of foreign currency.

The Security Council attempted to address these difficulties in resolution 787 and the revised guidelines which accompanied the new sanctions. This resolution strictly limited the types of commodities which could be transshipped and required transshipment to be approved by the Sanctions Committee under its no-objection procedure. The resolution further tightened the regime by requiring countries of destination to report to the Sanctions Committee upon completion of the transshipment.

While the language of resolution 787 did address many of the legal problems created by the imprecision of resolution 757, the transshipment regime continued to prove unworkable in practice. Most importantly, the Sanctions Committee, through the Sanctions Assistance Missions (SAMs) and authorities in the front-line states, was unable adequately to monitor and enforce the regime. Documents continued to be forged—approval letters themselves were often forged, but more frequently lists attached to approval letters (which themselves bore no official stamp or other markings) were changed to reflect items which were left behind or added to shipments.

Acknowledgment that the transshipment regime was unworkable, combined with escalated aggression by Bosnian Serbs against Bosnian Moslems in the spring of 1993, led to a growing consensus among states that transshipments should be totally banned. Accordingly, resolution 820—adopted on April 17, 1993, nearly one year after the establishment of the ban on imports and exports in resolution 757—established a complete ban on all land transfers of commodities into the territory of the FRY, and severely restricted transshipment on the Danube.

The failure of the transshipment regime can be attributed both to poorly constructed provisions and to practical problems. By failing adequately to establish limits on the types of commodities and products which could be transshipped, resolution 757 allowed considerable amounts of fuel, machinery, and other economic resources to enter the territory of the FRY, where they were frequently off-loaded (either by plan or against the wishes of the shippers) and used by the authorities of the FRY. Also, the earlier resolution did not provide any notification requirement upon completion of the transfer of commodities. Accordingly, there was no mechanism by which to verify that transshipment had been completed.

Most importantly, however, the regime as established was largely unworkable as a matter of practice. The international community was unable, or unwilling, to commit sufficient resources to monitor the implementation of the regime. First, with limited resources it proved impossible to verify the contents of shipments. Second, it was difficult for SAM teams to verify the authenticity of documents. Finally, the SAM teams were unable to monitor effectively the departure of conveyances in order to verify that goods which entered the FRY also departed the FRY.

### C. Imports from the FRY

At first blush, the sanctions provision prohibiting the importation of goods from the FRY appears to be among the most succinct and clear of those contained in the sanction resolutions. Specifically, resolution 757(4)(a) obligates states to prevent "the import into their territories of all commodities and products originating in the Federal Republic of Yugoslavia (Serbia and Montenegro) exported therefrom after the date of the present resolution." However, much in the same way that the Sanctions Committee identified and implemented "implied" exceptions to the sanctions regime's ban on exports to the FRY in the cases of the diplomatic exception and the informational materials exception, the Sanctions Committee also carved exceptions to the complete ban on imports for cases involving "religious objects" and for cases of "repatriation" from the FRY of goods belonging to other states.

The religious objects exception was established in October 1992, when the Sanctions Committee approved the importation from the FRY of a religious sculpture commissioned by a Serbian Orthodox Church in the United States. The Committee approved the shipment despite its recognition that "Resolution 757 did not specifically authorize such transactions" since the humanitarian exception only applied to exports to, not imports from, the FRY. In doing so, the Committee employed the peculiar rationale that the sculpture was a "religious object, not a commodity" and therefore not subject to the sanctions provisions. This rationale would exempt from the sanctions a host of other religious objects including paintings, figurines, bibles, and even religious text books.

In one of its first repatriation cases, the Sanctions Committee decided in July 1992 to authorize the return of a Turkish-registered aircraft which had been sent to the FRY for servicing prior to the adoption of resolution 757. Also in July, the Sanctions Committee authorized the return from the FRY of fabrics belonging to Liz Claiborne, Inc., which had not yet been processed into finished textile products.

The Sanctions Committee strictly confined its repatriation exception to cases in which the items (1) were only temporarily present in the FRY, and (2) were not in any way altered or processed while in the FRY. For example, the Committee refused Egypt's request for repatriation of equipment in the absence of more detailed information indicating "the exact nature and value" of the repairs rendered in the FRY. Nor was the Committee willing to authorize repatriation where goods had been bought and paid for prior to the imposition of sanctions under the repatriation exception. Thus, the Committee refused a request by Mongolia for repatriation of hotel furniture it had purchased from a FRY company before the Security Council's adoption of resolution 757 but which had not yet been shipped when the sanctions were imposed. Although several members of the Committee were sympathetic to the argument that this was merely a routine repatriation case since title had passed to Mongolia before the imposition of sanctions, authorization was denied because "without a mechanism to monitor and investigate such kinds of transactions, it would be impossible to verify claims that the goods to be exported from the FRY had been paid for before 30 May 1992."

A repatriation exception to the prohibition on imports from the sanctioned states makes good sense. The denial of repatriation claims only injures the property owners outside of the sanctioned state. Indeed, the sanctioned state could arguably refuse to release such property, in effect making a de facto expropriation, by shielding itself under the language of the sanctions. As such, future sanctions regimes would do well to include an explicit provision allowing the repatriation of property stranded in sanctioned states. This exception should also include cases in which title to property has passed prior to imposition of sanctions such as in the Mongolia furniture case, provided that the requesting state provides the Committee with specific information verifying that the merchandise in question was fully paid for prior to the imposition of sanctions.

### D. The Maritime Sanctions

### 1. FRY Vessels

After the imposition of the sanctions, the FRY continued to trade through its sizeable merchant fleet in circumvention of the Security Council resolutions. The application of the sanctions to FRY vessels thus became an increasingly important issue for the Sanctions Committee. While the language of resolution 757 does not explicitly cover such vessels, two of its provisions were potentially applicable: paragraph 4(c) provides that all states are required to prevent any activities in their territories which promote or are calculated to promote trade benefiting the FRY, and paragraph 5 provides that all states are required not to make available to the FRY "any funds or any other financial or economic resources."

In domestic litigation challenging the United States government's seizure of four FRY-owned, Maltese-flagged vessels which called at United States ports, the United States took the position that these provisions of resolution 757 authorized states to take appropriate action to prevent the continued operation of FRY vessels. In response to the United States' request for the Sanctions Committee's position on the matter—which the United States hoped to use to bolster its position in court—the Committee issued a ruling on August 28, 1992, stating: "in view of the fact that the vessels are apparently owned by majority interests in Montenegro, their continued operation and any payments related thereto would be in violation of the sanctions established under resolution 757 (1992)."

As is almost always the case with Sanctions Committee communications, the Committee did not explain the basis for its August 28, 1992 ruling. The ruling could be interpreted either (1) as requiring states to prohibit the provision of services to FRY vessels (which in most cases would effectively preclude their entry into or departure from port) as the European Community (EC) countries had done; or (2) as requiring states actively to seize and impound FRY vessels that enter their territorial waters—following the United States model. Although the question was largely rendered moot a year later when the Security Council adopted resolution 820, which explicitly provides that states "shall impound" all FRY-interest vessels as well as other vessels in their territories found to have been in violation of the sanctions, the ambiguity of paragraphs 4(c) and 5 of resolution 757 resulted in much disparity in the treatment of FRY vessels by states and consequently an uneven application of the sanctions in the interim. Moreover, while resolution 820 codifies the United States model, the rulings of the Sanctions Committee suggest that it had in mind the EC rule. For example, in one such case, the Committee emphasized that "the provision of supplies, services or payments to vessels of the Federal Republic of Yugoslavia is prohibited." The Committee has developed a rather broad definition of "vessels of the Federal Republic of Yugoslavia" (applicable under both interpretations). It has, for example, defined such vessels to include FRY-flagged vessels, as well as "vessel[s] owned wholly or partially by persons residing in or by companies registered in the Federal Republic of Yugoslavia (Serbia and Montenegro)." The Committee has explained that "the decisive question in determining whether sanctions should apply to a given vessel is who exercises effective control over the vessel, not simply what flag the vessel is flying." In another ruling, the Committee indicated that foreign owned and registered vessels under contract with entities in the FRY might be deemed to be FRY vessels for purposes of the sanctions.

The Committee has also carved out several exceptions to its prohibitions concerning FRY vessels. On December 17, 1992, for example, the Committee granted an exception "on the basis of humanitarian considerations" for the provision of "food, water and other humanitarian services to the crew" of FRY vessels. The Committee attempted to confine its exception by stating "the Committee does not authorize the unloading of the cargo, nor any maintenance or services to be provided to the vessel itself." In a later case, the Committee explained further that "in case of extreme, life-threatening emergencies of a humanitarian nature States may request the approval of the Sanctions Committee to permit on an exceptional basis such [FRY] vessels to enter their port waters or receive necessary services."

Soon thereafter, the Committee created an exception to its caveat prohibiting the unloading of cargo when it authorized the Netherlands to unload from the Crna Gora, a FRY-owned vessel, a cargo of 63,000 tons of hot coal, which was in danger of spontaneous ignition. The Committee's communication in that case explained that "the Committee's decision in this instance is founded solely upon an appreciation of the assessment by the Netherlands authorities that the continued confinement of the cargo in question represents a serious safety hazard" and the Committee's approval was made "on the condition that the cargo in question remains under impoundment by the Netherlands authorities for the duration of the sanctions." Later, the Committee reversed itself on the last of its conditions, ruling that the Crna Gora's cargo may be released provided "no funds or benefits related to the cargo should be made available to entities in or operating from the Federal Republic of Yugoslavia (Serbia and Montenegro)."

### 2. The Situation on the Danube

The Danube River flows 1,776 miles from Germany to the Black Sea through the countries of Austria, Slovakia, Hungary, Romania, Bulgaria and the FRY. Shipping on the river is regulated by the 1948 Danube Convention, which guarantees freedom of navigation on the Danube. The Danube constitutes a critical transportation link between Eastern Europe and Western Europe, and therefore became a central focus of the international community's efforts to disrupt trade with the FRY.

In response to the position of the Danubian states that their obligations under the Danube Convention prevented them from taking any action against FRY or other vessels violating the sanctions on the Danube, the Sanctions Committee informed the Danubian states that:

The special regime of the Danube under international conventions cannot affect the application of the sanctions regime since, under the Charter of the United Nations and the relevant resolutions of the Security Council, states must fulfill their Charter obligations to implement the sanctions regime notwithstanding the existence of any rights or obligations under any other international agreement.

In the face of continuing protestations by the Danubian states concerning the extent of their authority to act on the Danube, the Security Council adopted Security Council Resolution 787, which:

Reaffirms the responsibility of riparian states to take necessary measures to ensure that shipping on the Danube is in accordance with resolutions 713 (1991) and 757 (1992), including such measures commensurate with the specific circumstances as may be necessary to halt such shipping in order to inspect and verify their cargoes and destinations and to ensure strict implementation of the provisions of resolutions 713 (1991) and 757 (1992).

Later, in light of continuing intransigence on the part of the Danubian states to use force to enforce the Sanctions on the Danube, the Security Council issued a Presidential Statement calling on the Danubian states to enforce the Security Council resolutions "vigorously" with respect to vessels on the Danube and reminding them that "under Article 103 of the Charter, the obligations of the Members of the United Nations under the Charter shall prevail over their obligations under any other international agreement." In response, the members of the Danube Commission adopted a resolution which stated:

The states members of the Danube Commission deem it essential to confirm officially that, in implementing the Security Council resolutions, they are guided by the following notions: (a) All obligations relating to the regime of navigation on the Danube which are not affected by the sanctions must continue to be fulfilled strictly; (b) Measures adopted in implementation of the Security Council resolutions which establish some limits on the regime of free navigation on the Danube should be regarded as being solely of a temporary nature. Such measures related only to the actions taken with a view to the implementation of the relevant Security Council resolutions, and cannot influence the future regime of free navigation on the Danube.

After initial reluctance, the Danube states demonstrated through this resolution their intent to actively enforce the sanctions on the Danube.

When, consistent with the Sanctions Committee's August 1992 ruling, Ukraine, Romania, and Bulgaria began to detain FRY vessels and other vessels on the Danube suspected of violating the sanctions, a host of new issues arose. For example, in December 1992, Romania requested the Sanctions Committee's authorization to release empty FRY vessels from the port area of Galatzi on the Danube, where they were creating a dangerous situation due to the freezing of the river. The Committee apprised Romania that it could find no grounds upon which to approve that country's request. Two days later, the Committee reversed itself by approving the release of the empty vessels on the following conditions:

That the Sanctions Assistance Mission (SAM) in the area will be requested to verify that the vessels released for return to Serbia and Montenegro are indeed empty, further, that in approving the request to repatriate the vessels in question the Committee is doing so on humanitarian and health grounds in the present circumstances, and finally, that the present exception does not set a precedent for any future course of action in similar circumstances.

While explicitly denying the creation of precedent, the Sanctions Committee nevertheless in effect created a "safety exception" to the detention of FRY vessels as it had done earlier with respect to the prohibition on providing services to FRY vessels in the Crna Gora case. Three weeks later, the Sanctions Committee employed this same rationale in approving Romania's request to provide FRY authorities with fuel to ensure the functioning of FRY ice-breaking vessels on the Danube River.

The next month, the FRY retaliated against Romania for detaining its vessels by seizing Romanian vessels on the Danube and threatening to seize more Romanian vessels unless Romania allowed the passage of FRY vessels on the Danube. Soon thereafter, the FRY increased the pressure by using its vessels to blockade the Romanian "Iron Gates II" lock, halting all upstream and downstream traffic on the Danube. The FRY also reportedly threatened to blow up the levee at Prahovo with the purpose of changing the Danube's course and diverting traffic passing through the Romanian canal locks. In response, the Security Council issued a Presidential Statement demanding that the FRY immediately desist from such unlawful retaliatory measures taken in response to actions by states in fulfillment of their obligations under the Charter of the United Nations.

The members of the Sanctions Committee further urged Romania to deny FRY vessels use of the Iron Gates II Lock, which was on the Romanian side of the Danube. Romania argued, however, that "since the Romanian side does not impose any taxation on the Yugoslav vessels for the use of the locks, this activity cannot be assimilated as 'providing services' under paragraph 4 of Security Council Resolution 757 (1992)." The matter was settled a month later when the Security Council included in resolution 820 a provision confirming that:

[N]o vessels (a) registered in the FRY or (b) in which a majority or controlling interest is held by a person or undertaking in or operating from the FRY or (c) suspected of having violated or being in violation of resolutions 713 (1991), 757 (1992), 787 (1992) or the present resolution shall be permitted to pass through installations, including river locks or canals within the territory of member states.

### 3. Enforcement

In response to a request for the Committee's position on what actions could and should be undertaken with respect to vessels and their cargo in situations when violations of the sanctions have been established, the Committee stated:

In view of the fact that full responsibility for the implementation of the mandatory sanctions imposed by the Security Council rests with states and, where specifically indicated, international organizations, the Committee has noted that it is up to each State to institute the measures to meet its obligations set out in the relevant Security Council resolutions, including adoption of relevant national laws and/or procedures and their strict and effective implementation. The Committee felt that such action should, inter alia, envisage severe penal provisions, in accordance with appropriate norms of international law, so as to prevent the ship to deliver prohibited cargo and to ensure that prohibited cargo does not reach its final destination.

While a description of the measures taken by each country to enforce the sanctions against FRY vessels and other sanction-violating vessels is beyond the scope of this article, it is appropriate here to describe briefly those measures taken by the United States, which have served as a model for other countries.

On March 11, 1993, the United States Department of Treasury's Office of Foreign Assets Control named twenty-five maritime firms and fifty-five ships controlled, managed, or operated by these firms as "Specially Designated Nationals" of Yugoslavia. These vessels are presumed to be owned or controlled by the government of the FRY and, pursuant to Executive Order, are subject to "blocking" if they come within United States jurisdiction. Moreover, the regulatory prohibitions governing transactions by United States persons with the government of the FRY are automatically extended to these vessels. The United States Executive Orders also prohibit the import of any FRY-origin cargo into the United States and the export to the FRY of cargo from the United States, and vessels and their cargo found in violation of the Executive Orders are subject to seizure and forfeiture to the United States.

Though the United States enforcement actions appear quite sweeping, several gaps still exist. For example, the United States has no authority to take action against vessels that are not FRY vessels and have not engaged in illegal importation into or exportation from the United States, but have in the past engaged in third country trade with the FRY in violation of the Security Council sanctions. An effective way to ground such sanction-busting vessels is for the state of the vessel's registry to "de-flag" it and for other states to refrain from re-flagging the vessel since, under international law, ships without nationality are subject to arrest and detention by any state. Without new legislative authority, however, the United States is powerless to "de-flag" United States registered vessels that have violated the sanctions or to refrain from re-flagging vessels that other countries have de-flagged for this reason.

In light of the difficulties faced by individual states attempting to enforce the sanctions against non-FRY vessels engaged in illegal trade with the FRY, the North Atlantic Treaty Organization and the Western European Union placed a joint naval task force in the Adriatic Sea to deter violations of the sanctions. Under the terms of resolution 787, this multinational interdiction force was authorized to "use such measures commensurate with the specific circumstances as may be necessary under the authority of the Security Council to halt all inward and outward maritime shipping in order to inspect and verify their cargoes and destinations and to ensure strict implementation of the provisions of resolutions 713 (1991) and 757 (1992)." Because this measure proved to be subject to easy circumvention by vessels falsely declaring that the FRY was not their destination, the Security Council included in resolution 820 (1993) a provision "prohibit[ing] all commercial maritime traffic from entering the territorial sea of the [FRY] except when authorized on a case-by-case basis by the [Sanctions Committee]." This measure effectively imposed a naval blockade against the FRY.

### E. Sporting Events

Paragraph 8(b) of resolution 757 obligates states to "prevent the participation in sporting events on their territory of persons or groups representing the FRY." Immediately following the adoption of 757, the "Yugoslav" soccer team in Sweden for the European Cup Finals was informed by the Swedish government that it would not be allowed to participate. The United States government established guidelines for consular posts making eligibility determinations for athletes applying to come to the United States to participate in sporting events. FRY athletes already in the United States who did not meet the eligibility criteria were prohibited from competing.

Adopted on May 30, 1992, this sanction provision led to immediate questions concerning the extent to which athletes from the FRY would be able to participate in the Olympic Games scheduled to be held in Barcelona that summer. Initially, the International Olympic Committee (IOC) attempted to develop a plan which would allow athletes from the FRY to compete in the Olympics under the Olympic flag on a team fully funded by the IOC.

After considering the question of FRY participation at four meetings between July 16 and July 21, 1992, the Sanctions Committee arrived at its final decision on the participation of FRY athletes in the Summer Games. Noting that the Committee could be guided by no precedent or example, the Committee decided that participation of athletes as private individuals would not violate the provision, so long as: (1) it was clearly evident that the athletes competed solely in their personal and individual capacities; (2) the IOC assumed responsibility for the selection of participating athletes; (3) the athletes were accompanied only by trainers and not by any other personnel or officials; and (4) the athletes refrained from making any political statements or gestures.

The Sanctions Committee went on to state that athletes should be limited to participation in individual sports, because "participation ... in team events would inevitably evoke representation of their country, and therefore would be in violation of the relevant sanctions." The criteria established for participation in the Barcelona games have remained intact.

The reasoning underlying the Sanctions Committee's decision to limit participation to individual sports — that participation of more than one athlete "evoke[s] representation of" the FRY — is curious. Paragraph 8(b) of resolution 757 expressly determines that all states shall prevent participation in sporting events by persons or groups representing the FRY. The provision implicates an affirmative intention, either on the part of the athlete or the organization sponsoring the event, that the individual or group represents the FRY. Absent such a subjective intention, individuals — whether competing alone or as part of a group — should be allowed to participate. Allowing a figure skater to participate as an individual, while denying the participation of the two individuals forming the figure skating pair, seems to contradict the purpose of the provision.

## II. OBSERVATIONS AND RECOMMENDATIONS

### A. Security Council Drafting and the Role of the Sanctions Committee

The Security Council's sanctions resolutions contain a myriad of open-ended and undefined terms. The above discussion is replete with examples of such vaguely drafted terms, including resolution 713's reference to "military equipment," resolution 757's use of the phrase "economic resource," and resolution 760's exception for "products for essential humanitarian need." In some cases, such as with respect to the continued operation of FRY vessels, the Security Council has had to clarify the provisions of sanctions resolutions in subsequent resolutions or presidential statements. Sometimes this has followed the Sanctions Committee's inability to reach consensus on an appropriate interpretation, and other times the Council has merely ratified an earlier ruling by the Sanctions Committee to lend it increased visibility and support. Frequently, however, the subsequent resolutions of the Security Council have created confusion over whether the Council has promulgated a new obligation on states or has merely clarified an existing obligation. This, in turn, creates uncertainty over whether relevant rulings of the Sanctions Committee continue as good authority.

One of the principal reasons that the sponsors of the sanctions resolutions have tabled or agreed to such vague wording is to enable them to garner the maximum support of other members of the Council at the time of adoption of the sanctions resolutions. Frequently, disputes over technical terms are deferred by last minute substitution of less precise language — often language used in an earlier resolution concerning a different sanctions regime. Even though such horse-trading over technical terms is not usually essential for passage of the resolution, unanimous (or near unanimous) adoption by the Council is seen as important in cases of binding Chapter VII sanctions in order to signal wide-spread international support for sanctions.

Another reason for such vagueness is that Security Council resolutions are drafted in a time-sensitive, rather than deliberative, atmosphere. In the context of hurried negotiations, the Council is simply unable to consider fully the range of implications of its choice of language. Rather, the Security Council usually has at best a general idea of what it wants to accomplish through the adoption of a particular sanctions resolution, but it is not always certain about what specific conduct to prohibit.

The Council, therefore, is content to adopt (or recycle) vague terms in its sanctions resolutions and to defer to the Sanctions Committee for evolving application and clarification of the sanctions on a case-by-case basis. Moreover, the Council is usually not troubled by the potential for adverse Sanctions Committee interpretations because each member of the Council has an effective veto over any such interpretation. By allowing the Sanctions Committee to assume the function of interpreting the sanctions, the Council avoids the necessity of facing the difficult task of minute specification of what is and what is not to be permitted under the sanctions.

Surprisingly, with regard to some of the Sanctions Committee's most important rulings, such as on the existence of the "diplomatic," "safety," and "information materials" exceptions to the sanctions, the Security Council has taken no action to codify through subsequent resolution the Sanctions Committee's interpretations. On other questions, such as the application of the sanctions to FRY vessels and the obligation to freeze FRY assets, the Security Council has adopted the Sanctions Committee interpretations in subsequent "clarifying" resolutions. However, the Security Council has demonstrated a troubling tendency to overlook its previous clarifications when instituting a new sanctions regime based on the provisions of previous sanctions resolutions. For example, after the Security Council clarified in resolution 670 that states were required by resolution 661 to detain Iraqi ships and freeze Iraqi assets, the Council repeated the unclear language of resolution 661 in resolution 757 imposing sanctions on the FRY. The Council subsequently adopted resolution 820, which made the same clarifications that were made in resolution 670. To avoid unnecessary confusion, the Security Council should, to the extent possible, codify the important rulings of the Sanctions Committee in subsequent resolutions, and new sanctions regimes should take these clarifications fully into account.

The Sanctions Committee's March 16, 1992 ruling on the dual-use helicopter case defined the Committee as a body with a judicial function that was not explicitly delegated to it by the Security Council but with regard to which the Council has never objected. In this way, the Sanctions Committee fills a gap existing in the methodology of interpreting Security Council sanctions. Because the U.N.'s traditional judicial body—the International Court of Justice (ICJ)—is far too formal and cumbersome to provide speedy interpretation of the sanctions resolutions in cases that number in the hundreds per year, the Sanctions Committee acts as the only efficient forum to resolve ambiguity uniformly in sanctions resolutions. While the Security Council has acquiesced in the expanding judicial function of the Sanctions Committee, it has not taken advantage of subsequent sanctions resolutions to explicitly include this function in the Yugoslavia Sanctions Committee's mandate, nor has it included this function in the mandate of the subsequently established Haiti Sanctions Committee, suggesting that the status of the Sanctions Committee's judicial function is somewhat precarious. It would be unfortunate if the Council were to reign-in the Committee's judicial function, given the vital role that the Sanctions Committee plays in facilitating uniform interpretation of the sanctions. Consequently, the authors recommend that the mandate of future Sanctions Committees explicitly grant those Committees the authority "[t]o issue interpretations of the sanctions on a case-by-case basis in response to requests for fact-specific interpretations from governments."

## B. Consistency Among Sanctions Regimes

As revealed by comparing the texts reproduced in the notes below, the various U.N. sanctions regimes contain similar or identical provisions concerning: an embargo on arms to the sanctioned state (South Africa, Libya, the former Yugoslavia, Somalia, and Haiti); a prohibition of air flights of the sanctioned state (Iraq, Libya, and the FRY); the seizure of vessels and vehicles of the sanctioned state (Iraq and the FRY); an embargo on imports from the sanctioned state (Iraq and the FRY); an embargo on exports to the sanctioned State (Iraq, the FRY, and Haiti); a prohibition on making available funds or other resources to the sanctioned state (Iraq and the FRY); the freezing of assets of the sanctioned state (Iraq, the FRY, and Haiti); and the reduction of diplomatic ties with the sanctioned state (Libya and the FRY).

For reasons of fairness and predictability, identical provisions in different regimes should be construed as identical in scope. It logically follows that questions arising under one sanctions regime should not be addressed solely in terms of the precedent of that regime. Rather; recourse should be made to the precedent of the other regimes and each case should be viewed as a potential precedent for such other regimes including as yet unforeseen regimes that may be instituted in the future, using the provisions of the current Security Council resolutions as models. There is no mechanism, however, to ensure this consistency under the existing system.

Rather than create a single U.N. Sanctions Committee, separate Sanctions Committees have been established for each of the sanctions regimes. Although the several Sanctions Committees are composed of the same states (i.e., the members of the Security Council), frequently these states assign different personnel at their U.N. missions and at their capitals to participate in the proceedings of the different Committees and to make decisions regarding the different regimes. There is an obvious need for a coordinating mechanism between regimes. At a minimum, the U.N. Secretariat should publish a bi-annual "Sanctions Committee Digest," similar to Part I of this article, which would index and summarize the rulings of the several Sanctions Committees for easy reference.

## C. The Nature of the Sanctions Committee

Although it serves a judicial function, in many ways the Sanctions Committee differs from traditional judicial bodies or administrative agencies. These differences are discussed below, under the following categories: (1) composition and operation of the Bench; (2) form of decision; and, (3) decision-making process.

### 1. Composition and Operation of the Bench

Although the Sanctions Committee performs a judicial role, its composition and operation are unlike any other judicial entity. The Sanctions Committee, for example, is composed of diplomats rather than experienced lawyers or jurists. Because of their background, the Committee's members are accustomed to a problem-solving technique that stresses negotiation rather than legal reasoning. Moreover, unlike a traditional judicial body or administrative agency, the Sanctions Committee does not consist of a known bench. The composition of the Committee is in constant flux, changing as diplomats move on to other assignments and as "substitutes" sit in for their colleagues on a frequent basis, thereby disrupting the continuity of the bench. Finally, unlike a tribunal in which decisions are made by majority vote, in a consensus-based system, such as that employed by the Sanctions Committee, one Committee member (and hence state) can dominate the whole group. This also encourages horse-trading rather than principled decision-making. These factors greatly reduce the jural quality of the Committee's decisions. To remedy this defect the Sanctions Committee should make its decisions by vote, rather than consensus, and the members of the Committee should be persons of recognized competence in international law appointed by the members of the Security Council to serve fixed-year terms.

Perhaps the most significant distinction between the Sanctions Committee and most international tribunals and domestic courts in the common law tradition is that the Sanctions Committee does not employ adversary argument by Counsel to narrow and sharpen the decision process. Argument of Counsel can increase predictability by locating and pointing to significant issues, by gathering and focusing crucial authorities, by making facts clear and vivid, and by illuminating the probable consequences of potential decisions. Nor does the Sanctions Committee follow the informal rule-making procedure employed by United States administrative agencies, which provides for notice of a proposed rule and submission of views or arguments by interested parties. The efficacy of the Committee would be improved greatly if in important (as opposed to clearly routine) cases it were to entertain limited oral presentation by the state requesting an interpretation and brief written submissions by other states with a direct interest in the case.

### 2. Form of Decision

The form of the Sanctions Committee's decision also distinguishes it from other judicial entities. For example, the Sanctions Committee neither issues signed opinions nor records the vote of its members as do most judicial bodies. Anonymous decisions behind closed doors give rise to complaints that the Committee is acting like a "Star Chamber," whose members are insulated from even the barest measure of accountability for their rulings. Moreover, the Sanctions Committee does not issue a detailed opinion in the way a traditional court or administrative agency would — setting forth its findings of fact and application of law to those particular facts. Instead, the Committee issues brief conclusory communications, with the barest references to context.

In the common law tradition, in order to ascertain from a case the guiding(or binding) legal principle, one must identify the case's "ratio decidendi," which has been defined as "the material facts of the case plus the decision thereon." The Sanctions Committee frequently does not specify these material facts. One must read the Committee's rulings together with the incoming communications and the record of proceedings to even begin to ascertain what facts may have been considered material. Often it is simply impossible to determine from this record which of the various facts the Committee determined to be material or immaterial. Moreover, the Sanctions Committee rarely enunciates its legal reasoning in its communications. There is, therefore, no guide for determining which facts played a significant role in the Committee's decision.

Technically, the principle of stare decisis does not apply to the International Court of Justice and other international tribunals. Nevertheless, such international judicial bodies "are respectful of precedent" and frequently cite their previous decisions for authority and distinguish decisions when they are not being followed in similar cases. Although the record of the Sanctions Committee's deliberations are full of references to previous cases which the Committee Members considered to constitute precedent, Sanctions Committee formal communications rarely cite to the Committee's past precedent. Several of the Committee's communications, moreover, explicitly assert that they are not to be taken as precedent for future cases and the Committee has on occasion simply reversed itself without attempting to distinguish the previous decision or explain its change of course.

The absence of the doctrine of precedent leads inevitably to incoherent and unpredictable rulings. "Consistency is a prime value in a legal system" and justice requires that like cases be treated alike. Foreseeability as to what conduct is permissible or impermissible is especially critical in the area of sanctions implementation because of the many business relationships that are affected. In addition, if it is to function as a judicial body, the Committee has a duty to introduce into its work some degree of reason and some sense of fairness. By announcing that a particular decision shall not constitute precedent, the Committee undermines the international community's respect for and confidence in its decisions. Moreover, by adopting a politically expedient decision that does not fit into its precedent, the Committee impairs the rule of law. In contrast, one past president of the International Court of Justice lauded the ICJ's "remarkable unity of precedent [as] an important factor in the development of international law." At least with respect to important (as opposed to routine) cases, the Committee should issue brief written opinions that identify the material facts and application of law to those facts.

### 3. Decision Making Process

The Sanctions Committee does not have much recourse to one of the fundamental tools of legal interpretation: a detailed negotiating record. One would expect the function of the Sanctions Committee, as a quasi-judicial body, to be to interpret the provisions of the sanctions resolutions in the light of the purposes which the Security Council had in mind in adopting them. However, the members of the Security Council rarely use their "Explanations of Vote" (or, in U.N. parlance, EOVs) to give interpretive statements on specific provisions of resolutions. Instead, for the most part, EOVs are largely political statements, intended to send diplomatic signals rather than to clarify legal meaning. The debate on resolution 821, creating the Yugoslavia War Crimes Tribunal, was a notable exception. Many of the members of the Council explicitly provided detailed interpretive statements on the provisions of the Statute for the War Crimes Tribunal. It would be of great utility to the operation of the Sanctions Committee if the members of the Security Council continued to provide such interpretive statements, particularly with respect to the meaning of the provisions of sanctions resolutions.

### III. CONCLUSION

Although not originally intended for that purpose, the United Nations Sanctions Committees have come to play a vital role in issuing authoritative interpretations of U.N. sanctions resolutions. The analysis of the Yugoslavia Sanctions Committee's key decisions provided in this Article indicates that the Committee has issued a number of novel and surprising interpretations that at times greatly expand, and at others contract, the meaning of sanctions resolutions. Until now, the Committee has operated in obscurity, with its rulings and record familiar only to a handful of government officials, despite the fact that the interpretations of the Committee have a direct impact on the conduct of thousands of businesses around the world on a daily basis.

One principal purpose of this Article has been to demonstrate the need for the U.N. to publish a bi-annual digest of the rulings of its Sanctions Committees, which, like Part I of this Article, would analyze the Committees' cases in their context and group the decisions by topic for ease of reference. Such a digest would prove instrumental to governments and businesses, as well as to the Sanctions Committee itself. Throughout the Article, the authors have made several other recommendations to improve the operation of the Sanctions Committee and the interpretation of Security Council resolutions, which are summarized below:

(1) The Security Council should in future resolutions provide expressly that the Sanctions Committee's mandate include issuing interpretations of the sanctions resolutions, so that there can be no question of the Committee's continuing competence to undertake this function;

(2) The Security Council should take several steps to enhance the jural quality of the Sanctions Committee, including: (a) creating a single comprehensive Sanctions Com-

mittee to handle all of the U.N. sanctions regimes; (b) requiring that the members of the Sanctions Committee be experts with legal experience appointed by the members of the Security Council to serve fixed-year terms; (c) requiring that the Sanctions Committee make its decisions by vote, rather than consensus, and in important cases, that the Committee issue signed, written, opinions that identify the material facts and application of law to those facts; and (d) authorizing the Committee in important cases to allow limited oral presentation by the state requesting an interpretation and brief written submissions of interest by other states;

(3) In their Explanation of Votes, the Members of the Security Council should provide interpretive statements with respect to the meaning of the provisions of sanctions resolutions to aid the Sanctions Committee in interpreting the resolutions in the light of the purposes which the Security Council had in mind in adopting them; and

(4) The Security Council should, to the extent possible, codify the important rulings of the Sanctions Committee in subsequent resolutions, and should fully reflect these clarifications in new sanctions regimes.

In making these recommendations, the authors are sensitive to the view expressed by the United States Supreme Court in a similar context that "conserving scarce fiscal and administrative resources" should be taken into account in determining how judicial a decision-making process should be. The authors also recognize that some of these suggestions are likely to encounter initial political resistance. However, as the Security Council continues to intensify its reliance on comprehensive economic sanctions to respond to threats to international peace and security around the globe, the several U.N. Sanctions Committees will play an increasingly important role in interpreting those sanctions. Consequently, their work will come under heightened public scrutiny and there is likely to be increasing pressure to clarify the Sanctions Committees' authority to issue interpretations of the Sanctions resolutions, to legitimate the process by which such interpretations are rendered, and to make these interpretations readily available to the public.

## Authors' Note

Critics of the U.N. Sanctions Committee have argued that the use of collective sanctions can have disastrous repercussions for innocent parties who were not intended to be targets. The following three materials delve into the analysis of what the implication and effects of traditional sanctions are and what can be done to prevent unintended consequences. Material 3 addresses the potential harmful side effects of traditional sanctions. This article analyzes whether the collective U.N. sanctions can actually harm the exact people the sanctions were designed to protect. Materials 3 and 4 address a possible alternate approach to collective sanctions by analyzing the usage of targeted sanctions. It is argued that the use of targeted sanctions would put a greater weight of the burden of the sanctions on those individuals or groups of individuals that are committed the offensive acts.

## 6. Joy K. Fausey, Does the United Nations' Use of Collective Sanctions to Protect Human Rights Violate Its Own Human Rights Standards?

*Connecticut Journal of International Law*, 1994
[footnotes omitted by editors]

Coercion is an expensive means of social control, destructive of many of the values which it seeks to conserve.

### I. Introduction

The imposition of collective sanctions is a tool used increasingly by the United Nations (U.N.) in response to violations of international human rights law. Sanctions are intended to alter the policies of the government of a target nation and/or to exact a punishment for human rights violations. The recent increase in use of collective sanctions stems in large part from the perception of this technique as a more moderate approach, falling between the extremes of diplomacy and military intervention.

This Comment investigates whether the imposition of collective sanctions by the U.N. to punish or alter the behavior of a target nation's government results in the U.N. defying its own Charter. After examining precisely how collective sanctions are intended to work alongside specific U.N. human rights principles, this Comment suggests that the U.N. may be in violation of its own Charter for denying basic human rights with the application of most collective sanctions.

In discussing sanctions generally as a rehabilitative and/or punitive theory, this Comment focuses on the concept of how collective sanctions are supposed to effect their ultimate goal. In examining the means used to reach the end and the intended ramifications on the population of a nation, developments in Serbia and Iraq will be used to illustrate the practical realities of collective sanctioning.

The general theory of sanctions is multi-faceted and complex. I have attempted to reduce the present issue to its barest elements in order to avoid the interjection of other U.N. and sanctioning issues. For instance, this Comment does not address the effectiveness of sanctions in ultimately reaching a political or social goal. Also, the practical effects of sanctions are used only to enhance the basic tenets of sanctioning theory on which this Comment focuses.

In setting a foundation for analysis, section II of this Comment discusses the fundamentals of sanctioning. In particular, this section examines the means by which the imposer intends sanctions to effect a goal and how current situations demonstrate this proposition in practice. Section III addresses the portions of the U.N. Charter which are implicated by the use of sanctions and how sanctions are intended to work. Section IV analyzes justifications for U.N. sanction-imposition. This section addresses the issues of proportionality, humanitarian exemptions, and blameworthiness. Section V offers alternatives to collective sanctions.

### II. Sanctions

#### A. Generally

#### 1. Definition

To begin an analysis of the theory of sanction-imposition, a workable definition of "sanctions" is necessary. The following encompasses the generally accepted, traditional notions of the term: non-military measures used to influence a nation to conform to some desired behavior or to punish a nation for violating some international law. The encouraged behavior is usually derived from an international standard or obligation.

The above definition is inadequate for the purposes of this Comment. The definition suggests that the measures taken will somehow influence the target "nation." Also, the language implies that a "nation" behaves, or can be influenced by punishment for misbehavior. The above definition conforms with the traditional approach to sanctions which considers only sovereign nations to be recognized players within international law. The international legal community often focuses on the rights and obligations of nations in an effort to acknowledge the sovereign right of "nations" to conduct their own affairs. However, as recognition of individual rights in international law grows, deference to a nation's sovereignty consequently is diminished. This paper suggests an alternative, contemporary approach which accounts for the role of the individual in the international arena. Thus, a better definition of "sanctions" from which to proceed is: non-military measures used to influence the leaders of a nation to conform to some desired behavior or to punish the leaders of a nation for directing that nation in a certain way contrary to international human rights law. This contemporary/realistic approach recognizes the current direction of international law to recognize individual legal rights.

Proceeding from this approach, only people within a nation are influenced by "measures" taken against the "nation" and can be influenced by punishment for undesirable behavior. Likewise, only certain individuals within a nation can act on behalf of the nation. This conceptual and linguistic shift from sanctions against a nation to sanctions against the population of a nation follows from the broadening of international law to include individual human rights.

However, shifting from a use of the historical, more theoretical language of imposing sanctions against a "nation" would eliminate the "public relations" benefits such language confers on sanction-imposers. Since sanction-imposers can claim they are targeting an intangible "nation" rather than people, the effect of sanctions on individuals is less apparent. In most literature and debate regarding sanctions, sanctions rarely are said to be imposed against the people of a particular nation. Where sanctioning is concerned, however, a fixation on sovereignty results in the blind punishment of individuals not responsible for the behavior which prompted the sanctions.

This Comment is based on the premise that someone, not something (i.e., a nation), is the target of the "measures" mentioned in the traditional definition. If the behavior of an entire "nation" is to be affected or attacked, those controlling the behavior of the "nation" are those most likely meant to be influenced by the "measures."

Thus, this Comment proceeds from the proposed contemporary definition of sanctions in analyzing the international legal implications of U.N. collective sanctioning.

## 2. Types of Sanctions

The measures referred to in the definition of "sanctions" may take many forms. Collective economic measures are frequently used to attempt to influence a nation's leaders. Economic sanctions can be characterized as "(a) restrictions on the flow of goods, (b) restrictions on the flow of services, (c) restrictions on the flow of money and (d) control of markets themselves in order to reduce or nullify the target's chances of gaining access to them."

According to Makio Miyagawa in Do Economic Sanctions Work?, a lack of vital resources can destroy a nation's economy. No member of the population is exempted when a nation's economy is paralyzed. Economic sanctions typically are directed at the entire population of a country.

Cultural sanctions are another type of measure directed at the general population. These may include restrictions on participation in sporting events with teams of the target nation, on scientific exchanges or on travel to the target nation. These measures are less threatening to the livelihood of individuals than economic measures; however, the similarity between these two types of sanctions is important. Significantly, each is aimed at the general population as opposed to individuals within the country.

While this Comment focuses on collective economic and cultural sanctions imposed on a nation's population, the U.N. also imposes other types of sanctions. These other measures, such as individual sanctions, are not discussed here.

### B. How Sanctions Are Expected to Lead to a Goal

Little has been written about the basic way in which collective sanctions are expected to lead to their goal. That which has been written also uses language which focuses on the "nation" being influenced by sanctions. The purpose of this section is to explore exactly how the sanction-imposer anticipates that collective sanctions will prompt the leaders of a target nation into action. The issue is whether the sanctions are expected to cause the leaders of a nation to change their course of leadership.

The general thinking about how sanctions will lead to their goal is that "the burden of economic hardship imposed by sanctions will become intolerable." The next step in how this process will function is unclear. There appear to be a number of realistic ways in which collective sanctions, once they have produced hardship, can be expected to fulfill their goal. Under one approach, the sanctions directly impact the population and only indirectly influence the leaders to change. For example, the population is so deprived of goods and services that it forces the leaders to alter their behavior or overthrows those in power. Additionally, under this approach, the leaders may be compelled by guilt to comply with the goal of the sanctions. An alternative approach is one in which the collective sanctions lead to change by significantly depriving both the population and leaders of goods and services.

Thus, whatever the approach, the imposers intend that the hardship of sanctions on a population in some way increases the likelihood of the goal of the sanctions being reached. Alternatively, the imposer may see that the only way to be sure to reach the leaders is by including everyone in the nation within the scope of the sanctions.

Regardless of the reason why sanctions are directed at an entire population, when the U.N. imposes collective sanctions on a nation, the population is targeted with measures intended to affect a goal which most members of the population do not have the power to institute. Only a few members of the population are able to comply with the requirements necessary for the sanctions to be lifted. The remaining population is being targeted by the imposer to somehow encourage the leaders to alter their behavior on behalf of the nation. Alternatively, the U.N. may be encouraging the overthrow of the current government. Additional intentions of impoverishing the nation's population may be to create fear in the leaders of overthrow by the population because of the conditions, or to induce guilt in the leaders for the suffering of the population. In any event, in anticipating how the sanctions will reach their goal, the U.N. intentionally expects to cause deprivation within an entire population of a nation. This characteristic of sanctioning forms the basis of the argument that collective sanction imposition may defy the U.N. Charter.

### C. Practical Examples

If imposing sanctions doesn't accomplish the intended deprivation, the notion that this technique may be illegal would prove irrelevant. However, two recent examples of

U.N. sanction-imposition illustrate the effects of sanction implementation on the population. Developments in Iraq and Serbia demonstrate that collective sanction imposition can function as expected.

The sanctions which the U.N. imposed against the populations of these two nations are similar in both scope and outcome. This Comment focuses on the initial measures taken against those in Iraq and Serbia since these sanctions have not yet been lifted and the U.N. was among the first of the organizations, or groups, to impose sanctions in these areas following violent outbreaks.

## 1. The Scope of Sanctions Against Iraq and Serbia

### a. Iraq

The U.N. initially imposed sanctions against those in Iraq on August 6, 1990, following the Iraqi military's invasion and illegal occupation of Kuwait. The U.N. sanctions restricted the importation of products originating in Iraq and the exportation of all products to Iraq, except those used for humanitarian purposes. Also, the U.N. prohibit the remittance of any funds to Iraq, except funds for humanitarian purposes.

### b. Serbia

The U.N. adopted sanctions targeting Serbia's population on May 30, 1992, in response to Serbian military violence throughout Bosnia-Herzegovina. These sanctions forbade the importation and exportation of products from or to Serbia, except for supplies intended for humanitarian purposes. The sanctions also prohibited the provision of funds to Serbia, except payments made for humanitarian purposes.

## 2. Impact of Sanctions on Populations of Iraq and Serbia

Before investigating what effect sanctions may have had on the people within these nations, the difficulties of such an analysis must be acknowledged. There exists no exact method for measuring precisely what damage was caused by sanctions as opposed to other forces; or for measuring exactly how much of a problem is attributable to sanctions alone; or to sanctions combined with other forces. Nevertheless, the studies and reports cited below strongly suggest that sanctions have had a direct impact on the populations. Again, this Comment does not focus on the effectiveness of sanctions in reaching an ultimate political or social goal; rather, this Comment examines the effectiveness of the intermediate goal of sanctions, that of causing the deprivation of a population.

Regarding Iraq, the combination of the Gulf War and sanctions caused infant mortality rates to triple. Sanctions have reduced the standard of living in Iraq by about one-third.

The U.N. acknowledged the humanitarian crisis in Iraq by offering to allow the Iraqi export of oil if the payments could be used for humanitarian purposes. The U.N., however, refused to lift the collective sanctions.

With respect to Serbia, the economy has collapsed as a result of the war and sanctions and "a major public health catastrophe is unfolding...." Inflation in Serbia was approaching 25,000% near the end of December 1993 and the monthly income of the average Serb had dropped from five hundred dollars to fifteen dollars.

These summaries simply illustrate that so far as sanctions are intended to devastate the populations of the targeted nations, that principle of sanctioning works in practice.

This section has demonstrated how sanctions imposed against the entire population of a nation are intended to affect the whole population detrimentally. This deprivation of the entire population is somehow supposed to lead to a goal the U.N. has deemed important. Regardless of whether the goal is reached, however, this method of attaining the goal appears, at best, contradictory to the human rights principles set out in the U.N. Charter. The following section addresses the relevant U.N. Charter sections.

## III. U.N. Charter

As the constitution of the U.N. and the foundation from which the organization proceeds, the U.N. Charter is the document against which actions of the U.N. and its bodies are measured. The Charter is the single document which explicitly addresses the U.N. as an organization. The Charter states both the direction that the U.N. must take in its endeavors and the guiding principles and purposes under which the organization was created.

The following subsections address four issues involving the Charter and the premise of this Comment. The first is Charter-defined human rights which appear violated by the imposition of collective sanctions. The second is the U.N. justification for sanction-impositions taken from the Charter. The third issue encompasses the general question of whether the U.N. can violate its own Charter. The final issue addressed is whether two apparently conflicting U.N. Charter pieces can be reconciled.

### A. The Charter as Prohibiting U.N. Sanction-Imposition

The Preamble to the Charter states that one of the purposes for which the U.N. was created was "to promote social progress and better standards of life in larger freedom." In striving for this goal, the Preamble cautions that international machinery be used "for the promotion of the economic and social advancement of all peoples."

Article I states the purposes of the U.N. and indicates "the direction which the activities of the Organization are to take...." These purposes include settlement of situations involving a potential breach of the peace in conformity with principles of justice and international law. Another purpose is to promote and encourage respect for human rights.

Given the intended effects of sanctions on a population of a nation, these portions of the Charter support the argument that sanction-imposition contradicts the purposes of the U.N. However, the most persuasive language in the Charter against sanctions lies in Article 55, entitled "International Economic and Social Co-Operation." This article mandates that, in striving for peaceful and friendly relations among nations, the U.N. shall promote:

a. higher standards of living, full employment, and conditions of economic and social progress and development;

b. solutions of international economic, social, health, and related problems; and international cultural and educational cooperation; and

c. universal respect for, and observance of, human rights and fundamental freedoms for all without distinction as to race, sex language, or religion.

The human right to an adequate standard of living is that which is denied, and in some cases, destroyed in the face of sanctions. This human right is taken from an innocent group of people who are in the wrong place at the wrong time. Furthermore, as illustrated by the examples of Serbia and Iraq, with a decline in the standard of living go other human rights which the U.N. values, such as health and life.

### B. The Charter as Promoting U.N. Collective Sanctioning

To justify sanction imposition, the U.N. may rely on language from the Charter beginning with the first article. Article I, paragraph I, states that, in maintaining international peace and security, the U.N. may "take effective collective measures for the prevention and removal of threats to the peace and for the suppression of acts of aggression or other breaches of the peace...." In the second article, members agree to avoid the use of force in any manner inconsistent with the U.N.'s purposes. Both of these provisions can be used to argue that the Charter intended for sanctions to be a legal method for the U.N. to enforce the principles of the Charter. Yet these Articles do not point directly to economic sanctions.

Article 41 of the Charter directly addresses enforcement action. This article states that "the Security Council may decide what measures not involving the use of armed force are to be employed to give effect to its decisions ... including complete or partial interruption of economic relations and of ... communication, and the severance of diplomatic relations." Although the Charter fails to state against whom measures are to be taken, this section of the Charter appears to condone fully the imposition of sanctions as a Security Council response to a threat to international peace and security.

### C. U.N. Violation of Its Own Charter

Only one Charter purpose requires the Security Council to act affirmatively—the maintenance of peace and security. The Charter specifically instructs the Security Council to act in the face of threats to peace and security. On the other hand, the Charter offers no suggestions as to how the other purposes, including the promotion of higher living standards, are to be implemented. Such a lack of direction may suggest that the maintenance of peace and security outweighs all other purposes mentioned in the Charter and that the U.N. does not violate its Charter when it imposes collective sanctions in order to maintain peace and security. In analyzing this inference, this Comment presumes arguendo that the Charter requires no affirmative acts in furtherance of these other purposes. Specifically, the Charter does not require the U.N. to operate actively in the furtherance of higher living standards.

However, this presumption does not lead to the conclusion that the Charter implicitly permits the U.N. to act in complete contradiction to the other purposes. Such an analysis would render these purposes meaningless and the Charter itself senseless. The organization's existence would be a contradiction of its own constitution.

Nevertheless, this situation does currently exist in the U.N. In imposing collective sanctions, the organization has been unable to provide substance for each of the Charter's parts. The Security Council, in imposing sanctions following the mandate of Article 51, is denying another purpose of the organization: the promotion of higher standards of living. While Article 55 has not been used to invalidate Security Council actions previously, the Council nevertheless is bound to act within the confines of the Charter's other purposes and principles.

Furthermore, other divisions within the U.N. have condemned exactly the means by which the Security Council intends to reach its goals in imposing sanctions. For example, the General Assembly nearly annually adopts a resolution rejecting coercive economic measures as an instrument for exerting pressure against developing countries. These resolutions note the negative effect such measures have on external trade and the crucial part the measures play in the economies of developing countries. The General Assembly has recognized that the measures do not help to create the climate that peace needs for development and are at a variance with the U.N. Charter. While the reasons for imposing the measures addressed by these resolutions may differ from those of the Security Council in imposing sanctions, the effects of the collective sanctions and their compatibility with the Charter remain the same.

Ideally, the Security Council should change its sanctioning policies to conform with the Charter as it currently stands. However, if the Security Council continues to impose collective sanctions, the U.N.'s International Court of Justice has recently suggested that it has the power to declare Security Council acts illegal. Yet, a declaration by the Court of the illegality of a Security Council act may be unenforceable. As far back as 1971, the Court, referring to South African sanctions, stated that the duty of non-recognition of South Africa's administration of the territory should not deprive the people of Namibia of any advantage derived from international co-operation. Since the Security Council continues to impose collective sanctions, this statement by the Court evidently has gone unheeded; any subsequent pronouncements by the court may be ignored as well. Nevertheless, the Charter states that the Court is the principal judicial organ of the U.N. and that members must comply with its decisions. The Security Council, made up of U.N. members, is charged with enforcing the court's judgments. Thus, the Security Council could be placed in the unique situation of enforcing a judgment against itself.

Regardless of whether the Security Council chooses to follow a decision by the International Court of Justice, the presence of such a situation would be extremely embarrassing for the Security Council and for the U.N. as a whole. To avoid the risk of embarrassment, the Security Council may comply with the Charter before the U.N. court disagrees with it. Otherwise, the only way to induce the Security Council to alter its behavior would be to wait for it to recognize the need for change on its own. Given the current direction of international human rights law, such a change may soon be a reality.

The Charter should be read to give each of its parts meaning in order for the U.N. fully to strive for the Charter's purposes and principles. Charter provisions regarding human rights necessarily must restrict the broad Security Council powers of Chapter VII. Otherwise, the U.N. stands in violation of its own Charter.

### D. Reconciling Apparently Contradictory Charter Directives

The U.N. need not abandon one purpose to save the other. The seemingly divergent views of sanctions found in the Charter are not irreconcilable. Recall the focus of the contemporary approach is on the U.N.'s protection and promotion of individual human rights as opposed to sovereign rights or obligations. Through an application of this approach, coupled with a re-examination of the Charter directive, the U.N. more accurately and realistically can evaluate the breadth of the effects of collective sanction imposition.

For the collective sanctions to be legal within the Charter's standards, the Security Council must find that in order to restore international security, innocent people must "pay" for the crimes of their leaders. The Security Council must find that not only do the human rights of the population not deserve protection, but also that the rights may be denied for certain purposes. This result would contradict the Charter purposes relating to the promotion of human rights.

As a constitution, the Charter is an evolving document, as the framers of the document expected. While individual human rights were recognized at the time the Charter was written, the rights have developed substantially since that time. Individual rights are gaining more acceptance as the mystique of sovereignty fades. The Charter can be read in such a way to give meaning to the entire document. Sanctions should be imposed only against those responsible for the illegal behavior and those able to change this behavior.

### IV. Critique of Collective Sanctioning Justifications

This section analyzes and criticizes four arguments justifying the U.N. imposition of collective sanctions. These theories suggest that depending on the positioning of the "players" and the targeting of the blame, the U.N. may not have to answer for the human rights violated when collective sanctions are imposed.

## A. Proportionality

One argument that suggests why the U.N. may be justified in imposing sanctions against a population is that the Security Council has weighed the rights to be protected on both sides and decided that the rights violated by sanctions are less important than those which the sanctions seek to protect. Proportionality, as this balancing test is called, demands that an act bear some relation to its purpose. In determining the legality of sanctions, proportionality should be a consideration.

The concept of proportionality as a factor in deciding what measures to take against the leaders and/or population of a nation for violations of international law derives from the "just war" theory. The theory of proportionality has been applied over such a large number of years and in a variety of circumstances by many governments and organizations that it has gained the status of customary international law. The U.N.'s International Court of Justice has recognized the use of proportionality in nonwar situations. Additionally, the basis of proportionality, justice—that the punishment matches the crime—also finds support within the provisions of the U.N. Charter. However, the Charter itself does not require specifically that the Security Council impose proportionate measures in response to threats to peace and security.

The U.N. Charter gives the Security Council discretionary power to decide whether measures should be used and, if so, what measures to apply. However, in making this decision, the Security Council necessarily goes through a weighing process since it is required to discharge its duties "in accordance with the purposes and principles of the United Nations."

In principle, given the status of proportionality as customary international human rights law and its basis in justice, proportionality should be a factor considered by the Security Council in deciding whether to impose sanctions. In practice, even if the Security Council is presumed to consider proportionality in deciding whether and how to impose collective sanctions, the language used by the Council in evaluating proportionality would render such an analysis almost useless. As discussed in Section II, the Council uses historical international legal language to discuss the imposition of the sanctions, and refers to the sanctions as against a nation. The use of this historical language in considering the proportionality of collective sanctions defeats the purpose of the proportionality theory, and demonstrates a problem with this justification of collective sanctioning.

Proportionality in the application of collective sanctions must be analyzed within the true parameters of sanction imposition. In other words, the usual, detached language of describing sanctions must be exchanged for words which describe what is reality.

In order to reach a certain group within a population, the entire population is deprived under sanctions. Most of those deprived are not directly responsible for the behavior which prompted the sanctions. Thus, in terms of proportionality, a simple comparison of the rights of the violator of human rights versus those of the violatee is problematic.

With collective sanctions, the human rights deprived by the sanctions are not solely the human rights of those violating others' human rights. Thus, an additional step must be inserted in the proportionality analysis. The question to be answered is whether the human rights being violated by the target leaders are so important that they warrant depriving others within the target nation (not responsible for the initial violation) of their human rights. While the target leaders may not be able to protest a violation of their human rights from sanctions, the rest of the population deserves at least an acknowledgement that their human rights are being denied via the sanctions. In evaluating proportionality, the part of the population not directly responsible for the behavior which led to the sanctions should be considered separately from those in charge.

Thus, the language used in sanction-imposition is important. Referring to sanctions as "against a nation" denies the innocent population its human rights without taking proportionality into account separately where the population is concerned. Holding an entire nation to blame for the acts of a few of its members results in a disproportionate response by the U.N.

While the Security Council has acknowledged that leaders may be solely to blame, it nevertheless continues to impose collective sanctions in response to leaders' illegal acts. For example, with respect to Iraq, the Security Council noted the culpability of individuals who ordered breaches of humanitarian law, yet placed the responsibility on the nation of Iraq. Regarding Serbia, the Security Council again decided to impose collective sanctions, although it acknowledged that individuals were responsible for international human rights law violations. The Security Council possesses the information it needs in order to comply with the Charter, yet it continues to punish innocent populations.

A final consideration must be made in evaluating the proportionality problem if the target nation's leaders are depriving their own population of certain human rights. The Security Council should determine whether the rights it is seeking to protect (those being deprived by the target government) are so important to the population that the population should be deprived of additional human rights in order to gain those being deprived by the target government. This scenario highlights the inherent flaws of punishing a victim in order to get to the perpetrator.

One is hard-pressed to find a set of circumstances in which the U.N. Security Council may judge that one innocent group's rights may be extinguished in order to protect another's. Since the actual target of sanctions is typically one person or a specific group of people, the Security Council is responsible for examining the proportionality issue with a target nation's population addressed separately from its leaders. The fact that the target population was not responsible for the initial human rights violation and is not in a position (save rebellion) to remedy the situation to the U.N.'s satisfaction is crucial for the Security Council to include in its evaluation of proportionality. This responsibility is derived directly from the Charter which commands that the Security Council decide the appropriate measures to be taken in response to a threat to international peace. As stated by Article 24, these measures should be in accordance with the U.N.'s purposes and principles. This Article was included in the Charter to assure that the Security Council act purposefully and with reason in performing its functions.

Given the continued presence within the Council of historical international legal evaluations in which only nations are players, the proportionality justification is not helpful in responding to the violation of individual human rights by the U.N.'s collective sanctioning. A proportionality analysis by the Security Council does not automatically remove responsibility from the U.N. when human rights of an innocent population are violated in an effort to restore the human rights of others. Within a contemporary approach analysis, as described in Section II *supra*, collective sanctions are unlikely to meet the burden of proportionality.

## B. Humanitarian Exemptions

Another proposition suggested to justify the imposition of collective sanctions is that in adopting sanctions against a population, the U.N. exempts humanitarian goods and services from the restrictions. However, such a gesture by the U.N. does not negate the goal of the principle of collective sanctions regarding the target population. The sanctions still are kept in place in an effort to wear down the population so much that the leaders act or are removed.

Again, the practice of sanctioning demonstrates that the principle of sanctioning functions as intended, even with humanitarian exemptions in place. In the sanctions targeting the populations of both Iraq and Serbia, humanitarian items were exempted from the restrictions imposed by the sanctions. Yet, as a result of sanction-imposition, the populations of both nations have suffered tremendous declines in their standards of living as well as overall health deterioration. The humanitarian exemptions appear to be either a smoke-screen or a band-aid covering the major problems created by collective sanctions within a population. Humanitarian exemptions run contrary to the principle that collective sanctions are supposed to devastate a population.

The fact that humanitarian exemptions are included with the imposition of sanctions does not rectify the intention of the sanctions to deprive the population. The premise of this Comment is unaffected by the existence of exemptions of humanitarian items.

## C. Blame the Leaders

A third argument which is used to justify the imposition of sanctions by the U.N. is that the leaders of the nations against whom sanctions are levied are to blame for the suffering of their populations. If the leaders would comply with the wishes of the U.N., the sanctions against the population would be lifted.

To its detriment, this argument is a powerful demonstration of how sanctions are intended to affect the population. This argument admits the truth of the rationale of collective sanctioning which is proposed by this Comment. Specifically, arguing that until the sanctions are lifted, the leaders should be blamed for the suffering of the population acknowledges that the sanctions were intended to cause suffering within the population. Blaming the leaders functions as a call to arms for the population and a guilt-trip or fear-inducement for the leaders. In other words, the nation's population is to be exposed to the sanctions in order to motivate the leaders.

There are two possible responses to the argument that the leaders should be blamed for U.N. collective sanction imposition. The first is that the leaders do not choose for the U.N. the measures which it adopts in response to human rights violations. The U.N. ultimately decides to impose sanctions on a population.

The second response is that this same argument could be used to justify any measures the U.N. adopted in enforcing international law, including physically torturing a population. Using this justification, the U.N.'s use of torture against a nation's population would be blamed on the leaders who wouldn't comply with the U.N.'s wishes. However, such action is contrary to the Charter principles which require measures in accordance with the U.N.'s purposes and principles. Thus, diverting attention from the Security Council's actions by focusing on non-compliant leaders simply avoids recognition of those actually to blame—the sanction-imposers.

## D. Blame the Population

A final justification for the imposition of sanctions by the U.N. is that perhaps the population shares the blame with the leaders by supporting the leaders' actions. However, the population of a nation cannot be presumed to have consented to the leaders' actions. Further, as practice has shown, even if the population of a nation actively disagrees with its leader, the leader's illegal practices may continue. There is evidence in Iraq, for instance, that a significant minority or even a majority of citizens do not support their government and have tried to overthrow their government without success. Moreover, Iraq's President Saddam Hussein, has continually displayed an independence in decision-making which highlights the lack of connection between the acts of a nation's leader and the wishes of the nation's population. Hussein repeatedly has refused to accept the U.N.'s offer to allow Iraq to sell oil with the proceeds used for humanitarian needs within the Iraqi population.

Requiring a population to flee its homeland in order to express disagreement with its leaders is extreme and absurd. Non-participation in the illegal activity of its leaders should be sufficient to segregate the population from the punishment inflicted on its leaders.

None of the four arguments justifying the principles behind the U.N. imposition of collective sanctions is persuasive. To evaluate proportionality, the Security Council would have great difficulty in justifying the deprivation of human rights of one innocent group in favor of those of another innocent group. Regarding humanitarian effects, they do not, and are not intended to, reverse the detrimental effects of collective sanctions on a population. Finally, the blame for the effects of the sanctions cannot be transferred successfully from the U.N. to either the leaders or the target population.

## V. Conclusion

The use of collective sanctioning by the U.N. to respond to violations of international human rights law is intended to lead to further human rights violations. A large number of people within the population of a nation are sentenced for the crimes of a few of its members. This aspect of the concept of sanctioning is in direct conflict with human rights principles outlined in the U.N. Charter regarding living standards. The foundation of collective sanctioning makes the U.N. appear hypocritical at best when attempting to protect human rights.

In order to practice the human rights values it preaches, the U.N. should respond to human rights violations, by adopting alternative measures which are not meant to be detrimental to the innocent populations of target nations. The following two proposals are suggested as means of resolving international disputes in conformity with the U.N. Charter.

Just as collective sanctions have been turned to as alternatives to military solutions to international emergencies, alternatives to collective sanctions also exist which the U.N. should not ignore. Recognition of a target nation's population's human rights does not eliminate all possible responses to a leader's violation of international human rights laws.

One alternative has already been mentioned and is often used in conjunction with collective sanctions. Individual sanctions provide a means of targeting with precision the person or people responsible for the human rights violations and in a position to redirect the "nation's behavior." These sanctions eliminate the need for a middle-party to motivate leaders to change their behavior. An example of individual sanctions is the freezing of the leaders' funds wherever they may be located. Johan Galtung has suggested an even more extreme use of individual sanctions: arresting the key individuals. In whatever form, the principles of the U.N. Charter are in greater harmony with the practice of individual sanctions than with that of collective sanctions.

Another alternative to collective sanctions is positive sanctions or rewards. Since sanctions cost the imposers (who lose exports and may have to pay more to import certain goods from elsewhere) as well as the targets, perhaps a carrot would work better than a stick. Imposers are willing to pay for the enforcement of international obligations as is demonstrated by their participation in negative sanctions. Perhaps if identical amounts to those lost in negative sanctions were offered to the target nation through its leaders, as a reward for complying with international law, no populations would suffer. However, little is known about the operation of such a reward system.

Both of these suggestions remove the burden of paying for the illegal acts of a nation's leaders from the nation's general population. Before imposing collective sanctions in the future, the U.N. should re-examine the philosophy behind collective sanctioning and should consider alternative avenues of international law enforcement.

## 7. Gary C. Hufbauer and Barbara Oegg, Targeted Sanctions: A Policy Alternative?

*Law and Policy in International Business*, 2000
[footnotes omitted by editors]

### I. INTRODUCTION

Secretary-General Kofi Annan's 1997 report on the work of the United Nations stressed the importance of economic sanctions as the Security Council's tool to exert pressure without recourse to force. At the same time, the report expressed concern about the harm that sanctions inflict on vulnerable civilian groups and the collateral damage that they cause to third states. The Secretary-General encouraged the General Assembly and the Security Council to consider ways to "render sanctions a less blunt and more effective instrument" and reduce the humanitarian costs to civilian populations as far as possible.

Widely shared concerns about humanitarian and third country effects of sanctions can undermine the political unity required for the effective implementation of multilateral sanctions. Iraq is an example of such dangers. With the erosion of support for the economic embargo, it is becoming clear that the effectiveness of a sanctions regime partly depends on the manner in which it addresses humanitarian issues. Although virtually all sanctions regimes launched during the 1990s allow trade in humanitarian goods, the "blunt weapon" of a comprehensive embargo inevitably hurts those at the bottom of the economic heap. Given the historic inability of sanctions to achieve their foreign policy goals, the conventional wisdom that civilian pain leads to political gain is being questioned. Many analysts ask whether the results of sanctions warrant their costs. In response to these concerns, practitioners and scholars alike have been seeking ways to fine-tune sanctions to direct their force against those in power.

### II. TARGETED SANCTIONS

"Targeted sanctions" or "smart sanctions," like "smart bombs," are intended to focus their impact on leaders, political elites, and segments of society believed to be responsible for objectionable behavior, while simultaneously reducing collateral damage to the general population and to third countries. Growing emphasis on the individual accountability of those in power for the unlawful acts of states (highlighted by the Pinochet case and the Bosnian war crimes trials) has made the concept of targeted sanctions increasingly attractive.

Before engaging in a detailed analysis of specific measures, it may be useful to draw a distinction between "targeted" and "selective" sanctions. "Selective" sanctions, which are less broad than comprehensive embargoes, involve restrictions on particular products or financial flows. "Targeted" sanctions focus on certain groups or individuals within the targeted country and aim to impact these groups directly. As a result, there is some overlap between these two concepts.

#### A. *Arms Embargoes*

Arms embargoes are targeted sanctions in the sense that their stated purpose is to pressure military and political leaders by denying them access to weapons and other military equipment, while sparing the civilian population. More specifically, arms embargoes seek to reduce conflict by reducing access to weapons. In addition, arms embargoes help identify and stigmatize individuals and countries that violate international norms.

Since 1990, the U.N. Security Council has imposed ten arms embargoes designed to limit local conflicts. However, the effectiveness of arms embargoes in ending conflicts remains elusive. The use of force was necessary to convince the warring factions in Sierra Leone to lay down their arms, and the civil war in Angola continues unabated seven years after the Angolan arms embargo. Weak enforcement, poor monitoring, and dire conditions in bordering countries all work to effectively undermine arms embargoes.

Trafficking in small arms pays high profits even in normal times. Profits increase further with the imposition of an embargo, creating lucrative markets for illicit trade. These profits enrich precisely those people that the embargo is intended to hurt, creating a financial interest in prolonged conflict. This is particularly true when the targeted group controls valuable natural resources. Angola illustrates the problem. Realizing that National Union for the Total Independence of Angola (UNITA) rebels use diamond profits to finance their weapons purchases, the U.N. Security Council imposed an embargo on uncertified diamond exports from Angola. Despite additional efforts by the U.N. to tighten the implementation and enforcement of the arms and diamond embargoes, an end to Angola's civil war seems as remote as ever. This episode suggests that, as a stand-alone policy, arms embargoes are unlikely to curtail local conflicts if the political will to enforce them is lacking.

### B. *Travel Bans*

Travel or aviation bans fall into two categories: restrictions on all air travel to and from a target country, and restrictions on the travel of targeted individuals, groups, or entities. In the case of restrictions on air travel to and from a target country, or areas under the control of targeted groups (such as UNITA), the assumption is that the flight ban will affect people in power substantially more than members of the general population, thus minimizing the humanitarian impact.

The assumption that flight bans exert minimal humanitarian impact may not always hold true. In August 1996, the Security Council voted to impose a flight ban on the government of Sudan because of its suspected support of international terrorism. The United Nations delayed implementing the ban, however, and the U.N. Department of Humanitarian Affairs subsequently issued a report on its possible humanitarian effects. The report showed that even a selective flight ban could cause humanitarian suffering. Because the Sudanese national airline relies on international airports for its aircraft maintenance, a selective ban might have grounded the entire airline. This, in turn, would have created severe problems for relief organizations that relied on the airline to reach remote areas of the country. After evaluating these considerations, the U.N. Security Council refused to implement the flight ban. Similarly, the 1999 U.N. ban on all international flights by the Afghan airline has practically grounded the airline that relied on United Arab Emirates for maintenance. International aid agencies in Kabul have also criticized the ban, claiming that it affected their relief work and, due to the dependence of the postal service on the airline, cut off many poor Afghans from money sent by relatives abroad. Although it is difficult to draw general conclusions about the impact of flight bans on civilian populations from these examples, the bans do call attention to the complexities of "targeted" sanctions.

Travel bans and visa restrictions against individuals are useful in not only avoiding the possible humanitarian impacts of broader travel restrictions but also deny legitimacy to political leaders, military officials, and their supporters. The EU "blacklist" of Serbian President Milosevic's supporters is an interesting case study of this issue. The EU restrictions prohibited the 600 individuals on the blacklist from traveling in Europe and froze their assets in European banks. While Milosevic and his supporters benefited from the Serbian trade embargo by controlling the profitable black market, they appear to have felt the negative effects of this personal international isolation. They found themselves hobbled in conducting business abroad because the travel ban cuts them off from their companies and bank accounts.

With the exception of the EU blacklist and, possibly, the flight ban imposed on Libya in response to the Pan Am Flight 103 bombing, travel bans have had limited success. In the case of Libya, one should remember that Qaddafi handed over the Pan Am 103 suspects to an international court only after the United States and the United Kingdom, reacting to waning international support for the U.N. travel ban, were willing to compromise. The ban was crumbling because the Organization of African Unity called upon its members and others to suspend compliance with the ban. This sequence of events suggests that the travel ban itself had a minor impact on Qaddafi's decision to comply with U.N. Security Council demands. Nevertheless, Qaddafi's eventual compliance with U.N. demands indicates that a combination of travel ban, diplomatic, and other selective economic sanctions can contribute to the achievement of relatively modest policy goals.

Overall, travel sanctions appear to be primarily symbolic measures. While enforcing travel bans is easier than enforcing an arms embargo, some administrative challenges remain. For example, false passports and visas may allow targeted individuals to circumvent the sanctions. Also, it is often hard to identify the appropriate group or individuals that should be targeted. Deep knowledge of the country, the individuals, and the power structure is required to enforce effective individual travel bans.

## C. *Asset Freezes*

Recent studies have taken a closer look at the effectiveness of targeted financial sanctions (such as limiting access to financial markets, restricting economic assistance, and prohibiting new investment). Financial sanctions, in general, have a less immediate impact on trade flows and, therefore, cause less suffering than trade embargoes. Empirical evidence also suggests that financial sanctions may be more likely to achieve a policy change in the target country than restrictions on exports and/or imports. According to an analysis of economic sanctions cases in the second edition of *Economic Sanctions Reconsidered*, financial sanctions contributed to the achievement of foreign policy goals in forty-one percent of the cases, compared to only twenty-five percent for trade sanctions alone. However, financial sanctions have not typically been used as targeted measures. Preliminary data drawn from research completed for the third edition of *Economic Sanctions Reconsidered* suggests that only seven percent of the sanctions cases involving financial sanctions were targeted measures. Historically, asset freezes were imposed in episodes of severe hostility, often at the outbreak of war, and were part of a more comprehensive embargo.

In recent years, however, there have been a few instances of targeted financial sanctions. These include measures such as freezing the foreign assets of specifically designated individuals, state-owned companies, and governments. Selective asset freezes were imposed on Haiti, Serbia-Montenegro, the Bosnian Serbs, and UNITA. The primary challenge to the effectiveness of these asset freezes is the identification of funds belonging to the individuals, governments, and companies targeted. Although the means of tracking financial assets have greatly improved, so have the means of deception. Even when individual funds can be identified, secrecy and speed are critical to preventing targets from moving assets to numbered accounts in off-shore banking centers. Unfortunately, secrecy and speed are not easily reconciled with the need to build consensus among sender countries or within the U.N. Security Council. This point was illustrated by the recent U.N. sanctions imposed against the Taliban in Afghanistan, where the U.N. Security Council threatened to freeze its assets if U.N. demands were not met within one month; the Taliban had ample time to avoid the sanctions.

## III. SUPPORT FOR THE EFFECTIVENESS OF TARGETED MEASURES

The concept of targeted sanctions as an alternative to comprehensive trade embargoes is relatively new. Historically, asset freezes and travel bans were imposed in the context of broader economic sanctions. A survey of sanctions cases in the twentieth century shows that in only twenty cases were targeted sanctions (such as arms embargoes, asset freezes, and travel sanctions) imposed outside the framework of comprehensive embargoes (see Table 1). Moreover, even in these twenty cases, targeted sanctions were nearly always imposed in combination with selective export restrictions or aid suspensions.

The record indicates that targeted sanctions have been used either as a "warm-up" for broader measures or as the supposed "knock-out" punch. The sanctions taken against Haiti to restore democracy illustrate the "knock-out" approach. Initial comprehensive trade sanctions by the Organization of American States were succeeded by more targeted sanctions aimed directly at the Haitian military and its supporters to force them from power. Following the examples of the U.S. unilateral initiatives, the United Nations imposed a ban on private flights to and from Haiti, banned visas for Haitian military leaders, and urged its members to freeze targeted Haitian assets. UK and U.N. sanctions against Rhodesia illustrate the "warm-up" approach. An asset freeze, an arms embargo, and selective export bans did not persuade Ian Smith to allow majority rule in Rhodesia. After the targeted measures had been in place for two years, the U.N. Security Council resorted to a comprehensive embargo to compel the Rhodesian government to change its policy. The targeted measures against both Haiti and Rhodesia were unsuccessful, and it is worth noting that the imposition of targeted measures against Haiti was soon followed by military intervention.

The success rate of targeted sanctions, in the twenty cases where they were imposed outside of comprehensive embargoes, is relatively low when compared with economic sanctions in general. Only five of the twenty cases can be judged partially successful, indicating a success rate of twenty-five percent. This is slightly below the success rate of thirty-four percent for economic sanctions in general during the twentieth century. In two of the successful cases (Libya and Egypt), the goal was relatively limited and well defined. As a general proposition, targeted measures have the most success when modest goals are sought.

The recent EU proposal to lift the general flight ban on Serbia while, at the same time, tightening sanctions against the supporters of Serbia's President Milosevic illustrates a new use of targeted sanctions. As support for broader sanctions wanes, alternative measures that target the political elite offer a way to continue pressure on those people at the root of the problem, while simultaneously reducing the impact on the general population. During the long hostilities involving Serbia, the EU was able to identify entities and individuals linked to President Milosevic, thus increasing the accuracy of the targeted measures. The EU approach represented a compromise between the U.S. opposition to lifting sanctions and the more accommodating EU stance. In other words, targeted sanctions allowed the coalition to remain united. Sanctions diplomacy in Serbia may be a prelude to developments in Iraq and Cuba. Comprehensive sanctions against these two nations may be gradually replaced by targeted measures. For example, U.N. Secretary-General Kofi Annan has recently suggested a move in this direction for Iraq.

## IV. CONCLUSION

To summarize, targeted sanctions may satisfy the need in sender states to "do something." They may assuage humanitarian concerns, and they may serve to unify fraying coalitions. However, they are not a panacea for achieving foreign policy goals. To quote the U.N. Secretary-General:

> the international community should be under no illusion: these humanitarian and human rights policy goals cannot easily be reconciled with those of a sanctions regime. It cannot be too strongly emphasized that sanctions are a tool of enforcement and, like other methods of enforcement, they will do harm. This should be borne in mind when the decision to impose them is taken, and when the results are subsequently evaluated.

---

# 8. Making Targeted Sanctions Effective
## Guidelines for the Implementation of U.N. Policy Options
### [footnotes omitted by editors]

Edited by Peter Wallensteen, Carina Staibano, Mikael Eriksson
Results from the Stockholm Process on the Implementation of Targeted Sanctions
Uppsala University Department of Peace and Conflict Research (2003)
www.smartsanctions.se

### EXECUTIVE SUMMARY

**Background**

The international community is in need of peaceful ways to react to international threats against peace and security. There must be effective actions "between words and wars." The use of economic sanctions is one of the instruments available to the U.N. Security Council that has been used under Chapter VII of the U.N. Charter. Recent experiences of comprehensive sanctions have not been encouraging, however. The search has continued for more refined approaches and targeted sanctions is one such option. Targeted sanctions are directed against significant national decision-makers (political leaders and key supporters of a particular regimes) and resources that are essential for their rule.

Targeted sanctions have been the subject of an international diplomatic and academic process, which was initiated by Switzerland focusing on financial sanctions, the Interlaken Process. This was followed by the initiative of Germany, the Bonn-Berlin Process, dealing with arms embargoes, aviation sanctions and travel bans. These processes brought together experts, academic researchers, diplomats, practitioners and non-governmental organizations. Two volumes with practical suggestions were presented to the U.N. Security Council in October 2001. At this occasion, Sweden announced the start of a similar, third process, the Stockholm Process, concentrating on the implementation of targeted sanctions.

\* \* \*

### RECOMMENDATIONS

#### 1. Design Sanctions Resolutions with Implementation in Mind

It is important at the earliest stage of drafting a resolution to anticipate what will be required in order to implement the agreed measures. The purpose and the targets must be clear from the outset. Many participants in the Stockholm Process recommend an early assessment of the likely impact of the sanctions. This also means establishing a sanctions committee with necessary authority—in particular a reporting mechanism—to follow through on the decisions. The role of the chairperson of the sanction committee is important and requires considerable support from the Council and from the U.N. Secretariat.

## 2. Maintain International Support for the Sanctions Regime

Sanctions are to be implemented by Member States. Thus, it is important that they are fully informed of the rationale of the measures, from the early stages and throughout the sanctions regime. In this way, Member States are included in the sanctions policy, which will ensure political support and maintain their "political will" to implement measures. This helps to make clear that the sanctions regimes are "owned" by the international community. Furthermore, transparency is important so that the goals and measures are properly translated into action by all U.N. members. The media must also be kept updated on the sanctions and their implementation. Targeted sanctions are designed to minimize detrimental humanitarian effects. To maintain international support it is important to ensure that such effects are avoided.

## 3. Monitor, Follow Up and Improve the Measures throughout the Sanctions Regime

The Stockholm Report draws attention to the innovation of Expert Panels and Monitoring Mechanisms for the follow-up of sanctions implementation. Thus, specific and common guidelines are suggested for the work of such panels (Part II, Box 8). They point, inter alia, to the importance of Panels having the competence and authority to perform in-depth investigations and that Panel reports meet the highest evidentiary standards. The significance of such reporting is particularly evident when systematic sanctions evasion arises.

## 4. Strengthen the Sanctions Work of the U.N. Secretariat

The U.N. Secretariat has considerable experience in sanctions implementation. There is a need for an in-house information database on sanctions, as a service to Sanctions Committees, Member States, Expert Panels and Monitoring Mechanisms. This is a way of systematizing lessons learned. Also, the U.N. should operate a continuously updated, public research database on current sanctions regimes. The issue of a special U.N. sanctions coordinator is raised in this Report for further discussion. These measures for improving sanctions implementation will not occur without sufficient allocation of budgetary resources.

## 5. Although Different, Much Can Be Learned from the U.N. Counter-Terrorism Committee

The setting up of a special committee to inform and support Member States on how to counter terrorism suggests novel ways to conduct sanctions implementation. In particular the creation of contact points in all Member States, the continuous reporting of activities, and the development of ideas for capacity-building are directly relevant. Thus, the Stockholm Report suggests Practical Guidelines for Effective Implementation of Sanctions.

## 6. Effective Sanctions Requires Capacity-Building and Training Programs

The implementation of targeted sanctions is a strain on state capacity for many Member States. It requires training of staff and institutional development. In the long-run, improved government administration may also be beneficial for national development. Thus, national training programs—and support by Member States and international organizations—are encouraged in areas of sanctions implementation (police, customs, transportation services, financial controls, etc.).

## 7. Implementation Can Be Enhanced through a Model Law

The Reports suggest a model for sanctions legislation that can be useful for Member States when developing their legal frameworks for sanctions implementation. Two versions are presented, one for common law countries and one for civil law countries.

## 8. Implementation Will Vary Depending on the Type of Sanctions

Throughout the Stockholm Report targeted sanctions are discussed with respect to arms flows, financial resources, travel and aviation connections and specific export commodities. The measures needed to implement such sanctions will vary. Thus, recommendations are made for different types of sanctions with respect to national implementation (legal framework, administrative agency, information, monitoring, enforcement, etc.) and for strategies to counter evasion (by having precise definitions of targeted actors, maintaining commitment, considering complementary measures, etc.).

## 9. Maintaining Accuracy in Sanctions Targeting Is Crucial

A sanctions regime faces different challenges at different stages, but the actions in each stage can improve the performance in the next. The planning of sanctions is important for the operations of sanctions, which in turn requires vigilant follow-up procedures. It is necessary to expect retaliation against neighboring countries and thus positive inducements should be available. Also strategies of socially and politically isolating the targeted actors in their own state have to be considered. Processes for listing individuals and entities as targets and for removing them from such lists (delisting) are crucial.

## 10. Reporting on Sanctions Implementation

In order to assist Member States in their duties, this Report suggests a special questionnaire to be addressed to Member States on matters of sanctions implementation. It asks questions on contact points, specifies measures for particular types of sanctions, asks about the type of assistance that is needed and encourages Member States to identify available resources for such support.

\* \* \*

## PART I: CHOOSING TARGETED SANCTIONS

THIS REPORT IS devoted to the subject of targeted U.N. Security Council sanctions. The purpose is to suggest concrete improvements to this instrument, which can play a critical role in assisting the Security Council to maintain international peace and security. It focuses on the chain of needed actions to ensure that sanctions resolutions are implemented in as logical and as coherent a manner as possible. This increases the likelihood that sanctions will bring about compliance of the target with the relevant Security Council resolutions.

\* \* \*

The events of September 11, 2001, set in motion a number of extraordinary actions by the United Nations, such as the imposition of measures against global terrorism and the creation of a committee for overseeing such measures, the Counter-Terrorism Committee (CTC). Innovations related to the CTC have inspired new thinking regarding improvements to United Nations sanctions regimes. Thus, the experience of the CTC permeates the recommendations contained in this report.

### Targeted Sanctions Are Necessary

It is important to reiterate why targeted sanctions are needed, the significance of implementation and feedback, the conditions under which such sanctions are appropriate and plausible sanctions strategies.

Targeted sanctions are needed for the following reasons:

- The international community must have at its disposal the means to react and address situations that threaten international peace and security, other than military action or declaratory statements.

- Targeted sanctions, if applied effectively, can be less costly than other options (e.g. military) and can be tailored to specific circumstances.

- Comprehensive sanctions involve unintended negative effects, which the international community is unwilling to tolerate. The trend towards targeting sanctions shows that the international community has learned from this negative experience and is willing to move in new directions.
- Targeted sanctions are directed against particular political leaders and members of their regimes whose actions constitute a threat to international peace and security, in an effort to bring about behavioral change.

- Targeted sanctions, by affecting the leaders, as well as their key supporters, family members, important institutions under their control or specific flows of goods and services, can convey the message of the international community in a direct manner.

Since the end of the Cold War, the United Nations Security Council has gained experience in applying targeted sanctions, covering a vast array of measures, which are described in this report. Although this Report does not attempt to analyze the record of success and failure, it builds on the idea that such sanctions can be made increasingly effective.

A key lesson drawn from the Stockholm Process is the importance of ensuring that decisions involving sanctions are translated into action, that is, implementation. Actors against whom sanctions are imposed will be concerned only if they are personally exposed to pressure in the form of a direct impact on their bank accounts, prospects for travel, access to particular goods or diplomatic representation. In the absence of vigorous implementation of sanctions, targeted individuals are likely to dismiss the measures along with the need to change their behavior.

It follows, therefore, that for sanctions to have the desired effects and avoid unintended consequences, Member States must effectively pursue decisions of the Security Council, and the measures must be monitored by the United Nations system.

### Implementation Is as Strong as the Weakest Link

In order for targeted sanctions to have the intended effects and to increase the likelihood of compliance by the targeted actor, a chain of measures, stretching from the Security Council to the immediate surroundings of the targeted actor, and varying depending on the situation, must be in place. In the Stockholm Process, three Working Groups have been devoted to the key elements in the chain of implementation, each reporting in a separate part of the Report:

- The United Nations system: Sanctions Committees, Expert Panels, the Secretariat, other international organizations, non-governmental organizations and the private sector.

- Member States: principles of implementation and measures for particular types of sanctions; legal considerations, including the need for a model law for States and the strengthening of state capacity in implementation of sanctions.

- Accuracy of targeting: correct identification, measures to counter typical evasion strategies for types of sanctions, and ways for Member States to provide information to the Security Council and the Secretariat.

While for the most part, the three Working Groups dealt separately with their issues, some sessions were held with the participation of all Working Groups in order to facilitate information exchange. Plenary meetings were held in Gimo and Stockholm in Sweden. Two joint meetings of the Working Groups took place at Uppsala University. Separate Working Group meetings were held in New York and Brussels. For more information on the Process and other materials, see <www.smartsanctions.se>. The Index of this Report helps to identify the issues and proposals, as they were developed by the different Working Groups.

### Feedback Is Essential for Sanctions Efficiency

For sanctions regimes to be assessed and modified to ensure that objectives are properly met, an unhindered flow of information, transparency and a willingness to act early in the light of new events are required. Furthermore, all sanctions regimes require monitoring of their humanitarian effects in order to minimize their unintended consequences. Thus, the three Working Groups have, from different angles, explored the issues of feedback and information flow.

### Not All Situations Are Appropriate for Targeted Sanctions

While this Report aims to improve the utility of targeted sanctions as an instrument for international diplomacy and political action, it does not assume that sanctions will always be the appropriate course of action. Ascertaining whether or not the sanctions instrument is the appropriate one to be applied requires thorough analysis of each situation. Such an analysis should include the following general propositions, and build on empirical evidence and accumulated experience.

- The more credible the threat of sanctions, the less likely it will be that sanctions will have to be imposed.

- The more implementable the sanctions, the more impact they will have on the targeted actor, and thus the more likely that the targeted actor will comply.

- The more dependent the targeted actor on a particular commodity and international trade, the more likely that the targeted actor will comply.

- The more internally challenged a regime threatened by sanctions, or on which sanctions are imposed, the more likely that the target will comply.

- The more international and regional consensus surrounding threatened or imposed sanctions, the more likely that the target will comply.

### There Is a Choice among Different Types of Targeted Sanctions

In this Report targeted sanctions range from visa restrictions on particular individuals to arms embargoes on States. Such sanctions vary in terms of their "implementability" and accuracy. Some measures are easier to implement, as procedures and institutions already are in place in Member States and international organizations. Others may require special legislation, or even the creation of new institutions for implementation and monitoring. There is also variation in the ability of measures to actually hit the target. The accuracy achieved will depend on the type of measures used as well as their implementability. Some forms of sanctions are easier to evade than others. Thus, it is important for the international community when making decisions to consider the ease of implementing sanctions, their accuracy, the chances of quick feedback on the effects of sanctions and the ability to adjust sanctions as the real situation changes.

### There Is a Need for a Sanctions Strategy

There are arguments in favor of developing a strategy of flexible targeted sanctions, including a) gradually increasing the number of persons, institutions, etc. on the list of targeted actors, or b) gradually adding new types of sanctions to the original regime. If credible, such a strategy may provide incentives for earlier compliance. The use of sequencing of targeted sanctions has so far been rare, and might provide a new element in sanctions policy.

In sum, this Report focuses on choices to be made by the Security Council in reacting to threats to international peace and security. While sanctions (specifically targeted sanctions) should be high on its list of options, it should not always be the choice made. To date, the Security Council has imposed sanctions in fifteen conflict situations. At the same time, there have been more than one hundred armed conflicts, which the Council has discussed and decided on a course of action. Thus, sanctions are used selectively. The Stockholm Report provides guidance for how such a selection can be done at various phases of a crisis. It is done in the hope that targeted sanctions will be an effective measure in maintaining international peace and security.

## PARTII: MEASURES TO STRENGTHEN THE ROLE OF THE UNITED NATIONS IN THE IMPLEMENTATION OF TARGETED SANCTIONS

### 1. Introduction

THE PURPOSE OF Part II is to recommend practical and effective policy options that may contribute to strengthening the role of the Sanctions Committees of the Security Council and the U.N. Secretariat in the implementation of targeted sanctions. Thus, it seeks to identify major strengths and weaknesses for both the Secretariat and the Sanctions Committees that have an impact on their ability to contribute to the implementation, monitoring, and enforcement of targeted sanctions.

While primary responsibility for implementing targeted sanctions enacted by Security Council resolutions rests with Member States, effective implementation depends on strong coordination and communication between the U.N. and Member States. The Sanctions Committees of the Security Council and the U.N. Secretariat play a critical facilitating role, both in establishing a framework of procedures for sanctions implementation, and providing support to Member States. The Committees, increasingly assisted and strengthened by affiliated Panels of Experts and Monitoring Mechanisms, are the main bodies tasked with monitoring Member State compliance with U.N. Security Council sanctions resolutions, identifying violations of sanctions resolutions, and recommending to the Security Council ways to improve follow up action where poor compliance is discovered. Within the U.N. Secretariat, the role of providing substantive advice and technical and administrative support to the Sanctions Committees falls to the Security Council Subsidiary Organs Branch (SCSOB, Sanctions Branch) of the Security Council Affairs Division (SCAD), within the Department of Political Affairs (DPA).

Overall, there was a consensus among participants that improved implementation is both necessary and desirable. While various options were explored, it was generally agreed that the goal of enhancing implementation of U.N. targeted sanctions should proceed, wherever possible, by rationalizing and upgrading current capacities and working methods, rather than by the creation of a new and elaborate institutional apparatus. By better utilizing the existing capacity and resources of the U.N. system and by developing synergies among the Security Council, Sanctions Committees, the Secretariat, and specialized U.N. agencies and field operations, the U.N. can achieve more systematic and coordinated implementation.

### 2. The Security Council and Sanctions Committees

#### The Capacity and Working Methods of the Sanctions Committees

Sanctions Committees (SACOs) have the lead role in monitoring the implementation of Security Council resolutions on targeted sanctions. The tasks commonly assigned to the Sanctions Committees center on reviewing measures taken by Member States to implement sanctions (including through the solicitation and receipt of periodic reports), and monitoring sanctions violations. Sanctions Committees have also been tasked with maintaining lists of sanctioned individuals and entities. In those instances where an independent Panel of Experts or a Monitoring Mechanism is also established, the Sanctions Committees provide support to the experts, ensuring that their investigations proceed in accordance with relevant Security Council resolutions, receive and deliberate reports of their findings, and present those findings to the Security Council. They may also solicit the assistance of specialized U.N. agencies, such as requesting assessments of the humanitarian impact of specific sanctions regimes. Customarily, Sanctions Committees also are assigned the task of considering requests for humanitarian and other exemptions to the sanctions measures. Finally, the Sanctions Committees are the U.N.'s public face on sanctions, responsible for making available to the general public all relevant information regarding their respective sanctions mandates, including through Internet websites.

To their credit, Sanctions Committees have, in recent years, shown both ingenuity and dedication in their efforts to ensure these tasks are performed effectively. However, even under the best of circumstances, this is a tall order to fulfill. Like peacekeeping, sanctions are a key tool by which the Security Council seeks to maintain international peace and security under Chapter VII of the United Nations Charter. However, sanctions implementation has no institutional equivalent to the Department of Peacekeeping Operations (DPKO). Typically, Sanctions Committees must proceed with numerous political, administrative and time constraints, which are sometimes exacerbated by poorly specified or incomplete Security Council mandates. Most often, the core tasks of sanctions monitoring—soliciting and receiving reports of sanctions measures undertaken by Member States and reviewing the work of the independent Expert Panels—have taken priority over those of broader coordination and information dissemination.

### Coordination among U.N. Actors and Ownership by Member States

To promote effective implementation, sanctions should be integrated into a broader diplomatic strategy of conflict prevention and conflict resolution that includes, good offices, mediation, and where necessary, the threat or use of force in accordance with Chapter VII of the United Nations Charter. An integrated strategy requires more effective coordination both among the key sanctions bodies and between them and other relevant U.N. agencies and departments. Despite some notable exceptions, including the recent informal meetings between the Sanctions Committees concerning Sierra Leone, Liberia and Angola/UNITA, coordination among the Sanctions Committees remains sporadic. Coordination between Sanctions Committees, the Secretariat and other relevant U.N. agencies is likewise ad hoc. Among the Sanctions Committees and Expert Panels, this lack of systematic coordination can lead to unnecessary duplication of work, whereby Experts monitoring different sanctions regimes sometimes inadvertently pursue similar leads, make use of the same sources and make uncoordinated approaches to the same technical or regional organizations. While Sanctions Committees have undertaken periodic consultations with humanitarian agencies, the full potential of other U.N. agencies and departments to assist in sanctions implementation and the implications of sanctions implementation for their own work has not been fully explored.

Likewise sporadic are Sanctions Committee efforts to engage Member States, both directly, through briefings and consultations, and indirectly, through dissemination of information to the broader public and the mass media, in support of U.N. sanctions implementation. In the absence of continuous and effective public communication, U.N.

sanctions efforts remain vulnerable to myriad misperceptions including active anti-sanctions propaganda campaigns, which can erode commitment among Member States. Indeed, maximal transparency of all aspects related to the sanctions process (from imposition, through implementation, to lifting) was identified as one of the most critical components for improved sanctions implementation.

States that are not members of the Security Council feel excluded form a process which they are nonetheless bound to implement in accordance with the Charter of the United Nations. A resulting lack of Member State ownership over sanctions has had predictable consequences for effective implementation. While the decision to impose sanctions remains a prerogative of the Security Council, the sense of exclusion experienced by States not members of the Council can be reduced by more frequent information briefings and consultations which communicate, inter alia: (1) the rationale behind sanctions; (2) what is expected from Member States; (3) the complexity and difficulty of imposing targeted sanctions (including the problematic nature of managing lists, when information supplied by Member States is incomplete); (4) Security Council efforts to reduce untoward humanitarian and economic impacts including those affecting third-parties; and (5) instances of sanctions violations.

While briefings to the mass media are a useful way to disseminate this information they cannot substitute for direct interactions with non-Security Council Member States. Innovative lessons on promoting Member State communication and compliance could be drawn from the experience of the Counter-Terrorism Committee (CTC). For example, the CTC practice of conducting web-based consultation and information dissemination may offer an applicable model for use by Sanctions Committees. Ultimately, improved implementation depends upon more sustained engagement with Member States.

### Lessons of the Counter-Terrorism Committee for Sanctions Implementation

Under United Nations Security Council Resolution (UNSCR) 1373 (2001), the mandate of the Counter-Terrorism Committee renders it qualitatively distinct from Sanctions Committees. Properly speaking, the CTC is not yet charged with the implementation of sanctions, but with measures to identify and eliminate all sources of support for terrorist groups. Unlike the mandates underpinning Sanctions Committees, UNSCR 1373 has relatively straightforward requirements and does not have an end point. Sanctions mandates, on the other hand, have various objectives and varying levels of complexity, depending on the type of sanction involved: travel bans are relatively easier to implement than financial sanctions, while arms embargoes are rarely implemented effectively. Finally, because of the terrorist attack of September 11, 2001, the CTC enjoys an unprecedented level of political support, support that is no less critical to successful sanctions implementation, but which, for a variety of reasons, is typically lacking.

This said, several innovative aspects of the Counter-Terrorism Committee might be relevant to the goal of improved sanctions implementation. First, the high level of Member State reporting on compliance with UNSCR 1373 is a function not only of the compelling circumstances under which it was enacted, but also of innovations in the reporting requirements and formats that the CTC has developed for Member States. Second, the CTC facilitates the provision of technical assistance to Member States whose capacity for counterterrorism is weak. Third, the CTC has successfully established a solid working relationship with other relevant international and national bodies. Finally, the work of the CTC Chairperson has been assisted by the assignment of an expert on technical assistance. Consideration should be given to adapting these innovations to assist

Sanctions Committees and Member States to better comply with sanctions resolutions.

* * *

### 3. Coordination between the U.N. and Other Relevant Actors

Obviously the close cooperation between the U.N. and other international organizations, whether governmental, non-governmental or private, are important for the implementation of targeted sanctions. In this section, some linkages are identified and illustrated. Whether aimed at reducing the illicit flows of arms, finance, and commodities that sustain armed conflict or at deterring or punishing behavior that threatens international peace and security, targeted sanctions are a highly technical policy instrument. To be implemented effectively, they need the input and support of a wide range of specialized actors and agencies beyond the U.N..

### Relations with International Organizations

There have been several efforts by the Security Council, the Sanctions Committees and their affiliated Expert Panels and Monitoring Mechanisms to work more closely with selected specialized international agencies such as Interpol, to better utilize their respective assets and expertise, and coordinate policy initiatives for sanctions implementation. Understandably, the degree of U.N. interaction with outside actors in specific instances will vary, depending on, among other factors, the precise nature of the sanctions imposed, that is, whether they include travel bans, financial or arms embargoes, or commodity bans, and on the regions and interests affected. While flexibility is desirable, the ad hoc and limited nature of these partnerships reduces the potential to be gained by the U.N. from more sustained forms of communication and coordination on sanctions implementation as well as sanctions design. Consideration should be given to the creation of some kind of mechanism to ensure routine avenues for improved coordination on sanctions implementation.

### Relations with Regional and Sub-Regional Organizations

Likewise, much more work needs to be done in bringing regional and sub-regional organizations into a coordinated effort of sanctions implementation. Too often, these organizations are overlooked or insufficiently marshaled in support of U.N. targeted sanctions. The European Union (EU) is a partial exception, having developed its own role in the implementation of sanctions, particularly in the areas of international trade and finance, and having had more regular interactions with the Security Council and the Sanctions Committees through Member States, often via the good offices of a EU Member State holding the Presidency of the Union and through regular briefings in New York and Brussels on EU perspectives on sanctions.

Most other regional and sub-regional organizations, however, are not fully incorporated into the sanctions process. For example, despite recommendations by the Liberia Expert Panel to strengthen the ECOWAS moratorium, there has been little substantive engagement between the Security Council and ECOWAS. While many such regional actors and initiatives may require assistance in developing a full complement of technical expertise on arms embargoes, financial sanctions, commodity and aviation bans, they already possess strong regional knowledge of sanctions related behavior. Ways should be explored to ensure that the Sanctions Committees and the Sanctions Branch of the Secretariat more routinely utilize this knowledge.

### Relations with Non-Governmental Organizations

In recent years, the Security Council and the Sanctions Committees have taken great strides in bringing the perspectives and know-how of a range of NGO actors into the design and implementation of targeted sanctions. Under the Arria formula (the Arria formula is an informal arrangement that allows the Council greater flexibility to be briefed about international peace and security issues. It was first implemented in 1993 by Amb. Diego Arria of Venezuela), NGOs frequently give country and issue briefings to the Security Council. NGOs have also been the driving force in establishing the now widely accepted idea that the U.N. has a responsibility to prevent or reduce the humanitarian consequences of U.N. sanctions, and have lent their expertise to the design of impact assessment methods. A number of NGO practitioners have also served on Expert Panels. Most recently, NGOs have collaborated with U.N. Member States and the private sector in the Kimberley Process on the certification of rough diamonds, an initiative that flowed, in part, from the work of the Expert Panels in Angola and Sierra Leone in monitoring sanctions violations.

These interactions with NGOs should be continued and strengthened, especially on issues where NGOs enjoy a comparative functional advantage or regional presence. In particular, the Security Council should improve ways to ensure that sanctions policy take into account the views of indigenous civil society actors. The contribution of local NGOs in targeted countries should be treated with great sensitivity and verified given the possible failure safety nets from the parties affected, and the natural bias of NGOs (as with government officials). The Security Council should also consider exploring ways to bring in the expertise of human rights NGOs to bear upon the problem of ensuring that the procedures for identifying and managing sanctions targets are transparent and in conformity with international human rights norms and the rights of due process.

### Relations with the Private Sector

Private sector actors have become increasingly important to international peace and security, a fact which has been acknowledge by the creation of the U.N. Global Compact, an initiative of the Secretary-General to promote greater private sector commitment to conflict prevention and sustainable development. With the partial exception of the Kimberley Process for the certification of rough diamonds, there has been no concerted effort to engage the private sector in sanctions policy. Yet, many private sector actors, including financial institutions, insurance companies, and transportation companies, have both a capacity and expertise to bear on sanctions implementation. Ways should be explored, to increase opportunities for consultation with key representatives bodies of private sector actors on sanctions related issues, as well as to develop strategies and inducements for improved industry standards in ways that can be leveraged to complement the objectives of targeted sanctions and contribute to their implementation.

### Relations with Media

As both a source of information that may provide useful investigative leads and as a conduit for promoting well-informed public awareness of the course of U.N. sanctions efforts, the media are an indispensable partner for improved sanctions implementation. Given the wide room that exists for public misperception to undermine U.N. sanctions efforts, as well as the remedial potential of greater transparency, improved relations with the international media should be a priority area. Particular areas of priority include: improving the U.N.'s capacity to communicate with accredited U.N. correspondents, promoting transparency in the application of targeted sanctions; conveying a better understanding to a broader public regarding the scope and purpose of particular targeted sanctions regimes, particularly in sanctions-affected countries (see Part IV); improved public dissemination of the reports of Expert Panels and Monitoring Mechanisms, including efforts to prevent unauthorized leaks that undermine their credibility, and more skillful and systematized utilization of open information sources in on-going efforts to monitor and enforce targeted sanctions.

One way of accomplishing these objectives would be to improve the quality and profile of briefings on the work of Sanctions Committees and Expert Panels. The Secretary-General's spokesperson regularly informs the media of decisions made by the Security Council but is not expected to promote the implementation of sanctions. The designation of a Security Council spokesperson may be desirable in this regard. Currently, the Chairs of the Sanctions Committees act as spokespersons for the Committee, but their effectiveness could be enhanced if they were provided with adequate professional support or if the function of spokesperson were assigned to another specially designated individual.

**Recommendations:**

**Improve Coordination between the U.N. and Other Relevant Actors For the Security Council**

- Consideration should be given to the creation of a mechanism to ensure routine avenues for improved coordination and information sharing on sanctions implementation with relevant external agencies, such as Interpol, the Financial Action Task Force, and the World Customs Organization (WCO).

- Improve methods for routine engagement of regional and subregional organizations in support of sanctions implementation, both by inviting their regular input and by assisting them to build the technical capacity for coordinated sanctions monitoring and enforcement.

- Encourage greater interaction between relevant NGOs and the SACOs through more frequent NGO briefings on sanctions-related issues, perhaps through the use of the Arria formula of informal meetings between the SC members and key experts and actors. To make this an effective mechanism, schedules of relevant Security Council and SACO meetings should be provided to NGOs well in advance to allow them the needed preparation time.

- Ensure that a representative array of voices from civil society/NGOs are taken into account and included, where appropriate, in U.N.-led humanitarian evaluations of the impact of targeted sanctions regimes, including prior impact assessments and periodic follow up of actual sanctions impact on civilians. Establish a dual track interaction with large international NGOs that deal with international policy issues and NGOs in the field.

- Explore ways to bring the expertise of the Office of the High Commissioner for Human Rights (OHCHR) and human rights NGOs to bear on the problem of ensuring that procedures for compiling lists of sanctions targets are transparent and in conformity with international human rights norms and due process.

- Explore options to increase opportunities for consultation with key private sector actors on sanctions-related issues.

**Develop a Media Strategy**

**For the Security Council and Sanctions Committees**

- Establish a system of routine press briefings on the work of the Sanctions Committees to inform media, particularly in countries or regions where targeted sanctions are being applied, regarding the objectives, progress and challenges of sanctions implementation.

- Augment the liaison role of the Office of the Spokesman of the Secretary-General between the media, the UNSC Presidency, and the Sanctions Committees.

- Arrange for routine background press briefings by U.N. Expert Panels, timed to coincide with the formal release of Expert Panel reports.

- Ensure a coordinated and timely media message and reduce preemptive leaking of Expert Panel reports by introducing system of formal press embargoes and/or by establishing clear guidelines for all Sanctions Committees and Expert Panel members regarding disciplined procedures for public release of Expert Panel reports.

### For the Secretariat

- Develop strategies to assist the Security Council in providing better public information to Member States and the general public and to convey the message that targeted sanctions are a potentially valuable and useful instrument of deterrence and prevention.

## Authors' Note

In the aftermath of September 11th, the Security Council imposed sanctions against members of select groups and individuals, specifically targeting Osama bin Laden. The remaining materials in this chapter address the use of targeted sanctions against individuals, including travel bans and asset freezes.

## 9. Sanctions Targeting Individuals

### A. S.C. Res. 1267

The Security Council,

\* \* \*

*Acting* under Chapter VII of the Charter of the United Nations,

1. *Insists* that the Afghan faction known as the Taliban, which also calls itself the Islamic Emirate of Afghanistan, comply promptly with its previous resolutions and in particular cease the provision of sanctuary and training for international terrorists and their organizations, take appropriate effective measures to ensure that the territory under its control is not used for terrorist installations and camps, or for the preparation or organization of terrorist acts against other States or their citizens, and cooperate with efforts to bring indicted terrorists to justice;

2. *Demands* that the Taliban turn over Usama bin Laden without further delay to appropriate authorities in a country where he has been indicted, or to appropriate authorities in a country where he will be returned to such a country, or to appropriate authorities in a country where he will be arrested and effectively brought to justice;

3. *Decides* that on 14 November 1999 all States shall impose the measures set out in paragraph 4 below, unless the Council has previously decided, on the basis of a report of the Secretary-General, that the Taliban has fully complied with the obligation set out in paragraph 2 above;

4. *Decides further* that, in order to enforce paragraph 2 above, all States shall:

(a) Deny permission for any aircraft to take off from or land in their territory if it is owned, leased or operated by or on behalf of the Taliban as designated by the Committee established by paragraph 6 below, unless the particular flight has been approved in advance by the Committee on the grounds of humanitarian need, including religious obligation such as the performance of the Hajj;

(b) Freeze funds and other financial resources, including funds derived or generated from property owned or controlled directly or indirectly by the Taliban, or by any undertaking owned or controlled by the Taliban, as designated by the Committee established by paragraph 6 below, and ensure that neither they nor any other funds or financial resources so designated are made available, by their nationals or by any persons within their territory, to or for the benefit of the Taliban or any undertaking owned or controlled, directly or indirectly, by the Taliban, except as may be authorized by the Committee on a case-by-case basis on the grounds of humanitarian need;

5. *Urges* all States to cooperate with efforts to fulfil the demand in paragraph 2 above, and to consider further measures against Usama bin Laden and his associates;

6. *Decides* to establish, in accordance with rule 28 of its provisional rules of procedure, a Committee of the Security Council consisting of all the members of the Council to undertake the following tasks and to report on its work to the Council with its observations and recommendations:

(a) To seek from all States further information regarding the action taken by them with a view to effectively implementing the measures imposed by paragraph 4 above;

(b) To consider information brought to its attention by States concerning violations of the measures imposed by paragraph 4 above and to recommend appropriate measures in response thereto;

(c) To make periodic reports to the Council on the impact, including the humanitarian implications, of the measures imposed by paragraph 4 above;

(d) To make periodic reports to the Council on information submitted to it regarding alleged violations of the measures imposed by paragraph 4 above, identifying where possible persons or entities reported to be engaged in such violations;

\* \* \*

7. *Calls upon* all States to act strictly in accordance with the provisions of this resolution, notwithstanding the existence of any rights or obligations conferred or imposed by any international agreement or any contract entered into or any licence or permit granted prior to the date of coming into force of the measures imposed by paragraph 4 above;

8. *Calls upon* States to bring proceedings against persons and entities within their jurisdiction that violate the measures imposed by paragraph 4 above and to impose appropriate penalties;

\* \* \*

16. *Decides* to remain actively seized of the matter.

---

## B. COUNCIL REGULATION (EC) No 881/2002 of 27 May 2002

Article 2

1. All funds and economic resources belonging to, or owned or held by, a natural or legal person, group or entity designated by the Sanctions Committee and listed in Annex I shall be frozen.

2. No funds shall be made available, directly or indirectly, to, or for the benefit of, a natural or legal person, group or entity designated by the Sanctions Committee and listed in Annex I.

3. No economic resources shall be made available, directly or indirectly, to, or for the benefit of, a natural or legal person, group or entity designated by the Sanctions Committee and listed in Annex I, so as to enable that person, group or entity to obtain funds, goods or services.

---

## C. *Kadi* Case — Court of Justice of the European Union

Joined Cases C-402/05 P & C-415/05 P, *Kadi & Al Barakaat v. Council of the European Union*, 3 C.M.L.R. 41 (2008).

\* \* \*

13 On 15 October 1999 the Security Council adopted Resolution 1267 (1999), in which it, inter alia, condemned the fact that Afghan territory continued to be used for the sheltering and training of terrorists and planning of terrorist acts, reaffirmed its conviction that the suppression of international terrorism was essential for the maintenance of international peace and security and deplored the fact that the Taliban continued to provide safe haven to Usama bin Laden and to allow him and others associated with him to operate a network of terrorist training camps from territory held by the Taliban and to use Afghanistan as a base from which to sponsor international terrorist operations.

14 In the second paragraph of the resolution the Security Council demanded that the Taliban should without further delay turn Usama bin Laden over to appropriate authorities in a country where he has been indicted, or to appropriate authorities in a country where he will be arrested and effectively brought to justice. In order to ensure compliance with that demand, paragraph 4(b) of Resolution 1267 (1999) provides that all the States must, in particular, 'freeze funds and other financial resources, including funds derived or generated from property owned or controlled directly or indirectly by the Taliban, or by any undertaking owned or controlled by the Taliban, as designated by the Committee established by paragraph 6 below, and ensure that neither they nor any other funds or financial resources so designated are made available, by their nationals or by any persons within their territory, to or for the benefit of the Taliban or any undertaking owned or controlled, directly or indirectly, by the Taliban, except as may be authorised by the Committee on a case-by-case basis on the grounds of humanitarian need'.

15 In paragraph 6 of Resolution 1267 (1999), the Security Council decided to establish, in accordance with rule 28 of its provisional rules of procedure, a committee of the Security Council composed of all its members ('the Sanctions Committee'), responsible in particular for ensuring that the States implement the measures imposed by paragraph 4, designating the funds or other financial resources referred to in paragraph 4 and considering requests for exemptions from the measures imposed by paragraph 4.

16 Taking the view that action by the Community was necessary in order to implement Resolution 1267 (1999), on 15 November 1999 the Council adopted Common Position 1999/727/CFSP concerning restrictive measures against the Taliban (OJ 1999 L 294, p. 1).

17 Article 2 of that Common Position prescribes the freezing of funds and other financial resources held abroad by the Taliban under the conditions set out in Security Council Resolution 1267 (1999).

\* \* \*

30 On 8 March 2001 the Sanctions Committee published a first consolidated list of the entities which and the persons who must be subjected to the freezing of funds pursuant to Security Council Resolutions 1267 (1999) and 1333 (2000) (see the Committee's press

release AFG/131 SC/7028 of 8 March 2001). That list has since been amended and supplemented several times. The Commission has in consequence adopted various regulations pursuant to Article 10 of Regulation No 467/2001, in which it has amended or supplemented Annex I to that regulation.

31 On 17 October and 9 November 2001 the Sanctions Committee published two new additions to its summary list, including in particular the names of the following entity and person:

– 'Al-Qadi, Yasin (A.K.A. Kadi, Shaykh Yassin Abdullah; A.K.A. Kahdi, Yasin), Jeddah, Saudi Arabia', and

– 'Barakaat International Foundation, Box 4036, Spånga, Stockholm, Sweden; Rinkebytorget 1, 04, Spånga, Sweden'.

\* \* \*

39 Under Article 2 of Regulation No 881/2002:

'1. All funds and economic resources belonging to, or owned or held by, a natural or legal person, group or entity designated by the Sanctions Committee and listed in Annex I shall be frozen.

2. No funds shall be made available, directly or indirectly, to, or for the benefit of, a natural or legal person, group or entity designated by the Sanctions Committee and listed in Annex I.

3. No economic resources shall be made available, directly or indirectly, to, or for the benefit of, a natural or legal person, group or entity designated by the Sanctions Committee and listed in Annex I, so as to enable that person, group or entity to obtain funds, goods or services.'

\* \* \*

49 In support of his claims, Mr Kadi put forward in his application before the Court of First Instance three grounds of annulment alleging, in essence, breaches of his fundamental rights. The first alleges breach of the right to be heard, the second, breach of the right to respect for property and of the principle of proportionality, and the third, breach of the right to effective judicial review.

\* \* \*

280 The Court will now consider the heads of claim in which the appellants complain that the Court of First Instance, in essence, held that it followed from the principles governing the relationship between the international legal order under the United Nations and the Community legal order that the contested regulation, since it is designed to give effect to a resolution adopted by the Security Council under Chapter VII of the Charter of the United Nations affording no latitude in that respect, could not be subject to judicial review of its internal lawfulness, save with regard to its compatibility with the norms of jus cogens, and therefore to that extent enjoyed immunity from jurisdiction.

281 In this connection it is to be borne in mind that the Community is based on the rule of law, inasmuch as neither its Member States nor its institutions can avoid review of the conformity of their acts with the basic constitutional charter, the EC Treaty, which established a complete system of legal remedies and procedures designed to enable the Court of Justice to review the legality of acts of the institutions....

282 It is also to be recalled that an international agreement cannot affect the allocation of powers fixed by the Treaties or, consequently, the autonomy of the Community legal

system, observance of which is ensured by the Court by virtue of the exclusive jurisdiction conferred on it by Article 220 EC, jurisdiction that the Court has, moreover, already held to form part of the very foundations of the Community....

283 In addition, according to settled case-law, fundamental rights form an integral part of the general principles of law whose observance the Court ensures. For that purpose, the Court draws inspiration from the constitutional traditions common to the Member States and from the guidelines supplied by international instruments for the protection of human rights on which the Member States have collaborated or to which they are signatories. In that regard, the ECHR has special significance....

\* \* \*

314 In the instant case it must be declared that the contested regulation cannot be considered to be an act directly attributable to the United Nations as an action of one of its subsidiary organs created under Chapter VII of the Charter of the United Nations or an action falling within the exercise of powers lawfully delegated by the Security Council pursuant to that chapter.

315 In addition and in any event, the question of the Court's jurisdiction to rule on the lawfulness of the contested regulation has arisen in fundamentally different circumstances.

316 As noted above in paragraphs 281 to 284, the review by the Court of the validity of any Community measure in the light of fundamental rights must be considered to be the expression, in a community based on the rule of law, of a constitutional guarantee stemming from the EC Treaty as an autonomous legal system which is not to be prejudiced by an international agreement.

\* \* \*

324 The Guidelines of the Sanctions Committee, as last amended on 12 February 2007, make it plain that an applicant submitting a request for removal from the list may in no way assert his rights himself during the procedure before the Sanctions Committee or be represented for that purpose, the Government of his State of residence or of citizenship alone having the right to submit observations on that request.

325 Moreover, those Guidelines do not require the Sanctions Committee to communicate to the applicant the reasons and evidence justifying his appearance in the summary list or to give him access, even restricted, to that information. Last, if that Committee rejects the request for removal from the list, it is under no obligation to give reasons.

326 It follows from the foregoing that the Community judicature must, in accordance with the powers conferred on it by the EC Treaty, ensure the review, in principle the full review, of the lawfulness of all Community acts in the light of the fundamental rights forming an integral part of the general principles of Community law, including review of Community measures which, like the contested regulation, are designed to give effect to the resolutions adopted by the Security Council under Chapter VII of the Charter of the United Nations.

327 The Court of First Instance erred in law, therefore, when it held, in paragraphs 212 to 231 of Kadi and 263 to 282 of Yusuf and Al Barakaat, that it followed from the principles governing the relationship between the international legal order under the United Nations and the Community legal order that the contested regulation, since it is designed to give effect to a resolution adopted by the Security Council under Chapter VII of the Charter of the United Nations affording no latitude in that respect, must enjoy immunity from jurisdiction so far as concerns its internal lawfulness save with regard to its compatibility with the norms of jus cogens.

328 The appellants' grounds of appeal are therefore well founded on that point, with the result that the judgments under appeal must be set aside in this respect.

* * *

332 In the circumstances, the Court considers that the actions for annulment of the contested regulation brought by the appellants are ready for judgment and that it is necessary to give final judgment in them.

333 It is appropriate to examine, first, the claims made by Mr Kadi and Al Barakaat with regard to the breach of the rights of the defence, in particular the right to be heard, and of the right to effective judicial review, caused by the measures for the freezing of funds as they were imposed on the appellants by the contested regulation.

334 In this regard, in the light of the actual circumstances surrounding the inclusion of the appellants' names in the list of persons and entities covered by the restrictive measures contained in Annex I to the contested regulation, it must be held that the rights of the defence, in particular the right to be heard, and the right to effective judicial review of those rights, were patently not respected.

335 According to settled case-law, the principle of effective judicial protection is a general principle of Community law stemming from the constitutional traditions common to the Member States, which has been enshrined in Articles 6 and 13 of the ECHR, this principle having furthermore been reaffirmed by Article 47 of the Charter of fundamental rights of the European Union....

336 In addition, having regard to the Court's case-law in other fields ... it must be held in this instance that the effectiveness of judicial review, which it must be possible to apply to the lawfulness of the grounds on which, in these cases, the name of a person or entity is included in the list forming Annex I to the contested regulation and leading to the imposition on those persons or entities of a body of restrictive measures, means that the Community authority in question is bound to communicate those grounds to the person or entity concerned, so far as possible, either when that inclusion is decided on or, at the very least, as swiftly as possible after that decision in order to enable those persons or entities to exercise, within the periods prescribed, their right to bring an action.

337 Observance of that obligation to communicate the grounds is necessary both to enable the persons to whom restrictive measures are addressed to defend their rights in the best possible conditions and to decide, with full knowledge of the relevant facts, whether there is any point in their applying to the Community judicature (see, to that effect, Heylens and Others, paragraph 15), and to put the latter fully in a position in which it may carry out the review of the lawfulness of the Community measure in question which is its duty under the EC Treaty.

338 So far as concerns the rights of the defence, in particular the right to be heard, with regard to restrictive measures such as those imposed by the contested regulation, the Community authorities cannot be required to communicate those grounds before the name of a person or entity is entered in that list for the first time.

* * *

349 In addition, given the failure to inform them of the evidence adduced against them and having regard to the relationship, referred to in paragraphs 336 and 337 above, between the rights of the defence and the right to an effective legal remedy, the appellants were also unable to defend their rights with regard to that evidence in satisfactory conditions before the Community judicature, with the result that it must be held that their right to an effective legal remedy has also been infringed.

* * *

367 In addition, it must be considered whether, when that regulation was applied to Mr Kadi, his right to property was respected in the circumstances of the case.

368 It is to be borne in mind in this respect that the applicable procedures must also afford the person concerned a reasonable opportunity of putting his case to the competent authorities. In order to ascertain whether this condition, which constitutes a procedural requirement inherent in Article 1 of Protocol No 1 to the ECHR, has been satisfied, a comprehensive view must be taken of the applicable procedures (see, to that effect, the judgment of the European Court of Human Rights in *Jokela v. Finland* of 21 May 2002, Reports of Judgments and Decisions 2002-IV, § 45 and case-law cited, and § 55).

369 The contested regulation, in so far as it concerns Mr Kadi, was adopted without furnishing any guarantee enabling him to put his case to the competent authorities, in a situation in which the restriction of his property rights must be regarded as significant, having regard to the general application and actual continuation of the freezing measures affecting him.

370 It must therefore be held that, in the circumstances of the case, the imposition of the restrictive measures laid down by the contested regulation in respect of Mr Kadi, by including him in the list contained in Annex I to that regulation, constitutes an unjustified restriction of his right to property.

371 The plea raised by Mr Kadi that his fundamental right to respect for property has been infringed is therefore well founded.

372 It follows from all the foregoing that the contested regulation, so far as it concerns the appellants, must be annulled.

* * *

On those grounds, the Court (Grand Chamber) hereby:

1. Sets aside the judgments of the Court of First Instance of the European Communities of 21 September 2005 in Case T 315/01 Kadi v Council and Commission and Case T 306/01 Yusuf and Al Barakaat International Foundation v Council and Commission;

2. Annuls Council Regulation (EC) No 881/2002 of 27 May 2002 imposing certain specific restrictive measures directed against certain persons and entities associated with Usama bin Laden, the Al-Qaeda network and the Taliban, and repealing Council Regulation (EC) No 467/2001 prohibiting the export of certain goods and services to Afghanistan, strengthening the flight ban and extending the freeze of funds and other financial resources in respect of the Taliban of Afghanistan, in so far as it concerns Mr Kadi and the Al Barakaat International Foundation....

---

## 10. Bibliography of Additional Sources

- Steven R. Ratner, THE CIVILIAN IMPACT OF ECONOMIC SANCTIONS (1999).

- J.M. Willem and Van Genugten, UNITED NATIONS SANCTIONS: EFFECTIVENESS AND EFFECTS (1999).

- Paul Conlon, UNITED NATIONS SANCTIONS MANAGEMENT: A CASE STUDY OF THE IRAQ SANCTIONS COMMITTEE (2000).

- K. Gyeke-Dako, ECONOMIC SANCTIONS UNDER THE UNITED NATIONS (1973).

- David Cortright, THE SANCTIONS DECADE: ASSESSING U.N. STRATEGIES IN THE 1990S (2000).

- Jose E. Alvarez, Judging the Security Council, 90 AM. J. INT'L L. 1 (Jan. 1996).

- Mary E. Black, Collapsing Health Care in Serbia and Montenegro, BRIT.MED. J., Oct. 30, 1993, at 1135.

- Joe Glass, U.N. Set to Aid Detained Vessel: Cypriot-Flagged _Hanuman_ Held in Pakistan for Alleged Sanction Violation, LLOYD'S LIST, Dec. 4, 1993, at 10.

- Randy Harvey, Yugoslavia: This Year's Headache for I.O.C., LOS ANGELES TIMES, July 20, 1992, at 14.
- Christopher C. Joyner, Strengthening Enforcement of Humanitarian Law: Reflections on the International Criminal Tribunal for the Former Yugoslavia, 6 DUKE J. COMP. & INT'L L. 79 (Fall 1995).

- Frederick Kirgis, Jr., The U.N. at Fifty: The Security Council's First Fifty Years, 89 AM. J. INT'L L. 506 (Jul.1995).

- Paul Lewis, U.N. is Worried by Human Cost of Embargoes, THE NEW YORK TIMES, Dec. 19, 1993, at 21.

- Paul Magraph, Law Report: Freeze on Serbian Cash Upheld; *Regina v. HM Treasury and Another, Ex Parte Centro Com SRL*-Queens Bench Divisional Court (Lord Justice Watkins and, Mr. Justice Auld), THE INDEPENDENT (London), Nov. 5, 1993, at 28.

- Jean-Pierre Puessochet, The Court of Justice and International Action by the European Community: The Example of the Embargo Against the Former Yugoslavia, 20 FORDHAM INT'L L.J. 1557 (June 1997).

- Felicia Swindells, U.N. Sanctions in Haiti: A Contradiction Under Art. 41 and 55 of the U.N. Charter, 20 FORDHAM INT'L L.J. 1878 (June 1997).

- Paul C. Szasz, Peacekeeping, Peacemaking and Peace Building: The Role of the United Nations in Global Conflict: Peacekeeping in Operation: A Conflict Study of Bosnia, 28 CORNELL INT'L L.J. 685 (Spring 1995).

- Michael E. Brown, THE INTERNATIONAL DIMENSIONS OF INTERNAL CONFLICT (1996).

- Preston, Brown, THE KUWAIT/IRAQ SANCTIONS-U.S. REGULATIONS IN AN INTERNATIONAL SETTING (1991).

- Lori Fisher Damrosch, ENFORCING RESTRAINT: COLLECTIVE INTERVENTION IN INTERNAL CONFLICTS (1993).

- Louis Henkin, HOW NATIONS BEHAVE: LAW AND FOREIGN POLICY (1979).

- H.G. Schermers, INTERNATIONAL INSTITUTIONAL LAW (1980).

- Barry A. Burciul, UNITED NATIONS SANCTIONS: POLICY OPTIONS FOR CANADA DEPARTMENT OF FOREIGN AFFAIRS AND INTERNATIONAL TRADE (May 1998).

- Barry E. Carter, INTERNATIONAL ECONOMIC SANCTIONS: IMPROVING THE HAPHAZARD U.S. LEGAL REGIME (Cambridge: Cambridge University Press, 1988).

- Carter Center of Emory University, Working Paper Series, Final Report of the Meeting on the Viability of International Economic Sanctions (Atlanta: Carter Center, 1996).

- Center for Economic and Social Rights, U.N. SANCTIONED SUFFERING IN IRAQ (New York: CESR, 1996).

- Paul Conlon, Sanctions infrastructure and Activities of the United Nations: A Critical Assessment, Carnegie Commission on Preventing Deadly Conflict, Task Force on Economic Sanctions, September 20, 1995.

- David Cortright and George A. Lopez, ECONOMIC SANCTIONS: PANACEA OR PEACEBUILDING IN A POST-COLD WAR WORLD?

- M.S. Daoudi and M.S. Danjani, ECONOMIC SANCTIONS: IDEALS AND EXPERIENCE (London: Routledge & Kegan Paul, 1983).

- Margaret P. Doxey, INTERNATIONAL SANCTIONS IN CONTEMPORARY PERSPECTIVE (New York: St. Martin's Press, 1987).

- Kimberly Ann Elliott, TOWARDS A FRAMEWORK FOR MULTILATERAL SANCTIONS (Atlanta: Carter Center, 1996).

- Alexander George, FORCEFUL PERSUASION: COERCIVE DIPLOMACY AS AN ALTERNATIVE TO WAR (Washington: U.S. Institute for Peace, 1991).

- Elizabeth D. Gibbons, SANCTIONS IN HAITI: HUMAN RIGHTS AND DEMOCRACY UNDER ASSAULT (Washington: The CSIS Press, 1999).

- Eric Hoskins, THE IMPACT OF SANCTIONS: A STUDY OF UNICEF's PERSPECTIVE (New York: UNICEF Office of Emergency Programmes).

- Eric Hoskins and Samantha Nutt, THE HUMANITARIAN IMPACTS OF ECONOMIC SANCTIONS ON BURUNDI (Providence, RI: Watson Institute Occasional Paper #29, 1997).

- Gary Hufbauer and Jeffrey Schott, ECONOMIC SANCTIONS RECONSIDERED (Washington, 1985).

- Sister Mary Evelyn Jegen, Towards a Framework for International Sanctions Policy, 18 April 1996.

- David Leighton-Brown (ed.), THE UTILITY OF INTERNATIONAL ECONOMIC SANCTIONS (New York: St. Martin's Press, 1987).

- Michael P. Malloy, ECONOMIC SANCTIONS AND U.S. TRADE (Boston: Little, Brown, 1990).

- Larry Minear, David Cortright, Julia Wagler, George A. Lopez and Thomas G. Weiss, TOWARD MORE HUMANE AND EFFECTIVE SANCTIONS MANAGEMENT: ENHANCING THE CAPACITY OF THE UNITED NATIONS SYSTEM (Providence, RI: Watson Institute, Occasional Paper #31, 1998).

- Kim Richard Nossal, RAIN DANCING: SANCTIONS IN CANADIAN AND AUSTRALIAN FOREIGN POLICY (Toronto: University of Toronto Press, 1994).

- Pax Christi, INTERNATIONAL ECONOMIC SANCTIONS AND INTERNATIONAL RELATIONS (Brussels: Pax Christi, 1993).

- Secretary-General of the United Nations, Report on Economic Assistance to States Affected by the Implementation of the Security Council Resolutions Imposing Sanctions Against the Federal Republic of Yugoslavia. New York, United Nations, A/51/356, September 13, 1996.

- Security Council Non-Paper on Humanitarian Aspects of Sanctions, S/1995/300, April 1995.

- Stanley Foundation, POLITICAL SYMBOL OR POLICY TOOL: MAKING SANCTIONS WORK MUSCATINE (Iowa: The Stanley Foundation, 1993).

- John Stremlau, SHARPENING INTERNATIONAL SANCTIONS: TOWARDS A STRONGER ROLE FOR THE UNITED NATIONS (Washington, DC: Carnegie Commission on Preventing Deadly Conflict, 1996).

- Koenraad Van Brabant, Can Sanctions be Smarter?: The Current Debate, Report of a Conference Held in London, 16–17 December 1998. London: The Humanitarian Policy Group and the Relief and Rehabilitation Network at the Overseas Development Institute, May 1999.

- Koenraad Van Brabant (ed.), Sanctions: The Current Debate: A Summary of Selected Readings. London: The Humanitarian Policy Group and the Relief and Rehabilitation Network at the Overseas Development Institute, March 1999.

- Claudia von Braunmühl and Manfred Kulessa, The Impact of U.N. Sanctions on Humanitarian Assistance Activities: A Report on a Study Commissioned by the United Nations Department of Humanitarian Affairs. Berlin: Gesellschaft für Communication Management Interkultur Training, December 1995.

- Thomas G. Weiss, David Cortright, George A. Lopez and Larry Minear, POLITICAL GAIN AND CIVILIAN PAIN: HUMANITARIAN IMPACTS OF ECONOMIC SANCTIONS (Lanham, MD: Rowman and Littlefield, 1997).

- William M. McGlone, and Michael L. Burton, Economic Sanctions and Export Controls, 34 INT'L LAW 383 (2000).

- Sokol Braha, The Changing Nature of U.S. Sanctions Against Yugoslavia, 8 MICH. J. INT'L L. 273 (1999).

- Felicia Swindells, U.N. Sanctions in Haiti: A Contradiction Under Articles 41 and 55 of the U.N. Charter., 20 FORDHAM INT'L L.J. 1878 (1997).

- Peggy Kozal, Is the Continued Use of Sanctions As Implemented Against Iraq A Violation of International Human Rights?, 28 DENV. J. INT'L L. & POL'Y 383 (2000).

- Amy Howlett, Getting "Smart": Crafting Economic Sanctions That Respect All Human Rights, 73 FORDHAM L. REV. 1199 (2004).

- August Reinisch, Developing Human Rights and Humanitarian Law Accountability of the Security Council for the Imposition of Economic Sanctions, 95 AM. J. INT'L L. 851 (2001).

- Thihan Myo Nyun, Feeling Good or Doing Good: Inefficacy of the U.S. Unilateral Sanctions Against the Military Government of Burma/Myanmar, 7 WASH. U. GLOBAL STUD. L. REV. 455 (2008)

- Cassandra LaRae-Perez, Economic Sanctions As A Use of Force: Re-Evaluating the Legality of Sanctions from an Effects-Based Perspective, 20 B.U. INT'L L.J. 161 (2002).

- Padraic Foran, Why Human Rights Confuse the Sanctions Debate: Towards A Goal-Sensitive Framework for Evaluating United Nations Security Council Sanctions, 4 INTERCULTURAL HUM. RTS. L. REV. 123 (2009).

- Clemens A. Feinäugle, The U.N. Security Council al-Qaida and Taliban Sanctions Committee: Emerging Principles of International Institutional Law for the Protection of Individuals?, 9 GERMAN L.J. 1513 (2008).

# Chapter XI

# United Nations
# Peace Operations

## Introduction

Since the founding of the United Nations, the Security Council has authorized over sixty peacekeeping operations, with over fifty of them since 1988. There have been several notable successes, and in 1988 U.N. peacekeeping operations were awarded the Nobel Peace Prize. But failures in Somalia, Bosnia, and Rwanda in the 1990s raised questions concerning the U.N.'s proper peacekeeping role. This chapter examines the main issues involved in peacekeeping operations. Special emphasis is placed on the process for creating a mandate for a peacekeeping operation and the obstacles generally encountered during the negotiation of the mandate and during its implementation. The chapter will address varied issues, such as the nature and functions of peacekeeping, who has authority within the U.N. to establish peacekeeping operations, what the legal principles governing such operations are and what kind of quandaries peacekeepers frequently face in the field. As this chapter will illustrate, peacekeeping suffers from a variety of challenges. While the U.N. has been trying for several years to reform its peacekeeping activities, tangible improvements remain to be seen. In sum, this chapter provides a basis for discussing the main challenges facing U.N. peacekeeping operations and how those challenges might better be addressed.

## Objectives

- To understand the basic legal framework of establishing peacekeeping operations, specifically to understand the complexities of this framework.
- To understand the various types of peacekeeping operations, how they emerged over time, and what purposes they respectively fulfill.
- To understand the recurring quandaries that ought to be considered and, where possible, addressed when setting up a peacekeeping operation.

# Problems

Students should come to class prepared to discuss the following questions:

1. Why was the idea of a standing U.N. army shelved during the Cold War? What are the pros and cons of such a U.N. army?

2. What are the problems with relying on a system of volunteers to uphold collective security?

3. What are the functions of peacekeeping forces? In what types of situations are they most useful?

4. What and whose consent is necessary for a peacekeeping operation? Does it matter whether it is an internal or international armed conflict?

5. What does the principle of neutrality require? Can peacekeepers report war crimes or protect victims?

6. In what ways have peacekeeping operations become more complex, expensive, and dangerous?

7. What are the dangers when the mandate of U.N. peacekeeping forces is made more robust or when traditional peacekeeping functions are combined with enforcement functions?

8. Why did the U.N. peacekeeping operations fail in Somalia, Bosnia, and Rwanda?

9. What are the challenges faced by U.N. peacekeepers in the Democratic Republic of the Congo and in Darfur?

10. What are the prospects for future U.N. peacekeeping? Will a greater reliance on regional organizations solve some of the institutional and practical deficiencies of U.N. peacekeeping operations?

# Case Studies and Negotiation Simulations

### Negotiation Simulation: Democratic Republic of the Congo

After the Democratic Republic of Congo (DRC) (formerly Zaire) achieved independence in the 1960s, the country was ruled by Joseph Mobutu, a greed-driven dictator, who plundered the country of its wealth for decades. The 1994 genocide in neighboring Rwanda sparked the conflict in the DRC. Two million Rwandan Hutus sought refuge in the DRC, among whom many were Hutu *genocidaires*. From the refugee camps that were set up, Hutu militiamen organized and carried out military incursions in Rwanda to destabilize the new Tutsi-led government. In parallel, they allied themselves with Mobutu's regime and started attacking Congolese Tutsis living in eastern DRC. In turn, Rwanda and Uganda supported local Tutsi rival groups to fight against both the Hutu militias and the Congolese government army. Eventually, the Rwandan- and Ugandan-backed militias overthrew Mobutu and replaced him with their local ally, Laurent-Désiré Kabila. When Kabila failed to expel the Hutu militias and asked the Rwandan and Ugandan armies to leave the country, Rwanda and Uganda turned against him and his army. Zimbabwe, Namibia, and Angola then joined the conflict on Kabila's side. At Laurent Kabila's death, his son, Joseph, took power, and brokered a peace deal in 1999. Since 2003, all foreign armies have left the country except for Rwanda, which continues to wage a proxy war in the eastern part of the country, where violence remains endemic. Currently, the Congolese army, several factions, and foreign troublemakers fight each other over complex ethnic and political issues, as well as over control of the DRC's abundant resources, notably minerals.

Since 1998, approximately 5.4 million have died in the DRC, making it the deadliest conflict since World War II. Every day, approximately one thousand people die because of the war and its implications. Eastern DRC is characterized by recurring attacks on defenseless villages, the highest rate of sexual violence in the world, systematic looting, recruitment of child soldiers and child sex slaves, and forced labor. The situation has driven millions of Congolese into refugee camps plagued by insalubrity, destitution and insecurity. Rape has been the most appalling affliction of the conflict. It is estimated that more than 200,000 women and girls have been raped in the DRC since 1998. Violence against civilians is perpetrated by all parties to the conflict, including the Congolese army. Several humanitarian agencies and organizations are already on the ground to supply basic humanitarian relief and medical aid to civilians and internally displaced people (IDP's).

On request by the DRC, the Security Council has been scheduled for a special meeting to discuss the situation in the DRC and the potential creation of a peacekeeping operation. The debate will involve all five permanent members as well as three non-permanent members, Bangladesh, Sweden and Brazil, and the DRC as an observer. The participating states must decide whether there will be a peacekeeping operation in the DRC and, if so, what its mandate will be. For the purpose of this exercise, assume that there is no current peacekeeping mandate for the DRC.

As for all issues involving international peace and security, the five permanent members may exercise their veto when considering the creation of a peacekeeping operation. The positions and concerns of each participating state are listed below to guide you in representing your designated state during the class debate.

**China:** As a strong advocate of state sovereignty, China will only vote for the creation of a peacekeeping operation if the DRC gives its consent and if the peacekeepers are sent in support of the Congolese army and not as a neutral arbitrator between all forces. China also wants a mandate that strictly limits the use of force to the peacekeepers' individual self-defense.

**France:** Many French NGO's are in the DRC to provide help to the local population; as a result, France is concerned about the safe and unimpeded delivery of humanitarian aid as well as the safety of humanitarian workers. France will only consent to the creation of a peacekeeping operation if its mandate directs peacekeepers to actively protect humanitarian workers and facilitate the delivery of relief. France will support a mandate that authorizes the use of force beyond strict traditional self-defense but only if the DRC consents to it.

**Russia:** As a political maneuver and for the sake of appearances, Russia advocates an extensive mandate with a high number of peacekeepers and a significant budget. Knowing that the budget is tight, Russia's standards will purposefully not be met.

**United Kingdom:** As the front-runner of humanitarian intervention, the UK wants the peacekeepers to be granted extensive rules of engagement to protect civilians. While it understands that securing the DRC's consent is preferable, it does not perceive it as a prerequisite and the UK will not hesitate to bypass the DRC's consent through a Chapter VII resolution. The UK wants the peacekeeping operation to be an impartial force, treating and admonishing each side equally.

**United States:** Bearing in mind the Somalia debacle, the U.S. will only authorize a peace-keeping operation if its mandate is clearly defined and narrowly tailored to avoid mission creep. Securing the consent *of all parties* to the conflict is likewise a significant concern for the U.S. since it fears that without the rebel groups' consent, the mission's efficiency will be substantially jeopardized. The U.S. wants the peacekeeping operation to be a traditional peacekeeping operation rather than a peace-building or peace-making operation.

**Bangladesh:** As the second largest troop contributor to U.N. peacekeeping operations, Bangladesh is willing to contribute troops to a DRC mission so long as the peacekeepers are authorized to use force to defend themselves and their equipment but nothing more. Bangladesh will vote for a peacekeeping operation if the rules of engagement are clearly stated and if the mission remains limited to peacekeeping and does not include any aspects of peace enforcement.

**Sweden:** Sweden wants this peacekeeping operation to undertake enforcement activities but with the proper capacity to carry them out. It will not vote for an under-funded, under-staffed, and under-managed mission. Sweden feels it is time to implement some reform ideas that have been stalled for many years.

**Brazil:** As one of the states that is trying to secure a permanent seat in an expanded Security Council, Brazil has to show that it is committed to maintaining international peace and security. This entails that Brazil should take a strong stance in preventing mass violence against civilians. Despite this enhanced responsibility, Brazil is not convinced that the use of force will lead to the immediate end of violence and enhance the protection of civilians. Brazil is opposed to a mandate that would authorize enforcement activities as they fear these may exacerbate tensions on the ground and cause more harm than good to civilians.

**DRC:** Overwhelmed by the situation in the country and especially in its eastern part, the DRC has requested the creation of a peacekeeping operation to help it contain the conflict and combat the rebel groups and Rwandan combatants. It will only consent to a peacekeeping operation that supports the Congolese army in its operations against the rebels and militias. It wants assurances from the U.N. that the mandate will not be expanded to cover enforcement measures without its consent.

# Materials

1.  United Nations, Diagram of United Nations Peacekeeping Operations.

2.  U.N. Charter arts. 24(1), 37, 38, 39, 40, 41, 42, 43, 44, 47, 48, 52.

3.  Hilaire McCoubrey & Nigel White, THE BLUE HELMETS: LEGAL REGULATION OF UNITED NATIONS MILITARY OPERATIONS 18–20, 45–96 (1996).

4.  Trevor Findlay, *The New Peacekeeping and the New Peacekeepers Challenges for the New Peacekeepers*, *in* CHALLENGES FOR THE NEW PEACEKEEPERS 2, 7–11, 14–15 (Trevor Findlay ed., 1996).

5.  Hilaire McCoubrey & Nigel White, THE BLUE HELMETS: LEGAL REGULATION OF UNITED NATIONS MILITARY OPERATIONS 32–36 (1996).

6.  Michael W. Doyle & Nicholas Sambanis, *Conclusions, in* MAKING WAR AND BUILD-ING PEACE 337–342 (2006).

7.  Bibliography of Additional Sources

## Authors' Note

**Review of United Nations Peacekeeping Operations:** There are currently 15 peace operations directed and supported by the U.N. Department of Peacekeeping Operations (DPKO), 14 of which are peacekeeping missions. Expenditures on peacekeeping missions expanded greatly since the end of the Cold War. While U.N. peacekeeping spending averaged only $164 million per year from 1975–1980, and only $210.8 million for the 1981–88 period, spending rose to an average of $1.75 billion between the years 1989–96. While the U.N. peacekeeping budget reached almost $8 billion in 2010, the United Nations remains keen to point out that peacekeeping is far cheaper than full-blown military intervention. Studies provide empirical backing for the claim: the yearly cost of maintaining all U.N. peacekeeping operations is almost the same amount the U.S. spends on one month fighting in Afghanistan ($7 billion). A magazine article described one such study comparing U.N. and U.S. peace operations:

> Of the eight U.N.-led missions it examined, seven brought sustained peace (Namibia, El Salvador, Cambodia, Mozambique, Eastern Slavonia, Sierra Leone and East Timor), while one (in Congo) did not. An earlier RAND study had looked at eight American-led missions and found that only four of the nations involved (Germany, Japan, Bosnia and Kosovo), were now at peace, while the other four (Somalia, Haiti, Afghanistan and Iraq) were not, or at any rate, not yet.
>
> The comparison is not entirely fair. The Americans took on tougher targets: Iraq has more suicide-bombers than East Timor. On the other hand, the U.N. had punier forces and budgets at its disposal. The annual cost of all 11 U.N. peacekeeping operations [in 2006] is less than America spends in a month in Iraq.

U.N. peacekeeping operations have experienced successes and were awarded the Nobel Peace Prize in 1988. However, dramatic failures of the past, such as in Somalia, Rwanda, and Sierra Leone, as well as more recent difficulties, such as Eritrea's expulsion of peacekeeping forces, allegations of sexual abuse by peacekeepers, the ambush and murder of peacekeepers in DRC, and dire circumstances in Darfur, continue to raise questions concerning the U.N.'s proper peacekeeping role.

The evolution of the Westphalian system into widely accepted principles of state sovereignty has come into conflict with the desire of the international community, as expressed through the United Nations, to promote and protect universal human rights. The predicament the United Nations has been described as follows:

> The record of peacekeeping operations as detailed in the case studies and the sense of helplessness evident in Annan's comments and in the 'Lessons Report' and 'Comprehensive Review', serve as a reminder of the extraordinary character of the U.N.. It is not a security company competing with other organizations for 'business' and concerned about its performance and image. Neither is it a government elected by and answerable to, constituents. It cannot compel its members to engage in peacekeeping operations, and even those who do may opt out at any stage. It cannot be held to account for its actions or omissions. There is

## Diagram of United Nations Peacekeeping Operations

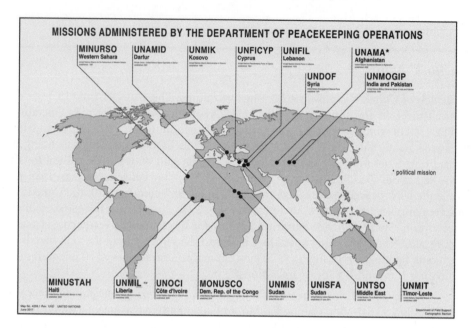

Source: UN.

no responsible body required to implement recommendations or to respond to criticism. Critics of the U.N., particularly those in the media, may expect or demand more from the larger powerful members, but those members may argue that if they exercise their 'muscle' they risk being accused by 'the U.N.' of the smaller states of neo-imperialism or of imposing alien values. 'The U.N.' of the powerful states may well perceive 'the U.N.' of the weaker states with its insistence on respect for sovereignty, as the creator of its own problems.

Inaction during the 1994 massacres in Rwanda might be widely regarded as the U.N.'s greatest failure, but who really was to blame? Was it the Secretary-General; the Security Council; the West; or the many African and other states which could have, but failed to provide contingents? And who then was entitled to level accusations or apportion blame? The reason for the U.N.'s perceived ineffectiveness in maintaining peace is, Ciechaski notes, that 'the doctrine of collective security embodied in the Charter is based on assumptions which are invalid in a world where states are not prepared to defend the existing order in situations where their national interests are not directly affected'.

This state of affairs led one commentator to argue that the U.N. should have a "fire brigade"—a small army of professionals with specialized skills, in order to avoid susceptibility to charges of neocolonialism and avoid the potentially catastrophic risks of delay.

Peacekeeping has traditionally been framed by the principles of consent, neutrality, and non-use of force. Since the end of the Cold War, intra-state conflicts have replaced inter-state conflicts as the main source of violence. Thus, peacekeepers have increasingly become involved in virulent internal conflicts and this has ultimately changed the nature of peace operations. Peacekeepers now have to face multiple non-state actors as well as governmental armies that sometimes act in disregard of international humanitarian law and human rights norms. As a result, some commentators have begun to question the "myth of neutrality."

As peace operations expand beyond monitoring cease-fires to include enforcing peace, the role of the United Nations must be reexamined in light of the traditional emphasis on consent, impartiality, and minimum force. Due to these expanded tasks, peacekeepers are asked to fulfill broader mandates with limited means and capabilities. Additionally, higher expectations among the public place further pressure on the peacekeepers.

There is no textual provision in the U.N. Charter providing for U.N. forces to keep the peace. As a result, the U.N. is limited to the use of Chapter VI and Chapter VII to maintain international peace and security. The basic difference between Chapters VI and VII is that under Chapter VII, the Security Council may impose measures on states that are legally binding. To do this, the Security Council must first determine that the situation constitutes a threat or breach of international peace. In contrast, Chapter VI provides for non binding recommendations. The following articles are pertinent for the study of U.N. peacekeeping.

# 1. U.N. Charter Articles 24, 37, 38–48, 52
## Chapter V: The Security Council

### Article 24

- In order to ensure prompt and effective action by the United Nations, its Members confer on the Security Council primary responsibility for the maintenance of international peace and security, and agree that in carrying out its duties under this responsibility the Security Council acts on their behalf.

\* \* \*

## Chapter VI: Pacific Settlement of Disputes

### Article 37

- Should the parties to a dispute of the nature referred to in Article 33 fail to settle it by the means indicated in that Article, they shall refer it to the Security Council.

- If the Security Council deems that the continuance of the dispute is in fact likely to endanger the maintenance of international peace and security, it shall decide whether to take action under Article 36 or to recommend such terms of settlement as it may consider appropriate.

\* \* \*

## Chapter VII: Action with Respect to Threats to the Peace, Breaches of the Peace, and Acts of Aggression

### Article 39

The Security Council shall determine the existence of any threat to the peace, breach of the peace, or act of aggression and shall make recommendations, or decide what measures shall be taken in accordance with Articles 41 and 42, to maintain or restore international peace and security.

### Article 40

In order to prevent an aggravation of the situation, the Security Council may, before making the recommendations or deciding upon the measures provided for in Article 39, call upon the parties concerned to comply with such provisional measures as it deems necessary or desirable. Such provisional measures shall be without prejudice to the rights, claims, or position of the parties concerned. The Security Council shall duly take account of failure to comply with such provisional measures.

### Article 41

The Security Council may decide what measures not involving the use of armed force are to be employed to give effect to its decisions, and it may call upon the Members of the United Nations to apply such measures. These may include complete or partial interruption of economic relations and of rail, sea, air, postal, telegraphic, radio, and other means of communication, and the severance of diplomatic relations.

### Article 42

Should the Security Council consider that measures provided for in Article 41 would be inadequate or have proved to be inadequate, it may take such action by air, sea, or land forces as may be necessary to maintain or restore international peace and security. Such action may include demonstrations, blockade, and other operations by air, sea, or land forces of Members of the United Nations.

### Article 43

- All Members of the United Nations, in order to contribute to the maintenance of international peace and security, undertake to make available to the Security Council, on its call and in accordance with a special agreement or agreements, armed forces, assistance, and facilities, including rights of passage, necessary for the purpose of maintaining international peace and security.

\* \* \*

### Article 47

- There shall be established a Military Staff Committee to advise and assist the Security Council on all questions relating to the Security Council's military requirements for the maintenance of international peace and security, the employment and command of forces placed at its disposal, the regulation of armaments, and possible disarmament.

### Article 48

- The action required to carry out the decisions of the Security Council for the maintenance of international peace and security shall be taken by all the Members of the United Nations or by some of them, as the Security Council may determine.

- Such decisions shall be carried out by the Members of the United Nations directly and through their action in the appropriate international agencies of which they are members.

\* \* \*

## Chapter VIII: Regional Arrangements

### Article 52

- Nothing in the present Charter precludes the existence of regional arrangements or agencies for dealing with such matters relating to the maintenance of international peace and security as are appropriate for regional action provided that such arrangements or agencies and their activities are consistent with the Purposes and Principles of the United Nations.

---

## *Authors' Note*

**Definition, History, and Typology of U.N. Peacekeeping:** The purpose if this section is to provide a succinct but comprehensive overview of the various types of peacekeeping operations, how they emerged over time, and what purposes they respectively fulfill.

### Initial intent of the U.N. Charter for collective security.

The original intention of the U.N. Charter was that Article 43 would be implemented. Under this article, Member States were supposed to keep at the Security Council's disposal armed forces and facilities for the maintenance of international peace and security. In parallel, Article 47 provided for the establishment of a Military Staff Committee that would serve as an advisor to the Security Council on the military aspects of collective security, including strategic planning. The prevailing dynamics of the Cold War made the conclusion of agreements under Article 43 impossible; the article was hence never implemented. Although the Military Staff Committee does exist, it is an inactive body that has never carried out its intended tasks.

### Peacekeeping as a practical bridge between Chapter VI and Chapter VII.

Because the collective security mechanisms initially envisaged proved unworkable, the practice of neutral peacekeeping was introduced as an acceptable alternative to prevent conflicts from escalating to full-scale wars. In dealing with matters of international peace and security, the U.N. was limited to the use of Chapter VI or Chapter VII. Thus, nowhere in the Charter was there an express provision providing for U.N. forces to keep the peace. Former U.N. Secretary-General Dag Hammarskjöld referred to peacekeeping as belonging to "Chapter Six and a Half" of the Charter, since it is neither a pure method of peaceful settlement of disputes under Chapter VI, nor a coercive action authorized under Chapter VII. Peacekeeping has hence been described as an "impartial intermediary in local wars or tense situations that serves to reduce the risk of escalation or resumption of violence and ensure an atmosphere 'conducive to constructive negotiations.'"

### Generations/types of peacekeeping operations: peace-keeping/peace-building/peace-making.

From their inception in the late 1940s, peacekeeping operations have undergone profound developments in terms of size, mandate, and purposes. Three types or "generations" of peacekeeping have traditionally been distinguished. The "first generation" of peacekeeping operations was limited to traditional mandates, such as observation missions, overseeing of cease-fires, border control, and demilitarization verification. Peacekeepers were sent as "buffer forces" in mostly inter-state conflicts, creating or securing the conditions for belligerents to resolve their dispute through diplomatic channels. The end of the Cold War led to a "second generation" of peacekeeping, also referred to as "peace-building" operations. These operations were not merely designed to maintain the status quo, but were created to actively help resolve conflicts and build peace by integrated, holistic means:

## Typology Chart on United Nations Peacekeeping

| Type/Examples | Functions | Requirements | Authority |
|---|---|---|---|
| 1. *Traditional*<br>1949 UNMOGIP-<br>India/Pakistan<br>1991 ONUSAL—<br>El Salvador | Act as buffer or pre-<br>ventive deployment<br>(Macedonia)<br>Monitor cease-fire de-<br>militarization<br>Verify troop with-<br>drawal | UN Command/<br>Control<br>Cease Fire<br>Consent (SOFAS)<br>Neutrality<br>Lightly Armed<br>International<br>Composition<br>UN Funded | S.C.-Ch. VI ½<br>Arts. 36(1), 24(1), 40<br>G.A.-Arts. 10, 11 |
| 2. *Integrated*<br>1991 UNTAC—<br>Cambodia | Election Supervision<br>Civilian Admin.<br>Train/Supervise<br>Police | UN Command/<br>Control<br>Cease Fire<br>Consent (SOFAS)<br>Neutrality<br>Lightly Armed<br>International<br>Composition<br>UN Funded | S.C.-Ch. VI ½<br>Arts. 36(1), 24(1), 40<br>G.A.-Arts. 10, 11 |

the organization and overseeing of elections (East Timor), or the rebuilding or strength-ening of state institutions (Nicaragua, Cambodia). However, with the proliferation of complex intra-state conflicts, first generation and even second generation of peacekeeping missions have proven inadequate if not altogether obsolete.

The growing impatience of the international community with these types of operations led to the development of a "third generation" of peacekeeping missions, referred to as "quasi-enforcement" operations or "peace-making." The latter combine traditional aspects of peacekeeping with enforcement actions provided under Chapter VII. Unlike traditional peacekeeping, third generation operations try to impose peace rather than maintain a peace that has already been established, and the parties' consent is not indispensable. The missions in Bosnia and in Somalia in the 1990s are examples of this third generation of peacekeeping.

### Blurring the boundaries between the types of peacekeeping operations

Ever since the end of the Cold War, almost all conflicts are based on intra-state conflicts or intra-state conflicts with regional implications. Thus, U.N. peacekeepers are ever more active in conflicts within states, although the U.N. Charter was designed to deal with inter-state conflicts. The growth of these peacekeeping missions is related to the need to address multiple humanitarian crises: new approaches are required to respond to the challenges faced. Today, peacekeepers often face numerous warring parties which have not yet reached a truce or peace agreement. The use of force becomes a necessary component. Moreover, complex peacebuilding efforts are required after the fighting has ceased.

The line between the need for enforcement and traditional peacekeeping was blurred in a number of conflicts since the Cold War like in Liberia, Sierra Leone, Cote d'Ivoire, Sudan, the Democratic Republic of Congo, Burundi, Haiti, and Sudan. Facing these complexities, often a linear or sequential approach is taken to deal with crises or humanitarian emergencies: conflict prevention, peacemaking, peacekeeping, and peace enforcement.

**Typology Chart on United Nations Peacekeeping, continued**

| Type/Examples | Functions | Requirements | Authority |
|---|---|---|---|
| 3. *Quasi Enforcement* 1992 UNPROFOR— Bosnia 1993 UNOSOM II— Somalia | Protect Aid Convoys Arrest War Criminals | UN Command/ Control Initial Consent S.C. Res. Delineates Scope Moderately Armed International Composition UN Funded | Ch. VII |
| 4. *Enforcement* 1950—Korea 1991—Iraq (Desert Storm) 1993—Somalia (Restore Hope) 1994—Haiti (Just Cause) 1994—Rwanda (Tourquise) 1995—Bosnia (IFOR) 1999— Kosovo (KFOR) | Enforce Economic Sanctions Compel Compliance with S.C. Res. Repel Aggression Prevent Human Rights Abuse Induce Peace Agreement Funded by Individual States | Not UN Controlled Consent Optional S.C. Res. delineates Scope (examples— Iraq and Yugo— Res. 770) Heavily Armed Led by Major Powers | Ch. VII "All necessary means …" |

Experience, however, has shown that these different steps should be seen as mutually reinforcing. If they are used in isolation and are not incorporated in a comprehensive approach, the root causes of conflict will hardly be addressed. At the same time, the boundaries of U.N. peacekeeping operations have become increasingly blurred because they are rarely limited to one type of activity. Often, a complex set of authorization to use force is incorporated in today's multidimensional peacekeeping operations that facilitate the political process, protect civilians, assist in the disarmament, demobilization and reintegration (DDR) of former combatants, support the organization of elections, protect and promote human rights and assist in restoring the rule of law.

Peacekeeping is inherently political in nature as the Security Council decides whether or not troops or police will be deployed. Often, a peace agreement or some kind of diplomatic process already happened before a peacekeeping operation is deployed. However, achieving an international consensus for political solutions to several current crises is not as strong today as in the immediate aftermath of the Cold War.

## 2. Hilaire McCoubrey and Nigel White, The Blue Helmets: Legal Regulation of United Nations Military Operations

### 1996
[footnotes omitted by editors]

### Peacekeeping by the U.N. Distinguished from Enforcement

Military enforcement action is essentially coercive action taken against a state or a faction within a state against the will of that state or faction. The aim is to force compliance with decisions of the Security Council, for instance to reveal aggression or to prevent human rights abuses. Military enforcement action is undertaken under Chapter VII as has been seen in the above section. The key to Chapter VII is article 39 which provides that the Security Council can utilize the economic and military enforcement provisions of Chapter VII after determining that there has been a "threat to the peace," "breach of the peace" or "act of aggression." In the above instances of military enforcement action, the Security Council had determined that the attacks against South Korea and Iraq were breaches of the peace, while the situations in Southern Rhodesia, Haiti and Rwanda were threats to the peace.

The exact legal and political nature of peacekeeping will be the subject of the next three chapters. The purpose here will be to define it briefly and contrast it with enforcement. Peacekeeping has been defined in the following fashion:

> As the United Nations practice has evolved over the years, a peacekeeping operation has come to be defined as an operation involving military personnel, but without enforcement powers, undertaken by the United Nations to help maintain or restore international peace and security in areas of conflict. These operations are voluntary and are based on consent and co-operation. While they involve the use of military personnel, they achieve their objectives not by force of arms, thus contrasting them with the "enforcement action" of the United Nations.

Although there is no express provision in the U.N. Charter providing for U.N. peacekeeping, it will be shown that it is more closely linked to the powers of the Security Council under Chapter VI which provides for a number of recommendatory powers designed to achieve a peaceful settlement of a conflict. The recommendations of the Security Council under Chapter VI must be accepted by the state or factions concerned. Similarly, peacekeeping forces which are designed to facilitate a cease-fire or a more general peaceful settlement are consented to by the former warring parties. In essence, this the fundamental difference between peacekeeping and enforcement. Peacekeeping is consensual whereas enforcement is non-consensual. From this basic principle the other tenets of peacekeeping have been established, namely neutrality and non-offensive force. Military enforcement actions on the other hand are fought against one of the parties and so are offensive operations in which the U.N. has taken sides. Further differences between peacekeeping and U.N. enforcement action, at least in practice, is in the fact that although member states volunteer forces for both types of U.N. military operations, peacekeeping and enforcement, peacekeeping operations are much more clearly under the command and control of the U.N. with regular Security Council review and day-to-day direction from the U.N. Secretary-General or his representative. Enforcement action, though it is supposed to be under U.N. command and control according to the wording of Chapter VII, has emerged as an essentially decentralized military operation receiving a Security Council blessing but little in the form of command and control.

In many ways traditional U.N. peacekeeping and U.N. authorized military enforcement actions are at opposite ends of the spectrum of U.N. military involvement in a conflict zone. However, as with all scales there comes a point in the middle where it becomes difficult to draw the line between peacekeeping and enforcement. The remainder of this chapter will contain an overview of the various types of peacekeeping force, from observation to quasi-enforcement. The core of peacekeeping forces is drawn from military units of member states, and this has led to a public perception that they should use more force when occasions demand. This perception has occasionally, and it must be said increasingly, had an effect on the political leaders of U.N. members with the result that on occasions, as shall be seen, traditional peacekeeping operations have been given enforcement mandates or have been supplemented or replaced by enforcement action. Such operations, as found in the Congo, Somalia and the former Yugoslavia for instance, will be included in this study. One issue to be discussed at a later stage is whether such a mixed approach actually undermines the credibility of U.N. peacekeeping.

* * *

### The Competence of the Security Council

The competence of the Security Council in the area of peacekeeping is much less controversial. Although there is no express power granted in the U.N. Charter allowing for the creation of peacekeeping forces, the arguments for recognizing that the Council has an implied or inherent power to create a peacekeeping force to adopt are much clearer than those put forward for the Assembly. First of all, according to article 24(1), "in order to ensure prompt and effective action by the United Nations, its members confer on the Security Council primary responsibility for the maintenance of international peace and security." Given the primary aim of the U.N. is to achieve intentional peace and security, it has been recognized, by the World Court in the Namibia case for instance, that article 24(1) confers upon the Council general powers to achieve these purposes.

An examination of the specific powers of the Security Council indicates that peacekeeping falls somewhere between Chapter VI, "Pacific Settlement of Disputes," and Chapter VII, "Action with Respect to Threats to the Peace, Breaches of the Peace, and Acts of Aggression." Peacekeeping constitutes a concrete military presence and therefore does not simply consist of mere recommendations for settlement or the establishment of basic fact-finding missions as is found in Chapter VI. However, peacekeeping is not pure military enforcement action as envisaged under Chapter VII. Sometimes peacekeeping is closer to or linked to pacific settlement and therefore can be seen as a power derived from article 36(1) of Chapter VI which provides that "the Security Council may, at any stage of a dispute [ ... ] recommend appropriate procedures or methods of adjustment."

On other occasions peacekeeping is solely concerned with overseeing provisional measures (cease-fires, withdrawals) in which case the Charter base can be seen as article 40 of Chapter VII which provides that "in order to prevent an aggravation of the situation, the Security Council may [ ... ] call upon the parties concerned to comply with such provisional measures it deems necessary or desirable." [ ... ] The power to call for provisional measures is contained in article 40, and generally peacekeeping forces are created to facilitate the observance of such measures, when they have been accepted by the parties to the conflict. Peacekeeping is often derived from Article 40, although its function does not vary with the nature of the obligation on the parties as regards the provisional measures. The nature of peacekeeping remains consensual and non-offensive whether or not the call for provisional measures is mandatory.

However, the Security Council has occasionally used peacekeeping forces to enforce provisional measures—a practice which dates back to the Congo in 1960. This is still reconcilable with article 40 in that the provision goes on to say that "the Security Council shall duly take account of failure to comply with provisional measures." In these instances then, although it is arguable that the peacekeeping force is not taking enforcement action in the full-blown sense, it is taking action which is closer to Chapter VII action in that it is enforcing provisional measures. This type of action has been taken much more readily in the post-Cold War era.

\* \* \*

### The Role of the Secretary-General

From the relatively narrow provisions of the U.N. Charter concerning the office of Secretary-General, the various holders of this post have developed an impressive set of powers to be used in the peaceful settlement of disputes and situations. Article 97 states that the Secretary-General "shall be the chief administrative officer of the Organization." However, unlike the Secretary-General of the League of Nations, who was simply a "civil servant," the Secretary-General is granted somewhat wider powers in the Charter. Article 98 provides that the Secretary-General "shall perform such other functions as are entrusted to him" by the Security Council, General Assembly, Economic and Social Council and the Trusteeship Council. Under this provision the Secretary-General carries out the mandates granted to him by the Security Council or the General Assembly. This may range from sending a fact-finding mission, to offering his good offices, to the organization and emplacement of a peacekeeping force.

The only autonomous power granted to him in the Charter is contained in article 99 which provides that "[t]he Secretary-General may bring to the attention of the Security Council any matter which in his opinion may threaten international peace and security." Given the importance of the concept of a "threat to the peace" in the workings of the Security Council, particularly as regards internal conflicts, this is potentially a very important provision. However, it has been little used by the office holders, although one notable exception was when Secretary-General Hammarskjold brought the deteriorating situation in the Congo to the attention of the Security Council in 1960 explicitly relying on article 99.

Nevertheless, despite the fact that the Charter explicitly only grants the Secretary-General the autonomous power to bring to the attention of the Security Council threats to international peace, over the years the office holder has developed an impressive set of inherent powers, such as good offices, mediation, even arbitration and fact finding. These powers have developed either with the acquiescence of the Security Council and General Assembly, or sometimes with their active encouragement in the sense that it has been recognized that the Secretary-General has inherent powers not dependent on a specific mandate from one of the other principal organs of the United Nations.

The Secretary-General's inherent powers seem to have stretched as far as to allow the office-holder, on his own authority, to send a fact finding mission to a conflict, but they have not extended as far as the authorization of an observer force or peacekeeping force; that still has to be mandated by the Security Council. However, greater activity by the United Nations in the late 1980s as the Cold War came to an end did see the possible extension of the Secretary-General's powers to at least the negotiation and emplacement of an observer force. Under a General Assembly mandate of 1980,44 the representative of the

Secretary-General helped negotiate the Geneva Accords of 1988 which, inter alia, provided for the withdrawal of Soviet troops from Afghanistan under U.N. supervision. The 50-strong observer team was quickly drawn from other U.N. operations and dispatched by the Secretary-General, with Perez de Cuellar simply informing the Security Council by letter. However, it was not until the end of October 1988, that the Security Council formally confirmed its agreement to the measures envisaged and executed by the Secretary-General, in particular the temporary dispatch to Afghanistan and Pakistan of military officers. No explanation was given in the Security Council. It appears that the Secretary-General had the consent of the Security Council to re-deploy existing U.N. observers to Afghanistan and Pakistan without formal authorization. Given the exigencies of the situation, and the fact that both superpowers wanted a U.N. presence, the need for a prior mandate from the Security Council was ignored and UNGOMAP (the United Nations Good Offices Mission in Afghanistan and Pakistan) was established under the inherent powers of the Secretary-General.

Such autonomy for the Secretary-General is only to be found in exceptional circumstances. Although the Secretary-General may negotiate the emplacement of a peacekeeping force with the parties, and may lay down a detailed plan for the establishment and functions of a peacekeeping force, it normally cannot be emplaced before the Security Council, or exceptionally the General Assembly, has authorized it. Nevertheless, the end of the Cold War has placed a much heavier burden on the Secretary-General, and overall his inherent competence has expanded to cope with the increasing involvement of the U.N. in conflict resolution.

\* \* \*

The Secretary-General's powers in the field of peacekeeping may have expanded over the years from being simply the administrator of forces to becoming the instigator and, as shall be seen in Chapter 7, the day-to-day political commander of the forces within the overall framework of the Security Council's mandate. It must be noted that this only applies to traditional peacekeeping forces and the new generation of integrated pacific settlement missions as found in Namibia and Cambodia. In the quasi-enforcement operations in Haiti, Rwanda and Somalia, and now with IFOR in Bosnia, the Secretary-General does not have any political control over the forces. In general, they are commanded, both politically and militarily, by a state or a group of states, operating under a loose Security Council mandate, although generally as with consensual peacekeeping forces, the Secretary-General is required by the Council to provide regular (usually at least biannual) reports on the progress of the force.

\* \* \*

### The U.N. and Regional Organizations

A genuinely consensual peacekeeping operation undertaken by an organization outside the U.N. does not require the permission of the U.N. before it is undertaken. The constitutional link between the U.N. and other organizations is to be found in Chapter VIII of the U.N. Charter. Article 52 actually encourages regional organizations or arrangements to "make every effort to achieve peaceful settlement of local disputes [ ... ] before referring them to the Security Council," as long as their activities in this field are consistent with the Purposes and Principles of the United Nations. Consensual, neutral peacekeeping conforms with the U.N. Charter and is a mechanism developed to facilitate the settlement of disputes.

A good example of a genuine peacekeeping operation undertaken outside the U.N. by another international body was the Commonwealth Force in Southern Rhodesia, which was part of the peace process established by the Lancaster House Agreement of 15 December 1979. The Agreement detailed, inter alia, the terms of a constitution for an independent Republic of Zimbabwe; arrangements for the immediate pre-independence period during which the country would return to the status of a British dependent territory under a Governor, while elections were held; and finally, the details of a cease-fire to end the fighting in the guerrilla war.

The cease-fire agreement entered into by the parties to the conflict stated that the British government was responsible for the establishment of a monitoring force under the Command of the Governor's Military Adviser, "to assess and monitor impartially all stages of the inception and maintenance of the cease-fire by the forces." The Commanders of the Rhodesian security forces and those of the Patriotic Front forces undertook to cooperate fully with the Commonwealth Force. The agreement also provided that "members of the monitoring force will carry weapons for their personal protection and will be provided with vehicles and aircraft carrying a distinctive marking." In a statement accompanying the cease-fire agreement, the Chairman of the conference, Lord Carrington, stated that the force would be 1,200 strong and would contain troops from Australia, New Zealand, Kenya, Fiji and the United Kingdom. His statement also made it clear that the Commonwealth Force's role was one of peacekeeping not enforcement.

* * *

The [Commonwealth Monitoring Force (CMF)] was clearly a neutral, consensual, peacekeeping force and, despite the fact that the Commonwealth has no express power to create such a force, it can be seen as a necessary implied or inherent power for an organization concerned with the peace and security of its members. However, when the activities or mandate of the force includes enforcement, then the constitutional position is changed, for article 53(l) of the U.N. Charter provides:

> The Security Council shall, where appropriate, utilize such regional arrangements or agencies for enforcement action under its authority. But no enforcement action shall be taken under regional arrangements or by regional agencies without the authorization of the Security Council.

This provision is effective for asserting the constitutional superiority of the U.N. over regional bodies in the field of enforcement action because of the near universal membership of the U.N. and because regional organizations, in their constituent documents, themselves do not claim superiority or indeed sometimes recognize U.N. superiority in this matter.

Nevertheless, there are several instances where the relevant regional organizations have, in practice undertaken enforcement action, without authorization from the Security Council, under the guise of a peacekeeping mandate.

The establishment of a small Symbolic Arab Security Force by the Arab League in June 1976, followed by the creation of a much larger Arab Deterrent Force (ADF) of 30,000 troops mainly from Syria in October 1976, in response to the civil war in Lebanon 17 is an example of a regional organization attempting peacekeeping operations in an environment unsuited to such actions, with the result that the operation became one of military intervention or enforcement.

Although there were aspects of the mandate of the ADF which appeared to be based on the peacekeeping concept—such as supervision of a cease-fire, withdrawal of troops and the collection of the weaponry belonging to the parties to the internal conflict— other aspects seemed to grant the force much wider powers of enforcement, such as maintaining internal security and assisting Lebanese authorities to take over public utilities." Although it is possible to argue that the U.N. gave a similarly wide mandate to ONUC in the Congo, as we have seen, that operation in reality became one of enforcement. In addition, if the performance of the Arab League Force is examined it can be seen that it became increasingly ruthless in its actions and was unafraid to use military coercion beyond that required in strict self-defense. Furthermore, even when the Lebanese government withdrew its consent to the ADF in 1982, the Force, which was by then entirely composed of Syrian troops, remained and increasingly aligned itself with the pro-Syrian factions in Lebanon.

On other occasions the Security Council has retrospectively endorsed regional organization quasi-enforcement operations as in the case of Liberia, where a civil war has raged since 1989 between the National Patriotic Forces of Liberia (NPFL) which rebelled against the corrupt and incompetent regime of Samuel Doe.

In July 1990, the Liberian government accepted a peace proposal put forward by the 16-member Economic Community of West African States (ECOWAS), consisting of a cease-fire, the deployment of a regional peacekeeping force, and the immediate formation of a government of national unity. Despite the fact that this proposal was rejected by the NPFL, on 25 August 1990, a 4,000 strong peacekeeping force known as the ECOWAS Monitoring Group (ECOMOG), arrived in Liberia. The NPFL saw this as military intervention on behalf of the beleaguered government. Although ECOMOG attempted to tread the neutral tightrope of a true peacekeeping force, it slowly became embroiled in the civil war, particularly after the death of President Doe in September 1990. ECOMOG started an offensive against the NPFL as well as increasing the already large Nigerian element of the force. The new Nigerian commander of the force was ordered by the Nigerian government to take offensive action against the rebels. Parallels can easily be drawn with the Syrian involvement in the ADF in Lebanon.

Various cease-fires were agreed to by the various factions culminating in the Yamoussoukra IV Accords of 30 October 1991, which also detailed procedures for disarmament of the various factions, the restructuring of ECOMOG to make it less dominated by Nigeria, the surrendering of territory to ECOMOG by the NPFL, and the holding of elections. The cease-fire did not hold, Taylor being angered by ECOWAS' recognition of Amos Sawyer, an exiled politician, as interim President. This led to fighting between the expanded 9,000 strong ECOMOG force and other rebels factions against the NPFL during 1992.

At this stage the U.N. Security Council became involved, adopting resolution 788 on 19 November 1992, which imposed a mandatory arms embargo against the whole of Liberia, except for ECOMOG. The resolution also expressed support for the Yamoussoukra IV Accords, whilst recalling the provisions of Chapter VIII of the U.N. Charter and commending "ECOWAS for its efforts to restore peace, security and stability in Liberia." From January 1993, ECOMOG went on the offensive against the NPFL pushing them back front the capital with the help of an extra 5,000 troops. On 26 March the Security Council adopted resolution 812 which threatened further measures if the peace accords were not complied with. The parties finally agreed to the implementation of the Cotonou peace agreement on 25 July, which contained provisions for the involvement of U.N. observers in the disarmament and elections process. In resolution 856 of 10 August 1993, the Security Council agreed to dispatch an advance team of 30 military observers to pave the way for the emplacement of a U.N. Observer Mission for Liberia (UNOMIL) to help implement the peace agreements. However, despite the presence of UNOMIL and ECOMOG, the disarmament process faltered and fighting continued to flare up in 1994. Indeed, the situation worsened with the detention of

UNOMIL observers by the NPFL, with the result that in September 1994, the Security Council requested that ECOMOG protect UNOMIL personnel's Despite a further cease-fire agreed in December 1994, the situation did not significantly improve in 1995, although the Security Council did renew and expand UNOMIL's mandate in November 1995 following a further cease-fire agreement and an agreement on a timetable for the implementation of the peace process.

It can be seen from this account that during its long involvement in Liberia, ECO-MOG had overstepped the boundary between neutral peacekeeping and military enforcement action. The U.N. Security Council has apparently retrospectively endorsed the action as corning with the provisions of Chapter VIII of the U.N. Charter in resolution 788. In other instances, the Security Council has, in accordance with article 53, prospectively authorized organizations to undertake enforcement action alongside a U.N. peacekeeping operation.

This "sub-contracting" is a new development caused by the need to back-up, or replace, peacekeeping operations by the use of force. This coincides with another post-Cold War development in the shape of the changing role of the North Atlantic Treaty Organization from defense organization to becoming a component of the wider collective security system. This has happened despite the fact that the NATO Treaty of 1949, remains clearly based on Article 51 of the U.N. Charter, which allows states to act in collective self-defense to an "armed attack." The basis of NATO, namely an attack on one party is an attack on all parties, has the advantage of not requiring Security Council authorization within the terms of article 53, but has the disadvantage of not expressly permitting NATO to take any enforcement, rather than defensive, action. Thus within the terms of its own treaty NATO could not, as an organization, take action beyond the defensive in a situation where a NATO member is not under attack. Yet this is exactly what it has done in Bosnia.

Despite the fact that the NATO Treaty has not been altered to allow it to take a wider security, as opposed to defensive, role, this has not prevented the Security Council calling on NATO to undertake certain enforcement tasks in Bosnia. While NATO clearly could not have undertaken this role unilaterally, it can do so under Security Council authority. Legally speaking this can be seen either as an authorization under article 53(1) of the Charter with the Security Council treating NATO as a regional arrangement, or as an authorization of the individual members of NATO to take enforcement action under Chapter VII of the Charter. The latter interpretation overcomes the defects in the NATO treaty by recognizing that the authorization is not directed at NATO but at individual states. Legally speaking, the individual members of NATO could have volunteered for the task, just as the French volunteered for limited enforcement action in Rwanda, and the United States in Haiti.

The Security Council started to bring NATO into the Bosnian theatre of war in resolution 770 of 13 August 1992, in which the Security Council, "acting under Chapter VII of the Charter of the United Nations," called "upon States to take nationally or through regional agencies [ … ] all measures necessary to facilitate in coordination with the United Nations the delivery by relevant United Nations humanitarian organizations and others of humanitarian assistance to Sarajevo and wherever needed in other parts of Bosnia." The phrase "all measures necessary" has been used in the past by the Security Council to authorize military operations.

* * *

The peace agreements secured at Dayton, Ohio in November 1995, as a result partly of NATO actions, provide for UNPROFOR in Bosnia to be replaced by a NATO-led Implementation Force (IFOR), which has the power to oversee and enforce the agreements, without the need to seek further approval from the Secretary-General.

* * *

The U.N. Security Council endorsed the creation and emplacement of IFOR in what amounted to a greater degree of delegation to NATO than had occurred in Bosnia before, but little different to the delegation to member states to undertake potentially offensive military operations in Rwanda, Haiti and Somalia. Resolution 1031 of 15 December 1995, authorized IFOR "to take all necessary measures to effect the implementation of and to ensure compliance with" the agreement and "stresses that the parties shall be held equally responsible for compliance [ ... ] and shall be equally subject to such enforcement action by IFOR as may be necessary to ensure implementation [ ... ] and takes note that the parties have consented to IFOR's taking of such measures." Although IFOR has been consented to by the parties, it is not a traditional form of peacekeeping. IFOR performs a traditional peacekeeping role while the accords are being complied with, but will become an offensive operation if the accords are broken. Indeed, even while it is performing a basic peacekeeping function, the threat of enforcement action if the peace is broken, combined with the much greater military capacity of IFOR, makes it a much more capable military operation that UNPROFOR, which for all practical purposes, despite Security Council attempts at tinkering with its mandate, was a traditional peacekeeping force.

It appears from this situation that the Security Council can use NATO, if NATO's members are willing, to carry out enforcement measures. Legally, article 53 states that NATO could not initiate enforcement action by itself, only action in collective self-defense. NATO members and others contributing to IFOR (including the Russian Federation) also require Security Council authorization under Chapter VII (articles 39 and 42) if they are not simply acting in self-defense. However, although these are the formal requirements of Chapters VII and VIII of the U.N. Charter, the practice of regional and other organizations, in Lebanon and Liberia for instance, shows that the provisions of the U.N. Charter asserting the supremacy of the Security Council in enforcement matters, are sometimes ignored, particularly when the organization in question has deployed a coercive military presence under the umbrella of a peacekeeping operation, relying on the spurious argument that neutral peacekeeping operations do not require the authorization of the Security Council.

* * *

## Authors' Note

Troop composition is another important aspect of U.N. peacekeeping operations. Because the U.N. does not have a standing army, it must rely on member states' willingness to contribute contingents for each peacekeeping operation. This dependence has given rise to a certain number of problems. The multinational composition of troops entails issues of language, lack of coordination, unclear chain of command, and unequal training, discipline, and experience. Additionally, the main troop contributors are developing states, which creates further challenges. The following excerpt from Trevor Findlay's article "The New Peacekeepers and the New Peacekeeping" in *Challenges for the New Peacekeepers* explains what motivates states to contribute troops and what the challenges created by this system are.

---

### 3. Trevor Findlay, The New Peacekeeping and the New Peacekeepers

*Challenges for the New Peacekeepers*, 1996
[footnotes omitted by editors]

U.N. peacekeeping traditionally relied on a handful of states to provide the bulk of the personnel required. These were mostly medium-sized developed states, principally Australia, Austria, Canada, Denmark, Finland, Ireland, New Zealand, Norway and Sweden, and larger developing states like India and Pakistan. A handful of smaller developing states, particularly Fiji, Ghana, Nepal and Senegal, were also prominent. However, beginning with the deployment of UNTAG in Namibia between April 1989 and March 1990, a period during which the cold war is widely considered to have ended, there has been an enormous increase in the number of states involved in U.N. peacekeeping. In 1988, before UNTAG, only 26 countries were involved. By November 1994 there were 76.

The main reason for the increasing involvement has been increased need. With the end of the cold war more of the world's armed conflicts became ripe for negotiated settlements as client states lost their superpower mentors and the Security Council achieved a new unity in actively seeking such settlements. The end of the cold war also unleashed new conflicts in the Balkan states and several of the former Soviet republics. The conflict resolution tool of choice in almost all cases has been peacekeeping or some variant thereof: more peacekeeping operations have been established since 1989 than in the previous 45 years of the U.N.'s history. While in 1988 the U.N. operated just 5 peacekeeping missions, by its peak year of 1993 it had 18.

\* \* \*

#### Motivations for participation

The motivations of the new peacekeepers probably differ little from those of the old, although a higher proportion of newcomers may be participating because of outside pressure, either from their allies or from the U.N. Secretary-General or Secretariat or some other international organization. For instance, many of the Caribbean states (and Israel), which participated in the MNF in Haiti and thereafter in UNMIH, were pressured to participate by the USA in order to lend a multilateral character to a U.S.-dominated mission. A similar process occurred in assembling the forces for UNITAF. Russia pressured fellow CIS members to join it in peacekeeping in Tajikistan.

Still, many states volunteer willingly. Although much is made of so-called peacekeeping fatigue, so keen have states been to participate in some of the 'safer' missions that a number of such missions have been 'over-subscribed'. More states were willing to volunteer troops for UNAVEM II and UNMIH, for instance, than could be accommodated.

Motives are invariably mixed. Altruism is one factor. Some of the 'old' peacekeepers like Canada, Norway and Sweden have regarded participation in peacekeeping as the quintessence of good inter-national citizenship. This may indeed have been a primary motivation in the days when peacekeeping was a relatively unpublicized backwater of international activity, but altruism is today more likely to be outweighed by other factors. Peacekeeping has acquired a certain cachet and participation is seen as enhancing national prestige and independence. Such factors appear especially important to the newly independent states of the former Soviet Union and former Warsaw Pact members whose foreign policies were essentially subordinated to that of the Soviet state for 40 years. Public opinion may, of course, still steal the altruism of governments and cause them to act, particularly in humanitarian crises, as in the case of Somalia.

For states which expect to be favoured candidates for permanent membership of the Security Council (if and when it is expanded), participation in peacekeeping has become a *sine qua non*. All the most widely touted candidates — Brazil, Germany, India, Indonesia, Japan, Nigeria and Pakistan — are now important contributors. Others hope their participation will increase their influence on the course of international events generally and more specifically in the areas in which peacekeeping operations are deployed. New Zealand's contribution to UNPROFOR during its term as a non-permanent member of the Security Council was at least partly inspired by a desire to enhance its credibility and influence in Council debates on the situation in the former Yugoslavia.

Some new peacekeepers, like Spain, see peacekeeping as contributing, inchoately, to their national security. Others see a more direct link. The members of the Association of South-East Asian Nations (ASEAN), all of which participated in UNTAC in Cambodia, saw that operation as being decidedly in their national security interests.

Some new peacekeepers may even view participation in peacekeeping as a down payment for the day when they themselves will need the assistance of the international community. This may be one of the principal motivations of the three Baltic states, Estonia, Latvia and Lithuania, which live in the shadow of Russia. The Baltic states also undoubtedly see participation in peacekeeping as demonstrating their ability to contribute to the purposes of the NATO alliance in which they ardently hope for membership. For others, such as Egypt, El Salvador, Greece, Israel, Jordan, Namibia, South Korea and Zimbabwe, participation in peacekeeping is a way of repaying a debt for the peacekeeping operations of which they have been beneficiaries in the past.

States in which the military is not entirely under civilian control, such as Argentina, may view peacekeeping as a means both of keeping their armed forces occupied outside the country rather than meddling in domestic affairs and of helping to rehabilitate them after an authoritarian era in which their integrity and professionalism were compromised. As Argentina's Defence Minister, Oscar Camilión, has diplomatically expressed it, Argentina's participation in peacekeeping 'not only gives members of the armed forces a deep feeling of professional pride, but also an international outlook which is very much helping to consolidate the military as a pillar of the constitutional system'.

A less edifying motivation for some of the new peacekeepers from the developing world may be a desire to profit from the reimbursements for the costs of troop contributions (over and above those they would have incurred if their forces had remained home). This is not confined to the new peacekeepers: Fiji's involvement in peacekeeping since 1978 has reportedly been a 'significant source of foreign exchange'. Some poorer states can indeed make a profit on such transactions, but the U.N. is usually so slow in paying and the amount so relatively niggardly that this cannot be a sole motivating factor. Even Fiji has threatened to quit peacekeeping unless it is 'reimbursed' more promptly.

The armed forces of some countries may also benefit by receiving equipment from better-equipped force contributors during peacekeeping operations, as happened in UNOSOM II in Somalia. In Bosnia and Herzegovina, Germany is supplying protective vehicles to the Pakistani contingent, while the Jordanians are receiving U.S. assistance.

Perhaps most important to all contributing militaries, whether from rich or poor countries, is the invaluable overseas experience that peacekeeping operations provide them in peacetime and the training and contacts with other military forces that may ensue. Some military establishments may not, however, favour excessive involvement in peacekeeping, either in general or in relation to particular missions. Many will take the view of the Australian military, which is that peacekeeping is a useful exercise, affording operational and training benefits, but that if over-emphasized it risks detracting from the nation's own defense needs.

In some cases it will not be the military (or only the military) that seeks a national role in peacekeeping but the foreign ministry, perhaps prodded by its mission to the U.N. in New York, in turn perhaps pressured by a U.N. Secretary-General and Secretariat desperately seeking contributors. The Secretary-General's attempts since 1993 to ensure the credibility of the new U.N. Standby Forces Arrangement by sending a military delegation to as many member states as possible to plead for and organize pledges of contributions may also have increased the number of actual participants in peacekeeping.

### Categories of new peacekeepers

Several categories of new peacekeepers are discernible. The first, perhaps surprisingly, comprises three of the five permanent members of the Security Council—China, Russia and the USA. All the five permanent members of the Security Council had largely forgone involvement during the cold war because of the danger that their rivalries would be injected into the very conflicts from which peacekeeping was designed to isolate them. France and the UK were partial exceptions. In contrast, China completely abjured participation in peacekeeping during the cold war, involving itself for the first time in 1989 in UNTAG. Since the end of the cold war both Russia and the USA have participated in several U.N. missions. Russia has even provided ground troops, as in UNPROFOR, and organized and taken the preponderant role in peacekeeping operations on its troubled periphery. The USA has dominated major non-U.N. (but U.N.-authorized) missions— UNITAF in Somalia and the MNF in Haiti. By 1995 it was also participating in a range of regular U.N. peacekeeping operations, including UNTSO, UNIKOM, MINURSO, UNPROFOR (in Croatia and Macedonia), UNMIH and UNOMIG. Its preference continues to be to provide support services rather than ground troops.

A second group of new peacekeepers comprises countries that were previously unacceptable because of their association with one of the cold war blocs or because of other political sensitivities: these include Bulgaria, Cuba, Israel, Romania, South Korea and Spain. A third group comprises the defeated World War II allies, called the 'enemy states' in the U.N. Charter. Germany and Japan, moving finally to assume all the rights and responsibilities of international citizenship, have begun incrementally to participate in peacekeeping. (Italy has participated in peacekeeping operations for some time, mostly by providing observers or air transport.) A fourth category of new peacekeepers includes newly independent states such as Estonia, Kyrgyzstan, Lithuania, Namibia and Ukraine, which never had the opportunity to participate before. A final group includes a wide variety of states which are participating for the first time simply because the current need for peacekeeping forces is so great. These include Brunei, Cape Verde, Costa Rica, Guyana, Luxembourg, Saudi Arabia, Singapore, Switzerland and Uganda. While their contributions may seem inconsequential compared to those of larger states, they broaden the support base for U.N. peacekeeping and the range of experience and capabilities available for future missions.

International organizations besides the U.N. are also becoming involved as new peace-keepers, as sponsors and organizers of peacekeeping missions, or at the very least as de-velopers of peacekeeping doctrine for missions to be employed in the future: these include the European Union (EU), the Organization for Security and Cooperation in Europe (OSCE), NATO, the North Atlantic Cooperation Council (NACC) and the CIS.

\* \* \*

The consequences of involvement in the new peacekeeping for states participating for the first time are immense. Political and constitutional complexities may delay, constrain or rule out their participation; the military or other personnel being offered may not be trained or equipped for peacekeeping; governments may not wish to accept U.N. com-mand and control of their forces; public opinion may not countenance casualties or tol-erate the subtleties, ambiguities and frustrations of peacekeeping; and, for a variety of reasons, the new peacekeepers on the ground may not shape up.

Lacking the experience and training of the 'old' peacekeepers, the newcomers have been thrown into the peacekeeping enterprise just as its boundaries have been widened, its content vastly expanded and some of its previous norms and assumptions called into question. In a sense all participants in the new peacekeeping are new peacekeepers since they are encountering a largely unfamiliar type of undertaking. The new peacekeepers have had to learn all the lessons of peacekeeping immediately. Since the traditional ethos of peacekeeping arguably remains the bedrock on which the new peacekeeping also op-erates this gives the old peacekeepers a decided advantage. This was most evident in So-malia, where unfamiliarity with or skepticism about the traditional approach to peacekeeping, particularly among U.S. personnel, was one of the factors which drew UN-OSOM II into peace enforcement operations for which it was not prepared. The report of the U.N. Commission of Enquiry into the débâcle in Mogadishu in 1993 recommended, as a consequence, that all future U.N. missions include experienced peacekeepers.

The new peacekeepers are, at least in theory, expected to carry out the same tasks as the more experienced. However, particular U.N. force commanders may assign new peacekeepers less demanding tasks, either at the request of their government, because of operational considerations or because it is known that the troops are unable to carry out more arduous assignments. The Japanese Self-Defense Forces (SDF) contingent in UNTAC, for instance, was not assigned to dangerous areas because of constitutional restrictions on its use of force in self-defense. This is not to imply that all the new peacekeepers are less capable as military forces than the old. Even the well-equipped and trained military of a highly developed country like Japan can flounder when con-fronted with the intricacies and subtleties of the new peacekeeping. In Cambodia Japanese troops reportedly experienced "initial confusion and a lengthy shakedown period."

\* \* \*

### In the field I: growing complexity and danger

Upon arrival in the field the new peacekeepers have had to face increasing complexity in conditions that test the mettle of even the best-trained troops and civilian personnel. Some of the complexity has been planned, the result of ambitious peace-building oper-ations as in El Salvador, Namibia and Cambodia. In other cases it evolved randomly and unexpectedly. In Bosnia and Herzegovina complexity came with deteriorating battlefield conditions, forcing ever more ingenious techniques on UNPROFOR to achieve delivery of humanitarian aid and inducing the Security Council to adopt over 100 resolutions and statements in its forlorn attempt to protect U.N. safe areas, dampen the conflict and achieve a lasting cease-fire and settlement. As U.N. Secretary-General Boutros Boutros-Ghali has noted, 'peacekeeping has to be reinvented every day'.

While not every post-cold war peacekeeping mission has included all of the following, the expanded repertoire of U.N. peacekeeping operations in 1993, for example, included: (a) election observation (Eritrea and Liberia) and organization (Cambodia); (b) humanitarian assistance and securing safe conditions for its delivery (Bosnia and Herzegovina, Somalia, Kurdish areas of Iraq); (c) observation and separation of combatants along a more or less demarcated boundary (Croatia, Kuwait-Iraq); (d) disarmament of military and paramilitary forces (Cambodia, Somalia and El Salvador); (e) promotion and protection of human rights (Cambodia and El Salvador); (f) mine clearance, training and mine awareness (Afghanistan and Cambodia); (g) military and police training (Cambodia and Haiti); (h) boundary demarcation (Kuwait-Iraq border); (i) civil administration (Cambodia); (j) provision of assistance to and repatriation of refugees (the former Yugoslavia, Cambodia and Somalia); (k) reconstruction and development (Cambodia and Somalia); and (l) maintenance of law and order (Cambodia and Somalia). Steven Ratner describes second generation U.N. missions as combining the three roles of administrator, mediator and guarantor.

Such complexity has troubled even experienced peacekeepers. As Canadian Major-General John MacInnis has noted, 'It is the aspect of complexity that poses challenges unthought of by peacekeepers only a few short years ago'. In traditional peacekeeping operations, the observation of a cease-fire line or other boundary was the principal purpose of the mission, towards which all other activities could be directed. In the multi-purpose missions of today not only may the peacekeeper be faced with several objectives, but some of them may be in conflict with each other. In Cambodia it was alleged by human rights groups that the pursuit of human rights violators was subordinated to the goal of holding an election. In Somalia the goal of a peaceful settlement was subordinated to the quest for justice against those responsible for killing U.N. troops.

Such complexity has been compounded by the failings of the U.N. in planning and managing peacekeeping operations, both at U.N. headquarters and in the field. The U.N. Secretariat was caught unprepared for the vast expansion in the number and complexity of new missions since 1989. The ad hoc, amateurish, almost casual methods of the past simply could not keep pace, resulting in disorganization, mismanagement and waste. While such characteristics had always been present to some extent in U.N. operations, the scale and complexity of the new missions magnified the consequences. In simple border patrol operations where there was a peace to keep, it mattered little if administration was lax and late. In operations where the U.N. itself was running elections, overseeing governmental functions and protecting human rights it mattered a great deal. The new peacekeepers were thus thrown on to their own resources in ways undreamed of in the old peacekeeping.

An arduous new role in which peacekeepers have become involved for the first time is the delivery of humanitarian aid and the management of huge refugee movements—sometimes in the midst of continuing armed conflict in which civilian populations themselves have become targets of the fighting. As a British colonel with extensive experience in Bosnia and Herzegovina has noted: 'It wasn't a task the British Army had done before … we were effectively sitting in the middle of somebody else's war' while trying to ensure the delivery of humanitarian aid. While at home military forces are often called upon to assist national authorities in disaster relief, few forces have the experience or training to handle the sheer volume of humanitarian relief supplies to millions of starving people during a civil conflict, as in Somalia, or the mass movement of terrified refugees, as in Rwanda, Croatia and Bosnia and Herzegovina. In some cases, as in Bosnia and Herzegovina, civilians may be hostile to the presence of the peacekeepers, or alternatively, so dependent on them as to threaten to use obstructionist tactics or violence against them if they attempt to depart. Although the best militaries are well disciplined, organized and resourceful, few of the new peacekeepers will have the flexibility and sensitivity (not to mention training and equipment) for handling in a foreign environment such delicate situations as crowd control or inter-communal violence. While atrocities do occur in war, few military personnel are likely to be well prepared for witnessing, as impartial by-standers, massive human rights violations such as massacres of innocent civilians or for the accompanying sense of helplessness at being unable to do anything to stop them.

Complexity is also introduced into the new peacekeeping by the multinational nature of the mission. UNTAC, the most international of any mission to date, along with its advance mission, UNAMIC, involved 34 nationalities among its military contingents and 32 among its civilian police. UNTAC's personnel in total were drawn from over 100 countries. UNIFIL, in contrast, in all its 17 years had no more than 14 participating countries, most of which were experienced old peacekeepers. New peacekeeping operations are therefore faced with multiple problems arising from a greater mix of capability, procedure, equipment, language, custom and ethos.

While in its older peacekeeping operations the U.N. could afford to be more selective in securing a judicious mix of capabilities and nationalities, today, when peacekeepers are in short supply for particular missions, there can be little choice but for the U.N. to accept whatever is offered. This has brought with it an inevitable lowering of standards. Sometimes the U.N. has been forced knowingly to accept contingents which were far from optimal in their training, experience or equipment. As the Secretary-General himself has lamented, 'You have to accept second-best and if not second-best you have to accept third-best' in the new peacekeeping. In some cases corruption, human rights violations and loutish behaviour have distinguished such forces, rather than their contribution to peace. The deployment of such troops necessitates greater ability and adaptability on the part of each component and national contingent and heightened diplomatic skills on the part of the head of mission and the force commander. An added complication is that U.N. commanders do not have disciplinary authority over the foreign forces under their command and must rely on the goodwill of each contingent commander to enforce discipline.

The Secretary-General has also been obliged to accept contributions from the great powers and from states which have a direct interest in the outcome of the conflict, which was not the case in most missions during the old era of peacekeeping. This is most notable in the former Yugoslavia, where Germany, Russia, Turkey, the USA and Muslim states such as Malaysia have biases towards or against parties to the conflict. Such older missions as UNIFIL and UNFICYP involved former colonial powers with at least a residual interest in the conflict, France and Britain respectively, but their presence was less problematic since they were acceptable to all the parties concerned and provided the U.N. with indispensable local knowledge and specialized capabilities. Today the involvement of the permanent members of the Security Council raises the profile of most missions, increases their political sensitivity, encourages greater press attention and heightens expectations—perhaps offsetting the advantages of greater force capability, stronger political backing and heightened prestige.

A further complication in the new peacekeeping is a diminution of what Sashi Tharoor calls its 'United Nations-ness'. Whereas peacekeeping missions during the cold war era were exclusively U.N. affairs, today the U.N. must share responsibilities in the field with regional organizations, as in Georgia where the CIS and OSCE are also operating, or, more problematically with a military alliance, as in the former Yugoslavia. The complexity of the 'dual-key' system for deciding when to use NATO air power in Bosnia and Herzegovina in furtherance of U.N. objectives was unprecedented in the history of U.N. peacekeeping. Similarly complex are arrangements in which the U.N. hands over authority and jurisdiction to a non-U.N. multilateral force, as in Somalia when UNOSOM I gave way to UNITAF, or when it takes over authority and jurisdiction from such a force, as at the end of UNITAF's mission and subsequently in Haiti. In the case of Iraq, UNIKOM was required to cooperate with and establish a peacekeeping operation on the border of a state which had been defeated in war by a U.N.-authorized coalition force. The new peacekeepers are thus required to coexist and cooperate with other entities in ways unheard of in the old peacekeeping—where the U.N. was usually the only player and perceived as benign by all sides.

Complexity is also introduced by the increasing civilianization of peacekeeping. There has been a civilian element in some traditional U.N. operations but they were present to administer operations rather than to participate in them. Since the end of the cold war there have been several U.N. operations with large civilian components which have played an integral role in the peacekeeping mission and have sometimes been its *raison d'être*. This is true of the missions in Angola, Cambodia, El Salvador, Mozambique, Namibia, Somalia and Western Sahara. The addition of such substantial civilian components has deemphasized the military character of peacekeeping, rendering the military component just one among many. Paradoxically it has also increased the range of tasks the military is called upon to perform, especially cooperative activities with civilian components, such as protection of and assistance with electoral activities. UNTAC was the epitome of this trend. It had seven components, only one of which was military. Other components had equally important roles and employed thousands of people. Alone, the Electoral Component's 62,000 employees, both local and international staff, dwarfed the military presence and a 3600-strong Civilian Police Component was also present. In addition there were several U.N. agencies such as the U.N. Development Programme (UNDP) or the U.N. High Commissioner for Refugees (UNHCR) and other foreign non-governmental organizations dealing with aid or human rights issues interacted with UNTAC. The local and international presses were ubiquitous and influential, comprising yet another civilian element with which the new peacekeepers must increasingly deal.

Finally, complexity is increased because of the nature of the intrastate conflicts in which peacekeepers find themselves. Such conflicts usually involve multiple parties, the territory held by each party may be unclear and subject to rapid change, rogue elements within factions may adopt independent positions and take independent action and outside states may be involved in supporting one side or other. Civil wars are often literally life or death struggles in which the alternative to total control of state power is political or physical oblivion. The forces involved are also often better armed than in the past and small ragtag armies may have more firepower than that available to the peacekeepers, even those from developed countries.

All these considerations make the new peacekeeping not only more complex but considerably more dangerous than the old. U.N. military casualties rose tenfold between 1991 and 1994, although the number of personnel deployed increased only eightfold. Of the 33 fatalities between January 1992 and December 1993, '16 were killed in areas where no government authorities existed de facto or where such authorities were unable to maintain order and hence to discharge their responsibilities by protecting persons within their jurisdiction ... 29 suffered from gunshot wounds, and there are grounds to believe that at least 6 were deliberately executed'. In 1993 there were 11 fatalities among civilian peace-keeping staff.

One consequence of these trends is an increase in 'the normal tendency of contin-gents to seek guidance from their own capitals'. This was seen at its worst in Somalia, where the Italians most famously, but also other contingents, sought instructions from home and then refused to act in accordance with the U.N. commander's directives. As experienced peacekeepers the Italians should have known better and their contingent commander was withdrawn at U.N. request. As Iqbal Riza notes, 'The anxieties of troop contributing countries for the safety of their troops are fully understandable, but it is evident that interference in operations only increases the danger to the personnel of the operation as a whole'. In Cambodia Japanese Government concern over retaining tight control of its troops meant that every task, request or order had to be referred to Tokyo for clearance.

A further consequence is disaffection at home with the peacekeeping mission, par-ticularly in these days of rapid communication and saturation television coverage. Fa-talities among the peacekeepers can trigger demands for withdrawal, debate about the nature of peacekeeping and calls for accountability. The reaction to the deaths of several Belgians in Rwanda was a case in point. Although Bulgarian opinion and the Bulgarian Parliament had been unanimous in supporting the dispatch of troops to Cambodia, the deaths of several of them brought strong pressure for their withdrawal. Actual with-drawal is rare but does happen. New peacekeepers Tanzania and Uganda have withdrawn from ECOMOG in Liberia. The best known withdrawal was that of the USA, followed by most of its Western allies, from Somalia after the killing of several of its troops in 1993 in Mogadishu.

A third consequence of the testing new environment is that it shows up more starkly the differences in the capabilities of different contingents. The better-equipped and trained troops, usually from Western states, are better able to defend themselves and to carry out other aspects of the new peacekeeping, whereas the less capable are both more vulnerable and less self-reliant. This mattered less in the less taxing environ-ment of the old peacekeeping but in the new peace-keeping it can strain relations be-tween contingents, jeopardize the integrity of the force and even imperil aspects of the mission.

### In the field II: challenges to traditional peacekeeping norms

Among the challenges that the new peacekeepers must cope with in second-generation missions are those that stretch to the limit the traditional peacekeeping norms relating to consent, impartiality and the use of force.

*Consent of the parties*

Consent may be shaky at the outset of a peacekeeping mission, perhaps because the parties have been inveigled against their will into a peace process or into agreeing to a U.N. presence, or it may degrade during a mission either because of the activities of the mission or because of factors beyond its control. In the worst case this leads to orga-nized violence against peacekeepers. No U.N. peacekeeping deployment has yet been greeted with armed force (although the original deployment of UNMIH to Haiti sailed away after local thugs brandished weapons at them from the quay) or had to fight its way out (although fire was exchanged with Somalis during the withdrawal of UNO-SOM II). During their deployment, however, many of the post cold war peacekeeping operations have come under fire from one or more of the local belligerents. This can restrict forces' movements, complicate their tasks, especially those of the more vulnerable civilian components, and give the U.N. presence a garrison appearance and mentality. Such an environment may undermine the morale of the mission and trigger calls for its withdrawal.

The principal challenge for peacekeepers in these circumstances is to attempt to establish or re-establish credibility and trust. The first requirement is to engage in persistent and painstaking negotiation with the parties. Since consent is weak, all manner of matters, from humanitarian aid convoy routes to the location of U.N. observer posts, must be negotiated and in many instances repeatedly renegotiated. The new peacekeepers also need to engage much more actively in so-called 'hearts and minds' campaigns to win over the civilian population and in 'civil information' campaigns designed to explain their presence. Lieutenant-General John Sanderson, the UNTAC force commander, claims that the success of his mission was due to its ability to 'forge an alliance' with the Cambodian people against those parties seeking to undermine the peace process and hence to conduct a free and fair election and democratic transfer of power.

In circumstances of doubtful or eroding consent the military component also needs to be better trained and equipped to defend itself and its mission (including the usually substantial civilian presence) and be at a higher stage of readiness and alert than in a situation of assured consent. The standard of such elements as communications and command and control also needs to be higher. U.N. command and control arrangements have traditionally been complicated by language problems, incompatible equipment and procedures, the lack of common training and staff structures and the need for geographical balance among participating states. They also suffer from multiple chains of command both in the theatre and between the military and civilian sides of the U.N..

An enhanced military capability may, depending on circumstances and the local culture, afford peacekeepers more authority and prestige. As Colonel Alistair Duncan has noted of Bosnia and Herzegovina: 'Very sadly the rule of the gun is what matters ... the man with the AK-47 is a big man. I had clout because with 56 Warriors [a tracked infantry combat vehicle] I was considered to be the most powerful man in Central Bosnia'. New peacekeepers from poorer, developing states will be more vulnerable in such situations unless provided with adequate protective equipment.

The most feared scenario is a complete loss of consent. This is most likely to occur after the U.N. has attempted punitive or retaliatory action against one of the parties as a result of non-cooperation or violation of agreements or international law. Following the NATO bombing of Bosnian Serb ammunition dumps near Pale in June 1995, after the Serbs refused to return heavy weapons seized from U.N. collection points, the Bosnian Serb leadership declared that all agreements with the U.N. were null and void, thereby explicitly withdrawing consent for the presence and activities of UNPROFOR. This was followed by the taking hostage of hundreds of UNPROFOR observers and troops. Such situations clearly place a peacekeeping mission in an impossible situation: with consent withdrawn the very vulnerability that is a condition of peacekeeping forces' succeeding permits their capture and use as political pawns.

When consent breaks down altogether the stark choices for the peacekeepers are then to withdraw, soldier on or convert to peace enforcement. While the transition from consent-based peacekeeping to consent-less peace enforcement is difficult, it is not impossible, as demonstrated by UNPROFOR in August 1995. It must, however, be well planned, be deliberate (rather than the result of 'mission creep') and be accompanied by the necessary changes in capability, mandate and commitment of force.

*Impartiality*

A second key tenet of traditional peacekeeping under challenge is the maintenance of an impartial, non-discriminatory stance towards all the parties to a conflict. Abandonment of impartiality, whether deliberate or inadvertent, runs the risk of turning the peacekeeping force into an enemy of one or more of the parties. Safeguarding the impartiality of the mission will be a constant preoccupation in situations where consent is fragile and will require some fine judgment on the part of the mission commander. A traditional U.N. border monitoring operation can proceed with its duties relatively unaffected by internal instability within a state, but a peacekeeping force in the midst of an intra-state conflict is invariably caught up in events and may through its actions pivotally affect their outcome. For instance, if only one party is breaking a cease-fire, impartiality is virtually impossible because U.N. forces may have to adopt defensive measures to protect themselves against that party. Even though a warring party has brought discrimination on itself it will accuse the U.N. of bias. The preferred situation may be that in Cambodia, where all parties accused the U.N. of partiality.

For the new peacekeepers the implications of the doctrine of impartiality include a need for greater care, awareness and sophistication in dealing with the parties. The new peacekeepers' roles of administrator, arbitrator and enforcer as well as keeper of the peace require special training in diplomacy, conflict resolution, mediation and other functions, which is not normally imparted to military personnel or even most civilian personnel recruited to U.N. missions.

*Use of force*

One of the main bones of contention between the old and new peacekeepers has been their differing attitudes to the use of military force. Traditionalists favoured persisting with the 'Scandinavian model' of strict adherence to the tried and true principles of peacekeeping, patient persuasion and negotiation and the minimum use of force, even in self-defense. Britain, relatively new to peacekeeping, recommended a 'wider peacekeeping' that was more robust but which basically retained the traditional peacekeeping ethos and practices. Some of the new peacekeepers, most notably the USA, supported by France, and even developing states like Malaysia on various occasions advocated greater use of force.

Greater use of force runs the risk of transforming a U.N. mission from peacekeeping to peace enforcement, either suddenly or through mission creep. As well as being dangerous to the forces on the ground, such a development is also fundamentally unfair to those nations which have contributed in good faith to what they supposed was a peacekeeping mission, and especially unfair to smaller contributors which usually have no say in such transformations unless they happen to be non-permanent members of the Security Council at the time. The withdrawal of their contingents may be not only politically embarrassing to effect but also physically impossible without the assistance of more powerful states. The fate of the Bangladeshi contingent trapped in Bihac in early 1995 is one example. Not only were they poorly equipped to defend themselves, being armed only with rifles, but they had not anticipated being in a situation of virtual all-out war in which withdrawal was impossible. In Somalia an even worse situation occurred when the Western states largely abandoned the U.N. mission to the non-Western contingents such as Egypt, India, Pakistan and Zimbabwe. While some of the contingents left behind were experienced old peacekeepers, the spectacle of the more technologically sophisticated and militarily capable states forsaking the mission after having led it into peace enforcement did nothing to promote enthusiasm for the new peacekeeping and made it more difficult to recruit contributors for future missions such as that in Rwanda.

After the Somalia débâcle a consensus appeared to emerge among the U.N., major troop contributors like the UK and the USA and new and old peacekeepers alike that, apart from self-defense or defense of the mission, military force can only be used for enforcement purposes, if at all, at a low tactical level, if a peacekeeping mission is not to be fatally jeopardized. It is now recognized that peace enforcement operations require a vastly different array of forces, command and control arrangements, military doctrine and political underpinning. The U.S. Army's field manual on peace operations now advises that:

> The proper use of force is critical in a peace operation. The use of force to attain a short-term tactical success could lead to a long-term strategic failure. The use of force may affect other aspects of the operation. The use of force may attract a response in kind, heighten tension, polarize public opinion against the operation and participants, foreclose negotiating opportunities, prejudice the perceived impartiality of the peace operation force, and escalate the overall level of violence ... In [peacekeeping], commanders should regard the use of force as a last resort.

The U.N. Commission of Enquiry into the events in Mogadishu recommended that the U.N. 'refrain from undertaking further peace enforcement actions within the internal conflicts of states', but that if peace enforcement was nevertheless undertaken the mandate of the force 'should be limited to specific objectives and the use of force should be applied as the ultimate means after all peaceful remedies have been exhausted'. Increased use of preventive diplomacy, peace building and emergency assistance was recommended.

UNPROFOR's at times surreal relationship with all the warring parties in the former Yugoslavia combined an enforcement role (with the assistance of NATO) with consent-based humanitarian activities, a mix that ultimately proved untenable. It produced a confusing operational environment for the new peacekeepers, where consent was present one day and not the next, in one situation and not another. However, the handling of the joint NATO/UNPROFOR peace enforcement bombing campaign against the Bosnian Serbs in August 1995, preceded by the deployment of a well-equipped Rapid Reaction Force and the withdrawal of peacekeepers to safe positions, indicated that the lessons of Somalia had been belatedly learned.

Even if the new peacekeepers avoid being drawn into peace enforcement, the chances of them being required to use force, if only in self-defense and defense of their mission, are higher than they were in the old peacekeeping.

Even when force is strictly limited to self-defense and not extended to the defense of the mission there may be ambiguities. Rules of engagement (ROEs) may lack detail, change over time or vary between national contingents. For instance, the right to self-defense may or may not, in the interpretation of a particular commander, include the right to a pre-emptive attack if peacekeepers believe a strike against them is imminent. In Cambodia, for example, the Dutch and French battalions were using completely different ROEs from those of the Bangladeshis, Bulgarians and Indonesians. This runs the risk of factional forces playing off one battalion against another, taking advantage of the less robust. A similar problem occurred in Somalia, where the Italians were much more willing than U.S. forces to negotiate rather than respond aggressively to provocation. Even the best ROEs will not cover all situations.

The peacekeeper's right to protect the peace process is also ambiguous and potentially open-ended. In regard to Rwanda it was argued by some that UNAMIR's forces should have positioned themselves between the Hutu killers and their victims and that any use of force which resulted could have been justified on the grounds of 'defending the mission'. Others regard the protection of populations in danger as going beyond protecting the mission unless specified in the mission mandate.

## Authors' Note

**The Scope of Self-Defense in the U.N. Charter Mandate:** A Chapter VI operation is assumed to be limited to self-defense, as it may use force beyond this only with the consent of the parties. In contrast, a Chapter VII operation may be authorized to use force beyond self-defense for enforcement purposes. The essential problem with the U.N. Charter in relation to the use of force by U.N. peacekeepers is that neither peacekeeping itself nor the problems which have attended its evolution were foreseen when it was drafted. The use of force in self-defense can only be a short-term palliative to a loss of consent and indeed may cause consent to deteriorate even faster. Lightly armed U.N. peacekeepers have thus traditionally stood no chance of deterring in a military sense. After 1973, the self-defense rule was expanded to encompass 'defense of the mission.' Although force can be strictly limited to self-defense, there might be ambiguities left: the rules of engagement are not detailed enough, change over time, or vary between national contingents. Importantly, the right to self-defense is in the interpretation of a particular commander and includes the right to a preemptive attack if peacekeepers believe a strike against them is imminent. The protection of the delivery of humanitarian aid established good civil-military information sharing systems with the Office of the Coordinator for Humanitarian Affairs (OCHA). The division of labor and working relationships between the new civilian components of the mission were not well established or negotiated with their non-mission counterparts such as UNHCR, UNICEF, and the numerous NGOs involved in protection tasks. Coordination mechanisms were slow to develop.

General Sir Michael Rose insisted that the U.N. Protection Force (UNPROFOR) in Bosnia should never "cross the Mogadishu line." When the Bosnian Serbs attacked U.N. "safe areas," Rose was reluctant to call on NATO air power. He did not want the U.N. to become a combatant, as it had in Somalia, where peacekeepers crossing the "Mogadishu Line" became party to the conflict during the U.S.-led intervention of the early 1990s. Back in 1994, the U.S. retreated from peacekeeping in Africa after 18 of its troops were killed in Somalia. An even bigger impact had the 'Mogadishu line' on Rwanda when the Clinton administration refused to intervene to stop the Rwandan genocide, not least because of the Somalia experience. The following excerpt from McCoubrey and White's *Blue Helmets* highlights the practical as well as conceptual problems that arise in quasi-enforcement peacekeeping such as the failed mission in Somalia.

## 4. Hilaire McCoubrey and Nigel White, The Blue Helmets: Legal Regulation of United Nations Military Operations

[footnotes omitted by editors]

### Quasi-enforcement in Intractable Conflicts

In the cases of Haiti and Rwanda, the emplacement of a consensual peacekeeping force was not sufficient for the achievement of a peaceful solution to the situation. As a result the Security Council additionally authorized the use of force by the United States and France in 1994 in an attempt to enforce a peaceful solution.

The recent conflicts in Haiti and Rwanda illustrate how the U.N. will sometimes replace or supplement ineffective peacekeeping operations, whose limited mandate proves inadequate for the task, with a U.N.-authorized enforcement operation. This technique whereby a U.N. peacekeeping force is replaced by a U.N.-authorized, but not a U.N.-commanded military operation, usually under the control of one state, seems to have been preferred to the re-mandating of a U.N. peacekeeping force into a U.N. enforcement action, as occurred in the Congo. It may be because the U.N. wishes to keep its peacekeeping and enforcement actions entirely separate, or it may be that the states wishing to contribute to an enforcement action do not want it to be under the control of the U.N.. This has certainly influenced the thinking of the United States, which is willing to receive U.N. authorization for its military actions, but is not willing to have them placed under the command and control of the U.N..

The Dayton Peace Accords on Bosnia signed by the leaders of Croatia, Serbia and Bosnia in November 1995 have led to the U.N. Security Council authorizing the replacement of the U.N. Protection Force (UNPROFOR) with a U.N.-authorized NATO-led operation in the form of a 60,000 strong, heavily armed, implementation force (IFOR), whose task is to enforce the peace agreement if the parties in Bosnia, as they so often have done, renege on the peace agreement.

* * *

The U.N. is much more willing to cross the threshold from peace enforcement after the end of the Cold War, simply because not so many or so great political restraints on the use of military force by the Security Council. The end of the Cold War has witnessed a great explosion in U.N. enforcement activity, both in the form of mandatory economic sanctions and in the form of military measures. However, this does not signify that the Council will authorize military force whenever it is faced with an apparently intractable situation. Although the U.N. was eventually successful in the Congo in the 1960s, the conflict nearly brought the Organization to its knees. The caution with which the U.N. approached the situation in the former Yugoslavia was in part due to its more recent failed experiment in forcible peacekeeping in Somalia.

The overthrow of the regime of Siad Barre in January 1991 signified a further deterioration in the civil war and anarchy in Somalia. The Security Council somewhat belatedly acted to try to combat the conflict which was exacerbating the famine in the drought-stricken country. It imposed a mandatory arms embargo and demanded that the various armed factions within the country observe a cease-fire. A cease-fire in Mogadishu was agreed by the two main warring factions on 3 March 1992, with provision for a small number of U.N. military observers (about 40) to monitor the cessation in hostilities. The leaders also agreed to develop a plan for the unimpeded delivery of humanitarian aid. However, the clans fell back into internecine conflict and the growing U.N. Operation in Somalia (UNOSOM), despite belligerent-sounding Security Council resolutions, became increasingly ineffective in helping to transport food to help feed the starving people.

In these desperate circumstances, the Security Council resorted to Chapter VII of the U.N. Charter in December 1992 and authorized a willing United States to lead a military operation "to use all necessary means to establish as soon as possible a secure environment for humanitarian relief operations in Somalia. The resolution contained very little concerning the command and control of the force, indeed it implicitly left it to the United

States by authorizing the Secretary-General and the Member states concerned to make the necessary arrangements for the unified command and control of the forces involved," which will reflect the United States' offer, although it did request the establishment of mechanism for coordination and liaison between UNOSOM and the new force which was later known as the Unified Task Force (UNITAF). UNOSOM was to be expanded up to 3,500 at the Secretary-General's discretion, but it was anticipated that it would be expanded so that it could eventually replace UNITAF. The resolution did not mention a time frame nor specific tasks for UNITAF beyond the establishment of a "secure environment for humanitarian relief operations in Somalia." The resolution ended by simply inviting the Secretary-General to continue his peaceful efforts to achieve a political settlement in Somalia.

Under the initial phase of "Operation Restore Hope," UNITAF was composed of 28,000 U.S. personnel, later to be supplemented by 17,000 personnel from 20 other states. As a result of their operations, food distribution had started to improve dramatically by January 1993. In his report, the Secretary-General suggested that UNITAF should also be neutralizing the heavy weapons of the various factions and inducing them to give up their small arms and begin the task of clearing mines. 70 This move beyond the essentially defensive protection of humanitarian aid convoys towards offensive action against the belligerents proved to be the downfall of UNITAF.

UNITAF adopted a fairly aggressive stance towards disarming the various factions in the country and in opening up humanitarian aid routes. It was not afraid to use substantial force beyond that required for self-defense. This tended to exacerbate the situation but was a policy continued by UNOSOM 11 when it replaced UNITAF in May 1993. Its failure resulted in UNOSOM II's withdrawal from Somalia in March 1995.

Although the use of force in Somalia was not of the same order as that used under U.N. authorization in the Gulf against Iraq in 1991, the level of force authorized and used by UNITAF and UNOSOM II goes well beyond that allowed for traditional peacekeeping operations, even those in dangerous intrastate conflicts such as UNIFIL in Lebanon. The new type of force, combining peacekeeping with enforcement where necessary, was envisaged by the Secretary-General in his report entitled Agenda for Peace adopted pursuant to the Summit Meeting of the Security Council on 31 January 1992, in which he proposed the establishment of peace enforcement units to be used in cases where a cease-fire has been agreed to but not yet complied with by the belligerents. The limited aim of these forces would be to secure a cease-fire, by the use of force if necessary. They would not be full enforcement measures under articles 42 and 43 designed to meet and repulse outright aggression such as committed by Iraq against Kuwait, nor would they be peacekeeping forces depending upon the consent and cooperation of the parties concerned, at least not initially. However, as the U.N. experience in the Congo shows, the enforcement of provisional measures can amount to the virtual imposition of a settlement on a country, or at least to the creation of conditions under which a settlement can emerge.

With the U.N. action in Somalia a relative failure (although mass starvation was temporarily averted) and its NATO-authorized operation in Bosnia hanging in the balance, all that can be said is that the development of a flexible peacekeeping/enforcement concept appears to be a dangerous step taken by the newly revitalized Security Council in that it clearly destroys the distinction between peacekeeping and enforcement which not only endangers genuine peacekeeping operations around the world but also the confidence of states or parties in requesting such forces simply because the U.N., in its peacekeeping role, is no longer seen as neutral, impartial and noninterventionist. However, it may be that such a risk has to be taken given the evidence that the integrated pacific approach to peacekeeping has not yet proved as successful as had been hoped, while the traditional approach to peacekeeping appears to involve far too long-term a commitment for the Security Council and troops contributors to tolerate any longer. It appears a strange paradox that at the time when peacekeeping appears so important, even fundamental to the world order, it has reached a crisis point. The next few years will dictate the future shape and perhaps even the continued existence of peacekeeping in an increasingly violent world.

## Authors' Note

**The Challenges of Peacebuilding:** Quasi enforcement peacekeeping operations are not the only type of peacekeeping fraught with challenges. The second generation of peacekeeping operations, deployed in post-conflict situations, is confronted with the many complexities that arise in state building. While fighting may be over, peacekeepers have been asked on a number of occasions to undertake missions of a more civilian nature, such as setting up and overseeing elections, strengthening institutions, supporting international administration, or assisting international tribunals. In the following excerpt, Doyle and Sambanis address the challenges that U.N. peacekeeping troops face in a post-conflict environment. They propose a seven-step plan to overcome the current constraints.

## 5. Michael W. Doyle and Nicholas Sambanis, Conclusions
### Making War and Building Peace, 2006

### A Seven-Step Plan

Given these general constraints and opportunities for success, let us explore difficult lessons about how to sequence the management of peacebuilding that emerge from our case studies and data analysis. The lessons of every case are different, but to understand those differences we need systematic comparisons that explore how they differ on comparable dimensions.

We should begin by recalling that successful peacebuilding is a counterrevolutionary or revolutionary event. A civil war revolutionizes the polity, society, economy, and culture. Civil wars, obviously, break up sovereignty and then sometimes create ferocious hierarchies in factions. Warriors, sometimes criminals, replace civil elites. Economies become geared to military production or looting. Hatred shapes interethnic or factional identity.

To create a self-sustaining peace, peacebuilding has to reverse all that. It must either divide a country, recognize a secession, and help establish two legitimate polities or establish a single legitimate polity. If there is no clear winner to the civil war or if international assistance from the West or the U.N. is going to be called upon, the polity will need to be participatory enough that factions previously at war become political parties that live with each other. Economies must be reoriented to civilian production and provide jobs for demobilized soldiers, and new terms of respect among diverse ethnic groups must be found. This last can often be done by punishing the perpetrators of the many abuses that civil wars inflict on innocent civilians in order that these communities can remove them from power and isolate the abusers, convincing each other that not everyone in the group was/is a war criminal and thereby helping to find the terms on which to live together as neighbors.

This is a revolutionary task that can be begun in two years, but will usually take a decade or more in some cases. The U.S. civil war took ten years—until the Compromise of 1876—to establish peace that allowed end of occupation, but then only on terms that were not sustainable in terms of American principles. We arrived at sustainable terms about a hundred years after the end of the war, with the victory of the civil rights movement. Cambodia has had its 1876 in two years (in 1990) with the U.N.-supervised elections; Bosnia is only now in "1873," considerably short of an "1876." Given the extent of the challenge of successful peacebuilding, getting the priorities right can make the difference between progress and stagnation. Staying the course is also important, as the sort of economic and political reconstruction that was necessary in Cambodia and Bosnia takes time. Peacebuilding operations with a sufficiently long horizon can help build peace.

The first step is security. A secure environment is the sine qua non of the beginning of peace. It precedes new courts, human rights, property laws, democracy, and so forth. There must be a new sovereign Leviathan, to borrow Thomas Hobbes's famous label for the state's legitimate monopoly of violence, in order to deter future acts of war and looting. If it is not available domestically, enforcement must be provided internationally.

* * *

Security is what allows people to begin to reconstruct the rest of their lives. It is the first step to building a state. The looting in Iraq immediately after the fall of Saddam Hussein's regime was costly not merely in material terms—it was if the United States indiscriminately bombed the country—it also signaled to the Fundamentalists, Baathists, and others that no one was in charge and that power was still up for grabs. In 2004, there were about 162,000 coalition troops in Iraq (150,000 U.S.). If Iraq had been as occupied (per capita) as Kosovo was, 500,000 would have been there. The gap was large and significant. A heavy entry is the first step to a faster exit.

Second, regional security must complement national security. It really helps if the international neighbors will stop intervening in order to allow the peace to proceed at home. A key achievement of the Cambodian peace was ensuring that China, Russia, Vietnam, the United States, and the Europeans were no longer supporting and financing rival armies. The U.N. can help, not least by mobilizing support through the "Friends" mechanism and ensuring regional cooperation with the peace process.

Third, quick "wins" will win support and time. Distributing food, medicine, turning the electricity back on, cleaning up the rubble: all send the message that a new order means a better life. It builds temporary support that is needed for longer term changes. But quick military wins need not translate into long political victories. The new polity will need more than security assistance, and enforcement missions alone will be unable to provide the foundations of a lasting peacebuilding process.

Fourth, the rule of law and constitutional consent are the foundations of all that follow. To build a legitimate state and to establish courts and police one needs locally and nationally legitimate delegations to decide the basic framework of rights and duties of citizens. In many respects a constitutional order should be designed to encourage both effective rule and to support moderate coalitions. Well-designed federal distributions of political authority, careful separations of power, judicial review, and parliamentary regimes—when tailored to local particularities—can be productive.

In a post-civil war situation, the consent often comes from a delicately negotiated peace treaty as in El Salvador and Cambodia that discovers the terms on which the factions are prepared to live with each other. In an international intervention, the "treaty" follows the imposed peace. If constitutional reform (or a new constitution) is necessary, it is key that a constituent assembly—a very broad group that can make credible claim to represent the major forces or elements of society—discusses and writes the framework of a constitution. How such delegates to a constitutional convention are selected and by whom is key. While the people (if one can have a "constitutional" agreement before the constitution) are best, an impartial international body is better at this than an international belligerent. A few weeks after the Taliban fell in the war in Afghanistan, the U.N. Special Representative Brahimi was already assembling the Bonn Conference at which these kinds of arrangements were developed for the political transition.

Fifth, not least among these rights that must be delimited is the right to property. This is a right the poor need even more than the rich. With ownership can come investment. As economists are wont to say "No one washes a renter car." Hernando de Soto has demonstrated that unless property is titled, it cannot be mortgaged and mortgage capital cannot be invested. The poor already have immense potential assets in their homes, businesses, and use of agricultural land. What they lack is a title to those assets that encourages investment and protects from extortion. With such ownership, then Smithian magic of the market can quickly come into play, and people will begin to earn themselves into sustainable livelihood. And the market can help diversify production beyond the natural resources such as oil and gems and logs that are the fuel of civil wars and corruption. Diversification of production and economic growth are the critical determinants of long-term war avoidance. With such growth in place, the U.N.'s task of rebuilding ailing polities will be easier and much more effective.

*  *  *

Sixth, democracy or wider participation is likely to be essential for longer run peace. Merely suppressing the other factions is difficult. But premature democracy is dangerous, and the transition process also carries new risks of renewed conflict. In the environment of intercommunal hostility that follows a civil war popular representation accurately represents antagonistic hostility. Overly delayed representation, on the other hand, will make the international peacebuilders into colonial oppressors. In Iraq, the U.S.-UK occupation could have been the precursor to an all-Iraqi Intifada, rather than a limited, if violent, insurgency, if the coalition had not effected a transition to an elected Iraqi transitional regime. It is with respect to this difficult but necessary transition that the U.N. can make a positive impact by marshaling both its legitimacy and its technical capacities and, by putting its lessons of experience to practice, help design the foundations of a stable participatory peace. Obviously a delicate balance is needed. In countries with the deepest political-ideological or ethnic rifts and legacies of very bloody civil wars, constitutional conventions and a legitimate transitional regime will buy time, and a U.N. mandate of transitional or executive authority may be the only viable option. Local village democracy takes time and is a necessary component of national democracy. The U.N. must plan for a national election that does not come too quickly. Elections must usually come after the institutional transformations that establish the foundations of the rule of law.

Seventh and last, genuine moral and psychological reconciliation comes after law and order is established, after the economy is again viable, after the trials of war criminals have taken place or the reports of reconciliation commissions [have] been made, and with the establishment of an education system in which all the children can be educated. In all countries, war stirs passions, and the more people have been affected (killed, displaced), the worse the postwar enmity and the more difficult will be the implementation of a peace settlement. Indeed, it is usually the next generation, if all goes well, that reconciles and establishes the beginnings of national or civic consciousness. Developing a common educational curriculum is immensely difficult. It still has not been achieved in the eastern part of Croatia or in Bosnia, where the teaching of history stops in 1990 and the pre-1990 history of the countries is being radically and incompatibly rewritten by each community.

The Seven Step plan need not be conducted in lockstep. Sometimes to achieve security factions will need to be assured and sometimes that assurance, as it was in El Salvador, will be promoted by establishing human rights monitoring (even before the war has ended) or starting reconstruction projects that employ demobilized soldiers and support former military commanders (as was done in Eastern Slavonia). But this list of priorities has an underlying logic. Skipping steps is costly, when, for example, due to lack of sovereign security, humanitarian and reconstruction projects merely fuel the rearmament of factions.

\* \* \*

## 6. Bibliography of Additional Sources

- Andreas Andersson, *Democracies and U.N. Peacekeeping Operations: 1990–1996*, 7 Int'l Peacekeeping 2 (2000).

- Séverine Autesserre, *Hobbes and the Congo: Frames, Local Violence, and International Intervention*, 63 Int'l Org. 249 (Spring 2009).

- Séverine Autesserre, The Trouble with the Congo: Local Violence and the Failure of International Peacebuilding (2010).

- Alex J. Bellamy, Paul D. Williams & Stuart Griffin, Understanding Peacekeeping (2010).

- Chris Bellamy, Knights in White Armour: The New Art of War and Peace (1997).

- Róisín Burke, *Status of Forces Deployed on U.N. Peacekeeping Operations: Jurisdictional Immunity*, 16 J. Conflict & Security L. 63 (2011).

- Michael Carnahan, Scott Gilmore & Monika Rahman, *Economic Impact of Peacekeeping: Interim Report Phase I*, U.N. Dep't Peacekeeping Ops. (2005).

- Robert M. Cassidy, Peacekeeping in the Abyss: British and American Peacekeeping Doctrine and Practice after the Cold War (2004).

- Jack Citrin, United Nations Peacekeeping Activities: A Case Study in Organizational Task Expansion (1965).

- Jocelyn Coulon, Soldiers of Diplomacy: The United Nations, Peacekeeping, and the New World Order (1998).

- Nicola Dahrendorf, *Sexual Exploitation and Abuse: Lessons Learned Study, Addressing Sexual Exploitation and Abuse in MONUC*, U.N. Peacekeeping (Mar. 2006).

- Francois Debrix, Re-envisioning Peacekeeping: The United Nations and the Mobilization of Ideology (1999).

- Paul F. Diehl, International Peacekeeping (1993).

- William J. Durch & Alison C. Giffin, *Challenges of Strengthening the Protection of Civilians in Multidimensional Peace Operations*, Apr. 8, 2010.

- William J. Durch et al., The Brahimi Report and the Future of U.N. Peace Operations (2003).

- Amy E. Eckert, *United Nations Peacekeeping in Collapsed States*, 5 J. Int'l L. & Prac. 273 (1996).

- Arvid Ekengard, *Coordination and Coherence in the Peace Operation in the Democratic Republic of Congo*, Swedish Defence Research Agency, Aug. 2009.

- The Evolution of U.N. Peacekeeping (William J. Durch ed., 1993).
- Larry Fabian, Soldiers Without Enemies: Preparing the United Nations for Peacekeeping (1971).
- B. Fetherston, Towards a Theory of United Nations Peacekeeping (1994).
- Frederick H. Fleitz, Peacekeeping Fiascoes of the 1990s: Causes Solutions and U.S. Interests (2002).
- Virginia Page Fortna, Does Peace Keeping Work? Shaping Belligerents' Choices After War (2008).
- Khusrav Gaibulloev, Todd Sandler & Hirofumi Shimizu, *Demands for U.N. and Non-U.N. Peacekeeping: Nonvoluntary versus Voluntary Contributions to a Public Good*, 53 J. Conflict Res. 827 (2009).
- David Gibbs, *Is Peacekeeping a New Form of Imperialism?*, 4 Int'l Peacekeeping 1 (1997).
- Michael J. Gilligan & Stephen J. Stedman, *Where Do the Peacekeepers Go?*, 5 Int'l Stud. Rev. 4 (2003).
- Stephen M.Hill & Shahin P. Malik, Peacekeeping and the United Nations (1996).
- Victoria Holt & Glyn Taylor, *Protecting Civilians in the Context of U.N. Peacekeeping Operations, Successes, Setbacks and Remaining Challenges*, Dep't Peacekeeping Ops. & Off. for Coordination Humanitarian Affs., Nov. 17, 2009.
- Victoria K. Holt & Tobias C. Berkman, The Impossible Mandate? Military Preparedness, the Responsibility to Protect and Modern Peace Operations (2006).
- Human Rights Watch, *Killings in Kiwanja: the U.N.'s Inability to Protect Civilians*, December 11, 2008.
- Dennis C. Jett, Why Peacekeeping Fails (1999).
- Bruce Jones, Richard Gowan & Jake Sherman, Building on Brahimi: Peacekeeping in an Era of Strategic Uncertainty (2009).
- Stian Kjeksrud & Jacob Aasland Ravndal, *Protection of Civilians in Practice — Emerging Lessons from the U.N. Mission in the DR Congo*, Norwegian Defence Res. Est., Dec. 15, 2010.
- Jean Krasno, Bradd C. Hayes & Donald C. Daniel, Leveraging For Success in United Nations Peace Operations (2003).
- Nicolas Lamp & Dana Trif, *United Nations Peacekeeping Forces and the Protection of Civilians in Armed Conflict* (Nov. 2009).
- Claudia Major, *EU-U.N. Cooperation in Military Crisis Management: The Experience of EUFOR RD Congo in 2006*, Inst. Sec. Stud. (Sept. 2008).
- Major Powers and Peacekeeping: Perspectives, Priorities and the Challenges of Military Intervention (Rachel E. Utley ed., 2006).
- Lise Morjé Howard, U.N. Peacekeeping in Civil Wars (2008).
- Emily Paddon, *Beyond Creed, Greed and Booty: Conflict in the Democratic Republic of Congo, Africa*, 80 J. Int'l Afr. Inst. 322 (2010).
- Peacekeeping and Conflict Resolution (Tom H. Woodhouse and Oliver Ramsbotham eds., 2001).

- Todd Sandler & Hirofumi Shimizu, *Peacekeeping and Burden-Sharing, 1994–2000*, 39.2 J. PEACE RES. 651 (2002).

- Danesh Sarooshi, THE UNITED NATIONS AND THE DEVELOPMENT OF COLLECTIVE SECURITY: THE DELEGATION BY THE U.N. SECURITY COUNCIL OF ITS CHAPTER VII POWERS (1999).

- Hurofumi Shimizu, *Peacekeeping and Burden-Sharing 1994–2000*, 39 J. PEACE RES. 6 (2002).

- James Sloan, *The Use of Offensive Force in U.N. Peacekeeping: A Cycle of Boom and Bust?*, 30 HASTINGS INT'L & COMP. L. REV. 385 (Spring 2007).

- Michael G. Smith, PEACEKEEPING IN EAST TIMOR: THE PATH TO INDEPENDENCE (2003).

- Astri Suhrke, *Peacekeepers as Nation-builders: Dilemmas of the U.N. in East Timor*, 8 INT'L PEACEKEEPING 4 (2001).

- Richard Synge, MOZAMBIQUE: U.N. PEACEKEEPING IN ACTION, 1992–94 (1997).

- John Terence O'Neill & Nicholas Rees, UNITED NATIONS PEACEKEEPING IN THE POST-COLD WAR ERA (2005).

- N.D. WHITE, KEEPING THE PEACE: THE UNITED NATIONS AND THE MAINTENANCE OF INTERNATIONAL PEACE AND SECURITY (1997).

- U.N. DEP'T PUB. INFO., UNITED NATIONS: 50 YEARS OF U.N. PEACEKEEPING (1998).

- U.N. DEPARTMENT OF PEACEKEEPING & DEPARTMENT OF FIELD SUPPORT, A NEW PARTNERSHIP AGENDA: CHARTING A NEW HORIZON FOR U.N. PEACEKEEPING (2009).

- U.N. PEACEKEEPING, AMERICAN POLICY, AND THE UNCIVIL WARS OF THE 1990S (William J. Durch ed., 1996).

- U.N. Secretary-General, *Global Field Support Strategy: Rep. of the Secretary-General*, U.N. Doc. A/64/633 (Jan. 26, 2010).

- U.N. Secretary-General, *Protection of Civilians in Armed Conflict: Rep. of the Secretary-General*, U.N. Doc. S/1999/957 (Sept. 8, 1999).

- U.N. Secretary-General, *Strengthening the Capacity of the United Nations to Manage and Sustain Peace Operations: Rep. of the Secretary-General*, U.N. Doc. A/61/858 (Apr. 13, 2007).

- UNITED NATIONS INTERVENTIONISM: 1991–2004 (Mats Berdal & Spyros Economides eds., 2007).

- Thierry Vircoulon, *After MONUC, Should MONUSCO Continue to Support Congolese Military Campaigns?*, INTERNATIONAL CRISIS GROUP, July 19, 2010.

- Valorie K.Vojdik, *Sexual Abuse and Exploitation of Women and Girls by U.N. Peacekeeping Troops*, 15 MICH. ST. J. INT'L L. 157 (2007).

- James Wall & Daniel Druckman, *Mediation in Peacekeeping Missions*, 47.5 J. CONFLICT RESOL. 693 (2003).

- Michael Wallace Nest & Emizet F. Kisangani, DEMOCRATIC REPUBLIC OF CONGO: ECONOMIC DIMENSIONS OF WAR AND PEACE (2005).

- Erin A. Weir, GREATER EXPECTATIONS: U.N. PEACEKEEPING & CIVILIAN PROTECTION (2009).

# Chapter XII

# International Organizations and the Use of Force

## Introduction

This chapter examines the role of international organizations in authorizing or legitimizing the use of force. There are several legal bases for the use of force, among them international treaties and conventions, customary international law, and the United Nations Charter. The U.N. Charter places a general prohibition on the use of force, subject only to exceptions in the Charter. One exception is Security Council authorization under Chapter VII, though states, regional organizations, and ad hoc coalitions of states have in the past resorted to force without explicit authorization. These actions have sparked considerable debate over the role of the United Nations in international armed conflict. Through the lens of the Gulf War in 1990, the Iraq War in 2003, and the NATO campaign in Libya in 2011, this chapter will examine the role of the United Nations in authorizing the use of force.

## Objectives

- To understand the role of United Nations Charter in authorizing the use of force in international conflicts.
- To understand the international legal framework for the use of force.
- To become familiar with the United Nations Charter and its role in limiting and authorizing a state's use of force.
- To gain a critical perspective on the debate between state sovereignty and intervention.
- To be able to critically analyze current and future conflicts vis-à-vis international organizations and their role in authorizing or limiting the use of force.

## Problems

Students should come to class prepared to discuss the following questions:

1. Was the use of force against Iraq in 1990 legal?
2. Was the use of force against Iraq in 2003 legal?

3. What were the legal consequences of the NATO-led intervention in Libya in 2011?

4. Does implied authorization to use force exist? Or, must it be explicit?

5. May a country or coalition of countries enforce Security Council resolutions without specific Security Council authorization to do so?

6. What elements or factors should be present before a State engages in the use of force? Who has the ultimate say in determining those factors or elements?

7. How effective is the framework created by the United Nations Charter in deterring or preventing the use of force?

8. What are states authorized to do in order to protect civilians under attack? What is the scope of that authority?

9. How does Security Council Resolution 1970, authorizing the use of force against the Qadhafi regime, compare to the Security Council's actions in the Gulf War and the Iraq War in 2003? Why is the phrase "including Benghazi" in article 4 significant?

10. Come to class prepared to participate in the following simulation of a case before the ICJ between Tangoon (Applicant) and Samutra (Respondent).

    Members of Group A will represent Tangoon.

    Members of Group B will represent Samutra.

    Members of Group C will role play the ICJ Panel.

# Case Studies and Negotiation Simulations

Case Concerning the October 2012 Typhoon
and the Samutran Use of Force
[Based on the 2011 Niagara Moot Court Competition
Problem written by Michael Scharf]

1. This case involves two States which are located on a single island about the size of Haiti and the Dominican Republic, located near the equator in the Pacific Ocean: the State of Tangoon (Applicant) to the west, and the Republic of Samutra (Respondent) to the east. Each is composed primarily of ethnic Tanmutrans, an ancient seafaring people who settled on the island over a thousand years ago and are adherents of the Tanmutra religion. The two States were once a single political entity but separated in 1960, when an ultra-orthodox Tanmutran religious faction seized control of the western part of the island, declared the creation of an independent State called Tangoon, and erected a twenty-foot high concrete wall dividing the island in two. With the exception of the negotiation of this Compromis, there have been no diplomatic relations between the two governments since the split. The current political and military leader of Tangoon is the Tanmutran High Priest, 57 year-old Ismail Omar, who has served as head of state for the past ten years.

2. In 1961 Tangoon was admitted into the United Nations, while Samutra retained the island country's original membership in the organization, dating back to 1946. Both states have accepted the compulsory jurisdiction of the International Court of Justice under Article 36(2) of the Court's Statute. While Samutra accepted the compulsory jurisdiction of the ICJ in 1946 without reservation, Tangoon's 1961 declaration accepting the ICJ's compulsory jurisdiction contained the following reservation: "This declaration shall not

apply to disputes arising under a multilateral treaty, unless all parties to the treaty affected by the decision are also parties to the case before the Court."

3. In addition, both States are party to the Genocide Convention, the International Covenant on Economic, Social and Cultural Rights, and the International Covenant on Civil and Political Rights. In 2003, Samutra became a party to the Rome Treaty establishing the International Criminal Court (ICC). Tangoon is not a party to the ICC Treaty.

4. Due to the efforts of its stable democratic and secular government, in the last twenty-five years Samutra has prospered as a world-class tourist destination, known for its fine sand beaches, spectacular reefs, abundant sports fishing, and ancient Tanmutran temples that resemble those at Ankgor Wat. With ample foreign investment and tourist dollars, the five million Tanmutran people of Samutra enjoy one of the highest standards of living and life expectancies in the world. The Samutra University School of Medicine is internationally renowned for its work in the control and eradication of tropical diseases. Samutra has a modern navy and a relatively large and well-equipped army, numbering 200,000 troops, which frequently participates in U.N. peacekeeping missions.

5. Tangoon, on the other hand, continues to be ruled by an ultra-orthodox religious regime which has isolated its population of two million from the outside world, including Samutra. Although the ruling religious elite live in lavish hill-top temple compounds and enjoy a high standard of living, the ordinary people of Tangoon are among the poorest and least healthy in the world.

6. On October 10–11, 2012, a massive "category 5" typhoon known as "Kodo" swept through the area of the Pacific Ocean where Samutra and Tangoon are located, battering the island with winds as strong as 160 mph, over 40 inches of rain, and waves as high as 30 feet. The government of Samutra had issued timely warnings and taken effective steps to protect its population from the storm, while the government of Tangoon did nothing to warn its civilian population of the imminent danger. According to the October 22, 2012 Report of the U.N. Secretary General, in the aftermath of the storm, most of the population of Tangoon was rendered homeless and without potable drinking water, and diseases were rapidly spreading, with thousands of unburied corpses present throughout the countryside.

7. At the urging of the U.N. Secretary-General, on October 14, 2012, the government of Samutra sent an emissary to Tangoon to offer immediate humanitarian assistance to its devastated population. The emissary was denied entry at the border-wall, and all subsequent attempts by Samutra to establish communications with the Tangoon government have been rebuffed.

8. On October 21, 2012, the government of Samutra requested an emergency session of the U.N. Security Council to address the crisis in Tangoon. After meeting late into the night, the Security Council adopted Resolution 1901 (October 23, 2012), which is appended at **Tab 1**.

9. Despite Resolution 1901, the government of Tangoon continued to refuse Samutra's assistance. Meanwhile, satellite photographs dated November 1, 2012, indicated that most of the people of Tangoon were still without shelter and that hundreds of thousands of corpses could be seen lying on the fields and floating on the lakes throughout the country.

10. On November 10, 2012, at the request of the ICC Prosecutor, the International Criminal Court issued an arrest warrant for Tangoon head of state Ismail Omar, charging him with crimes against humanity on the basis of Tangoon's decision to deny humanitarian aid in the aftermath of the typhoon to the civilian population of Tangoon, resulting in hundreds of thousands of deaths.

11. The next day, the United Kingom circulated a draft Security Council resolution which would have authorized Samutra "to use all necessary means to enter Tangoon and deliver vital humanitarian aid to its suffering people." China, however, indicated that it would veto the resolution if brought to a vote, and no further action was taken to push it forward.

12. A week later, on November 18, 2012, Samutra used its military to demolish several portions of the concrete wall separating the island, through which it sent convoys of aid trucks accompanied by armed troops into Tangoon in order to distribute food, clothing, medicine, and temporary shelters to the surviving Tangoon population. During the operation, the Samutran troops apprehended Ismail Omar and brought him back to Samutra where he now awaits extradition to the International Criminal Court. In a letter to the Security Council dated November 19, 2012, Samutra fully briefed the Council as to its actions. The Council has not subsequently taken any action in regard to this matter

13. On December 15, 2012, the State of Tangoon filed a complaint against the Republic of Samutra before the International Court of Justice, invoking the compulsory jurisdiction of the Court. The complaint alleged that Samutra violated Tangoon's territorial sovereignty under Article 2(4) of the U.N. Charter when the Samutran army broke through the security barrier and entered Tangoon's territory, employing deadly force against the Tangoon defense forces. The Complaint further alleges that Samutra violated international law when it abducted the Tangoon High Priest, and that the doctrine of head of state immunity precludes Samutra from subjecting Ismail Omar to extradition proceedings. The complaint requested 100 million dollars in compensation for the damages stemming from this breach of international law and the immediate repatriation of Ismail Omar.

14. In its reply, Samutra asserted that its actions were justified to protect it from the spread of disease from Tangoon's side of the island and were consistent with the "responsibility to protect" doctrine and therefore did not violate international law. Finally, Samutra asserted that the apprehension of Ismail Omar was permissible because the ICC had issued an international warrant for his arrest.

15. This *Compromis* was agreed to by the parties in an effort to frame the factual and legal issues before the Court. The Court has scheduled oral argument in this case for May 1, 2010.

United Nations

**Tab 1**

**United Nations
Security Council**
SC/1901

Department of Public Information • News and Media Division • New York

**Resolution 1901: The Situation in Tangoon**
Adopted by the Security Council at is 6232rd Meeting on 23 October 2012

*The Security Council,*

*Welcoming* the Report of the Secretary General on the situation in Tangoon, dated 22 October 2012,

*Recalling* its resolution 1674 of 28 April 28, 2006, reaffirming the responsibility to protect doctrine,

*Determining* that the situation in Tangoon constitutes a threat to international peace and security,

*Acting* under Chapter VII of the U.N. Charter,

1. *Expresses* its grave concern about the humanitarian catastrophe unfolding in Tangoon in the aftermath of Typhoon Kodo;

2. *Welcomes* Samutra's offers of humanitarian assistance and calls on the government of Tangoon to immediately accept and facilitate Samutra's aid before millions die;

3. *Warns* the government of Tangoon that denial of humanitarian aid in these circumstances could constitute an international crime triggering individual criminal responsibility, and that it will face serious consequences if it does not comply with this Resolution without delay;

4. *Decides* to refer the situation in Tangoon since 10 October 2012 to the Prosecutor of the International Criminal Court for investigation and possible prosecution, and urges all States, whether party or not to the Rome Statute to cooperate fully with the Court;

5. *Decides* to remain seized of this matter.

# Materials

1. U.N. Charter, art. 2.

2. U.N. Charter, arts. 39, 41–42, 48–49, 51.

3. S.C. Res. 678, U.N. Doc. S/RES/678 (Nov. 29, 1990).

4. President George H.W. Bush, Address on the Invasion of Iraq (Jan. 16, 1991).

5. S.C. Res. 687, U.N. Doc. S/RES/687 (Apr. 3, 1991).

6. President George W. Bush, Address on Iraq, (Oct. 7 2002).

7. S.C. Res. 1441, U.N. Doc. S/RES/1441 (Nov. 8, 2002).

8. Joint Declaration by Russia, Germany and France on War with Iraq (Mar. 5, 2003).

9. William H. Taft, Remarks by the Legal Adviser of the Department of State Before the National Association of Attorneys General (Mar. 20, 2003).

10. Thomas M. Franck, *Future Implication Of The Iraq Conflict: What Happens Now? The United Nations After Iraq*, 97 Am. J. Int'l. L. 590, 607–620 (July 2003).

11. Michael P. Scharf, *Is Invasion of Iraq Lawful Under International Law*, 57 International Bar News 2–5 (Mar. 2003).

12. Richard A. Falk, *Future Implication of the Iraq Conflict: What Future for the U.N. Charter System of War Prevention?*, 97 Am. J. Int'l L. 590, 590–598 (July 2003).

13. S.C. Res. 1973, U.N. Doc. S/RES/1973 (Mar. 17, 2011).

14. Bibliography of Additional Sources

## Authors' Note

The United Nations Charter is clear in its prohibition of the use of force, subject only to specific exceptions detailed in the Charter. Many legal scholars argue that, absent general principles of international law, such as the right to self-defense enshrined in the Charter, the only basis for the use of force is U.N. authorization under Chapter VII. Some scholars contend, however, that absent explicit U.N. authorization, there may still be a legal basis for the use of force.

# 1. U.N. Charter, Article 2

Article 2

The Organization and its Members, in pursuit of the Purposes stated in Article 1, shall act in accordance with the following Principles.

1. The Organization is based on the principle of the sovereign equality of all its Members.

2. All Members, in order to ensure to all of them the rights and benefits resulting from membership, shall fulfill in good faith the obligations assumed by them in accordance with the present Charter.

3. All Members shall settle their international disputes by peaceful means in such a manner that international peace and security, and justice, are not endangered.

4. All Members shall refrain in their international relations from the threat or use of force against the territorial integrity or political independence of any state, or in any other manner inconsistent with the Purposes of the United Nations.

5. All Members shall give the United Nations every assistance in any action it takes in accordance with the present Charter, and shall refrain from giving assistance to any state against which the United Nations is taking preventive or enforcement action.

6. The Organization shall ensure that states which are not Members of the United Nations act in accordance with these Principles so far as may be necessary for the maintenance of international peace and security.

7. Nothing contained in the present Charter shall authorize the United Nations to intervene in matters which are essentially within the domestic jurisdiction of any state or shall require the Members to submit such matters to settlement under the present Charter; but this principle shall not prejudice the application of enforcement measures under Chapter VII.

# 2. U.N. Charter, Articles 39, 41–42, 48–49, 51

### Chapter VII: Action With Respect To Threats To The Peace, Breaches Of The Peace, And Acts Of Aggression

Article 39

The Security Council shall determine the existence of any threat to the peace, breach of the peace, or act of aggression and shall make recommendations, or decide what measures shall be taken in accordance with Articles 41 and 42, to maintain or restore international peace and security.

Article 41

The Security Council may decide what measures not involving the use of armed force are to be employed to give effect to its decisions, and it may call upon the Members of the United Nations to apply such measures. These may include complete or partial interruption of economic relations and of rail, sea, air, postal, telegraphic, radio, and other means of communication, and the severance of diplomatic relations.

## Article 42

Should the Security Council consider that measures provided for in Article 41 would be inadequate or have proved to be inadequate, it may take such action by air, sea, or land forces as may be necessary to maintain or restore international peace and security. Such action may include demonstrations, blockade, and other operations by air, sea, or land forces of Members of the United Nations.

## Article 48

1. The action required to carry out the decisions of the Security Council for the maintenance of international peace and security shall be taken by all the Members of the United Nations or by some of them, as the Security Council may determine.

2. Such decisions shall be carried out by the Members of the United Nations directly and through their action in the appropriate international agencies of which they are members.

## Article 49

The Members of the United Nations shall join in affording mutual assistance in carrying out the measures decided upon by the Security Council.

## Article 51

Nothing in the present Charter shall impair the inherent right of individual or collective self-defense if an armed attack occurs against a Member of the United Nations, until the Security Council has taken measures necessary to maintain international peace and security. Measures taken by Members in the exercise of this right of self-defense shall be immediately reported to the Security Council and shall not in any way affect the authority and responsibility of the Security Council under the present Charter to take at any time such action as it deems necessary in order to maintain or restore international peace and security.

---

## Authors' Note

On August 2, 1990, Iraq invaded Kuwait, prompting the United Nations Security Council to pass a series of resolutions condemning Iraq's actions, imposing penalties on Iraq (including an economic embargo), and affirming the right of collective self-defense as a response to Iraq's invasion of Kuwait. Iraq's continued non-compliance with United Nations resolutions led the Security Council to authorize collective force to "restore international peace and security" in the region. On January 16, 1991, the United States and coalitions forces invaded Iraq (hereinafter called the Gulf War), ultimately forcing Iraq into a cease-fire with Kuwait, subject to the terms of U.N. Security Council Resolution 687. In the Gulf War, the United States and coalition forces thus received explicit U.N. authorization to use force in Iraq.

---

# 3. Resolution 678

United Nations Security Council, 1990
Adopted by the Security Council at its 2963rd meeting on 29 November 1990

*The Security Council,*

* * *

*Noting* that, despite all efforts by the United Nations, Iraq refuses to comply with its obligation to implement resolution 660 (1990) and the above-mentioned subsequent relevant resolutions, in flagrant contempt of the Security Council,

*Mindful* of its duties and responsibilities under the Charter of the United Nations for the maintenance and preservation of international peace and security,

*Determined* to secure full compliance with its decisions,

*Acting* under Chapter VII of the Charter,

1. *Demands* that Iraq comply fully with resolution 660 (1990) and all subsequent relevant resolutions, and decides, while maintaining all its decisions, to allow Iraq one final opportunity, as a pause of goodwill, to do so;

2. *Authorizes* Member States co-operating with the Government of Kuwait, unless Iraq on or before 15 January 1991 fully implements, as set forth in paragraph 1 above, the above-mentioned resolutions, to use all necessary means to uphold and implement resolution 660 (1990) and all subsequent relevant resolutions and to restore international peace and security in the area;

3. *Requests* all States to provide appropriate support for the actions undertaken in pursuance of paragraph 2 of the present resolution;

4. *Requests* the States concerned to keep the Security Council regularly informed on the progress of actions undertaken pursuant to paragraphs 2 and 3 above;

5. *Decides* to remain seized of the matter.

---

# 4. President George H.W. Bush, Address on Invasion of Iraq
## 1991

Just two hours ago, allied air forces began an attack on military targets in Iraq and Kuwait. These attacks continue as I speak. Ground forces are not engaged.

This conflict started August 2nd when the dictator of Iraq invaded a small and helpless neighbor. Kuwait—a member of the Arab League and a member of the United Nations—was crushed; its people, brutalized. Five months ago, Saddam Hussein started this cruel war against Kuwait. Tonight, the battle has been joined.

This military action, taken in accord with United Nations resolutions and with the consent of the United States Congress, follows months of constant and virtually endless diplomatic activity on the part of the United Nations, the United States, and many, many other countries. Arab leaders sought what became known as an Arab solution, only to conclude that Saddam Hussein was unwilling to leave Kuwait. Others traveled to Baghdad in a variety of efforts to restore peace and justice. Our Secretary of State, James Baker, held an historic meeting in Geneva, only to be totally rebuffed. This past weekend, in a last-ditch effort, the Secretary-General of the United Nations went to the Middle East with peace in his heart—his second such mission. And he came back from Baghdad with no progress at all in getting Saddam Hussein to withdraw from Kuwait.

Now the 28 countries with forces in the Gulf area have exhausted all reasonable efforts to reach a peaceful resolution—have no choice but to drive Saddam from Kuwait by force. We will not fail.

As I report to you, air attacks are underway against military targets in Iraq. We are determined to knock out Saddam Hussein's nuclear bomb potential. We will also destroy his chemical weapons facilities. Much of Saddam's artillery and tanks will be destroyed. Our operations are designed to best protect the lives of all the coalition forces by targeting Saddam's vast military arsenal. Initial reports from General Schwarzkopf are that our operations are proceeding according to plan.

Our objectives are clear: Saddam Hussein's forces will leave Kuwait. The legitimate government of Kuwait will be restored to its rightful place, and Kuwait will once again be free. Iraq will eventually comply with all relevant United Nations resolutions, and then, when peace is restored, it is our hope that Iraq will live as a peaceful and cooperative member of the family of nations, thus enhancing the security and stability of the Gulf.

Some may ask: Why act now? Why not wait? The answer is clear: The world could wait no longer. Sanctions, though having some effect, showed no signs of accomplishing their objective. Sanctions were tried for well over five months, and we and our allies concluded that sanctions alone would not force Saddam from Kuwait.

While the world waited, Saddam Hussein systematically raped, pillaged, and plundered a tiny nation, no threat to his own. He subjected the people of Kuwait to unspeakable atrocities—and among those maimed and murdered, innocent children.

While the world waited, Saddam sought to add to the chemical weapons arsenal he now possesses, an infinitely more dangerous weapon of mass destruction—a nuclear weapon. And while the world waited, while the world talked peace and withdrawal, Saddam Hussein dug in and moved massive forces into Kuwait.

While the world waited, while Saddam stalled, more damage was being done to the fragile economies of the Third World, emerging democracies of Eastern Europe, to the entire world, including to our own economy.

The United States, together with the United Nations, exhausted every means at our disposal to bring this crisis to a peaceful end. However, Saddam clearly felt that by stalling and threatening and defying the United Nations, he could weaken the forces arrayed against him.

While the world waited, Saddam Hussein met every overture of peace with open contempt. While the world prayed for peace, Saddam prepared for war.

I had hoped that when the United States Congress, in historic debate, took its resolute action, Saddam would realize he could not prevail and would move out of Kuwait in accord with the United Nation resolutions. He did not do that. Instead, he remained intransigent, certain that time was on his side.

Saddam was warned over and over again to comply with the will of the United Nations: Leave Kuwait, or be driven out. Saddam has arrogantly rejected all warnings. Instead, he tried to make this a dispute between Iraq and the United States of America.

Well, he failed. Tonight, 28 nations—countries from 5 continents, Europe and Asia, Africa, and the Arab League—have forces in the Gulf area standing shoulder to shoulder against Saddam Hussein. These countries had hoped the use of force could be avoided. Regrettably, we now believe that only force will make him leave.

Prior to ordering our forces into battle, I instructed our military commanders to take every necessary step to prevail as quickly as possible, and with the greatest degree of protection possible for American and allied service men and women. I've told the American people before that this will not be another Vietnam, and I repeat this here tonight. Our troops will have the best possible support in the entire world, and they will not be asked to fight with one hand tied behind their back. I'm hopeful that this fighting will not go on for long and that casualties will be held to an absolute minimum.

This is an historic moment. We have in this past year made great progress in ending the long era of conflict and cold war. We have before us the opportunity to forge for ourselves and for future generations a new world order—a world where the rule of law, not the law of the jungle, governs the conduct of nations. When we are successful—and we will be—we have a real chance at this new world order, an order in which a credible United Nations can use its peacekeeping role to fulfill the promise and vision of the U.N.'s founders.

We have no argument with the people of Iraq. Indeed, for the innocents caught in this conflict, I pray for their safety. Our goal is not the conquest of Iraq. It is the liberation of Kuwait. It is my hope that somehow the Iraqi people can, even now, convince their dictator that he must lay down his arms, leave Kuwait, and let Iraq itself rejoin the family of peace-loving nations.

\* \* \*

## Authors' Note

United Nations Security Council Resolution 687 was issued at the end of open hostilities in the Gulf War in 1991. Resolution 687 set up a framework for international teams to monitor Iraq's military infrastructure with respect to the development of weapons of mass destruction. This document also became part of the legal basis for the invasions in 2003, as you will note below in the section on the Iraq War in 2003.

## 5. Resolution 687

### United Nations Security Council, 1991

Adopted by the Security Council at its 2981st meeting, on 3 April 1991

*The Security Council,*

\* \* \*

*Welcoming* the restoration to Kuwait of its sovereignty, independence and territorial integrity and the return of its legitimate Government,

\* \* \*

*Reaffirming* the need to be assured of Iraq's peaceful intentions in the light of its unlawful invasion and occupation of Kuwait,

\* \* \*

*Aware* of the use by Iraq of ballistic missiles in unprovoked attacks and therefore of the need to take specific measures in regard to such missiles located in Iraq,

\* \* \*

*Conscious* of the threat that all weapons of mass destruction pose to peace and security in the area and of the need to work towards the establishment in the Middle East of a zone free of such weapons,

\* \* \*

*Bearing in mind* its objective of restoring international peace and security in the area as set out in recent resolutions of the Security Council,

*Conscious* of the need to take the following measures acting under Chapter VII of the Charter,

1. *Affirms* all thirteen resolutions noted above, except as expressly changed below to achieve the goals of this resolution, including a formal cease-fire;

\* \* \*

8. *Decides* that Iraq shall unconditionally accept the destruction, removal, or rendering harmless, under international supervision, of:

(a) All chemical and biological weapons and all stocks of agents and all related subsystems and components and all research, development, support and manufacturing facilities;

(b) All ballistic missiles with a range greater than 150 kilometres and related major parts, and repair and production facilities;

9. *Decides*, for the implementation of paragraph 8 above, the following:

(a) Iraq shall submit to the Secretary-General, within fifteen days of the adoption of the present resolution, a declaration of the locations, amounts and types of all items specified in paragraph 8 and agree to urgent, on-site inspection as specified below;

(b) The Secretary-General, in consultation with the appropriate Governments and, where appropriate, with the Director-General of the World Health Organization, within forty-five days of the passage of the present resolution, shall develop, and submit to the Council for approval, a plan calling for the completion of the following acts within forty-five days of such approval:

(i) The forming of a Special Commission, which shall carry out immediate on-site inspection of Iraq's biological, chemical and missile capabilities, based on Iraq's declarations and the designation of any additional locations by the Special Commission itself;

(ii) The yielding by Iraq of possession to the Special Commission for destruction, removal or rendering harmless, taking into account the requirements of public safety, of all items specified under paragraph 8 (a) above, including items at the additional locations designated by the Special Commission under paragraph 9 (b) (i) above and the destruction by Iraq, under the supervision of the Special Commission, of all its missile capabilities, including launchers, as specified under paragraph 8 (b) above;

(iii) The provision by the Special Commission of the assistance and cooperation to the Director-General of the International Atomic Energy Agency required in paragraphs 12 and 13 below;

10. *Decides* that Iraq shall unconditionally undertake not to use, develop, construct or acquire any of the items specified in paragraphs 8 and 9 above and requests the Secretary-General, in consultation with the Special Commission, to develop a plan for the future ongoing monitoring and verification of Iraq's compliance with this paragraph, to be submitted to the Security Council for approval within one hundred and twenty days of the passage of this resolution;

\* \* \*

32. *Requires* Iraq to inform the Security Council that it will not commit or support any act of international terrorism or allow any organization directed towards commission of

such acts to operate within its territory and to condemn unequivocally and renounce all acts, methods and practices of terrorism;

\* \* \*

34. *Decides* to remain seized of the matter and to take such further steps as may be required for the implementation of the present resolution and to secure peace and security in the area.

## Authors' Note

The 2003 invasion of Iraq has been the subject of considerable debate. Some scholars argue that the invasion violated the United Nations Charter and was illegal under international law. Others assert that the United States and coalition forces acted in accordance with general principles of international law, and more specifically, in accordance with United Nations Security Council resolutions on Iraq, which gave them the implicit authority to use force in Iraq.

## 6. President George W. Bush, Address on Iraq
### 2002

Thank you for that very gracious and warm Cincinnati welcome. I'm honored to be here tonight. I appreciate you all coming. Tonight I want to take a few minutes to discuss a grave threat to peace and America's determination to lead the world in confronting that threat.

The threat comes from Iraq. It arises directly from the Iraqi regime's own actions, its history of aggression and its drive toward an arsenal of terror.

Eleven years ago, as a condition for ending the Persian Gulf War, the Iraqi regime was required to destroy its weapons of mass destruction, to cease all development of such weapons and to stop all support for terrorist groups. The Iraqi regime has violated all of those obligations. It possesses and produces chemical and biological weapons. It is seeking nuclear weapons. It has given shelter and support to terrorism and practices terror against its own people. The entire world has witnessed Iraq's 11-year history of defiance, deception and bad faith.

\* \* \*

Members of Congress of both political parties, and members of the United Nations Security Council, agree that Saddam Hussein is a threat to peace and must disarm. We agree that the Iraqi dictator must not be permitted to threaten America and the world with horrible poisons and diseases and gases and atomic weapons.

\* \* \*

Iraq's weapons of mass destruction are controlled by a murderous tyrant who has already used chemical weapons to kill thousands of people. This same tyrant has tried to dominate the Middle East, has invaded and brutally occupied a small neighbor, has struck other nations without warning and holds an unrelenting hostility toward the United States. By its past and present actions, by its technological capabilities, by the merciless nature of its regime, Iraq is unique.

As a former chief weapons inspector of the U.N. has said, "The fundamental problem with Iraq remains the nature of the regime itself." Saddam Hussein is a homicidal dictator who is addicted to weapons of mass destruction.

\* \* \*

Knowing these realities, America must not ignore the threat gathering against us. Facing clear evidence of peril, we cannot wait for the final proof, the smoking gun that could come in the form of a mushroom cloud.

* * *

Some believe we can address this danger by simply resuming the old approach to inspections and applying diplomatic and economic pressure. Yet this is precisely what the world has tried to do since 1991.

The U.N. inspections program was met with systematic deception. The Iraqi regime bugged hotel rooms and offices of inspectors to find where they were going next. They forged documents, destroyed evidence and developed mobile weapons facilities to keep a step ahead of inspectors. Eight so-called presidential palaces were declared off-limits to unfettered inspections. These sites actually encompass 12 square miles, with hundreds of structures both above and below the ground where sensitive materials could be hidden.

The world has also tried economic sanctions and watched Iraqi's billions of dollars in illegal oil revenues to fund more weapons purchases rather than provide for the needs of the Iraqi people.

The world has tried limited military strikes to destroy Iraq's weapons of mass destruction capabilities, only to see them openly rebuilt while the regime again denies they even exist.

The world has tried no-fly zones to keep Saddam from terrorizing his own people, and in the last year alone the Iraqi military has fired upon American and British pilots more than 750 times.

After 11 years during which we've tried containment, sanctions, inspections, even selected military action, the end result is that Saddam Hussein still has chemical and biological weapons and is increasing his capabilities to make more. And he is moving ever closer to developing a nuclear weapon.

Clearly, to actually work, any new inspections, sanctions or enforcement mechanisms will have to be very different. America wants the U.N. to be an effective organization that helps keep the peace. And that is why we are urging the Security Council to adopt a new resolution setting out tough, immediate requirements.

Among those requirements the Iraqi regime must reveal and destroy, under U.N. supervision, all existing weapons of mass destruction. To ensure that we learn the truth, the regime must allow witnesses to its illegal activities to be interviewed outside the country. And these witnesses must be free to bring their families with them, so they are all beyond the reach of Saddam Hussein's terror and murder.

And inspectors must have access to any site, at any time without pre-clearance, without delay, without exceptions.

The time of denying, deceiving and delaying has come to an end. Saddam Hussein must disarm himself, or, for the sake of peace, we will lead a coalition to disarm him.

Many nations are joining us and insisting that Saddam Hussein's regime be held accountable. They are committed to defending the international security that protects the lives of both our citizens and theirs.

And that's why America is challenging all nations to take the resolutions of the U.N. Security Council seriously. These resolutions are very clear. In addition to declaring and destroying all of its weapons of mass destruction, Iraq must end its support for terrorism. It must cease the persecution of its civilian population. It must stop all illicit trade outside the oil-for-food program. It must release or account for all Gulf War personnel, including an American pilot whose fate is still unknown.

By taking these steps and by only taking these steps, the Iraqi regime has an opportunity to avoid conflict.

\* \* \*

I hope this will not require military action, but it may. And military conflict could be difficult. An Iraqi regime faced with its own demise may attempt cruel and desperate measures. If Saddam Hussein orders such measures, his generals would be well advised to refuse those orders. If they do not refuse, they must understand that all war criminals will be pursued and punished.

If we have to act, we will take every precaution that is possible. We will plan carefully. We will act with the full power of the United States military. We will act with allies at our side and we will prevail.

\* \* \*

Failure to act would embolden other tyrants, allow terrorists access to new weapons and new resources, and make blackmail a permanent feature of world events.

The United Nations would betray the purpose of its founding and prove irrelevant to the problems of our time. And through its inaction, the United States would resign itself to a future of fear.

\* \* \*

If military action is necessary, the United States and our allies will help the Iraqi people rebuild their economy and create the institutions of liberty in a unified Iraq, at peace with its neighbors.

Later this week, the United States Congress will vote on this matter. I have asked Congress to authorize the use of America's military if it proves necessary to enforce U.N. Security Council demands.

Approving this resolution does not mean that military action is imminent or unavoidable. The resolution will tell the United Nations, and all nations, that America speaks with one voice and it is determined to make the demands of the civilized world mean something.

\* \* \*

Saddam Hussein's actions have put us on notice, and there's no refuge from our responsibilities.

\* \* \*

## Authors' Note

The following United Nations Security Council resolution was a response to Iraq's continued non-compliance with international weapons inspections. This resolution is viewed by some as sufficient legal basis for authorizing the United States to use force against Saddam Hussein. However, many states and scholars disagree.

# 7. Resolution 1441

United Nations Security Council, 2002

*The Security Council,*

\* \* \*

*Recognizing* the threat Iraq's noncompliance with Council resolutions and proliferation of weapons of mass destruction and long-range missiles poses to international peace and security,

*Recalling* that its resolution 678 (1990) authorized Member States to use all necessary means to uphold and implement its resolution 660 (1990) of 2 August 1990 and all relevant resolutions subsequent to Resolution 660 (1990) and to restore international peace and security in the area,

*Further recalling* that its resolution 687 (1991) imposed obligations on Iraq as a necessary step for achievement of its stated objective of restoring international peace and security in the area,

*Deploring* the fact that Iraq has not provided an accurate, full, final, and complete disclosure, as required by resolution 687 (1991), of all aspects of its programmes to develop weapons of mass destruction and ballistic missiles with a range greater than one hundred and fifty kilometres, and of all holdings of such weapons, their components and production facilities and locations, as well as all other nuclear programmes, including any which it claims are for purposes not related to nuclear-weapons-usable material,

*Deploring further* that Iraq repeatedly obstructed immediate, unconditional, and unrestricted access to sites designated by the United Nations Special Commission (UNSCOM) and the International Atomic Energy Agency (IAEA), failed to cooperate fully and unconditionally with UNSCOM and IAEA weapons inspectors, as required by resolution 687 (1991), and ultimately ceased all cooperation with UNSCOM and the IAEA in 1998,

\* \* \*

*Deploring also* that the Government of Iraq has failed to comply with its commitments pursuant to resolution 687 (1991) with regard to terrorism, pursuant to resolution 688 (1991) to end repression of its civilian population and to provide access by international humanitarian organizations to all those in need of assistance in Iraq, and pursuant to resolutions 686 (1991), 687 (1991), and 1284 (1999) to return or cooperate in accounting for Kuwaiti and third country nationals wrongfully detained by Iraq, or to return Kuwaiti property wrongfully seized by Iraq,

*Recalling* that in its resolution 687 (1991) the Council declared that a ceasefire would be based on acceptance by Iraq of the provisions of that resolution, including the obligations on Iraq contained therein,

*Determined* to ensure full and immediate compliance by Iraq without conditions or restrictions with its obligations under resolution 687 (1991) and other relevant resolutions and recalling that the resolutions of the Council constitute the governing standard of Iraqi compliance,

\* \* \*

*Acting* under Chapter VII of the Charter of the United Nations,

1. *Decides* that Iraq has been and remains in material breach of its obligations under relevant resolutions, including resolution 687 (1991), in particular through Iraq's failure to

cooperate with United Nations inspectors and the IAEA, and to complete the actions required under paragraphs 8 to 13 of resolution 687 (1991);

2. *Decides*, while acknowledging paragraph 1 above, to afford Iraq, by this resolution, a final opportunity to comply with its disarmament obligations under relevant resolutions of the Council; and accordingly decides to set up an enhanced inspection regime with the aim of bringing to full and verified completion the disarmament process established by resolution 687 (1991) and subsequent resolutions of the Council;

* * *

4. *Decides* that false statements or omissions in the declarations submitted by Iraq pursuant to this resolution and failure by Iraq at any time to comply with, and cooperate fully in the implementation of, this resolution shall constitute a further material breach of Iraq's obligations and will be reported to the Council for assessment in accordance with paragraph 11 and 12 below;

* * *

9. *Requests* the Secretary-General immediately to notify Iraq of this resolution, which is binding on Iraq; demands that Iraq confirm within seven days of that notification its intention to comply fully with this resolution; and demands further that Iraq cooperate immediately, unconditionally, and actively with UNMOVIC and the IAEA;

* * *

11. *Directs* the Executive Chairman of UNMOVIC and the Director-General of the IAEA to report immediately to the Council any interference by Iraq with inspection activities, as well as any failure by Iraq to comply with its disarmament obligations, including its obligations regarding inspections under this resolution;

12. *Decides* to convene immediately upon receipt of a report in accordance with paragraphs 4 or 11 above, in order to consider the situation and the need for full compliance with all of the relevant Council resolutions in order to secure international peace and security;

13. *Recalls*, in that context, that the Council has repeatedly warned Iraq that it will face serious consequences as a result of its continued violations of its obligations;

14. *Decides* to remain seized of the matter.

## Authors' Note

The following material is a response by Russia, Germany, and France to the United States' aggressive push for action against Iraq. Facing strong opposition in the Security Council, the United States began a campaign to "sell" the war internationally and garner support for military action. However, with strong opposition from veto holding members in the Security Council like France and Russia, the United States had little chance of passing a resolution that authorized them to use force against Saddam Hussein.

# 8. Joint Declaration by Russia, Germany and France, War with Iraq

## 2003

Our common objective remains the full and effective disarmament of Iraq, in compliance with UNSCR 1441.

We consider that this objective can be achieved by the peaceful means of the inspections.

Moreover, we observe that these inspections are producing increasingly encouraging results:

—The destruction of the al-Samoud missiles has started and is making progress;

—The Iraqis are providing biological and chemical information;

—The interviews with Iraqi scientists are continuing.

Russia, Germany and France resolutely support Messrs. Blix and El-Baradei and consider the meeting of the Council on 7 March to be an important stage in the process put in place.

We firmly call for the Iraqi authorities to cooperate more actively with the inspectors to fully disarm their country. These inspections cannot continue indefinitely.

We consequently ask that the inspections now be speeded up, in keeping with the proposals put forward in the memorandum submitted to the Security Council by our three countries. We must:

—Specify and prioritize the remaining issues, program by program

—Establish, for each point, detailed timelines.

Using this method, the inspectors have to present without any delay their work programme accompanied by regular progress reports to the Security Council. This schedule could provide for a meeting clause to enable the Council to evaluate the overall results of this process.

In these circumstances, we will not let a proposed resolution pass that would authorize the use of force. Russia and France, as permanent members of the Security Council, will assume all their responsibilities on this point.

We are at a turning point. Since our goal is the peaceful and full disarmament of Iraq, we have today the chance to obtain through peaceful means a comprehensive settlement for the Middle East, starting with a move forward in the peace process, by:

—Publishing and implementing the roadmap;

—Putting together a general framework for the Middle East, based on stability and security, renunciation of force, arms control and trust building measures.

## Authors' Note

After several months of intense international debate, the United States launched a massive military campaign against Iraq on March 20, 2003. The following material is an excerpt from a speech given by William H. Taft, the legal advisor to the Department of State, the day the war began.

## 9. William H. Taft, Remarks by the Legal Adviser of the Department of State before the National Association of Attorneys General

### 2003

\* \* \*

Finally, let me say a few words about the legal basis for our actions in Iraq. First, it goes without saying that the President's authority to use force under U.S. law is clear. Under the Constitution he has not simply the authority but the responsibility to use force to protect our national security. Congress has confirmed in two separate resolutions in 1991 and again last fall that the President has authority to use our armed forces in the specific case of Iraq.

Under international law, the basis for use of force is equally strong. There is clear authorization from the Security Council to use force to disarm Iraq. The President referred to this authority in his speech to the American people on Monday night. The source of this authority is UNSCR 678, which was the authorization to use force for the Gulf War in January 1991. In April of that year, the Council imposed a series of conditions on Iraq, including most importantly extensive disarmament obligations, as a condition of the ceasefire declared under UNSCR 687. Iraq has "materially breached" these disarmament obligations, and force may again be used under UNSCR 678 to compel Iraqi compliance.

Historical practice is also clear that a material breach by Iraq of the conditions for the cease-fire provides a basis for use of force. This was established as early as 1992. The United States, the U.K. and France have all used force against Iraq on a number of occasions over the past twelve years. Just last November, in Resolution 1441, the Council unanimously decided that Iraq has been and remains in material breach of its obligation. 1441 then gave Iraq a "final opportunity" to comply, but stated specifically that violations of the obligations, including the obligation to cooperate fully, under 1441 would constitute a further material breach. Iraq has clearly committed such violations and, accordingly, the authority to use force to address Iraq's material breaches is clear.

This basis in international law for the use of force in Iraq today is clear. The Attorney General of the United Kingdom has considered the issue and reached the same conclusion we have. The President may also, of course, always use force under international law in self-defense.

## Authors' Note

The following materials reflect the academic debate over the use of force under the United Nations Charter. Scholars have disagreed, as they often do, on whether the invasion of Iraq was a violation of the United Nations Charter or whether it was a unilateral action that was supported by previous resolutions and international law.

## 10. Thomas M. Franck, Future Implication of the Iraq Conflict: What Happens Now? The United Nations after Iraq

American Journal of International Law, 2003
[footnotes omitted by editors]

### I. Who Killed Article 2(4) Again?

Thirty-three years ago I published an article in this *Journal* entitled *Who Killed Article 2(4)? or: Changing Norms Governing the Use of Force by States*, which examined the phenomenon of increasingly frequent resort to unlawful force by Britain, France, India, North Korea, the Soviet Union, and the United States. The essay concluded with this sad observation:

> The failure of the U.N. Charter's normative system is tantamount to the inability of any rule, such as that set out in Article 2(4), in itself to have much control over the behavior of states. National self-interest, particularly the national self-interest of the super-Powers, has usually won out over treaty obligations. This is particularly characteristic of this age of pragmatic power politics. It is as if international law, always something of a cultural myth, has been demythologized. It seems this is not an age when men act by principles simply because that is what gentlemen ought to do. But living by power alone ... is a nerve-wracking and costly business.

The recent recourse to force in Iraq recalls this observation, which again seems all too apt. All that has changed is that we now have on offer proposed models for interstatal relations that seem even worse than the dilapidated system to which, by 1970, state misbehavior had reduced the postwar world. That once shiny new postwar system, embodied in the United Nations Charter, had been based on the assumption of states' reciprocal respect for law as their sturdy shield against the prospect of mutual assured destruction in an uncharted nuclear era. The 1970 essay regretted the loss of that vision in a miasma of so-called realpolitik.

\* \* \*

There is one major difference, however, between then and now. The unlawful recourses to force, during the period surveyed in the 1970 essay, were accompanied by a fig leaf of legal justification, which, at least tacitly, recognized the residual force of the requirement in Charter Article 2(4) that states "refrain in their international relations from the threat or use of force against the territorial integrity or political independence of any state." Then, the aggressors habitually defended the legality of their recourse to force by asserting that their actions, taken in response to an alleged prior attack or provocation, were exercises of the right of self-defense under the terms of Charter Article 51. Now, however, in marked contrast, they have all but discarded the fig leaf. While a few government lawyers still go through the motions of asserting that the invasion of Iraq was justified by our inherent right of self-defense, or represented a collective measure authorized by the Security Council under Chapter VII of the Charter, the leaders of America no longer much bother with such legal niceties. Instead, they boldly proclaim a new policy that openly repudiates the Article 2(4) obligation. What is remarkable, this time around, is that once-obligatory efforts by the aggressor to make a serious effort to stretch law to legitimate state action have given way to a drive to repeal law altogether, replacing it with a principle derived from the Athenians at Melos: "the strong do what they can and the weak suffer what they must."

\* \* \*

## V. Did the Iraq Invasion Violate the Charter?

Any prognosis regarding the future of world order must begin by addressing the question whether recent events have indeed had a transformative effect on the law of the international system and, if so, what that transformation portends. As in 1970, one must begin by making a clear-eyed appraisal of what has been happening. If the invasion of Iraq was nothing but an act of self-defense by the United States and its allies, or merely an exercise of police power previously authorized by the Security Council, these events would serve only to verify the continued efficacy of the Charter system. There would have been no violation of the cardinal principle of Article 2(4), as that no-first-use pledge is always subordinate to both the right of self-defense recognized by Article 51 and the right of the Security Council, under Chapter VII, to authorize action against a threat to the peace. If, however, the invasion cannot thus be reconciled with the rules of the Charter, does the invasion of Iraq constitute a simple violation of the rules—one of many and thus of no more legal significance than a holdup of the neighborhood grocery—or should it be celebrated as a deliberate and salutary move toward U.N. reform? Or should these recent events be understood, more apocalyptically, as the final burial of the Charter's fundamental rules? At this point in our analysis of the systemic significance of these events, it becomes essential to focus not only on facts but also on motives for action. Needless to say, this is swampy terrain; but one must try.

The invasion of Iraq can be positioned in each of these explanatory contexts, but just barely. It can be argued that the invasion was lawful (and thus neither violative nor transformative of the Charter). It can also be argued that, while the attack on Iraq may have been technically illegal, its transformative effect on the law has been wholly benevolent. Finally, it can be argued that these events have repealed a legal regime far beyond its prime and, at last, have ushered in a new doctrine of preventive use of force that is far more responsive to the real dangers of our times.

The argument that recent events have not challenged, or have violated only *de minimis*, the Charter law pertaining to recourse to force is very difficult to sustain, although it enjoys the enthusiastic support of some American academics and the rather less enthusiastic support of State Department lawyers. Abroad, it has been advanced only by the British attorney general, supported by a prominent academic lawyer. As enunciated by Legal Adviser William Howard Taft IV of the Department of State, the argument has two prongs. The first is that the president may, "of course, always use force under international law in self-defense." The problem with that rationale is that, even if it were agreed that the right of self-defense "against an armed attack" (Charter, Art. 51) had come, through practice, to include a right of action against an imminent (as opposed to an actual) armed attack, the facts of the situation that existed in March 2003 are hard to fit within *any* plausible theory of imminence. This was a time, after all, when U.N. and International Atomic Energy Agency inspectors were actively engaged in situ in an apparently unrestricted search for weapons of mass destruction (WMDs) undertaken with full authorization by the Security Council. Whatever the inspectors did or did not learn about Iraqi WMDs, nothing in their reports lends any credibility to the claim of an imminent threat of armed aggression against anyone. Indeed, the memorandum of the attorney general of the United Kingdom, while supporting the right to use force, wisely omits all reference to this rationale for its exercise.

The second prong of the *de minimis* argument is more sophisticated than the plea to have acted in self-defense. It avers that the attack led by Britain and the United States had already been sanctioned by the Security Council. Essential to the success of this assertion is a creative, and ultimately unsustainable, reading of three Security Council resolutions—678, 687, and 1441—and of their "legislative history." According to Legal Adviser Taft, Resolution 678:

> Was the authorization to use force for the Gulf War in January 1991. In April of that year, the Council imposed a series of conditions on Iraq, including most importantly extensive disarmament obligations, as a condition of the ceasefire declared under UNSCR 687. Iraq has "materially breached" these disarmament obligations, and force may again be used under UNSCR 678 to compel Iraqi compliance.
>
> ... Just last November, in resolution 1441, the Council unanimously decided that Iraq has been and remains in material breach of its obligation. 1441 then gave Iraq a "final opportunity" to comply, but stated specifically that violations of the obligations, including the obligation to cooperate fully, under 1441 would constitute a further material breach. Iraq has clearly committed such violations and, accordingly, the authority to use force to address Iraq's material breaches is clear.

The British government developed this same thesis, claiming that, by Resolution 678 the Security Council had authorized "Member States to use all necessary means to restore international peace and security in the area" and that, while that authorization "was suspended but not terminated by Security Council resolution (SCR) 687 (1991)," it was "revived by SCR 1441 (2002)."

This version of the meaning and intent of these three resolutions is highly problematic, and appears to have caused the resignation, on a matter of principle, of the deputy legal adviser of the British Foreign Office. Resolution 678 culminated a series of resolutions by the Security Council that condemned Iraq's invasion of Kuwait, called for the immediate withdrawal of the aggressor, imposed mandatory sanctions on Iraq until Kuwaiti sovereignty was restored, and declared the Iraqi annexation of Kuwait to be null and void. In each instance, the purpose of the resolution was solely to liberate Kuwait. Only when these measures failed to secure Iraqi withdrawal did the Council in Resolution 678, citing Chapter VII of the Charter, "authorize[] Member States co-operating with the Government of Kuwait ... to use all necessary means to uphold and implement resolution 660 (1990) and all subsequent relevant resolutions and to restore international peace and security in the area."

This sequence readily demonstrates that the restoration of Kuwaiti sovereignty was the leitmotif of Council action. That the authorization of collective measures by Resolution 678 additionally refers to the restoration of "international peace and security in the area" does not connote some expansive further mandate for contingent action against Iraq at the discretion of any individual member of the coalition of the willing. President George Bush Sr. acknowledged as much in explaining why the American military had not pursued Saddam Hussein's defeated forces to Baghdad. They were not authorized to do so.

The resolution, however, certainly does signal that Iraq was to be subject to further post-conflict intrusive controls: those imposed by the Council in Resolution 687, as part of the cease-fire. These additional obligations are made binding by reference to Chapter VII of the Charter and they were designed, implemented, and meant to be monitored by the Security Council as a whole, not by any individual member acting at its own pleasure. Resolution 687, sometimes referred to as the "mother of all cease-fires," is not only a binding decision of the Security Council, but also an international agreement between the United Nations and Iraq, made effective only "upon official notification by Iraq to the

Secretary-General and to the Security Council of its acceptance" of the provisions set out therein. In legal form, then, as also in substance, this proviso manifests that it is the Security Council and the United Nations, and not individual members, who are the parties, with Iraq, to the cease-fire agreement. It is they who are entitled in law to determine whether Iraq is complying with its commitments to the Council, how long these are to remain in effect, and what is to be done in the event of their violation.

* * *

Neither the text nor the debates on the adoption of Resolution 687 reveal the slightest indication that the Council intended to empower any of its members, by themselves, to determine that Iraq was in material breach. Much less can the resolution be read to authorize any state to decide unilaterally to resume military action against Iraq, save in the event of an armed attack. That deduction is supported by the architecture of the Charter. For the Council to have made a prospective grant of unilateral discretion to states to deploy armed force, in the absence of an actual (or imminent) armed attack, would have been an unprecedented derogation from the strictures of Article 2(4). At the least, to be plausible, such a derogation would have had to be explicit. Moreover, such a delegation of unlimited discretion to individual states cannot be assumed because it could not have been implemented alongside the Council's institution of an extensive system of inspections under *its* authority and control.

* * *

Thus, neither Resolution 678 nor Resolution 687 helps Washington or London make a convincing case that they acted with, rather than against, the law. Nor are their difficulties in any way alleviated by Resolution 1441. While that instrument does deplore "that the Government of Iraq has failed to comply with its commitments pursuant to resolution 687," it addresses that failure exclusively by deciding "to set up an enhanced inspection regime." Anticipating further Iraqi noncompliance, the resolution makes provision for the Council to be convened immediately "in order to consider the situation and the need for full compliance ... in order to secure international peace and security," and it warns Iraq "in that context ... that it will face serious consequences as a result of its continued violations of its obligations." It once again decides that the Council will "remain seized of the matter." The British attorney general somehow concluded from these words that even though the Council is to convene to "consider the matter before any action is taken," no matter what the Council does or does not do, "further [military] action can be taken [by a member] without a new resolution of the Council." From this he deduces that "all that resolution 1441 requires is reporting to and discussion by the Security Council of Iraq's failures, but not an express further decision to authorise force." This conclusion is at best a creative interpretation. In fact, what Resolution 1441 did was to purchase unanimity for the return of the inspectors by postponing to another day, which the sponsors hoped might never be reached, the argument as to whether Resolutions 678 and 687 had authorized further enforcement at the sole discretion of one or more of the Council's members.

Perhaps to its credit, the Taft statement does not tread this tortuous path. Instead, it argues that since the Council had recognized several times that Iraq had committed a "material breach" of Resolution 687, recourse to force rested within the sole discretion of each Council member in accordance with the provision of the law of treaties on the consequences of such a "material" violation of obligations. This tack moves the argument away from a parsing of Council resolutions to the Vienna Convention on the Law of Treaties. But it is the United Nations, not the United States, that is the offended "party" to Resolution 687, and thus it is the Council, not the United States, that has the option under the Convention to regard the resolution as voided by Iraq's material breaches. Additionally, even if the United States were regarded as a "party" to the commitments made by Iraq in agreeing to Resolution 687, a material breach would not release Washington, as the offended party, from the obligation under the Vienna Convention "to fulfil any obligation embodied in the treaty to which it would be subject under international law independently of the [materially breached] treaty." That provision, it would appear, places the United States squarely back under the obligation of Charter Article 2(4), which, in the absence of any provision in Resolution 687 to the contrary, must be regarded as an essential part of its legal context and which requires states to abstain from the use of force in the absence either of an armed attack or of prior authorization by the Security Council.

These British and U.S. justifications do not fare well under close examination, however benevolent their intent to demonstrate compliance with the Charter. Consequently, the effect of those nations' unauthorized recourse to force against Iraq must be seen as either revising or undermining the provisions limiting the discretion of states to resort to force.

## VI. A Charter Revised

Well, if the Iraq invasion did not exactly conform with the law of the Charter, should it not, at least, be celebrated as a violation that has the capacity to reform the law and make it more realistic?

In international law, violators do sometimes turn out to be lawgivers. I have argued elsewhere that the Charter, as a quasi-constitutional instrument, is capable of evolving through the interpretive practice of its principal organs. That interpretive practice may sometimes be led by states with an interest in outcomes that cannot be legitimated by a narrowly originalist reading of the text. In such circumstances, violation shades into revision, sometimes to the benefit of the law and the institution charged with its implementation. The phenomenon is not unknown, also, to domestic law, though it occurs much more frequently in the international arena. The International Court has confirmed, for example, that the abstention of a permanent member of the Security Council in a vote on a substantive resolution is no longer to be taken to constitute a veto as a result of "abundant evidence" of members' practice to that effect. The Court reached this conclusion despite the text of Charter Article 27(3), which requires that substantive resolutions receive "the concurring votes of the permanent members." In a similar example of the interpretive power of institutional practice, extensive U.N. peacekeeping operations have long been based on an evolutionary reading of the Charter's imagined "Chapter 6½." Nothing in the text actually authorizes these by-and-large salubrious activities. In recent years, too, practice has seemed to legitimate such humanitarian interventions as those undertaken by regional organizations in West Africa and Kosovo, even though they had not received the requisite (Art. 53) prior authorization of the Security Council. Further evidence of this important interpretive change is afforded by the Constitutive Act of the African Union, Article 4(h) of which recognizes "the right of the Union to intervene in a Member State pursuant to a decision of the Assembly in respect of grave circumstances, namely: war crimes, genocide and crimes against humanity," when such intervention is authorized by two-thirds of the members.

Even allowing that the Charter text is subject to reinterpretation in practice, it is difficult to chart the direction in which it could be said to be evolving under the impetus of the Middle Eastern events of March and April, 2003. Nevertheless, a courageous attempt to divine that direction has been made by the dean of Princeton's Woodrow Wilson School, Professor Anne-Marie Slaughter. Seeking to close the gap between Charter norms and U.S. practice, she has proposed that the Security Council:

Adopt a resolution recognizing that the following set of conditions would constitute a threat to the peace sufficient to justify the use of force: 1) possession of
weapons of mass destruction or clear and convincing evidence of attempts to
gain such weapons; 2) grave and systematic human rights abuses sufficient to
demonstrate the absence of any internal constraints on government behavior;
and 3) evidence of aggressive intent with regard to other nations.

* * *

While it is altogether admirable to seek to make the invasion of Iraq an opportunity to
strengthen the U.N. system, this analysis, alas, takes far too optimistic a view of what the administration in Washington and the governments of most other countries have concluded
from this angry episode. For the Bush administration, it has underscored the danger of subordinating the policy discretion of the world's only superpower to the perceptions and interests of institutions in which other, mostly minor and sometimes venal, governments are
able to project a degree of power entirely incommensurate with reality. This view is particularly troublesome when the issue pertains to a matter, such as international terrorism, that
holds far greater interest for America than for most other governments. For almost all other
members of the United Nations, on the other hand, the events leading up to the invasion of
Iraq demonstrated the folly of embarking upon any renegotiation of the rules pertaining to
the deployment of force, however sensible, when they knew full well that Washington would
ultimately apply the agreed standards unilaterally. That, to most states, was the message of
Resolution 1441, which ultimately became the legal justification for the invasion of Iraq. As
the British attorney general put it, agreed standards are a sound basis for multilateral discussion, but not for multilateral control over action. The world's governments, their advice
on Iraq spurned, now understand that the sole superpower's administration is not in the
least interested in rules, old or new, if they are to be applied case by case through "a genuine
multilateral decision-making process." It has no intention of subordinating its sole responsibility for protecting what it perceives to be its national security to the judgment of others.

A "genuine multilateral decision-making process" requires the willingness of each participant to accept views, perceptions, and policies it does not share, but that prevail within
the institution engaging in the process. In the run-up to the Iraq invasion, it became clear
that the overwhelming majority of nations—not, as some have said, just a power-jealous
President Jacques Chirac of France and the feckless Chancellor Gerhard Schröder of Germany—believed either that Iraq did not have a significant number of weapons of mass destruction or, if such weapons and the necessary delivery systems existed, that they could
be found by the instituted system of inspections. Very few nations accepted that credible
evidence could be shown of either WMDs or an operational link between Al Qaeda and
the regime in Baghdad. This was a judgment call, pure and simple, and there are indications that the majority may have been right, and the United States and Britain wrong, as
to both the evidence at hand and what to do about it. But the nub of the matter is not
who was right and who wrong but *who gets to decide what to do*. The U.N. system did not
"fail" because of differences of opinion about what to do if the facts were, indeed, as asserted by Washington. Saddam Hussein had no do-or-die defenders in the Council chamber. To the extent the Council can be said to have "failed," it failed because most states had
"misunderstood" the role assigned to them under the Charter and the applicable resolutions. They expected, or naively hoped, to be the jury to which evidence and arguments
as to the facts would be presented and that, collegially, they would then make the final decision about what should be done; whereas the British and U.S. governments took the
view that, after the discourse ended, the decision would be up to them, alone. The problem is not one of devising new rules but of reaching agreement on who gets to apply them.

In essence, the Iraqi crisis was not primarily about what to do but, rather, who decides. There is an answer to that problem, of course, one clearly set out in Article 27 of the Charter. Through the veto, the United States, with the other four permanent members, has the right to block collective action and it takes frequent advantage of this prerogative. On the other hand, the Charter does not give the United States, or any other state, sole power to *initiate* action, except in response to an armed attack. While this deal may have seemed acceptable to America in 1945, it is apparently no longer satisfactory to the protectors of American preeminence. Nowadays, the U.S. government does not wish to be limited in this way. Thus, the invasion of Iraq is more accurately seen as a repudiation of the central decision-making premise of the Charter system than as a genuine opening to reform, unless by reform is meant the reconstitution of the international system along the lines of an American global protectorate.

This is a sad conclusion to offer well-meaning champions of the Charter system. Unfortunately, however, this is not a time for optimistic speculation about how to make the United Nations more responsive to new challenges. Rather, reformers need first to understand that the system stands in mortal jeopardy of being destroyed altogether. If, and only if, something can be done about *that* will there be another time to talk about improving the rules.

## VII. Repudiating the U.N. System

The U.S. government (without, in this instance, the acquiescence of Britain) is out to disable the United Nations. Oh, yes, on its present tangent Washington will keep its membership, but primarily to block by its veto any action by others thought to be inimical to American interests. From time to time, the Bush administration may find it convenient to use the Organization to fix a famine, relocate some refugees, share some costs, even train a police force. What recent events make clear, however, is that the United States no longer considers itself subordinated in any way to the treaty rules that lie at the heart of the United Nations Charter. An anomalous situation therefore faces the Organization, which cannot expel a veto-bearing scofflaw state against its will, but which, in those circumstances, is doomed to encounter great difficulty in carrying out the wishes of its other members. Only three alternatives seem to offer themselves at present: the United States could change its policy, it could withdraw from the Organization, or the other members could withdraw to form a new system of international relations, a coalition of the *seriously* willing. None of these options are easy or probable.

Some see the present impasse as an opportunity to be rid of an international regime that is insufficiently responsive to both America's needs and the reality of our disproportionate power. The most creative of these "realist" intellectuals link the demise of the United Nations as a viable peace-and-security system to the invention of something more amenable to U.S. interests. But *what?* According to Michael Glennon, "Ad hoc coalitions of the willing will effectively succeed it." [ ... ] In practice, this prescription would require the United States to do everything alone, with Britain in tow ...

\* \* \*

At the heart of the debate about the future of American foreign policy is not this or that strategy toward one or another rogue regime. It is the role of institutions and law in policymaking generally. Glennon reflects the views of many in the current U.S. administration when he launches this bold assertion: "States are not bound by rules to which they do not agree." Significantly, he deletes the Westphalian concomitant: States *are* bound by rules to which they do agree. The United States, in full compliance with its own complex constitutional process, accepted the regime of the U.N. Charter, which includes limitations on the right of unilateral recourse to force.

* * *

While the usual U.S. response to such inhibiting entanglements is to reject the treaty, the administration understands that for the United States to withdraw from the U.N. system would leave its machinery intact but in the hands of others, an unpalatable outcome. Thus, we now see the effort to incapacitate what Washington can neither abide nor abandon.

* * *

## IX. What Can Be Done?

It is not within the purchase of the lawyer to make, or to change, national policy. That, in a democracy, falls within the purview of the voters and their representatives. If the voters want the United States to play the imperial superpower, it is for the historians to warn of the discouraging precedents and for the economists to count the costs. It is for the press to portray fairly and fearlessly how that policy affects the people and societies at which it is directed.

* * *

## 11. Michael P. Scharf, Is Invasion of Iraq Lawful under International Law?
### *International Bar News*, 2003

The United States and United Kingdom have just launched a war against Iraq, with the objective of overthrowing the regime of Saddam Hussein, which is alleged to be producing weapons of mass destruction. Does this attack against a sovereign state, aimed at removing its internationally recognized government, in the absence of specific authorisation from the U.N. Security Council, violate international law? In the coming days, this question will be subject to extensive debate in the opinion pages of the world's newspapers as well as in the halls of the United Nations and foreign ministries across the globe. A great deal rides on the answer to this question. If the military intervention is judged to have violated international law, the United States and United Kingdom will suffer diplomatically, most notably through an erosion of international support for their continuing war against al-Qaeda. To avoid this, the United States and United Kingdom have articulated three legal justifications for their action. This article examines the merits of their case.

### Justification No 1: Iraq's Failure to Disarm

Article 2(4) of the U.N. Charter, which has been likened to the First Commandment of modern international law, prohibits any nation from using force against another. The Charter contains only two exceptions to this prohibition: a nation can attack another (1) when such action is authorized by the U.N. Security Council, or (2) when it is acting in self-defense in the face of an armed attack. The United States and United Kingdom have argued that an invasion of Iraq is permissible under both of these exceptions. Their first argument is that the invasion is legally justified because of Iraq's failure to disarm as required by Security Council Resolution 687, which established the cease-fire at the end of the Gulf War in 1991. Under the terms of Security Council Resolution 687, Iraq agreed to discontinue its weapons of mass destruction programme in return for a cessation of hostilities. Since Iraq has failed to live up to its promise, the argument goes, the cease-fire is no longer in effect and the members of the international community can rely on Security Council Resolution 678, which was adopted in 1990, authorising U.N. member states to use 'all necessary means' to expel the Iraqi occupiers from Kuwait and 'to restore international peace and security in the area'. Under this view, the 1991 Gulf War is not over, and military operations could be resumed by the United States and its allies under the original Security Council authorisation to use force.

The problem with this argument is that Resolution 687 did not authorise individual states to break the cease-fire in the future based on their belief that Iraq has violated the terms of the cease-fire by producing chemical, biological or nuclear weapons. Instead, the Resolution states that the Security Council 'decides to remain seized of the matter and to take such further steps as may be required for the implementation of the present resolution and to secure peace and security in the area'. This language suggests that the responsibility for overseeing and enforcing the cease-fire was left with the Security Council itself, not with individual states. It is notable that three of the permanent members of the Security Council—France, Russia and China—have taken the position that this clause means that another Security Council resolution would be needed to authorize a resumption of the war against Iraq. It is also significant that the Administration of Bush the elder did not view Resolution 678 as a broad enough grant of authority to invade Baghdad and topple Saddam Hussein. It is ironic, critics assert, that the current Bush Administration would now argue that this Resolution could be used ten years later to justify a forcible regime change.

### Justification No 2: Iraq's Failure to Cooperate Fully with Weapons Inspections

The second U.S./U.K. argument is that an invasion of Iraq can be justified under international law in light of Iraq's failure to cooperate fully with weapons inspections as required by Security Council Resolution 1441. Resolution 1441 was adopted on 8 November 2002, after eight weeks of intense negotiation. The final text of the Resolution represents a compromise between the French/Russian view and the American/British perspective. The Security Council acquiesced to the United States by deciding that Iraq 'was and remains in material breach' of prior resolutions, and recalling that the Council has repeatedly warned Iraq that it will face 'serious consequences' as a result of its continued violation of its obligations. Further, the Resolution does not explicitly require another Security Council vote on authorisation of military force as France and Russia had proposed, although it does provide that any breach must be reported by the Chairman of the Inspection Team to the Security Council, which shall convene immediately to consider the situation and decide what to do.

'The lawfulness of the U.S./U.K. action will be judged not in a court of law, but in the court of world opinion' the use of force if it concludes that Iraq is not fully cooperating with inspections or if the inspections provide evidence that Iraq is producing weapons of mass destruction—without the need for further Security Council action. But it is significant that France, Russia, China, and other members of the Council made clear at the time they voted in favour of the Resolution that it 'excludes an automaticity in the use of force' and that the use of force is only valid 'with the prior, explicit authorization of the Security Council'. The United States has made similar implied authorization arguments twice in the past. The first was in the context of Operation Desert Fox, a series of air strikes on Iraq in December 1988. The second was with respect to its 1999 intervention against Serbia. On both occasions, Russia and China objected to the U.S. interpretation. If the United States once again insists on an implied authorisation argument despite the opposition of Russia and China, it is likely that the long-term result will be their increased use of the veto to prevent the Council from adopting Chapter VII resolutions, thus undercutting the possibility of useful political consensus being expressed in those instruments.

**Justification No 3: An Act of Self-Defence**

The third argument is that the attack is legally justified as an act of pre-emptive self-defence as permitted by Article 51 of the U.N. Charter. Article 51 provides that 'nothing in the present charter shall impair the inherent right of individual or collective self-defense in an armed attack occurs against a Member of the United Nations'. A literal interpretation of this clause would rule out using force until another state had actually launched its attack which, in the modern age of weapons of mass destruction, would often be too late to respond successfully. Arguing that the U.N. Charter was not meant to be a 'suicide pact', governments and legal scholars have long maintained that Article 51 should be read as permitting 'anticipatory' or 'pre-emptive' self-defence in the context of an imminent and overwhelming threat. It is noteworthy that the equally authentic French version of Article 51 uses the phrase 'aggression armée', meaning 'armed aggression', instead of the more restrictive term 'armed attack' contained in the English version. The right to respond to armed aggression would include the right to respond to credible threats, since aggression can exist separate from and prior to an actual attack.

While its origins can be traced back to the diplomatic correspondence between the United States and Britain following the 1837 'Caroline incident', the contours of the modern right to pre-emptive self-defence were mapped by the international response to two actions by Israel. The first was Israel's 1967 air strikes against Egyptian military airfields, which were launched after several weeks of frantic diplomacy while hostile troops were massing against Israel in the Sinai, the Golan Heights, and the West Bank. Many countries supported Israel's right to conduct defensive strikes prior to armed attack and draft resolutions condemning the Israeli action were soundly defeated in both the U.N. Security Council and the General Assembly. The second action occurred 14 years later, on 7 June 1981, when Israeli aircraft bombed the Iraqi Osirik nuclear reactor. In a statement released after the air strike, the Israeli Government justified its action as an act of self-defence, claiming that 'sources of unquestioned reliability told us that the reactor was intended for the production of atomic bombs, which were to be used against Israel'. This time, the U.N. Security Council (including the United States) and General Assembly responded by adopting resolutions condemning Israel for the strike, largely on the basis that Israel had failed to prove that the Iraqi threat was sufficiently immediate to justify pre-emptive self-defence.

**No imminent threat**

Now flash forward to 2003. The Bush Administration has said that an attack against Iraq is justified because: (1) Iraq possesses chemical and biological weapons and is on the verge of possessing nuclear weapons; (2) Iraq has used weapons of mass destruction in the past (against Iran and the Kurds of northern Iraq); and (3) Iraq has manifested its hostile intentions towards the United States and its allies (especially Israel).

On its face, this case would seem to be more like the widely condemned 1981 Israeli bombing of the Osirik reactor than the widely accepted 1967 Israeli air strikes against Egypt. As explained below, in the case of Iraq in 2003, the imminence of the threat is just not present. Although the Bush Administration claims that Iraq could get nuclear weapons soon, most experts, including the U.S. Central Intelligence Agency and the International Atomic Energy Agency, have concluded that it would take Iraq several years or more to develop nuclear weapons. Further, it is generally acknowledged that Iraq has no missiles, planes, or other means to hit the United States or even Israel with chemical or biological weapons. And, as former U.S. National Security Adviser Brent Scowcroft and others have pointed out, Saddam Hussein, for all his evils, has not had a record of cooperating with terrorist groups who might utilize unconventional means of delivering such weapons. (In contrast, al-Qaeda has received support from Kurd controlled northern Iraq which is protected from Saddam Hussein by the U.S. and British-patrolled no-fly zone.) Baghdad has been deterred from taking any provocative action over the course of the last decade, and Saddam Hussein's military strength has been substantially diminished by years of sanctions and periodic bombings by U.S. and British air forces. Even if the U.N. inspectors had uncovered evidence that Iraq was producing agents for use in chemical or biological weapons, it seems unlikely for logistical reasons that such weapons will be used imminently in attacks on the United States or the United Kingdom. However, it should not be forgotten that Iraq has used chemical weapons in the past against the Iranians and the Kurds. But none of Iraq's neighbours, including Israel, has appealed for protection from an imminent attack by Iraq—something the International Court of Justice has held is a prerequisite for the use of collective self-defence. In its National Security Strategy, issued by the White House in September 2002, the Bush Administration argued for a relaxation of the imminent threat requirement for pre-emptive self-defence in the aftermath of the deadly attacks of 11 September, for which the United States had no warning. In President Bush's words, since 'unbalanced dictators with weapons of mass destruction can deliver those weapons on missiles or secretly provide them to terrorists allies[,] if we wait for threats to fully materialize, we will have waited too long'. It is noteworthy in this regard that, subsequent to Iraq's 1990 invasion of Kuwait and its use of chemical weapons against the Iranians and Kurds, there has been a reappraisal of the legality of Israel's 1981 action by many diplomats and legal scholars. In hindsight, Israel's justification does not look far-fetched, after all.

**Stability of the International System Under Threat**

But critics of an expanded notion of pre-emptive self-defence maintain that a nation's capacity alone should not be sufficient to trigger defensive strikes against it. The world is full of other countries, such as North Korea, that possess weapons of mass destruction and have been generally hostile toward the United States, but they have not been seen as legitimate targets for preemptive attacks. And if the law is interpreted as permitting any country that feels threatened to attack any country from which it feels the threat is emanating, the international taboo against using force will be severely diminished and the international system will be dangerously destabilised. International law is governed by the principle of reciprocity: what is good for the goose is good for the gander. Critics worry that the example set by the invasion of Iraq will undoubtedly be invoked by others pressing for war, such as Russia against Georgia, India against Pakistan, China against Taiwan, or North Korea against South Korea. The precedent would encourage nations to strike first under the pretext of pre-emption.

After World War II, German and Japanese leaders were tried and convicted for planning and participating in an aggressive war. But there is no international court existing today with jurisdiction to consider the issue of the legality of the U.S./U.K. invasion of Iraq. While the newly established International Criminal Court (ICC) does have jurisdiction over any specific war crimes committed during the invasion by British troops by virtue of the United Kingdom's Ratification of the Court's statute, unlike the Nuremberg tribunal, the ICC's jurisdiction does not extend to the crime of aggression. Consequently, the lawfulness of the U.S./U.K. action will be judged not in a court of law, but in the court of world opinion. Whatever that court's ultimate judgment, the debate itself has advanced the cause of international law. It should be acknowledged that international law is not a static instrument, but one that is fluid and which may change under the influence of consistent state practice and the stated opinions of governments. By articulating a legal case, the United States and the United Kingdom have acknowledged the relevance of international law, and have interpreted it, they believe, to offer greater opportunity for international peace and security.

## 12. Richard A. Falk, Future Implication of the Iraq Conflict: What Future for the U.N. Charter System of War Prevention?

*American Journal of International Law*, July 2003
[footnotes omitted by editors]

### I. Framing an Inquiry

President George W. Bush historically challenged the United Nations Security Council when he uttered some memorable words in the course of his September 12, 2002, speech to the General Assembly: "Will the U.N. serve the purpose of its founding, or will it be irrelevant?" In the aftermath of the Iraq war there are at least two answers to this question. The answer of the U.S. government would be to suggest that the United Nations turned out to be irrelevant due to its failure to endorse recourse to war against the Iraq of Saddam Hussein. The answer of those who opposed the war is that the U.N. Security Council served the purpose of its founding by its refusal to endorse recourse to a war that could not be persuasively reconciled with the U.N. Charter and international law. This difference of assessment is not just factual, whether Iraq was a threat and whether the inspection process was succeeding at a reasonable pace; it was also conceptual, even jurisprudential. The resolution of this latter debate is likely to shape the future role of the United Nations, as well as influence the attitude of the most powerful sovereign state as to the relationship between international law generally and the use of force as an instrument of foreign policy.

These underlying concerns antedate the recent preoccupation with Iraq, and were vigorously debated during the Cold War era, especially during the latter stages of the Vietnam War. But the present context of the debate regarding the interplay between sovereign discretion on matters of force and U.N. authority was framed in the late 1990s around the topic of humanitarian intervention, especially in relation to the Kosovo war. The burning issue in the Kosovo setting was whether "a coalition of the willing" acting under the umbrella of NATO was legally entitled to act as a residual option, given the perceived U.N. Security Council unwillingness to mandate a use of force despite the urgent humanitarian dangers facing the Albanian Kosovars. In that instance, a formal mandate was sought and provided by NATO, but without what seemed to be textually required by Article 53(1) of the U.N. Charter, that is, lacking some expression of explicit authorization by the U.N. Security Council. Legal apologists for the initiative insisted that such authorization could be derived from prior U.N. Security Council resolutions, as well as from the willingness of the United Nations to manage the post-conflict civil reconstruction of Kosovo that amounted to a tacit assent, providing the undertaking with a retroactive certification of legality. To similar effect were arguments suggesting that the failure of the Security Council to adopt a resolution of censure introduced by those members opposed to the Kosovo war amounted to an implied acknowledgment of legality.

But the tension with the Charter rules on the use of force was so clear that these efforts at legalization seemed ineffectual, and a far preferable approach was adopted by the Independent International Commission on Kosovo, which concluded that the intervention in Kosovo was "illegal, but legitimate." The troublesome elasticity of this doctrine was conditioned in two ways, first by suggesting the need for the intervening side to bear a heavy burden of persuasion as to the necessity of intervention to avoid an impending or ongoing humanitarian catastrophe. Second, there was a checklist of duties that need to be fulfilled by the intervenors to achieve legitimacy, emphasizing the protection of the civilian population, adherence to the international laws of war, and a convincing focus on humanitarian goals, as distinct from economic and strategic aims. In Kosovo the moral and political case for intervention seemed strong: a vulnerable and long abused majority population facing an imminent prospect of ethnic cleansing by Serb rulers, a scenario for effective intervention with minimal risks of unforeseen negative effects or extensive collateral damage, and the absence of significant nonhumanitarian motivations on the intervening side. As such, the foundation for a principled departure under exceptional circumstances from a strict rendering of Charter rules on the use of force seemed present. The legality/legitimacy gap, however, was recognized to be unhealthy, eroding the authority of international law over time, and the Commission recommended strongly that it be closed at the earliest possible time by U.N. initiative. Its report urged, for example, that the permanent members of the Security Council consider agreeing not to cast adverse votes in the setting of impending humanitarian catastrophes. The adoption of such a practice would have enabled the Kosovo intervention to be approved by the Security Council even in the face of Russian and Chinese opposition, which would have been registered in the debate and by way of abstentions.

More ambitiously, the Commission proposed a three-step process designed to acknowledge within the United Nations Charter system the enforcement role of the organization in contexts of severe human rights violations. The first step consists of a framework of principles designed to limit claims of humanitarian intervention to a narrow set of circumstances, and to assure that the dynamics of implementation adhere to international humanitarian law and promote the well-being of the people being protected. The second step is to draft a resolution for adoption by the General Assembly in the form of a Declaration on the Right and Responsibility of Humanitarian Intervention that seeks to reconcile respect for sovereign rights, the duty to implement human rights, and the responsibility to prevent humanitarian catastrophes. The third step would be to amend the Charter to incorporate these changes as they pertain to the role and responsibility of the U.N. Security Council, and other multilateral frameworks and coalitions that undertake humanitarian interventions. It should be noted that no progress toward closing this legitimacy/legality gap by formal or informal action within the United Nations can be anticipated at this time. There exists substantial opposition, especially among Asian countries, to any expansion of the interventionary mandate of the United Nations and other political actors in the setting of human rights. This opposition has deepened since Kosovo because of the controversial uses of force claimed by the United States in its antiterrorism campaign that have combined security and human rights arguments.

Iraq tested the U.N. Charter system in a way complementary to that associated with the Kosovo controversy. The Iraq test was associated with the impact of the September 11 attacks and the challenge of mega-terrorism. The initial American military response to the Qaeda attack and continuing threat was directed at Afghanistan, a convenient territorial target both because it seemed to be the nerve center of the terrorist organization and a country ruled by the Taliban regime that allowed Al Qaeda to operate extensive terrorist training bases within its territory, and because it lacked some crucial attributes needed for full membership in international society, including widespread diplomatic recognition. The reasonableness of waging war to supplant the Taliban regime and destroy the Qaeda base of operations in Afghanistan was widely accepted by the entire spectrum of countries active in world politics, although there was only the most minimal effort by the U.S. government to demonstrate that it was acting within the U.N. framework. The

Qaeda responsibility for September 11 was amply demonstrated, the prospect of future attacks seemed great and possibly imminent, and the American capability to win the war at a proportional cost seemed convincing. There was no significant international opposition to the American initiation and conduct of the Afghanistan war, and there were varying levels of support from all of America's traditional allies. International law was stretched in these novel circumstances to provide a major state with the practical option of responding with force to one important source of mega-terrorist warfare.

But when the Iraq phase of the September 11 response beyond Afghanistan began to be discussed by American leaders, most reactions around the world were highly critical, generating a worldwide peace movement dedicated to avoiding the war and a variety of efforts by governments to urge an alternative to war. The main American justification for proceeding immediately against Iraq was articulated in the form of a claimed right of preemptive warfare, abstractly explained as necessary conduct in view of the alleged interface between weaponry of mass destruction and the extremist tactics of the mega-terrorists. It was argued that it was unacceptable in these circumstances for the United States to wait to be attacked, and that preemptive warfare was essential to uphold the security of the "civilized" portion of the world. In his talk at the United Nations, Bush said, "We cannot stand by and do nothing while dangers gather." It was this claim that was essentially rejected by the U.N. Security Council's refusal to go along with U.S./U.K. demands for a direct endorsement of recourse to war. The precise American contention was more narrowly and multiply framed in relation to the failures of Iraq to cooperate fully with the U.N. inspectors, the years of nonimplementation of earlier Security Council resolutions imposing disarmament obligations on Iraq after the Gulf War, and, above all, by the supposedly heightened threat posed by Iraq's alleged arsenal of weapons of mass destruction.

\* \* \*

At this stage, it is impossible to predict how the Iraq war will impact upon the Charter system with respect to the international regulation of force. It will depend on how principal states, especially the United States, treat the issue. International law, in this crucial sense, is neither more nor less than what the powerful actors in the system, and to a lesser extent the global community of international jurists, say it is. International law in the area of the use of force cannot by itself induce consistent compliance because of sovereignty-oriented political attitudes combined with the gross disparities in power that prevent the logic of reciprocity and the benefits of mutuality from operating with respect to the security agenda of states. The "realist" school has dominated the foreign policy process of major countries throughout the existence of the modern state system, having been challenged only marginally by a Wilsonian approach that is more reliant on legalism and moralism. To the extent that restraint with respect to the use of force is advocated by realists, it is based on cost-benefit assessments, including the diplomatic virtue of prudence and the avoidance of over-extension that has been blamed throughout history for the decline of major states.

\* \* \*

## II. The Iraq War and the Future of the Charter System

Against the jurisprudential background depicted in the previous section, an interpretation of the Iraq precedent is necessarily tentative. It depends, in the first analysis, on whether the American battlefield victory in the Iraq war can be converted into a political victory, which will be measured in Iraq by such factors as stability, democratization, recovery of Iraqi sovereignty, and economic development. If the American occupation is viewed as successful, then the intervention is likely to be treated as "legitimate," despite being generally regarded as "illegal." Such a perception will be viewed by some as adding a needed measure of flexibility in the application of the Charter system in a world where the possible interplay of mega-terrorist tactics and weaponry of mass destruction validates recourse to anticipatory self-defense, but it will be dismissed by others as an opportunistic repudiation of legal restraints by the world's sole superpower.

There are two main conceptual explanations of this likely divergence of opinion. The first relates to issues of *factual plausibility*. The doctrine of preemption, as such, is less troublesome than its unilateral application in circumstances where the burden of persuasion as to the imminence and severity of the threat is not sustained. The diplomatic repudiation of the United States in the Security Council resulted mainly from the factual unpersuasiveness of the U.S. arguments about the threats associated with Iraqi retention of weaponry of mass destruction and the claims of linkage between the Baghdad regime and the Qaeda network, and the alleged failures of deterrence and containment. There were no doubts about the brutality of Saddam Hussein's rule, but there was little support for recourse to war on such grounds. This skepticism has been heightened by the failure so far to uncover weaponry of mass destruction in the aftermath of the war, despite total access to suspicious sites and the cooperation of Iraqi scientists and weapons personnel.

The second ground of divergence relates to arguments of *retroactive justification*. Here the focus is on whether a war opposed because its side effects seemed potentially dangerous, and its advance rationale was not convincing enough to justify stretching the Charter system of restraint, could be justified after the fact. The justifications combine the quick military victory with relatively low casualty figures, as reinforced by the documentation of Saddam Hussein's criminality as an Iraqi leader. Such an argument would seem more convincing if the American-led coalition forces had been more clearly welcomed as "liberators" rather than viewed as "occupiers," and if the post-combat American presence in Iraq was less marred by violent incidents of resistance and further American casualties. It remains too early to pass judgment. If the occupation is relatively short, and is generally perceived to benefit the Iraqi people and not the American occupiers, arguments based on retroactive justification are likely to gain support, and the Iraqi precedent would be viewed not so much as destructive of the Charter system, as an extension of it based on the emerging enlargement of the role of the international community to protect societies vulnerable to abusive governments.

\* \* \*

### III. The Charter System, Mega-Terrorism, and Humanitarian Intervention

In the 1990s there was a definite trend toward accepting a more interventionary role for the United Nations with respect to the prevention of ethnic cleansing and genocide. The Security Council, as supported by the last three secretaries-general, reflecting a greater prominence for the international protection of human rights and less anxiety about risks of escalation than were operative during the Cold War, narrowed the degree of deference owed to the territorial supremacy of sovereign governments. As such, the domestic jurisdiction exclusion of U.N. intervention expressed in Article 2(7) was definitely under challenge from the widespread grassroots and governmental advocacy of humanitarian intervention in the years following the Cold War. Although the pattern of claims and practice remained contested, being resisted especially by China and other Asian countries, there was considerable support for humanitarian intervention. The U.N. was more insistently attacked for doing too little, as in Bosnia and Rwanda, than in doing too much.

A variant on this debate is connected with the instances of uses of force under American leadership in the post-September 11 world. In both Afghanistan and Iraq recourse to force rested on defensive claims against the new threats of mega-terrorism, but the effect in both instances was to liberate captive populations from extremely oppressive regimes, establishing patterns of governance and potential self-determination that seemed virtually impossible for the oppressed citizenry to achieve by normal modes of resistance. Even though the humanitarian *motivations* of the United States are suspect in both instances, due to a past record of collaboration with these regimes while their abusive conduct was at its worst, the effect of the interventions was emancipatory, and the declared intention of the occupation is to support human rights and democratization. Undoubtedly, such forcible liberations would not have taken place without the pressures mounted and the climate created by the September 11 attacks. Nevertheless, to the extent that mega-terrorism is associated with criminal forms of governmental authority, would it not be reasonable to construe uses of force that accomplished "regime change" as part of an enlarged doctrine of humanitarian intervention?

\* \* \*

But a pro-intervention argument should not be treated as acceptable in circumstances where the use of force is associated with alleged security threats posed by the menace of mega-terrorism, but the justification tendered after the fact emphasizes humanitarian intervention. In Afghanistan the security argument was sufficiently convincing as to make the humanitarian benefits of the war a political and moral bonus, but without bearing on the legal case for recourse to force, which was already convincing on the defensive grounds claimed. In Iraq, by contrast, the security and related anti-Qaeda arguments were unconvincing, and the claimed humanitarian benefits resulting from the war were emphasized by American officials as a way to circumvent the illegality of the American-led recourse to force. Such post hoc efforts at legalization should not be accorded much respect, especially in the context of a major war where prior efforts to obtain a mandate for the use of force were not endorsed by the Security Council even in the face of major diplomatic pressures mounted by Washington in the several months prior to the Iraq war.

### IV. A Constructivist Future for the U.N. Charter System

The position favored here is that the United States would be best served by adhering to the U.N. Charter system. This system is flexible enough to accommodate new and genuine security imperatives as well as changing values, including a shifting balance between sovereign rights and world community responsibilities. In both settings of humanitarian intervention and responses against mega-terrorism the Charter system can be *legally* vindicated *in appropriate factual circumstances*.

\* \* \*

It is not the Charter system that is in disarray, providing sensible grounds for declaring the project of regulating recourse to war by states a failed experiment that should now be abandoned. It is rather leading states, and above all the United States, that need to be persuaded that their interests are served and their values realized by a more diligent pursuit of a law-oriented foreign policy.

\* \* \*

## Authors' Note

In early 2011, thousands of demonstrators took to the streets in Libya to protest poor economic and political conditions under the four-decade regime of Mummar Qadhafi. Qadhafi responded with force as the protests increased in intensity. Targeting civilians and civilian controlled areas, Qadhafi ordered the military, militias, and mercenaries to quell the protests. Hundreds of civilians were killed in air raids by the Libyan Air Force. Many protesters and military personnel were also killed as the fighting intensified. Despite the loss of several key cities in the east of Libya, Qadhafi continued to order attacks against civilians and civilian targets.

On February 26, 2011, the United Nations Security Council passed resolution 1970 in response to the use of force by the Libyan government against Libyan citizens. Resolution 1970 implemented an arms embargo and authorized states to freeze Libyan assets in an attempt to pressure Qadhafi to stop targeting civilians and civilian controlled areas. The resolution also issued a travel ban against numerous Libyan officials. Qadhafi rejected the resolution and failed to comply with the demand to stop targeting civilians. On March 17, 2011, in response to the impending fall of Benghazi, Qadhafi's rhetoric that the streets would run with the blood of the rebels, and the failure of Resolution 1970, the United Nations Security Council passed Resolution 1973, authorizing the use of force against the Qadhafi regime.

## 13. Resolution 1973
### United Nations Security Council, 2011

*The Security Council*

*Recalling* its resolution 1970 (2011) of 26 February 2011,

*Deploring* the failure of the Libyan authorities to comply with resolution 1970 (2011),

*Expressing* grave concern at the deteriorating situation, the escalation of violence, and the heavy civilian casualties,

*Reiterating* the responsibility of the Libyan authorities to protect the Libyan population and *reaffirming* that parties to armed conflicts bear the primary responsibility to take all feasible steps to ensure the protection of civilians,

*Condemning* the gross and systematic violation of human rights, including arbitrary detentions, enforced disappearances, torture and summary executions,

\* \* \*

*Expressing its determination* to ensure the protection of civilians and civilian populated areas and the rapid and unimpeded passage of humanitarian assistance and the safety of humanitarian personnel,

\* \* \*

*Determining* that the situation in the Libyan Arab Jamahiriya continues to constitute a threat to international peace and security,

*Acting* under Chapter VII of the Charter of the United Nations,

1. *Demands* the immediate establishment of a cease-fire and a complete end to violence and all attacks against, and abuses of, civilians;

2. *Stresses* the need to intensify efforts to find a solution to the crisis which responds to the legitimate demands of the Libyan people and *notes* the decisions of the Secretary-General to send his Special Envoy to Libya and of the Peace and Security Council of the African Union to send its ad hoc High Level Committee to Libya with the aim of facilitating dialogue to lead to the political reforms necessary to find a peaceful and sustainable solution;

3. *Demands* that the Libyan authorities comply with their obligations under international law, including international humanitarian law, human rights and refugee law and take all measures to protect civilians and meet their basic needs, and to ensure the rapid and unimpeded passage of humanitarian assistance;

**Protection of civilians**

4. *Authorizes* Member States that have notified the Secretary-General, acting nationally or through regional organizations or arrangements, and acting in cooperation with the Secretary-General, to take all necessary measures, notwithstanding paragraph 9 of resolution 1970 (2011), to protect civilians and civilian populated areas under threat of attack in the Libyan Arab Jamahiriya, including Benghazi, while excluding a foreign occupation force of any form on any part of Libyan territory, and *requests* the Member States concerned to inform the Secretary-General immediately of the measures they take pursuant to the authorization conferred by this paragraph which shall be immediately reported to the Security Council;

\* \* \*

**No fly zone**

6. *Decides* to establish a ban on all flights in the airspace of the Libyan Arab Jamahiriya in order to help protect civilians;

7. *Decides further* that the ban imposed by paragraph 6 shall not apply to flights whose sole purpose is humanitarian, such as delivering or facilitating the delivery of assistance, including medical supplies, food, humanitarian workers and related assistance, or evacuating foreign nationals from the Libyan Arab Jamahiriya, nor shall it apply to flights authorised by paragraphs 4 or 8, nor other flights which are deemed necessary by States acting under the authorisation conferred in paragraph 8 to be for the benefit of the Libyan people, and that these flights shall be coordinated with any mechanism established under paragraph 8;

8. *Authorizes* Member States that have notified the Secretary-General and the Secretary-General of the League of Arab States, acting nationally or through regional organizations or arrangements, to take all necessary measures to enforce compliance with the ban on flights imposed by paragraph 6 above, as necessary, and requests the States concerned in cooperation with the League of Arab States to coordinate closely with the Secretary General on the measures they are taking to implement this ban, including by establishing an appropriate mechanism for implementing the provisions of paragraphs 6 and 7 above,

\* \* \*

**Enforcement of the arms embargo**

13. *Decides that* paragraph 11 of resolution 1970 (2011) shall be replaced by the following paragraph: "Calls upon all Member States, in particular States of the region, acting nationally or through regional organisations or arrangements, in order to ensure strict implementation of the arms embargo established by paragraphs 9 and 10 of resolution 1970 (2011), to inspect in their territory, including seaports and airports, and on the high seas, vessels and aircraft bound to or from the Libyan Arab Jamahiriya, if the State concerned has information that provides reasonable grounds to believe that the cargo contains items the supply, sale, transfer or export of which is prohibited by paragraphs 9 or 10 of resolution 1970 (2011) as modified by this resolution, including the provision of armed mercenary personnel, *calls upon* all flag States of such vessels and aircraft to cooperate with

such inspections and authorises Member States to use all measures commensurate to the specific circumstances to carry out such inspections";

\* \* \*

28. *Reaffirms* its intention to keep the actions of the Libyan authorities under continuous review and underlines its readiness to review at any time the measures imposed by this resolution and resolution 1970 (2011), including by strengthening, suspending or lifting those measures, as appropriate, based on compliance by the Libyan authorities with this resolution and resolution 1970 (2011).

29. *Decides* to remain actively seized of the matter.

\* \* \*

## 14. Bibliography of Additional Sources

- Jonathan I. Charney, *The Use of Force Against Terrorism and International Law*, 95 Am. J. Int'l L. 835 (2001).

- Thomas Franck, Recourse to Force (2002).

- Judith G. Gardam, *Legal Restraints on Security Council Military Enforcement Action*, 17 Mich. J. Int'l L. 285 (1996).

- Judith G. Gardam, *Proportionality and Force in International Law*, 87 Am. J. Int'l L. (1993).

- Thomas D. Grant, *Agora: Future Implication of the Iraq Conflict: The Security Council and Iraq: An Incremental Practice*, 97 Am. J. Int'l L. 823 (Oct. 2003).

- Christine Gray, *President Obama's 2010 United States National Security Strategy and International Law on the Use of Force*, 10 Chinese J. Int'l L. 35 (2011).

- Christopher Greenwood, *International Law and the Pre-emptive Use of Force: Afghanistan, Al-Qaida, and Iraq*, 4 San Diego Int'l L. J. (2003).

- Christopher Greenwood, *New World Order or Old? The Invasion of Kuwait and the Rule of Law*, 55 Mod. L. Rev. 153 (1992).

- The Iraq Crisis and World Order: Structural and Normative Challenges (W. P. S. Sidhu & Ramesh Thakur eds.) (2006).

- Craig Martin, *Taking War Seriously: A Model for Constitutional Constraints on the Use of Force, in Compliance with International Law*, 76.2 Brook. L. Rev. 611 (2011).

- Sean D. Murphy, *Assessing the Legality of Invading Iraq*, 92 Geo. L.J. 173 (2004).

- New Killing Fields: Massacre and the Politics of Intervention (Nicolaus Mills & Kira Brunner eds.) (2002).

- Mary O'Connell, International Law and the Use of Force, (2005).

- Nicholas Rostow, *International Law and the 2003 Campaign against Iraq, in Issues in International Law and Military Operations*, 80 Int'l L. Stud. 21 (Richard B. Jaques ed.) (2006).

- Ken Roth, *War in Iraq: Not a Humanitarian Intervention*, Human Rights Watch World Report 2004 (2004).

- Oscar Schachter, *The Right of States to Use Armed Force*, 82 Mich. L. Rev. 1620 (1984).

# Chapter XIII

# The International Nuclear Nonproliferation Regime

## Introduction

This chapter introduces the reader to the major instruments, bodies, and states of the nuclear nonproliferation regime. In 1957, the International Atomic Energy Agency (IAEA) was created to promote the spread of peaceful uses for nuclear technology and to promote nuclear disarmament. As such, the IAEA built a framework within which states were permitted to use nuclear power for peaceful purposes. The efforts of the IAEA were augmented in 1970 with the adoption of the Nuclear Nonproliferation Treaty (NPT), which serves as the cornerstone of nuclear non-proliferation efforts. The nuclear non-proliferation regime has come under increasing pressure in the past few years as the nuclear states of Israel, India, and Pakistan continue to operate outside the treaty framework, and North Korea and Iran have made substantial progress in the development of nuclear weapons. This chapter provides a basis to discuss the challenges posed to nuclear weapons regulation, the effectiveness of existing mechanisms, and the nature of the debate concerning efforts to constrain North Korea's and Iran's efforts.

## Objectives

- To form a basic understanding of the nuclear nonproliferation legal regime.
- To evaluate and identify the strengths and weaknesses of the nonproliferation regime.
- To explore how the current regime for nuclear non-proliferation may be improved.
- To understand how the situations in Iran and North Korea may be addressed within the existing framework of legal mechanisms.

# Problems

Students should come to class prepared to discuss the following questions:

1.  Is the Nuclear Nonproliferation Treaty (NPT) effective? What modifications or measures would make the NPT more effective?

2.  Is the International Atomic Energy Agency (IAEA) effective? What modifications or measures would make the IAEA more effective?

3.  Do you agree with the International Court of Justice's (ICJ) conclusions on the legality of the threat or use of nuclear weapons? Are nuclear weapons legitimate under Article 51 of the U.N. Charter? Are they compatible with the laws of armed conflict, and international humanitarian law in particular?

4.  What factors have influenced states to abandon their nuclear weapons programs? Can these factors be applied to non-nuclear weapons states with suspected nuclear weapons development programs?

5.  Given the developments concerning the case of Iran, does Iran still have the right to develop a peaceful nuclear energy program?

6.  Do non-signatories to the NPT (e.g., Israel, India, and Pakistan) have the right to develop nuclear weapons programs? Given that North Korea is no longer part of the NPT, does North Korea now have the right to develop a nuclear weapons program?

7.  What legitimate countermeasures (e.g., diplomatic negotiations, sanctions, use of force) can states apply in response to suspected nuclear weapons programs? Discuss the pros and cons of each. Which method is the most or least effective?

8.  Can we live with emerging nuclear-armed states? What effects will emerging nuclear-armed states have on the nonproliferation regime? What implications will emerging nuclear-armed states have for the future?

# Case Studies and Negotiation Simulations

Drawing from the materials in this chapter, students should come to class prepared to participate in the following case studies:

Iran: For the purposes of this study, assume that the International Atomic Energy Agency (IAEA) has just confirmed that Iran has developed a medium-range ballistic missile that is capable of reaching Jerusalem. In a statement released by Iran's Ministry of Foreign Affairs, Iran has announced its withdrawal from the Nuclear Non-Proliferation Treaty (NPT) and confirmed its nuclear missile capability. Iran has also stated that because they are no longer bound by the provisions of the NPT, their nuclear weapons program is legitimate and lawful. The IAEA Director General has convened an emergency meeting on the matter with the following states: Iran, the United States, China, Russia, the United Kingdom, France, Germany, and Israel. Propose courses of action for continuing relations with Iran from the perspective of each that address national and international security.

North Korea and South Korea: For the purposes of this study, assume that North Korea has just threatened to detonate a nuclear warhead in South Korea in response to perceived territorial aggression by the South. In response, the US has convened an emergency meeting with South Korea, Japan, China and Russia to discuss potential ways to avoid the implementation of this threat. From these various perspectives propose courses of action for dealing with this situation.

# Materials

1. Statute of the International Atomic Energy Agency, arts. I–IV, VII, IX–X, XII, Oct. 26, 1956, 8 U.S.T. 1093, 276 U.N.T.S. 3.

2. Treaty on the Non-proliferation of Nuclear Weapons, Jul. 1, 1968, 21 U.S.T. 483, 729 U.N.T.S. 161.

3. Legality of the Threat or Use of Nuclear Weapons, Advisory Opinion, 1996 I.C.J. 226 (Jul. 8) 90–92, 95–97, 105.

4. Liz Heffernan, *The Nuclear Weapons Opinions: Reflections on the Advisory Procedure of the International Court of Justice*, 28.1 STETSON L. REV. 133 (1998).

5. Barack Obama, U.S. President, Address at Hradcany Square, Prague, Czech Republic (Apr. 5, 2009).

6. Sergio Duarte, U.N. High Representative for Disarmament Affairs, Address at the Fordham International Law Journal Symposium: Nuclear Weapons and International Law: A Nuclear Nonproliferation Regime for the 21st Century (Feb. 25, 2010).

7. Greg Bruno, *Iran's Nuclear Program: A CFR.org Backgrounder*, Council on Foreign Relations (Mar. 10, 2010).

8. Greg Bruno, *CFR.org Interview with Manouchehr Mottaki: What Iran Wants*, Council on Foreign Relations (Sept. 20, 2009).

9. *Deputy Foreign Minister: Iran Determined to Continue Peaceful Nuclear Activities*, Islamic Republic News Agency, May 21, 2009.

10. *Implementing Tougher Sanctions on Iran: A Progress Report: Hearing Before the H. Comm. on Foreign Affairs* (2010) (statement of U.S. Undersecretary of State William Burns).

11. Catherine Ashton, Eur. Union High Representative, Address in Istanbul, Turkey (Jan. 22, 2011).

12. Director General of the International Atomic Energy Agency (IAEA), *Implementation of the N.P.T. Safeguards Agreement and Relevant Provisions of Security Council Resolutions in the Islamic Republic of Iran*, GOV/2011/7 (Feb. 25, 2011).

13. P5+1 Group, Iran's Nuclear Program, Statement at IAEA Board of Governors Meeting, Mar. 9, 2011.

14. Erica Downs & Suzanne Maloney, *Getting China to Sanction Iran*, 90.2 Foreign Aff. 15 (Mar.–Apr. 2011).

15. Israel Ministry of Foreign Affairs, *Israel's Response to U.N. Security Council Resolution 1929 on Sanctions Against Iran*, June 9, 2010.

16. Ronen Bergman, *Letter from Tel Aviv: Netanyahu's Iranian Dilemma*, Foreign Aff. (June 10, 2009).

17. Center for Arms Control and Non-Proliferation, *Risky Business: Why Attacking Iran Is a Bad Idea*, (Apr. 12, 2007).

18. *KCNA "Detailed Report" Explains NPT Withdrawal*, Korean Central News Agency, Jan. 22, 2003.

19. Jayshree Bajoria & Carin Zissis, *The Six-Party Talks on North Korea's Nuclear Program: A CFR.org Backgrounder*, Council on Foreign Relations (Jul. 1, 2009).

20. U.N. Panel of Experts on DPRK Nuclear Armament, Rep. to the Security Council from the Panel of Experts Established Pursuant to Resolution 1874 (2009) (S/2010/517) (May 12, 2010).

21. Republic of Korea Ministry of Foreign Affairs and Trade, *Making Efforts Toward a Peaceful Resolution of the North Korean Nuclear Issue* (May 17, 2010).

22. Director General of the International Atomic Energy Agency (IAEA), *Application of Safeguards in the Democratic People's Republic of Korea (DPRK)*, GOV/2010/45-GC(54)/12 (Aug. 31, 2010).

23. Jayshree Bajoria, *The China-North Korea Relationship*, Council on Foreign Relations (Oct. 7, 2010).

24. *Breaking the Cycle of North Korea Provocations: Hearing Before the S. Comm. on Foreign Relations* (2011) (statement of Special Representative for North Korea Policy Stephen Bosworth).

25. Bibliography of Additional Sources

## Authors' Note

The following three materials are the main sources upon which current rules for states' nuclear activities are based. The 1957 Statute of the International Atomic Energy Agency (IAEA) established the IAEA, the world agency for governing nuclear affairs. The IAEA's primary goals are to promote the spread of peaceful uses for nuclear technology and to promote nuclear disarmament. Though the IAEA is independent of the United Nations, it reports to the U.N. General Assembly and Security Council. The 1970 Treaty on the Non-Proliferation of Nuclear Weapons also aims to promote disarmament and peaceful applications of nuclear technology. The Treaty has been signed by 190 states. The 1996 ICJ Advisory Opinion on the Legality of the Threat or Use of Nuclear Weapons is one of few authoritative legal decisions concerning nuclear weapons. The Court found that, while international law does not expressly prohibit the use of nuclear weapons, the use of nuclear weapons generally contradicts international law of armed conflict, particularly norms of humanitarian law. The Court did not address whether the use of nuclear weapons would be legal in extreme circumstances.

# 1. Statute of the International Atomic Energy Agency, Articles I–IV, VIII, XII

### 1957

### Article I: Establishment of the Agency

The Parties hereto establish an International Atomic Energy Agency (hereinafter referred to as "the Agency") upon the terms and conditions hereinafter set forth.

### Article II: Objectives

The Agency shall seek to accelerate and enlarge the contribution of atomic energy to peace, health and prosperity throughout the world. It shall ensure, so far as it is able, that assistance provided by it or at its request or under its supervision or control is not used in such a way as to further any military purpose.

### Article III: Functions

A. The Agency is authorized:

1. To encourage and assist research on, and development and practical application of, atomic energy for peaceful uses throughout the world; and, if requested to do so, to act as an intermediary for the purposes of securing the performance of services or the supplying of materials, equipment, or facilities by one member of the Agency for another; and to perform any operation or service useful in research on, or development or practical application of, atomic energy for peaceful purposes;

2. To make provision, in accordance with this Statute, for materials, services, equipment, and facilities to meet the needs of research on, and development and practical application of, atomic energy for peaceful purposes, including the production of electric power, with due consideration for the needs of the under-developed areas of the world;

3. To foster the exchange of scientific and technical information on peaceful uses of atomic energy;

4. To encourage the exchange of training of scientists and experts in the field of peaceful uses of atomic energy;

5. To establish and administer safeguards designed to ensure that special fissionable and other materials, services, equipment, facilities, and information made available by the Agency or at its request or under its supervision or control are not used in such a way as to further any military purpose. [ ... ]

\* \* \*

B. In carrying out its functions, the Agency shall:

1. Conduct its activities in accordance with the purposes and principles of the United Nations to promote peace and international co-operation, and in conformity with policies of the United Nations furthering the establishment of safeguarded worldwide disarmament and in conformity with any international agreements entered into pursuant to such policies;

2. Establish control over the use of special fissionable materials received by the Agency, in order to ensure that these materials are used only for peaceful purposes;

\* \* \*

4. Submit reports on its activities annually to the General Assembly of the United Nations and, when appropriate, to the Security Council: if in connection with the activities of the Agency there should arise questions that are within the competence of the Security Council. [ ... ]

5. Submit reports to the Economic and Social Council and other organs of the United Nations on matters within the competence of these organs.

\* \* \*

D. Subject to the provisions of this Statute and to the terms of agreements concluded between a State or a group of States and the Agency which shall be in accordance with the provisions of the Statute, the activities of the Agency shall be carried out with due observance of the sovereign rights of States.

### Article IV: Membership

A. The initial members of the Agency shall be those States Members of the United Nations or of any of the specialized agencies which shall have signed this Statute within ninety days after it is opened for signature and shall have deposited an instrument of ratification.

B. Other members of the Agency shall be those States, whether or not Members of the United Nations or of any of the specialized agencies, which deposit an instrument of acceptance of this Statute after their membership has been approved by the General Conference upon the recommendation of the Board of Governors. [ ... ]

C. The Agency is based on the principle of the sovereign equality of all its members, and all members, in order to ensure to all of them the rights and benefits resulting from membership, shall fulfill in good faith the obligation assumed by them in accordance with this Statute.

\* \* \*

### Article VIII: Exchange of information

A. Each member should make available such information as would, in the judgment of the member, be helpful to the Agency.

B. Each member shall make available to the Agency all scientific information developed as a result of assistance extended by the Agency pursuant to article XI.

C. The Agency shall assemble and make available in an accessible form the information made available to it under paragraphs A and B of this article. It shall take positive steps to encourage the exchange among its members of information relating to the nature and peaceful uses of atomic energy and shall serve as an intermediary among its members for this purpose.

\* \* \*

### Article XII: Agency safeguards

A. With respect to any Agency project, or other arrangement where the Agency is requested by the parties concerned to apply safeguards, the Agency shall have the following rights and responsibilities to the extent relevant to the project or arrangement:

1. To examine the design of specialized equipment and facilities, including nuclear reactors, and to approve it only from the view point of assuring that it will not further any military purpose, that it complies with applicable health and safety standards, and that it will permit effective application of the safeguards provided for in this article;

\* \* \*

3. To require the maintenance and production of operating records to assist in ensuring accountability for source and special fissionable materials used or produced in the project or arrangement;

4. To call for and receive progress reports;

5. To approve the means to be used for the chemical processing of irradiated materials solely to ensure that this chemical processing will not lend itself to diversion of materials for military purposes. [ ... ]

6. To send into the territory of the recipient State or States inspectors, designated by the Agency after consultation with the State or States concerned, who shall have access at all times to all places and data and to any person who by reason of his occupation deals with materials, equipment, or facilities which are required by this Statute to be safeguarded, as necessary to account for source and special fissionable materials supplied and fissionable products and to determine whether there is compliance with the undertaking against use in furtherance of any military purpose referred. [ ... ].

7. In the event of non-compliance and failure by the recipient State or States to take requested corrective steps within a reasonable time, to suspend or terminate assistance and

withdraw any materials and equipment made available by the Agency or a member in furtherance of the project.

B. The Agency shall, as necessary, establish a staff of inspectors. The Staff of inspectors shall have the responsibility of examining all operations conducted by the Agency itself to determine whether the Agency is complying with the health and safety measures prescribed by it for application to projects subject to its approval, supervision or control, and whether the Agency is taking adequate measures to prevent the source and special fissionable materials in its custody or used or produced in its own operations from being used in furtherance of any military purpose. [ … ]

C. [ … ] The inspectors shall report any non-compliance to the Director General who shall thereupon transmit the report to the Board of Governors. The Board shall call upon the recipient State or States to remedy forthwith any non-compliance which it finds to have occurred. The Board shall report the non-compliance to all members and to the Security Council and General Assembly of the United Nations. In the event of failure of the recipient State or States to take fully corrective action within a reasonable time, the Board may take one or both of the following measures: direct curtailment or suspension of assistance being provided by the Agency or by a member, and call for the return of materials and equipment made available to the recipient member or group of members. The Agency may also, in accordance with article XIX, suspend any non-complying member from the exercise of the privileges and rights of membership.

## 2. Treaty on the Non-Proliferation of Nuclear Weapons
### 1970

The States concluding this Treaty, hereinafter referred to as the "Parties to the Treaty",

Considering the devastation that would be visited upon all mankind by a nuclear war and the consequent need to make every effort to avert the danger of such a war and to take measures to safeguard the security of peoples,

Believing that the proliferation of nuclear weapons would seriously enhance the danger of nuclear war,

In conformity with resolutions of the United Nations General Assembly calling for the conclusion of an agreement on the prevention of wider dissemination of nuclear weapons,

Undertaking to co-operate in facilitating the application of International Atomic Energy Agency safeguards on peaceful nuclear activities,

Expressing their support for research, development and other efforts to further the application, within the framework of the International Atomic Energy Agency safeguards system, of the principle of safeguarding effectively the flow of source and special fissionable materials by use of instruments and other techniques at certain strategic points,

Affirming the principle that the benefits of peaceful applications of nuclear technology, including any technological by-products which may be derived by nuclear-weapon States from the development of nuclear explosive devices, should be available for peaceful purposes to all Parties to the Treaty, whether nuclear-weapon or non-nuclear-weapon States,

Convinced that, in furtherance of this principle, all Parties to the Treaty are entitled to participate in the fullest possible exchange of scientific information for, and to contribute alone or in co-operation with other States to, the further development of the applications of atomic energy for peaceful purposes,

Declaring their intention to achieve at the earliest possible date the cessation of the nuclear arms race and to undertake effective measures in the direction of nuclear disarmament,

Urging the co-operation of all States in the attainment of this objective,

Recalling the determination expressed by the Parties to the 1963 Treaty banning nuclear weapon tests in the atmosphere, in outer space and under water in its Preamble to seek to achieve the discontinuance of all test explosions of nuclear weapons for all time and to continue negotiations to this end,

Desiring to further the easing of international tension and the strengthening of trust between States in order to facilitate the cessation of the manufacture of nuclear weapons, the liquidation of all their existing stockpiles, and the elimination from national arsenals of nuclear weapons and the means of their delivery pursuant to a Treaty on general and complete disarmament under strict and effective international control,

Recalling that, in accordance with the Charter of the United Nations, States must refrain in their international relations from the threat or use of force against the territorial integrity or political independence of any State, or in any other manner inconsistent with the Purposes of the United Nations, and that the establishment and maintenance of international peace and security are to be promoted with the least diversion for armaments of the world's human and economic resources,

*Have agreed as follows:*

### Article I

Each nuclear-weapon State Party to the Treaty undertakes not to transfer to any recipient whatsoever nuclear weapons or other nuclear explosive devices or control over such weapons or explosive devices directly, or indirectly; and not in any way to assist, encourage, or induce any non-nuclear-weapon State to manufacture or otherwise acquire nuclear weapons or other nuclear explosive devices, or control over such weapons or explosive devices.

### Article II

Each non-nuclear-weapon State Party to the Treaty undertakes not to receive the transfer from any transferor whatsoever of nuclear weapons or other nuclear explosive devices or of control over such weapons or explosive devices directly, or indirectly; not to manufacture or otherwise acquire nuclear weapons or other nuclear explosive devices; and not to seek or receive any assistance in the manufacture of nuclear weapons or other nuclear explosive devices.

### Article III

1. Each Non-nuclear-weapon State Party to the Treaty undertakes to accept safeguards, as set forth in an agreement to be negotiated and concluded with the International Atomic Energy Agency. [ ... ]

2. Each State Party to the Treaty undertakes not to provide: *(a)* source or special fissionable material, or *(b)* equipment or material especially designed or prepared for the processing, use or production of special fissionable material, to any non-nuclear-weapon State for peaceful purposes, unless the source or special fissionable material shall be subject to the safeguards required by this Article.

3. The safeguards required by this Article shall be implemented in a manner designed to comply with Article IV of this Treaty, and to avoid hampering the economic or technological development of the Parties or international co-operation in the field of peaceful nuclear activities. [ ... ]

4. Non-nuclear-weapon States Party to the Treaty shall conclude agreements with the International Atomic Energy Agency to meet the requirements of this Article either individually or together with other States in accordance with the Statute of the International Atomic Energy Agency. [ … ]

## Article IV

1. Nothing in this Treaty shall be interpreted as affecting the inalienable right of all the Parties to the Treaty to develop research, production and use of nuclear energy for peaceful purposes without discrimination and in conformity with Articles I and II of this Treaty.

* * *

## Article V

Each Party to the Treaty undertakes to take appropriate measures to ensure that, in accordance with this Treaty, under appropriate international observation and through appropriate international procedures, potential benefits from any peaceful applications of nuclear explosions will be made available to non-nuclear-weapon States Party to the Treaty on a non-discriminatory. [ … ]

## Article VI

Each of the Parties to the Treaty undertakes to pursue negotiations in good faith on effective measures relating to cessation of the nuclear arms race at an early date and to nuclear disarmament, and on a treaty on general and complete disarmament under strict and effective international control.

## Article VII

Nothing in this Treaty affects the right of any group of States to conclude regional treaties in order to assure the total absence of nuclear weapons in their respective territories.

## Article VIII

1. Any Party to the Treaty may propose amendments to this Treaty.

2. Any amendment to this Treaty must be approved by a majority of the votes of all the Parties to the Treaty, including the votes of all nuclear-weapon States Party to the Treaty and all other Parties which, on the date the amendment is circulated, are members of the Board of Governors of the International Atomic Energy Agency.

## Article IX

3. This Treaty shall enter into force after its ratification by the States, the Governments of which are designated Depositaries of the Treaty, and forty other States signatory to this Treaty and the deposit of their instruments of ratification. For the purposes of this Treaty, a nuclear weapon State is one which has manufactured and exploded a nuclear weapon or other nuclear explosive device prior to 1 January, 1967.

## Article X

1. Each Party shall in exercising its national sovereignty have the right to withdraw from the Treaty if it decides that extraordinary events, related to the subject matter of this Treaty, have jeopardized the supreme interests of its country. [ … ] Such notice shall include a statement of the extraordinary events it regards as having jeopardized its supreme interests.

2. Twenty-five years after the entry into force of the Treaty, a conference shall be convened to decide whether the Treaty shall continue in force indefinitely, or shall be extended for an additional fixed period or periods. This decision shall be taken by a majority of the Parties to the Treaty.

\* \* \*

## 3. Legality of the Threat or Use of Nuclear Weapons, Advisory Opinion
### International Court of Justice, 1996

\* \* \*

90. Although the applicability of the principles and rules of humanitarian law and of the principle of neutrality to nuclear weapons is hardly disputed, the conclusions to be drawn from this applicability are, on the other hand, controversial.

91. According to one point of view, the fact that recourse to nuclear weapons is subject to and regulated by the law of armed conflict does not necessarily mean that such recourse is as such prohibited. As one State put it to the Court:

> "Assuming that a State's use of nuclear weapons meets the requirements of self-defence, it must then be considered whether it conforms to the fundamental principles of the law of armed conflict regulating the conduct of hostilities"

> "the legality of the use of nuclear weapons must therefore be assessed in the light of the applicable principles of international law regarding the use of force and the conduct of hostilities, as is the case with other methods and means of warfare"

and

> "the reality is that nuclear weapons might be used in a wide variety of circumstances with very different results in terms of likely civilian casualties. In some cases, such as the use of a low yield nuclear weapon against warships on the High Seas or troops in sparsely populated areas, it is possible to envisage a nuclear attack which caused comparatively few civilian casualties. It is by no means the case that every use of nuclear weapons against a military objective would inevitably cause very great collateral civilian casualties."

92. Another view holds that recourse to nuclear weapons could never be compatible with the principles and rules of humanitarian law and is therefore prohibited. In the event of their use, nuclear weapons would in all circumstances be unable to draw any distinction between the civilian population and combatants, or between civilian objects and military objectives, and their effects, largely uncontrollable, could not be restricted, either in time or in space, to lawful military targets. Such weapons would kill and destroy in a necessarily indiscriminate manner, on account of the blast, heat and radiation occasioned by the nuclear explosion and the effects induced; and the number of casualties which would ensue would be enormous. The use of nuclear weapons would therefore be prohibited in any circumstance, notwithstanding the absence of any explicit conventional prohibition. That view lay at the basis of the assertions by certain States before the Court that nuclear weapons are by their nature illegal under customary international law, by virtue of the fundamental principle of humanity.

95. Nor can the Court make a determination on the validity of the view that the recourse to nuclear weapons would be illegal in any circumstance owing to their inherent and total incompatibility with the law applicable in armed conflict. Certainly, as the Court has already indicated, the principles and rules of law applicable in armed conflict—at the heart of which is the overriding consideration of humanity—make the conduct of armed hos-

tilities subject to a number of strict requirements. Thus, methods and means of warfare, which would preclude any distinction between civilian and military targets, or which would result in unnecessary suffering to combatants, are prohibited. In view of the unique characteristics of nuclear weapons, to which the Court has referred above, the use of such weapons in fact seems scarcely reconcilable with respect for such requirements. Nevertheless, the Court considers that it does not have sufficient elements to enable it to conclude with certainty that the use of nuclear weapons would necessarily be at variance with the principles and rules of law applicable in armed conflict in any circumstance.

96. Furthermore, the Court cannot lose sight of the fundamental right of every State to survival, and thus its right to resort to self-defense, in accordance with Article 51 of the Charter, when its survival is at stake. Nor can it ignore the practice referred to as "policy of deterrence", to which an appreciable section of the international community adhered for many years. The Court also notes the reservations which certain nuclear-weapon States have appended to the undertakings they have given, notably under the Protocols to the Treaties of Tlatelolco and Rarotonga, and also under the declarations made by them in connection with the extension of the Treaty on the Non-Proliferation of Nuclear Weapons, not to resort to such weapons.

97. Accordingly, in view of the present state of international law viewed as a whole, as examined above by the Court, and of the elements of fact at its disposal, the Court is led to observe that it cannot reach a definitive conclusion as to the legality or illegality of the use of nuclear weapons by a State in an extreme circumstance of self-defence, in which its very survival would be at stake.

105. For these reasons, THE COURT,

(1) *Decides* to comply with the request for an advisory opinion;

(2) *Replies* in the following manner to the question put by the General Assembly:

A. Unanimously, there is in neither customary nor conventional international law any specific authorization of the threat or use of nuclear weapons;

B. By eleven votes to three, there is in neither customary nor conventional international law any comprehensive and universal prohibition of the threat or use of nuclear weapons as such;

C. Unanimously, a threat or use of force by means of nuclear weapons that is contrary to Article 2, paragraph 4, of the United Nations Charter and that fails to meet all the requirements of Article 51, is unlawful;

D. Unanimously, a threat or use of nuclear weapons should also be compatible with the requirements of the international law applicable in armed conflict, particularly those of the principles and rules of international humanitarian law, as well as with specific obligations under treaties and other undertakings which expressly deal with nuclear weapons;

E. By seven votes to seven, by the President's casting vote, it follows from the above-mentioned requirements that the threat or use of nuclear weapons would generally be contrary to the rules of international law applicable in armed conflict, and in particular the principles and rules of humanitarian law; However, in view of the current state of international law, and of the elements of fact at its disposal, the Court cannot conclude definitively whether the threat or use of nuclear weapons would be lawful or unlawful in an extreme circumstance of self-defence, in which the very survival of a State would be at stake;

F. Unanimously, there exists an obligation to pursue in good faith and bring to a con-clusion negotiations leading to nuclear disarmament in all its aspects under strict and effective international control.

* * *

## 4. Liz Heffernan, The Nuclear Weapons Opinions: Reflections on the Advisory Procedure of the International Court of Justice

*Stetson Law Review*, 1998
[footnotes omitted by editors]

### I. Introduction

On July 8, 1996, in response to a request by the United Nations (U.N.) General Assembly, the International Court of Justice (ICJ) delivered an advisory opinion on the legality of nuclear weapons. On the same day, it refused a similar request made by the World Health Organization (WHO). These events represent a significant development in the recent his-tory of the ICJ. Although the legality of nuclear weapons has been the subject of ongo-ing and occasionally heated debate in diplomatic and academic circles, judicial pronouncements relating to nuclear weapons have been rare, particularly at the interna-tional level. This was the first occasion on which the ICJ directly addressed the funda-mental issue of the status of nuclear weapons under international law. On such an emotive and divisive topic, the publication by the ICJ of an opinion of any hue was destined to prove controversial.

The ICJ's views on the legality of nuclear weapons have already inspired considerable comment. But even putting aside the substantive findings, the Nuclear Weapons Opin-ions raise many intriguing issues. Principal among them are questions relating to the ICJ's working practices and its role in the international community. The Nuclear Weapons Opinions cast a quizzical light on the process of judicial consensus-building and decision-making. They reveal a bench that is deeply divided in its vision of the theory and prac-tice of international law and of its own role in its development. In addition, the Nuclear Weapons Opinions send mixed messages regarding the wisdom and propriety of judicial intervention into the politically-charged domain of nuclear weapons policy and practice. In short, the ICJ has turned a secondary spotlight on itself, adding fuel to a fire ignited by recent criticisms of its working practices.

* * *

### III. The Nuclear Weapons Opinions

* * *

On May 14, 1993, the World Health Assembly, the plenary body of the WHO, adopted a resolution deciding to request an advisory opinion of the ICJ on the following question: "In view of the health and environmental effects, would the use of nuclear weapons by a State in war or other armed conflict be a breach of its obligations under international law including the WHO Constitution?" On December 15, 1994, a similar resolution was adopted by the U.N. General Assembly seeking an advisory opinion addressing the question: "Is the threat or use of nuclear weapons in any circumstance permitted under international law?"

On July 8, 1996, the ICJ delivered the Nuclear Weapons Opinions in response to the requests made by the WHO and the U.N. General Assembly, respectively. With regard to

Article 65 of its Statute, the ICJ declined to deliver an advisory opinion on the substantive question raised by the WHO. While recognizing that the WHO does possess the power to request advisory opinions, the ICJ held that the WHO was not competent to submit the particular request. In the ICJ's view, the subject-matter of the request fell outside the scope of the WHO's activities, as contemplated by Article 96(2) of the U.N. Charter.

In contrast, the ICJ, by thirteen votes to one, decided to comply with the General Assembly's request for an advisory opinion. In addition to holding that the request was within the competence of the General Assembly, the ICJ found that there were no compelling reasons that would justify the exercise of its discretion not to render an advisory opinion. The decision of the ICJ to accept jurisdiction was virtually unanimous. The sole dissenting voice was that of Judge Oda who, in a lengthy opinion, set out his view that the ICJ should have exercised its discretion to refuse jurisdiction in this case on grounds of "judicial propriety and economy." Judge Oda raised several objections to the exercise of advisory jurisdiction, principally that the request was not based on any meaningful consensus within the General Assembly, that it was inadequate in a number of respects, and that "there was ... no imminent need to raise the question of the legality or illegality of nuclear weapons."

In response to the substantive question raised by the General Assembly, the ICJ made several findings. First, it unanimously determined that "[t]here is in neither customary nor conventional international law any specific authorization of the threat or use of nuclear weapons." Second, "[b]y eleven votes to three," the ICJ found that "[t]here is in neither customary nor conventional international law any comprehensive and universal prohibition of the threat or use of nuclear weapons."

Third, the ICJ unanimously determined that a threat or use of nuclear weapons must comply with three categories of international legal rules: the rules regarding non-use of force contained in Articles 2(4) and 51 of the U.N. Charter; the rules regarding armed conflict, particularly the rules and principles of humanitarian law; and the specific obligations contained in treaties and other undertakings which address nuclear weapons.

In light of these findings, by the slimmest of majorities—seven votes to seven with the President's vote cast in favor—the ICJ concluded:

> "that the threat or use of nuclear weapons would generally be contrary to the rules of international law applicable in armed conflict, and in particular the principle and rules of humanitarian law; However, in view of the current state of international law, and of the elements of fact at its disposal, the Court cannot conclude definitively whether the threat or use of nuclear weapons would be lawful or unlawful in an extreme circumstance of self-defense, in which the very survival of a State would be at stake...."

Finally, the ICJ unanimously found the existence of an "obligation to pursue in good faith and to bring to a conclusion negotiations leading to nuclear disarmament in all its aspects under strict and effective international control."

\* \* \*

## VII. The Scope of the ICJ's Adjudication

\* \* \*

## C. The Applicable Law

Before addressing the question put to it by the General Assembly, the ICJ gave some consideration to the relevant applicable law that might be drawn from "the great corpus of international law norms available to it....." The ICJ considered the following: human rights (specifically the right to life), the prohibition against genocide, rules relating to the use of force, and the law of armed conflict and specific treaties dealing with nuclear weapons. As among these rules, the ICJ concluded that "the most directly relevant applicable law" is the law relating to the use of force, and the law applicable in armed conflict and specific treaties dealing with nuclear weapons. The relevance of rules relating to human rights, genocide, and the environment were largely discounted by the ICJ. This conclusion is contrary to the suggestion of a number of states in their submissions to the ICJ. Moreover, such rules exercised considerable influence over the dissenting opinions of Judges Koroma, Shahabuddeen, and Weeramantry.

Several states had cited the relevance of international human rights norms. Particular reliance was placed on the International Covenant on Civil and Political Rights (Covenant), Article 6(1) of which protects the right to life. The ICJ acknowledged the non-derogable status of this right which precludes any state party from denying its application in times of war or public emergency. However, in the view of the ICJ, the test of what constitutes an arbitrary deprivation of life in times of hostilities is a matter for the law of armed conflict. This analysis led the ICJ to conclude that the issue of whether loss of life through the use of a certain weapons in warfare constitutes a violation of Article 6 "can only be decided by reference to the law applicable in armed conflict and not deduced from the terms of the Covenant itself."

The ICJ's reading of Article 6 is troubling. The suggestion that, in times of hostilities, the application of Article 6 is controlled exclusively by the law of armed conflict, undermines the standing of the Covenant guarantee and its potential development by the Human Rights Committee. It suggests that Article 6 is susceptible to different meanings, based on an assumption that a bright line exists between times of hostilities and times of peace. Yet, these concepts do not coincide with the Covenant's notion of derogation and are at odds with the non-derogable character of Article 6. In effect, the ICJ excludes the possibility that Article 6 may provide a greater level of protection than the customary notion of arbitrary deprivation of life.

The lack of discussion of other human rights norms is also regrettable. Over the past several decades, the development of these norms has extended the substantive reach of international law and influenced legal thinking. Despite the ICJ's intimation that the law of armed conflict conditions the law of rights, evidence also exists supporting the reverse trend. One positive aspect of the U.N. response to the recent conflict in the Former Yugoslavia was the recognition of the formal link between the U.N.'s human rights monitoring and the actions of the Security Council.

Similar reflections surface regarding the ICJ's treatment on the prohibition on genocide. Genocide is prohibited by custom, and arguably by *jus cogens* and is at the center of international and national regimes directed toward the prosecution of war crimes. The consequences of the use of nuclear weapons suggest that the threshold of genocide could be readily crossed by a use of nuclear weapons, or, indeed, by a threat to use such weapons. Yet, even if it is assumed that not every use of nuclear weapons would invariably constitute genocide, this does not render the prohibition against genocide irrelevant to the ICJ's analysis, anymore than the law of the Charter or the rules of armed conflict do. The ICJ's holding would have been stronger if it had stated that, if applied with the requisite intent and direction, a use of nuclear weapons would contravene the prohibition against genocide.

Finally, the rapidly developing field of international law governing environmental concerns has placed additional limitations on the conduct of hostilities. Certain limitations stem from the general corpus of international environmental law. Additional limitations result from the incorporation of environmental concerns into international treaties concerning armed conflict. The contribution of these rules was deemed relevant to the Nuclear Weapons Opinions only to the extent that they have been subsumed into the law of armed conflict. Environmental rules are mere factors which may be taken into account in the application of that law, just as genocide is embodied in the criminalization of the laws of war, and as the right to life protected by human rights treaties is overshadowed by the protection against arbitrary life contained in humanitarian law.

\* \* \*

## Authors' Note

The following two materials are speeches on nuclear weapons by President Barack Obama and Sergio Duarte, the U.N.'s head for disarmament and nuclear affairs. President Obama advocates nuclear disarmament and outlines several measures that the United States will undertake to advance this objective. Duarte lauds the US-Russia agreement to establish a new nuclear security framework, discussed by President Obama, but addresses several challenges to the actualization of global nuclear disarmament.

## 5. Speech by President Barack Obama on Nuclear Weapons
### 2009

\* \* \*

One of those issues that I'll focus on today is fundamental to the security of our nations and to the peace of the world, that's the future of nuclear weapons in the 21st century. The existence of thousands of nuclear weapons is the most dangerous legacy of the Cold War. No nuclear war was fought between the United States and the Soviet Union, but generations lived with the knowledge that their world could be erased in a single flash of light. Cities like Prague that existed for centuries, that embodied the beauty and the talent of so much of humanity, would have ceased to exist.

Today, the Cold War has disappeared but thousands of those weapons have not. In a strange turn of history, the threat of global nuclear war has gone down, but the risk of a nuclear attack has gone up. More nations have acquired these weapons. Testing has continued. Black market trade in nuclear secrets and nuclear materials abound. The technology to build a bomb has spread. Terrorists are determined to buy, build or steal one. Our efforts to contain these dangers are centered on a global non-proliferation regime, but as more people and nations break the rules, we could reach the point where the center cannot hold.

Now, understand, this matters to people everywhere. One nuclear weapon exploded in one city, be it New York or Moscow, Islamabad or Mumbai, Tokyo or Tel Aviv, Paris or Prague, could kill hundreds of thousands of people. And no matter where it happens, there is no end to what the consequences might be, for our global safety, our security, our society, our economy, to our ultimate survival.

Some argue that the spread of these weapons cannot be stopped, cannot be checked, that we are destined to live in a world where more nations and more people possess the ultimate tools of destruction. Such fatalism is a deadly adversary, for if we believe that the spread of nuclear weapons is inevitable, then in some way we are admitting to ourselves that the use of nuclear weapons is inevitable.

Just as we stood for freedom in the 20th century, we must stand together for the right of people everywhere to live free from fear in the 21st century. And as nuclear power, as a nuclear power, as the only nuclear power to have used a nuclear weapon, the United States has a moral responsibility to act. We cannot succeed in this endeavor alone, but we can lead it, we can start it.

So today, I state clearly and with conviction America's commitment to seek the peace and security of a world without nuclear weapons. I'm not naive. This goal will not be reached quickly, perhaps not in my lifetime. It will take patience and persistence. But now we, too, must ignore the voices who tell us that the world cannot change. We have to insist, "Yes, we can."

Now, let me describe to you the trajectory we need to be on. First, the United States will take concrete steps towards a world without nuclear weapons. To put an end to Cold War thinking, we will reduce the role of nuclear weapons in our national security strategy, and urge others to do the same. Make no mistake: As long as these weapons exist, the United States will maintain a safe, secure and effective arsenal to deter any adversary, and guarantee that defense to our allies, including the Czech Republic. But we will begin the work of reducing our arsenal.

To reduce our warheads and stockpiles, we will negotiate a new Strategic Arms Reduction Treaty with the Russians this year. President Medvedev and I began this process in London, and will seek a new agreement by the end of this year that is legally binding and sufficiently bold. And this will set the stage for further cuts, and we will seek to include all nuclear weapons states in this endeavor.

To achieve a global ban on nuclear testing, my administration will immediately and aggressively pursue US ratification of the Comprehensive Test Ban Treaty. After more than five decades of talks, it is time for the testing of nuclear weapons to finally be banned.

And to cut off the building blocks needed for a bomb, the United States will seek a new treaty that verifiably ends the production of fissile materials intended for use in state nuclear weapons. If we are serious about stopping the spread of these weapons, then we should put an end to the dedicated production of weapons-grade materials that create them. That's the first step. Second, together we will strengthen the Nuclear Non-Proliferation Treaty as a basis for cooperation.

The basic bargain is sound: Countries with nuclear weapons will move towards disarmament, countries without nuclear weapons will not acquire them, and all countries can access peaceful nuclear energy. To strengthen the treaty, we should embrace several principles. We need more resources and authority to strengthen international inspections. We need real and immediate consequences for countries caught breaking the rules or trying to leave the treaty without cause.

And we should build a new framework for civil nuclear cooperation, including an international fuel bank, so that countries can access peaceful power without increasing the risks of proliferation. That must be the right of every nation that renounces nuclear weapons, especially developing countries embarking on peaceful programs. And no approach will succeed if it's based on the denial of rights to nations that play by the rules. We must harness the power of nuclear energy on behalf of our efforts to combat climate change, and to advance peace opportunity for all people.

But we go forward with no illusions. Some countries will break the rules. That's why we need a structure in place that ensures when any nation does, they will face consequences.

Just this morning, we were reminded again of why we need a new and more rigorous approach to address this threat. North Korea broke the rules once again by testing a rocket that could be used for long range missiles. This provocation underscores the need for action—not just this afternoon at the U.N. Security Council, but in our determination to prevent the spread of these weapons.

Rules must be binding. Violations must be punished. Words must mean something. The world must stand together to prevent the spread of these weapons. Now is the time for a strong international response, now is the time for a strong international response, and North Korea must know that the path to security and respect will never come through threats and illegal weapons. All nations must come together to build a stronger, global regime. And that's why we must stand shoulder to shoulder to pressure the North Koreans to change course.

Iran has yet to build a nuclear weapon. My administration will seek engagement with Iran based on mutual interests and mutual respect. We believe in dialogue. But in that dialogue we will present a clear choice. We want Iran to take its rightful place in the community of nations, politically and economically. We will support Iran's right to peaceful nuclear energy with rigorous inspections. That's a path that the Islamic Republic can take. Or the government can choose increased isolation, international pressure, and a potential nuclear arms race in the region that will increase insecurity for all.

So let me be clear: Iran's nuclear and ballistic missile activity poses a real threat, not just to the United States, but to Iran's neighbors and our allies. The Czech Republic and Poland have been courageous in agreeing to host a defense against these missiles. As long as the threat from Iran persists, we will go forward with a missile defense system that is cost-effective and proven. If the Iranian threat is eliminated, we will have a stronger basis for security, and the driving force for missile defense construction in Europe will be removed.

So, finally, we must ensure that terrorists never acquire a nuclear weapon. This is the most immediate and extreme threat to global security. One terrorist with one nuclear weapon could unleash massive destruction. Al Qaeda has said it seeks a bomb and that it would have no problem with using it. And we know that there is unsecured nuclear material across the globe. To protect our people, we must act with a sense of purpose without delay.

So today I am announcing a new international effort to secure all vulnerable nuclear material around the world within four years. We will set new standards, expand our cooperation with Russia, pursue new partnerships to lock down these sensitive materials.

We must also build on our efforts to break up black markets, detect and intercept materials in transit, and use financial tools to disrupt this dangerous trade. Because this threat will be lasting, we should come together to turn efforts such as the Proliferation Security Initiative and the Global Initiative to Combat Nuclear Terrorism into durable international institutions. And we should start by having a Global Summit on Nuclear Security that the United States will host within the next year.

Now, I know that there are some who will question whether we can act on such a broad agenda. There are those who doubt whether true international cooperation is possible, given inevitable differences among nations. And there are those who hear talk of a world without nuclear weapons and doubt whether it's worth setting a goal that seems impossible to achieve.

But make no mistake: We know where that road leads. When nations and peoples allow themselves to be defined by their differences, the gulf between them widens. When we fail to pursue peace, then it stays forever beyond our grasp. We know the path when we choose fear over hope. To denounce or shrug off a call for cooperation is an easy but also a cowardly thing to do. That's how wars begin. That's where human progress ends.

There is violence and injustice in our world that must be confronted. We must confront it not by splitting apart but by standing together as free nations, as free people. I know that a call to arms can stir the souls of men and women more than a call to lay them down. But that is why the voices for peace and progress must be raised together.

Those are the voices that still echo through the streets of Prague. Those are the ghosts of 1968. Those were the joyful sounds of the Velvet Revolution. Those were the Czechs who helped bring down a nuclear-armed empire without firing a shot.

Human destiny will be what we make of it. And here in Prague, let us honor our past by reaching for a better future. Let us bridge our divisions, build upon our hopes, accept our responsibility to leave this world more prosperous and more peaceful than we found it. Together we can do it.

\* \* \*

## 6. Sergio Duarte, A Nuclear Nonproliferation Regime for the 21st Century
### Address at the Fordham International Law Journal Symposium, 2010

\* \* \*

In many respects, this year has the potential to mark a turning point in the history of global efforts to achieve nuclear disarmament. After all, the Presidents of the countries with the largest nuclear arsenals, the Russian Federation and the United States, have both jointly and individually voiced their support for the goal of eliminating nuclear weapons. The two countries are now finalizing a treaty to replace the expired START, one that will further reduce deployments of strategic nuclear weapons and their delivery vehicles. Other nuclear-weapon States party to the Nuclear Non-Proliferation Treaty (NPT) have taken various steps to limit their own nuclear weapons capabilities—including such actions as closing down nuclear test sites, halting production of fissile material for use in weapons, and eliminating entire classes of nuclear weapons and delivery vehicles. Overall, declared global nuclear weapon stockpiles have dropped considerably since the height of the Cold War.

Reinforcing these activities by governments is a groundswell of new initiatives from individuals and groups in civil society to achieve a nuclear-weapon-free world. Former senior statesmen now in at least ten countries have authored opinion-editorials voicing their support for nuclear disarmament, following the first of a series of such "op-eds" originally published in the Wall Street Journal by George Shultz, William Perry, Henry Kissinger, and Sam Nunn. Another major initiative, the International Commission on Nuclear Non-Proliferation and Disarmament, jointly organized by Australia and Japan, has just issued a massive study containing a detailed step-by-step proposal for achieving global nuclear disarmament. Earlier this month, over 200 international political, military, business, and faith leaders gathered in Paris for the Global Zero Summit to launch the next phase of the Global Zero Campaign focused on the phased elimination of all nuclear weapons. Countless additional civil society initiatives are underway around the world today, and nuclear disarmament is also a goal that is increasingly cited as a priority by world leaders attending the plenary sessions of the U.N. General Assembly.

With all of these activities going on, one is tempted to follow the advice of the great reggae singer Bobby McFerrin, who famously urged, "Don't worry, be happy."

Yet, unfortunately, there are some legitimate grounds for worrying, both about the future of nuclear disarmament and the role of international law in achieving it.

First, let us look at some numbers. Here we are in the year 2010—64 years after the U.N. General Assembly first identified the goal of eliminating nuclear weapons; 48 years after the Soviet Union and the United States agreed at the U.N. on a joint proposal for "general and complete disarmament" (the McCloy-Zorin joint statement); 40 years after the NPT entered into force, which committed its parties to "pursue negotiations in good faith" on nuclear disarmament; and 10 years after the nuclear-weapon states at the 2000 NPT Review Conference made their "unequivocal undertaking" to accomplish the total elimination of their nuclear arsenals—after all these years, and there are still reportedly over 20,000 nuclear weapons in the world today, with many still on high-alert status. The fact that we do not know the exact number only testifies to another problem—the extremely limited transparency over these arsenals and their associated stocks of fissile materials.

Second, let us consider the problem of the double standard. Critics of the NPT have often termed the treaty "discriminatory" because it establishes a legal distinction between nuclear have and have-not states. Though nuclear disarmament has obviously not been achieved, the nuclear-weapon states have been asking the non-nuclear-weapon states to agree to increased, more intrusive controls over their own peaceful nuclear activities. This certainly contrasts with U.N. General Assembly resolution 2028, which in 1965 endorsed the negotiation of the NPT, saying that "the treaty should embody an acceptable balance of mutual responsibilities and obligations of the nuclear and non-nuclear Powers."

Furthermore, in 1995, the states parties agreed to extend the NPT indefinitely, as part of a "package deal" that contained several important elements—including efforts to establish a nuclear-weapon-free zone in the Middle East, a "programme of action" to achieve the "full realization" of article VI of the treaty dealing with disarmament, and a strengthened review process. Yet today, there have been no efforts whatsoever to establish the Middle East zone, large nuclear stockpiles remain, and the treaty review process continues to face difficulties in eliciting hard facts about the status of existing nuclear arsenals. These are just some of the difficult issues that will no doubt be taken up at the 2010 NPT Review Conference which opens next May.

Third, let us consider what is often called "modernization" of the nuclear arsenals. In the face of numerous political and legal commitments to eliminate nuclear weapons, all of the nuclear-weapon states have various programmes to improve, modernize, or refurbish their nuclear arsenals and their associated delivery systems. Experts often refer to this as the phenomenon of "vertical proliferation," involving the continued qualitative improvement of existing arsenals. Some nuclear-weapon states have tried to reconcile these goals with disarmament by claiming that modernization will allow the retirement of older, less safe weapon systems, or by asserting that a more reliable nuclear arsenal will discourage allies covered by the nuclear umbrella from acquiring their own nuclear weapons.

Fourth, let us consider what is happening with the nuclear deterrence doctrine governing the use of such weapons. While there are some differences among the nuclear-weapon states in the specific circumstances that they have declared would lead to the use of such weapons, the great common denominator of all of these doctrines is the claim that nuclear weapons are both an effective and legitimate means for these states to deter nuclear attacks upon them. Secretary-General Ban Ki-moon has referred to this doctrine as "contagious" because of the historical tendency of the deterrence doctrine to proliferate along with their associated weapons.

Fifth, let us consider just some of the formidable challenges facing the "rule of law" today in the field of disarmament. Though opened for signature in 1996, the Comprehensive Nuclear-Test-Ban Treaty has still not entered into force. And though the 1995 NPT Review and Extension Conference agreed to "the immediate commencement and early conclusion of negotiations" on a fissile material treaty, such negotiations have still not taken place despite strong support for such a treaty worldwide. In other areas, the nuclear-weapon states have still not ratified all the protocols to four of the five treaties establishing regional nuclear-weapon-free zones—and none has ratified the protocols to the treaties establishing such zones in Central Asia and Southeast Asia. There are also no multilateral treaties governing missiles or other nuclear weapon delivery systems, and, with the abrogation of the Anti-Ballistic Missile Treaty, no international treaties regulating missile defenses.

* * *

The world community, through such means as U.N. General Assembly resolutions and Final Documents at NPT Review Conferences, has over the years identified at least five criteria to use in assessing progress in disarmament. Verification is one of these—it is not sufficient for states simply to declare unilaterally that they do not have nuclear weapons, and this must be confirmed by highly reliable and objective means. Another criterion is irreversibility; confidence in compliance grows if controls are sufficient to make it extremely difficult if not impossible for a state to abandon a disarmament commitment and build or reconstruct a nuclear arsenal. Transparency is also essential in gauging progress in disarmament, for nuclear disarmament will never be achieved if the world does not have hard facts about the size of nuclear arsenals and concrete progress being made in eliminating them. Another criterion is universality; any agreement to achieve global nuclear disarmament must be fully "global" in geographic scope, with no exceptions. Lastly, the world community expects disarmament commitments to be legally binding.

Of these, the last actually also applies to the other criteria, for how can one realistically expect verification or irreversibility to be reliably achieved if they are purely discretionary or optional? Is universality simply to be achieved as a result of a straw poll, or must it be registered in a somewhat more binding form? Similarly, the world should not have to rely upon voluntary declarations by states about their nuclear weapons. This is not the way that nuclear nonproliferation policy is enforced, so why should it be any different for disarmament?

In this sense, law is a vital ingredient in any scheme for achieving a world free of nuclear weapons. If the international community were viewed as on a boat heading to a world without nuclear weapons, political will and politics would constitute its sail, and law its anchor—and both are essential in reaching that destination.

It is precisely because of this indispensability of law that Secretary-General Ban Ki-moon included the goal of negotiating a nuclear weapon convention, or a framework of mutually reinforcing agreements with the same goal, as the first of his five-part nuclear disarmament proposal, which he announced on 28 October 2008. Speaking just days earlier at Harvard University, he reminded his audience, that "The United Nations has long stood for the rule of law and disarmament. Yet it also stands for the rule of law in disarmament, which we advance through our various statements, resolutions, and educational efforts."

* * *

The Conference on Disarmament in Geneva is the world's single forum for negotiating multilateral disarmament treaties. [ ... ] The Conference was able to reach agreement on a substantive program of work last year, but was unable to implement it due to differences amongst some of its members over some key issues and priorities. Virtually all members want to proceed immediately with negotiations on a fissile material treaty, but there is still no consensus among its 65 members on this. Other items on the conference's agenda for substantive discussions, but not negotiations, are nuclear disarmament, negative security assurances, and the prevention of an arms race in outer space.

Let me say that I do not believe that the obstacles to negotiations encountered in the Conference on Disarmament are due to any fundamental flaw in the CD as an institution. These obstacles are due rather to differences in the policies of its Member States. Some want a treaty to cut off production of fissile material for weapons, while others want such a treaty to include stocks of previously produced material—and at least one member has voiced its concern that, as proposed, the fissile material cut-off treaty would seriously threaten its security. There are persisting differences in priorities as well. Some want negotiations dealing with nuclear disarmament and security assurances, while others want to commence negotiations on a treaty banning the deployment or use of weapons in space. Progress in these areas will require some changes in state policies.

It is of course true that there can be incremental progress in nuclear disarmament and nonproliferation without the need for new multilateral treaties. States can voluntarily decide on their own—as did Libya and South Africa—to abandon nuclear weapon programs. In 1991, the Russian Federation and the United States undertook a series of unilateral actions that resulted in a substantial reduction in deployments of certain types of short-range nuclear weapons. The many difficulties of treaty negotiation and ratification—such as we are now seeing with respect to the CTBT—have prompted some commentators to dismiss the need for treaties in the field of arms control, or have inspired the negotiation of extremely brief agreements, like the Strategic Offensive Reductions Treaty of 2002, which was about one page in length.

Yet despite the difficulty of negotiating arms-control and disarmament treaties, the world community still recognizes their value, as illustrated by the very fact that the Russian Federation and the United States chose to negotiate a treaty to succeed the START treaty and they have also announced they intend to negotiate additional reductions by means of future treaties.

In his famous speech to the General Assembly in September 1961 announcing a detailed US proposal for "general and complete disarmament," President Kennedy stressed the importance to disarmament of both verification and of international law. He said, "For disarmament without checks is but a shadow, and a community without law is but a shell."

As for the next logical steps forward in filling in the "shell" of disarmament, I would of course point to the large unfinished agenda of bringing the CTBT into force, negotiating a fissile material treaty, completing ratifications of the Protocols to the regional nuclear weapon-free zone treaties, and starting the process of developing multilateral legal norms for controlling missiles and outlawing space weapons.

But looking further down the road, I think Secretary-General Ban Ki-moon got it quite right by drawing attention to the need for a nuclear-weapon convention or framework of agreements with a similar objective. Long-term planning should be a near-term priority, not a long-term goal, and I think there is much indeed to be gained just by doing some serious thinking about what exactly would have to be included in such a convention. The mere act of identifying these elements would help in clarifying the work that needs to be done to conclude and implement such a treaty. This is why I believe the "Model Nuclear Weapon Convention" being circulated by the governments of Malaysia and Costa Rica—which was drafted by nongovernmental experts—is a good step in the right direction. In my opinion, it is never "too early" to start thinking about the architecture and legal obligations that will be needed to achieve global nuclear disarmament—it is far better to do this work early than too late.

So let me conclude not only by thanking you for having me, but also challenging all of you here today to use your skills to contribute in some way to the great cause of nuclear disarmament. You can conduct in-depth research. You can investigate. You can advocate. You can educate others. And you can establish networks of exchanging ideas on how to advance disarmament and the rule of law together. This is my call to action today, for there are few things more rewarding than in contributing to a truly great cause, and nuclear disarmament is one of the greatest.

## *Authors' Note*

The following three materials discuss the current status of Iran's nuclear programs and policy. Material 7 provides an overview of Iran's nuclear program and related issues of concern to the international community. Materials 8 and 9 present the viewpoints of Iran's Minister and Deputy Minister for Foreign Affairs. The ministers defend Iran's right to develop a nuclear program, maintaining that Iran's nuclear activity is legal and in compliance with international nuclear standards.

## 7. Greg Bruno, Backgrounder: Iran's Nuclear Program
### Council on Foreign Relations, 2010

### Introduction

Iran's leaders have worked to pursue nuclear energy technology since the 1950s, spurred by the launch of US President Dwight D. Eisenhower's Atoms for Peace program. It made steady progress, with Western help, through the early 1970s. But concern over Iranian intentions followed by the upheaval of the Islamic Revolution in 1979 effectively ended outside assistance. Iran was known to be reviving its civilian nuclear programs during the 1990s, but revelations in 2002 and 2003 of clandestine research into fuel enrichment and conversion raised international concern that Iran's ambitions had metastasized beyond peaceful intent.

Iran has consistently denied allegations it seeks to develop a bomb. Yet many in the international community remain skeptical. Despite a US intelligence finding in November 2007 that concluded Iran halted its nuclear weapons program in 2003, the Bush administration warned that Iran sought to weaponize its nuclear program, concerns the Obama administration shares. Nonproliferation experts note Iran's ability to produce enriched uranium continues to progress but disagree on how close Iran is to mastering capabilities to weaponize.

The September 2009 revelation of a second uranium enrichment facility near the holy city of Qom, constructed under the radar of international inspectors, deepened suspicion surrounding Iran's nuclear ambitions. The West's fears were confirmed in mid-February 2010 when the IAEA released a report that detailed Iran's potential for producing a nuclear weapon, including further fuel enrichment and plans for developing a missile-ready warhead.

* * *

## Known Capabilities

The withdrawal of Western support after the Islamic Revolution slowed Iran's nuclear progress. And a confluence of factors, opposition to nuclear technology by Ayatollah Ruhollah Khomeini, the exodus of nuclear scientists, and the destruction of Iraq's nuclear facility by Israel in 1981, which removed an immediate threat, sent Iran's nuclear program into a tailspin. But many nonproliferation experts believe Iran became interested again in a nuclear program by the mid-1980s. Leonard S. Spector, deputy director of the Center for Nonproliferation Studies, writes there is evidence Iran received assistance from Pakistani nuclear scientist AQ Khan as early as 1985, though it wasn't until the death of Khomeini in 1989 that Tehran's efforts reached critical mass. [Khan, speaking to a Pakistani television journalist in August 2009, confirmed that his network assisted Iran in contacting suppliers of nuclear technology].

Unlike his predecessor, Ayatollah Ali Khamenei held a more favorable view of nuclear energy and military technology, and set out to rebuild Tehran's program. Analysts also believe the discovery of Iraq's clandestine nuclear weapons program during the 1991 Gulf War, as well as a growing US presence in the region, pushed Tehran to ramp up its research. In a boost to the civilian nuclear effort, Russia in January 1995 picked up where Germany left off, signing a contract with Iran to complete two 950-megawatt light-water reactors at Bushehr (with fuel supplied by Russia). In September 2008, the Russian company building the power plant reiterated its commitment to finishing the project, while Moscow has said it hopes to fire up the reactor by the end of 2009. Iranian officials have also announced that the Darkhovin project has resumed, and plans call for a 360-megawatt reactor to be operational there by 2016. Iran, which has also turned to China, Pakistan, and North Korea for nuclear technology and assistance, claims it wants to build nuclear power plants to diversify its energy portfolio.

With an eye toward fueling these facilities with domestically produced fuel, and, many experts say, to develop a weapon, Iran has built a vast network of uranium mines, enrichment plants, conversion sites, and research reactors. Of these facilities, about a dozen are considered major nuclear sites. For instance, the Isfahan Nuclear Technology Center employs as many as three thousand scientists and is suspected of housing Iran's weapons program, according to the US-funded nonpartisan Congressional Research Service. Isfahan is also the location of Iran's uranium-conversion efforts, where approximately 366 tons of uranium hexafluoride has been produced since March 2004. This so-called feedstock is fed into centrifuges at another central site: the Natanz enrichment facility.

* * *

David Albright, an expert on Iran's nuclear program and president of the Institute for Science and International Security, estimates Iran is producing roughly 2.77 kg of LEU per day, a rate that has remained consistent throughout 2009. Mark Fitzpatrick, senior fellow for nonproliferation at the International Institute for Strategic Studies in London, says if Iran were to stockpile sufficient LEU they would be able to produce 25 kg of weapons-grade uranium for production of a single bomb "within a couple of months," a timeline. [ ... ]

## Unanswered Questions

International skepticism of Iranian intentions was first aroused in August 2002 when a London-based Iranian opposition group disclosed details about a secret heavy-water production plant at Arak, as well as the underground enrichment facility at Natanz. In

May 2003, State Department spokesman Richard Boucher said the disclosure of Arak and Natanz raised serious questions about Iran's nuclear intentions. "We believe Iran's true intent is to develop the capability to produce fissile material for nuclear weapons," Boucher said, "using both the plutonium route (supported ultimately by a heavy-water research reactor) and the highly enriched uranium route (supported by a gas centrifuge enrichment plant)." These revelations, coupled with subsequent admissions from Iran that it has concealed aspects of its program, prompted the IAEA to intensify inspections.

While international inspectors have never found concrete evidence linking Iran's nuclear program to weapons development, Iran's concealment of its program, like the partially constructed enrichment facility near Qom, which Western officials say was under construction for years before Iran's disclosure in the fall of 2009, has fed concerns. In a June 2003 report, IAEA inspectors concluded that Iran had failed to meet obligations under its Safeguards Agreement signed in 1974. Failures included withholding construction and design details of new facilities, and not reporting processed and imported uranium. Some undeclared shipments dated to 1991, the IAEA said.

International pressure following the revelations led Iran to temporarily cease its enrichment-related activities, and in late 2003 Tehran signed an Additional Protocol allowing the atomic agency greater access to nuclear sites. Negotiations with members of the European Union quickly followed. But on August 8, 2005, Iran announced it was resuming uranium conversion at Isfahan. By early 2006, IAEA inspectors confirmed that Iran had once again resumed its enrichment program. [ ... ]

Under the terms of the NPT, signatories have the "inalienable right" to produce fuel for civilian energy production, either by enriching uranium or separating plutonium. But the United States and other Western governments accuse Iran of failing to abide by NPT safeguards, and of pursuing technology to produce nuclear weapons. [ ... ]

Albright, of ISIS, says Iranian enrichment capabilities are improving, a troubling development given Iran's continued refusal to answer IAEA questions about past activities. In February 2008, the IAEA presented Iran with intelligence collected by the United States that US officials say proves Tehran worked to develop nuclear weapons in the recent past. The intelligence is believed to have been smuggled out of Iran on a laptop computer in 2004 and handed over to the Central Intelligence Agency (CIA). The data included alleged evidence of the so-called Green Salt project, a secret uranium-processing program; high-explosives testing; and design of a reentry vehicle "which could have a military nuclear dimension," the IAEA says. Iranian officials claim the data is fake. But the November 2007 US National Intelligence Estimate (NIE) concluded that while Iran likely halted its weapons program in fall 2003, "Tehran at a minimum is keeping open the option to develop nuclear weapons" in the future. IAEA Director General Mohamed ElBaradei, speaking in September 2009, said Iran continues to be uncooperative on many fronts, making it impossible to determine Tehran's intent. "Iran has not cooperated with the Agency in connection with the remaining issues," he said, "which need to be clarified in order to exclude the possibility of there being military dimensions to Iran s nuclear program."

### Sanctions and Saber Rattling

The United States has imposed unilateral economic sanctions on Iran for nearly three decade, but international efforts to cripple Iran's nuclear program have coalesced more recently. In September 2005, the IAEA Board of Governors expressed an "absence of confidence that Iran's nuclear program is exclusively for peaceful purposes." Five months later, the board voted to refer Iran to the U.N. Security Council, and in December 2006, the U.N. Security Council adopted the first of a series of resolutions imposing sanctions to punish Iran for continued uranium enrichment. Resolution 1737 initiated a block on the sale or transfer of sensitive nuclear technology. Subsequent resolutions, the most recent in September 2008, which reaffirmed past mandates, added financial and travel sanctions on Iranian individuals and companies. In June 2008, the European Union imposed its own set of sanctions, freezing the assets of nearly forty individuals and entities doing business with Bank Melli, Iran's largest bank. Western officials have accused Bank Melli of supporting Iran's nuclear and missile programs.

Now some members of Congress are backing a bill that would authorize the White House to penalize foreign companies for selling refined petroleum to Iran. Some analysts support this approach, but former US Ambassador to the U.N. John R. Bolton suggests only the threat of force can prevent an Iran nuclear bomb. CFR's Micah Zenko says Israel may be prepared to act in that regard if the United States doesn't.

Despite increasing calls for a military solution, international diplomacy continues apace. In mid-2008, the European Union resubmitted a 2006 offer of incentives for Iran to give up its enrichment activities. In October 2009, talks between Iran, the United States, and other world powers ended in failure as Iran's leadership rejected a plan to send its uranium to the West, hours after Iranian negotiators agreed to the deal.

Iran continues to send mixed signals regarding cooperation with the IAEA, though considerable evidence suggests Iran's defiance. In November 2009, the Iranian government approved ten new uranium enrichment plants. In February 2010, escalation mounted when Iran announced plans to heighten the enrichment levels of existing uranium stockpiles and Ahmadinejad declared, on the Islamic Republic's thirty-first anniversary, Iran to be a "nuclear state." These developments and Iran's continued intransigence led the IAEA's new director general, Yukiya Amano, to publicly announce IAEA fears that Iran was working on nuclear weaponization. A February 2010 report read, "Iran has not provided the necessary cooperation to permit the agency to confirm that all nuclear material in Iran is in peaceful activities."

Russia and China traditionally have resisted calls for a fourth round of U.N. sanctions, but in March 2010 President Medvedev signaled that Russia was warming to the possibility of sanctions. China, however, continues to resist stronger sanctions, and its foreign minister announced in early March that sanctions will not solve the Iran nuclear issue.

US officials remain committed to a bilateral, dual-track approach of both international sanctions and incentives. An example of this tactic is the March 2010 decision to allow the export of internet services like instant messaging and file sharing to Iran. These services are intended to facilitate the free flow of information and undermine the regime's control over the media and communications.

## 8. Greg Bruno, Interview with Manouchehr Mottaki: What Iran Wants

### Council on Foreign Relations, 2009

Revelations of a secret uranium-enrichment plant near the city of Qom have renewed fears that Iran's nuclear endeavors are designed to produce an atomic bomb, a claim Iranian officials vehemently dispute. In an interview with CFR.org, Iranian Foreign Minister Manouchehr Mottaki says Tehran has always operated within international legal boundaries, and seeks acknowledgement of this fact. Iran is hoping the October 1 talks in Geneva will trigger a broader dialogue of cooperation, from expanding economic partnerships to shaping new security frameworks. These issues will in turn serve as a bridge to more specific issues. "We have given three topics in the proposed package and that makes it possible for all parties to enter into discussions," he says, "even about the nuclear program."

**Iran meets with the international community tomorrow in Geneva. Is Iran ready to talk about its nuclear program and address demands that Western governments have made regarding the halting of uranium enrichment?**

First of all, we hope that we will have constructive discussions. By presenting a package of proposals, we wanted to show that Iran is serious for these negotiations. We have given three topics in the proposed package and that makes it possible for all parties to enter into discussions even about the nuclear program. That also includes political and security issues, economic matters, and international cooperation. And in the international part, some matters can be dedicated to the nuclear programs and nuclear issues. We are optimistic about the talks tomorrow. Because the negotiations are taking place after a long time, we should not have much expectation. Maybe that requires formation of some committees to continue the process. [With such committees] a different level can be done and continuation of dialogue can be defined and determined.

**A senior member of parliament, Hassan Ghafourifard, has suggested that Iran would be willing to withdraw from the Nonproliferation Treaty if the international community doesn't drop its demands that Iran stop enriching uranium. Is this something Iran is considering doing?**

We are not going to compromise our legal rights under any circumstances toward the enjoyment of legal activities. And we have no plan at the moment to withdraw from the NPT.

**How about allowing expanded inspections of Iran's nuclear facilities? A recent public opinion poll suggests your public favors an approach that would allow for Iran to continue enriching uranium, but would give the International Atomic Energy Agency (IAEA) expanded access. Is that a possible solution?**

We provide complete cooperation with the agency within the framework of our commitments in accordance with NPT and within the framework of the international law regulations.

**Can you map out for us what a successful framework would look like based on talks tomorrow? Specifically, what is Iran looking for?**

If you go to the nuclear issue, we believe that the rights of all member states to the IAEA and NPT must be respected within the framework of international laws and regulations. Recognition of such rights by these countries should not be only on paper. It must be fulfilled on the ground. That is what we are arguing. And we believe that must be respected and recognized in practice.

* * *

**When President Obama, President Nicolas Sarkozy of France, and Prime Minister Gordon Brown of Britain disclosed the facility in Pittsburgh last week, one of their main concerns was of transparency and trust. We've had a long discussion in the media over the last couple of days about the legal responsibilities that Iran has on disclosure. But is there a moral responsibility to be more transparent with its facilities?**

Iran has always laid emphasis on the legal framework of the question. But unfortunately from the other side, especially during the former US administration [of George W. Bush], they always tried to take a political attitude toward the question. During the years of our membership in the agency, Iran has always [gone] beyond its commitments in the IAEA. While we had no obligation to suspend our legal activities, we did it for confidence building, given the fact that [the] Additional Protocol is not mandatory and it was not approved by the parliament in Iran. We implemented the Additional Protocol for two years for confidence building. But the Americans have never told or informed the international community of the new generation of nuclear bombs they have built. We always act based on transparent methods. And the basis of our work is legal and international frameworks. And we think there should be a balance between your rights and your obligations. We cannot just focus on obligations without considering or recognizing the rights of the members. Or countries cannot say we only want our rights to be recognized but we have no obligations. So, we do everything based on the legal framework, and our activities are transparent and within the framework of international law and regulations.

**But the question is Iran's responsibility. You made reference to American responsibilities, but just yesterday, the secretary-general of the U.N. expressed concern that Iran wasn't meeting its responsibility to be transparent. Indeed he had a conversation with you on that very subject. So it's not just the United States that is calling for transparency. The secretary-general of the U.N. is saying the same thing.**

In your previous question you referred to the statements in Pittsburgh. I would like to add a few things to that and then we can deal with the statements of the secretary-general. We think in Pittsburgh, President Obama was misled based on wrong information and wrong analysis. The wrong analysis was provided by the British. Wrong information by certain terrorist groups.

**Which terror groups are you referring to?**

Usually you know these channels of wrong information. It seems to me that President Obama should be very mindful of these issues and statements. He's very much interested in starting or introducing a new approach in his work. He can be regarded as an opportunity for the people of the United States in trying to change the face of America before the world. So he must be very cautious. It [would have been] very easy for him to ask all these things from the agency.

About the statements of the U.N. secretary-general. In a meeting with him, we encouraged the secretary-general to take a position based on the United Nations frameworks and the international laws and regulations because there shouldn't be the impression that he always takes positions after members of the Security Council take positions about Iran. We have done everything and we have carried out all our obligations as a member state to the IAEA. Of course we have never accepted and implemented the resolutions of the Security Council for suspension of Iran's legal activities. We believe that according to the United Nations charter, the Security Council has no right to deny other nations of their own rights or exercising their rights. For this reason we believe that the United Nations needs to be restructured. For this reason, we believe that the secretary-general must be elected by [the] GA [General Assembly], not by the Security Council. Certain countries are looking for having a weak secretary-general within the framework of the United Nations. A former secretary-general of the United Nations once told me that some countries are trying to delete the word "general" from his position.

**And yes the perception question remains, the perception that the facility at Qom was kept secret.**

Some told us we announced that late. Others told us we announced early. Some others asked why we announced before October 1. We did everything according to our obligations. We never lied beyond our obligations, if not going beyond the obligations and [doing] more.

# 9. Ali Ahani, Iran Determined to Continue Peaceful Nuclear Activities

### Statement of Iranian Deputy Foreign Minister, 2009

Deputy Foreign Minister in Training and Research Affairs said here Wednesday evening Iran, as an NPT member, is determined to continue peaceful nuclear activities within framework of international regulations, under agency's full supervision.

Ali Ahani added in reply to Russian media reporters and university students at the Russian Foreign Ministry's Diplomatic Academy, "Iran is among the first signatories of the NPT, and as a responsible country, abides by its entire commitments towards the International Atomic Energy Agency (IAEA)."

Pointing out that the agency has full supervision over Iran's nuclear activities, he said, "The IAEA Sec Gen Muhamed Elbaradei has thus far issued over 15 reports on Iran's nuclear activities in all of which he is stressed that NO deviation from the peaceful path has been observed in Iran's nuclear program."

The IRI deputy FM added, "Enriched uranium at Iran's nuclear centers is sealed immediately after getting out of the centrifuges under the direct and full supervision of the IAEA, and no activity is concealed from the eyes of the agency's careful inspectors." Ahani said, "Therefore, we expect Russia, the Russian experts and technicians, and this country's news media not to look at the matter through the lenses of the biased Western media."

The Iranian deputy foreign minister said, "It is our right as a member of the agency to be benefited from our defined rights within the NPT framework and to take advantage of the peaceful nuclear technology along with its nuclear fuel production cycle and complete with its low level enrichment facilities."

He emphasized Iran's determination to keep up pursing its nuclear activities while fully respecting the international regulations, arguing, "We are by no means interested in worrying the others with our nuclear activities and we believe relying on cooperation with the IAEA it is possible to seek a formula to ensure the others of the unlimited peaceful nature of Iran's nuclear activities."

Ahani said, "There is one precondition for doing so and that is that the 5+1 Group should have trust in the agency and to permit that international foundation to continue its technical work, since Iran, too, is completely ready for full cooperation with the agency."

He then criticized the conduct of some 5+1G members towards Iran, calling it "irrational", arguing, "In response to the proposals made by that group for Iran we, too, presented a package, but keeping in mind that the conditions have changed, we are now updating that package, which will be handed over to the 5+1G as soon as it is prepared."

The IRI Deputy FM in response to a question by the reporter of Nezavisimaya Gazetta emphasized that Iran has no need for nuclear weapons, adding, "In this respect we are agreed with the stand adopted by some countries, such as Russia, that believe Iran should not get access to nuclear arms, assuring everyone that in the military doctrine of the IR of Iran there is no room for nuclear arms."

Ahani added, "And let me remind you the fact that Iran was the initiator of the idea of declaring the Middle East as a nuclear weapons free zone (NWFZ)."

Pointing out that Iran also favors the idea of global nuclear disarmament, he said, "Iran once presented the draft of a resolution to the United Nations, which was unfortunately rejected with the negative votes of the United States and the European Union."

About the Bushehr Nuclear Power Reactor (BNPR), Ahani said, "That rector that the Russian experts have accepted the responsibility of its completion ten years ago is going to be competed in near future and I hope that would be completed, as it has been lastly declared, within the next few months, when it would also be actually hopefully put to use."

He said, "Any further elongation of the process of the completion of the BNPR would have a negative effect on the reputation of the Russian Federation not only at the IRI Parliament, Majlis, but also in the public opinion of the Iranian nation."

The deputy Iranian FM said, "The BNPR is both a test and a symbol for cooperation and friendship between Iran and Russia, and will be marked as thus also in the history of the two countries' relations."

The Russian Federation Foreign Ministry's Diplomatic Academy was established in the year 1934 and 2,000 students are currently studying there.

## Authors' Note

The following four materials, presented chronologically, demonstrate the international community's stance toward Iran's nuclear program. Material 10, congressional testimony of US Deputy Secretary of State William Burns, focuses on the strong US opposition to Iran's development of a nuclear weapons program. Burns asserts that Iranian development of nuclear weapons is illegal and discusses sanctions that the US has implemented in response to Iran's evolving nuclear activities. Material 11 is a statement from Catherine Ashton, the European Union High Representative for Foreign Affairs and Security Policy, following a meeting with Iranian representatives. Ashton affirms the EU's recognition of Iran's right to develop a nuclear energy program. She says that Iran has not demonstrated that its program is for peaceful purposes, however, so sanctions against Iran will continue. Material 12 is a report from the IAEA director general detailing Iran's compliance with Nonproliferation Treaty (NPT) safeguard measures and provisions of relevant Security Council resolutions. The report finds that Iran has not complied with all of its duties in demonstrating the peaceful nature of its nuclear activities. Material 13 is the response of the P5+1 Group, composed of China, France, Germany, Russia, the United Kingdom, and the United States, to the IAEA director general's report on Iran. In the letter, the P5+1 Group conveys its concern with regard to Iran's nuclear program and its openness to support Iran's effort to comply with international rules governing its nuclear activity.

## 10. William Burns, Implementing Tougher Sanctions on Iran: A Progress Report

US Deputy Secretary of State Testimony to House
Foreign Affairs Committee, 2010

\* \* \*

We meet today at a moment of great consequence in the long and complicated history of international concerns about Iran and its nuclear ambitions. In recent months, working closely together, the Administration, Congress and our international partners have put in place the strongest and most comprehensive set of sanctions that the Islamic Republic of Iran has ever faced. It is a set of measures that we are determined to implement fully and aggressively. It is a set of measures that is already producing tangible results. And it is a set of measures that reinforces our collective resolve to hold Iran to its international obligations.

A great deal is at stake, for all of us. A nuclear-armed Iran would severely threaten the security and stability of a part of the world crucial to our interests and to the health of the global economy. It would seriously undermine the credibility of the United Nations and other international institutions, and seriously weaken the nuclear nonproliferation regime at precisely the moment when we are seeking to strengthen it. These risks are only reinforced by the wider actions of the Iranian leadership, particularly its longstanding support for violent terrorist groups like Hizballah and Hamas; its opposition to Middle East peace; its repugnant rhetoric about Israel, the Holocaust, 9/11, and so much else; and its brutal repression of its own citizens.

In the face of those challenges, American policy is straightforward. We must prevent Iran from developing nuclear weapons. We must counter its destabilizing actions in the region and beyond. And we must continue to do all we can to advance our broader interests in democracy, human rights, peace and economic development across the Middle East. President Obama has made clear repeatedly that we will stand up for those rights that should be universal to all human beings, and stand with those brave Iranians who seek only to express themselves freely and peacefully. The simple truth is that a government that does not respect the rights of its own people will find it increasingly difficult to win the respect that it professes to seek in the international community.

We have emphasized from the start that what is at issue between Iran and the rest of the world is not its right to a peaceful nuclear program, but rather its decades-long failure to live up to the responsibilities that come with that right. If Iran is sincere, it should not be hard to show the rest of the international community that its nuclear program is aimed at exclusively peaceful purposes. Facts are stubborn things, however, and it is a telling fact that Iran, alone among signatories of the NPT, continues to fail year after year to convince the IAEA and the United Nations of its peaceful nuclear intentions.

Nearly two years ago, President Obama began an unprecedented effort at engagement with Iran. We did so without illusions about whom we were dealing with, or the scope of our differences over the past thirty years. We sought to create early opportunities for Iran to pursue a different path and to build confidence in its intentions. This was both a serious demonstration of our good faith, and also an investment in partnership with a growing coalition of countries profoundly concerned about Iran's nuclear ambitions.

When, regrettably, those early efforts made little headway, we and our partners were left with no choice but to respond to Iran's intransigence by employing another tool of diplomacy, political and economic pressure. The cornerstone of this campaign was U.N. Security Council resolution 1929, passed early last June. By far the toughest of the four Chapter Seven resolutions enacted in recent years, 1929 broke important new ground in curbing arms transfers to Iran; targeting the central role of the IRGC in Iran's proliferation efforts; banning for the first time all Iranian activities related to ballistic missiles that could deliver a nuclear weapon; sharply limiting Iran's ability to use the international financial system to fund and facilitate nuclear and missile proliferation; and for the first time highlighting formally potential links between Iran's energy sector and its nuclear ambitions. Russia's partnership was particularly crucial to passage of such an effective resolution, which led directly to its enormously important cancellation of the S-300 surface-to-air missile sale to Iran.

The significance of 1929 is only partly about its content. It is also about the message of international solidarity that it sent, and the platform that its carefully-crafted language has provided for subsequent steps. Barely a week after passage of 1929, the European Union announced by far its most sweeping collection of measures against Iran, including a full prohibition of new investment in Iran's energy sector, bans on the transfer of key technology, and the strictest steps to date against Iranian banks and correspondent banking relationships. [ ... ]

None of this is accidental. We have worked intensively with our partners, in conversation after conversation and trip after trip around the world, to produce an unprecedented package of measures, and to ensure robust enforcement.

Central to our strategy have been the efforts made by the Congress, by all of you, to sharpen American sanctions. When the President signed into law the Comprehensive Iran Sanctions Accountability and Divestment Act (CISADA) in early July, the Administration and the Congress sent an unmistakable signal of American resolve and purpose, expanding significantly the scope of our domestic sanctions and maximizing the impact of new multilateral measures.

We are enforcing the law rigorously and energetically. Already, more foreign investment in Iran has been curbed than at any time since Congress enacted the original Iran Sanctions Act nearly fifteen years ago. In late September, Secretary Clinton imposed sanctions for the first time in the history of the ISA, on a Swiss-based, Iranian-owned firm involved in hundreds of millions of dollars worth of deals in Iran. [ ... ] According to reliable estimates, Iran may be losing as much as $50–60 billion overall in potential energy investments, along with the critical technology and know-how that comes with them.

Faced with new international concerns, and the choice between doing business with Iran and doing business with America, more and more foreign companies are pulling out of the Iranian market. Major energy traders like Lukoil, Reliance, Vitol, Glencore, IPG, Tupras and Trafigura have stopped sales of refined petroleum products to Iran. [ ... ]

* * *

I cannot honestly predict for you with any certainty how all these collective and individual measures will affect the choices that Iran's leadership makes. We will continue to sharpen those choices. We will show what's possible if Iran meets its international obligations and adheres to the same responsibilities that apply to other nations. We will intensify the costs of continued non-compliance and show Iran that pursuit of a nuclear weapons program will make it less secure, not more secure. And in the meantime we will continue to reassure our friends and partners in the Gulf of our long-term commitment to their security. [ ... ]

Let me conclude by emphasizing two simple but important realities. First, Iran is not ten feet tall. Its economy is badly mismanaged. Iran's leaders have tried very hard to deflect or divert the international pressures building all around them—itself an acknowledgement of their potential effect.

Second, and just as significant, sanctions and pressure are not an end in themselves. They are a complement, not a substitute, for the diplomatic solution to which we and our partners are still firmly committed. [ ... ]

The P5+1, led by EU High Representative Ashton, will approach next week's meeting with Iran with seriousness of purpose and a genuine readiness to engage constructively on international concerns about Iran's nuclear program. The door is open to serious negotiation, if Iran is prepared to walk through it.

## 11. Catherine Ashton, Address in Istanbul
### Statement by EU High Representative, 2011

\* \* \*

The countries I represent remain united in seeking a swift resolution of the international community's concerns regarding Iran's nuclear programme, on the basis of successive Security Council Resolutions and Resolutions of the IAEA Board of Governors. That remains the central purpose of these talks.

In Geneva, we agreed that at this meeting in Istanbul we would discuss practical ideas and ways of cooperating towards resolution of our core concerns about the nuclear issue.

We came here with specific practical proposals which would build trust. We put forward detailed ideas including on an updated version of the TRR fuel exchange arrangement and ways to improve transparency through IAEA monitoring measures accepted by the international community. We came without preconditions, and made every effort to secure agreement.

We have had a series of meetings with Iran, including a separate meeting of the Vienna Group countries with Iran.

We had hoped to have a detailed and constructive discussion of those ideas. But it became clear that the Iranian side was not ready for this, unless we agreed to pre-conditions relating to enrichment and sanctions.

Both these pre-conditions are not a way to proceed. On the fuel cycle we have said many times, including today, that we recognize Iran's right to a civil nuclear energy programme. It remains essential that Iran demonstrates that its programme is exclusively for peaceful purposes.

But so far the IAEA has not been able to certify the exclusively peaceful nature of Iran's programme, given what the Agency states is a lack of sufficient cooperation by Iran.

As far as the removal of sanctions is concerned, it remains our united position that this would accompany the re-establishment of confidence in the Iranian nuclear programme rather than be a precondition for discussing it. We also note that UNSC Resolution 1929 specifies the requirements for removal of sanctions, and those do not exist today.

This is not the conclusion I had hoped for. We had hoped to embark on a discussion of practical ways forward, and have made every effort to make that happen. I am disappointed to say that this has not been possible. The E3+3 reaffirmed their continued commitment to pursuing a diplomatic solution. We expect Iran to demonstrate a pragmatic attitude and to respond positively to our openness toward dialogue and negotiations. The door remains open, the choice remains in Iran's hands.

I have made personally clear to Dr Jalili that our proposals remain on the table and that we are ready to start talking without preconditions the moment Iran is ready.

## 12. Implementation of the NPT Safeguards Agreement and Relevant Provisions of Security Council Resolutions in the Islamic Republic of Iran

Report by Director General of the IAEA, 2011

### A. Introduction

1. This report of the Director General to the Board of Governors and, in parallel, to the Security Council, is on the implementation of the NPT Safeguards Agreement, and relevant provisions of Security Council resolutions in the Islamic Republic of Iran (Iran).

2. The Security Council has affirmed that the steps required by the Board of Governors in its resolutions are binding on Iran. The relevant provisions of the aforementioned Security Council resolutions were adopted under Chapter VII of the United Nations Charter, and are mandatory, in accordance with the terms of those resolutions.

3. By virtue of its Relationship Agreement with the United Nations, the Agency is required to cooperate with the Security Council by furnishing to it at its request such information and assistance as may be required by the Security Council in the exercise of its responsibility for the maintenance or restoration of international peace and security. [ ... ]

4. In a letter dated 26 May 2011, H.E. Dr Fereydoun Abbasi, Vice President of Iran and Head of the Atomic Energy Organization of Iran (AEOI) informed the Director General that Iran would be prepared to receive relevant questions from the Agency on it nuclear activities after a declaration by the Agency that the work plan had been fully implemented and that the Agency would thereafter implement safeguards in Iran in a routine manner. In his reply of 3 June 2011, the Director General informed Dr Abbasi that the Agency was neither in a position to make such a declaration, nor to conduct safeguards in Iran in a routine manner, in light of concerns about the existence in Iran of possible military dimensions to Iran's nuclear programme. [ ... ]

\* \* \*

### B. Facilities Declared under Iran's Safeguards Agreement

6. Under its Safeguards Agreement, Iran has declared to the Agency 15 nuclear facilities and nine locations outside facilities where nuclear material is customarily used (LOFs). The Agency continues to verify the non-diversion of declared nuclear material at these facilities and LOFs. Notwithstanding, certain of the activities being undertaken by Iran at some of the facilities are contrary to relevant resolutions of the Board of Governors and the Security Council, as indicated below, the Agency continues to implement safeguards at these facilities and LOFs.

### C. Enrichment Related Activities

7. Contrary to the relevant resolutions of the Board of Governors and the Security Council, Iran has not suspended its enrichment related activities in the following declared facilities, all of which are nevertheless under Agency safeguards.

\* \* \*

### D. Reprocessing Activities

28. Pursuant to the relevant resolutions of the Board of Governors and the Security Council, Iran is obliged to suspend its reprocessing activities, including R&D. In a letter to the Agency dated 15 February 2008, Iran stated that it "does not have reprocessing activities".

[ ... ] It is only with respect to TRR, the MIX Facility and the other facilities to which the Agency has access that the Agency can confirm that there are no ongoing reprocessing related activities in Iran.

### E. Heavy Water Related Projects

29. Contrary to the relevant resolutions of the Board of Governors and the Security Council, Iran has not suspended work on all heavy water related projects, including the construction of the heavy water moderated research reactor, the IR-40 Reactor, which is under Agency safeguards.

\* \* \*

### F. Uranium Conversion and Fuel Fabrication

32. Although it is obliged to suspend all enrichment related activities and heave water related projects, Iran is conducting a number of activities at UCF and the Fuel Manufacturing Plant (FMP) at Esfahan which, as described below, are in contravention of those obligations, although both facilities are under Agency safeguards.

\* \* \*

### G. Possible Military Dimensions

38. Previous reports by the Director General have identified outstanding issues related to possible military dimensions to Iran's nuclear programme and actions required of Iran to resolve these. Since 2002, the Agency has become increasingly concerned about the possible existence in Iran of undisclosed nuclear related activities involving military related organizations, including activities related to the development of a nuclear payload for a missile, about which the Agency has regularly received new information.

39. The Board of Governors has called on Iran on a number of occasions to engage with the Agency on the resolution of all outstanding issues in order to exclude the existence of possible military dimensions to Iran's nuclear programme. [ ... ] Since August 2008, Iran has not engaged with the Agency in any substantive way on this matter.

\* \* \*

43. The information indicates that Iran has carried out the following activities that are relevant to the development of a nuclear device:

- Efforts, some successful, to procure nuclear related and dual use equipment and materials by military related individuals and entities;
- Efforts to develop undeclared pathways for the production of nuclear material;
- The acquisition of nuclear weapons development information and documentation from a clandestine nuclear supply networks; and
- Work on the development of an indigenous design of a nuclear weapon including the testing of components.

44. While some of the activities identified in the Annex have civilian as well as military applications, others are specific to nuclear weapons.

\* \* \*

### I. Additional Protocol

48. Contrary to the relevant resolutions of the Board of Governors and the Security Council, Iran is not implementing its Additional Protocol. The Agency will not be in a position to provide credible assurance about the absence of undeclared nuclear material and

activities in Iran unless and until Iran provides the necessary cooperation with the Agency, including by implementing its Additional Protocol.

* * *

## K. Summary

52. While the Agency continues to verify the non-diversion of declared nuclear material at the nuclear facilities and LOFs declared by Iran under its Safeguards Agreement, as Iran is not providing the necessary cooperation, including by not implementing its Additional Protocol, the Agency is unable to provide credible assurance about he absence of undeclared nuclear material and activities in Iran, and therefore to conclude that all nuclear material in Iran is in peaceful activities.

53. The Agency has serious concerns regarding possible military dimensions to Iran's nuclear programme. After assessing carefully and critically the extensive information available to it, the Agency finds the information to be, overall, credible. The information indicates that Iran has carried out activities relevant to the development of a nuclear explosive device. The information also indicates that prior to the end of 2003, these activities took place under a structured programme, and that some activities may still be ongoing.

* * *

## 13. P5+1 Group, Iran's Nuclear Program

Read by the Governor of the Russian Federation

Mr. Chairman,

I have the honor to make this statement on behalf of China, France, Germany, Russia, the United Kingdom and the United States.

Our six countries wish to thank Director General Amano for his latest report on the "Implementation of the NPT Safeguards Agreement and relevant provisions of the UNSC Resolutions in the Islamic Republic of Iran". We commend the Secretariat for its efforts to pursue its verification mission and reaffirm that the IAEA plays an essential role in establishing confidence in the exclusively peaceful nature of Iran's nuclear program.

We recall that our six countries, with the support of the EU High Representative, are determined and committed to find a comprehensive negotiated long-term solution which restores international confidence in the exclusively peaceful nature of Iran's nuclear program, while respecting Iran's legitimate right under the NPT to the peaceful use of nuclear energy.

Iran's obligations under the relevant UNSC and the IAEA Board of Governors Resolutions are explicitly set out in the latest IAEA report. Full implementation by Iran of these international obligations is needed to establish confidence in the exclusively peaceful nature of Iran's nuclear program. The implementation of the NPT Safeguards Agreement, and relevant provisions of UNSC Resolutions in the Islamic Republic of Iran, which were adopted under Chapter VII of the U.N. Charter, is mandatory.

We call on Iran to cooperate fully with the Agency, including prompt implementation and ratification of the Additional Protocol, applying the modified Code 3.1 of the subsidiary arrangements to its Safeguards Agreement, and implementing all transparency measures, as requested by the Agency. Outstanding issues need to be resolved in order to exclude the existence of possible military dimensions to Iran's nuclear program.

We, together with the EU High Representative, held two meetings with Iran in the last few months, one in Geneva in December, and another in Istanbul in January. At that meeting, it was not possible to reach any substantive result. We came to Geneva and to Istanbul with a constructive spirit and proposed in Istanbul several practical ideas aimed at building confidence and to facilitate the engagement of a constructive dialogue with Iran on the basis of reciprocity and step-by-step approach. We look to Iran to engage in future in a similarly constructive spirit.

We reaffirm our June 2008 offer and the proposals we made in Istanbul. It remains our wish to establish a cooperative relationship with Iran in many fields including that of peaceful nuclear technology—where of course we fully recognize Iran's rights under the NPT. We invite Iran to consider our proposals seriously.

We remain ready to participate actively in the E3+ 3 process with Iran. We expect Iran to demonstrate a pragmatic attitude and to respond positively to our proposals and to our openness toward dialogue and negotiations. The door remains open.

## Authors' Note

The following material addresses the positions of two super powers, China and Russia, concerning Iran's developing nuclear program. Material 14, an article from *Foreign Affairs*, considers issues that factor into the Chinese take on Iran sanctions, including the Chinese-Iranian relationship. The piece also addresses strategy that may facilitate US diplomacy with China concerning Iran sanctions.

## 14. Erica Downs and Suzanne Maloney, Getting China to Sanction Iran,

*Foreign Affairs*, 2011

### The Chinese-Iranian Oil Connection

For more than three decades, the United States has tried to persuade the international community to counter the threat posed by Iran's Islamic regime. The results have often been underwhelming, with even Washington's closest allies resisting tough measures against Iran because of strategic considerations and commercial interests.

Recently, however, that landscape has changed. Last June, the United Nations Security Council penalized Tehran for failing to suspend its uranium-enrichment program by adopting strict new sanctions, including an arms embargo and tough restrictions on Iranian banks and the Revolutionary Guard Corps. Resolution 1929 also paved the way for individual states to adopt even more stringent penalties. Australia, Canada, Japan, Norway, South Korea, and the European Union implemented unprecedented curbs on investment in Iran. The US Congress passed new sanctions against any company selling gasoline to Iran or investing in Iran's refining capacity. Collectively, these measures have squeezed Iran's economy.

Yet one uncertainty still looms large: China's commitment to such policies. Driven by economic interests, as well as sympathy for Iran's grievances, China is the only major player still active in the Iranian oil patch. Whereas firms from most other countries have retreated due to international pressure and Iran's unfavorable business climate, China and its companies adhere only to the letter of Resolution 1929, which contains no explicit restrictions on energy investment or trade. China has thus emerged as the linchpin of the international sanctions regime against Iran and, by extension, of the effort to fore-stall Iran from acquiring a nuclear capability.

This situation presents US policymakers with tough choices. Even as the US political climate has turned more rancorous toward both Iran and China, the Obama adminis-tration will need to build a more positive partnership with China on the Iran issue while attempting to stabilize the broader bilateral relationship. One option is to exploit the un-derlying fissures that exist between Beijing and Tehran despite their strong ideological and commercial links.

### The Chinese Exception

The sanctions regime targeting Iran is now more muscular than ever, but the gap be-tween the U.N. Security Council measures and the much harsher sanctions adopted by the United States and other countries has created an uneven playing field in Iran. In con-trast to virtually all major Western governments, Beijing still allows its companies to do business there. However, some activities considered acceptable by Beijing are punishable under the new, extraterritorial US sanctions.

Two likely flash points concern Chinese investments to recover and produce Iran's oil and natural gas (upstream activities) and China's sale of gasoline to Iran. First, Tehran is likely to continue to seek upstream investments from China's national oil companies (NOCs) to compensate for the departure of other firms. Chinese companies have moved carefully so far because of the tough operating environment and diplomatic sensitivities, but the prospect of gaining a larger position in Iran's upstream market will prove in-creasingly tempting: it is a rare opportunity to secure huge fields that might have gone to Western companies in the absence of sanctions. These NOCs, which are powerful po-litical actors, may try to convince Beijing that gaining access to Iran's hydrocarbon re-serves is worth the risk of US sanctions against Chinese companies. Second, Chinese oil traders may want to continue supplying gasoline to Iran even as many European companies voluntarily stop selling in order to avoid new penalties on their business dealings in the United States. The incentives of Chinese firms are both financial (Tehran reportedly buys the gasoline at a 25 percent premium above the market rate) and political (Beijing opposes US sanctions as extraterritorial legislation that harms the Iranian people).

China's posture toward Iran and the US response will have implications for both the global energy business and international diplomacy. If China refuses to stop its upstream investments or gasoline sales, the Obama administration will have to choose between ap-plying US sanctions to Chinese firms and waiving them. Either move would be costly, but the price of inaction might be higher. With Chinese companies expanding their stakes in Iran, competitors that have voluntarily pulled out might return, and others might start pressuring their governments to relax the sanctions or might skirt them altogether by creeping back into Iran.

Washington must balance persuasive and dissuasive tools in order to strengthen Beijing's cooperation on Iran and continue to work with it on other priorities, such as North Korea, climate change, and reforming the international economic order. Sanctioning Chinese companies would only complicate bilateral relations, heighten-ing the tensions that grew during 2010. Like its predecessors, the Obama administra-tion has thus far declined to enforce a 1996 measure penalizing third-country companies that invest in Iran's energy sector. However, this wink-and-nod approach might not satisfy congressional hawks seeking to raise the cost of defiance for Tehran. The Re-publican Party's resurgence in Congress in the November 2010 elections will put pres-sure on the White House to turn up the heat on both Iran and China. Congress can make its preferences felt through tough rhetoric, hearings, investigations, and reporting requirements. Proposals for new penalties against Tehran, including sanctions against any company that purchases Iranian crude oil, are already circulating on Capitol Hill.

Ultimately, the Obama administration will have to find a middle ground. It must avoid slapping sanctions on US allies and fragmenting the hard-won international coalition on Iran while maintaining robust economic pressure on Tehran and enhancing the credibility of US policy. Outreach toward Beijing should thus reinforce the intrinsic limitations of Chinese-Iranian cooperation and reduce the chances of a confrontation between Washington and Beijing over Iran.

### Dangerous Liaisons

In order to secure Beijing's cooperation, Washington must appreciate the full scope of the Chinese-Iranian relationship. China is the world's second-largest oil importer. Iran's oil and natural gas reserves rank among the world's largest, making the country an attractive destination for China's NOCs, which are increasingly looking for opportunities abroad. Already, Iran is China's third-largest supplier of crude oil.

\* \* \*

### The Ties That Bind

Yet ties between China and Iran are hardly ironclad. Beijing takes a more cautious approach to Iran than sensational press headlines and political rhetoric in the United States often imply. The amount of money that China's NOCs have committed to projects in Iran, let alone actually invested, is considerably smaller than the $100–$120 billion frequently cited. Chinese firms are not entirely immune to the checks that have hindered other companies. They have also been deliberately prudent in finalizing their investments. Their strategy is to negotiate agreements but delay major spending in the hope of securing access to Iran's resources over the long term while minimizing the immediate risks of taking on legal and financial commitments in an unpredictable environment.

\* \* \*

## Authors' Note

The following two excerpts consider an issue of pressing concern regarding Iran's nuclear development: the impact on Israel. Material 15 is a statement from the Israeli Minister of Foreign Affairs, who condemns Iran's nuclear program and calls for international pressure on Iran to curb nuclear development. Material 16 is an analysis from *Foreign Affairs* that addresses the perceived threat of the Iranian nuclear program, from the perspectives of the Israeli public and intelligence community. The article also discusses US-Israeli diplomacy on the issue and the approach of Prime Minister Binyamin Netanyahu.

## 15. Israel's Response to U.N. Security Council Resolution 1929 on Sanctions against Iran

### Statement by the Israeli Minister of Foreign Affairs, 2010

Israel views U.N. Security Council Resolution 1929 as an important step in the efforts to get Iran to acquiesce to international demands: suspension of uranium enrichment, including enriching to 20%; cessation of construction of the facility in Qom; full cooperation with IAEA investigation into the military aspect of the nuclear program; and granting the agency full access [to the facility].

This is the sixth resolution calling for Iran to suspend uranium enrichment and to cooperate with the IAEA. Iran is in blatant violation of all the resolutions that have been adopted to date, demonstrating its scorn for the international community and its institutions.

It is of high importance to implement the resolution fully and immediately. At the same time, it should be recognized that this resolution is not sufficient in and of itself and should be accompanied by significant steps in additional international frameworks as well as on a national level. Only sanctions that focus on a variety of sectors in Iran are likely to influence Iran's calculations.

Broad, determined international action is needed in order to make clear to the Iranian regime the price tag for continuing to violate international demands. The combination of Iran's extremist ideology together with nuclear weapons will have catastrophic consequences.

---

## 16. Ronen Bergman, Letter from Tel Aviv: Netanyahu's Iranian Dilemma

*Foreign Affairs*, 2009

At a recent symposium at Tel Aviv University, Major General Aharon Zeevi Farkash, the former chief of military intelligence, described Israel's public perception of the Iranian nuclear threat as "distorted." His view, which is shared by many in Israel's security and intelligence services, is that Israel is not Iran's primary target, and therefore, Israel must not attack Iran unilaterally. Members of the audience took issue with his analysis. One woman, speaking with a heavy Farsi accent, said of the Iranian regime, "They're crazy, and they will drop a bomb on us the moment they can. We need to deal with them now!"

Her sentiment reflects the public mood in Israel, where many are convinced that Iranian President Mahmoud Ahmadinejad wants to annihilate them and is willing to risk the destruction of his own country to do so. For most Israelis, the question is not whether Iran will attack but when. Polls consistently show that Israelis are overwhelmingly in favor of striking Iran's nuclear facilities. A recent survey commissioned by Tel Aviv University's Center for Iranian Studies found that three out of four Israelis believe the United States will not be able to stop Iran from acquiring nuclear weapons, and one in two supports taking immediate military action.

It is impossible to separate such convictions from their historical context. The fear that Jews, having escaped the furnaces of the Holocaust, could face annihilation in Israel has always haunted the public psyche. Long before Ahmadinejad's outbursts, therefore, Israelis were already attuned to hearing echoes of the Wannsee Conference in Tehran's inflammatory rhetoric. Historical comparisons between Tehran and Nazi-controlled Berlin are common, as is linking the Allied forces' refusal to bomb the concentration camps with the present international reluctance to take effective action against Iran. In April 2008, Benjamin Netanyahu, then leader of the opposition, made such an explicit comparison in a conversation with Stephen Hadley, then national security adviser in the Bush administration. "Ahmadinejad is a modern Hitler," Netanyahu told Hadley, "and the mistakes that were made prior to the Second World War must not be repeated."

But this visceral fear of Iran among the public and elected politicians is not shared by the intelligence community. Experts on the Iranian regime are quick to point out that

Ahmadinejad does not call the shots in Iran; the real power lies with Ayatollah Ali Khamenei, the country's supreme religious leader. Furthermore, these experts note, throughout its 30 years of existence, the Iranian regime has shown pragmatism and moderation whenever its survival was at stake. And the Iranians clearly understand that a nuclear attack against Israel would lead to a devastating Israeli counterstrike that, among other things, would mean the end of the revolutionary regime. Finally, the Mossad and the Military Intelligence believe that the real reason the Iranians are intent on acquiring nuclear weapons, aside from the obvious considerations of prestige and influence, is to deter US intervention and efforts at regime change.

Despite its assessment of Iran's motives, the Israeli intelligence community nonetheless believes that everything must be done to prevent Iran from becoming a nuclear power. To begin with, Israel cannot afford to risk nuclear weapons falling into the hands of someone less pragmatic than Khamenei; given its tiny size, Israel would be unlikely to recover from even a single nuclear blast. This makes the risk of relying on the rationality of the Iranian regime intolerable. In addition, a nuclear Tehran could provide assistance to terror organizations, especially those active against Israel, without fear of reprisal. Lastly, an Iranian bomb would draw key regional players such as Egypt, Jordan, and Saudi Arabia into a regional nuclear arms race.

But ultimately, the intelligence community believes that Israel's military options are limited. No matter how great a success in tactical terms, even under the rosiest scenario, an air strike against Iran's nuclear installations would set its nuclear program back by only two or three years. Moreover, intelligence suggests that Iran would retaliate to such a strike by using its proxy forces, in particular, Hamas and Hezbollah, to unleash a wave of terrorist attacks against Israeli and Jewish targets around the world.

Israel's isolation on the question of Iran haunts both the public and the experts. If anything is to be done to thwart the nuclear ambitions of the regime in Tehran, Jerusalem will have to do so unilaterally, and bear the consequences. As Ariel Levite, the former deputy director general of the Israel Atomic Energy Commission, told a closed forum in April 2007, "The worst scenario of all would be if the president of the United States tells us: 'If you want to attack, then go ahead and attack. I won't stop you. But if you do attack, you will pay the price. It's up to you.'"

Israeli policymakers, then, are left to parse exactly how far President Barack Obama is willing to support Israel in its efforts to counter the Iranian threat. For the moment, Obama has made it clear that his focus is on talking with Iran. An Israeli attack would seriously undermine any hope of substantive dialogue. But the parameters of this dialogue are largely unknown, which makes Israel worried. Does the administration have clearly defined criteria for success? How will it decide that talks have failed, and how long will it tolerate a lack of progress? And perhaps the most worrisome question of all: Is a successful outcome of dialogue, as judged by Washington, compatible with Israel's security needs?

For now, Washington wants Israel to sit on its hands, and Israel has apparently agreed to do so. It is clear to all in Jerusalem that if Israel were to launch an unauthorized attack while the possibility of dialogue is still alive, the Obama administration might retaliate punitively, both diplomatically and economically. Indeed, some government officials in Jerusalem believe that any Israeli attack, even after diplomacy has failed, would require explicit American authorization.

Others, however, especially in Netanyahu's inner circle, believe that the statements made by members of the US administration, including Obama himself, provide the wink and the nod that Israel needs in order to take action farther down the road. [ ... ]

Netanyahu himself still appears to be undecided. He has repeatedly stated over the years that Israel cannot countenance a nuclear Iran. In an interview I conducted with him in late 2007, he said: "We need to prepare for a situation in which we have failed and Iran has succeeded in acquiring a bomb. Against lunatics, deterrence must be absolute, total. The lunatics must understand that if they raise their hand against us, we will hit them in a way that will eviscerate any desire to harm us."

Some political analysts believe that this sort of language reflects Netanyahu's profound personal convictions and his sense of duty as a national leader. Others maintain that his tough-guy rhetoric is just a façade, part of his political persona. [ ... ]

And yet campaign promises, if repeated often enough, have a tendency to create their own momentum. Public pressure to act is considerable. Netanyahu knows that a successful Iranian nuclear test could destroy his political future. Moreover, the immediate political environment in which Netanyahu operates is conducive to authorizing a preemptive strike. His senior coalition partner, Foreign Minister Avigdor Lieberman, has made threats against Iran on numerous occasions. And, unlike many of the country's mid-level intelligence analysts and security officials, the current leaders of the Mossad and the Shin Bet believe in solving problems by force.

As Iran approaches nuclear weapons capability, sometime in 2010, according to current Mossad estimates, an increasing number of people in Netanyahu's circle will adopt the view that Israel needs to take action and that the United States will be understanding of Israel's needs. And if the Obama administration is not so understanding? Israel may decide that the existential danger posed by a potential second Holocaust warrants risking even a serious rift with the United States. Ultimately, the fear of a nuclear-armed state whose leader talks openly of destroying Israel may outweigh the views of the country's intelligence experts.

---

## Authors' Note

The following article posits that the United States should not preemptively attack Iran, citing several negative consequences of such an action. The article considers potential military, economic, political, and humanitarian repercussions.

---

## 17. Center for Arms Control and Non-Proliferation, Risky Business: Why Attacking Iran Is a Bad Idea

### 2007

This fact sheet explains why a preemptive US military strike against Iran would be a catastrophic mistake. A host of unknown variables make measurable success highly unlikely and the risks the US would incur far outweigh any possible benefits. The military, economic, humanitarian, and political consequences of attacking Iran would damage American strategic interests across the globe for years to come.

### Military Risks

**Iran could attack US naval forces and commercial oil tankers operating in the Persian Gulf, especially in the Strait of Hormuz.**

Tehran could use mines, submarines, small surface vessels, and land-based anti-ship missiles in the narrow waterway of the Strait of Hormuz. Iran is also believed to possess roughly 100 HY-2/C-201 Silkworm or Seersucker missiles on 8–10 mobile launchers currently deployed near the Strait.

**Iran could attack US forces stationed in Iraq, Afghanistan, and elsewhere.**

Tehran could launch Shahab-3 medium-range missiles, possibly armed with chemical, biological, or radiological warheads, against American forces stationed in the Middle East. Iran could also persuade radical Iraqi cleric Moqtada al-Sadr, a Shia who has pledged support to Tehran in the event of a US attack, to have his Mahdi Army attack American soldiers in Iraq.

**Iran could use its proxy forces such as Hezbollah to attack Israel, topple the fragile Lebanese government, or terrorize soft targets like embassies, commercial centers, or American citizens.**

Iran could attack Israel directly using its Shahab-3 missiles or prod Hezbollah militants to launch short-range rockets from southern Lebanon. Other Iranian-influenced groups such as Palestine Islamic Jihad, the Hezbollah-financed al-Aqsa Brigades, or the Damascus-controlled Hamas militants could also attack Israel or destroy the nascent Palestinian national unity government.

**A truly effective military strike would be a time-consuming and extensive operation, thus increasing the risk of retaliation against American forces.**

The Iranians have fortified their nuclear facilities with blast proof doors, extensive divider walls, hardened ceilings, 20 cm-thick concrete walls, and double concrete ceilings with earth-fill between layers. While American GBU-28 "bunker-buster" conventional weapons might be able to destroy these hardened targets, the US would need to hit them many times to ensure total destruction. Retired Air Force Colonel Sam Gardiner, an expert in strategic war gaming, estimated that there are at least 400 "aim points" in Iran, 75 of which would require penetrating weapons to destroy.

**Any setback to the Iranian nuclear program would be only temporary.**

Without a long-term diplomatic solution consistent with international nonproliferation standards, a military strike on Iran amounts to an open-ended military commitment. The Israeli attack against Iraq's Osirak nuclear reactor in 1981 did not end Saddam Hussein's WMD activity and an American attack against Iran would assuredly not end Mahmoud Ahmadinejad's nuclear aspirations.

Economic Risks

**Oil prices would go sky high, experts predict over $200 per barrel and $5 per gallon.**

According to a tally by Oil and Gas Journal, Iran has the second-highest supply of untapped oil reserves in the world, an estimated 125.8 billion barrels. With these vast petroleum resources and its concurrent ability to disrupt shipments in the Strait of Hormuz, through which 40 percent of the world's daily oil exports pass, Iran could severely destabilize global financial markets.

**A global economic recession could be triggered if Moqtada al-Sadr got involved.**

Moqtada al-Sadr, a staunch Iranian ally, controls Iraq's 140,000-member Facilities Protection Service responsible for guarding oil pipelines and refineries. He could easily cut the oil flow off from Iraq in response to an American military strike on Iran. The loss of exports from Iraq and Iran combined would cripple the global economy. This would not only harm the most industrialized countries but also hinder development efforts in critically impoverished areas of Africa, Asia, and Latin America.

Humanitarian Risks

**Conventional attacks would kill thousands of Iranian civilians.**

Tehran purposefully built its nuclear facilities near population centers to deter potential attackers. Any claim that an attack on Iran could be accomplished in one day or that it would be "limited" or "surgical" ignores the enormity of the operation. There is no such thing as a "clean" strike on Iranian facilities located so close to population centers.

**Should the US use nuclear "bunker busters," civilian casualties would be incalculable and international condemnation would be universal.**

The Bush administration has contemplated using B61-11 nuclear "bunker busters" against Iranian underground facilities to ensure absolute target destruction. Using a nuclear bunker buster would create massive clouds of radioactive fallout that could spread far from the site of the attack. More than a hundred thousand civilian casualties could easily result, according to nuclear experts.

**Political Risks**

**Global determination to build nuclear weapons would be reinforced, possibly leading to a renewed arms race.**

The unmistakable message of a military strike would be that the US is willing to attack countries that do not possess nuclear weapons. North Korea has clearly indicated that its revived plutonium reprocessing activity and its nuclear test are a reaction to the American invasion of Iraq and a strike against Iran would likely strengthen Pyongyang's resolve.

**An attack on Iran would undoubtedly strengthen hard line extremists.**

President Mahmoud Ahmadinejad would consolidate his power to the detriment of moderate reformers like former President Mohammad Khatami. Long sought-after opportunities to undermine the radical clerics and encourage Iranian democracy would be lost.

**The attacks would unite the Iranian population against the US**

The Iranian population, which remains generally pro-American, would vehemently turn against the US following a military strike. The US would lose a priceless opportunity to nurture a friendly ally in a troubled region.

**Unknown Variables**

**American intelligence about Iranian facilities is inconclusive.**

The International Atomic Energy Agency (IAEA) has identified at least 18 Iranian nuclear facilities, but reliable sources suggest there may be more than 70. It is possible that Iran possesses buried nuclear facilities that have escaped detection by American intelligence. After all, the US did not find out about North Korea's underground facilities until much later, and Iranian nuclear activity at Esfahan, Natanz, and Arak was a secret until dissidents revealed it in 2002.

**American intelligence estimates that Iran is at least five to ten years away from building nuclear weapons.**

Taking military action against Iran would be a repeat of the mistake the US made in Iraq in response to misestimates of Saddam's WMD program.

\* \* \*

## Authors' Note

The following material is a report by the state-run Korean Central News Agency that explains North Korea's reasons for withdrawing from the Nonproliferation Treaty (NPT). The report states that North Korea's withdrawal from the NPT is permissible due to North Korea's unique status as a result of US threats to its sovereignty.

## 18. Detailed Report Explains NPT Withdrawal

Korean Central News Agency, 2003

To cope with the grave situation where our state security and national sovereignty are being threatened due to the United States and forces following the United States and the US tyrannical nuclear crushing policy toward the DPRK, the DPRK Government took an important measure to immediately withdraw from the NPT.

KCNA [Korean Central News Agency] issues the following detailed report relating the circumstances where the Republic government declared its withdrawal from the NPT.

### Details on becoming a NPT member

Our country's purpose for entering the NPT lay in removing the US nuclear threat and importantly, in smoothly resolving the country's energy issue with nuclear power.

We have actively encouraged hydroelectric and thermoelectric generation capabilities to meet the increasing energy demand in the people's economy. However, this was limited in its potential power. Accordingly, we decided to develop the nuclear power industry, which is the best method for resolving the electricity issue in our country's conditions. Thus, we adopted the atomic power law in 1974 and legally restricted the usage of atomic power to only peaceful purposes.

We promoted scientific research tasks to develop our country's nuclear power industry. At the same time, we exerted efforts to receive an atomic power plant on a turnkey basis from other countries. This is because at that time, the worldwide trend for nuclear power plants was on LWRs, based on low-enriched uranium, and [a nuclear power plant] was too much for us to [build] by ourselves due to the technological complexity.

We decided to introduce LWRs and make them the pillars in our country's energy production, so we negotiated with some developed countries. However, this project did not develop smoothly, and no country wanted to sell us LWRs.

The only countries that were exporting atomic power plant facilities in the 1960s and 1970s were Western countries, including the former Soviet Union and the United States, and some countries in West Europe. First, we tried to purchase developed LWRs by paying money to the Western countries, including Canada, Sweden, and France. However, this could not be realized due to hampering by the US COCOM [Coordinating Committee for Export Control to Communist Areas].

Thus, we negotiated the LWR supply issue with the former Soviet Union, although it was not as technologically developed as the Western countries. At that time, the Soviet Union said that if we were to receive nuclear-related technologies, we must enter the NPT and sign safeguard agreements with the International Atomic Energy Agency [IAEA].

We prudently studied the issue of entering the NPT. In particular, the basic spirit of the NPT drew our, who are receiving the US nuclear threat under conditions where the state land is divided, natural attention. The NPT's basic spirit notes that countries possessing nuclear weapons should not threaten or use nuclear weapons on other countries, should not create an emergency situation that endangers the basic interests of non-nuclear countries, and should exert all efforts to avoid a nuclear war.

On 12 December 1985, we entered the NPT with the purpose to realize international cooperation in the nuclear power industry sector, remove nuclear threats toward us, and make the Korean peninsula a non-nuclear zone.

\* \* \*

## Background of Our Withdrawal from the NPT

\* \* \*

To defend the country's sovereignty and security in response to the created situation, we entered a semi-war situation and on 12 March 1993, took a measure to withdraw from the NPT to defend our supreme interests.

Article 10 of the NPT clearly states that each treaty participant may withdraw when a special situation is created in which its supreme interests are threatened. Therefore, our measure was an exercise of our legitimate right, which no one could contradict.

On 13 June 1994, we took the measure of withdrawing from the IAEA in the aftermath of the adoption of the "resolution" that stated "IAEA cooperation" with us "would be suspended," and demanding, in the 10 June 1994 Board of Governors meeting, the opening of our military facilities with regards to our "nuclear issue."

From then on, all the unjust IAEA "resolutions" taken in connection with us became nullified, and we were not bound by any IAEA rules and decisions.

### The DPRK's Unique Status

When our statement on the withdrawal from the Nuclear Non-Proliferation Treaty [NPT] was announced, the world expressed grave concerns about the creation of a dangerous touch-and-go situation on the Korean peninsula due to the United States' arbitrariness and demanded a peaceful resolution of the Korean peninsula's nuclear issue through dialogue and negotiations.

Our Republic's sincere efforts to prevent the danger of the outbreak of a war on the Korean peninsula and to ensure regional peace and stability, and the strong demands of the peace-loving people of the world compelled the United States to come to the negotiating table for a peaceful resolution of the Korean peninsula's nuclear issue.

The DPRK-US Joint Statement was adopted on 11 June 1993, after several rounds of bilateral negotiations.

In the Joint Statement, the United States promised not to use or threaten us with force, including nuclear weapons, but to respect our sovereignty and refrain from interfering in our internal affairs. We decided to temporarily suspend the effect of our withdrawal from the NPT as long as we deemed necessary.

And thus, we came to be placed in a unique status regarding our relations with the NPT.

\* \* \*

Since the Bush administration came to office, anti-DPRK stifling maneuvers have reached an extreme and DPRK-US relations have fallen into the worst situation.

As soon as the Bush administration officials took power, they made it a policy to crush the DPRK with force of arms, and completely blocked the already-begun DPRK-US dialogue.

Even before they faced us, they labeled the DPRK a "dictatorial state," "rogue state," and the like, and openly declared they would "break down" our system. Moreover, they threw cold water on progress in North-South relations.

In February 2001, the new US administration's diplomatic and security team went so far as to say North Korea dragged around the former Clinton administration, only giving in charity, and that unlike the Clinton administration's intent, the new administration would implement a "policy of strength," openly raving about its so-called "hard-line stance" toward the DPRK.

Bush even spoke ill of our supreme leadership. Not content with that, he went so far as to make harsh remarks, describing us as part of "axis of evil" in his "State of the Union Address" to Congress on 30 January 2002.

There is no such case in the history of recent DPRK-US relations as the US President personally making an open aggressive threat against our nation, an independent and sovereign state, through his policy speech. This is, in fact, little short of declaring war against us.

\* \* \*

Thus, the United States undisguisedly abolished the DPRK-US Agreed Framework and internationalized its anti-DPRK stifling maneuvers by mobilizing even the IAEA. The United States began executing a declaration of war against us. As this was the case, we were forced to withdraw from the NPT, which has been used as a tool for implementing the United States' anti-DPRK hostile policy, in order to cope its declaration of war, and defend and safeguard the nation's sovereignty and right to existence.

As we can see from the aforementioned facts, the nuclear problem on the Korean peninsula is a product of the US anti-DPRK hostile policy. At the same time, it is thoroughly an issue between the DPRK and the United States and a problem that should be resolved between the DPRK and the United States by sitting face to face with each other.

Therefore, the most realistic measure for basically resolving the nuclear problem on the Korean peninsula and peacefully breaking through the prevailing grave situation is only to conclude a non-aggression treaty between the DPRK and the United States.

In the event that the United States legally pledges non-aggression, including the non-use of nuclear [weapons] against us, through a non-aggression treaty, we will disperse the US security worries.

Although we withdrew from the NPT, our nuclear activities will be limited to the peaceful purpose of electricity production at the present stage.

If the United States discards its hostile policy against the DPRK and discontinues making nuclear threats, we will be ready to prove, through a separate verification between the DPRK and the United States, that we will not make nuclear weapons.

It is a consistent stance of the DPRK Government to peacefully resolve the nuclear problem on the Korean peninsula on equal footings between the DPRK and the United States through just and fair negotiations that will simultaneously dispel the two sides' worries.

## Authors' Note

The following six materials present the international community's perspective on North Korea's nuclear activities. Material 19 discusses the Six-Party Talks, a diplomatic effort to achieve North Korean disarmament through negotiations among North and South Korea, the United States, China, Japan, and Russia. The article provides an overview of the negotiation framework, discusses the progress and setbacks that have taken place since the talks began in 2003, and presents the interests of the involved parties. Material 20 is a report of the U.N.-appointed panel of experts that convened according to Security Council Resolution 1874. The report discusses the status of North Korea disarmament efforts, with regard to trade-related and diplomatic mechanisms that have encouraged disarmament. Material 21 is a statement of the South Korean Ministry of Foreign Affairs. The statement condemns North Korea's development of nuclear weapons and advocates continued international efforts geared toward disarmament. Material 22 is a report of the IAEA director general, which outlines North Korea's implementation of IAEA safeguards. While North Korea has prohibited the IAEA from implementing safeguards since 2002, the IAEA has been able to monitor North Korea's nuclear activities to a limited extent. Material 23 discusses the strong diplomatic and economic relationship between North Korea and China, analyzing how this relationship factors into China's approach to the international effort to disarm North Korean. Material 24 is congressional testimony of Stephen Bosworth, the US Special Representative for North Korea. Bosworth discusses the US approach to North Korea's nuclear program, including focus on maintaining sanctions and promoting diplomacy between North and South Korea.

## 19. Jayshree Bajoria and Carin Zissis, The Six-Party Talks on North Korea's Nuclear Program
### Council on Foreign Relations, 2009

### Introduction

The Six-Party Talks are aimed at ending North Korea's nuclear program through a negotiating process involving China, the United States, North and South Korea, Japan, and Russia. Since the talks began in August 2003, the negotiations have been bedeviled by diplomatic standoffs among individual Six-Party member states, particularly between the United States and North Korea. In April 2009, North Korea quit the talks and announced that it would reverse the ongoing disablement process called for under at the Six-Party agreements and restart its Yongbyon nuclear facilities. Because Pyongyang appears intent on maintaining its nuclear program, some experts are pessimistic the talks can achieve anything beyond managing the North Korean threat. The Obama administration has been pursuing talks with the other four countries in the process to bring Pyongyang back to the negotiation table. Alongside the United Nations' effort to sanction North Korea's nuclear and missile tests, "this regional partnership between the United States and the countries of Northeast Asia remains the best vehicle … for building stable relationships on and around the Korean peninsula," writes CFR's Sheila Smith.

### The Framework

The Six-Party Talks began in August 2003. Numerous rounds of negotiations resulted in a September 2005 agreement in which Pyongyang agreed to abandon its quest to become a nuclear power. The talks came after a policy reversal in the presidency of George W. Bush, who had initially ended the policy of direct engagement with Pyongyang endorsed by President Bill Clinton before him. Bush included North Korea in the "Axis of Evil" during his 2002 State of the Union address and, that October, the Central Intelligence Agency (CIA) concluded that Pyongyang was pursuing a uranium-enrichment program. According to Washington, this violated the spirit of the 1994 Agreed Framework, in which the United States pledged to provide fuel oil and construct two light-water reactors while North Korea promised to end a plutonium enrichment program in exchange.

North Korea admitted to the uranium-enrichment program but refused to end it unless the United States agreed to hold bilateral talks and normalize relations. When Washington rebuffed these demands, North Korea withdrew from the Nuclear Nonproliferation Treaty (NPT), forced International Atomic Energy Agency (IAEA) inspectors to leave, and restarted its plutonium-enrichment program. With tensions mounting, including the March 2003 interception of a US spy plane by North Korean fighter aircraft over the

Sea of Japan, the United States, North Korea, and China held trilateral talks in Beijing in April 2003. These negotiations served as a prelude to the first round of Six-Party Talks, which brought other regional players, South Korea, Japan, and Russia, into the fold.

### Stop-and-Go Negotiations

According to the September 2005 pact, Pyongyang would eventually abandon its nuclear program, rejoin the NPT, and allow IAEA monitors to return. In exchange, North Korea would receive food and energy assistance from the other members. The statement also paved the way for Pyongyang to normalize relations with both the United States and Japan, and for the negotiation of a peace agreement for the Korean peninsula.

However, negotiations hit a roadblock in November 2005 after the US Treasury Department placed restrictions on Macao-based Banco Delta Asia, which Washington accused of laundering $25 million in North Korean funds. The Macanese government subsequently froze Pyongyang's roughly fifty accounts held in the bank. As the talks fell apart, North Korea stepped up its provocative behavior, conducting missile tests in July 2006 and a nuclear test in October 2006.

After the nuclear crisis came to a head, Beijing pressed North Korea to rejoin the talks. In February 2007, during the sixth round of talks, members hammered out a denuclearization plan, seen by Washington as a means to jump-start the September 2005 statement, involving a sixty-day deadline for North Korea to freeze its nuclear program in exchange for aid and the release of the Banco Delta Asia funds. The deal also involved a series of bilateral talks, including between North Korea and the United States.

In July 2007, the denuclearization program gained momentum with Pyongyang shutting down its main plutonium-producing nuclear plant at Yongbyon. In October, Pyongyang agreed to end its nuclear program in exchange for aid and diplomatic concessions and started to disable the Yongbyon plant by removing eight thousand fuel rods from the nuclear reactor under the guidance of US experts.

In May 2008, North Korea handed over around eighteen thousand pages of documents to the United States detailing production records of its nuclear programs. This handover was followed by a declaration a month later, as agreed in the Six-Party Talks. In June, it imploded the cooling tower of the Yongbyon nuclear plant and the Bush administration responded by removing restrictions on North Korea from the Trading with the Enemy Act. Following Pyongyang's agreement to some verification measures in October, Washington took North Korea off the State Sponsors of Terrorism list.

Critics of the Bush administration's policy toward North Korea said Washington had capitulated to Pyongyang, asserting the North Korean declaration from June 2008 fell short on three important counts:

- It did not include details of suspected uranium enrichment;
- It did not address Pyongyang's proliferation activities to countries like Syria and Libya;
- It failed to give an account of the nuclear weapons already produced.

By the end of the Bush administration, Pyongyang failed to agree to a verification protocol for its nuclear program. The new Obama administration in Washington signaled early on that it would be ready to engage Pyongyang. However, North Korea's multiple missile tests, followed by a nuclear test in May 2009, resulted in the United States pushing for tougher sanctions through a new U.N. Security Council Resolution. During a visit by South Korean President Lee Myung-bak to Washington in June, Obama said he was still willing to engage in negotiations with North Korea, "but belligerent, provocative behavior that threatens neighbors will be met with significant, serious enforcement of sanctions that are in place."

## Objectives for Parties Involved

*United States:* For Washington, the Six-Party Talks serve as a means to make North Korea's nuclear weapons program a multinational problem rather than an issue to be solved through bilateral discussion. Although Washington worries about the Communist state's poor human rights record, the chief US concern remains Pyongyang's nuclear program and possible sale of nuclear materials and technology to hostile states and terrorist groups. As part of any agreement, Washington wants the reclusive state to accept IAEA monitors in the country.

*North Korea:* The regime of Kim Jong-Il seeks a nonaggression security pledge from the United States, which deploys more than twenty-five thousand troops in South Korea. Pyongyang also wants normalized relations with Washington. North Korea wants unfettered access to economic aid from other Six-Party countries and hopes for the completion of the two light-water reactors promised in the 1994 Agreed Framework.

*South Korea:* Frozen in an unresolved conflict with North Korea, South Korea's ultimate goal is the denuclearization and reunification of the Korean peninsula. Seoul also wishes to avoid a sudden regime change in Pyongyang that would force it to bear the economic burden of a large, sudden influx of refugees across its border.

*China:* Beijing serves as Pyongyang's long-standing ally and main trade partner, and has used its influence with the Kim regime to bring North Korea to the Six-Party negotiating table. China's ability to play such a role in the talks boosts its relations with Washington. Like South Korea, China fears a rush of refugees across its border and has provided North Korea with energy and food assistance. Beijing has been resistant to implementing stringent U.N. resolutions imposing sanctions against Pyongyang. North Korea also serves as a buffer zone between China and US troops in South Korea.

*Russia:* Moscow's position at the table allows Russia, also concerned with refugee flows, to reassert its influence in Northeast Asia. Russia has joined China in warning against cornering North Korea with harsh sanctions.

*Japan:* Tokyo worries about North Korea's testing of missiles that could reach Japan's population centers or US military bases there. But Japan also sees the Six-Party Talks as a forum for negotiating an admission of Pyongyang's guilt in the 1970s and 1980s abductions of Japanese citizens by North Korean spies. The issue serves as a divisive point in the US-Japan alliance; Tokyo did not want Washington to remove North Korea from its state sponsors of terrorism list until the abduction question was resolved. Meanwhile, Pyongyang has demanded at times that Tokyo not participate in the talks.

Obstacles to the Talks

*An unpredictable North Korean regime:* Despite shifting ground on holding bilateral talks, the United States has found North Korea erratic in negotiations and actions. "They know that we have a tough time figuring out what really motivates them," said Christopher Hill, Washington's former chief envoy to the talks.

*Differing approaches by Six-Party governments:* CFR Adjunct Senior Fellow Scott Snyder says the Six-Party Talks and other regional efforts preceding it failed to meet the North Korean challenge because the participating states "placed their own immediate priorities and concerns above the collective need to halt North Korea's nuclear program." While Japan and the United States consistently have pushed for strong sanctions in response to North Korean weapons testing, China, South Korea, and Russia often have pushed for less stringent sanctions out of fear that a sudden toppling of the regime would lead to major refugee influxes.

*US Resistance to Bilateral Negotiations:* For much of the Bush administration's tenure, Washington resisted holding one-on-one talks with Pyongyang, preferring the Six-Party

Talks so that any compromises with the Kim regime were framed as part of multilateral negotiations. Yet North Korea repeatedly demanded direct talks as a condition for stopping its nuclear program. In June 2007, former envoy Hill made a surprise visit to Pyongyang to push forward the February deal, finalizing a reversal in the US stance on dealing directly with North Korea.

*Regime Succession in Pyongyang:* After Kim Jong-Il reportedly suffered a stroke in August 2008, experts say North Korea's actions have been driven by domestic politics. CFR's Paul B. Stares, director of the Center for Preventive Action, argues that for future diplomatic initiatives to be successful, "they must adjust for the likelihood that the nuclear weapons program is being driven primarily out of considerations of 'regime survival' as distinct from national security." Thus, he writes, it may be necessary for Washington "to consider active measures to reassure the Kim family regime of its future."

## Solving the Policy Puzzle

So far, the Six-Party Talks have failed to denuclearize North Korea and have brought few results. Several experts think North Korea is now determined to be recognized as a nuclear weapons state rather than to negotiate an end to its nuclear program. Former Secretary of State Henry A. Kissinger writes in the *Washington Post* that "the issue for diplomacy has become whether the goal should be to manage North Korea's nuclear arsenal or to eliminate it." He argues any policy that does not eliminate the North's nuclear military capability "in effect acquiesces in its continuation."

After Pyongyang walked out of the Six-Party Talks in May 2009, the Obama administration has pursued negotiations with the other parties in the forum to signal that it hasn't abandoned the goal of North Korea's denuclearization. In testimony to a House Foreign Affairs subcommittee in June 2009, CFR's Snyder said this new process "provides the best available means by which to increase pressure on North Korea to return to the Six-Party Talks and to honor its commitments to denuclearization."

However, on trying to restore the negotiating track with North Korea, the Obama administration could also offer strictly bilateral US-North Korea negotiations, notes a May 2009 report (PDF) by the Congressional Research Service. Some experts say that even though a multilateral approach may be the best option, it has produced few results. Charles Pritchard, former ambassador and special envoy for negotiations with North Korea from 2001–2003, writes that "it is a bilateral approach between the United States and North Korea that has worked the best, that has produced the most results in the shortest period of time." But in the end, few analysts believe North Korea has any intention of giving up its nuclear program. Victor Cha, deputy chief of the US delegation to the Six-Party Talks during the Bush administration, writes in the Washington Post that "since the talks will never achieve what either Washington or Pyongyang wants, they serve as a way to manage the problem, contain the proliferation threat and run out the clock on the regime."

---

# 20. Report to the Security Council from the Panel of Experts Established Pursuant to Resolution 1874
### U.N. Panel of Experts on DPRK Nuclear Armament, 2010

\* \* \*

## II. Introduction

11. In response to the continuing non-compliance of the Democratic People's Republic of Korea (DPRK) with its international obligations and following the nuclear test conducted

by the Democratic People's Republic of Korea on 25 May 2009, the Security Council adopted resolution 1874 (2009) on 12 June 2009. With that resolution the Council strengthened measures previously adopted in resolution 1718 (2006) and stressed that the Democratic People's Republic of Korea must abandon all its nuclear-related, other existing weapons of mass destruction-related and ballistic missile-related programmes and return to full compliance with its international obligations.

\* \* \*

13. Faced with the DPRK's announced withdrawal from the NPT and its renunciation of its obligations under the Safeguards Agreement between the International Atomic Energy Agency (IAEA) and the Democratic People's Republic of Korea (INFCIRC/403), the Security Council, on 11 May 1993, adopted resolution 825 (1993), formally calling upon the Democratic People's Republic of Korea to honour its non-proliferation obligations and to comply with its IAEA Safeguards Agreement. In addition, concerned countries undertook numerous and repeated demarches to persuade the DPRK to return to full compliance with its treaty obligations, and the DPRK agreed to "suspend" its announced withdrawal from the NPT. After a short period of cooperation, the Democratic People's Republic of Korea again increased tension in the region on 31 August 1998, by launching an object propelled by a missile over the territory of Japan, which fell into the sea in the vicinity of Japan. [ ... ]

14. The DPRK expelled all remaining IAEA inspectors on 27 December 2002, and informed the Security Council on 10 January 2003 that it had decided "to revoke the 'suspension' on the effectuation of the withdrawal from the NPT."

15. In an effort to defuse growing tension stemming from these DPRK actions, and to return the DPRK to NPT- and IAEA-related and other international obligations, China, Japan, Republic of Korea, Russian Federation and the United States on 27 August 2003, entered into joint talks with the DPRK ("Six-Party talks"). The Six-Party talks continued over the next two years without producing the desired results. [ ... ] In November 2005, however, the DPRK ceased its participation in this Six-Party process. On 5 July 2006, the DPRK, in defiance of previous undertakings and Security Council pronouncements, launched seven ballistic missiles, including a long range ballistic missile. Condemning these actions, the Security Council, on 15 July 2006, adopted resolution 1695 (2006) demanding that the DPRK "suspend all activities related to its ballistic missile programme, and in this context re-establish its pre-existing commitments to a moratorium on missile launching." The resolution also "requires" all Member States to prevent the provision to, or acquisition from, the DPRK of "missile and missile-related items, materials, goods and technology." The Council also urged the DPRK to abandon all nuclear weapons and existing nuclear programmes, and to return immediately to the Six-Party talks without precondition.

16. Despite these efforts to bring the DPRK back to the Six-Party talks, on 3 October 2006, the Democratic People's Republic of Korea announced its intention to conduct a nuclear test, and, in disregard of the Security Council Presidential Statement of 6 October 2006 (S/PRST/2006/41) urging the DPRK not to proceed, the DPRK announced that it had conducted a nuclear test on 9 October 2006. [ ... ]

\* \* \*

18. The Six-Party talks were resumed in December 2006, and on 13 February 2007 the parties announced agreement on first phase actions aimed at DPRK denuclearization. That was followed, on 3 October 2007, with the agreement on "Second-Phase Actions for the Implementation of the Joint Statement." Under these agreements, the DPRK undertook,

in return for 50,000 tons of fuel oil aid and other economic assistance, to shut down its Yongbyon reactor within 60 days, and plans were subsequently laid for the return of IAEA inspectors. However, the Six-Party talks reached a new impasse soon thereafter. And, in September 2008, the DPRK reversed its position on the closing of Yongbyon nuclear facilities, requested IAEA to remove seals and surveillance equipment, and prohibited further IAEA access to the site.

19. International tensions were further increased in April 2009, as the DPRK, acting in contravention of Security Council resolution 1718 (2006), launched a multi-stage ballistic missile again, which the DPRK claimed was an effort to place an experimental communications satellite into orbit. [ ... ]

20. On 25 May 2009, the DPRK conducted a second underground nuclear test, leading the Security Council, on 12 June 2009, to adopt resolution 1874 (2009), strengthening the measures previously adopted in resolution 1718 (2006). [ ... ] These and other decisions taken under Chapter VII have imposed legally binding obligations on the DPRK.

### III. Background

21. An understanding of the measures adopted by the Security Council, their application, implementation and impact, requires some discussion of the context in which these measures have been applied. This includes a review of the principal reasons cited by the DPRK for its nuclear, other WMD and ballistic missile-related programmes as well as the prevailing economic situation in the country.

22. While the decision-making process with regard to the DPRK's nuclear, other WMD and ballistic missile-related programmes remains unclear, many experts with whom the DPRK's conduct was discussed believe that it is influenced by a mixture of perceived security concerns and domestic factors. The DPRK believes also that its nuclear programme can provide the country a way to achieve its stated goal of becoming a "strong and prosperous country" (kangsongdaeguk) by the year 2012 without succumbing to what they view as "foreign influences." They also consider their nuclear capability as a valuable asset which provides them important leverage in dealing with the rest of the world.

23. Two elements which stand out in the DPRK's calculations are its "military first" (Songun) policy and its emphasis on "self reliance" (Juche). It has broadly been reported that the DPRK amended its constitution in 2009 to elevate this "military-first" policy into a national guiding principle, thereby solidifying the military's preeminent role. [ ... ]

24. While few reliable economic statistics are published by the DPRK, several recent reports produced by credible foreign sources indicate that the DPRK's state directed economy is suffering from a number of serious setbacks. The DPRK's continuous trade deficits, the lack of foreign currency reserves, chronic food shortages and the recent currency restructuring have had a substantial negative impact on the overall economy and the well being of large segments of the DPRK's general population. [ ... ]

25. The DPRK government has placed special emphasis on the development of a military-industrial complex including a significant armaments industry and an industry capable of supporting the country's nuclear, other WMD and ballistic missile-related programmes. DPRK's military-related industries (which also manufacture dual use items) are virtually indistinguishable from those supplying civilian needs. [ ... ]

26. While the DPRK releases no official statistics concerning its export trade, estimates prior to resolution 1874 (2009) placed it in the range of US $1.5 and US $3 billion, with the DPRK running an annual trade deficit in excess of US $1 billion. [ ... ]

\* \* \*

## IV. Security Council measures

28. The Security Council, in resolution 1874 (2009) sought to strengthen and build upon the measures previously adopted by the Council in resolution 1718 (2006) with a view of convincing the DPRK to comply with its Security Council imposed obligations, to return to the Six-Party talks, and to take significant irreversible steps to carry out its undertakings pursuant to previous Six-Party talks agreements. The measures adopted were also designed to inhibit the DPRK's ability to acquire equipment, material, technology and financial and other resources related to its nuclear, other weapons of mass destruction and ballistic missile programmes. These measures now include:

- A ban on the provision to the DPRK of all items, materials, equipment, goods and technology as specified in the resolution, as well as other items, material, equipment, goods and technology, determined by the Security Council or the Committee, which could contribute to the DPRK's nuclear-related, other weapons of mass destruction related, or ballistic missile-related programmes;
- A ban on the provision of all arms and related materiel to the DPRK (with the exception, subject to notification requirements, of small arms and light weapons and their related materiel);
- A ban on the procurement from the DPRK of listed and other items determined by the Security Council or the Committee, which could contribute to nuclear-related, other weapons of mass destruction-related, or ballistic missile-related programmes;
- A ban on the procurement from the DPRK of all arms and related materiel, including, small arms and light weapons and their related materiel;
- A ban on the transfer to and from the DPRK of financial transaction, technical training, advice, services or assistance related to the provision, manufacture, maintenance or use of all the items cited above (except for small arms and light weapons provided to the DPRK);
- A ban on the provision of luxury goods to the DPRK

29. In addition, Member States (and relevant international financial and credit institutions) are also called upon:

- To prevent the provision of financial services [ ... ];
- To refrain from entering into new commitments for grants, financial assistance, or concessional loans to the DPRK, except for humanitarian and developmental purposes directly addressing the needs of the civilian population, or the promotion of denuclearization;
- Not to provide public financial support for trade with the ... where such financial support could contribute to the DPRK's nuclear-related, other WMD-related, or ballistic missile-related programmes or activities; and,
- To exercise vigilance and prevent specialized teaching or training of DPRK nationals within their territories or by their nationals, of disciplines which could contribute to the DPRK's proliferation sensitive nuclear activities and the development of nuclear weapon delivery systems.

\* \* \*

## VII. Trade-Related Measures Compliance Related to Nuclear, Other Weapons of Mass Destruction and Ballistic Missile Activities

\* \* \*

58. No official allegations have been presented to the Committee concerning the provision of proscribed nuclear related or ballistic missile-related items, technology or know-how to or from the DPRK since the adoption of U.N. Security Council resolution 1874 (2009).

59. Nevertheless, the Panel of Experts has reviewed several government assessments, IAEA reports, research papers and media reports indicating continuing DPRK involvement in nuclear and ballistic missile related activities in certain other countries including Iran, Syria and Myanmar

\* \* \*

## 21. Making Efforts Toward a Peaceful Resolution of the North Korean Nuclear Issue

Ministry of Foreign Affairs and Trade Republic of Korea, 2010

The North Korean nuclear issue is a matter which concerns not only the Korean Peninsula but also the international community since it poses a serious threat to peace and stability in Northeast Asia and undermines the foundation of the international non-proliferation regime. The Korean government has remained engaged in diplomatic efforts aimed at reaching a peaceful resolution of the North Korean nuclear issue through the Six-Party Talks, which involve the two Koreas, the United States, Japan, China and Russia.

\* \* \*

However, the Six-Party Talks have fallen into a stalemate since December 2008, following a failure to reach an agreement on how to verify the completeness and correctness of the declaration of nuclear programs submitted by North Korea in June 2008.

In early 2009, North Korea carried out a series of provocative acts in spite of the calls of the international community: they launched a long-range rocket and started reversing disablement measures at the Yongbyon facilities in April, while refusing to participate in the Six-Party Talks. They even conducted a second nuclear test in May. Such provocations represent clear violations of relevant U.N. Security Council resolutions as well as all outstanding Six-Party Talks agreements.

The international community has demonstrated a unified and resolute response to North Korea's provocations, particularly, by fully implementing U.N. Security Council resolution 1874 which was adopted on June 12, 2009.

Despite diplomatic efforts aimed at bringing North Korea back to the Six-Party Talks North Korea has thus far refused to change its position toward the nuclear issue while continuing its nuclear activities, heightening the international community's concern. Further, through a Foreign Ministry Statement issued on January 11, 2010, North Korea demanded the lifting of U.N. Security Council sanctions as a precondition to its return to the Six-Party Talks and proposed to hold negotiations on a peace treaty before discussions on denuclearization.

Regarding North Korea's demands, the Korean government shares with the related countries the position that the lifting of sanctions can be reviewed only after progress is made in North Korea's denuclearization as stipulated in the U.N. Security Council resolution. As for a peace arrangement, the directly related parties will negotiate at an appropriate separate forum after the Six-Party Talks resume and substantial progress is made in the denuclearization process of North Korea.

The Korean government will never accept North Korea as a nuclear weapon state in any case. Thus, we will exert efforts to realize North Korea's complete and verifiable denuclearization in a peaceful manner through the Six-Party Talks, which is the most viable framework for addressing the North Korean nuclear issue. This position is widely and strongly supported by the international community.

The Korean government will continue to pursue a Two-Track Approach. The door for diplomatic negotiations remains open, while sanctions on North Korea under the relevant U.N. Security Council resolutions are faithfully implemented. This Two-Track Approach is supported by other Five Parties as well.

In addition, President Lee Myung-bak proposed a 'Grand Bargain' initiative in September 2009, in order to resolve the North Korean nuclear issue in a comprehensive manner. The initiative aims at encompassing in a single agreement all steps related to North Korea's irreversible denuclearization and the Five Parties' corresponding measures, departing from the partial and incremental agreements of the past. Based on a common understanding, the Five Parties are continuing consultations to elaborate this initiative.

Given the difficulties of substantially improving inter-Korean relations without genuine progress in denuclearization of North Korea, the Korean government also places high priority on the nuclear issue as part of the agenda of future inter-Korean dialogues.

In close cooperation with the international community which is supportive of the peaceful resolution of the North Korean nuclear issue, the Korean government will spare no effort to make progress in the complete and verifiable denuclearization of North Korea through inter-Korean dialogue as well as the Six-Party Talks.

---

## 22. Report of the IAEA Director General, Application of Safeguards in the Democratic People's Republic of Korea
### 2010
* * *

### C. Conclusion

9. Since December 2002, the DPRK has not permitted the Agency to implement safeguards in the country and, therefore, the Agency cannot draw any safeguards conclusion regarding the DPRK. Nor has the DPRK implemented the relevant measures called for in United Nations Security Council resolutions 1718 (2006) and 1874 (2009). At the behest of the DPRK, the Agency ceased the implementation of the ad hoc monitoring and verification arrangement in the DPRK on 15 April 2009. As a result, since that date the Agency has not been able to carry out any monitoring and verification activities in the DPRK and thus cannot provide any conclusions regarding the DPRK's nuclear activities.

---

## 23. Jayshree Bajoria, The China-North Korea Relationship
### Council on Foreign Relations, 2010

### Introduction

China is North Korea's most important ally; biggest trading partner; and main source of food, arms, and fuel. China has helped sustain Kim Jong-Il's regime and opposed harsh international economic sanctions in the hope of avoiding regime collapse and an uncontrolled influx of refugees across its eight-hundred-mile border with North Korea. After Pyongyang tested a nuclear weapon in October 2006, experts say that China has reconsidered the nature of its alliance to include both pressure and inducements. North

Korea's second nuclear test in May 2009 further complicated its relationship with China, which has played a central role in the Six Party Talks, the multilateral framework aimed at denuclearizing North Korea. CFR's Scott Snyder and See-won Byun of the Asia Foundation argue the nuclear tests highlight the tensions between China's "emerging role as a global actor with increasing international responsibilities and prestige and a commitment to North Korea as an ally with whom China shares longstanding historical and ideological ties." Beijing continues to have more leverage over Pyongyang than any other nation, say analysts. The economic leverage in particular, some point out, has only grown as a result of North Korea's declining relations with South Korea and the international community. But most experts agree that Beijing is unlikely to exercise its leverage given its concerns regarding regional stability and the uncertainty surrounding regime succession in North Korea.

### Strong Allies

China has supported North Korea ever since Chinese fighters flooded onto the Korean peninsula to fight for their comrades in the Democratic People's Republic of Korea (DPRK) in 1950. Since the Korean War divided the peninsula between the North and South, China has lent political and economic backing to North Korea's leaders: Kim Il-Sung and his son and successor, Kim Jong-Il.

In recent years, China has been one of the authoritarian regime's few allies. But this long-standing relationship suffered a strain when Pyongyang tested a nuclear weapon in October 2006 and China agreed to U.N. Security Council Resolution 1718, which imposed sanctions on Pyongyang. By signing off on this resolution, as well as earlier U.N. sanctions that followed the DPRK's July 2006 missile tests — Beijing departed from its traditional relationship with North Korea, changing from a tone of diplomacy to one of punishment. China also agreed to stricter sanctions after Pyongyang's second nuclear test in May 2009. Alan Romberg, a former US State Department official with the Henry L. Stimson Center in Washington, told *TIME*, "Pyongyang has spit in the [People's Republic of China's] eye." Despite their long alliance, experts say Beijing does not control Pyongyang. "In general, Americans tend to overestimate the influence China has over North Korea," says Daniel Pinkston, a Northeast Asia expert at the International Crisis Group.

Some experts say China's frustrations with the Kim Jong-Il regime seem to be growing, due to Pyongyang's continued brinkmanship, the regime's succession plans, and North Korea's growing economic crisis. China refused to take a stance against North Korea, despite evidence that Pyongyang sunk a South Korean naval vessel in March 2010. But in meetings with Kim following the incident, Chinese President Hu Jintao asked Kim to refrain from future provocations, says John S. Park, director of the Korea Working Group at the US Institute of Peace. Hu also reportedly insisted on long-overdue market reforms, notes Aidan Foster-Carter, a Korea expert at Leeds University.

At the same time, China has too much at stake in North Korea to halt or withdraw its support entirely. "The idea that the Chinese would turn their backs on the North Koreans is clearly wrong," says CFR Senior Fellow Adam Segal. Beijing only agreed to U.N. Resolution 1718 after revisions removed requirements for tough economic sanctions beyond those targeting luxury goods, and China's trade with North Korea has continued to increase. Bilateral trade between China and North Korea reached $2.79 billion in 2008, up 41.3 percent compared to 2007. Park writes that much of China's economic interactions with North Korea are not actually prohibited by the current U.N. sanctions regime, as Beijing characterizes them as economic development and humanitarian activities. China's enforcement of the U.N. sanctions is also unclear, says a January 2010 report from the US Congressional Research Service, which notes that Chinese exports of banned luxury goods averaged around $11 million per month in 2009.

### Pyongyang's Gains

Pyongyang is economically dependent on China, which provides most of its food and energy supplies. Nicholas Eberstadt, a consultant at the World Bank, says that since the early 1990s, China has served as North Korea's chief food supplier and has accounted for nearly 90 percent of its energy imports. By some estimates, China provides 80 percent of North Korea's consumer goods and 45 percent of its food. North Korea's economic dependence on China is rapidly increasing, as indicated by a significant trade imbalance. [ ... ]

China also provides aid directly to Pyongyang. "It is widely believed that Chinese food aid is channeled to the military," reports the Congressional Research Service. That allows the World Food Program's food aid to be targeted at the general population "without risk that the military-first policy or regime stability would be undermined by foreign aid policies of other countries." China is also a strong political ally. "As an authoritarian regime that reformed, they understand what Kim Jong-Il is most concerned with, survival," Segal says.

### China's Priorities

China's support for Pyongyang ensures a friendly nation on its northeastern border, and provides a buffer zone between China and democratic South Korea, which is home to around twenty-nine thousand US troops and marines. This allows China to reduce its military deployment in its northeast and "focus more directly on the issue of Taiwanese independence," Shen Dingli of the Institute of International Studies at Fudan University in Shanghai writes in *China Security*. North Korea's allegiance is important to Beijing as a bulwark against US military dominance of the region as well as against the rise of Japan's military.

China also gains economically from its association with North Korea; growing numbers of Chinese firms are investing in North Korea and gaining concessions like preferable trading terms and port operations. Chinese companies have made major investments aimed at developing mineral resources in North Korea's northern region. The January 2010 Congressional Research Service report says this "is part of a Chinese strategy" of stabilizing the border region it shares with North Korea, lessening the pressure on North Koreans to migrate to China, and raising the general standard of living in North Korea. USIP's Park writes these economic development plans also further China's national interests in developing its own chronically poor northeastern provinces by securing mineral and energy resources across the border.

"For the Chinese, stability and the avoidance of war are the top priorities," says Daniel Sneider, the associate director for research at Stanford's Asia-Pacific Research Center. "From that point of view, the North Koreans are a huge problem for them, because Pyongyang could trigger a war on its own." The specter of hundreds of thousands of North Korean refugees flooding into China is a huge worry for Beijing. "The Chinese are most concerned about the collapse of North Korea leading to chaos on the border," CFR's Segal says. If North Korea does provoke a war with the United States, China and South Korea would bear the brunt of any military confrontation on the Korean peninsula. Yet both those countries have been hesitant about pushing Pyongyang too hard, for fear of making Kim's regime collapse.

\* \* \*

### Beijing's Leverage

Beijing has been successful in bringing North Korean officials to the negotiating table at the Six Party Talks many times. "It's clear that the Chinese have enormous leverage over North Korea in many respects," Sneider, of Stanford's Asia-Pacific Research Center, says. "But can China actually try to exercise that influence without destabilizing the regime? Probably not." Pinkston says that for all of North Korea's growing economic ties with China, Kim still makes up his own mind: "At the end of the day, China has little influence over the military decisions."

Also, China does not wish to use its leverage except for purposes consistent with its policy objectives and strategic interests, say experts. Choo writes, "After all, it is *not* about securing influence over North Korean affairs but is about peaceful management of the relationship with the intent to preserve the status quo of the peninsula."

**Looking Forward**

And even though China may be angry at North Korea's nuclear brinkmanship, analysts say it will avoid moves that could cause a sudden collapse of the regime. Given the competition for influence in preparation for the eventual passing of a physically weak Kim Jong-Il, China may feel even more restrained from pressuring North Korea for fear of alienating a future power base.

But Asian military affairs expert Andrew Scobell writes, "No action by China should be ruled out where North Korea is concerned." According to Scobell, Beijing might stop propping up Pyongyang and allow North Korea to fail if it believed a unified Korea under Seoul would be more favorably disposed toward Beijing. A January 2008 report by the Center for Strategic and International Studies and the US Institute of Peace, two Washington-based think tanks, says China has its own contingency plans [ ... ] to dispatch troops to North Korea in case of instability. According to the report, the Chinese army could be sent into North Korea on missions to keep order if unrest triggers broader violence, including attacks on nuclear facilities in the North or South.

---

## 24. Stephen Bosworth, Testimony to the US Senate Committee on Foreign Relations, Breaking the Cycle of North Korea Provocations

### Special Representative for North Korea Policy, 2011

[ ... ] The North Korea issue is one of the most important foreign policy challenges of our time. North Korea's nuclear and ballistic missile program and proliferation activity pose an acute threat to a region of enormous economic vitality as well as to our global nonproliferation efforts and to our security interests more generally.

North Korea has repeatedly reneged on its commitments under the September 2005 Joint Statement made in the context of the Six-Party Talks. It has also failed to comply with a number of U.N. Security Council Resolution (UNSCR) obligations. At the beginning of his administration, President Obama expressed a willingness to engage North Korea. It responded by conducting missile tests, expelling IAEA inspectors, announcing a nuclear test, disclosing its uranium enrichment program, and stating that the Six-Party Talks were "dead." It also expelled the US personnel delivering food aid to the North Korean people. The United States has been a leader of a unified international response to these North Korean provocations. The U.N. Security Council adopted UNSCRs 1718 and 1874, calling on North Korea to immediately cease its nuclear activities and provocative actions.

North Korea's provocative actions have continued this past year, with its sinking of the Republic of Korea (ROK) corvette *Cheonan* in March and its artillery attack of South Korean Yeonpyong Island in November. [ ... ].

Following the attack on Yeonpyong Island, President Obama reaffirmed our commitment to the defense of the ROK and emphasized that we will stand "shoulder to shoulder" with our ally. The United States continues to demonstrate our commitment to deter North Korean provocations through joint military exercises with the ROK. [ ... ] We also continue to strengthen our non-proliferation efforts with regard to North Korea, including the adoption of new unilateral sanctions targeting DPRK illicit activities.

We strongly believe that North-South dialogue that takes meaningful steps toward reducing inter-Korean tensions and improving relations should precede a resumption of the Six-Party Talks. We believe North-South talks are an important opportunity for North Korea to demonstrate its sincerity and willingness to engage in dialogue. Ultimately, if North Korea fulfills its denuclearization commitments, the Five Parties are prepared to provide economic assistance and help to integrate North Korea into the international community.

In November, North Korea disclosed a uranium enrichment program and claimed that it was building a light-water nuclear reactor. These activities clearly violate North Korea's commitments under the 2005 Joint Statement and its obligations under UNSCRs 1718 and 1874. [ ... ]

Looking into the future, we continue to firmly believe that a dual-track approach to North Korea offers the best prospects for achieving denuclearization and a stable region. We are open to meaningful engagement but will continue to pursue the full and transparent implementation of sanctions. We are looking for demonstrable steps by North Korea that it is prepared to meet its international obligations and commitments to achieve the goal of the 2005 Joint Statement: the verifiable denuclearization of the Korean Peninsula in a peaceful manner.

In the meantime, the United States is continuing to consult closely with our partners in the Six-Party process. President Obama and Secretary Clinton have been at the forefront of this effort, reaching out to leaders in Japan, South Korea, China, and Russia. [ ... ]

During a mid-January visit to the United States by PRC President Hu Jintao, we made progress on greater cooperation with the Chinese on North Korea issues. In a Joint Statement issued during the visit, both sides agreed that the complete denuclearization of the Korean Peninsula remains our paramount goal. The United States and China also jointly "expressed concern regarding the DPRK's claimed uranium enrichment program," "opposed all activities inconsistent with the 2005 Joint Statement and relevant international obligations and commitments," and "called for the necessary steps that would allow for the early resumption of the Six-Party Talks process to address this and other relevant issues." [ ... ]

In addition, we have further solidified our alliances with the ROK and Japan and have improved trilateral cooperation among the three countries in responding to the DPRK's provocative and belligerent behavior. [ ... ]

In the meantime, the United States continues to improve the implementation of unilateral and international sanctions on North Korea to constrain its nuclear and missile programs. On August 30, the President signed Executive Order (E.O.) 13551, giving the US government new authorities to target North Korea's conventional arms proliferation and illicit activities. [ ... ] At the same time, we have stated unequivocally that we will not lift sanctions on the DPRK just for their returning to talks.

In March 2009, the DPRK terminated the US food aid program, ordering our humanitarian personnel out of the country and requiring that they leave behind 20,000 metric tons of undelivered US food items. The United States remains deeply concerned about the well-being of the North Korean people, particularly in light of continuing reports of chronic food shortages. The US government policy on humanitarian assistance and food aid is based on three factors: (1) level of need; (2) competing needs in other countries; and (3) our ability to ensure that aid is reliably reaching the people in need. [ ... ]

The United States also remains deeply concerned about the human rights situation in North Korea. We work closely with the United Nations, including the Human Rights Council, other international and non-governmental organizations, and other governments to try to improve the human rights situation in North Korea. The State Department's 2009 Country Report on Human Rights Practices for North Korea reports that the DPRK government continued to commit numerous serious abuses. [ ... ]

We are also working closely with the U.N. and other organizations to protect North Korean refugees. The United States has urged China to adhere to its international obligations as a party to the 1951 Refugee Convention and its 1967 Protocol, including by not expelling or *refouling* North Koreans protected under those treaties and undertaking to co-operate with UNHCR in the exercise of its functions. [ ... ] We support increasing the flow of balanced information into the DPRK through independent broadcasters based in the ROK and in collaboration with the Broadcasting Board of Governors and its partners Voice of America and Radio Free Asia. [ ... ] In conclusion, we continue to work closely with our Six-Party partners in an effort to promote peace and stability on the Peninsula and achieve the goals of the 2005 Six-Party Joint Statement. We believe we can make progress in cooperation with our partners in Tokyo, Beijing, Moscow, and Seoul. We are also working with our partners and the United Nations to advance human rights in North Korea, protect the status of North Korean refugees, and monitor the need for humanitarian assistance in North Korea. The door is open to Pyongyang to join and benefit from such an effort but only if it abandons the misguided notion that violence, threats, and provocation are the path toward achievement of its goals.

We face enormous challenges when dealing with North Korea. The denuclearization of the Korean Peninsula will not be easy to achieve, but we cannot abandon the goal. Through a strategy that combines openness to dialogue with a continuation of bilateral and multilateral sanctions, we believe we have an opportunity to bring about important improvements to the global nonproliferation regime and to regional and global security. We believe that our partners in the Six-Party process share this assessment and we will continue to work closely with them as we move forward.

* * *

## 25. Bibliography of Additional Sources

- African Nuclear-Weapon-Free Zone Treaty (Treaty of Pelindaba), Apr. 11, 1996, 35 I.L.M. 698.

- Arms Control Association, *Chronology of U.S.-North Korean Nuclear and Missile Diplomacy.*

- Greg Bruno, Council on Foreign Relations, *The Lengthening List of Iran Sanctions* (July 28, 2010).

- Desmond Butler, *Promises, Promises: Obama's Mixed Results on Nukes,* Associated Press (Apr. 5, 2011).

- Central Asian Nuclear Free Zone Treaty (Treaty of Semipalatinsk), Sept. 8, 2008.

- Comprehensive Test Ban Treaty, Sept. 24, 1996, U.N. Doc. A/50.1027.

- Council on Foreign Relations, *Meeting with His Excellency Lee Myung-bak* (Sept. 21, 2009).

- James A. Green & Francis Grimal, *The Threat of Force As an Action in Self-Defense Under International Law*, 44 Vand. J. Transnat'l L. 285 (2011).

- Michael Hamel-Green, Regional Initiatives on Nuclear- and WMD-Free Zones: Cooperative Approaches to Arms Control and Non-Proliferation (2005).

- Melissa Hanham, Nuclear Threat Initiative, *Impact of the Cheonan Incident on the Six-Party Talks* (May 17, 2010).

- Toni Johnson, Council on Foreign Relations, *Fifteen Nuclear Agendas to Watch* (May 27, 2010).

- David S. Jonas, *The New U.S. Approach to the Fissile Material Cutoff Treaty: Will Deletion of a Verification Regime Provide the Way out of the Wilderness?*, 18 Fla. J. Int'l L. 597 (Aug. 2006).

- Jeffery Lewis & Jayshree Bajoria, Council on Foreign Relations, *Interview: North Korea-Iran Nuclear Cooperation* (Dec. 14, 2010).

- Model Protocol Additional to the Agreement(s) Between State(s) and the International Atomic Energy Agency for the Application of Safeguards, IAEA Doc. INFCIRC/540 (corrected) (Sept. 1997).

- North Korea and Nuclear Weapons: The Declassified U.S. Record, National Security Archive Electronic Briefing Book No. 87 (Robert A. Wampler ed., 2003).

- Sammy Salama, Nuclear Threat Initiative, *Was Libyan WMD Disarmament a Significant Success for Nonproliferation?* (Sept. 2004).

- Janene Sawers, U.S. Inst. for Peace, *Nuclear Weapon Free-Zones as a New Deterrent?* (Apr. 2010).

- South Pacific Nuclear Free Zone Treaty (Treaty of Rarotonga), Aug. 6, 1985, 24 I.L.M. 1440.

- Treaty for the Prohibition of Nuclear Weapons in Latin America and the Caribbean (Treaty of Tlatelolco), Feb.14, 1967, 634 U.N.T.S. 326.

- *United States Pursues Nonproliferation Agenda at Npt Review Conference, Agrees to 2012 Conference on Nuclear-Free Middle East*, 104 Am. J. Int'l L. 520 (2010).

# Part V
# Protection of Human Rights and Enforcement of International Criminal Law

# Chapter XIV

# Self-Determination

## Introduction

This chapter addresses the role of international organizations in resolving self-determination based conflicts. A number of international organizations, including the U.N., Organization for Security and the Co-operation in Europe, and the International Court of Justice, have played significant roles in establishing the relevant legal principles governing the conflict between sovereignty and self-determination, and in seeking to resolve specific conflicts.

There are three primary concepts of self-determination that will be addressed in this chapter. Internal self-determination refers to the right of people to exercise the right of self-government with an existing state. External self-determination addresses the ability of a group of people and associated territory to become independent, and is usually associated with the consent of the parent state. Remedial self-determination provides that when a people's rights are so abused the only viable option to exercise their right of self-government is independence. The concept of remedial self-determination is not fully settled in international law or state practice, nor is the relationship between self-determination and sovereignty.

The chapter also addresses the emerging conflict resolution approach of earned sovereignty, which is based upon the extensive engagement of international organizations, and provides a basis for evaluating its utility as a viable approach to resolving self-determination based conflicts.

## Objectives

- To understand the complex relationship between sovereignty and self-determination.
- To understand the concept of self-determination, where the right is derived and how it is interpreted in international law.
- To understand the role of international organizations in promoting self-determination while preserving sovereignty.
- To understand the development of the concept of remedial self-determination and its legal status.
- To explain the basis of earned sovereignty and its potential role for promoting the resolution of self-determination based conflicts.

# Problems

Students should come to class prepared to discuss the following questions:

1. Should self-determination disputes be resolved by domestic institutions in the state in question, or should the international community be involved?

2. How should courts and international organizations handle the tension between the sovereignty of a state and the right of its people to self-determination?

3. How did the ICJ interpret the concepts of self-determination in its advisory opinion on Kosovo? Do you agree with this reasoning?

4. Do you agree with the ICJ's reasoning in its Advisory Opinion on the compliance of Kosovo's declaration of independence with international law? Does it matter that Serbia and other states refuse to recognize Kosovo, even after the ICJ's advisory opinion?

5. What constitutes a "people" for the purposes of self-determination?

6. Are you persuaded by the argument that Nagorno Karabakhos should be internationally recognized as an independent state? Why or why not?

7. What distinguishes Kosovo from Nagorno Karabakh, in terms of each region's argument for self-determination?

8. What are the arguments for and against the existence of the Trusteeship Council?

9. Should the U.N. consider reviving the Trusteeship Council or creating something like it to assist with self-governance or to mediate controversial claims like those of South Ossetia and the Palestinian Territories?

# Case Studies and Negotiation Simulations

Drawing from the materials in this chapter, students should come to class prepared to participate in the following case studies:

**Nagorno-Karabakh**: Through referendum on December 10, 1991, Armenians in Nagorno-Karabakh approved the creation of an independent state, separate from Azerbaijan. Armenians in Nagorno-Karabakh had long sought autonomy, alleging systematic persecution under the Soviet Azerbaijani government. Influenced by Nagorno-Karabakh's declaration of independence, the dissolution of the Soviet Union, and the independence of Azerbaijan, the conflict soon grew into a full scale war between Azerbaijan and Nagorno-Karabakh/Armenia. The bloody conflict ended on May 12, 1994, after Russian mediation of a ceasefire that left Nagorno-Karabakh in the control of large swaths of territory. Still, few states have recognized the independence of Nagorno-Karabakh. As you read the following materials, consider why this might be. From the Armenian perspective, argue for Nagorno-Karabakh's right to self-determination. From the Azerbaijani perspective, argue for Azeri sovereignty and territorial integrity.

**Kosovo**: This chapter includes a number of materials that focus on the events leading up to and including Kosovo's declaration of independence from Serbia in February 2008. The legality of Kosovo's unilateral decision to declare itself an independent sovereign state was disputed, but in 2010, the International Court of Justice (ICJ) issued an advisory opinion stating that the Kosovo declaration did not violate international law. The ICJ was careful to note that the specific circumstances leading up to the declaration, particularly Serbia's persecution of several ethnic groups in Kosovo, distinguished the Kosovo declaration from other states. Should a unilateral declaration of independence be allowed under international law? Should the circumstances surrounding such declarations influence their legality? From the perspective of Kosovo, argue for self-determination in support of the ICJ's opinion. From the Serbian perspective, argue why Kosovo's declaration of independence was illegal under international law.

**South Sudan:** The Sudan People's Liberation Army (SPLA) and the Sudan Armed Forces (SAF) were engaged in conflict with each other from 1983 until July 2002, when they signed the Protocol of Machakos, leading to the Comprehensive Peace Agreement (CPA) between the Sudan People's Liberation Movement (SPLM) and the Government of Sudan. The CPA, signed in September 2003, stipulated that a referendum will determine whether Sudan would remain one state or be separated along a controversial east-west line, dividing the state into distinct northern and southern states. On February 7, 2011, the referendum in Southern Sudan occurred and Southerners overwhelmingly voted for independence. On July 9, 2011, South Sudan became independent. Did this declaration of independence violate international law? What if, despite the referendum, the Republic of Sudan had withdrawn its consent prior to the declaration of independence? Alternatively, what would have happened if the Republic of Sudan had withdrawn its consent before or after the referendum? Discuss these questions from the perspectives of the Northerners and Southerners.

# Materials

1. Conference on Security and Co-Operation in Europe Final Act, Aug. 1, 1975, 14 I.L.M. 1292.

2. The Comprehensive Peace Agreement Between the Government of the Republic of Sudan and the Sudanese People's Liberation Movement/Sudanese People's Liberation Army, Jan. 9, 2005.

3. KONSTITUTSIYA (1974) [KONST.] [SOCIALIST FEDERAL REPUBLIC OF YUGOSLAVIA CONSTITUTION].

4. KONSTITUTSIIA RSFSR (1977) [KONST. RSFSR] [RSFSR CONSTITUTION] art. 72.

5. New England Ctr. for Int'l Law and Policy & PILPG, A Blueprint for Resolving the Nagorno-Karabakh Crisis (2000).

6. S.C. Res. 1244, U.N. Doc. S/RES/1244 (June 10, 1999).

7. Accordance with International Law of the Unilateral Declaration of Independence in Respect of Kosovo, Advisory Opinion, 2010 I.C.J. 141 (July 22).

8. Paul R. Williams, *Earned Sovereignty: Bridging the Gap Between Sovereignty and Self-Determination*, 40 STAN. J. INT'L L. 347 (2004).

9. U.N. Charter, arts. 86–91.

10. Tom Parker, Centre for European and Asian Studies, Norwegian School of Management, The Ultimate Intervention: Revitalizing The U.N. Trusteeship Council For The 21st Century (2003).

11. Bibliography of Additional Sources

## *Authors' Note*

The Conference on Security and Co-operation in Europe's Final Act (hereafter "Helsinki Final Act") aimed to ameliorate relations between Communist states and the West by establishing accords concerning state sovereignty, peaceful dispute resolution, and human rights. At the close of the Conference, almost all of the European states, as well as the United States and Canada, signed the Helsinki Final Act, which articulated fundamental human rights, including the right to self-determination, while still recognizing the concept of sovereignty and its essential role in state security.

# 1. Conference on Security and Co-Operation in Europe, Final Act

### Helsinki Declaration, 1975

The Conference on Security and Co-Operation in Europe, which opened at Helsinki on 3 July 1973 and continued at Geneva from 18 September 1973 to 21 July 1975, was concluded at Helsinki on 1 August 1975 by the High Representatives of Austria, Belgium, Bulgaria, Canada, Cyprus, Czechoslovakia, Denmark, Finland, France, the German Democratic Republic, the Federal Republic of Germany, Greece, the Holy See, Hungary, Iceland, Ireland, Italy, Liechtenstein, Luxembourg, Malta, Monaco, the Netherlands, Norway, Poland, Portugal, Romania, San Marino, Spain, Sweden, Switzerland, Turkey, the Union of Soviet Socialist Republics, the United Kingdom, the United States of America and Yugoslavia.

\* \* \*

Motivated by the political will, in the interest of peoples, to improve and intensify their relations and to contribute in Europe to peace, security, justice and co-operation as well as to rapprochement among themselves and with the other States of the world,

Determined, in consequence, to give full effect to the results of the Conference and to assure, among their States and throughout Europe, the benefits deriving from those results and thus to broaden, deepen and make continuing and lasting the process of détente,

The High Representatives of the participating States have solemnly adopted the following:

\* \* \*

**Declaration on Principles Guiding Relations between Participating States**

\* \* \*

*I. Sovereign equality, respect for the rights inherent in sovereignty*

The participating States will respect each other's sovereign equality and individuality as well as all the rights inherent in and encompassed by its sovereignty, including in particular the right of every State to juridical equality, to territorial integrity and to freedom and political independence. They will also respect each other's right freely to choose and develop its political, social, economic and cultural systems as well as its right to determine its laws and regulations.

Within the framework of international law, all the participating States have equal rights and duties. They will respect each other's right to define and conduct as it wishes its relations with other States in accordance with international law and in the spirit of the present Declaration. They consider that their frontiers can be changed, in accordance with international law, by peaceful means and by agreement. They also have the right to belong or not to belong to international organizations, to be or not to be a party to bilateral or multilateral treaties including the right to be or not to be a party to treaties of alliance; they also have the right to neutrality.

## II. Refraining from the threat or use of force

The participating States will refrain in their mutual relations, as well as in their international relations in general, from the threat or use of force against the territorial integrity or political independence of any State, or in any other manner inconsistent with the purposes of the United Nations and with the present Declaration. No consideration may be invoked to serve to warrant resort to the threat or use of force in contravention of this principle.

Accordingly, the participating States will refrain from any acts constituting a threat of force or direct or indirect use of force against another participating State.

Likewise they will refrain from any manifestation of force for the purpose of inducing another participating State to renounce the full exercise of its sovereign rights. Likewise they will also refrain in their mutual relations from any act of reprisal by force.

No such threat or use of force will be employed as a means of settling disputes, or questions likely to give rise to disputes, between them.

## III. Inviolability of frontiers

The participating States regard as inviolable all one another's frontiers as well as the frontiers of all States in Europe and therefore they will refrain now and in the future from assaulting these frontiers.

Accordingly, they will also refrain from any demand for, or act of, seizure and usurpation of part or all of the territory of any participating State.

## IV. Territorial integrity of States

The participating States will respect the territorial integrity of each of the participating States.

Accordingly, they will refrain from any action inconsistent with the purposes and principles of the Charter of the United Nations against the territorial integrity, political independence or the unity of any participating State, and in particular from any such action constituting a threat or use of force.

The participating States will likewise refrain from making each other's territory the object of military occupation or other direct or indirect measures of force in contravention of international law, or the object of acquisition by means of such measures or the threat of them. No such occupation or acquisition will be recognized as legal.

## V. Peaceful settlement of disputes

The participating States will settle disputes among them by peaceful means in such a manner as not to endanger international peace and security, and justice.

They will endeavor in good faith and a spirit of cooperation to reach a rapid and equitable solution on the basis of international law.

For this purpose they will use such means as negotiation, enquiry, mediation, conciliation, arbitration, judicial settlement or other peaceful means of their own choice including any settlement procedure agreed to in advance of disputes to which they are parties.

In the event of failure to reach a solution by any of the above peaceful means, the parties to a dispute will continue to seek a mutually agreed way to settle the dispute peacefully.

Participating States, parties to a dispute among them, as well as other participating States, will refrain from any action which might aggravate the situation to such a degree as to endanger the maintenance of international peace and security and thereby make a peaceful settlement of the dispute more difficult.

*VI. Non-intervention in internal affairs*

The participating States will refrain from any intervention, direct or indirect, individual or collective, in the internal or external affairs falling within the domestic jurisdiction of another participating State, regardless of their mutual relations.

They will accordingly refrain from any form of armed intervention or threat of such intervention against another participating State.

They will likewise in all circumstances refrain from any other act of military, or of political, economic or other coercion designed to subordinate to their own interest the exercise by another participating State of the rights inherent in its sovereignty and thus to secure advantages of any kind.

Accordingly, they will, inter alia, refrain from direct or indirect assistance to terrorist activities, or to subversive or other activities directed towards the violent overthrow of the regime of another participating State.

*VII. Respect for human rights and fundamental freedoms, including the freedom of thought, conscience, religion or belief*

The participating States will respect human rights and fundamental freedoms, including the freedom of thought, conscience, religion or belief, for all without distinction as to race, sex, language or religion.

They will promote and encourage the effective exercise of civil, political, economic, social, cultural and other rights and freedoms all of which derive from the inherent dignity of the human person and are essential for his free and full development.

Within this framework the participating States will recognize and respect the freedom of the individual to profess and practice, alone or in community with others, religion or belief acting in accordance with the dictates of his own conscience.

The participating States on whose territory national minorities exist will respect the right of persons belonging to such minorities to equality before the law, will afford them the full opportunity for the actual enjoyment of human rights and fundamental freedoms and will, in this manner, protect their legitimate interests in this sphere.

The participating States recognize the universal significance of human rights and fundamental freedoms, respect for which is an essential factor for the peace, justice and well-being necessary to ensure the development of friendly relations and co-operation among themselves as among all States.

They will constantly respect these rights and freedoms in their mutual relations and will endeavour jointly and separately, including in co-operation with the United Nations, to promote universal and effective respect for them.

They confirm the right of the individual to know and act upon his rights and duties in this field.

In the field of human rights and fundamental freedoms, the participating States will act in conformity with the purposes and principles of the Charter of the United Nations and with the Universal Declaration of Human Rights. They will also fulfill their obligations as set forth in the international declarations and agreements in this field, including inter alia the International Covenants on Human Rights, by which they may be bound.

*VIII. Equal rights and self-determination of peoples*

The participating States will respect the equal rights of peoples and their right to self-determination, acting at all times in conformity with the purposes and principles of the Charter of the United Nations and with the relevant norms of international law, including those relating to territorial integrity of States.

By virtue of the principle of equal rights and self-determination of peoples, all peoples always have the right, in full freedom, to determine, when and as they wish, their internal and external political status, without external interference, and to pursue as they wish their political, economic, social and cultural development.

The participating States reaffirm the universal significance of respect for and effective exercise of equal rights and self-determination of peoples for the development of friendly relations among themselves as among all States; they also recall the importance of the elimination of any form of violation of this principle.

* * *

**X. Fulfillment in good faith of obligations under international law**

The participating States will fulfill in good faith their obligations under international law, both those obligations arising from the generally recognized principles and rules of international law and those obligations arising from treaties or other agreements, in conformity with international law, to which they are parties.

In exercising their sovereign rights, including the right to determine their laws and regulations, they will conform with their legal obligations under international law; they will furthermore pay due regard to and implement the provisions in the Final Act of the Conference on Security and Co-operation in Europe.

The participating States confirm that in the event of a conflict between the obligations of the members of the United Nations under the Charter of the United Nations and their obligations under any treaty or other international agreement, their obligations under the Charter will prevail, in accordance with Article 103 of the Charter of the United Nations.

All the principles set forth above are of primary significance and, accordingly, they will be equally and unreservedly applied, each of them being interpreted taking into account the others.

* * *

## *Authors' Note*

The Machakos Protocol, one of the several separate agreements that comprise the Comprehensive Peace Agreement (CPA) between the government of the Republic of Sudan and the Sudanese People's Liberation Movement/Sudanese People's Liberation Army (SPLM/A), provided for the referendum that would enable the people of South Sudan to exercise their right of self-determination to decide whether they would become independent or remain part of Sudan. The CPA's umbrella section gave effect to the separate agreements, including the Machakos Protocol, and bound the two parties to abide by the agreements. The CPA included an annex that detailed the implementation modalities of the Machakos Protocol's referendum and associated preparation and follow-up actions.

In a referendum held in January 2011, more than ninety-eight percent of the electorate of South Sudan chose to secede from the Republic of Sudan. On July 9, 2011, South Sudan became an independent state.

# 2. The Comprehensive Peace Agreement between the Government of the Republic of Sudan and the Sudanese People's Liberation Movement/Sudanese People's Liberation Army

## 2005

### SIGNED AT MACHAKOS, KENYA ON 20TH JULY, 2002

\* \* \*

### Part A: Agreed Principles

1.1 That the unity of the Sudan, based on the free will of its people, democratic governance, accountability, equality, respect, and justice for all citizens of the Sudan is and shall be the priority of the Parties and that it is possible to redress the grievances of the people of South Sudan and to meet their aspirations within such a framework.

1.2 That the people of South Sudan have the right to control and govern affairs in their region and participate equitably in the National Government.

1.3 That the people of South Sudan have the right to self-determination, *inter alia*, through a referendum to determine their future status.

\* \* \*

1.5.5 Design and implement the Peace Agreement so as to make the unity of the Sudan an attractive option especially to the people of South Sudan.

\* \* \*

### Part B: The Transition Process

\* \* \*

2.5 At the end of the six (6) year Interim Period there shall be an internationally monitored referendum, organized jointly by the GOS and the SPLM/A, for the people of South Sudan to: confirm the unity of the Sudan by voting to adopt the system of government established under the Peace Agreement; or to vote for secession.

2.6 The Parties shall refrain from any form of unilateral revocation or abrogation of the Peace Agreement.

\* \* \*

2.10.1 The National Constitutional Review Commission, as detailed in Section 2.12 herein, shall also detail the mandate and provide for the appointment and other mechanisms to ensure the independence of the following institutions:

\* \* \*

2.10.1.5 An ad-hoc Commission to monitor and ensure accuracy, legitimacy, and transparency of the Referendum as mentioned in the Machakos Protocol on Self-Determination for the People of South Sudan, which shall also include international experts;

\* \* \*

## Authors' Note

The Canadian Supreme Court addressed the legality of Quebec's prospective unilateral secession from Canada in its opinion in *Reference re Secession of Quebec*. In its decision, the Court analyzed and applied Canadian and international law relating to self-determination, ultimately finding that international and domestic law would not allow Quebec to exercise the right to self-determination via unilateral secession.

# 3. Constitution of the Russian Federation, Article 74
## (1977)

III. The National-State Structure of the USSR

*Chapter Eight*: The USSR—A Federal State

74. Each union republic retains the right to freely secede from the USSR.

# 4. Constitution of the Socialist Federal Republic of Yugoslavia
## (1974)
### BASIC PRINCIPLES

The nations of Yugoslavia, proceeding from the right of every nation to self-determination, including the right to secession, on the basis of their will freely expressed, in the common struggle of all nations and nationalities in the National Liberation War and Socialist Revolution, and in conformity with their historic aspirations, aware that further consolidation of their brotherhood and unity is in the common interest, have, together with the nationalities with which they live, united in a federal republic of free and equal nations and nationalities and founded a socialist federal community of working people—the Socialist Federal Republic of Yugoslavia, in which, in the interests of each nation and nationality separately and of all of them together they shall realize and ensure.

## Authors' Note

Nagorno-Karabakh's declaration of independence from Azerbaijan has not been embraced by the international community. The following excerpt makes the case for the independence of Nagorno-Karabakh in light of the customary international law of self-determination and the precedent set by the dissolution of Yugoslavia.

## 5. New England Center for International Law and Policy and the Public International Law and Policy Group, A Blueprint for Resolving the Nagorno-Karabakh Crisis

### 2000

\* \* \*

### III. The Right of Self-Determination

Possessing the right of self-determination is a legal question, while accomplishing self-determination is a question of power and diplomacy. This section examines the former, while Section IV presents a formula for attaining the latter.

### A. The Meaning of Self-Determination

#### 1. International Recognition of the Principle of Self-Determination.

The principle of self-determination is included in Articles 1, 55, and 73 of the United Nations Charter. The right to self-determination has also been repeatedly recognized in a series of resolutions adopted by the U.N. General Assembly, the most important of which is Resolution 2625(XXV) of 1970. While these resolutions are not in themselves binding, they do constitute an authoritative interpretation of the U.N. Charter. In the Western Sahara case in 1975, the Frontier Dispute case in 1986, and the case Concerning East Timor in 1995, the International Court of Justice held that the principle of self-determination has crystallized into a rule of customary international law, applicable to and binding on all States.

The principle of self-determination was further codified in the International Covenant on Civil and Political Rights, and the International Covenant on Economic, Social and Cultural Rights — which are considered to constitute the international "Bill of Rights." Before its break up, the Soviet Union was a party to both of these human rights treaties, and the U.N. Human Rights Commission confirmed in 1993 that the former Soviet Republics continue to be bound by these treaty obligations.

Under the principle of self-determination, all self identified groups with a coherent identity and connection to a defined territory are entitled to collectively determine their political destiny in a democratic fashion and to be free from systematic persecution. For such groups, the principle of self-determination may be implemented by a variety of means, including autonomy within a federal entity, a confederation of states, free association, or, in certain circumstances, outright independence. Moreover, in accordance with the Charter on European Security accepted by the OSCE in Istanbul in November 1999, it is now widely held that conflict concerning ethnic minorities can only be positively resolved within democratic entities, and that in instances where states are undemocratic the principle of self-determination takes greater priority over the principle of territorial integrity.

#### 2. Who is Entitled to Self-Determination?

For a group to be entitled to a right to collectively determine its political destiny, it must possess a focus of identity sufficient for it to attain distinctiveness as a people.

The traditional two part test examines first "objective" elements of the group to ascertain the extent to which its members share a common racial background, ethnicity, language, religion, history and cultural heritage. Another important "objective" factor is the territorial integrity of the area which the group is claiming.

The second "subjective prong" of the test requires an examination of the extent to which individuals within the group self-consciously perceive themselves collectively as a distinct "people." It necessitates that a community explicitly express a shared sense of values and a common goal for its future. Another "subjective" factor is the degree to which the group can form a viable political entity.

## 3. Self-Determination and the Right to Independence

Traditionally, the right to pursue independence as an exercise of the principle of self-determination was applied to people under "colonial" or "alien" domination, and under the principle known as *uti possi detis* states were permitted to become independent only within their former colonial boundaries.

However, the modern trend, supported by the writing of numerous scholars, U.N. General Assembly resolutions, declarations of international conferences, judicial pronouncements, decisions of international arbitral tribunals, and state practice since the fall of communism in Eastern Europe, has supported the right of a non-colonial "people" to secede from an existing state when the group is collectively denied civil and political rights.

The denial of the exercise of the right of democratic self-government as a precondition to the right of a non-colonial people to dissociate from an existing state is supported most strongly by the United Nations' 1970 Declaration on Principles of International Law Concerning Friendly Relations, which frames the proper balance between self-determination and territorial integrity as follows:

> Nothing in the foregoing paragraphs shall be construed as authorizing or encouraging any action which would dismember or impair, totally or in part, the territorial integrity or political unity of sovereign and independent States conducting themselves in compliance with the principle of equal rights and self-determination of peoples as described above and thus possessed of a government representing the whole people belonging to the territory without distinction as to race, creed or color.

By this Declaration, the General Assembly indicated that the right of territorial integrity takes precedence over the right to self-determination only so long as the state possesses "a government representing the whole people belonging to the territory without distinction as to race, creed or color." Where such a representative government is not present, "peoples" within existing states will be entitled to exercise their right to self-determination through secession.

* * *

If a government is at the high end of the scale of representative government, the only modes of self-determination that will be given international credence are those with minimal destabilizing effect, such as internal autonomy. If a government is extremely unrepresentative, then much more potentially destabilizing modes of self-determination, including secession, may be recognized as legitimate.

The case for secession becomes even stronger when the claimant group has attained *de facto* independence. In one of the first cases involving the right of self-determination, the Commission of Jurists on the Aaland Islands dispute recognized *de facto* independence as a special factor:

> From the point of view of both domestic and international law, the formation, transformation and dismemberment of States as a result of revolutions and wars

create situations of fact which, to a large extent, cannot be met by the application of the normal rules of positive law.... This transition from a de facto situation to a normal situation de jure cannot be considered as one confined entirely within the domestic jurisdiction of a State. It tends to lead to readjustments between the members of the international community and to alterations in their territorial and legal status.

Thus, if pursuant to the situation on the ground, the entity satisfies the criteria for independent statehood, the conflict between the principles of self-determination and territorial integrity evaporates. The applicable criteria for statehood are: (1) a permanent population; (2) a defined territory; (3) a government; and (4) capacity to enter into relations with other states.

Finally, some commentators have taken the position that the right of a people to secede must further be based on a "balancing of conflicting principles," considering such factors as "the nature of the group, its situation within its governing state, its prospects for an independent existence, and the effect of its separation on the remaining population and the world community in general."

### 4. The Process for Exercising the Right of Self-Determination

In acknowledging the independence of Slovenia, Croatia, Bosnia-Herzegovina and Macedonia, the international community, and in particular the European Union, established a number of preconditions, such that their attainment of international status would be exercised consistent with the principles of *uti possi detis* and respect for territorial integrity. To that end, the international community recognized these states within the borders that they possessed as constituent territorial units of the former Yugoslavia. The international community also required these states to hold a referendum confirming the wishes of the general public to seek independence, and to demonstrate their commitment to respect fundamental principles of international law, including those relating to the protection of minority rights, democratic processes of governance and economic organization, and the protection of human rights.

### B. Nagorno Karabakh's Legal Entitlement to Independence

Nagorno Karabakh has a right of self-determination, including the attendant right to independence, according to the criteria recognized under international law set forth above.

### 1. The Armenians of Nagorno Karabachos are a Group Entitled to Self-Determination

The Armenians of Nagorno Karabachos possess the objective and subjective factors required of a group entitled to the right to self-determination.

The Armenians of Nagorno Karabachos are objectively distinct from the Azerbaijanis. The Nagorno Karabachos Armenians speak a dialect of Armenian, an Indo-European language, while the Azerbaijanis speak a Turkic dialect, which is part of the Altaic language group. The Nagorno Karabachos Armenians are Christians, while the Azerbaijanis are predominantly Shi'i Muslims. And the Nagorno Karabachos Armenians share the ancient culture and historical experience of the Armenian people, while the Azerbaijanis are now developing a national identity and share the historical experience of Turkic peoples.

Nagorno Karabachos also has a long tradition of being a distinct territorial unit. The region of Nagorno Karabachos (Artsakh) was organized as one of the fifteen provinces of historical Armenia and was also a separate "Melikdom" under the Persian Empire. Nagorno Karabachos distinct territorial identity was recognized by the Soviet Union when it was designated an "autonomous region" (1923 through 1989) and later as an "ethno-territorial administrative division" administered directly from Moscow rather than by Azerbaijan (January through November 1989).

With respect to the subjective prong of the test, the Armenian population of Nagorno Karabachos responded to the decision of Azerbaijan to remove the autonomy of Nagorno Karabachos and to place the region under Azerbaijan's direct administration in November 1991, by holding an internationally monitored referendum on the independence of the region. On December 10, 1991, 82 percent of the Nagorno Karabachos electorate (as determined by the January 1989 USSR census) took part in this vote in which a 99.7 percent majority supported secession. Since this time, the Nagorno Karabachos Republic has essentially operated as a de facto state.

## 2. Nagorno Karabachos Right to Self-Determination Includes the Right to Independence

The Azerbaijanis argue that political independence for Nagorno Karabachos violates the right of Azerbaijan to territorial integrity. But the claim to territorial integrity can be negated where a state does not conduct itself "in compliance with the principle of equal rights and self-determination of peoples" and does not allow a subject people "to pursue their economic, social and cultural development" as required by United Nations General Assembly Resolution 2625(XXV). Moreover, it should be noted that when Azerbaijan declared independence from the Soviet Union, it claimed to be the successor state to the Azerbaijani Republic of 1918–1920. The League of Nations, however, did not recognize Azerbaijan's inclusion of Nagorno Karabachos within Azerbaijan's claimed territory.

Prior to 1988, Azerbaijan's human rights record with respect to the Armenian people of Nagorno Karabachos was dismal. During the seven decades of the USSR's existence, the government of Soviet Azerbaijan conducted a systematic policy of repression and removal of Karabachos Armenians from their historic homeland. During this time, the Armenian population in Nagorno Karabachos was reduced from ninety-five percent of the total population of the region in 1926, to seventy-five percent of the population in 1976.

Subsequent to the Karabachos movement for independence in 1988, the human rights violations against the Armenians of Nagorno Karabachos intensified, including "pogroms, deportations, and other atrocities." Azerbaijan began a blockade of food and fuel into Nagorno Karabachos which continues to the present. In view of these developments, Nobel Peace Prize laureate Andrei Sakharov warned in November of 1988 that the "Armenian people are again facing the threat of genocide," and that "for Nagorno Karabachos this is a question of survival, for Azerbaijan—just a question of ambitions." Hence, the prospects for guaranteeing human rights and allowing the Karabachos Armenians to pursue their "economic, social and cultural development" under Azerbaijani rule, even with Azerbaijani assurances of local autonomy, are not very promising. Under these circumstances, the Nagorno Karabachos claim to self-determination through independence may supersede Azerbaijan's claim to territorial integrity.

That Nagorno Karabachos has had to resort to force to protect itself, to break the Azerbaijani blockade by opening the Lachin Corridor to Armenia and the world, and to establish defensible borders does not disqualify it from the right to independence. In fact, the tension between the right of Nagorno Karabachos to self-determination and the right of Azerbaijan to maintain its territorial integrity must be analyzed in view of the de facto independence Nagorno Karabachos has achieved and maintained for the past six years by virtue of the success of its armed forces, and its development of civil and political institutions.

Nagorno Karabachos now meets all of the traditional requirements for statehood set forth by the Montevideo Convention. It has control over a defined territory, which encompasses over 5,000 sq. kilometers. Its permanent population of 150,000 is greater than that of other States that have been admitted into the United Nations since 1990, including Andorra (66,000), Liechtenstein (32,000), Marshall Islands (66,000), The Federated States of Micronesia (132,000), Monaco (32,000), Nauru (11,000), Palau (18,000), and San Marino (25,000). Nagorno Karabachos has its own democratically elected president and legislature. Its government commands the armed forces, and engages in discussions with foreign states. Through its government institutions, Karabachos has the capacity to conduct international relations and has represented the people of the region at international peace negotiations under the mediation of the Organization on Security and Co-operation in Europe, as well as established representative offices in the United States, France, Russia, Lebanon, Australia, and Armenia.

Finally, Nagorno Karabachos right to independence is also consistent with the balancing-of-factors approach advocated by some commentators. That the vast majority of the people in Nagorno Karabachos constitute a unique group, with its own government and defense forces and a historic tie to the territory, has been discussed above. That the group has achieved de facto independence after an overwhelming vote for secession and after withstanding a military assault indicates its prospects for an independent existence. As a result of the armed conflict, the current population of Nagorno Karabachos is approximately 95% Armenian, with the other five percent of the population being made up of Russian, Greek, Azerbaijani and Tatar minorities. The government of Nagorno Karabachos is ensuring minority rights and continued political participation of these ethnic minorities and others who may wish to return. The government of Nagorno Karabachos has expressed its willingness to establish bilateral contacts with the government of Azerbaijan on matters relating to refugee return and minority rights protections, as well as on a range of other subjects relevant to their bilateral relationship.

As for its effect on Azerbaijan, the de jure secession of Nagorno Karabachos would have little effect. Azerbaijan would lose only two percent of its total population and it would neither lose a part of its oil fields nor be cut off from important connecting roads or waterways. The end of oppression and the avoidance of a further escalation of violence would be in the international interest. And as discussed in more detail below, a negotiated exchange of territories could improve the security of both Nagorno Karabachos and Azerbaijan and substantially reduce the current level of instability in the region.

Thus, international law provides a firm basis for Nagorno Karabachos pursuit of independence from Azerbaijan.

\* \* \*

## Authors' Note

In 1999, UNSCR 1244 established the Interim Administration in Kosovo (UNMIK), effectively transferring sovereignty over Kosovo from Serbia to the U.N.. This arrangement was initially established for a period of twelve months. During the interim period, Kosovo would neither be under Serbian control, nor under the control of Kosovar institutions, but would negotiate its final status while being governed by the U.N.. The resolution also provided for the deployment of NATO forces to provide security during the interim period. The interim period was repeatedly extended until Kosovo declared independence in February 2008.

# 6. Resolution 1244

## U.N. Security Council, 1999

Adopted by the Security Council at its 4011th meeting, on 10 June 1999

The Security Council,

\* \* \*

*Determined* to resolve the grave humanitarian situation in Kosovo, Federal Republic of Yugoslavia, and to provide for the safe and free return of all refugees and displaced persons to their homes,

\* \* \*

*Welcoming* the general principles on a political solution to the Kosovo crisis adopted on 6 May 1999 (S/1999/516, annex 1 to this resolution) and welcoming also the acceptance by the Federal Republic of Yugoslavia of the principles set forth in points 1 to 9 of the paper presented in Belgrade on 2 June 1999 (S/1999/649, annex 2 to this resolution), and the Federal Republic of Yugoslavia's agreement to that paper,

*Reaffirming* the commitment of all Member States to the sovereignty and territorial integrity of the Federal Republic of Yugoslavia and the other States of the region, as set out in the Helsinki Final Act and annex 2,

*Reaffirming* the call in previous resolutions for substantial autonomy and meaningful self-administration for Kosovo,

*Determining* that the situation in the region continues to constitute a threat to international peace and security,

*Determined* to ensure the safety and security of international personnel and the implementation by all concerned of their responsibilities under the present resolution, and acting for these purposes under Chapter VII of the Charter of the United Nations,

1. Decides that a political solution to the Kosovo crisis shall be based on the general principles in annex 1 and as further elaborated in the principles and other required elements in annex 2;

2. Welcomes the acceptance by the Federal Republic of Yugoslavia of the principles and other required elements referred to in paragraph 1 above, and demands the full cooperation of the Federal Republic of Yugoslavia in their rapid implementation;

3. Demands in particular that the Federal Republic of Yugoslavia put an immediate and verifiable end to violence and repression in Kosovo, and begin and complete verifiable phased withdrawal from Kosovo of all military, police and paramilitary forces according to a rapid timetable, with which the deployment of the international security presence in Kosovo will be synchronized;

4. Confirms that after the withdrawal an agreed number of Yugoslav and Serb military and police personnel will be permitted to return to Kosovo to perform the functions in accordance with annex 2;

5. Decides on the deployment in Kosovo, under United Nations auspices, of international civil and security presences, with appropriate equipment and personnel as required, and welcomes the agreement of the Federal Republic of Yugoslavia to such presences;

6. Requests the Secretary-General to appoint, in consultation with the Security Council, a Special Representative to control the implementation of the international civil

presence, and further requests the Secretary-General to instruct his Special Representative to coordinate closely with the international security presence to ensure that both presences operate towards the same goals and in a mutually supportive manner;

7. Authorizes Member States and relevant international organizations to establish the international security presence in Kosovo as set out in point 4 of annex 2 with all necessary means to fulfill its responsibilities under paragraph 9 below;

8. Affirms the need for the rapid early deployment of effective international civil and security presences to Kosovo, and demands that the parties cooperate fully in their deployment;

9. Decides that the responsibilities of the international security presence to be deployed and acting in Kosovo will include:

   a. Deterring renewed hostilities, maintaining and where necessary enforcing a cease-fire, and ensuring the withdrawal and preventing the return into Kosovo of Federal and Republic military, police and paramilitary forces, except as provided in point 6 of annex 2;

   b. Demilitarizing the Kosovo Liberation Army (KLA) and other armed Kosovo Albanian groups as required in paragraph 15 below;

   c. Establishing a secure environment in which refugees and displaced persons can return home in safety, the international civil presence can operate, a transitional administration can be established, and humanitarian aid can be delivered;

   d. Ensuring public safety and order until the international civil presence can take responsibility for this task;

   e. Supervising demining until the international civil presence can, as appropriate, take over responsibility for this task;

   f. Supporting, as appropriate, and coordinating closely with the work of the international civil presence;

   g. Conducting border monitoring duties as required;

   h. Ensuring the protection and freedom of movement of itself, the international civil presence, and other international organizations;

10. Authorizes the Secretary-General, with the assistance of relevant international organizations, to establish an international civil presence in Kosovo in order to provide an interim administration for Kosovo under which the people of Kosovo can enjoy substantial autonomy within the Federal Republic of Yugoslavia, and which will provide transitional administration while establishing and overseeing the development of provisional democratic self-governing institutions to ensure conditions for a peaceful and normal life for all inhabitants of Kosovo;

11. Decides that the main responsibilities of the international civil presence will include:

   a. Promoting the establishment, pending a final settlement, of substantial autonomy and self-government in Kosovo, taking full account of annex 2 and of the Rambouillet accords (S/1999/648);

   b. Performing basic civilian administrative functions where and as long as required;

   c. Organizing and overseeing the development of provisional institutions for democratic and autonomous self-government pending a political settlement, including the holding of elections;

d.  Transferring, as these institutions are established, its administrative responsibilities while overseeing and supporting the consolidation of Kosovo's local provisional institutions and other peace-building activities;

e.  Facilitating a political process designed to determine Kosovo's future status, taking into account the Rambouillet accords (S/1999/648);

f.  In a final stage, overseeing the transfer of authority from Kosovo's provisional institutions to institutions established under a political settlement;

g.  Supporting the reconstruction of key infrastructure and other economic reconstruction;

h.  Supporting, in coordination with international humanitarian organizations, humanitarian and disaster relief aid;

i.  Maintaining civil law and order, including establishing local police forces and meanwhile through the deployment of international police personnel to serve in Kosovo;

j.  Protecting and promoting human rights;

k.  Assuring the safe and unimpeded return of all refugees and displaced persons to their homes is Kosovo;

\* \* \*

19. *Decides* that the international civil and security presences are established for an initial period of 12 months, to continue thereafter unless the Security Council decides otherwise;

\* \* \*

### Annex 2

Agreement should be reached on the following principles to move towards a resolution of the Kosovo crisis:

1.  An immediate and verifiable end of violence and repression in Kosovo.

2.  Verifiable withdrawal from Kosovo of all military, police and paramilitary forces according to a rapid timetable.

3.  Deployment in Kosovo under United Nations auspices of effective international civil and security presences, acting as may be decided under Chapter VII of the Charter, capable of guaranteeing the achievement of common objectives.

4.  The international security presence with substantial North Atlantic Treaty Organization participation must be deployed under unified command and control and authorized to establish a safe environment for all people in Kosovo and to facilitate the safe return to their homes of all displaced persons and refugees.

5.  Establishment of an interim administration for Kosovo as a part of the international civil presence under which the people of Kosovo can enjoy substantial autonomy within the Federal Republic of Yugoslavia, to be decided by the Security Council of the United Nations. The interim administration to provide transitional administration while establishing and overseeing the development of provisional democratic self-governing institutions to ensure conditions for a peaceful and normal life for all inhabitants in Kosovo.

\* \* \*

8.  A political process towards the establishment of an interim political framework agreement providing for substantial self-government for Kosovo, taking full ac-

count of the Rambouillet accords and the principles of sovereignty and territorial integrity of the Federal Republic of Yugoslavia and the other countries of the region, and the demilitarization of UCK. Negotiations between the parties for a settlement should not delay or disrupt the establishment of democratic self-governing institutions.

\* \* \*

## Authors' Note

In 2010, the International Court of Justice (ICJ) issued an advisory opinion concerning Kosovo's 2008 declaration of independence. The Court found that the declaration was permissible since it was not prohibited by Security Council Resolution 1244, the Constitutional Framework established under the U.N. interim mission in Kosovo, or general international law.

## 7. Accordance with International Law of the Unilateral Declaration of Independence in Respect of Kosovo, Advisory Opinion
### International Court of Justice, 2012

\* \* \*

On the accordance with international law of the unilateral declaration of independence in respect of Kosovo, THE COURT, composed as above, *gives the following Advisory Opinion*:

1. The question on which the advisory opinion of the Court has been requested is set forth in resolution 63/3 adopted by the General Assembly of the United Nations (hereinafter the General Assembly) on 8 October 2008.

\* \* \*

The resolution reads as follows: "The General Assembly,

\* \* \*

*Decides,* in accordance with Article 96 of the Charter of the United Nations to request the International Court of Justice, pursuant to Article 65 of the Statute of the Court, to render an advisory opinion on the following question:

"Is the unilateral declaration of independence by the Provisional Institutions of Self-Government of Kosovo in accordance with international law?"

\* \* \*

### III. Factual Background
### C. The events of 17 February 2008 and thereafter

\* \* \*

75. In its operative part, the declaration of independence of 17 February 2008 states:

1. We, the democratically-elected leaders of our people, hereby declare Kosovo to be an independent and sovereign state. This declaration reflects the will of our people and it is in full accordance with the recommendations of U.N. Special Envoy Martti Ahtisaari and his Comprehensive Proposal for the Kosovo Status Settlement.

2. We declare Kosovo to be a democratic, secular and multi-ethnic republic, guided by the principles of non-discrimination and equal protection under the

law. We shall protect and promote the rights of all communities in Kosovo and create the conditions necessary for their effective participation in political and decision-making processes.

*  *  *

5. We welcome the international community's continued support of our democratic development through international presences established in Kosovo on the basis of U.N. Security Council resolution 1244 (1999). We invite and welcome an international civilian presence to supervise our implementation of the Ahtisaari Plan, and a European Union-led rule of law mission.

*  *  *

10. We hereby undertake the international obligations of Kosovo, including those concluded on our behalf by the United Nations Interim Administration Mission in Kosovo (UNMIK),

*  *  *

12. We hereby affirm, clearly, specifically, and irrevocably, that Kosovo shall be legally bound to comply with the provisions contained in this Declaration, including, especially, the obligations for it under the Ahtisaari Plan [ ... ] We declare publicly that all states are entitled to rely upon this declaration[ ... ]"

76. The declaration of independence was adopted at a meeting held on 17 February 2008 by 109 out of the 120 members of the Assembly of Kosovo, including the Prime Minister of Kosovo and by the President of Kosovo (who was not a member of the Assembly). [ ... ] It was not transmitted to the Special Representative of the Secretary-General and was not published in the Official Gazette of the Provisional Institutions of Self-Government of Kosovo.

77. After the declaration of independence was issued, the Republic of Serbia informed the Secretary-General that it had adopted a decision stating that that declaration represented a forceful and unilateral secession of a part of the territory of Serbia, and did not produce legal effects either in Serbia or in the international legal order. Further to a request from Serbia, an emergency public meeting of the Security Council took place on 18 February 2008, in which Mr. Boris Tadić, the President of the Republic of Serbia, participated and denounced the declaration of independence as an unlawful act which had been declared null and void by the National Assembly of Serbia.

### IV. The question whether the declaration of independence is in accordance with international law

*  *  *

### A. General international law

79. During the eighteenth, nineteenth and early twentieth centuries, there were numerous instances of declarations of independence, often strenuously opposed by the State from which independence was being declared. Sometimes a declaration resulted in the creation of a new State, at others it did not. In no case, however, does the practice of States as a whole suggest that the act of promulgating the declaration was regarded as contrary to international law. On the contrary, State practice during this period points clearly to the conclusion that international law contained no prohibition of declarations of independence. During the second half of the twentieth century, the international law of self-determination developed in such a way as to create a right to independence for the peoples of non-self-governing territories and peoples subject to alien subjugation, domination

and exploitation (cf. Legal Consequences for States of the Continued Presence of South Africa in Namibia (South West Africa) notwithstanding Security Council Resolution 276 (1970)). A great many new States have come into existence as a result of the exercise of this right. There were, however, also instances of declarations of independence outside this context. The practice of States in these latter cases do not point to the emergence in international law of a new rule prohibiting the making of a declaration of independence in such cases.

* * *

81. Several participants have invoked resolutions of the Security Council condemning particular declarations of independence: see, inter alia, Security Council resolutions 216 (1965) and 217 (1965), concerning Southern Rhodesia; Security Council resolution 541 (1983), concerning northern Cyprus; and Security Council resolution 787 (1992), concerning the Republika Srpska. The Court notes, however, that in all of those instances the Security Council was making a determination as regards the concrete situation existing at the time that those declarations of independence were made; the illegality attached to the declarations of independence thus stemmed not from the unilateral character of these declarations as such, but from the fact that they were, or would have been, connected with the unlawful use of force or other egregious violations of norms of general international law, in particular those of a peremptory character (*jus cogens*). In the context of Kosovo, the Security Council has never taken this position. The exceptional character of the resolutions enumerated above appears to the Court to confirm that no general prohibition against unilateral declarations of independence may be inferred from the practice of the Security Council.

82. A number of participants in the present proceedings have claimed, although in almost every instance only as a secondary argument, that the population of Kosovo has the right to create an independent State either as a manifestation of a right to self-determination or pursuant to what they described as a right of "remedial secession" in the face of the situation in Kosovo. The Court has already noted (see paragraph 79 above) that one of the major developments of international law during the second half of the twentieth century has been the evolution of the right to self-determination. Whether, outside the context of non-self-governing territories and peoples subject to alien subjugation, domination and exploitation, the international law of self-determination confers upon part of the population of an existing State a right to separate from that State is, however, a subject on which radically different views were expressed by those taking part in the proceedings and expressing a position on the question. Similar differences existed regarding whether international law provides for a right of "remedial secession" and, if so, in what circumstances. There was also a sharp difference of views as to whether the circumstances which some participants maintained would give rise to a right of "remedial secession" were actually present in Kosovo.

83. The Court considers that it is not necessary to resolve these questions in the present case. [ ... ]

84. For the reasons already given, the Court considers that general international law contains no applicable prohibition of declarations of independence. Accordingly, it concludes that the declaration of independence of 17 February 2008 did not violate general international law. Having arrived at that conclusion, the Court now turns to the legal relevance of Security Council resolution 1244, adopted on 10 June 1999.

## B. Security Council resolution 1244 (1999) and the UNMIK
## Constitutional Framework created thereunder

85. Within the legal framework of the United Nations Charter, notably on the basis of Articles 24, 25 and Chapter VII thereof, the Security Council may adopt resolutions imposing obligations under international law. The Court has had the occasion to interpret and apply such Security Council resolutions on a number of occasions and has consistently treated them as part of the framework of obligations under international law. [ ... ] Resolution 1244 (1999) was expressly adopted by the Security Council on the basis of Chapter VII of the United Nations Charter, and therefore clearly imposes international legal obligations. The Court notes that none of the participants has questioned the fact that resolution 1244 (1999), which specifically deals with the situation in Kosovo, is part of the law relevant in the present situation.

\* \* \*

87. A certain number of participants have dealt with the question whether regulations adopted on behalf of UNMIK by the Special Representative of the Secretary-General, notably the Constitutional Framework (see paragraph 62 above), also form part of the applicable international law within the meaning of the General Assembly's request.

88. In particular, it has been argued before the Court that the Constitutional Framework is an act of an internal law rather than an international law character. According to that argument, the Constitutional Framework would not be part of the international law applicable in the present instance and the question of the compatibility of the declaration of independence therewith would thus fall outside the scope of the General Assembly's request. The Court observes that UNMIK regulations, including regulation 2001/9, which promulgated the Constitutional Framework, are adopted by the Special Representative of the Secretary-General on the basis of the authority derived from Security Council resolution 1244 (1999), notably its paragraphs 6, 10, and 11, and thus ultimately from the United Nations Charter. The Constitutional Framework derives its binding force from the binding character of resolution 1244 (1999) and thus from international law. In that sense it therefore possesses an international legal character.

89. At the same time, the Court observes that the Constitutional Framework functions as part of a specific legal order, created pursuant to resolution 1244 (1999), which is applicable only in Kosovo and the purpose of which is to regulate, during the interim phase established by resolution 1244 (1999), matters which would ordinarily be the subject of internal, rather than international, law.

> "[f]or the purposes of developing meaningful self-government in Kosovo pending a final settlement, and establishing provisional institutions of self-government in the legislative, executive and judicial fields through the participation of the people of Kosovo in free and fair elections."

The Constitutional Framework therefore took effect as part of the body of law adopted for the administration of Kosovo during the interim phase. The institutions which it created were empowered by the Constitutional Framework to take decisions which took effect within that body of law. In particular, the Assembly of Kosovo was empowered to adopt legislation which would have the force of law within that legal order, subject always to the overriding authority of the Special Representative of the Secretary-General.

\* \* \*

91. The Court notes that Security Council resolution 1244 (1999) and the Constitutional Framework were still in force and applicable as at 17 February 2008. Paragraph 19 of Security Council resolution 1244 (1999) expressly provides that "the international civil and

security presences are established for an initial period of 12 months, to continue thereafter unless the Security Council decides otherwise". No decision amending resolution
1244 (1999) was taken by the Security Council at its meeting held on 18 February 2008,
when the declaration of independence was discussed for the first time, or at any subsequent meeting. [ ... ] Furthermore, Chapter 14.3 of the Constitutional Framework sets
forth that "[t]he SRSG ... may effect amendments to this Constitutional Framework".
Minor amendments were effected by virtue of UNMIK regulations UNMIK/REG/2002/
9 of 3 May 2002, UNMIK/REG/2007/29 of 4 October 2007, UNMIK/REG/2008/1 of 8
January 2008 and UNMIK/REG/2008/9 of 8 February 2008. Finally, neither Security
Council resolution 1244 (1999) nor the Constitutional Framework contains a clause providing for its termination and neither has been repealed; they therefore constituted the
international law applicable to the situation prevailing in Kosovo on 17 February 2008.

* * *

93. From the foregoing, the Court concludes that Security Council resolution 1244 (1999)
and the Constitutional Framework form part of the international law which is to be considered in replying to the question posed by the General Assembly in its request for the
advisory opinion.

1. Interpretation of Security Council resolution 1244 (1999)

* * *

97. First, resolution 1244 (1999) establishes an international civil and security presence in
Kosovo with full civil and political authority and sole responsibility for the governance of
Kosovo. As described above (see paragraph 60), on 12 June 1999, the Secretary-General
presented to the Security Council his preliminary operational concept for the overall organization of the civil presence under UNMIK. On 25 July 1999, the Special Representative
of the Secretary-General promulgated UNMIK regulation 1999/1, deemed to have entered
into force as of 10 June 1999, the date of adoption of Security Council resolution 1244
(1999). Under this regulation, "[a]ll legislative and executive authority with respect to Kosovo,
including the administration of the judiciary", was vested in UNMIK and exercised by the
Special Representative. Viewed together, resolution 1244 (1999) and UNMIK regulation
1999/1 therefore had the effect of superseding the legal order in force at that time in the territory of Kosovo and setting up an international territorial administration. For this reason,
the establishment of civil and security presences in Kosovo deployed on the basis of resolution 1244 (1999) must be understood as an exceptional measure relating to civil, political and security aspects and aimed at addressing the crisis existing in that territory in 1999.

98. Secondly, the solution embodied in resolution 1244 (1999), namely, the implementation of an interim international territorial administration, was designed for humanitarian
purposes: to provide a means for the stabilization of Kosovo and for the re-establishment
of a basic public order in an area beset by crisis. This becomes apparent in the text of resolution 1244 (1999) itself which, in its second preambular paragraph, recalls Security
Council resolution 1239, adopted on 14 May 1999, in which the Security Council had
expressed "grave concern at the humanitarian crisis in and around Kosovo". The priorities which are identified in paragraph 11 of resolution 1244 (1999) were elaborated further in the so-called "four pillars" relating to the governance of Kosovo described in the
Report of the Secretary-General of 12 June 1999 (paragraph 60 above). By placing an
emphasis on these "four pillars", namely, interim civil administration, humanitarian affairs, institution building and reconstruction, and by assigning responsibility for these
core components to different international organizations and agencies, resolution 1244
(1999) was clearly intended to bring about stabilization and reconstruction. The interim

administration in Kosovo was designed to suspend temporarily Serbia's exercise of its authority flowing from its continuing sovereignty over the territory of Kosovo. The purpose of the legal régime established under resolution 1244 (1999) was to establish, organize and oversee the development of local institutions of self-government in Kosovo under the aegis of the interim international presence.

99. Thirdly, resolution 1244 (1999) clearly establishes an interim régime; it cannot be understood as putting in place a permanent institutional framework in the territory of Kosovo. This resolution mandated UNMIK merely to facilitate the desired negotiated solution for Kosovo's future status, without prejudging the outcome of the negotiating process.

100. The Court thus concludes that the object and purpose of resolution 1244 (1999) was to establish a temporary, exceptional legal régime which, save to the extent that it expressly preserved it, superseded the Serbian legal order and which aimed at the stabilization of Kosovo, and that it was designed to do so on an interim basis.

## 2. The question whether the declaration of independence is in accordance with Security Council resolution 1244 (1999) and the measures adopted thereunder

101. The Court will now turn to the question whether Security Council resolution 1244 (1999), or the measures adopted thereunder, introduces a specific prohibition on issuing a declaration of independence, applicable to those who adopted the declaration of independence of 17 February 2008. In order to answer this question, it is first necessary, as explained in paragraph 52 above, for the Court to determine precisely who issued that declaration.

### (a) The identity of the authors of the declaration of independence

102. The Court needs to determine whether the declaration of independence of 17 February 2008 was an act of the "Assembly of Kosovo", one of the Provisional Institutions of Self-Government, established under Chapter 9 of the Constitutional Framework, or whether those who adopted the declaration were acting in a different capacity.

* * *

104. The Court notes that, when opening the meeting of 17 February 2008 at which the declaration of independence was adopted, the President of the Assembly and the Prime Minister of Kosovo made reference to the Assembly of Kosovo and the Constitutional Framework. The Court considers, however, that the declaration of independence must be seen in its larger context, taking into account the events preceding its adoption, notably relating to the so-called "final status process" (see paragraphs 64 to 73). Security Council resolution 1244 (1999) was mostly concerned with setting up an interim framework of self-government for Kosovo (see paragraph 58 above). Although, at the time of the adoption of the resolution, it was expected that the final status of Kosovo would flow from, and be developed within, the framework set up by the resolution, the specific contours, let alone the outcome, of the final status process were left open by Security Council resolution 1244 (1999). Accordingly, its paragraph 11, especially in its subparagraphs (d), (e) and (f), deals with final status issues only in so far as it is made part of UNMIK's responsibilities to "facilitate a political process designed to determine Kosovo's future status, taking into account the Rambouillet accords" and "in a final stage, [to oversee] the transfer of authority from Kosovo's provisional institutions to institutions established under a political settlement".

105. The declaration of independence reflects the awareness of its authors that the final status negotiations had failed and that a critical moment for the future of Kosovo had been reached. The Preamble of the declaration refers to the "years of internationally-sponsored

negotiations between Belgrade and Pristina over the question of our future political status" and expressly puts the declaration in the context of the failure of the final status negotiations, inasmuch as it states that "no mutually-acceptable status outcome was possible" (tenth and eleventh preambular paragraphs). Proceeding from there, the authors of the declaration of independence emphasize their determination to "resolve" the status of Kosovo and to give the people of Kosovo "clarity about their future" (thirteenth preambular paragraph). This language indicates that the authors of the declaration did not seek to act within the standard framework of interim self-administration of Kosovo, but aimed at establishing Kosovo "as an independent and sovereign state." The declaration of independence, therefore, was not intended by those who adopted it to take effect within the legal order created for the interim phase, nor was it capable of doing so. On the contrary, the Court considers that the authors of that declaration did not act, or intend to act, in the capacity of an institution created by and empowered to act within that legal order but, rather, set out to adopt a measure the significance and effects of which would lie outside that order.

106. This conclusion is reinforced by the fact that the authors of the declaration undertook to fulfill the international obligations of Kosovo, notably those created for Kosovo by UNMIK, and expressly and solemnly declared Kosovo to be bound vis-à-vis third States by the commitments made in the declaration. [ ... ]

107. Certain features of the text of the declaration and the circumstances of its adoption also point to the same conclusion. Nowhere in the original Albanian text of the declaration (which is the sole authentic text) is any reference made to the declaration being the work of the Assembly of Kosovo. The words "Assembly of Kosovo" appear at the head of the declaration only in the English and French translations contained in the dossier submitted on behalf of the Secretary-General. The language used in the declaration differs from that employed in acts of the Assembly of Kosovo in that the first paragraph commences with the phrase "We, the democratically-elected leaders of our people ...", whereas acts of the Assembly of Kosovo employ the third person singular.

Moreover, the procedure employed in relation to the declaration differed from that employed by the Assembly of Kosovo for the adoption of legislation. In particular, the declaration was signed by all those present when it was adopted, including the President of Kosovo, who (as noted in paragraph 76 above) was not a member of the Assembly of Kosovo. In fact, the self-reference of the persons adopting the declaration of independence as "the democratically-elected leaders of our people" immediately precedes the actual declaration of independence within the text "hereby declare Kosovo to be an independent and sovereign state." It is also noticeable that the declaration was not forwarded to the Special Representative of the Secretary-General for publication in the Official Gazette.

108. The reaction of the Special Representative of the Secretary-General to the declaration of independence is also of some significance. The Constitutional Framework gave the Special Representative power to oversee and, in certain circumstances, annul the acts of the Provisional Institutions of Self-Government. On previous occasions, in particular in the period between 2002 and 2005, when the Assembly of Kosovo took initiatives to promote the independence of Kosovo, the Special Representative had qualified a number of acts as being incompatible with the Constitutional Framework on the grounds that they were deemed to be "beyond the scope of [the Assembly's] competencies" (United Nations dossier No. 189, 7 February 2003) and therefore outside the powers of the Assembly of Kosovo.

The silence of the Special Representative of the Secretary-General in the face of the declaration of independence of 17 February 2008 suggests that he did not consider that the declaration was an act of the Provisional Institutions of Self-Government designed to take effect within the legal order for the supervision of which he was responsible. As the practice shows, he would have been under a duty to take action with regard to acts of the Assembly of Kosovo which he considered to be *ultra vires*. [ ... ]

109. The Court thus arrives at the conclusion that, taking all factors together, the authors of the declaration of independence of 17 February 2008 did not act as one of the Provisional Institutions of Self-Government within the Constitutional Framework, but rather as persons who acted together in their capacity as representatives of the people of Kosovo outside the framework of the interim administration.

(b) *The question whether the authors of the declaration of independence acted in violation of Security Council resolution 1244 (1999) or the measures adopted thereunder*

110. Having established the identity of the authors of the declaration of independence, the Court turns to the question whether their act in promulgating the declaration was contrary to any prohibition contained in Security Council resolution 1244 (1999) or the Constitutional Framework adopted thereunder.

\* \* \*

113. The question whether resolution 1244 (1999) prohibits the authors of the declaration of 17 February 2008 from declaring independence from the Republic of Serbia can only be answered through a careful reading of this resolution.

114. First, the Court observes that Security Council resolution 1244 (1999) was essentially designed to create an interim régime for Kosovo, with a view to channeling the long-term political process to establish its final status. The resolution did not contain any provision dealing with the final status of Kosovo or with the conditions for its achievement.

In this regard the Court notes that contemporaneous practice of the Security Council shows that in situations where the Security Council has decided to establish restrictive conditions for the permanent status of a territory, those conditions are specified in the relevant resolution. For example, although the factual circumstances differed from the situation in Kosovo, only 19 days after the adoption of resolution 1244 (1999), the Security Council, in its resolution 1251 of 29 June 1999, reaffirmed its position that a "Cyprus settlement must be based on a State of Cyprus with a single sovereignty and international personality and a single citizenship, with its independence and territorial integrity safeguarded". The Security Council thus set out the specific conditions relating to the permanent status of Cyprus.

By contrast, under the terms of resolution 1244 (1999) the Security Council did not reserve for itself the final determination of the situation in Kosovo and remained silent on the conditions for the final status of Kosovo.

Resolution 1244 (1999) thus does not preclude the issuance of the declaration of independence of 17 February 2008 because the two instruments operate on a different level: unlike resolution 1244 (1999), the declaration of independence is an attempt to determine finally the status of Kosovo.

115. Secondly, turning to the question of the addressees of Security Council resolution 1244 (1999), as described above, it sets out a general framework for the "deployment in Kosovo, under United Nations auspices, of international civil and security presences." It is mostly concerned with creating obligations and authorizations for United Nations Member States as well as for organs of the United Nations such as the Secretary-General and his Special Representative. The only point at which resolution 1244 (1999) expressly

mentions other actors relates to the Security Council's demand, on the one hand, "that the KLA and other armed Kosovo Albanian groups end immediately all offensive actions and comply with the requirements for demilitarization" and, on the other hand, for the "full cooperation by all concerned, including the international security presence, with the International Tribunal for the Former Yugoslavia." There is no indication, in the text of Security Council resolution 1244 (1999), that the Security Council intended to impose, beyond that, a specific obligation to act or a prohibition from acting, addressed to such other actors.

116. The Court recalls in this regard that it has not been uncommon for the Security Council to make demands on actors other than United Nations Member States and intergovernmental organizations. [ ... ]

117. Such reference to the Kosovo Albanian leadership or other actors, notwithstanding the somewhat general reference to "all concerned" is missing from the text of Security Council resolution 1244 (1999). When interpreting Security Council resolutions, the Court must establish, on a case-by-case basis, considering all relevant circumstances, for whom the Security Council intended to create binding legal obligations. The language used by the resolution may serve as an important indicator in this regard. The approach taken by the Court with regard to the binding effect of Security Council resolutions in general is, mutatis mutandis, also relevant here. [ ... ]

118. Bearing this in mind, the Court cannot accept the argument that Security Council resolution 1244 (1999) contains a prohibition, binding on the authors of the declaration of independence, against declaring independence; nor can such a prohibition be derived from the language of the resolution understood in its context and considering its object and purpose. The language of Security Council resolution 1244 (1999) is at best ambiguous in this regard. The object and purpose of the resolution, as has been explained in detail (see paragraphs 96 to 100), is the establishment of an interim administration for Kosovo, without making any definitive determination on final status issues. [ ... ]

119. The Court accordingly finds that Security Council resolution 1244 (1999) did not bar the authors of the declaration of 17 February 2008 from issuing a declaration of independence from the Republic of Serbia. Hence, the declaration of independence did not violate Security Council resolution 1244 (1999). [ ... ]

120. The Court therefore turns to the question whether the declaration of independence of 17 February 2008 has violated the Constitutional Framework established under the auspices of UNMIK. Chapter 5 of the Constitutional Framework determines the powers of the Provisional Institutions of Self-Government of Kosovo. It was argued by a number of States which participated in the proceedings before the Court that the promulgation of a declaration of independence is an act outside the powers of the Provisional Institutions of Self-Government as set out in the Constitutional Framework.

121. The Court has already held, however (see paragraphs 102 to 109 above), that the declaration of independence of 17 February 2008 was not issued by the Provisional Institutions of Self-Government, nor was it an act intended to take effect, or actually taking effect, within the legal order in which those Provisional Institutions operated. It follows that the authors of the declaration of independence were not bound by the framework of powers and responsibilities established to govern the conduct of the Provisional Institutions of Self-Government. Accordingly, the Court finds that the declaration of independence did not violate the Constitutional Framework.

* * *

## V. General conclusion

122. The Court has concluded above that the adoption of the declaration of independence of 17 February 2008 did not violate general international law, Security Council resolution 1244 (1999) or the Constitutional Framework. Consequently the adoption of that declaration did not violate any applicable rule of international law.

123. For these reasons, THE COURT,

(1) Unanimously,

*Finds* that it has jurisdiction to give the advisory opinion requested;

(2) By nine votes to five,

*Decides* to comply with the request for an advisory opinion;

* * *

(3) By ten votes to four,

*Is of the opinion* that the declaration of independence of Kosovo adopted on 17 February 2008 did not violate international law.

* * *

## Authors' Note

The following article discusses the concept of earned sovereignty, its main elements, and its application in recent peace processes. The article distinguishes the earned sovereignty method from traditional approaches to resolving sovereignty-based disputes.

## 8. Paul R. Williams, Earned Sovereignty: Bridging the Gap between Sovereignty and Self-Determination

*Stanford Journal of International Law*, 2004

### Introduction

* * *

The intensity and severity of sovereignty-based conflicts, their relationship to increasing levels of terrorism, and the lack of effective legal norms and principles have given rise to the need for a new approach to resolving sovereignty-based conflicts. This need is increasingly being met by the emerging conflict resolution approach of earned sovereignty. In seven recent peace agreements concerning sovereignty-based conflicts, the parties have relied upon the approach of earned sovereignty. In two of the major outstanding conflicts, earned sovereignty forms the basis of the proposed agreement. The approach of earned sovereignty has been aided in its development by the increasing efforts of international organizations and powerful states to undertake global conflict management, including a willingness to aid states in conflict resolution and undertake institution building in conflict-affected areas.

Despite the increasing ad hoc reliance on the approach of earned sovereignty by mediators and parties to conflict, there is scant scholarly commentary as to the precise nature of the approach, the political debate surrounding its use, and its utility for resolving sovereignty-based conflicts. To initiate the debate, the Public International Law & Policy

Group, in cooperation with the Denver University School of Law, hosted a daylong round-table discussion focused on the emerging trend of earned sovereignty and its potential utility for resolving ongoing sovereignty-based conflicts. The Denver Journal of International Law and Policy published the preliminary observations presented during the round-table. This Article draws from that series of papers in an effort to further refine the understanding of the approach of earned sovereignty.

In particular this article extends the debate by parsing out and clearly defining the various elements of the earned sovereignty approach as they have been developed and employed in previous peace agreements. A clear understanding of the elements of the approach and how they have been employed to facilitate the peaceful resolution of previous conflicts will enhance the ability of peace negotiators and parties to effectively apply the approach in future conflicts where relevant. To facilitate a comprehensive understanding of the earned sovereignty approach and its potential utility in future conflict resolution efforts, this Article also seeks to provide a sense of the political debate surrounding the advantages and risks associated with the approach.

Earned sovereignty, as developed in recent state practice, entails the conditional and progressive devolution of sovereign powers and authority from a state to a substate entity under international supervision. Earned sovereignty most naturally develops within a peace process as a multistage approach to address the issue of the final political status of the substate entity. As an emerging conflict resolution approach, earned sovereignty is defined by three core elements: shared sovereignty, institution building, and a determination of final status. To increase the flexibility necessary to deal with the political fragilities of peace processes, and with the historical diversity of different conflicts, earned sovereignty may also encompass three additional elements: phased sovereignty, conditional sovereignty, and constrained sovereignty. These optional elements further enhance the applicability of earned sovereignty to the circumstances of a particular conflict and allow for the modification or development of the approach as necessary to meet the needs of the parties.

* * *

## I. The Traditional Approaches to Resolving Sovereignty-Based Conflicts: Sovereignty vs. Self-Determination

Traditional approaches to resolving sovereignty-based conflicts may be characterized as falling within the spectrum of the "sovereignty first" approach, based primarily upon the principles of sovereignty, territorial integrity, and political independence, or the "self-determination first" approach, based upon the legal principles relating to self-determination and the protection of human rights.

The predominant "sovereignty first" approach is generally relied upon by states wishing to preserve their territorial integrity, or by third-party states that fear that the creation of too many new states may undermine international stability or set a precedent that may be used by secessionist movements within their state. In this approach, sovereignty is regarded as the essential element of the political existence of a state, and forms the basis for international relations. A core attribute of sovereignty is the exclusive jurisdiction of a state to exercise political power and authority within its own borders and to exercise all rights necessary to preserve its territorial integrity from external and internal threats. Mediators adopting the "sovereignty first" approach often find themselves in a position of accommodating, and in some instances appeasing, aggressor regimes.

The "self-determination first" approach is frequently relied upon by secessionist movements, and has been sympathetically received by small states without significant minority populations. This approach, which evolved within the context of decolonization, is based upon the principle that dependent peoples are entitled to exercise self-government. Under this approach, all self-identified groups with a coherent identity and connection to a defined territory are entitled to collectively determine their political destiny in a democratic fashion and to be free from systematic persecution. Self-government is generally attained through the creation of an autonomous province within the parent state, although it may in some limited circumstances be attained through secession.

Increasingly, these two approaches fail to offer satisfactory options for structuring the peaceful resolution of sovereignty-based conflicts, as they frequently result in political gridlock and continued violence. The "sovereignty first" approach is relied upon by the parent state, and frequently the international community, to argue for the retention of the substate entity within the parent state and to justify the use of force to accomplish that objective. For instance, the mantra of sovereignty has been used by states to shield themselves from international action resulting from human rights abuses committed as part of their attempts to stifle self-determination movements. Examples of this include the Iraqi Anfal campaigns against the Kurds, the violation of Kurdish human rights in Turkey, the Russian campaign in Chechnya, the targeting of Christians in southern Sudan, and Indonesia's brutal occupation of East Timor, as well as its recent campaign in Aceh. Despite the non-absolute nature of sovereignty, the international community also frequently clings to the misconception of absolute sovereignty in the context of sovereignty-based conflicts—with dire consequences.

The "self-determination first" approach is relied upon by the substate entity to support a claim for heightened autonomy or secession, and to justify the use of force to defend its people against the national army or police force. For instance, the mantra of self-determination has been used to justify the use of armed force, and frequently terrorism, by groups such as the Tamil Tigers, the Free Aceh Movement, the Moro Islamic Liberation Front, and the Jammu Kashmir Liberation Front in their efforts to achieve greater autonomy within or independence from the parent state.

Given the rather exclusive nature of the two primary approaches, their utility has been reduced to little more than legal and political shields behind which states and substate entities justify their actions. The approach of earned sovereignty is an attempt to bridge the impasse between the two approaches of "sovereignty first" and "self-determination first," and to create an opportunity to resolve the conflicts and reduce the accompanying human rights violations and spread of terrorism.

## II. Earned Sovereignty: An Emerging Conflict Resolution Approach

Earned sovereignty is designed to create an opportunity for resolving sovereignty-based conflicts by providing for the managed devolution of sovereign authority and functions from a state to a substate entity. In some instances, the substate entity may acquire sovereign authority and functions sufficient to enable it to seek international recognition, while in others the substate entity may only acquire authority to operate within a stable system of heightened autonomy.

Earned sovereignty seeks to promote peaceful coexistence between a state and a substate entity by establishing an equitable and acceptable power sharing arrangement; it is not intended solely to promote self-determination claims. Earned sovereignty is a neutral approach that attempts to end conflicts by reestablishing security and promoting democracy and institution building war torn territories.

As a conflict resolution approach, earned sovereignty has developed as an inherently flexible process implemented over a variable time period. As noted in the Introduction, this approach is defined by three core elements: shared sovereignty, institution building, and a determination of final status. The process may also encompass three optional elements: phased sovereignty, conditional sovereignty, and constrained sovereignty. These optional elements are employed to tailor the earned sovereignty approach to the unique circumstances of each conflict and to the particular needs of the parties.

## A. The Elements of Earned Sovereignty

The first core element is shared sovereignty. Each case of earned sovereignty is characterized by an initial stage of shared sovereignty, whereby the state and substate entity may both exercise some sovereign authority and functions over a defined territory. Sometimes international institutions may also exercise sovereign authority and functions in addition to, or in lieu of, the parent state. In rare cases, the international community may exercise shared sovereignty with an internationally recognized state. In almost all instances, an international institution is responsible for monitoring the parties' exercise of their authority and functions.

The second core element is institution building. During the period of shared sovereignty, prior to the determination of final status, the substate entity, frequently with the assistance of the international community, undertakes to construct new institutions for self-government, or modify those already in existence. The substate entity also works with the international community to develop the institutional capacity for exercising increased sovereign authority.

The third core element is the eventual determination of the final status of the substate entity and its relationship to the parent state. In many instances the status will be determined by a referendum. In others, it may involve a negotiated settlement between the state and substate entity, often with international mediation. Invariably, the determination of final status for the substate entity is conditioned on the consent of the international community in the form of international recognition.

The first optional element is phased sovereignty. Phased sovereignty entails the accumulation by the substate entity of increasing sovereign authority and functions over a specified period of time prior to the determination of final status. The accumulation of sovereign authority and functions may be correlated with the ability of the substate entity to assume these powers, as a reward for responsible state behavior, or a combination of both.

The second optional element is conditional sovereignty. Conditional sovereignty may be applied to the accumulation of increased sovereign authority by the substate entity, or it may be applied as a set of standards to be achieved prior to the determination of the substate entity's final status. These benchmarks vary depending on the characteristics of the conflict and generally include conditions, such as protecting human and minority rights, halting terrorism, developing democratic institutions, instituting the rule of law, and promoting regional stability. In most cases, the relationship between the attainment of certain benchmarks and the devolution of authority is not automatic—it is subject to evaluation by a monitoring authority that often involves international institutions. Such evaluation allows for a margin of discretion to determine when and how to successfully push forward the process of devolving authority.

The third optional element, constrained sovereignty, consists of applying limitations on the sovereign authority and functions of the new state. Constrained sovereignty is often required as a guarantee for the parent state and the international community. For instance, the new entity may be placed under a continued international administrative and/ or military presence, or its sovereign authority may be limited with respect to the right of undertaking territorial association with other states.

The state and substate entities almost always adopt the elements of earned sovereignty by mutual agreement, but in some cases the international community may support or initiate one or more of the elements of earned sovereignty against the preferences of the state or substate entity, as in the case of Kosovo.

\* \* \*

## Conclusion

\* \* \*

By following a measured process for the resolution of a sovereignty-based dispute, the earned sovereignty approach creates an opportunity for states to minimize many of the destabilizing factors associated with immediate secession. The application of conditions to the increased assumption of sovereign authority and functions by a substate entity creates a highly effective means for influencing the behavior of the substate entity in order to ensure the protection of legitimate interests of the parent state and the international community.

The ability to determine the final status of the substate entity years after the initial peace agreement provides an opportunity for the parties to make a decision on final status at a time when passions are not inflamed by an ongoing armed conflict. The approach also permits a more rational, deliberative process, which may involve the international community in some form. Similarly, the involvement of the international community in institution building benefits the state and substate entity by enabling the creation of institutions necessary to ensure the stable operation of the substate entity, either as a new state or as a province with heightened autonomy. The creation of domestic institutions also provides the state and the international community with an additional point of contact to pressure the substate entity, which facilitates the protection of legitimate interests, such as the protection of minority rights, and responsible regional behavior.

Like any approach to conflict resolution, there are risks associated with earned sovereignty. The approach may create an irreversible expectation of independence on the part of the substate entity, as reflected in experiences in Northern Ireland, southern Sudan, and Montenegro. In addition, the conditions may not be taken seriously and may only be minimally met. Alternately, the conditions may be so difficult to attain that a substate entity finds itself locked in an unending effort to meet unachievable goals, with the consequence that tensions are exacerbated rather than relieved. This dynamic describes in part the unstable, yet politically adaptive, developments in Kosovo, and may even offer insight into the difficulties moving ahead in the Israel/Palestine negotiations. These concerns may be effectively managed, however, by the good faith involvement of international actors and by a precise drafting of the peace agreement. In the end, the approach of earned sovereignty provides an additional tool for parties and mediators to structure the resolution of sovereignty-based disputes in a manner that promotes regional stability, minimizes human rights violations, and removes an impetus for the further spread of increasingly destructive terrorist organizations.

## *Authors' Note*

The U.N. has been directly involved in the transition to self-determination for a number of states. From 1945 until 1994, the U.N. Trusteeship Council was responsible for administering territories as they transitioned from colonial rule to self-governance. The major goals of the Trusteeship Council were to promote the advancement of the inhabitants of Trust Territories and their progressive development towards self-government or independence. Although the Trusteeship Council continues to exist as a U.N. organ, it no longer has any active trusteeships. The last trusteeship ended in 1994 when Palau became an independent state.

Despite the shuttering of the Trusteeship Council, a number of modern disputes have arisen that required international intervention. U.N. Security Council Resolution 1244 made the U.N. the interim sovereign of Kosovo and culminated with Kosovo's declaration of independence from Serbia in 2008. Although this was not a transition from colonial rule, the interim assistance of the U.N. was essential to the stability of the region and helped end serious human rights and humanitarian law violations.

Failed states and states whose independence is controversial face significant challenges in achieving self-determination and stability. Although the number of states that fit in this category is unlikely to be widely agreed upon, since the end of the Cold War, numerous entities are currently in or have gone through situations of ambiguous sovereignty and self-determination. For example, East Timor has struggled with its independence from Portugal and Indonesia despite substantial long-term support from the U.N.. Relatively peaceful transitions, such as the dissolution of the Soviet Union into fifteen states and Czechoslovakia into the Czech Republic and the Slovak Republic peacefully in 1992, can happen, but conflict appears to be the norm when controversial issues of self-determination arise.

## 9. United Nations Charter, Articles 86–91

### Chapter XIII: The Trusteeship Council

#### Composition

#### Article 86

The Trusteeship Council shall consist of the following Members of the United Nations:

a. Those Members administering trust territories;

b. Such of those Members mentioned by name in Article 23 as are not administering trust territories; and

c. As many other Members elected for three-year terms by the General Assembly as may be necessary to ensure that the total number of members of the Trusteeship Council is equally divided between those Members of the United Nations which administer trust territories and those which do not.

Each member of the Trusteeship Council shall designate one specially qualified person to represent it therein.

## Functions and Powers

### Article 87

The General Assembly and, under its authority, the Trusteeship Council, in carrying out their functions, may:

  a. consider reports submitted by the administering authority;

  b. accept petitions and examine them in consultation with the administering authority;

  c. provide for periodic visits to the respective trust territories at times agreed upon with the administering authority; and

  d. take these and other actions in conformity with the terms of the trusteeship agreements.

### Article 88

The Trusteeship Council shall formulate a questionnaire on the political, economic, social, and educational advancement of the inhabitants of each trust territory, and the administering authority for each trust territory within the competence of the General Assembly shall make an annual report to the General Assembly upon the basis of such questionnaire.

## Voting

### Article 89

Each member of the Trusteeship Council shall have one vote.

Decisions of the Trusteeship Council shall be made by a majority of the members present and voting.

## Procedure

### Article 90

The Trusteeship Council shall adopt its own rules of procedure, including the method of selecting its President.

The Trusteeship Council shall meet as required in accordance with its rules, which shall include provision for the convening of meetings on the request of a majority of its members.

### Article 91

The Trusteeship Council shall, when appropriate, avail itself of the assistance of the Economic and Social Council and of the specialized agencies in regard to matters with which they are respectively concerned.

---

## *Authors' Note*

Tom Parker argues that the U.N.'s long dormant Trusteeship Council should be revived and charged with managing the U.N.'s dispute resolution activities. The following excerpt from Parker's article details the Trusteeship Council's theoretical and historical bases.

## 10. Tom Parker, The Ultimate Intervention: Revitalizing the U.N. Trusteeship Council for the 21st Century
Centre for European and Asian Studies,
Norwegian School of Management, 2003

### Introduction

After forty-seven years of operation the U.N. Trusteeship Council successfully completed the job it was created to do with the termination of the trusteeship of Palau in December 1994. In all the Trusteeship Council and its proxies shepherded eleven territories to independence or voluntary association with a state. Created to oversee the progressive development of Trust Territories towards self-government or independence the Trusteeship Council now lies dormant and awaiting termination. Meanwhile the U.N. paradoxically finds itself increasingly involved on an ad hoc basis in state building and governance projects around the world.

As the U.N. struggles to meet new Post-Cold War challenges such as those posed by failed and disintegrating states and to find answers to more traditional threats to international peace and security such as territorial disputes there is a need to establish some form of framework within which to respond. The need for something of this nature was envisaged by former U.N. Secretary General Boutros-Boutros Ghali in his seminal paper Agenda for Peace but all responses so far have been rooted in the actions of an increasingly overburdened Security Council.

\* \* \*

### Part I: The Historical Context

*a) The Origins of the Idea of Trusteeship*

It has been argued that the essence of the International Trusteeship System is the protection of native rights. Although they exercised little influence on their more mercenary contemporaries, early legal theorists such as Jean Lopez de Palacios Rubios and Franciscus de Vitoria first raised this issue in response to the discovery and exploration of the New World. In *De Indis* de Vitoria argued that the New World should be developed in the interests of its native peoples and not just for the profit of Spaniards: "The property of the wards, is not part of the guardian's property ... the wards are its owners." Although de Vitoria did not see the Indians as equals he did characterize them as belonging to the same social universe. De Vitoria's ideas were taken up by, among others, Jean Bodin, Domingo Soto and Balthasar de Ayala. In *Mare Liberum* Hugo Grotius applied de Vitoria's arguments to refuting Portuguese claims over the East Indes.

The concept of trusteeship became more explicitly developed during the era of British colonial expansion and consolidation. The development of British parliamentary democracy was driven in part by the political philosopher John Locke's identification of the "social contract" that exists between the people and the legislature. It was perhaps inevitable that this theory would also eventually color Britain's relationship with its colonial territories. The prominent conservative theorist and politician Edmund Burke is widely credited as being the first to invoke the concept of "trust" in speeches addressing British policy in India and North America in the last decades of the 18th Century. It was Burke who coined the phrase "sacred trust" which appears in Article 22(1) of the Covenant of the League of Nations and Article 73 of the U.N. Charter. Burke's paternalistic vision of Britain's civilizing mission became an essential part of the mythology of British Imperialism perhaps best typified by Colonial Secretary Joseph Chamberlain's declaration in 1898 that in acquiring new territory the British were acting as the "trustees of civilization for the commerce of the world."

Interest in the concept of trusteeship was certainly not confined to the British Empire. At the same time that British imperialists such as Sir Thomas Stamford Raffles and Sir Thomas Munro were exploring ideas of trusteeship within the context of Britain's colonial possessions, Americans were exploring the concept at home in their relations with the Native American peoples. In 1831 Chief Justice Marshall of the Supreme Court held that the Cherokee nation had an undisputed right to the lands they occupied observing: "They are in a state of pupilage; their relation to the United States resembles that of a ward to his guardian."

Other nations began to adopt similar policies. At the Berlin Conference of 1884–1885 fifteen European Powers met to alleviate the friction generated between them as a result of the rush to secure the remaining unclaimed territories of Africa as colonial dependencies. The conference produced a groundbreaking General Act which bound the signatories to "care for the improvement of the conditions of the moral and material well-being" of the natives of the Congo Basin which is generally regarded as the first treaty of its sort.

By the dawn of the 20th Century the concept of trusteeship took on an added dimension as a number of statesman and radical thinkers began to look at the principle of international accountability. As early as 1902 the left-wing British economist J. A. Hobson suggested in his influential study of Imperialism that the right to exercise control over dependent peoples should only be granted to a nation on condition that it so be accredited by a body "genuinely representative of civilization." However, the real shift in attitudes was to come with the outbreak of the First World War during which the concept of trusteeship became increasingly linked with plans to create an international body to regulate and oversee international affairs.

The carnage of the First World War bred widespread discontent with old idea that peace in Europe could be ensured by maintaining a balance of power between the major powers. As the war dragged on more and more people embraced the idea of, in the words of Lord Robert Cecil, "an organization ... in essence universal, not to protect the national interest of this or that country ... but to abolish war." The idea attracted powerful advocates from across the political spectrum. In the United States Democrats and Republicans both flocked to join the League to Enforce Peace. In Britain a special committee was formed under Sir Walter Phillimore to look at the idea and in France a commission chaired by former Prime Minister Léon Bourgeois drew up plans for an international organization with its own army to police the peace.

U.S. President Woodrow Wilson caught the public mood when he unveiled his Fourteen Points for peace in an address to a Joint Session of Congress on 8th January 1918. For the purposes of this paper, two Points in particular stand out:

> Point V, which promised "a free, open-minded, and absolutely impartial adjustment of all colonial claims, based upon a strict observance of the principle that in determining all such questions of sovereignty the interests of the populations concerned must have equal weight with the equitable claims of the government whose title is to be determined."

and

> Point XIV, which called for the creation "a general association of nations ... for the purpose of affording mutual guarantees of political independence and territorial integrity to great and small states alike."

Across Europe squares and streets were named after the U.S. President. Posters appeared demanding "A Wilson Peace." By the end of the war public expectations had grown to such a pitch that the British Prime Minister Lloyd George told the Imperial War Cabinet in December 1918 that it would be nothing less than "a political disaster" to return from the Peace Conference without a League of Nations.

The idea of some form of international oversight for the colonies of the Western powers gathered pace in tandem with this new spirit of internationalism, particularly in the United States (the only major power essentially without colonial ambitions) and amongst European socialist parties. With the declaration of an armistice thoughts inevitably turned to the coming peace settlement.

In December 1918 The South African soldier-statesman Jan Smuts set out to bring Wilson's "rather nebulous ideas" more form in a paper (later released as a pamphlet) entitled "The League of Nations: A Practical Suggestion." In addition, to sketching out a possible administrative structure for the League, Smuts also suggested that it should provide for the mandated administration of the territories belonging to Austria, Russia and Turkey by the victorious powers. Smuts did not believe such a scheme should be extended to the German colonies of Africa and the Pacific which he felt were inhabited by "barbarians" more suited to annexation and direct colonial rule. President Wilson was given a copy of Smut's paper by Lloyd George and when the President finally sat down in January 1919 to expand on his original ideas the draft he produced borrowed heavily from Smuts.

### b) The Mandates System

*"Conceived in generosity but born in sin, it had grown up in repentance."*

On 25 January 1919 the Paris Peace Conference formally approved the establishment of a Commission on the League of Nations under the chairmanship of President Wilson. Right from the start the issue of mandates was one of the principal, and most contentious, items on the agenda. None of the victorious powers believed Germany should get back its colonial possessions — it was felt that Germany had demonstrated by her behavior that she was unfit to rule other peoples. The question was what to do with them.

President Wilson's vision went much further than that of Smuts and it was Wilson's vision that prevailed in Article 22 of the Covenant of the League of Nations. Article 22 extended the "Mandates System" to those colonies and territories belonging to Germany and Turkey "inhabited by peoples not yet able to stand by themselves under the strenuous conditions of the modern world."

Wilson made it plain from the start that he expected the League to assume responsibility for all Germany's former colonies. He argued forcibly that the League would be a laughing stock if the annexation of enemy territory by the victorious powers were not invested with some "quality of trusteeship." Wilson's first draft of the League System also included the principle of direct international administration — he originally intended for the League to entrust the task of administration to "some single state or organized agency."

Britain and Canada broadly supported Wilson's suggestions. However, Wilson did not get it all his own way. Ranged against him were France and the increasingly independent British Dominions of South Africa, Australia and New Zealand who all favored annexation. Wilson refused to condone what he termed "dividing the swag" and battle lines were drawn with Australia and New Zealand leading the charge over German islands in the Pacific.

It was Smuts and Cecil who came up with a compromise solution: a three tier Mandates System. 'A' class mandates for nations which were nearly ready to run their own affairs. 'B' class mandates which would be run by the mandatory power. 'C' class mandates for territories contiguous or close to the mandatory power which would be run as an extension of its own territory subject to certain restrictions. The Australian Prime Minster Billy Hughes was privately satisfied with this outcome commenting that although he had not secured a freehold on New Guinea and the Solomon Islands he had at least acquired a 999-year lease.

Smuts also put paid to the idea of promoting international administrations as an alternative to a mandatory power which he argued would inevitably lead to "paralysis tempered by intrigue." Smuts was strongly supported by the French Minister for Colonies Henri Simon who noted somewhat disingenuously that tentative experiments in international administration had "failed ignominiously." However, some degree of international participation in the process was secured by the British that an expert Commission be created to assist the League Council in the supervision of the Mandatory Administrations. This was incorporated into the League Covenant.

In the end, despite the wrangling of the colonial powers, the final draft of Article 22 of the League Covenant retained much of Wilson's original vision of "a quality of trusteeship". Article 22(1) stated that the Mandates System should apply "the principle that the well-being and development of such peoples form a sacred trust of civilization" and that "securities for the performance of this trust" should be embodied within it. Article 22(2) talked of the "tutelage" of such peoples "entrusted" to advanced nations. In Article 22(5) the Mandatory Powers for class 'B' and 'C' mandates were charged with responsibility for ensuring that territories were administered "under conditions which will guarantee freedom of conscience and religion, subject only to the maintenance of public order and morals."

However, it should be noted that one final concession made to the colonial powers that were to administer the Mandates System was that Article 22 of the League Covenant made no mention of self-determination. In marked contrast to Wilson's espousal of self-determination in his Fourteen Points the right of mandates to self-governance was not established as a legal right within the System but as a question of fact—mandates' ability "to stand by themselves."

At its inception in 1920 fourteen former German and Turkish territories encompassing some 20 million inhabitants were placed under mandate. Three 'A' class mandates were established in the Middle East (Iraq, Syria-Lebanon and Palestine), six 'B' class mandates were carved out of the former German colonies of Togoland-Cameroons and German East Africa and five 'C' class Mandates created from former German colonies in South West Africa and the Pacific. The Administering Powers were Britain (including the Dominions of Australia, South Africa and New Zealand), France, Belgium and Japan.

Unfortunately, as the attitude of the Australian Prime Minister indicated, in the inter-war years the manner in which the administration of the 'B' and 'C' class mandates was approached looked very similar in consequence to direct annexation. However, for all its failings the Mandates System can lay claim to two important achievements. By the time the System was wound up in 1946 all but one class 'A' mandate—Palestine—had achieved independence, powerful reinforcement of the implied but unstated principle that the ultimate objective of all Mandatory Powers should be to prepare the territories under their "tutelage" for self-government.

Furthermore, the provision made in Article 22(7) of the League Covenant obliging the Mandatory Powers to submit annual reports to the Permanent Mandates Commission concerning the administration of the territories under their control created established a body of practice and precedent relating to international oversight. It is true that there was not much the Commission could do in the face of blatant breaches of the principles of Trusteeship by some of the Mandatory Powers—such as the Japan's decision to fortify its Pacific Island Mandates in 1937. However, the Commission was able to establish an international standard of best practice against which recalcitrant states could be held up to public condemnation. In the words of A. J. R. Groom with the establishment of the Mandates System: "The genie of international accountability could not be put back into the bottle of untrammeled colonial possession."

### c) The International Trusteeship System

The creation of the United Nations at the end of the Second World War presented the international community with an opportunity to address the shortcomings that had become apparent in the Mandates System. The dramatic events of the inter-war years and the trauma of a second global conflagration ensured that the international climate had changed substantially since the Paris Peace Conference, not least because the practice of colonialism was now under fire from all sides.

In the Joint Declaration known as the Atlantic Charter issued in August 1941 British Prime Minister Winston Churchill and U.S. President Franklin D. Roosevelt stated publicly that they would respect the right of all peoples to choose the form of government under which they would live. Churchill later sought to limit the scope of this declaration to Axis-dominated Europe but expectations had already been raised in the colonies. The Atlantic Charter was subsequently endorsed by the Declaration of the United Nations made by 24 different nations in January 1942.

The debate on the future of the Mandates System and of colonial territories in general was to set ally against and ally and create unusual alliances between competing powers. Despite their ideological differences the United States and Soviet Union both wanted to see the dismemberment of the old European Empires and to this end they held bilateral talks on how best to tackle the colonial issue as early as May 1942. At the so-called Big Three Conferences held in Cairo and Tehran in 1943 Roosevelt actually proposed to Churchill and Soviet Premier Josef Stalin that all French dependent territories be placed under International Trusteeship. Roosevelt's suggestion was vehemently opposed by Churchill who saw an implicit threat to the British Empire in the proposal.

In the colonial territories themselves independence movements were gaining in strength supported by pressure groups in the West—particularly in the United States—made up of vocal members from the immigrant communities. Public opinion was increasingly important. In part, colonial commitment to the Allied cause had been brought with hints and promises of changes to come and by the end of the war pressure was building for evidence of this. Furthermore, Japan's initial military success in Far East Asia against the European Powers had destroyed the myth of European invincibility and given hope to the more militant national liberation movements throughout the colonial world as the Dutch were to discover in Indonesia.

In addition to the 'enemy without', some of the European nations, exhausted by war or occupation, had lost the will to continue as colonial powers. Progressive development and legislation at home sat uneasily with the autocratic rule of subject peoples abroad. In November 1944 the governments of Australia and New Zealand held a conference in Wellington at which they officially accepted the principles of trusteeship and international oversight. Churchill's defeat by Clement Attlee's Labor Party in the British Gen-

eral Election was another key development in this regard although it came too late to affect the discussions surrounding the creation of the international Trusteeship System. In
1943 the British Labor Party had issued a colonial policy statement in which it called for
the development of self-government and "the attainment of political rights not less than
those enjoyed or claimed by those of British democracy" for the colonial peoples of the
Empire. The statement also proclaimed the Party's acceptance of the principle of international supervision and accountability. Once in power, the Labor Party more or less remained true to this policy goal.

The question of an International Trusteeship System had not come up at the Dumbarton
Oaks conference in August–October 1944 when the framework of a general International
Organization to replace the League of Nations was first sketched out. However, it was
discussed at the "Big Three" conference held in Yalta in February 1945 and an American
proposal based on a draft plan produced by Leo Pasvolsky of the U.S. State Department
in 1942 was adopted. At both Churchill and De Gaulle's insistence there was to be no discussion of the actual territories to be affected at the forthcoming San Francisco Conference on the creation of the United Nations Charter.

Like the Mandates System before it, the evolution of the International Trusteeship System at the San Francisco Conference was shaped by the need to find a suitable compromise between a variety of competing interests and, perhaps inevitably, it became one of
the most contentious issues of the conference. Equally inevitably, states' experience of
the Mandates System informed their approach to the issue—indeed Duncan Hall has argued that the main contribution of the text of the U.N. Charter was to spell out in detail
much of what was already implicit but undeveloped in the sparsely worded League
Covenant.

The International Trusteeship System was expounded in Chapters XII and XIII of the
Charter and was uncoupled from the issue of colonial administration which was dealt
with separately in the Declaration Regarding Non-Self-Governing Territories that
formed Chapter XI. Chapter XII imposed a much more detailed set of obligations on
Administering States than the Mandates System and the Trusteeship Territories were
accorded a much more sophisticated personality than under the League Covenant. The
Charter also identified the promotion of political, economic, social and educational development towards self-government as one of the System's principle objectives. The
text of U.N. Charter made it perfectly clear that Trusteeship Agreements were no 999-
year leases.

The main departures from the Mandates System were substantial changes in the oversight mechanisms and in the security and economic relationship between the Administering Power and the Trusteeship Territory. Under Article 7(1) of the U.N. Charter the
Trusteeship Council was accorded the enhanced status of being designated a "Principal
Organ" of the United Nations. The Council was to be composed of government representatives
rather than private members as had been the case with the Mandates Commission. The
idea was that government representatives would perforce be better informed about what
was going on in the Trusteeship Territories than any private individual and would be able
to speak in the Council backed by the full authority of his or her government. The membership of the Council was to be evenly divided between Administering Powers and non-
Administering Powers. Finally, to emphasize the importance attached to the Trusteeship
provisions of the Charter Article 87 accorded ultimate authority on Trusteeship matters
to the General Assembly.

In the field of security and defense Article XII reflected the post-war obsession with preventing further conflict by charging the Administering Powers with ensuring the Trust Territory played its part in the maintenance of "international peace and security"—a sharp contrast with the effective demilitarization sought under the League Covenant. Chapter XII went even further in Articles 82 and 83 creating the concept of Special Strategic Areas—an American proposal which had its roots in lobbying by the U.S. Navy—under which all or part of a Trust Territory can be placed under the jurisdiction of the Security Council instead of the General Assembly. Articles 82 and 83 were fairly opaque and it was not until the first Strategic Trust Agreement between the United States and Japan's former Pacific Mandate Territories in 1947 that the potentially far reaching implications of this exemption became clear. Ultimately, this enabled the United States to establish a string of military bases in the Pacific where it had had none before.

The Mandates System was officially terminated on 18 April 1946 with the dissolution of the League of Nations. Article 77 of the U.N. Charter identified territories held under mandate as being suitable candidates for Trusteeship Agreements. However, the Charter made no definite provision for the future of the mandated territories as it was anticipated that the Mandatory States would automatically place their charges under the new system. The majority of Mandatory Powers voluntarily submitted their remaining Mandates to the Trusteeship System.

At the opening session of the Trusteeship Council on 26 March 1947 U.N. Secretary General Trygve Lie told the Council that it would be working towards its own demise: "[the] ultimate goal is to give the Trust Territories full statehood ... A successful Trusteeship System will afford a reassuring demonstration that there is a peaceful and orderly means of achieving the difficult transition from backward and subject status to self-government or independence, to political and economic self-reliance." Held up to this standard, when the Trusteeship Council effectively suspended its operations after December 1994 it could reasonably claim to have discharged its obligations successfully.

\* \* \*

## 11. Bibliography of Additional Sources

- ANNE F. BAYEFSKEY, SELF-DETERMINATION IN INTERNATIONAL LAW: QUEBEC AND LESSONS LEARNED (2000).
- ANTONIO CASSESE, SELF-DETERMINATION OF PEOPLES (1995).
- Conference for Peace in Yugoslavia, Arbitration Commission Opinion No. 10, 31 I.L.M. 1525 (July 4, 1992).
- Declaration of the Council of Ministers of the European Community on Guidelines on the Recognition of New States in Eastern Europe and the Soviet Union (Dec. 16, 1991).
- Raymond Detrez, *The Right to Self-Determination and Secession in Yugoslavia: A Hornets' Nest of Inconsistencies, in* Contextualizing Secession 112 (Bruno Coppieters & Richard Sakwa eds., 2003).
- Karl Doehring, *Self-Determination, in* The Charter of the United Nations: A Commentary (Bruno Simma ed., 1994).
- Richard Falk, *The Kosovo Advisory Opinion: Conflict Resolution and Precedent*, 105 AM. J. INT'L. L. 50 (Jan. 2011).

- Michael Freeman, *The Right to Self-Determination in International Politics: Six Theories in Search of a Policy*, 25 REV. INT'L. STUD. 355 (1999).

- Hurst Hannum, Autonomy, Sovereignty, and Self-Determination (1990).

- Karen Heymann, *Earned Sovereignty for Kashmir: The Legal Methodology to Avoiding a Nuclear Holocaust*, 19 AM. U. INT'L L. REV. 153 (2003).

- International Crisis Group, *North Kosovo: Dual Sovereignty in Practice*.

- F. L. Kirgis, Jr., *Editorial Comment: The Degrees of Self-Determination in the United Nations Era*, 88 AM. J. INT'L. L. 304 (1994).

- Nathan P. Kirschner, *Making Bread From Broken Eggs: A Basic Recipe For Conflict Resolution Using Earned Sovereignty*, 28 WHITTIER L. REV. 1131 (2007).

- Heribert Franz Koeck et al., From Protectorate to Statehood (2009).

- *Report of the International Committee of Jurists on the Legal Aspects of the Aaland Islands Question*, League of Nations Off. J., Spec. Supp. No. 3, 5 (1920).

- Michael J. Matheson, *United Nations Governance of Postconflict Societies* 95 AM. J. INT'L L. 76 (Jan. 2001).

- Diane F. Orentlicher, *International Responses to Separatist Claims: Are Democratic Principles Relevant?*, *in* Secession and Self-Determination (2003).

- Milena Sterio, *On The Right To External Self-Determination: "Selfistans," Secession, And The Great Powers' Rule*, 19 MINN. J. INT'L L. 137 (Winter 2010).

- Strobe Talbott, *Self-Determination in an Interdependent World*, FOREIGN POL'Y 152 (Spring 2000).

- Patrick Thornberry, *Self-Determination, Minorities, Human Rights: A Review of International Instruments*, 38 INT'L. & COMP. L.Q. 867 (1989).

- Declaration on Principles of International Law Concerning Friendly Relations and Co-operation Among States in Accordance with the Charter of the United Nations, G.A. Res. 2625 (XXV), U.N. Doc. A/8082 (Oct. 24, 1970).

- High Level Panel on Threats, Challenges and Change, *A More Secure World: Our Shared Responsibility*, *transmitted by note of the Secretary General*, U.N. Doc. A/59/565 (Dec. 5, 2004).

- MARC WELLER, CONTESTED STATEHOOD: KOSOVO'S STRUGGLE FOR INDEPENDENCE (2009).

- Ralph Wilde, *Accordance with International Law of the Unilateral Declaration of Independence in Respect of Kosovo*, 105 AM. J. INT'L. L. 301 (2011).

- Paul Williams, Janusz Bugajski, & R. Bruce Hitchner, Ctr. Strategic & Intl. Stud., Achieving a Final Status Settlement for Kosovo (2003).

- Paul R. Williams, *Earned Sovereignty: The Road to Resolving the Conflict Over Kosovo's Final Status*, 31 DENV. J. INT'L L. & POL'Y 387 (2003).

- Jane Wright, *Minority Groups, Autonomy, and Self-Determination*, 19 OXFORD J. LEGAL STUD. 605 (1999).

- John Young, *Sudan: Not More Diplomacy but Popular National Struggles*, 34 R. AFR. POL. ECON. 165 (2007).

# Chapter XV

# The International Human Rights Framework

## Introduction

U.N. bodies have been instrumental in the promulgation, monitoring, and enforcement of international human rights law. Often thought of in the abstract, the idea of international human rights is a complex issue that does not always translate into a practical definition. Not only do states differ on the definition of human rights, academics and policy makers often differ on the fundamental question of what right is a human right. As the world becomes smaller and people grow more and more interconnected, the question of human rights becomes more pressing. This chapter aims to provide a solid understanding of international human rights norms through the examination of major international treaties, their monitoring bodies, and the academic debate surrounding the topic. The following chapter (XVI) will provide details regarding the corresponding enforcement mechanisms.

## Objectives

- To be able to recognize fundamental human rights and their relation to international organizations.
- To understand the legal basis of the global human rights protection system.
- To become familiar with regional human rights instruments.
- To gain a critical perspective on derogation from treaty obligations during times of crisis, states of emergency, and inter-governmental organization accountability for human rights abuses.
- To understand the main debates surrounding the human rights concept in regard to the status of socio-economic rights, minority rights, and cultural relativism.

# Problems

Students should come to class prepared to discuss the following questions:

1. What is a "human right"?

2. What rights are fundamental, which are socio-economic rights, and which, if any, are not "human rights" at all?

3. How does each regional human rights charter or treaty reflect regional attitudes towards human rights?

4. Is the right to life and property the same as the right to potable drinking water or the right to rest and leisure?

5. What rights do citizens have concerning the political process?

6. How do states balance protecting political interests with protecting the rights of citizens?

7. Are the international human rights discussed in this chapter biased toward democratic ideals?

# Case Studies and Negotiation Simulations

Students should come to class prepared to participate in a discussion on how the following policies or practices in each case relate to human rights. Students should draw from concepts and ideas found in the materials, as well as in any other international human right instrument not mentioned here. For each case, the class should be prepared to answer the following questions:

- Does the legislation or custom violate international human rights standards?

- Does the legislation or custom violate the International Covenant on Civil and Political Rights (ICCPR)? **The text of the Covenant is available at: http://www1.unm/humanrts/instree/b3ccp.htm**

- Does the legislation or custom violate cultural rights?

- How should states balance national security with the protection of human rights?

- What should be the outcome of each situation?

- What defenses could each state raise to defend their law or policy?

**Iran:** Iran bases its law in the Islamic Penal Code outlined in the Quran. Iranian law imposes upon women a number of penalties that are not similarly imposed upon men. Women convicted of adultery may be stoned to death. A woman who fails to wear a veil in public may be flogged with one hundred lashes. Women convicted of theft or assault may have their limbs amputated.

**France:** Since 2010, French law bans the *burqa* and other Islamic face coverings in public places. The law imposes as punishment a fine of 150 Euros and/or a citizenship course. In addition, forcing a woman to wear a *niqab* or *burqa* is punishable by a 15,000 Euro fine or a one-year prison term. France considers these garments a form of enslavement and a public safety risk. Immediately after the law came into force in April 2011, several women were arrested.

**Sudan:** Sudanese law is governed by both Islamic Sharia law and by local tribal customs. The Sudanese Penal Code legalizes capital punishment for juveniles, the elderly, third-time offenders of the law against homosexual activity, violators of certain labor regulations and certain political opponents of the State.

**Ghana:** Ghanaian local tribal custom requires parents guilty of crimes or torts under local tribal law to turn over their minor daughters as servants to the victim or the victim's family for a certain period of time based upon the severity of the infraction. These punishments often include required sexual conduct. Ghana argues that these ancient tribal customs do not violate international human rights standards.

**Sri Lanka:** The civil war between the Tamil Tigers and the Government of Sri Lanka ended in 2009. At the end of the war, under a national state of emergency, the Government placed hundreds of thousands of men, women, and children fleeing Tiger-controlled areas into camps surrounded by barbed wire and guarded by military personnel. The Government argued that the protective measures were necessary to screen the internally displaced persons for potential Tamil combatants in order to protect national security. Despite government assurances that civilians would be allowed freedom of movement, months after the end of the war, between 20,000 and 30,000 people were in the camps. Many people who left the camps ended up in similarly restrictive "transit camps;" and others were told to give a date of their return, otherwise authorities would treat them as fugitives.

**United States:** A series of classified documents were released that contained internal Bush Administration legal arguments defending the use of torture and harsh treatment of detainees following September 11, 2001. The narrow definition in the memoranda of what constituted torture caused a political firestorm. The legal advice concluded that many interrogation techniques, including water boarding, sleep deprivation, and physiological torment, did not constitute torture.

# Materials

1. Universal Declaration of Human Rights. G.A. res 217A (III), U.N. Doc A/810 (1948).

2. Frank Newman & David Weissbrodt, INTERNATIONAL HUMAN RIGHTS 13–19, 91–97, 130–141 (1994).

3. U.N. Hum. Rts. Comm., General Comment No. 28 on the Equality of Rights Between Men and Women, U.N. Doc. CCPR/C/21/Rev.1/Add.10 (Mar. 29, 2000).

4. European Convention on Human Rights and Fundamental Freedoms, preamble, Nov. 4, 1955, 213 U.N.T.S 221.

5. American Convention on Human Rights, preamble, Nov. 22, 1969, 1144 U.N.T.S. 123.

6. African Charter on Human and People's Rights, preamble, June 27, 1981, 21 I.L.M. 58.

7. Charter of the Association of South-East Asian Nations (ASEAN), Nov. 20, 2007.

8. Council of Arab League States, Arab Charter on Human Rights, Sept. 15, 1994, *reprinted in* 18 HUM. RTS. L.J. 151 (1997).

9. U.N. Econ. & Soc. Council, Siracusa Principles on the Limitation and Derogation of Provisions in the International Covenant on Civil and Political Rights, U.N. Doc. E/CN.4/1985 (Sept. 28, 1984).

10. U.N. Hum. Rts. Comm., General Comment 29 on States of Emergency, U.N. Doc. CCPR/C/21/Rev.1/Add.11 (Aug. 31, 2001).

11. International Convention on Civil and Political Rights, art 4, Dec 16, 1966, G.A. Res 2200A (XXI).

12. United Nations, Report of the Secretary-General's Panel of Experts On Accountability in Sri Lanka (Mar. 31, 2011).

13. U.S. Department of Justice, Memorandum for John Rizzo-Interrogation of Al Qaeda Operative, August 1, 2002.

14. Karen Kenny, *U.N. Accountability for its Human Rights Impact: Implementation Through Participation, in* THE U.N., HUMAN RIGHTS, AND POST-CONFLICT SITUATIONS (Nigel D. White & Dirk Klaasen eds., 2005).

15. Makau Mutua, *The Big Idea: Are Human Rights Universal? Or Is the West Imposing Its Philosophy on the Rest of the World,* BOSTON GLOBE, Apr. 29, 2001.

16. John Shattuck, *Dignity and Freedom are for Everyone,* BOSTON GLOBE, Apr. 29, 2001.

17. Rhona K.M. Smith, *The Fate of Minorities-Sixty Years On,* 1 WEB J. CURRENT L. ISSUES (2009).

18. Eric C. Christiansen, *Adjudicating Non-Justiciable Rights: Socio-Economic Rights and the South African Constitutional Court,* 38 COLUM. HUM. RTS. L. REV. 321 (2007).

19. G.A. Res. 64/292, U.N. Doc. A/RES/64/292 (Aug. 2, 2010).

20. Universal Declaration of Human Rights, G.A. Res. 217(III), U.N. Doc. A/RES/217(III), arts. 19–21, 28 (Dec. 10, 1948).

21. U.N. High Commissioner for Human Rights, Twenty-Five Years of the Right to Development: Achievements and Challenges (Feb. 24, 2011).

22. Bibliography of Additional Sources

---

# 1. Universal Declaration of Human Rights
## Table of Contents, 1948

The Universal Declaration of Human Rights is often regarded as the primary instrument in defining international human rights. Excerpted below is the table of contents. The Declaration includes rights that are universally considered fundamental, like the right to life, liberty and personal security, and it includes rights that some argue are not rights at all, like the right to rest and leisure.

*Universal Declaration of Human Rights-Table of Contents*

Article 1: Right to Equality

Article 2: Freedom from Discrimination

Article 3: Right to Life, Liberty, Personal Security

Article 4: Freedom from Slavery

Article 5: Freedom from Torture and Degrading Treatment

Article 6: Right to Recognition as a Person before the Law

Article 7: Right to Equality before the Law

Article 8: Right to Remedy by Competent Tribunal

Article 9: Freedom from Arbitrary Arrest and Exile

Article 10: Right to Fair Public Hearing

Article 11: Right to be Considered Innocent until Proven Guilty

Article 12: Freedom from Interference with Privacy, Family, Home and Correspondence

Article 13: Right to Free Movement in and out of the Country

Article 14: Right to Asylum in other Countries from Persecution

Article 15: Right to a Nationality and Freedom to Change Nationality

Article 16: Right to Marriage and Family

Article 17: Right to Own Property

Article 18: Freedom of Belief and Religion

Article 19: Freedom of Opinion and Information

Article 20: Right of Peaceful Assembly and Association

Article 21: Right to Participate in Government and Free Elections

Article 22: Right to Social Security

Article 23: Right to Desirable Work and Join Trade Unions

Article 24: Right to Rest and Leisure

Article 25: Right to Adequate Living Standard

Article 26: Right to Education

Article 27: Right to Participate in the Cultural Life of the Community

Article 28: Right to a Social Order that Articulates this Document

Article 29: Community Duties Essential to Free and Full Development

Article 30: Freedom from State or Personal Interference in the above Rights

## Authors' Note

International Human Rights Instruments Overview: The following materials describe the legal basis of the global human rights protection system, providing a broad overview of international human rights and relevant treaties.

# 2. Newman and Weisbrodt, International Human Rights
## 1994

### 1. The U.N. and International Human Rights Law

Treaties constitute the primary sources of international human rights law. The United Nations Charter is both the most prominent treaty and contains seminal human rights provisions. Charter Article 103 establishes the primacy of the U.N. Charter: "In the event of a conflict between the obligations of the Members of the United Nations under the present Charter and their obligations under any other international agreement, their obligations under the present Charter shall prevail."

### a. Human Rights under the U.N. Charter

The Charter identifies the promotion and encouragement of respect for human rights as among the principal objectives of the United Nations:

Article 1: The Purposes of the United Nations are: ... To achieve international cooperation in solving international problems of an economic, social, cultural, or humanitarian character, and in promoting and encouraging respect for human rights and for fundamental freedoms for all without distinction as to race, sex, language or religion.

* * *

Articles 55 and 56 of the Charter establish the primary human rights obligations of all 185 U.N. member states:

**Article 55**: With a view to the creation of conditions of stability and well-being which are necessary for peaceful and friendly relations among nations based on respect for the principle of equal rights and self-determination of peoples, the United Nations shall promote:

> a. higher standards of living, full employment, and conditions of economic and social progress and development;

> b. solutions of international economic, social, health, and related problems; and international cultural and educational cooperation; and

> c. universal respect for, and observance of, human rights and fundamental freedoms for all without distinction as to race, sex, language, or religion.

**Article 56**: All members pledge themselves to take joint and separate action in cooperation with the Organization for the achievement of the purposes set forth in Article 55.

### b. International Bill of Human Rights

The United Nations General Assembly defined the human rights obligations of member states in the International Bill of Human Rights, which is comprised of:

- Universal Declaration of Human Rights
- International Covenant on Economic, Social and Cultural Rights
- International Covenant on Civil and Political Rights
- Optional Protocol to the International Covenant on Civil and Political Rights

The Covenant on Civil and Political Rights establishes an international minimum standard of conduct for all participating governments, ensuring the rights of self-determination; legal redress; equality; life; liberty; freedom of movement; fair, public, and speedy trial of criminal charges; privacy; freedom of expression, thought, conscience, and religion; peaceful assembly; freedom of association (including trade union rights); family; and participation in public affairs; but forbidding torture; "cruel, inhuman or degrading treatment or punishment"; slavery; arbitrary arrest; double jeopardy; and imprisonment for debt.

By ratifying the Covenant on Economic, Social and Cultural Rights, a government agrees to take steps for the progressive realization of the following rights to the full extent of its available resources: the right to gain a living by work; to have safe and healthy working conditions; to enjoy trade union rights; to receive social security; to have protection for the family; to possess adequate housing and clothing; to be free from hunger; to receive health care; to obtain free public education; and to participate in cultural life, creative activity, and scientific research. [ … ]

### c. Other U.N. Treaties

The U.N. has further codified and more specifically defined international human rights law in a number of treaties relating to various subjects initially identified by the International Bill of Human Rights. Treaties create legal obligations for those nations that are party to them, but are generally not binding on the international community as a whole. Treaties may, however, create general international law when such agreements are intended for adherence by states generally, are in fact widely accepted, and restate general principles of law.

Once drafted by the United Nations, treaties are adopted by General Assembly and are then opened for ratification or other forms of acceptance by governments, often including those governments not involved in the drafting process. For example, the United States participated in drafting and adopting the International Covenant on Civil and Political Rights, which the U.S. ratified in 1992, albeit with several significant reservations as to its application. The U.S. also participated in drafting and adopting, but has only signed and has not yet ratified the International Covenant on Economic, Social and Cultural Rights.

Aside from the Charter and the International Bill of Human Rights, the most significant U.N. treaties that have received enough ratifications or accessions to enter into force include (in order of their date of entry into force):

- Convention on the Prevention and Punishment of the Crime of Genocide
- Convention relating to the Status of Refugees
- Protocol relating to the Status of Refugees
- International Convention on the Elimination of All Forms of Racial Discrimination
- Convention on the Elimination of All Forms of Discrimination Against Women
- Convention Against Torture and Other Cruel, Inhuman or Degrading Treatment or Punishment
- Convention on the Rights of the Child
- Second Optional Protocol to the International Covenant on Civil and Political Rights, aiming at the abolition of the death penalty
- International Convention on the Protection of the Rights of All Migrant Workers and Their Families-entered into force in 2003
- International Convention for the Protection of all Persons from Enforced Disappearance-entered into force December 2010
- Convention on the Rights of Persons with Disabilities-entered into force 2008

Treaties so drafted are interpreted as international legislation. The most authoritative collection of rules concerning the interpretation of treaties is the Vienna Convention on the Law of Treaties. The principal sources of interpretation include the terms of the treaty, agreements or instruments made in connection with conclusion of the treaty, subsequent agreements between the parties, subsequent practice in the application of the treaty, relevant rules of international law applicable to relations between the parties, and any special meaning intended by the parties. Article 32 of the Vienna Convention provides that supplementary means of interpretation include preparatory work (traveaux preparatoires), which is similar to legislative history for statutes.

Pursuant to nine of the principal human rights treaties, committees have been established to provide authoritative interpretive materials. Those nine treaty bodies are the Human Rights Committee (under the Civil and Political Covenant); the Committee on Economic, Social and Cultural Rights; the Committee on the Elimination of Racial Discrimination; the Committee on the Elimination of Discrimination Against Women; the Committee Against Torture and Optional Protocol to the Convention Against Torture; the Committee on the Rights of the Child, the Committee on Migrant Workers, the Committee on the Rights of Persons with Disabilities, the Committee on Enforced Disappearance. The nine treaty bodies regularly review reports by States parties as to their compliance with the respective treaties and most issue general comments and recommendations that reflect their experience in reviewing the States reports and thus provide authoritative interpretations of the treaty provisions. The treaty bodies also issue conclusions as to each State report that provide useful interpretive indications. Further, three of the treaty bodies—the Human Rights Committee, the Committee on the Elimination of Racial Discrimination, and the Committee Against Torture—may receive communications complaining about violations of those treaties and thus issue adjudicative decisions interpreting and applying treaty provisions.

### d. Related U.N. Instruments

In addition to treaties, the United Nations has promulgated dozens of declarations, codes, rules, guidelines, principles, resolutions, and other instruments that interpret the general human rights obligations of member states under Articles 55 and 56 of the U.N. Charter and may reflect customary international law. The Universal Declaration of Human Rights is the most prominent of those human rights instruments, which not only provides an authoritative, comprehensive, and nearly contemporaneous interpretation of the human rights obligations under the U.N. Charter, but also has provisions which have been recognized as reflective of customary international law. Among the other prominent human rights instruments are:

- Standard Minimum Rules for the Treatment of Prisoners
- Declaration on the Rights of Disabled Persons
- Code of Conduct for Law Enforcement Officials
- Declaration on the Right to Development
- Body of Principles for the Protection of All Persons under Any Form of Detention or Imprisonment
- Principles on the Effective Prevention and Investigation of Extralegal, Arbitrary and Summary Executions
- Declaration on the Protection of All Persons from Enforced Disappearances
- Declaration on the Rights of Persons Belonging to National or Ethnic, Religious or Linguistic Minorities
- Declaration on the Elimination of Violence Against Women
- Beijing Declaration and Platform of Action

### 2. Other Worldwide Treaties and Instruments

The United Nations is not the only global organization which has issued or facilitated the issuance of worldwide human rights standards. Others include U.N. specialized agencies (such as the International Labor Organization (ILO) and the U.N. Educational, Scientific, and Cultural Organization (UNESCO)) as well as the International Committee of the Red Cross.

As the oldest intergovernmental organization, the International Labor Organization (ILO) has promulgated 183 recommendations and 176 conventions, including several treaties relating to human rights. For example, the ILO has promulgated the following treaties:

- Convention concerning Forced or Compulsory Labor (ILO No. 29)
- Convention concerning Freedom of Association and Protection of the Right to Organize (ILO No. 87)
- Convention concerning the Application of the Principles of the Right to Organize and to Bargain Collectively (ILO No. 98)

- Convention concerning Equal Remuneration for Men and Women Workers for Work of Equal Value (ILO No. 100)
- Abolition of Forced Labor Convention (ILO No. 105)
- Discrimination (Employment and Occupation) Convention (ILO No. 111)
- Convention concerning the Promotion of Collective Bargaining (ILO No. 154)
- Forced Labor Convention (ILO No. 155)
- Convention concerning Indigenous and Tribal Peoples in Independent Countries (ILO No. 169)

Those treaties are principally interpreted by the ILO's Committee on Freedom of Association, which adjudicates complaints by trade unions that their rights have been infringed, and the ILO Committee of Experts, which reviews periodic states reports under the ILO standard-setting treaties.

The U.N. Educational, Scientific and Cultural Organization (UNESCO) has promulgated several treaties related to human rights, for example, the Convention against Discrimination in Education.

The International Committee of the Red Cross has since the mid-19th century convened governmental conferences to draft treaties protecting soldiers and sailors wounded in armed conflict, prisoners of war, and civilians in times of war. These treaties constitute the core of international humanitarian law which is designed to limit human rights violations during periods of international and non-international armed conflict. In the context of armed conflicts, international humanitarian law provides a stronger and far more detailed basis for the protection of human rights than the International Bill of Human Rights and other U.N. human rights instruments.

The principal multilateral treaties that legislate international humanitarian law—the four Geneva Conventions of 1949—have been ratified by more governments than other human rights treaties aside from the U.N. Charter and the Convention on the Rights of the Child. The four Geneva Conventions are:

- Geneva Convention for the Amelioration of the Condition of the Wounded and Sick in Armed Forces in the Field
- Geneva Convention for the Amelioration of the Condition of Wounded, Sick and Shipwrecked Members of Armed Forces at Sea
- Geneva Convention Relative to the Treatment of Prisoners of War
- Geneva Convention Relative to the Protection of Civilian Persons in Time of War
- The two Geneva Protocols of 1977 extend and make more specific the protections of the 1949 Geneva Conventions to international and non-international armed conflicts:
- Protocol Additional to the Geneva Conventions of 12 August 1949 Relating to the Protection of Victims of International Armed Conflicts (Protocol I)
- Protocol Additional to the Geneva Conventions of 12 August 1949, and Relating to the Protection of Victims of Non-International Armed Conflicts (Protocol II)

Many provisions of the four Geneva Conventions, the two Protocols, and the Hague Conventions of 1899 and 1907 are broadly accepted as restating customary international humanitarian law applicable to all countries. Humanitarian law applies specifically to emergency situations; international human rights law permits significant derogations during these same periods.

Since there are inconsistencies and gaps between the protections afforded by various human rights and humanitarian law instruments, as well as by national and local laws, the individual should be entitled to the most protective provisions of applicable international, national, or local laws. Accordingly, if humanitarian law affords better rights protections than human rights law, humanitarian law should be applied—and vice versa. [ … ]

### 3. Customary International Law

International custom is a source of international law where it is evidence of a general practice accepted as law. Only widespread, rather than unanimous, acquiescence is needed, and acquiescence may occur in a short period of time. Often there is disagreement as to precisely when a rule has ripened into a norm, but consensus that a norm in fact has evolved does emerge. For example, the U.S. Court of Appeals in *Filartiga v. Pena-Irala*, determined that the right to be free from torture had become customary international law.

Governmental practice in negotiating and approving international instruments has been accorded an increasingly important role in the development of customary law. In the human rights field widespread acceptance of treaties, declarations, resolutions, and other instruments arguably has become more significant than actual practice in creating binding law. Authority for that development seems to adhere in Article 38(1)(c) of the International Court's Statute, which directs the Court to apply "the general principles of law recognized by civilized nations."

A customary norm binds all governments, including those that have not recognized the norm, so long as they have not expressly and persistently objected to its development. The Restatement of the Foreign Relations Law of the United States lists several 77 prohibitions as giving rise to customary international law: (a) genocide; (b) slavery or slave trade; (c) the murder or causing the disappearance of individuals; (d) torture or other cruel, inhuman or degrading treatment or punishment; (e) prolonged arbitrary detention; (f) systematic racial discrimination; or (g) consistent patterns of gross violations of internationally recognized human rights.

A *jus cogens* norm is a peremptory rule of international law that prevails over any conflicting international rule or agreement. A *jus cogens* norm permits no derogation, and can be modified only by a subsequent international law norm of the same character.

The concept of *jus cogens* is of relatively recent origin, although it is incorporated in the Vienna Convention on the Law of Treaties. Its content is disputed, and thus far, only the U.N. Charter's principles prohibiting the use of force are generally agreed to be *jus cogens*. The International Court of Justice appeared to find that a peremptory norm of international law establishes the inviolability of envoys and embassies in its judgment concerning Iranian treatment of the U.S. diplomatic and consular staff in Tehran. Commentators have suggested that prohibitions against genocide, slavery, racial discrimination, and other gross human rights violations also have acquired *jus cogens* status.

* * *

## *Authors' Note*

Since the Newman and Weisbrodt article was published, three new conventions and two Optional Protocols entered into force, along with the respective enforcement bodies: International Convention for the Protection of the Rights of All Migrant Workers and Their Families (2003); International Convention for the Protection of All Persons from Enforced Disappearance (2010); Convention on the Rights of Persons with Disabilities (2008); Optional Protocol to the Convention Against Torture (2002); Optional Protocol to the

Covenant on Economic, Social, and Cultural Rights (2008). A complete list of the U.N. human rights documents can be found online.

---

### 3. General Comment No. 28, Article 3, The Equality of Rights Between Men and Women
Human Rights Committee, 2000

\* \* \*

3. The obligation to ensure to all individuals the rights recognized in the Covenant, established in articles 2 and 3 of the Covenant, requires that State parties take all necessary steps to enable every person to enjoy those rights. These steps include the removal of obstacles to the equal enjoyment each of such rights, the education of the population and of state officials in human rights and the adjustment of domestic legislation so as to give effect to the undertakings set forth in the Covenant. The State party must not only adopt measures of protection but also positive measures in all areas so as to achieve the effective and equal empowerment of women. States parties must provide information regarding the actual role of women in society so that the Committee may ascertain what measures, in addition to legislative provisions, have been or should be taken to give effect to these obligations, what progress has been made, what difficulties are encountered and what steps are being taken to overcome them.

4. State parties are responsible for ensuring the equal enjoyment of rights without any discrimination. Articles 2 and 3 mandate States parties to take all steps necessary, including the prohibition of discrimination on the ground of sex, to put an end to discriminatory actions both in the public and the private sector which impair the equal enjoyment of rights.

5. Inequality in the enjoyment of rights by women throughout the world is deeply embedded in tradition, history and culture, including religious attitudes. The subordinate role of women in some countries is illustrated by the high incidence of prenatal sex selection and abortion of female fetuses. States parties should ensure that traditional, historical, religious or cultural attitudes are not used to justify violations of women's right to equality before the law and to equal enjoyment of all Covenant rights. States parties should furnish appropriate information on those aspects of tradition, history, cultural practices and religious attitudes which jeopardize, or may jeopardize, compliance with article 3, and indicate what measures they have taken or intend to take to overcome such factors.

\* \* \*

13. States parties should provide information on any specific regulation of clothing to be worn by women in public. The Committee stresses that such regulations may involve a violation of a number of rights guaranteed by the Covenant, such as: article 26, on non-discrimination; article 7, if corporal punishment is imposed in order to enforce such a regulation; article 9, when failure to comply with the regulation is punished by arrest; article 12, if liberty of movement is subject to such a constraint; article 17, which guarantees all persons the right to privacy without arbitrary or unlawful interference; articles 18 and 19, when women are subjected to clothing requirements that are not in keeping with their religion or their right of self-expression; and, lastly, article 27, when the clothing requirements conflict with the culture to which the woman can lay a claim.

\* \* \*

28. The obligation of States parties to protect children (article 24) should be carried out equally for boys and girls. States parties should report on measures taken to ensure that

girls are treated equally to boys in education, in feeding and in health care, and provide the Committee with disaggregated data in this respect. States parties should eradicate, both through legislation and any other appropriate measures, all cultural or religious practices which jeopardize the freedom and well being of female children.

* * *

31. [ ... ] The Committee has also often observed in reviewing States parties' reports that a large proportion of women are employed in areas which are not protected by labor laws and that prevailing customs and traditions discriminate against women, particularly with regard to access to better paid employment and to equal pay for work of equal value. States parties should review their legislation and practices and take the lead in implementing all measures necessary to eliminate discrimination against women in all fields, for example by prohibiting discrimination by private actors in areas such as employment, education, political activities and the provision of accommodation, goods and services. States parties should report on all these measures and provide information on the remedies available to victims of such discrimination.

32. The rights which persons belonging to minorities enjoy under article 27 of the Covenant in respect of their language, culture and religion do not authorize any State, group or person to violate the right to the equal enjoyment by women of any Covenant rights, including the right to equal protection of the law. States should report on any legislation or administrative practices related to membership in a minority community that might constitute an infringement of the equal rights of women under the Covenant (communication No. 24/1977, *Lovelace v. Canada*, Views adopted July 1981) and on measures taken or envisaged to ensure the equal right of men and women to enjoy all civil and political rights in the Covenant. Likewise, States should report on measures taken to discharge their responsibilities in relation to cultural or religious practices within minority communities that affect the rights of women. In their reports, States parties should pay attention to the contribution made by women to the cultural life of their communities.

## *Authors' Note*

Regional Human Rights Instruments: This section contains descriptions of and selected excerpts from regional human rights instruments: the European Union Charter of Fundamental Rights, the European Convention of Human Rights, the American Convention of Human Rights, the African Charter on Human and People's Rights, the Association of Southeast Asian Nations (ASEAN) Charter, and the Arab Charter on Human Rights. Because the EU Charter has a supranational aspect, an explanatory paragraph from the European Union is provided. For the remaining charters, excerpts from the preambles and/or explanatory articles are included in order to provide insight into how different regions conceptualize and formulate human rights. Every regional human rights instrument provides a framework to protect rights, but each does so in a slightly different manner.

European Union Charter of Fundamental Rights: In June 1999, the Cologne European Council concluded that the fundamental rights applicable at the European Union (EU) level should be consolidated in a charter to give them greater visibility. The heads of state/government aspired to include in the charter the general principles set out in the 1950 European Convention on Human Rights and those derived from the constitutional traditions common to EU countries. In addition, the charter was to include the fundamental rights that apply to EU citizens, as well as the economic and social rights contained in the Council of Europe Social Charter and the Community Charter of Fundamental

Social Rights of Workers. The charter would also reflect the principles derived from the case law of the Court of Justice and the European Court of Human Rights. The charter was drawn up by a convention consisting of a representative from each EU country and the European Commission, as well as members of the European Parliament and national parliaments. The charter was formally proclaimed in Nice in December 2000 by the European Parliament, Council and Commission. In December 2009, with the entry into force of the Lisbon Treaty, the charter was given binding legal effect equal to the Treaties. To this end, the charter was amended and proclaimed a second time in December 2007.

The charter brings together in a single document rights previously found in a variety of legislative instruments, such as in national and EU laws, as well as in international conventions from the Council of Europe, the United Nations (U.N.) and the International Labor Organization (ILO). By making fundamental rights clearer and more visible, the charter creates in the EU legal certainty concerning human rights.

---

## 4. European Convention on Human Rights and Fundamental Freedoms
### 1969

The governments signatory hereto, being members of the Council of Europe,

Considering the Universal Declaration of Human Rights proclaimed by the General Assembly of the United Nations on 10th December 1948;

Considering that this Declaration aims at securing the universal and effective recognition and observance of the Rights therein declared;

Considering that the aim of the Council of Europe is the achievement of greater unity between its members and that one of the methods by which that aim is to be pursued is the maintenance and further realization of human rights and fundamental freedoms;

Reaffirming their profound belief in those fundamental freedoms which are the foundation of justice and peace in the world and are best maintained on the one hand by an effective political democracy and on the other by a common understanding and observance of the human rights upon which they depend;

Being resolved, as the governments of European countries which are like-minded and have a common heritage of political traditions, ideals, freedom and the rule of law, to take the first steps for the collective enforcement of certain of the rights stated in the Universal Declaration.

\* \* \*

---

## 5. American Convention on Human Rights
### 1969

**Preamble**

The American states signatory to the present Convention,

*Reaffirming* their intention to consolidate in this hemisphere, within the framework of democratic institutions, a system of personal liberty and social justice based on respect for the essential rights of man;

*Recognizing* that the essential rights of man are not derived from one's being a national of a certain state, but are based upon attributes of the human personality, and that they therefore justify international protection in the form of a convention reinforcing or complementing the protection provided by the domestic law of the American states;

*Considering* that these principles have been set forth in the Charter of the Organization of American States, in the American Declaration of the Rights and Duties of Man, and in the Universal Declaration of Human Rights, and that they have been reaffirmed and refined in other international instruments, worldwide as well as regional in scope;

*Reiterating* that, in accordance with the Universal Declaration of Human Rights, the ideal of free men enjoying freedom from fear and want can be achieved only if conditions are created whereby everyone may enjoy his economic, social, and cultural rights, as well as his civil and political rights; and

*Considering* that the Third Special Inter-American Conference (Buenos Aires, 1967) approved the incorporation into the Charter of the Organization itself of broader standards with respect to economic, social, and educational rights and resolved that an inter-American convention on human rights should determine the structure, competence, and procedure of the organs responsible for these matters.

* * *

## 6. African Charter on Human and Peoples' Rights
### Preamble, June 27, 1981

**Preamble**

The African States members of the Organization of African Unity, parties to the present convention entitled "African Charter on Human and Peoples' Rights",

*Recalling* Decision 115 (XVI) of the Assembly of Heads of State and Government at its Sixteenth Ordinary Session held in Monrovia, Liberia, from 17 to 20 July 1979 on the preparation of a "preliminary draft on an African Charter on Human and Peoples' Rights providing inter alia for the establishment of bodies to promote and protect human and peoples' rights";

*Considering* the Charter of the Organization of African Unity, which stipulates that "freedom, equality, justice and dignity are essential objectives for the achievement of the legitimate aspirations of the African peoples";

*Reaffirming* the pledge they solemnly made in Article 2 of the said Charter to eradicate all forms of colonialism from Africa, to coordinate and intensify their cooperation and efforts to achieve a better life for the peoples of Africa and to promote international cooperation having due regard to the Charter of the United Nations and the Universal Declaration of Human Rights;

*Taking into consideration* the virtues of their historical tradition and the values of African civilization which should inspire and characterize their reflection on the concept of human and peoples' rights;

*Recognizing* on the one hand, that fundamental human rights stem from the attributes of human beings which justifies their national and international protection and on the other hand that the reality and respect of peoples rights should necessarily guarantee human rights;

*Considering* that the enjoyment of rights and freedoms also implies the performance of duties on the part of everyone;

*Convinced* that it is henceforth essential to pay a particular attention to the right to development and that civil and political rights cannot be dissociated from economic, social and cultural rights in their conception as well as universality and that the satisfaction of economic, social and cultural rights is a guarantee for the enjoyment of civil and political rights;

*Conscious* of their duty to achieve the total liberation of Africa, the peoples of which are still struggling for their dignity and genuine independence, and undertaking to eliminate colonialism, neo-colonialism, apartheid, Zionism and to dismantle aggressive foreign military bases and all forms of discrimination, particularly those based on race, ethnic group, color, sex, language, religion or political opinions;

*Reaffirming* their adherence to the principles of human and peoples' rights and freedoms contained in the declarations, conventions and other instrument adopted by the Organization of African Unity, the Movement of Non-Aligned Countries and the United Nations;

*Firmly convinced* of their duty to promote and protect human and people' rights and freedoms taking into account the importance traditionally attached to these rights and freedoms in Africa.

\* \* \*

# 7. Charter of the Association of Southeast Asian Nations (ASEAN)
## 2007

\* \* \*

**Article 1:** (7) To strengthen democracy, enhance good governance and the rule of law, and to promote and protect human rights and fundamental freedoms, with due regard to the rights and responsibilities of the Member States of ASEAN.

\* \* \*

**Article 2:** (2) ASEAN and its Member States shall act in accordance with the following Principles:

\* \* \*

(i) respect for fundamental freedoms, the promotion and protection of human rights, and the promotion of social justice;

(j) upholding the United Nations Charter and international law, including international humanitarian law, subscribed to by ASEAN Member States;

\* \* \*

**Article 14:** (1) In conformity with the purposes and principles of the ASEAN Charter relating to the promotion and protection of human rights and fundamental freedoms, ASEAN shall establish an ASEAN human rights body.

\* \* \*

# 8. Arab Charter on Human Rights
## Council of Arab League States, 1994

\* \* \*

**Part One**

**Article 1**

A. All peoples have the right to self determination and to have control over their wealth and natural resources. By virtue of that right, they have the right to freely determine their political status and to freely pursue their economic, social and cultural development.

B. Racism, Zionism, occupation and foreign control constitute a challenge to human dignity and are a fundamental obstacle to the human rights of peoples. It is a duty to condemn all such practices and to work towards their abolishment.

## Part Two

### Article 2

Each State party to the present Charter undertakes to ensure that every individual located within its territory and subject to its jurisdiction, shall have the right to enjoy all the rights and freedoms recognised in this [Charter], without distinction on the basis of race, colour sex, language, religion, political opinion, national or social origin, wealth, birth or other status, and without any discrimination between men and women.

### Article 3

A. There will be no restriction of any basic human right which is recognised or existent in any State party to this Charter, by virtue of law, treaties or custom. Nor may [these rights] be derogated from under the pretext that they have not been recognised in this Charter, or recognised to a lesser degree.

B. No State party to this Charter shall derogate from the basic freedoms contained in [this Charter] and from which the citizens of another state benefit, which affords those freedoms to a lesser degree.

### Article 4

A. It is prohibited to impose limitations on the rights and freedoms guaranteed by virtue of this Charter unless where prescribed by law and considered necessary to protect national and economic security, or public order, or public health, or morals, or the rights and freedoms of others.

B. State Parties may, in times of public emergencies which threaten the life of the nation, take measures that exonerate them from their obligations in accordance with this Charter to the extent strictly required by the circumstances.

C. The limitations or derogations shall not affect the prohibition from torture and degrading [treatment], the return to [one's] country, political asylum, trial, the prohibition against retrial of the same act, and the principle of the legality of the crime and punishment.

### Article 5

Everyone has the right to life, liberty, and security of person; these rights are protected by law.

### Article 6

There can be no crime, or punishment, except for what is stipulated in law. Nor can there be any punishment for any acts committed previous to the enactment of that law. The accused benefits from a subsequent law, if it is in his interest.

### Article 7

The accused is presumed innocent until proven guilty in a lawful trial where defence rights are guaranteed.

### Article 8

Every person has the right to liberty and security of person. No one shall be subjected to arrest or detention or stopped without legal basis and must be brought before the judiciary without delay.

## Article 9

Everyone is equal before the judiciary, and the right to judicial recourse is guaranteed for every person, on the territory of a State.

## Article 10

Sentence of death will be imposed only for the most serious crimes; every individual sentenced to death has the rights to seek pardon or commutation of the sentence.

## Article 11

Under no circumstances may the death sentence be imposed for a political offence.

## Article 12

Sentences of death shall not be carried-out on persons below eighteen years of age, or a pregnant woman, until she gives birth, or a nursing mother, until two years have passed from the date of [her child's] birth.

## Article 13

A. The State parties shall protect every person in their territory from physical or psychological torture, or from cruel, inhuman, degrading treatment. [The State parties] shall take effective measures to prevent such acts; performing or participating in them shall be considered a crime punished by law.

B. No medical or scientific experimentation shall be carried-out on any person without his free consent.

## Article 14

No one shall be imprisoned for proven inability to repay a debt or another civil obligation.

## Article 15

Those punished with deprivation of liberty must be treated humanely.

## Article 16

No person can be tried twice for the same crime. Anyone against whom such a measure is taken has the right to challenge its legality and request his release. Anyone who is the victim of an illegal arrest or detention has the right to compensation.

## Article 17

Private life is sacred, and violation of that sanctity is a crime. Private life includes family privacy, the sanctity of the home, and the secrecy of correspondence and other forms of private communication.

## Article 18

The recognition of a person before the law is a character attached to every person.

## Article 19

The people are the source of authority. Political capacity is a right for every citizen of a legal age to be exercised in accordance with the law.

## Article 20

Everyone residing on the territory of a State shall have freedom of movement and freedom to choose the place of residence in any part of the territory, within the limits of the law.

### Article 21

Citizens shall not be arbitrarily or illegally deprived from leaving any Arab country, including their own, or their residency restricted to a particular place, or forced to live in any area of their country.

### Article 22

No citizen can be expelled from his own country, or deprived of the right to return to it.

### Article 23

Every citizen has the right to seek political asylum in other countries, fleeing persecution. A person who was pursued for a common crime does not benefit from this right. Political refugees shall not be extradited.

### Article 24

No citizen shall be arbitrarily denied of his original nationality, nor denied his right to acquire another nationality without legal basis.

### Article 25

The right to private ownership is guaranteed to every citizen. Under no circumstances shall a citizen be arbitrarily or illegally deprived of all or part of his property.

### Article 26

The freedom of thought, conscience and opinion is guaranteed to everyone.

### Article 27

Persons from all religions have the right to practice their faith. They also have the right to manifest their opinions through worship, practice or teaching without jeopadising the rights of others. No restrictions of the exercise of the freedom of thought, conscience and opinion can be imposed except through what is prescribed by law.

### Article 28

Citizens have the freedom of assembly and association in peaceful manner. No restrictions shall be imposed on either of these two freedoms except when it is necessary for national security, or public safety, or the protection of the rights and freedoms of others.

### Article 29

The State shall ensure the right to form trade unions and the right to strike within the limits prescribed by law.

### Article 30

The State shall ensure every citizen the right to work which guarantees a standard of living that provides the basic life necessities and ensures the rights to a comprehensive social security.

### Article 31

The freedom to choose employment is guaranteed, and forced labour is prohibited. Forced labour does not include compelling a person to carry out work in execution a judicial decision.

### Article 32

The State shall ensure to citizens equal opportunity in employment, and equal pay for work of equal value.

## Article 33

Every citizen has the right to occupy public office in his country.

## Article 34

Eradicating illiteracy is a commitment and an obligation. Education is a right for every citizen. Elementary education is compulsory and free. Secondary and university education shall be accessible to all.

## Article 35

Citizens have the right to live in an intellectual and cultural atmosphere that reveres Arab nationalism and cherishes human rights. Racial, religious and other forms of discrimination are rejected, while international cooperation and world peace are upheld.

## Article 36

Everyone has the right to participate in the cultural life, enjoy literary and artistic production, and be given the chance to advance his artistic thought and creative talent.

## Article 37

Minorities shall not be deprived of their right to enjoy their own culture or follow their own religious teachings.

## Article 38

A. The family is the fundamental unit of society, and enjoys its protection.

B. The State shall ensure special care and protection for the family, mothers, children and the elderly.

## Article 39

The youth has the right to have greater opportunity to develop physical and mental abilities.

* * *

## *Authors' Note*

**Practical Application of Human Rights Principles:** This section provides a perspective on states' practical application of human rights principles. State application of human rights principles often diverges from the theoretical principle. As evidenced in the following materials, states often find exceptions to universal principles of human rights when it best suits their needs. In times of crisis, states seek to narrowly define human rights in order to increase their power to act without "violating" a human right.

There are five materials in this section. Reading 9 is a set of principles, agreed upon by the international community, that elaborate each basis for derogating from the ICCPR, revealing that states are limited in their capacity to derogate from treaty obligations. Reading 10 is the Human Rights Committee's general comment on the ICCPR's Article 4, which sets rules for states that declare a state of emergency, by placing limits on emergency powers to ensure that the protection of national needs is balanced with the protection of individual human rights. These principles should be kept in mind when analyzing Materials 12 and 13, which describe violations undertaken by states fighting asymmetrical wars. Material 12 contains excerpts from the recently released U.N. report on Sri Lanka's actions during the civil war. Material 13 in an excerpt from a Bush Administration legal memo concerning treatment of detainees. Finally, Reading 13 analyzes the United Nations and accountability for human rights abuses committed by its own staff.

## 9. Siracusa Principles on the Limitation and Derogation of Provisions in the International Covenant on Civil and Political Rights

United Nations Economic and Social Council, U.N. Sub-Commission on Prevention of Discrimination and Protection of Minorities, 1985

\* \* \*

### Part I. The Limitation Clauses in the Covenant

A. <u>General Interpretative Principles Relating to the Justification of Limitations</u>

1. No limitations or grounds for applying them to rights guaranteed by the Covenant are permitted other than those contained in the terms of the Covenant itself.

2. The scope of a limitation referred to in the Covenant shall not be interpreted so as to jeopardize the essence of the right concerned.

3. All limitation clauses shall be interpreted strictly and in favor of the rights at issue.

4. All limitations shall be interpreted in the light and context of the particular right concerned.

5. All limitations on a right recognized by the Covenant shall be provided for by law and be compatible with the objects and purposes of the Covenant.

6. No limitation referred to in the Covenant shall be applied for any purpose other than that for which it has been prescribed.

7. No limitation shall be applied in an arbitrary manner.

8. Every limitation imposed shall be subject to the possibility of challenge to and remedy against its abusive application.

9. No limitation on a right recognized by the Covenant shall discriminate contrary to Article 2, paragraph 1.

10. Whenever a limitation is required in the terms of the Covenant to be "necessary," this term implies that the limitation:

   (a) Is based on one of the grounds justifying limitations recognized by the relevant article of the Covenant,

   (b) Responds to a pressing public or social need,

   (c) Pursues a legitimate aim, and

   (d) Is proportionate to that aim.

Any assessment as to the necessity of a limitation shall be made on objective considerations.

11. In applying a limitation, a State shall use no more restrictive means than are required for the achievement of the purpose of the limitation.

12. The burden of justifying a limitation upon a right guaranteed under the Covenant lies with the State.

13. The requirement expressed in Article 12 of the Covenant, that any restrictions be consistent with other rights recognized in the Covenant, is implicit in limitations to the other rights recognized in the Covenant.

14. The limitation clauses of the Covenant shall not be interpreted to restrict the exercise of any human rights protected to a greater extent by other international obligations binding upon the State.

## B. Interpretative Principles Relating to Specific Limitation Clauses

### *"Prescribed by law"*

15. No limitation on the exercise of human rights shall be made unless provided for by national law of general application which is consistent with the Covenant and is in force at the time the limitation is applied.

16. Laws imposing limitations on the exercise of human rights shall not be arbitrary or unreasonable.

17. Legal rules limiting the exercise of human rights shall be clear and accessible to everyone.

18. Adequate safeguards and effective remedies shall be provided by law against illegal or abusive imposition or application of limitations on human rights.

### *"In a democratic society"*

19. The expression "in a democratic society" shall be interpreted as imposing a further restriction on the limitation clauses it qualifies.

20. The burden is upon a State imposing limitations so qualified to demonstrate that the limitations do not impair the democratic functioning of the society.

21. While there is no single model of a democratic society, a society which recognizes and respects the human rights set forth in the Charter of the United Nations and the Universal Declaration of Human Rights may be viewed as meeting this definition.

### *"Public order (ordre public)"*

22. The expression "public order (*ordre public*)" as used in the Covenant may be defined as the sum of rules which ensure the functioning of society or the set of fundamental principles on which society is founded. Respect for human rights is part of public order (*ordre public*).

23. Public order (*ordre public*) shall be interpreted in the context of the purpose of the particular human right which is limited on this ground.

24. State organs or agents responsible for the maintenance of public order (*ordre public*) shall be subject to controls in the exercise of their power through the parliament, courts, or other competent independent bodies.

### *"Public health"*

25. Public health may be invoked as a ground for limiting certain rights in order to allow a State to take measures dealing with a serious threat to the health of the population or individual members of the population. These measures must be specifically aimed at preventing disease or injury or providing care for the sick and injured.

26. Due regard shall be had to the International Health Regulations of the World Health Organization.

### *"Public morals"*

27. Since public morality varies over time and from one culture to another, a state which invokes public morality as a ground for restricting human rights, while enjoying a certain margin of discretion, shall demonstrate that the limitation in question is essential to the maintenance of respect for fundamental values of the community.

28. The margin of discretion left to States does not apply to the rule of non-discrimination as defined in the Covenant.

*"National security"*

29. National security may be invoked to justify measures limiting certain rights only when they are taken to protect the existence of the nation or its territorial integrity or political independence against force or threat of force.

30. National security cannot be invoked as a reason for imposing limitations to prevent merely local or relatively isolated threats to law and order.

31. National security cannot be used as a pretext for imposing vague or arbitrary limitations and may only be invoked when there exists adequate safeguards and effective remedies against abuse.

32. The systematic violation of human rights undermines true national security and may jeopardize international peace and security. A State responsible for such violation shall not invoke national security as a justification for measures aimed at suppressing opposition to such violation or at perpetrating repressive practices against its population.

*"Public safety"*

33. Public safety means protection against danger to the safety of persons, to their life or physical integrity, or serious damage to their property.

34. The need to protect public safety can justify limitations provided by law. It cannot be used for imposing vague or arbitrary limitations and may only be invoked when there exist adequate safeguards and effective remedies against abuse.

*"Rights and freedoms of others" or the "Rights or reputations of others"*

35. The scope of the rights and freedoms of others that may act as a limitation upon rights in the Covenant extends beyond the rights and freedoms recognized in the Covenant.

36. When a conflict exists between a right protected in the Covenant and one which is not, recognition and consideration should be given to the fact that the Covenant seeks to protect the most fundamental rights and freedoms. In this context especial weight should be afforded to the rights from which no derogation may be made under article 4 of the Covenant.

37. A limitation to a human right based upon the reputation of others shall not be used to protect the state and its officials from public opinion or criticism.

*"Restrictions on public trial"*

38. All trials shall be public unless the Court determines in accordance with law that:

The press or the public should be excluded from all or part of a trial on the basis of specific findings announced in open court showing that the interest of the private lives of the parties or their families or of juveniles so requires; or

The exclusion is strictly necessary to avoid publicity (a) prejudicial to the fairness of the trial or (b) endangering public morals, public order (*ordre public*), or national security in a democratic society.

\* \* \*

# 10. General Comment 29, States of Emergency Article 4
United Nations Human Rights Committee, 2001

1. Article 4 of the Covenant is of paramount importance for the system of protection for human rights under the Covenant. On the one hand, it allows for a State party unilater-

ally to derogate temporarily from a part of its obligations under the Covenant. On the other hand, article 4 subjects both this very measure of derogation, as well as its material consequences, to a specific regime of safeguards. The restoration of a state of normalcy where full respect for the Covenant can again be secured must be the predominant objective of a State party derogating from the Covenant. In this general comment, replacing its General Comment No 5, adopted at the thirteenth session (1981), the Committee seeks to assist States parties to meet the requirements of article 4.

2. Measures derogating from the provisions of the Covenant must be of an exceptional and temporary nature. Before a State moves to invoke article 4, two fundamental conditions must be met: the situation must amount to a public emergency which threatens the life of the nation, and the State party must have officially proclaimed a state of emergency. The latter requirement is essential for the maintenance of the principles of legality and rule of law at times when they are most needed. When proclaiming a state of emergency with consequences that could entail derogation from any provision of the Covenant, States must act within their constitutional and other provisions of law that govern such proclamation and the exercise of emergency powers; it is the task of the Committee to monitor the laws in question with respect to whether they enable and secure compliance with article 4. In order that the Committee can perform its task, States parties to the Covenant should include in their reports submitted under article 40 sufficient and precise information about their law and practice in the field of emergency powers.

* * *

5. The issues of when rights can be derogated from, and to what extent, cannot be separated from the provision in article 4, paragraph 1, of the Covenant according to which any measures derogating from a State party's obligations under the Covenant must be limited "to the extent strictly required by the exigencies of the situation". This condition requires that States parties provide careful justification not only for their decision to proclaim a state of emergency but also for any specific measures based on such a proclamation. If States purport to invoke the right to derogate from the Covenant during, for instance, a natural catastrophe, a mass demonstration including instances of violence, or a major industrial accident, they must be able to justify not only that such a situation constitutes a threat to the life of the nation, but also that all their measures derogating from the Covenant are strictly required by the exigencies of the situation. In the opinion of the Committee, the possibility of restricting certain Covenant rights under the terms of, for instance, freedom of movement (article 12) or freedom of assembly (article 21) is generally sufficient during such situations and no derogation from the provisions in question would be justified by the exigencies of the situation.

* * *

7. Article 4, paragraph 2, of the Covenant explicitly prescribes that no derogation from the following articles may be made: article 6 (right to life), article 7 (prohibition of torture or cruel, inhuman or degrading punishment, or of medical or scientific experimentation without consent), article 8, paragraphs 1 and 2 (prohibition of slavery, slave-trade and servitude), article 11 (prohibition of imprisonment because of inability to fulfill a contractual obligation), article 15 (the principle of legality in the field of criminal law, i.e. the requirement of both criminal liability and punishment being limited to clear and precise provisions in the law that was in place and applicable at the time the act or omission took place, except in cases where a later law imposes a lighter penalty), article 16 (the recognition of everyone as a person before the law), and article 18 (freedom of thought, conscience and religion). The rights enshrined in these provisions are non-

derogable by the very fact that they are listed in article 4, paragraph 2. The same applies, in relation to States that are parties to the Second Optional Protocol to the Covenant, aiming at the abolition of the death penalty, as prescribed in article 6 of that Protocol. Conceptually, the qualification of a Covenant provision as a non-derogable one does not mean that no limitations or restrictions would ever be justified. The reference in article 4, paragraph 2, to article 18, a provision that includes a specific clause on restrictions in its paragraph 3, demonstrates that the permissibility of restrictions is independent of the issue of derogability. Even in times of most serious public emergencies, States that interfere with the freedom to manifest one's religion or belief must justify their actions by referring to the requirements specified in article 18, paragraph 3. On several occasions the Committee has expressed its concern about rights that are non-derogable according to article 4, paragraph 2, being either derogated from or under a risk of derogation owing to inadequacies in the legal regime of the State party.

8. According to article 4, paragraph 1, one of the conditions for the justifiability of any derogation from the Covenant is that the measures taken do not involve discrimination solely on the ground of race, color, sex, language, religion or social origin. Even though article 26 or the other Covenant provisions related to non-discrimination (articles 2, 3, 14, paragraph 1, 23, paragraph 4, 24, paragraph 1, and 25) have not been listed among the non-derogable provisions in article 4, paragraph 2, there are elements or dimensions of the right to non-discrimination that cannot be derogated from in any circumstances. In particular, this provision of article 4, paragraph 1, must be complied with if any distinctions between persons are made when resorting to measures that derogate from the Covenant.

9. Furthermore, article 4, paragraph 1, requires that no measure derogating from the provisions of the Covenant may be inconsistent with the State party's other obligations under international law, particularly the rules of international humanitarian law. Article 4 of the Covenant cannot be read as justification for derogation from the Covenant if such derogation would entail a breach of the State's other international obligations, whether based on treaty or general international law. This is reflected also in article 5, paragraph 2, of the Covenant according to which there shall be no restriction upon or derogation from any fundamental rights recognized in other instruments on the pretext that the Covenant does not recognize such rights or that it recognizes them to a lesser extent.

* * *

12. In assessing the scope of legitimate derogation from the Covenant, one criterion can be found in the definition of certain human rights violations as crimes against humanity. If action conducted under the authority of a State constitutes a basis for individual criminal responsibility for a crime against humanity by the persons involved in that action, article 4 of the Covenant cannot be used as justification that a state of emergency exempted the State in question from its responsibility in relation to the same conduct. Therefore, the recent codification of crimes against humanity, for jurisdictional purposes, in the Rome Statute of the International Criminal Court is of relevance in the interpretation of article 4 of the Covenant.

13. In those provisions of the Covenant that are not listed in article 4, paragraph 2, there are elements that in the Committee's opinion cannot be made subject to lawful derogation under article 4. Some illustrative examples are presented below.

   (a) All persons deprived of their liberty shall be treated with humanity and with respect for the inherent dignity of the human person. Although this right, prescribed in article 10 of the Covenant, is not separately mentioned in the list of non-derogable rights in article 4, paragraph 2, the Committee believes that here the Covenant expresses a norm of general international law not subject to derogation. This is supported by the reference to the inherent dignity of the human person in the preamble to the Covenant and by the close connection between articles 7 and 10.

(b) The prohibitions against taking of hostages, abductions or unacknowledged detention are not subject to derogation. The absolute nature of these prohibitions, even in times of emergency, is justified by their status as norms of general international law.

(c) The Committee is of the opinion that the international protection of the rights of persons belonging to minorities includes elements that must be respected in all circumstances. This is reflected in the prohibition against genocide in international law, in the inclusion of a non-discrimination clause in article 4 itself (paragraph 1), as well as in the non-derogable nature of article 18.

(d) As confirmed by the Rome Statute of the International Criminal Court, deportation or forcible transfer of population without grounds permitted under international law, in the form of forced displacement by expulsion or other coercive means from the area in which the persons concerned are lawfully present, constitutes a crime against humanity. The legitimate right to derogate from article 12 of the Covenant during a state of emergency can never be accepted as justifying such measures.

(e) No declaration of a state of emergency made pursuant to article 4, paragraph 1, may be invoked as justification for a State party to engage itself, contrary to article 20, in propaganda for war, or in advocacy of national, racial or religious hatred that would constitute incitement to discrimination, hostility or violence.

14. Article 2, paragraph 3, of the Covenant requires a State party to the Covenant to provide remedies for any violation of the provisions of the Covenant. This clause is not mentioned in the list of non-derogable provisions in article 4, paragraph 2, but it constitutes a treaty obligation inherent in the Covenant as a whole. Even if a State party, during a state of emergency, and to the extent that such measures are strictly required by the exigencies of the situation, may introduce adjustments to the practical functioning of its procedures governing judicial or other remedies, the State party must comply with the fundamental obligation, under article 2, paragraph 3, of the Covenant to provide a remedy that is effective.

15. It is inherent in the protection of rights explicitly recognized as non-derogable in article 4, paragraph 2, that they must be secured by procedural guarantees, including, often, judicial guarantees. The provisions of the Covenant relating to procedural safeguards may never be made subject to measures that would circumvent the protection of non-derogable rights. Article 4 may not be resorted to in a way that would result in derogation from non-derogable rights. Thus, for example, as article 6 of the Covenant is non-derogable in its entirety, any trial leading to the imposition of the death penalty during a state of emergency must conform to the provisions of the Covenant, including all the requirements of articles 14 and 15.

16. Safeguards related to derogation, as embodied in article 4 of the Covenant, are based on the principles of legality and the rule of law inherent in the Covenant as a whole. As certain elements of the right to a fair trial are explicitly guaranteed under international humanitarian law during armed conflict, the Committee finds no justification for derogation from these guarantees during other emergency situations. The Committee is of the opinion that the principles of legality and the rule of law require that fundamental requirements of fair trial must be respected during a state of emergency. Only a court of law

may try and convict a person for a criminal offence. The presumption of innocence must be respected. In order to protect non-derogable rights, the right to take proceedings before a court to enable the court to decide without delay on the lawfulness of detention, must not be diminished by a State party's decision to derogate from the Covenant.

17. In paragraph 3 of article 4, States parties, when they resort to their power of derogation under article 4, commit themselves to a regime of international notification. A State party availing itself of the right of derogation must immediately inform the other States parties, through the United Nations Secretary-General, of the provisions it has derogated from and of the reasons for such measures. Such notification is essential not only for the discharge of the Committee's functions, in particular in assessing whether the measures taken by the State party were strictly required by the exigencies of the situation, but also to permit other States parties to monitor compliance with the provisions of the Covenant. In view of the summary character of many of the notifications received in the past, the Committee emphasizes that the notification by States parties should include full information about the measures taken and a clear explanation of the reasons for them, with full documentation attached regarding their law. Additional notifications are required if the State party subsequently takes further measures under article 4, for instance by extending the duration of a state of emergency. The requirement of immediate notification applies equally in relation to the termination of derogation. These obligations have not always been respected: States parties have failed to notify other States parties, through the Secretary-General, of a proclamation of a state of emergency and of the resulting measures of derogation from one or more provisions of the Covenant, and States parties have sometimes neglected to submit a notification of territorial or other changes in the exercise of their emergency powers. Sometimes, the existence of a state of emergency and the question of whether a State party has derogated from provisions of the Covenant have come to the attention of the Committee only incidentally, in the course of the consideration of a State party's report. The Committee emphasizes the obligation of immediate international notification whenever a State party takes measures derogating from its obligations under the Covenant. The duty of the Committee to monitor the law and practice of a State party for compliance with article 4 does not depend on whether that State party has submitted a notification.

## Authors' Note

**United Nations Human Rights Committee:** The Human Rights Committee is a United Nations group with the mandate to observe the implementation of the International Covenant on Civil and Political Rights (ICCPR). States are obliged to submit to the Committee reports detailing their implementation of ICCPR provisions. Although the principles of international human rights may be simply stated, it is often difficult for states to practically apply those principles.

## 11. International Covenant on Civil and Political Rights, Article 4
### General Assembly Resolution 2200A XXI, 1966

### Article 4

1. In time of public emergency which threatens the life of the nation and the existence of which is officially proclaimed, the States Parties to the present Covenant may take measures derogating from their obligations under the present Covenant to the extent strictly

required by the exigencies of the situation, provided that such measures are not inconsistent with their other obligations under international law and do not involve discrimination solely on the ground of race, color, sex, language, religion or social origin.

2. No derogation from articles 6, 7, 8 (paragraphs I and 2), 11, 15, 16 and 18 may be made under this provision.

3. Any State Party to the present Covenant availing itself of the right of derogation shall immediately inform the other States Parties to the present Covenant, through the intermediary of the Secretary-General of the United Nations, of the provisions from which it has derogated and of the reasons by which it was actuated. A further communication shall be made, through the same intermediary, on the date on which it terminates such derogation.

## 12. Report of the Secretary-General's Panel of Experts on Accountability in Sri Lanka
### United Nations, 2011

### Executive Summary

On 22 June 2010, the Secretary-General announced the appointment of a Panel of Experts to advise him on the implementation of the joint commitment included in the statement issued by the President of Sri Lanka and the Secretary-General at the conclusion of the Secretary-General's visit to Sri Lanka on 23 March 2009. In the Joint Statement, the Secretary-General "underlined the importance of an accountability process", and the Government of Sri Lanka agreed that it "will take measures to address those grievances". The Panel's mandate is to advise the Secretary-General regarding the modalities, applicable international standards and comparative experience relevant to an accountability process, having regard to the nature and scope of alleged violations of international humanitarian and human rights law during the final stages of the armed conflict in Sri Lanka. The Secretary-General appointed as members of the Panel Marzuki Darusman (Indonesia), Chair; Steven Ratner (United States); and Yasmin Sooka (South Africa). The Panel formally commenced its work on 16 September 2010 and was assisted throughout by a secretariat.

### Framework for the Panel's work

In order to understand the accountability obligations arising from the last stages of the war, the Panel undertook an assessment of the "nature and scope of alleged violations" as required by its Terms of Reference. The Panel's mandate however does not extend to fact-finding or investigation. The Panel analyzed information from a variety of sources in order to characterize the extent of the allegations, assess which of the allegations are credible, based on the information at hand, and appraise them legally. The Panel determined an allegation to be credible if there was a reasonable basis to believe that the underlying act or event occurred. This standard gives rise to a legal responsibility for the State or other actors to respond. Allegations are considered as credible in this report only when based on primary sources that the Panel deemed relevant and trustworthy. In its legal assessment, the Panel proceeded from the long-settled premise of international law that during an armed conflict such as that in Sri Lanka, both international humanitarian law and international human rights law are applicable. The Panel applied the rules of international humanitarian and human rights law to the credible allegations involving both of the primary actors in the war, that is, the Liberation Tigers of Tamil Eelam (LTTE) and the Government of Sri Lanka. Neither the publicly expressed aims of each side (combating terrorism, in the case of the Government, and fighting for a separate homeland, in the case of the LTTE), nor the asymmetrical nature of the tactics employed affects the applicability of international humanitarian and human rights law.

Sri Lanka is a party to several human rights treaties which require it to investigate alleged violations of international humanitarian and human rights law and prosecute those responsible; customary international law applicable to the armed conflict also includes such obligations. In addition to underscoring these legal obligations, in providing its advice to the Secretary-General, the Panel has drawn heavily on the international standards expressed in various United Nations documents and views of treaty bodies. These sources express the core understanding that achieving accountability for crimes under international law involves the right to the truth, the right to justice and the right to reparations, including through institutional guarantees of non-recurrence. The Panel has also drawn on the diverse practical approaches, consistent with these standards, which have been developed in numerous other countries that have faced similar challenges for ensuring accountability. The Panel has used this framework as the basis both for assessing the domestic policy, measures and institutions, which are relevant to the approach to accountability taken by the Government of Sri Lanka to date, and for developing its recommendations to the Secretary-General. Finally, in formulating its advice, the Panel has given priority to the rights and needs of the victims who suffered tragic consequences from the actions of both parties in the protracted armed conflict in Sri Lanka; women, children, and the elderly usually bear the brunt of suffering and loss in wars, and the Sri Lankan case is no exception.

Allegations found credible by the Panel:

The Panel's determination of credible allegations reveals a very different version of the final stages of the war than that maintained to this day by the Government of Sri Lanka. The Government says it pursued a "humanitarian rescue operation" with a policy of "zero civilian casualties." In stark contrast, the Panel found credible allegations, which if proven, indicate that a wide range of serious violations of international humanitarian law and international human rights law was committed both by the Government of Sri Lanka and the LTTE, some of which would amount to war crimes and crimes against humanity. Indeed, the conduct of the war represented a grave assault on the entire regime of international law designed to protect individual dignity during both war and peace.

Specifically the Panel found credible allegations associated with the final stages of the war. Between September 2008 and 19 May 2009, the Sri Lanka Army advanced its military campaign into the Vanni using large-scale and widespread shelling, causing large numbers of civilian deaths. This campaign constituted persecution of the population of the Vanni. Around 330,000 civilians were trapped into an ever decreasing area, fleeing the shelling but kept hostage by the LTTE. The Government sought to intimidate and silence the media and other critics of the war through a variety of threats and actions, including the use of white vans to abduct and to make people disappear.

The Government shelled on a large scale in three consecutive No Fire Zones, where it had encouraged the civilian population to concentrate, even after indicating that it would cease the use of heavy weapons. It shelled the United Nations hub, food distribution lines and near the International Committee of the Red Cross (ICRC) ships that were coming to pick up the wounded and their relatives from the beaches. It shelled in spite of its knowledge of the impact, provided by its own intelligence systems and through notification by the United Nations, the ICRC and others. Most civilian casualties in the final phases of the war were caused by Government shelling.

The Government systematically shelled hospitals on the frontlines. All hospitals in Vanni were hit by mortars and artillery, some of them were hit repeatedly, despite the fact that their locations were well-known to the Government. The Government also systematically deprived people in the conflict zone of humanitarian aid, in the form of food and medical supplies, particularly surgical supplies, adding to their suffering. To this end, it purposefully underestimated the number of civilians who remained in the conflict zone. Tens of thousands lost their lives from January to May 2009, many of whom died anonymously in the carnage of the final few days.

The Government subjected victims and survivors of the conflict to further deprivation and suffering after they left the conflict zone. Screening for suspected LTTE took place without any transparency or external scrutiny. Some of those who were separated were summarily executed, and some of the women may have been raped. Others disappeared, as recounted by their wives and relatives during the LLRC hearings. All IDPs were detained in closed camps. Massive overcrowding led to terrible conditions, breaching the basic social and economic rights of the detainees, and many lives were lost unnecessarily. Some persons in the camps were interrogated and subjected to torture. Suspected LTTE were removed to other facilities, with no contact with the outside world, under conditions that made them vulnerable to further abuses.

Despite grave danger in the conflict zone, the LTTE refused civilians permission to leave, using them as hostages, at times even using their presence as a strategic human buffer between themselves and the advancing Sri Lankan Army. It implemented a policy of forced recruitment throughout the war, but in the final stages greatly intensified its recruitment of people of all ages, including children as young as fourteen. The LTTE forced civilians to dig trenches and other emplacements for its own defenses, thereby contributing to blurring the distinction between combatants and civilians and exposing civilians to additional harm. All of this was done in a quest to pursue a war that was clearly lost; many civilians were sacrificed on the altar of the LTTE cause and its efforts to preserve its senior leadership.

From February 2009 onwards, the LTTE started point-blank shooting of civilians who attempted to escape the conflict zone, significantly adding to the death toll in the final stages of the war. It also fired artillery in proximity to large groups of internally displaced persons (IDPs) and fired from, or stored military equipment near, IDPs or civilian installations such as hospitals. Throughout the final stages of the war, the LTTE continued its policy of suicide attacks outside the conflict zone. Even though its ability to perpetrate such attacks was diminished compared to previous phases of the conflict, it perpetrated a number of attacks against civilians outside the conflict zone.

Thus, in conclusion, the Panel found credible allegations that comprise five core categories of potential serious violations committed by the Government of Sri Lanka: (i) killing of civilians through widespread shelling; (ii) shelling of hospitals and humanitarian objects; (iii) denial of humanitarian assistance; (iv) human rights violations suffered by victims and survivors of the conflict, including both IDPs and suspected LTTE cadre; and (v) human rights violations outside the conflict zone, including against the media and other critics of the Government.

The Panel's determination of credible allegations against the LTTE associated with the final stages of the war reveal six core categories of potential serious violations: (i) using civilians as a human buffer; (ii) killing civilians attempting to flee LTTE control; (iii) using military equipment in the proximity of civilians; (iv) forced recruitment of children; (v) forced labor; and (vi) killing of civilians through suicide attacks.

Accountability

Accountability for serious violations of international humanitarian or human rights law is not a matter of choice or policy; it is a duty under domestic and international law. These credibly alleged violations demand a serious investigation and the prosecution of those responsible. If proven, those most responsible, including Sri Lanka Army commanders and senior Government officials, as well as military and civilian LTTE leaders, would bear criminal liability for international crimes.

At the same time, accountability goes beyond the investigation and prosecution of serious crimes that have been committed; rather it is a broad process that addresses the political, legal and moral responsibility of individuals and institutions for past violations of human rights and dignity. Consistent with the international standards mentioned above, accountability necessarily includes the achievement of truth, justice and reparations for victims. Accountability also requires an official acknowledgement by the State of its role and responsibility in violating the rights of its citizens, when that has occurred. In keeping with United Nations policy, the Panel does not advocate a "one-size-fits-all" formula or the importation of foreign models for accountability; rather it recognizes the need for accountability processes to be defined based on national assessments, involving broad citizen participation, needs and aspirations. Nonetheless, any national process must still meet international standards. Sri Lanka's approach to accountability should, thus, be assessed against those standards and comparative experiences to discern how effectively it allows victims of the final stages of the war to realize their rights to truth, justice and reparations.

The Government has stated that it is seeking to balance reconciliation and accountability, with an emphasis on restorative justice. The assertion of a choice between restorative and retributive justice presents a false dichotomy. Both are required. Moreover, in the Panel's view, the Government's notion of restorative justice is flawed because it substitutes a vague notion of the political responsibility of past Government policies and their failure to protect citizens from terrorism for genuine, victim-centered accountability focused on truth, justice and reparations. A further emphasis is clearly on the culpability of certain LTTE cadre; the Government's plan, in this regard, contemplates rehabilitation for the majority and lenient sentences for the "hard core" among surviving LTTE cadre. The Government's two-pronged notion of accountability, as explained to the Panel, focusing on the responsibility of past Governments and of the LTTE, does not envisage a serious examination of the Government's decisions and conduct in prosecuting the final stages of the war or the aftermath, nor of the violations of law that may have occurred as a result.

The Panel has concluded that the Government's notion of accountability is not in accordance with international standards. Unless the Government genuinely addresses the allegations of violations committed by both sides and places the rights and dignity of the victims of the conflict at the centre of its approach to accountability, its measures will fall dramatically short of international expectations.

The Lessons Learnt and Reconciliation Commission

The Government has established the Lessons Learnt and Reconciliation Commission as the cornerstone of its policy to address the past, from the ceasefire agreement in 2002 to the end of the conflict in May 2009. The LLRC represents a potentially useful opportunity to begin a national dialogue on Sri Lanka's conflict; the need for such a dialogue is illustrated by the large numbers of people, particularly victims, who have come forward on their own initiative and sought to speak with the Commission.

Nonetheless, the LLRC fails to satisfy key international standards of independence and impartiality, as it is compromised by its composition and deep-seated conflicts of interests of some of its members. The mandate of the LLRC, as well as its work and methodology to date, are not tailored to investigating allegations of serious violations of international humanitarian and human rights law, or to examining the root causes of the decades-long ethnic conflict; instead these focus strongly on the wider notion of political responsibility mentioned above, which forms part of the flawed and partial concept of accountability put forth by the Government. The work to date demonstrates that the LLRC has: not conducted genuine truth-seeking about what happened in the final stages of the armed conflict; not sought to investigate systematically and impartially the allegations of serious violations on both sides of the war; not employed an approach that treats victims with full respect for their dignity and their suffering; and not provided the necessary protection for witnesses, even in circumstances of actual personal risk.

In sum, the LLRC is deeply flawed, does not meet international standards for an effective accountability mechanism and, therefore, does not and cannot satisfy the joint commitment of the President of Sri Lanka and the Secretary-General to an accountability process.

## Other domestic mechanisms

The justice system should play a leading role in the pursuit of accountability, irrespective of the functioning or outcomes of the LLRC. However, based on a review of the system's past performance and current structure, the Panel has little confidence that it will serve justice in the existing political environment. This is due much more to a lack of political will than to lack of capacity. In particular, the independence of the Attorney-General has been weakened in recent years, as power has been more concentrated in the Presidency. Moreover, the continuing imposition of Emergency Regulations, combined with the Prevention of Terrorism Act in its current form, present a significant obstacle for the judicial system to be able to address official wrongdoing while upholding human rights guarantees. Equally, the Panel has seen no evidence that the military courts system has operated as an effective accountability mechanism in respect of the credible allegations it has identified or other crimes committed in the final stages of the war.

Other domestic institutions that could play a role in achieving accountability also demonstrate serious weaknesses. Over three decades, commissions of inquiry have been established to examine a number of serious human rights issues. While some have served important fact-finding goals, overwhelmingly these commissions have failed to result in comprehensive accountability for the violations identified. Many commissions have failed to produce a public report, and recommendations have rarely been implemented. The Human Rights Commission of Sri Lanka could also potentially contribute to advancing certain aspects of accountability, but the Panel still has some serious reservations and believes that the Commission will need to demonstrate political will and resourcefulness in following up on cases of mission persons and in monitoring the welfare of detained persons.

## Other obstacles to accountability

During the course of its work, the Panel observed that there are several other contemporary issues in Sri Lanka, which if left unaddressed, will deter efforts towards genuine accountability and may undermine prospects for durable peace in consequence. Most notably, these include: (i) triumphalism on the part of the Government, expressed through its discourse on having developed the means and will to defeat "terrorism", thus ending Tamil aspirations for political autonomy and recognition, and its denial regarding the human cost of its military strategy; (ii) on-going exclusionary policies, which are particularly deleterious as political, social and economic exclusion based on ethnicity, perceived or real, have been at the heart of the conflict; (iii) the continuation of wartime measures, including not only the Emergency Regulations and the Prevention of Terrorism Act, mentioned above, but also the continued militarization of the former conflict zone and the use of paramilitary proxies, all of which perpetuate a climate of fear, intimidation and violence; (iv) restrictions on the media, which are contrary to democratic governance and limit basic citizens' rights; and (v) the role of the Tamil Diaspora, which provided vital moral and material support to the LTTE over decades, and some of whom refuse to acknowledge the LTTE's role in the humanitarian disaster in the Vanni, creating a further obstacle to accountability and sustainable peace.

An environment conducive to accountability, which would permit a candid appraisal of the broad patterns of the past, including the root causes of the long-running ethnonationalist conflict, does not exist at present. It would require concrete steps towards building an open society in which human rights are respected, as well as a fundamental shift away from triumphalism and denial towards a genuine commitment to a political solution that recognizes Sri Lanka's ethnic diversity and the full and inclusive citizenship of all of its people, including Tamils, as the foundation for the country's future.

International role in the protection of civilians

During the final stages of the war, the United Nations political organs and bodies failed to take actions that might have protected civilians. Moreover, although senior international officials advocated in public and in private with the Government that it protect civilians and stop the shelling of hospitals and United Nations or ICRC locations, in the Panel's view, the public use of casualty figures would have strengthened the call for the protection of civilians while those events in the Vanni were unfolding. In addition, following the end of the war, the Human Rights Council may have been acting on incomplete information when it passed its May 2009 resolution on Sri Lanka.

\* \* \*

## 13. Memorandum for John Rizzo-Interrogation of Al Qaeda Operative

U.S. Department of Justice Office of Legal Counsel, 2002

You have asked for this Office's views on whether certain proposed conduct would violate the prohibition against torture found at Section 2340A of title 18 of the United States Code. You have asked for this advice in the course of conducting interrogations of Abu Zubaydah. As we understand it, Zubaydah is one of the highest ranking members of the Al Qaeda terrorist organization, with which the United States is currently engaged in an international armed conflict following the attacks on the World Trade Center and the Pentagon on September 11, 2001. This letter memorializes our previous oral advice, given on July 24, 2002 and July 26, 2002, that the proposed conduct would not violate this prohibition.

\* \* \*

As part of this increased pressure phase, Zubaydah will have contact only with a new interrogation specialist, whom he has not met previously, and the Survival, Evasion, Resistance, Escape ("SERE") training psychologist who has been involved in the interrogations since they began. This phase will likely last no more than several days but could last up to thirty days. In this phase, you would like to employ ten techniques that you believe will dislocate his expectations regarding the treatment he believes he will receive and encourage him to disclose the crucial information mentioned above. These techniques are: (1) attention grasp, (2) walling, (3) facial hold, (4) facial slap (insult slap), (5) cramped confinement, (6) wall standing, (7) stress positions, (8) sleep deprivation, (9) insects placed in a confinement box, and (10) the waterboard. You have informed us that the use of these techniques would be on an as-needed basis and that not all of these techniques will necessarily be used. The interrogation team would use these techniques in some combination to convince Zubaydah that the only way he can influence his surrounding environment is through cooperation. You have, however, informed us that you expect these techniques to be used in some sort of escalating fashion, culminating with the waterboard, though not necessarily ending with this technique. Moreover, you have also orally informed us that although some of the techniques may be used more than once, that repetition will not be substantial because the techniques generally lose their effectiveness after several repetitions. [ ... ]

Based on the facts you have given us, we understand each of these techniques to be as follows. The attention grasp consists of grasping the individual with both hands, one hand on each side of the collar opening, in a controlled and quick motion. In the same motion as the grasp, the individual is drawn toward the interrogator.

For walling, a flexible false wall will be constructed. The individual is placed with his heels touching the wall. The interrogator pulls the individual forward and then quickly and firmly pushes the individual into the wall. It is the individual's shoulder blades that hit the wall. During this motion, the head and neck are supported with a rolled hood or towel that provides a c-collar effect to prevent whiplash. To further reduce the probability of injury, the individual is allowed to rebound from the flexible wall. You have orally informed us that the false wall is in part constructed to create a loud sound when the individual hits it, which will further shock or surprise in the individual. In part, the idea is to create a sound that will make the impact seem far worse than it is and that will be far worse than any injury that might result from the action.

The facial hold is used to hold the head immobile. One open palm is placed on either side of the individual's face. The fingertips are kept well away from the individual's eyes.

With the facial slap or insult slap, the interrogator slaps the individual's face with fingers slightly spread. The hand makes contact with the area directly between the tip of the individual's chin and the bottom of the corresponding earlobe. The interrogator invades the individual's personal space. The goal of the facial slap is not to inflict physical pain that is severe or lasting. Instead, the purpose of the facial slap is to induce shock, surprise, and/or humiliation.

Cramped confinement involves the placement of the individual in a confined space, the dimensions of which restrict the individual's movement. The confined space is usually dark. The duration of confinement varies based upon the size of the container. For the larger confined space, the individual can stand up or sit down; the smaller space is large enough for the subject to sit down. Confinement in the larger space can last up to eighteen hours; for the smaller space, confinement lasts for no more than two hours.

Wall standing is used to induce muscle fatigue. The individual stands about four to five feet from a wall, with his feet spread approximately to shoulder width. His arms are stretched out in front of him, with his fingers resting on the wall. His fingers support all of his body weight. The individual is not permitted to move or reposition his hands or feet.

A variety of stress positions may be used. You have informed us that these positions are not designed to produce the pain associated with contortions or twisting of the body. Rather, somewhat like walling, they are designed to produce the physical discomfort associated with muscle fatigue. [ ... ]

Sleep deprivation may be used. You have indicated that your purpose in using this technique is to reduce the individual's ability to think on his feet and, through the discomfort associated with lack of sleep, to motivate him to cooperate. [ ... ]

You would like to place Zubaydah in a cramped confinement box with an insect. You have informed us that he appears to have a fear of insects. In particular, you would like to tell Zubaydah that you intend to place a stinging insect into the box with him. You would, however, place a harmless insect in the box. You have orally informed us that you would in fact place a harmless insect such as a caterpillar in the box with him. [ ... ]

Finally, you would like to use a technique called the "waterboard." In this procedure, the individual is bound securely to an inclined bench, which is approximately four feet by seven feet. The individual's feet are generally elevated. A cloth is placed over the forehead and eyes. Water is then applied to the cloth in a controlled manner. As this is done, the cloth is lowered until it covers both the nose and the mouth. Once the cloth is saturated and completely covers the mouth and nose, air now is slightly restricted for 20 to 40 seconds due to the presence of the cloth. This causes an increase in carbon dioxide level in the individual's blood. This increase in the carbon dioxide level stimulates increased effort to breathe. This effort plus the cloth produces the perception of "suffocation and incipient panic," i.e., the perception of drowning. The individual does not breathe any water into his lungs. During those 20 to 40 seconds, water is continuously applied from a height of twelve to twenty-four inches. After this period, the cloth is lifted, and the individual is allowed to breathe unimpeded for three or four full breaths. The sensation of drowning is immediately relieved by the removal of the cloth. The procedure may then be repeated. The water is usually applied from a canteen cup or small watering can with a spout. You have orally informed us that this procedure triggers an automatic physiological sensation of drowning that the individual cannot control even though he may be aware that he is in fact not drowning. You have also orally informed us that it is likely that this procedure would not last more than 20 minutes in any one application.

We also understand that a medical expert with SERE experience will be present throughout this phase and that the procedures will be stopped if deemed medically necessary to prevent severe mental or physical harm to Zubaydah. [ ... ]

* * *

## 14. Karen Kenny, U.N. Accountability for its Human Rights Impact: Implementation Through Participation

The U.N., Human Rights, and Post-Conflict Situations, 2005

The U.N.'s principal organs include the SC and the GA with a secretariat and a complex tapestry of subsidiary bodies and specialized agencies in varying degrees of consanguinity with the organization. It has offices and programs in more than one hundred and fifty countries and *ad hoc* peace-related field missions, variously comprising military, police and civilian personnel in dozens more. It is under-resourced and its management culture is frequently pared unfavorably with that of the private sector. Its member states place the U.N. under pressure to be seen to be doing something (or not) when good sense would suggest different priorities or timing.

Until recently, the budget of the Secretariat for human rights has been less than 1 per cent of the U.N.'s total budget. Moved in the mid-1980s from New York to Geneva, the Secretariat became more remote from the high seat of policy and political decision-making at U.N. headquarters in New York. But with the end of the Cold War has come increased understanding of human rights and of the roles of international organizations in safeguarding them. While the primary responsibility for ensuring respect for human rights still resides with states, the U.N. itself has come to be seen as having a key role in securing the implementation of human rights, which touch almost all aspects of its own direct work.

The U.N. is one of the subjects of a trend which sees non-state actors as potentially liable for the human rights consequences of their actions. In the case of corporations, the World Bank and IMF are now advocating 'corporate social responsibility' and the U.N. advocates its 'global compact' with business. There is relatively ready acceptance that profit-seeking enterprises are to be held accountable. As yet, however, a different expectation seems at play in the case of the U.N. as an organization—in part, it seems, due to the perception that the organization always intends to 'do good'.

Some might suggest that to regard the U.N. as legally responsible for its impact on the enjoyment of human rights may be contrary to international public policy as it risks stunting work which is overall in the public interest. However, this suggestion becomes less compelling when it is recalled the U.N. actions cover a very broad spectrum of activities and interests. Indeed, it might be likened to confusing *jus in bellum* with *jus ad bello*. In fact, the question is one of general application in human rights law: should generally praiseworthy motivation or a lack of intent to impact negatively on human rights immunize one from legal responsibility? The trend of human rights law suggests that good intentions are not the issue when it comes to human rights—the impact and actual effects of actions are what matter. As it is, states are already potentially subject to international legal responsibility for inadvertent, unintended human rights violations or those resulting from the incompetence of their state agents.

* * *

### The nature of the U.N. obligation: to respect and ensure respect for human rights

Two of the traditional categories of human rights obligations: to respect and to ensure respect, are used here to examine implementation in practice by the U.N. of the law applicable.

It is submitted that the U.N.'s human rights responsibility encompasses the spectrum of decisions, acts or omissions which, on their face, violate international human rights law—the obligation to respect. It also encompasses those actions which have this *effect*—as part of the obligation to ensure respect, at least if negative effect is foreseeable.

Examples of U.N. human rights concerns are mentioned below. This chapter does not elaborate upon examples with a view to determining whether or not actual violations of the law applicable occurred—rather they illustrate the type of issues which arise when considering the implementation of its law applicable by the U.N.. U.N. practitioners, the source of these examples, indicate a vacuum of legal accountability which is a cause of grave concern.

The vacuum extends beyond the decisions of its political organs to the bureaucratic level, with the spectrum of decisions, acts or omissions which, on their face, violate international human rights law, or which have this foreseeable effect.

### The U.N. Obligation to Respect Human Rights

The main focus of public international lawyers in this area has been SC resolutions as part of the spectrum of relevant U.N. decisions, acts or omissions which, on their face, may violate international human rights law. This is illustrated by the recent controversy regarding the series of SC resolutions concerning Iraq and whether they provided sufficient authorization for the use of force or whether a so-called second resolution was needed. In contrast, very little attention is focused on the internal day-to-day decision-making within the U.N. which may violate its applicable law. Illustrative examples follow which relate to U.N. activity from peace building, humanitarian aid and human rights operations.

*Alleged torture; rape; summary, arbitrary or extra-judicial executions by U.N. personnel*

Allegations of torture and executions of Somalis by Belgian, Italian and U.N. troops were made during the term of the 1992–95 intervention Operation Restore Hope. In 1993, the U.N. Special Rapporteur for such executions addressed his urgent letter of concern, as he would to a state, to Admiral Jonathan Howe as the U.N. Force Commander. It sought clarification of the allegations and reassurance that the matter was being independently investigated. A judicial inquiry was instigated in Canada, *inter alia,* regarding the murder of two Somalis by Canadian soldiers and the subsequent cover up. This led to the resignation of the then defense minister as well as his successor. Given the many serious allegations, it is not clear that in Canada or elsewhere the required standard has been met not only with justice being done, but being seen to be done. Similarly, the issue of respect for applicable law arises when U.N. military or police personnel arrest and detain persons. The U.N. Special Rapporteur on Violence against Women, Radhika Coomaraswamy, has also voiced concern over reported increases in the trafficking of women for prostitution in areas where U.N. peacekeepers are stationed. Allegations have also been made regarding the sexual abuse of women survivors of the Rwanda genocide by staff and officers of the ICTR. The Memorandum of Understanding between the Department of Peacekeeping Operations and the Office of the High Commissioner for Human Rights reiterates the understanding that U.N. peacekeeping forces will themselves directly respect the Geneva Conventions.

*Peace agreements—endorsing human rights violations on their face*

In the case of Bosnia-Hervegovina, the U.N. expressly endorsed ethnic discrimination in the Dayton Peace Agreement establishing the post-war order in 1995.

*Humanitarian Action*

In 2000 a study of eight key U.N. 'actors' in humanitarian action was undertaken by this author. Beneficiaries of humanitarian action are rights-holders, no less when life is at risk from lack of food, shelter or medical care than when they are tortured or denied their right to vote. In practice, under pressure of emergencies, rights are often reduced to needs, and public international law is perceived as moot. It needs to be recognized that the application of human rights law involves challenging the prevalent needs-based orthodoxy in humanitarian action. The study also found that the Department of Political Affairs and the DPKO have very limited views of their own human rights roles. Numerous instances are cited in which specific activities in the delivery of aid have been pursued in isolation from a human rights framework. A classical illustration of this arises in negotiating access. In 1999, a delegation of U.N. negotiators led by a senior official (now the U.N. High Commissioner for Human Rights) purported to conclude a U.N.-Afghanistan treaty which, on its face, violated both that state's and the U.N.'s human rights obligations under the Convention on the Rights of the Child and the Convention for the Elimination all Forms of Discrimination Against Women. By the agreement, the U.N. agreed to discriminate against women and girl-children in the provision of humanitarian aid (regarding access to healthcare, employment in local U.N. jobs, etc). Non-discrimination was expressly stated to be a matter for 'gradual' achievement.

* * *

*Human rights effects of SC sanctions*

The issue of the human rights effects of SC sanctions received particular attention in 1999—drawn to the attention of the SC by operational agencies, the WHO and UNICEF. Based on their research relating to Iraq, UNICEF Director Carol Bellamy noted in 1999 that without sanctions there would have been half a million fewer deaths of children under-5 in the country during the eight-year period from 1991 to 1998. She cited the SC's Panel on Humanitarian Issues: 'Even if not all suffering in Iraq can be imputed to external factors, especially sanctions, the Iraqi people would not be undergoing such deprivations in the absence of the prolonged measures imposed by the Security Council and the effects of war.'

*Inequalities in the U.N. response to different human rights crises*

This issue was raised with respect to Kosovo and Sierra Leone by the then UNHCHR in 1999. However, in contrast to the attention which the effects of some formal decisions (or omissions) by the U.N.'s political organs receive from international lawyers, there is relatively little attention to the effects of its internal operational decisions.

* * *

*Failure to act to prevent, prosecute, genocide*

In the case of the Rwanda genocide of 1994, the then secretary-general failed to present to the SC the legal imperative to prevent genocide, in spite of information provided by his U.N. force commander there three months before the killing started. The force commander had requested permission to take control of arms dumps, which he was informed had been hidden for the purpose of genocide. Then, once the predicted mass killing started, the SC was not expressly alerted by the secretary-general that genocide was occurring.

In the past, the U.N. also failed to make the necessary preparations to facilitate future prosecution of acts of genocide. In one example, the blocking of U.N. humanitarian access to vulnerable populations in Bosnia and Herzegovina was systematically used as a weapon of war over several years. 'Deliberately inflicting ... conditions of life calculated to bring about [the group's] physical destruction in whole or in part.' There were some 30,000 U.N. personnel present there from 1991 to 1995 while convoys were being routinely blocked. The ICTY was established to prosecute such crimes. Those U.N. actors did not systematically and reliably document the phenomenon to facilitate the ICTY in prosecuting those shown to be responsible. In the result, charges such as genocide have not yet been brought for those who blocked access in any of the conflicts of the former Yugoslavia. The opportunity to deter others, elsewhere, from such crimes was not taken. Today, it remains unclear whether the secretary-general has clarified instructions to staff and other U.N. personnel regarding operational support to the ICC.

* * *

## Authors' Note

**The Human Rights Concept:** This section focuses on the debate surrounding the concept of fundamental human rights. Among government officials, human rights activists, and academics there is a strong debate as to the fundamental idea of human rights. The debate centers around which rights are fundamental and which rights are non-justiciable. The following materials cover this debate. Materials 15 and 16 exemplify two opposing views on the legitimacy of the cultural relativist argument. Material 17 provides perspectives on the status of minority/group rights. Material 18 offers opposing perspectives on the justiciability and enforcement of economic and social rights. The last material in this section is a U.N. General Assembly Resolution regarding the right to water and sanitation.

## 15. Makau Mutua, The Big Idea: Are Human Rights Universal? Or Is the West Imposing Its Philosophy on the Rest of the World?
### *The Boston Globe*, 2001

The adoption in 1948 by the United Nations of the Universal Declaration of Human Rights sought to give universal legitimacy to a doctrine that is fundamentally Eurocentric in its construction. Sanctimonious to a fault, the Universal Declaration underscored its arrogance by proclaiming itself the "common standard of achievement for all peoples and nations."

The fact that human rights have since become a central norm of global civilization does not prove their universality. It is rather a testament to the conceptual, cultural, economic, military, and philosophical domination of the European West over non-European peoples and traditions.

No one familiar with Western liberal traditions of political democracy and free market capitalism would find international human rights law unusual.

Its emphasis on the individual egoist as the center of the moral universe underlines its European orientation. The basic human rights texts drew heavily from the American Bill of Rights and the French Declaration of the Rights of Man. There is no evidence of inspiration from Asian, Islamic, Buddhist, Hindu, African, or any other non-European traditions.

The West was able to impose its human rights philosophy on the rest of the world because in 1948 it dominated the U.N.. Most Asian and African societies at the time were European colonies. The two non-Westerners who were at the table, Charles Malik of Lebanon and Peng-chun Chang of China, were educated in the West and firmly rooted in the European intellectual traditions of the day.

There is no doubt that the current human rights corpus is well meaning. But that is beside the point. International human rights fall within the historical continuum of the European colonial view in which whites pose as the saviors of a benighted and savage non-European world. The white human rights zealot joins the unbroken chain that connects him to the colonial administrator, the Bible-wielding missionary, and the merchant of free enterprise. Salvation is presented as possible only through the holy trinity of human rights, political democracy, and free markets.

To the official guardians of human rights—the U.N., Western governments, and human rights activists—calls for the multicultural reconstruction of human rights are demonized as the hypocritical cries of cultural relativists, an evil species of humans who are apologists for savage cultures.

What these guardians seek is the remaking of non-Europeans into little dark, brown, and yellow Europeans, in effect dumb copies of the original. This view of human rights reinforces the hierarchy of race and color in which whites, who are privileged globally, are the models and saviors of nonwhites, who are victims and savages.

This cultural arrogance is perhaps best exemplified by human rights advocacy over the practice labeled in the West as female genital mutilation. "Mutilation" implies the willful, savage, and sadistic infliction of pain on a hapless victim. It is language that stigmatizes as barbaric cultures that condone the practice and dehumanizes the women who are subjected to it.

No consideration is given to the cultural foundation of the practice. Instead, we are presented with the racist stereotype of barbaric, machete-wielding natives only too eager to inflict pain on women in their own societies. The human rights movement should step back from this arrogant approach. It should respect cultural pluralism as a basis for finding common ground. In the case of female genital mutilation, for example, a new approach would first excavate the social meaning and purposes of the practice, as well as its effects, and then investigate the conflicting positions over the practice in that society. Rather than demonizing practitioners, solutions to the issue could be found through intercultural dialogue and introspection. Such solutions might range from modifying the practice to discarding it.

In the area of political governance—and in particular on the rights to political participation and religious freedom—the practices of Western states are used as the yardstick. Political democracy may be inevitable, but non-Western political traditions must be allowed to evolve their own distinctive systems conducive to their demographic, historical, and cultural traditions.

On religious freedom, it is wrongheaded simply to protect the right of missionary Christianity to proselytize and decimate non-Western spiritual traditions and cultures at will. Western knee-jerk reactions to restrictions on Christians in non-Western countries such as China or India must be balanced against the duty of those societies to protect their spiritual heritages.

Like earlier crusades, the human rights movement lacks the monopoly of virtue that its advocates claim. If human rights are to represent a higher human intelligence, they must overcome the seemingly incurable desire to universalize Eurocentric values by repudiating that which is different and non-European. Human rights are not bad per se, nor is the human rights corpus irredeemable. But we must realize that the current human rights declaration represents a single tradition, that of the West. It will remain incomplete and illegitimate in non-European societies unless it is reconstructed to create a truly multicultural mosaic. Ideas do not become universal merely because powerful interests declare them to be so. Inclusion—not exclusion—is the key to legitimacy.

## 16. John Shattuck, Dignity and Freedom Are for Everyone
### *The Boston Globe*, 2001

At the June 1993 U.N. World Conference on Human Rights, delegates from China, Indonesia, Cuba, Iran, and Libya tried to push through a resolution recognizing cultural relativism as a limitation on human rights. They argued that different cultures, religions, and political systems naturally have different ideas about the meaning of human rights and that any assertion that rights are universal is a subversive power play by Western governments.

As head of the U.S. delegation, I was not surprised by this maneuver. Governments are always wary of human rights, especially if they are suppressing them, in which case they often try to hide behind a veil of cultural difference. Fortunately, delegates from South Africa, Poland, South Korea, Brazil, and many other countries representing different cultures and religions that had all recently thrown off the shackles of repressive regimes were quick to see through the Chinese resolution. They united to defeat it.

The Universal Declaration of Human Rights was adopted in 1948 by countries all over the world that banded together to forswear the scourge of World War II and the horrors that accompanied it. Genocide, slavery, torture, forced starvation, and other crimes against humanity were the targets of the U.N. declaration. Its principles were drawn from the world's many philosophical and religious traditions, and it was meant both to celebrate cultural diversity and to shield culture from being used as an excuse for government repression.

Human rights are claims of dignity and integrity by individuals and groups against the governments that rule over them. These claims should not be limited by accident of birth. The fact that a person is Chinese should not mean that his government can torture him, any more than the government of South Africa should be able to use apartheid to separate South Africans on the basis of race or the U.S. government should impose inhumane prison conditions on Americans.

Since the assertion of cultural differences by governments does not justify their abuse of basic rights, repressive regimes often resort to claims of sovereignty to try to shield themselves from international scrutiny. Because sovereignty is a core principle of international law, tyrants often try to transform it into a weapon to use against universality. Under the banner of sovereignty, for example, Slobodan Milosevic organized the violent expulsion of hundreds of thousands of ethnic Albanians from Serbian Kosovo, the Chinese leadership killed thousands of peacefully demonstrating students and workers in Tiananmen Square, and the Indonesian military slaughtered people in East Timor after they had voted for independence.

If sovereignty is the last resort of tyrants seeking to avoid the reach of human rights, it is also sometimes the instrument of leaders in a democracy who want to define human rights to suit their own ideas. When Republican Senator Jesse Helms of North Carolina used a claim of U.S. sovereignty to warn that he would block the Senate from even considering a treaty establishing an International Criminal Court, his position was no more justifiable than that of the Turkish prime minister who used a claim of Turkish sovereignty to block the U.N. from investigating torture in Turkish prisons.

A more subtle argument against universality is that there is a distinction between the political and economic rights recognized in the U.N. declaration. Western democracies with strong economies tend to emphasize political rights, while poorer countries with developing economies emphasize economic rights. What does this distinction mean? Political rights are the basic freedoms of speech and association, while economic rights are the less well-defined but equally basic freedoms from need. As the World Conference on Human Rights recognized, however, these two sets of rights should be indivisible, since economic growth is far more likely to occur under conditions of political freedom and political freedom is most likely to be stable when people's basic economic needs continue to be met.

Universality is not undermined by linking these two sets of rights; it is reinforced.

A final argument against universality is that it intrudes on long-established cultural or religious practices. Cultures and religions cannot be changed by appeals to human rights, but those who are subject to severe persecution because of such practices should be protected by the Universal Declaration of Human Rights. For example, women who flee from female genital mutilation, long practiced in some cultures, should receive asylum in other countries.

Human rights are for everyone. They are not a Western construct, nor an assertion of cultural hegemony, but a set of aspirations that people the world over should be treated with dignity in a climate of freedom by their own governments.

## 17. Rhona K.M. Smith, The Fate of Minorities-Sixty Years On
### Web Journal of Current Legal Issues, 2009

### Summary

The General Assembly Resolution by which the Universal Declaration of Human Rights was adopted noted that 'the United Nations cannot remain indifferent to the fate of minorities.' However, the complexities of the subject precluded agreement at that time on a text ensuring the rights of minorities are protected and thus the matter was referred to the Economic and Social Council (ECOSOC). ECOSOC was instructed to request its Commission on Human Rights and the Sub-Commission on the Prevention of Discrimination and the Protection of Minorities 'to make a thorough study of the problem of minorities'. This article seeks to provide a synopsis of the fate of minorities, set against their historical context, after all, as Nowak notes '[p]rotection of minorities represents one of the most important predecessors to modern, international human rights protection.' It is remarkable that while international human rights have attained global acclaim and universal acceptance, 'the fate of minorities' has, arguably, yet to be satisfactorily resolved.

\* \* \*

### The problem of definition

It is axiomatic that for the rights of minorities to be protected, agreement on who falls within the term 'minority' is essential. The absence of a universally accepted definition is an impediment which appears insurmountable. Both states and the potential minorities themselves obstruct the process of defining the scope of the term. States are reluctant to have so broad a definition that large tranches of their population fall within the definition, secession is a major (and in some instances all too realistic) fear. Minority people often object to the inferiority connotations of 'minority' and most find difficulty agreeing objective (or subjective) characteristics of 'minority-ness' which can be accurately encapsulated in law. Even a purely subjective test is problematic as not all minorities wish to be identified as such.

\* \* \*

This lack of an acceptable definition of 'minority' has long plagued proponents of minority rights. Similarly with 'peoples' rights': definition proved an intractable problem 'the people cannot decide until someone decides who are the people.' A failure to determine the scope of 'minority' means that even were rights to be determined, they would be ineffectual, as states could obviate responsibility through definition-selection.

\* \* \*

### Minorities and the United Nations

Human rights have been a key feature of the work of the United Nations. Minority rights, in vogue between the two World Wars, were superseded by the new notion of universal human rights—a system of law intended to solve minority issues by guaranteeing equality to all peoples, thus alleviating the need for special treatment of certain groups within a State. In the words of Brownlie, the 'assumption lying behind the classical formulation of standards of human rights, …, has been that group rights would be taken care of automatically as the result of the protection of the rights of individuals.' The reality has not proven this to be the case. Many vulnerable groups have found the international provisions to be woefully inadequate and, as a consequence, have suffered gross violations of their human rights. Minority groups find themselves in the position of having to individually claim overtly 'group' or community 'minority rights' as individual rights: the right to speak a minority language as an individual rather than a collective right exercisable by the minority group, for example.

\* \* \*

Encapsulating universal rights in a legal treaty proved more problematic than anticipated and it was not until 1966 that the International Covenant on Civil and Political Rights (ICCPR) and the International Covenant on Economic, Social and Cultural Rights (ICESCR) were adopted (both taking ten further years to enter into force). These offer the prospect of the rhetoric of protection becoming a reality, though in the case of minorities, this is indeed a thorny issue. Many States remain reluctant to address minority issues due to fear of encouraging dissidence and secession. Genocide in Rwanda, the dissolution of the Soviet Union and Yugoslavia as well as Sudan and DR Congo are obvious embodiments of those fears although infringements of minority rights remain part of the problem. As Asbjorn Eide notes:

> 'a substantial portion of the human rights violations that come to the attention of the United Nations are related to some kind of group conflict, to majority-minority relations. And yet, the United Nations has been singularly ill-equipped to deal with these issues. Initially, there was great hesitance within the organization with regard to minorities and group relations inside state, due in part to a widespread feeling that the experience with minority rights in the period of the League of Nations (from 1919 until the eruption of World War II) had been rather disastrous and had contributed to the outbreak of World War II. It was also widely thought that the international protection of individual human rights would make it unnecessary to deal specifically with minority protection'

Individual rights, as enshrined in the Declaration and Covenants, undoubtedly can be deployed in protection of minorities. However, they are ultimately weak when being applied to the collective enjoyment of rights, a key element of minority claims. The individual has hope, the group despair.

### Enforcing and monitoring rights: Article 27 of the ICCPR

\* \* \*

Remarkably, one article of the ICCPR explicitly provides for minority rights: Article 27:

> 'In those States in which ethnic, religious or linguistic minorities exist, persons belonging to such minorities shall not be denied the rights, in community with the other members of their group, to enjoy their on culture, to profess and practice their own religion, or to use their own language.'

On the face of it, this appears to afford protection to groups. However, as the Human Rights Committee makes clear, 'it establishes and recognizes a right which is conferred on individuals belonging to minority groups' and is additional to the other rights in the covenant. Thus it can be claimed by individual members of the group, not the group itself, despite the fact that Article 27 was viewed as plugging an identified gap in the sequence of internationally recognized human rights. In *Ballantyne, Davidson and MacIntyre* v. *Canada*, a numerical criteria was deployed by the Committee meaning those belonging to an English speaking minority in a Quebec town could not rely on Article 27 as English speakers were a numerical majority in Canada as a whole. Thus francophones could potentially invoke the minority provisions in Quebec. The same applied under the minority guarantees of the League of Nations—these were sometimes applied to 'minority' people who were a majority in the area in which they lived but a minority in the State as a whole.

\* \* \*

## Advancing minority rights-U.N. developments

\* \* \*

Political reality gave impetus to developments on minority rights in the early 1990s. Mounting ethnic tensions (the dissolution of the Soviet Union and the break-up of Yugoslavia) hastened the adoption of the U.N. Declaration on the Rights of Persons Belonging to National or Ethnic, Religious and Linguistic Minorities in 1992—itself the product of more than ten years of protracted negotiations and debate. The Declaration provides that:

> 'persons belonging to national or ethnic, religious and linguistic minorities [(.)] have the right to enjoy their own culture, to profess and practice their own religion, and to use their own language, in private and in public, freely and without interference or any form of discrimination.'

The Declaration owes its existence to the inspiration provided by Article 27 of the ICCPR but aims at promoting peace and stability. The basic provisions of the declaration target discrimination and, 'where appropriate' encourage States to actively promote aspects of minority culture. The latter includes provision of minority language education, cultural and historical education of all and political participation.

\* \* \*

## 18. Eric C. Christiansen, Adjudicating Non-Justiciable Rights: Socio-Economic Rights and the South African Constitutional Court
*Columbia Human Rights Law Review*, 2007
[footnotes omitted by editors]

### I. Introduction

It has historically been argued and traditionally accepted that socio-economic rights are non-justiciable. Advocates of this position have asserted that, while rights to housing, health care, education, and other forms of social welfare may have value as moral statements of a nation's ideals, they should not be viewed as a legal declaration of enforceable rights. Adjudication of such rights requires an assessment of fundamental social values that can only be carried out legitimately by the political branches of government, and the proper enforcement of socio-economic rights requires significant government resources that can only be adequately assessed and balanced by the legislature. Judges and courts, according to this argument, lack the political legitimacy and institutional competence to decide such matters.

Nevertheless, a steadily increasing number of countries have chosen to include socio-economic rights in their constitutions-with varying (and sometimes unclear) levels of enforcement. At the core of such "social rights" are rights to adequate housing, health care, food, water, social security, and education. Each of these rights is enumerated in the 1996 South African Constitution. Moreover, most of them have been the subject of full judicial proceedings before the South African Constitutional Court. This makes the South African situation unparalleled in international constitutional jurisprudence. Although some other countries' constitutions enumerate socio-economic rights, few countries' courts have found such rights to be fully and directly justifiable, and even fewer have multiple, affirmative social rights opinions. No other country has developed their case law sufficiently to outline a comprehensive jurisprudence.

As a consequence, South Africa's role in the social rights adjudication debate is seen as revolutionary and heroic by proponents of justiciablility and as irresponsible and doomed by its detractors. Now, as the first generation of justices leaves the Court, sufficient judgments exist to articulate a novel but coherent jurisprudence. What is revealed is a Court that has been both less revolutionary and less irresponsible than commentators expected (and continue to allege). This is because the Court's jurisprudence has incorporated the concerns of the jurists who argue that courts lack the legitimacy and competence to decide such matters, even while the Court is performing the affirmative review and remediation functions desired by the jurists who favor judicial enforcement of social rights. The Court maintains an affirmative social rights jurisprudence tempered by internalized justiciablility concerns.

\* \* \*

## III. Overview of Non-Justiciablility Arguments

When the abstract question of the justifiability of social rights reached the Constitutional Court in July 1996, the issue had already been widely debated. Any court would have been aware of the traditional consensus that social rights were not justiciable. [ ... ]

### A. Non-Justiciability Arguments

The arguments typically marshaled in opposition to judicial enforcement of socio-economic rights are manifold and confusing. In the most simplistic presentation of these arguments, the special nature of socio-economic rights and the institutional limitations of courts make adjudication of these rights impossible. To provide an overview of these arguments, this Article focuses first on the difficulties arising from the supposed differences between negative political rights and positive social rights. Many of the alleged distinctions between these two types of rights are historical and descriptive rather than inherent and normative. Second, this Article examines viewpoints opposing adjudication of such rights, that is, arguments about the legitimate and competent enforcement of social rights by judges and courts.

\* \* \*

### 1. Fundamentally Different Fundamental Rights

The tension between civil and political rights and social and economic rights has a long history—a history that more often burdens rather than aids an understanding of their genuine differences. These differences were presumptively evidenced by the twentieth-century division of the rights in the Universal Declaration of Human Rights (UDHR) into two distinct binding Covenants—the International Covenant on Civil and Political Rights (lCCPR) and the International Covenant of Economic, Social and Cultural Rights (ICESCR).

This division is certainly neither an originally-intended nor a necessary separation. The post-war UDHR envisions and expressly identifies the inherent and necessary interrelationship of the two types of rights. But in the years following the drafting of the UDHR, global politics (most importantly the rise of Cold War tensions) and the formation of the first-generation factions in the United Nations led to a division of the rights promoted in the UDHR into the two distinct Covenants. Nevertheless, the indivisibility of social and political rights has been repeatedly affirmed by the international community. The 1993 Vienna Declaration reasserts the international law consensus:

> All human rights are universal, indivisible and interdependent and interrelated. The international community must treat human rights globally in a fair and equal manner, on the same footing, and with the same emphasis.... [I]t is the duty of States, regardless of their political, economic and cultural systems, to promote and protect all human rights and fundamental freedoms.

Although the initial distinction between ICCPR rights, so-called "negative rights," and ICESCR rights, "positive rights," grew out of post-war political tensions, in more recent decades the division has been presumed to reflect fundamental differences in the nature of the rights themselves. Traditional political rights such as freedom of expression, equal protection, and due process are considered negative rights because they only require that the state refrain from interfering in the individual's exercise of the right; they are rights to be free from government interference. Socio-economic rights are identified as positive rights because they impose affirmative obligations upon the state to advance particular areas of social welfare. Under the dominant thinking that supports and encourages this separation, negative rights are justiciable because they involve discrete cases, they examine precise rights, and their remedies implicate only a cessation of action by government beyond the scope of judicial authority. Positive rights are merely (and necessarily) hortatory because they are vaguely worded, involve more complex issues, and would assign unacceptable positive obligations to government.

Because the manner in which most academics and practitioners discuss rights and rights adjudication has been fundamentally shaped by systems in which only traditional civil and political rights have been justiciable, it becomes difficult to distinguish between inherent characteristics of social rights and their socially-constructed limitations. In classic arguments against the justiciability of social rights, these distinctions, often presented as a set of inviolable maxims, are coupled with arguments about the political legitimacy and institutional competence of courts in order to reject judicial enforcement of social welfare rights. For these reasons, discussions about the justiciability of social rights are inherently difficult.

Increasingly, academics and commentators have recognized the invalidity of this positive-negative distinction. A typical negative right (e.g., freedom of expression) is equally imprecise and gives rise to a comparable need for interpretation (e.g., what limits exist, is there differential treatment for political, commercial, religious, hate-based or pornographic speech, what is the interrelationship with other political rights, etc.) as much as a typical positive right (e.g., right to education). Paradoxically, the argument that social rights are less precise than political rights may primarily rest on their extremely limited history of adjudication.

Similarly, political rights can require assessment of significant factual or social phenomena. Consider, for example, the information reviewed to make a decision about the validity of voting procedures or disparate impact discrimination claims. And, even negative rights impose substantial affirmative obligations on states. After all, a voting rights decision can require expensive new procedures or materials or may vastly increase voter rolls, placing a huge financial burden on the state.

In these ways, an *a priori* distinction between negative and positive rights is inconsistent with a genuine understanding of the rights. This is not to assert that there are no differences between political and social rights. Indeed there are; even at an abstract level, social rights are more frequently related to social policy, a more volatile area of govern-ment policy for most nations. In theory, the social rights remedies imposed by a court could be overwhelming to a state, such as if a court were to require the government to provide universal employment, universal education through to the university level, free unlimited health care, etc. But this is the enforcement issue, not the justiciability issue. The nature of the rights themselves is not a legitimate basis for rejecting their justiciability. The South African Court has recognized this as well. A valid rejection of social rights justiciability must rely on their inability to be properly or effectively adjudicated. Hence, the real area of concern is not the nature of the rights but what some commentators fear judges and courts will do with such rights.

\* \* \*

### a. Legitimacy: Overreaching Courts?

Legitimacy arguments focus on the inappropriateness of assigning the task of interpreting social values to an unelected judiciary, and, most critically, of allowing judicial interfer-ence in the allocation of state monies — a core legislative task. The primary concern is that crafting and assigning a remedy in a social rights case is too similar to the legislature's traditional role of deciding policy and creating and implementing programs. To view such rights as justiciable would necessarily and impermissibly intrude on the province of the legislative branch — most glaringly when a court overrides a legislative act regarding social welfare and asserts a different course of action for the state.

\* \* \*

---

## 19. Resolution 64, The Human Right to Water and Sanitation
United Nations General Assembly, Aug. 3, 2010

*The General Assembly,*

\* \* \*

*Deeply concerned* that approximately 884 million people lack access to safe drinking water and that more than 2.6 billion do not have access to basic sanitation, and alarmed that approximately 1.5 million children under 5 years of age die and 443 million school days are lost each year as a result of water- and sanitation-related diseases,

\* \* \*

1. *Recognizes* the right to safe and clean drinking water and sanitation as a human right that is essential for the full enjoyment of life and all human rights;

2. *Calls upon* States and international organizations to provide financial resources, capacity-building and technology transfer, through international assistance and cooperation, in particular to developing countries, in order to scale up efforts to provide safe, clean, ac-cessible and affordable drinking water and sanitation for all;

3. *Welcomes* the decision by the Human Rights Council to request that the independent expert on human rights obligations related to access to safe drinking water and sanitation submit an annual report to the General Assembly, and encourages her to continue work-ing on all aspects of her mandate and, in consultation with all relevant United Nations agencies, funds and programs, to include in her report to the Assembly, at its sixty-sixth session, the principal challenges related to the realization of the human right to safe and clean drinking water and sanitation and their impact on the achievement of the Millen-nium Development Goals.

## Authors' Note

Political Transitions and Human Rights: The final two materials for this chapter highlight the issue of democratic and political transitions within states. Reading 20 is a selection of articles from the Universal Declaration of Human Rights that specifically relate to democratic rights. Reading 21 is a recent statement by the U.N. High Commissioner for Human Rights, where the Commissioner draws a connection between the right to development and political, economic, and social rights.

## 20. Universal Declaration of Human Rights, Articles 19, 20, 21, 28
### 1948

### Article 19

Everyone has the right to freedom of opinion and expression; this right includes freedom to hold opinions without interference and to seek, receive and impart information and ideas through any media and regardless of frontiers.

### Article 20

(1) Everyone has the right to freedom of peaceful assembly and association.

(2) No one may be compelled to belong to an association.

### Article 21

(1) Everyone has the right to take part in the government of his country, directly or through freely chosen representatives.

(2) Everyone has the right of equal access to public service in his country.

(3) The will of the people shall be the basis of the authority of government; this will shall be expressed in periodic and genuine elections which shall be by universal and equal suffrage and shall be held by secret vote or by equivalent free voting procedures.

### Article 28

Everyone is entitled to a social and international order in which the rights and freedoms set forth in this Declaration can be fully realized.

## 21. Statement by the U.N. High Commissioner for Human Rights, Twenty-Five Years of the Right to Development: Achievements and Challenges
### 2011

\* \* \*

I am very pleased to commemorate with you the twenty-fifth anniversary of the adoption of the United Nations Declaration on the Right to Development. I wish to convey my sincere appreciation to the Friedrich Ebert foundation for the excellent cooperation we enjoyed in organizing this important gathering. The Friedrich Ebert foundation has been a leader in the promotion of the realization of the right to development and an active participant in the work of the United Nations in this field as we heard just now.

* * *

The constituent elements of the right to development are rooted in the provisions of the Charter of the United Nations, the Universal Declaration of Human Rights and the International Covenants of Civil and Political Rights and Economic, Social and Cultural Rights as well as other United Nations instruments.

* * *

The primary inspiration for the modern articulation of the right to development comes from Judge Keba M'Baye of Senegal, who in 1972 argued that development should be viewed as a right. He was able to secure a General Assembly resolution in 1977 which authorized a study of the issue and resulted ultimately in the adoption, in 1986, of the U.N. Declaration on the Right to Development, approved by 146 out of the then 159 U.N. Member States.

The logic of the right to development, as expressed in the Declaration itself, is unassailable: Everyone has the right to participate in, contribute to and enjoy economic, social, cultural and political development. The Declaration sets out the particular requirements of the right to development itself, and, by extension, human rights-based development, and these are the requirements:

- Putting the human person at the centre of development,
- To ensuring active and meaningful participation,
- Securing non-discrimination,
- Fairly distributing the benefits of development,
- Respecting self-determination, and sovereignty over natural resources, and
- Informing all processes that advance other civil, political economic, social and cultural rights.

* * *

Rampant poverty and stark inequalities that continue to confront the world are affronts to human dignity, and a violation of human rights. According to the latest UNDP Human Development Report, an estimated one-third of the population in 104 developing countries, or about 1.75 billion people, experience multidimensional poverty. More than half live in South Asia. Rates are highest in Sub-Saharan Africa, with significant variation across regions, groups and indigenous peoples. The absolute number of malnourished people — defined by minimal energy consumption — which stood at 850 million in 1980 has now increased to around 1 billion worldwide.

* * *

At the same time, democratic deficits and weak governance at the national level, combined with the lack of an enabling international environment for development, continue to prevent full implementation of the right to development.

* * *

Then and now, still, people are taking to the streets because of rampant poverty and inequalities, rising unemployment, a lack of opportunities, and the chronic denial of their economic, social and cultural rights, as well as civil and political rights. They have no regular channels to express their discontent; they are deprived of the benefits arising from the natural resources of their countries, and they cannot meaningfully participate in the decision-making process to change the situation. These are exactly the kind of issues addressed by the U.N. Declaration on the Right to Development. The right to development not only helps address these root causes, the Declaration also guides our efforts to find sustainable solutions because it puts people at the very heart of development.

So once again let me wish you well in your deliberations. Thank you.

## 22. Bibliography of Additional Sources

- Philip Alston, THE U.N. AND HUMAN RIGHTS: A CRITICAL APPROACH (1992).
- Matthew G. St. Amand, *Public Committee Against Torture in Israel v. The State of Israel et al.: Landmark Human Rights Decision by the Israeli High Court of Justice or Status Quo Maintained?*, 25 N.C. J. INT'L L. & COM. REG. 655 (Summer 2000).
- Jacqueline Bhabha, *Arendt's Children: Do Today's Migrant Children Have a Right to Have Rights?*, HUM. RTS. Q. (2009).
- Ian Brownlie, BASIC DOCUMENTS ON HUMAN RIGHTS (1992).
- Kristen D.A. Carpenter, *The International Covenant on Civil and Political Rights: A Toothless Tiger?*, 26 N.C. J. INT'L L. & COM. REG. 1 (Fall 2000).
- James Crawford, *The Rights of Peoples: Some Conclusions, in* THE RIGHTS OF PEOPLES 159 (James Crawford ed., 1988).
- Jack Donnelly, UNIVERSAL HUMAN RIGHTS IN THEORY AND PRACTICE (1988).
- John Dugard & Christine Van den Wyngaert, *Reconciling Extradition with Human Rights*, 92 AM. J. INT'L L. 187 (Apr. 1998).
- Thomas M. Franck, *Is Personal Freedom a Western Value?*, 91 AM. J. INT'L L. 593 (Oct. 1997).
- Michael Freeman, *Are There Collective Human Rights?*, 43 POL. STUD. 25 (1995).
- James A. Graff, *Human Rights, Peoples, and the Right to Self-Determination, in* GROUP RIGHTS 186 (Judith Baker ed., 1994).
- Catherine M. Grosso, *International Law in Domestic Arena: The Case of Torture in Israel*, 86 IOWA L. REV. 305 (Oct. 2000).
- INTERIGHTS & COMMONWEALTH SECRETARIAT, DEVELOPING HUMAN RIGHTS JURISPRUDENCE, VOLUME 7: SEVENTH JUDICIAL COLLOQUIUM ON THE DOMESTIC APPLICATION OF INTERNATIONAL HUMAN RIGHTS NORMS, GEORGETOWN, GUYANA, 3–5 (1998).
- Kelly Kollman & Matthew Waites, *The Global Politics of Lesbian, Gay, Bisexual, and Transgender Human Rights: an Introduction*, 15.1 CONTEMP. POL. 1 (2009).
- Richard B. Lillich & Frank C. Newman, INTERNATIONAL HUMAN RIGHTS: PROBLEMS OF LAW AND POLICY (1979).
- Marc Limon, *Human Rights and Climate Change: Constructing a Case for Political Action*, 33.2 HARV. ENV. L. REV. 439 (2009).
- Ann Elizabeth Mayer, *Universal Versus Islamic Human Rights: A Clash of Cultures or a Clash with a Construct?*, 15 MICH. J. INT'L L. 307 (Winter 1994).
- Frederic Megret, *The Disabilities Convention: Human Rights of Persons with Disabilities or Disability Rights?*, 30.2 HUM. RTS. Q. 494 (May 2008).

- Theodor Meron, *The Humanization of Humanitarian Law*, 94 Am. J. Int'l L. 239 (Apr. 2000).

- Johan Nordenfelt, *Human Rights—What They Are and What They Are Not*, 56 Nordic J. Int'l L. 3 (1987).

- Richard Pierre Claude & Burns H. Weston, Human Rights in the World Community: Issues and Action (1992).

- William A. Schabas, *Sentencing by International Tribunals: A Human Rights Approach*, 7 Duke J. Comp. & Int'l L. 461 (1997).

- Arjun Sengupta, *On the Theory and Practice of the Right to Development*, 24.4 Hum. Rts. Q. 837 (Nov. 2002).

- Zelim Skurbaty, As If People Mattered: Critical Appraisal of "Peoples" and "Minorities" from the International Human Rights Perspective and Beyond (2000).

- Karen E. Smith, *Speaking With One Voice? European Union Co-ordination on Human Rights Issues at the United Nations*, 44.1 J. Common Market Stud. 113 (2006).

- Henry J. Steiner, International Human Rights in Context (2000).

- Abdulrahim P. Vijapur, Essays on International Human Rights (2000).

- Marie Vlachova, *Trafficking in Humans: The Slavery of Our Age*, 4.4 Partnership for Peace Consortium Q.J. 1 (Winter 2005).

- Johan D. Van Der Vyver & John Witte Jr., Religious Human Rights in Global Perspective (1996).

- Ton J.M. Zuijdwijk, Petitioning the United Nations: A Study in Human Rights (1982).

# Chapter XVI

# Human Rights Violations: Mechanisms for Protection

## Introduction

This chapter takes the reader beyond the international human rights covenants and treaties presented in the previous chapter and explores the mechanisms and bodies established to enforce and protect those rights. While efforts to protect human rights began as a national endeavor pursued by states and their national institutions, the protection of human rights has become an international concern since World War II. A number of regional and global institutions have been developed to enforce the obligations of states to protect human rights. Many of these institutions have met with mixed success. This chapter will provide a basis for investigating the degree to which various institutions are effective, why this might be the case, and how those institutions might be improved. The chapter also provides a foundation for exploring the controversial nature of human rights enforcement and the debate over regional versus international enforcement of human rights obligations.

## Objectives

- To understand the jurisdiction and operation of various regional and international human rights mechanisms.

- To understand the basic procedures for utilizing the various human rights mechanisms.

- To understand how to identify the appropriate channels of action for particular circumstances.

- To be able to analyze the effectiveness of various human rights mechanisms and consider how they might be improved.

# Problems

Students should come to class prepared to discuss the following questions:

1.  Why did the United Nations transition from the Commission on Human Rights to the Human Rights Council?

2.  What are the contentious issues concerning the creation of the Human Rights Council? Why are they contentious?

3.  Discuss the arguments for and against Israeli and Palestinian violation of international law during the Gaza War.

4.  What conditions apply to the right of signatory states to declare reservations to the International Covenant on Civil and Political Rights?

5.  Which regional human rights mechanism is the most effective? Why?

6.  What are the respective strengths and weaknesses of the regional human rights mechanisms discussed in this chapter? What solutions or modifications would you recommend to address the weaknesses?

7.  Do you agree with the opinion of the European Court of Human Rights concerning the constitution of Bosnia and Herzegovina? Why, or why not?

8.  Under what circumstances is it appropriate for the international community to intervene in a state's domestic affairs to protect human rights? Do you agree with the argument that international humanitarian intervention, rather than intervention by the African Union, would have been a more effective, appropriate response in the case of Darfur?

# Simulation

### Case Study: Darfur

Conflict in the Darfur region of Sudan began in 2003 and escalated to become one of the world's greatest humanitarian crises. Darfur is a region in the western part of Sudan, just south of Egypt. Before crisis struck the region, the population stood at about 6 million people, consisting of nearly 100 different ethnic and tribal groups. In the spring of 2003, conflict enveloped Darfur when two Darfuri rebel movements—the Sudan Liberation Movement (SLM) and Justice and Equality Movement (JEM)—attacked government installations in defiance of political and economic marginalization. The Sudanese government responded swiftly, and viciously, through the government armed militia known as the Janjaweed. The militia raided nearly 400 villages, killing as many as 300,000 civilians between 2003 and 2005.

The fighting has internally displaced 2.7 million people that live in large camps across Darfur, and are plagued with famine and infectious diseases, while another 300,000 Darfuris are estimated to have fled to neighboring Chad. With government backing and instructions to clear civilians from areas in support of rebel groups, the Janjaweed have indiscriminately killed women and children, looted, and participated in mass rapes, all in violation of the 1949 Geneva Convention. Overall, the U.N. estimates that 4.7 million of the 6 million people in Darfur have been impacted by the conflict.

In April 2004 a fact-finding team from the Office of the High Commissioner for Human Rights began missions to Chad and Sudan to investigate human rights abuses. During the same time period, the African Union assumed leadership in brokering an end to the conflict. Along with support from the U.N. Security Council, the AU brokered two cease-fires, but neither was observed.

The United States Congress declared in July 2004 that genocide was occurring in Sudan, and then Secretary of State Colin Powell publicly asserted that the Sudanese government was responsible for the genocide. However, the U.N. Report of the International Commission of Inquiry on Darfur concluded that the Sudanese government had not committed genocide, but rather certain government officials had committed genocidal acts. In June 2005, the International Criminal Court launched investigations into human rights abuses in Darfur, but the Sudanese government failed to cooperate, as it is not a signatory of the ICC and does not recognize its authority. The U.N. Human Rights Council expressed concern over the situation in Sudan for the first time in March 2007, but failed to condemn Sudan's actions. This resolution came one year after the Council was founded.

A combined United Nations-African Union peacekeeping force (UNAMID) replaced an underfunded and underequipped African Union force in January 2006. The ICC indicted Sudanese President Omar al Bashir, but the Sudanese government refused to remove him from office or send him to The Hague. While the Human Rights Council voted in 2009 to maintain close scrutiny of the situation, fighting continued and the government remained centrally responsible for the mass murders, chaos, and injustice. It refused to allow a robust international peacekeeping force into the region, to prosecute any individuals responsible for crimes against humanity, and even expelled international humanitarian aid groups. Darfuri civilians were left unprotected and dispossessed from their most basic human rights.

You are a lawyer representing Darfurians who have been subject to countless human rights abuses. Assuming Sudan abides by the treaty-based bodies, develop a strategy for navigating the regional and international institutions to pursue justice for your clients. Bear in mind the time frame of each mechanism, as well as the limited resources available to you. What options do you have? Draft a step-by-step proposal. What would be the objective—to establish grievances, or to obtain compensation?

# Materials

1. *Report of the Task Force on Reform of the U.N. Commission on Human Rights*, A.B.A. Sec. Int'l L. (2005).

2. Scott R. Lyons, *ASIL Insight: The New United Nations Human Rights Council*, Am. Soc. Intl. L. (Mar. 27, 2006).

3. U.N. Hum. Rts. Council, Media Summary Rep. on the Goldstone U.N. Fact Finding Mission (Sept. 15, 2009).

4. Peter Berkowitz, *The Goldstone Report and International Law*, Pol'y Rev. (Aug.–Sept. 2010).

5. Dinah PoKempner, *Valuing the Goldstone Report*, 16.2 Global Governance (Apr.–June 2010).

6. U.N. Off. of the High Comm'n for Hum. Rts., General Comment 24 on its 52nd Sess., U.N. Doc. CCPR/C/21/Rev.1/Add.6 (Apr. 11, 1994).

7. Observations by the United States on General Comment 24, U.N. Doc. CCPR/A/50/40/Vol.1 Annex VI (1995).

8. Celine Tran, *Striking a Balance Between Human Rights and Peace and Stability: A Review of the ECtHR's Decision in* Sejdić *and Finci v.* Bosnia and Herzegovina *and Its Implications*, 18.2 Hum. Rts. Br. 3 (2011).

9. Tim Curry et al., *Updates from the Regional Human Rights Systems*, 12 Hum. Rts. Br. 23, 25–26 (2005).

10. Inter-American Commission on Human Rights, *What is the IACHR?*

11. Anna Meijknecht & Byung Sook Patinaje-de Vries, *Is There a Place for Minorities' and Indigenous People's Rights within ASEAN?: Asian Values, ASEAN Values and the Protection of Southeast Asian Minorities and Indigenous Peoples*, 17.1 Int'l J. on Minority & Group Rts. 75 (2010).

12. Paul D. Williams & Alex J. Bellamy, *The Responsibility to Protect and the Crisis in Darfur*, 36.1 Security Dialogue 27 (2005).

13. Bibliography of Additional Sources

---

## Authors' Note

**United Nations Human Rights Council:** International law includes a number of instruments for enforcing customary law. One such mechanism is the Human Rights Council, which replaced the Commission on Human Rights in March 2006. The Council is an inter-governmental body established to address human rights violations. It is comprised of 47 states responsible for upholding and protecting human rights through a Universal Periodic Review process that evaluates all 192 U.N. member states. The Council has an Advisory Committee that provides it with expertise and understanding of human rights issues. A Complaints Procedure mechanism gives individuals and organizations the opportunity to file reports.

---

# 1. Report of the Task Force on Reform of the U.N. Commission on Human Rights
### American Bar Association Section of International Law, 2005

The American Bar Association Section of International Law's Task Force on Reform of the United Nations Commission on Human Rights was established in January of 2004. During the course of that year, the Task Force held monthly meetings at which it heard from a wide variety of individuals, including officials of the U.S. Government, think tanks, nongovernmental organizations, and former Ambassadors of the U.S. to the Commission, all of whom contributed to our understanding of the issues and needed reforms. The Section of International Law, along with the Center for Human Rights, Section of Individual Rights and Responsibilities, and Standing Committee on Law and National Security, have approved these principles as outlined by the Task Force summary below.

Our review had as its focus the role of the Commission in contributing to the promotion and protection of human rights. As the recent report of the Secretary-General's High-level Panel on Threats, Challenges and Change stated, the "Commission on Human Rights is entrusted with promoting respect for human rights globally, fostering international cooperation in human rights, responding to violations in specific countries and assisting countries in building their human rights capacity."

At bottom, these are concerns of lawyers charged by our professional calling with promoting and protecting human rights. As we reviewed the performance of the Commission, particularly in recent years, and considered needed reforms, we focused on issues of particular relevance to lawyers, such as replacing the Commission with a Human Rights Council; the need to reemphasize fundamental human rights; promotion of the rule of law; development of the Democracy Caucus; strengthening the investigative processes of the Commission; and adopting a Code of Conduct committing the members to honor their human rights undertakings and cooperate with the Commission.

* * *

On the whole, the Task Force found that the Commission on Human Rights, particularly in recent years, has failed to fulfill its mission to promote and protect human rights. While there are a number of reasons why this is the case, a primary cause is the increasingly politicized nature of the Commission, which has severely compromised the capacity of the Commission to take action in response to serious human rights violations.

The Commission, it should be understood, is an intergovernmental body (as opposed to a body of independent experts), whose membership reflects the overall composition of the U.N.. In the early years of its existence, this intergovernmental status contributed importantly to the legitimacy of human rights norms as set out in the Universal Declaration of Human Rights and other key instruments. In recent years, however, a number of states with severely compromised human rights records have sought to exploit the political nature of the Commission, resulting from its intergovernmental status, to prevent exposure and criticism of their transgressions, as well as the violations of other states. As the Secretary-General noted in his Larger Freedom report, "the Commission's capacity to perform its tasks has been increasingly undermined by its declining credibility and professionalism. In particular, States have sought membership on the Commission not to strengthen human rights but to protect themselves against criticism or to criticize others." The standing of the Commission was severely compromised by the selection of Libya as Chair and the re-election of Sudan as a member in the midst of the genocide in Darfur. Perhaps, the most shameful failure of the Commission in recent years was the refusal last year to adopt a resolution clearly condemning that genocide.

Notwithstanding its criticism of the Commission, the Task Force recognizes that the Commission has done important work in exposing, through its rapporteurs, cases of serious human rights violations. This work is especially important in countries with poor human rights records, which have ratified few human rights treaties and are therefore not subject to oversight by treaty monitoring bodies. Such exposure, on occasion, has resulted in prisoners being freed.

The Task Force recognizes that the inherently political nature of an intergovernmental body such as the Commission inevitably limits its ability to function as the beacon of human rights envisioned when it was created in 1946. These limitations are reinforced by its size (53 Member States), status as a subsidiary of the Economic and Social Council (ECOSOC), and restricted meeting schedule (once a year, apart from special sessions).

The Task Force endorses the Secretary-General's proposal of a smaller, standing Human Rights Council, whose members would be elected by the General Assembly subject to a two-thirds majority. As compared with the Commission, the Council would have the status, the time, and smaller and more committed membership to fulfill its responsibilities as the leading human rights intergovernmental body in the U.N. structure. And, the Council will provide a much-needed opportunity for a fresh start.

The Task Force recommends guidelines for the new Council designed to focus its mission on fundamental human rights and the rule of law, promote responsible behavior by Member States, strengthen the role of the Democracy Caucus of Member States, and enhance the professionalism of the investigative processes. The Task Force further, and in line with the recommendations of the Secretary-General, proposes reforms to enrich the contribution of the High Commissioner for Human Rights.

This report assumes the creation of a Human Rights Council on the basis proposed by the Secretary-General and, as indicated above, offers guidance drawn from the experience of the Commission to be drawn upon in establishing necessary rules, operations and processes. The Task Force notes that its recommendations would be equally applicable in the event the General Assembly determines to retain the existing Commission. In the end, no proposed set of legal and institutional reforms will succeed unless the U.S. and the other democratic Member States undertake to treat the Council with a seriousness of purpose and commitment at least equal to that of the Member States whose agenda has been to prevent the Commission from doing its job of protecting human rights. The Task Force offers specific recommendations in that regard.

The ABA recommendation also calls for enhanced coordination with human rights treaty bodies. These are some of the most legally oriented and least politically charged parts of the U.N. human rights system. Attention could also be given to the extent to which there should be greater resources for individual complaint mechanisms. These mechanisms have been used effectively in contexts where national legal systems are not willing or able to provide relief for serious human rights abuses.

During the course of deliberations of the Task Force, the Secretary-General's High-level Panel on Threats, Challenges and Change issued its final report, which addressed many issues facing the U.N., including the performance of the Human Rights Commission. The report confirmed a number of the findings of the Task Force, including its findings that the Commission's capacity to meet its mandate has been "undermined by eroding credibility and professionalism," and that "standard-setting to reinforce human rights cannot be performed by states that lack a demonstrated commitment to their promotion and protection." Moreover, the High-level Panel expressed a similar concern to that of the Task Force that "in recent years states have sought membership of the Commission not to strengthen human rights but to protect themselves against criticism or to criticize others."

* * *

The High-level Panel also made a number of recommendations. The Task Force endorses the recommendations concerning the designation of experienced human rights figures as heads of their delegations, creating an advisory council, having the High Commissioner for Human Rights prepare an annual report on the situation of human rights worldwide, regular reporting to the Security Council, and increased funding. The Task Force, however, does not agree with the recommendation of universal membership in the Commission. As discussed in Appendix A, Section II of this report, the Task Force concluded that opening the membership to all members of the U.N. would make it even more difficult than at present for the Commission to take action in response to human rights violations. The example set by U.N. bodies that have universal membership, such as the General Assembly and its third committee, does not inspire confidence that expanding the membership of the Commission so that it includes all members of the U.N. will lead to more responsible behavior.

As noted above, the Secretary-General also rejected the High-level Panel's recommendation of universal membership and proposed instead that the Commission be replaced by a smaller, standing Human Rights Council, whose members would be elected by a two-thirds majority of the General Assembly and would "undertake to abide by the highest human rights standards." The Secretary-General's report makes recommendations also for strengthening the role and capacity of the High Commissioner. The Task Force supports these proposals of the Secretary-General.

A number of governmental and nongovernmental organizations (NGOs) have issued reports calling for improved effectiveness and making appropriate recommendations. To add value, the Task Force, in fashioning its recommendations for guidelines for the Council, focused its efforts on recommendations designed to depoliticize the work of the Commission, improve its performance, and refocus its resources on the protection of fundamental human rights.

The analysis and recommendations of the Task Force are divided into the following sections in Appendix A:

**A Human Rights Council**

The first section of Appendix A presents the rationale for creating a Human Rights Council to replace the Commission and recommends:

- The General Assembly should create a Human Rights Council, whose members would be elected by a two-thirds majority of the General Assembly. The Council should be substantially smaller than the 53 member Commission.

- The Council should be a standing body of the U.N..

- The resolution establishing the Council should commit all Member States of the U.N. to cooperate with the Council, particularly with its investigative processes.

**Mission**

The second section of Appendix A reviews the evolution of the Commission's mandate and its failure in recent years to adequately focus on its core mandate. Taking account of the failings of the Commission, the Task Force recommends that the Council:

- Assign special priority to protecting and promoting fundamental human rights.

- Establish a highly professional investigative processes, and in particular a strong rapporteur process, and improve coordination with other U.N. human rights treaty bodies.

- Reject any discriminatory, exclusive agenda items aimed at specific countries, such as the standing agenda item created by the Commission with respect to Israel, the only country so treated.

- Focus world attention on conflicts that may result in ethnic cleansing, genocide, or other mass violations of human rights.

The Task Force welcomes and applauds the efforts of the High Commissioner and the Secretary-General to develop initiatives to promote the rule of law in post conflict and transitional states and to establish a democracy fund as a source of support. The Task Force further encourages the High Commissioner to establish a task force of experts to provide advice in formulating plans for, and providing rule of law assistance to states wishing to improve their compliance with international human rights norms, as well as other related issues. Such an advisory body could also assist in identifying and disseminating "best practices" and in generating support for actions of the High Commissioner.

### Process for Selecting Members of the Council

The third section of Appendix A addresses the selection of members of the Council. The Task Force preferred limiting membership to states that met minimal human rights standards but concluded that such an approach would not likely find acceptance in the U.N.. While a majority of states might be prepared to exclude other states that are subject to sanctions imposed by the Security Council or the censure of the new Human Rights Council, the current Member States would be hard pressed to reach a consensus on the appropriate standards to determine membership on the Commission.

Therefore, the Task Force agreed with the Secretary-General's recommendation that the members be elected by the General Assembly on the basis of a two-thirds majority vote, a requirement intended to limit membership to those countries which, by virtue of their qualifications, are able to garner the support of a super-majority of the General Assembly. If the members determine, as seems likely, that seats on the Council should be allocated among the regional groups, that should be allowed only on the basis that all regional groups reserve the right to reject any candidates on the basis of their human rights records. The Task Force is examining the procedures for best assuring that the super-majority voting requirement functions as intended by the Secretary-General.

In addition, the Secretary-General and High Commissioner should exercise moral suasion with respect to the selection of Commission members by regional groups, the U.S., and other members of the Democracy Caucus should more effectively exert their influence over the selection process. The Council should adopt a Code of Conduct (Recommendation, Appendix I) under which members would, inter alia, pledge to honor their human rights obligations and to cooperate fully with the Commission's investigations. Certain breaches of the Code could result in the imposition of sanctions.

Specifically the Task Force makes the following recommendations:

- Regional groups should reserve the right to oppose the candidacy of a state that has a poor human rights record, even if such a candidacy has the support of the sponsoring regional group.

- Any Member State subject to action taken by the Security Council under Chapter VII of the U.N. Charter or the censure of the Human Rights Council should be prohibited from serving on the Council until the sanctions or censure are lifted.

- The Secretary-General and High Commissioner for Human Rights should use their good offices to persuade the Member States of the Regional Groups to select for membership in the Human Rights Council only states with good human rights records.

- The U.S. and democratic states should seek to strengthen and activate the emerging "Democracy Caucus" so as to promote the effective operation of the Council by, among other actions, supporting for membership on the Council only states with good human rights records.

- The Council should adopt a Code of Conduct pledging members to comply with their obligations to protect human rights imposed by treaty, to use their membership on the Council to promote international efforts to protect human rights, to designate prominent persons with substantial human rights expertise to head their delegations to the Council, and to cooperate with the investigative mechanisms of the Council, including the work of rapporteurs charged with investigating allegations of human rights abuses. Serious violations of a member's obligations of good citizenship of the Council as defined in Article IV of the Code could give rise to the imposition of sanctions, including removal from membership and disqualification from re-election for at least one term.

\* \* \*

### Relationship with NGOs

The final section in Appendix A addresses the relationship between the Council and NGOs and makes proposals for enhancing the role and contribution of NGOs to the work of the Council, as compared with the Commission. Specifically, the Task Force recommends that the Council should appoint a coordinator to facilitate NGO communication and interaction with the Council, and do away with the strict requirement that NGOs may only have half the speaking time allotted to Member States. The replacement of the Commission by a standing Council will also provide a greater opportunity for constructive NGO involvement in the work of the Council.

\* \* \*

## APPENDIX A

### Section 1
### Replacing the Commission on Human Rights with a Human Rights Council

**With respect to the need to replace the Commission on Human Rights with a Human Rights Council, the Task Force found:**

The inherently political nature of an intergovernmental body such as the Commission inevitably limits its ability to function as the beacon of human rights envisioned when it was created in 1946. This situation is exacerbated by its relatively large size (53 Member States), status as a subsidiary of ECOSOC and limited meeting schedule (once a year apart from special sessions).

As the Secretary-General noted in his Larger Freedom report, "the Commission's capacity to perform its tasks has been increasingly undermined by its declining credibility and professionalism. In particular, States have sought membership of the Commission not to strengthen human rights, but to protect themselves against criticism or to criticize others."

The standing of the Commission was severely compromised by the selection of Libya as Chair, the re-election of Sudan as a member in the midst of the genocide in Darfur, and the shameful failure of the Commission last year to adopt a resolution clearly condemning that genocide.

The credibility deficit of the Commission has, according to the Secretary-General, cast a shadow on the reputation of the U.N. system as a whole.

The Secretary-General has appropriately identified the reform of U.N. human rights mechanisms as a central component of the entire U.N. reform effort. As such, the protection of human rights is on par with the U.N. interests in promoting security and fostering political and economic development.

As will be discussed in greater detail below, the primary focus for protecting human rights has shifted from standards formulation to implementation. The focus on implementation requires a smaller body than one charged with standards development, and requires a standing committee.

The creation of a Council will enable the U.N. to begin anew with a clean slate and avoid many of the limitations seemingly irrevocably imbedded in the operating system of the Commission.

**The Task Force recommends that in order to more effectively promote the protection of human rights, the Human Rights Commission should be replaced by a new Human Rights Council established on the following basis:**

The Task Force endorses the Secretary-General's proposal of a standing and smaller Human Rights Council, whose members would be elected by the General Assembly subject to a two-thirds majority. As compared with the Commission, the Council would have the status, the time, and smaller and more credible membership to fulfill its responsibilities as the leading human rights intergovernmental body in the U.N. structure.

1. The General Assembly should create a Human Rights Council.

The number of members should be substantially smaller than the 53-member Commission.

2. The Council members should be elected by a two-thirds majority of the General Assembly. The Chair of the Council should be elected by a two-thirds majority of the Council.

The super-majority voting requirement is intended to assure that members are broadly approved by the overwhelming majority of the members of the General Assembly.

3. The Council should be a standing body of the U.N..

The creation of a standing body will enable the Council to devote the necessary time and resources to protecting human rights, and will prohibit states from running out the clock in order to escape censure for human rights violations.

4. The Council should have co-equal status with the other major organs of the U.N. — ECOSOC and the General Assembly.

This will likely require that the Charter be amended, a lengthy and difficult process. In the interim, it may be necessary to establish the Council as a subsidiary body of the General Assembly, with the objective of converting it to a free standing body when charter amendments are next presented to the members.

5. The resolution or amendment establishing the Council should commit all Member States of the U.N. to cooperate with the Council, particularly with its investigative processes.

### Section II
### Setting the Mission of the Human Rights Council

**With respect to the mission of the Human Rights Council, the Task Force found:**

The Commission's original priority was to submit proposals to the General Assembly relating to an international bill of rights, the protection of minorities, the status of women and other human rights norms. The Commission was also charged with making studies and providing information at the request of ECOSOC. Over the years, the Commission has interpreted its broad mandate to encompass the establishment of standards for the protection of human rights, the investigation of systematic abuses, and the recommendation of affirmative measures to protect human rights. During its first twenty years, the Commission emphasized its responsibility for standard setting and successfully produced a number of important draft conventions. While the Commission continues to undertake standard setting work (e.g., the draft text on disappearances), its focus in recent years has shifted to the implementation of existing standards.

To promote the ability of the Commission to investigate systematic human rights abuses, the ECOSOC authorized the Commission to carry out special investigative procedures. Of these procedures, certain ones were subject to strict rules of confidentiality, which have undermined their effectiveness. The Commission has developed a monitoring system but has never adequately fulfilled its potential to protect fundamental civil and political rights.

In particular, the increasingly politicized nature of the Commission has severely compromised its capacity to take action in response to serious human rights violations. Some states have used the Commission's recognition of social and economic rights to deflect attention from the violation of civil and political rights.

The Commission has often remained silent in the face of gross violations of human rights, or has adopted ineffectual resolutions without urging further, meaningful steps. A recent instance of this failure was the Commission's weak response to the genocide in Darfur, Sudan during the 60th Session.

The Commission's efforts to investigate or censure human rights violators are frequently stifled through bloc voting, no-action motions, and other procedural maneuvers by regional groups and by alliances of non-democratic states. For instance, certain notorious violators of human rights successfully banded together in the 60th Session of the Commission to defeat important resolutions. Only the most politically isolated states are subject to censure by the Commission, which means that Middle Eastern and African States, as well as Russia and China, enjoy a near-immunity. On the other hand, the Commission spends a disproportionate amount of its time on Israel, which is the only state with its own agenda item and is the subject of repeated resolutions.

The Commission's emphasis on consensus decision-making ultimately protects human rights violators by enabling them and their allies to drastically water down country-specific resolutions or chairperson's statements.

As the Secretary-General has noted, the human rights priority in the coming years is on effective implementation of the by now well-established international norms.

**The Task Force recommends that to fulfill its mission and avoid the failings of the Commission, the Human Rights Council should follow the following guidelines:**

> 1. The Council should assign special priority to protecting and promoting fundamental human rights that form the foundation of human dignity by protecting all human beings against abusive state action. Member states should not be allowed to use protection of economic and social rights as a pretext to detract from protection of civil and political rights.

> The Council should establish procedures and implement a program of strong initiatives to ensure the protection of these fundamental human rights, including aggressive investigations, public hearings, and reports to the Security Council when there is evidence that an egregious violation has occurred. These efforts should not detract from the attention given to other human rights abuses within the jurisdiction of the Council.

> 2. Efforts should be undertaken to establish a highly professional investigative process, and in particular a strong rapporteur system.

> Discriminatory, exclusive agenda items, such as the agenda item for Israel, the only country so treated, should not be continued. While no country should avoid

scrutiny when it is warranted, the exclusive focus of an entire agenda item on a single country is discriminatory.

3. The Council should bring attention quickly to conflicts that could result in ethnic cleansing and genocide, and should mobilize international action to resolve these conflicts and prevent atrocities.

### Section III
### Selection Process for the Members of the Council and Code of Conduct

This section addresses the selection of members of the Council and the adoption of a Code of Conduct. The Task Force found that efforts to establish binding criteria for the selection of members of the Council, while highly desirable, would not be feasible, except in the instance of countries that are under Chapter VII actions imposed by the Security Council or the censure by new Human Rights Council. However, there are a variety of other, less contentious means to improve the selection process and promote more responsible behavior by members. The Task Force recommends that the Secretary-General and the High Commissioner informally bring their influence to bear in protecting the credibility of the Council from being compromised by the selection of known human rights violators. Further, the U.S. and other democratic states should more effectively organize the participation of democratic states across the regional groups so as to promote the selection of states with commendable human rights records. In addition, the Task Force recommends the adoption by the Council of a Code of Conduct whereby all Member States would pledge to comply with obligations imposed under human rights agreements to which they are party, to cooperate with the investigative mechanisms of the Council, and to designate prominent persons with substantial human rights expertise to head their delegations. Serious violations of a member's obligations of good citizenship of the Council imposed under Article IV of the Code could result in removal and disqualification from future membership.

**With respect to the selection process for the members of the Council and the Chairperson, the Task Force found:**

Membership in the Council brings with it the responsibility to conform to a standard of good citizenship as members of the body, including a commitment to honor human rights obligations assumed under treaties and a pledge to cooperate with the Council, particularly with respect to investigations. Membership in the Council should provide an avenue for states to engage in setting and elaborating standards, reinforcing the protection of human rights, responding to serious violations, promoting human rights, and contributing to the clarification of their conceptual underpinnings. These tasks cannot be meaningfully performed by states that lack credibility in human rights matters.

Member States would have great difficulty reaching a consensus in support of objective membership criteria, although they might be prepared to exclude countries currently sanctioned by the Security Council or censured by the Human Rights Council.

Adopting universal membership, as recommended by the High-level Panel, would likewise not make the Commission more effective. Opening the membership to all members of the U.N. could make it even more difficult for the Commission to respond to human rights violations. Those U.N. bodies that do have universal membership, such as the General Assembly and its third committee, are not particularly effective.

Similarly, the effectiveness of the Commission has been greatly influenced by the independence and professionalism of the Chairperson.

Particular concerns raised by the Task Force include:

- Many Member States fail to uphold the standards embodied in the major human rights instruments and either commit or fail to respond to serious human rights violations;

- Some states become members of the Commission with the purpose of protecting themselves against international criticism for serious human rights violations committed by their own authorities. This finding in particular was highlighted in the observations of the High-level Panel;

- Recently the credibility of the Commission has been substantially degraded as key officers have been selected from some Member States (e.g., Libya) that have a track record of severe human rights violations. Other countries (e.g., Sudan) have been accepted as members notwithstanding egregious and on-going human rights violations:

If the above concerns remain unaddressed in the selection process for the Council, its credibility and relevance will be undercut profoundly.

**The Task Force recommends that in order to promote a representative and effective Council, and ensure the selection of a responsible and independent chairperson, the following reforms should be adopted:**

1. Members of the Council should be elected by the General Assembly on the basis of a two-thirds majority.

2. While the members can be expected to insist that traditional standards of geographic representation be applied, the requirement for a super-majority vote should lead to the rejection of the candidacies of human rights abusers, particularly given the limited number of available memberships.

3. Regional groups should refuse to enter into voting protocols or other procedures, which call for the automatic acceptance of candidates by the appropriate regional group.

4. Assuming that the seats on the Council are allocated among the regional groups, the non-sponsoring regional groups, and in particular the Western European and Other States Group (WEOG), must reserve the right to reject candidates with poor human rights records.

5. Any Member State under Security Council action taken under Chapter VII of the U.N. Charter or censure of the Human Rights Council should be prohibited from serving on the Council.

6. The Secretary-General and the High Commissioner should seek to persuade Member States of the regional groups to reject the candidacies of known human rights violators for membership and leadership in the Council.

7. The U.S. and other democratic states should work together to support candidates for membership and leadership that support human rights and oppose others and develop an agenda for meaningful action by the Council.

8. The U.S. and other democratic states should seek to strengthen and energize the emerging "Democracy Caucus," which is currently chaired by Chile.

   To this end, the U.S. should work with other democracies to build upon the work of the Council for a Community of Democracies to promote a coalition of democratic states that will act in concert to pass key resolutions in response to crises and to develop effective operating mechanisms within the Human Rights Council. The Democracy Caucus should also undertake efforts to ensure that democratic states are selected for membership in the Council and should work to prevent the selection of non-democratic states.

9. To promote the effective development and implementation of a Democracy Caucus agenda and participate effectively in the work of the Council as a standing body, the U.S. should appoint a full time Ambassador to the Council and do so as early as possible. This Ambassador should be instructed to initiate consultations with Democracy Caucus Member State ambassadors in Washington to formulate an agenda and plan of action for the Council meetings. This activity should be coordinated with similar efforts by U.S. Embassies. Particular emphasis should be placed on encouraging the Democracy Caucus member countries of Africa, Eastern Europe, and Latin America to take leadership roles.

10. The Council should adopt a Code of Conduct committing the Member States to promote international protection of human rights; to honor international human rights efforts; to cooperate with the investigative mechanisms of the Council (specifically including cooperation with the rapporteurs charged with investigating allegations of human rights abuses); and to appoint as heads of their delegations persons with substantial human rights expertise. The obligation to appoint as head of delegation persons with human rights experience would go far to enhance the overall professionalism of the Council.

The Code would not impose new human rights obligations on the Member States; rather it would pledge the members to honor existing human rights responsibilities in their capacity as members of the Council. (See Recommendation, Appendix I for Proposed Code.) Since all of these responsibilities are logically related to membership in the Council, a strong case can be made for their acceptability.

A Member State's serious breach of its obligations of good citizenship of the Council imposed under Article IV of the Code could lead to its censure, suspension of membership, or ineligibility for future membership. These obligations arise out of the relationship between every member and the Council and, for that reason, the Code provides for sanctions in the event of serious violations. As a necessary complement to the Code, the Council should create a "Membership Committee" to make determinations of serious breaches of the good citizenship obligations and recommend appropriate sanctions. The Council should adopt rules governing the work of the Membership Committee.

* * *

## Section VI
## Enhancing the Role of NGOs

**With respect to the future relationship of the Council with NGOs, the Task Force found:**

NGOs play an important role in the work of the Commission, serving as a reality check on the rhetoric and political maneuverings of Member States. Yet their access to the Commission has been limited, thereby minimizing their ability to provide the Commission with useful information. According to a long-standing decision of the Commission, representatives of Member States are allotted twice the speaking time permitted to NGOs. Due to this time constraint, in many instances NGOs have been forced to give joint statements before the Commission, which some groups have found to be unacceptable. Moreover, limits on speaking time and on the length of written submissions have required NGOs to make short, hasty arguments. In addition, NGOs have sometimes been arbitrarily barred from the proceedings of the Commission and working groups. The transformation of the Commission into a standing Council will provide greater opportunity for constructive NGO involvement in the work of the Council.

**The Task Force recommends that in order to enhance the participation of NGOs, the Human Rights Council should adopt the following policies:**

1. NGOs should maintain, at a minimum, the same degree of access to the Council as now exists with the Commission.

2. The High Commissioner recently appointed an NGO liaison official, whose responsibilities should be continued and expanded to include coordination between NGOs and the Council.

3. Consistent with its status as a standing body, the Council should enlarge the opportunity of NGOs to provide information to it. Requirements, such as the Commission imposes, restricting NGOs to half the speaking time allotted to Member States, should not be adopted.

4. The Council should recognize and support the valuable contributions NGOs make with respect to the follow-up of field visits and implementation of recommendations.

---

## Authors' Note

The following article discusses the creation of the United Nations Human Rights Council. The article provides an overview of the debates that arose concerning the Council's characteristics and functions, namely its size and representation, voting procedure, term limits, periodic review, and standing sessions. The article considers the viewpoints of strong proponents of the Council and its detractors, including the United States.

---

## 2. Scott R. Lyons, The New United Nations Human Rights Council

### American Society of International Law, 2006

After five months of contentious negotiations to develop a new entity to replace the ineffective Commission on Human Rights, the United Nations General Assembly overwhelmingly approved the creation of a Human Rights Council on March 15, 2006. The vote approved a draft resolution, put forth as a compromise proposal on February 23, 2006, by General Assembly President Jan Eliasson. The outcome is recognized as being imperfect due to efforts to reach consensus among Member States. However, supporters of the Human Rights Council consider this agreement to be a significant accomplishment for U.N. Reform.

Secretary-General Kofi Annan, High Commissioner for Human Rights Louise Arbour, the United Nations Association-USA, the human rights non-governmental organizations (NGOs), and several Nobel Peace Prize laureates publicly supported the new compromise proposal. The common sentiment among them was that the new Human Rights Council represents a substantial improvement over the Commission in many ways, while preserving some of the Commission's best features, including NGO access, use of independent rapporteurs, and the authority to adopt individual country resolutions.

John Bolton, the United States Permanent Representative to the U.N., voiced strong opposition and voted against the proposal because the compromise included a fundamental concession among the many problems in the view of the U.S.: the text dropped the requirement for election to the Council from a minimum two-thirds of U.N. Member States present and voting, to a simple majority of all Member States. The U.S. argued that this provision, along with the failure to include a clause excluding States sanctioned for human rights abuses by the Security Council, may permit abusive regimes to participate in the Human Rights Council.

## The Debate Concerning the Human Rights Council and Its New Provisions

### Criteria for Membership

*Criteria for Membership*

The NGO community, the Secretary-General, the U.S., and many other states were strong advocates of excluding States with atrocious human rights records from participating in the new Human Rights Council. This position responded to prior or current membership by countries accused of gross human rights abuses, including Zimbabwe, the Sudan, the Republic of the Congo, Cuba, Ethiopia, and Saudi Arabia, as well as Libya, which chaired the Commission in 2003. There has been concern that some States previously sought membership on the Commission to shield themselves from public condemnation or to have a platform to criticize others. The new Human Rights Council includes the criterion that membership "shall take into account candidates' contribution to the promotion and protection of human rights." An earlier draft prohibited membership to any State found responsible for human rights abuses or violations by U.N. bodies. However, the new Council opens participation to all Member States regardless of Security Council sanctions, something strongly opposed by the U.S. Contention will remain as to how the U.N. defines and evaluates the "contribution" requirement, as the language is ambiguous and could still permit States that abuse human rights to gain membership.

*Size/Representation*

The Commission on Human Rights had 53 members, or over 25% of U.N. Member States. The U.S. continuously advocated that that number was too large to be effective, with Ambassador Bolton indicating a preference for 20 members in the new Council, and 30 as an absolute maximum. The new Council includes 47 members, which is a greater number than even than the original amount suggested by General Assembly President Eliasson. A larger Council increases the opportunity for small developing States to have access to the world stage. However, there is also a greater possibility of inefficiency and diplomatic wrangling. The new Council also includes widespread geographic representation based upon regional groups, with the largest number of seats going to Africa and Asia. The U.S. expressed concern that the regional allocation does not properly take into account a State's human rights performance, but the "contribution" clause and secret balloting (which would not allow regional groups to select their own Council members, but would enable States to vote against neighboring powers without risking retaliation) may address this problem.

There was originally contention around whether the permanent five members of the Security Council (the United Kingdom, France, the Russian Federation, China, and the U.S.) would have an enhanced opportunity for membership on the Council. Ambassador Bolton originally advocated for the five permanent members to have permanent seats on the Human Rights Council, but backed away from this position in response to widespread opposition. It was not included in the final version.

*Election Process*

The most controversial issues stemmed from electoral requirements. The debate centered on whether a two-thirds (2/3) vote or a simple majority should be required to obtain membership. The U.S., the European Union, and the NGO community originally endorsed a two-thirds (2/3) requirement in order to make it easier to exclude states that are gross violators of human rights. An interesting note was that this rule could have excluded the U.S. from a seat, which happened a few years ago, by a united Islamic Conference vote (the 56 Islamic states) or by states seeking retribution. The new Council only requires a simple majority directly elected through secret ballots by the General Assembly. As noted above, though, the simple majority must be a majority of *all* Member States. In some cases, that could set a higher standard for election than a standard of two-thirds of the Member States actually present and voting at the time the election is held.

### Term Limits

Another disputed provision was the inclusion of term limits. Council members will serve for a three-year period and are not eligible for re-election after two consecutive terms. The U.S. opposed this provision since it precludes the U.S. from always being eligible to sit on the Human Rights Council.

### Periodic Review

An important provision is that all States sitting on the new Council will be subject to a "universal periodic review mechanism" that examines their human rights records. The intention of this clause is to keep States from using the Council to shield their own human rights records from scrutiny or from "hiding out" while criticizing other States.

### Standing Sessions

An issue of previous concern had been the inactivity of the Human Rights Commission, stemming from both its short session and its infrequent meetings. The Commission met only six weeks a year in a single session. As a result, it was often not able to address human rights concerns that arose because of the delay in response time and a possible backlog by the time it actually sat. The new Council must meet regularly and for at least three sessions a year, one of them to be no less than ten weeks. An important additional feature that the U.S. advocated and was included is that the Human Rights Council will be able to have "special sessions" if the need arises, at the request of a Member of the Council with support from one-third of the Council.

### Conclusion

The new Human Rights Council is widely acknowledged to be imperfect. However, there were risks in the failure to create a new Council, which would have been be an embarrassment for the U.N., or to create one that showed no semblance of reform or lessons learned from the Commission on Human Rights, which would have been a different type of embarrassment for the U.N.. To succeed, the new Human Rights Council must truly be "transparent, fair and impartial," as the text indicates, "and uphold the highest standards in the promotion and protection of human rights." The test will be whether the U.N. General Assembly elects members with respectable human rights records which truly want to confront those States that are responsible for human rights abuses, regardless of geo-strategic or border relationships.

## *Authors' Note*

**Goldstone Report:** In 2009, the U.N. Human Rights Council commissioned Justice Richard Goldstone to lead a fact-finding mission to investigate violations of international human rights law and international humanitarian law during the Gaza War that occurred from December 2008 to January 2009. The mandate of the U.N. Fact Finding

Mission on the Gaza Conflict was "[t]o investigate all violations of international human
rights law and international humanitarian law that might have been committed at any
time in the context of the military operations that were conducted in Gaza during the
period from 27 December 2008 and 18 January 2009, whether before, during or after."
The report is considered to be highly controversial, as it initially only called for an investigation of Israeli violations. Yet, Goldstone's team reported that both Israel and
Hamas had violated laws of war. Both Israel and Hamas dismissed the findings of the report. Material 3 is the media summary issued after the release of the full report. The
following materials highlight the debate and controversy behind the report and speak to
the effectiveness of the Human Rights Council.

---

## 3. Goldstone U.N. Fact Finding Mission Summary Report
### U.N. Human Rights Council, 2009

*Findings*:

   The Mission found that, in the lead up to the Israeli military assault on Gaza, Israel
imposed a blockade amounting to collective punishment and carried out a systematic
policy of progressive isolation and deprivation of the Gaza Strip. During the military operation, houses, factories, wells, schools, hospitals, police stations and other public buildings were destroyed, with families, including the elderly and children, left living amid the
rubble of their former dwellings long after the attacks ended, as no reconstruction has
been possible due to the continuing blockade. Significant trauma, both immediate and
long-term, has been suffered by the population of Gaza. More than 1,400 people were
killed. The Gaza military operations were directed by Israel at the people of Gaza as a
whole, in furtherance of an overall policy aimed at punishing the Gaza population, and
in a deliberate policy of disproportionate force aimed at the civilian population. The destruction of food supply installations, water sanitation systems, concrete factories and
residential houses was the result of a deliberate and systematic policy to make the daily
process of living, and dignified living, more difficult for the civilian population. Israeli
forces also humiliated, dehumanized and carried out an assault on the dignity of the people in Gaza, through the use of human shields, unlawful detentions, unacceptable conditions of detention, the vandalizing of houses, the treatment of people when their houses
were entered, graffiti on the walls, obscenities and racist slogans. The Israeli operations
were carefully planned in all their phases as a deliberately disproportionate attack designed to punish, humiliate and terrorize a civilian population, radically diminish its local
economic capacity both to work and to provide for itself, and to force upon it an ever
increasing sense of dependency and vulnerability. Responsibility lies in the first place with
those who designed, planned, ordered and oversaw the operations.

   Israel failed to take feasible precautions required by international law to avoid or minimize loss of civilian life, injury to civilians and damage to civilian objects. The firing of
white phosphorus shells over the UNRWA compound, the intentional strike at the Al
Quds hospital using high explosive artillery shells and white phosphorous, the attack
against Al Wafa hospital, were violations of international humanitarian law. The kinds of
warnings issued by Israel in Gaza cannot be considered as sufficiently effective in the circumstances to comply with customary law. There were numerous instances of deliberate
attacks on civilians and civilian objects (individuals, whole families, houses, mosques)
in violation of the fundamental international humanitarian law principle of distinction,
resulting in deaths and serious injuries. Israeli attacks were also launched with the in-

tention of spreading terror among the civilian population. In several cases, Israeli armed forces did not allow humanitarian organisations access to the wounded and medical relief, as required by international law. In one incident investigated, involving the deaths of at least 35 Palestinians, the Mission found that Israeli forces launched an attack which a reasonable commander would have expected to cause excessive loss of civilian life. By deliberately attacking police stations and killing large numbers of policemen, most of whom were civilian non-combatants, Israel violated international humanitarian law.

The Mission found that Israel used white phosphorous, flechettes and heavy metal weapons. The use of white phosphorous, flechettes and heavy metal (such as tungsten) is restricted or even prohibited in certain circumstances. Flechettes, as an area weapon, are particularly unsuitable for use in urban settings while the Mission is of the view that the use of white phosphorous as an obscurant should be banned. The Mission also investigated several incidents in which Israeli armed forces used local Palestinian residents as human shields. Israel's questioning of Palestinian civilians under threat of death or injury to extract information constitutes a violation of the Fourth Geneva Convention. Israeli forces in Gaza rounded up and detained large groups of persons protected under the Fourth Geneva Convention. Severe beatings, humiliating and degrading treatment and detention in foul conditions suffered by individuals in the Gaza Strip under the control of the Israeli forces and in detention in Israel, constitute a violation of international humanitarian and human rights law. Israel's treatment of women during detention was contrary to the requirements of international law. Israel's rounding-up of large groups of civilians and their prolonged detention under the circumstances described in the Report constitute a collective penalty and amounts to measures of intimidation or terror prohibited the Fourth Geneva Convention. Israel's attacks against the Palestinian Legislative Council building and the main prison in Gaza constituted deliberate attacks on civilian objects in violation of international humanitarian law. Israeli armed forces unlawfully and wantonly attacked and destroyed without military necessity a number of food production facilities, drinking water installations, farms and animals. Israeli forces carried out widespread destruction of private residential houses, water wells and water tanks unlawfully and wantonly. Israel also disregarded the inviolability of United Nations premises, facilities and staff, and this is unacceptable.

Israel's blockade of Gaza amounts to a violation of Israel's obligations as an Occupying Power under the Fourth Geneva Convention. The deliberate actions of the Israeli forces and the declared policies of the Government indicate the intention to inflict collective punishment on the people of the Gaza Strip. Israel violated its obligation to allow free passage of all consignments of medical and hospital objects, food and clothing that were needed to meet the urgent humanitarian needs of the civilian population.

There is strong evidence that Israeli forces committed grave breaches of the Fourth Geneva Convention in Gaza, including: willful killing, torture or inhuman treatment, willfully causing great suffering or serious injury to body or health, and extensive destruction of property. As grave breaches, these acts give rise to individual criminal responsibility. The use of human shields also constitutes a war crime under the Rome Statute of the International Criminal Court. Israeli acts that deprive Palestinians in the Gaza Strip of their means of subsistence, employment, housing and water, that deny their freedom of movement and their right to leave and enter their own country, that limit their rights to access a court of law and an effective remedy, could lead a competent court to find that the crime of persecution, a crime against humanity, has been committed.

In the West Bank, with acts of violence by settlers against Palestinians (which have increased), Israel failed to protect the Palestinians, and sometimes acquiesced to the

acts of violence. Israel used excessive force against Palestinian demonstrators, including the use of firearms, including live ammunition, and the use of snipers resulting in
the deaths of demonstrators, in violation of international law. Israel has discriminatory
"open fire regulations" for security forces dealing with demonstrations, based on the
presence of persons with a particular nationality, violating the principle of non-
discrimination in international law. Israel has failed to investigate, and when appropriate prosecute, acts by its agents or by third parties involving serious violations of
international humanitarian law and human rights law. Israel's removal of residential
status from Palestinians could lead to virtual deportation and entail additional violations
of other rights.

Israeli practices of detention of Palestinians in Israeli prisons before and during the
military operations are generally inconsistent with human rights requirements. The practice of administrative detention by Israel contravenes the right not to be arbitrarily detained, and Israel's use of secret evidence as a basis for the administrative detention is
inconsistent with the ICCPR. The detention of members of the Palestinian Legislative
Council by Israel is in violation of the ICCPR also constitutes an instance of collective
punishment prohibited under article 33 of the GC IV. The same can be said about the
massive detention of adults and children, often in inhuman or degrading conditions and
without the guarantees required by international law.

Israeli checkpoints are often a site of humiliation. The extensive destruction and appropriation of property, including land confiscation and house demolitions in the West
Bank including East Jerusalem, not justified by military necessity and carried out unlawfully and wantonly, amounts to a grave breach of the Geneva Conventions. The continued
construction of settlements constitutes a violation of article 49 of the Fourth Geneva Convention. As movement and access restrictions, the settlements and their infrastructure,
demographic policies vis-à-vis Jerusalem and Area C of the West bank, as well as the separation of Gaza from the West Bank, prevent a viable, contiguous and sovereign Palestinian state from arising, they are in violation of the *jus cogens* right to self-determination.

The prolonged situation of impunity has created a justice crisis in the OPT that warrants action. Israel's system of investigation and prosecution of serious violations of
human rights and humanitarian law, in particular of suspected war crimes and crimes against
humanity, has major structural flaws that make the system inconsistent with international
standards. The few investigations conducted by the Israeli authorities on alleged serious
violations of international human rights and humanitarian law and, in particular, alleged
war crimes, lack the required credibility and conformity with international standards.
There is little potential for accountability for serious violations of international humanitarian and human rights law through domestic institutions in Israel.

Inside Israel, there has been intolerance for dissent against the war, the authorities
placed obstacles in the way of protesters, there were instances of physical violence against
protesters, and hostile retaliatory actions against civil society organisations by the Government. Activists were also compelled to attend interviews with the General Security
Services. Israel's denial of media access to Gaza and the continuing denial of access to
human rights monitors are an attempt to remove the Government's actions from public
scrutiny and to impede investigations and reporting.

Palestinian armed groups have launched rockets and mortars into Israel since April
2001. Between 27 December 2008 and 18 January 2009, these attacks have left 4 people
dead and hundreds injured, while causing terror, psychological trauma, and erosion of
the educational, social, cultural and economic lives of the communities in southern Is-

rael. For its part, Israel has not provided the same level of protection from rockets and mortars to affected Palestinian citizens as it has to Jewish citizens.

In firing rockets and mortars into Southern Israel, Palestinian armed groups operating in the Gaza Strip failed to distinguish between military targets and the civilian population and civilian objects in Southern Israel. Where there is no intended military target and the rockets and mortars are launched into civilian areas, they constitute a deliberate attack against the civilian population, which would constitute war crimes and may amount to crimes against humanity. The rocket and mortars attacks have caused terror in the affected communities of southern Israel, causing loss of life and physical and mental injury to civilians as well as damage to buildings and property. Israeli soldier Gilad Shalit meets the requirements for prisoner-of-war status under the Third Geneva Convention and should be protected, treated humanely and be allowed external communication. The Mission found no evidence to suggest that Palestinian armed groups in Gaza either directed civilians to areas where attacks were being launched or that they forced civilians to remain within the vicinity of the attacks. The Mission also found no evidence that members of Palestinian armed groups engaged in combat in civilian dress. In the one incident the Mission investigated, of an Israeli attack on a mosque, the Mission found that there was no indication that that mosque was used for military purposes or to shield military activities.

The Gaza authorities carried out extrajudicial executions, arbitrary arrest, detention and ill treatment of people, in particular political opponents, which constitute serious violations of human rights. The Palestinian Authority's actions against political opponents in the West Bank also constitute violations of human rights. Detentions on political grounds violate the rights to liberty and security of person, to a fair trial and the right not to be discriminated against on the basis of one's political opinion. Reports of torture and other forms of ill treatment during arrest and detention require prompt investigation and accountability. Finally, conflict between Fatah and Hamas is having adverse consequences for the human rights of the Palestinian population.

International law sets obligations on States to ensure compliance by other States (in this case, Israel) with international humanitarian law, and to help protect populations from war crimes and crimes against humanity. The international community has been largely silent and has to-date failed to act to ensure the protection of the civilian population in the Gaza Strip and generally in the OPT. The isolation of the Gaza authorities and the sanctions against the Gaza Strip have negatively impacted on the protection of the population. Protection of civilian populations requires respect for international law and accountability for violations.

To deny modes of accountability reinforces impunity. Allegations of violations of international humanitarian law falling within the jurisdiction of responsible Palestinian authorities in Gaza have also not been investigated. Where domestic authorities are unable or unwilling to comply with this obligation, international justice mechanisms must be activated to prevent impunity. There is little potential for accountability for serious violations of international humanitarian and human rights law through domestic institutions in Israel and even less in Gaza. Longstanding impunity has been a key factor in the perpetuation of violence in the region. Several of the violations referred to in this report amount to grave breaches of the Fourth Geneva Convention, and there is a duty imposed by the Geneva Conventions on all High Contracting Parties to search for and bring before their courts those responsible for the alleged violations. The serious violations of International Humanitarian Law recounted in this report fall within the subject-matter jurisdiction of the International Criminal Court (ICC). The prosecution of persons responsible for serious violations of international humanitarian law would contribute to ending such violations, to the protection of civilians and to the restoration and maintenance of peace.

*Recommendations*

- *To the Human Rights Council, that it* Request the Secretary-General to bring this report to the attention of the Security Council under Art. 99 of the Charter so that the Security Council may consider action; and that it Submit the report to the General Assembly with a request that it should be considered.

- *To the United Nations Security Council, with regard to Israel, that it* require the Government of Israel, under Article 40 of the Charter of the United Nations: To take all appropriate steps, within a period of three months, to launch appropriate investigations that are independent and in conformity with international standards; Inform the Security Council, within a further period of three months, of actions taken; Establish an independent committee of experts in International Humanitarian and Human Rights Law to monitor and report on any domestic legal or other proceedings undertaken by the Government of Israel; Upon receipt of the committee's report the Security Council consider the situation and, in the absence of good faith investigations that are independent and in conformity with international standards, again acting under Chapter VII of the Charter of the United Nations, refer the situation in Gaza to the Prosecutor of the International Criminal Court.

- *To the United Nations Security Council, with regard to the relevant Palestinian authorities, that it:* require the independent committee of experts (referred to in previous paragraph) to monitor and report on any domestic legal or other proceedings undertaken by the relevant authorities in the Gaza Strip; Upon receipt of the committee's report the Security Council consider the situation and, in the absence of good faith investigations that are independent and in conformity with international standards, acting under Chapter VII of the Charter of the United Nations, refer the situation in Gaza to the Prosecutor of the International Criminal Court.

- *To the Prosecutor of the International Criminal Court,* With reference to the declaration under article 12 (3) received by the Office of the Prosecutor of the ICC from the Government of Palestine, the legal determination should be made by the Prosecutor as expeditiously as possible; The Mission further recommends that the United Nations Human Rights Council formally submit this report to the Prosecutor of the ICC.

- *To the General Assembly,* The Mission recommends that the General Assembly request the Security Council to report to it on measures taken with regard to ensuring accountability for serious violations of international humanitarian and human rights law; The GA may consider whether additional action within its powers is required in the interests of justice, including under resolution 377 (V) Uniting for Peace; Establish an escrow fund to be used to pay adequate compensation to Palestinians who have suffered loss and damage, and that the Government of Israel pay the required amounts into such fund; Ask the Government of Switzerland to convene a conference of the High Contracting Parties to the Fourth Geneva Convention of 1949 on measures to enforce the Convention in the OPT.

- *To Israel,* The Mission recommends that Israel immediately cease the border closures and restrictions of passage through border crossings with the Gaza Strip; Cease the restrictions on access to the sea for fishing purposes; Review its rules of engagement, standard operating procedures, open fire regulations and other guidance for military and security personnel; Allow freedom of movement for Palestinians within the OPT—within the West Bank including East Jerusalem, between the Gaza Strip and the West Bank and between the OPT and the outside world; Lift travel bans currently in place on Palestinians for their human rights or political activities; Release Palestinians who are detained in Israeli prisons in connection with the occupation; Cease the discriminatory treatment of Palestinian detainees; Release all members of the Palestinian Legislative Council currently in detention; Cease actions aimed at limiting the expression of criticism by civil society and members of the public; Refrain from any action of reprisal against individuals and organizations that have cooperated with the U.N. Fact Finding Mission; Respect the inviolability of U.N. premises and personnel; Provide reparation to the United Nations fully and without further delay.

- *To Palestinian armed groups,* The Mission recommends that Palestinian armed groups undertake forthwith to respect international humanitarian law, and that Palestinian armed groups who hold Israeli soldier Gilad Shalit in detention release him on humanitarian grounds.

- *To responsible Palestinian authorities,* Ensure prompt and independent investigation of all allegations of serious human rights violations by security forces under its control; Release without delay all political detainees currently in their power and refrain from further arrests on political grounds.

- *To the international community, States Parties to the Geneva Conventions of 1949* start criminal investigations in national courts, using universal jurisdiction, where there is sufficient evidence of the commission of grave breaches of the Geneva Conventions of 1949; Support the work of Palestinian and Israeli human rights organizations in documenting and publicly reporting on violations of human rights and international humanitarian law; States involved in peace negotiations between Israel and representatives of the Palestinian people, especially the Quartet, ensure that respect for the rule of law, international law and human rights assume a central role in internationally sponsored peace initiatives; Initiate a programme of environmental monitoring under the auspices of the United Nations.

- *To the international community and responsible Palestinian authorities,* Establish appropriate mechanisms to ensure that the funds pledged by international donors for reconstruction activities in the Gaza strip are smoothly and efficiently disbursed.

- *To the international community, Israel and Palestinian authorities,* Actors involved in the peace process should involve Israeli and Palestinian civil society and women in devising sustainable peace agreements based on respect for international law.

- *To the United Nations Secretary General,* Develop a policy to integrate human rights in peace initiatives in which the United Nations is involved, especially the Quartet.

- *To the Office of the High Commissioner for Human Rights,* Monitor the situation of persons who have cooperated with the U.N. Fact Finding Mission and pay attention to follow up to the Mission's recommendations in its periodic reporting on the OPT to the Human Rights Council.

---

## 4. Peter Berkowitz, The Goldstone Report and International Law
*Policy Review*, 2010
[footnotes omitted by editors]

The controversy over the "Report of the United Nations Fact Finding Mission on the Gaza Conflict" (September 15, 2009), more commonly known as the Goldstone

Report, seems to have died down. But its larger significance has yet to be appreciated. For the most part, the controversy has swirled around the reliability of the Goldstone Report's factual findings and the validity of its legal findings concerning Operation Cast Lead, which Israel launched on December 27, 2008, and concluded on January 18, 2009. But another and more far-reaching issue, which should be of great significance to those who take seriously the claims of international law to govern the conduct of war, has scarcely been noticed. And that pertains to the disregarding of fundamental norms and principles of international law by the United Nations Human Rights Council (HRC), which authorized the Goldstone Mission; by the Mission members, who produced the Goldstone Report; and by the HRC and the United Nations General Assembly (of which the HRC is a subsidiary organ), which endorsed the report's recommendations. Their conduct combines an exaltation of, and disrespect for, international law. It is driven by an ambition to shift authority over critical judgments about the conduct of war from states to international institutions. Among the most serious political consequences of this shift is the impairment of the ability of liberal democracies to deal lawfully and effectively with the complex and multifarious threats presented by transnational terrorists.

Notwithstanding a veneer of equal interest in the unlawful conduct of both Israel and the Palestinians, the Goldstone Report—informally named after the head of the U.N. Mission, Richard Goldstone, former judge of the Constitutional Court of South Africa and former prosecutor of the International Criminal Tribunals for the former Yugoslavia and Rwanda—overwhelmingly focused on allegations that in Operation Cast Lead Israel committed war crimes and crimes against humanity. The purpose of Israel's three-week operation was to substantially reduce the rocket and mortar fire that Hamas, long recognized by the United States and European Union as a terrorist organization, had been unlawfully raining down upon civilian targets in southern Israel for eight years, and which Hamas had intensified after its bloody takeover of Gaza from the Palestinian Authority in 2007. While the Goldstone Report indicated that here and there Palestinian armed groups may have committed war crimes, it purported to find substantial evidence—based primarily on the testimony of Palestinians either affiliated with, or subject to, Hamas—that Israel had repeatedly violated international law by using disproportionate force. At its most incendiary, the Goldstone Report purported to find solid evidence that Israel had committed crimes against humanity—among the gravest breaches of international law—by implementing a deliberate policy of terrorizing Palestinian civilians, both by targeting civilian noncombatants and destroying civilian infrastructure.

Israel has provided three major responses to the Goldstone Report. The most recent came from the Intelligence and Terrorism Information Center (ITIC), an Israeli NGO that works closely with the Israel Defense Forces (IDF). In March 2010, the ITIC published and posted online a 349-page study, "Hamas and the Terrorist Threat from the Gaza Strip: The Main Findings of the Goldstone Report Versus the Factual Findings." Like the two previously published accounts by the Israeli government of the country's continuing investigations of allegations of unlawful conduct committed by its armed forces during the three weeks of Operation Cast Lead—"The Operation in Gaza: Factual and Legal Aspects" (July 29, 2009), and "Gaza Operation Investigations: An Update'" (January 29, 2010)—it garnered next to no attention in the press, from international human rights organizations, from the HRC, or from the General Assembly. Nor have the Goldstone Report's champions in the international human rights community or Judge Goldstone and his colleagues dealt seriously with the incisive criticisms published by scholars and journalists concerning both the report's factual findings and legal findings.

But the deeper issue for international law concerns the right and the responsibility of states to make lawful judgments, under the international law of armed conflict, about the conduct of war, including the crucial judgments in asymmetric warfare concerning what constitutes a proportional use of force. That issue cannot be resolved by showing that the Goldstone Report's findings of fact about the Gaza operation are severely biased, or by demonstrating that the report misapplied or misunderstood the test for determining whether Israel exercised force in a proportional manner, although such showings and demonstrations are highly relevant. Nor can it be resolved by bringing to light how the Goldstone Mission itself—as conceived and authorized by the Human Rights Council, carried out by Goldstone and his colleagues, and endorsed by the United Nations General Assembly—disregarded basic norms and principles of international law, even though this multifarious disregard of law is of great significance. In the end, whether nation-states or international authorities should have primary responsibility for enforcing the lawful conduct of war turns on conflicting opinions about armed conflict, politics, and justice. Even those many conservatives and progressives who share a commitment to the freedom and dignity of the individual may come to different conclusions grounded in conflicting opinions about the best means for securing individual rights while maintaining international order.

Authoritative sources in international law assign primary responsibility for judgments about whether war has been conducted in accordance with the law of armed conflict to the judicial and other relevant organs of nation-states. That assignment is rooted in the larger liberal tradition's teaching that nation-states—particularly those based on the consent of the governed and devoted to securing individual rights—are the best and most legitimate means of securing peace, exercising authority over the individual, and preserving political freedom. That teaching is bound up with the view that states are likely to be more sober in assessing the actions of other states than international organizations because states must bear the burden of any proposed reform or rule. In contrast, the Goldstone Report and its supporters appear to be animated by the conviction that judgments about the lawful conduct of war are best and primarily vindicated by international institutions, because of their superior objectivity, impartiality, and expertise. And they have shown themselves willing to disregard international law as it is in order to remake it as they believe it should be. One reason to prefer the allocation of responsibilities in international law as it currently stands to the Goldstone Report's efforts to transform it are the report's stunning defects. They illustrate that those who are responsible for the operation of international institutions are no less subject to the passions and prejudices that thwart the impartial and objective administration of law than the government officials in civilized nations, and in some cases may be more subject to such passions and prejudices.

\* \* \*

## 5. Dinah PoKempner, Valuing the Goldstone Report
*Global Governance*, 2010

The Goldstone Report had a politicized and emotional reception that has colored its evaluation to date. There have been so many attacks on the report, both before and after its release, that the campaign took on a life and logic of its own. Most of the attacks allege bias in some way without seriously contesting the actual findings of the report. Given that Justice Richard Goldstone revised the mission's mandate to apply equally to all sides, and found serious crimes on the part of both Hamas and Israel, these attacks are ill-founded at best and sometimes just efforts to change the subject. But calls of bias strongly resonate, given Israel's sense of continual siege and the mission's sponsorship by the U.N. Human Rights Council, hardly a neutral broker in the conflict. Another frequent contention is that the report passes judgment on Israel's right to defend itself, or pronounces standards that make effective self-defense impossible. This angle plays into both Jewish anxiety over the threat to the existence of Israel, and Western worries about fighting asymmetrical war. The few critiques that go to real substance tend to rely on the inadequately documented assertions of Israeli officials or reflect disagreements on the proper legal standards to apply to the conflict. So far, there has been virtually no well-sourced, transparent response by either side to the report's very serious allegations.

The scuffling obscures a longer perspective: will the report accomplish its mission; namely, to impel the parties in conflict to examine their conduct and hold those responsible for violations to account? A functional assessment of the report on its own terms, compliance with human rights and international humanitarian law (IHL), is most relevant to those who suffered violations and to the development of law, practices, and institutions in this area. From this vantage point, there is a mixed picture, with some success.

As an example of U.N. fact-finding, the mission followed the best U.N. efforts, and its findings are consistent with that of other independent analysts. Although it might have been more explicit as to the evidentiary standards it employed, the mission did consider facts on each side and explained how it discounted or credited evidence. Its legal analysis follows current international legal interpretation while opening new questions to debate and development. The report provided a detailed template against which to judge progress in investigation and accountability.

*  *  *

### The Context of the Controversy

By any measure, the civilian toll of Operation Cast Lead (OCL) was severe. Casualties on the Palestinian side were in the neighborhood of 1,400 lives, with the Israeli human rights group B'Tselem estimating more than half of these civilian deaths, even excluding the killing of police. The IDF inflicted enormous destruction of the civilian infrastructure on top of the deprivations already produced from Israel's blockade, resulting in tens of thousands of persons displaced, approximately 4,000 residences destroyed and 3,000 seriously damaged, in addition to tremendous damage to farms, factories, and water and sanitation works. Reconstruction is largely at a standstill due to Israel's refusal to allow cement and iron through its blockade. On the Israeli side, in contrast, the war is widely assessed as having accomplished its purpose—halting the rocket attacks against an increasing circle of civilian areas within range from Gaza. The children of Sderot can sleep better, and the economies of the Israeli communities nearest Gaza are reviving. The military operation produced few casualties on the Israeli side, and was overwhelmingly supported by the Israeli public.

The operation, though "successful" in terms of Israeli government objectives, was perceived as disproportionate and punitive by many other nations. The Human Rights Council mandated a one-sided investigation into the humanitarian law and human rights violations of Israel, a mandate Justice Goldstone initially rejected and then revised to extend to violations on all sides of the conflict, which was approved by the president of the council. Goldstone indeed found war crimes and possible crimes against humanity on the part of both Israel and Hamas. He urged that thorough legal investigations be taken up in timely fashion by both sides and, if not, then by the international community, including possible referral to the International Criminal Court.

Israel chose not to cooperate with the investigation. This was an opportunity missed, as it had in Justice Goldstone an exceptionally experienced and eminent jurist and investigator with personal ties to Israel who was committed to ensuring a fair hearing. As it had done on the occasion of the International Court of Justice's consideration of the legality of the "separation barrier," the Israeli government refused to provide information or otherwise cooperate, and then condemned the outcome as uninformed and biased. Although this maneuver is hardly unique to Israel, it is both damaging to the international system and the uncooperative state's reputation. It suggested that Israel had something to hide and did not want a credible investigation.

\* \* \*

### The Arguments of Delegitimation

The report's legitimacy has been questioned even by critics of Israel's government because it was mandated by the Human Rights Council, a body that has shown an extreme institutional bias against Israel to the detriment of its focus on serious human rights problems elsewhere. It is hard to say whether one investigation, however well conducted, could reverse the ways of the council, but some have condemned Goldstone for even trying.

\* \* \*

Both the Israeli and U.S. governments rejected the Goldstone Report on the claim that it undermined Israel's right of self-defense. The self-defense argument is tricky because there are two very different issues that can come packaged this way: first, whether the Goldstone Report in fact condemns Israel for aggression and, second, whether its reading of international humanitarian law puts states confronting terrorism at an impossible disadvantage. Neither argument has merit, but they are easily and often confused.

\* \* \*

### The Goldstone Report as a U.N. Fact-finding Mission

Fact-finding occurs all over the U.N. system, but the full-fledged investigation into violations of IHL and human rights in the course of armed conflict is more rare, taking place more often under the mandate of the Security Council. The purpose of such fact-finding is usually to document whether there is evidence of crimes and recommend measures for accountability. Further action is expected on the completion of the report, in the nature of Security Council resolutions, establishment of tribunals, or criminal investigations. Fact-finding missions are not adjudicatory in force, but they do typically set out a legal framework and legal conclusions. Moreover, fact-finding with respect to ongoing or recent armed conflicts presents particular challenges; among them, access to the battlefield; the need for forensic, ballistic, and other technical evaluations; issues of security, credibility, and partiality of witnesses; and the obtainment of sensitive internal information that is relevant to weighing the lawfulness of attacks such as anticipated military advantage, intelligence on opposing forces, or command level knowledge or authorization of unlawful attacks. Some missions founder for lack of state cooperation, and all struggle with this aspect.

\* \* \*

[T]he International Inquiry on Darfur, headed by Antonio Cassesse and including a future member of the Goldstone team (Hina Jilani), was mandated to investigate violations of international humanitarian and human rights law, determine whether acts of genocide had taken place, identify perpetrators, and suggest means of ensuring accountability. The inquiry visited the region several times over three months and interviewed a wide range of sources on all sides, including secondary sources such as NGOs, diplomats, and other experts. It concluded that the government of Sudan and the Janjaweed were responsible for a wide range of international crimes and identified perpetrators for competent judicial authorities to investigate, but did not release their names publicly. The report made extensive recommendations to both Sudan and the international community, including recommending the exercise of universal jurisdiction. The report also noted the degree of cooperation with its mission on the part of both government and rebels, and the fact that in some situations witnesses may have been under pressure or planted.

\* \* \*

... [T]he Goldstone inquiry did not identify particular perpetrators, but it did draw conclusions on the culpability of each side for particular offenses based on available evidence. The team drew on a wide range of sources, including 188 individual interviews, field visits to Gaza, satellite and other images, and medical and forensic evaluations. And it relied primarily on information it gathered firsthand.

\* \* \*

## Contested Findings

The actual findings that have been most disputed are a mix. Some present difficult issues that are open to debate. Although the NGOs that tried to investigate the operation often avoided these, Goldstone took them on, and the report's conclusions, while not beyond debate, are at least reasonable in view of the law. One such issue is the status of the Gaza police who were targeted and killed at the outset in great numbers in a premeditated strategy. Israel argues that, under Hamas, many members of the civilian police were drawn from military units and asserted, based on Hamas statements, that the civilian police would assume military functions in the course of the conflict. The Palestinian narrative was quite different: while some of the police had been drawn from the ranks of resistance fighters and others had non-Hamas affiliations, their function was civilian law and order, even in the event of Israeli ground attack. Faced with this conflict, the report found Israel's evidence insufficient to conclude that the police generally were part of the armed forces or supporting combat, or that enough of them played a dual role to justify attacking the whole corps. This was a factual call, involving analysis of evidence and credibility. The thrust of the law, however, is to resolve doubts in favor of a presumption of civilian status for people and objects that normally would be so classified, and this appears to have guided the determination.

\* \* \*

Other issues, although disputed, are less gray. Many have praised the lengths to which Israel goes to give warnings to Palestinians of impending attacks, and the IDF routinely invokes this fact in defense of its observance of IHL. While it is true that the numbers of leaflets and telephone calls were massive, many of these were legally flawed in that they were ineffective, giving no indication of the place of impending attack, the time, or genuinely safe areas.

\* \* \*

## The Report's Impact

The report as a fact-finding exercise followed appropriate standards and produced a voluminous account of serious crimes, no small accomplishment given the six-month period from the inception of the mission to the publication of its report. As an account, it suffers from the lack of input from Israel, but it cannot be faulted for that, or for refusing to keep silent or omit issues because the alleged offender withheld cooperation. It is still within Israel's power to put forward to the public facts that would change the conclusions.

But does the report do what it is supposed to do—impel the parties to investigate violations and hold perpetrators responsible? Its immediate history is discouraging. The United States kept silent for a few days following the report's release, and then pronounced it "unfair" without contesting its findings, leaving the impression of a political decision, not a legal or intelligence assessment. The U.S. House of Representatives passed a resolution condemning the report that was as one-sided in its own way as the original Human Rights Council mandate. The Human Rights Council endorsed the report on October 15, 2009, and the final version of the resolution was revised to explicitly call on both sides to rectify violations, a small victory for Goldstone and his effort to make his mandate a fair one. The General Assembly overwhelmingly endorsed the report and called on both sides to mount credible investigations. The Security Council has discussed the report, but is not expected to make a resolution, given U.S. determination to keep the issue confined to the Human Rights Council and the General Assembly.

While momentum seems to have fizzled at the U.N., the issue of international prosecution is still alive, with Israel pressuring the UK to change its laws that allow private parties to initiate arrest warrants for foreign officials accused of war crimes. The Goldstone Report also recommends that the Security Council set a six-month deadline for referral to the International Criminal Court (ICC) should the parties not make good-faith efforts to investigate cases and hold individuals to account. There are reports that the IDF has completed its second tier of investigations into allegations of criminal conduct, this time interviewing Palestinian witnesses, and has concluded there is no basis to any of the incidents brought to its attention.

\* \* \*

There are no perfect fact-finding exercises, and this one operated under heavy constraints due to Israel's noncooperation. Many of the report's shortcomings derive from this, but the mission cannot be faulted for setting forth conclusions from an incomplete picture. To empower noncooperating parties would be to defeat international fact-finding entirely. Justice Goldstone created an alternate narrative to those of the governments of the region. His introduction of public sessions to showcase the impact of the conflict on victims on each side, a technique borrowed from South Africa's Truth and Reconciliation Commission, presented the rare opportunity for the opposing communities to hear each other, and may become a useful feature of future exercises. Some acknowledgment of crimes committed on each side will be needed if there is ever to be a mutual reconciliation. The report may yet produce that acknowledgment and impel justice, the cornerstone of peace.

## *Authors' Note*

**Human Rights Committee:** The Human Rights Committee monitors compliance with the International Covenant on Civil and Political Rights (ICCPR). The Committee meets three times a year in Geneva and New York and has four monitoring functions, including the examination of reports submitted by states parties and the adoption of general comments on articles of the covenant. Under its optional protocol, the Committee considers individual complaints. Article 1 of the Optional Protocol states:

> "A State Party to the Covenant that becomes a Party to the present Protocol recognizes the competence of the Committee to receive and consider communications from individuals subject to its jurisdiction who claim to be victims of a violation by that State Party of any of the rights set forth in the Covenant. No

communication shall be received by the Committee if it concerns a State Party to the Covenant which is not a Party to the present Protocol."

Moreover, the Committee assesses inter-state complaints. Articles 41–43 of ICCPR set out a more elaborate procedure for the resolution of disputes between States parties over a State's fulfillment of its obligations under the Covenant through the establishment of an *ad hoc* Conciliation Commission. The procedure applies only to States parties to the ICCPR, which have made a declaration accepting the competence of the Committee in this regard. Finally, all state parties are obliged to submit a report to the Committee about how human rights are being implemented, first within one year of acceding to the Covenant, and then approximately every four years thereafter.

Materials 6 and 7 discuss signatories' reservations to the Covenant, explaining that generally, signatories may make reservations as long as the reservations do not contradict the objectives of the Covenant.

---

# 6. General Comment on Issues Relating to Reservations Made upon Ratification or Accession to the Covenant or the Optional Protocols thereto, or in Relation to Declarations under Article 41 of the Covenant

## U.N. Office of the High Commission for Human Rights, 1994

1. As of 1 November 1994, 46 of the 127 States parties to the International Covenant on Civil and Political Rights had, between them, entered 150 reservations of varying significance to their acceptance of the obligations of the Covenant. Some of these reservations exclude the duty to provide and guarantee particular rights in the Covenant. Others are couched in more general terms, often directed to ensuring the continued paramountcy of certain domestic legal provisions. Still others are directed at the competence of the Committee. The number of reservations, their content and their scope may undermine the effective implementation of the Covenant and tend to weaken respect for the obligations of States parties.

\* \* \*

5. The Covenant neither prohibits reservations nor mentions any type of permitted reservation. The same is true of the first Optional Protocol.

\* \* \*

6. The absence of a prohibition on reservations does not mean that any reservation is permitted. The matter of reservations under the Covenant and the first Optional Protocol is governed by international law. Article 19(3) of the Vienna Convention on the Law of Treaties provides relevant guidance. It stipulates that where a reservation is not prohibited by the treaty or falls within the specified permitted categories, a State may make a reservation provided it is not incompatible with the object and purpose of the treaty. Even though, unlike some other human rights treaties, the Covenant does not incorporate a specific reference to the object and purpose test, that test governs the matter of interpretation and acceptability of reservations.

7. In an instrument which articulates very many civil and political rights, each of the many articles, and indeed their interplay, secures the objectives of the Covenant. The object and purpose of the Covenant is to create legally binding standards for human rights by defining certain civil and political rights and placing them in a framework of obliga-

tions which are legally binding for those States which ratify; and to provide an efficacious supervisory machinery for the obligations undertaken.

8. Reservations that offend peremptory norms would not be compatible with the object and purpose of the Covenant. Although treaties that are mere exchanges of obligations between States allow them to reserve *inter se* application of rules of general international law, it is otherwise in human rights treaties, which are for the benefit of persons within their jurisdiction. Accordingly, provisions in the Covenant that represent customary international law (and *a fortiori* when they have the character of peremptory norms) may not be the subject of reservations.

* * *

12. The intention of the Covenant is that the rights contained therein should be ensured to all those under a State's party's jurisdiction. To this end certain attendant requirements are likely to be necessary. Domestic laws may need to be altered properly to reflect the requirements of the Covenant; and mechanisms at the domestic level will be needed to allow the Covenant rights to be enforceable at the local level. Reservations often reveal a tendency of States not to want to change a particular law. And sometimes that tendency is elevated to a general policy. Of particular concern are widely formulated reservations which essentially render ineffective all Covenant rights which would require any change in national law to ensure compliance with Covenant obligations. No real international rights or obligations have thus been accepted. And when there is an absence of provisions to ensure that Covenant rights may be sued on in domestic courts, and, further, a failure to allow individual complaints to be brought to the Committee under the first Optional Protocol, all the essential elements of the Covenant guarantees have been removed.

* * *

16. The Committee finds it important to address which body has the legal authority to make determinations as to whether specific reservations are compatible with the object and purpose of the Covenant. As for international treaties in general, the International Court of Justice has indicated in the *Reservations to the Genocide Convention Case* (1951) that a State which objected to a reservation on the grounds of incompatibility with the object and purpose of a treaty could, through objecting, regard the treaty as not in effect as between itself and the reserving State. Article 20, paragraph 4, of the Vienna Convention on the Law of Treaties 1969 contains provisions most relevant to the present case on acceptance of and objection to reservations. This provides for the possibility of a State to object to a reservation made by another State. Article 21 deals with the legal effects of objections by States to reservations made by other States. Essentially, a reservation precludes the operation, as between the reserving and other States, of the provision reserved; and an objection thereto leads to the reservation being in operation as between the reserving and objecting State only to the extent that it has not been objected to.

17. As indicated above, it is the Vienna Convention on the Law of Treaties that provides the definition of reservations and also the application of the object and purpose test in the absence of other specific provisions. But the Committee believes that its provisions on the role of State objections in relation to reservations are inappropriate to address the problem of reservations to human rights treaties. Such treaties, and the Covenant specifically, are not a web of inter-State exchanges of mutual obligations. They concern the endowment of individuals with rights. The principle of inter-State reciprocity has no place, save perhaps in the limited context of reservations to declarations on the Committee's competence under article 41. And because the operation of the classic rules on reservations is so inadequate for the Covenant, States have often not seen any legal interest in or

need to object to reservations. The absence of protest by States cannot imply that a reservation is either compatible or incompatible with the object and purpose of the Covenant. [ ... ]

18. It necessarily falls to the Committee to determine whether a specific reservation is compatible with the object and purpose of the Covenant. This is in part because, as indicated above, it is an inappropriate task for States parties in relation to human rights treaties, and in part because it is a task that the Committee cannot avoid in the performance of its functions. In order to know the scope of its duty to examine a State's compliance under article 40 or a communication under the first Optional Protocol, the Committee has necessarily to take a view on the compatibility of a reservation with the object and purpose of the Covenant and with general international law. Because of the special character of a human rights treaty, the compatibility of a reservation with the object and purpose of the Covenant must be established objectively, by reference to legal principles, and the Committee is particularly well placed to perform this task. The normal consequence of an unacceptable reservation is not that the Covenant will not be in effect at all for a reserving party. Rather, such a reservation will generally be severable, in the sense that the Covenant will be operative for the reserving party without benefit of the reservation.

19. Reservations must be specific and transparent, so that the Committee, those under the jurisdiction of the reserving State and other States parties may be clear as to what obligations of human rights compliance have or have not been undertaken. Reservations may thus not be general, but must refer to a particular provision of the Covenant and indicate in precise terms its scope in relation thereto. When considering the compatibility of possible reservations with the object and purpose of the Covenant, States should also take into consideration the overall effect of a group of reservations, as well as the effect of each reservation on the integrity of the Covenant, which remains an essential consideration. States should not enter so many reservations that they are in effect accepting a limited number of human rights obligations, and not the Covenant as such. So that reservations do not lead to a perpetual non-attainment of international human rights standards, reservations should not systematically reduce the obligations undertaken only to the presently existing in less demanding standards of domestic law. Nor should interpretative declarations or reservations seek to remove an autonomous meaning to Covenant obligations, by pronouncing them to be identical, or to be accepted only insofar as they are identical, with existing provisions of domestic law. States should not seek through reservations or interpretative declarations to determine that the meaning of a provision of the Covenant is the same as that given by an organ of any other international treaty body.

20. States should institute procedures to ensure that each and every proposed reservation is compatible with the object and purpose of the Covenant. It is desirable for a State entering a reservation to indicate in precise terms the domestic legislation or practices which it believes to be incompatible with the Covenant obligation reserved; and to explain the time period it requires to render its own laws and practices compatible with the Covenant, or why it is unable to render its own laws and practices compatible with the Covenant. States should also ensure that the necessity for maintaining reservations is periodically reviewed, taking into account any observations and recommendations made by the Committee during examination of their reports. Reservations should be withdrawn at the earliest possible moment. Reports to the Committee should contain information on what action has been taken to review, reconsider or withdrawn reservations.

# 7. Observations by the United States on General Comment 24
## 1995

* * *

## 2. Acceptability of reservations: governing legal principles

The question of the status of the Committee's views is of some significance in light of the apparent lines of analysis concerning the permissibility of reservations in paragraphs 8–9. Those paragraphs reflect the view that reservations offending peremptory norms of international law would not be compatible with the object and purpose of the Covenant, nor may reservations be taken to Covenant provisions which represent customary international law.

It is clear that a State cannot exempt itself from a peremptory norm of international law by making a reservation to the Covenant. It is not at all clear that a State cannot choose to exclude one means of enforcement of particular norms by reserving against inclusion of those norms in its Covenant obligations.

The proposition that any reservation which contravenes a norm of customary international law is *per se* incompatible with the object and purpose of this or any other convention, however, is a much more significant and sweeping premise. It is, moreover, wholly unsupported by and is in fact contrary to international law.

* * *

In fact, a primary object and purpose of the Covenant was to secure the widest possible adherence, with the clear understanding that a relatively liberal regime on the permissibility of reservations should therefore be required.

## 5. Effect of invalidity of reservations

It seems unlikely that one can misunderstand the concluding point of this General Comment ... Since this conclusion is so completely at odds with established legal practice and principles and even the express and clear terms of adherence by many States, it would be welcome if some helpful clarification could be made.

The reservations contained in the United States instrument of ratification are integral parts of its consent to be bound by the Covenant and are not severable. If it were to be determined that any one or more of them were ineffective, the ratification as a whole could thereby be nullified.

* * *

The general view of the academic literature is that reservations are an essential part of a State's consent to be bound. They cannot simply be erased. This reflects the fundamental principle of the law of treaties: obligation is based on consent. A State which does not consent to a treaty is not bound by that treaty. A State which expressly withholds its consent from a provision cannot be presumed, on the basis of some legal fiction, to be bound by it. It is regrettable that General Comment 24 appears to suggest to the contrary.

## *Authors' Note*

The United Nations has created numerous other committees designed to address specific human rights issues.

**The Committee on Economic, Social, and Cultural Rights:** The Committee on Economic, Social, and Cultural Rights is a group of independent experts that monitors progress of countries working to implement the International Covenant on Economic, Social, and Cultural Rights (ICESCR). The committee meets twice a year, and all state parties must submit regular reports about their efforts to adhere to the Covenant. The Committee responds to each report with "concluding observations." There is an optional protocol, which allows for individual complaints.

**The Committee on the Elimination of Racial Discrimination** is a group of independent experts that monitors implementation of the Convention on the Elimination of All Forms of Racial Discrimination. The Committee monitors compliance via an early-warning procedure, examination of inter-state complaints, and investigation of individual complaints. States are required to submit a report one year after acceding and then every two years thereafter.

**The Committee on the Elimination of Discrimination against Women** was established in 1982. The committee consists of 23 experts on women's issues from around the world, and monitors implementation of national measures to fulfill its obligation to the Convention on the Elimination of All Forms of Discrimination Against Women. The Committee investigates the progress of each member state in implementing the convention and then makes recommendations.

**The Committee Against Torture** is a group of ten independent experts monitoring implementation of the Convention Against Torture and Other Cruel, Inhuman or Degrading Treatment or Punishment by state parties. All state parties are obliged to submit regular reports about how they are adhering to the Covenant. The committee then responds with "concluding observations." The Committee also considers individual complaints, undertakes inquiries, and considers inter-state complaints. The Optional Protocol to the Convention against Torture allows for an international presence in interrogation and detention facilities.

**The Committee on the Rights of the Child** is a group of independent experts that monitors implementation of the Convention on the Rights of the Child by its state parties. It also monitors two optional protocols of the Convention: the involvement of children in armed conflict, and the sale of children, child prostitution, and child pornography.

**The Committee on Migrant Workers** is a group of independent experts that monitors implementation of the International Convention on the Protection of the Rights of All Migrant Workers and Members of Their Families. All state parties are obliged to submit regular reports about how they are adhering to the Covenant. The Committee then responds with "concluding observations." Under certain circumstances, the body considers individual complaints or communications from individuals claiming that their rights under the Convention have been violated.

**The Committee on the Rights of Persons with Disabilities** is a group of independent experts that monitors implementation of the Convention on the Rights of Persons with Disabilities. The optional protocol gives the Committee the option to examine individual complaints of alleged violations by state parties.

**The Committee on Enforced Disappearances** is a group of independent experts that monitors implementation by state parties of the Convention. In accordance with Article 31, a State Party may at the time of ratification of this Convention or at any time afterwards declare that it recognizes the competence of the Committee to receive and consider communications from or on behalf of individuals subject to its jurisdiction claiming to be victims of a violation by this State Party of provisions of this Convention.

**European Court of Human Rights:** The European Court of Human Rights was created in 1959 by the European Convention on Human Rights. The Court is based in Strasbourg, France and rules on cases brought forward by individuals or states alleging violations of civil and political rights delineated in the Convention. In its fifty years, the Court has delivered approximately 10,000 judgments concerning the human rights of the 800 million Europeans in the forty-seven Council of Europe member states that have ratified the Convention. Each year, nearly 50,000 new applications are filed with the Court.

The Council of Europe selects the Court's judges for non-renewable nine-year terms. Individuals, companies, and NGO's can bring complaints at the Court. Alternatively, one state can bring an inter-state application against another state. Individual parties bring the majority of the Court's cases. Sixty-four percent of the Court's cases pertain to Article 6 (right to a fair hearing) or Article 1 (protection of property). Once the Court delivers a judgment of a violation, the Committee of Ministers of the Council of Europe receives the file and then works with the relevant state to decide how to execute the judgment and how to prevent future similar violations. The end result of this process is usually the implementation of legal mechanisms and remedies, including legislative amendments.

The following article provides a more specific view of the European Court of Human Rights, by focusing on a case concerning whether the constitution of Bosnia and Herzegovina discriminated against elected officials on the basis of ethnicity. The article discusses the parties' arguments, the Court's opinion, and the opinion's potential impact on Bosnia and Herzegovina.

---

## 8. Céline Tran, Striking a Balance between Human Rights and Peace and Stability: A Review of the European Court of Human Rights Decision *Sejdić and Finci v. Bosnia and Herzegovina*
### Human Rights Brief, 2011

### Introduction

On December 22, 2009, the European Court of Human Rights issued its judgment in the *Case of Sejdic and Finci v. Bosnia and Herzegovina*, finding certain provisions of the Constitution of Bosnia and Herzegovina (BiH) in breach of the European Convention on Human Rights (ECHR) because they created ethnically discriminatory requirements for certain elected positions. The Court's willingness to address ethnic discrimination in a post-conflict constitution, like BiH's, broke new ground in Europe's human rights framework. The legal significance of the decision is three-fold: 1) it marked the first time that the Court applied the general prohibition of discrimination prescribed by Article 1 of Protocol No. 12 to the ECHR; 2) it addressed intricate political considerations pertaining to peace and stability in deciding whether or not to uphold the ECHR; and 3) it confronted the sensitive issue of the ECHR's compatibility with a Member State's constitution, an issue with which it has rarely had to deal. The Court held that finding the respondent state in violation of the ECHR was a sufficient remedy for the petitioners, but the legal significance of finding a power-sharing provision in a post-conflict constitution in violation of the ECHR remains.

BiH has a distinctive political system by which the three largest ethnic groups are equally represented in the state's institutions. The Constitution of BiH distinguishes between "constituent peoples" (Bosniacs, Serbs, and Croats) and "Others" (members of all other ethnic minorities). Under the Constitution, only members of the constituent peoples are eligible to run for the Presidency and for the House of Peoples — one of two chambers in the Parliamentary Assembly. As of 2000, BiH was composed of 48 percent Bosniacs, 37.1 percent Serbs, 14.3 percent Croats, and 0.6 percent other minorities.

The Presidency of BiH is a three member collective composed of one Bosniac, one Serb, and one Croat. The three Members of the Presidency are elected by popular vote for a four-year term. Every eight months, one of the three Members assumes the chair of the Presidency. Chairmanship does not entail any additional powers or functions, but instead serves to convey an image of leadership. Decisions are made by consensus among the three Members of the Presidency. However, when a consensus is not reached, the majority may take a decision and the third Member may challenge the decision by declaring it against his constituent peoples' best interests. Similarly, each of the constituent peoples is represented by five members in the House of Peoples.

This system of representation was established in the Constitution of BiH to ensure that none of the constituent peoples could dominate the government and override the other groups. [ ... ]

This article reviews the *Sejdić and Finci* judgment, focusing on how the Court reconciled the interests of human rights versus those of peace and stability. This dichotomy continues to be intensely controversial and the outcome of the case was anything but self-evident. As the recent elections in BiH have shown, ethnic tensions and mistrust still pervade Bosnian society. However, while there are legitimate concerns and even fears that changing the Constitution to include the Others in the government will only spark tensions, there are ways to integrate minorities without encroaching on the representation of the three major ethnic groups. Denying certain categories of people one of the most fundamental rights is neither sustainable nor acceptable within European standards. While BiH is currently under European pressure to reform its constitution, the long term implications of the Court's decision for BiH are likely to be far reaching.

### Bosnia's Breach of the Prohibition of Discrimination

In 2006, M. Sejdić, a Roma, and M. Finci, of Jewish descent, filed an application to the Court, contending that the Constitution of BiH deprives them of their right to run for public office on the sole basis of their ethnic origins in violation of several articles of the ECHR. Sejdić and Finci, both prominent Bosnian politicians were ineligible to run for the Presidency and the House of Peoples, respectively. The two men challenged the Constitution under Article 14 of the ECHR, which prohibits discrimination in the exercise of any right set forth in the ECHR, in conjunction with Article 3 of Protocol No. 1, guaranteeing free and fair legislative elections. They also relied on Article 1 of Protocol No. 12, which prescribes a general prohibition of discrimination rather than specific discrimination related to another right under Article 14. While petitioners were not affected by an individual measure, they were nonetheless considered victims for purposes of admissibility because they were particularly at risk of being affected by the provisions in question.

Supporting their claim that ethnic discrimination amounts to racial discrimination that can never be justified, the petitioners looked to the Court's extensive jurisprudence on discrimination. Specifically, the petitioners cited the case of *Timishev v. Russia*, where an ethnic Chechen was denied registration of his permanent residence in Nalchik (Kabardino-Balkaria Republic) on the basis of his former residence in the Chechen Republic, the Court found that a difference in treatment based exclusively on a person's ethnic origin cannot be objectively justified in a contemporary democratic society. The Court has consistently applied the long-standing "objective and reasonable" test when considering claims of Article 14 violations. Under the law of the Council of Europe, not every difference in treatment amounts to discrimination. A difference in treatment violates Article 14 of the ECHR only if it has "no objective and reasonable justification," namely, if it does not pursue a "legitimate aim" or if there is no "reasonable relationship of proportionality between the means employed and the aim sought to be reali[z]ed." Because differences in treatment are not all objectionable, states are granted a certain margin of appreciation "in assessing whether and to what extent differences justify a different treatment in law." The scope of this margin of appreciation varies according to the subject matter of the discrimination and the circumstances of a particular case.

In its defense, BiH argued that the discriminatory provisions contained in the Constitution were objectively and reasonably justified. It relied on the case of *Zdanoka v. Latvia* in which the Court declared that:

> [S]tates enjoy considerable latitude in establishing constitutional rules on the status of members of parliament, including criteria governing eligibility to stand for election ... these criteria vary in accordance with the historical and political factors specific to each State.

\* \* \*

Nevertheless, the Court concluded that ethnic-based discrimination is a form of racial discrimination, which is a "particularly egregious kind of discrimination." As a result, the Court strictly applied the "objective and reasonable" test in considering the petitioners' claim. It found that the provisions at stake had been legitimate at the time they were drafted because they aimed to restore peace in BiH. However, the Court avoided the question of whether the provisions were *still* legitimate and instead, focused on the criterion of proportionality. To decide the proportionality prong, the Court first examined BiH's political progress and then considered whether other means exist to achieve proper power-sharing that do not discriminate against the Others.

\* \* \*

Another significant factor in the Court's reasoning was that BiH had voluntarily agreed, through membership in the Council of Europe, to abide by its standards. In fact, when BiH joined the Council of Europe in 2002, it agreed to review its electoral legislation for compliance with the ECHR within one year. Moreover, BiH had undertaken the same promise upon entering the Stabilization and Association Agreement with the EU. BiH knew that its Constitution was not in conformity with the ECHR, and therefore, it had the responsibility to reform it. Following this analysis of the political and legal situation of BiH, the Court concluded that the discriminatory provisions were not proportional to the aim sought.

Lastly, and most importantly, the findings of the European Commission for Democracy through Law (Venice Commission) showed that alternative means exist for a state to successfully maintain power-sharing mechanisms without discriminating against certain categories of people. The Court agreed with the Bosnian government that nothing in the ECHR commanded BiH to completely change its power-sharing mechanisms. In fact, the Court shared the belief that the time was not ripe for BiH to adopt a system reflecting majority rule, echoing what the Venice Commission had recommended in its 2005 opinion. However, as long as there are other, non-discriminatory means to achieve power-sharing, the constitutional provisions cannot be objectively and reasonably justified, as they are not proportional to the aim sought.

\* \* \*

The Court decided to strike the balance in favor of human rights, but did not do so in complete disregard of wider peace and stability considerations. On the contrary, the Court carefully assessed the situation, taking into account various amicus curiae briefs, and concluded that BiH was ready to move away from its post-conflict government structure, without completely abolishing it. Specifically, the Court found that other minorities could be integrated in the government without jeopardizing the protection of the constituent peoples' interests, which it recognized as paramount.

\* \* \*

### Implications for the Government of Bosnia and Herzegovina

The Court's judgment is a serious condemnation of BiH's Constitution and requires active measures to be taken by the government to fulfill its obligations under the ECHR. Although the Court did not expressly order BiH to change its Constitution, the ruling implies that BiH must do so because it is the state's responsibility to avoid another violation of the ECHR on the same grounds. Consequently, the execution of this judgment requires BiH to enact amendments to the constitutional provisions governing the elections to the Presidency and the House of Peoples. As of this writing, the government of BiH has yet to take the necessary measures to ensure execution of the judgment. The government's inaction is hardly surprising given that constitutional reform in BiH has always proven a delicate matter. BiH faces two major constitutional reform issues: the discriminatory electoral system on the one hand, and wider state structure reforms on the other hand. While all political stakeholders recognize the need to change the discriminatory provisions in the light of the Court's decision, they consistently fail to reach a consensus on the broader state reforms.

\* \* \*

### Conclusion

The Court's ruling does not compel BiH to completely disassemble its power-sharing mechanisms because a government based on purely majority rule is currently unrealistic for BiH. In its judgment, the Court referred to the Venice Commission's recommendations, which proposed ways to circumvent the exclusion of the Others while maintaining a balance of power between the three main ethnic groups. Both of the Venice Commission's proposals are reasonable and acceptable for political stakeholders. Therefore, nothing should continue to impede the execution of the Court's judgment. As the Council of Europe and other experts have stated, changing the discriminatory provisions should be BiH's first priority.

There are various factors motivating BiH to adhere to the Court's judgment. Compliance with the human rights standards of the Council of Europe is essential not only to ensure that BiH respects its international obligations, but also as a prerequisite for EU integration. Furthermore, EU accession is one of the few common grounds that Bosnian political leaders share. What remains to be seen is how proactive the Council of Europe will be in urging BiH to implement the Court's ruling. While the Council has issued reports and statements on the situation in BiH, noting the state's obligation to enforce the ruling, no coercive measures in the form of fines or suspension of rights in the Council of Europe have been taken. While this lack of pressure may be frustrating, it would be unrealistic for the Council to adopt a stricter position, as changing a state's constitution is altogether more challenging than striking down an individual measure. The EU may have more leverage to enforce compliance with the Court's judgment, especially since it has identified BiH as the Balkan state lagging most in the EU integration process.

While the Court's decision is a positive step, as far as human rights are concerned, it does not directly address the more sensitive and challenging issue of the ethnic divide within the BiH government. The Court was neither asked, nor does it have the jurisdiction to decide upon this deeper issue. Yet, it is widely acknowledged that BiH needs to overcome these wider divisions in order to have a better functioning government and a cohesive society. As previously mentioned, the DPA intended to end a war by providing sufficient ethnic safeguards in the constitution. Thus, the DPA was never designed to be an efficient instrument of government. In effect, the DPA enabled fifteen years of political deadlock and unmanageable bureaucratic expenses.

Although BiH is still struggling to recover from the effects of civil war and Bosnians remain in some parts of the country profoundly divided and distrustful, the only way to achieve sustainable peace and stability is by fostering a sense of nationhood. The persistence of institutionalized ethnic differentiation is an obstacle to building a country based on citizens, instead of peoples. Under the current constitution, BiH cannot avoid nationalistic divide, which is its greatest obstacle to peace and stability. Accordingly, any reference to ethnicity in the government should be eliminated, as national unity begins with internal government unity. To overcome its many institutional defects, BiH should adopt a piecemeal and progressive approach as opposed to one that is more comprehensive and immediate. However, it may be a long time before Serbs, Bosniacs or Croats agree to be ruled by a unified government, and it is not difficult to understand why.

## *Authors' Note*

**Inter-American Commission on Human Rights and the Inter-American Court of Human Rights:** The next two articles discuss the Inter-American system for protecting human rights. Under the auspices of the Organization of American States (OAS), these two institutions were created to provide a supra-national mechanism to protect the rights of people within the member states. The articles below provide a brief overview of the Commission as well as the Court.

## 9. Tim Curry and Nerina Cevra and Erin Palmer, Updates from the Regional Human Rights Systems
### Human Rights Brief, 2005

* * *

### Inter-American System

THE INTER-AMERICAN Human Rights System was created with the adoption of the American Declaration of the Rights and Duties of Man (Declaration) in 1948. In 1959, the Inter-American Commission on Human Rights (Commission) was established as an independent organ of the Organization of the American States (OAS) and it held its first session one year later. In 1969, the American Convention on Human Rights (Convention) was adopted. The Convention further defined the role of the Commission and created the Inter-American Court of Human Rights (Inter-American Court). According to the Convention, once the Commission determines the case is admissible and meritorious, it will make recommendations and, in some cases, present the case to the Court for adjudication. The Court hears these cases, determines responsibility under relevant regional treaties and agreements, and assesses and awards damages and other forms of reparation to victims of human rights violations.

* * *

## 10. Inter-American Commission on Human Rights, What Is the IACHR?

The Inter-American Commission on Human Rights (IACHR) is one of two bodies in the inter-American system for the promotion and protection of human rights. The Commission has its headquarters in Washington, D.C. The other human rights body is the Inter-American Court of Human Rights, which is located in San José, Costa Rica.

The IACHR is an autonomous organ of the Organization of American States (OAS). Its mandate is found in the OAS Charter and the American Convention on Human Rights. The IACHR represents all of the member States of the OAS. It has seven members who act independently, without representing any particular country. The members of the IACHR are elected by the General Assembly of the OAS.

The IACHR is a permanent body, which meets in ordinary and special sessions several times a year. The Executive Secretariat of the IACHR carries out the tasks delegated to it by the IACHR and provides legal and administrative support to the IACHR as it carries out its work.

### Brief History of the Inter-American Human Rights System

The Inter-American human rights system was born with the adoption of the American Declaration of the Rights and Duties of Man in Bogotá, Colombia in April of 1948. The American Declaration was the first international human rights instrument of a general nature. The IACHR was created in 1959 and held its first session in 1960. Since that time and until December 2011, the Commission has held 143 sessions, some of them at its headquarters, others in different countries of the Americas.

By 1961, the IACHR had begun to carry out on-site visits to observe the general human rights situation in a country or to investigate specific situations. Since that time, the IACHR has carried out 92 visits to 23 member States. In relation to its visits for the observation of the general human rights situation of a country, the IACHR has published 60 special country reports to date.

In 1965, the IACHR was expressly authorized to examine complaints or petitions regarding specific cases of human rights violations. The IACHR has received thousands of petitions, which have resulted in 19,423 petitions and cases which have been processed or are currently being processed. (The procedure for the processing of individual cases is described below). The final published reports of the IACHR regarding these individual cases may be found in the Annual Reports of the Commission or independently by country.

In 1969, the American Convention on Human Rights was adopted. The Convention entered into force in 1978. As of August of 1997, it has been ratified by 25 countries: Argentina, Barbados, Brazil, Bolivia, Chile, Colombia, Costa Rica, Dominica, Dominican Republic, Ecuador, El Salvador, Grenada, Guatemala, Haiti, Honduras, Jamaica, Mexico, Nicaragua, Panama, Paraguay, Peru, Suriname, Trinidad and Tobago, Uruguay and Venezuela. The Convention defines the human rights which the ratifying States have agreed to respect and ensure. The Convention also creates the Inter-American Court of Human Rights and defines the functions and procedures of both the Commission and the Court. The IACHR also possesses additional faculties which pre-date and are not derived directly from the Convention, such as the processing of cases involving countries which are still not parties to the Convention.

**What are the Functions and Powers of the Commission?**

The IACHR has the principal function of promoting the observance and the defense of human rights. In carrying out its mandate, the Commission:

a) Receives, analyzes and investigates individual petitions which allege human rights violations, pursuant to Articles 44 to 51 of the Convention. This procedure will be discussed in greater detail below.

b) Observes the general human rights situation in the member States and publishes special reports regarding the situation in a specific State, when it considers it appropriate.

c) Carries out on-site visits to countries to engage in more in-depth analysis of the general situation and/or to investigate a specific situation. These visits usually result in the preparation of a report regarding the human rights situation observed, which is published and sent to the General Assembly.

d) Stimulates public consciousness regarding human rights in the Americas. To that end, carries out and publishes studies on specific subjects, such as: measures to be taken to ensure greater independence of the judiciary; the activities of irregular armed groups; the human rights situation of minors and women, and; the human rights of indigenous peoples.

e) Organizes and carries out conferences, seminars and meetings with representatives of Governments, academic institutions, non-governmental groups, etc ... in order to disseminate information and to increase knowledge regarding issues relating to the inter-American human rights system.

f) Recommends to the member States of the OAS the adoption of measures which would contribute to human rights protection.

g) Requests States to adopt specific "precautionary measures" to avoid serious and irreparable harm to human rights in urgent cases. The Commission may also request that the Court order "provisional measures" in urgent cases which involve danger to persons, even where a case has not yet been submitted to the Court.

h) Submits cases to the Inter-American Court and appears before the Court in the litigation of cases.

i) Requests advisory opinions from the Inter-American Court regarding questions of interpretation of the American Convention.

## *Authors' Note*

**African Court of Justice and Human Rights:** The African Court on Human and Peoples' Rights merged with the Court of Justice of the African Union at an African Union Summit on July 1, 2008. The Court is based in Tanzania and is the main judicial body of the African Union, with sixteen judges from distinct member states, representing each geographic region of the continent. The Court is divided into two sections: the General

Affairs Section, presided over by eight judges, and the Human Rights Section, also with eight judges.

State parties to the Protocol to the Statute of the African Court of Justice and Human Rights, may submit cases to the court, as well as the Assembly of the Heads of States and Government of the Union, and the Parliament of the African Union. Staff members of the Union also may bring cases to the Court. Moreover, the African Commission on Human and Peoples' Rights, the African Committee of Experts on the Rights and Welfare of the Child, African Intergovernmental Organizations, African National Human Rights Institutions, NGO's accredited by the AU or its organs, and individuals are all entitled to submit cases to the Court. However, individuals and NGO's may only bring cases against a particular state if that state has signed an additional special declaration that permits the Court to hear cases brought by individuals or NGO's against the state. This caveat presents a challenge for most individuals and groups seeking access to the Court's mechanisms.

Moreover, the Court does not accept cases from states that are not members of the Union or states that have not ratified the Protocol. Additionally, the Court does not receive cases brought against leaders. The Court's judgment is final. If a judgment is not properly executed, the Court refers the non-compliance to the Assembly, which will decide measures to address the non-compliance.

**Association of Southeast Asian Nations Intergovernmental Commission on Human Rights:** Article 14 of the ASEAN Charter created the Intergovernmental Commission on Human Rights in July 2009. The Commission meets twice a year in Jakarta and reaches decisions by consensus. Authoritarian regimes that historically repress and violate human rights maintain veto power, which limits the Commission's efficacy. Each ASEAN member state appoints one representative who is accountable to its appointing government. However, the Commission does not have the mandate to investigate human rights abuse cases or to prosecute offenders, despite its mission to promote and protect fundamental human rights.

The following article considers minority and indigenous rights within the ASEAN system, considering the approaches of various international legal mechanisms to this group of rights and the approach of the ASEAN community.

---

## 11. Anna Meijknecht and Byung Sook Patinaje-de Vries, Is There a Place for Minorities' and Indigenous People's Rights within ASEAN?: Asian Values, ASEAN Values and the Protection of Southeast Asian Minorities and Indigenous Peoples

*International Journal on Minority and Group Rights*, 2010
[footnotes omitted by editors]

### 1. Introduction

In 1993, the Ministers and representatives of Asian states, meeting in Bangkok in the context of preparations for the World Conference on Human Rights, adopted a Declaration, known as 'The Bangkok Declaration'. It contained the aspirations and commitments of the Asian region. One of these commitments emphasized by the Asian states was "the importance of guaranteeing the human rights and fundamental freedoms of vulnerable groups such as ethnic, national, racial, religious and linguistic minorities, migrant workers, disabled persons, indigenous peoples, refugees and displaced persons".

Strangely enough, in subsequent documents adopted by Southeast Asian states cooperating in the framework of the Association of Southeast Asian Nations (ASEAN), virtually no reference was made to minorities or indigenous peoples. Instead, most ASEAN documents seem to emphasize and to promote the (cultural) diversity of the Southeast Asian region. For instance, in an ASEAN document called 'ASEAN Vision 2020', adopted during the 30th anniversary of ASEAN in 1997, it was stated: "Our rich diversity has provided the strength and inspiration to us to help one another foster a strong sense of community" and that "we envision our rich human and natural resources contributing to our development and shared prosperity." In 2003, this vision was reaffirmed in a subsequent ASEAN document called Bali Concord II. The new ASEAN Charter, which entered into force in December 2008, also omits to refer to minorities and indigenous peoples, but acknowledges the potential of ASEAN's cultural diversity. One of the principles mentioned in the ASEAN Charter is: "respect for the different cultures, languages and religions of the peoples of ASEAN." However, the same sentence also emphasizes "their common values in the spirit of unity in diversity." ASEAN's motto, also proclaimed in the Charter, further tempers the optimism with regard to the protection of diversity. The motto, "One Vision, One Identity, One Community", indicates that the emphasis of ASEAN is on strengthening unity rather than on promoting diversity.

\* \* \*

## 2. Diversity in Southeast Asia

### 2.1. Introduction

Southeast Asia is characterized by great ethnic, cultural and religious diversity, and is home to a large number of migrants from China and India, dominant groups of Malays and Indonesians, as well as indigenous peoples, hill tribes and many minority groups. Vietnam, for instance, has 54 official ethnic groups.

As noted and regretted by many experts in the field of minority rights, there are no generally accepted definitions of minorities and indigenous peoples in international law. On the one hand, to a certain extent, minorities, indigenous peoples, states and legal scholars seem to have accepted this situation and even appear to be able to develop rights for minorities and indigenous peoples without such a generally accepted definition, or on the basis of working definitions. On the other hand, some uncertainty persists, for instance, with regard to the distinction between ethnic minorities and indigenous peoples. Scholars like Duncan, who has dealt with this issue in the Southeast Asian context, combines the two categories and uses one notion: "indigenous (ethnic) minorities." Clarke developed short working definitions of both groups which are applicable to the Southeast Asian context; he describes 'indigenous peoples' as "autochthonous, or descendants of the earliest known habitants of a territory" and 'minorities' as "settler populations with more recent links (often stretching back hundreds of years), who share a common identity with groups in at least one other country."

Several Southeast Asian states seem to use their large ethnic diversity, and the accompanying lack of conceptual clarity, for political purposes. Laos and Vietnam, for instance, have a highly developed system of ethnic classification, which they use for census purposes. Moreover, as was pointed out by Hadden, "the main focus of official policy is on the development of national unity by assimilation rather than by providing separate or autonomous structures."

## 2.2. Policy and Practice

In general, at the level of nation states, the picture with regard to the protection of minorities and indigenous peoples appears to be somewhat diffuse. For instance, a statement by the Asian Forum for Human Rights and Development (Forum Asia) that the policy of none of the nation-states of ASEAN "reflects an ethos that celebrates and promotes this diversity, or empowers and protects the rights of its national, ethnic, religious and linguistic minorities/nationalities" might be somewhat refined by the fact that some Southeast Asian states, e.g. Vietnam, Laos and Cambodia, did develop programmes in the field of education and agriculture with the aim of improving the situation of their respective minorities. Notwithstanding, Forum Asia keeps pointing out that, in Asian societies, particular attention must be paid to the marginalized minority groups, especially minority women and children. Moreover, even if attention is being paid by states to minorities and indigenous peoples, several scholars warn that official programmes bringing development assistance, healthcare and education are often a cover for states for (forced) acculturation, assimilation and resettlement and often contribute to the degeneration of minorities and indigenous peoples.

* * *

It could be stated that the problem underlying the conceptual issue is a lack of formal recognition of, and respect for, the identity and culture of minority communities and indigenous peoples. According to the conclusions of the Sub-Regional Seminar on Minority Rights held in Thailand in 2003, this lack of formal recognition often results in a "denial of the rights to citizenship, to effective participation in government and to the recognition of their distinctive histories, cultures and lifestyles, notably in the context of national development policies".

## 2.3. Conclusion

The silence with regard to minorities and indigenous peoples in the documents of ASEAN has been interpreted by Forum Asia as "an indication of the denial of human rights for [ethnic minorities] and [indigenous peoples] in member countries, or even an outright denial of their existence". Notwithstanding some examples of states which did develop policies and projects supporting minority education and the agricultural sector, the overall picture in most Southeast Asian states is rather dispiriting: the enormous cultural and religious diversity in Southeast Asia created by the different indigenous peoples and minorities is often considered as a hindrance to national progress or as a threat to national security by governments. Many Southeast Asian governments seem to aim at minimizing diversity within their country, thereby developing programmes that have the objective of assimilating and controlling indigenous people and ethnic minorities. These policies can often be traced back to the governments' ambition to modernize and develop into an industrialized economy, which means that social change is necessary to reach higher levels of economic development.

According to Forum Asia, the violations of human rights and of the rights of minorities and indigenous peoples are due to a "prevailing culture of impunity for human rights violators", as well as "a renewed emphasis on cultural specific cities to justify human rights violations." In the following section, a closer look will be taken at those 'cultural specific cities' and describe how the concept of the universality of human rights works out in the Southeast Asian context.

* * *

## 5. Asian Minorities and Indigenous Peoples and the United Nations: A Last Resort?

### 5.1. Introduction

The lack of domestic or regional mechanisms sends Asia's minorities and indigenous peoples to the United Nations (U.N.) for redress. Fortunately, the bulk of the core international human rights documents are ratified by the majority of ASEAN member states. Consequently, these states are bound by internationally recognized human rights, and they are obliged to submit periodic reports to the monitoring Committees of that particular treaty.

In general, there are the principles of equality and non-discrimination in the enjoyment of all human rights that are codified in different U.N. human rights documents. Additionally, there are a number of U.N. documents that are of special importance for minorities and indigenous peoples. To what extent have Southeast Asian states embraced these international documents?

### 5.2. Minorities

### 5.2.1. Article 27 of the International Covenant on Civil and Political Rights

Article 27 of the International Covenant on Civil and Political Rights (ICCPR) is the most widely accepted legally binding provision on minorities. The Human Rights Committee (HRC) observed that "this article establishes and recognizes a right which is conferred on individuals belonging to minority groups and which is distinct from, and additional to, all the other rights which, as individuals in common with everyone else, they are already entitled to enjoy under the [ICCPR]." Although the HRC has never defined the concepts of 'peoples' or 'minorities' used in Articles 1 and 27, respectively, indigenous peoples are in most cases bound to fit under the concept of 'ethnic, religious or linguistic minorities.' For instance, minorities' right to enjoy their own culture has been widely interpreted so as to include "a particular way of life associated with the use of land resources, especially in the case of indigenous peoples. That right may include such traditional activities as fishing or hunting and the right to live in reserves protected by law."

Only half of the ASEAN member states have ratified or acceded to the ICCPR; Brunei Darussalam, Malaysia, Burma and Singapore have neither signed nor ratified this Convention and Laos only signed the ICCPR. None of the ratifying states have, however, made a reservation to Article 27, which implies recognition of the existence of minorities. Although Article 18 ICCPR does not explicitly refer to minorities, the Article is also relevant because it protects the freedom of thought, conscience and religion. Next to this, Article 1 ICCPR (and ICESR—International Covenant on Economic, Social and Cultural Rights) should be mentioned. Minorities have tried to invoke this right, but the Human Rights Committee as the monitoring body of the ICCPR has decided that no claim for self-determination may be brought under the Optional Protocol. Of the ASEAN member states, Cambodia has signed this Protocol and only the Philippines has also ratified this Protocol. This low acceptance of the possibility of individual complaints seems to follow from the idea that the implementation of human rights is a matter of domestic jurisdiction according to Asian governments. In general, it could be concluded with regard to the ICCPR that because of the low acceptance of the Treaty and the First Optional Protocol, the protection of Southeast Asian minorities based on these documents is rather limited.

\* \* \*

*5.2.1. Declaration on the Rights of Persons Belonging to National or Ethnic, Religious and Linguistic Minorities*

Finally, the Declaration on the Rights of Persons Belonging to National or Ethnic, Religious and Linguistic Minorities (UNDM) should be mentioned, which was inspired by the provisions of Article 27 of the ICCPR and adopted by the General Assembly of the United Nations in 1992. The UNDM, which is a non-binding instrument, contains several rights of minorities, such as the right to enjoy their own culture, profess and practice their own religion, and use their own language freely in public and in private; the right to participate effectively in cultural, religious, social, economic, and public life, and in decisions on the national and, where appropriate, regional level concerning their minority group or region. The UNDM also formulated several obligations for states with regard to minorities, such as the obligation to protect their existence and their national or ethnic, cultural, religious, and linguistic identity, and the obligation to consider legitimate interests of minorities in developing national policies and programmes, as well as in planning and implementing programmes of cooperation and assistance. Southeast Asian states are obliged (albeit only politically) to abide by the standards set in this U.N. minority instrument.

*5.3. Indigenous Peoples*

As far as indigenous peoples are concerned, two documents should be mentioned: Convention No. 169 Concerning Indigenous and Tribal Peoples in Independent Countries, adopted by the International Labour Organization in 1989 (ILO Convention No. 169), and the United Nations Declaration on the Rights of Indigenous Peoples, adopted by the General Assembly in September 2007.

*5.3.1. ILO Convention No. 169*

ILO Convention No. 169 is the most comprehensive binding international document dealing with indigenous peoples' rights. In its Preamble, the Convention draws attention to "the distinctive contributions of indigenous and tribal peoples to the cultural diversity and social and ecological harmony of humankind and the international co-operation and understanding." Many provisions in ILO Convention No. 169 are aimed at national governments and contain obligations to take specific measures with regard to indigenous peoples. Maybe deterred by the binding nature of this Convention, none of the Southeast Asian or even Asian states have ratified this Convention. However, as described by Alexandra Xanthaki, this Convention has served as a model in the drafting of national legislation in the region, such as the Indigenous Peoples' Rights Act 1997 (the Philippines) and the new Land Law 2001 (Cambodia).

*5.3.2. United Nations Declaration on the Rights of Indigenous Peoples*

Considering this lack of official enthusiasm for ILO Convention No. 169, it is remarkable that all Southeast Asian states voted in favour of the United Nations Declaration on the Rights of Indigenous Peoples in 2007. This Declaration was hailed as "a triumph for justice and human dignity following more than two decades of negotiations between governments and indigenous peoples' representatives." The General Assembly of the United Nations affirmed in the Preamble that "all people contribute to the diversity and richness of civilizations and cultures, which constitute the common heritage of mankind" and is convinced that "control by indigenous peoples over developments affecting them and their lands, territories and resources will enable them to maintain and strengthen their institutions, cultures and traditions, and to promote their development in accordance with their aspirations and needs." The articles of the Declaration address both individual and collective rights and deal extensively with cultural rights and identity rights of indigenous peoples, such as their right to education, health, employment and language. The Declaration also promotes the full and effective participation of indigenous peoples in all matters that concern them. As said, all Southeast Asian and Asian states voted in favour of the Declaration, but the statements of the different representatives reveal some common concerns, mainly in relation to the scope of the right to self-determination of indigenous peoples and to the use of natural resources.

* * *

### 5.5. Southeast Asian States and the United Nations: Conclusion

Most Southeast Asian states have exercised restraint towards legally binding U.N. and ILO documents dealing with the protection of minorities, indigenous peoples and even cultural diversity in general. The 1992 U.N. Declaration on the Rights of Persons Belonging to National or Ethnic, Religious and Linguistic Minorities and especially the U.N. Declaration on the Rights of Indigenous Peoples, however, have been welcomed with more enthusiasm. The latter even seems to have triggered some change in the Southeast Asian attitude towards the protection of indigenous peoples. Notwithstanding certain concerns — which Asian states share with many non-Asian states — with regard to the scope of the right to self-determination of indigenous peoples and the use of natural resources, most Asian states are positive to the U.N. Declaration on the Rights of Indigenous Peoples. It remains to be seen whether this change was triggered by the nonbinding nature of the U.N. Declaration, or by a sincere appreciation of its value.

Considering the chronology of the adoption of the Declaration in September 2007, and the adoption of the ASEAN Charter in November 2007, it could be stated in the first place that the relevant provisions in the ASEAN Charter, like the principle mentioned in Article 2(2)(l), should be seen in the light of the U.N. Declaration. More generally, a confirmation of this approach can be found in Article 2(2)(j) of the Charter which refers to "upholding the United Nations Charter and international law, including international humanitarian law, subscribed to by ASEAN Member States." This means that the intentions of the ASEAN member states with regard to "respect for the different cultures, languages and religions of the peoples of ASEAN" as laid down in the Charter can be taken seriously and might even become the starting point for the further development of indigenous peoples' rights, and hopefully also for minorities in Southeast Asia. In the second place, conversely, the comments and support of most Southeast Asian representatives at the adoption of the U.N. Declaration by the General Assembly can — in retrospective — also be taken more seriously.

### 5.6. Practice: The Problems Remain

Notwithstanding these hesitant, though positive, first signs, the atmosphere was far from optimistic during the 1st Regional Workshop on Minority Issues in Southeast Asia organised by several non-governmental organizations (NGOs) in January 2008, where "with extreme concern the situation of national or ethnic, religious and linguistic minorities, and the similarity and interrelationship with the situation of indigenous peoples" was noted. The following general problems were pointed out: non-recognition of the diversity of ethnic, racial, religious and other identities within states in the region by national governments; discriminating laws and policies often combined with the imposition of exclusivist national identities by states, often based on the ethnicity and identity of the ethnic majority; statelessness and the denial or deprivation of citizenship; disadvantaged situations such as poverty and exclusion generally experienced by minorities and indigenous peoples; lack of effective participation and representation in all stages of decision-making; the continuing serious situation faced by many minority women and children; the need for effective state compliance and domestic application of international human rights standards on minorities and indigenous peoples.

Subsequently, the human rights situations of minorities and indigenous peoples by country were raised and it became clear that no Southeast Asian state had a truly clean slate. Therefore, the subsequent reaffirmation of "the state's primary responsibility to promote and protect the human rights of minorities and indigenous peoples in accordance with international human rights standards" sounded rather unconvincing and perfunctory. The NGOs who participated in this workshop seem to have placed their hopes on the United Nations, especially the U.N. Independent Expert on Minority Issues, the United Nations Forum on Minority Issues, and the Durban Review Conference in 2009, which they consider to be "a new opportunity to look into human rights issues related to racism, racial discrimination, xenophobia and related intolerance." As far as ASEAN is concerned, the development of effective Terms of Reference for an ASEAN human rights body (the ASEAN Inter-Governmental Commission on Human Rights) is called for "in accordance with international human rights standards, with full and meaningful participation by civil society and, in particular, representatives of minorities and indigenous peoples."

## Authors' Note

The chapter's final article focuses on the human rights crisis in Darfur. The article discusses the situation and the response of NGO's, state governments, the United Nations, and other international groups. The article argues that international humanitarian action would have been a more effective and appropriate response than the actual response, which was to charge the African Union with the humanitarian mission.

## 12. Paul D. Williams and Alex J. Bellamy, The Responsibility to Protect and the Crisis in Darfur

### Security Dialogue, 2005

Speaking shortly after the U.N. Security Council passed Resolution 1556 on the crisis in the Sudanese province of Darfur, the Philippines ambassador to the U.N. remarked that 'sovereignty also entails the responsibility of a State to protect its people. If it is unable or unwilling to do so, the international community has the responsibility to help that State achieve such capacity and such will and, in extreme necessity, to assume such responsibility itself'. Similarly, the UK representative suggested that the adoption of Resolution 1556 'underlines the commitment of the Security Council to ensure that all Governments fulfill that most basic of obligations—the duty to protect their own citizens'. These sentiments echoed those of the International Commission on Intervention and State Sovereignty (ICISS) and advocates of the 'sovereignty as responsibility' approach.

* * *

The parallels between this conception of sovereignty and the views put forward in the Security Council by the Philippines and the UK in relation to Darfur are striking. During the first half of 2004, the situation in Darfur was repeatedly described as representing a 'supreme humanitarian emergency', that is, a situation where 'the only hope of saving lives depends on outsiders coming to the rescue'. According to the ICISS, there are two threshold criteria—'large scale loss of life' and 'large scale ethnic cleansing'—that must be met before the 'responsibility to protect' can be invoked to override state sovereignty.

Since there can be little doubt that these threshold conditions were met in the Darfur case, armed intervention to halt human suffering would have been legitimate.

And yet, international society failed to even seriously contemplate military intervention. Although Resolution 1556 was passed under Chapter VII of the U.N. Charter, the Security Council chose not to assume responsibility for alleviating human suffering in Darfur by authorizing a humanitarian intervention. Instead, it imposed an arms embargo on the region, demanded that the Sudanese government disarm the so-called janjaweed militias and facilitate the delivery of humanitarian aid, and supported the envisaged African Union (AU) Protection Force. This Protection Force constitutes the only foreign troops deployed to Darfur. The problem for the civilian victims in the province is twofold. First, until late October 2004, the AU troops were only mandated to protect the Union's small Observer Mission, which deployed to the region in June 2004. Second, by the end of October only some 597 out of the envisaged 3,300 AU peacekeepers had actually arrived in the region.

*　*　*

### The Crisis in Darfur and International Responses

In our opinion, the crisis in Darfur represented a supreme humanitarian emergency. It therefore provides an important test case of international society's commitment to an emerging norm of humanitarian intervention and the ideas set out in *The Responsibility to Protect* report. The current war in Darfur began in earnest in February 2003, when first Sudan Liberation Army (SLA) and then Justice and Equality Movement (JEM) forces attacked government military installations in frustration at decades of political marginalization and economic neglect. The rebels initially appeared to take the government by surprise and enjoyed some successes, notably the destruction of half a dozen military aircraft and the capture of an air force general at El Fasher Airport in April 2003. The government responded to the insurgency by deploying some of its own troops (notably the air force), but more significantly by arming and supporting the janjaweed militias (an umbrella term popularly encompassing outlaws/bandits, Arab tribal militias and the Popular Defence Forces). The janjaweed subsequently engaged in killings, abductions, forced expulsions, systematic sexual violence, and deliberate destruction of crops, livestock and important cultural and religious sites.

After several attempts to negotiate a ceasefire during late 2003, the government launched a major ground and air offensive in late January 2004. Shortly afterwards, President Bashir declared that 'law and order' had been restored and that the government had 'established control in all theatres' (Justice Africa, 2004). However, hostilities continued and another round of ceasefire negotiations began in late March in Chad's capital, N'Djamena. By 25 April, these negotiations had produced two rather confused agreements (the first was signed on 8 April). The confusion stemmed in part from the inexperience and rifts within the rebel movements during the negotiations, and partly from the Chadian government's inability to act as a neutral mediator. The result was a ceasefire agreement riddled with poor drafting and serious discrepancies between its English and Arabic versions. It was not surprising that the ceasefire failed to hold, and a pattern developed of government and janjaweed attacks followed by the rebels responding in kind.

By this stage, Khartoum's counter-insurgency operations had spilled across the border into Chad, resulting in the deaths of approximately 30,000 people (mainly civilians) and forcing approximately 1.2 million to flee their homes. Around 200,000 of these were estimated to have crossed into Chad, while the majority remained internally displaced within camps in Darfur (which remained vulnerable to continued janjaweed attack and

780 XVI · HUMAN RIGHTS VIOLATIONS

exploitation, and sealed off from most international relief agencies). By mid-2004, the World Health Organization was estimating that between 240 and 440 people were dying every day as a result of the conflict. USAID predicted that, if left unchecked, by October–December 2004 this number could increase to as many as 2,400 per day. Whatever the true statistics, the situation was commonly described within the U.N. system and Western states as 'the most serious humanitarian emergency in the world today'. By September 2004, the situation had deteriorated further. The number of estimated deaths had risen to 70,000 and the U.N. Secretary-General's Special Representative on Sudan, Jan Pronk, reported that the overall number of people requiring relief had increased by at least 10% (to around 2 million) since the Security Council had become engaged in the problem in June 2004.

Not surprisingly, Darfur's crisis attracted various labels. The U.N. Security Council, the EU and a variety of NGOs (including Amnesty International, Human Rights Watch and the International Crisis Group) all acknowledged that the government of Sudan was complicit in large-scale crimes against humanity and ethnic cleansing in Darfur. Other NGOs, such as Physicians for Human Rights and Justice Africa, went further, calling the crisis genocide. Inevitably, the use of the word 'genocide' invited comparisons with the slaughter in Rwanda during 1994 and highlighted the need to avoid a repeat of international society's feeble response there. Speaking at the U.N.'s Human Rights Commission on the tenth anniversary of the Rwandan genocide, Kofi Annan (2004) had said that events in Darfur left him 'with a deep sense of foreboding. Whatever terms it uses to describe the situation, the international community cannot stand idly by ... [but] must be prepared to take swift and appropriate action. By "action" in such situations I mean a continuum of steps, which may include military action.' On 9 September 2004, following a similar determination in the U.S. Congress, Secretary of State Colin Powell made the unprecedented announcement to the Senate Foreign Relations Committee that his government also believed genocide had been committed in Darfur. However, Powell went on to endorse a restrictive interpretation of the 1948 Genocide Convention and to insist that, despite his determination, no new action would be required on the part of the U.S. government.

As a result, alongside the usual array of NGO activities, international society's responses to Darfur's crisis have come primarily in the form of humanitarian assistance through the U.N. and its specialized programmes and agencies (such as the World Food Programme, UNHCR and the WHO), the USA and the EU. In political terms, however, the responses have been slow, tepid and divided.

* * *

The reluctance of the U.N., the EU and the USA to threaten military intervention in Darfur meant that the AU assumed centre stage in the international response. However, despite clear evidence of government complicity in attacks upon civilians, like the West, the AU has refused to act without the consent of the Sudanese government. Darfur's crisis presented the AU with a genuine opportunity to find an African solution to this African problem through the invoking of Article 4(h) of its new charter, which permits collective intervention in 'grave circumstances', namely, when there is evidence of war crimes, crimes against humanity and genocide. However, in this case, the slogan of 'African solutions to African problems' provided a convenient façade behind which Western powers could wash their hands of committing their own soldiers to Darfur.

Given our argument that a humanitarian intervention would have been legitimate in Darfur's case, what should have been done in practical terms? In our opinion, would-be interveners would have faced a spectrum of options along the following lines:

1. Stop further deaths from slaughter, disease and hunger by providing troops to (a) ensure delivery of humanitarian assistance to the various camps for refugees and internally displaced persons (IDPs) within Darfur; (b) protect the camps from the various militias; and (c) set up a no-fly zone and provide aerial reconnaissance.

2. Carry out (1), but also provide troops to help police a ceasefire agreement while talks continue between the government and rebels.

3. Carry out (1) and (2), and ensure the resettlement of IDPs and refugees.

4. Carry out (1), (2) and (3), and provide troops to help manage the transition period after the government/janjaweed and SLA/JEM conclude a political agreement.

\* \* \*

## 13. Bibliography of Additional Sources

- Anne Bayefsky, HOW TO COMPLAIN TO THE U.N. HUMAN RIGHTS TREATY SYSTEM (2003).

- Anne F. Bayefsky, ENFORCING INTERNATIONAL HUMAN RIGHTS LAW: THE U.N. TREATY SYSTEM IN THE 21ST CENTURY (2000).

- Michael Bowman, *Towards a Unified Treaty Body for Monitoring Compliance with U.N. Human Rights Conventions? Legal Mechanisms for Treaty Reform*, 7 HUM. RTS. L. REV. 225–49 (2007).

- Thomas Buergenthal, *The Normative and Institutional Evolution of International Human Rights*, 19 HUM. RTS. Q. 703–23 (1997).

- Patrick James Flood, THE EFFECTIVENESS OF U.N. HUMAN RIGHTS INSTITUTIONS (Jan. 1998).

- THE FUTURE OF U.N. HUMAN RIGHTS TREATY MONITORING (Philip Alston & James Crawford eds., 2000).

- Jeroen Gutter, *Special Procedures and the Human Rights Council: Achievements and Challenges Ahead*, 7 HUM. RTS. L. REV. 93 (2007).

- Françoise J. Hampson, *An Overview of the Reform of the U.N. Human Rights Machinery*, 7 HUM. RTS. L. REV. 7 (2007).

- Hurst Hannum, *Reforming the Special Procedures and Mechanisms of the Commission on Human Rights*, 7 HUM. RTS. L. REV. 73 (2007).

- Christof Heyns, *The African Regional Human Rights System: The African Charter*, 108 PENN ST. L. REV. 679–702 (2004).

- Rachael Lorna Johnstone, *Cynical Savings or Reasonable Reform? Reflections on a Single Unified U.N. Human Rights Treaty Body*, 7 HUM. RTS. L. REV. 173–200 (2007).

- Ann E. Kent, CHINA, THE UNITED NATIONS AND HUMAN RIGHTS, THE LIMITS OF COMPLIANCE (1999).

- John J. Mearsheimer, *The False Promise of International Institutions*, 19 INT'L SECURITY 5 (Winter 1994).

- Michael O'Flaherty, Human Rights and the U.N. (M. Nijhoff Publishers 2002).
- Michael O'Flaherty, The U.N. and Human Rights: Practice Before the Treaty Bodies (2nd edn Nijhoff The Hague 2002).
- Michael O'Flaherty & Claire O'Brien, *Reform of U.N. Human Rights Treaty Monitoring Bodies: A Critique of the Concept Paper on the High Commissioner's Proposal for a Unified Standing Treaty Body*, 7 Hum. Rts. L. Rev. 141–72 (2007).
- Thomas Pegram, *Diffusion Across Political Systems: The Global Spread of National Human Rights Institutions*, 32.3 Hum. Rts. Q. 729 (Aug. 2010).
- The United Nations and Human Rights, A Critical Appraisal (Philip Alston ed., 1992).
- Hao Duy Phan, *Institutions for the Protection of Human Rights in Southeast Asia*, 31.3 Contemporary Southeast Asia (Dec. 2009).
- Clemens Rieder, *Protecting Human Rights Within the European Union: Who Is Better Qualified to Do the Job — The European Court of Justice or the European Court of Human Rights*, 20 Tul. Eur. & Civ. L.F. 73–107 (2005).
- Naomi Roht-Arriaza, Impunity and Human Rights in International Law and Practice (1995).
- Patrizia Scannella & Peter Splinter, *The United Nations Human Rights Council: A Promise to Be Fulfilled*, 7 Hum. Rts. L. Rev. 41–72 (2007).
- Hanna Beate Schöpp-Schilling, *Treaty Body Reform: The Case of the Committee on the Elimination of Discrimination Against Women*, 7 Hum. Rts. L. Rev. 201–24 (2007).
- Wouter Vandenhole, The Procedures before the U.N. Human Rights Treaty Bodies: Divergence or Convergence? (2004).
- Kirsten Young, The Law and Process of the U.N. Human Rights Committee (2002).

# Chapter XVII

# The WTO, Human Rights Sanctions, and Treatment of Detainees in the War on Terror

## Introduction

This chapter introduces the World Trade Organization (WTO), an international institution created in 1995 to adjudicate cases relating to the General Agreement on Tariffs and Trade (GATT). It also examines one of the most important issues of our time—the balance between protecting human rights and effectively fighting the war on terrorism. In this context, the materials explore whether the WTO would permit a State to unilaterally impose economic sanctions to induce another State to comply with international human rights law and international humanitarian law.

## Objectives

- To understand the purpose and structure of the WTO.
- To examine the role of Member States in the WTO structure.
- To understand the tools available to the WTO and Member States for enforcing trade agreements and punishing violators.
- To understand the exceptions that exist for Member States to justify discriminating against other countries in trade practices.
- To debate whether an exception should exist for Member States to be able to discriminate as a punishment against States that commit human rights violations.

## Problems

1. The WTO was established to facilitate free trade through the elimination of quotas, tariffs, subsidies, and other trade barriers and unfair trade practices. Assume you were a State Representative at the negotiations leading to the creation of the WTO and

GATT. Would you be in favor of including an explicit exception to the Agreement, permitting human rights sanctions? Come to class prepared to debate the pros and cons of such an exception.

2.  Come to class prepared to participate in the following simulation of a case before the WTO between the United States (Applicant) and Canada (Respondent).

    Members of Group A will represent the United States.

    Members of Group B will represent Canada.

    Members of Group C will role play the WTO Panel.

# Simulation

Case Concerning the Guantanamo Bay Detainees
and the Canadian Tariff on U.S. Beef Products
[Based on the 2006 Niagara Moot Court Competition
Problem written by Michael Scharf]

Author's Note: The following problem is fictional, but it is based loosely on events described in Jane Mayer, *Outsourcing Torture*, THE NEW YORKER, February 14, 2005.

1.  Since the overthrow of the Taliban government in Afghanistan, the United States government has maintained on-going intelligence and military cooperation with the government of Pakistan in an effort to capture al Qaeda and former Taliban officials who might be seeking refuge in that country. This operation has resulted in numerous captures and arrests over the past three years. Some of those captured are apprehended by U.S. forces, and others are captured by Pakistani forces.

2.  Mr. Mohamed Aziz is a dual Canadian and Pakistani citizen. He was born is Pakistan in 1978 and moved to Canada with his parents when he was 6 years old. After living in Canada for 10 years, he took all the necessary steps to gain Canadian citizenship and in 1994 became a dual citizen. In 1996, he graduated in 1996 from Degrassi High School in Toronto, and in 2000 he earned a degree in Business Administration from Ryerson University in Toronto. Thereafter, Mr. Aziz started an import business to take advantage of his connections with extended family in Pakistan. Mr. Aziz determined that there was a market in Canada for Pakistani rugs, furniture, textiles and faux jewel home accessories. He annually made numerous trips between Canada and Pakistan and by 2004 his business was grossing over a million dollars (U.S.) per year.

3.  One of the "most wanted" al Qaeda leaders is Shakat Zacoui, a deputy to Osama bin Laden. In May 2004, the Pakistani intelligence agency (the Inter Services Intelligence, or "ISI") photographed Mr. Zacoui having coffee at an outdoor café in Islamabad with Mohamed Aziz.

4.  On June 1, 2004, the government of Pakistan notified the United States CIA Section Chief in Islamabad (referred to for purposes of this case as "Agent Smith") that ISI had that day apprehended Mohamed Aziz at the Islamabad airport while he was waiting to board a flight to Toronto (via London). Mr. Aziz had in his possession at the time of his arrest both his Canadian and Pakistani passports. Although it had no other evidence to suggest that Mr. Aziz was himself a member of the al Qaeda terrorist network, the government of Pakistan suspected that Mr. Aziz might have ma-

terial information related to the whereabouts of the elusive Mr. Zacoui, who it considered "a ticking bomb, likely to strike with devastating consequences at any moment." Neither the government of Pakistan nor the government of the United States notified Canada about the arrest of Mr. Aziz at this time.

5. Without consulting with his superiors, Agent Smith suggested that his Pakistani counterparts should subject Mr. Aziz to "extraordinary methods of interrogation" in order to compel him to identify where Mr. Zacoui could be found. Agent Smith was present as an observer at, but did not actively participate in, the five-hour interrogation of Mr. Aziz, which took place on the evening of June 1. During the interrogation, Mr. Aziz was subject to "water-boarding," a technique in which a suspect is bound and repeatedly immersed in water until he nearly drowns. Throughout the ordeal, Mr. Aziz claimed that he had not known Mr. Zacoui before Mr. Zacoui struck up an innocent conversation with Mr. Aziz at the café in Islamabad. Mr. Aziz further insisted that he had no idea that Mr. Zacoui was a member of the al Qaeda terrorist organization. And he denied any knowledge of Mr. Zacoui's likely whereabouts.

6. After the interrogation, Agent Smith remarked to the Pakistani officials that he found it suspicious that Mr. Aziz made no attempt to confess during "water-boarding." He observed that normally, individuals subjected to water-boarding will say and admit to anything as a way of gaining relief from the ordeal, and suggested that it appeared that Mr. Aziz may have received special training to resist forceful interrogation methods.

7. On June 3, 2004, the Pakistani authorities turned Mr. Aziz over to Agent Smith, who arranged for Mr. Aziz to be transferred to the U.S. detention center known as Camp X-Ray in Guantanamo Bay, Cuba. The United States did not notify the Government of Canada that it had taken custody of Mr. Aziz nor that it had transferred Mr. Aziz to Camp X-Ray. Upon arrival at Guantanamo Bay, Mr. Aziz was classified as "an unlawful enemy combatant" and placed in solitary confinement and subjected to frequent interrogations accompanied by "moderate physical and psychological pressure," including sleep deprivation, prolonged questioning, the use of stress positions, exposure to loud music, yelling at the detainee, deprivation of light, introducing unpleasant odors, removal of clothing, exposure to uncomfortable cell temperatures, using dogs to induce stress, mistreatment of religious objects, and the use of scenarios designed to convince the detainee that death or severely painful consequences are imminent. Mr. Aziz was not charged with any crime, nor given access to counsel.

8. The Pentagon's Combatant Status Review Tribunal (CSRT) was established on July 7, 2004, in response to the U.S. Supreme Court's holding in *Rasul v. Bush*, 124 S. Ct. 2686 (June 28, 2004), that detainees at Guantanamo Bay have a right to challenge their imprisonment. The CSRT is composed of U.S. military officers, and is empowered by Executive Order to review the validity of a given prisoner's continued detention. As of the date of this Compromis, the CSRT had rejected 387 of 393 petitions it had received from detainees at Guantanamo Bay.

9. On August 5, 2004, Mr. Aziz was brought before the CSRT. Mr. Aziz was not allowed access to counsel before or during the proceeding. During the CSRT proceeding, Mr. Aziz told the tribunal what he had repeatedly told his interrogators: that he was a Canadian citizen, that he was in Pakistan in June 2004 to visit his cousins and to purchase rugs for his Toronto-based import/export business, that he had never before met Shakat Zacoui, that he did not know Zacoui was a member of al Qaeda, and that he had no knowledge of Zacoui's whereabouts.

10. Without setting forth reasons, the CSRT rejected Mr. Aziz's plea. Although he has been charged with no crime, and continues to maintain that he has no information about the whereabouts of Shakat Zacoui, Mr. Aziz remains in solitary confinement at the U.S. detention center in Guantanamo Bay.

11. In January 2005, "confidential governmental sources" related the story of Mr. Aziz's plight to a reporter for *News Day*, which included the tale of Mr. Aziz in a story entitled "Torture and the War on Terror," published on February 14, 2005. Thereafter, Samantha Rayburn, the member of Parliament (NDP) and Foreign Affairs Critic representing Mr. Aziz's district, requested the Canadian Department of Foreign Affairs to seek Mr. Aziz's release to the custody of the Government of Canada with the assurances that the Government of Canada would detain Mr. Aziz under Canada's Anti-Terrorism Act and that the Canadian legal system would adjudicate the case if there was sufficient evidence that he had committed a crime.

12. In February 2005, the Canadian Department of Foreign Affairs, through the Canadian Embassy, raised the issue in a demarche in Washington, D.C. The United States Administration rejected the Canadian request for the surrender of Mr. Aziz, stating that the Government and courts of Canada could not be trusted to make correct legal decisions and adequately protect the national interests of the United States in this case.

13. By March 2005, the Aziz story had become a *cause celebre* in Canada. The continuing U.S. refusal to surrender Mr. Aziz to Canada prompted Ms. Rayburn to introduce a Private Member's Bill in the Canadian House of Commons to enact the "Canadian Torture Victim Protection Act, which became law on April 15, 2005. The Act provides:

> Whereas the United States failed to notify Canada in a timely manner of the arrest and detention of Canadian citizen Mohamed Aziz.

> Whereas the United States is responsible for the inhuman and degrading treatment of Mohamed Aziz at the hands of Pakistani authorities, in violation of U.S. obligations under the Torture Convention, the International Covenant on Civil and Political Rights, and the Geneva Conventions of 1949;

> Whereas the United States has subjected Mohamed Aziz to prolonged solitary confinement without charging him with any crime, and without providing him access to counsel, at its detention center in Guantanamo Bay in violation of the International Covenant on Civil and Political Rights and the Geneva Conventions of 1949;

> Whereas the Government of Canada has requested the United States to return Mohamed Aziz to Canada, where he would be face criminal charges if the United States provides sufficient evidence to warrant prosecution;

> Whereas the United States has rejected Canada's request;

> The Government of Canada hereby imposes a ten percent tariff on imports of U.S. produced beef and live cattle until such time as the Governor in Council has certified that the United States has repatriated Canadian citizen Mohamed Aziz and any other Canadian citizens being held by the United States without charge as unlawful enemy combatants.

14. On April 16, 2005, Canadian Prime Minister Paul Martin sent a diplomatic note to President George Bush of the United States, which stated in relevant part:

> In an effort to persuade the United States to release Canadian citizen Mohamed Aziz and other Canadians being held in violation of international law at Guantanamo Bay, Parliament has decided to impose a ten percent tariff on beef and cattle imports

from the United States, which I signed into law today. Canada believes this action is permissible as a legitimate human rights sanction under Article XX of the WTO/ GATT. The tariff will be immediately rescinded upon the repatriation of the unlawfully detained Canadian citizens. We hope this matter can be promptly resolved.

15. President Bush responded in a diplomatic note, dated April 21, 2005, which stated in relevant part:

The United States is disappointed with Canada's implementation of the so called "Canadian Torture Victim Protection Act." The United States firmly denies that it has violated international law in the treatment of Canadian citizen Mohamed Aziz. Under the law of state responsibility, the United States is not liable for the actions carried out by Pakistani authorities in Pakistan against Mr. Aziz. Moreover, as an unlawful enemy combatant now detained at Guantanamo Bay, the Geneva Conventions do not apply to Mr. Aziz. Finally, U.S. obligations under the International Covenant on Civil and Political Rights and the Torture Convention do not apply to actions taken by U.S. authorities outside of the territory of the United States. The United States has no obligation to return Mr. Aziz, who we are holding because he has material information about the al Qaeda terrorist organization. Canada, on the other hand, has violated international law by imposing a ten percent tariff on imports of U.S. produced beef and cattle. Article XX of GATT does not permit this type of unilateral "human rights sanction." While I place great importance on the U.S.-Canada relationship, the United States will not be coerced into releasing a known associate of one of the world's most dangerous terrorists.

16. Over the next several months, Canada and the United States engaged in a series of high level bilateral consultations in an effort to resolve the matter of Mohamed Aziz to no avail. Ultimately, the United States decided to submit the "Case of the Canadian Beef Tariff" to the WTO for adjudication. Accordingly, the United States submitted two questions for the WTO to hear and resolve:

(a) whether the United States violated international human rights law and/or international humanitarian law with respect to the treatment and detention of Mohamed Aziz; and if so,

(b) whether Canada's ten percent tariff on U.S. produced beef and cattle is permissible as a unilateral human rights sanction under Article XX of the GATT.

# Materials

1. Understanding the World Trade Organization http://www.wto.org/english/ thewto_e/ whatis_e/tif_e/fact1_e.htm.

2. Michael P. Scharf, *2006 Niagara Moot Court Bench Memo.*

3. General Agreements on Tariffs and Trade (GATT), Articles I, III, XX.

4. Convention Against Torture, Articles 1–16, 30.

5. International Covenant on Civil and Political Rights, Articles 2, 3, 4, 7, and 9.

6. ILC Draft Articles on State Responsibility for Internationally Wrongful Acts, Articles 1–3, 5, 6, 26.

7. Jay S. ByBee, *White House Torture Memo*, August 1st, 2002.

8. Bibliography of Additional Sources

788    XVII · THE WTO, SANCTIONS, AND TREATMENT OF DETAINEES

# 1. Understanding the World Trade Organization

### What Is the World Trade Organization?

Simply put: the World Trade Organization (WTO) deals with the rules of trade between nations at a global or near-global level. But there is more to it than that.

There are a number of ways of looking at the WTO. It's an organization for liberalizing trade. It's a forum for governments to negotiate trade agreements. It's a place for them to settle trade disputes. It operates a system of trade rules. (But it's not Superman, just in case anyone thought it could solve—or cause—all the world's problems!)

Above all, it's a negotiating forum ...

Essentially, the WTO is a place where member governments go, to try to sort out the trade problems they face with each other. The first step is to talk. The WTO was born out of negotiations, and everything the WTO does is the result of negotiations. The bulk of the WTO's current work comes from the 1986–94 negotiations called the Uruguay Round and earlier negotiations under the General Agreement on Tariffs and Trade (GATT). The WTO is currently the host to new negotiations, under the "Doha Development Agenda" launched in 2001.

Where countries have faced trade barriers and wanted them lowered, the negotiations have helped to liberalize trade. But the WTO is not just about liberalizing trade, and in some circumstances its rules support maintaining trade barriers—for example to protect consumers or prevent the spread of disease.

It's a set of rules ...

At its heart are the WTO agreements, negotiated and signed by the bulk of the world's trading nations. These documents provide the legal ground-rules for international commerce. They are essentially contracts, binding governments to keep their trade policies within agreed limits. Although negotiated and signed by governments, the goal is to help producers of goods and services, exporters, and importers conduct their business, while allowing governments to meet social and environmental objectives.

The system's overriding purpose is to help trade flow as freely as possible—so long as there are no undesirable side-effects. That partly means removing obstacles. It also means ensuring that individuals, companies and governments know what the trade rules are around the world, and giving them the confidence that there will be no sudden changes of policy. In other words, the rules have to be "transparent" and predictable.

And it helps to settle disputes ...

This is a third important side to the WTO's work. Trade relations often involve conflicting interests. Agreements, including those painstakingly negotiated in the WTO system, often need interpreting. The most harmonious way to settle these differences is through some neutral procedure based on an agreed legal foundation. That is the purpose behind the dispute settlement process written into the WTO agreements.

The WTO began life on 1 January 1995, but its trading system is half a century older. Since 1948, the General Agreement on Tariffs and Trade (GATT) had provided the rules for the system. (The second WTO ministerial meeting, held in Geneva in May 1998, included a celebration of the 50th anniversary of the system.)

It did not take long for the General Agreement to give birth to an unofficial, de facto international organization, also known informally as GATT. Over the years GATT evolved through several rounds of negotiations.

The last and largest GATT round, was the Uruguay Round which lasted from 1986 to 1994 and led to the WTO's creation. Whereas GATT had mainly dealt with trade in goods, the WTO and its agreements now cover trade in services, and in traded inventions, creations and designs (intellectual property).

## Trade Without Discrimination

### 1. Most-favoured-nation (MFN): treating other people equally

Under the WTO agreements, countries cannot normally discriminate between their trading partners. Grant someone a special favour (such as a lower customs duty rate for one of their products) and you have to do the same for all other WTO members.

This principle is known as most-favoured-nation (MFN) treatment. It is so important that it is the first article of the General Agreement on Tariffs and Trade (GATT), which governs trade in goods. MFN is also a priority in the General Agreement on Trade in Services (GATS) (Article 2) and the Agreement on Trade-Related Aspects of Intellectual Property Rights (TRIPS) (Article 4), although in each agreement the principle is handled slightly differently. Together, those three agreements cover all three main areas of trade handled by the WTO.

Some exceptions are allowed. For example, countries can set up a free trade agreement that applies only to goods traded within the group — discriminating against goods from outside. Or they can give developing countries special access to their markets. Or a country can raise barriers against products that are considered to be traded unfairly from specific countries. And in services, countries are allowed, in limited circumstances, to discriminate. But the agreements only permit these exceptions under strict conditions. In general, MFN means that every time a country lowers a trade barrier or opens up a market, it has to do so for the same goods or services from all its trading partners — whether rich or poor, weak or strong.

### 2. National treatment: Imported and locally-produced goods should be treated equally —

at least after the foreign goods have entered the market. The same should apply to foreign and domestic services, and to foreign and local trademarks, copyrights and patents. This principle of "national treatment" (giving others the same treatment as one's own nationals) is also found in all the three main WTO agreements (Article 3 of GATT, Article 17 of GATS and Article 3 of TRIPS), although once again the principle is handled slightly differently in each of these.

National treatment only applies once a product, service or item of intellectual property has entered the market. Therefore, charging customs duty on an import is not a violation of national treatment even if locally-produced products are not charged an equivalent tax.

## Freer Trade: Gradually, Through Negotiation

Lowering trade barriers is one of the most obvious means of encouraging trade. The barriers concerned include customs duties (or tariffs) and measures such as import bans or quotas that restrict quantities selectively. From time to time other issues such as red tape and exchange rate policies have also been discussed.

Since GATT's creation in 1947–48 there have been eight rounds of trade negotiations. A ninth round, under the Doha Development Agenda, is now underway. At first these focused on lowering tariffs (customs duties) on imported goods. As a result of the negotiations, by the mid-1990s industrial countries' tariff rates on industrial goods had fallen steadily to less than 4%.

But by the 1980s, the negotiations had expanded to cover non-tariff barriers on goods, and to the new areas such as services and intellectual property.

Opening markets can be beneficial, but it also requires adjustment. The WTO agreements allow countries to introduce changes gradually, through "progressive liberalization". Developing countries are usually given longer to fulfill their obligations.

### Predictability: Through Binding and Transparency

Sometimes, promising not to raise a trade barrier can be as important as lowering one, because the promise gives businesses a clearer view of their future opportunities. With stability and predictability, investment is encouraged, jobs are created and consumers can fully enjoy the benefits of competition—choice and lower prices. The multilateral trading system is an attempt by governments to make the business environment stable and predictable.

#### The Uruguay Round increased bindings

#### Percentages of tariffs bound before and after the 1986–94 talks

|                       | Before | After |
|-----------------------|--------|-------|
| Developed countries   | 78     | 99    |
| Developing countries  | 21     | 73    |
| Transition economies  | 73     | 98    |

(These are tariff lines, so percentages are not weighted according to trade volume or value)

In the WTO, when countries agree to open their markets for goods or services, they "bind" their commitments. For goods, these bindings amount to ceilings on customs tariff rates. Sometimes countries tax imports at rates that are lower than the bound rates. Frequently this is the case in developing countries. In developed countries the rates actually charged and the bound rates tend to be the same.

A country can change its bindings, but only after negotiating with its trading partners, which could mean compensating them for loss of trade. One of the achievements of the Uruguay Round of multilateral trade talks was to increase the amount of trade under binding commitments. In agriculture, 100% of products now have bound tariffs. The result of all this: a substantially higher degree of market security for traders and investors.

The system tries to improve predictability and stability in other ways as well. One way is to discourage the use of quotas and other measures used to set limits on quantities of imports—administering quotas can lead to more red-tape and accusations of unfair play. Another is to make countries' trade rules as clear and public ("transparent") as possible. Many WTO agreements require governments to disclose their policies and practices publicly within the country or by notifying the WTO. The regular surveillance of national trade policies through the Trade Policy Review Mechanism provides a further means of encouraging transparency both domestically and at the multilateral level.

### Principles of the Trading System

The WTO agreements are lengthy and complex because they are legal texts covering a wide range of activities. They deal with: agriculture, textiles and clothing, banking, telecommunications, government purchases, industrial standards and product safety, food sanitation regulations, intellectual property, and much more. But a number of simple, fundamental principles run throughout all of these documents. These principles are the foundation of the multilateral trading system.

## Promoting fair competition

The WTO is sometimes described as a "free trade" institution, but that is not entirely accurate. The system does allow tariffs and, in limited circumstances, other forms of protection. More accurately, it is a system of rules dedicated to open, fair and undistorted competition.

The rules on non-discrimination—MFN and national treatment—are designed to secure fair conditions of trade. So too are those on dumping (exporting at below cost to gain market share) and subsidies. The issues are complex, and the rules try to establish what is fair or unfair, and how governments can respond, in particular by charging additional import duties calculated to compensate for damage caused by unfair trade.

Many of the other WTO agreements aim to support fair competition: in agriculture, intellectual property, services, for example. The agreement on government procurement (a "plurilateral" agreement because it is signed by only a few WTO members) extends competition rules to purchases by thousands of government entities in many countries.

## Encouraging development and economic reform

The WTO system contributes to development. On the other hand, developing countries need flexibility in the time they take to implement the system's agreements. And the agreements themselves inherit the earlier provisions of GATT that allow for special assistance and trade concessions for developing countries.

Over three quarters of WTO members are developing countries and countries in transition to market economies. During the seven and a half years of the Uruguay Round, over 60 of these countries implemented trade liberalization programmes autonomously. At the same time, developing countries and transition economies were much more active and influential in the Uruguay Round negotiations than in any previous round, and they are even more so in the current Doha Development Agenda.

At the end of the Uruguay Round, developing countries were prepared to take on most of the obligations that are required of developed countries. But the agreements did give them transition periods to adjust to the more unfamiliar and, perhaps, difficult WTO provisions—particularly so for the poorest, "least-developed" countries. A ministerial decision adopted at the end of the round says better-off countries should accelerate implementing market access commitments on goods exported by the least-developed countries, and it seeks increased technical assistance for them. More recently, developed countries have started to allow duty-free and quota-free imports for almost all products from least-developed countries. On all of this, the WTO and its members are still going through a learning process. The current Doha Development Agenda includes developing countries' concerns about the difficulties they face in implementing the Uruguay Round agreements.

## Settling Disputes: The priority is to settle disputes, not to pass judgment.

Dispute settlement is the central pillar of the multilateral trading system, and the WTO's unique contribution to the stability of the global economy. Without a means of settling disputes, the rules-based system would be less effective because the rules could not be enforced. The WTO's procedure underscores the rule of law, and it makes the trading system more secure and predictable. The system is based on clearly-defined rules, with timetables for completing a case. First rulings are made by a panel and endorsed (or rejected) by the WTO's full membership. Appeals based on points of law are possible.

However, the point is not to pass judgment. The priority is to settle disputes, through consultations if possible. By July 2005, only about 130 of the 332 cases had reached the full panel process. Most of the rest have either been notified as settled "out of court" or remain in a prolonged consultation phase—some since 1995.

### Principles: equitable, fast, effective, mutually acceptable

Disputes in the WTO are essentially about broken promises. WTO members have agreed that if they believe fellow-members are violating trade rules, they will use the multilateral system of settling disputes instead of taking action unilaterally. That means abiding by the agreed procedures, and respecting judgments.

A dispute arises when one country adopts a trade policy measure or takes some action that one or more fellow-WTO members considers to be breaking the WTO agreements, or to be a failure to live up to obligations. A third group of countries can declare that they have an interest in the case and enjoy some rights.

A procedure for settling disputes existed under the old GATT, but it had no fixed timetables, rulings were easier to block, and many cases dragged on for a long time inconclusively. The Uruguay Round agreement introduced a more structured process with more clearly defined stages in the procedure. It introduced greater discipline for the length of time a case should take to be settled, with flexible deadlines set in various stages of the procedure. The agreement emphasizes that prompt settlement is essential if the WTO is to function effectively. It sets out in considerable detail the procedures and the timetable to be followed in resolving disputes. If a case runs its full course to a first ruling, it should not normally take more than about one year—15 months if the case is appealed. The agreed time limits are flexible, and if the case is considered urgent (e.g. if perishable goods are involved), it is accelerated as much as possible.

The Uruguay Round agreement also made it impossible for the country losing a case to block the adoption of the ruling. Under the previous GATT procedure, rulings could only be adopted by consensus, meaning that a single objection could block the ruling. Now, rulings are automatically adopted unless there is a consensus to reject a ruling—any country wanting to block a ruling has to persuade all other WTO members (including its adversary in the case) to share its view. Although much of the procedure does resemble a court or tribunal, the preferred solution is for the countries concerned to discuss their problems and settle the dispute by themselves. The first stage is therefore consultations between the governments concerned, and even when the case has progressed to other stages, consultation and mediation are still always possible.

### How are disputes settled?

Settling disputes is the responsibility of the Dispute Settlement Body (the General Council in another guise), which consists of all WTO members. The Dispute Settlement Body has the sole authority to establish "panels" of experts to consider the case, and to accept or reject the panels' findings or the results of an appeal. It monitors the implementation of the rulings and recommendations, and has the power to authorize retaliation when a country does not comply with a ruling.

- First stage: consultation (up to 60 days). Before taking any other actions the countries in dispute have to talk to each other to see if they can settle their differences by themselves. If that fails, they can also ask the WTO director-general to mediate or try to help in any other way.

- Second stage: the panel (up to 45 days for a panel to be appointed, plus 6 months for the panel to conclude). If consultations fail, the complaining country can ask for a panel to be appointed. The country "in the dock" can block the creation of a panel once, but when the Dispute Settlement Body meets for a second time, the appointment can no longer be blocked (unless there is a consensus against appointing the panel).

Officially, the panel is helping the Dispute Settlement Body make rulings or recommendations. But because the panel's report can only be rejected by consensus in the Dispute Settlement Body, its conclusions are difficult to overturn. The panel's findings have to be based on the agreements cited.

The panel's final report should normally be given to the parties to the dispute within six months. In cases of urgency, including those concerning perishable goods, the deadline is shortened to three months.

The agreement describes in some detail how the panels are to work. The main stages are:

- Before the first hearing: each side in the dispute presents its case in writing to the panel.

- First hearing: the case for the complaining country and defense: the complaining country (or countries), the responding country, and those that have announced they have an interest in the dispute, make their case at the panel's first hearing.

- Rebuttals: the countries involved submit written rebuttals and present oral arguments at the panel's second meeting.

- Experts: if one side raises scientific or other technical matters, the panel may consult experts or appoint an expert review group to prepare an advisory report.

- First draft: the panel submits the descriptive (factual and argument) sections of its report to the two sides, giving them two weeks to comment. This report does not include findings and conclusions.

- Interim report: The panel then submits an interim report, including its findings and conclusions, to the two sides, giving them one week to ask for a review.

- Review: The period of review must not exceed two weeks. During that time, the panel may hold additional meetings with the two sides.

- Final report: A final report is submitted to the two sides and three weeks later, it is circulated to all WTO members. If the panel decides that the disputed trade measure does break a WTO agreement or an obligation, it recommends that the measure be made to conform with WTO rules. The panel may suggest how this could be done.

- The report becomes a ruling: The report becomes the Dispute Settlement Body's ruling or recommendation within 60 days unless a consensus rejects it. Both sides can appeal the report (and in some cases both sides do).

## Appeals

Either side can appeal a panel's ruling. Sometimes both sides do so. Appeals have to be based on points of law such as legal interpretation—they cannot reexamine existing evidence or examine new issues.

Each appeal is heard by three members of a permanent seven-member Appellate Body set up by the Dispute Settlement Body and broadly representing the range of WTO membership. Members of the Appellate Body have four-year terms. They have to be individuals with recognized standing in the field of law and international trade, not affiliated with any government. The appeal can uphold, modify or reverse the panel's legal findings and conclusions. Normally appeals should not last more than 60 days, with an absolute maximum of 90 days.

The Dispute Settlement Body has to accept or reject the appeals report within 30 days—and rejection is only possible by consensus.

## *Authors' Note*

The following selection presents a comprehensive analysis of the simulation material concerning the fictional incident between the U.S. and Canada in the WTO. The material addresses whether the U.S. violated international law with its treatment of the suspected terrorist detainee. The selection then analyzes whether Canada's response is lawful under GATT.

The materials that follow are meant to aid in simulation preparation. Material 3 provides an excerpt of GATT so as to provide the legal framework in which the parties operate. The remaining materials address state responsibility and provide relevant law surrounding international human rights law. These excerpts are meant to aid the parties in determining whether the U.S. violated international human rights law and whether Canada was legally justified in leveling a tariff in response.

## 2. Michael P. Scharf, 2006 Niagara Moot Court Bench Memo

Legal Analysis

### I. Has the United States Violated International Law in Relation to the Treatment of Mohamed Aziz?

#### A. Is the United States Responsible for the Inhumane Treatment of Aziz by the Pakistani Intelligence Agency?

##### 1. Does "Water-boarding" constitute torture?

The United Nations Convention Against Torture and Other Cruel, Inhuman or Degrading Treatment or Punishment defines torture as: "any act by which severe pain or suffering, whether physical or mental, in intentionally inflicted on a person for such purposes as obtaining from him or a third person information or a confession, punishing him for an act he or a third person has committed or is suspected of having committed, or intimidating or coercing him or a third person, or for any reason based on discrimination of any kind, when such pain or suffering is inflicted by or at the instigation of or with the consent or acquiescence of a public official or other person acting in an official capacity. It does not include pain or suffering arising only from, inherent in or incidental to lawful sanctions."

This definition and the ban on torture has been held to constitute customary international law, applicable even to non-parties of the Torture Convention.[1] The prohibition of torture has also achieved the status of *jus cogens*: it is a non-derogable norm of international law which holds the highest hierarchical position among other norms and principles.[2]

---

1. See *Prosecutor v. Furundzija*, IT-95-17/IT, ICTY Trial Chamber II, 1 December 1998, at para 160.
2. See *Al Adsuani v. United Kingdom*, Eur. Ct. H.R., Judgment of 21 November 2001, paras. 60–61; *Ireland v. United Kingdom*, Eur. Ct. H.R., Judgment of 18 January 1978, para 163; *Prosecutor v. Furundzija*, ICTY, 1 December 1998.

The Torture Convention draws a distinction between "torture" and "other cruel, inhuman or degrading treatment," which may determine the outcome of the present case. For example, as discussed in section B below, the extraterritorial application of the Torture Convention is limited to prosecuting nationals for acts of torture committed abroad; the duty to prosecute does not apply to inhuman or degrading treatment. In addition, as discussed below, the necessity defense may be foreclosed for acts rising to the level of torture but may be a legitimate defense for acts constituting inhuman or degrading treatment.

The leading case focusing on the distinction between torture and inhuman or degrading treatment is *Ireland v. United Kingdom*, decided by the European Court of Human Rights in 1978.[3] In that case, the European Court found that the five techniques in question (wall standing, hooding, subjection to noise, deprivation of sleep, and reduced diet) constituted inhuman and degrading treatment, but did not rise to the level of torture under the Convention. In subsequent cases, the European Court for Human Rights has been extremely reluctant to attach what it calls the "special stigma to deliberate inhuman treatments causing very serious and cruel suffering" which accompanies a finding of "torture." Drawing from this precedent, the United States could argue that acts must cross an extremely high threshold to meet the definition of torture; and that in the absence of bodily injuries, the infliction of physical pain that does not leave permanent marks or impair organs would not constitute torture.

Canada may respond by calling the Court's attention to the more recent case law of the European Court of Human Rights, in which the Court appears to have lowered its very high threshold for finding "torture." Thus, in the 1996 case of *Aksoy v. Turkey*, the European Court determined that subjecting the accused to prolonged hanging by the arms, which resulted in temporary paralysis of both arms, constituted torture; in the 1997 case of *Aydin v. Turkey*, the European Court found that rape by an official during incarceration constituted torture; and in the 1999 case of *Selmouni v. France*, the European Court found that blows to the body, sexual humiliation, and threats of bodily harm with a blowtorch constituted torture.[4] In making these determinations, the European Court stated that the European Convention (which contains the same definition of torture as the Torture Convention) was a "living instrument" and that the *Ireland v. United Kingdom* severity test must be adapted to reflect contemporary understanding and evolution of the law."[5]

Canada may also point to the case law of the Inter-American Commission and Court, which have applied a lower threshold for finding torture than the European Court of Human Rights did in the case of *Ireland v. United Kingdom*. They have found the following measures to constitute torture: "prolonged incommunicado detention, keeping detainees hooded and naked in cells, interrogating them under the drug pentothal, *holding a person's head in water until the point of drowning,* standing or walking on top of individuals, cutting with pieces of broken glass, putting a hood over a person's head and burning him or her with lighted cigarettes, rape; mock burials, mock executions, beatings, deprivation of food and water, threats of removal of body parts, and death threats."[6] The U.N. Human Rights Committee has found similar acts or conduct to constitute torture, including: electric shocks, mock executions, forcing prisoners to remain standing for

---

3. *Ireland v. United Kingdom*, Eur. Ct. H.R., Judgment of 18 January 1978.

4. *Aksoy v. Turkey*, 1996-VI Eur. Ct. H.R. 2260; *Aydin v. Turkey; 1997-V Eur. Ct. H.R. 1866; Selmouni v. France 1999-V Eur. Ct. H.R. 155.*

5. *Selmouni v. France 1999-V Eur. Ct. H.R. 155, 183.*

6. Robert Goldman, "Trivializing Torture: The Office of Legal Counsel's 2002 Opinion Letter and International Law Against Torture," 12 Hum. Rts. Br. 1 (2004).

extremely long periods of time, and holding persons incommunicado for more than three months while keeping that person blindfolded with hands tied together resulting in limb paralysis, leg injuries, substantial weight loss, and eye infection.[7] The U.N. Special Rapporteur on Torture has listed several acts determined to be torture, including beating; extraction of nails or teeth; burns; electric shocks; suspension; suffocation; exposure to excessive light or noise; sexual aggression; prolonged denial of rest or sleep, food, sufficient hygiene, or medical assistance; total isolation and sensory deprivation; and simulated executions.[8]

### 2. Does the Torture Convention Apply Extraterritorially?

Article 2 of the Torture Convention requires State Parties to prevent torture "in any territory under its jurisdiction." The United States may argue that it has not violated this obligation because the conduct in this case was committed at a Pakistan government detention center, not in the United States or on a U.S. base.

Article 5 of the Torture Convention, in contrast, requires State Parties to assert criminal jurisdiction over acts of torture committed by their nationals even if that conduct occurs on foreign territory. Canada will argue that the United States has breached Article 5 by failing to prosecute Agent Smith for his involvement in the torture of Mohamed Aziz. The United States may respond that the Convention does not criminalize the act of observing torture, only actively participating in torture—which Agent Smith did not do. In addition, the United States will point out that the extraterritorial obligation under Article 5 only applies to prosecution of acts rising to the level of torture, not acts constituting inhuman or degrading treatment that fall short of torture as in this case.

### 3. Are the Actions of the Pakistani Intelligence Agents Attributable to the United States?

The Rules of State responsibility and attribution are laid out in the International Law Commission's Draft Articles on State Responsibility, which have been cited by the International Court of Justice and the International Criminal Tribunal for the Former Yugoslavia as reflecting binding rules of customary international law.[9] Article 1 of the Articles on State Responsibility provides that "every internationally wrongful act of a State entails the international responsibility of that State." Article 2 provides that a State commits an internationally wrongful act of a State when conduct consisting of an action or omission is attributable to it and constitutes a breach of its international obligations. Article 3 states that how a state characterizes an act under its domestic law is immaterial if international law provides that it is unlawful.[10]

Article 5 of the Articles on State Responsibility attributes conduct to a state by a person or entity "which is empowered by the law of that State to exercise elements of the governmental authority ... provided the person or entity is acting in that capacity in the particular instance."[11] The Commentary to Article 5 states that the Article is intended to take para-State entities into account. Examples given include private security firms contracted by the government to act as prison guards and airlines which may be given powers related to immigration control or quarantine laws.

---

7. *Id.*

8. *Id.*

9. See Case Concerning the Gabcikovo-Nagymaros Project, 1997 I.C.J. 7, at paras. 47–52; *Prosecutor v. Blaskic*, IT-95-14-AR108bis, ICTY Appeals Chamber, 29 Oct. 1997.

10. Draft Articles on Responsibility of States for Internationally Wrongful Acts, International Law Commission, 53rd sess., G.A. Supp. No. 10 (A/56/10) (Nov. 2001).

11. *Id.*

Similarly, Article 6 of the Draft Articles on State Responsibility attributes conduct to a state by an organ placed at the disposal of a State by another State if the organ is acting in the exercise of elements of the governmental authority of the State at whose disposal it is placed.

Canada may argue that under either Article 5 or Article 6 of the Draft Articles, the Pakistani Intelligence Agents became agents of the United States government when they subjected Mohamed Aziz to waterboarding at the suggestion of the U.S. CIA Station Chief (Agent Smith), while the Station Chief observed.

The United States may respond that the International Law Commission's Commentaries on the Draft Articles provide that a State must have directed or controlled the specific operation and the "conduct complained of must be an integral part of that operation."[12] "Suggesting" is not the same thing as "directing." In addition, the United States may argue, based on the ICJ holding in the case of *Military and Paramilitary Activities in and against Nicaragua*[13] that for the conduct of the Pakistani government personnel to be attributed to the United States "it would in principle have to be proved that that State had effective control of the military or paramilitary operations in the course of which the alleged violations were committed."[14] Canada may argue that the *Nicaragua* precedent has been overtaken by the decision of the ICTY Appeals Chamber in *Tadic*, which applied a looser "overall control" test.[15] The U.S. will point out, however, that the ICTY itself stated that the *Tadic* opinion was not meant to displace *Nicaragua*. Rather, *Tadic* was confined to the question of what level of foreign state involvement is necessary for the Court to apply the Grave Breaches provision of the Geneva Conventions in establishing individual criminal responsibility, and the *Nicaragua* test continues to be appropriate for finding state responsibility.

In the alternative, the United States may argue that since Agent Smith did not specify that the Pakistani Intelligence Agents should employ "water-boarding," the United States cannot be responsible for any actions by the Pakistanis that went beyond Agent Smith's suggestion. Canada may respond that a number of cases have found liability even if the act was allegedly *ultra vires*. For example, in the *Thomas H. Youmans Case* before the Mexican-American Claims Commission,[16] Mexico could not escape responsibility for murders committed by Mexican soldiers on the ground that these acts were outside the scope of the soldiers' competency given that the soldiers at the time were on duty and their commander was present. In the *Jean-Baptiste Caire Cases*,[17] Mexico was again held responsible for murders committed by two soldiers as part of an extortion scheme even though their commanders had no knowledge of what they had done because they acted as "apparent officers" of the Mexican State and/or "exercised powers or measures connected with their official character." The United States will seek to distinguish these cases from the present case, where the perpetrators are members of a foreign State's intelligence agency, rather than members of the U.S. military.

---

12. Commentaries on Responsibilities of States for Internationally Wrongful Acts, International Law Commission, 53rd sess., G.A. Supp. No. 10 (A/56/10) (Nov. 2001), 101.
13. *Military and Paramilitary Activities in and Against Nicaragua (Nicar. v. U.S.)*, 1986 I.C.J. 14, 114 (Jun. 27).
14. *Id.* at para. 115.
15. *Prosecutor v. Tadic*, IT-94-1, ICTY Appeals Chamber, 15 July 1999, at para. 114.
16. *Thomas H. Youmans Case* (U.S. v. Mex.) 4 RIAA 110 (1926)
17. *Jean-Baptiste Caire Cases*, (Fr. & Mex. Mixed Claims Commission 1929), 5 Ann. Digest 146.

As an alternative theory of State liability, Canada may rely on the joint criminal enterprise doctrine. It has been a long-standing principle in international law, at least since the end of World War II, that when two or more people act in concert to further a common criminal purpose, the acts of one person or entity are attributable to the other members of the group. The common purpose notion applies even where a co-perpetrator committed an act that was outside of the common design, but was a natural and foreseeable consequence of the common purpose.[18] In the present case, Agent Smith shared a common design with the Pakistani Intelligence agents to employ "extraordinary methods of interrogation in order to compel [Mohamed Aziz] to identify where Mr. Zacoui could be found." Even if Agent Smith did not have water-boarding specifically in mind, it was among the foreseeable techniques that the Pakistanis were likely to employ given that broad mandate. As such, the inhumane treatment can be attributable to Agent Smith, and consequently, the United States since Smith was a government official acting within the scope of his employment.

### 4. Can the Mistreatment of Aziz be Justified under the Doctrine of Necessity?

Echoing the analysis contained in the controversial August 1, 2002, memo prepared by Assistant Attorney General Jay S. Bybee, the United States may argue that under international law the "necessity defense" permits extraordinary interrogation techniques such as water-boarding in some circumstances notwithstanding the general prohibition on torture. The necessity defense has been recognized in Article 26 of the Draft Articles on State Responsibility. In making this argument, the United States will point out the overriding interest in discovering the location of most-wanted al Qaeda leader Shakat Zacoui, who, according to the Compromis, is considered "a ticking bomb, likely to strike with devastating consequences at any moment."

The United States is not the only country that has taken this position in the aftermath of 9/11. The European Commission has opined that there is room for a "balancing act" between the interests of national security and that of an individual to be free from torture and ill-treatment, despite the status of the prohibition of torture in international law.[19] Authority for such an approach can also be found in the Israeli Supreme Court's decision denying judicial authorization for physical torture while acknowledging that the necessity defense could be used to exonerate government agents who take part in such acts.[20]

Canada, in turn, may point out that the necessity defense was repeatedly rejected as excusing liability for inhumane treatment at Nuremberg and subsequent WWII war crimes trials.[21] Canada may also point out that the U.N. Committee Against Torture, which is the treaty body created to facilitate enforcement of the Torture Convention, issued a statement following the attacks on 9/11 in which it reminded States parties to the Convention of the non-derogable nature of the obligations contained in the Convention, even in times of crisis.[22] The jurisprudence of the European Court of Human Rights has similarly ruled

---

18. See Tadic, *supra*, at paras. 195–198.

19. See European Commission Working Document, "The Relationship between Safeguarding Internal Security and Complying with International Protection Obligations and Instruments," http://www.statewatch.org/news/2001/dec/immcom743.pdf.

20. Supreme Court of Israel, Judgment Concerning the Legality of the General Security Service's Interrogation Methods, 38 I.L. M. 1471 (1999).

21. See e.g., *United States v. Alstoetter*, 3 Trials of War Criminals Before the Nuremberg Military Tribunals Under Control Council Law No. 10, at 1086 (rejecting defense by Sclegelberger that his actions prevented an even worse approach to the administration of justice).

22. Statement of the Committee Against Torture, 22 November 2001, CAT/C/XXVII/Misc.7, para 79.

out the possibility of a balancing act between interests of national security and the interests of the individual to be protected against torture or cruel, inhuman or degrading treatment and punishment. In making this point, the European Court in *Soering v. The United Kingdom*, stressed "the absolute prohibition of torture and of inhuman or degrading treatment or punishment under the terms of the Convention."[23]

One obstacle to raising the necessity defense is that the doctrine is not available "if the issue of the competing values has been previously foreclosed by a deliberate legislative choice.[24] Canada could argue that the absolute character of the ban on torture leaves no room for the necessity defense, precisely because there can be no exceptions. Thus, the Torture Convention provides in Article 2: "No exceptional circumstances whatsoever, whether a state of war or threat of war, internal political instability or any other public emergency, may be invoked as a justification of torture." The United States will point out that this non-derogation clause applies only to torture. While State Parties must "undertake to prevent" cruel, inhuman, or degrading treatment, the "no exceptional circumstances" provision does not explicitly apply to such conduct. Thus, if water-boarding is deemed to be "inhuman or degrading treatment," but not "torture," then the language of the Convention does not foreclose the necessity defense in this case.

### 5. Is Release of Aziz the Required Remedy?

Canada may cite the Yugoslavia Tribunal Appeals Chamber decision in the *Nikolic* case for the proposition that an accused person must be released "in circumstances where an accused is very seriously mistreated, maybe even subject to inhuman, cruel or degrading treatment, or torture, before being handed over...."[25] But the United States will point out that the Yugoslavia Tribunal, citing the Eichmann precedent, stressed that the individual's rights must be weighed against the international community's interest in punishing "universally condemned offenses."[26] The United States will characterize terrorism as falling within that category. Canada will respond that unlike Nikolic, who had been charged by an international criminal tribunal with war crimes and crimes against humanity, Mohamed Aziz has been charged with no crime.

### B. Did the United States violate International Law in the treatment of Aziz in Guantanamo Bay?

Canada will argue that the treatment of Mr. Aziz at Guantanamo Bay violated the Torture Convention and also the following provisions of the International Covenant on Civil and Political Rights (ICCPR): inhuman or degrading treatment under Article 7; and arbitrary arrest and unlawful detention under Article 9. The United States has four potential defenses: First, the United States may argue that under the doctrine of *lex specialis*, the provisions of the Geneva Conventions and not the ICCPR and Torture Convention apply to detainees at Guantanamo Bay. Second, unlike the non-derogable nature of torture, the rights under Article 7 and 9 of the Covenant may be suspended in "time of pub-

---

23. *Soering v. United Kingdom*, Eur. Ct. H.R., Judgment of 7 July 1989, para. 88.

24. See ILC Draft Articles on State Responsibility, Article 25; *United States v. Oakland Cannabis Buyer's Coop*, 532 U.S. 483, 491 (2001) (assuming necessity is an available defense to federal criminal charges but holding that Congress made a determination that marijuana has no medical benefits worthy of an exception and thus necessity was not available as a defense to distributing a controlled substance).

25. *Prosecutor v. Nikolic*, Decision on Interlocutory Appeal Concerning Legality of Arrest, IT-94-2-AR73, ICTY Appeals Chamber, 5 June 2003, at para. 28 (The ICTY declined to dismiss the case notwithstanding the illegality of Nikolic's arrest because he had not been subject to severe abuse during his abduction).

26. Id. at Para. 25.

lic emergency which threatens the life of the nation" under Article 4 of the Covenant. See the discussion of the necessity defense in Subsection II(d) above. Third, the United States may argue that the ICCPR does not apply to actions by U.S. personnel undertaken outside of the United States. Finally, the United States may argue that the Court should apply the principle *mala captus bene detentus*, meaning that a person improperly seized may nevertheless properly be detained, especially where that person may constitute a threat to a country's security.

### 1. The Doctrine of *Lex Specialis* and the Geneva Conventions

Pursuant to the doctrine of *lex specialis*, the United States has taken the position that International Humanitarian Law, rather than International Human Rights Law, applies to persons detained pursuant to its Global War on Terrorism. To quote the United States submission to the Inter-American Commission on Human Rights in the *Case relating to prisoners detained at Guantanamo Bay*:

> The law of armed conflict is the *lex specialis* governing the status and treatment of persons detained during armed conflict.... The consequences of conflating the two bodies of law would be dramatic and unprecedented. For instance, application of principles developed in the context of human rights law would allow all enemy combatants detained in armed conflict to have access to courts to challenge their detention, a result directly at odds with well-settled law of war that would throw the centuries-old, unchallenged practice of detaining enemy combatants into complete disarray. As Professor Meron, currently President of the International Criminal Tribunal for the Former Yugoslavia, concludes: "The two systems, human rights and humanitarian norms, are thus distinct."[27]

Canada will respond by pointing to the Inter-American Commission's decision in the *Detainees at Guantanamo Bay* case.[28] While recognizing that the concept of *lex specialis* applies where there is a specific conflict between the rules of International Humanitarian Law and Human Rights law in the context of armed conflict, the Commission held that Human Rights Law nonetheless complements and reinforces International Humanitarian Law during armed conflict, such that no one may fall into a law-free zone. The International Court of Justice similarly ruled in the *Advisory Opinion on the Israeli Wall Being Built in Palestine*, that "the protection offered by human rights conventions does not cease in case of armed conflict, save through the effect of provisions for derogation of the kind to be found in Article 4 of the International Covenant on Civil and Political Rights."[29] Consequently, Canada will argue that international human rights law and international humanitarian law apply concurrently, and the United States must afford Mr. Aziz the fundamental protections under both regimes.

Although the United States has characterized its ongoing world-wide conflict with al Qaeda as an armed conflict, the U.S. Government has concluded that the Geneva Convention Relative to the Treatment of Prisoners of War (POW Convention)[30] does not

---

27. Statement by Andre Surena at Hearing of the Inter-American Commission on Human Rights on Issues Relating to Prisoners Detained at Guantanamo Bay, Cuba (October 20, 2003), available at: http://www.state.gov/s/1/2003/44385.htm.

28. Inter-American Commission on Human Rights, Detainees at Guantanamo Bay, Cuba, March 12, 2002, available at: http://www.photius.com/rogue_nations/guantanamo.html.

29. Consequences of the Construction of a Wall in the Occupied Palestinian Territory, ICJ Advisory Opinion, 2004 ICJ Rep; Human Rights Committee, General Comment No. 31 [80], U.N. Doc. CCPR/C/21/Rev.1/Add.13, para. 106.

30. Third Geneva Convention of 1949.

apply to the conflict with al Qaeda—a stance the United States is likely to repeat in the present case. It reaches that conclusion based on the fact that al Qaeda is not a state, and even if it were, it has neither declared its acceptance of the Geneva Prisoner of War Convention nor applied its provisions. Further, the United States has taken the position that even if members of al Qaeda were covered by the POW Convention, as "unlawful combatants" they would still not be entitled to prisoner of war status, a determination that was in the present case confirmed by a competent tribunal (the CSRT) pursuant to Article 5 of the POW Convention.[31] The United States has further taken the position that the Geneva Convention on the Protection of Civilian Persons (Civilian Convention) does not apply to members of al Qaeda because the Convention was not intended to apply to irregular belligerents.[32] In the alternative, the United States may argue that the Convention permits the government to detain civilians where, as in this case, "the security of the Detaining Power makes it absolutely necessary."[33]

Canada will respond by pointing out that the Pictet Commentary to the Geneva Conventions states that "every person in enemy hands must have some status under international law; he is either a prisoner of war and, as such, covered by the Geneva Prisoner of War Convention, or a civilian covered by the Geneva Convention on the Protection of Civilian Persons.... There is no intermediate status."[34] The authoritative U.S. Army Field Manual 27–10 on the Law of Land Warfare takes the same position, and the ICRC has always maintained that those not qualifying for POW status should be viewed as civilians and consequently fall under the protection of article 4 of the Civilians Convention.[35] In accord with this view, the International Criminal Tribunal for the Former Yugoslavia recently held in the *Celebici Camp Case* that "there is no gap between the Third and Fourth Geneva Convention and that if an individual is not entitled to protections of the Third Convention ... he or she necessarily falls within the ambit of Convention IV.[36]

If the POW Convention applies, Canada will assert that the treatment of Mr. Aziz does not comport with the requirements of the Convention. In particular, Article 17(4) of the Convention states that no physical or mental torture, nor any other form of coercion may be inflicted on prisoners of war to secure from them information of any kind whatsoever. Articles 31 and 32 of the Civilian Convention contain the same language. Moreover, if the Civilian Convention applies, Canada will point out that the Convention requires that "internment shall cease as soon as possible after the close of hostilities." It is unreasonable, Canada will assert, for the United States to be able to hold civilians indefinitely just because it has defined its war on terrorism as a war with no end."

Finally, Canada may argue that the term war on terrorism is appropriately only used in a metaphoric sense, and consequently the "war" between the United States and al Qaeda cannot trigger the application of the laws of war outside the territory of Afghanistan and Iraq. This is consistent with the holding of the U.S. court in the *Pan-Am Inc. v. Aetna*

---

31. Memorandum of William H. Taft, IV, the Legal Adviser of the Department of State, dated March 22, 2002, available at http://www.humanrightsfirst.org/us_law/etn/gov_rep/gov_memo_int-law.htm.

32. Id.

33. Fourth Geneva Convention, Art. 42.

34. Commentary on Geneva Convention IV, J.S. Pictet, ed. ICRC, 1958, at 51 (the Pictet Commentary is considered the definitive record of the negotiations of the Geneva Conventions).

35. See H.P. Gasser, "Act of Terror, Terrorism and International Humanitarian Law," 84 Int'l Rev. Red Cross, No. 847, September 2002, at 568.

36. *Prosecutor v. Delalic*, Celbici Camp case, Judgment, IT-96-21-T, 16 November 1998, at para. 271.

*Casualty and Surety Co. case*, in which the court ruled that the United States could not have been at war with the terrorist group known as the PFLP because it had engaged in terrorist acts as a non-state, non-belligerent, non-insurgent actor."[37] In such a case, Human Rights Law, rather than International Humanitarian Law, governs this case.

### 2. The Extraterritorial Application of the ICCPR and Torture Convention

When the United States ratified the International Covenant on Civil and Political Rights it included a reservation providing that the prohibition on cruel, inhuman, or degrading treatment or punishment means only whatever is barred under the Fifth, Eighth, or Fourteenth Amendments to the U.S. Constitution."[38] Since then, the United States has maintained consistently that the Covenant does not apply to U.S. conduct outside the United States. It is one of the core principles of international law that in treaty relations a nation is not bound without its consent, and is only bound to the extent of its consent. Under international law, a reservation made when ratifying a multilateral Convention validly alters or modifies the treaty obligation, unless reservations are disallowed by the Convention or if the reservation in question is inconsistent with the Convention's object and purpose.[39] Therefore, the United States reservation prevents the Court from finding that the ICCPR applies to U.S. actions in Guantanamo Bay, which is in Cuba, not the United States.

(Note, the United States included an identical reservation in the Torture Convention, and would make the same argument that the reservation prevents the extraterritorial application of that Convention to this Case).

In making this argument, the United States may draw on the case law of the European Court of Human Rights, which has taken the view that the European Convention on Human Rights is regionally bounded. Thus, in the *2001 Bankovic* case, the European Court noted that "the Convention was not designed to be applied throughout the world, even in respect of the conduct of Contracting States."[40] Canada may point out, however, that the European Court's jurisdiction is in flux with respect to this issue. In *Issa v. Turkey*, a November 2004 judgment concerning the conduct of Turkish forces during cross-border incursions to route out terrorists who had taken refuge in northern Iraq, the Court indicated that once individuals come within an area under the control of a Contracting State, those individuals are deemed to be within the legal space of that State.[41]

Canada may further respond by drawing the WTO's attention to the ICJ's Advisory opinion in the *Construction of a Wall in the Occupied Palestinian Territory* case, and to the General Comments of the Human Rights Committee, which affirm that the ICCPR extends to "those within the power or effective control of the forces of a State party act-

---

37. *Pan-Am Inc. v. Aetna Casualty and Surety Co.*, 505 F.2d 989, 1013–1015 (2nd Cir. 1974).

38. US Senate Resolution of Advice and Consent to Ratification of the International Covenant on Civil and Political Rights, 138 Cong. Rec. 8070 (1992).

39. Vienna Convention on the Law of Treaties, May 23, 1969, 1155 U.N.T.S. 331 (US recognizes this treaty as reflecting customary international law).

40. *Bankovic and Others v. Certain NATO Member States*, Grand Chamber Decision as to the Admissibility of Application no. 52207/99, 12 December 2001 (holding that Convention did not apply to NATO bombing of Belgrade TV station since Serbia was not a party to the Convention).

41. *Issa and Others v. Turkey*, Application no. 31821/96, Judgment, 6 November 2004 (The Court noted that if Turkey "could be considered to have exercised, temporarily, effective overall control of a particular portion of the territory of northern Iraq" and if it could be shown that "at the relevant time, the victims were within that specific area," then "it would follow logically that they were within the jurisdiction of Turkey).

ing outside its territory."[42] Since the ICCPR reflects customary international law, and as such is binding on even non-parties, it is also binding when the United States acts extraterritorially notwithstanding the U.S. reservation.

Finally, Canada may cite the U.S. Supreme Court's decision in *Rasul v. Bush*[43] where the U.S. Supreme Court held that the federal habeas corpus statute confers on the District Court jurisdiction to hear petitioners' habeas corpus challenges to the legality of their detention at Guantanamo Bay. The Court pointed out that the United States occupies the base under the terms of a 1903 Lease Agreement, which stipulates that the U.S. "shall exercise complete jurisdiction and control over and within" the leased territory; and in 1934, the United States and Cuba concluded a treaty providing that "the lease would remain in effect so long as the United States of America shall not abandon the ... naval station of Guantanamo." Thus, the Court in Rasul concluded that the presumption against extraterritorial application of U.S. law did not restrict the application of U.S. law in Guantanamo, because the naval base is, for all practical purposes, within the territorial jurisdiction of the United States. Canada will argue that the same analysis compels the conclusion that the ICCPR should also apply to U.S. acts at Guantanamo.

### 3. The ICCPR and the Mala captus Bene Detentus Principle

Article 9 of the 1966 International Covenant on Civil and Political Rights provides that everyone has the right to liberty and security of person, that "no one shall be subjected to arbitrary arrest or detention," and that "no one shall be deprived of his liberty except on such grounds and in accordance with such procedure as are established by law."[44] The Human Rights Committee, which was established to monitor the implementation of the Covenant, has ruled on several occasions that transborder abductions violate Article 9 of the Covenant.[45] Interpreting a similar provision in the 1950 European Convention for the Protection of Human Rights, the European Court of Human Rights has stated that where state authorities are involved in a luring or abduction, the rights of the individual are violated.[46] Drawing from this precedent, Canada may argue that a country must release a detainee where custody over the person has been obtained in circumvention of the normal procedures. Since the United States did not obtain custody over Mr. Aziz via the 1942 U.S.-Pakistan Extradition Treaty, but rather through "irregular rendition," his continuing detention violates Article 9 of the Covenant.

In response, the United States will point out that several countries, including the United States, apply the principle *mala captus bene detentus*, meaning that a person improperly seized may nevertheless properly be detained. The United States Supreme Court applied the principle in the 1992 Alvarez-Machain case, in holding that U.S. courts had jurisdiction to try an individual forcibly abducted from Mexico.[47] As discussed above, the Yugoslavia Tribunal applied the principle in deciding not to release an accused Serb war

---

42. Consequences of the Construction of a Wall in the Occupied Palestinian Territory, ICJ Advisory Opinion, 2004 ICJ Rep; Human Rights Committee, General Comment No. 31 [80], U.N. Doc. CCPR/C/21/Rev.1/Add.13, para. 10.

43. 124 S.Ct. 2686, June 28, 2004.

44. 1966 International Covenant on Civil and Political Rights, 23 March 1976, 999 UNTS 171, Art. 9(1).

45. See Views of the Human Rights Committee Under Article 5(4) of the Optional Protocol to the International Covenant on Civil and Political Rights, UN Doc. A/36/40 (1981), at 176 and 185.

46. See *Stocke v. Germany*, Judgment of 19 March 1991, Eur. Ct. H.R. (Ser. A). No. 199 (Annex, Opinion of the Commission, para. 167).

47. *United States v. Alvarez-Machain*, 504 U.S. 655, at 669 (1992).

criminal despite finding that he had been abducted from Serbia in circumvention of the Extradition Agreement between Serbia and the Tribunal.[48] Canada may distinguish ICTY *Nikolic* decision on the basis that Nikolic was an indicted war criminal whereas Mr. Aziz has not been charged with any offense.

In addition, Canada may point out that the *Alvarez-Machain* case was met with widespread criticism throughout the international community. Less than a year after the decision, the United Kingdom's House of Lords emphatically rejected the mala captus bene detentus rule as inconsistent with evolving standards of human rights.[49] Meanwhile, the U.N. Working Group on Arbitrary Detention concluded that "the detention of Humberto Alvarez-Machain is declared to be arbitrary, being in contravention of ... Article 9 of the International Covenant on Civil and Political Rights."[50] Canada would then urge this WTO Panel to use the present case to settle the issue of whether the mala captus bene detentus principle is no longer acceptable as a matter of international law.

## II. Is Canada's Ten Percent Tariff on U.S.-Produced Beef Unlawful under the GATT?

### A. The Exceptions contained in Article XX of the GATT 1994

Canada and the United States are parties to the Agreement Establishing the World Trade Organization,[51] which incorporates the current version of GATT, designated as GATT 1994. A Canadian ten percent tariff on U.S.-produced beef would violate the free trade provisions of GATT 1994 unless it fell within the exceptions set forth in Article XX. Among the exceptions listed in that article are measures "(a) necessary to protect public morals," and "(b) necessary to protect human, animal or plant life or health." Article XX reflects an express policy decision to allow measures considered harmful to market access when a sufficient social or economic policy justification exists. The WTO has never had occasion to determine whether Article XX could be used to justify a unilateral human rights sanction. (Note, unilateral sanctions are to be contrasted with multilateral sanctions imposed by the U.N. Security Council, which override the GATT by virtue of Article 103 of the U.N. Charter).

In interpreting Article XX, the core interpretive tools are:

An assessment of the ordinary meaning to be given to the terms.

Their context, including the preamble to the treaties and WTO case law.

Any applicable rules of international law between the parties.

Supplementary means of interpretation, including the preparatory work of the treaty.

According to their ordinary meaning, the terms "public morals" and "human life or health" could be interpreted to include human rights against torture and degrading and inhumane treatment.

---

48. *Prosecutor v. Nikolic*, Decision on Interlocutory Appeal Concerning Legality of Arrest, IT-94-2-AR73, ICTY Appeals Chamber, 5 June 2003, at para. 28 (The ICTY declined to dismiss the case notwithstanding the illegality of Nikolic's arrest because he had not been subject to severe abuse during his abduction).

49. See *Regina v. Horseferry Road Magistrates' Court (Ex parte Bennett)*, [1994] 1 App. Cas. 42 (Eng. HL 1993) (holding that a New Zealand citizen, forcibly returned to England from South Africa, could obtain a stay of the criminal proceedings against him in England).

50. Report of the Working Group on Arbitrary Detention, UN Commission on Human Rights, 50th Session, Agenda Item 10, UN Doc. E/CN.4/1994/27 (1993), at 139–140.

51. April 15, 1994, 33 I.L.M. 1144 (1995).

Relevant WTO case Law: In *United States—Gambling and betting services*,[52] the WTO Panel stated that the terms "public morals" and "public order" could vary in time and space, depending on prevailing social, cultural, ethical and religious values, and that WTO members "should be given some scope to define and apply for themselves [these concepts] in their respective territories according to their own systems and scales of values." Similarly, in *United States—Import prohibition of certain shrimp and shrimp products*,[53] the WTO adopted an "evolutionary approach" to the interpretation of the Article XX exceptions. The WTO thus ruled that the term "exhaustible natural resources" under Article XX(g) included endangered species such as the sea turtle, basing its ruling on international environmental law, as it had developed since the negotiation of the original GATT. An "evolutionary approach" could allow the WTO to interpret the Article XX exceptions in light of modern international human rights norms and standards. The *Shrimp/Sea Turtle case* also stands for the proposition that the Article XX exceptions are not limited to protecting the morals or health of those in the importing State, but rather can include concern for those located in the exporting State or subject to the actions of the exporting State.

Applicable rules of international law between the parties: In *United States—Standards for reformulated and conventional gasoline*,[54] the WTO held that WTO law cannot be read in "clinical isolation from public international law." In the *Shrimp/Turtle* case cited above, for example, the WTO relied upon the Convention on International Trade in Endangered Species of Wild Fauna and Flora and other multilateral environmental agreements as a means of interpreting the term "exhaustible natural resources." Canada could argue that international human rights treaties, such as the Torture Convention and the International Covenant on Civil and Political Rights, would similarly be valid tools to interpret the terms "public morals," "human life or health" and "public order" under Article XX. Reading the Article XX exceptions to include torture would enable WTO members comply with their other international legal responsibilities without creating a conflict between obligations originating from WTO and human rights treaties.

Supplementary means of interpretation (negotiating history): There was no debate on the meaning of article XX(a) during the GATT negotiations because the term "public morals" had already had an established meaning with respect to prior commercial treaties. In that context, the public morals exception had been used to include slavery, weapons, narcotics, liquor, pornography, compulsory labor, and animal welfare. The GATT negotiating record indicates that the "protection of human life or health exception" of Article XX(b) was understood to justify discrimination against foreign products on the basis of "sanitary regulations." While the United States will argue for a strict reading that confines the exceptions to the original intent of the negotiators, Canada will argue that torture is sufficiently similar to slavery and compulsory labor, thus warranting application of the Article XX exception in this case.

In making its case, Canada may point out that the United States, itself, has a long history of using unilateral trade restrictions to pursue humanitarian goals. In 1974, the United States conditioned eligibility of non-market countries for most-favored-nation

---

52. In *United States—Gambling and betting services*, Report of the Panel, 10 Nov. 2004, paras. 6.461, and 6.465–6.468.

53. *United States—Import prohibition of certain shrimp and shrimp products*, Report of the Appellate Body, 12 October 1998, paras 129–130.

54. *United States—Standards for reformulated and conventional gasoline*, Report of the Appellate Body, 29 April 1996.

status on whether the country provided its citizens the right to emigrate. In 1978, the United States prohibited the importation of any product of Ugandan origin until the President certified that Uganda is no longer committing a consistent pattern of gross violations of human rights. In 1982, the United States withdrew most-favored-nation status from Poland because of the crackdown against the Solidarity labor union. In 1985, the United States banned the importation of Krugerrands from South Africa because of its objections to the policies and practices of Apartheid. In 1987, the United States banned the importation of sugars, syrups, and molasses from Panama until the President certified that freedom of the press, due process of law, and other constitutional guarantees have been restored to the Panamanian people.[55]

## B. The Requirement of Necessity

The Article XX exceptions are each subject to the requirement of necessity. The WTO Appellate Body has noted that the standard of necessity is an objective standard, based on weighing and balancing the relative importance of the particular interest at stake, the contribution of the measure to the realization of the ends pursued by it, and the restrictive impact of the measure on international commerce.[56] The burden of proof is on the State invoking the Article XX exception to make a prima facie case that its measure is necessary to protect public morals or human life or health. The State invoking the exception, in this case Canada, must demonstrate that the measure in question falls somewhere between "indispensable to" and "making a contribution to" the policy interest being pursued by it.[57]

In *Thailand—Restrictions on importation of and internal taxes on cigarettes*,[58] the WTO Panel stated: "The import restrictions imposed by Thailand could be considered to be 'necessary' in terms of Article XX(b) only if there were no alternative measure consistent with the General Agreement, or less inconsistent with it, which Thailand could reasonably be expected to employ to achieve its health policy objectives." In the present Case, Canada exhausted diplomatic avenues before enacting the tariff on U.S.-produced beef, and it had few options other than use of a trade sanction to employ to induce the United States to release Mohamed Aziz. Because the United States has a veto on the Security Council, action in that body is not practicable. While several human rights bodies, such as the Human Rights Committee, the Inter-American Commission on Human Rights, and the Inter-American Court of Human Rights, could consider Canada's complaint, these bodies can do no more than condemn U.S. human rights violations as they have no authority to impose economic or other sanctions against violators. The United States, in turn, may argue that since the tariff has little chance of affecting U.S. policy in this case, it will not "make a contribution to" the policy interest being pursued by it.

## C. The Chapeau Requirements

Any measure asserted under Article XX must also pass the requirements of the introductory clause of Article XX, which provides a means of ensuring that the exceptions are not used for a protectionist purpose. The introductory clause provides that the exceptions are "subject to the requirement that such measures are not applied in a manner which would constitute a means of arbitrary or unjustifiable discrimination between

---

55. See Steve Charnovitz, "The Moral Exception in Trade Policy," 38 Va. J. Int'l L. 689, 697 (1998).

56. *See United States—Gambling and betting services*, Report of the Appellate Body, para 304.

57. *Id.* at paras. 306, 307, 309.

58. *Thailand—Restrictions on importation of and internal taxes on cigarettes*, Report of the Panel, 7 November 1990, para. 174.

countries where the same conditions prevail, or a disguised restriction on international trade."

Arbitrary or unjustifiable discrimination: The main purpose of this condition is to restrict attempts to legitimize discrimination against certain countries, but the provision does not outlaw every kind of discrimination — just arbitrary and unjustifiable discrimination. The provision is especially important in cases where a tariff, quota, or import ban is applied against a single country, as in the present case. But singling a country out is not arbitrary or unjustifiable where the target country is the only country where the objectionable practice exists. The United States may argue that since many countries employ similar interrogation techniques in the war against terrorism, the Canadian tariff on only U.S.-produced beef is arbitrary and unjustifiable. Canada may respond that other countries may engage in torture and inhumane acts, but only the United States is committing such acts against Canadian citizens whom it alleges are unlawful enemy combatants.

Disguised Restriction: The goal of this second requirement is to ensure that a contracting party does not invoke the Article XX exceptions as a pretext for protectionist pursuits. In one of the earliest cases concerning this requirement, the Tuna 1 Panel noted that a publicly announced trade measure could not be considered "disguised."[59] Canada's tariff on U.S.-produced beef would meet this test since it was publicly announced a year before it was to be implemented. But the United States, echoing the criticism of many commentators, may argue that overemphasis on publication risks misuse of Article XX, where blatantly protectionist measures might pass the disguised regulation test precisely because of their blatancy.

The United States may argue that the Canadian tariff on U.S.-produced beef is in reality a measure intended to prop up the ailing Canadian beef industry, which had been hard hit by the 2003 U.S. ban on imports of Canadian cattle following the disclosure that a Canadian cow had come down with "mad cow disease" (bovine spongiform encephalopathy), a degenerative nerve illness linked to the rare and fatal human nerve disorder Cretzfeldt-Jakob Disease. Before the ban, Canada exported far more beef products than it imported, with over ninety percent of Canadian beef exports going to the United States. Meanwhile over fifty percent of Canada's beef imports are from the United States. The U.S. ban was costly for Canadian ranchers, who lost more than 5.7 billion dollars, setting back the ranching industry ten years. The ban also affected employment in several related sectors, including meat packing, food processing and the transportation industry. Under GATT and NAFTA, Canada was unable to introduce an import ban, quotas, or tariffs on foreign beef products for the purpose of ameliorating the domestic oversupply caused by the closure of the U.S. market to Canadian beef exports. In July 2005, the U.S. ban was partially lifted, but it continues to apply to Canadian cattle older than thirty months, based on scientific findings that levels of infection from mad cow disease increase with age.[60]

Based on this background, the United States may argue that the Canadian tariff on U.S.-produced beef is a disguised measure whose real objective is to protect the Canadian beef industry, which was suffering from an oversupply of beef caused by the combination of the U.S. ban and continuing imports of beef from the United States. Canada, in turn, may argue that it singled out U.S. beef imports because a large percentage of those imports originate from Texas, the U.S. President's home state, and thus the sanc-

---

59. *United States—Restrictions on imports of tuna, 16 August 1991, para. 108.*

60. See CBS News, US To Lift Canadian Cattle Ban, November 18, 2005, www.cbsnews.com/stories/2005/11/16/national/main1050500.shtml.

tion is likely to affect some of the President's most important GOP political and financial backers. It therefore has a greater chance of prompting the President to release Mohamed Aziz than if the tariff had been imposed on something like automobiles, which are produced in a predominantly democratic region of the country.

---

# 3. General Agreements on Tariffs and Trade (GATT)
## 1947

### Article I

*General Most-Favored-Nation Treatment*

1. With respect to customs duties and charges of any kind imposed on or in connection with importation or exportation or imposed on the international transfer of payments for imports or exports, and with respect to the method of levying such duties and charges, and with respect to all rules and formalities in connection with importation and exportation, and with respect to all matters referred to in paragraphs 2 and 4 of Article III, any advantage, favor, privilege or immunity granted by any contracting party to any product originating in or destined for any other country shall be accorded immediately and unconditionally to the like product originating in or destined for the territories of all other contracting parties.

\* \* \*

### Article III

*National Treatment on Internal Taxation and Regulation*

4. The products of the territory of any contracting party imported into the territory of any other contracting party shall be accorded treatment no less favorable than that accorded to like products of national origin in respect of all laws, regulations and requirements affecting their internal sale, offering for sale, purchase, transportation, distribution or use. The provisions of this paragraph shall not prevent the application of differential internal transportation charges which are based exclusively on the economic operation of the means of transport and not on the nationality of the product.

\* \* \*

### Article XX

*General Exceptions*

Subject to the requirement that such measures are not applied in a manner which would constitute a means of arbitrary or unjustifiable discrimination between countries where the same conditions prevail, or a disguised restriction on international trade, nothing in this Agreement shall be construed to prevent the adoption or enforcement by any contracting party of measures:

   (*a*)  necessary to protect public morals;

   (*b*)  necessary to protect human, animal or plant life or health;

   (*c*)  relating to the importations or exportations of gold or silver;

   (*d*)  necessary to secure compliance with laws or regulations which are not inconsistent with the provisions of this Agreement, including those relating to customs enforcement, the enforcement of monopolies operated under paragraph 4 of Article II and Article XVII, the protection of patents, trade marks and copyrights, and the prevention of deceptive practices;

(*e*) relating to the products of prison labor;

(*f*) imposed for the protection of national treasures of artistic, historic or archaeological value;

(*g*) relating to the conservation of exhaustible natural resources if such measures are made effective in conjunction with restrictions on domestic production or consumption;

(*h*) undertaken in pursuance of obligations under any intergovernmental commodity agreement which conforms to criteria submitted to the CONTRACTING PARTIES and not disapproved by them or which is itself so submitted and not so disapproved;

(*i*) involving restrictions on exports of domestic materials necessary to ensure essential quantities of such materials to a domestic processing industry during periods when the domestic price of such materials is held below the world price as part of a governmental stabilization plan; *Provided* that such restrictions shall not operate to increase the exports of or the protection afforded to such domestic industry, and shall not depart from the provisions of this Agreement relating to non-discrimination;

(*j*) essential to the acquisition or distribution of products in general or local short supply; *Provided* that any such measures shall be consistent with the principle that all contracting parties are entitled to an equitable share of the international supply of such products, and that any such measures, which are inconsistent with the other provisions of the Agreement shall be discontinued as soon as the conditions giving rise to them have ceased to exist. The CONTRACTING PARTIES shall review the need for this sub-paragraph not later than 30 June 1960.

---

# 4. Convention against Torture and Other Cruel, Inhuman or Degrading Treatment or Punishment

## 1984

*Adopted and opened for signature, ratification and accession by General Assembly resolution 39/46 of 10 December 1984*

*Entry into force 26 June 1987, in accordance with article 27 (1)*

The States Parties to this Convention,

Considering that, in accordance with the principles proclaimed in the Charter of the United Nations, recognition of the equal and inalienable rights of all members of the human family is the foundation of freedom, justice and peace in the world,

Recognizing that those rights derive from the inherent dignity of the human person,

Considering the obligation of States under the Charter, in particular Article 55, to promote universal respect for, and observance of, human rights and fundamental freedoms,

Having regard to article 5 of the Universal Declaration of Human Rights and article 7 of the International Covenant on Civil and Political Rights, both of which provide that no one shall be subjected to torture or to cruel, inhuman or degrading treatment or punishment,

Having regard also to the Declaration on the Protection of All Persons from Being Subjected to Torture and Other Cruel, Inhuman or Degrading Treatment or Punishment, adopted by the General Assembly on 9 December 1975,

Desiring to make more effective the struggle against torture and other cruel, inhuman or degrading treatment or punishment throughout the world,

Have agreed as follows:

## PART I

### Article 1

1. For the purposes of this Convention, the term "torture" means any act by which severe pain or suffering, whether physical or mental, is intentionally inflicted on a person for such purposes as obtaining from him or a third person information or a confession, punishing him for an act he or a third person has committed or is suspected of having committed, or intimidating or coercing him or a third person, or for any reason based on discrimination of any kind, when such pain or suffering is inflicted by or at the instigation of or with the consent or acquiescence of a public official or other person acting in an official capacity. It does not include pain or suffering arising only from, inherent in or incidental to lawful sanctions.

2. This article is without prejudice to any international instrument or national legislation which does or may contain provisions of wider application.

### Article 2

1. Each State Party shall take effective legislative, administrative, judicial or other measures to prevent acts of torture in any territory under its jurisdiction.

2. No exceptional circumstances whatsoever, whether a state of war or a threat of war, internal political in stability or any other public emergency, may be invoked as a justification of torture.

3. An order from a superior officer or a public authority may not be invoked as a justification of torture.

### Article 3

1. No State Party shall expel, return ("refouler") or extradite a person to another State where there are substantial grounds for believing that he would be in danger of being subjected to torture.

2. For the purpose of determining whether there are such grounds, the competent authorities shall take into account all relevant considerations including, where applicable, the existence in the State concerned of a consistent pattern of gross, flagrant or mass violations of human rights.

### Article 4

1. Each State Party shall ensure that all acts of torture are offences under its criminal law. The same shall apply to an attempt to commit torture and to an act by any person which constitutes complicity or participation in torture.

2. Each State Party shall make these offences punishable by appropriate penalties which take into account their grave nature.

### Article 5

1. Each State Party shall take such measures as may be necessary to establish its jurisdiction over the offences referred to in article 4 in the following cases:

(a) When the offences are committed in any territory under its jurisdiction or on board a ship or aircraft registered in that State;

(b) When the alleged offender is a national of that State;

(c)  When the victim is a national of that State if that State considers it appropriate.

2. Each State Party shall likewise take such measures as may be necessary to establish its jurisdiction over such offences in cases where the alleged offender is present in any territory under its jurisdiction and it does not extradite him pursuant to article 8 to any of the States mentioned in paragraph I of this article.

3. This Convention does not exclude any criminal jurisdiction exercised in accordance with internal law.

## Article 6

1. Upon being satisfied, after an examination of information available to it, that the circumstances so warrant, any State Party in whose territory a person alleged to have committed any offence referred to in article 4 is present shall take him into custody or take other legal measures to ensure his presence. The custody and other legal measures shall be as provided in the law of that State but may be continued only for such time as is necessary to enable any criminal or extradition proceedings to be instituted.

2. Such State shall immediately make a preliminary inquiry into the facts.

3. Any person in custody pursuant to paragraph I of this article shall be assisted in communicating immediately with the nearest appropriate representative of the State of which he is a national, or, if he is a stateless person, with the representative of the State where he usually resides.

4. When a State, pursuant to this article, has taken a person into custody, it shall immediately notify the States referred to in article 5, paragraph 1, of the fact that such person is in custody and of the circumstances which warrant his detention. The State which makes the preliminary inquiry contemplated in paragraph 2 of this article shall promptly report its findings to the said States and shall indicate whether it intends to exercise jurisdiction.

## Article 7

1. The State Party in the territory under whose jurisdiction a person alleged to have committed any offence referred to in article 4 is found shall in the cases contemplated in article 5, if it does not extradite him, submit the case to its competent authorities for the purpose of prosecution.

2. These authorities shall take their decision in the same manner as in the case of any ordinary offence of a serious nature under the law of that State. In the cases referred to in article 5, paragraph 2, the standards of evidence required for prosecution and conviction shall in no way be less stringent than those which apply in the cases referred to in article 5, paragraph 1.

3. Any person regarding whom proceedings are brought in connection with any of the offences referred to in article 4 shall be guaranteed fair treatment at all stages of the proceedings.

\* \* \*

## Article 10

1. Each State Party shall ensure that education and information regarding the prohibition against torture are fully included in the training of law enforcement personnel, civil or military, medical personnel, public officials and other persons who may be involved in the custody, interrogation or treatment of any individual subjected to any form of arrest, detention or imprisonment.

2. Each State Party shall include this prohibition in the rules or instructions issued in regard to the duties and functions of any such person.

### Article 11

Each State Party shall keep under systematic review interrogation rules, instructions, methods and practices as well as arrangements for the custody and treatment of persons subjected to any form of arrest, detention or imprisonment in any territory under its jurisdiction, with a view to preventing any cases of torture.

### Article 12

Each State Party shall ensure that its competent authorities proceed to a prompt and impartial investigation, wherever there is reasonable ground to believe that an act of torture has been committed in any territory under its jurisdiction.

### Article 13

Each State Party shall ensure that any individual who alleges he has been subjected to torture in any territory under its jurisdiction has the right to complain to, and to have his case promptly and impartially examined by, its competent authorities. Steps shall be taken to ensure that the complainant and witnesses are protected against all ill-treatment or intimidation as a consequence of his complaint or any evidence given.

### Article 14

1. Each State Party shall ensure in its legal system that the victim of an act of torture obtains redress and has an enforceable right to fair and adequate compensation, including the means for as full rehabilitation as possible. In the event of the death of the victim as a result of an act of torture, his dependents shall be entitled to compensation.

2. Nothing in this article shall affect any right of the victim or other persons to compensation which may exist under national law.

### Article 15

Each State Party shall ensure that any statement which is established to have been made as a result of torture shall not be invoked as evidence in any proceedings, except against a person accused of torture as evidence that the statement was made.

### Article 16

1. Each State Party shall undertake to prevent in any territory under its jurisdiction other acts of cruel, inhuman or degrading treatment or punishment which do not amount to torture as defined in article I, when such acts are committed by or at the instigation of or with the consent or acquiescence of a public official or other person acting in an official capacity. In particular, the obligations contained in articles 10, 11, 12 and 13 shall apply with the substitution for references to torture of references to other forms of cruel, inhuman or degrading treatment or punishment.

2. The provisions of this Convention are without prejudice to the provisions of any other international instrument or national law which prohibits cruel, inhuman or degrading treatment or punishment or which relates to extradition or expulsion.

---

## 5. International Covenant on Civil and Political Rights, Articles 2, 3, 4, 7, and 9

### 1966

### Article 2

1. Each State Party to the present Covenant undertakes to respect and to ensure to all individuals within its territory and subject to its jurisdiction the rights recognized in the

present Covenant, without distinction of any kind, such as race, colour, sex, language, religion, political or other opinion, national or social origin, property, birth or other status.

2. Where not already provided for by existing legislative or other measures, each State Party to the present Covenant undertakes to take the necessary steps, in accordance with its constitutional processes and with the provisions of the present Covenant, to adopt such laws or other measures as may be necessary to give effect to the rights recognized in the present Covenant.

3. Each State Party to the present Covenant undertakes:

(a) To ensure that any person whose rights or freedoms as herein recognized are violated shall have an effective remedy, notwithstanding that the violation has been committed by persons acting in an official capacity;

(b) To ensure that any person claiming such a remedy shall have his right thereto determined by competent judicial, administrative or legislative authorities, or by any other competent authority provided for by the legal system of the State, and to develop the possibilities of judicial remedy;

(c) To ensure that the competent authorities shall enforce such remedies when granted.

## Article 3

The States Parties to the present Covenant undertake to ensure the equal right of men and women to the enjoyment of all civil and political rights set forth in the present Covenant.

## Article 4

1. In time of public emergency which threatens the life of the nation and the existence of which is officially proclaimed, the States Parties to the present Covenant may take measures derogating from their obligations under the present Covenant to the extent strictly required by the exigencies of the situation, provided that such measures are not inconsistent with their other obligations under international law and do not involve discrimination solely on the ground of race, colour, sex, language, religion or social origin.

2. No derogation from articles 6, 7, 8 (paragraphs I and 2), 11, 15, 16 and 18 may be made under this provision.

3. Any State Party to the present Covenant availing itself of the right of derogation shall immediately inform the other States Parties to the present Covenant, through the intermediary of the Secretary-General of the United Nations, of the provisions from which it has derogated and of the reasons by which it was actuated. A further communication shall be made, through the same intermediary, on the date on which it terminates such derogation.

\* \* \*

## Article 7

No one shall be subjected to torture or to cruel, inhuman or degrading treatment or punishment. In particular, no one shall be subjected without his free consent to medical or scientific experimentation.

\* \* \*

## Article 9

1. Everyone has the right to liberty and security of person. No one shall be subjected to arbitrary arrest or detention. No one shall be deprived of his liberty except on such grounds and in accordance with such procedure as are established by law.

2. Anyone who is arrested shall be informed, at the time of arrest, of the reasons for his arrest and shall be promptly informed of any charges against him.

3. Anyone arrested or detained on a criminal charge shall be brought promptly before a judge or other officer authorized by law to exercise judicial power and shall be entitled to trial within a reasonable time or to release. It shall not be the general rule that persons awaiting trial shall be detained in custody, but release may be subject to guarantees to appear for trial, at any other stage of the judicial proceedings, and, should occasion arise, for execution of the judgment.

4. Anyone who is deprived of his liberty by arrest or detention shall be entitled to take proceedings before a court, in order that court may decide without delay on the lawfulness of his detention and order his release if the detention is not lawful.

5. Anyone who has been the victim of unlawful arrest or detention shall have an enforceable right to compensation.

# 6. Draft Articles on State Responsibility for Internationally Wrongful Acts

International Law Commission, 2001

### Part I
### The Internationally Wrongful Act of a State

#### Chapter I
#### General principles

## Article 1

Responsibility of a State for its internationally wrongful acts

Every internationally wrongful act of a State entails the international responsibility of that State.

## Article 2

Elements of an internationally wrongful act of a State

There is an internationally wrongful act of a State when conduct consisting of an action or omission:

(a)  Is attributable to the State under international law; and

(b)  Constitutes a breach of an international obligation of the State.

## Article 3

Characterization of an act of a State as internationally wrongful

The characterization of an act of a State as internationally wrongful is governed by international law. Such characterization is not affected by the characterization of the same act as lawful by internal law.

\* \* \*

#### Chapter II
#### Attribution of conduct to a State

## Article 5

Conduct of persons or entities exercising elements of governmental authority

The conduct of a person or entity which is not an organ of the State under article 4 but which is empowered by the law of that State to exercise elements of the governmental authority shall be considered an act of the State under international law, provided the person or entity is acting in that capacity in the particular instance.

### Article 6

Conduct of organs placed at the disposal of a State by another State

The conduct of an organ placed at the disposal of a State by another State shall be considered an act of the former State under international law if the organ is acting in the exercise of elements of the governmental authority of the State at whose disposal it is placed.

* * *

## Chapter V
## Circumstances precluding wrongfulness

### Article 26

Compliance with peremptory norms

Nothing in this Chapter precludes the wrongfulness of any act of a State which is not in conformity with an obligation arising under a peremptory norm of general international law.

---

# 7. The White House Torture Memo
## U.S. Department of Justice, 2002

Office of Legal Counsel
Office of the Assistant Attorney General
Washington, D.C. 20530
August 1, 2002

**Memorandum for Alberto R. Gonzales**
**Counsel to the President**

*Re. Standards of Conduct for Interrogation under 18 U.S.C. §§ 2340–2340A*
[footnotes omitted by editors]

You have asked for our Office's views regarding the standards of conduct under the Convention Against Torture and Other Cruel, Inhuman and Degrading Treatment or Punishment as implemented by Sections 2340–2340A of title 18 of the United States Code. As we understand it, this question has arisen in the context of the conduct of interrogations outside of the United States. We conclude below that Section 2340A proscribes acts inflicting, and that are specifically intended to inflict, severe pain or suffering, whether mental or physical. Those acts must be of an extreme nature to rise to the level of torture within the meaning of Section 2340A and the Convention. We further conclude that certain acts may be cruel, inhuman, or degrading, but still not produce pain and suffering of the requisite intensity to fall within Section 2340A's proscription against torture. We conclude by examining possible defenses that would negate any claim that certain interrogation methods violate the statute.

In Part I, we examine the criminal statute's text and history. We conclude that for an act to constitute torture as defined in Section 2340, it must inflict pain that is difficult to endure. Physical pain amounting to torture must be equivalent to intensity to the pain accompanying serious physical injury, such as organ failure, impairment of bodily function, or even death. For purely mental pain or suffering to amount to torture under Section 2340, it must result in significant psychological harm of significant duration, e.g., lasting for months or even years. We conclude that the mental harm also must result from one of the predicate acts listed in the statute, namely: threats of imminent death; threats of infliction of the kind of pain that would amount to physical torture; infliction of such physical pain as a means of psychological torture; use of drugs or other procedures designed to deeply disrupt the senses, or fundamentally alter an individual's personality; or threatening to do any of these things to a third party. The legislative history simply reveals that Congress intended for the statute's definition to track the Convention's definition of torture and the reservations, understandings, and declarations that the United States submitted with its ratification. We conclude that the statute, taken as a whole, makes plain that it prohibits only extreme acts.

In Part II, we examine the text, ratification history, and negotiating history of the Torture Convention. We conclude that the treaty's text prohibits only the most extreme acts by reserving criminal penalties solely for torture and declining to require such penalties for "cruel, inhuman, or degrading treatment or punishment." This confirms our view that the criminal statute penalizes only the most egregious conduct. Executive branch interpretations and representations to the Senate at the time of ratification further confirm that the treaty was intended to reach only the most extreme conduct.

In Part III, we analyze the jurisprudence of the Torture Victims Protection Act, 28 U.S.C. §§ 1350 note (2000), which provides civil remedies for torture victims, to predict the standards that courts might follow in determining what actions reach the threshold of torture in the criminal context. We conclude from these cases that courts are likely to take at totality-of-the-circumstances approach, and will look to an entire course of conduct, to determine whether certain acts will violate Section 2340A. Moreover, these cases demonstrate that most often torture involves cruel and extreme physical pain. In Part IV, we examine international decisions regarding the use of sensory deprivation techniques. These cases make clear that while many of these techniques may amount to cruel, inhuman and degrading treatment, they do not produce pain or suffering of the necessary intensity to meet the definition of torture. From these decisions, we conclude that there is a wide range of such techniques that will not rise to the level of torture.

* * *

## 18 U.S.C. §§ 2340–2340A

Section 2340A makes it a criminal offense for any person "outside the United States [to] commit[] or attempt[] to commit torture." (1) Section 2340 defines the act of torture as an:

> act committed by a person acting under the color of law specifically intended to inflict severe physical or mental pain or suffering (other than pain or suffering incidental to lawful sanctions) upon another person with his custody or physical control.

18 U.S.C.A. §§ 2340(1); see id. §§ 2340A. Thus, to convict a defendant of torture, the prosecution must establish that (1) the torture occurred outside the United States; (2) the defendant acted under the color of law; (3) the victim was within the defendant's custody or physical control; (4) the defendant specifically intended to cause severe physical or mental pain or suffering, and (5) that the act inflicted severe physical or mental pain or suffering. See also S. Exec. Rep. No. 101-30, at 6 (1990) ("For an act to be 'torture,' it must ... cause severe pain and suffering, and be intended to cause severe pain and suffering.")....

## B. "Severe Pain or Suffering"

The key statutory phrase in the definition of torture is the statement that acts amount to torture if they cause "severe physical or mental pain or suffering." In examining the meaning of a statute, its text must be the starting point. *See INS v. Phinpathya*, 464 U.S. 183, 189 (1984) ("This Court has noted on numerous occasions that in all cases involving statutory construction, our starting point must be the language employed by Congress, ... and we assume that the legislative purpose is expressed by the ordinary meaning of the words used.") (internal quotations and citations omitted). Section 2340 makes plain that the infliction of pain or suffering per se, whether it is physical or mental, is insufficient to amount to torture. Instead, the text provides that pain or suffering must be "severe." The statute does not, however, define the term "severe." "In the absence of such a definition, we construe a statutory term in accordance with its ordinary or natural meaning." *FDIC v. Meyer*, 510 U.S. 471, 476 (1994). The dictionary defines "severe" as "[u]nsparing in exaction, punishment, or censure" or "[I]nflicting discomfort or pain hard to endure; sharp; afflictive; distressing; violent; extreme; as severe pain, anguish, torture." Webster's New International Dictionary 2295 (2d ed. 1935); see American Heritage Dictionary of the English Language 1653 (3d ed. 1992) ("extremely violent or grievous: severe pain") (emphasis in original); IX The Oxford English Dictionary 572 (1978) ("Of pain, suffering, loss, or the like: Grievous, extreme" and "of circumstances ... hard to sustain or endure"). Thus, the adjective "severe" conveys that the pain or suffering must be of such a high level of intensity that the pain is difficult for the subject to endure.

Congress's use of the phrase "severe pain" elsewhere in the United States Code can shed more light on its meaning. *See, e.g., West Va. Univ. Hosps., Inc. v. Casey*, 499 U.S. 83, 100 (1991) ("[W]e construe [a statutory term] to contain that permissible meaning which fits most logically and comfortably into the body of both previously and subsequently enacted law."). Significantly, the phrase "severe pain" appears in statutes defining an emergency medical condition for the purpose of providing health benefits. See, e.g., 8 U.S.C. § 1369 (2000); 42 U.S.C. § 1395w-22 (2000); *id.* § 1395x (2000); *id.* § 1395dd (2000); *id.* § 1396b (2000); *id.* § 1396u-2 (2000). These statutes define an emergency condition as one "manifesting itself by acute symptoms of sufficient security (including severe pain) such that a prudent lay person, who possesses an average knowledge of health and medicine, could reasonably expect the absence of immediate medical attention to result in — placing the health of the individual ... (i) in serious jeopardy, (ii) serious impairment to bodily functions, or (iii) serious dysfunction of any bodily organ or part." Id. § 1395w-22(d)(3)(B) (emphasis added). Although these statutes address a substantially different subject from Section 2340, they are nonetheless helpful for understanding what constitutes severe physical pain. They treat severe pain as an indicator of ailments that are likely to result in permanent and serious physical damage in the absence of immediate medical treatment. Such damage must rise to the level of death, organ failure, or the permanent impairment of a significant body function. These statutes suggest that "severe pain," as used in Section 2340, must rise to a similarly high level — the level that would ordinarily be associated with a sufficiently serious physical condition or injury such as death, organ failure, or serious impairment of body functions — in order to constitute torture.

\* \* \*

## II. U.N. Convention Against Torture and Other Cruel Inhuman or Degrading Treatment or Punishment.

Because Congress enacted the criminal prohibition against torture to implement CAT, we also examine the treaty's text and history to develop a fuller understanding of the context of Sections 2340–2340A. As with the statute, we begin our analysis with the treaty's text. *See Eastern Airlines Inc. v. Floyd*, 499 U.S. 530, 534–35 (1991) (When interpreting a treaty, we begin with the text of the treaty and the context in which the written words are used.) (quotation marks and citations omitted). CAT defines torture as:

> any act by which severe pain or suffering, whether physical or mental, is intentionally inflicted on a person for such purposes as obtaining from him or a third person information or a confession, punishing him for an act he or a third person has committed or is suspected of having committed, or intimidating or coercing him or a third person, or for any reason based on discrimination of any kind, when such pain or suffering is inflicted by or at the instigation of or with the consent or acquiescence of a public official or other person acting in an official capacity.

Article 1(1) (emphasis added). Unlike Section 2340, this definition includes a list of purposes for which such pain and suffering is inflicted. The prefatory phrase "such purposes as" makes clear that this list is, however, illustrative rather than exhaustive. Accordingly, severe pain or suffering need not be inflicted for those specific purposes to constitute torture; instead, the perpetrator must simply have a purpose of the same kind. More importantly, like Section 2340, the pain and suffering must be severe to reach the threshold of torture. Thus, the text of CAT reinforces our reading of Section 2340 that torture must be an extreme act.

CAT also distinguishes between torture and other acts of cruel, inhuman, or degrading treatment or punishment. Article 16 of CAT requires state parties to "undertake to prevent ... other acts of cruel, inhuman or degrading treatment or punishment which do not amount to torture as defined in article 1." (Emphasis added). CAT thus establishes a category of acts that are not to be committed and that states must endeavor to prevent, but that states need not criminalize, leaving those acts without the stigma of criminal penalties. CAT reserves criminal penalties and the stigma attached to those penalties for torture alone. In so doing, CAT makes clear that torture is at the farthest end of impermissible actions, and that it is distinct and separate from the lower level of "cruel, inhuman, or degrading treatment or punishment." This approach is in keeping with CAT's predecessor, the U.N. Declaration on the Protection from Torture. That declaration defines torture as "an aggravated and deliberate form of cruel, inhuman or degrading treatment or punishment." Declaration on Protection from Torture, U.N. Res. 3452, Art. 1(2) (Dec. 9, 1975).

## A. Ratification History

Executive branch interpretation of CAT further supports our conclusion that the treaty, and thus Section 2340A, prohibits only the most extreme forms of physical or mental harm. As we have previously noted, the "division of treaty-making responsibility between the Senate and the President is essentially the reverse of the division of law-making authority, with the President being the draftsman of the treaty and the Senate holding the authority to grant or deny approval." *Relevance of Senate Ratification History to Treaty Interpretation*, 11 Op. O.L.C. 28, 31 (Apr. 9, 1987) ("Sofaer Memorandum"). Treaties are negotiated by the President in his capacity as the "sole organ of the federal government in the field of international relations." *United States v. Curtiss-Wright Export Corp.*, 299 U.S. 304, 320 (1936). Moreover, the President is responsible for the day-to-day interpretation of a treaty and retains the power to unilaterally terminate a treaty. *See Goldwater v. Carter*, 617 F.2d 697, 707–08 (D.C Cir.) (en banc) vacated and remanded with instructions to dismiss on other grounds, 444 U.S. 996 (1979). The Executive's interpretation is to be accorded the greatest weight in ascertaining a treaty's intent and meaning.

*See, e.g., United States v. Stuart*, 489 U.S. 353, 369 (1989) ("'the meaning attributed to treaty provisions by the Government agencies charged with their negotiation and enforcement is entitled to great weight'") (quoting *Sumitomo Shoji America, Inc. v. Avagliano*, 457 U.S. 176, 184–85 (1982)); *Kolovrat v. Oregon*, 366 U.S. 187, 194 (1961) ("While courts interpret treaties for themselves, the meaning given them by the department of government particularly charged with their negotiation and enforcement is given great weight."); *Charlton v. Kelly*, 229 U.S. 447, 468 (1913) ("A construction of a treaty by the political departments of the government, while not conclusive upon a court..., is nevertheless of much weight.").

A review of the Executive branch's interpretation and understanding of CAT reveals that Congress codified the view that torture included only the most extreme forms of physical or mental harm. When it submitted the Convention to the Senate, the Reagan administration took the position that CAT reached only the most heinous acts. The Reagan administration included the following understanding:

> The United States understands that, in order to constitute torture, an act must be a deliberate and calculated act of an extremely cruel and inhuman nature, specifically intended to inflict excruciating and agonizing physical or mental pain or suffering.

S. Treaty Doc. No. 100-20, at 4–5. Focusing on the treaty's requirement of "severity," the Reagan administration, concluded, "The extreme nature of torture is further emphasized in [this] requirement." S. Treaty Doc. No. 100-20, at 3 (1988); S. Exec. Rep. 101-30, at 13 (1990). The Reagan administration also determined that CAT's definition of torture fell in line with "United States and international usage, [where it] is usually reserved for extreme deliberate and unusually cruel practices, for example, sustained systematic beatings, application, of electric currents to sensitive parts of the body and tying up or hanging in positions that cause extreme pain." S. Exec. Rep. No. 101-30, at 14 (1990). In interpreting CAT's definition of torture as reaching only such extreme acts, the Reagan administration underscored the distinction between torture and other cruel, inhuman, or degrading treatment or punishment. In particular, the administration declared that article 1's definition of torture ought to be construed in light of article 16. See S. Treaty Doc. No. 100-20, at 3. Based on this distinction, the administration concluded that: "'Torture' is thus to be distinguished from lesser forms of cruel, inhuman, or degrading treatment or punishment, which are to be deplored and prevented, but are not so universally and categorically condemned as to warrant the severe legal consequences that the Convention provides in case of torture." S. Treaty Doc. 100-20, at 3. Moreover, this distinction was "adopted in order to emphasize that torture is at the extreme end of cruel, inhuman and degrading treatment or punishment." S. Treaty Doc. No. 100-20, at 3. Given the extreme nature of torture, the administration concluded that "rough treatment as generally falls into the category of 'police brutality,' while deplorable, does not amount to 'torture.'" S. Treaty Doc. No. 100-20, at 4.

Although the Reagan administration relied on CAT's distinction between torture and "cruel, inhuman, or degrading treatment or punishment," it viewed the phrase "cruel, inhuman, or degrading treatment or punishment" as vague and lacking in a universally accepted meaning. Of even greater concern to the Reagan administration was that because of its vagueness this phrase could be construed to bar acts not prohibited by the U.S. Constitution. The administration pointed to Case of *X v. Federal Republic of Germany* as the basis for this concern. In that case, the European Court of Human Rights determined that the prison officials' refusal to recognize a prisoner's sex change might constitute degrading treatment. See S. Treaty Doc. No. 100-20, at 15 (citing European Commission on Human Rights, Dec. on Adm., Dec. 15, 1977, *Case of X v. Federal Republic of Ger-*

*many* (No. 6694/74), 11 Dec. & Rep. 16)). As a result of this concern, the Administration added the following understanding:

> The United States understands the term, 'cruel, inhuman or degrading treatment or punishment,' as used in Article 16 of the Convention, to mean the cruel, unusual, and inhumane treatment or punishment prohibited by the Fifth, Eighth and/or Fourteenth Amendments to the Constitution of the United States."

S. Treaty Doc. No. 100-20, at 15–16. Treatment or punishment must therefore rise to the level of action that U.S. courts have found to be in violation of the U.S. Constitution in order to constitute cruel, inhuman, or degrading treatment or punishment. That which fails to rise to this level must fail, a fortiori, to constitute torture under Section 2340.

The Senate did not give its advice and consent to the Convention until the first Bush administration. Although using less vigorous rhetoric, the Bush administration joined the Reagan administration in interpreting torture as only reaching extreme acts. To ensure that the Convention's reach remained limited, the Bush administration submitted the following understanding:

> The United States understands that, in order to constitute torture, an act must be specifically intended to inflict severe physical or mental pain or suffering and that mental pain or suffering refers to prolonged mental pain caused by or resulting from (1) the intentional infliction or threatened infliction of severe physical pain or suffering; (2) administration or application, or threatened administration or application, of mind altering substances or other procedures calculated to disrupt profoundly the senses or the personality; (3) the threat of imminent death; or (4) the threat that another parson will imminently be subjected to death, severe physical pain or suffering, or the administration or application of mind-altering substances or other procedures calculated to disrupt profoundly the senses or personality.

S. Exec. Rep. No. 101-30, at 36. This understanding accomplished two things. First, it ensured that the term "intentionally" would be understood as requiring specific intent. Second, it added form and substance to the otherwise amorphous concept of mental pain or suffering. In so doing, this understanding ensured that mental torture would rise to a severity seen in the context of physical torture. The Senate ratified CAT with this understanding, and as is obvious from the text, Congress codified this understanding almost verbatim in the criminal statute.

To be sure, it might be thought significant that the Bush administration's language differs from the Reagan administration understanding. The Bush administration said that it had altered the CAT understanding in response to criticism that the Reagan administration's original formulation had raised the bar for the level of pain necessary for the act or acts to constitute torture. See Convention Against Torture: Hearing Before the Senate Comm. On Foreign Relations, 101st Cong. 9–10 (1990) ("1990 Hearing") (prepared statement of Hon. Abraham D. Sofaer, Legal Adviser, Department of State). While it is true that there are rhetorical differences between the understandings, both administrations consistently emphasize the extraordinary or extreme acts required to constitute torture. As we have seen, the Bush understanding as codified in Section 2340 reaches only extreme acts. The Reagan understanding, like the Bush understanding, ensured that "intentionally" would be understood as a specific intent requirement. Though the Reagan administration required that the "act be deliberate and calculated" and that it be inflicted with specific intent, in operation there is little difference between requiring specific intent alone and requiring that the act be deliberate and calculated. The Reagan understanding also made express what is obvious from the plain text of CAT: torture is an extreme form of cruel and inhuman treatment. The Reagan administration's understanding that the pain be "excruciating and agonizing" is in substance not different from the Bush administration's proposal that the pain must be severe.

The Bush understanding simply took a rather abstract concept—excruciating and agonizing mental pain—and gave it a more concrete form. Executive branch representations made to the Senate support our view that there was little difference between these two understandings and that the further definition of mental pain or suffering merely sought remove the vagueness created by concept of "agonizing and excruciating" mental pain. See 1990 Hearing, at 10 (prepared statement of Hon. Abraham D. Sofaer, Legal Adviser, Department of State) ("no higher standard was intended" by the Reagan administration understanding than was present in the Convention or the Bush understanding); *id.* at 13–14 (statement of Mark Richard, Deputy Assistant Attorney General; Criminal Division, Department of Justice) ("In an effort to overcome this unacceptable element of vagueness [in the term "mental pain"], we have proposed an understanding which defines severe mental pain constituting torture with sufficient specificity ... to protect innocent persons and meet constitutional due process requirements.") Accordingly, we believe that the two definitions submitted by the Reagan and Bush administrations had the same purpose in terms of articulating a legal standard, namely, ensuring that the prohibition against torture reaches only the most extreme acts. Ultimately, whether the Reagan standard would have been even higher is a purely academic question because the Bush understanding clearly established a very high standard.

Executive branch representations made to the Senate confirm that the Bush administration maintained the view that torture encompassed only the most extreme acts. Although the ratification record, i.e., testimony, hearings, and the like, is generally not accorded great weight in interpreting treaties, authoritative statements made by representatives of the Executive Branch are accorded the most interpretive value. See Sofaer Memorandum, at 35–36. Hence, the testimony of the executive branch witnesses defining torture, in addition to the reservations, understandings and declarations that were submitted to the Senate by the Executive branch, should carry the highest interpretive value of any of the statements in the ratification record. At the Senate hearing on CAT, Mark Richard, Deputy Assistant Attorney General, Criminal Division, Department of Justice, offered extensive testimony as to the meaning of torture. Echoing the analysis submitted by the Reagan administration, he testified that "[t]orture is understood to be that barbaric cruelty which lies at the top of the pyramid of human rights misconduct," 1990 Hearing, at 16 (prepared statement of Mark Richard). He further explained, "As applied to physical torture, there appears to be some degree of consensus that the concept involves conduct, the mere mention of which sends chills down one's spine[.]" *Id.* Richard gave the following examples of conduct satisfying this standard: "the needle under the fingernail, the application of electrical shock to the genital area, the piercing of eyeballs, etc." Id. In short, repeating virtually verbatim the terms used in the Reagan understanding, Richard explained that under the Bush administration's submissions with the treaty "the essence of torture" is treatment that inflicts "excruciating and agonizing physical pain." *Id.* (emphasis added).

As to mental torture, Richard testified that "no international consensus had emerged [as to] what degree of mental suffering is required to constitute torture[,]" but that it was nonetheless clear that severe mental pain or suffering "does not encompass the normal legal compulsions which are properly a part of the criminal justice system[:] interrogation, incarceration, prosecution, compelled testimony against a friend, etc,—notwithstanding the fact that they may have the incidental effect of producing mental strain." *Id.* at 17. According to Richard, CAT was intended to "condemn as torture intentional acts such as those designed to damage and destroy the human personality." *Id.* at 14. This description of mental suffering emphasizes the requirement that any mental harm be of significant duration and lends further support for our conclusion that mind-altering substances must have a profoundly disruptive effect to serve as a predicate act.

Apart from statements from Executive branch officials, the rest of a ratification record is of little weight in interpreting a treaty. See generally Sofaer Memorandum. Nonetheless, the Senate understanding of the definition of torture largely echoes the administrations' views. The Senate Foreign Relations Committee Report on CAT opined: "[f]or an act to be 'torture' it must be an extreme form of cruel and inhuman treatment, cause severe pain and suffering and be intended to cause severe pain and suffering." S. Exec. Rep. No. 101-30, at 6 (emphasis added). Moreover, like both the Reagan and Bush administrations, the Senate drew upon the distinction between torture and cruel, inhuman or degrading treatment or punishment in reaching its view that torture was extreme. Finally, the Senate concurred with the administrations' concern that "cruel, inhuman, or degrading treatment or punishment" could be construed to establish a new standard above and beyond that which the Constitution mandates and supported the inclusion of the reservation establishing the Constitution as the baseline for determining whether conduct amounted to cruel, inhuman, degrading treatment or punishment. See 136 Cong. Rec. 36,192 (1990); S. Exec. Rep. 101-30, at 39.

### B. Negotiating History

CAT's negotiating history also indicates that its definition of torture supports our reading of Section 2340. The state parties endeavored to craft a definition of torture that reflected the term's gravity. During the negotiations, state parties offered various formulations of the definition of torture to the working group, which then proposed a definition based on those formulations. Almost all of these suggested definitions illustrate the consensus that torture is an extreme act designed to cause agonizing pain. For example, the United States proposed that torture be defined as "includ[ing] any act by which extremely severe pain or suffering ... is deliberately and maliciously inflicted on a person." J. Herman Burgees & Hans Danelius, *The United Nations Convention Against Torture: A Handbook on the Convention Against Torture and Other Cruel Inhuman and Degrading Treatment or Punishment,* 41 (1988) ("CAT Handbook"). The United Kingdom suggested an even more restrictive definition, i.e., that torture be defined as the "systematic and intentional infliction of extreme pain or suffering rather than intentional infliction of severe pain or suffering." *Id.* at 45 (emphasis in original). Ultimately, in choosing the phrase "severe pain," the parties concluded that this phrase "sufficient[ly] ... convey[ed] the idea that only acts of a certain gravity shall ... constitute torture." *Id.* at 117.

In crafting such a definition, the state parties also were acutely aware of the distinction they drew between torture and cruel, inhuman, or degrading treatment or punishment. The state parties considered and rejected a proposal that would have defined torture merely as cruel, inhuman or degrading treatment or punishment. *See Id.* at 42. Mirroring the Declaration on Protection From Torture, which expressly defined torture as an "aggravated and deliberate form of cruel, inhuman or degrading treatment or punishment," some state parties proposed that in addition to the definition of torture set out in paragraph 2 of article 1, a paragraph defining torture as "an aggravated and deliberate form of cruel, inhuman or degrading treatment or punishment" should be included. *See Id.* at 41; see also S. Treaty Doc. No. 100-20, at 2 (the U.N. Declaration on Protection from Torture (1975) served as "a point of departure for the drafting of [CAT]"). In the end, the parties concluded that the addition, of such a paragraph was superfluous because Article 16 "impl[ies] that torture is the gravest form of such treatment or punishment." CAT Handbook at 80; see S. Exec. Rep. No. 101-30, at 13 ("The negotiating history indicates that [the phrase 'which do not amount to torture'] was adopted in order to emphasize that torture is at the extreme end of cruel, inhuman and degrading treatment or punishment and that Article 1 should be construed with this in mind").

Additionally, the parties could not reach a consensus about the meaning of "cruel, inhuman, or degrading treatment or punishment." See CAT Handbook at 47. Without a consensus, the parties viewed the term as simply "'too vague to be included in a convention which was to form the basis for criminal legislation in the Contracting States.'" *Id.* This view evinced by the parties reaffirms the interpretation of CAT as purposely reserving criminal penalties for torture alone.

CAT's negotiating history offers more than just support for the view that pain or suffering must be extreme to amount to torture. First, the negotiating history suggests that the harm sustained from the acts of torture need not be permanent. In fact, "the United States considered that it might be useful to develop the negotiating history which indicates that although conduct resulting in permanent impairment of physical or mental faculties is indicative of torture, it is not an essential element of the offence." *Id.* at 44. Second, the state parties to CAT rejected a proposal to include in CAT's definition of torture the use of truth drugs, where no physical harm or mental suffering was apparent. This rejection at least suggests that such drugs were not viewed as amounting to torture per se. *See Id.* at 42.

## C. Summary

The text of CAT confirms our conclusion that Section 2340A was intended to proscribe only the most egregious conduct. CAT not only defines torture as involving severe pain and suffering, but also it makes clear that such pain and suffering is at the extreme end of the spectrum of acts by reserving criminal penalties solely for torture. Executive interpretations confirm our view that the treaty (and hence the statute) prohibits only the worst forms of cruel, inhuman, or degrading treatment or punishment. The ratification history further substantiates this interpretation. Even the negotiating history displays a recognition that torture is a step far-removed from other cruel, inhuman or degrading treatment or punishment. In sum, CAT's text, ratification history and negotiating history all confirm that Section 2340A reaches only the most heinous acts.

## IV. International Decisions

International decisions can prove of some value in assessing what conduct might rise to the level of severe mental pain or suffering. Although decisions by foreign or international bodies are in no way binding authority upon the United States, they provide guidance about how other nations will likely react to our interpretation of the CAT and Section 2340. As this Part will discuss, other Western nations have generally used a high standard in determining whether interrogation techniques violate the international prohibition on torture. In fact, these decisions have found various aggressive interrogation methods to, at worst, constitute cruel, inhuman, and degrading treatment, but not torture. These decisions only reinforce our view that there is a clear distinction between the two standards and that only extreme conduct, resulting in pain that is of an intensity often accompanying serious physical injury, will violate the latter.

## A. European Court of Human Rights

An analogue to CAT's provisions can be found in the European Convention on Human Rights and Fundamental Freedoms (the "European Convention"). This convention prohibits torture, though it offers no definition of it. It also prohibits cruel, inhuman, or degrading treatment or punishment. By barring both types of acts, the European Convention implicitly distinguishes between them and further suggests that torture is a grave act beyond cruel, inhuman, or degrading treatment or punishment. Thus, while neither the European Convention nor the European Court of Human Rights decisions interpreting that convention would be authority for the interpretation of Sections 2340–2340A, the European Convention decisions concerning torture nonetheless provide a useful barometer of the international view of what actions amount to torture.

The leading European Court of Human Rights case explicating the differences between torture and cruel, inhuman, or degrading treatment or punishment is *Ireland v. the United Kingdom* (1978). In that case, the European Court of Human Rights examined interrogation techniques somewhat more sophisticated than the rather rudimentary and frequently obviously cruel acts described in the TVPA cases. Careful attention to this case is worthwhile not just because it examines methods not used in the TVPA cases, but also because the Reagan administration relied on this case in reaching the conclusion that the term torture is reserved in international usage for "extreme, deliberate, and unusually cruel practices." S. Treaty Doc. 100-20, at 4.

The methods at issue in Ireland were:

(1) Wall Standing. The prisoner stands spread eagle against the wall, with fingers high above his head, and feet back so that he is standing on his toes such that his all of his weight falls on his fingers.

(2) Hooding. A black or navy hood is placed over the prisoner's head and kept there except during the interrogation.

(3) Subjection to Noise. Pending interrogation, the prisoner is kept in a room with a loud and continuous hissing noise.

(4) Sleep Deprivation. Prisoners are deprived of sleep pending interrogation.

(5) Deprivation of Food and Drink. Prisoners receive a reduced diet during detention and pending interrogation.

The European Court of Human Rights concluded that these techniques used in combination, and applied for hours at a time, were inhuman and degrading but did not amount to torture. In analyzing whether these methods constituted torture, the court treated them as part of a single program. *See Ireland*, ¶ 104. The court found that this program caused "if not actual bodily injury, at least intense physical and mental suffering to the person subjected thereto and also led to acute psychiatric disturbances daring the interrogation." *Id.* ¶ 167. Thus, this program "fell into the category of inhuman treatment[.]" *Id.* The court further found that "[t]he techniques were also degrading since they were such as to arouse in their victims feeling of fear, anguish and inferiority capable of humiliating and debasing them and possible [sic] breaking their physical or moral resistance." *Id.* Yet, the court ultimately concluded:

> Although the five techniques, as applied in combination, undoubtedly amounted to inhuman and degrading treatment, although their object was the extraction of confession, the naming of others and/or information and although they were used systematically, they did not occasion suffering of the particular intensity and cruelty implied by the word torture ...

*Id.* (emphasis added). Thus, even though the court had concluded that the techniques produce "intense physical and mental suffering" and "acute psychiatric disturbances," they were not sufficient intensity or cruelty to amount to torture.

The court reached this conclusion based on the distinction the European Convention drew between torture and cruel, inhuman, or degrading treatment or punishment. The court reasoned that by expressly distinguishing between these two categories of treatment, the European Convention sought to "attach a special stigma to deliberate inhuman treatment causing very serious and cruel suffering." *Id.* ¶ 167. According to the court, "this distinction derives principally from a difference in the intensity of the suffering inflicted." *Id.* The court further noted that this distinction paralleled the one drawn in the U.N. Declaration on the Protection From Torture, which specifically defines torture as "'an aggravated and deliberate form of cruel, inhuman or degrading treatment or punishment.'" *Id.* (quoting U.N.. Declaration on the Protection From Torture).

The court relied on this same "intensity/cruelty" distinction to conclude that some physical maltreatment fails to amount to torture. For example, four detainees were severely beaten and forced to stand spread eagle up against a wall. *See id.* ¶ 110. Other detainees were forced to stand spread eagle while an interrogator kicked them "continuously on the inside of the legs." *Id.* ¶ 111. Those detainees were beaten, some receiving injuries that were "substantial" and others received "massive" injuries. See id. Another detainee was "subjected to ...'comparatively trivial' beatings" that resulted in a perforation of the detainee's eardrum and some "minor bruising." *Id.* ¶ 115. The court concluded that none of these situations "attain[ed] the particular level [of severity] inherent in the notion of torture." *Id.* ¶ 174.

## B. Israel Supreme Court

The European Court of Human Rights is not the only other court to consider whether such a program of interrogation techniques was permissible. In Public Committee Against Torture in *Israel v. Israel*, 38 LLM 1471 (1999), the Supreme Court of Israel reviewed a challenge brought against the General Security Service ("GSS") for its use of five techniques. At issue in Public Committee Against Torture In Israel were: (1) shaking, (2) the Shabach, (3) the Frog Crouch, (4) the excessive tightening of handcuffs, and (5) sleep deprivation. "Shaking" is "the forceful shaking of the suspect's upper torso, back and forth, repeatedly, in a manner which causes the neck and head to dangle and vacillate rapidly." *Id.* ¶ 9. The "Shabach" is actually a combination of methods wherein the detainee is seated on a small and low chair, whose seat is tilted forward, towards the ground. One hand is tied behind the suspect, and placed inside the gap between the chair's seat and back support. His second hand is tied behind the chair, against its back support. The suspect's head is covered by an opaque sack, falling down to his shoulders. Powerfully loud music is played in the room. *Id.* ¶ 10.

The "frog crouch"' consists of "consecutive, periodical crouches on the tips of one's toes, each lasting for five minute intervals." *Id.* ¶ 11. The excessive tightening of handcuffs simply referred to the use {of} handcuffs that were too small for the suspects' wrists. *See id.* ¶ 12. Sleep deprivation occurred when the Shabach was used during "intense nonstop interrogations." *Id.* ¶ 13.

While the Israeli Supreme Court concluded that these acts amounted to cruel, and inhuman treatment, the court did not expressly find that they amounted to torture. To be sure, such a conclusion was unnecessary because even if the acts amounted only to cruel and inhuman treatment the GSS lacked authority to use the five methods. Nonetheless, the decision is still best read as indicating that the acts at issue did not constitute torture. The court's descriptions of and conclusions about each method indicate that the court viewed them as merely cruel, inhuman or degrading but not of the sufficient severity to reach the threshold of torture. While its descriptions discuss necessity, dignity, degradation, and pain, the court carefully avoided describing any of these acts as having the seventy of pain or suffering indicative of torture. *See id.* at ¶¶ 24–29. Indeed, in assessing the Shabach as a whole, the court even relied upon the European Court of Human Right's Ireland decision, for support and it did not evince disagreement with that decision's conclusion that the acts considered therein did not constitute torture. *See id.* ¶ 30.

Moreover, the Israeli Supreme Court concluded that in certain circumstances GSS officers could assert a necessity defense. CAT, however, expressly provides that "[n]o exceptional circumstance whatsoever, whether a state of war or a threat of war, internal political instability or any other public emergency may be invoked as a justification of torture." Art 2(2). Had the court been of the view that the GSS methods constituted torture, the Court could not permit this affirmative defense under CAT. Accordingly, the court's decision is best read as concluding that these methods amounted to cruel and inhuman treatment, but not torture.

In sum, both the European Court on Human Rights and the Israeli Supreme Court have recognized a wide array of acts that constitute cruel, inhuman, or degrading treatment or punishment, but do not amount to torture. Thus, they appear to permit, under international law, an aggressive interpretation as to what amounts to torture, leaving that label to be applied only where extreme circumstances exist.

## VI. Defenses

In the foregoing parts of this memorandum, we have demonstrated that the ban on torture in Section 2340A is limited to only the most extreme forms of physical and mental harm. We have also demonstrated that Section 2340A, as applied to interrogations of enemy combatants ordered by the President pursuant to his Commander-in-Chief power would be unconstitutional. Even if an interrogation method, however, might arguably cross the line drawn in Section 2340, and application of the statute was not held to be an unconstitutional infringement of the President's Commander-in-Chief authority, we believe that under the current circumstances certain justification defenses might be available that would potentially eliminate criminal liability. Standard criminal law defenses of necessity and self-defense could justify interrogation methods needed to elicit information to prevent a direct and imminent threat to the United States and its citizens.

### A. Necessity

We believe that a defense of necessity could be raised, under the current circumstances, to an allegation of a Section 2340A violation. Often referred to as the "choice of evils" defense, necessity has been defined as fellows:

> Conduct that the actor believes to he necessary to avoid a harm or evil to himself or to another is justifiable, provided that:
>
> (a) the harm or evil sought to be avoided by such conduct is greater than that sought to be prevented by the law defining the offense charged; and
>
> (b) neither the Code nor other law defining the offense provides exceptions or defenses dealing with the specific situation involved; and
>
> (c) a legislative purpose to exclude the justification claimed does not otherwise plainly appear.

Model Penal Code § 3.02. See also Wayne R. LaFave & Austin W. Scott, 1 Substantive Criminal Law § 5.4 at 627 (1986 & 2002 supp.) ("LaFave & Scott"). Although there is no federal statute that generally establishes necessity or other justifications as defenses to federal criminal laws, the Supreme Court has recognized the defense. See *United States v.*

*Bailey*, 444 U.S. 394, 410 (1980) (relying on LaFave & Scott and Model Penal Code definitions of necessity defense).

The necessity defense may prove especially relevant in the current circumstances. As it has been described in the case law and literature, the purpose behind necessity is one of public policy. According to LaFave and Scott, "the law ought to promote the achievement of higher values at the expense of lesser values, and sometimes the greater good for society will be accomplished by violating the literal language of the criminal law." *LaFave & Scott*, at 629. In particular, the necessity defense can justify the intentional killing of one person to save two others because "it is better that two lives be saved and one lost than that two be lost and one saved." *Id.* Or, put in the language of a choice of evils, "the evil involved in violating the terms of the criminal law ( … even taking another's life) may be less than that which would result from literal compliance with the law ( … two lives lost)." *Id.*

Additional elements of the necessity defense are worth noting here. First, the defense is not limited to certain types of harms. Therefore, the harm inflicted by necessity may include intentional homicide, so long as the harm avoided is greater (i.e., preventing more deaths). *Id.* at 634. Second, it must actually be the defendant's intention to avoid the greater harm: intending to commit murder and then learning only later that the death had the fortuitous result of saving other lives will not support a necessity defense. *Id.* at 635. Third, if the defendant reasonably believed that the lesser harm was necessary, even if, unknown to him, it was not, he may still avail himself of the defense. As LaFave and Scott explain, "if A kills B reasonably believing it to be necessary to save C and D, he is not guilty of murder even though, unknown to A, C and D could have been rescued without the necessity of killing B." Id. Fourth, it is for the court, and not the defendant to judge whether the harm avoided outweighed the harm done. *Id.* at 636. Fifth, the defendant cannot rely upon the necessity defense if a third alternative is open and known to him that will cause less harm.

It appears to us that under the current circumstances the necessity defense could be successfully maintained in response to an allegation of a Section 2340A violation. On September 11, 2001, al Qaeda launched a surprise covert attack on civilian targets in the United States that led to the deaths of thousands and losses in the billions of dollars. According to public and governmental reports, al Qaeda has other sleeper cells within the United States that may be planning similar attacks. Indeed, al Qaeda plans apparently include efforts to develop and deploy chemical, biological and nuclear weapons of mass destruction. Under these circumstances, a detainee may possess information that could enable the United States to prevent attacks that potentially could equal or surpass the September 11 attacks in their magnitude. Clearly, any harm that might occur during an interrogation would pale to insignificance compared to the harm avoided by preventing such an attack, which could take hundreds or thousands of lives.

Under this calculus, two factors will help indicate when the necessity defense could appropriately be invoked. First, the more certain that government officials are that a particular individual has information needed to prevent an attack, the more necessary interrogation will be. Second, the more likely it appears to be that a terrorist attack is likely to occur, and the greater the amount of damage expected from such an attack, the more that an interrogation to get information would become necessary. Of course, the strength of the necessity defense depends on the circumstances that prevail, and the knowledge of the government actors involved, when the interrogation is conducted. While every interrogation that might violate Section 2340A does not trigger a necessity defense, we can say that certain circumstances could support such a defense.

Legal authorities identify an important exception to the necessity defense. The defense is available "only in situations wherein the legislature has not itself, in its criminal statute, made a determination of values." *Id.* at 629. Thus, if Congress explicitly has made clear that violation of a statute cannot be outweighed by the harm avoided, courts cannot recognize the necessity defense. LaFave and Israel provide as an example an abortion statute that made clear that abortions even to save the life of the mother would still be a crime; in such cases the necessity defense would be unavailable. *Id.* at 630. Here, however, Congress has not explicitly made a determination of values vis-a-vis torture. In fact, Congress explicitly removed efforts to remove torture from the weighing of values permitted by the necessity defense.

## B. Self-Defense

Even if a court were to find that a violation of Section 2340A was not justified by necessity, a defendant could still appropriately raise a claim of self-defense. The right to self-defense, even when it involves deadly force, is deeply embedded in our law, both as to individuals and as to the nation as a whole. As the Court of Appeals for the D.C. Circuit has explained:

> More than two centuries ago, Blackstone, best known of the expositors of the English common law, taught that "all homicide is malicious, and of course amounts to murder, unless ... excused on the account of accident or self-preservation...." Self-defense, as a doctrine legally exonerating the taking of human life, is as viable now as it was in Blackstone's time.

*United States v. Peterson*, 483 F.2d 1222, 1228–29 (D.C. Cir. 1973). Self-defense is a common-law defense to federal criminal law offenses, and nothing in the text, structure or history of Section 2340A precludes its application to a charge of torture. In the absence of any textual provision to the contrary, we assume self-defense can be an appropriate defense to an allegation of torture.

The doctrine of self-defense permits the use of force to prevent harm to another person. As LaFave and Scott explain, "one is justified in using reasonable force in defense of another person, even a stranger, when he reasonably believes that the other is in immediate danger of unlawful bodily harm from his adversary and that the use of such force is necessary to avoid this danger." *Id.* at 663–64. Ultimately, even deadly force is permissible, but "only when the attack of the adversary upon the other person reasonably appears to the defender to be a deadly attack." *Id.* at 664. As with our discussion of necessity, we will review the significant elements of this defense. According to LaFave and Scott, the elements of the defense of others are the same as those that apply to individual self-defense.

First, self-defense requires that the use of force be necessary to avoid the danger of unlawful bodily harm. *Id.* at 649. A defender may justifiably use deadly force if he reasonably believes that the other person is about to inflict unlawful death or serious bodily harm upon another, and that it is necessary to use such force to prevent it. *Id.* at 652. Looked at from the opposite perspective, the defender may not use force when the force would be as equally effective at a later time and the defender suffers no harm or risk by waiting. See Paul H. Robinson, 2 Criminal Law Defenses § 131(c) at 77 (1984). If, however, other options permit the defender to retreat safely from a confrontation without having to resort to deadly force, the use of force may not be necessary in the first place. *LaFave and Scott* at 659–60.

Second, self-defense requires that the defendant's belief in the necessity of using force be reasonable. If a defendant honestly but unreasonably believed force was necessary, he will not be able to make out a successful claim of self-defense. *Id.* at 654. Conversely, if a defendant reasonably believed an attack was to occur, but the facts subsequently showed no attack was threatened he may still raise self-defense. As LaFave and Scott explain, "one may be justified in shooting to death an adversary who, having threatened to kill him, reaches for his pocket as if for a gun, though it later appears that he had no gun and that he was only reaching for his handkerchief." *Id.* Some authorities, such as the Model Penal Code, even eliminate the reasonability element, and require only that the defender honestly believed—regardless of its unreasonableness—that the use of force was necessary.

Third, many legal authorities include the requirement that a defender must reasonably believe that the unlawful violence is "imminent" before he can use force in his defense. It would be a mistake, however, to equate imminence necessarily with timing—that an attack is immediately about to occur. Rather, as the Model Penal Code explains, what is essential is that, the defensive response must be "immediately necessary." Model Penal Code §3.04(1). Indeed, imminence may be merely another way of expressing the requirement of necessity. Robinson at 78. LaFave and Scott, for example, believe that the imminence requirement makes sense as part of a necessity defense because if an attack is not immediately upon the defender, the defender has other options available to avoid the attack that do not involve the use of force. *LaFave and Scott* at 656. If, however, the fact of the attack becomes certain and no other options remain, the use of force may be justified. To use a well-known hypothetical, if A were to kidnap and confine B, and then tell B he would kill B one week later, B would be justified in using force in self-defense, even if the opportunity arose before the week had passed. *Id.* at 656; see also Robinson at §131(c)(1) at 78. In this hypothetical, while the attack itself is not imminent, B's use of force becomes immediately necessary whenever he has an opportunity to save himself from A.

Fourth, the amount of force should be proportional to the threat. As LaFave and Scott explain, "the amount of force which [the defender] may justifiably use must be reasonably related to the threatened harm which he seeks to avoid." *LaFave and Scott* at 651. Thus, one may not use deadly force in response to a threat that does not rise to death or serious bodily harm. If such harm may result, however, deadly force is appropriate. As the Model Penal Code §3.04(2)(b) states, "[t]he use of deadly force is not justifiable ... unless the actor believes that such force is necessary to protect himself against death, serious bodily injury, kidnapping or sexual intercourse compelled by force or threat."

Under the current circumstances, we believe that a defendant accused of violating Section 2340A could have, in certain circumstances, grounds to properly claim the defense of another. The threat of an impending terrorist attack threatens the lives of hundreds if not thousands of American citizens. Whether such a defense will be upheld depends on the specific context within which the interrogation decision is made. If an attack appears increasingly likely, but our intelligence services and armed forces cannot prevent it without the information from the interrogation of a specific individual, then the more likely it will appear that the conduct in question will be seen as necessary. If intelligence and other information support the conclusion that an attack is increasingly certain, then the necessity for the interrogation will be reasonable. The increasing certainty of an attack will also satisfy the imminence requirement. Finally, the fact that previous al Qaeda attacks have had as their aim the deaths of American citizens, and that evidence of other plots have had a similar goal in mind, would justify proportionality of interrogation methods designed to elicit information to prevent such deaths.

To be sure, this situation is different from the usual self-defense justification, and, indeed, it overlaps with elements of the necessity defense. Self-defense as usually discussed involves using force against an individual who is about to conduct the attack. In the current circumstances, however, an enemy combatant in detention does not himself present a threat of harm. He is not actually carrying out the attack; rather, he has participated in the planning and preparation for the attack, or merely has knowledge of the attack through his membership in the terrorist organization. Nonetheless, leading scholarly commentators believe that interrogation of such individuals using methods that might violate Section 2340A would be justified under the doctrine of self-defense, because the combatant by aiding and promoting the terrorist plot "has culpably caused the situation where someone might get hurt. If hurting him is the only means to prevent the death or injury of others put at risk by his actions, such torture should be permissible, and on the same basis that self-defense is permissible." Michael S. Moore, *Torture and the Balance of Evils*, 23 Israel L. Rev. 280, 323 (1989) (symposium on Israel's Landau Commission Report). Thus, some commentators believe that by helping to create the threat of loss of life, terrorists become culpable for the threat even though they do not actually carry out the attack itself. They may be hurt in an interrogation because they are part of the mechanism that has set the attack in motion, *id*. at 323, just as is someone who feeds ammunition or targeting information to an attacker. Under the present circumstances, therefore, even though a detained enemy combatant may not be the exact attacker—he is not planting the bomb, or piloting a hijacked plane to kill civilians—he still may be harmed in self-defense if he has knowledge of future attacks because he has assisted in their planning and execution.

Further, we believe that a claim by an individual of the defense of another would be further supported by the fact that, in this case, the nation itself is under attack and has the right to self-defense. This fact can bolster and support an individual claim of self-defense in a prosecution, according to the teaching of the Supreme Court in *In re Neagle*, 135 U.S. 1 (1890). In that case, the State of California arrested and held deputy U.S. Marshal Neagle for shooting and killing the assailant of Supreme Court Justice Field. In granting the writ of habeas corpus for Neagle's release, the Supreme Court did not rely alone upon the marshal's right to defend another or his right to self-defense. Rather, the Court found that Neagle, as an agent of the United States and of the executive branch, was justified in the killing because, in protecting Justice Field, he was acting pursuant to the executive branch's inherent constitutional authority to protect the United States government. Id. at 67 ("We cannot doubt the power of the president to take measures for the protection of a judge of one of the courts of the United States who, while in the discharge of the duties of his office, is threatened with a personal attack which may probably result in his death."). That authority derives, according to the Court, from the President's power under Article II to take care that the laws are faithfully executed. In other words, Neagle as a federal officer not only could raise self-defense or defense of another, but also could defend his actions on the ground that he was implementing the Executive Branch's authority to protect the United States government.

If the right to defend the national government can be raised as a defense in an individual prosecution, as Neagle suggests, then a government defendant, acting in his official capacity, should be able to argue that any conduct that arguably violated Section 2340A was undertaken pursuant to more than just individual self-defense or defense of another. In addition, the defendant could claim that he was fulfilling the Executive Branch's authority to protect the federal government, and the nation, from attack. The September 11 attacks have already triggered that authority, as recognized both, under domestic and international law. Following the example of In re Neagle, we conclude that a government defendant may also argue that his conduct of an interrogation, if properly authorized, is justified on the basis of protecting the nation from attack.

There can be little doubt that the nation's right to self-defense has been triggered under our law. The Constitution announces that one of its purposes is "to provide for the common defense." U.S. Const., Preamble. Article I, § 8 declares that Congress is to exercise its powers to "provide for the common Defence." See also 2 Pub. Papers of Ronald Reagan

920, 921 (1988–89) (right of self-defense recognized by Article 51 of the U.N. Charter) The President has a particular responsibility and power to take steps to defend the nation and its people. *In re Neagle*, 135 U.S. at 64. See also U.S. Const., art. IV, § 4 (The United States shall ... protect [each of the States] against Invasion"). As Commander-in-Chief and Chief Executive, he may use the armed forces to protect the nation and its people. *See, e.g., United States v. Verdugo-Urquidez*, 494 U.S. 259, 273 (1990). And he may employ secret agents to aid in his work as Commander-in-Chief. *Totten v. United States*, 92 U.S. 105, 106 (1876). As the Supreme Court observed in The Prize Cases, 67 U.S. (2 Black) 635 (1862), in response to an armed attack on the United States "the President is not only authorized but bound to resist force by force ... without waiting for any special legislative authority." *Id.* at 668. The September 11 events were a direct attack on the United States, and as we have explained above, the President has authorized the use of military force with the support of Congress.

As we have made clear in other opinions involving the war against al Qaeda, the nation's right to self-defense has been triggered by the events of September 11. If a government defendant were to harm an enemy combatant during an interrogation in a manner that might arguably violate Section 2340A, he would be doing so in order to prevent further attacks on the United States by the al Qaeda terrorist network. In that case, we believe that he could argue that his actions were justified by the executive branch's constitutional authority to protect the nation from attack. This national and international version of the right to self-defense could supplement and bolster the government defendant's individual right.

### Conclusion

For the foregoing reasons, we conclude that torture as defined in and proscribed by Sections 2340–2340A, covers only extreme acts. Severe pain is generally of the kind difficult for the victim to endure. Where the pain is physical, it must be of an intensity akin to that which accompanies serious physical injury such as death or organ failure. Severe mental pain requires suffering not just at the moment of infliction but it also requires lasting psychological harm, such as seen in mental disorders like posttraumatic stress disorder. Additionally, such severe mental pain can arise only from the predicate acts listed in Section 2340. Because the acts inflicting torture are extreme, there is significant range of acts that though they might constitute cruel, inhuman, or degrading treatment or punishment fail to rise to the level of torture.

Further, we conclude that under the circumstances of the current war against al Qaeda and its allies, application, of Section 2340A to interrogations undertaken pursuant to the President's Commander-in-Chief powers may be unconstitutional. Finally, even if an interrogation method might violate Section 2340A, necessity or self-defense could provide justifications that would eliminate any criminal liability.

Please let us know if we can be of further assistance.

Jay S. Bybee
Assistant Attorney General

---

## 8. Bibliography of Additional Sources

• William Bradford, *Article: International Legal Compliance: Surveying The Field*, 36 Geo. J. Int'l L. 495 (2006).

• Yishai Blank, *Symposium: Comparative Visions of Global Public Order (Part 2): Localism in the New Global Legal Order*, 47 Harv. Int'l L.J. 263 (2006).

- Andrew T. Guzman, *Article: Global Governance and the WTO*, 45 Harv. Int'l L.J. 303 (2004).

- Christopher J. Borgen, *Article: Resolving Treaty Conflicts*, 37 Geo. Wash. Int'l L. Rev. 573 (2005).

- Colin B. Picker, *Essay: Neither Here Nor There—Countries that are Neither Developing Nor Developed in the WTO: Geographic Differentiation as Applied to Russia and the WTO*, 36 Geo. Wash. Int'l L. Rev. 147 (2004).

- *Article: U.S. May Be Sidestepping U.N. Convention Against Torture in War on Terror*, Posted March 20, 2003, http://www.law.virginia.edu/home2002/html/news/2003_spr/torture_ps.htm.

- Judicial and Similar Proceedings, European Court of Human Rights Grand Chamber: *Ocalan v. Turkey*, Number 5, 44 I.L.M. 1058 (2005).

- Geoffrey R. Watson, *Article ICJ Advisory opinion on Construction of a Wall in the Occupied Palestinian Territory: the "Wall" Decisions in Legal and Political Context*, 99 A.J.I.L. 6 (2005).

- Edward R. Fluet, *Article: Conflict Diamonds: U.S. Responsibility and Response*, 7 San Diego Int'l L.J. 103 (2005).

- Edited by John R. Crook, *Contemporary Practice of the United States Relating to International Law: Attorney General Nominee's Views on Compliance with U.S. Treaty Obligations, Torture, Protocol I to the Geneva Conventions, Revising the Geneva Convention*, 2005, 99 A.J.I.L. 481, 1374 words (2005).

- Christopher Greenwood, *New orders? New norms? International Law and the 'War on Terrorism,'* International Affairs, Volume 78 Issue 2 (2002).

# Chapter XVIII

# International Criminal Police Organization: Interpol

## Introduction

This chapter serves as an introduction to the purposes and structure of Interpol. As the largest international police organization in the world, Interpol deals with many complex and important issues. The questions and simulations are designed to elicit discussion and debate on Interpol's effort to protect priceless works of art and to recover stolen works of art.

## Objectives

- To understand the history and purpose of Interpol.
- To examine the difficulties of combating the illicit trade of cultural property.
- To understand the purpose of the Object ID in combating the illicit trade of cultural objects.
- To understand Interpol's role in the recovering stolen works of art.
- To understand the steps taken by the international community to prevent the illicit trade of cultural property.
- To demonstrate the unique relationship Interpol maintains with numerous international organizations.

## Problems

1. Come prepared to discuss the following questions:
    a. What is Interpol? What kind of organization is it? What is its relation to the United Nations?
    b. What purposes and functions does Interpol serve?
    c. What are the similarities and differences between Interpol and a federal domestic police force? Are those differences benefits or drawbacks?

    d.   How does Interpol make policy decisions? Why is this approach best suited for Interpol's aims?

2.   Come prepared to discuss the *Convention on the Means of Prohibiting and Preventing the Illicit Import, Export and Transfer of Ownership of Cultural Property* and the *Convention on Stolen or Illegally Exported Cultural Objects*, and answer the following questions:

    a.   What is "Cultural Property"? What would qualify as cultural property and what would not qualify?

    b.   Can the possessor of the stolen property be entitled to compensation? If so, what are the requirements?

    c.   Is the Convention on Stolen Objects retroactive? What are the ramifications of this distinction?

3.   Come prepared to critique "Object ID," and answer the following questions:

    a.   What is "Object ID"?

    b.   What are the benefits of and possible problems with "Object ID"?

4.   Come prepared to participate in the following simulation:

    In January 2011, mass protests broke out in Egypt against the heavy-handed rule of former Egyptian President Hosni Mubarak. After eighteen days of protest Mubarak stepped down, ending his thirty years of autocratic rule. During the chaos and protests, the famed Museum of Egyptian Antiquities (aka. Egyptian Museum) was vandalized and looted. The vandals destroyed many priceless relics from Egyptian past, including the beheading of two mummies that were on display. The most significant relic taken was the scarab of King Tutankhamun. Along with the mask of King Tutankhamun, the scarab is one of the most valuable relics discovered in King Tutankhamun's tomb and essential to the history of Egypt. The scarab has been located in North Korea, which is not a member of Interpol. Egypt, with its newly established government, desperately wishes to recover King Tutankhamun's scarab. What are Egypt's options? What can Interpol do to aid in the recovery?

    a.   Members of Group A will represent Egypt

    b.   Members of Group B will represent North Korea

    c.   Members of Group C will represent Interpol

# Materials

1.  Colin McLaughlin, An Introduction to Interpol (2005).

2.  Alia Szopa, *Hoarding History: A Survey of Antiquity Looting and Black Market Trade*, 13 U. Miami Bus. L. Rev. 55, 64–70 (Fall/Winter 2004).

3.  Interpol, *Stolen Works of Art: Object ID*, at http://www.interpol.int/Public/WorksOfArt/Partnership/objectid.asp (last modified on May 19, 2004).

4.  Christopher Andreae, *Art Museums Balance Access Against Security*, The Christian Science Monitor, Aug. 27, 2004, at Arts 12.

5.  Kenneth Hamma, *Symposium: V. The New Millennium Finding Cultural Property Online*, 19 Cardozo Arts & Ent. L.J. 125, 128–132 (2001).

6. Brian Braiker, *Art Cops*, Newsweek, Jan. 21, 2005.

7. CNN.com, *Interpol Hunts Stolen Iraqi Art*, at http://www.cnn.com/2003/WORLD/ europe/04/18/sprj.nilaw.artifacts.interpol/index.html (Apr. 18, 2003).

8. *Convention on the Means of Prohibiting and Preventing the Illicit Import, Export and Transfer of Ownership of Cultural Property*, UNESCO (14 November 1970)

9. *Convention on Stolen or Illegally Exported Cultural Objects*, UNIDROIT (June 24, 1995).

10. *Co-operation agreement between the United Nations and the International Criminal Police Organization-Interpol*, Interpol (July 8, 1997).

11. *Co-operation agreement between the United Nations Educational, Scientific and Cultural Organization and the International Criminal Police Organization-Interpol*, Interpol (Oct. 5, 1999).

12. *Memorandum of understanding with the International Council of Museums on countering the theft and trafficking in cultural property*, Interpol (Apr. 11, 2000).

13. Interpol, *Interpol Member Countries (190)*, at: http://www.interpol.int/Public/Icpo/ Members/default.asp (last visited August 15, 2012).

14. Bibliography of Additional Sources

# 1. Colin McLaughlin, An Introduction to Interpol
## 2005
[footnotes omitted by editors]

### Historical Background

Interpol is the oldest wide-scale mechanism for international police cooperation. Prior to World War I, international cooperation between police agencies was only used to combat violent political opponents. Overall, State police agencies rarely cooperated, due to concern of individual state sovereignty. This lack of cooperation greatly concerned many top level police personnel from around the world. Therefore, in September 1923, police chiefs from twenty countries met in Vienna to discuss the problem. The result of this conference was the International Criminal Police Commission (ICPC), better known as Interpol.

Interpol opened its membership to any country wishing to join and abide by its Constitution. It was thought of as an unconventional agency since police officers would now be able to communicate on official business with officers of other governments, outside of diplomatic channels, and without the traditional formalities set by an international treaty or convention. Even though this was an "unconventional agency," there were many aspects of the organization that were very common. For instance, countries still had to apply for membership, pay dues, and follow the rules set forth by the organization.

In the beginning, it was decided that Vienna would headquarter the organization. At the time, Austria was known for having the best central record system on international offenders, and the Austrian government agreed to provide financial assistance to and supply the officers for the new organization. This changed, though, in 1930, when the members decided to be independent from Austria, and to elect officers by a majority vote rather than having them appointed by Austria. However, this sense of independence soon changed when Nazi Germany came to power. Fearing that Hitler would take over Interpol, the member states voted to have Interpol's officers appointed by the Austrian government in 1934. This resolution was reaffirmed in 1937 at the General Assembly in

London. Unfortunately, this plan completely backfired when Germany invaded and annexed Austria. The Nazi government took over all officer positions in Interpol and, in 1941, relocated Interpol's headquarters to Berlin.

After World War II ended, Interpol members Sweden, Belgium, France, Switzerland, and England worked to reform the organization. After much debate, the members decided in 1946 to move Interpol's headquarters to France. Then, in 1948, the United Nations (U.N.) gave Interpol the status of Non-Governmental Organization (NGO) and it was to work with the U.N.'s Economic and Social Council (ECOSOC). Working with ECOSOC as an NGO was a great achievement for Interpol as the process of obtaining this status is rigorous. First, an organization must be in existence for at least two years in order to apply, it must have a democratic decision making mechanism, and it must receive must of its funding through contributions from national affiliates, individual members or other non-governmental components. After meeting all of the prerequisite requirements, an organization must file a letter of intent. Then, it must complete an application and questionnaire, along with supplying supporting documents. After this, the organization's application is screened and passed on to the Committee on Non-Governmental Organizations. If the committee recommends the organization obtain NGO status then the members of ECOSOC making the final decision.

With this designation by the U.N., Interpol continued to increase its membership, and by 1955, the ICPC had 50 members. Concerned that the ICPC did not have a more permanent-sounding name, Interpol's official name was changed to the International Criminal Police Organization (ICPO), though it kept its shortened name of Interpol. Changing the organization's name was not enough for its members, though, as it aimed for more respect. First, Interpol wanted to create a permanent headquarters, as it had been moving from place to place in France since 1946. Thus, Interpol decided to build a permanent headquarters in Lyon, France, a suburb of Paris. Also, Interpol applied to the U.N. for the status of Inter-Governmental Organization (IGO). Interpol's wish was granted in 1971 when ECOSOC named Interpol an IGO.

An IGO differs from an NGO in several ways. First, and most importantly, an IGO is an institution that is created by a treaty or agreement and joined by governments. This gives an IGO international legal status and allows it to make collective decisions concerning particular problems on the global agenda. This greatly differs from an NGO which is independent from government. Also, an IGO must have a permanent staff which meets regularly, and have specific decision making process, which is not always true of an NGO. Because of the differences in IGOs and NGOs, IGO carry more power and prestige then NGOs.

Interpol continued to gain respect in the international community in 1983 when United States President Ronald Reagan signed an Executive Order naming Interpol "a public international organization entitled to all the privileges, exemptions and immunities conferred by standing U.S. legislation on such organizations." Interpol works with the National Central Bureau of the United States Department of Justice, which includes such agencies as: Secret Service; Customs Service; Drug Enforcement Administration; Bureau of Alcohol, Tobacco and Firearms; Immigration and Naturalization Service; Postal Service; Marshals Service; Comptroller of the Currency; Internal Revenue Service; and the Federal Bureau of Investigation.

**Purposes and Core Functions**

Article 2 of Interpol's Constitutions states that its aims are:

(a) To ensure and promote the widest possible mutual assistance between all criminal police authorities within the limits of the laws existing in the different countries and in the spirit of the "Universal Declaration of Human Rights"; and

(b)  To establish and develop all institutions likely to contribute effectively to the prevention and suppression of ordinary law crimes

It is evident, from Article 2 that Interpol's main function is to assist member states in fighting international crime. It must also be noted that Interpol's Constitution also addresses other important state issues as well. First, Article 2 reiterates the importance of sovereignty as it provides that all interactions must be "within the limits of the laws existing in the different countries." Moreover, Interpol limits its utilization to "criminal police authorities." This prevents other state agencies from interfering with Interpol's aims.

Another important aspect of Interpol is that it does not discriminate in its membership. Today, with 188 Members, the organization includes "democracies, limited monarchs, dictatorships, and countries that are governed according to capitalist, socialist, and mixed philosophies." In fact, Interpol now has four official languages: Arabic, English, French, and Spanish. Also, each member is considered equal in Interpol. Unlike the U.N. Security Council, there is no select group of members with special powers, such as a veto. Instead, Interpol is run more like the U.N. General Assembly, as each member has one vote no matter its size or financial contribution to the organization.

Interpol has many functions on which to concentrate its efforts and resources. The first is securing global police communications services. To meet this function, Interpol created a global police communications system known as I-24/7, so named because its information is available at all times.

Another vital function of Interpol is providing operational data services and databases. According to Interpol, "once police can communicate across borders, they need access to information that can assist investigations or help prevent crime." Interpol has massive databases which permit members to conduct searches of known international criminals (including fingerprints, photographs, and DNA profiles), stolen travel documents (commonly used for illicit activities), identification details on stolen vehicles, as well as information relating to stolen artwork and cultural heritage. Interpol states that this information "is Interpol's lifeblood and a critical tool for disseminating information to police around the world." With this information, Interpol aids in such areas as fugitive apprehension, public safety and terrorism, drugs and organized crime, trafficking in human beings, financial and high tech crime, corruption, environmental crime and property crime.

Even though it is not embedded in an international political structure such as the United Nations or the Council of Europe, Interpol has gained much respect since World War II. Interpol still provides a far-reaching communications network for the exchange of criminal intelligence and other important information between its members. There are many positive aspects to Interpol, including its large and diverse membership. Interpol's biggest weakness is that it can only be effective when the participating States are willing to cooperate and fully engage in the activities of the organization, as some Member States lack a complete commitment to Interpol. Regardless, Interpol remains a vital tool in fighting international crime.

## Authors' Note

The following two excerpts detail the illicit trade of cultural property. Material 2 describes Interpol's role in monitoring the black market of the import, export, and transfer of ownership of cultural property. The article discusses the restrictions designed by the international community to prevent the illicit art trade. Material 3 is a statement by Interpol that describes the formalization of a standard for the identification of cultural objects. In particular, the material details the use of the Object ID in the organization's attempt to curb the illicit trade of cultural objects.

## 2. Alia Szopa, Hoarding History: A Survey of Antiquity Looting and Black Market Trade

*University of Miami Business Law Review*, 2004
[footnotes omitted by editors]

\* \* \*

The first international response to the looting of antiquities to gain worldwide acceptance came in 1970 when UNESCO held the Convention on the Means of Prohibiting and Preventing the Illicit Import, Export, and Transfer of Ownership of Cultural Property ("Convention"). The goal of this Convention was to protect the cultural property of countries against "theft, pillage or misappropriation," as well as to provide for the requisition of such property in times of war and peace. The reason for protecting this property is found in the fact that "cultural property constitutes one of the basic elements of civilization and national culture, and that its true value can be appreciated only in relation to the fullest possible information regarding its origin, history, and traditional setting." When antiquities are moved illegally, much valuable information regarding the object is lost forever. The purpose of the Convention was to preserve this priceless information by lessening the ease with which antiquity thieves can liquidate antiquities. If thieves cannot export and import artifacts to exchange their takings for money, the incentive for looters in taking artifacts in the first place will be significantly lessened.

The Convention lays out a multi-pronged plan. The General Assembly of all signatories to the Convention first selects which members will compose the World Heritage Committee, a group of twenty-one signatory states. This decision-making committee determines what cultural property is "important for [a country's] archaeology, prehistory, history, literature, art or science," and designates this property as protected. Next, each signatory implements special services to protect their designated cultural property, drafts laws against illicit import and export, establishes inventories of their nationally protected property, and promotes the principles of the Convention to museums, libraries, archives, and laboratories in order to ensure the preservation and presentation of cultural property. The Convention acquires legal status only after it is signed by a nation. As of May 1, 2004, 178 nations had signed the Convention. Many of the signatories are Third World countries and source nations, but large art importing nations such as Canada, France, the United States, Switzerland, and Germany have also signed.

Particularly important to the Convention is Article 7, which provides for the restitution of cultural objects. Import and export regulation attack illicit art trade as artifacts are being exported out of the source nation and into a new country, whereas restitution provides a remedy (return to the rightful owner) once the objects have already crossed borders. Import and export regulations alone will not curb illegal art trade effectively. Countries must implement import and export regulations along with a provision for the restitution of cultural objects. Thus, a provision like Article 7 completes the Convention's multi-pronged plan. Nevertheless, Article 7 creates no official international tribunal to handle disputes between parties over restitution, and instead leaves this responsibility to the individual states. In theory, such disputes could go before the International Court of Justice in The Hague, but there are many difficulties with this, and restitution is not likely to follow. Critics view this shortcoming as a major weakness to the Convention because laws attempting to curb illicit antiquities trade are only as strong as the mechanism in place to uphold the law. Here the mechanism is missing.

Additional criticisms of the Convention are numerous. First, most of the signatory nations only agreed to its conditions in limited ways. This circumstance tends to water down the ideas of the Convention and makes its pursuit of objectives less vigorous. Second, the Convention itself is restricted only to artifacts stolen from museums, public monuments, and similar institutions. Therefore, antiquities yet to be unearthed and artifacts which are unearthed but held by private individuals are effectively excluded from the Convention. Third, there is a disconnection between definitions of important terminology. For example, each signatory is allowed to "define the cultural property that is to be protected." Finally, the term "owner in good faith" is never defined by the Convention, leaving interpretation up to the individual member countries. Without harmonization of important nomenclature and some level of unification in the way such terminology is interpreted, the possibility of curbing illicit trade does not exist.

In light of such problems, UNESCO approached the International Institute for the Unification of Private Law ("UNIDROIT") to help it improve the recovery of stolen and otherwise illegally removed cultural artifacts. In June 1995, UNIDROIT completed a treaty that would greatly expand protection of cultural entities. The treaty, however, is not retroactive and does not apply to pieces stolen from the host country before its ratification. Currently, twenty-two countries have signed the treaty, eleven of which have ratified it, and thirteen countries have acceded to it. The majority of the countries which have signed the treaty are source nations. Many market nations, including the United States, have yet to sign. One reason market nations, particularly the United States, are apprehensive to sign is due to the negative response from art dealers. These dealers are concerned that they will no longer be able to exhibit or sell pieces in countries that have ratified the treaty because the source nations may be able to legally confiscate their artifacts.

In addition to UNIDROIT, several international, nongovernmental bodies have been established to help counter difficulties faced by UNESCO. The two main organizations which focus on these efforts are INTERPOL and the International Council of Museums ("ICOM"). INTERPOL, headquartered in Lyon, France, is the organization actually charged with patrolling the illicit traffic of antiquities. Created "to facilitate cross-border criminal police cooperation," INTERPOL focuses on providing reliable communication to police around the globe in order to ease information transmission on stolen property and wanted suspects. In addition, it coordinates international investigations.

Specifically, INTERPOL's stolen art unit keeps track of all notices of major art thefts. Notices include date and place of theft, description of the work, a photograph, and details of local authorities to contact with information. INTERPOL then sends this information to all relevant agencies such as law enforcement and customs. These agencies are responsible for circulating the information to other members of the art industry.

INTERPOL faces a multitude of difficulties in accomplishing its mission. First, INTERPOL has other responsibilities. Because there are other pressing international crimes aside from art crimes, valuable resources and manpower must be shared. Thus, art theft, and subsequently antiquity theft, is not a top priority. Second, in order for INTERPOL to get involved, the theft must involve the artifact being transported across national borders. Third, the majority of information submitted to INTERPOL on art thefts and losses of cultural property comes from an array of geographically and culturally disperse nations, not from a single source or area. This factor, in effect, causes fluctuation in the volume of art and cultural property crimes reported by various countries. For example, in 1999, Jean-Pierre Jouanny of INTERPOL stated that close to 6,000 art thefts were reported in France, the location of INTERPOL's headquarters, whereas only 2,000 reports each from Russia, Germany, the Czech Republic, and Italy. Due in part to the modernization in transportation and communications, non-French reports were up from previous years. Still, fewer than 100 tips per year are received from non-European nations. Fourth, the agency has been criticized for being slow to disseminate information on thefts, failing to update records, and keeping incomplete records.

Unlike INTERPOL, ICOM has targeted the problem of illicit antiquities trade by applying pressure on museums to promote professional ethics internally. "ICOM is an international organization of museums and museum professionals which is committed to the conservation, continuation, and communication to society of the world's natural and cultural heritage, present and future, tangible and intangible." The French-based council seeks to carry out this objective in three ways. First, ICOM provides guidelines for the training of museum personnel. Second, it helps museums improve their security by establishing inventories. The inventory index is extremely useful in museum security as it can prove a museum's ownership of an object and aid in the object's identification. ICOM has established a committee, the International Committee for Documentation ("ICDOC"), which aids various museums in setting up these inventories. Third, ICOM published a Professional Code of Ethics ("ICOM Code") consisting of twenty recommendations and ethical principles to govern museums and museum professionals and established a committee to police museums' adherence to the ICOM Code.

Of particular importance in the ICOM Code is its policy outlining the procedures that museum professionals must follow when acquiring a new piece of art. This policy states that museums shall acquire pieces only in cooperation with and in observance of the laws of the source nation. Ramifications of the acquisition policy have been felt by museums in Australia, Canada, Israel, New Zealand, the United Kingdom, and the United States.

Communication with the international art community is of the utmost importance in curbing illicit art trade, and, thus, it is a central tenant to ICOM. For this reason, ICOM holds workshops around the world aimed at educating antiquity professionals. Past workshops have been held in Thailand, Cambodia, Hungary, Tanzania, and Western Africa. ICOM also publishes a quarterly bulletin which is distributed to its thirteen thousand members in one hundred forty-five countries. These bulletins announce missing objects that have been reported to INTERPOL and, in the past, have assisted in the location and restitution of several antiquities, such as Japanese objects stolen from a museum in Israel and a bronze head stolen from the Nigerian National Museum. Stemming from the success of the bulletin, ICOM created a publication entitled "A Hundred Missing Objects." The first edition featured items from a Cambodian site in Ankor which were recently the subject of systematic pillaging. Immediately after the series went to publication, one of the featured objects was found with a Parisian antique dealer and was successfully returned to Cambodia.

---

## 3. Interpol, Stolen Works of Art: Object ID

In 1993, discussions between the Getty Information Institute and leading national and international umbrella agencies and government bodies established that there was a consensus on the need to collectively address issues relating to documentation practices and the implementation of international standards. In July of that year the Institute convened a meeting in Paris to discuss the possibility of developing an international collaborative project to define documentation standards for identifying cultural objects. The meeting was attended by representatives of the Conference for Security and Co-operation in Europe (now the Organization for Security and Co-operation in Europe), the Council of Europe, the International Council of Museums, Interpol, UNESCO, and the U.S. Information Agency. The participants agreed on the need for such an initiative and recommended that it focus on developing a standard for the information required to identify cultural objects, and on the mechanisms for encouraging the implementation of the standard. As a result of these consultations, a project was defined and initiated, one of the objectives of which was to recommend an international 'core' documentation standard for the identification of cultural objects.

The findings of the surveys and recommendations of the roundtable meetings established that there was strong agreement on the categories of information that should constitute the standard. The result is Object ID, a standard that is best defined in terms of the ways in which it can be implemented:

- to provide a checklist of the information required to identify stolen or missing objects,
- as a documentation standard that establishes the minimum level of information needed to describe an object for purposes of identification,
- as a key building block in the development of information networks that will allow divers organizations to exchange descriptions of objects rapidly,
- to provide a solid basis for training programmes to teach the documentation of objects.

The standard has been developed in response to an identified need, and is designed to be used by non-specialists and to be capable of being implemented in traditional, non-computerized ways of making inventories and catalogues as well as in more sophisticated computerized databases. Because Object ID is designed to be used by a number of communities, and by specialists and non-specialists alike, it identifies broad concepts rather than specific fields and uses simple, non-technical language. Similarly, its function as a checklist usable by the public led to the decision to present the definitions of the information categories in the form of questions—such as 'What materials is the object made of?'—an approach that was found to be more comprehensible to non-specialists than definitions in the form of statements.

From the outset, the project recognized the need to work collaboratively with organizations in six key communities:

- Cultural heritage organizations (including museums, national inventories, and archaeological organizations)
- Law enforcement agencies
- Customs agencies
- The art trade
- Appraisers
- The insurance industry

The information needs of these users vary, but all need documentation that makes it possible to identify individual objects. Building a broad consensus across these communities on the categories of information essential for identifying objects was the essential precondition to a successful outcome for this initiative.

The first step toward establishing consensus on this core information was to identify and compare the information requirements of each of these communities, to understand the purposes for which their information is collected, and to determine how it is used and with whom it is shared. These requirements were identified by a combination of background research, interviews, and, most importantly, major international question-naire surveys.

The first of these surveys was carried out between July and December 1994 by the Getty Information Institute, with the endorsement of the Council of Europe, ICOM, and UNESCO. The survey elicited responses from organizations in 43 countries, including many major museums and galleries, heritage documentation centres, Interpol, and a number of national law enforcement agencies. The survey also took into account exist-ing standards and standard setting initiatives in the museum world, including those of the International Council of Museums, the Museum Documentation Association (UK), and the Canadian Heritage Information Network.

The results of this preliminary survey—published in July 1995 as Protecting Cultural Objects through International Documentation Standards: A Preliminary Survey—demon-strated that there did, indeed, exist a broad consensus on many of the categories of information that are candidates for inclusion in the proposed standard. Encouraged by these findings, the project went on to survey the information needs of the other key communities, namely dealers in art, antiques, and antiquities; appraisers of personal property; art insurance spe-cialists; and customs agencies. Over 1,000 responses were received from organizations in 84 countries and territories, making this survey the largest of its kind ever carried out.

It is important to point out that Object ID is not an alternative to existing standards; rather it is a core standard created for a very specific purpose—that of describing cultural objects to enable them to be identified. As such, it can be incorporated into existing sys-tems and nested within existing standards. For example, in August 1997 the Executive Council of the International Council of Museums (ICOM) adopted a resolution that "A museum should be able to generate from its collection information system such data (preferably according to the 'Object ID' standard) that can identify an object in case of theft or looting." Similarly, it has been nested within the Spectrum standard for museum in-formation developed by the Museum Documentation Association (United Kingdom). It has also been incorporated into a number of law enforcement databases, including the Na-tional Stolen Art File of the Federal Bureau of Investigation (United States).

Combating the illicit trade in cultural objects requires international collaboration among a variety of types of organizations in both the public and private sectors. The con-tribution of the Object ID project has been to identify a minimum standard for describ-ing cultural objects, to encourage the making of descriptions of objects in both private and public ownership, and to bring together organizations that can encourage the im-plementation of the standard, as well as those that will play a part in developing networks along which this information can circulate.

Object ID has been translated into 13 languages.

When supplying descriptions of works of art, the National Central Bureaus of Inter-pol's 181 member countries use standardized forms called CRIGEN/ART forms. These forms exist in Arabic, English, French and Spanish and are used to enter data on stolen works of art into Interpol's database at the General Secretariat. This ensures that all police de-partments use the same vocabulary to describe the same objects.

## Authors' Note

The next four materials provide a glimpse into the illicit trade involving works of art and the international community's attempt thwart it. Material 4 is an article from *The*

*Christian Science Monitor* that details a number of high-profile art thefts as well as the magnitude of international art thefts. Material 5 is a journal article that utilizes the tracking of artwork stolen during World War II to illustrate the difficulties in providing a standardized identification system for stolen artwork. Material 6, an article from *Newsweek*, details the steps taken by the United States in the formation of a new FBI unit to specifically track stolen artwork. Material 7 outlines the plundering of artwork in Iraqi National Museum during the onset of the U.S. invasion in 2003. These materials provide insight into the challenges that are faced by Interpol and national police forces in the prevention of the theft artwork and other cultural property.

---

## 4. Christopher Andreae, Art Museums Balance Access against Security
### *The Christian Science Monitor*, 2004

Since "The Scream" by Norwegian angst-artist Edvard Munch was stolen by armed robbers last Sunday, the media have been asking every art expert in sight, Why does this keep happening?

Art thefts, though not often as high-profile as the broad daylight robbery in Oslo, are persistently on the increase worldwide. This latest heist once again spotlights the holes in international law, the high costs of insurance and security, and the delicate balance that institutions must strike between protecting works of art and displaying them openly.

One question of course is: What do the thieves hope to gain by stealing "The Scream," an iconic image plastered on dorm-room walls and used in television and print advertisements?

The simple answer, according to Karl-Heinz Kind, who specializes in the recovery of artworks for Interpol, is money. "This is easier [for thieves] to achieve with items that are not so well known. But [it's] nearly impossible with very well known items like the Leonardo da Vinci [stolen a year ago from a Scottish country house, and still not recovered.]" The same is true for the Munch paintings.

Mr. Kind says the first step for thieves is, relatively speaking, the easiest — stealing the item by stealth or by force. "But then they are suddenly faced with a big problem that they didn't foresee: how to get rid of it and make money out of it."

The most likely scenario, he adds, in the case of a famous painting, is that the thieves will try to obtain money from the owner or the insurers.

Demanding a ransom (as of press time, no demands for money had been made for the Munch paintings) or attempting to sell an artwork can be a dangerous game for thieves. Burglars have been known to wait as long as 10 or 20 years before seeking payment for the painting's return, in the (often mistaken) assumption that the police are less likely to prosecute many years later.

The situation is complicated by the fact that museums often aren't able to devote sufficient resources to insuring their art, which continues to climb in value, according to Julian Radcliffe, chairman of the Art Loss Register, speaking on National Public Radio.

Museums, he told NPR's "Talk of the Nation," actually file more insurance claims for fire damage, accidents, and vandalism than for theft. And institutions that count on funding by municipalities are limited in how much insurance — and security — they can afford.

Sadly, the city of Oslo recently gave the Munch Museum additional funds for security, but the daytime theft occurred before improvements could be made. And besides, cultural institutions are reluctant to make their buildings into fortresses, or to arm their guards.

Few museums are even willing to discuss their protective measures. Security at the Museum of Fine Arts, Boston, for example, is so secret, that few staff members know anything about it. Dawn Griffin, head of public relations, won't comment, naturally, but says that even in times of tight budgets, security is one thing museums like the MFA will not compromise.

Art museums are not the only institutions concerned with preventing theft.

In Europe, for example, a number of historic properties contain important works of art.

Security is even more of a test for historic houses than for museums. Many of England's National Trust properties, for example, are country houses in remote places. Sian Evans, spokeswoman for the Trust, says that the organization is "reluctant to put the contents of their houses in glass cases." But, she says, "there is a constant effort to achieve a balance between the safety of such objects and making them appropriate to the ambience of the house." She, too, declines to talk about security.

While safeguarding information is important, secrecy on the part of some collectors and institutions can actually hamper recovery of stolen artwork.

One organization noted for art-crime investigation is London's Metropolitan Police Service, known as the Met, whose arts and antiques squad has achieved some fame.

In fact, this small bunch of experts was involved in trapping the thieves of another version of Munch's "The Scream" stolen from Norway's National Gallery in 1994. (The painting was recovered and put back on display two years later.)

The Met's website shows photos of recently stolen works. Currently the list includes an astronomically valuable Rubens called "Landscape with a Rainbow," but the Met's policy is not to divulge where or when this — or any other — painting was stolen.

Interpol, on the other hand, in Lyon, France, makes maximum use of publicity. With 181 member countries, Interpol is not an investigative body, but it coordinates information. It also features recently stolen works of art on its website and on a regularly updated CD-ROM. More than 26,000 stolen items are featured (many of these, however, are surprisingly small, such as individual coins or books).

However eager Interpol is to provide information on stolen art, it is dependent on member countries' willingness to share information. Many are less than cooperative. Some thefts are not even properly registered, or the owner does not, or cannot, provide a good description of the item. In that case, Interpol can't list those stolen works.

"What is needed is to improve the information flow," says Kind. The way to start this, is having a reliable inventory before a theft occurs.

"This is a very basic problem for all the third-world countries," he says. "Even in museums, they sometimes have no basic inventories, no photographs of works, so what can you do? Also," he adds, "this is valid for private owners: They need to make inventories of their property."

Despite such difficulties, Interpol has had many successes. One of the most remarkable, considering the time it took, was the recovery of several paintings stolen from a Romanian museum in 1968. The art, discovered in New York, had been missing for 30 years.

Maybe the Munch will be back, screaming, on its wall in Oslo, somewhat sooner than that.

Other high-profile art heists across the world:

The two Munch paintings stolen in Oslo are just the most recent example of high-profile thefts of paintings that have yet to be recovered. Others include: July 31, 2004, In Rome, 10 paintings worth $5 million belonging to a collection housed in a historic hospital were stolen from an unguarded restoration room. Among those lost: "La Sacra Famiglia" by the 16th-century artist Parmigianino; "Flagellazione" by Caravaggio mentor Cavalier D'Arpino; and "Testa di Vecchio" by Lanfranco, a master of the High Baroque.

May 19, 2004, Pablo Picasso's "Nature Morte a la Charlotte," worth $3 million, was reported missing from a restoration studio in Paris's Pompidou Center.

Dec. 16, 2003, "Special 21 (Palo Duro Canyon)" by Georgia O'Keeffe was stolen from the New Mexico Museum of Fine Arts in Santa Fe. Valued in excess of $500,000.

Aug. 27, 2003, In Scotland, thieves posing as tourists overpowered a lone guide in Drumlanrig Castle to steal da Vinci's "Madonna with the Yarnwinder," valued between $40 million and $80 million.

July 20, 2002, In Paraguay, thieves tunneled into the National Fine Arts Museum and stole a dozen paintings, including a self-portrait by Tintoretto, "The Virgin Mary and Jesus" by Esteban Murillo, "Landscape" by Gustave Coubert, and "Woman's Head" by Adolphe Piot. Police say the 80-foot tunnel took months to dig.

July 17, 2001, In Germany, an Andy Warhol portrait of Lenin disappears from a Cologne warehouse. It had just been sold to a gallery owner for around $700,000.

Dec. 22, 2000, In Stockholm, three armed and hooded men snatch two Renoirs and a Rembrandt from Sweden's National Museum and then escape by speedboat. Police later recover Renoir's "Conversation" by accident during a drug raid.

March 18, 1990, In Boston, two men disguised as police officers pulled off what remains the biggest art heist in history—handcuffing security guards inside the Isabella Stewart Gardner Museum, and then taking an estimated $ 300 million in art. Among them were three Rembrandts, a Vermeer, a Manet, and five by Degas.

---

# 5. Kenneth Hamma, Symposium: V. The New Millennium Finding Cultural Property Online

*Cardozo Arts & Entertainment Law Journal*, 2001
[footnotes omitted by editors]

\* \* \*

## I. Online provenance for works transferred in Europe during the Holocaust-era

The current state of research in the area of the online provenance for works transferred in Europe during the Holocaust-era exists almost entirely as digital information. There are hundreds of websites, representing the investigative "publishing" work of thousands of collection curators, archivists, historians, librarians, and etcetera. These websites have the potential to become an enormous virtual resource, unlike anything ever created in the domain of the visual arts. Today, we see a very small percentage of what we will see in a year, or even in a month. What seems to be guiding this development is a shared set of goals centered on easier, more transparent access to information. Sometimes, the steps to realizing these goals are expressly stated—as in the consortium of national museums in the UK referred to previously. Further, the UK museums have even agreed on the format of presentation. For example, the posted lists of works with problematic provenance all contain the same elements of information in the same order. Along these lines, numerous suggestions have been made in the United States to go one step further. This suggestion proposes that museums contribute to a single database, thus allowing searching to be both quicker and more effective.

This is a model we understand from print publications. However, in the world of the Internet, this congruency is not needed. In fact, one can say this is neither the best, nor the most financially reasonable course. Nor is it likely to produce results quickly, and the issue of timeliness weighs heavily on the survivors of the Holocaust.

It is likely that you are all well acquainted with searching the Internet for resources that exist in an invisible realm in which underlying commonalities may be discovered first and only through a search. For the topic at issue here, you might conduct an Internet search using the keywords "art" and "restitution" or "museum" and "spoliation." The results of this online search create a 'virtual' database of resources pulled from many different Internet sites, all of which are somehow related to art restitution.

Not so long ago, the recovery of a lost painting relied, and generally still relies, on the serendipitous discovery of it in a printed catalogue, the accidental discovery of it in the public market, or by its appearance on a museum wall. These kinds of discovery processes have been known to be modestly effective, as the exceptional rather than normal result. With the kind of Internet search previously described, it seems that we are on the threshold of a world in which the discovery of a single painting may rely on the confluence of easily discoverable resources, pulled together in an intentional pattern, from resources available around the world from the moment they are published. This type of activity was unimaginable even three or four years ago. Several years ago, art purchases could be checked at the International Foundation for Art Research ("IFAR"), in addition to the usual and normally well-known printed resources. These traditional resources are becoming a smaller percent, albeit remaining an important percent, of the resources that are always available on our desks at work or home.

In the world of creating printed resources we are all well acquainted with the process of researching, then writing, then indexing. This sequence is fundamental. First, you must gather the most comprehensive resources. Then, you must document your findings. And finally, you must index all of the resources before publishing them. The same is not true in the online world—where there is tremendous potential for asynchronous development of individual resources that can, and will, act as one resource when it is queried or searched. What will permit this online effort to be effective is our reliance on common language standards in our digital communications.

II. Standards

To see how the online effort will evolve, let me back up a bit into the realm of standards. Standards are a vital part of the infrastructure that supports the world of online information.

In October 1999, Interpol issued the first of its CD-ROMs offering searchable lists of stolen works of art. The information was recorded in three languages and accompanied by pictures of the stolen works. Subscribers then receive quarterly updates. The first of the CD-ROMs contains over 14,000 works organized in relatively few categories. This CD-ROM was light years ahead of the communications system that existed prior to its October 1999 release. As a means of communication, the CD-ROM is like the Internet model that I suggested earlier, but it is obviously several orders of magnitude smaller. In order to get to this kind of service, one of the difficulties that must be overcome is the use of words. This difficulty can be illustrated by describing a museum label and a police report. A painting in a museum might be described as: "Anthony van Dyck; Flemish, 1599–1641; Portrait of Agostino Pallavicini; Oil on canvas; 216 x 141 cm." In a police report, the same painting would likely be described as: "a large painting of a bald man in a red dress." With luck, the police report description may include the name of the artist.

The Interpol CD-ROM product addresses this mismatch of language and expectations. This is done by focusing on a single product, and by employing communication techniques based on common assumptions and shared vocabularies. The name that has been given to this approach is "Object ID." Object ID was created under the leadership of the Getty Information Institute several years ago with the participation of galleries, law-enforcement agencies, standards organizations and museums. It is essentially an information guide that includes about a dozen specific fields. The product responds effectively to both museum reports and police reports equally. In addition, Object ID also includes several suggestions on how to go about filling out such reports. For example, when writing about the medium of a work of art, Object ID suggests including further details. Thus, the user would be prompted to write "oil on canvas" rather than just "oil." This seemingly simple set of suggestions went a long way in making this particular CD-ROM successful.

In addition to creating a mutually agreeable convention for what to describe, there remained the need to accommodate differences in the use of terms and the unavoidable misuse of terms. How many of us would be able to easily distinguish a highly-patinated bronze sculpture from a highly-patinated copper sculpture? Many of us say Florence, when referring to the city others know as Firenze. Also, it possible to call the Greek mythological giant Titan by his Italian name, Tiziano. The enormity of the problem may not be comprehended initially because — in conversation — these synonyms are usually taken in stride. However, in the world of digital resources, this situation does not arise because computers cannot make the necessary connections between the synonyms. The differences in usage cause a database or Internet search to return with 'nothing found.'

To remedy this problem, additional Getty tools were put to use in compiling the CD-ROM and cataloguing mechanisms around the world. These tools include three well-structured and hierarchical vocabularies that effectively make information storage and retrieval smart. They are the Art and Architecture Thesaurus ("AAT"), the Union List of Artist Names ("ULAN"), and the Thesaurus of Geographic Names ("TGN").

The Art and Architecture Thesaurus knows the relationships among millions of terms commonly used to describe works of art and architecture. It knows about object names and their relationships. For example, it knows that 'commode' can refer to a chest of drawers or a necessary convenience. In addition, when 'commode' is meant to refer to a chest of drawers, AAT knows what other types of furniture to which the word 'commode' is related. The AAT also knows other descriptive terms. For example, it knows that orange is a color, and it is able to discern objects and personal names. Lastly, AAT also knows about historical periods and other events related to art and architecture.

The Union List of Artist Names knows the variant spellings of artist names currently in use or known from the literature, in addition to the other various names given to individual artists.

The Thesaurus of Geographic Names contains the variant common spellings of cities, provinces, states, countries, and other places. It also includes the hierarchical relationship among these entities, as well as their latitudinal and longitudinal coordinates. A key component for art and architecture, it also includes historical place names. Consequently, the TGN understands Flemish as an historical and geographic concept.

These tools were originally developed to provide a common way to catalogue books and articles in the domain of the visual arts. They are the children of the Bibliography of the History of Art, the Avery Index to Architectural Periodicals, and the Provenance Index.

---

## 6. Brian Braiker, Art Cops
### *Newsweek*, 2005

If you were looking forward to placing a bid on "The Mocking of Christ" in New York this coming Wednesday, Christie's may have some unwelcome news: the international auction house has pulled it off the block. It appears that the 16th-century Mirabello Cavalori oil painting, valued at $80,000–$100,000, was stolen from an art shop in Rome on Oct. 4. The storeowner spotted the painting on the Christie's Web site (attributed to Bartolomeo Passarotti) earlier this month and contacted the art-theft squad of the Carbinieri, Italy's version of the FBI. "This was such a recent theft, it wasn't on any [stolen art] databases," says the auction house's Andree Corroon, who says Christie's acquired the painting on good faith from a client they have worked with in the past. "We would never knowingly sell a stolen work of art."

The Italian shopkeeper was lucky. Usually stolen art goes unfound for a decade or more—if it gets recovered at all: up to 90 percent of all stolen art is gone for good, according to the FBI. Interpol, the international police agency, considers art theft one of the biggest global crimes, behind only the drug trade, international arms dealing and money laundering. Hard statistics are all but impossible to come by since art tends to appreciate in value, and some missing works might even be classified as priceless. But estimates from the FBI, Interpol and the Los Angeles Police Department's Art Theft Detail put the value of fine art stolen every year between $5 billion and $8 billion. "The numbers are incredible," Assistant U.S. Attorney Bob Goldman tells NEWSWEEK.

The FBI has decided to do something about it. Last November, the bureau announced that it is forming a new team to deal explicitly with art theft. The brand-new unit has already had its first taste of success. Just last month it recovered some pieces of more than $2 million in art stolen from a Missouri storage unit last October. More than 100 pieces, including paintings, prints and sculptures by Pablo Picasso, Willem de Kooning, Mark Rothko and others, were discovered stashed away in a St. Louis suburb. Robert K. Wittman, the new team's senior investigator, has been on the art-theft beat for 15 years and says he has had a hand in recovering some of the $100 million of art and artifacts by the FBI over the last four years. "The fact that you can put something back into a museum and kids can look at it, that's what's neat," he says. "That's why this is important."

Still, the U.S. is late getting into the art-recovery game. Countries from France to Britain to Germany have long had law-enforcement teams specializing in art theft. Italy's Carbinieri boasts a squad of more than 200 officers and is helmed by a colonel in epaulettes. The FBI's new team is eight men strong, with each agent covering a swath of territory and working with local police to provide resources and expertise that may be lacking in, say, Omaha, Neb. Several incidents precipitated the creation of the squad: first was the brazen 1990 burglary of Boston's Isabella Stewart Gardner Museum in which two men ripped paintings from their frames, making off with nearly $400 million of artwork, including three Rembrandts, a Vermeer, a Manet and five works by Degas. Sen. Ted Kennedy subsequently pushed through the Theft of Major Artwork statute, making it a felony punishable by up to 10 years in prison for stealing any museum art more than a century old or worth at least $100,000.

The second event that spurred the unit's creation was looting in Iraq following the ouster of Saddam Hussein. "Past history does show if there's theft of significant objects, some of the objects will end up in the States because there are big-money collectors here," says Goldman, one of two federal prosecutors on the team, which is currently training in Philadelphia. "It's taken a while to show there is a significant need for this [unit]." The Art Loss Register, the world's largest database of stolen art and antiques, is a list of 140,000 missing artifacts that, according to art historian Amanda Hannon, grows by 10,000 new entries every year.

Where, exactly, does all this stolen art go? Last year armed thieves burst into an Oslo, Norway, museum and made off with one version of Edvard Munch's masterpiece, "The Scream." Police have made one arrest in the case, but the whereabouts of the painting is still unknown. "The Scream" is so famous, though, that no legitimate art dealer or gallery would ever touch it. "You'll never see 'The Scream' come to auction," says Corroon of Christie's. The movies offer the Dr. No myth — that art ends up in the hands of some nefarious private collector like the James Bond villain who displays a stolen Goya in his lair — but experts stress that reality (surprise, surprise) belies the Hollywood portrayal. "There's no legitimate market for stolen art," says Sharon Flescher of the International Foundation for Art Research, a nonprofit research and education group. "It might, in theory, be used for money-laundering purposes or as collateral in the criminal world. Or thieves might try to ransom or barter the art back or try to claim a reward, if there is one."

Be that as it may, one itinerant French waiter, Stephane Breitwieser, received a 26-month prison sentence this month for stealing hundreds of works of art worth more than $1 billion from galleries in France, Germany and Switzerland, which he says he merely wanted to hang on his own walls. He lived with his mother, who destroyed them because she was afraid the police would find them.

Indeed, the execution of theft is rarely the sophisticated stuff of "The Thomas Crown Affair." The Isabella Stewart Gardner thieves used cheesy mustache disguises and brute force to pry paintings out of their frames, ripping the canvas of Rembrandt's "The Sea of Galilee" and probably reducing its value in the process. Most art theft in the United States is committed during a burglary, almost always of private residences, or by the falsification of paperwork. In 2001, a Beverly Hills, Calif., ophthalmologist was sentenced to 37 months in prison after being fingered by the LAPD and FBI in an art-insurance scam. Steven Cooperman was convicted of faking the 1992 theft of Pablo Picasso's "Nude Before a Mirror" and Claude Monet's "The Customs Officer's Cabin in Pourville" and collecting $17.5 million from his insurance companies. "I love Hollywood's idea of theft," chuckles Detective Don Hrycyk of the LAPD, which before the creation of the FBI team was the only law-enforcement agency in the country with an art-theft detail. Over time, through careful paperwork forgery, through fake prints or smuggling, he says, stolen art can end up in private collections or even museums.

Hrycyk, who has led the recovery of $53 million in stolen art since 1993, is currently on the lookout for a first-edition Superman comic book valued at $191,000. "In the manual for my unit, it states that we are supposed to handle paintings, limited-edition prints and sculptures," he says. "Over the years, suddenly we have to handle a case involving an expensive tapestry or dinosaur bones."

Before his unit was formed, he says the police tended to look at stolen art as just another type of property theft. But a stolen piece of art, whether it's famous or not, is something more than a stolen car or a swiped television set. Art is a reflection of our better nature, a permanent one-of-a-kind expression of what makes us human. Through his years on the job, Hrycyk has learned that a special expertise is required for dealing with stolen cultural artifacts. And the FBI is not the only other agency now subscribing to this idea; Ohio State University is planning an invitation-only training initiative for local law-enforcement representatives from across the country to learn about the issues unique to stolen art. With new initiatives like these, perhaps fewer masterpieces will disappear into the chiaroscuro of crime.

## 7. Interpol Hunts Stolen Iraqi Art
### CNN.com, 2003

Interpol has formed a team to track down art and antiquities dating back thousands of years that have been stolen from Iraqi cultural institutions, including the country's national museum in Baghdad.

The international police agency made the announcement Friday, the day after a panel of antiquities experts said it suspected some of the looting had been "commissioned" by collectors who had anticipated the fall of Saddam Hussein's regime.

The team will meet officials in Kuwait later this month to determine exactly what has been stolen before traveling on to Baghdad. FBI agents from the U.S. are also being sent to Iraq to assist with criminal investigations against anyone suspected of involvement in the looting.

Interpol, based in Lyon, France, said it had told police in its 181 member countries to make border guards, customs authorities, art dealers, auction houses, and the wider public aware of the situation.

"The conflict in Iraq has unfortunately resulted in large-scale destruction and theft of the cultural heritage of the country," said Karl-Heinz Kind, the agency's specialist in the theft of art and antiquities.

"Interpol is calling on organizations and institutions involved in conservation and trade of antiquities to categorically decline any offers of cultural property originating from Iraq," he added.

"In case of doubts concerning the origin of certain items, these bodies should immediately contact Interpol and seek expert evaluation of what is being offered for sale."

A meeting of experts and other interested parties, including representatives from the United Nations, the International Council of Museums and the World Customs Organization, will take place in Lyon between May 5 and May 6, to determine a strategy to deal with the thefts, Interpol said.

Much of the looted treasures could surface in London, one of the world's largest centers for trade in Islamic art, said Dick Ellis, an expert in recovering stolen art.

"The first thing to do is to assess what has been stolen and create a circular of the key objects and get it into the marketplace to close down the market," he said.

U.N. officials say they warned the United States government several months in advance of the war that the museum and other cultural institutions were at risk.

The U.S. has also been widely criticized for having taken steps to protect Iraqi oil fields but failing to take similar steps to protect the Iraqi National Museum.

The chairman of a committee that advises the White House on protecting antiquities around the world has resigned over what he says is the U.S. failure to stop the looting.

In a letter sent to U.S. President George W. Bush, Martin Sullivan, who headed the White House Cultural Property Advisory Committee said the "tragedy was foreseeable and preventable."

"While our military forces have displayed extraordinary precision and restraint in deploying arms — and apparently in securing the Oil Ministry and oil fields — they have been nothing short of impotent in failing to attend to the protection of (Iraq's) cultural heritage," Sullivan said in his letter.

## Authors' Note

The following two materials provide examples of the international community's attempt to establish standards for international cooperation in prohibiting and preventing the illicit trade of cultural property. These excerpts detail the conventions convened by UNESCO and UNIDROIT in order to provide guidance and regulation for States in the area of preserving cultural property.

## 8. Convention on the Means of Prohibiting and Preventing the Illicit Import, Export and Transfer of Ownership of Cultural Property

### 1970

The General Conference of the United Nations Educational, Scientific and Cultural Organization, meeting in Paris from 12 October to 14 November 1970, at its sixteenth session,

Recalling the importance of the provisions contained in the Declaration of the Principles of International Cultural Co-operation, adopted by the General Conference at its fourteenth session,

Considering that the interchange of cultural property among nations for scientific, cultural and educational purposes increases the knowledge of the civilization of man, enriches the cultural life of all peoples and inspires mutual respect and appreciation among nations,

Considering that cultural property constitutes one of the basic elements of civilization and national culture, and that its true value can be appreciated only in relation to the fullest possible information regarding its origin, history and traditional setting,

Considering that it is incumbent upon every State to protect the cultural property existing within its territory against the dangers of theft, clandestine excavation, and illicit export,

Considering that, to avert these dangers, it is essential for every State to become increasingly alive to the moral obligations to respect its own cultural heritage and that of all nations,

Considering that, as cultural institutions, museums, libraries and archives should ensure that their collections are built up in accordance with universally recognized moral principles,

Considering that the illicit import, export and transfer of ownership of cultural property is an obstacle to that understanding between nations which it is part of Unesco's mission to promote by recommending to interested States, international conventions to this end,

Considering that the protection of cultural heritage can be effective only if organized both nationally and internationally among States working in close co-operation,

Considering that the Unesco General Conference adopted a Recommendation to the effect in 1964;

Having before it further proposals on the means of prohibiting and preventing the illicit import, export and transfer of ownership of cultural property, a question which is on the agenda for the session as item 19.

Having decided, at its fifteenth session, that this question should be made the subject of an international convention,

Adopts the Convention on the fourteenth day of November 1970.

### Article 1

For the purposes of this Convention, the term 'cultural property' means property which, on religious or secular grounds, is specifically designated by each State as being of importance for archaeology, prehistory, history, literature, art or science and which belongs to the following categories:

    (a) Rare collections and specimens of fauna, flora, minerals and anatomy, and objects of palacontological interest;

    (b) property relating to history, including the history of science and technology and military and social history, to the life of national leaders, thinkers, scientists and artists and to events of national importance;

    (c) products of archaeological excavations (including regular and clandestine) or of archaeological discoveries;

    (d) elements of artistic or historical monuments or archaeological sites which have been dismembered;

    (e) antiquities more than one hundred years old, such as inscriptions, coins and engraved seals;

    (f) objects of ethnological interest;

    (g) property of artistic interest, such as;

    (i) pictures, paintings and drawings produced entirely by hand on any support and in any material (excluding industrial designs and manufactures articles decorated by hand);

    (ii) original works of statuary art and sculpture in any material;

    (iii) original engravings, prints and lithographs;

    (iv) original artistic assemblages and montages in any material;

    (h) rare manuscripts and incunabula, old books, documents and publications of special interest (historical, artistic, scientific, literary, etc.) singly or in collections;

    (i) postage, revenue and similar stamps, singly or in collections;

    (j) archives, including sound, photographic and cinematographic archives;

    (k) articles of furniture more than one hundred years old and old musical instruments.

### Article 2

1. The States Parties to this Convention recognize that the illicit import, export and transfer of ownership of cultural property is one of the main causes of the impoverishment of the cultural heritage of the countries of origin of such property and that international co-operation constitutes one of the most efficient means of protecting each country's cultural property against all the dangers resulting therefrom.

2. To this end, the States parties undertake to oppose such practices with the means at their disposal, and particularly by removing their causes, putting a stop to current practices, and by helping to make the necessary reparations.

## Article 3

The import, export or transfer of ownership of cultural property effected contrary to the provisions adopted under this Convention by the States Parties thereto, shall be illicit.

## Article 4

The States parties to this Convention recognize that for the purpose of the Convention property which belongs to the following categories forms part of the cultural heritage of each State:

(a) Cultural property created by the individual or collective genius of nationals of the State concerned, and cultural property of importance to the State concerned created within the territory of that State by foreign nationals or stateless persons resident within such territory;

(b) cultural property found within the national territory;

(c) cultural property acquired by archaeological, ethnological or natural science missions, with the consent of the competent authorities of that country or origin of such property;

(d) cultural property which has been the subject of a freely agreed exchange;

(e) cultural property received as a gift or purchased legally with the consent of the competent authorities of the country of origin of such property.

## Article 5

To ensure the protection of their cultural property against illicit import, export and transfer of ownership, the States parties to this Convention, undertake, as appropriate for each country, to set up within their territories one or more national services, where such services do not already exist, for the protection of the cultural heritage, with a qualified staff sufficient in number for the effective carrying out of the following functions:

(a) contributing to the formation of draft laws and regulations designed to secure the protection of the cultural heritage and particularly prevention of the illicit import, export and transfer of ownership of important cultural property;

(b) establishing and keeping up to date, on the basis of a national inventory of protected property, a list of important public and private cultural property whose export would constitute an appreciable impoverishment of the national cultural heritage;

(c) promoting the development or the establishment of scientific and technical institutions (museums, libraries, archives, laboratories, workshops....) required to ensure the preservation and presentation of cultural property;

(d) organizing the supervision of archaeological excavations, ensuring the preservation 'in situ' of certain cultural property, and protecting certain areas reserved for future archaeological research;

(e) establishing, for the benefit of those concerned (curators, collectors, antique dealers, etc.) rules in conformity with the ethical principles set forth in this Convention; and taking steps to ensure the observance of those rules;

(f) taking educational measures to stimulate and develop respect for the cultural heritage of all States, and spreading knowledge of the provisions of this Convention;

(g) seeing that appropriate publicity is given to the disappearance of any items of cultural property.

### Article 6

The States Parties to this Convention undertake:

(a) To introduce an appropriate certificate in which the exporting State would specify that the export of the cultural property in question is authorized. The certificate should accompany all items of cultural property exported in accordance with the regulations;

(b) to prohibit the exportation of cultural property from their territory unless accompanied by the above-mentioned export certificate;

(c) to publicize this prohibition by appropriate means, particularly among persons likely to export or import cultural property.

### Article 7

The States Parties to this Convention undertake:

(a) To take the necessary measures, consistent with national legislation, to prevent museums and similar institutions within their territories from acquiring cultural property originating in another State party which has been illegally exported after entry into force of this Convention, in the States concerned. Whenever possible, to inform a State of origin Party to this Convention of an offer of such cultural property illegally removed from that State after the entry into force of this Convention in both States;

(b) (i) to prohibit the import of cultural property stolen from a museum or a religious or secular public monument or similar institution in another State Party to this Convention after the entry into force of this Convention for the States concerned, provided that such property is documented as appertaining to the inventory of that institution; (ii) at the request of the State party of origin, to take appropriate steps to recover and return any such cultural property imported after the entry into force of this Convention in both States concerned, provided, however, that the requesting State shall pay just compensation to an innocent purchaser or to a person who has valid title to that property. Requests for recovery and return shall be made through diplomatic offices. The requesting Party shall furnish, at its expense, the documentation and other evidence necessary to establish its claim for recovery and return. The Parties shall impose no customs duties or other charges upon cultural property returned pursuant to this Article. All expenses incident to the return and delivery of the cultural property shall be borne by the requesting Party.

### Article 8

The States Parties to this Convention undertake to impose penalties or administrative sanctions on any person responsible for infringing the prohibitions referred to under Articles 6(b) and 7(b) above.

### Article 9

Any State Party to this Convention whose cultural patrimony is in jeopardy from pillage of archaeological or ethnological materials may call upon other States Parties who are affected. The States Parties to this Convention undertake, in these circumstances, to participate in a concerted international effort to determine and to carry out the necessary concrete measures, including the control of exports and imports and international commerce in the specific material concerned. Pending agreement each State concerned shall take provisional measures to the extent feasible to prevent irremediable injury to the cultural heritage of the requesting State.

## Article 10

The State Parties to this Convention undertake:

(a) To restrict by education, information and vigilance, movement of cultural property illegally removed from any State Party to this Convention and, as appropriate for each country, oblige antique dealers, subject to penal or administrative sanctions, to maintain a register recording the origin of each item of cultural property, names and addresses of the supplier, description and price of each item sold and to inform the purchaser of the cultural property of the export prohibition to which such property may be subject;

(b) to endeavour by educational means to create and develop in the public mind a realization of the value of cultural property and the threat to the cultural heritage created by theft, clandestine excavations and illicit exports.

## Article 11

The export and transfer of ownership of cultural property under compulsion arising directly or indirectly from the occupation of a country by a foreign power shall be regarded as illicit.

## Article 12

The States Parties to this Convention shall respect the cultural heritage within the territories for the international relations of which they are responsible, and shall take all appropriate measures to prohibit and prevent the illicit import, export and transfer of ownership of cultural property in such territories.

## Article 13

The States Parties to this Convention also undertake, consistent with the laws of each State:

(a) To prevent by all appropriate means transfers of ownership of cultural property likely to promote the illicit import or export of such property;

(b) to ensure that their competent services co-operate in facilitating the earliest possible restitution of illicitly exported cultural property to its rightful owner;

(c) to admit actions for recovery of lost or stolen items of cultural property brought by or on behalf of the rightful owners;

(d) to recognize the indefeasible right of each State Party to this Convention to classify and declare certain cultural property as inalienable which should therefore ipso facto not be exported, and to facilitate recovery of such property by the State concerned in cases where it has been exported.

## Article 14

In order to prevent illicit export and to meet the obligations arising from the implementation of this Convention, each State Party to the Convention should, as far as it is able, provide the national services responsible for the protection of its cultural heritage with an adequate budget and, if necessary, should set up a fund for this purpose.

## Article 15

Nothing in this Convention shall prevent States Parties thereto from concluding special agreements among themselves or from continuing to implement agreements already concluded regarding the restitution of cultural property removed, whatever the reason, from its territory of origin, before the entry into force of this Convention for the States concerned.

## Article 16

The States Parties to this Convention shall in their periodic reports submitted to the General Conference of the united Nations Educational, Scientific and Cultural Organization on dates and in a manner to be determined by it, give information on the legislative and administrative provisions which they have adopted and other action which they have taken for the application of this Convention, together with details of the experience acquired in this field.

## Article 17

1. The States Parties to this Convention may call on the technical assistance of the United Nations Educational, Scientific and Cultural organization, particularly as regards:

    (a)  Information and education;

    (b)  consultation and expert advice;

    (c)  co-ordination and good offices.

2. The United Nations Educational, Scientific and Cultural Organization may, on its own initiative conduct research and publish studies on matters relevant to the illicit movement of cultural property.

3. To this end, the United Nations Educational, Scientific and Cultural Organization may also call on the co-operation of any competent non-governmental organization.

4. The United Nations Educational, Scientific and Cultural Organization may, on its own initiative, make proposals to States Parties to this Convention for its implementation.

5. At the request of at least two States parties to this Convention which are engaged in a dispute over its implementation, Unesco may extend its good offices to reach a settlement between them.

∗  ∗  ∗

## Article 22

The States Parties to this Convention recognize that the Convention is applicable not only to their metropolitan territories but also to all territories for the international relations of which they are responsible; they undertake to consult, if necessary, the governments or other competent authorities of these territories on or before ratification, acceptance or accession with a view to securing the application of the Convention to those territories and to notify the Director-General of the United Nations Educational, Scientific and Cultural Organization of the territories to which it is applied, the notification to take effect three months after the date of its receipt.

# 9. Convention on Stolen or Illegally Exported Cultural Objects
## 1995

THE STATES PARTIES TO THIS CONVENTION,

ASSEMBLED in Rome at the invitation of the Government of the Italian Republic from 7 to 24 June 1995 for a Diplomatic Conference for the adoption of the draft Unidroit Convention on the International Return of Stolen or Illegally Exported Cultural Objects,

CONVINCED of the fundamental importance of the protection of cultural heritage and of cultural exchanges for promoting understanding between peoples, and the dissemination of culture for the well-being of humanity and the progress of civilization,

DEEPLY CONCERNED by the illicit trade in cultural objects and the irreparable damage frequently caused by it, both to these objects themselves and to the cultural heritage of national, tribal, indigenous or other communities, and also to the heritage of all peoples, and in particular by the pillage of archaeological sites and the resulting loss of irreplaceable archaeological, historical and scientific information,

DETERMINED to contribute effectively to the fight against illicit trade in cultural objects by taking the important step of establishing common, minimal legal rules for the restitution and return of cultural objects between Contracting States, with the objective of improving the preservation and protection of the cultural heritage in the interest of all,

EMPHASISING that this Convention is intended to facilitate the restitution and return of cultural objects, and that the provision of any remedies, such as compensation, needed to effect restitution and return in some States, does not imply that such remedies should be adopted in other States,

AFFIRMING that the adoption of the provisions of this Convention for the future in no way confers any approval or legitimacy upon illegal transactions of whatever kind which may have taken place before the entry into force of the Convention,

CONSCIOUS that this Convention will not by itself provide a solution to the problems raised by illicit trade, but that it initiates a process that will enhance international cultural co-operation and maintain a proper role for legal trading and inter-State agreements for cultural exchanges,

ACKNOWLEDGING that implementation of this Convention should be accompanied by other effective measures for protecting cultural objects, such as the development and use of registers, the physical protection of archaeological sites and technical co-operation,

RECOGNISING the work of various bodies to protect cultural property, particularly the 1970 UNESCO Convention on illicit traffic and the development of codes of conduct in the private sector,

HAVE AGREED as follows:

## Chapter I — Scope of Application and Definition

### Article 1

This Convention applies to claims of an international character for:

(a)  the restitution of stolen cultural objects;

(b)  the return of cultural objects removed from the territory of a Contracting State contrary to its law regulating the export of cultural objects for the purpose of protecting its cultural heritage (hereinafter "illegally exported cultural objects").

### Article 2

For the purposes of this Convention, cultural objects are those which, on religious or secular grounds, are of importance for archaeology, prehistory, history, literature, art or science and belong to one of the categories listed in the Annex to this Convention.

## Chapter II — Restitution of Stolen Cultural Objects

### Article 3

(1) The possessor of a cultural object which has been stolen shall return it.

(2) For the purposes of this Convention, a cultural object which has been unlawfully excavated or lawfully excavated but unlawfully retained shall be considered stolen, when consistent with the law of the State where the excavation took place.

(3) Any claim for restitution shall be brought within a period of three years from the time when the claimant knew the location of the cultural object and the identity of its possessor, and in any case within a period of fifty years from the time of the theft.

(4) However, a claim for restitution of a cultural object forming an integral part of an identified monument or archaeological site, or belonging to a public collection, shall not be subject to time limitations other than a period of three years from the time when the claimant knew the location of the cultural object and the identity of its possessor.

(5) Notwithstanding the provisions of the preceding paragraph, any Contracting State may declare that a claim is subject to a time limitation of 75 years or such longer period as is provided in its law. A claim made in another Contracting State for restitution of a cultural object displaced from a monument, archaeological site or public collection in a Contracting State making such a declaration shall also be subject to that time limitation.

(6) A declaration referred to in the preceding paragraph shall be made at the time of signature, ratification, acceptance, approval or accession.

(7) For the purposes of this Convention, a "public collection" consists of a group of inventoried or otherwise identified cultural objects owned by:

(a)  a Contracting State

(b)  a regional or local authority of a Contracting State;

(c)  a religious institution in a Contracting State; or

(d)  an institution that is established for an essentially cultural, educational or scientific purpose in a Contracting State and is recognised in that State as serving the public interest.

(8) In addition, a claim for restitution of a sacred or communally important cultural object belonging to and used by a tribal or indigenous community in a Contracting State as part of that community's traditional or ritual use, shall be subject to the time limitation applicable to public collections.

## Article 4

(1) The possessor of a stolen cultural object required to return it shall be entitled, at the time of its restitution, to payment of fair and reasonable compensation provided that the possessor neither knew nor ought reasonably to have known that the object was stolen and can prove that it exercised due diligence when acquiring the object.

(2) Without prejudice to the right of the possessor to compensation referred to in the preceding paragraph, reasonable efforts shall be made to have the person who transferred the cultural object to the possessor, or any prior transferor, pay the compensation where to do so would be consistent with the law of the State in which the claim is brought.

(3) Payment of compensation to the possessor by the claimant, when this is required, shall be without prejudice to the right of the claimant to recover it from any other person.

(4) In determining whether the possessor exercised due diligence, regard shall be had to all the circumstances of the acquisition, including the character of the parties, the price paid, whether the possessor consulted any reasonably accessible register of stolen cultural objects, and any other relevant information and documentation which it could reason-

ably have obtained, and whether the possessor consulted accessible agencies or took any other step that a reasonable person would have taken in the circumstances.

(5) The possessor shall not be in a more favourable position than the person from whom it acquired the cultural object by inheritance or otherwise gratuitously.

## Chapter III—Return of Illegally Exported Cultural Objects

### Article 5

(1) A Contracting State may request the court or other competent authority of another Contracting State to order the return of a cultural object illegally exported from the territory of the requesting State.

(2) A cultural object which has been temporarily exported from the territory of the requesting State, for purposes such as exhibition, research or restoration, under a permit issued according to its law regulating its export for the purpose of protecting its cultural heritage and not returned in accordance with the terms of that permit shall be deemed to have been illegally exported.

(3) The court or other competent authority of the State addressed shall order the return of an illegally exported cultural object if the requesting State establishes that the removal of the object from its territory significantly impairs one or more of the following interests:

  (a)  the physical preservation of the object or of its context;

  (b)  the integrity of a complex object;

  (c)  the preservation of information of, for example, a scientific or historical character;

  (d)  the traditional or ritual use of the object by a tribal or indigenous community, or establishes that the object is of significant cultural importance for the requesting State.

(4) Any request made under paragraph 1 of this article shall contain or be accompanied by such information of a factual or legal nature as may assist the court or other competent authority of the State addressed in determining whether the requirements of paragraphs 1 to 3 have been met.

(5) Any request for return shall be brought within a period of three years from the time when the requesting State knew the location of the cultural object and the identity of its possessor, and in any case within a period of fifty years from the date of the export or from the date on which the object should have been returned under a permit referred to in paragraph 2 of this article.

### Article 6

(1) The possessor of a cultural object who acquired the object after it was illegally exported shall be entitled, at the time of its return, to payment by the requesting State of fair and reasonable compensation, provided that the possessor neither knew nor ought reasonably to have known at the time of acquisition that the object had been illegally exported.

(2) In determining whether the possessor knew or ought reasonably to have known that the cultural object had been illegally exported, regard shall be had to the circumstances of the acquisition, including the absence of an export certificate required under the law of the requesting State.

(3) Instead of compensation, and in agreement with the requesting State, the possessor required to return the cultural object to that State, may decide:

    (a)  to retain ownership of the object; or

    (b)  to transfer ownership against payment or gratuitously to a person of its choice residing in the requesting State who provides the necessary guarantees.

(4) The cost of returning the cultural object in accordance with this article shall be borne by the requesting State, without prejudice to the right of that State to recover costs from any other person.

(5) The possessor shall not be in a more favourable position than the person from whom it acquired the cultural object by inheritance or otherwise gratuitously.

### Article 7

(1) The provisions of this Chapter shall not apply where:

    (a)  the export of a cultural object is no longer illegal at the time at which the return is requested; or

    (b)  the object was exported during the lifetime of the person who created it or within a period of fifty years following the death of that person.

(2) Notwithstanding the provisions of sub-paragraph (b) of the preceding paragraph, the provisions of this Chapter shall apply where a cultural object was made by a member or members of a tribal or indigenous community for traditional or ritual use by that community and the object will be returned to that community.

### Chapter IV—General Provisions

### Article 8

(1) A claim under Chapter II and a request under Chapter III may be brought before the courts or other competent authorities of the Contracting State where the cultural object is located, in addition to the courts or other competent authorities otherwise having jurisdiction under the rules in force in Contracting States.

(2) The parties may agree to submit the dispute to any court or other competent authority or to arbitration.

(3) Resort may be had to the provisional, including protective, measures available under the law of the Contracting State where the object is located even when the claim for restitution or request for return of the object is brought before the courts or other competent authorities of another Contracting State.

### Article 9

(1) Nothing in this Convention shall prevent a Contracting State from applying any rules more favourable to the restitution or the return of stolen or illegally exported cultural objects than provided for by this Convention.

(2) This article shall not be interpreted as creating an obligation to recognise or enforce a decision of a court or other competent authority of another Contracting State that departs from the provisions of this Convention.

### Article 10

(1) The provisions of Chapter II shall apply only in respect of a cultural object that is stolen after this Convention enters into force in respect of the State where the claim is brought, provided that:

    (a)  the object was stolen from the territory of a Contracting State after the entry into force of this Convention for that State; or

(b)   the object is located in a Contracting State after the entry into force of the Convention for that State.

(2) The provisions of Chapter III shall apply only in respect of a cultural object that is illegally exported after this Convention enters into force for the requesting State as well as the State where the request is brought.

(3) This Convention does not in any way legitimise any illegal transaction of whatever nature which has taken place before the entry into force of this Convention or which is excluded under paragraphs (1) or (2) of this article, nor limit any right of a State or other person to make a claim under remedies available outside the framework of this Convention for the restitution or return of a cultural object stolen or illegally exported before the entry into force of this Convention.

* * *

## Chapter V — Final Provisions

### Article 13

(1) This Convention does not affect any international instrument by which any Contracting State is legally bound and which contains provisions on matters governed by this Convention, unless a contrary declaration is made by the States bound by such instrument.

(2) Any Contracting State may enter into agreements with one or more Contracting States, with a view to improving the application of this Convention in their mutual relations. The States which have concluded such an agreement shall transmit a copy to the depositary.

(3) In their relations with each other, Contracting States which are Members of organizations of economic integration or regional bodies may declare that they will apply the internal rules of these organizations or bodies and will not therefore apply as between these States the provisions of this Convention the scope of application of which coincides with that of those rules.

### Article 14

(1) If a Contracting State has two or more territorial units, whether or not possessing different systems of law applicable in relation to the matters dealt with in this Convention, it may, at the time of signature or of the deposit of its instrument of ratification, acceptance, approval or accession, declare that this Convention is to extend to all its territorial units or only to one or more of them, and may substitute for its declaration another declaration at any time.

(2) These declarations are to be notified to the depositary and are to state expressly the territorial units to which the Convention extends.

(3) If, by virtue of a declaration under this article, this Convention extends to one or more but not all of the territorial units of a Contracting State, the reference to:

(a)   the territory of a Contracting State in Article 1 shall be construed as referring to the territory of a territorial unit of that State;

(b)   a court or other competent authority of the Contracting State or of the State addressed shall be construed as referring to the court or other competent authority of a territorial unit of that State;

(c)   the Contracting State where the cultural object is located in Article 8 (1) shall be construed as referring to the territorial unit of that State where the object is located;

(d) the law of the Contracting State where the object is located in Article 8 (3) shall be construed as referring to the law of the territorial unit of that State where the object is located; and

(e) a Contracting State in Article 9 shall be construed as referring to a territorial unit of that State.

(4) If a Contracting State makes no declaration under paragraph 1 of this article, this Convention is to extend to all territorial units of that State.

\* \* \*

### Article 18

No reservations are permitted except those expressly authorised in this Convention.

\* \* \*

### Article 20

The President of the International Institute for the Unification of Private Law (Unidroit) may at regular intervals, or at any time at the request of five Contracting States, convene a special committee in order to review the practical operation of this Convention.

## *Authors' Note*

The next three materials illustrate Interpol's cooperation with other international organizations in the protection of cultural property. Materials 10 and 11 are excerpts of co-operation agreements between Interpol and the United Nations and UNESCO, respectively. Material 12 is a Memorandum of Understanding (MOU) between Interpol and the International Council of Museums on efforts taken to counter the theft of cultural property.

## 10. Co-Operation Agreement between the United Nations and the International Criminal Police Organization-Interpol
### Interpol, 1997

### Article 1

Areas of cooperation

The United Nations and Interpol undertake to cooperate in the following fields, through their appropriate bodies:

a.  Responding to the needs of the international community in the face of both national and transnational crime;

b.  Assisting the international community in achieving the goals of preventing crime within and among States and improving the response to crime, in particular, through police training and public awareness campaigns aimed at alerting the public to the considerable threat posed by certain types of crime;

c.  Assisting States, in particular in their efforts to combat organized criminal groups involved in such forms of crime as money-laundering, illicit traffic in human beings, offenses against minors, drug trafficking, as well as violations of international environmental and humanitarian laws;

d.  Cooperating, where appropriate, in the implementation of the mandates of international judicial institutions, such as the International Tribunal for the Prosecution of Persons Responsible for Serious Violations of International Humanitarian Law Committed in the Territory of the Former Yugoslavia since 1991 and the International Criminal Tribunal for the Prosecution of Persons Responsible for Genocide and Other Serious Violations of International Humanitarian Law Committed in the Territory of Rwanda and Rwandan Citizens Responsible for Genocide and Other Such Violations Committed in the Territory of Neighbouring States between 1 January and 31 December 1994, which have been or may be established by the United Nations;

e.   Cooperating, when requested by the United Nations and as appropriate, in respect of carrying out investigations and any other police-related matters in the context of peace-keeping and similar operations;

f.   Examining the possibility of establishing through special arrangements with Offices and Programmes concerned common or linked computerized databases relating to penal law, to avoid undesirable duplication between them with respect to the collection and analysis of such information.

## Article 2

Consultation and cooperation

1.   The United Nations and Interpol shall exchange views, when appropriate, on policy issues within their respective competence and consult regularly on matters of common interest with a view to achieving their objectives and coordinating their positions and activities. When appropriate, they will also hold consultations on the most effective way of organizing particular activities of common interest related to their respective mandates and on the optimum use of their resources in connection with such activities.

2.   To this end, the United Nations and Interpol shall set up appropriate structures for such consultations as and when necessary.

## Article 3

Exchange of information and documents

The United Nations and Interpol shall make every effort to achieve the best use of available information related to the issues of common interest. To that end, and subject to necessary limitations and their internal regulations concerning the safeguarding of confidential or semi-confidential material and information, they shall arrange for the exchange of information and documents of common interest.

## Article 4

Technical cooperation

1.   Should the activities of the United Nations and of Interpol in fields of common interest so dictate, either Organization may request the cooperation of the other whenever the latter Organization is in a position to help develop the former's activities.

2.   The United Nations and Interpol shall endeavour, insofar as possible and in compliance with their constituent instruments and the decisions of their competent bodies, to respond favourably to such requests for cooperation in accordance with procedures and arrangements to be mutually agreed upon.

3.   The United Nations and Interpol shall cooperate, when appropriate and to the extent possible, in evaluating projects and programmes of common interest that relate to the areas of their respective competence. Interpol agrees in this regard to assist the United Nations upon request in reviewing national, regional or global crime pre-

vention and criminal justice projects and programmes falling within the area of its expertise.

4. The United Nations and Interpol shall deepen their dialogue and promote the undertaking of joint studies and the provision of advisory services and technical assistance, regarding the mutually-reinforcing interrelationship between crime prevention, administration of justice and respect for human rights.

## Article 5

Joint action

The United Nations and Interpol may, through special arrangements, decide to act jointly in the implementation of projects that are of common interest. The special arrangements shall define the modalities for the participation of each Organization in such projects and shall determine the expenses payable by each of them.

## Article 6

Reciprocal representation

1. In conformity with General Assembly resolution 51/l of 22 October 1996, Interpol may participate in the sessions and work of the General Assembly of the United Nations as an observer.

2. Subject to such decisions as may be taken by its other competent bodies concerning the attendance of its meetings by observers, the United Nations shall, subject to the rules of procedure of the bodies concerned, invite Interpol to send representatives to United Nations meetings and conferences where observers are allowed, whenever matters of interest to Interpol are discussed. The provisions of this paragraph shall, in particular, be observed with regard to United Nations meetings and seminars and conferences on the prevention of crime.

3. Subject to such decisions as may be taken by its competent bodies concerning the attendance of its meetings by observers, Interpol shall invite the United Nations to send representatives to all its meetings and conferences where observers are allowed, whenever matters of interest to the United Nations are discussed.

4. The United Nations and Interpol shall make every effort to ensure that if one of them is involved in organizing an international meeting for the consideration of the issues which fall within the competence of the other, representatives of the latter will be invited to attend that meeting.

## Article 7

Cooperation between the Secretariats

1. The Secretary-General of the United Nations and the Secretary-General of Interpol shall consult from time to time regarding the implementation of their respective responsibilities under this Agreement and other issues of common interest.

2. The Secretary-General of the United Nations and the Secretary-General of Interpol shall make appropriate administrative arrangements to ensure effective cooperation and liaison between the Secretariats of the two Organizations.

## Article 8

Personnel arrangements

Subject to their relevant internal regulations, the United Nations and Interpol shall examine the possibility of organizing the exchange of personnel on a temporary basis. They will enter into special arrangements, if necessary, for that purpose.

## Article 9

Implementation of the Agreement

The United Nations and Interpol may, if necessary, enter into supplementary arrangements for the implementation of the present Agreement.

## Article 10

Entry into force, amendments and duration

1. This Agreement shall enter into force following the exchange of written notifications confirming the completion by both Organizations of their internal requirements in this respect.

2. This Agreement may be amended by mutual consent between the United Nations and Interpol expressed in writing.

3. Either of the Organization may terminate this Agreement by giving six months' written notice to the other party.

---

# 11. Co-Operation Agreement between the United Nations Educational, Scientific and Cultural Organization and the International Criminal Police Organization-Interpol

Interpol, 1999

The International Criminal Police Organization-Interpol (hereinafter referred to as INTERPOL) and The United Nations Educational, Scientific and Cultural Organization (hereinafter referred to as UNESCO),

Wishing to co-ordinate their efforts within the framework of the missions assigned to them,

Recognizing that INTERPOL is responsible for ensuring and promoting the widest possible mutual assistance between all the criminal police authorities within the limits of the laws existing in the different countries and in the spirit of the Universal Declaration of Human Rights,

Recognizing that the purpose of UNESCO is to contribute to peace and security by promoting collaboration among the nations through education, science and culture in order to further universal respect for justice, for the rule of law and for human rights and fundamental freedoms,

Recognizing the desirability of UNESCO's co-operating with Interpol in combating, among other things, illicit traffic in cultural properties and crime taking advantage of new technology, such as cybercrime and child pornography,

Have agreed on the following:

## Article 1

Mutual consultation

INTERPOL and UNESCO shall consult regularly on policy issues and matters of common interest for the purpose of realizing their objectives and co-ordinating their respective activities.

INTERPOL and UNESCO shall exchange information on developments in any of their fields and projects that are of mutual interest and shall reciprocally take observations concerning such activities into consideration with a view to promoting effective co-operation.

When appropriate, consultation shall be arranged at the required level between representatives of UNESCO and INTERPOL to agree upon the most effective way in which to organize particular activities and to optimize the use of their resources in compliance with their respective mandates.

### Article 2

Exchange of information

INTERPOL and UNESCO shall combine their efforts to achieve the best use of all available information relevant to trafficking of cultural properties and crime taking advantage of new technology.

Subject to such arrangements as may be necessary for the safeguarding of confidential information, INTERPOL and UNESCO shall ensure full and prompt exchange of information and documents concerning matters of common interest.

Communication of police information by INTERPOL to UNESCO shall be subject to INTERPOL's internal regulations. If an item of information communicated by INTERPOL to UNESCO is modified or deleted, INTERPOL shall inform UNESCO so that the latter may keep its own archives up-to-date. INTERPOL shall not be liable in the event that the use by UNESCO of an item of information is prejudicial to an individual's or entity's interests, if INTERPOL has informed UNESCO that that item of information has been modified or deleted. Police information communicated by INTERPOL to UNESCO shall be used by UNESCO exclusively for the purposes of prevention or suppression of transnational ordinary law crime, with due respect for national laws and international treaties.

Communication of information by UNESCO to INTERPOL shall be subject to the provisions of UNESCO's internal regulations.

### Article 3

Reciprocal representation

Representatives of INTERPOL and representatives of UNESCO shall be invited to attend meetings convened under their respective auspices and participate, as observers without vote, in the deliberations thereof, with respect to matters of mutual interest and competence. Additional arrangements for reciprocal representation may be made if and when necessary.

The Director General of UNESCO and the Secretary-General of INTERPOL shall each designate a person to act as a focal point with a view to ensuring the implementation of the provisions of the present Co-operation Agreement.

### Article 4

Technical co-operation

INTERPOL and UNESCO shall, in the interest of their respective activities, seek and share each other's expertise and experience to optimize the effects of such activities.

UNESCO shall review, at INTERPOL's request, projects at national, regional and global levels in order to provide comments and suggestions appropriate to its domain of expertise.

By mutual agreement, UNESCO and INTERPOL shall co-operate in the development and execution of programmes, projects and activities relating particularly to crimes and offences concerning cultural properties and information and communications technologies.

Joint activities to be conducted under the present Co-operation Agreement shall be subject to the approval of individual project documents by both parties and shall be monitored under an agreed mechanism.

INTERPOL and UNESCO shall co-operate in evaluating such programmes, projects and activities of common interest, subject to mutual agreement on a case-by-case basis.

### Article 5

Personnel arrangements

Subject to their relevant internal regulations, UNESCO and INTERPOL shall examine the possibility of organizing the exchange of personnel on a temporary basis. They will enter into special arrangements, if necessary, for that purpose.

### Article 6

Entry into force, modification and duration

1.  The present Co-operation Agreement shall enter into force on the date on which it is signed by the Secretary-General of INTERPOL and the Director General of UNESCO, subject to the approval of the INTERPOL Executive Committee and of the Executive Board of UNESCO.

2.  The present Co-operation Agreement may be modified by mutual consent expressed in writing. It may also be revoked by either party by giving six months' notice to the other party.

## 12. Memorandum of understanding with the International Council of Museums on Countering the Theft and Trafficking in Cultural Property
### Interpol, 2000

The International Criminal Police Organization — Interpol (hereinafter referred to as Interpol) and the International Council of Museums (hereinafter referred to as ICOM):

Recognizing that the protection of the cultural heritage must be the subject of international co-operation,

Noting that the looting of cultural property is a worldwide phenomenon and that it gives rise to a large amount of illicit trafficking,

Considering that the illicit trafficking in cultural property constitutes a crime against the world's cultural heritage,

Considering that Interpol's aims are to ensure and promote the widest possible mutual assistance between all criminal police authorities within the limits of the laws existing in the different countries and in the spirit of the Universal Declaration of Human Rights, and to establish and develop all institutions likely to contribute effectively to the prevention and suppression of ordinary law crimes,

Aware that the ICPO-Interpol plays a fundamental role in combating the theft of and illicit traffic in cultural property,

Aware that ICOM also plays a vital role in protecting cultural property,

Considering that strengthening co-operation at international level between bodies responsible for protecting and conserving the cultural heritage, on the one hand, and police authorities on the other will increase the effectiveness of the fight against the illicit trafficking in this heritage,

Have agreed on the following:

## Article 1

Mutual consultation

Interpol and ICOM shall consult regularly on matters of common interest for the purpose of realizing their objectives.

When appropriate, consultation shall be arranged at the required level between representatives of ICOM and of Interpol to agree upon the most effective way in which to organize particular activities and to optimize the use of their available resources in compliance with their respective mandates.

## Article 2

Exchange of information

Subject to such arrangements as may be necessary for the safeguarding of confidential information, Interpol and ICOM shall ensure full and prompt exchange of information and documents concerning matters of common interest.

The two Parties shall communicate to each other any information they may have concerning modus operandi used in the illicit traffic of cultural property and statistics they may have on this form of crime.

Subject to its internal regulations, Interpol shall consider authorizing ICOM to consult its information on stolen works of art.

ICOM shall communicate to Interpol information it has on cases of theft of and illicit traffic in cultural property. The appropriate supporting documents shall be attached to such information.

In conformity with its internal regulations, Interpol shall make the necessary arrangements for the use of information communicated in application of paragraph 4. In this respect, ICOM shall authorize Interpol to reproduce and circulate, for crime prevention purposes, the information it receives from ICOM.

## Article 3

Reciprocal representation

Where appropriate, arrangements shall be made for reciprocal representation at Interpol and ICOM meetings convened under their respective auspices and dealing with matters in which the other party has an interest or technical competence.

The Secretary-General of ICOM and the Secretary-General of Interpol shall each designate a person to act as a focal point with a view to ensuring the implementation of the provisions of the present Memorandum of understanding.

## Article 4

Technical Co-operation

Each Party shall, at the request of the other Party, review projects to be implemented at national, regional and international level, in order to provide comments and suggestions which are appropriate to their area of concern.

By mutual agreement and within the limits of their resources, the Parties shall work together to set up and implement programmes, projects and activities, in particular those linked to combating the theft of, and traffic in, cultural property.

Within the limits of their resources, each Party shall take part in cultural property training activities for staff involved in combating illicit traffic in cultural property organized by the other Party and shall work closely with the other Party so that museum professionals and police services combating this form of trafficking may share experience and expertise.

**Article 5**

Entry into force, modification and duration

The present Memorandum of understanding shall enter into force on the date on which it is signed by the Secretary-General of Interpol and the Secretary-General of ICOM, subject to the approval of the Interpol General Assembly and the Executive Council of ICOM.

The present Memorandum of understanding may be modified by mutual consent expressed in writing. It may also be revoked by either party by giving six months' notice to the other party.

# 13. Interpol, Interpol Member Countries (190)

**A**

Afghanistan | Albania | Algeria | Andorra | Angola | Antigua & Barbuda | Argentina | Armenia | Aruba | Australia | Austria | Azerbaijan

**B**

Bahamas | Bahrain | Bangladesh | Barbados | Belarus | Belgium | Belize | Benin | Bhutan | Bolivia | Bosnia and Herzegovina | Botswana | Brazil | Brunei | Bulgaria | Burkina-Faso | Burundi

**C**

Cambodia | Cameroon | Canada | Cape Verde | Central African Republic | Chad | Chile | China | Colombia | Comoros | Congo | Congo (Democratic Rep.) | Costa Rica | Côte d'Ivoire | Croatia | Cuba | Curaçao | Cyprus | Czech Republic

**D**

Denmark | Djibouti | Dominica | Dominican Republic

**E**

Ecuador | Egypt | El Salvador | Equatorial Guinea | Eritrea | Estonia | Ethiopia

**F**

Fiji | Finland | Former Yugoslav Republic of Macedonia | France

**G**

Gabon | Gambia | Georgia | Germany | Ghana | Greece | Grenada | Guatemala | Guinea | Guinea Bissau | Guyana

**H**

Haiti | Honduras | Hungary

**I**

Iceland | India | Indonesia | Iran | Iraq | Ireland | Israel | Italy

**J**

Jamaica | Japan | Jordan

**K**

Kazakhstan | Kenya | Korea (Rep. of) |Kuwait | Kyrgyzstan

**L**

Laos | Latvia | Lebanon | Lesotho | Liberia | Libya | Liechtenstein | Lithuania | Luxembourg

**M**

Madagascar | Malawi | Malaysia | Maldives | Mali | Malta | Marshall Islands | Mauritania | Mauritius | Mexico | Moldova | Monaco | Mongolia | Montenegro | Morocco | Mozambique | Myanmar

**N**

Namibia | Nauru | Nepal | Netherlands | New Zealand | Nicaragua | Niger | Nigeria | Norway

**O**

Oman

**P**

Pakistan | Panama | Papua New Guinea | Paraguay | Peru | Philippines | Poland | Portugal

**Q**

Qatar

**R**

Romania | Russia | Rwanda

**S**

Samoa | San Marino | Sao Tome & Principe | Saudi Arabia | Senegal | Serbia | Seychelles | Sierra Leone | Singapore | Sint Maarten | Slovakia | Slovenia | Somalia | South Africa | South Sudan (Rep. of) | Spain | Sri Lanka | St Kitts & Nevis | St Lucia | St Vincent & Grenadines | Sudan | Suriname | Swaziland | Sweden | Switzerland | Syria

**T**

Tajikistan | Tanzania | Thailand | Timor Leste | Togo | Tonga | Trinidad & Tobago | Tunisia | Turkey | Turkmenistan

**U**

Uganda | Ukraine | United Arab Emirates | United Kingdom | United States | Uruguay | Uzbekistan

\* \* \*

**V**

Vatican City State | Venezuela | Vietnam

**Y**

Yemen

**Z**

Zambia | Zimbabwe

## 14. Bibliography of Additional Sources

- About Object ID, available at http://www.object-id.com/about.html (last visited Apr. 19, 2001).

- Malcolm Anderson et al., Policing the European Union 52 (1995).

- Art and Architecture Thesaurus Browser (Getty Research), available at http://www.getty.edu/research/tools/vocabulary/aat/index.html (last visited Apr. 18, 2001).

- Art and Architecture Thesaurus Browser (Getty Research), available at http://www.getty.edu/research/tools/vocabulary/ulan/index.html (last visited Apr. 19, 2001).

- Art and Architecture Thesaurus Browser (Getty Research), available at http://www.getty.edu/research/tools/vocabulary/tgn/index.html (last visited Apr. 19, 2001).

- Avery Index to Architectural Periodicals (Avery Index to Architectural Periodicals CD-ROM, Cumulative ed., 1930–2001).

- Bibliography of the History of Art (Bibliography of the History of Art CD-ROM, 1973–2001).

- Monica den Boer & Neil Walker, European Policing After 1992, 31 J. COMMON MKT. STUD., at 4–5.

- Robert Cailliau, A Short History of the Web, available at http://www.inria.fr/Actualites/Cailliau-fra.html (last visited Apr. 19, 2001).

- John Conklin, Art Crime 280 (1994).

- Council for the Prevention of Art Theft: Object ID Finds a New Home at CoPAT, available at http://www.copat.co.uk/news1.html (last visited Apr. 18, 2001).

- Executive Order 12425 of 16 June 1983.

- Michael Fooner, Interpol: Issues in World Crime and International Criminal Justice 48 (New York: Plenum Press 1989).

- The Getty Provenance Index (Getty Provenance Index CD-ROM, Cumulative ed., 1999).

- Sabine Gimbrere, Illicit Traffic in Cultural Property and National and International Law, in Illicit Traffic in Cultural Property: Museums Against Pillage 53, 54 (Harrie Leyten ed., 1995).

- Jeanette Greenfield, The Return of Cultural Treasurers 216 (1989).

- ICOM Website, What is ICOM, at http://icom.museum/organization.html (last updated Jan. 27, 2005).

- ICOM Website, ICOM News Thematic Files, at http://icom.museum/thematic.html (last updated Aug. 5, 2004).

- International Foundation for Art Research (IFAR), available at http://www.ifar.org/ (last visited Apr. 19, 2001).

- 11 September Task Force at Interpol Headquarters (Sept. 14, 2001), at http://www.interpol.int/Public/ICPO/PressReleases/PR2001/PR200119.asp (last visited Jan. 27, 2005).

- Interpol, Constitution and General Regulations (St.-Cloud, France, 1983).

- Interpol, Interpol—An Overview (2005), at http://www.interpol.int/Public/Icpo/FactSheets/FSgi01.asp (last modified April 2005).

- Introduction to Interpol, at http://www.interpol.com/Public/Icpo/introduction.asp (last visited Jan. 25, 2005).

- R.B. Jensen, The International Anti-Anarchist Conference of 1889 and the Origins of Interpol, 16 J. CONTEMP. HIST. 323 (1981).

- Michael Kelly, Conflicting Trends in the Flourishing International Trade of Art and Antiquities: Restitutio in Integrum and Possessio animo Ferundi/Lucrandi, Dick. J. Int'l L. 31, 44 (1995).

- Harrie Leyten, Illicit Traffic in Collections of Western Museums of Ethnography, in Illicit Traffic in Cultural Property: Museums Against Pillage 14, 18 (Harrie Leyten ed., 1995) (quoting the 1970 UNESCO Convention).

- National Museum Directors Conference: Spoliation of works of art during the Holocaust and World War, available at http://www.nationalmuseums.org.uk/spoliation/spoliation. (last visited Apr. 19, 2001).

- C. Noonan & J. Raskin, Intellectual Property Crimes, 38(3) Am. Crim. L. Rev. 971, 1016 (2001).

- Elizabeth des Portes, The Fight Against Illicit Traffic in Cultural Property: a Priority for Museum Professionals, in Illicit Traffic in Cultural Property: Museums Against Pillage 34, 35 (Harrie Leyten ed., 1995).

- Howard N. Spiegler & Lawrence M. Kaye, American Litigation to Recover Cultural Property: Obstacles, Options, and a Proposal, in Trade in Illicit Antiquities: The Destruction of the World's Archeological Heritage 121, 125 (Neil Brodie, Jennifer Doole & Colin Renfrew eds., 2001).

- UNESCO, 30th Anniversary of UNESCO Convention on the Means of Prohibiting and Preventing the Illicit Import, Export and Transfer of Ownership of Cultural Property, at http://www.unesco.org/bpi/eng/unescopress/2000/00–116e.shtml (last visited February 4, 2005).

- UNESCO, Launch of Code of Ethics for Art Dealers at Anniversary Celebration of Convention on Ending Illicit Trade in Cultural Property (Nov. 16, 2000), at http//:www.unesco.org/bpi/eng/unescopress/ 2000/00–119e.shtml (last visited Jan. 25, 2005).

- UNESCO, Prevention of the Illicit Import, Export and Transfer of Ownership of Cultural Property, at http://www.unesco.org/culture/legalprotection/theft/html eng/indexen.shtml (last visited Jan. 21, 2005).

- UNESCO, World Heritage Committee, at http://whc.unesco.org/committ.htm (last visited February 22, 2005).

- UNESCO Resolution E/RES/1579(L), Special Arrangement between the International Criminal Police Organization and the Economic and Social Council, 20 May 1971.

- UNIDROIT, Status Report: Unidroit Convention on Stolen or Illegally Exported Cultural Objects (June 6, 1995, updated 2004), at http://www.unidroit.org/english/implement/i–95.htm (last visited Jan. 23, 2005).

- U.S. Federal Register (Washington, D.C.) 48, no. 119 (20 June 1983), 28069.

- World Heritage Website, States Parties, at http://whc.unesco.org/pg.cfm?cid=246 (last visited February 22, 2005).

# Chapter XIX

# U.N. Conference to Define Terrorism

## Introduction

One of the ways the United Nations promotes the creation of international law is by convening diplomatic conferences to adopt international conventions, usually based on drafts developed by U.N. bodies. Despite the best of intentions, the final product of such multinational negotiations is often an instrument riddled with exceptions and ambiguities and lacking in effective enforcement. To help the reader understand the challenges inherent in the multinational negotiating process, this chapter examines the current proposal for a U.N. conference to define terrorism and differentiate it from the legitimate struggle for national liberation.

## Objectives

- To begin to understand the need for an internationally accepted definition of terrorism.
- To understand why the international community cannot agree on a definition of terrorism.
- To investigate possible suggestions on developing a cohesive definition of terrorism.
- To understand the evolution of the United States' own definition of terrorism in relation to members of al Qaeda and the Taliban.
- To understand the recent developments in jurisprudence related to terrorism.

## Simulation

1.  Come to class prepared to participate in a simulated U.N. Conference to define terrorism and distinguish it from legitimate action pursuant to self-determination.

    - Members of Group A will represent the United States, Canada, or Germany (countries vulnerable to terrorist acts abroad).
    - Members of Group B will represent Israel, Iraq, Russia, or Peru (countries with active insurgent groups in their territory).

873

- Members of Group C will represent Syria, Iran, or North Korea (countries that have been accused of participating in state-sponsored terrorism).

2. You should come to the session ready to propose language for a treaty containing an international definition of terrorism that would be acceptable to your country given its unique interests.

# Materials

1. Paust, Bassiouni, Williams, Scharf, Gurule, and Zagaris, INTERNATIONAL CRIMINAL LAW: CASES AND MATERIALS (1996), pp. 1175–90.

2. Nicholas Rostow, *Before and After: The Changed U.N. Response to Terrorism Since September 11th*, 35 CORNELL INT'L L.J. 475.

3. Susan Tiefenbrun, *A Semiotic Approach to a Legal Definition of Terrorism*, 9 ILSA J. INT'L. & COMP. L. 357 (2003).

4. Jennifer Trahan, *Terrorism Conventions: Existing Gaps and Different Approaches*, 8 NEW ENG. INT'L & COMP. L. ANN. 215 (2002).

5. Michael P. Scharf, *Defining Terrorism as the Peacetime Equivalent of War Crimes: Problems and Prospects*, 37 CASE W. RES. J. INT'L L. 359 (2005).

6. William J. Haynes, Enemy Combatants, Council on Foreign Relations, Dec. 12, 2002, at http://www.cfr.org/publication/5312/enemy_combatants.html.

7. Combatant Status Review Tribunals: Factsheet, United States Department of Defense, at http://www.defenselink.mil/news/Jul2004/d20040707factsheet.pdf (July 7, 2004).

8. Kathleen T. Rhem, DoD to Review Status of All Guantanamo Detainees, American Forces Press Service, July 8, 2004, at http://www.defenselink.mil/transcripts/2004/tr20040707-0981.html.

9. *Interlocutory Decision on the Applicable Law: Terrorism, Conspiracy, Homicide, Perpetration, Cumulative Charging*, STL-11-01/1, Special Tribunal for Lebanon, 16 February 2011, available at http://www.unhcr.org/refworld/docid/4d6280162.html.

10. Michael P. Scharf, INTRODUCTORY NOTE TO THE DECISION OF THE APPEALS CHAMBER OF THE SPECIAL TRIBUNAL FOR LEBANON ON THE DEFINITION OF TERRORISM, 50 ILM 509 (2011).

11. Bibliography of Additional Sources

---

## 1. Paust, Bassiouni, Williams, Scharf, Gurule, and Zagaris, International Criminal Law: Cases and Materials
### 1996

Terrorism
The Problem of Definition
Introductory Problem

In sweeping language in 1985, the United Nations General Assembly "unequivocally" condemned, "as criminal, all acts, methods and practices of terrorism wherever and by whomever committed". The Security Council also "resolutely" condemned "'all acts of terrorism'... in all its forms, wherever and by whomever committed," while endorsing a similar statement of the Secretary-General that same year. Nonetheless, none of the resolutions actually defined that which is so resolutely condemned.

For years, the international community has tried unsuccessfully to arrive at a common definition of terrorism. Proposals have repeatedly been made to convene an international conference to draft a convention defining terrorism. If you were representing the United States or Canada at such a conference, what definition of terrorism would you propose? If you were representing Israel, Libya, Syria, Cuba, or China, in what ways would your proposed definition differ, and why? What are likely to be the major sticking points in arriving at a widely agreeable definition of terrorism?

**Patterns of Global Terrorism: 1988**
**(U.S. Dep't of State, March 1989), pp. iii–v**
**Introduction**

Over the past 20 years terrorism has been a major issue on the international agenda. Television has brought terrorist atrocities live and in color into our living rooms. Through their actions, terrorists have forced our attention to them. Although we may look at terrorism as a uniquely contemporary phenomenon, terrorism has been with us for centuries.

The group whose name gave us our word for assassin arose in Persia about 900 years ago and later flourished in Syria. The assassins recognized that a tiny group of men prepared to die could paralyze a larger foe, and that fear of such attacks could give them power beyond their size.

By the late nineteenth century, the telegraph, newspapers, and rising literacy led Russian anarchists to recognize the shock value of violence. They referred to their terrorist attacks as "propaganda by deed." They knew that the audience for their acts was wider than the immediate victims.

Given the persistence of terrorism over centuries, it is unreasonable to expect we can eliminate it completely. But our government can, and must, take vigorous action to limit terrorism.

**U.S. Counterterrorism Policy**

The U.S. Government has developed a comprehensive strategy to respond to the problem of international terrorism. The first element of our counterterrorism policy is that we do not make concessions of any kind to terrorists. We do not pay ransom, release convicted terrorists from prison, or change our policies to accommodate terrorist demands — such actions would only lead to more terrorism. And we vigorously encourage other countries to be firm with terrorists, for a solid international front is essential to overall success.

The second element of our strategy is to make state sponsors of terrorism pay a price for their actions. This policy was most graphically demonstrated by the April 1986 bombing raids on terrorist support facilities in Libya. But there are also political, diplomatic and economic actions, public diplomacy and sanctions that can be employed — that is, peaceful measures that can be crafted to discourage states from persisting in their support of terrorism.

Third, the U.S. Government has developed a program of action based on practical measures. It is designed to bring terrorists to justice, to disrupt their operations, and to destroy their networks. The program includes aggressive measures, working with our friends and allies, to identify, track, apprehend, prosecute, and punish terrorists by using the rule of law. It also includes measures designed to protect U.S. citizens abroad by strengthening security and research toward developing equipment to prevent terrorist incidents.[1]

* * *

This strategy has made possible a number of successes. Individually they are modest, but collectively they do suggest that we are gaining ground. The margins between success and failure are thin; they depend greatly on the diligence and persistence of the individuals here and in friendly governments charged with responsibility for intelligence collection, law enforcement, and diplomatic efforts directed against terrorism.

* * *

## Definitions

No one definition of terrorism has gained universal acceptance. For the purposes of this report, however, we have chosen the definition commonly used by the U.S. Government for the past 20 years, which also is widely accepted and one which we have used in previous reports.

Accordingly, "terrorism" is premeditated, politically motivated violence perpetrated against noncombatant targets by subnational groups or clandestine state agents, usually intended to influence an audience. "International terrorism" is terrorism involving the citizens or territory of more than one country.

### Notes and Questions

1. Use of intent and political purpose elements in defining terrorism now seems common (i.e., that the actions must be intentional and engaged in for a political purpose). Indeed, "terrorism" should be viewed as a strategy or tactic—thus, one intentionally engaged in for certain political purposes. Should the threat of violence against persons also be covered—e.g., a bombing of a building coupled with an intentional threat of future violence against persons?

2. Is the word "violence," or even the phrase "politically motivated violence," too broad? To be realistic and descriptive, should a definition of "terrorism" involve a terror outcome? Would such an element involve intense fear or anxiety in the primary target? See, e.g., Paust, An Introduction to and Commentary on Terrorism and the Law, 19 CONN. L. REV. 697, 703–05 (1987). Also recall the elements contained in Article 51(2) of Protocol I to the Geneva Conventions (in Chapter Nine) ("Acts or threats of violence the primary purpose of which is to spread terror among the civilian population....").

3. "Terror" has been defined as "The state of being terrified or greatly frightened; intense fear, fright or dread." 11 THE COMPACT EDITION OF THE OXFORD ENGLISH DICTIONARY 3268 (1971). Why is a dictionary definition relevant to the interpretation of international agreements or customary international norms? See, e.g., Vienna Convention on the Law of Treaties, art. 31(1) ("the ordinary meaning to be given to the terms"); Chapter One, Sections 1 and 2.

4. Note that the U.S. definition above excludes strategies or tactics directed against combatant targets. Under Geneva law, terroristic targetings of noncombatants to which the Conventions or Protocols apply are prohibited. E.g., 1949 Geneva Civilian Conven-

---

1. The final element of US counterterrorism policy is the Department of Homeland Security. This Department is a combined agency with the goal of fighting terror by using the resources of the FBI, CIA and others. Soon after September 11, 2001, President Bush instituted this department and signed into law the PATRIOT Act for the purpose of fighting terror.

tion, art. 33 ("all measures of ... terrorism"); Protocol 1, art. Sl (acts or threats of vio-lence "the primary purpose of which is to spread terror among the civilian population'); Protocol 11, art. 4 (2) ("acts of terrorism" against noncombatants and others "who do not take a direct part ... in hostilities"). Terror is not unusual and it is even foreseeable on the battlefield or near and around hostilities. Is there and should there be an exclu-sion from what is ordered impermissible terrorism of terroristic tactics directed against combatants and lawful military targets during an armed conflict? See J. Paust, An Intro-duction, *supra*, at 705–10; Terrorism and the International Law of War, 64 MIL. L. REV. 1, 27–31 (1974).

* * *

7. The first international attempt to define terrorism was undertaken by the League of Nations, which in 1937 drafted a Convention for the Prevention and Punishment of Terrorism. The League of Nations Convention defined terrorism as "criminal acts directed against a State and intended or calculated to create a state of terror in the minds of par-ticular persons, or a group of persons or the general public." League of Nations Conven-tion, Art. 1(2), League of Nations Doc. C.547 M.384 1937 V (1937). The League of Nations Convention never entered into force as only one nation, India, ratified it before the out-break of World War 11 and the demise of the League of Nations. See Geoffrey Levitt, Is "Terrorism" Worth Defining?, 13 Ohio N.U.L. REV. 97, 98 n.3 (1986). What acts would the League of Nations Convention cover? Is the Convention's definition too broad, or too narrow? Does the word "criminal" beg an important question?

8. For some, the major problem in defining terrorism has been distinguishing "ter-rorists' from "freedom fighters" or "revolutionaries." During the 1980s, the U.S. Govern-ment labeled the rebels in El Salvador "agents of subversion," while referring to the Afghan guerrillas as "resisters" and the Contras in Nicaragua as "freedom fighters" who in Presi-dent Reagan's words were "the moral equivalent of the Founding Fathers." Newsweek, January 6, 1986, at 39. Do these labels reflect a double standard or are the distinctions jus-tified? According to one author:

To make the struggle with terrorism more successful, we should at least attempt to distinguish between "terrorists" and "revolutionaries." Although there is no unanimity among writers on international law concerning the right to fight against the constituted government, one argument should be spelled out more clearly. The very essence of democ-racy provides for the power of the majority, the protection of the rights of the minority, and legally recognized, nonviolent methods for the exchange of ruling teams. To recog-nize a right to the violent change of the legally constituted government as inherent in democracy would undermine the sense of democracy itself. As Victoria Toensing cor-rectly pointed out, "we must make our position unmistakable to terrorists: in a democ-ratic society dissidents cannot use bullets when they have both freedom of expression and the ballot box."

Rett R. Ludwikoski, Political and Legal Instruments in Supporting and Combating Terrorism: Current Developments, 11 TERRORISM, 197, 206 (1988).

Do you agree with this distinction? Does it confuse two separate questions: the legit-imacy of an overall struggle or process and that of particular tactics utilized? Is, for ex-ample, a member of a revolutionary group in a country with a non-democratic regime who blows up a school bus full of children with the intent to terrorize others any less a "terrorist" than one who commits the same act with the same intent in a democracy? Fur-ther, is the perpetrator of such a tactic any less a terrorist if he/she happens to be an of-ficial in a dictatorial or democratic process? Do all democracies provide full protection with respect to the rights of minorities? Consider, for example, the United Kingdom's treatment of members of the IRA in Northern Ireland during the 1970s and 1980s and Israel's treatment of the Palestinians in the occupied territories. Would an objective focus on terrorism as a strategy or tactic help to avoid confusion between the legitimacy of a general struggle and that of a terroristic tactic? Are not even "freedom fighters" bound to refrain from war crimes, acts of genocide, and impermissible strategies of terrorism? Recall the 1919 list of war crimes in Chapter Two, Section 1.

9. In 1991, a U.S. Representative to the United Nations explained the United States Government's continuing objection to the convening of an international conference to define terrorism and distinguish it from the legitimate struggle for self-determination as follows:

The [U.N. Sixth] Committee has before it the suggestion that a conference be convened or a working group established to define terrorism and differentiate it from the struggle for self-determination. We agree with those delegations who have stated that such an exercise should not be undertaken unless it is supported by consensus. That there is no such consensus is clear from the debate so far.

It seems to us equally clear that there are compelling reasons why such a conference or working group is neither necessary nor useful. In the first place, abstract definitions are notoriously difficult to achieve and dangerous in what all but the most perfect of definitions excludes by chance. In the same place, the history of the effort to deal with the problem of terrorism under the League of Nations and in the United Nations indicates that the difficulty of an abstract definition is, as a practical matter, insurmountable. All that prior efforts at a general definition achieved was to distract attention from the concrete achievements which lay within our grasp. . . .

If then, a general definition is all but impossible and a distraction from concrete action, are there nevertheless reasons why it should be pursued? Does support for fundamental human rights including the right to self-determination require us to pursue a definition? Does the measure of disagreement as to whether the condemnation of terrorism includes State conduct and, if so to what extent, require us to pursue a definition or parameters of the concept? The United States answers both of these questions in the negative.

It is not necessary to define terrorism in order to safeguard basic human rights including the right to self-determination. It is a profound insult to the right of self-determination to suggest a dichotomy between condemning terrorism and affirming basic human rights including the right of all peoples to enjoy the rights enunciated in the Charter of the United Nations, and the Universal Declaration of Human Rights resolution of the General Assembly relevant to equal rights and self-determination. We speak as a nation which fought for its independence and as a nation which has aided others in their struggle to achieve self-determination. But that does not mean there are no limits to the permissible methods. No cause can justify the random violence of interference with civil aviation, attacks on diplomats, hostage-taking, the use of plastic explosives. The delegation of Romania told us earlier of the tragic kidnapping of one of its diplomats. Is there anyone who wondered whether the cause justified this flagrant violation of the Convention on the Protection of Diplomats and the Convention Against Hostage-Taking? Of course not. To the extent there was any awareness of the goal being sought, the cause was tarnished in all our minds. Whatever some of us may incline to contemplate in the abstract, when confronted with a specific case we are driven to reaffirm the blanket condemnation of such acts as unjustifiable. Considering how long the international community has accepted the notion that there are acts so heinous that States may not resort to them in the exercise of their right to self-defense no matter how dire their situation, it is not surprising that there are similar inhumane acts that groups and individuals may not engage in no matter how just their cause.

If then a definition is neither necessary nor desirable to preserve fundamental human rights, is it necessary to resolve the issue as to whether the term includes State conduct-so-called State terrorism? We answer this question in the negative because it is unnecessary to denominate State conduct as terrorism in order to establish its illegality. A solid body of law already exists. State conduct is governed by a variety of rules, the most salient of which, in relation to the uses of violence, is Article 2 paragraph 4 of the [U.N.] Charter [which prohibits the use of force against the territorial integrity or political independence of any State]. Bearing in mind the Charter, the Declaration of Principles of International Law Concerning Friendly Relations, and the Geneva Conventions of 1949, we cannot imagine any State conduct which can reasonable be called terrorism that is not a violation of the law already. State support of terrorist acts by individuals and groups is a clear violation of Article 2(4) of the Charter with all the legal consequences attendant thereon. Likewise, we do not believe it is necessary or desirable to apply the term to common crimes pursued for private gain since each of our societies has an adequate legal framework to deal with such conduct. The term terrorism is however of enormous utility when applied to acts of violence of a particularly heinous nature by individuals or groups that are more than common crimes for private gain but less than action by a State. There are some of the reasons we do not believe a definition is necessary or useful.

Statement of Michael P. Scharf, United States Adviser to the forty-sixth General Assembly, in the Sixth Committee, on Item 125, Terrorism, October 21, 1991, Press Release USUN 63-(91).

Do you agree? In light of this statement, can you think of any reasons why an international definition of terrorism would nonetheless be desirable? Are there core areas of agreed legal prohibition (e.g., human rights prohibitions and protections)? Cf. Question 14 *infra*. But if there are, can terrorism be met by more adequate implementation of core area prohibitions without defining terrorism as such? Yet, if others persist, shouldn't we arrive at an objective definition and stress the core prohibitions already extant in international law?

10. The International Law Commission (ILC), a group of 34 international legal experts elected by the U.N. General Assembly with a mandate to encourage "the progressive development of the international law and its codification," has drafted a Code of Crimes Against the Peace and Security of Mankind (Report of the International Law Commission, 43rd Sess., 29 April–19 July 1991, 46th Sess., Supp. (No. 10), U.N. Doc. A/46/10). The ILC's Draft Code contains the following provision on terrorism:

**Article 24: International Terrorism**

An individual who as an agent or representative of a State commits or orders the commission of any of the following acts:

- undertaking, organizing, assisting, financing, encouraging or tolerating acts against another State directed at persons or property and of such a nature as to create a state of terror in the minds of public figures, groups of persons or the general public shall, on conviction thereof, be sentenced to [ ].

How does this definition differ from those contained in U.S. legislation and in the League of Nations Convention for the Prevention and Punishment of Terrorism discussed above? Also recall Chapter Eight, Section 2, concerning norms of non-intervention. What criticisms would you expect to be raised with respect to the ILC's definition of terrorism? Would such a definition cover acts of economic coercion authorized by the Security Council designed to provide a nearly immediate and effective impact? Would it cover legitimate bombing by aircraft of legitimate military targets during war? Should the state of terror be an intended outcome? More generally, should intent and terror outcome be part of an adequate definition?

11. In its official comments on Article 24 of the ILC's draft Code of Crimes, Australia wrote:

Australia has difficulties with the drafting of this article. It notes in particular that the definition is not expressed to include an element of violence. Is therefore the offence intended to encompass non-physical acts of terror such as propaganda? Further, it is uncertain whether the agents or representatives need to be acting in their official capacity. The absence of intention or motive from the definition also needs explanation.

In its comments on the draft article, the United States wrote:

Article 24 purports to punish international terrorism, even though there is no generally accepted definition of "terrorism" and no adequate definition of terrorism is given by the Code. The Code attempts to define terrorism through the use of a tautology. The Code defines terrorism as the "undertaking, organizing, assisting, financing, encouraging or tolerating [by agents or representatives of a State of acts against another State directed at persons or property and of such a nature as to create a state of terror in the minds of public figures, groups of persons or the general public." This definition is patently defective because "terror" is not defined....

Another fundamental problem with article 24 of the Code is that it limits the crime of terrorism to acts committed by "agents or representatives of a State." In fact, many terrorist acts are committed by individuals acting in their private capacity. The United States cannot accept a definition of terrorism that excludes acts committed by persons who are either not acting as agents of a State, or whose affiliation with a State cannot be definitively proved in a court of law.

Switzerland provided the following comments:

It would appear that the elements constituting the crime of international terrorism might not, depending on circumstances, be clearly distinguished from those constituting intervention, defined as the act of intervening in the internal or external affairs of a State by fomenting subversive or terrorist activities. Does the act, when carried out by agents of a State, of financing or training armed bands for the purposes of sowing terror among the population and thus encouraging the fall of the Government of another State come under this provision?

International Law Commission, Thirteenth Report on the Draft Code of Crimes Against the Peace and Security of Mankind (Observations of Governments), 47 Sess., 2 May–21 July 1995, U.N. Doc. A/CN.4/466 (24 March 1995), at 28–30.

12. For some, it may be useful to analyze different definitions in view of the following:

1.   Does the definition limit terrorism to an intranational or international character?

2.   Does it matter whether victim's are innocents or persons directly involved in the situation sought to be affected by the act?

3.   Does it matter whether the instrumental target (persons or property) are protected by national or international law?

4. Does it matter whether the act is committed during or outside an armed conflict?

5. Does the definition allow for the distinction between legitimate and illegitimate types and degrees of force?

Boire, Terrorism Reconsidered As Punishment. Toward an Evaluation of the Acceptability of Terrorism as a Method of Societal Change or Maintenance, 20 Stanford J. Int'l L. 4S (1984).

13. For others, it should not be determinative whether instrumental or primary targets are "innocent" or the tactic is used in an armed conflict or any other social context, and the two questions of what is "terrorism" and whether any particular use of the tactic is "legitimate" should definitely be considered separately. See, e.g., Paust, An Introduction, *supra*, at 701–10, and references cited.

14. In the concurring opinion dismissing plaintiffs' tort actions against certain alleged terrorists responsible for an attack on a bus in Israel in *Tel-Oren v. Libyan Arab Republic*, 726 F.2d 79S (D.C. Cir. 1984), Judge Harry Edwards stated:

"While this nation unequivocally condemns all terrorist attacks, that sentiment is not universal. Indeed, the nations of the world are so divisively split on the legitimacy of such aggression as to make it impossible to pinpoint an area of harmony or consensus. Unlike the issue of individual responsibility, which much of the world has never even reached, terrorism has evoked strident reactions and sparked strong alliances among numerous nations. Given this division, I do not believe that under current law terrorist attacks [outside of those prohibited by international conventions] amount to law of nations violations."

See also id. at 807 (Bork, J., concurring) (otherwise misleadingly citing claims and viewpoints of Professor Paust in "Nonprotected" Persons or Things, in LEGAL ASPECTS OF INTERNATIONAL TERRORISM 341, 354–58 (Bork citing 355–561 (A. Evans & J. Murphy eds. 1978)). Did judge Edwards "throw the baby out with the bath water"? Can't one find a core area of accepted prohibition? See also RESTATEMENT SS 404, Comm. a, 702(c), (d), (e), (g); *Ireland v. United Kingdom*, 25 Eur. Ct. H.R. (Sen A), para. 149 (1978) (dictum: 'terrorist activities … of individuals or of groups … are in clear disregard of human rights."); Paust, The Link Between Human Rights and Terrorism and Its Implications for the Law of State Responsibility, 11 Hast. Int'l & Comp. L. Rev. 41 (1987); Paust, An Introduction, *supra*.

15. Professor Paust has suggested the following as a descriptive and objective definition: "'terrorism' involves the intentional use of violence, or the threat of violence, by a precipitator (the accused) against an instrumental target in order to communicate to a primary target a threat of future violence, so as to coerce the primary target through intense fear or anxiety in connection with a demanded political outcome"; Paust, An Introduction, *supra*, at 701. Do you agree? If not, what would you change?

### The Multilateral Legal Framework

### Introductory Note

Historically, progress in countering terrorism through application of the rule of law was blocked by a seemingly inexorable international disagreement over whether violent acts committed in furtherance of national liberation struggles should be encompassed within the definition of terrorism. As an alternative to the debate over a general definition of terrorism, the international community has concluded over the last twenty years a series of individual conventions that identify specific acts which all Parties agree are inherently unacceptable. By agreeing that the offenses enumerated in these instruments are criminal regardless of motivation or context, this approach avoids the controversy over who is a "terrorist" and who is a "freedom fighter."

## A. U.N. Terrorism Resolutions

Reproduced below is the 1991 United Nations General Assembly resolution which "unequivocally condemns, as criminal and unjustifiable, all acts, methods and practices of terrorism wherever and by whoever committed." (A nearly identical resolution was adopted by the United Nations by consensus in 1989 and 1993). Rather than attempt to define terrorism, the resolution simply lists the Coexisting international conventions relating to various aspects of the problem of international terrorism." These international "anti-terrorist" conventions require States Parties to criminalize specified conduct, to either initiate prosecution of or to extradite the transgressors, and to cooperate with other States for effective implementation.

### U.N. G.A. Resolution 46/51, 9 Dec. 1991, U.N. Doc. A/46/654

The General Assembly ...

Recalling moreover the existing international conventions relating to various aspects of the problem of international terrorism, inter alia, the Convention on Offenses and Certain Other Acts Committed on Board Aircraft, signed at Tokyo on 14 September 1963, the Convention for the Suppression of Unlawful Seizure of Aircraft, signed at The Hague on 16 December 1970, the Convention for the Suppression of Unlawful Acts against the Safety of Civil Aviation, concluded at Montreal on 23 September 1971, the Convention on the Prevention and Punishment of Crimes against Internationally Protected Persons, including Diplomatic Agents, adopted in new York on 14 December 1973, the International Convention against the Taking of Hostages, adopted in New York on 17 December 1979, the Convention on the Physical Protection of Nuclear Material, adopted at Vienna on 3 March 1980, the Protocol for the Suppression of Unlawful Acts of Violence at Airports Serving International Civil Aviation, supplementary to the Convention for the Suppression of Unlawful Acts against the Safety of Civil Aviation, signed at Montreal on 24 February 1988, the Convention for the Suppression of Unlawful Acts against the Safety of Maritime Navigation, done at Rome on 10 March 1988, the Protocol for the Suppression of Unlawful Acts against the Safety of Fixed Platforms located on the Continental Shelf, done at Rome on 10 March 1988, and the Convention on the Marking of Plastic Explosives for the Purpose of Detection, done at Montreal on 1 March 1991,

Convinced that a policy of firmness and effective measures should be taken in accordance with international law in order that all acts, methods and practices of international terrorism may be brought to an end,

Taking note of Security Council resolution 638 (1989) of 31 July 1989 on the taking of hostages,

Deeply disturbed by the world-wide persistence of acts of international terrorism in all its forms, including those in which States are directly or indirectly involved, which endanger or take innocent lives, have a deleterious effect on international relations and may jeopardize the territorial integrity and security of States,

Calling attention to the growing connection between terrorist groups and drug traffickers,

Convinced of the importance of the observance by States of their obligations under the relevant international conventions to ensure that appropriate law enforcement measures are taken in connection with the offenses addressed in those conventions,

Convinced also of the importance of expanding and improving international cooperation among States, on a bilateral, regional and multilateral basis, which will contribute to the elimination of acts of international terrorism and their underlying causes and to the prevention and elimination of this criminal scourge,

Convinced further that international cooperation in combating and preventing terrorism will contribute to the strengthening of confidence among States, reduce tensions and create a better climate among them,

Mindful of the need to enhance the role of the United Nations and the relevant specialized agencies in combating international terrorism,

Mindful also of the necessity of maintaining and protecting the basic rights of, and guarantees for, the individual in accordance with the relevant international human rights instruments and generally accepted international standards,

Reaffirming the principle of self-determination of peoples as enshrined in the Charter of the United Nations,

Reaffirming also the inalienable right to self-determination and independence of all peoples under colonial and racist regimes and other forms of alien domination and foreign occupation, and upholding the legitimacy of their struggle, in particular the struggle of national liberation movements, in accordance with the purposes and principles of the Charter and the Declaration on Principles of International Law concerning Friendly Relations and Cooperation among States in accordance with the charter of the United Nations,

Recognizing that the effectiveness of the struggle against terrorism could be enhanced by the establishment of a generally agreed definition of international terrorism,

Taking note of the report of the Secretary-General,

1. Once again unequivocally condemns, as criminal and unjustifiable, all acts, methods and practices of terrorism wherever and by whomever committed, including those which jeopardize the friendly relations among States and their security;

2. Deeply deplores the loss of human lives which results from such acts of terrorism, as well as the pernicious impact of these acts on relations of cooperation among States;

3. Calls upon all States to fulfil their obligations under international law to refrain from organizing, instigating, assisting or participating in terrorist acts in other States, or acquiescing in or encouraging activities within their territory directed towards the commission of such acts;

4. Urges all States to fulfil their obligations under international law and take effective and resolute measures for the speedy and final elimination of international terrorism and to that end, in particular:

    (a) To prevent the preparation and obligations in their respective territories, for commission within or outside their territories, of terrorist and subversive acts directed against other States and their citizens;

    (b) To ensure the apprehension and prosecution or extradition or perpetrators of terrorist acts;

    (c) To endeavor to conclude special agreements to that effect on a bilateral, regional and multilateral basis;

    (d) To cooperate with one another in exchanging relevant information concerning the prevention and combating of terrorism;

    (e) to take promptly all steps necessary to implement the existing international conventions on this subject to which they are parties, including the harmonization of their domestic legislation with those conventions;

5. Appeals to all States that have not yet done so to consider becoming party to the international conventions relating to various aspects of international terrorism referred to in the preamble to the present resolution;

6. Urges all States, unilaterally and in cooperation with other States, as well as relevant United Nations organs, to contribute to the progressive elimination of the causes underlying international terrorism and to pay special attention to all situations, including colonialism, racism and situations involving mass and flagrant violations of human rights and fundamental freedoms and those involving alien domination and foreign occupation, that may give rise to international terrorism and may endanger international peace and security;

7. Firmly calls for the immediate and safe release of all hostages and abducted persons, wherever and by whomever they are being held;

8. Calls upon all States to use their political influence in accordance with the Charter of the United Nations and the principles of international law to secure the safe release of all hostages and abducted persons and to prevent the commission of acts of hostage-taking and abduction;

9. Expresses concern at the growing and dangerous links between terrorist groups, drug traffickers and their paramilitary gangs, which have resorted to all types of violence, thus endangering the constitutional order of States and violating basic human rights;

10. Welcomes the efforts undertaken by the International Civil Aviation Organization aimed at promoting universal acceptance of, and strict compliance with, international air security conventions, and welcomes the recent adoption of the Convention on the Marking of Plastic Explosives for the Purpose of Detection;

11. Requests the other relevant specialized agencies and intergovernmental organizations, in particular the International Maritime Organization, the Universal Postal Union, the World Tourism Organization, the International Atomic Energy Agency and the United Nations Educational, Scientific and Cultural Organization, within their respective spheres of competence, to consider what further measures can usefully be taken to combat and eliminate terrorism;

12. Requests the Secretary-General to continue seeking the views of Member States on international terrorism in all its aspects and on ways and means of combating it, including the convening at an appropriate time, under the auspices of the United Nations, of an international conference to deal with international terrorism in the light of the proposal referred to in the penultimate preambular paragraph of General Assembly resolution 44/29 [calling for an international conference to define terrorism]; ...

\* \* \*

15. Considers that nothing in the present resolution could in any way prejudice the right to self-determination, freedom and independence, as derived from the Charter of the United Nations, of peoples forcibly deprived of that right referred to in the Declaration of Principles of International Law concerning Friendly Relations and Cooperation among States in accordance with the Charter of the United Nations, particularly peoples under colonial and racist regimes or other forms of alien domination, or the right of these peoples to struggle legitimately to this end and to seek and receive support in accordance with the principles of the Charter, the above-mentioned Declaration and the relevant General Assembly resolutions, including the present resolution.

*Notes and Questions*

1. The General Assembly's resolution does not define the term "terrorism." It does, however, refer to human rights and it refers to the acts covered by the several international conventions and protocols listed in the preamble. Those conventions prohibit the following: aircraft hijacking, aircraft sabotage, attacks against ships and fixed platforms in the ocean, attacks at airports, violence against officials and diplomats, hostage-taking, theft of nuclear material, and use of unmarked plastic explosives. Would resort to other forms of terror-violence not covered by the conventions such as placing a bomb in a market place or attacking a school bus with a machine gun for political purposes and with an intent to produce a terror outcome fit within the resolution's unequivocal condemnation of terrorism?

2. Paragraph 3 of the resolution states that it is a violation of international law for states to organize, instigate, assist or participate in terrorist acts in other States, or acquiesce in or encourage activities within their territory directed towards the commission of such acts. Would the mere act of providing financial assistance to a terrorist organization be a violation of international law? What about the provision of other forms of logistical support such as passports and weapons? Would permitting a terrorist organization to maintain a headquarters or training facility in a State's territory be a violation of international law? Would refusing to extradite a person charged with acts of terrorism on the basis of the political offense exception to extradition (discussed in Chapter Five, Section 1) be a violation of international law? In answering these questions, consider the International Court of justice's opinion in the Case of Military and Paramilitary Activities in and Against Nicaragua (*Nicaragua v. United States of America*) in Chapter Eight, Section 2. In that case, the ICJ held that, by arming, training, and directing the Contras, the United States violated the customary international law principle of the non use of force by "organizing or encouraging the organization of irregular forces or armed bands ... for incursion into the territory of another State." Id. at para. 22 8. The Court stressed, however, that neither Nicaragua's provision of arms to the opposition in El Salvador nor the United States' provision of funds to the Contras in Nicaragua, by themselves, amounted to a prohibited use of force. Id. at paras. 228, 230. But see Chapter Eight, Sections 1 and 2, concerning impermissible intervention and violations of neutrality laws; JOHN F. MURPHY, PUNISHING INTERNATIONAL TERRORISTS: THE LEGAL FRAMEWORK FOR POLICY INITIATIVES 59 (1985), quoting I.L.C. resolution on International Terrorism: " 'No situation could be envisaged in which state support for persons or groups engaged or preparing to engage in the acts ... of international terrorism would not violate basic rules of international law.' "

3. In 1986, the United States bombed targets in Tripoli, the capital of Libya, partly in response to a series of terrorist attacks in Europe culminating in the bombing of a Berlin disco in which two Americans were killed and over 100 people injured. The United States justified its action on the basis of evidence that the persons responsible for the terrorist attacks had traveled on Libyan passports and that Libya was likely to continue to support acts of terrorism against the United States unless something was done. At the time, the President of the United States, Ronald Reagan, stated: "By providing material support to terrorists groups which attack U.S. citizens, Libya has engaged in armed aggression against the United States under established principles of international law, just as if it had used its own armed forces." Secretary of State George Shultz elaborated:

"A nation attacked by terrorists is permitted to use force to prevent or preempt future attacks, to seize terrorists, or to rescue its citizens when no other means is available. The law requires that such actions be necessary and proportionate. But this nation has consistently affirmed the rights of states to use force in exercise of their right of individual or collective self-defense. The U.N. Charter is not a suicide pact."

Abraham D. Sofaer, International Law and the Use of Force, THE NATIONAL INTEREST 53, 57 (Fall 1988). See also Sofaer, Terrorism, the Law, and National Defense, 126 MIL. L. REV. 89 (1989). Do you agree? Was the 1986 bombing in Tripoli consistent with the International Court of justice's holding in the Nicaragua Case? More generally, is "pre-emptive" self-defense permissible and was the armed conflict, however short, nonetheless permissible under international law? Compare Paust, Responding Lawfully to International Terrorism: The Use of Force Abroad, 8 Whittier L. Rev. 711 (1986) with Boyle, Preserving the Rule of Law in the War Against Terrorism, id.

4. Does the last paragraph of the U.N. Terrorism Resolution preserve the right of peoples struggling against alien or colonial domination to resort to acts of "terrorism"? Does the phrase "the right of these peoples to struggle legitimately to this end" mean that resort to terrorism can never be justified since "terrorism" is not a legitimate means? Can some terrorist acts be legitimate and distinguished from acts that are unacceptable under any circumstances? With respect to terroristic tactics utilized against combat-Ants and other lawful military targets during an armed conflict, see Paust, An Introduction, *supra*, at 705–10, and references cited. Recall the 1919 list of war crimes, in Chapter Two, Section 1.

5. In 1994, the General Assembly adopted the Declaration on Measures to Eliminate International Terrorism, contained in the annex to resolution 49/60. The Declaration states, inter alia, that "criminal acts intended or calculated to provoke a state of terror in the general public, a group of persons or particular persons for political purposes are in any circumstances unjustifiable, whatever the considerations of political, philosophical, ideological, racial, ethnic, religious or any other nature that may be invoked to justify them." Does this constitute an internationally agreed definition of terrorism? What acts would fall within this definition? What acts would the definition exclude? Would the fact that this definition only covers "criminal acts" exempt violence committed as part of a struggle for national liberation or pursuant to concerted activities designed to achieve self-determination?

## *Authors' Note*

The international community has been unable to come to a general consensus on the appropriate definition of terrorism. There are a number of stumbling blocks that have precluded a cohesive approach to the issue, including the difficulty in distinguishing between a terrorist and a freedom fighter. The following material provides a glimpse into the international community's shift in attention on terrorism after the events of September 11th. Material 2 addresses a number of the impediments that plague both the General Assembly and Security Council's plan to combat terrorism. Material 3 provides an overview of the myriad of definitions of terrorism that exist throughout the world community and the implications of such differences. Finally, Material 4 details the role of conventions in addressing and combating terrorism. This article discusses the discrepancies and gaps that exist between the conventions as they exist now.

## 2. Nicholas Rostow, Before and After: The Changed U.N. Response to Terrorism Since September 11th

*Cornell International Law Journal*, 2002
[footnotes omitted by editors]

\* \* \*

### II. Before and After September 11, 2001

There is no doubt that the attacks against the United States on September 11, 2001, have changed the context of U.N. activities. Before September 11, the U.N. treated the general subject of terrorism as a General Assembly issue. Specifically, the matter mainly fell within the jurisdiction of the Sixth (Legal) Committee of the General Assembly. Through the Sixth Committee and other U.N. bodies, the U.N. has played a part in elaborating conventions addressing specific crimes committed by terrorists, although most of the Conventions omit the word "terrorism." The conventions address the handling of nuclear material, plastic explosives, aviation, maritime navigation, protected persons, and hostage-taking. The goal was to create a basis for universal jurisdiction over, and condemnation and criminalization of, the types of crimes that terrorists commit, but not terrorism per se. Although non-lawyers decided what the conventions would or would not cover, lawyers negotiated the texts.

At the same time as negotiators made progress on acceptable texts in these areas, the Sixth Committee was unable to agree on a definition of terrorism. Since the May 1972 terrorist killings of 28 airline passengers in Israel and of 11 Israeli athletes at the Munich Olympic Games in September 1972, the General Assembly has debated how to define terrorism and has been unable to reach a consensus. Some do not want to label people terrorists when they use tactics, which, in other contexts would make them terrorists. Advocates of this perspective would exempt from the definition of terrorism all activities done in resistance to "foreign occupation" and activities by those "engaged in the struggle for national liberation." Despite the efforts of then Secretary-General Waldheim in the wake of the killings at the Munich Olympics and subsequent attempts by others after September 11, 2001, it has proved so far impossible to achieve a comprehensive definition of terrorism. The effort to define terrorism has foundered because some want to be able to use terrorism to advance their political or social agendae. To this end, in the U.N. arena, those that would use terrorism insist on consideration of the causes of terrorism and other distracting and difficult matters that derogate from treating terrorism as a means to an end. As a result, there is no U.N.-originated convention on the subject (yet).

After the Sixth Committee failed, the General Assembly decided to change the forum (however slightly, given the participation). In 1996, the General Assembly established an ad hoc committee to elaborate an international convention for the suppression of terrorist bombings. The General Assembly subsequently charged that committee with elaborating new international conventions for the suppression of acts of nuclear terrorism and a comprehensive legal framework for dealing with international terrorism. The General Assembly has renewed the committee's mandate every year since then, and the committee has issued annual reports since 1997. Delegates have been able to agree on the criminality of certain activities without ever having agreed on a definition of terrorism.

After September 11, 2001, the Security Council weighed in on terrorism—"took charge" probably is not too strong a term—and became the locus of action. That the larger world could not agree on a definition of terrorism or condemnation of terrorism in all circumstances became irrelevant; or, if not irrelevant, a symptom of political disagreement all could understand. As a first step, the Security Council adopted Resolution 1368. The Resolution unequivocally condemned the terrorist attacks of September 11, called on all states to "work together urgently to bring to justice the perpetrators, organizers and sponsors" of the attacks, and called on the international community to "redouble their efforts to prevent and suppress terrorist acts including by increased cooperation and full implementation of the relevant international anti-terrorist conventions and Security Council resolutions." The Resolution also reaffirmed the inherent right of self-defense in accordance with Article 51 of the U.N. Charter. Given the circumstances, this affirmation was significant: it implied that the attacks triggered the right even if, at the time of adoption, the U.N. Security Council knew almost nothing about who or what had launched them.

## A. Capacity-Building: The CTC

Resolution 1373 followed shortly after Security Council Resolution 1368. In the resolution, the Council decided to impose a number of binding obligations on States. They require that States prohibit both active and passive support for terrorists. As a result, not only are States to punish financial transactions on behalf of terrorists and freeze the asset of terrorists and their supporters, but also States must tighten their border controls, increase their vigilance against passport and identification forgery, deny safe haven to terrorists, and work toward enhancing international cooperation against terrorism. As compared to previous resolutions, Resolution 1373 is far-reaching. It imposes on all States legal obligations of the kind usually contained only in treaties developed through the normal treaty-making process. The Security Council was able to adopt such a resolution under the immediate pressure of the September 11 attacks. Effective implementation of this Resolution will increase capabilities to fight terrorism all over the world.

To help assure implementation, the Security Council applied a practice normally reserved for keeping the Security Council's hands on the details of sanctions and established a committee of the whole Security Council to monitor implementation. The new committee, known as the Counter-Terrorism Committee (CTC), operates by consensus, meaning that all Committee Member States have a veto. The Resolution calls on all States to report to the CTC on their implementation of the Resolution no later than 90 days from the date of adoption, and thereafter according to a CTC-mandated timetable. The mandate in this Resolution carries no expiration date or completion point.

The CTC Chair has often remarked that the U.N. Member State response shows the degree of shared understanding of the importance of the issue, and acceptance of, and support for, the Resolution and the CTC. The Chair's actions have contributed to this acceptance and support. The Chair regularly briefs the entire U.N. membership on the CTC's activities. He believes in maximum transparency as a good in itself and, in the case of the CTC, necessary to maintain its legitimacy within the U.N. community. He uses these occasions to stress the CTC's fidelity to Resolution 1373, often noting that document is the CTC's "Bible."

The Resolution calls on States to report the steps they are taking to implement the Resolution. These reports generally cover counter-terrorism measures in seven areas: legislation, financial asset controls, customs, immigration, extradition, law enforcement, and illegal arms trafficking. Almost all Members of the U.N. reported to the CTC in the first year. To expedite analysis of these reports, the CTC divided itself into three sub-committees. Each of the sub-committees works toward processing five reports a week. Experts in relevant subjects aid the sub-committees by, among other things, drafting the CTC response to the initial reports. The experts have proved invaluable and integral to the CTC process, assisting with the continuing need to fully probe countries' responses. For example, when a country asserts, "money laundering is illegal so no money laundering takes place," the experts reply, "we need to know how this law is implemented," or "how do you monitor to ensure that no money laundering takes place?" The experts' external, non-political role helps the CTC obtain real answers.

The sub-committees draft (and the full Committee approves) letters back to the reporting States, saying, "Thank you for the information you provided; we still need additional information on the following issues…" Thus, the response letters vary greatly by State, depending on the specificity of the first report. For example, one country submitted a single-spaced, 58-page report, with relevant appendices. The CTC response was able to discuss intricate details of the country's banking system. In contrast, some reports have been sketchy. In such cases, the CTC has responded with a tutorial on how to understand the obligations of Resolution 1373 and how to meet the needs of the CTC. This practice has prompted some criticism about whether the CTC treats some states unfairly by holding them to a different standard based on their level of development. However, disparities are an inevitable and a necessary aspect of the CTC's work. There is no point of completion when the committee will issue a certificate of compliance that a State has become "Terrorism-Proof." The CTC's task has been to ensure, to the extent possible given its resources, that each State is making its best efforts to eliminate opportunities for terrorists to establish themselves in its territory. The CTC's work with Member States through the review process has helped individual States learn how best to strengthen their counter-terrorism capabilities and has gone far in creating a more universal, "best practices" in the global fight against terrorism.

The open-ended dialogue between the CTC and the Member States has evolved and matured. The Committee has developed standardized questions. These are not published. But the responses are public, available on the internet. As a result, the CTC has created the basis for anyone independently to develop a matrix evaluating every State's assessment of its implementation of Resolution 1373. Such action ought to help the international community increase incentives for fulfilling 1373 obligations, thus strengthening the world's capacity to combat terrorists and terrorism.

Resolution 1373 does not include a definition of terrorism. As a result, every country is left to define terrorism for itself, and the Resolution can instead focus on raising the capacity and the capability to fight terrorism — leaving other U.N. bodies and multi-lateral groups to argue about what is and what is not terrorism. The CTC fulfills its mandate by trying to make countries honestly assess their own counter-terrorism policies and capacities. In the case of States that are unwilling to characterize as terrorist activities in pursuit of certain goals, the CTC is able to highlight the inconsistencies such an approach can engender. For example, the CTC can call attention to tensions arising from a State's different international obligations, particularly conflicts between obligations under U.N. conventions and provisions in regional conventions that address the same subject.

The Office of the U.N. High Commissioner for Human Rights has expressed concern that the war on terrorism not be exploited for political advantage by allowing governments wrongly to incarcerate political opponents. The Office has asked the CTC to monitor respect for human rights in connection with States' implementation of Resolution 1373. As the CTC Chair told the Security Council in public session in January and July 2002, the CTC is mindful of human rights in its work and values communication with the Office of the High Commissioner. But, the Chairman said, the CTC cannot and must not stray from its mandate in Resolution 1373. Therefore, the CTC does not view itself as a human rights monitoring body and leaves such work to others. In addition, as some representatives on the CTC have noted, Resolution 1373 is, in essence, a call to implement a regime of law. If Resolution 1373 is properly implemented, the rule of law will be strengthened. In turn, human rights, which depend on the rule of law for their consistent vindication, will be strengthened.

After one year in operation, the CTC's future direction and goals remain in a process of step-by-step clarification. The CTC could be enormously effective. Its influence extends from helping countries adopt laws regarding the abuse of charitable institutions and other devices to elude financial regulations, to encouraging enhanced border security training using multilateral fora, to assisting governmental organizations in the counter-terrorism area, among other things. Conceivably, the CTC could help the international community reach agreement on a constructive definition of terrorism. On the other hand, even States that strongly oppose terrorism express concern from time to time about the CTC's potential to scour deeply into a government's innermost activities.

In monitoring implementation, the CTC aims to improve worldwide counter-terrorism capabilities and to help match countries that need assistance in this area with assistance providers. Thus, it serves as a switchboard. Even countries with substantial counter-terrorism capacity need help, if only in the area of understanding their own vulnerabilities. Through the CTC process and interactions with regional and sub-regional groups, countries that have not thought of themselves as capable of providing counter-terrorism assistance are now looking at their capabilities in a new light. For example, some small countries have great expertise in regulating and monitoring financial transactions. Other countries need training in these fields. A match may be possible, fostered by the CTC. In addition, the dialogue between States and the CTC may allow the CTC to indicate areas in which the CTC believes a State needs assistance, even if the State does not view itself in that light. Further, the CTC believes that it can help regional and sub-regional organizations leverage scant assistance resources, in part because these organizations can help tailor such resources to the needs of their particular region.

As part of the process of building a database on worldwide, counter-terrorism assistance capabilities, in November 2001 the CTC invited all States with the capacity to do so to contribute to the compilation of a database of sources of advice and expertise in the areas of legislative and administrative practice. Using this information, the Committee created a web-based directory for assistance in the areas of activity covered by Resolution 1373: drafting counter-terrorism legislation, financial law and practice, extradition law and practice, police and law enforcement work, and (illegal) arms trafficking.

### B. Sanctions

The Security Council was ready to respond to the terrorist acts of September 11 because it had already decided that terrorism constitutes an appropriate subject for its consideration and action. The Council had already spent several years addressing issues related to terrorism in Taliban-ruled Afghanistan and, before that, in Libya after the bombing of Pan Am Flight 103 in December 1988. In August 1998, the Security Council condemned the attacks on U.N. personnel in the Taliban-held territories of Afghanistan. Later that year, the Council demanded that the Taliban stop providing sanctuary and training to international terrorists and halt the cultivation and production of, and trafficking in, illegal drugs. Then, in October 1999, under the Presidency of Russia, the Security Council acted in response to several bombings of apartment buildings in Moscow for which the Russian government blamed Chechen terrorists.

On October 15, 1999, the Security Council adopted Resolution 1267, imposing sanctions on Usama bin Laden and Taliban-controlled Afghanistan, and the Security Council created a Committee of the Whole Council to administer the resolution's implementation. This Resolution obligated all States to freeze Taliban assets and to deny permission for any Taliban-affiliated aircraft to depart or land from their territory. The Resolution directed the Committee to designate funds to be frozen and aircraft to be denied take-off or landing rights. Because these measures are decision of the Security Council under Chapter VII of the U.N. Charter, they are mandatory on all States. After the removal of the Taliban from power in Afghanistan and the apparent destruction of Al-Qaida's bases there, the Security Council on January 6, 2002, adopted Resolution 1390, removing the territorial basis for the sanctions on the Taliban — instead of sanctioning Afghanistan in order to change its policies, measures would now be directed against "Usama bin Laden, members of the Al-Qaida organization and the Taliban and other individuals, groups, undertakings and entities associated with them" wherever they happened to be.

The Security Council broke new ground in adopting such an approach. In tackling the realities of transnational terrorists who employ all means of transportation, communication, and finance, the Council has had growing pains. In particular, the Council has discovered that its mandatory sanctions regime can create administrative difficulties if the targeted individuals or entities claim to have been victim of mistaken identity. The Council has tried to be practical while avoiding judicial functions or otherwise usurping the legal obligations of governments with respect to persons suspected of terrorism.

### III. The Moral Imperative

The Security Council resolutions on terrorism adopted since September 11, 2001, frame the work of U.N. organs on terrorism. For most Member States they also provide a framework and guide for action. Even without consensus on the criminal wrongfulness of terrorism in all circumstances much can be accomplished in such areas as capacity-building, implementation of sanctions against terrorists, their accomplices and supporters, and international cooperation generally. Most successful anti-terrorist efforts have resulted from multi-lateral cooperation. In working on these goals step-by-step, U.N. institutions and the broader international community may help bring about a global consensus on a definition of terrorism. Direct progress to that end now remains stalled by those who find terrorism a convenient, powerful, and available weapon. These people and entities do not accept that the activities they advocate are terrorist.

The U.N. Secretary-General, Kofi Annan, has used his global moral authority, enhanced when he received the Nobel Peace Prize in 2001, to condemn terrorist acts, and call for worldwide unity against terrorism. In a speech the day after the attacks of September 11, the Secretary-General said, "All nations of the world must be united in their solidarity with the victims of terrorism, and in their determination to take action, both against the terrorists themselves and against all those who give them any kind of shelter, assistance or encouragement." On October 1, 2001, while urging States to conclude a Comprehensive Convention on Terrorism, he said:

It will also be important to obtain agreement on a comprehensive convention on international terrorism. In the post-11 September era, no one can dispute the nature of the terrorist threat, nor the need to meet it with a global response. I understand that there are outstanding issues, which until now have prevented agreement on this convention. Some of the most difficult issues relate to the definition of terrorism. I understand and accept the need for legal precision. But let me say frankly that there is also a need for moral clarity. There can be no acceptance of those who would seek to justify the deliberate taking

of innocent civilian life, regardless of cause or grievance. If there is one universal principle that all peoples can agree on, surely it is this.

His speech became the basis for his personal engagement in an effort, in late autumn
2001, to push States to reach agreement. That effort so far has failed.

The international effort to combat terrorism is over thirty years old. It came close to
agreement on a generally applicable definition of terrorism in the immediate aftermath
of the attacks of September 11, 2001. Despite the personal efforts of the Secretary-General
acting as a facilitator, prod, and moral conscience, the Organization of the Islamic Conference (OIC), consisting of 57 Islamic Member States of the U.N., could not agree with
the rest of the international community on what terrorism is. The differences are em-
blematic of the history of international discussions on terrorism. First, the OIC wants to
exclude acts directed against foreign occupation from the terrorist label. In 2001, the reasons did not need to be declared: the OIC wanted to exempt terrorism against Israel and
terrorism against India over Kashmir. Second, the OIC wanted to brand violations of the
laws of war by State military forces as terrorist. This goal is aimed at the Israel Defense
Forces. All countries with large armies objected. Violations of the laws of war are war
crimes; they are not ipso facto acts of terrorism. The OIC could not accept language of
a proposed compromise on these two issues, even though the compromise bowed in the
direction of struggles by "peoples" under international law and contained a reference to
international law in the provisions regarding a State's regular armed forces.

The conventional wisdom concludes that the international community will not succeed in this area until the conflicts in the Middle East and over Kashmir come to an end.
Once the international community can agree on a definition, then it can move ahead on
measures against terrorist use of nuclear and other weapons of mass destruction. Indeed,
it could even bring to the counter-terrorism effort the array of international institutions
operating in geographical areas traditionally hospitable to terrorists. By such time, of
course, the utility and impact of achieving agreement on a generally applicable definition may have diminished: those conflicts have prevented agreement to date and have
provided at least nominal justifications for many terrorist acts.

---

## 3. Susan Tiefenbrun, A Semiotic Approach to a Legal Definition of Terrorism

*ILSA Journal of International & Comparative Law*, 2003
[footnotes omitted by editors]

\* \* \*

### III. The Many Definitions of Terrorism

Even though there are many definitions of terrorism available for legislative purposes,
"terrorism" per se has never been explicitly defined in any of the seventeen existing multilateral anti-terrorism conventions. Moreover, the multilateral conventions are not applicable to state-sponsored terrorism. They apply only to terrorism committed by individual
actors. The absence of a universally-accepted definition of terrorism and the inapplica-
bility of multilateral anti-terrorism legislation to state-sponsored terrorism reflect the
deeply political nature of the term terrorism and the absence among nations of commonly shared values about the rule of law, the legitimacy of goals, and the means to
achieve these goals. For example, the international community cannot agree on whether
"innocent civilian" is a necessary or simply a sufficient element of the definition. It also

cannot agree on who should be included in the category of "innocent civilians" or "diplomats" or "civilian installations" or "legitimate targets." The international community cannot agree on whether terrorism is illegal under all situations or whether it is sometimes permissible in order to achieve a legitimate goal. Some international organizations proclaim that the right to self-rule legitimizes the use of the most appropriate means, including terrorism, to achieve the goals of liberation and independence.

## A. United States' Definitions of Terrorism

In the United States there is a general confusion about what constitutes terrorism. The United States has shifted its conception of terrorism as a "crime" to terrorism as an "act of war." In the past, the United States classified international terrorism as a crime and applied legal means as the primary tool to fight it. More recently, however, the United States has moved away from reactive counter-terrorism law enforcement methods towards more proactive techniques to fight international terrorism. This shift has occurred because the United States now perceives terrorist acts as acts of war. In its war against terrorism, the United States now uses expanded law enforcement and intelligence agencies like the FBI and the CIA to fight terrorism, and these agencies have their own definitions of terrorism.

In the United States federal system, each state determines what constitutes an offense under its domestic criminal or penal code. States define terrorism generically as a crime. For example, the Arkansas Criminal Code provides that "a person commits the offense of terroristic[sic] threatening if, with the purpose of terrorizing another person, he threatens to cause death or serious physical injury or substantial property damage to another person."

The United States Congress has not been able to reach a consensus on a working definition of terrorism. The executive branch has also not developed a coordinated position on the meaning of the term. The absence of a generally-accepted definition of terrorism in the United States allows the government to craft variant or vague definitions which can result in an erosion of civil rights and the possible abuse of power by the state in the name of fighting terrorism and protecting national security.

## 1. United States 1996 Anti-Terrorism Act's Definition of Terrorism

In the 1996 United States Antiterrorism Act and Effective Death Penalty Act, the United States defines international terrorism as:

> the unlawful use of violence against the United States, citizens of the United States or any other nation, outside the boundaries of the United States, apparently intended to intimidate or coerce a civilian population, influence government policy, or to affect the conduct of a government for political or social objectives.

This definition includes the five basic elements outlined above, but does not list specific terrorist acts that can be classified as criminal. The advantage of not listing specific acts as "terrorist acts" is that as new forms of technology are created, new forms of terrorist acts are likely to develop, and this law will still cover these news modalities. The disadvantage of not listing specific acts as "terrorist acts" is that the decision will be left up to policy makers to determine who is and who is not committing "terrorist acts." A subjective definition leaves too much room for political bias to affect the decision.

Despite the presence of a definition of terrorism in the United States 1996 Antiterrorism Act, some civil libertarians have attacked this law, basing their objection on a dubious claim that the Act does not contain a definition of terrorism. A more valid claim might be that the United States Antiterrorism Act of 1996 does not explicitly designate specific acts that constitute terrorism. Civil libertarians have expressed a legitimate fear that the alleged absence of a definition will have the following deleterious result: "'Terrorism' is whatever the Secretary of States decides it is … the Secretary of State may designate a foreign group as a terrorist organization if the Secretary of State finds that the group 'engages in terrorist activity' that threatens the security of United States nationals or the national security of the United States." The absence of a universally-accepted definition of terrorism and the failure to list specific acts as terrorist acts could cause this bad result to happen in other countries besides the United States.

### 2. The 2001 United and Strengthening America by Providing Appropriate Tools Required to Intercept and Obstruct Terrorism Act (United States Patriot Act)

The President of the United States has defined terrorism in a recent anti-terrorism act known as the United States Patriot Act. The definition is as follows: "For crimes to be defined as 'terrorist acts' the government must show that they were calculated to influence or affect the conduct of government by intimidation or coercion or to retaliate against government conduct."

This definition requires insight into the mental state of the perpetrator, does not specifically identify the necessary element of violence, and reduces the purpose clause to achieving political goals (i.e., influencing government conduct).

Some civil libertarians have objected to the erosion of civil liberties in the 2001 United States Patriot Act because it authorizes executive detention on the mere suspicion that an immigrant has at some point engaged in a violent crime or provided humanitarian aid to a proscribed organization. This provision authorizes guilt by association and gives the government the power to deny entry to aliens for reasons that are arguably "pure speech" acts.

### 3. The International Money Laundering Abatement and Financial Anti-Terrorism Act of 2001

The United States Financial Anti-Terrorism Act of 2001, which is the counterpart of the United Nations International Convention for the Suppression of the Financing of Terrorism (1999), was signed into law on October 26, 2001, as Title III of the United States Patriot Act. This statute requires the Secretary of the Treasury to implement numerous changes under a strict timetable in order to follow the trail of those who finance terrorism. Due diligence measures require the identification of beneficial owners of bank accounts.

The United States has designated a variation on the domestic form of "terrorism" called "global terrorism." For example, President Bush signed Executive Order 13244 on September 23, 2001, requiring United States persons to block the assets of a new category of sanctioned parties, known as "specially designated global terrorists (SDGTS)." This category includes individuals, organizations, charities, and business entities. It includes United States persons, United States citizens and permanent residents, United States corporations, and their non-United States branches. The Office of Foreign Assets Control of the United States Department of the Treasury will implement the executive order. The President has threatened to freeze assets and transactions of banks and other financial institutions that refuse to share information about terrorists. An action to freeze assets was also taken by the United Nations Security Council in Resolution 1267 on October 15, 1999, under Chapter VII of the United Nations Charter. Similar actions were taken against Osama bin Laden on December 19, 2000 pursuant to Security Council Resolution 1333.

### 4. FBI's Definition of Terrorism

Since 1980, the Federal Bureau of Investigation (FBI) has defined terrorism as: "the unlawful use of force or violence against persons or property to intimidate or coerce a government, the civilian population, or any segment thereof, in the furtherance of political or social objectives."

The FBI's definition does not include the basic five elements because it omits the necessary element of intent and limits the purpose to the achievement of "political or social objectives." Moreover, the definition does not specifically include or exclude state-sponsored terrorism. If the definition of terrorism does not include the element of intent to coerce or intimidate, then any criminal, like the Son of Sam, who kills just for the sake of bloodthirsty violence, could be deemed a terrorist.

### 5. United States State Department's Definition of Terrorism

The United States Department of State defines the term "terrorism" as: "premeditated, politically motivated violence perpetrated against noncombatant targets by sub-national groups or clandestine agents, usually intended to influence an audience."

This definition includes all five elements and the requisite intent, but it limits the purpose to "politically motivated" goals. The United States State Department's definition arguably excludes terrorism committed by a state because it lists only "sub-national groups or clandestine agents." However, if the term "agents" refers to "agents of the state," then state-sponsored terrorism is included in this definition.

### 6. United States State Department Definition of International Terrorism

The United States Department of State defines the term "international terrorism" as: "terrorism involving citizens of the territory of more than one country."

The requirement of more than one country in the United States State Department definition refers to both perpetrators and victims. The State Department also defines the term "terrorist group" to mean "any group practicing, or that has significant subgroups that practice international terrorism." Since international terrorism refers back to "terrorism," which includes only sub-national groups or clandestine agents, arguably the United States State Department definition of international terrorism does not cover state-sponsored terrorist acts, unless the term "agents" refers to the state.

### B. English Definition of Terrorism

The United Kingdom has undergone an evolutionary process in the definition of terrorism. The English defined terrorism in the English Prevention of Terrorism (Temporary Provision) Act of 1984 and in the English Prevention of Terrorism (Temporary Provision) Act of 1989: "Terrorism means the use of violence for political ends and includes any use of violence for the purpose of putting the public or any section of the public in fear."

This definition is overly broad, does not include the element of intent, expansively includes "civilians" in the category of "any section of the public" (which could include combatants), and limits the goal to "political" benefit. The perpetration of violence without a requirement of intent could produce odd results. For example, demonstrators for a political cause that end up in a brawl might be deemed "terrorists." An accidental killing by the police or by the army, which is hardly an act of terror, might fall within this definition of terrorism.

In 1996 Lord Lloyd defined terrorism as: "The use of serious violence against persons or property or the threat to use such violence, to intimidate or coerce a government, the public, or any section of the public, in order to promote political, social, or ideological objectives."

This definition remedies the earlier one that placed limitations on goals, modifies the act of violence by describing it as "serious violence," maintains the element of "civilians" in the broad category of "any section of the public" but still falls short of including an element of intent.

In the 1999 Prevention of Terrorism Bill, the British government defined terrorism even more broadly to include expressions of extremism by groups such as the Animal Liberation Front that had only one issue as its cause. The more recent United Kingdom Terrorism Act of 2000 defines terrorism in Section l(1):

Terrorism means the use or threat of action where the action falls within subsection (2) (i.e. violence, serious damage, endangering life, etc.) and (b) the use or threat is designed to influence the government or to intimidate the public or a section of the public, and (c) the use or threat is made for the purpose of advancing a political, religious or ideological cause.

Terrorist action is further defined in Section 1 (2) as:

Acts involving serious violence against a person, serious damage to property, acts that endanger a person's life, other than that of the person committing the action; acts that create a serious risk to the health or safety of the public or a section of the public, or acts designed seriously to interfere with or disrupt an electronic system.

Thus, English law continues to omit the element of intent in its definition of terrorism. United Kingdom law specifically lists certain acts that are terrorist acts, like environmental terrorism, biological terrorism, and even computer hacking. English law on terrorism is extraterritorial and covers terrorist actions outside the United Kingdom and committed by governments of a country outside the United Kingdom.

As a matter of comparative law, United States law and United Kingdom law are quite different with regard to the definition of terrorism. The United Kingdom Terrorism Act of 2000 provides a broad definition of the criminal act of terrorism ("serious violence against a person, serious damage to property, acts that endanger a person's life") and also specifically names certain terrorist acts ("acts that create a serious risk to the health or safety of the public ... or disrupt an electronic system"). In contrast, the United States 1996 Antiterrorism Act includes the element of intent but softens the requirement by adding the adverb "apparently" to the element of intent ("apparently intended to intimidate or coerce a civilian population."). The United States law on terrorism does not specifically list the acts that constitute terrorist criminal acts.

The English approach to terrorism may have odd but beneficial results. If Greenpeace were to threaten to disrupt a government computer system (e.g. in order to put pressure on Iraq for dealing with its Kurd population in an inhumane manner), the Greenpeace movement would be committing an act of terrorism. As odd as this result may seem given its laudable purpose, in my view the identification of the Greenpeace organization's act as a terrorist act would be correct in this instance because terrorist acts are not justified, even if they are committed for humanitarian purposes.

### C. French Definition of Terrorism

The French coined the term "terrorism" during the French revolution, in the period that followed the fall of Robespierre in 1793–1794, under the infamous Reign of Terror. The French define terrorism in the dictionary as "violence committed by an organization in order to create a climate of insecurity or in order to overthrow the established government." This definition eliminates the elements of intent and harm to innocent civilians and limits the purpose to the achievement of political goals. In France the term terrorism is also included under the definition of crimes against humanity. As a result of the famous Klaus Barbie case, a new law defining crimes against humanity had to be adopted in the French Criminal Code. The term "terrorism" is also specifically defined in the French Criminal Code:

"Acts are terrorist acts when they are intentionally committed by an individual entity or by a collective entity in order to seriously disturb law and order by intimidation or by terror."

Unlike the United States law, which does not list particular acts as terrorist acts, the French law specifically names and describes the acts that constitute terrorism. Article 421-1 of the French Criminal Code lists the following acts as terrorist acts:

Attempted murder, assault, kidnapping, hostage-taking on airplanes, ships, all means of transport, theft, extortion, destructions, and crimes committed during group combat, the production or ownership of weapons of destruction and explosives including the production, sale, import and export of explosives, the acquisition, ownership, transport of illegal explosive substances, the production, ownership, storage, or acquisition of biological or chemical weapons, and money laundering.

Article 421-2 of the French Criminal Code continues the list of terrorist acts to include environmental terrorism: "... Placing in the air, on the ground, under the ground and in the water (including territorial water) any substance that would put the health of man and animals or the environment in danger."

Article 421-2-1 of the French Criminal Code makes it illegal to belong to or participate in a group that is formed for the purpose of planning one of the terrorist acts named above.

Article 421-2-2 of the French Criminal Code makes it illegal for anyone to finance a terrorist organization by intentionally providing funds, collecting funds, or managing funds of any value whatsoever, or by giving advice for the purpose of financing terrorism, if that person knows that these funds are going to be used fully or partially for the purpose of committing terrorist acts, and whether or not the terrorist act actually occurs.

Article 421-3 of the French Criminal Code sets forth penalties ranging from six years to life imprisonment for the commission of a terrorist act. Article 421-4 of the French Criminal Code adds monetary penalties to the prison sentence. For example, if the terrorist is convicted to fifteen years of imprisonment, he or she might also be required to pay a monetary penalty of 225,000 Euros. If an alleged terrorist is convicted of killing one or several people, he or she would be sentenced to imprisonment for life and would be required to pay a penalty of 750,000 Euros. Article 421-5 of the French Criminal Code provides that an alleged terrorist who is convicted for ten years of imprisonment must also pay a penalty of 225,000 Euros.

Article 422-1 of the French Criminal Code provides an exemption for informants. Anyone who had attempted to commit a terrorist act and who, having informed the administrative and judicial authorities in advance of the commission of the act, facilitated the avoidance of the terrorist act and the identification of the other guilty parties will be immune from imprisonment and penalties.

Article 422-2 of the French Criminal Code permits the reduction of a prison sentence by half for anyone who committed a terrorist act or aided in a terrorist act if that person, by warning or informing the administrative or judiciary authorities, enabled the terrorist act to be avoided, or enabled anyone's death or permanent injury to be avoided, or provided the names of the other guilty parties. A life sentence will be reduced to twenty years for such assistance.

Article 422-5 of the French Criminal Code expressly requires that corporations ("personnes morales") engaging in terrorist activities pay monetary penalties. Article 422-6 of the French Criminal Code includes confiscation of property as a penalty for any person or corporation engaging in terrorist activity.

Article 422-7 of the French Criminal Code provides that any financial penalties imposed on the terrorists will be given to the victims' funds.

Article 434-2 of the French Criminal Code imposes five years of imprisonment and a fine of 75,000 Euros on anyone attempting to harm the fundamental interests of the nation by a terrorist act.

Article 434-6 of the French Criminal Code imposes a penalty of three years imprisonment and 45,000 Euros for anyone aiding a terrorist convicted of ten years of imprisonment. Aiding and abetting may be simply offering a terrorist lodging, subsidies, means of subsistence or any other form of assistance. The penalty for aiding and abetting can be increased to five years of imprisonment and 75,000 Euros. However, relatives of the terrorist (parents, brothers, sisters and their spouse) and the spouse of the terrorist or the person with whom the terrorist is living are not included in the list of aiders and abetters.

### D. European Nations' Definition of Terrorism

The European Convention on the Suppression of Terrorism was signed by 17 out of 19 member states of the Council of Europe in January 1977. According to this treaty, all states must treat assassination, hostage taking, bomb attacks, and hijacking (major terrorist offenses), as "common crimes" and cannot refuse extradition. However, an escape clause was inserted into the European Convention on the Suppression of Terrorism permitting the contacting state to reserve the right to regard a certain offense as a political one. This escape clause would enable that state to withhold extradition. The member states of the European Union strengthened this provision by the European Convention on Extradition.

### E. Canadian Definition of Terrorism

Canada has recently made strong legislative proposals in an attempt to combat terrorism. The Canadian Anti-terrorism Act takes aim at terrorist groups, but also seeks to strike an appropriate balance between respecting Canadian values of fairness and respect for human rights while protecting Canadians and the global community from terrorism. This balance is accomplished by providing what the Canadian Department of Justice refers to as checks and balances in the form of "clear definitions" of terrorism.

Terrorist activities in Canada have always been treated as criminal offenses. Under the Canadian Criminal Code terrorists can be prosecuted for hijacking, murder, and other acts of violence. The Government of Canada has signed all 12 United Nations Conventions and Protocols related to terrorism and has ratified 10, including those that protect against harming aircraft, civil aviation and airports, international shipping, internationally protected persons and diplomats, the safety of nuclear material, and the prevention of the taking of hostages and terrorist bombings. According to the Justice Department, Canada plans to ratify the remaining two United Nations counter-terrorism conventions dealing with the suppression of terrorist financing and the suppression of terrorist bombings. Canada also expects to ratify the Convention on the Safety of United Nations and Associated Personnel Convention (1994), ensuring the safety of United Nations personnel, including peacekeepers, from attacks against their person, official premises, private accommodation and modes of transport. Canada proposes to amend its Criminal Code to implement these United Nations Conventions and to establish provisions aimed at disabling and dismantling the activities of terrorist groups and those who support them.

Canadian law defines a "terrorist activity" in the Criminal Code as an action that takes place either within or outside of Canada that "is an offense under one of the ten United Nations anti-terrorism conventions and protocols; or is an action": "taken or threatened for political, religious, or ideological purposes and threatens the public or national security by killing, seriously harming or endangering a person, substantial property damage that is likely to seriously harm people or by interfering with or disrupting an essential service, facility or system."

This Canadian definition of terrorism does not explicitly include the words "violence," but it is implied in the descriptive term "seriously harming or endangering." While the element of "innocent civilians" is not designated with particularity, the broad term "a person" and "people" implies civilians.

The element of intent is also not specified but merely implied vaguely in the words "an action is taken." Some insight into the element of intent implied in these words can be gleaned by looking at the list of specific acts of terrorism which Canadian law provides. Unlike the terrorism definition in United States law, the Canadian law lists specific terrorist acts, including the disruption of an essential service, facility or system. It is interesting to note that in an effort to balance civil rights with the protection of national security, Canadian law does not include under the definition of a terrorist act the disruption of an essential service during a lawful protest or a work strike, if the action does not intend to cause serious harm to persons. Therefore, the emphasis on intent as a condition of terrorist activity in this context strongly supports the view that the element of intent is implied in the definition of terrorism under Canadian law. The element of "fear, coercion or intimidation" is not specified explicitly but implied in the term "threatens." The Canadian definition specifically designates the purpose of the terrorist action as political, religious, or ideological and omits "military" and "ethnic."

Canadian law permits the designation of groups as "terrorist groups" if their activities meet the definition of terrorist activity.

The Canadian Criminal Code makes it a crime to knowingly collect or provide funds, either directly or indirectly, in order to carry out terrorist crimes. The maximum sentence for this offense would be ten years. It is a crime to knowingly participate in, contribute to or facilitate the activities of a terrorist group. Participation or contribution could include knowingly recruiting into the group new individuals for the purpose of enhancing the ability of the terrorist group to aid, abet, or commit indictable offences. The maximum sentence for the offense of participating or contributing would be ten years of imprisonment. The maximum sentence for facilitating would be fourteen years of imprisonment. Anyone who instructs another to carry out a terrorist act or an activity on behalf of a terrorist group ("leadership" offense) carries a maximum life sentence. Anyone knowingly harboring or concealing a terrorist would receive a maximum sentence of ten years.

A careful analysis of the Canadian definition of terrorism with respect to the five necessary elements shows that the definition is not as "clear" as the Canadian Department of Justice would have us believe. It is, however, more specific than United States law which does not list with particularity any acts of terrorism.

\* \* \*

### VIII. The Paradoxes Inherent in the Meaning of Terrorism

The main problem in defining the term "terrorism" is not its overlap with other crimes but the paradox inherent in the meaning of the word. President Ronald Reagan has coined this paradox in the proverbial statement: "One man's terrorism is another man's freedom fighter" or the poetic parallelism articulated by the international law scholar Cherif Bassiouni: "What is terrorism to some is heroism to others." The paradox is related to the distinction between illegal terrorism and legal revolutionary violence. The antinomy in the term "terrorism" is based on the coexistence of conflicting rights of self-defense and self-determination, on the one hand, and the fundamental right to the protection of human rights, on the other hand.

Another manifestation of this paradox is the state's obligation to protect the national security of its people, which, if zealously enforced through overly broad legislation, may be in direct conflict with the state's obligation to protect its citizens' civil liberties.

Article 51 of the United Nations Charter provides the right to individual or collective self-defense if an armed attack occurs against a member of the United Nations. Moreover, every nation has a right to self-determination. In l979 Algeria, Libya and a few other countries wanted the United Nations to make an exception in one of its multilateral conventions against hostage taking for national liberation movements in which peoples are fighting against colonial domination and alien occupation and against racist regimes in the exercise of their right of self-determination. However, the Western countries rejected this demand on the grounds that even armies may not take civilian hostages because such an act would violate the Geneva Convention. There must be a balance established between the right of a democracy to defend itself against terrorism and the preservation of civil liberties and human rights. The difficulty to achieve this delicate balance has resulted in the proliferation of global treaties and declarations aimed at combating international terrorism and the abysmal failure by the international community to define terrorism and to prohibit state-sponsored terrorist acts. The time has come to take a more active approach to defining the term terrorism.

\* \* \*

## 4. Jennifer Trahan, Terrorism Conventions: Existing Gaps and Different Approaches
*New England International & Comparative Law Annual*, 2002
[footnotes omitted by editors]

\* \* \*

## I. EXISITING MULTILATERAL TERRORISM CONVENTIONS AND PROTOCOLS

### A. Piecemeal Coverage

There are ten multilateral conventions and two protocols addressing a variety of terrorist acts, but no convention covering terrorism generally.

Specifically, existing multilateral conventions and protocols cover:

*Airplane hijacking and airports.* Airplane hijacking is covered by three conventions, known as the Tokyo, Hague and Montreal Conventions. The conventions apply to acts occurring while a civilian aircraft is in flight, destroying or endangering the safety of such an aircraft, or damaging or destroying international air navigation facilities. An additional protocol to the Montreal Convention covers acts against persons at airports, airport facilities and aircraft not in service.

*Attacking "internationally protected persons."* The Convention on the Prevention and Punishment of Crimes Against Internationally Protected Persons, Including Diplomatic Agents covers terrorist acts against (a) a head of state, a head of government or a minister of foreign affairs, whenever such person is in a foreign state, as well as any accompanying family members, and (b) any representative or official of a state or an international organization of an intergovernmental character, who is entitled to special protection from attack under international law.

*Theft of nuclear materials.* The Convention on the Physical Protection of Nuclear Material covers unlawful receipt, possession, use, transfer, alteration, disposal, dispersal, theft, embezzlement or fraudulently obtaining nuclear materials; demanding such materials by use of force; and threatening to use such materials.

*Taking hostages.* The International Convention Against the Taking of Hostages covers "any person who seizes or detains and threatens to kill, to injure or to continue to detain another person ... in order to compel ... a State, an international intergovernmental organization, a natural or juridical person, or a group of persons, to do or abstain from doing any act as an explicit or implicit condition for the release of the hostage."

*Unlawful acts against maritime navigation and fixed platforms on the continental shelf.* The Convention for the Suppression of Unlawful Acts Against the Safety of Maritime Navigation covers acts committed on board a ship, destroying a ship, endangering persons on the ship, or destroying or seriously damaging maritime navigation facilities. A protocol extends coverage to fixed platforms on the continental shelf.

*Terrorist bombing.* The International Convention for the Suppression of Terrorist Bombings covers a person who "unlawfully and intentionally delivers, places, discharges or detonates an explosive or other lethal device in, into or against a place of public use, a State or government facility, a public transportation system or an infrastructure facility."

*Financing terrorism.* The International Convention for the Suppression of the Financing of Terrorism covers "directly or indirectly, unlawfully and willfully" providing or collecting funds to terrorist organizations or persons engaged in terrorism.

*Marking plastic explosives.* The Convention on the Marking of Plastic Explosives for the Purpose of Identification obligates states to mark plastic explosives with certain detection agents, and destroy existing stockpiles of explosives that lack those detection agents.

Most of these conventions and protocols requires states to: (a) criminalize the acts covered and make them "punishable by appropriate penalties which take into account the grave nature of those offences"; (b) establish jurisdiction over offenses committed in certain contexts and permit states to establish jurisdiction over offense committed in other contexts; (c) take alleged offenders into custody and make a preliminary factual inquiry; (d) notify, either through the U.N. Secretary-General or directly, certain potentially interested states of the actions taken; (e) submit the case for prosecution if the state does not extradite the alleged offender; (f) deem the offence to be an "extraditable offence" for the purpose of any extradition treaty between states parties; and (g) assist each other in connection with criminal proceedings regarding the offences covered.

While these international conventions and protocols are clearly of tremendous importance, addressing terrorism in this topical fashion leaves obvious gaps in coverage. For example, terrorist acts committed using biological, chemical or nuclear weapons, which are the subject of another draft convention, currently are not covered by any multilateral terrorism convention. The three conventions addressing airplane hijacking cover acts committed "in flight" and destroying the aircraft, but do not appear to cover destruction and deaths caused on the ground. Terrorist acts in civilian locations other than airports—for instance, a shopping mall or restaurant—are not addressed, except to the extent a "protected person" happens to be present, or the acts are covered by the convention on terrorist bombings. Addressing terrorism topically is necessarily a responsive approach in that it responds to the types of terrorist methods currently in use or used in the past, but fails to address new methods of terrorism. One way to eliminate such gaps in coverage would be to adopt a multilateral terrorism convention criminalizing terrorism generally—a topic discussed further below.

## B. Little Preventive Focus

As detailed above, most provisions of existing terrorism conventions and protocols focus on apprehension and prosecution of terrorists who have committed terrorist acts. By and large, the conventions, with two notable exceptions, do not focus on prevention. The conventions generally devote only one article to the topic of preventing terrorism, and usually address the subject only in very broad language. For instance, the Montreal Convention mandates that "Contracting States shall, in accordance with international and national law, endeavour to take *all practicable measures* for the purpose of preventing the offences" mentioned in the convention. The Convention on the Prevention and Punishment of Crimes Against Internationally Protected Persons additionally requires states to cooperate by "exchanging information and co-ordinating the taking of administrative and other measures as appropriate to prevent the commission of those crimes." A concern arises as to the majority of the conventions and protocols whether the language used, which fails to explain what specific actions states are required to undertake, will result in states taking any action with respect to those obligations.

Certain conventions also require states to share information about possible terrorist attacks. Yet, at least one convention has no such requirement, and two others only require sharing "accurate and verified" information. One concern is that if a state waits until information is "accurate and verified" before sharing it, the information may be communicated too late to be useful. The Convention on the Physical Protection of Nuclear Material obligates sharing of information and cooperation only once nuclear materials have been stolen or threats have been made to steal such material.

Only two conventions detail the steps states are required to take in attempting to prevent terrorism—the Convention on the Marking of Plastic Explosives for the Purpose of Identification and the International Convention for the Suppression of the Financing of Terrorism. The former convention, which was implemented in response to the bombing of Pan Am 103 in midair over Lockerbie, Scotland, mandates that plastic explosives contain certain chemicals that make them more readily detectible with the goal of preventing such bombings. Under the convention, states must prohibit and prevent the manufacture of unmarked explosives, destroy or render permanently ineffective existing stockpiles of unmarked explosives not in military use within three years of the convention's entry into force, and destroy or render ineffective military stockpiles of unmarked explosives within fifteen years. Unfortunately, the convention's benefits are to some extent diminished by that lengthy phase-in process.

The only other convention detailing specific steps states should take to prevent terrorism is the International Convention for the Suppression of the Financing of Terrorism, which has been ratified by twenty-eight states. A person commits an offence within the meaning of that convention if the person

> by any means, directly or indirectly, unlawfully and willfully, provides or collects funds with the intention that they should be used or in the knowledge that they are to be used, in full or in part, in order to carry out:
>
> (a) An act which constitutes an offence within the scope of [one of the existing multilateral terrorism conventions and protocols]; or

(b) Any other act intended to cause death or serious bodily injury to a civilian, or to any other person not taking an active part in the hostilities in a situation of armed conflict, when the purpose of such act, by its nature or context, is to intimidate a population, or to compel a government or an international organization to do or to abstain from doing any act.

The convention is aimed at striking at the assets of terrorist organizations, with the goal of undermining such organizations. Thus, in addition to requiring prosecution of persons and entities that finance terrorist organizations, is inherently designed to try to prevent terrorism.

As to specific obligations to prevent the financing of terrorism, the convention obligates states to: (a) undertake measures to prohibit persons in a state's territory who encourage, instigate, organize or engage in the crimes covered; (b) require financial institutions to utilize measures to identify customers, and pay special attention to unusual or suspicious financial transactions; (c) consider prohibiting the opening of accounts the holders of which are unidentified; (d) consider requiring financial institutions to verify the legal existence of all customers; (e) consider reporting obligations regarding unusually large financial transactions; (f) consider requiring financial institutions to maintain all transaction records for at least five years; (g) cooperate with other states parties on measures to supervise the licensing of money-transmission agencies; and (h) cooperate in measures to detect or monitor cross-border transportation of cash and bearer negotiable instruments. Arguably, only with such explicit articulations can states know what types of cooperation and prevention measures international conventions are requiring them to undertake. Thus, because—with two notable exceptions—most terrorist conventions contain only broadly worded language geared to preventing terrorism, there is certainly room to improve on states' obligations to prevent terrorism.

## C. Exclusion For Acts In One State

Another interesting feature of the existing terrorism conventions and protocols is that under several conventions, acts occurring solely in one state are omitted from coverage. For instance, under the International Convention for the Suppression of Terrorist Bombings and the International Convention Against the Taking of Hostages, if the offence is committed within a single state, the alleged offender and victims are nationals of that state, and the alleged offender is still within that state, the conventions do not apply. Similarly, under the International Convention for the Suppression of the Financing of Terrorism, if the offence is committed in one state and the offender is a national of that state, the convention would not apply. For instance, the Montreal Convention does not apply unless (a) "the place of take-off or landing, actual or intended, of the aircraft is situated outside the territory" of the state where the aircraft is registered, or (b) the offence is committed in a state other than the aircraft's state of registration, unless the alleged offender is located in a state other than the aircraft's state of registration.

While the exclusions undoubtedly were designed to afford states sovereignty in dealing with matters solely occurring within their own territory and pertaining to their own nationals, these exclusions may have unintended consequences. For instance, under the Hostages Convention, if a Saudi national and al-Qaeda member took other Saudi nationals hostage in Saudi Arabia, demanding release, for instance, of convicted al-Qaeda terrorist Ramzi Ahmed Yousef by the United States, the Hostages Convention would not apply even though Saudi Arabia has ratified it. While that result makes sense at a certain level since Saudi Arabia has the closest nexus to and presumably interest in prosecuting that crime, because it is increasingly apparent that terrorist organizations such as al-Qaeda operate on a global bases, some consequences might be problematic.

**For example:**

- There would be no obligation upon Saudi Arabia to inform other states of the actions taken unless otherwise mandated by a mutual assistance treaty. This could be problematic if, for instance, the hostage taking were part of a larger plot and the crime did not otherwise receive widespread or prompt publicity.

- Saudi Arabia would be under no obligation to deem the offence extraditable under existing extradition treaties. Thus, if, for instance, another nation — such as the United States — wanted to prosecute the alleged perpetrator, for instance, for hostage-taking committed in the United States, the accused might not be subject to extradition unless an extradition treaty between the United States and Saudi Arabia happened to cover hostage taking.

- States would have no obligation to provide Saudi Arabia assistance regarding the criminal proceedings unless an assistance obligation were created by another treaty.

- States would be under no treaty obligation to take actions designed to prevent such hostage taking.

Similarly, in the context of September 11 — because the hijacked aircraft departed from and were intended to land within the United States — if the aircraft were registered in the United States, the Montreal Convention would not apply to any alleged offender found in the United States — at least regarding acts committed in the United States. That is probably not problematic regarding the crimes committed on September 11 because, even without convention obligations, the United States would undertake the obligations imposed under the Montreal Convention, such as taking into custody any alleged perpetrators found in the United States, investigating the crime, and commencing prosecutions.

This exclusion could be problematic, however, if a country does not take such prosecution obligations as seriously. For instance, had the events occurred in Syria or Libya and the aircraft been registered in those countries, even though both countries are parties to the Montreal Convention, none of the Montreal Convention obligations to prosecute the perpetrators would apply.

Thus, the exclusions built into the conventions pertaining to acts occurring within a single state arguably should be reconsidered. Given the increasingly global reach of terrorist organizations, terrorists acts occurring within a single state may have broad ramifications, and all states arguably have an interest in having convention obligations apply and seeing terrorists active within a single state prosecuted.

### D. Little Obligation to Combat Domestic Terrorism

Because many terrorism conventions fail to require states to take specific measures to prevent terrorism and also exclude acts occurring within a single state, there are limited obligations requiring states to take action against terrorist organizations active within a single state that have not yet perpetrated international terrorism.

As discussed above, only two conventions detail measures that states should undertake to prevent terrorism — the Convention on the Marking of Plastic Explosives for the Purpose of Identification and the International Convention for the Suppression of the Financing of Terrorism. Because most conventions also exclude acts occurring within a single state, even the broad prevention language they contain fails to address terrorist activity occurring in a single state. Thus, there is very little specific language in the conventions and protocols that mandates states to attempt to combat domestic terrorism.

Another effect of international terrorism conventions paying limited attention to the issue of preventing terrorism is that, to the extent states undertake measures aimed at preventing terrorism, the actions taken could be too severe in terms of harming individual liberties. For example, there has been concern that in the wake of September 11, some states have justified more generalized repression under the guise of fighting terrorism, or otherwise infringed upon human rights protections. Thus, ironically, the failure to address terrorism prevention more fully can cause two quite divergent problems: (a) states that are not serious about combating terrorism within their borders may not do enough, or may do nothing at all, to attempt to detect and prevent terrorism; and (b) states that take steps to combat terrorism may do so without any international mechanism to check their actions, which could have an adverse cost especially to individuals who are non-citizens and whose rights may be insufficiently protected under national or international law.

### E. Avoiding Extradition by Professing Political Motives

The terrorism conventions and protocols are also inconsistent on whether a suspect can avoid extradition by professing that the actions taken were politically motivated. Certain of the later conventions explain that extradition may not be avoided on that ground. For instance, the International Convention for the Suppression of the Financing of Terrorism provides:

> None of the offences [covered] shall be regarded for the purposes of extradition or mutual legal assistance as a political offence or as an offence connected with a political offence or as an offence inspired by political motives. Accordingly, a request for extradition or for mutual legal assistance based on such an offence may not be refused on the sole ground that it concerns a political offence or an offence connected with a political offence or an offence inspired by political motives.

The failure of many of the earlier conventions to contain similar provisions raises the troubling suggestion that extradition may be avoided under those conventions by claiming the offence was politically motivated. This is yet another issue that the comprehensive terrorism convention could resolve.

\* \* \*

## Authors' Note

As the international community has failed to develop a common definition of terrorism, politicians and legal scholars alike have investigated a wide variety of potential solutions. The following material provides an analysis of one such proposed solution: defining acts of terrorism as 'peacetime equivalents of war crimes.'

## 5. Michael P. Scharf, Defining Terrorism as the Peacetime Equivalent of War Crimes: Problems and Prospects

*Case Western Reserve Journal of International Law*, 2005
[footnotes omitted by editors]

### I. Introduction

The problem of defining "terrorism" has vexed the international community for decades. The United Nations General Assembly has repeatedly called for the convening of an international conference to define terrorism and distinguish it from legitimate acts in furtherance of national liberation struggles. Twelve years ago, representing the United States, I delivered a speech in the U.N. Sixth (Legal) Committee, in which I pointed out that general definitions of terrorism "are notoriously difficult to achieve and dangerous in what all but the most perfect of definitions excludes by chance." I concluded that the history of the effort to deal with the problem of terrorism under the League of Nations and in the United Nations indicates that "the difficulty of an abstract definition is, as a practical matter, insurmountable."

A few months after I gave that speech at the United Nations, Alex Schmid, the Senior Crime Prevention and Criminal Justice Officer at the U.N.'s Terrorism Prevention Branch in Vienna, proposed a novel approach to the problem of defining terrorism which would draw on the existing consensus of what constitutes a war crime. After circulating without much interest through the United Nations during the last decade, Schmid's proposal suddenly gained world-wide attention in April 2004, when it was cited by the Supreme Court of India as a way around what the Court characterized as the Gordian definitional knot. In *Singh v. Bihar*, the Indian Supreme Court explained: "If the core of war crimes-deliberate attacks on civilians, hostage-taking and the killing of prisoners is extended to peacetime, we could simply define acts of terrorism veritably as 'peacetime equivalents of war crimes.'"

This article examines the proposal to define terrorism as the peacetime equivalent of war crimes in the context of answering two questions: First, why might it be useful to define terrorism by reference to the existing laws of war? And second, what are the potential negative consequences which might counsel against such an approach? Before addressing these questions, however, it is useful to provide a brief history of the modern international effort to define terrorism.

## II. The International Quest for a General Definition of Terrorism

In 1987, the United Nations General Assembly adopted Resolution 42/159, recognizing that the effectiveness of the struggle against terrorism could be enhanced by the establishment of a generally agreed definition of international terrorism. The issue was initially assigned to the U.N. Sixth (Legal) Committee, which had over the years drafted a number of conventions addressing specific crimes committed by terrorists, although none of these conventions ever used the word "terrorism" let alone provided a definition of the term. When the Sixth Committee failed to make progress in reaching a consensus definition of terrorism, the General Assembly in 1996 established an ad hoc committee to develop a comprehensive framework for dealing with international terrorism.

Foremost among its accomplishments, the ad hoc committee developed the International Convention for the Suppression of the Financing of Terrorism, which defined terrorism as (1) any activity covered by the twelve anti-terrorism treaties; and (2) "any other act intended to cause death or serious bodily injury to a civilian, or to any other person not taking an active part in the hostilities in a situation of armed conflict, when the purpose of such act, by its nature or context, is to intimidate a population, or to compel a Government or an international organization to do or to abstain from doing any act." 129 States have so far ratified this multilateral treaty. This was as close as the international community has ever come to adopting a widely accepted general definition of terrorism.

Immediately after the events of September 11, 2001, the General Assembly established a working group to develop a comprehensive convention on international terrorism. In the spirit of cooperation that marked the early days after the September 11 attacks, the members of the working group nearly reached consensus on the following definition of terrorism:

> [Terrorism is an act] intended to cause death or serious bodily injury to any person; or serious damage to a State or government facility, a public transportation system, communication system or infrastructure facility … when the purpose of such act, by its nature or context, is to intimidate a population, or to compel a Government or an international organization to do or abstain from doing an act.

The effort hit a snag, however, when Malaysia, on behalf of the 56-member Organization of the Islamic Conference (OIC), proposed the addition of the following language:

> Peoples' struggle including armed struggle against foreign occupation, aggression, colonialism, and hegemony, aimed at liberation and self-determination in accordance with the principles of international law shall not be considered a terrorist crime.

According to Nicholas Rostow, General Counsel to the U.S. Mission to the United Nations, the OIC's proposal intended to exempt acts against Israel over the occupied territories and acts against India over Kashmir from the definition of terrorism, and to brand violations of the laws of war by State military forces such as the Israel Defense Forces as terrorist acts. When neither side was willing to compromise on this issue, the project was shelved indefinitely.

With work on a general definition of terrorism once again stalled in the General Assembly, the U.N. Security Council stepped in to the fray. Acting under Chapter VII of the U.N. Charter, the Council adopted Resolution 1373, which in essence transformed the Terrorism Financing Convention into an obligation of all U.N. member States, requiring them to prohibit financial support for persons and organizations engaged in terrorism. The Council missed an opportunity, however, to adopt a universal definition of terrorism when it decided not to include the Terrorism Financing Convention's definition of terrorism in Resolution 1373, but rather to leave the term undefined and to allow each State to ascertain its own definition of terrorism. Further, the Council created a committee (The Counter-Terrorism Committee) to oversee the implementation of the resolution, but it did not give the Committee the mandate to promulgate a list of terrorists or terrorist organizations to whom financial assistance would be prohibited under the resolution.

The Security Council's most recent statement on terrorism came in response to a bloody terrorist attack at an elementary school in Russia in October 2004. Upon Russia's insistence, the Security Council adopted Resolution 1566, which provides:

> criminal acts, including against civilians, committed with the intent to cause death or serious bodily injury, or taking of hostages, with the purpose to provoke a state of terror in the general public or in a group of persons or particular persons, intimidate a population or compel a government or an international organization to do or to abstain from doing any act, which constitute offenses within the scope of and as defined in the international conventions and protocols relating to terrorism, are under no circumstances justifiable by considerations of a political, philosophical, ideological, racial, ethnic, religious, or other similar nature, and calls upon all States to prevent such acts and, if not prevented, to ensure that such acts are punished by penalties consistent with their grave nature [ … ].

At first blush this clause seems to be a general definition of terrorism, similar to that contained in the Terrorist Financing Convention. But due to the inclusion of the italicized language (which was required to gain consensus), this clause actually does no more than reaffirm that there can be no justification for committing any of the acts prohibited in the twelve counter-terrorism conventions; a sentiment that was expressed in numerous past General Assembly and Security Council resolutions.

### III. The Case for Defining Terrorism as the Peacetime Equivalent of War Crimes

Terrorism can occur during armed conflict or during peacetime (defined as the non-existence of armed conflict). When terrorism is committed in an international or internal armed conflict (including a guerrilla war or insurgency), it is covered by the detailed provisions of the four 1949 Geneva Conventions and their Additional Protocols of 1977. These International Humanitarian law ("IHL") conventions provide very specific definitions of a wide range of prohibited conduct; they apply to both soldiers and civilian perpetrators; they trigger command responsibility; and they create universal jurisdiction to prosecute those who engage in prohibited acts. The Conventions prohibit use of violence against non-combatants, hostage taking, and most of the other atrocities usually committed by terrorists. In addition, the Conventions and Additional Protocols contain several provisions aimed specifically at acts of terrorism committed during armed conflict.

The key to whether the IHL conventions apply to acts of terrorism is the "armed conflict threshold." By their terms, these IHL conventions do not apply to "situations of internal disturbances and tensions such as riots and isolated and sporadic acts of violence." In those situations, terrorism is not covered by the laws of war, but rather by a dozen anti-terrorism conventions, which outlaw hostage-taking, hijacking, aircraft and maritime sabotage, attacks at airports, attacks against diplomats and government officials, attacks against U.N. peacekeepers, use of bombs or biological, chemical or nuclear materials, and providing financial support to terrorist organizations. These peacetime anti-terrorism Conventions establish universal jurisdiction to prosecute perpetrators, require states where perpetrators are found to either prosecute them or extradite them, and establish a duty to provide judicial cooperation for other states.

While some of the anti-terrorism Conventions are widely ratified, only fifty countries have ratified all twelve treaties. Moreover, there are significant gaps in the regime of the peacetime anti-terrorism conventions. For example, assassinations of businessmen, engineers, journalists and educators are not covered, while similar attacks against diplomats and public officials are prohibited. Attacks or acts of sabotage by means other than explosives against a passenger train or bus, or a water supply or electric power plant, are not covered; while similar attacks against an airplane or an ocean liner would be included. Placing anthrax into an envelope would not be covered; nor would most forms of cyber-terrorism. Additionally, acts of psychological terror that do not involve physical injury are not covered, even though placing a fake bomb in a public place or sending fake anthrax through the mails can be every bit as traumatizing to a population as an actual attack.

Defining terrorism as the peacetime equivalent of war crimes would fill most of these gaps. Moreover, it would make it clearer that States have a right to use military force in self-defense against a terrorist group physically located within the boundaries of another state. As described below, some domestic and international judicial bodies have already applied the laws of war to peacetime acts of terrorism, thereby setting a precedent for an approach that lowers the armed conflict threshold to equate acts of terrorism with war crimes.

## A. The Juan Carlos Abella Human Rights Case

An international body first considered this question in the *Juan Carlos Abella v. Argentina* case, decided by the Inter-American Commission on Human Rights in 1997. The case concerned the January 23, 1989, attack by forty-two civilians, armed with civilian weapons, on the La Tablada military barracks in Argentina during peacetime. The Argentine government sent 1,500 troops to subdue this terrorist attack. Allegedly, after four hours of fighting, the civilian attackers tried to surrender by waiving white flags, but the Argentine troops refused to accept their surrender and the fighting raged on for another thirty hours until most of the attackers were killed or badly wounded by incendiary weapons.

The Inter-American Commission first held that international humanitarian law (the laws of war) was part of its subject matter jurisdiction by implied reference in Article 27(1) of the Inter-American Convention on Human Rights. Next, the Commission held that the confrontation at the La Tablada barracks was not merely an internal disturbance or tension (in which case it would not qualify as an armed conflict subject to the laws of war). The Commission stated that international humanitarian law "does not require the existence of large scale and generalized hostilities or a situation comparable to a civil war in which dissident armed groups exercise control over parts of national territory." The Commission found the confrontation at the La Tablada barracks to qualify as an armed conflict because it involved a carefully planned, coordinated and executed armed attack against a quintessential military objective—a military base, notwithstanding the small number of attackers involved and the short time frame of the fighting. The Commission thus stated that had the Argentinean troops in fact refused to accept the surrender of the civilian attackers, or had they in fact used weapons of a nature to cause superfluous injury or unnecessary suffering; this would have constituted a war crime. However, "because of the incomplete nature of the evidence," the Commission was unable to find against Argentina concerning these allegations.

The Juan Carlos Abella case is an important precedent because it lowers the armed conflict threshold so that many terrorist situations could now trigger the standard of the laws of war. But it also highlights several potential problems with applying the laws of war to terrorist attacks. First, by confining their attack to a military barracks, the terrorists (who in this case carried their arms openly) acted lawfully under the laws of war. Conversely, the laws of war would constrain the methods the government could use to quell the attack.

## B. The United States' Response to the 9/11 Attacks

In testimony before the Senate Judiciary Committee, Scott Silliman, the Executive Director of the Center on Law, Ethics and National Security at Duke University School of Law, explained that since the United States was not in a state of armed conflict with al Qaeda on the morning of September 11, 2001, the attacks by al Qaeda could not be considered violations of the laws of war. Although al Qaeda had been responsible for a few prior sporadic attacks against the United States, including the bombings of the U.S. embassies in Kenya and Tanzania in 1998 and the attack on the U.S.S. Cole in 2000, and the United States had attacked al Qaeda's Afghan training bases with cruise missiles in 1998, these did not rise to the level of protracted armed violence between governmental authorities and organized armed groups as required to trigger the laws of war.

Nevertheless, in promulgating the instruments governing the prosecution of al Qaeda members before U.S. military commissions, the United States made clear that in its view, ongoing mutual hostilities were not required to qualify the attacks of September 11 as an armed conflict. Rather, "a single hostile act or attempted act may provide sufficient basis for the nexus [between the conduct and armed hostilities] so long as its magnitude or severity rises to the level of an 'armed attack'... or the number, power, stated intent or organization of the force with which the actor is associated is such that the act or attempted act is tantamount to an attack by an armed force." Applying this novel definition which reduces the armed conflict threshold to require merely a single severe terrorist act, the Military Commissions have charged several members of al Qaeda with committing war crimes in relation to the attacks of September 11.

## C. The Fawaz Yunis Prosecution

In other contexts, U.S. courts have applied the laws of war to even minor terrorist acts committed during peacetime. Consider the case of *United States v. Yunis*. Fawaz Yunis was a member of the Amal militia which opposed the presence of the PLO in Lebanon. On June 11, 1985, Yunis hijacked a Jordanian airliner from Beirut and attempted to fly it to the PLO Conference in Tunis to make a political statement. At his trial in the United States for committing acts of terrorism (hijacking and hostage taking), Yunis sought to use the obedience to orders defense. This is the defense made famous in the case of Lieutenant William L. Calley who was tried for the My Lai massacre in Vietnam. According to U.S. law, "acts of a subordinate done in compliance with an unlawful order given him by his superior are excused ... unless [the order] is one which a man of ordinary sense and understanding would ... know to be unlawful ..."

The Yunis court instructed the jury that Yunis could prevail on the obedience to orders defense if it found that the Amal Militia was a "military organization." To make that finding, however, the judge indicated that the jury had to determine that (1) the Amal Militia had a hierarchical command structure; (2) it generally conducted itself in accordance with the laws of war; and (3) its members had a distinctive symbol and carried their arms openly. Although the jury did not find that the Amal Militia met this test, at least some terrorist organizations would qualify as a "military organization" under it, and thus have the right to rely on the obedience to orders defense.

## D. The Ahmed Extradition Case

In the Mahmoud El-Abed Ahmed Extradition case, the U.S. court used the rules of armed conflict by analogy to determine whether a peacetime terrorist act could qualify for the political offense exception to extradition. In 1986, Ahmed attacked an Israeli passenger bus near Tel Aviv, and then fled to the United States. At his extradition hearing, his lawyer, former U.S. Attorney-General Ramsey Clark, argued that this was a non-extraditable political offense.

The Court held that a person relying on the political offense exception must prove the acceptability of his offense under the laws of war, even when an armed conflict did not exist as such at the time of the offense. The Court found that Ahmed's acts did not qualify for the political offense exception because they violated Additional Protocol II's prohibition on targeting civilians. While this result ensured that Ahmed would be prosecuted in Israel, the implication of the holding is that if a terrorist targets military personnel or a government installation, the terrorist would be protected by the political offense exception.

## IV. Negative Implications of Applying the Laws of War to Peacetime Acts of Terrorism

The Abella, Yunis, Ahmed, and al Qaeda cases show that domestic and international judicial bodies are beginning to apply the laws of war to terrorist acts outside the traditional concept of armed conflict. These cases thus provide a precedent for treating terrorism as the peacetime equivalent of war crimes. But these cases also indicate some of the problems inherent to this approach, which stem from the fact that the laws of war establish rights as well as obligations for those over whom they apply.

## A. Unlawful Versus Lawful Combatants

The terms "lawful" and "unlawful-combatants" are designed to draw a distinction between armed forces, which are a legitimate target of war, and the civilian population, which is not. To promote the distinction, only lawful combatants are entitled to the protection afforded by the laws of war, including the combatant's privilege and Prisoner of War status.

Under the 1949 Geneva Conventions, to qualify as a lawful combatant members of a militia had to inter alia have a fixed distinctive sign recognizable at a distance, something most terrorists would not have. In recognition of the realities of modern guerrilla warfare, however, the 1977 Protocol I to the Geneva Conventions provides that, while combatants should clearly distinguish themselves from civilians, it may be that "the nature of hostilities" will in some cases effectively preclude such distinction. In such case, members of a fighting force will nevertheless retain "combatant" status and be entitled to POW status upon capture, provided they "carry arms openly" during actual military engagements.

It is for this reason that the United States has not ratified Additional Protocol I, which it felt gave too much protection to terrorist groups. But the Protocol has been ratified by 155 countries, including seventeen of the nineteen members of NATO and three of the Permanent Members of the Security Council. The Protocol has been invoked as reflecting customary international law in various conflicts by governments, U.N. investigative bodies, and the International Committee of the Red Cross. The United States, itself, argued that the Protocol represented customary international law in advocating that the International Criminal Tribunal for the former Yugoslavia should have jurisdiction over breaches of the Protocol. U.S. soldiers are subject to arrest and prosecution/extradition for breaches of the Protocol when they are present in the territory of any State Party. When the U.S. deploys troops on a U.N. peace-keeping mission, the United Nations requires that they be subject to Protocol I. Finally, as a matter of policy on the conduct of hostilities during coalition actions, the United States has implemented the rules of the Protocol because of the need to coordinate rules of engagement with its coalition partners.

Consequently, if the laws of war are extended to peacetime acts of terrorism, than many terrorists would be able to qualify for the rights of combatants under the less stringent standard of Additional Protocol I.

## B. The Combatant's Privilege and Collateral Damage Doctrine

If terrorism is defined as the peacetime equivalent of war crimes, terrorists could rely on the "combatant's privilege," under which combatants are immune from prosecution for certain common crimes. For example, killing a combatant is justified homicide, not murder. This means that terrorist attacks on military, police, or other government personnel would not be prosecutable or extraditable offenses. Similarly, kidnapping combatants constitutes a lawful taking of prisoners. Consequently, taking military or government personnel hostage would generally not constitute a crime.

Moreover, under the combatant's privilege, government installations are a lawful target of war. Though citing Alex Schmid's definitional approach with approval, the recent judgment of the Indian Supreme Court cautioned that "if terrorism is defined strictly in terms of attacks on non-military targets, a number of attacks on military installations and soldiers' residences could not be included." Thus, terrorist attacks on military, police, or government buildings would not be regarded as criminal; nor would attacks on navy vessels or aircraft. The collateral damage doctrine would apply, such that injury or deaths to civilians would not be regarded as criminal so long as the target was a government installation, and reasonable steps were taken to minimize the risk to innocent civilians.

Thus, under the proposal to define terrorism as the peacetime equivalent of war crimes, if al Qaeda had attacked the Pentagon not with airliners full of innocent passengers, but with a truck bomb, that would have been a lawful act of war, not terrorism.

### C. Assassination

Another problem with the proposal is that it would permit assassination of political leaders while they are within their own borders. The Internationally Protected Person Convention only protects heads of state, high level officials, and diplomats when they are on a mission outside of their home state. The laws of war, which would apply to such persons while within their country, make it a war crime to kill "treacherously," — understood as prohibiting assassination. But this prohibition has been narrowly interpreted to, for example, permit targeting military or civilian commanders during a conflict. Executive Order 12,333, which prohibits U.S. government personnel from engaging in assassination, has been subject to a similarly narrowly interpretation.

Shortly after the 1986 bombing of Libyan leader Colonel Muammar Qaddafi's personal quarters in Tripoli, Senior Army lawyers made public a memorandum that concluded that Executive Order 12,333 was not intended to prevent the United States from acting in self-defense against "legitimate threats to national security" even during peacetime. More recently, the United States has begun to use unmanned Predator drone aircraft, equipped with Helfire missiles, to hunt down members of the al Qaeda terrorist organization throughout the world, even outside the zone of conflict. If the laws of war apply to terrorists in peacetime it would logically follow that they have the same right as governments to target military or civilian commanders and others who pose a threat to the security of their insurgency or self-determination movement.

### D. POW Status

Another problem is that defining terrorism as the peacetime equivalent of war crimes might entitle some terrorists to POW status, which requires that they be given special rights beyond those afforded to common prisoners. By way of analogy, one might examine the case of *United States v. Noriega*, in which General Noriega argued that Article 22 of the Third Geneva Convention required that he not be interned in a penitentiary. Although the District Court held that Article 22 did not apply to POWs convicted of common crimes, it agreed that General Noriega was entitled to POW status and therefore entitled to the protections of Article 13 ("humane treatment"); Article 14 ("respect for their persons and their honour"); and Article 16 ("equal treatment"). The members of al Qaeda being tried by the U.S. Military Commissions in Guantanamo Bay have made a similar argument in their habeas petitions, contending that as POWs under the Geneva Conventions they cannot lawfully be tried by military commission.

Even if they are ultimately denied POW status, under the Geneva Conventions the al Qaeda detainees are still entitled to fundamental guarantees of humane treatment and may not be tortured or degraded. In contrast, if the members of al Qaeda were deemed common criminals not subject to the protections of the laws of war, the United States would actually have more leeway in how it treats al Qaeda members that are captured and detained outside of its borders.

### E. The Obedience to Orders Defense

Finally, as the Fawas Yunis Case demonstrated, defining terrorism as the peacetime equivalent of war crimes would enable terrorists to rely on the obedience to orders defense. This may be a fair tradeoff for providing the prosecution with the use of the doctrine of command responsibility, but at least in some cases it will render it more difficult to obtain a conviction of accused terrorists. While the defense is not available with respect to acts that our manifestly unlawful, such as intentionally targeting civilians or taking hostages, it would apply to those lower down in the chain of command who are ordered to perform specific tasks, such as procuring explosives or an airline schedule or a fake passport which are not in themselves manifestly war crimes.

## V. Conclusion

The proposal to define terrorism as the peacetime equivalent of war crimes necessitates application of the laws of war to terrorists. The approach would fill some of the gaps of the current anti-terrorism treaty regime. It might permit the exercise of more forceful measures that might not be permissible under the rubric of law enforcement. It would give the prosecution the ability to argue the doctrine of command responsibility, which was not previously applicable to peacetime acts. It will also encourage terrorist groups to play by the rules of international humanitarian law. Conversely, the approach virtually declares open season for attacks on government personnel and facilities. It would encourage insurrection by reducing the personal risks of rebels, and it would enhance the perceived standing of insurgents by treating them as combatants rather than common criminals.

It is important that those advocating this new approach to the definition of terrorism be fully aware of all the legal consequences that arise from the approach. It is no panacea, and in the final analysis the negative consequences may render it another dead end in the enduring struggle to define terrorism.

---

## Authors' Note

The following three materials chronicle the evolution of America's policy toward terrorists in the aftermath of September 11th. Material 6 conveys the initial categorization of all al Qaeda and Taliban members as "unlawful combatants" as determined by President George W. Bush. This classification has important implications for the application of protections afforded under the Geneva Convention and its Additional Protocols. Material 7 represents the shift in U.S. policy and the implementation of Combat Status Review Tribunals to allow detainees at Guantanamo Bay to challenge the legality of the detainee's confinement. Material 8 conveys the processes of the Status Review Tribunals and discusses some direct effect of the U.S. Supreme Court's decisions in *Rasul v. Bush* and *Odah v. Rumsfeld*. These materials depicts the state of tumult that exists even within America's own definition of terrorism and enemy combatants, as well as determining the appropriate approach to combating international terrorism.

---

## 6. William J. Haynes, Enemy Combatants
### Council on Foreign Relations, 2002

MEMORANDUM

To: Members of the ASIL-CFR Roundtable
From: William J. Haynes II, General Counsel of the Department of Defense
Subject: Enemy Combatants

There is no doubt that the attacks of September 11, 2001, constituted acts of war. They possessed the intensity and scale of war. They involved at least one military target, the Pentagon, and they came on the heels of a decade of attacks by al Qaida on U.S. military and civilian targets. Congress on September 18, 2001, authorized the President to use force in response to the attacks. And both the United Nations and NATO recognized that the attacks were "armed attacks" within the meaning of the U.N. Charter and NATO treaty. Since September 11th (and perhaps before then), we have been at war—both legally and in fact.

War implies legal powers and rules that are not available during peacetime. Among other things, the war context gives the President the authority to detain enemy combatants at least until hostilities cease.

### Enemy Combatant

An "enemy combatant" is an individual who, under the laws and customs of war, may be detained for the duration of an armed conflict. In the current conflict with al Qaida and the Taliban, the term includes a member, agent, or associate of al Qaida or the Taliban. In applying this definition, the United States government has acted consistently with the observation of the Supreme Court of the United States in Ex parte Quirin, 317 U.S. 1, 37–38 (1942): "Citizens who associate themselves with the military arm of the enemy government, and with its aid, guidance and direction enter this country bent on hostile acts are enemy belligerents within the meaning of the Hague Convention and the law of war."

"Enemy combatant" is a general category that subsumes two sub-categories: lawful and unlawful combatants. See Quirin, 317 U.S. at 37–38. Lawful combatants receive prisoner of war (POW) status and the protections of the Third Geneva Convention. Unlawful combatants do not receive POW status and do not receive the full protections of the Third Geneva Convention. (The treatment accorded to unlawful combatants is discussed below).

The President has determined that al Qaida members are unlawful combatants because (among other reasons) they are members of a non-state actor terrorist group that does not receive the protections of the Third Geneva Convention. He additionally determined that the Taliban detainees are unlawful combatants because they do not satisfy the criteria for POW status set out in Article 4 of the Third Geneva Convention. Although the President's determination on this issue is final, courts have concurred with his determination.

---

## 7. Combatant Status Review Tribunals: Factsheet
### United States Department of Defense, 2004

In response to last week's decisions by the Supreme Court, the Deputy Secretary of Defense today issued an order creating procedures for a Combatant Status Review Tribunal to provide detainees at Guantanamo Bay Naval Base with notice of the basis for their detention and review of their detention as enemy combatants. Each of these individuals has been determined to be an enemy combatant through multiple levels of review by the Department of Defense. The procedures for the Review Tribunal are intended to reflect the guidance the Supreme Court provided in its decisions last week.

### The Supreme Court's Decisions

- The Supreme Court held that the federal courts have jurisdiction to hear challenges to the legality of the detention of enemy combatants held at Guantanamo Bay. In a separate decision—involving an American citizen held in the United States—the Court also held that due process would be satisfied by notice and an opportunity to be heard, and indicated that such process could properly be provided in the context of a hearing before a tribunal of military officers.

- The Court specifically cited certain existing military regulations, Army Regulation 190–8, which it suggested might be sufficient to meet the standards it articulated. The tribunals established under those regulations are relatively informal and occur without counsel or a personal representative. The process is a streamlined process designed to allow for expeditious determinations; in citing it, the Court recognized the military's need for flexibility and indicated that the process might provide all that was needed even for a citizen. Even in a traditional conflict, such a hearing is not provided to everyone who is detained, but only in cases of doubt as to the basis for detention.

**The Process**—The order issued today creates tribunals very much like those cited favorably by the Court to meet the unique circumstances of the Guantanamo detainees, and will provide an expeditious opportunity for non-citizen detainees to receive notice and an opportunity to be heard. It will not preclude them from seeking additional review in federal court.

- *Notice.* By July 17, each detainee will be notified of the review of his detention as an enemy combatant, of the opportunity to consult with a personal representative, and of the right to seek review in U.S. courts.

- *Personal Representative.* Each detainee will be assigned a military officer as a personal representative to assist in connection with the Tribunal process. This person is not a lawyer but provides assistance to the detainee that is not normally offered in the process cited favorably by the Supreme Court or required by the Geneva Conventions.

- Tribunals. Detainees will be afforded an opportunity to appear before and present evidence to a Tribunal composed of three neutral commissioned military officers, none of whom was involved in the apprehension, detention, interrogation, or previous determination of status of the detainee.

- *Hearings.*

- The detainee will be allowed to attend all proceedings of the Tribunal except for those involving deliberation and voting or which would compromise national security if held in the presence of the detainee.

- The detainee will be provided with an interpreter and his personal representative will be available to assist at the hearing.

- The detainee will be allowed to present evidence, to call witnesses if reasonably available, and to question witnesses called by the Tribunal.

- The detainee will have the right to testify or otherwise address the Tribunal in oral or written form, but may not be compelled to testify.

- *Decision.* The Tribunal will decide whether a preponderance of evidence supports the detention of the individual as an enemy combatant, and there will be a rebuttable presumption in favor of the Government's evidence.

- *Non-Enemy Combatant Determination.* If the Tribunal determines that the detainee should no longer be classified as an enemy combatant, the Secretary of Defense will advise the Secretary of State, who will coordinate the transfer of the detainee for release to the detainee's country of citizenship or other disposition consistent with domestic and international obligations and U.S. foreign policy.

## 8. Kathleen T. Rhem, DoD to Review Status of All Guantanamo Detainees

American Forces Press Service, 2004

Within 10 days, all 594 detainees held at the U.S. naval base at Guantanamo Bay, Cuba, will be informed of their right to contest their status under new procedures.

Defense officials announced July 7 that they are setting up a series of hearings to give all detainees a forum to plead their case to a panel of three U.S. military officers, officially called a Combatant Status Review Tribunal.

"Each of the detainees at Guantanamo has been determined to be an enemy combatant through multiple layers of review by the department," a senior Defense Department official said in a background briefing in the Pentagon.

He said the new procedures, which were provided for in an order signed July 7 by Deputy Defense Secretary Paul Wolfowitz, are designed to reflect guidance handed down by the U.S. Supreme Court in two recent decisions.

The tribunal panel will not look at guilt or innocence. The defense official said the tribunals are being set up only "to provide an opportunity for the detainee to contest the determination that's been made that he is an enemy combatant."

The Supreme Court ruled June 28 in two consolidated cases, *Rasul v. Bush*, No. 03-334, and *al Odah v. Rumsfeld*, No. 03-343, that enemy combatants held by the U.S. government had the right to contest their status before a judge or other neutral decision maker. Government officials believe the Combatant Status Review Tribunal meets that requirement.

The senior defense official and an accompanying senior Justice Department official did not brief on other areas of the Supreme Court's decision, such as the requirement that detainees be given the opportunity to protest their detention in U.S. federal courts. The officials said such procedures are still being worked out, and they wouldn't speculate.

Officials are still working on a timeline for the review tribunals but did release some details. Within 10 days, all detainees will be notified of the tribunal proceedings and of their right to request an appearance before a federal judge to seek a writ of habeas corpus. Habeas corpus is an order for a person in custody to be brought before a court to decide the legality of detention.

Also within 10 days from the order's signing, all detainees will be appointed a "personal representative" in the form of a U.S. military officer who has access to the detainees' case information and will help them prepare presentations for the tribunal. The personal representative may also participate in the tribunal on the detainee's behalf.

The tribunals will convene within 30 days after the personal representatives are given the detainees' personal files and meet with the detainees for the first time.

Detainees will be afforded the opportunity to present evidence, make statements on their own behalf and call witnesses "that are reasonably available." The defense official said the implementing authority, Navy Secretary Gordon England, will determine what "reasonably available" entails.

Detainees will not be compelled to testify at the tribunals if they choose not to.

Translators will be available at all stages of this process, the officials said.

The tribunal will consist of a voting panel of three military officers, with a minimum of one attorney. A second military attorney will serve as a non-voting recorder. The panel's deliberations on each case will be done in private.

XIX · UN CONFERENCE TO DEFINE TERRORISM

The officials explained that should the panel decide a detainee is not an enemy combatant, Defense Secretary Donald Rumsfeld would notify Secretary of State Colin Powell. Powell would, in turn, work with the detainee's home country to coordinate release to that country.

## Authors' Note

The Special Tribunal for Lebanon ("STL"), established in 2007 by the United Nations Security Council to prosecute those responsible for the 2005 bombings that killed former Lebanese Prime Minister Rafiq Hariri and twenty-two others, is the world's first international court with jurisdiction over the crime of terrorism. *See* Statute of the Special Tribunal for Lebanon, *appended to* S.C. Res. 1757, U.N. Doc. S/RES/1757 (May 30, 2007). On January 17, 2011, the Tribunal's Prosecutor, Daniel Bellemare, submitted a sealed indictment for the pre-trial judge to confirm. The pre-trial judge, in turn, requested that the Appeals Chamber resolve fifteen questions relating to the substantive criminal law to be applied by the STL, the applicable modes of criminal responsibility, and guidance regarding whether the STL should charge crimes cumulatively or in the alternative. In response, the STL Appeals Chamber handed down a landmark ruling on February 16, 2011. Material 9 presents the *Interlocutory Decision on the Applicable Law: Terrorism, Conspiracy, Homicide, Perpetration, Cumulative Charging, Special Tribunal for Lebanon Appeals Chamber*, Case No. STL-11-01/I (Feb. 16, 2011). This selection provides the definition of terrorism as applied by the STL. Material 10 provides a summarization of the Appeals Chamber judgment in an excerpt from Michael P. Scharf. This excerpt addresses the implications of this decision on international terrorism jurisprudence.

## 9. Interlocutory Decision on the Applicable Law: Terrorism, Conspiracy, Homicide, Perpetration, Cumulative Charging

Special Tribunal for Lebanon, 2011

\* \* \*

### B. The Notion of Terrorism To Be Applied by the Tribunal

The Tribunal shall apply the Lebanese domestic crime of terrorism, interpreted in consonance with international conventional and customary law that is binding on Lebanon.

Under Lebanese law the objective elements of terrorism are as follows: (i) an act whether constituting an offence under other provisions of the Criminal Code or not; and (ii) the use of a means "liable to create a public danger". These means are indicated in an illustrative enumeration: explosive devices, inflammable materials, poisonous or incendiary products, or infectious or microbial agents. According to Lebanese case law, these means do not include such non-enumerated implements as a gun, a machine-gun, a revolver, a letter bomb or a knife. The subjective element of terrorism is the special intent to cause a state of terror.

Although Article 2 of the Statute enjoins the Tribunal to apply Lebanese law, the Tribunal may nevertheless take into account international law for the purpose of interpreting Lebanese law. In this respect, two sets of rules may be taken into account: the Arab Convention against Terrorism, which has been ratified by Lebanon, and customary international law on terrorism in time of peace.

The Arab Convention enjoins the States Parties to cooperate in the prevention and suppression of terrorism and defines terrorism for that purpose, while leaving each contracting party freedom to simultaneously pursue the suppression of terrorism on the basis of its own national legislation.

A comparison between Lebanese law and the Convention shows that the two notions of terrorism have in common two elements: (i) the both embrace acts; and (ii) they require the intent of spreading terror or fear. However, the Convention's definition is broader than that of Lebanese law in that it does not require the underlying act to be carried out by specific means, instrumentalities or devices. In other respects the Arab Convention's notion of terrorism is narrower: it requires the underlying act to be violent, and it excludes acts performed in the course of a war of national liberation (as long as such war is not conducted against an Arab country).

On the basis of treaties, U.N. resolutions and the legislative and

On the basis of treaties, U.N. resolutions and the legislative and judicial practice of States, there is convincing evidence that a customary rule of international law has evolved on terrorism *in time of peace*, requiring the following elements: (i) the intent (*dolus*) of the underlying crime and (ii) the special intent (*dolus specialis*) to spread fear or coerce authority; (iii) the commission of a criminal act, and (iv) that the terrorist act be transnational. The very few States still insisting on an exception to the definition of terrorism can, at most, be considered persistent objectors. A comparison between the crime of terrorism as defined under the Lebanese Criminal Code and that envisaged in customary international law shows that the latter notion is broader with regard to the means of carrying out the terrorist act, which are not limited under international law, and narrower m that (i) it only deals with terrorist acts in time of peace, (ii) it requires both an underlying criminal act and an intent to commit that act and (iii) it involves a transnational element.

While fully respecting the Lebanese jurisprudence relating to cases of terrorism brought before Lebanese courts, the Tribunal cannot but take into account the unique gravity and transnational dimension of the crimes at issue and the Security Council's consideration of them as particularly grave international acts of terrorism justifying the establishment of an international court. As a result, for the purpose of adjudicating these facts, the Tribunal is justified in applying, at least in one respect, a construction of the Lebanese Criminal Code's definition of terrorism more extensive that than suggested by Lebanese case law. While Lebanese courts have held that a terrorist attack must be carried out through one of the means enumerated in the Criminal Code, the Code itself suggests that its list of implements is illustrative, not exhaustive, and might therefore include also such implements as handguns, machine-guns and so on, depending on the circumstances of each case. The only firm requirement is that the means used to carry out the terrorist attack also be liable to create a common danger, either by exposing bystanders or onlookers to harm or by instigating further violence in the form of retaliation or political instability. This interpretation of Lebanese law better addresses contemporary forms of terrorism and also aligns Lebanese law more closely with the relevant international law that is binding on Lebanon.

This interpretation does not run counter to the principle of legality (*nullum crimen sine lege*) because (i) this interpretation is consistent with the offence as explicitly defined under Lebanese law; (ii) it was accessible to the accused, especially given the publication of the Arab Convention and other international treaties ratified by Lebanon in the Official Gazette (none of which limits the means or implements by which terrorist acts may be performed); (iii) hence, it was reasonably foreseeable by the accused.

In sum, and in light of the principles enunciated above, the notion of terrorism to be applied by the Tribunal consists of the following elements: (i) the volitional commission of an act; (ii) through means that are liable to create a public danger; and (iii) the intent of the perpetrator to cause a state of terror. Considering that the elements of the notion of terrorism do not require an underlying crime, the perpetrator of an act of terrorism that results in deaths would be liable for terrorism, with the deaths being an aggravating circumstance; additionally, the perpetrator may also, and *independently*, be liable for the underlying crime if he had the requisite criminal intent for that crime.

\* \* \*

## 10. Michael P. Scharf, Introductory Note to the Decision of the Appeals Chamber of the Special Tribunal for Lebanon on the Definition of Terrorism
### International Legal Materials, 2011

Although the STL's Statute stipulates that the court is to apply the crime of terrorism as defined by Lebanese law, the Appeals Chamber held that the STL is authorized to construe Lebanese law defining terrorism with the assistance of international treaty and customary law. Interlocutory Decision, paras 45, 62. This was a departure from the traditional approach of treaty interpretation, as reflected in Article 32 of the Vienna Convention on the Law of Treaties, in which the Tribunal would apply the "ordinary meaning" of the terms of the Statute unless the text was found to be either ambiguous or obscure or would lead to an interpretation which is manifestly absurd or unreasonable. Since the Statute of the STL clearly stated that the Court was to apply the Lebanese domestic law on terrorism, under the traditional approach, resort to supplementary means of interpretation would be appropriate only if the Court had found that there was an inconsistency or gap in the applicable Lebanese law.

In diverging from the traditional approach, the Appeals Chamber stated that "the old maxim *in claris non fit interpretation* (when a text is clear there is no need for interpretation) is in truth fallacious," explaining that "it overlooks the spectrum of meanings that words, and especially a collection of words, may have and misses the truth that context can determine meaning." Interlocutory Decision, para. 19. Instead, the Appeals Chamber adopted a "semiotic" approach to interpretation. Semiotics begins with the assumption that terms such as "terrorism" are not historic artifacts whose meaning remains static over time. Rather, the meaning of such terms changes along with the interpretative community or communities. As the STL Appeals Chamber explained, this interpretative approach "recognizes the reality that society alters over time and interpretation of a law may evolve to keep pace." Interlocutory Decision, para. 21.

The Appeals Chamber thus held that it was appropriate to read the Lebanese law in the context of "international obligations undertaken by Lebanon with which, in the absence of very clear language, it is presumed any legislation complies." Interlocutory Decision, paras. 19–20. This interpretive approach opened the door for the Appeals Chamber to determine whether a defined offense of terrorism exists under customary international law. To that end, the Appeals Chamber found that "although it is held by many scholars and other legal experts that no widely accepted definition of terrorism has evolved in the world society because of the marked difference of views on some issues, closer scrutiny reveals that in fact such a definition has gradually emerged." Interlocutory Decision, paras. 83 and 102.

Based on its review of state practice and indicators of *opinio juris*, the Appeals Chamber declared that the customary international law definition of terrorism consists of the following three key elements: (i) the perpetration of a criminal act (such as murder, kidnapping, hostage-taking, arson, and so on), or threatening such an act; (ii) the intent to spread fear among the population (which would generally entail the creation of public danger) or directly or indirectly coerce a national or international authority to take some action, or to refrain from taking it; (iii) when the act involves a transnational element. Interlocutory Decision at para 85.

Reading the Lebanese law on terrorism together with the definition of terrorism under customary international law, the Appeals Chamber concluded that the particular means used in an attack were not dispositive in determining whether an attack was terrorism or simply murder. Interlocutory Decision at para. 147. In other words, contrary to Lebanese case law, the Appeals Chamber opined that attacks committed by rifles or handguns, which are not likely per se to cause a danger to the general population, are nevertheless within the jurisdiction of the STL. Interlocutory Decision at paras. 59, 138, 145.

Yet, the significance of this aspect of the Appeals Chamber opinion is far broader than its application to the case before the STL. This is the first time in history that an international tribunal has authoritatively confirmed the crystallization of a general definition of terrorism under customary international law. The decision will almost certainly spark a debate about whether the STL's conclusion is correct in light of the conventional view that the international community has not yet reached consensus on a general definition of terrorism. Since the decision has been issued by an international tribunal, and penned by a highly respected jurist, it is possible that the decision itself will be seen as "a Grotian moment," crystallizing a customary international law definition of terrorism. If so, the decision will have a momentous effect on the decades-long effort of the international community to develop a broadly acceptable definition of terrorism.

## 11. Bibliography of Additional Sources

- Yonah Alexander, INTERNATIONAL TERRORISM: NATIONAL, REGIONAL, AND GLOBAL PERSPECTIVES (1976).

- United States, Congress. Senate. Select Committee on Intelligence. Current and projected national security threats to the United States: Hearing before the Select Committee on Intelligence of the United States Senate, One Hundred Sixth Congress, second session (February 2, 2000).

- Paul Wilkinson, TERRORISM VERSUS DEMOCRACY: THE LIBERAL STATE RESPONSE (2000).

- United States. General Accounting Office. Combating terrorism: Action taken but considerable risks remain for forces overseas: Report to the Ranking Minority Member, Committee on Armed Services, House of Representatives/United States General Accounting Office. Washington, D.C. (P.O. Box 37050, Washington, D.C. 20013): The Office (2000).

- Acts of Terror?, THE CHRISTIAN SCIENCE MONITOR, May 13, 1986, at 19.

- Another U.N. Obscenity, THE JERUSALEM POST, July 20, 1998, at 8.

- Ayaz R. Shaikh, A Theoretic Approach to Transnational Terrorism, 80 GEO. L.J. 2131 (1992).

- David Ott, Ineffectual and an Affront to the Principles of Justice, THE HERALD (Glasgow), September 2, 1998, at 15.

- Douglas J. Ende, Reaccepting the Compulsory Jurisdiction of the International Court of Justice, 61 WASH. L. REV. 1145 (1986).

- Gregory M. Travalio, Terrorism, International Law, and the Use of Military Force, 18 Wis. Int'l L.J. 145 (2000).

- John P. Egan, Defining "Terrorism" in Political Terms, Chicago Tribune, March 8, 1986, at 10.

- Louis Rene Beres, The Legal Meaning of Terrorism for the Military Commander, 11 Conn. J. Int'l L. 1 (1995).

- Matthew H. James, Keeping the Peace—British, Israeli, and Japanese Legislative Responses to Terrorism, 15 Dick. J. Int'l L. 405 (1997).

- Roberta Smith, America Tries to Come to Terms With Terrorism: The United States Anti-Terrorism and Effective Death Penalty Act of 1996 v. British Anti-Terrorism Law and International Response, 5 Cardozo J. Int'l & Comp. L. 249 (1997).

- Ross E. Schreiber, Ascertaining Opinio Juris of States Concerning Norms Involving the Prevention of International Terrorism: A Focus on the U.N. Process, 16 B.U. Int'l L.J. 309 (1998).

- Terrorism: Dubious evidence, The Economist, May 9, 1981, at 28.

- Todd M. Sailer, The International Criminal Court: An Argument to Extend Its Jurisdiction to Terrorism and a Dismissal of U.S. Objections, 13 Temp. Int'l & Comp. L.J. 311 (1999).

- Tyler Raimo, Winning at the Expense of Law: The Ramifications of Expanding Counter-Terrorism Law Enforcement Jurisdiction Overseas, 14 Am. U. Int'l L. Rev. 1473 (1999).

- Keith E. Sealing, "State Sponsors of Terrorism" Are Entitled to Due Process Too: The Amended Foreign Sovereign Immunities Act is Unconstitutional, 15 Am. U. Int'l L. Rev. 395 (2000).

- Antonio Vercher, Terrorism in Europe: An International Comparative Legal Analysys (Clarendon Press, 1992).

- Cindy C. Combs, Terrorism in the Twenty-First Century (Prentice Hall, 2000).

- Howard S. Levie, Terrorism in War, The Law of War Crimes (Oceana Publications, 1993).

- James X. Dempsey, Terrorism and the Constitution (First Amendment Foundation, 1999).

- Joseph J. Lambert, Terrorism and Hostages in International Law: A Commentary of the Hostages Convention of 1979 (Grotius Publications, 1990).

- Raphael Perl, Terrorism, The Future and U.S. Foreign Policy (Congressional Research Office, 1996).

- Robert H. Kupperman, Terrorism: threat, Reality, Response (Hoover Institution Press, 1979).

- Henry H. Han (ed.), Terrorism & Political Violence: Limits & Possibilities of Legal Control (Oceana Publications, 1993).

# Chapter XX

# International War Crimes Tribunals

## Introduction

Among the most important new bodies within the United Nations system are the international war crimes tribunals. This chapter examines four current tribunals, the International Criminal Tribunal for the Former Yugoslavia (ICTY), the International Criminal Tribunal for Rwanda (ICTR), the Special Court for Sierra Leone (SCSL), and the Iraqi High Tribunal (IHT). This chapter compares these new tribunals to the first international criminal tribunal, the Nuremberg Tribunal. It also addresses the challenges of setting up a new United Nations body and, in the case of the IHT, setting up a non-U.N. body. The chapter also addresses the question of whether the members of the Security Council were serious about bringing major perpetrators to justice or whether these tribunals constitute little more than a public relations ploy, as some critics maintain.

## Objectives

- To understand the reasons and circumstances surrounding the convening of the Nuremberg Tribunal.

- To understand the complexities of establishing an international criminal tribunal.

- To understand the difficult choices that must be resolved in order to determine the appropriate composition and jurisdiction of an international criminal tribunal.

- To understand the utility of the various ad hoc tribunals and international domestic courts.

- To examine and understand the establishment, composition, procedures, and jurisdiction of the ICTY, ICTR, SCSL, and IHT, including the similarities and differences.

# Problems

1.  Come to class prepared to discuss the following issues:

    (a) What were the motives/interests of the Allies relevant to establishing the Nuremberg Tribunal following World War II?

    (b) What were the criticisms of the Nuremberg Tribunal?

    (c) What were the motives/interests of the members of the Security Council relevant to establishing the Yugoslavia Tribunal?

    (d) Did the Yugoslavia Tribunal avoid the shortcomings of Nuremberg?

    (e) What are the weaknesses of the Yugoslavia War Crimes Tribunal? Were the major powers serious about enforcing the Tribunal's mandate?

    (f) What are the comparative advantages of a hybrid tribunal (like the Special Court for Sierra Leone) or an internationalized domestic tribunal (like the Iraqi High Tribunal) compared to the Security Council-created tribunals?

2.  Come to class prepared to participate in a simulated pre-trial session before the Iraqi High Tribunal. Students will be assigned to represent the Defense or Prosecution, who will be arguing the following motions:

    (a) Defense Motion challenging the legitimacy of the Tribunal.

    (b) Defense Motion to dismiss charges of genocide related to the Anfal Campaign and ecological attacks against the Marsh Arabs.

    (c) Prosecution Motion to Bar the Defendant from Representing Himself in Court.

    (d) Prosecution Motion to Bar the Defense from Raising the "Tu Quoque" Defense.

# Materials

1.  The Nuremberg Tribunal, excerpts from [Virginia Morris and Michael P. Scharf, THE INTERNATIONAL CRIMINAL TRIBUNAL FOR RWANDA, 2–7 (Transnational Publishers, Inc. 1998); Michael P. Scharf and William A. Schabas, Slobodan Milosevic on Trial: A Companion, 39–43 (Continuum, 2002); Virginia Morris and Michael P. Scharf, THE INTERNATIONAL CRIMINAL TRIBUNAL FOR RWANDA, 7–17 (Transnational Publishers, Inc. 1998); and Principles of the Nuremberg Charter and Judgment Formulated by the International Law Commission and adopted by G.A. Res. 177(11)(a), 5 U.N. GAOR, Supp. No. 12, at 11–14, para. 99, U.N. Doc. A/1316 (1946)].

2.  Michael Scharf, BALKAN JUSTICE, pp. xi–xvii, 3–17, 37–90, and 207–228.

3.  Press Conference from ICTY Prosecutor, The Hague, March 12, 2006.

4.  *The ICTR Must Achieve Justice for Rwandans*, 13 AM. U. INT'L L. REV. 1469 (1998).

5.  Michael P. Scharf, The Special Court for Sierra Leone, ASIL Insight, Oct. 2000.

6.  Rena L. Scott, *Moving From Impunity to Accountability in Post-War Liberia: Possibilities, Cautions, and Challenges*, 33 IJLI 345 (2005).

7.  Marlise Simons and J. David Goodman, *Ex-Liberian Leader Gets 50 Years for War Crimes*, THE NEW YORK TIMES, May 30, 2012.

8. Various Essays from *Grotian Moment: The Saddam Hussein Trial Blog*, http://www. law.case.edu/saddamtrial/.

9. Bibliography of Additional Sources

---

# 1. The Nuremberg Tribunal
### *Establishment of the Nuremberg Tribunal*
**Virginia Morris and Michael P. Scharf, THE INTERNATIONAL CRIMINAL TRIBUNAL FOR RWANDA, 2–7 (Transnational Publishers, Inc. 1998)**
[footnotes omitted by editors]

The possibility of establishing an international criminal court with jurisdiction over war crimes and crimes against humanity was seriously considered for the first time in relation to the atrocities committed during the First World War. At the end of the war, the Allied Powers established the Commission on the Responsibility of the Authors of the War and on Enforcement of Penalties to investigate and recommend action on war crimes committed by the personnel of the defeated Central Powers. The Commission documented thirty categories of offenses against the laws and customs of war ranging from the deliberate bombardment of undefended places and attacks against hospital ships by the Germans to the massacre of over a million Armenians by Turkish authorities and by the Turkish populace supported by the public policy of the State.

After the war, the Treaty of Sevres and the Treaty of Versailles, respectively, provided for the prosecution of Turkish and German war criminals (including Kaiser Wilhelm II) before international tribunals. However, no international tribunals were ever established for this purpose. Instead, Kaiser Wilhelm was given sanctuary in the Netherlands and the Allied Powers consented to the trial of accused Germans before the German Supreme Court sitting at Leipzig. Of the 896 Germans accused of war crimes by the Allied Powers, only twelve were tried and of those only six were convicted (and given token sentences). The Turks fared even better by receiving amnesty for their crimes in the Treaty of Lausanne, which replaced the Treaty of Sevres.

Despite the unsatisfactory experience with the attempt to conduct international war crimes trials after the First World War, the Allies were determined to conduct such trials at the end of the Second World War. In the midst of this worldwide conflagration, the Allies took a number of decisive measures in order to ensure that the persons who were responsible for the outbreak of the war and the atrocities that followed would be brought to justice. In 1943, the Allies set up the United Nations War Crimes Commission to collect evidence with a view to conducting trials at the end of the war. Furthermore, the Allies solemnly declared and gave full warning of their unequivocal intention to bring to justice the German political and military leaders who were responsible for the atrocities committed during the war. In 1945, the victorious Allied Governments of the United States, France, the United Kingdom and the Soviet Union concluded the London Agreement providing for the establishment of the International Military Tribunal at Nuremberg (Nuremberg Tribunal) to try the most notorious of the Germans accused of crimes against peace, war crimes and crimes against humanity. The Charter of the International Military Tribunal (Nuremberg Charter) was annexed to the London Agreement.

The Nuremberg Charter was the constitutive instrument of the Nuremberg Tribunal. Thus, the Nuremberg Charter established the structure and governed the functions of the Nuremberg Tribunal. Each State Party to the Nuremberg Charter was to appoint one of the four judges and one of their alternates. The members of the Nuremberg Tribunal were to select from among themselves a President for the first trial, with the presidency rotating among the members in successive trials. A conviction and a sentence could be imposed only by an affirmative vote of at least three members of the Nuremberg Tribunal. All other questions would be decided by majority vote, with the President having the decisive vote in the event of a tie. Each State Party was also to appoint one of the four Chief Prosecutors. The Chief Prosecutors were to act as a committee in designating the major war criminals to be tried by the Nuremberg Tribunal and in preparing the indictments. The Chief Prosecutors were also responsible for drafting the rules of procedure for the Nuremberg Tribunal, which were subject to the approval of the judges. The Nuremberg Tribunal was not bound by technical rules of evidence and was at liberty to admit any evidence which it deemed to have probative value. Moreover, the Nuremberg Tribunal was given the power to compel the presence of witnesses, to interrogate defendants, to compel the production of documents and other evidence, to administer oaths, and to appoint officers to take evidence on commission. The Nuremberg Tribunal was also authorized, upon conviction of a defendant, to impose any punishment it considered just, including the death penalty. The Nuremberg Tribunal judgments were not subject to review.

As regards jurisdiction and applicable law, the Nuremberg Charter determined the subject matter jurisdiction of the Nuremberg Tribunal and provided the definitions of the three categories of crimes with which the defendants were charged:

> *Crimes Against Peace*: namely, planning, preparation, initiation or waging of a war of aggression, or a war in violation of international treaties, agreements or assurances, or participation in a Common Plan or Conspiracy for the accomplishment of any of the foregoing;

> *War Crimes*: namely, violations of the laws or customs of war. Such violations shall include, but not be limited to, murder, ill-treatment or deportation to slave-labor or for any other purpose of civilian population of or in occupied territory, murder or ill-treatment of prisoners of war or persons on the seas, killing of hostages, plunder of public or private property, wanton destruction of cities, towns or villages, or devastation not justified by necessity;

> *Crimes Against Humanity*: namely, murder, extermination, enslavement, deportation, and other inhumane acts committed against any civilian population, before or during the war, or persecutions on political, racial, or religious grounds, in execution of or in connection with any crime within the jurisdiction of the Tribunal, whether or not in violation of domestic law of the country where perpetrated.

....

As regards due process, the Nuremberg Charter guaranteed certain fundamental rights of the accused in order to ensure that every accused received a fair trial, namely: (1) the right to be furnished with the indictment in a language which the accused understands at a reasonable time before trial; (2) the right to give any explanation relevant to the charges against the accused; (3) the right to translation of proceedings before the Nuremberg Tribunal in a language which the accused understands; (4) the right to have the assistance of counsel; and (5) the right to present evidence and to cross-examine any witness called by the prosecution. At the same time, the Nuremberg Charter provided for trials in absentia, authorized the Nuremberg Tribunal to interrogate the accused, limited the defenses available to the accused by excluding the act of State defense and the defense of superior orders; and precluded any challenges to the jurisdiction or the composition of the Nuremberg Tribunal.

....

In terms of procedure, the Nuremberg Charter and Rules of Procedure provided an innovative blend and balance of various elements of the Continental European inquisitorial system and the Anglo-American adversarial system in order to create a tailor-made international criminal procedure which would be generally acceptable to the States Parties representing both systems.... The Nuremberg Tribunal was governed by simplified evidentiary rules which constituted another unique feature of the Nuremberg Charter. The technical rules of evidence developed under the common law system of jury trials to prevent the jury from being influenced by improper evidence were considered to be unnecessary for trials conducted in the absence of a jury. Accordingly, the Nuremberg Charter provided that the Nuremberg Tribunal was not bound by technical rules of evidence and could admit any evidence which it deemed to have probative value. Consequently, the Nuremberg Tribunal allowed the prosecutors to introduce ex parte affidavits against the accused over the objections of their attorneys.

### The Rationale for Creating the Nuremberg Tribunal
### Michael P. Scharf and William A. Schabas, Slobodan Milosevic on Trial: A Companion, 39–43 (Continuum, 2002)

The events that prompted the formation of the Nuremberg Tribunal in 1945 are probably more familiar to most than those which led to the creation of the Yugoslavia War Crimes Tribunal a half century later. Between 1933 and 1940, the Nazi regime established concentration camps where Jews, Communists and opponents of the regime were incarcerated without trial; it progressively prohibited Jews from engaging in employment and participating in various areas of public life, stripped them of citizenship, and made marriage or sexual intimacy between Jews and German citizens a criminal offense; it forcibly annexed Austria and Czechoslovakia; invaded and occupied Poland, Denmark, Norway, Luxembourg, Holland, Belgium, and France; and then it set in motion "the final solution to the Jewish problem" by establishing death camps such as Auschwitz and Treblinka, where six million Jews were exterminated.

As Allied forces pressed into Germany and an end to the fighting in Europe came into sight, the Allied powers faced the challenge of deciding what to do with the surviving Nazi leaders who were responsible for these atrocities. Holding an international trial, however, was not their first preference. The British Government opposed trying the Nazi leaders on the ground that their "guilt was so black" that it was "beyond the scope of judicial process." British Prime Minister Winston Churchill, therefore, proposed the summary execution of the Nazi leaders. Soviet leader Joseph Stalin, however, urged that Nazi leaders be tried, much as he had done with dissidents in his own country during the purges of the 1930s. United States President Franklin D. Roosevelt initially appeared willing to go along with Churchill's proposal. But upon Roosevelt's death in April 1945, President Harry Truman made it clear that he opposed summary execution. Instead, at the urging of U.S. Secretary of War, Henry Stimson, Truman pushed for the establishment of an international tribunal to try the Nazi leaders.

The arguments for a judicial approach were compelling, and soon won the day. First, judicial proceedings would avert future hostilities which would likely result from the execution, absent a trial, of German leaders. Legal proceedings, moreover, would bring German atrocities to the attention of all the world, thereby legitimizing Allied conduct during and after the war. They would individualize guilt by identifying specific perpetrators instead of leaving Germany with a sense of collective guilt. Finally, such a trial would permit the Allied powers, and the world, to exact a penalty from the Nazi leadership rather than from Germany's civilian population.

*The Legacy of the Nuremberg Tribunal*
Virginia Morris and Michael P. Scharf, THE INTERNATIONAL CRIMINAL
TRIBUNAL FOR RWANDA, 7–17 (Transnational Publishers, Inc. 1998)
(footnotes omitted)

After a trial that lasted 284 days, the Nuremberg Tribunal convicted nineteen of the twenty-two German officials and sentenced twelve of the major war criminals to death by hanging. In the course of the lengthy trial, the Nuremberg Tribunal documented the Nazi atrocities "with such authenticity and in such detail that there can be no responsible denial of these crimes in the future and no tradition of martyrdom of the Nazi leaders can arise among informed people." The judgment of the Nuremberg Tribunal also paved the way for the trial of over a thousand other German political and military officers, businessmen, doctors, and jurists under Control Council Law No. 10 by military tribunals in occupied zones in Germany and in the liberated or Allied Nations. Moreover, the Charter and the Judgment of the Nuremberg Tribunal established the fundamental principles of individual responsibility for crimes under international law which provide the cornerstones of the legal foundation for all subsequent international criminal proceedings.

A year after the Nuremberg trial, the major Japanese war criminals were tried before the International Military Tribunal for the Far East (Tokyo Tribunal). The Charter of the International Military Tribunal for the Far East (Tokyo Charter) was based largely on the Nuremberg Charter. Nonetheless, the Charter and the Judgment of the Tokyo Tribunal are generally considered to be less authoritative than those of the Nuremberg Tribunal. Whereas the Nuremberg Charter was adopted as part of an international agreement after extensive multilateral negotiations, the Tokyo Charter was promulgated as an executive order by the Supreme Allied Commander for Japan following the war, General Douglas MacArthur, without the prior approval of the other Allied Powers. Furthermore, in contrast to the Nuremberg Tribunal whose judges and prosecutors were selected by four different countries, the prosecutor and the judges of the Tokyo Tribunal were personally selected by General MacArthur. In his dissenting opinion, the French judge of the Tokyo Tribunal, Henri Bernard, expressed the view that "so many principles of justice were violated during the trial that the Court's judgment certainly would be nullified on legal grounds in most civilized countries." Thus, the United Nations General Assembly expressly affirmed the principles of international law recognized in the Charter and the Judgment of the Nuremberg Tribunal and merely took note of the Charter and the Judgment of the Tokyo Tribunal.

Although the Nuremberg Tribunal has been hailed as one of the most important developments in international law in this century, it has also been subject to three major criticisms. While these criticisms are not entirely justified, they deserve consideration because they are also not entirely without some foundation. It is important to consider the shortcomings of the Nuremberg precedent in order to avoid them in the future. At the same time, it is important to judge the Nuremberg precedent—not by contemporary standards—but by the standards of its time.

First, the Nuremberg Tribunal has been criticized as a victor's tribunal before which only the vanquished were called to account for violations of international humanitarian law committed during the war. The victorious States created the Nuremberg Tribunal and appointed their nationals to serve as its judges. The ability of the judges to objectively perform their judicial functions was questioned due to their nationality and the various roles which they performed. In particular, two of the Nuremberg judges had earlier served on the committee of prosecutors that negotiated the Nuremberg Charter, selected the defendants for trial, and drafted the indictments against these defendants. In addition, during the Nuremberg trial the defense counsel argued that the judges were not qualified to pass judgment on the accused because the States which tried the Nuremberg defendants were guilty of many of the same crimes for which their representatives on the bench would judge their former adversaries.

The first criticism of the Nuremberg Tribunal as victor's justice is without any foundation in terms of the existing international law at the time and ignores the fact that the only other alternative that was seriously considered was far less desirable, namely, victor's vengeance. At the conclusion of the Second World War, the victorious parties to the armed conflict were fully competent as a matter of international law to try the members of the vanquished armed forces for violations of the laws and customs of war. The history of war has sadly demonstrated that vengeance often prevails on the battlefield during the war and impunity often prevails at the negotiating table after the war. It was an extraordinary triumph of justice and the rule of law that the major German war criminals were brought to trial before a court of law, rather than being summarily executed (as proposed by Winston Churchill and Joseph Stalin at the Yalta Conference in 1945) or being allowed to go unpunished (as after the First World War). As the Chief Prosecutor for the United States at Nuremberg, Supreme Court Justice Robert H. Jackson, observed in his opening remarks for the prosecution: "That four great nations, flushed with victory and stung with injury, stay the hands of vengeance and voluntarily submit their captive enemies to the judgment of the law, is one of the most significant tributes that Power has ever paid to Reason." Clearly, it would have been preferable to bring the major German war criminals before a permanent international criminal court which had been established previously by the international community and whose judiciary excluded nationals of the parties to the armed conflict. This ideal solution was quite simply not an option at the end of the Second World War. Yet few, if any, have suggested that the characteristics of the Nuremberg Tribunal as a "victor's tribunal" resulted in the conviction of a single innocent man. The documentary evidence alone was overwhelming.

The second criticism of the Nuremberg Tribunal was that the defendants were prosecuted and punished for crimes expressly defined as such for the first time in an instrument adopted by the victors at the conclusion of the war. In particular, the Nuremberg Tribunal was perceived by some as applying ex poste facto law because it held individuals responsible for waging a war of aggression for the first time in history. Senator Robert Taft of Ohio was one of the first to voice this criticism in 1946. His views became part of the public legacy of Nuremberg when his speech was included by John F. Kennedy in his 1956 Pulitzer Prize winning book Profiles in Courage. To this day, articles appear in the popular press deriding Nuremberg as "a retroactive jurisprudence that would surely be unconstitutional in an American court."

This second criticism of the Nuremberg Tribunal minimizes the existing law at the time. The war crimes for which the defendants were tried and punished were violations of well established rules of law governing the conduct of war. The crimes against humanity for which the defendants were tried and punished were contrary to the national law of every civilized nation. No reasonable individual could possibly doubt the serious criminal nature of such crimes which were clearly malum in se. The crimes against peace for which the defendants were tried and punished were contrary to a panoply of legal instruments that prohibited aggressive warfare at the time. Nazi Germany initiated an aggressive war—not because it believed that this was permitted under international law—but because it believed that it could do so with impunity. The fact that a law has not been enforced in the past is no guarantee that it will not be enforced in the future. In this regard, there were specific warnings of individual responsibility for violations of international law at the end of the First World War and during the Second World War, as discussed previously. Furthermore, the defendants had the opportunity to raise this legal challenge which was considered and rejected by the Nuremberg Tribunal.

The third criticism of the Nuremberg Tribunal was that it functioned on the basis of limited procedural rules which did not provide sufficient protection of the rights of the accused. More specifically, the Nuremberg Charter is criticized for providing insufficient due process guarantees for the accused which were circumscribed by several rulings of the Nuremberg Tribunal in favor of the prosecution. In particular, the Nuremberg Tribunal allowed the prosecutors to introduce the ex parte affidavits of persons who were available to testify at trial as evidence against the defendants. As one of the Nuremberg prosecutors, Telford Taylor, wrote: "Total reliance on ... untested depositions by unseen witnesses is certainly not the most reliable road to factual accuracy.... Considering the number of deponents and the play of emotional factors, not only faulty observation but deliberate exaggeration must have warped many of the reports." The procedural rulings in favor of the prosecution were considered to be particularly troubling since the Nuremberg Charter did not provide for a right of appeal. It has further been argued that the defendants who were acquitted by the Nuremberg Tribunal did not fare much better than those who were convicted since the Nuremberg Charter failed to provide any guarantee of the non bis in idem principle (known in the United States as the prohibition of double jeopardy). Consequently, the defendants Schacht, von Papen and Fritzsche were acquitted by the Nuremberg Tribunal only to be subsequently tried and convicted by German national courts for similar crimes.

The third criticism of the limited procedural guarantees provided by the Nuremberg Charter ignores the fact that this was the first attempt to establish an international standard of due process and fair trial. Notwithstanding the absence of any internationally recognized standard of fair trial, the Nuremberg Charter endeavored to guarantee the minimum rights of the accused which were considered to be essential for a fair trial based on general principles of procedural fairness and due process recognized in various national criminal justice systems at the time. It is generally recognized that the defendants who were tried by the Nuremberg Tribunal were entitled to the essential procedural guarantees required for a fair trial even if there were some procedural imperfections.

The Nuremberg Tribunal was unquestionably a significant achievement for its time notwithstanding its shortcomings. Telford Taylor recognized that the Nuremberg Tribunal was not free from what he referred to as its "political warts." Even Justice Jackson acknowledged at the conclusion of the Nuremberg trial that "many mistakes have been made and many inadequacies must be confessed." But he went on to say that he was "consoled by the fact that in proceedings of this novelty, errors and missteps may also be instructive to the future." In this regard, the Nuremberg precedent provides an important benchmark for evaluating the subsequent international criminal tribunals.

Despite its shortcomings, the Nuremberg precedent has had an enduring impact on the development of international criminal law and jurisdiction. The principles of international law recognized in the Charter and the Judgment of the Nuremberg Tribunal constitute the fundamental principles of international criminal law today. The Nuremberg precedent also contributed to the further development of international criminal law after the Second World War. In 1948, the Nuremberg precedent with respect to persecution as a crime against humanity led to the adoption of the Convention on the Prevention and Punishment of the Crime of Genocide. In 1949, the Nuremberg precedent with respect to war crimes was codified and further developed in the Geneva Conventions for the protection of war victims. In terms of international criminal jurisdiction, the Nuremberg Tribunal demonstrated for the first time the feasibility of establishing an international criminal tribunal to replace the historical tradition of impunity and vengeance by a new world order based on justice and the rule of law. In doing so, the Nuremberg Tribunal laid the foundation for all subsequent international criminal jurisdictions.

### Principles of the Nuremberg Charter and Judgment Formulated by the International Law Commission(1950)

I. Any person who commits an act which constitutes a crime under international law is responsible therefor and liable to punishment.

II. The fact that internal law does not impose a penalty for an act which constitutes a crime under international law does not relieve the person who committed the act from responsibility under international law.

III. The fact that a person who committed an act which constitutes a crime under international law acted as Head of State or responsible Government official does not relieve him from responsibility under international law.

IV. The fact that a person acted pursuant to order of his Government or of a superior does not relieve him from responsibility under international law, provided a moral choice was in fact possible to him.

V. Any person charged with a crime under international law has the right to a fair trial on the facts and law.

VI. The crimes hereinafter set out are punishable as crimes under international law: (a) Crimes against peace, (b) War crimes, (c) Crimes against humanity....

VII. Complicity in the commission of a crime against peace, a war crime, or a crime against humanity as set forth in Principle VI is a crime under international law.

## Authors' Note

The following selection discusses establishment of the ad hoc tribunal for the International Criminal Tribunal for the Former Yugoslavia. Material 2 analyzes the matters most important to the tribunal in its creation and function, including an emphasis of cases that had important implications for the ICTY and future tribunals. The material explains the difficulties behind establishing a court of the ICTY's size and magnitude. Material 3 provides a press release from the ICTY Prosecutor upon the death of Slobodan Milosevic.

## 2. Michael Scharf, Balkan Justice

June 18, 1992
Omarska Detention Center
Prijedor, Northern Bosnia

This is not a tale for the faint of heart. In the summer of 1992, ethnic violence engulfed Bosnia-Herzegovina (Bosnia). Thousands of Muslim men and women were forced from their homes and incarcerated in Serb-run concentration camps. The worst of these was located at the Omarska iron ore mine in northeast Bosnia. Omarska was known as a "death camp" and, in fact, more than half of those interned there never left alive. Sanitary conditions were appalling. Food was scarce. Medical care was nonexistent. The jailers were brutal. One in particular Dusko Tadic (pronounced DOO-shko TAH-ditch) became widely known as "The Butcher."

Survivors of Omarska report that Tadic personally raped one woman detainee, murdered thirteen men, and tortured scores of others. It is said that he used a large hammer to smash inmates' heads; that he beat other prisoners with iron bars, wooden clubs, and the butt of his rifle; that he forced prisoners to drink motor oil and mud from puddles; and, on one occasion, that he discharged the contents of a fire extinguisher into the mouth of one of the inmates. Then, on the afternoon of June 18, Tadic is alleged to have participated in an act so vile that news of it quickly spread throughout the world.

That day, five prisoners were summoned to Omarska's garage building, known as "the hangar." Among these prisoners was a Muslim policeman named Fikret Harambasic (Han). When Han arrived at the hangar, Tadic and a group of Serbs allegedly beat him and the other prisoners with truncheons and forced them to wallow naked and bloody in the sump oil collected in the garage service pits. Two of the prisoners died in the course of the beatings; Han lapsed in and out of consciousness. But the Serbs soon grew bored and decided to try something new, something dreadfully new.

According to witnesses, one of the prisoners was ordered at knife point to bite off Han's testicles. The Serbs were yelling, "Bite, harder, harder," as Han was sexually mutilated; all the while a tape recorder insidiously played the popular Muslim song, "Let Me Live, Don't Take Away My Happiness." Dozens of witnesses throughout the camp heard Han's inhuman screams of pain over the music and the cheering of his Serb tormentors. Han did not survive the night. The next morning his body was tossed with dozens of others onto a garbage truck destined for a mass grave somewhere in the nearby countryside.

This vicious incident has become a symbol for the entire Bosnian Muslim experience at the hands of their Serb neighbors during the bloody summer of 1992. It was the one documented atrocity that, more than any other, defined the horrors of Omarska. And it was the revelation of those horrors that finally prodded the international community to action in Bosnia.

Four years later, Dusko Tadic, a forty-year-old Bosnian Serb pub owner and karate instructor, would find himself in a similar situation to that of Hermann Goering following the Second World War. He would become the first person in fifty years to stand trial before an international tribunal for crimes against humanity. Millions around the world tuned in to the televised proceedings billed by the media as "the trial of the century" — to find out whether Tadic was the sadistic instrument of the Serb policy of "ethnic cleansing" that the prosecution made him out to be, or just a scapegoat for people who had suffered terribly and were looking for revenge as the defense contended. At stake was no less than the future of international humanitarian law. This is the true story behind this landmark trial.

## Introduction

The wrongs which we seek to condemn and punish have been so calculated, so malignant and so devastating, that civilization cannot tolerate their being ignored, because it cannot survive their being repeated.

ROBERT H. JACKSON
**Opening Speech for the Prosecution**
**at Nuremberg, 21 November 1945**

During the twentieth century, four times as many civilians have been victims of war crimes and crimes against humanity than the number of soldiers killed in all the international wars combined. After the Nazis exterminated six million Jews during the Holocaust, the world community said "never again." The victorious Allied powers set up an international tribunal at Nuremberg to prosecute the Nazi leaders for their monstrous deeds. There was hope that the legacy of Nuremberg would be the institutionalization of a judicial response to atrocities committed by anyone, anywhere around the globe.

Yet, the pledge of "never again" quickly became the reality of "again and again" as the world community failed to take action to bring those responsible to justice when 4 million people were murdered in Stalin's purges (1937–1953), 5 million were annihilated in China's Cultural Revolution (1966–1976), 2 million were butchered in Cambodia's killing fields (1975–1979), 30,000 disappeared in Argentina's Dirty War (1976–1983), 200,000 were massacred in East Timor (1975–1985), 750,000 were exterminated in Uganda (1971–1987), 100,000 Kurds were gassed in Iraq (1987–1988), and 75,000 peasants were slaughtered by death squads in El Salvador (1980–1992). The U.N. High Commissioner for Human Rights summed up the state of affairs when he recently said, "A person stands a better chance of being tried and judged for killing one human being than for killing 100,000."

Then, in the summer of 1992, the world learned of the existence of Serb-run concentration camps in Bosnia-Herzegovina, with conditions reminiscent of the Nazi-run camps of World War II. Daily reports of acts of unspeakable barbarity committed in the Balkans began to fill the pages of our newspapers. The city of Sarajevo, which had recently impressed the world as host of the 1984 Winter Olympics, was transformed from a symbol of ethnic harmony into a bloody killing ground. For the first time since World War II, genocide had returned to Europe. The international outcry was deafening.

I was, at the time, the Attorney—Adviser for United Nations Affairs at the U.S. Department of State. I had previously served as counsel to the Counter-Terrorism Bureau and when I was promoted to my new position in 1991, I requested to work on the hot issue of the day the Persian Gulf War. But my superior felt that I should first gain some experience in a "less critical area," and accordingly assigned me responsibility for the situation in Yugoslavia. In this capacity, over the next two years, I participated in and observed first-hand the policy formulation, negotiation, and compromises that shaped the United States' and United Nations' responses to the unfolding crisis in the former Yugoslavia. During this time, it fell on me to draft the Security Council resolution that established a War Crimes Commission to investigate and document the Yugoslav atrocities, the U.S. proposal for the statute of an International War Crimes Tribunal, and ultimately the Security Council resolution establishing the Tribunal and the crucial interpretive statement delivered by Ambassador Madeleine Albright at the time that resolution was adopted.

\* \* \*

### Establishing the Tribunal

In a December 1992 Press Conference following his controversial "naming names" speech, U.S. Secretary of State Lawrence Eagleburger added his voice to a growing international chorus publicly calling for the creation of a Nuremberg-like tribunal to try persons believed to be responsible for atrocities in the former Yugoslavia. Later that week, I attended a meeting of the U.S. Human Rights Delegation to prepare for the upcoming session of the U.N. Commission on Human Rights scheduled to meet in Geneva from February 1 to March 12, 1993. At the meeting, the head of our delegation, Ambassador Morris Abrahms, asked how we might be able to implement Eagleburger's mandate at the Human Rights Commission. After much discussion, it was agreed that the United States could propose the formation of an expert working group to prepare the statute for an ad hoc international tribunal. Once completed, the statute would be provided to the Security Council for approval.

By the time the U.S. delegation had arrived in Geneva in late January, we had obtained all of the "clearances" necessary to proceed with our war crimes tribunal initiative. Little did we know that France was about to pull the rug out from under us and steal our thunder. At the same time we began consulting our allies on our proposal at the Human Rights Commission, France circulated a draft Security Council resolution in New York calling for the creation of a Yugoslavia war crimes tribunal. The French draft was accompanied by a report prepared by a committee of French jurists containing a detailed analysis of the legal issues involved in the endeavor.

I received a cable from the State Department ordering my early return from Geneva so that I could help craft a response to the French initiative. The cable could not have come at a worse time. I was at that very moment trying to broker a deal between the Islamic countries and the Europeans on a Human Rights Commission resolution entitled the "Rape and Abuse of Women in the Territory of the Former Yugoslavia." The resolution was in response to reports that as many as twenty thousand Muslim women had been systematically raped in Bosnia by Serb forces. Britain had proposed a text which was perceived as too soft by the Islamic countries. They, in turn, circulated a competing resolution which stated that the "systematic practice of rape is being used as a weapon of war against Muslim women and children and as an instrument of ethnic cleansing by the Serbian forces." Their resolution further stated that the rapes in Bosnia constituted genocide—a determination the Europeans were not ready to make. The two sides threatened to vote against each other's resolutions. For our part, the U.S. delegation was not satisfied with either text, since our main objective was the adoption of a resolution that would for the first time in history state that rape in an armed conflict is an international crime.

I requested a meeting of the European and Islamic delegations, at which I argued that it was important that a single resolution on rape in Yugoslavia be adopted by consensus in order to demonstrate to the Serbs that the international community was united in its opposition to the practice of systematic rapes and was willing to act to halt its continuation. To try to bridge the gap, I offered to draft a compromise text, which I would circulate the next day. My compromise text began with a clause stating that rape was a war crime. It also contained some of the strong language contained in the Islamic draft, and at the same time it incorporated the key British clauses requesting a U.N. investigation into the rape and abuse of women in the former Yugoslavia and assistance to the victims of such acts. Finally, it sought to skirt the genocide issue by simply "noting General Assembly Resolution 47/121 of 18 December 1992 in which the Assembly stated, inter alia, that the abhorrent policy of ethnic cleansing is a form of genocide."

The negotiations had reached a critical juncture just when I was informed that I would be returning to Washington on the next plane out. The tide was turned when the deputy head of our delegation, Geraldine Ferraro, made a compelling speech urging the two sides to put aside their differences. By describing her experiences working with rape victims as a prosecutor in New York City, the former Democratic vice-presidential candidate was able to transform what had been mainly an academic debate into an emotional appeal that was hard to reject. Minutes before I had to leave, a deal was struck and my compromise text was ultimately adopted without dissent by the Human Rights Commission as Resolution 1993/8.

Upon my return to Washington, I learned that the French draft Security Council resolution proposed an innovative two-step approach to the establishment of a Yugoslavia

War Crimes Tribunal under which the Security Council would initially commit itself to the establishment of such a tribunal and later approve the statute for the Tribunal. The process proscribed for drafting the statute was the subject of intense negotiations between the members of the council. During the course of these negotiations, Italy submitted a report prepared by a commission of Italian jurists and Sweden submitted a report prepared by the three distinguished rapporteurs appointed by the Conference on Security and Cooperation in Europe (CSCE), each containing a draft statute for the Yugoslav War Crimes Tribunal. Two weeks later, on February 22, 1993, the Security Council adopted Resolution 808 in which it decided in principle to establish an international tribunal "for the prosecution of persons responsible for serious violations of international humanitarian law committed in the territory of the former Yugoslavia since 1991. Rather than assign the task of drafting the statute for the Tribunal to a committee of government representatives as the United States had proposed in Geneva, the resolution requested the Secretary-General of the United Nations to prepare a report within sixty days "on all aspects of this matter, including specific proposals and where appropriate options for the effective and expeditious implementation of [this decision], taking into account suggestions put forward in this regard by Member States.

At the time of the vote on the resolution, Ambassador Madeleine Albright delivered perhaps her most stirring address ever to the Security Council. "There is an echo in this Chamber today," she began. "The Nuremberg Principles have been reaffirmed. We have preserved the long-neglected compact made by the community of civilized nations forty-eight years ago in San Francisco to create the United Nations and enforce the Nuremberg Principles." Looking each member of the council squarely in the eye, Albright continued, "The lesson that we are all accountable to international law may have finally taken hold in our collective memory" "This will be no victor's tribunal," she concluded. "The only victor that will prevail in this endeavor is the truth."

Resolution 808 was artfully crafted. It reflected a commitment by the Security Council to establish a tribunal, but it did not indicate the shape the Tribunal would take. It guaranteed that the members of the council could have input into the drafting of the Tribunal's statute, but it left the final draft up to the Secretary-General, thereby avoiding the prospect of drawn out and contentious negotiations. And the resolution dodged the most potentially explosive issue of all by leaving it to the Secretary-General to recommend how the Tribunal would be established.

There were basically two options for establishing the Tribunal. One, advocated by the CSCE Report submitted by Sweden, was to draft a convention that would then be opened to all governments to ratify. Given that governments would need to pass implementing legislation to provide evidence and surrender suspects to the Tribunal, there was a strong argument for allowing states to individually exercise their consent to the Tribunal through ratification of a treaty. On the other hand, it would take time to negotiate a treaty and possibly years before enough governments ratified it. In addition, it was highly unlikely that Serbia would participate, and Serbia's participation was critical.

The other option was for the Security Council to establish the Tribunal itself, as a subsidiary body, acting under the peace enforcement provisions of the United Nations Charter (Chapter VII). This option offered two important advantages. First, it would ensure that the Tribunal was quickly established, since all it would take was a majority vote of the Security Council, including the affirmative vote of the five permanent members. Second, the Security Council's decision to establish the Tribunal under its Chapter VII powers would create binding obligations on all states. But this approach, too, had major drawbacks. There was a real possibility that one of the permanent members of the council, perhaps China or Russia, would veto the draft statute. In addition, the Security Council had never before created a subsidiary judicial body, and there were concerns that such action would be beyond the council's competence.

The United States was one of eighteen governments and international organizations to submit proposals to the Secretary-General for the Tribunal's statute. The United States' draft statute was prepared at the Department of State by a team of three lawyers—James O'Brien, Attorney-Adviser for Political-Military Affairs; Robert Kushen, Attorney-Adviser for Law Enforcement and Intelligence; and me. We worked around the clock for two weeks on our proposed statute, which was refined through an extensive interdepartmental and interagency process. Ultimately, our proposals on the general organization of the Tribunal, the rights of the accused, the double jeopardy principle, and the standard for appeals found their way into the Secretary-General's draft statute. In addition, our proposal that rape be listed for the first time in the history of humanitarian law as an international crime was also accepted. However, two novel suggestions we made, which were not adopted, are worthy of note.

The first concerned the law that the Tribunal would apply. War crimes are generally viewed as applicable only during international armed conflicts, and it was not clear that the conflict in Bosnia between the Bosnian Serbs and the Bosnian Muslims would necessarily meet that criteria. To ensure that the Tribunal "got it right," we proposed that the Statute stipulate that "for this purpose, the conflict in the former Yugoslavia on or after 25 June 1991 shall be deemed to be of an international character." The Secretary-General evidently thought such a clause would be an encroachment on the independence of the Tribunal's judicial function and omitted it from the proposed Statute.

The second suggestion was contained in paragraph 4 of the U.S. proposal, which read: "The Security Council should create a subordinate body, comprised of the members of the Security Council, to be known as the Administrative Council. This body would, among other things, exercise general administrative control over the staffing and operation of the chief prosecutor and the tribunal, and approve recommendations for financing the tribunal's operations." This proposal, which was modeled after the Iraqi Compensation Commission established by Security Council Resolution 687, was meant to ensure some Security Council control over the Tribunal. Moreover, in light of the problems encountered by the 780 Commission, we frankly did not trust the U.N. Secretariat on its own to provide the necessary budget and staff. In hindsight, given the Tribunal's similar administrative problems, our proposal might have made good sense. But at the time it was viewed as "singularly insensitive." Cherif Bassiouni, the chairman of the 780 Commission, described it as a "Kneejerk reaction—keep out the General Assembly," and the Secretary-General apparently agreed.

The report of the Secretary-General was prepared by a working group within the United Nations Office of Legal Affairs (OLA), consisting of Larry Johnson, Winston Tubman, Daphna Shraga, and Virginia Morris, working under the direction of the then Legal Counsel, Carl August Fleischhauer, and the Deputy Legal Counsel, Ralph Zacklin. The report, containing a draft statute for the Tribunal, was sent to the Security Council on May 3. For the reader's reference, the statute is reproduced in Appendix B in the back of this book. Under the draft statute, the Yugoslavia Tribunal would be establish by a decision of the Security Council under its Chapter VII powers. The Tribunal would be composed of three organs—the tubers (comprising two trial chambers and an appeals chamber), the prosecutor, and the registry—which would be located at The Hague be funded by the General Assembly. The statute does not establish office of defense counsel, but it does provide for a right to counsel and for appointment of counsel in the event that the accused lacks sufficient means" to pay for it.

Under Articles 2 through 5 of the draft statute, the Tribunal would have jurisdiction over four different international crimes committed in the territory of the former Yugoslavia after January 1, 1991:

> Grave Breaches of the Geneva Conventions of 12 August 1949—which include the willful killing, torture or inhumane treatment, causing great suffering or serious injury to people protected by the conventions, and the extensive destruction and appropriation of property, not justified by military necessity and carried out unlawfully and wantonly. Grave breaches of the Geneva Convention further include compelling prisoners of war or civilians to serve in the forces of a hostile power, willfully depriving a prisoner of war or a civilian of the rights to a fair and regular trial, the unlawful deportation or transfer or unlawful confinement of civilians, and the taking of civilian hostages.

> Violations of the laws or customs of war—which include the employment of weapons calculated to cause unnecessary suffering; the wanton destruction of population centers not justified by military necessity; the attack of undefended population centers; the seizure of, destruction or willful damage done to institutions of religion, charity, education, and the arts and science; historic monuments and works of art and science; and the plunder of public or private property.

> Genocide—which is defined as the intentional attempt to destroy, in whole or in part, a national, ethnic, racial or religious group by killing members of the group, causing serious bodily or mental harm to members of the group, deliberately inflicting on its members conditions of life calculated to bring about the group's physical destruction in whole or in part, imposing measures to prevent births within the group, or forcibly transferring children of the group to another group. Punishable crimes of genocide also include conspiracy to commit genocide, direct and public incitement to commit genocide, attempts to commit genocide, and complicity in genocide.

> Crimes against humanity—which include the following acts committed against any civilian population in times of international or internal armed conflict: murder, extermination, enslavement, deportation, imprisonment, torture, rape, persecution on political, racial and religious grounds, and other inhumane acts.

The statute provides for criminal liability of persons who planned, instigated, ordered, committed, or otherwise aided and abetted in these offenses. It expressly incorporates the theory of command responsibility and bans the obedience-to-orders defense. The Tribunal would have primacy over national court proceedings concerning persons indicted of these crimes, and persons tried by the Tribunal could not later be tried before national courts for the same crime. Finally, the statute stipulated that there would be no in absentia trials or imposition of the death penalty.

My colleagues and I at the State Department received the Secretary-General's report with mixed impressions. On balance, we thought OLA had done an excellent job, though we were not completely satisfied with every clause of the statute. We were troubled, for example, by the statute's very narrow approach to the applicable law According to the Secretary-General's report, the jurisdiction of the Tribunal was strictly limited to "rules of international humanitarian law which are beyond any doubt part of customary law." Applying this cautious standard, the Secretary-General omitted from the Tribunal's jurisdiction the two Additional Protocols to the 1949 Geneva Conventions, which apply the laws of war to "internal conflicts." Having rejected our proposal that the statute stipulate that the war in Bosnia was an international armed conflict, we viewed the inclusion of the protocols as critical to the successful prosecution of atrocities in Bosnia. Although the two protocols had been ratified by well over a hundred governments including the former Yugoslavia, OLA determined that there was not yet sufficient acceptance of them to constitute customary international law Ironically, the fact that the United States had not yet ratified the protocols was probably the major reason for OLA's position.

We were also concerned about the Secretary-General's definition of crimes against humanity contained in Article 5 of the statute. While the Secretary-General's report stated that international law now prohibits crimes against humanity "regardless of whether they are committed in an armed conflict," the proposed statute gave the Tribunal jurisdiction over crimes against humanity only "when committed in armed conflict." This qualification could make it difficult for a prosecutor to win convictions for atrocities committed at Bosnian concentration camps if the prosecutor had to prove such acts were committed in connection with armed conflict. This was a curious limitation given that none of the countries or organizations that submitted proposals suggested that the Tribunal's jurisdiction over crimes against humanity should be so restricted.

In addition, my colleagues at the Pentagon, in particular, had strong objections to the statute's provisions on command responsibility and the defense of superior orders. Article 7(3) of the statute provided that a commander was responsible for the acts committed by a subordinate "if he knew or had reason to know that the subordinate was about to commit such acts or had done so and the superior failed to take the necessary and reasonable measures to prevent such acts or to punish the perpetrators thereof." We had favored a broader formulation, as reflected in the judgment of a military commission under the auspices of the International Military Tribunal for the Far East in the Yamashita case. In that case, General Yamashita was found to be criminally liable for atrocities committed by the Japanese forces under his command, not on the ground that he knew or had reason to know of these acts, but on the ground that he condoned a general atmosphere of lawlessness that pervaded the troops under his command. With regard to the statute's prohibition of the defense of superior orders found in Article 7(4), the Department of Defense felt that there should be a limited exception to this rule as recognized in United States law for circumstances in which a subordinate lacks information necessary to adjudge the legality of an act ordered by his superior.

Finally, we were puzzled by the Secretary-General's provision on sentencing which stated, "in determining the terms of imprisonment, the trial Chambers shall have recourse to the general practice regarding prison sentences in the courts of the former Yugoslavia." The problem was that the former Yugoslavia had employed the death penalty and its criminal code reflected a policy of "twenty years or death." In other words, since the code favored capital punishment for serious cases, it stipulated that imprisonment for not more than twenty years could be imposed for a capital offense. Since the Secretary-General's statute forbade the imposition of capital punishment, we were concerned that it might be read as requiring that twenty years be the maximum penalty — which would be too lenient for the types of crimes committed in Bosnia.

We considered a variety of possible ways to pursue modification of the statute. The most obvious method would be to entertain amendments to the draft on the floor of the Security Council. A second tactic would be to propose certain modifications in an annex to the statute. These could be informally agreed upon by the members of the council in advance. A third strategy would be to specify certain revisions in the Security Council resolution approving the statute. Each of these tactics, however, would have likely resulted in lengthy negotiations and undesirable political compromises.

Our sense of urgency stemmed from the fact that since February 22, when the council had decided in principle to establish the Yugoslavia War Crimes Tribunal, the war in Bosnia had greatly intensified. Fighting had begun between the Bosnian Muslims and Croats, who had been allies against the Serbs in the first year of the war. The same week the Secretary-General submitted his proposed statute, we received reports that the Croatian defense forces had rounded up thousands of Muslim men in raids on the city of Mostar and had deported them to detention centers which were little better than the Serb-run concentration camps. Meanwhile, the Bosnian Serbs were conducting a fierce assault on the Muslim towns of Zepa and Srebrenica which had swollen with thousands of refugees from surrounding villages. With these events as a backdrop, the five permanent members of the Security Council agreed during informal meetings that there should be no amendments and no further discussion on the Secretary-General's statute for the Tribunal.

In an innovative approach to this dilemma, at the last minute we were able to persuade France, the United Kingdom, and Russia to join in making similar statements interpreting certain key provisions of statute when they voted on the resolution. These statements, for ample, would express the understanding of the four countries that jurisdiction of the Tribunal covered the Additional Protocols to Geneva Conventions and that crimes against humanity under the statute need only be committed "during," rather than "in connection with," armed conflict.

On other matters in which the four countries could not reach agreement, we decided to make unilateral "additional clarifications." Thus, on the issues of command responsibility and the defense of obedience to superior orders, Ambassador Albright, reading from a speech I drafted, stated: "It is our understanding that individual liability arises in the case of ... the failure of a superior — whether political or military — to take reasonable steps to prevent or punish such crimes by persons under his or her authority. It is, or course, a defense that the accused was acting pursuant to orders where he or she did not know the orders were unlawful and a person of ordinary sense and understanding would not have known the orders to be unlawful." And on the issue of sentencing, she said, "We also understand that the Tribunal may impose a sentence of life imprisonment or consecutive sentences for multiple offenses, in any appropriate case.

At the time, I was skeptical that our plan would work. I was worried that the international tribunal would not give much weight to the "pre-cooked" interpretive statements since only four of the fifteen members of the Security Council had participated in making similar statements. In addition, the four interpretive statements were not worded identically and, in fact, could be read quite differently. Moreover, Britain, France and Russia limited their interpretive statements to a few select provisions of the statute, while the United States alone made "clarifications" on several other provisions. One of my colleagues has argued that it was significant that none of the members of the council at the time took issue with our "additional clarifications." But this argument ignores the nature of formal proceedings in the Council. The representatives are generally not lawyers and for the most Part act as mouthpieces for speeches cabled to them from their capitals. No delegate was authorized to jump up and "object" when remarks were made by the United States. Moreover, the statement was given after the delegates had already voted on the resolution, and the delegates had no notice of the United States' additional clarifications until it was too late to vote "no." For added insurance, we later tried to codify our interpretive statements in the Tribunal's Rules of Procedure, but our attempt was rejected by the Tribunal's judges. Ironically, the United States' creative approach to this problem was reminiscent of its unsuccessful attempt to expand the concept of conspiracy in the context of the Nuremberg Tribunal some fifty years earlier, which was discussed in Chapter 1.

Our creative approach also risked alienating the other members of the Security Council. The representative of Venezuela, Diego Arria, said the non-aligned countries felt the resolution "was rammed down our throats." "They said to us: 'If you object, you'll be responsible for damaging the war crimes Tribunal,'" he added. Echoing these sentiments, the representative of Brazil told the council that "We would certainly have preferred that an initiative bearing such far reaching political and legal implications had received a much deeper examination in a context that allowed a broader participation by all States Members of the United Nations." China, which as permanent member could have vetoed the resolution, told the council that it had serious reservations and that it believed the approach envisaged in the Secretary-General's report "is not in compliance with the principle of State judicial sovereignty" Yet with the situation in the former Yugoslavia spinning out of control, no country was willing to be seen as the spoiler.

On May 25, 1993, Resolution 827 approving the Secretary-General's statute for the Tribunal was adopted by a unanimous vote of the fifteen members of the Security Council. This resolution, which I had a hand in drafting, contained several other clauses worthy of note. The most important clause provided that all states were required to comply with the orders of the Tribunal. This would obligate countries to provide judicial assistance and arrest and transfer accused persons to the Tribunal. Ambassador Albright warned that noncompliance with this obligation would subject a state to Security Council sanctions or, in the case of Serbia, to continuing or heightened sanctions. Having learned our lesson from the financial difficulties suffered by the 780 Commission, we included a clause authorizing a voluntary fund for the Tribunal and urging states to contribute funds, equipment, and personnel. Since the statute was not particularly detailed as to the intention, trial, and appeals process, we viewed the Tribunal's Rules of Procedure as critical to the success of the Tribunal. Accordingly, in draft for the resolution we proposed that the judges should submit rules to the council for approval. Other members of the council such a clause would undermine the independence of the Tribunal, however. As a compromise, Resolution 827 invited states to submit proposals for the Tribunal's rules for the judges' consideration. Finally, the statute did not give the Tribunal the power to award victim compensation, we included a clause in the resolution declaring that the creation of the Tribunal was without prejudice to the future establishment of a victim compensation program. What we had in mind was a procedure similar to that devised for the victims of the Iraqi invasion of Kuwait, in which frozen Iraqi assets and proceeds from Iraq oil sales would be dispersed to victims through a U.N. Compensation Commission. To date, however, no such institution for Bosnia has been set up by the Security Council.

The first step in transforming the Yugoslavia War Crimes Tribunal from a paper court to an operational judicial institution was to appoint the eleven judges that would sit in two three-member trial panels and a five-member appeals chamber. Shortly after the Security Council's decision to establish the international tribunal, the Secretary-General initiated the election process by inviting states to submit nominations. The Security Council considered forty-one candidates from thirty-eight countries and came up with a list of twenty-three candidates which was submitted to the General Assembly in late August 1993.28 In mid-September 1993, in ten contentious rounds of voting over three days, the General Assembly elected eleven judges from this list. Gabrielle Kirk McDonald, a former federal court judge of the United States, garnered the largest number of votes (137) on the assembly's first ballot on which six other judges were chosen. The vote totals for the other six judges were as follows: Italian international law Professor Antonio Cassese (123); Egyptian law professor Georges Michel Abi-Saab (116); Chinese Foreign Ministry legal adviser Li Haopei (111); Germain le Foyer de Costil, presiding judge of the French Court of Major Jurisdiction of Nanterrer (107); and Lal Chand Vohrah, a senior Malaysian high court judge (96). No candidates obtained the required absolute majority of 94 votes needed for election on either the second or the third ballot. On the fourth ballot the assembly elected Sir Ninian Stephen, former governor-general of Australia and judge of the Australian High Court (97 votes). No candidates obtained the required number of votes on the fifth or the sixth ballot. On the seventh ballot, the assembly elected Adolphus Godwin Karibi-Whyte, former Nigerian Supreme Court judge (95 votes). The last two judges, Elizabeth Odio Benito of Costa Rica and Rustam Sidhwa of Pakistan, were selected on the tenth round of balloting. By the time of the Tadic trial, pursuant to a provision in the Tribunal's statute allowing the Secretary-General unilaterally to fill vacancies, Judge Sidhwa was replaced by fellow Pakistani Saood Jan, Judge Abi-Saab was replaced by fellow Egyptian Fouad Riad, and Judge de Costil was replaced by fellow Frenchman Claude Jorda.

The nine men and two women elected to the bench were from both civil and common law countries: three from Asia, two from Europe, two from Africa, two from North America and one each from Latin America and Australia. There were several striking characteristics about the composition of the panel selected. The first was the absence of a Muslim on the bench, especially since Muslims constituted by far the largest portion of the victims of atrocities in the former Yugoslavia. "It is absurd that most of the victims are Muslim, yet they have no representatives on the Tribunal," lamented Mohamed Sacirbey, Bosnia's ambassador to the U.N.

On the other hand, four of the eleven judges did come from countries with predominantly Muslim populations — Malaysia, Nigeria, Egypt, and Pakistan — and might therefore be uniquely sympathetic to the Muslim victims. Indeed, an opposite argument could be made — that there was a far greater number of Muslim countries represented on the bench than would be warranted by the percentage of Muslims to the total world population or the percentage of Muslim countries to the total number of countries in the world. In contrast, the nominee for the Tribunal's bench from Russia (the state with the closest historic ties to Serbia), Valentin G. Kisilez, a member of the Presidium of the Kahiningrad Regional Court, was defeated ostensibly to avoid a pro-Serb bias. This drew Russia's ire in light of the Unwritten rule that all permanent members of the Security Council are represented on important U.N. institutions.

Also notable was the absence of a British judge. The official British explanation was that they did not put forward a candidate in order not to prejudice the possible selection of Scottish Attorney General John Duncan Lowe, who was then among the leading candidates for the position of the Tribunal's prosecutor. However, it has been suggested by U.N. diplomats that the real reason was Britain's fear that, like Russia, its candidate might suffer an embarrassing defeat because of Britain's prominent and controversial role in the Bosnian crisis. In at the time of these elections, Bosnia was preparing a submission the International Court of Justice which would charge Britain with complicity in genocide for having opposed the lifting of the arms embargo on Bosnia and the U.S. proposal for airstrikes against Serb bases.

The judge who would preside over the panel trying Dusko Tadic was Gabrielle Kirk McDonald, a fifty-three-year-old former federal district judge known for a breezy Texas style that mixed directness with humor. McDonald was born in St. Paul, Minnesota, but grew up just outside Manhattan in Riverside, New York, and in Teaneck, New Jersey where she was one of two African-American students in her high school class. She attended Boston

University and then Howard Law School. After graduation, she joined the NAACP legal defense fund as staff attorney, where she met Conrad Harper, who would twenty-five years later become State Department Legal Adviser. McDonald made a same for herself as a civil rights lawyer in the 1960s and 1970s, and at age thirty-seven was appointed by President Jimmy Carter to be the third black woman on the federal bench.

She resigned from the judiciary in 1988 to pursue a career in private practice. In 1993 she had accepted an appointment to the faculty of the Thurgood Marshall School of Law in Houston when her old friend Conrad Harper called to see if she would consider being the United States candidate for the Yugoslavia Tribunal. Although she had no prior experience in international law, Harper told one reporter that "McDonald was well qualified as a former federal judge who had heard criminal matters, but she offered more as a woman, an African-American, and someone with a deep interest in civil rights." He added that "the Clinton Administration was interested in nominating a woman for the job on the tribunal because of the Use of rape as an instrument of warfare in the Bosnian conflict." A divorced mother with two kids in college, McDonald said it was an offer she could not refuse. "It was an opportunity to participate in something new," she explained. "It was wonderful to be a part of this because I consider myself to be a civil rights lawyer at heart." McDonald compared her new role with her experience working with the newly drafted Civil Rights Act of 1964. "There was little precedent," she said, "so we had to borrow precedent. That is what we're doing at The Hague, we're borrowing precedent from other legal systems."

At their first meeting at The Hague on November 17, 1993, the judges elected Antonio Cassese from Italy, an authority on international law, as president of the Tribunal. He was to administer the chambers, including assigning judges to cases, and was himself the head of the five-judge appeals chamber. At the time, there were no premises for the Tribunal and no permanent staff. "There was zero!" Cassese says. "Nothing! We had four secretaries, a few computers, and the U.N. had rented a meeting room and three small offices in the Peace Palace. The rent was paid for two weeks." The General Assembly had not yet made a formal decision on the Tribunal's budget, and it would be nearly a year before a prosecutor would take office. A motion was made that the judges adjourn until the General Assembly had provided for "the indispensable minimum infrastructure." But at Cassese's urging, the judges decided instead to begin work immediately on the Rules of Procedure so that they would be ready by the time the office of the prosecution was up and running.

Two months later, on February 11, 1994, the Yugoslavia Tribunal adopted 125 rules, covering some 72 pages. (By way of comparison, it took a committee of American judges and law professors four years to draft the federal Rules of Criminal Procedure in the early 1940s.) The judges decided to embrace a largely adversarial approach to their of Procedure, rather than the inquisitorial system prevailing in Continental Europe. Yet there were three significant deviations from adversarial system. First, as at Nuremberg, there was no rule against hearsay evidence. Second, during a trial, the Tribunal itself could order the production of additional evidence to ensure that it was satisfied with the evidence on which its judgments were based and to minimize the possibility of a charge being dismissed for lack of evidence. Third, the practices of plea-bargaining and granting of immunity were not included.

This last departure became a point of heated debate. To induce accused war criminals to testify against higher level officials, the United States proposed a provision for the rules that would have allowed the prosecutor to grant them either full or limited testimonial immunity in exchange for their cooperation. In arguing for its proposal, the United States said, "We recognize that many other legal systems have difficulty with these concepts, but we believe that these tools would be helpful in the war crimes context for leading prosecutors up the chain of command from the foot soldier who directly committed an atrocity to the military or political leader who had knowledge of or commanded it." The president of the Tribunal, Antonio Cassese responded: "The persons appearing before us will be charged with genocide, torture, murder, sexual assault, wanton destruction, persecution and other inhuman acts. After due reflection, we have decided that no one should be immune from prosecution for crimes such as these, no matter how useful their testimony may otherwise be." Yet, in a partial concession to the U.S. position, the Tribunal provided that cooperation was a factor to be taken into account in imposing sentence. This provision was to become critical in the case of Drazen Erdemovic who, on May 30, 1996, became the first person to plead guilty before the Tribunal. He admitted to machine-gunning seventy unarmed Muslim civilians at Srebrenica. In return for his testimony against Radovan Karadzic and Ratko Mladic, the prosecutor agreed to ask the Court to give Erdemovic a reduced sentence.

Two other important matters addressed in the rules are worth mentioning here. The first has become known as the Rule 61 "super indictment" procedure. Despite the statute's requirement that an accused be present at trial, the judges gave serious consideration to providing for in absentia trial, or "trial by default" as the Tribunal put it, in cases where a state refused to hand over a suspect. As a compromise, the judges crafted Rule 61, which provided for a mini-trial, at which the accused was not present or represented, to enable the prosecutor to introduce in open court (and thus preserve) testimony of witnesses, documentation, physical evidence, and video recordings of witness interviews. The trial chamber would then request the prosecutor to provide an account of the efforts made to arrest the accused. If a majority of the three trial chamber judges determined that the information presented a prima facie case of guilt and that the warrant was not executed due to a refusal to cooperate by the state concerned, it would transmit a certification of this to the Security Council as a basis for possible sanctions. As described below, the Tadic trial was interrupted from June 27–July 14 so that the Tribunal could hold a Rule 61 proceeding concerning Radovan Karadzic and Ratko Mladic.

The second important issue concerned the protection of witnesses. As Judge Cassese remarked, the judges were "very much aware that there may be considerable reluctance on the part of witnesses to come to the Tribunal to testify. One of our overriding concerns has been how to encourage witnesses to do this." To remedy this, the rules provided for the use of depositions (subject to cross-examination of the deponent) ; measures for shielding the identity of witnesses from the public and even from the defendant "until such time as the witness can be brought under the protection of the Tribunal"; the establishment of a "Victims and Witnesses unit" within the registry; and the promulgation of a sweeping rape shield provision.

The purpose of the rape shield provision was to protect a victim of sexual abuse from unreasonable harassment, intimidation, or invasions of privacy by precluding the defendant from raising and trying to prove the defense of consent. Although the provision was applauded by women's groups, it engendered strong criticism from groups worried about safeguarding the rights of defendants. At the insistence of the Australian judge, Sir Ninian Stephen, the judges amended the rape shield provision to allow for the defense of consent if the accused first satisfied the trial chamber in camera (in closed proceedings) that evidence was relevant and credible.

It may prove helpful to the reader at this point to set out the main steps of the proceedings as detailed in the Rules of Procedure. Proceedings are initiated when the prosecutor issues an indictment, which submitted to the judge who has been designated to review indictments for that particular month. If the judge confirms the indictment, arrest order or order for the transfer of the accused is sent to the authorities of the state in which the accused is located. After arrest, the accused is transferred to the Tribunal's detention center at The Hague. Immediately upon his arrival, he is brought before a trial chamber and charged. Before trial, the prosecution and defense must reciprocally disclose to one another the evidence in their possession.

The trial proceeds as follows: After opening statements by the parties, the prosecutor presents his case. Each witness may be cross-examined by counsel for the defense after he/she has testified and then re-examined by the prosecutor. Next the defense presents its case, and the prosecution cross-examines the defense witnesses, who are then re-examined by the defense. The prosecutor may then present rebuttal evidence. The judges may ask questions of the witnesses at any time during the trial. After the presentation of evidence, the two sides make their closing arguments. Thereafter, the trial chamber deliberates privately and pronounces its findings in public. If two of the three judges determine that the defendant is guilty beyond a reasonable doubt, then sentencing proceedings are initiated. An appeal against the judgment may be lodged within thirty days by either the prosecution or the defense. Finally, the sentence is served in one of the countries that has indicated to the Security Council its willingness to accept convicted persons.

The drafters of the Yugoslavia Tribunals statute and rules were determined to prevent the Tribunal from being subjected to the kinds of criticisms that have tarnished the legacy of Nuremberg. The Yugoslavia Tribunal itself acknowledged in its first annual report that "one can discern in the statute and the rules a conscious effort to avoid some of the often-mentioned flaws of Nuremberg and Tokyo." And yet at least one commentator has concluded that the Yugoslavia Tribunal "will likely invite much of the same criticisms that followed the first international war crimes trials."

In some respects, the Yugoslavia Tribunal is a vast improvement over its predecessor. Its detailed Rules of Procedure and Evidence, for example, represent a tremendous advancement over the scant set of rules that were fashioned for the Nuremberg Tribunal. In further contrast to the Nuremberg Tribunal, the Yugoslavia Tribunal prohibits trials in absentia, since these are inherently unfair and are likely to be seen as empty gestures (although the Tribunal's Rule 61 procedure might be susceptible to similar criticisms). In addition, whereas the defense attorneys at Nuremberg were prevented from full access to the Nuremberg Tribunal's evidentiary archives, defendants before the Yugoslavia Tribunal are entitled to any exculpatory evidence in the possession of the prosecutor; and both the prosecution and the defense are reciprocally bound to disclose all documents and witnesses prior to trial. Finally, since the Nuremberg Tribunal has been criticized for compelling defendants to make incriminating statements, the statute of the Yugoslavia Tribunal guarantees every accused the right "not to be compelled to testify against himself or to confess guilt," in addition to a panoply of other rights not recognized under the Nuremberg Charter.

As discussed above, the most often heard criticism of Nuremberg was its perceived application of ex post facto laws, by holding persons responsible for the first time in history for the "crime of aggression" and by applying the concept of conspiracy which had never been recognized in Continental Europe. The creators of the Yugoslavia Tribunal went to great lengths to avoid a similar perception with regard to the international tribunal. The Security Council adopted a series of resolutions that put the people of the former Yugoslavia on notice that they were bound by existing international humanitarian law, in particular the Geneva Conventions. The resolutions enumerated the various types of reported acts that would amount to breaches of this law and warned that persons who committed or ordered the commission of such breaches would be held individually responsible. Moreover, the jurisdiction of the international tribunal was defined on the basis of the highest standard of applicable law, namely rules of law which are beyond any doubt part of customary law to avoid any question of full respect for the principle nullem crimen sine lege. It is particularly noteworthy that the crime of waging a war of aggression, which engendered so much criticism after Nuremberg, is not within the Yugoslavia Tribunal's jurisdiction.

In other respects, the Yugoslavia Tribunal may be more susceptible to criticism. Let us begin with the criticism that Nuremberg constituted "victor's justice." In contrast to Nuremberg, the Yugoslavia Tribunal was created neither by the victors nor by the parties involved the conflict, but rather by the United Nations, representing the international community of states. The judges of the Yugoslavia Tribunal come from all parts of the world and are elected by the General-Assembly.

On the other hand, the decision to establish the Yugoslavia Tribunal was made by the U.N. Security Council, which cannot truly be characterized as a neutral third party; rather, it has itself become deeply involved and taken sides in the conflict. As detailed in Chapter 2, the Security Council has imposed sanctions on the side perceived to be most responsible for the conflict, authorized the use of force and airstrikes, and sent in tens of thousands of peacekeeping personnel. Its numerous resolutions have been ignored and many of its peacekeeping troops have been injured or killed; some have even been held hostage. Moreover, throughout the conflict, the Security Council has (justifiably) favored the Bosnian Muslims and Croats over the Serbs. Although it imposed sweeping economic sanctions on Serbia and the Bosnian Serbs, such action was never even proposed when Croatian forces committed similar acts of "ethnic cleansing" in Bosnia in October 1993. Throughout the conflict, the council had been quite vocal in its condemnation of Serb atrocities, but its criticisms of those committed by Muslims and Croats were muted. When the deputy head of UNPROFOR began to raise concerns about the uneven response to violations of international humanitarian law in 1993, he was told by a colleague at U.N. headquarters in New York, "Take cover — the fix is on."

While the Yugoslavia Tribunal is designed to be independent from the Security Council, one cannot ignore the fact that the statute provides that the Tribunal's prosecutor is selected by the Security Council and its judges are selected by the General Assembly from a short list proposed by the Security Council. Indeed, given that the battle for control of Bosnia was in large measure a religious war between Bosnian Muslims and Bosnian Serbs, it is somewhat astonishing that four of the eleven judges elected by the General Assembly upon the nomination of the council come from states with predominantly Muslim populations, while the nominee from the state with the closest historic ties to Serbia (Russia) was defeated to avoid a pro-Serb bias. Not surprisingly, the Tribunal proved unacceptable to the government of Serbia, which sent a letter to the council warning that the Tribunal would not be impartial, given the Security Council's "one sided approach" to the Balkans war.

Another criticism of Nuremberg was that those acquitted by the Tribunal were retried and convicted in subsequent proceedings before national courts. The statute of the Yugoslavia Tribunal, in contrast, expressly protects defendants against double jeopardy by prohibiting national courts from retrying persons who have been tried by the international tribunal. However, by permitting the Tribunal's prosecutor to appeal an acquittal, the Tribunal itself may infringe the accuser's interest in finality which underlies the double jeopardy principle.

A final criticism of Nuremberg was that it did not provide for the of appeal. The statute of the Yugoslavia Tribunal has been recognized as constituting a major advancement over Nuremberg by guaranteeing the right of appeal and providing for a separate court of al. However, the procedure for the selection of judges by the General Assembly did not differentiate between trial and appellate judges, leaving the decision to be worked out by the judges themselves. When they arrived at The Hague, this became the subject of acrimonious debate. Nearly all the judges wished to be appointed to appeals chamber, which was viewed to be the more prestigious assignment. As a compromise, the judges agreed that assignments would for an initial period of one year and subject to "rotat[ion] on a regular basis" thereafter.

The rotation principle adopted by the judges is at odds with the provisions of the Tribunal's statute intended to maintain a clear distinction between the two levels of jurisdiction. Article 12 provides that there shall be three judges in each trial chamber and five judges in the appeals chamber, and Article 14(3) expressly states that a judge shall serve only in the chamber to which he or she is assigned. These provisions were intended to ensure the right of an accused to have an adverse judgment and sentence in a criminal case reviewed by "a higher tribunal according to law," as required by Article 14 of the International Covenant on Civil and Political Rights. The purpose of the principle of the double degree of jurisdiction under which judges of the same rank do not review each other's decisions is to avoid undermining the integrity of the appeals process. It was feared that judges might be hesitant to reverse decisions in order to avoid a future reversal of their own decisions. The adoption of the rotation rule is not the kind of decision one would expect from a Tribunal keenly aware of the need to be perceived as above reproach. In light of this action, the comment made by my colleague at the State Department about the "water at The Hague" might not have been so far off the mark, after all.

* * *

### Epilogue and Assessment (pp. 207–228)

Despite the mixed verdict, historians are likely to rank the trial of Dusko Tadic among the most important trials of the century. Unlike other renowned criminal trials such as the treason trials of Esther and Julius Rosenberg, the Chicago Seven trial, the Watergate trials, the Rodney King case, and the O.J. Simpson trial, the importance of the Tadic case lies not in the status of the defendant or even the nature of his alleged crimes, but in the fact that the proceedings constituted an historic turning point for the world community. Just as the Nuremberg trials following World War II launched the era of human rights promulgation fifty years ago, the Tadic trial has inaugurated a new age of human rights enforcement.

As the Yugoslav Tribunal itself reflected in its first annual report: "The United Nations, which over the years has accumulated an impressive corpus of international standards enjoining States and individuals to conduct themselves humanely, has now set up an institution to put those standards to the test, to transform them into living reality. A whole body of lofty, if remote, United Nations ideals will be brought to bear upon human beings. Through the Tribunal, those imperatives will be turned from abstract tenets into inescapable commands."

At the opening session of the Yugoslav Tribunal in November 1993, U.N. Under-Secretary-General for Legal Affairs Carl-August Fleischhauer said that in setting up the Tribunal, the Security Council had demonstrated a determination to achieve three aims: "First, to put an end to the crimes being committed in the former Yugoslavia; second, to take effective measures to bring to justice the persons who are responsible for those crimes;

and, third, to break the seemingly endless cycle of ethnic violence and retribution." It is no overstatement to suggest that the success or failure of the Yugoslav Tribunal in meeting these goals of deterrence, justice, and peace will decide the direction of human rights enforcement into the next century.

With respect to the first of these goals, the trial of Dusko Tadic should be seen as an effort not merely to bring an individual to justice but to understand the most barbarous butchery to blight Europe in fifty years—and perhaps prevent a repetition of recent history. The record of the trial provides an authoritative and impartial account to which future historians may turn for truth, and future leaders for warning. While there are various means to achieve an historic record of abuses after a war, the most authoritative rendering is possible only through the crucible of a trial that accords full due process.

If, to paraphrase American writer and philosopher George Santayana, we are condemned to repeat our mistakes if we have not learned the lessons of the past, then we must establish a reliable record of those mistakes if we wish to prevent their recurrence. The chief prosecutor at Nuremberg, Robert Jackson, underscored the logic of this proposition when he reported to President Truman that one of the most important legacies of the Nuremberg trials was that they documented the Nazi atrocities "with such authenticity and in such detail that there can be no responsible denial of these crimes in the future and no tradition of martyrdom of the Nazi leaders can arise among informed people." Similarly, the Tadic trial has generated a comprehensive record of the nature and extent of international crimes in the Balkans, how they were planned and executed, the fate of individual victims, who gave the orders, and who carried them out. By carefully establishing these facts one witness at a time in the face of vigilant cross-examination by distinguished defense counsel, the Tadic trial produced a definitive account that can endure the test of time and resist the forces of revisionism.

A half century after Nuremberg, historians like Daniel Jonah Goldhagen continue to address the question of how so many ordinary people could be so readily enlisted to participate in atrocities. Goldhagen's recent work, Hitler's Willing Executioners, hypothesizes that the Holocaust was a product of the German people's unique cultural pre-disposition to "eliminationist antisemitism." But the Tadic case suggests a different answer. Lead prosecutor Grant Niemann believes the trial proved that "human beings are universally capable of doing the things Tadic has done." The most extraordinary hallmark of the Yugoslav carnage was its intimacy. Torturers knew their victims and had often grown up alongside them as neighbors and friends. Perhaps the real lesson of the Tadic trial is that given the right set of circumstances, many of us can become willing executioners. It is what the American historian Hannah Arendt, in her classic account of the Eichman trial, referred to as the "banality of evil." Four centuries earlier, the philosopher Thomas Hobbes hypothesized that there is everywhere a thin line between civilization and barbarism.

What are the circumstances that can lure out this dark side of human nature and push us across that thin line? "That is one of the mysteries of the Yugoslav conflict," says deputy prosecutor Graham Lewitt. "What transforms ordinary people into savages? The Tadic case gave us a glimpse of how provocation, incitement, and propaganda can raise hatred and fear to such an extent that ordinary people turn on their neighbors in a bloodthirsty way," he added. Throw in official sanction, a bit of coercion by persons in authority, pressure from assenting comrades, and opportunities for personal gain. Then add a long history of ethnic tension and you have the active ingredients of ethnic cleansing—Bosnian style.

What is most shocking about the Balkan conflict is not that atrocities were committed, but that the rest of the world did so little to prevent them or bring them to an end. As the Court TV anchor, Terry Moran, observed during the trial, "The Tadic trial proved once again how very difficult it is for people to care about evil in countries and places that are far from their personal experiences. Whether we are humankind in fact as well as in name is an open question in light of what happened in Bosnia and the international community's continuing inadequate response."

Unfortunately, worldwide ethnic nationalism has not likely reached its peak with events in the former Yugoslavia. As Senator Daniel Patrick Moynihan recently observed, "Of the next fifty states which will come into being in the next fifty years, ethnic conflict will almost [always] be the defining characteristic by which that process will take place." Consequently, the questions raised by the savagery in the Balkans—how to preserve minority rights, when to recognize claims to self-determination, how to apply preventive strategies, and when to use force—are likely to confront us again and again in the coming years. More than anything else, the record of the Balkan hostilities generated by the Tadic trial should stand as a reminder to the international community of the perils of unchecked ethnic conflict.

If the fate of the victims of Bosnia stands as a lesson to the international community, the image of Dusko Tadic in the dock, transmitted throughout the world by satellite, sends a message to would-be war criminals and human rights abusers around the globe that in the future those who commit such acts may be held accountable for their actions. As Judge McDonald, who presided over the Tadic trial, succinctly put it: "We are here to tell people that the rule of law has to be respected."

The vehicle of a televised trial is an especially potent one both for attaining respect for the rule of law and for deterring future violations. Throughout the summer of 1996, live television coverage of the Tadic trial was carried throughout Bosnia, while private cable TV transmission in Belgrade made the trial accessible to at least a limited Serbian audience. As chief prosecutor Richard Goldstone told me in an interview, "People don't relate to statistics, to generalizations. People can only relate and feel when they hear somebody that they can identify with telling what happened to them. That's why the public broadcasts of the Tadic case can have a strong deterrent effect."

While Nuremberg came too late to help the Nazis' victims, the Tadic trial and the subsequent trials before the Yugoslav Tribunal at least have a chance of deterring Serbs and others from continuing to commit atrocities. There is particular benefit to exposing the unscathed Serbian population in Belgrade to the ghastly consequences of blood-curdling nationalistic rhetoric. Even for those who support Karadzic and Milosevic, "it will be much more difficult to dismiss live testimony given under oath than simple newspaper reports," Graham Blewitt points out. "The testimony will send a reminder in a very dramatic way that these crimes were horrendous."

Although there is ongoing debate about the general deterrent value of criminal punishment, prosecutor Grant Niemann believes "deterrence has a better chance of working with these kinds of crimes than it does with ordinary domestic crimes because the people who commit these acts are not hardened criminals; they're politicians or leaders of the community that have up until now been law abiding people." Richard Goldstone adds, "If people in leadership positions know there's an international court out there, that there's an international prosecutor, and that the international community is going to act as an international police force, I just cannot believe that they aren't going to think twice as to the consequences. Until now they haven't had to. There's been no enforcement mechanism at all."

Indeed, Richard Goldstone believes the existence of the Tribunal may have already deterred human rights violations in the former Yugoslavia during the Croatian army offensive against Serb rebels in August 1995. "Fear of prosecution in The Hague," he said, "prompted Groat authorities to issue orders to their soldiers to protect Serb civilian rights when Croatia took control of the Krajina and Western Slavonia regions of the country."

Unfortunately, it did not have a similar deterrent effect when the Serbs massacred over ten thousand civilians in the "safe area" of Srebrenica the previous month. Perhaps this was because, at the time, the Bosnian Serb leaders responsible for the Srebrenica atrocities (Radovan Karadzic and General Ratko Mladic) had no reason to believe there was a real possibility that they would be brought to trial before the Tribunal.

The Tribunal's deterrent value may ultimately be linked to the eventual fate of these two men. "The international community, acting through the Security Council, has raised the victims' expectations that war criminals would be brought to account for the terrible atrocities they have suffered," Goldstone has said. "If the accused are left free to continue to flout international agreements and international law is there really less likelihood of further violence in the former Yugoslavia?" He adds, "The failure to make arrests also risks destroying the broader deterrent value of the Tribunal. Future tyrants will be given notice that they also have nothing to fear from international justice for as long as they are surrounded by armed guards."

In a sense, four trials were simultaneously held in that compact, high-tech courtroom at The Hague from May through November 1996. First, and most obviously, there was the trial of Dusko Tadic, whose fate was in the hands of the Tribunal. Second, there was the trial of the Bosnian Serb leadership and even the authorities in Belgrade, who were implicitly in the dock with Tadic. In fact, during the first six weeks of the trial, there was nearly as much evidence introduced into the record of Slobodan Milosevic's responsibility for ethnic cleansing as about the particular crimes Tadic had committed. Third, there was the trial of the international community, which had failed to prevent or halt the bloodshed in the former Yugoslavia. The trial made clear that the fate of Bosnia could have been avoided if only the major powers had possessed the political will and judgment to take vigorous actions when the time was right. And fourth, perhaps most importantly, the Tribunal was itself on trial. For in assessing the Tadic trial one must ask, did the Tribunal discharge its duty in a way that will create confidence and faith that guilt and innocence can be adjudicated by an international war crimes tribunal?

"Whatever amounts from this Tribunal," deputy prosecutor Graham Blewitt told me, "there will always be debates about whether it has been successful or not. It's difficult to quantify success. It's not just a matter of looking at the number of indictments, the number of persons tried, and the number of convictions. To me, the best measure of success is if it can achieve the prosecution of individuals fairly, regardless of whether they are convicted or acquitted." Clearly, this international tribunal, with its detailed rules of procedure, represents an advance on its Nuremberg predecessor—notably by forswearing in absentia trials, by making better provisions for the defense, and by providing a right of appeal. Still, at times, the Tribunal tread dangerously close to denying Tadic a fair trial, most conspicuously by its decision to allow certain prosecution witnesses to testify anonymously and by permitting the prosecution to base so much of its case on hearsay. "For those who would respond to criticisms of the Tribunal by saying you have to start somewhere," Tadic's lawyer Michail Wladiniiroff told me, "I say that's not good enough when you're dealing with a person whose life and liberty are at stake."

In contrast to most televised trials, the Tadic proceedings were marked by a great deal of substance and very little sensationalism. The rhetoric was restrained, objections were few and the cross-examination was forceful but seldom insulting. Perhaps this is one of the inherent benefits of a jury-less trial. Then again, the effort to ensure an absolutely fair trial may have cut against the goal of deterrence, for the world media (and viewers) soon lost interest in the orderly, unenthralling proceedings. Reflecting this development, over the course of the trial, the number of print journalists covering the case dwindled from over a hundred to less then a handful. When I visited the Tribunal in July, the only other person in the entire three hundred-seat public gallery was Ed Vulliamy from The Guardian. While prosecutor Goldstone repeatedly extolled the educational benefits of the world-wide coverage of the trial and its potential deterrent value, Grant Niemann told me that "the popular appeal and educational aspect of the trial was not part of our consideration at all. Our prosecution strategy, including the order of our witnesses, was designed to secure a conviction, not boost the ratings of Court TV" But, as Fred Graham, the chief anchor and managing editor of Court TV, pointed out, "The prosecutors should have realized that if they presented an airtight case at the cost of boring the world into tuning them out, they had failed to accomplish an important part of their mission."

In addition to deterrence and justice, there is the issue of peace and reconciliation. The Yugoslav Tribunal was created, in the words of Security Council Resolution 827, "to contribute to the restoration and maintenance of peace." As with Nuremberg, the sight of leading war crimes suspects—from all sides of the ethnic divide—standing trial and receiving sentences is supposed to enable a population scarred by the war to apportion blame on individuals and not on the collective. "Avoiding collective guilt will greatly strengthen the peace process in Bosnia," says the Tribunal's press spokesman, Christian Chartier. "We have an obligation to carry forward the lessons of Nuremberg," President Clinton stated. "Those accused of war crimes, crimes against humanity, and genocide must be brought to justice. There must be peace for justice to prevail, but there must be justice when peace prevails," he added. In a similar vein, on the day the Dayton Peace Agreement was signed, the president of the Tribunal, Judge Antonio Cassese, said: "Justice is an indispensable ingredient of the process of national reconciliation. It is essential to the restoration of peaceful and normal relations especially for people who have had to live under a reign of terror. It breaks the cycle of violence, hatred and extrajudicial retribution. Thus peace and justice go hand-in-hand."

If it achieves its aims, the Tribunal will do far more to secure lasting peace in Bosnia than the sixty thousand NATO troops stationed there as part of the Dayton Accords. "If the trials fail," Justice Gold stone warns, "so will any attempt at peace." "It is nonsensical to expect that hundreds of thousands of victims could forgive or forget. And if there is a peace treaty in former Yugoslavia or anywhere else in which the architects of atrocities are left unpunished in leading positions, then all it will be is an interval between cycles of violence," he adds. For this reason, Goldstone insists, the arrest of the indicted Bosnian Serb leader Radovan Karadzic, "is not only in the interests of justice but in the interests of peace."

To some extent, the Dayton Accords transformed the role of the Tribunal. After Dayton, its function was not just to punish the guilty, but through the issuance of indictments, to identify persons who, under the agreement, were prohibited from being elected or appointed members of government in Bosnia. In this way, official accusation became a means of removing from the political scene men like Karadzic who were viewed as the greatest impediment to peace.

Dusko Tadic stood trial for the murder of thirteen people and the torture of nineteen others. In the United States, he would have been considered among the nation's worst mass murderers, rivaling the likes of Charles Manson, Albert DeSalvo ("the Boston Strangler"), Kenneth Bianchi ("the Hillside Strangler"), David Berkowitz ("Son of Sam"), Ted Bundy, and Jeffrey Dahmer. And yet, in the context of the former Yugoslavia, he is persistently referred to as just a bit player.

A number of critics have even questioned whether the Tribunal was right to focus on such a minor sadist for its first case, whereas Nuremberg tried the key Nazi leaders themselves. If, as one newspaper put it, "Mr. Tadic was no more than a monstrous tadpole in a pool of sharks," why should he have been the subject of the Tribunal's first prosecution? Elanne Sophie Gre, the Norwegian judge who served on the 780 Commission, remarked that "he is not the level of person I would like to see at The Hague I think they should have aimed higher up."

There are several reasons, however, why Dusko Tadic turned out to be an ideal subject for the first trial. First, Tadic fell into the hands of the international community when he was arrested in Germany in 1994. Given the nature of his alleged offenses and the evidence pointing to his guilt, the Tribunal could not turn a blind eye to the allegations. Second, through the Tadic case, the Tribunal has begun to build a pyramid of evidence leading to the principals ultimately responsible for the horrors in Bosnia. Third, to the victims of Dusko Tadic and his colleagues, to those who suffered as a result of the actions of ordinary prison guards and police officials, it is very important that some of their torturers be bought to justice. Only by prosecuting individuals at all levels of responsibility can the victims see that justice has been done. Finally, the Tadic case has provided an opportunity for the Tribunal to work out the kinks in its procedures before turning to more important and more difficult cases.

Asked whether the Tadic case was a good one to begin with, Richard Goldstorn replied, "If one had a choice, clearly not. Instead one would have vaunted to start with a higher profile defendant. It is highly unsatisfied that someone at the level of Dusko Tadic should face trial and that those who incited and facilitated his conduct should escape justice and remain unaccountable. But it's really an academic question because yet had no choice; Tadic was the only accused available to bring before the Tribunal at a time when the judges, the media, and the international community were clamoring for us to begin prosecution."

At the time of the Tadic trial, there were just six other indicted Yugoslav war criminals in custody at The Hague: Croatian General Tihomir Blaskic, Bosnian Groat Zdravko Mucic, Serbian Army member Drazen Erdenovic, and three Bosnian Muslims — Zejnil Delalic, Hazim Delic, am Esad Landzo. (The number in custody was at one time eight, but Bosnian Serb general Djordje Djukic had been released for medical reasons prior to his death and Bosnian Serb Goran Lajic was released why it was determined by the prosecution that he was the wrong Goran Lajic.) "If we don't get more arrests for the Tribunal in the fairly near future," laments Richard Goldstone, "then I think people with justification will be able to conclude that we've been effectively prevented from doing the work that we've been set up to do. What worries me about the failure to effect arrests," Goldstone continues, "is that the public perception of the success of the Tribunal is inextricably linked to the resources we are given. The politicians won't want to spend scarce dollars on what the public regards as a failure." Tadic's trial alone cost the Tribunal some twenty million dollars. "Ultimately," Goldstone adds, "credibility is going to depend on whether we are able to put on trial in The Hague the major people who have been indicted."

The challenge for the Tribunal is to work backwards from the likes of Tadic to those who fanned the flames of hatred. Goldstone did not hesitate to indict Karadzic and Mladic, despite criticism at the time that such indictments would derail the peace process. But will the Tribunal's prosecutor have the fortitude to indict Slobodan Milosevic if the mounting evidence establishes his culpability? From a political point of views such action in the near future would seem to be folly. But from the point of view of justice, it might be indispensable. Despite Goldstone's insistence that the indictment process is immune from politics, there is reason to believe that global diplomacy, for better or worse, affects the Tribunal's policies.

Even bringing Karadzic and Mladic to justice has turned into an uphill battle for the Tribunal. In its resolution conditionally lifting the trade sanctions on Serbia and Republika Srpska (Resolution 1022), the Security Council reiterated that compliance with the orders of the Tribunal was integral to the obligations of Serbia and Republika Srpska under the Dayton agreement. Under the resolution, if either the commander of IFOR, Admiral Leighton Smith of the United States, or United Nations High Representative Carl Bildt of Sweden, had reported that those governments had significantly failed to carry out their obligations, then the sanctions were to be automatically reimposed within five days. However, in another indication of the relationship between international politics and the functioning of the Tribunal, no action was taken when General Ratko Mladic boasted of his freedom in front of television cameras on a ski slope and then appeared in public in Belgrade at the funeral of indicted war criminal, pjordje Djukic. In May 1996, Tribunal president Antonio Cassese called for the re-imposition of sanctions against Serbia for failing to execute arrest warrants. That request was elevated to a demand in June following the Rule 61 hearing on Karadzic and Mladic. The Security Council responded by stating that it "deplores the failure to date of the Federal Republic of Yugoslavia (Serbia and Montenegro) to execute the arrest warrants," but it neither threatened nor took any further action.

Goldstone places much of the blame on the NATO led IFOR for Karadzic and Tadic's evasion of justice. "There is no moral, legal or political justification for a military authority to grant effective immunity to persons whom the prosecutor, on behalf of the Security Council, has determined should be brought to trial," he says.43 "That IFOR, with its force of 60,000 troops, its sophisticated weaponry and intelligence capability, is able to effect such arrests must be beyond question. From a political point of view, can IFOR's men in uniform legitimately argue that they can avoid certain duties because they are potentially dangerous? On a national level, policemen are not infrequently obliged to arrest people who are armed and dangerous. Yet, it is inconceivable that an attorney general would call off the arrests because of the risks to the lives of the arresting officers." Expressing a similar sentiment, Chief Judge Casscse threatened that the Tribunal judges would resign en masse in the summer of 1997 unless the attempt was made to bring Karadzic and Mladic to justice.

Others felt that dispatching NATO troops to hunt down Serbs would be a tragic mistake. They feared it would fuel the conflict by handing the two sides more scores to settle when NATO was scheduled to depart at the end of the year. General Mladic, himself has said that NATO-led military forces would pay heavily if they tried to arrest him. "They have to understand one thing, that I am very expensive and that my people support me," Mladic told an interviewer. Serbian President Slobodan Milosevic has similarly warned that Bosnia "could blow up" if top Bosnian Serb indicted war criminals were arrested.

The U.S. Joint Chiefs of Staff have told Congress that even if IFOR had orders to arrest the indicted war criminals who are at large in Bosnia, the NATO force just does not have enough intelligence information on their whereabouts. Yet, based on the addresses printed on the Tribunal's "Most Wanted" poster and other leads, a Washington-based group called the Coalition for International Justice easily located thirty-six of the seventy-five indicted war criminals.

According to Richard Goldstone, the trials before the Tribunal are likely to continue for at least the next three to four years. Whether men like Karadzic and Mladic will ever face justice before the Tribunal remains to be seen. Even if they do, however, Goldstone will not have the satisfaction of overseeing their prosecution. At the end of the Tadic trial, the Tribunal's venerated prosecutor resigned from his post to resume his position on South Africa's Constitutional Court. He was succeeded by Justice Louise Arbour, a rising star in the Canadian court system who has presided over some of her country's most politically charged civil rights and war crimes cases. Like Goldstone, Arbour had no previous prosecutorial experience. Yet Goldstone's strengths were his vision and his diplomatic acumen, rather than his administrative or trial skills. Arbour is relatively unknown in legal or human-rights circles outside Canada, but I had the opportunity to speak with her at an international conference in Brussels the week before she was to move her family and belongings to The Hague. Where Goldstone had been tenacious in his quest to launch the prosecutions and obtain resources for the Tribunal, Arbour struck me as somewhat more cautious in her approach, though no less personally committed to the success of the Tribunal. Only time will tell whether she will be able to insure that the Tribunal maintains momentum at a critical period in its history.

The Yugoslavia tribunal was meant as a one-time-only ad hoc institution. But soon after the Tribunal had been established, the Security Council found itself faced with an even greater genocide when over half a million Tutsis were massacred by the Hutus in Rwanda during a one hundred-day period in the spring of 1994. Comparing the scale of the crimes committed in Rwanda to Nazi Germany and Bosnia, Rwanda's Prime Minister-designate queried the United Nations Security Council, "Is it because we're Africans that a [similar] court has not been set up?" With the justifiable charge of Eurocentricity ringing through the Security Council, the Council was compelled to establish a Rwanda Tribunal, which has its own trial chambers but shares the appeals chamber and the office of the prosecutor of the Yugoslavia Tribunal.

The creation of the Rwanda Tribunal showed that the machinery designed for the Yugoslavia Tribunal could be employed for other specific circumstances and offenses, thereby avoiding the need to reinvent the wheel in response to each global humanitarian crisis. Why then, one might inquire, has a Tribunal not been set up for the Iraqi violations of international humanitarian law committed during the Gulf War? These violations included the taking of civilian hostages, the use of hostages as human shields, rape and willful killing of civilians, torture of prisoners of war, pillage of Kuwaiti hospitals, indiscriminate Scud missile attacks against civilians in Saudi Arabia and Israel, intentional release of oil into the Persian Gulf, igniting oil fields in Kuwait, and the use of poisonous gas against the Kurds in Northern Iraq. After all, the Security Council has condemned these violations, warned that individuals, as well as the government of Iraq, would be liable for them, and called on member states to submit information on Iraqi atrocities to the council for further action.

There would seem to be a moral imperative to make the attempt to bring such persons to justice before an international Tribunal in light of the scale, brutality, and depravity of their violations of international humanitarian law (which followed the Security Council's warning that individuals would be held accountable). At the very least, an international tribunal for Iraqi war crimes could help develop and preserve the historical record and express international outrage by issuing indictments. And yet, the Security Council shows no signs of taking such action. Nor is there serious consideration of setting up a tribunal for the genocide in Cambodia, the terrorism committed by Libya, or the crimes against humanity recently committed in El Salvador, Haiti, East Timor, or Burundi.

There are several reasons why the Security Council has proven unwilling or unable to continue with the ad hoc approach that was employed for Yugoslavia and Rwanda. The first reason, which is sometimes referred to as "tribunal fatigue," is that the process of reaching a consensus on the tribunal's statute, electing judges, selecting a prosecutor, and appropriating funds has turned out to be extremely time-consuming and politically exhausting for the members of the Security Council. At least one permanent member of the Security Council—China—has openly expressed concern about using the Yugoslavia Tribunal as a precedent for the creation of other ad hoc criminal tribunals, perhaps out of fear that its own human rights record might subject it to the proposed jurisdiction of such future international criminal courts. In addition, the creation of ad hoc tribunals by the council is viewed as inherently unfair by the vast majority of countries of the world that do not possess permanent membership and a veto on the council because the permanent members are able to shield themselves and their allies from the jurisdiction of such tribunals, notwithstanding atrocities that may be committed within their borders. The final reason for hesitance in creating additional ad hoc tribunals is purely economic; that is, the expense of establishing tribunals is simply seen as too much for an organization whose budget is already stretched too thin.

## 3. Press Conference from ICTY Prosecutor
### The Hague, 2006

Ladies and Gentlemen,

I deeply regret the death of Slobodan Milosevic. It deprives the victims of the justice they need and deserve.

In the indictment which was judicially confirmed in 2001, Milosevic was accused of 66 counts of genocide, crimes against humanity and war crimes committed in Croatia, Bosnia and Herzegovina and Kosovo between 1991 and 1999. These crimes affected hundreds of thousands of victims throughout the former Yugoslavia.

During the prosecution case, 295 witnesses testified and 5000 exhibits were presented to the court. This represents a wealth of evidence that is on the record. After the presentation of the prosecution case, the Trial Chamber, on 16 June 2004, rejected a defense motion to dismiss the charges for lack of evidence, thereby confirming, in accordance with Rule 98 *bis*, that the prosecution case contains sufficient evidence capable of supporting a conviction on all 66 counts. The Defense was given the same amount of time as the prosecution to present its case. There were in total **466** hearing days. **4 hours** per day. Only **40 hours** were left in the Defense case, and the trial was likely to be completed by the end of the spring.

It is a great pity for justice that the trial will not be completed and no verdict will be rendered. However, other senior leaders have been indicted for the crimes for which Slobodan Milosevic was also accused. Later this year, the trial of eight senior leaders accused of the Srebrenica genocide will begin. Furthermore, also this year, six most senior former Serbian leaders will be tried for crimes committed in Kosovo. But the most senior perpetrators are still at large. Now more than ever, I expect Serbia to finally arrest and transfer Ratko Mladic and Radovan Karadzic to The Hague as soon as possible.

The death of Slobodan Milosevic makes it even more urgent for them to face justice. Finally, I would like to share a thought for Zoran Dindić, his wife and his family. Exactly three years ago, he was murdered in Belgrade. He is the man who had the courage to bring Slobodan Milosevic to The Hague so that he could face justice.

## Authors' Note

The next selection addresses the specific issues that plagued the formation and operation for the International Criminal Tribunal for Rwanda. Material 4 provides a firsthand perspective from Bernard Muna, the Deputy Prosecutor for International Criminal Tribunal for Rwanda. The material explains the investigation and logistics of convening the ad hoc tribunal.

## 4. Bernard Muna, The ICTR Must Achieve Justice for Rwandans
*American University International Law Review*, 1998

### THE ICTR MUST ACHIEVE JUSTICE FOR RWANDANS
Presentation by Bernard Muna
Deputy Prosecutor for International Criminal Tribunal for Rwanda

### Introduction

First of all, I wish to thank those who organized this conference, because I believe it is important towards the end of this century that the international community start to sign treaties and pass conventions that protect human rights. Therefore, I am grateful to be able to participate with the ongoing trials. I believe that we are making a definite statement that humanity, collectively in the future, will not stand by and watch when other people violate human rights. To me, that is the real reason that I would support the International Criminal Court.

That being said, I have the privilege of participating in the trials that are going on in the Rwanda Tribunal. I would like to start by giving you the picture of the enormous task that lies in front of us. You have heard that the genocide in Rwanda was five times faster than the one in Germany, even though the German genocide had gas chambers. If you take the lower figure of 500,000 people killed you are looking at 5,000 people a day. If you take the higher figure of one million people killed, you are looking at 10,000 people killed a day without guillotines or gas chambers. Instead, most of the killings were done with match heads and spears. This meant that a large proportion of the population were implicated for this to succeed.

This is the real drama. When Judge Pillay was giving you the statistics of the fact that there were 120,000 people in jails, I saw some of you shaking your head. More than 120,000 people were needed to kill 5,000 to 10,000 people a day in all different parts of Rwanda. That is the real tragedy. That is the real complication for the prosecution because you are looking at a situation in which there was a government, army, and police. All the structures of government were present and yet this wholesale killing took place.

The real tragedy is that with the government, police, and the army all participating in this killing, those who died had nobody to protect them. No government structure. No police. Yet, within the drama, those who were close will know there were heroes. There were those who hid their friends, those who tried to save some of them by taking them to safe houses. By and large, it was a telling thing for human nature when neighbor turned against neighbor. Further, there were situations where women were asked to kill their own children.

I think as we look forward our task in the Rwanda Tribunal is to simply hurry up. I believe that it is a very difficult task. Justice requires time and in our case we must administer justice as justice, but unfortunately it is often seen as a political tool. So what then do we sacrifice? These are the tasks and the difficulties that the Office of the Prosecutor must meet.

## I. The Prosecution's Investigation

Evidently, from what I have told you, the thrust of our investigation when I arrived had to be refocused on the conspiracy theory. The question becomes how did this tragedy occur if there was a government and an army in place. There must have been either a conspiracy of silence, a conspiracy of inactivity or inaction, or a conspiracy of participation to allow them to do the killing.

Our investigation at this stage, which is the main thrust of the policy of the Office of the Prosecutor, is based on the fact that we have firmly established that it was an act of conspiracy. Those who were called upon as government officials, government departments, and police actually turned against the people and killed them. This is the main thrust of the Rwanda investigations.

It is important for the future to ask people what they want. In the future, this should not happen again. The only way we can stop it is to show why it happened. This is also a main thrust of the investigation policy. We must be able to establish how the killing was organized and how this tragedy was realized.

I think for posterity and for history, we have the duty to record it. The judges are there to bring the full story out and to sift the truth from the untruth. But, it is the job of the prosecutor, I believe, to be able to bring all this together and put it before the judges so that they are able to finally decide and put in the annals of history what really happened in Rwanda.

You have already heard about how many people we are prosecuting. I will not go into more detail but I will give just a general observation on our policy. I have met a lot of very well meaning people, such as ambassadors and ministers, who come to Rwanda and express concern about the Rwandan justice system. My answer is this: any justice system can only administer justice according to their own means. When I say their own means I am talking about manpower, finances, and so on.

## II. Logistical Issues When Mounting a Prosecution

If you went into Rwanda right now and attempted to administer justice as you would administer it here in the United States, it would be impossible. Where would they get the money to pay for the defense counsel, to build the jails, or to feed the prisoners? As we are judging the Rwandan justice system, we must remember that Rwanda can only administer justice according to the means available. For example, most of their magistrates were killed and others left the country. Therefore, you have a society without magistrates.

So what can Rwanda do? Send potential magistrates back to school for three years, and then have them get four or five years of experience while these guys are in jail? This is a drama. That is the reality. You have 130,000 people in jail that are to be tried. What do they do? These are the questions that we must examine before we rush to criticize, judge, and moralize the Rwandan system. The reality is there. Therefore, you administer justice according to your own means. It may not be perfect, but human justice is never perfect no matter what we may pretend or what we may think.

## III. Rape Prosecuted as Genocide

Now, in moving forward on some of the new ground that we are breaking we must address the use of rape charges. We have been able to see clearly in our investigations that apart from the rape, other forms of sexual violence exist. Rape is actually a means of committing genocide because when you are causing serious physical or mental harm to members of the group, you are deliberately inflicting on them conditions of life which are diminishing their lives. If you are humiliating the females in a racial group, then these women in the future cannot be expected to be mentally stabilized to bring up a family. So, rape in itself can be a means of committing genocide. Of course, we also see rape as torture, as a crime against humanity. These views, however, are not reflected in the charges, which we are putting before the court.

## IV. Challenges Faced by the ICTR

I believe that the real challenge of the Rwanda Tribunal is twofold. First, we must administer justice. We are a court of law. Justice must be fair and it must be done by the people. But at the same time it must also meet with the political atmosphere in Rwanda. The people are waiting for justice. The question is do we rush justice or do we administer justice at the pace it requires.

As we look at the Rwandan experience, I think that one of the lessons we must learn is that a court cannot be a bureaucratic organization. One of the things our court system is presently suffering from is that it has a very strong umbilical cord tied to one of the biggest bureaucrats in the world, the United Nations system. This means that those who are setting the guidelines are always thinking bureaucratically. If we are to create a new court, we must look at it as a court of law with professionals, people who know what law is about and not just bureaucracy. These are the people who know that a court is to administer justice. These are the people who know what the system is all about. To me, this is the first thing we have to do when we establish a court.

Second, we must reexamine the purpose of this court. If the court is going to administer justice, then we must give it the manpower, and thus the capability of administering justice.

We have come under a lot of criticism as being slow, and comparisons have been made to the Nuremberg trials. Yet people forget that in the Nuremberg trial the Department of the Prosecutor had about 2,000 or more people. Additionally, it was a military court and not a civilian court with 180 eyes of the United Nations looking at us with different interests. Therefore, we are under a different pressure of reestablishing a civil court. In essence, we must go very carefully and make sure that we are planting a firm foundation for the future and hope that if we succeed then the new international court can be successful.

## Conclusion

I would like to wind up by saying that one of the tragedies in Rwanda is that there is still conflict. In the time that we are taking to go to court, there is still fighting in the northwest part of the country near the border between Zaire and Rwanda. As we speak here today, there are still people who believe that the war must continue. Unless that country can increase its security, a judge might adjudicate fifty or even one hundred cases. That, however, will not solve the problem of Rwanda.

Rwanda's problems will finally be solved when justice is done, when the people are satisfied that justice was done, and when all of humanity accepts that we must live together as a community. We must allow everybody to live his own life within that society without interference or threat from another person. To me, this is the challenge. A court will come and go, but the real challenge for the international community is whether we will be able to make that point and make it clear. Everyone must understand that when people are being killed because they belong to a political party or to a religious group, this court means business. The international community must not only insist that these cases go before a judge, but they must act beforehand to see that there is prevention.

## Authors' Note

The following three selections introduce the Special Court for Sierra Leone, considered a hybrid international domestic court. Material 5 provides a background analysis of the SCSL and illustrates the differences between the SCSL and previous ad hoc tribunals. Material 6 discusses the implications for the indictment of Charles Taylor, including the international efforts to end impunity. Material 7, a *New York Times* article, details SCSL sentencing of former Liberian leader Charles Taylor in 2012.

## 5. Michael P. Scharf, The Special Court for Sierra Leone
### ASIL Insight, 2000
### [footnotes omitted by editors]

### Introduction

The United Nations and Sierra Leone are about to establish a hybrid international-domestic Court to prosecute those allegedly responsible for atrocities in the Sierra Leone civil war. This will be the third ad hoc international criminal court to be created by the United Nations over the last decade, following the establishment of the war crimes tribunals for the former Yugoslavia (ICTY) in 1993 and Rwanda (ICTR) in 1994.

### Background

Since March 1991, the western African country of Sierra Leone has been caught in a bloody civil war. The fighting was temporarily suspended when the Lome Peace Agreement was reached on July 7, 1999, between the democratically elected government of President Ahmed Tejan Kabbah and the rebel Revolutionary United Front (RUF), led by Foday Sankoh. The peace agreement, which was signed by the parties as well as the Special Representative of the U.N. Secretary-General, granted amnesty to the members of the RUF and set up a Truth Commission to document violations of international humanitarian law in lieu of prosecutions.

Soon afterward, however, Foday Sankoh and his followers resumed attacks on the government's forces, as well as on the civilian population. Sankoh was recently captured by government forces and is currently in custody in the Sierra Leonean capital of Freetown.

In an effort to break the cycle of violence and begin the process of reconciliation, the government of Sierra Leone requested the United Nations to establish an international court to prosecute those responsible for atrocities during the civil war. On August 14, 2000, the U.N. Security Council adopted Resolution 1315, which requested "the Secretary-General to negotiate an agreement with the Government of Sierra Leone to create an independent special court," whose subject matter jurisdiction "should include notably crimes against humanity, war crimes and other serious violations of international humanitarian law," and whose personal jurisdiction would be "over persons who bear the greatest responsibility" for these crimes "including those leaders who, in committing such crimes, have threatened the establishment of and implementation of the peace process in Sierra Leone." The Council asked the Secretary-General to produce a detailed blueprint for the special court.

### The Report of the Secretary-General: A Blueprint for the Special Court

Following the successful completion of negotiations with the Government of Sierra Leone, on October 4, 2000, Secretary-General Kofi Annan issued his report to the Security Council on the Special Court for Sierra Leone. As specified in the Agreement between the United Nations and Sierra Leone, the Special Court would differ from the ICTY and ICTR in several notable respects. First, unlike the ICTY and ICTR, which were established by Chapter VII Resolution of the Security Council, the Special Court is a treaty-based court established by the Agreement between the United Nations and Sierra Leone. As a consequence, while it has primacy over domestic prosecutions in Sierra Leone and can issue binding orders to the government of Sierra Leone, the Special Court lacks the power of the ICTY and ICTR to assert primacy over national courts of third States or to order the surrender of an accused located in any third State. This is not expected to hinder the Court's operation since most of the suspected perpetrators are now in custody in Sierra Leone.

A second difference concerns the composition of the Special Court. Unlike the ICTY and ICTR, which are composed exclusively of international judges elected by the U.N. General Assembly, and a Prosecutor selected by the Security Council, the Special Court is to be composed of both international and Sierra Leonean judges, prosecutors and staff. The Special Court is to have two Trial Chambers, each with two judges appointed by the Secretary-General and one judge appointed by the Government of Sierra Leone; and a five-member Appeals Chamber with three judges appointed by the Secretary-General and two judges appointed by the Government of Sierra Leone. The Secretary-General decided against the sharing of the ICTY/R's single Appeals Chamber because this would be "legally unsound and practically not feasible." The Special Court is to have a Chief Prosecutor appointed by the Secretary-General and a Deputy Prosecutor appointed by Sierra Leone in consultation with the United Nations. The Court's Registrar would be appointed by the Secretary-General.

A third difference concerns the Special Court's subject matter jurisdiction. While the subject matter jurisdiction of the ICTY/R is made up of violations of international humanitarian law which are beyond doubt part of customary international law, the Special Court's subject matter jurisdiction extends (in addition to war crimes and crimes against humanity) to certain crimes under Sierra Leonean law, including abusing a girl under 14 years of age, abduction of a girl for immoral purposes, and setting fire to dwelling-houses or public buildings. But unlike the ICTY and ICTR, the Special Court does not have jurisdiction over the crime of genocide, since there was no evidence that the mass killing in Sierra Leone was at any time perpetrated against an identifiable national, ethnic, racial or religious group with the intent to annihilate the group as such. Despite these differences, the Special Court is to be guided by the decisions of the appeals chamber of the Yugoslav and Rwanda Tribunals, and to apply the Rules of Procedure of the ICTR, though the judges have the power to amend or adopt additional rules, where a specific situation is not provided for.

The Special Court's temporal jurisdiction runs from November 30, 1996 to a date to be decided by a subsequent agreement between the parties. Although the civil war and attendant atrocities go back to 1991, the Secretary-General concluded that extending the temporal jurisdiction back that far would create too heavy a burden for the prosecution and the Court. The 1996 starting date (which corresponded with the first failed peace agreement between the Government and RUF) was selected as this "would have the benefit of putting the Sierra Leone conflict in perspective without unnecessarily extending the temporal jurisdiction of the Special Court."

Asked during a press conference at U.N. Headquarters about how the Court's subject matter and temporal jurisdiction could be reconciled with the amnesty granted under the Lome Agreement, Assistant Under-Secretary-General for Legal Affairs, Ralph Zacklin said that the amnesty given by the Sierra Leone Government was for crimes under Sierra Leone law, whereas "international crimes were a different matter." He also pointed out that during the signing of the Lome Agreement, the Special Representative of the Secretary-General had entered a reservation on the amnesty provision. Given that the Special Court's subject matter jurisdiction includes crimes under Sierra Leone Law that are not international crimes, the better answer would be that the amnesty applied only to domestic prosecutions, and has no application to prosecution before a hybrid international-national judicial body.

The most difficult dilemma for the Secretary-General was how to deal with juvenile offenders, children as young as 14 who committed acts of extreme barbarity. The government of Sierra Leone had initially insisted that those responsible for the most egregious atrocities be brought to trial and punished if found guilty no matter their age. Human Rights groups, on the other hand, were opposed to trials of anyone under 18. Under the compromise that was reached, no one under 15 may be tried by the Special Court, and 15–18-year-old defendants will receive separate anonymous hearings and special counseling and will serve out their terms under parole in demobilization camps or foster homes, rather than a prison.

Unlike the ICTY and ICTR which are not located in the states where the atrocities were committed, the Special Court is expected to be located at the headquarters of the U.N. peacekeeping operation in Freetown, Sierra Leone. This will enable the Court to have ready access to witnesses and evidence. The Special Court is also expected to move more quickly than the ICTY and ICTR, which each took more than two years to become fully operational, in part because the Special Court will have a narrower mandate and fewer defendants, and because the Special Court has the full backing of the government of Sierra Leone. U.N. officials have said that they expect to start hiring court staff, including prosecutors and defense lawyers by the end of the year.

The cost of the Special Court is estimated at U.S. $22 million for its first year of operation, compared to the ICTY and ICTR whose annual budgets each exceed $90 million. This estimated cost does not, however, include funding for detention facilities, investigations, translators, or defense counsel. While Security Council Resolution 1315 had suggested the mechanism of voluntary contributions to fund the Special Court, the Secretary-General has opted instead for assessed contributions from U.N. member states (in which case the United States will be assessed twenty-five percent of the costs) on the grounds that "voluntary contributions will not provide the assured and continuous source of funding which would be required to appoint the judges, the Prosecutor and the Registrar, to contract the services of all administrative and support staff and to purchase the necessary equipment."

## 6. Rena L. Scott, Moving From Impunity to Accountability in Post-War Liberia: Possibilities, Cautions, and Challenges
*International Journal of Legal Information*, 2005
[footnotes omitted by editors]

\* \* \*

### A. The Special Court for Sierra Leone: The New Path Forward

\* \* \*

The SCSL is a unique mechanism for war crimes law enforcement. The SCSL was created as an agreement between the U.N. and Sierra Leone, with the specific mandate to bring to justice those "who bear the greatest responsibility" for serious violations of international humanitarian law and Sierra Leonean law, committed in the territory of Sierra Leone since November 30, 1996. The Court's main focus is to try those who held leadership and command positions, that is, those who planned and instigated attacks. The government and civil society of Sierra Leone have concluded that lower level perpetrators of human rights violations and victims of these violations will have their opportunity for justice through Sierra Leone's Truth and Reconciliation Commission.

The SCSL has indicted thirteen people for war crimes, including former Liberian president Charles Taylor and former Sierra Leone government minister Hinga Norman. The surviving indictees are being charged with war crimes, crimes against humanity, and serious violations of international humanitarian law.

The Special Court is more flexible than a fully international court because the Court can apply both international law as well as Sierra Leonean law, allowing the Court to address crimes specific to the Sierra Leonean conflict. Yet the reach of the Special Court is limited to the national courts of Sierra Leone and does not extend to the courts of third states. Unlike Sierra Leone, the International Criminal Tribunal for Rwanda (ICTR) and the International Criminal Tribunal for Yugoslavia (ICTY) Tribunals were mandatory in nature because the U.N. determined under Chapter VII of the U.N. charter that the wars in those countries were a threat to international peace and security.

The Court has issued a number of precedent-setting decisions on international law, including a ruling in 2004 that heads of state are not immune from prosecution before an international court. Crimes under Sierra Leonean law are limited to offences relating to the abuse of girls and damage to property under two Sierra Leonean statutes. This ability of the Court to decide cases under Sierra Leonean law reinforces Sierra Leone's rules of law alongside the international rules that will be applied.

Some would argue that the most pressing issue facing the court relates to its financing mechanism. The government of Sierra Leone is unable to contribute in any significant manner to the operational costs of the Special Court, which means that the Court relies primarily on contributions from nongovernmental sources. Institutions created by the Security Council, such as the ICTR and the ICTY, are funded by scaled assessments, in which each country's contribution is proportionate to its size and wealth. However, because the U.N. did not directly establish by the SCSL, the Sierra Leone court is financed through voluntary contributions. One should note, however, that a major obstacle for funding the Court is its relative inability to collect the funds that donor states have pledged.

Yet it is highly unlikely that the international community will let this effort fail. By the end of 2003, the United States, through its United States Agency for International Development (USAID) program, provided the Special Court a total of $15 million to pursue its operations. The organization's rationale for support of the Court is that the nation's fragile peace will depend heavily on sustained external support. Furthermore, given the United Kingdom's unique connection to Sierra Leone, British aid for Sierra Leone is more than likely.

The critiques of the SCSL have been offset by its promises. The hope is that trials taking place in Freetown will send a powerful message to the people of Sierra Leone that justice is being done within the framework of the rule of law. There are signs that these goals are being achieved. The special court has trained local attorneys and sent teams to explain legal concepts to villagers, soldiers, and students. Additionally, the simple fact that the SCSL has indicted Charles Taylor sends the message that Sierra Leone is committed to changing its legal landscape.

## B. Dominant Methods of Addressing the Aftermath of Violence, Just as Many Unanswered Questions and Possibly the Wrong Target: Amnesty, Truth and Reconciliation Commissions, and Traditional Mechanisms for Peace and Reconciliation in Liberia

The problem of how many and who to punish, and an ethic of reconciliation and forgiveness, permeate discourse on international peace and justice. Professors Laurel Fletcher and Martha Minow have considered the question of why countries address past episodes of mass violence, and the goals they seek to achieve. These goals include:

(1) discovering and publicizing the truth;

(2) making a symbolic break with the past;

(3) promoting the rule of law and strengthening democratic institutions;

(4) deterrence;

(5) punishment of perpetrators; and

(6) healing victims and achieving social reconstruction.

As part of the discussion on which of these goals should be privileged over others, there is a growing debate as to whether trials are useful in the reconciliation process at all.

Although I discuss both the utility and the problems with trials in the next section, I assert first that in arguing for less punitive measures, some scholars and policymakers question the effectiveness of law in promoting peace in these ruined societies. First, some suggest that although trials have the potential to be effective and efficient, there is no hard proof that they actually promote rule of law goals or peace. At worst, trials may detract from rule of law goals because they lead to further instability in the country. This is so because trials focus on punishing instead of bringing about economic justice and political change. Second, some suggest that trials as an exclusive means to promoting peace and justice do not deal adequately with the need for all members of a society to be reconciled. Finally, trials and other reconstruction efforts are too expensive considering the amount of infrastructure and training needed to get them running.

In response to claims about the disadvantages of trials, transitional justice scholars focus primarily on three types of less punitive mechanisms. Scholars have offered alternatives such as amnesty in exchange for truth and reconciliation, or using traditional courts and other traditional dispute mechanisms to dispense more quickly with less serious violations. The use of these mechanisms suggests that, to move from a society of violence and to rehabilitate the masses, the society and the international community must promote mechanisms that target society at large instead of individual perpetrators.

* * *

## CONCLUSION

Liberia's civil war is officially over, yet the war criminals are free and some are even help-ing run the transitional government under CPA authority. Meanwhile, Charles Taylor re-laxes in Nigeria's resort city of Calabar. By contrast, Sierra Leone's brave step to implement the SCSL is commendable because it signals a desire to begin the transition to rule of law and the end of rule by impunity. Sierra Leone can be a model for Liberia.

Legal mechanisms do have their limits and cannot function alone. It goes without say-ing that tribunals are not and should not be a substitute for early global intervention. An effective post-war regime must include institutions for monitoring abuses, conflict avoid-ance measures, sustainable peace, protection of minority rights, election supervision, and other functions. Legal mechanisms will not work without strong political mechanisms and economic support to combat Africa's post-colonial weak state syndrome. Still, by re-visiting the colonial period and the growth of the post-colonial African political ruling style, we can see the growth of a culture of impunity. Rule by African elites without answering to their own people has directly caused a failure of their states.

Liberia has become the quintessential example of an African failed state. The goal of this article has been to show that Liberia can begin to end the culture of impunity and ring in a sustainable peace. This will happen if the intervention of the transitional gov-ernment of Liberia and the international community focuses on changing the behavior of political elites instead of focusing exclusively on reconciliation among the masses. Un-fortunately, Liberia's present CPA does precisely that; it focuses exclusively on reconcili-ation. Ultimately, positive change is far more likely in Liberia through the use of judicially punitive mechanisms such as prosecution in a hybrid Special Court of law.

---

## 7. Marlise Simons and J. David Goodman, Ex-Liberian Leader Gets 50 Years for War Crimes
### *The New York Times*, 2012

Charles G. Taylor, the former president of Liberia and a once-powerful warlord, was sen-tenced on Wednesday to 50 years in prison for his role in atrocities committed in Sierra Leone during its civil war in the 1990s.

In what was viewed as a watershed case for modern human rights law, Mr. Taylor was the first former head of state convicted by an international tribunal since the Nuremberg trials in Germany after World War II.

Mr. Taylor was found guilty of "aiding and abetting, as well as planning, some of the most heinous and brutal crimes recorded in human history," said Richard Lussick, the judge who presided over the sentencing here in an international criminal court near The Hague. He said the lengthy prison term underscored Mr. Taylor's position as a govern-ment's leader during the time the crimes were committed.

"Leadership must be carried out by example, by the prosecution of crimes, not the com-mission of crimes," the judge said in a statement read before the court.

If carried out, the sentence is likely to mean that Mr. Taylor, 64, will spend the rest of his life in prison. He looked at the floor after he was asked to stand as the sentence was read.

The chief prosecutor, Brenda Hollis, told a news conference that could be viewed in West Africa: "The sentence today does not replace amputated limbs; it does not bring back those who were murdered," she said. "It does not heal the wounds of those who were raped or forced to become sexual slaves."

Mr. Taylor's legal team said it would file an appeal. "The sentence is clearly excessive, clearly disproportionate to his circumstances, his age and his health, and does not take into account the fact that he stepped down from office voluntarily," said Morris Anya, one of Mr. Taylor's lawyers.

The prosecution, which had sought an even longer sentence of 80 years, said it was considering its own appeal, to raise the level of responsibility attributed to Mr. Taylor for crimes committed under his leadership.

Two rebel commanders tried earlier were handed similar prison sentences of 50 and 52 years, and a prosecutor said Mr. Taylor's overall responsibility for the atrocities was considerably greater. He did not freely leave office, but was pushed out in 2003 as rebels marched on his capital and a delegation of African leaders urged him to prevent further bloodshed and seek exile in Nigeria.

The court must set a precise prison term; it is not allowed to impose a life sentence or the death penalty.

Outside the courthouse, Salamba Silla, who works with victims' groups in Sierra Leone, pleaded for more help for former child soldiers, orphans, people whose limbs were hacked off and other victims of the country's war. "You can see hundreds of them begging on the streets of Freetown," the capital, she said. "Many who suffered horrendously need help to return to the provinces, they think they cannot survive there."

Ibrahim Sorie, a lawmaker from Sierra Leone who had been seated in the court's gallery, said the sentence was fair. "It restores our faith in the rule of law, and we see that impunity is ending for top people," Mr. Sorie said.

By previous agreement, Mr. Taylor will serve his sentence in a British prison, but since the appeals process is expected to last at least a year, he will remain in the relative comfort of the United Nations' detention center at The Hague.

After more than a year of deliberations, the Special Court for Sierra Leone found Mr. Taylor guilty in late April of crimes against humanity and war crimes for his part in fomenting widespread brutality that included murder, rape, the use of child soldiers, the mutilation of thousands of civilians and the mining of diamonds to pay for guns and ammunition. Prosecutors have said that Mr. Taylor was motivated in these gruesome actions not by any ideology but rather by "pure avarice" and a thirst for power.

The United Nations-backed tribunal began it work in Sierra Leone, where it tried its other cases, but out of concern that hearings in West Africa would cause unrest among those who still support Mr. Taylor, his trial was moved to the Netherlands.

In Liberia, where Mr. Taylor began a civil war and amassed a record of human rights atrocities during his dictatorial rule, there has not been the political will or the resources to set up a tribunal. The mandate of the Special Court for Sierra Leone covers only crimes between 1996 and 2002, and because the tribunal is to be shut down, critics say that a number of people close to Mr. Taylor have escaped prosecution.

Witnesses who testified at the Taylor trial—which lasted more than twice as long as planned—included men whose hands had been chopped off and women who had been raped. Associates and aides of Mr. Taylor also testified. One aide described a secret bonding ritual in Liberia during which he and others joined Mr. Taylor in eating a human heart.

Diamonds, as well as atrocities, also came up repeatedly in the 2,500-page judgment. The judges agreed with the prosecution that diamonds mined in Sierra Leone were used to pay for arms and ammunition for Mr. Taylor's proxy army, and that rough diamonds were delivered to Mr. Taylor's house in Monrovia, the Liberian capital.

One diamond story that received a lot of attention during the trial involved the court appearance of the model Naomi Campbell. Prosecutors said Ms. Campbell had been sent uncut diamonds as a gift from Mr. Taylor after they attended a charity dinner hosted by Nelson Mandela when he was the president of South Africa.

Two of Ms. Campbell's companions who recounted the episode in court—her agent, Carole White, and the actress Mia Farrow—were repeatedly called "liars" during cross-examination by the defense.

But the judges wrote that the two women were "frank and truthful witnesses," and contrasted them with Ms. Campbell. They called her a "reluctant witness" who "deliberately omitted certain details out of fear." They added that Ms. Campbell "said she came to the realization that the diamonds were sent by Taylor."

Eight other leading members of different forces and rebel groups have already been sentenced by the tribunal. Mr. Taylor is the special court's last defendant. Since his trial began, 115 witnesses have testified.

The three-panel bench, made up of judges from Uganda, Samoa and Ireland, gave Mr. Taylor leeway during his defense. He spent seven months—covering 81 days of the trial—in the witness chair, telling his life story without ever being cut off for digressions or political statements. He said he had heard about atrocities—"that nobody on this planet would not have heard about the atrocities in Sierra Leone"—but that he would "never, ever" have permitted them.

## Authors' Note

The following material analyzes a wide range of issues surrounding the convening of the Iraqi High Tribunal. The selections discuss the composition, jurisdiction, and choice of laws of the IHT. Material 8 further discusses the prosecution of Saddam Hussein and assesses the similarities and differences between the Hussein trial and that of Slobodan Milosevic.

## 8. Various Essays from Grotian Moment: The Saddam Hussein Trial Blog

Basic Information about the Iraqi High Tribunal
by Michael Scharf

[The Statute and Rules of Procedure of the IHT are located at http://www.law.case.edu/saddamtrial]

### What is the Iraqi High Tribunal?

The Iraqi High Tribunal (IHT) is an independent judicial body established by the U.S.-appointed Iraqi Governing Council on December 10, 2003, and approved by the Iraqi Transitional National Assembly on August 11, 2005, to prosecute high level members of the former Iraqi regime who are alleged to have committed war crimes, crimes against humanity, genocide, and aggression. It is composed of two, five-person Trial Chambers, and a nine-person Appeals Chamber. The IST has been called an "internationalized domestic court" since its statute and rules of procedure are modeled upon the U.N. war crimes tribunals for the former Yugoslavia, Rwanda, and Sierra Leone, and its statute requires the IHT to follow the precedent of the U.N. tribunals. Its judges and prosecutors are to be assisted by international experts. But it is not fully international, since its seat is Baghdad, its Prosecutor is Iraqi, and its bench is composed exclusively of Iraqi judges.

### Why not an international court?

The Statute of the International Criminal Court (ICC) precludes that Court from trying cases that involved crimes committed prior to July 2002; most of Saddam Hussein's crimes were committed before that time. And creating a new U.N. ad hoc war crimes tribunal, like the tribunals for the former Yugoslavia and Rwanda, requires the approval of the U.N. Security Council. Several countries that wield a veto on the Council made it known that they would not vote for an ad hoc tribunal to try Saddam Hussein.

### What are the specific charges against Saddam Hussein?

Rather than join the defendants and offenses and hold a single, comprehensive trial like at Nuremberg, the IST has decided to proceed with a dozen mini-trials. The first case to be brought against Saddam Hussein involves his role in the 1982 execution of around 150 Iraqi civilians in Dujail, a predominantly Shiite town north of Baghdad, in response to a failed assassination attempt on Saddam. Several of his top deputies have also been charged in the massacre. Among other charges, Saddam Hussein stands accused of ordering the slaughter of some 5,000 Kurds with chemical gas in Halabja in 1988, killing or deporting more than 10,000 members of the Kurdish Barzani tribe in the 1980s, invading Kuwait in 1990, and drying rivers, killing hundreds of thousands of Marsh Arabs in response to their 1991 uprising. In addition to Saddam, eleven high-ranking Iraqi officials are in custody awaiting indictments, including Abid Hamid al-Tikriti, a former presidential secretary, Ali Hassan al-Majid ("Chemical Ali"), Saddam's cousin and adviser, and Tariq Aziz, the former deputy prime minister.

### Under which body of laws will they be tried?

The IHT has jurisdiction over crimes committed in Iraq or abroad (e.g., in Iran or Kuwait) between 1968 and 2003 by former regime members. The IHT's subject matter jurisdiction is comprised of a mix of international law crimes and domestic law crimes that existed prior to Saddam's ascension to power in 1968. The international law offenses are (1) war crimes, (2) the crime of aggression, and (3) the crime of genocide. The domestic law crimes are (1) manipulation of the judiciary; (2) wastage of national resources and squandering of public assets and funds; and (3) acts of aggression against an Arab country. The IST's procedural law is comprised of a mix of international law procedures set forth in the IST's Rules of Procedures, supplemented by the Rules of Procedure of the Iraqi Criminal Code. Traditional Islamic Law, "sharia," is not applied by the IST. The IST is empowered to imprison convicted persons for up to life or subject them to capital punishment.

### Who are the judges on the tribunal?

The IHT is comprised of about fifty investigative, trial, and appellate judges, all of them native Iraqis mostly of Shiite or Kurdish ethnic origin. The IHT Statute prohibits anyone from serving as a judge who was a member of the Baath party. Each judge was nominated and vetted by the Iraqi Governing Council with the assistance of the 20,000 member Iraqi Bar Association. Five judges will preside over each trial, and nine different judges will preside over each appeal. The names of most of the judges have not been disclosed for security reasons.

### What is the U.S. role in the trial?

The IHT, whose costs are covered by the new government of Iraq, was originally established with $75 million in U.S. funds. The United States established the "Regime Crimes Liaison Office" (RCLO) in Baghdad to help the IHT with investigations, translation of legal materials, and training. RCLO is run by the U.S. Department of Justice, and has worked in partnership with international NGOs such as the International Bar Association (based in London), the International Legal Assistance Consortium (based in Stockholm), the International Association of Penal Law (based in Siracusa, Sicily), and an Academic Consortium (including Case Western Reserve University School of Law, William and Mary School of Law, and University of Connecticut School of Law).

### Why has the tribunal taken two years to get off the ground?

Two years is about how long it took the U.N. created ad hoc tribunals to become fully operational. The IHT investigative judges and prosecutors have spent the bulk of their time examining over two million documents, collecting testimony from some 7,000 witnesses, and reading reports by forensic experts from roughly 200 mass graves throughout Iraq. Meanwhile, the IST judges have been busy developing the Rules of Procedure and undergoing training in the specialized area of war crimes, crimes against humanity, and genocide.

### Issue: Does Saddam Hussein have a right to represent himself before the Iraqi Special Tribunal like Slobodan Milosevic has done at The Hague?

#### YES *by William Schabas*

Inspired by the example of Slobodan Milosevic, Saddam Hussein may choose to represent himself in court. He seems to have no shortage of lawyers. One report says that as many as 2,000 attorneys claim to be retained. But Saddam is surely an intelligent and articulate advocate, and can probably do a competent job.

Article 14 of the International Covenant on Civil and Political Rights, the principal human rights treaty governing Iraq, a person accused of a criminal offence 'to defend himself in person or through legal assistance of his own choosing'. There can be no ambiguity about the text of this provision. However, in its rulings on the Milosevic case, the International Criminal Tribunal for the former Yugoslavia has held that this is not an unlimited right, and that there are implicit exceptions.

One exception, of course, is the defendant who disrupts the proceedings. This should not be confused with an accused who undertakes an aggressive and vigorous defense. But where a defendant does not comport in an appropriate manner, he or she may be removed from the courtroom. Really, the rule is no different whether the defendant is represented by counsel or not. Nor is it any different with respect to any other individual in the courtroom.

Assuming, for the sake of argument, that Saddam is mature enough to behave appropriately, are there any other grounds allowing the court to deny him the right of self-representation?

The ICTY seems to have endorsed the idea that an accused person's ill health, at a level rendering him or her unable to put in a full day's work, might be a good reason. However, in the Milosevic case the Appeals Chamber did not seem to think that the medical problems of the accused, which had reduced the pace of the trial significantly, were so important as to justify counsel being imposed. It seems unfair, indeed discriminatory, to deny the right of self-defense because of poor health, which is, in effect, a form of disability. Would a blind man be denied the right of self-defense? The ICTY Appeals Chamber found one isolated decision in the United States that denied the right of self-defense to a stuttering defendant.

The Special Court for Sierra Leone has also ruled that the right of self-defense can be denied in the interests of a speedy trial. This is only one of several questionable decisions by that body. The ICTY Appeals Chamber passed in silence over the Special Court's ruling; if it had anything positive to say about it, surely the judgment would have been mentioned.

There is no support in the case law for the proposition that an important accused, like Saddam Hussein or Slobodan Milosevic, forfeits the right of self-defense because of his or her position, although this idea seems to have been entertained by some academic writers. Their logic is hard to follow. If they are right, why doesn't it apply to the right to defense generally? After all, the accused is certainly required to instruct defense counsel. How does denying an important accused the right of self-defense differ from denying such a person the right of defense altogether?

The right of self-defense is set out unambiguously in article 14 of the International Covenant, and any limitations have been applied very strictly by the ICTY Appeals Chamber. So while Saddam Hussein might forfeit this right by behaving inappropriately, as long as he follows the rules the right can't be taken away from him.

I have never believed the tired old saw about a man who defends himself having a fool for a client. Saddam Hussein knows the facts and the issues. No person can be more familiar with the case and the charges. He may well prove to be his best lawyer. Good luck to him!

## NO: *By Michael P. Scharf*

At the start of the Slobodan Milosevic trial before the International Criminal Tribunal for the Former Yugoslavia in February 2002, the presiding judge, Britain's Richard May, ruled that "under international law, the defendant has a right to counsel, but he also has a right not to have counsel." Judge May's ruling gave Milosevic the chance to make unfettered speeches throughout the trial. In contrast, a defendant is ordinarily able to address the court only when he takes the stand to give testimony during the defense's case-in-chief, and in the usual case, the defendant is limited to giving evidence that is relevant to the charges, and he is subject to cross examination by the prosecution. The decision to permit Milosevic to represent himself in court also affected the ability of the judges to control the dignity of the proceedings. As his own defense counsel, Milosevic has been able to treat the witnesses, prosecutors and judges in a manner that would earn ordinary defense counsel a citation or incarceration for contempt of court. In addition to regularly making disparaging remarks about the court and browbeating witnesses, Milosevic digresses at length during cross-examination of every witness, despite repeated warnings from the bench. Milosevic, who spends his nights at the tribunal's detention center, has no incentive to heed the judges' admonitions.

To the extent that he is playing not to the court of law in The Hague, but to the court of public opinion back home in Serbia, Milosevic's tactics are proving quite effective. The daily broadcasts of his trial (paid for by the U.S. Agency for International Development) have consistently ranked among the most popular television shows in Serbia. His approval rating in Serbia doubled during the first weeks of his trial. A poll taken half way through the trial found that thirty-nine percent of the Serb population rated Milosevic's trial performance as "superior," while less than twenty-five percent felt that he was getting a fair trial, and only thirty-three percent thought that he was actually responsible for war crimes. Milosevic has gone from the most reviled individual in Serbia to number four on the list of most admired Serbs, and in December 2003, Milosevic easily won a seat in the Serb parliament in a nation-wide election. The decision to permit Milosevic to represent himself has thus undermined one of the most important aims the Security Council sought to achieve in creating the Yugoslavia Tribunal: to educate the Serb people, who were long misled by Milosevic's propaganda, about the acts of genocide, crimes against humanity, and war crimes committed by his regime.

Like Milosevic, Saddam Hussein is also an attorney by training, with his law degree from the prestigious Cairo University. Taking a page out of Milosevic's play book, Saddam Hussein's legal staff is likely to file a pre-trial motion, asserting that Saddam Hussein has a right to represent himself before the IST. Must the IST grant Hussein's motion, thereby enabling Hussein to appear on the nightly news throughout the Middle East, riling against the illegal U.S. invasion of Iraq, insisting that the United States was complicit in Iraqi war crimes against Iran, and encouraging his followers to step up the acts of violence against the United States and new Iraqi government? The answer is no.

When the Iraqi Transitional National Assembly repromulgated the IST Statute on August 11, 2005, it replaced the clause from the December 10, 2003 version of the IST Statute (Article 20(d)(4)) that had provided that the accused has a right "to defend himself in person or through legal assistance of his own choosing" with a new provision (Article 19(4)(d)) that states only that the accused has a right "to procure legal counsel of his choosing." Based on the Milosevic precedent, Saddam Hussein's lawyers are likely to argue that fundamental human rights law, enshrined in the Covenant on Civil and Political Rights, an international treaty to which Iraq is a party, requires that Hussein be allowed to represent himself, notwithstanding this change to the IST Statute. Like the original wording of the IST Statute, Article 14(3)(d) of the Covenant provides that a defendant has the right "to defend himself in person or through legal assistance of his own choosing." But the negotiating record of the Covenant indicates that the drafters' concern was with effective representation, not self-representation. Based on the negotiating record, distinguished commentators such as Cherif Bassiouni have concluded that "whenever it is in the best interest of justice and in the interest of adequate and effective representation of the accused, the court should disallow self-representation and appoint professional counsel." It is also significant that most civil law countries including France, Germany, Denmark, and Belgium, among others, require that defendants be represented by counsel in serious criminal cases. Interpreting the clause in the European Convention on Human Rights with the same language as Article 14(d)(3) of the Covenant, the European Court of Human Rights has affirmed the right of States to assign a defense against the will of the accused in the administration of justice.

Even if there is an international right to self-representation, it would be at most a qualified right. In its 1975 ruling in *Feratta v. California*, the U.S. Supreme Court held that there is a right to self-representation in U.S. courts, but that the "a right of self-representation is not a license to abuse the dignity of the courtroom." U.S. appellate courts have subsequently held that the right of self-representation is subject to exceptions—such as when the defendant acts in a disruptive manner or when self-representation interferes with the dignity or integrity of the proceedings (as would be the case with Saddam Hussein). Drawing on this precedent, in September 2004, the Yugoslavia Tribunal reversed Judge May's earlier ruling, and held instead that Milosevic had to have trial counsel for the remainder of his trial. In the Yugoslavia Tribunal's view: "If at any stage of a trial there is a real prospect that it will be disrupted and the integrity of the trial undermined with the risk that it will not be conducted fairly, then the Trial Chamber has a duty to put in place a regime which will avoid that. Should self-representation have that impact, we conclude that it is open to the Trial Chamber to assign counsel to conduct the defense case, if the Accused will not appoint his own counsel." This decision was affirmed by the Appeals Chamber of the Yugoslavia Tribunal in November 2004. Other international tribunals, including the Rwanda Tribunal in the Barayagwiza case and the Special Court for Sierra Leone in the Norman case have also assigned counsel over the objections of a defendant who wished to represent himself.

International Law requires that Saddam Hussein be afforded a fair trial, which can best be achieved by ensuring that he is vigilantly represented by distinguished legal counsel, not by permitting him to represent himself.

For a fuller treatment of this issue, See Michael P. Scharf and Christopher M. Rassi, Do Former Leaders have an International Right to Self-Representation in War Crimes Trials? OHIO STATE JOURNAL ON DISPUTE RESOLUTION 3–42 (2005).

**Issue: Is the Iraqi Special Tribunal, which was established on December 10, 2003 by the Occupying Power and the unelected Iraqi Governing Council, a legitimate judicial institution?**

**YES: By Linda Malone[1]**

The Geneva Conventions mandate that the laws of an occupied state be changed only in cases of military necessity. Therefore, a narrow interpretation of occupation law under the Geneva Conventions would require finding that the Iraqi Special Tribunal (IST) was not a legitimate judicial institution, solely in regard to its status as a creation of an occupying power without a military reason for its establishment. The trend among legal scholars, however, is to recognize the need for an occupying power to be permitted to change the laws of an occupied state in order to render humanitarian aid. This broader interpretation of occupation law under the Geneva Conventions, allowing both occupation and the alteration of an occupied state"s laws for humanitarian purposes, would legitimize the IST as a judicial institution, despite its formation by an occupying power with or without military necessity.

The IST may also be a legitimate judicial institution because of its approval by the unelected Iraqi Governing Council (IGC). The IGC, although unelected, is recognized by the international community as having been a legitimate governing body. The recognition and approval of the IST by the IGC thereby legitimizes the IST as a legitimate judicial body, because it was created by a legitimate governing body.

Finally, the newly elected Iraqi government has the power to either formally or informally legitimize the IST. The Iraqi government may choose to formally legitimize the IST through its legislative process, or by executive mandate. Either action would legitimize not only the future actions of the IST, but its past actions, as well. If the Iraqi government chooses to informally legitimize the IST, it may do so by simply continuing to operate the IST, recognizing its jurisdiction and the binding power of its decisions. This continued operation would grant tacit approval to the IST and would legitimize its actions. Such recognition by an elected government would be the best method of solidifying the legitimacy of the IST, and would leave the least room for doubt regarding the authority of the IST.

**YES: *By Christopher M. Rassi***

The Iraqi Governing Council promulgated the Statute of the Iraqi Special Tribunal (the "IST") on December 10, 2003 (the "2003 Statute"). On March 8, 2004 the Iraqi Gov-

---

1. All information presented in this answer was taken from a Memorandum for the Iraqi Special Tribunal regarding the legality of the IST, prepared by Heidi M. Brown and Tarek Z. Shuman in April 2005.

erning Council promulgated the Law of Administration for the State of Iraq for the Transitional Period (the "TAL"). The TAL, established by the Iraqi Governing Council before the restoration of Iraqi sovereignty, is Iraq"s Interim Constitution and preserves and continues the 2003 Statute in force and effect. Article 48 of the TAL confirms the 2003 Statute as "issued on 10 December 2003." It also declares that the 2003 Statute "exclusively defines the [IST's] jurisdiction and procedures, notwithstanding the provisions of [the TAL.]"

On August 11, 2005, the Transitional National Assembly instituted a revised Statute for the IST (the "2005 Statute") which abrogated in full the 2003 Statute. Despite the TAL's Article 48, the Iraqi Transitional Government has the power to replace the 2003 Statute with a revised Statute without amending the TAL itself. The TAL only confirmed the 2003 Statute, and refers back to the 2003 Statute itself for exclusive interpretive authority, which gives power to the new elected Government of Iraq. Article 37 of the 2003 Statute states that "[t]he Governing Council or the Successor Government has the powers to establish other rules and procedures in order to implement this [2003] Statute." Article 32 of the 2003 Statute further states that "[t]he powers conferred on the Governing Council in this Statute shall be transferred to the executive authority in any future government (the "Successor Government") established following the disbanding of the Governing Council." Not only did the Transitional National Authority have the Constitutional power to replace the Statute, but this act lends legitimacy to the very institution of the IST. Commentators have questioned the legitimacy of the IST, which was initially created and designed by occupiers and an unelected government. The 2005 Statute, established by the Transitional National Assembly, should alleviate the fears of those that believe that the IST is not the work and will of the elected Iraqi Government. Further, such an act ensures that the IST will continue to operate even though its founding Government has been replaced.

### The IST should fulfill its promise as a true hybrid domestic-international court
*by Laura Dickinson*

HARNESSING THE IST'S POTENTIAL AS A "HYBRID" COURT: Iraq Should Consider Appointing Foreign Judges to the IST to Enhance the Legitimacy and Capacity of the Court

The Iraqi Special Tribunal is poised to begin some of the most important war crimes trials of this century, both for Iraq and the world at large. Whatever one may think about the legality and morality of the Iraq war, it is difficult to dispute that Saddam Hussein and his associates should be brought to trial for the widespread atrocities they are accused of having committed. Criminal prosecutions have the potential not only to adjudicate individual responsibility, but also to create a historical record, to send a message that Iraq is committed to the rule of law, and to pave the way for broader societal healing. Yet these worthy goals are imperiled by the ongoing conflict in the country, by the real risks such conflict poses to the courageous judges who have stepped forward to serve on the tribunal, and by concerns that the tribunal will not be independent or impartial. It is my view, therefore, that the Iraqi government should seriously consider exercising its authority under the IST statute to appoint foreign judges in order to enhance the legitimacy and capacity of the court, and thereby fulfill its promise as a "hybrid" domestic-international court.

Iraq chose to create a "hybrid" domestic-international court to address the atrocities committed during the regime of Saddam Hussein. Some policy-makers and scholars had argued that only a purely international tribunal—composed entirely of foreign judges trying cases under international law in a courtroom safely outside the territory of Iraq—could mete out fair justice in the Iraqi cases. Others had suggested that a domestic court was more appropriate, in order to enable Iraqi participation in the process and to prevent any overtones of imperialism. Yet in the end Iraq chose create a hybrid of the two, a court that has some international and some domestic components (although to be sure, in its current structure it more closely resembles a domestic court). For example, the court has the authority to apply both domestic and international law. In addition, the IST Statute requires the appointment of international advisors, who will advise the judges and prosecutors on international law and will "monitor" the Tribunal's observance of due process principles. The Statute includes no formal role for the United Nations, but the judge who serves as President of the Tribunal may request assistance from the U.N. in appointing the non-Iraqi experts. And while the judges of the court are currently all Iraqi nationals, the Statute provides that the government can appoint non-Iraqi judges if such a move is deemed "necessary." The court thus resembles, and has the capacity to resemble even more closely, a growing number of hybrid domestic-international courts around the world—from East Timor, to Sierra Leone, to Kosovo, to Cambodia—that hold special promise in the adjudication of war crimes.

Scholars and policy-makers have paid less attention to hybrid domestic-international courts than to purely international or purely domestic tribunals, but such courts offer distinct advantages. Such courts are "hybrid" because both the institutional apparatus and the applicable law consist of a blend of the international and the domestic. Foreign judges sit alongside their domestic counterparts to try cases prosecuted and defended by teams of local lawyers working with those from other countries. This hybrid model has developed in a range of settings, generally post-conflict situations where no politically viable full-fledged international tribunal exists, as in East Timor or Sierra Leone, or where an international tribunal exists but cannot cope with the sheer number of cases, as in Kosovo. Most recently, an agreement to create a hybrid court in Cambodia has been reached. Because of their hybrid character, such courts have special advantages in gaining legitimacy among multiple populations, as well as in promoting capacity-building and the rule of law.

With respect to legitimacy—which I am here defining quite broadly to mean those factors that tend to make the decisions of a juridical body acceptable to various populations observing its procedures "on the ground"—hybrid courts have advantages over purely domestic tribunals on the one hand, and purely international tribunals on the other. Not surprisingly, the perceived legitimacy of domestic judicial institutions in post-conflict situations is often in question. To the extent that such institutions exist at all, they typically will have suffered severely during the conflict. The physical infrastructure often will have sustained extensive, crippling damage, and the personnel is likely to be severely compromised or lacking in essential skills. Judges and prosecutors may remain in place from the prior regime, which may have backed the commission of widespread atrocities. Thus, the state may continue to employ the very people who failed to prosecute or convict murderers or torturers or ethnic cleansers. Alternatively, the new regime may replace the old personnel almost completely, resulting in an enormous skill and experience deficit, as well as the danger of show trials and overly zealous prosecution for past crimes. At the same time, broad acceptance of purely international processes may be difficult to establish as well. For example, in light of the continuing ethnic tensions within the region, the ICTY was established at the Hague, far removed from the scene of the atrocities, and the court was staffed by international judges and staff. However, the lack of connection to local populations has been problematic.

Hybrid courts can solve some of these legitimacy problems. In Kosovo and East Timor, the addition of international judges and prosecutors to cases involving serious human rights abuses may have enhanced the perceived legitimacy of the process, at least to some degree. In both contexts, the initial failure of U.N. authorities to consult with the local population in making governance decisions generally, and decisions about the judiciary specifically, sparked public outcry. Thus, in both Kosovo and East Timor the appointment of foreign judges to domestic courts to sit alongside local judges and the appointment of foreign prosecutors to team up with local prosecutors helped to create a framework for consultation.

The appointment of international judges to the local courts in these highly sensitive cases may also have helped to enhance the perception of the independence of the judiciary. In Kosovo this was most apparent, as the previous attempts at domestic justice had failed to win any support among Serbs. Indeed, Serbian judges refused to cooperate in the administration of justice, and the verdicts in the cases tried by ethnic Albanians were regarded by the ethnic Serbian population as tainted. In contrast, the verdicts of the hybrid tribunals garnered considerable support, even among Serbs.

As compared to purely domestic and purely international institutions, hybrid courts may also better promote local capacity-building, which is often an urgent priority in post-conflict situations. The conflicts in Kosovo and East Timor virtually eliminated the physical infrastructure of the judiciary, including court buildings, equipment, and legal texts. But even more devastating than the physical loss was the loss in human resources. In Kosovo, only Serbs had the experience and training to work as judges and prosecutors; yet these Serbs often refused to work in the new system because doing so would constitute a betrayal of their ethnic heritage. There were some Albanians with legal training, but they had been almost completely excluded from the system for many years and therefore had little experience. In East Timor, the capacity deficit was even more severe because the Indonesians, who had staffed the judiciary had evacuated, and few Timorese possessed any legal training or experience. Yet a purely international process that largely bypasses the local population does little to help support local capacity.

The hybrid process thus offers advantages in the arena of capacity-building as well. The side-by-side working arrangements allow for on-the-job training that is likely to be more effective than abstract classroom discussions of formal legal rules and principles. And the teamwork can allow for sharing of experiences and knowledge in both directions. Foreign actors have the opportunity to gain greater sensitivity to local issues, local culture, and local approaches to justice at the same time that local actors can learn from foreign actors. In addition, hybrid courts can serve as a locus for international funding efforts, thereby pumping needed funds into the rebuilding of local infrastructure.

In view of the potential threats to the IST's legitimacy, both inside and outside Iraq, the Iraqi government should seriously consider drawing from the lessons of the other hybrid courts and further develop the IST's hybrid character. Specifically, by appointing foreign judges, the Iraqi government might enhance perceptions, both within Iraq and in the broader international community, of the court's independence. Specifically, the addition of foreign judges might serve as a shield for the domestic judges, as was the case in Kosovo, and help to create a sense of each panel's neutrality as to all ethnic groups within Iraq. At the same time, the appointment of foreign judges with experience in international human rights or humanitarian law might provide a welcome infusion of expertise in these areas, while at the same time offer opportunities for these experts to develop knowledge of Iraqi law and Iraqi approaches to these issues.

Thus, by taking advantage of the potentially hybrid nature of the court, the IST could both lend greater legitimacy to its process and help build the expertise and capacity of the local Iraqi justice sector. And, to combat any potential nationalist fears about the imposition of "western" justice on Iraqis, the foreign judges might be drawn from Arab or Muslim countries. For example, judges or lawyers involved in recent human rights trials in Indonesia might be willing to serve. And while making the court a true hybrid is obviously not a panacea, I believe it would place the IST and the emerging Iraqi justice system on firmer footing than it is today.

### "What If" a Different U.S. Strategy Had Built a Different Court for Iraq?
*by David Scheffer*

The trials of former Iraqi President Saddam Hussein and many of his regime's top officials will demonstrate whether the Bush administration's judicial strategy for post-war Iraq is likely to work. Will it compensate for an intervention and occupation that so boldly challenged fundamental principles of international law? I need not make the case for how serious the situation is in Iraq today or how the U.S. performance there might fare with any reasonable cost-benefit analysis or scrutiny under the law of war (particularly with respect to detainees). But it is fair to ask whether in the realm of rule of law challenges a different judicial and Security Council strategy could have been pursued prior to Operation Iraqi Freedom in March 2003. After all, an alternative U.S. strategy, particularly with respect to accountability for atrocity crimes (genocide, crimes against humanity, serious war crimes, aggression), had developed steadily during the Clinton Administration, from 1993 through 2000. So I will indulge in a "what if" exercise on accountability. The Iraqi experience of recent years desperately needs such an alternative perspective—a Plan B, if you will—so that we might better understand the merits and flaws of current policies.

Imagine where we would be today if, in September 2002 when President George W. Bush challenged the United Nations General Assembly to be "relevant" and confront Iraq's alleged non-compliance with Security Council resolutions, particularly those pertaining to weapons of mass destruction (WMDs), he had coupled that challenge with a far more persuasive evidentiary case: the quarter century record of the Iraqi regime's alleged atrocity crimes against its own people and other countries. Bush had the standing and leverage at that moment in history to achieve what had been a critical goal of the Clinton Administration and should have been pursued (despite all of Bush's "anything but Clinton" policies) with the changing of the guard in January 2001.

The critical moment in history had arrived when President Bush stepped up to the podium of the U.N. General Assembly on September 12, 2002, to seek Security Council action on Iraq. I contended then and I would maintain today that the stars were aligned on that day to achieve the objective we, with strong bipartisan support, had spent almost eight years of the Clinton Administration striving to build support for among key governments. President Bush, who made reference to the alleged atrocities of the Iraqi regime but focused his call for action on Iraq's disarmament obligations under Security Council resolutions, could have called on the Security Council to create immediately a powerful international criminal tribunal to investigate, indict, and when possible apprehend and bring to trial those officials of the Iraqi regime responsible for atrocity crimes. Branding properly investigated Iraqi officials as indicted fugitives of an international criminal tribunal would have done far more to isolate and discredit them (both internally and abroad) than any political condemnation from western capitals or the United Nations on what has proven to be a false reading of any WMD threat from Iraq.

There likely would have been support for such an initiative during the fall of 2002 when Security Council members were prepared to get tough with Baghdad, but wanted the basis for their action to be both credible and lawful and to be viewed as such by the public. With American and British military intervention looming, France and Germany could have pointed to the judicial cases unfolding against Iraqi officials as the stronger basis to support ultimate action to replace the regime, particularly after a further phase of WMD inspections. The legal memoranda prepared by lawyers in the British Government in 2002 and early 2003, reported in recent months, might have read somewhat differently if there had been a basis in law to apprehend Iraqi officials indicted by an international criminal tribunal established under U.N. Charter Chapter VII authority. The U.S. Congress, which had long sought the indictment of Saddam Hussein, might have strengthened the use of force authorization in the much-debated language of the Authorization for Use of Military Force Against Iraq Resolution of 2002 by including a law enforcement component to it, drawing, in fact, on prior Congressional resolutions seeking to bring Saddam Hussein to justice. The preparation for judicial investigations and prosecutions would have been much further advanced and strengthened with international participation and support by the time of an intervention than proved to be the case once the largely American cast of investigators finally began their work in earnest during the occupation.

By September 2002 the evidence of atrocities was significant and far more convincing than all the so-called intelligence about suspected WMD capabilities. It was remarkable following the March 2003 intervention when journalists, the Coalition Provisional Authority, the White House, and the Pentagon reported the discovery of mass graves and torture chambers as if these had never been anticipated and the allegedly criminal actions of the Iraqi regime were being exposed thanks to the Anglo-American intervention. Anyone who worked the Iraq account during the 1990's had reason to believe that torture chambers existed and that mass graves had to dot the landscape of Iraq to account for the reported hundreds of thousands of victims of the regime during the 1980's and 1990's. The real question was where the torture chambers and mass graves would be located and how many bodies of what identity would be found within the graves. The discovery of such sites is important as evidence for trials and for the historical record in Iraq, but the discoveries themselves should have nothing to do with ex post facto justifications for the intervention.

Whatever evidence of atrocity crimes might have justified—at least to some—a humanitarian intervention or law enforcement intervention into Iraq in 2003 already existed on the public record at the time. The critical issue would have been, if raised, whether there was sufficient political will to rely, to a significant degree, on that kind of evidence backed up by the investigations of an international criminal tribunal rather than only WMD suspicions to authorize military action. The political will to act based on the extensive record of atrocity crimes as the target of an international criminal tribunal and some of which reportedly were continuing in Iraq, may not have emerged by March 2003. However, the international tribunal's mandate and initial investigations might have provided the additional justification to garner enough Security Council support (or acquiescence) for an alternative path, proposed by (non-permanent Security Council member) Chile in early March 2003, to give the U.N. weapons inspectors a final though limited opportunity to complete their work within a deadline set by the Council, failing which coalition action would have been authorized.

Perhaps that is too much of a "what if" stretch. But in my view the alternative U.S. strategy should have been to seize the day in September 2002 to build the court that would have created a law enforcement context for the Security Council's further deliberations on Iraq and its WMD capabilities. The debate in the Council and the final Anglo-American decision to intervene relied instead on a fundamentally flawed WMD assessment of Iraq. It was only in the aftermath when, several months later and lacking any WMD discoveries, the alleged criminal character of the Iraqi regime emerged in

Bush Administration briefings as a growing and perhaps primary rationale for the intervention, as if such news was a discovery we should all credit to the intervention and occupation, and then somehow deduce that it was the rationale all along for Operation Iraqi Freedom.

So "what if" an international criminal tribunal on Iraq had been established by the Security Council? It could have been structured to include significant participation by Iraqi judges, prosecutors, investigators, and defense counsel following the intervention. It could have authorized that trials ultimately to be held or continued in Iraq when the security situation permitted. It could have attracted technical and financial support from Europe, Latin America, and the United Nations rather than be dependent on the support of one of the occupation powers, the United States. It would have been independent of any meddling domestic political influence or perceptions of victor's justice.

But "what if" is a strictly historical perspective. The Iraqi Higher Criminal Court is here to stay and it deserves the best efforts of all who are invested in its pursuit of justice.

### Issue: Did the Iraqi regime's actions to dam rivers, leading to the destruction of the habitat of the Marsh Arabs, constitute a form of genocide?

### YES: By Linda Malone[2]

The term genocide is applied to prohibited actions taken against a specific protected group, with the intent of destroying that group. The prohibited act taken against the Marsh Arabs was the degradation of their environment to the point of "deliberately inflicting upon the group conditions of life calculated to bring about its physical destruction in whole or in part" within the meaning of the Genocide Convention.

The action the Iraqi regime took in order to bring about this destruction was to dam and drain the natural wetlands essential to the culture, livelihoods, and lives of the Marsh Arabs. This action was taken, along with bombing raids, torture, and mass public executions, in retaliation for the Shi'a uprising against the Iraqi Regime. Ninety-three percent of the marshland upon which the Marsh Arabs were dependent was destroyed by the dam and drainage project. Of the 250,000 Marsh Arabs residing in the marshland in 1991, only 40,000 remain.

It is always possible that a government's environmental actions could have unforeseen and tragic consequences, and such could be the case in this instance. The destruction of the marshland, however, took place alongside other government-sponsored actions, namely bombing raids, torture, and executions, meant to bring about the immediate deaths of members of the Marsh Arabs as punishment for an uprising against the Iraqi Regime. In this context, the destruction of the marshland appears much more likely to have been an intentional, slow execution of a group by its government, bringing the damming and draining of the marshlands within the definition of genocide as defined by the Genocide Convention, to which Iraq is a party-state.

If the Iraqi Special Tribunal finds that the damming and draining of the marshland was a deliberate action taken by the Iraqi regime in order to bring about the destruction of the Marsh Arabs, then it may conclude that this action constituted an act of genocide against the Marsh Arabs, and may prosecute the members of the regime accordingly.

---

2. All information presented in this answer was taken from a Memorandum for the Iraqi Special Tribunal regarding the crimes against the Marsh Arabs by the Iraqi regime, prepared by Katherine Allnutt and Jennifer Evans in April 2005.

## Issue: Did the Anfal Operations constitute Genocide?

### PERHAPS: By Linda Malone[3]

The Iraqi constitution recognizes and protects the separate nationality of the Kurdish population within the Iraqi state. Military activities by the Iraqi government conducted from February through September of 1988 ("Operation Anfal") along the Iranian border ("cordon sanitaire") under the leadership of Saddam Hussein, nevertheless targeted certain Kurdish population centers and subjected them to gross violations of human rights.

Estimates from Human Rights Watch indicates that upwards of 100,000 Kurdish men, women, and children were killed by mass executions, chemical attacks against dozens of Kurdish villages, systematic firing squads, the destruction of approximately 2,000 villages near to the border of Iran and elsewhere in Iraq, the destruction of residential structures in civilian areas, looting of civilian property and farm animals, arbitrary arrest of villagers captured in designated "prohibited areas," and mass deportations and relocations from the northern part of Iraq to camps located in non-Kurdish areas of Iraq. These actions not only denied particular groups of Kurdish Iraqis security within Iraq"s borders, but affirmatively victimized them in particular, as a regional population.

Article II of the convention on the Prevention and Punishment of Genocide ("Genocide Convention" or "Convention"), defines genocide:

In the present Convention, genocide means any of the following acts committed with intent to destroy, in whole or in part, a national, ethnical, racial, or religious group, as such:

   (a)  Killing members of the group;

   (b)  Causing serious bodily or mental harm to members of the group;

   (c)  Deliberately inflicting on the group conditions of life calculated to bring about is physical destruction in whole or in part;

   (d)  Imposing measures intended to prevent births within the group;

   (e)  Forcibly transferring children of the group to another group.

Article 3 of the Convention makes the international crime punishable.

Although it is clear that numerous human rights abuses occurred within the cordon sanitaire, the prosecution of genocide is complicated by the lack of a coordinated national policy by the Iraqi government to persecute the Kurds as a nationality through the territory of Iraq. Indeed, evidence tends to show that people initially placed into relocation centers were subsequently released to their families, and that others who complied with Iraqi Government orders were left unharmed. Indeed, the various Anfal Operations appears somewhat limited to the rural border regions between Iraq and Iran with major population centers remaining mostly unscathed.

The Kurds, as a distinct minority nationality within Iraq, should be protected as a group by the Genocide Convention. Likewise, the acts of the Iraqi government in the cordon sanitaire, (mass exterminations, etc.) appear to be actus reus within the definition of genocide. For the actors to be liable for apparent human rights abuses under the Genocide Convention in particular, however, they must have had the specific genocidal "intent to destroy, in whole or in part, a national, ethnical, racial, or religious group, as such." This is the most difficult analysis because it involves both subjective and objective determinations.

---

3. All information presented in this answer was taken from a Memorandum for the Iraqi Special Tribunal prepared by Dominique Callins, Heather Johnson, and Jennifer Lagerquist in April 2005.

Preliminary to the finding of specific genocidal intent, judges sitting for the Iraqi Tribunal considering cases of genocide will need to first define objectively, the group that was allegedly targeted. In this case, Iraqi Kurds as a national group would clearly be protected groups within the Convention, and may have been victimized "in part." Iraqi Kurds of the cordon sanitaire might also be recognized as an "ethnical" sub-group of the larger Kurdish nationality. Multiple ethnical sub-groups might exist in the region, and this finding might lead to different conclusions of whether smaller groups were targeted "in whole" or "part". Once the group has been defined, judges will assess the specific intent of alleged perpetrators.

The intent must be to destroy the group "in part." The numbers of intended victims must be substantial, either quantitatively or qualitatively. The quantitative analysis might consider a raw numeric total of victims, or a proportional one assessed in relation to the total number of individuals of the group under the control of the perpetrators. The qualitative assessment would focus on whether the target for destruction was picked because of its importance to the group such that its elimination would be likely to destroy the group. It will be for the judges to determine in light of the examples presented by Rwanda and Yugoslavia, whether substantial destruction, either qualitatively or quantitatively, occurred.

Finally, intent must be directed towards the group "as such." That a separate motive exists for the persecution of the group is irrelevant, as long as it is membership in the group that drives the destruction, and that the destruction was committed because of its tendency to destroy the group.

Finding that genocide occurred in Iraq will be an exhaustive consideration of the facts of each case; any consideration of genocidal intent must be carefully considered based on a totality of the circumstances.

### Issue: The Significance of the Anfal Campaign Indictment
### An Ambitious but Risky Move
*by Michael P. Scharf*

As the Dujail trial was nearing an end, on April 4, 2006, the Iraqi High Tribunal announced the referral of its second case to the Trial Chamber. The case concerns the Anfal campaign, a series of eight military operations launched against the Northern Kurds in 1988, which resulted in an estimated 100,000 deaths. (See also Issue #6).

The IHT had been criticized for beginning with the Dujail Case, which involved 150 casualties, rather than the far more weighty Anfal case, whose casualty figures were 100 times greater. Since many experts were opining that Saddam would be promptly executed following the verdict in the Dujail trial, comparisons were made to the 1931 trial of Chicago mob boss Al "Scarface" Capone, who was prosecuted for tax evasion rather than for the thousands of murders he orchestrated in a series of gang wars in the 1920s. While Saddam might pay the ultimate price for Dujail, his victims would be robbed of seeing him face justice for his much greater atrocities.

The announcement of the Anfal referral changed all that. Since the Anfal case is scheduled to begin immediately after the close of the Dujail trial (while the Dujail verdict is being appealed to the Appeals chamber of the IHT), this means that whatever the Dujail verdict, Saddam Hussein will be available to face his accusers in the Anfal trial.

The Anfal referral is important in a second respect. The IHT announced that Saddam and his co-defendants, including Ali Hassan Al-Majid ("Chemical Ali"), would be charged with the crime of genocide. Genocide has been called "the crime of crimes." It is the worst crime known to humankind, and it is the hardest crime to prove. Charging Saddam with genocide suggests that his atrocities rank with those committed by Adolf Hitler, Pol Pot, Idi Amin, and Slobodan Milosevic.

The problem, however, is that it will be extremely difficult to prove the genocide charge in relation to the Anfal campaign, and thus there is a great risk that Saddam will be acquitted, leaving the world to wonder whether he was no more than a petty thug as opposed to a genocidal dictator, after all.

The 1948 Genocide Convention defines genocide as mass killing and other similar actions "committed with intent to destroy, in whole or in part, a national, ethnical, racial or religious group, as such." It is significant that the drafters of the Genocide Convention deliberately excluded acts directed against "political groups," or "opponents of the regime" from the definition of Genocide. This exclusion was due to the fact that the Convention was drafted during the height of the cold war, during which the Soviet Union and other totalitarian governments feared that they would face interference in their internal affairs if genocide was defined to include such acts. Thus, history has not labeled the murder of four million Russians in Stalin's purges (1937–1953) or of five million Chinese in Mao's Cultural Revolution (1966–1976) as acts of genocide.

With their distinct language and culture, the Iraqi Kurds obviously constitute an ethnic group under the Genocide Convention. Moreover, the large number of victims in a distinct geographic area is more than sufficient for a finding of genocide. The challenge for the Tribunal will be finding the necessary "specific intent" to destroy the Kurds "as such"—in other words for no predominant reason other than because they are Kurds. As described below, there are two alternative theories, having nothing to do with ethnocentrism, xenophobia, or hatred of Kurds, for why Saddam ordered the Anfal operations.

First, in 1986, the two main Kurdish parties, the KDP and PUK, united with the help of Iran (which was then at war with Iraq), to attempt to topple Saddam's government. Thus, the Anfal campaign may have been aimed at punishing the Kurds for their acts of treason and at suppressing the continuing threat of an Iranian-backed insurgency. It is noteworthy that Kurds who cooperated with Iraqi officials, dissociated themselves from Kurdish nationalists, and accepted deportation to southern Iraq, were not otherwise persecuted.

Second, parts of Kurdistan in northern Iraq contained vast quantities of oil that Saddam's government desired. The Kurdish claims to these oil fields in the 1980s would have been perceived as a significant threat that required a response. It is significant in this regard that the Anfal campaign did not target all Kurdish populated towns throughout Iraq, just those in oil-rich Kurdistan in northern Iraq, and that the people killed in the Anfal campaign included non-Kurds, as well as Kurds, who refused to vacate the targeted towns.

These motivations would not absolve Saddam for liability for crimes against humanity and war crimes (for using chemical weapons and indiscriminately killing mass numbers of Kurdish civilians). But if the Tribunal concludes that the Anfal operations predominantly reflected Saddam's intent to retaliate against the Kurds for treason, to suppress insurgency, or to gain access to oil, Saddam must be acquitted of the genocide charge. Thus, the genocide charge represents an ambitious but risky move for the Tribunal.

### Issue: Does Saddam Hussein Have a Viable Defense Based on the Necessity to Combat Insurgents and Terrorists?

#### NO: *By Michael Scharf*

In the first trial of the Iraqi Special Tribunal scheduled to start on October 19, 2005, Saddam Hussein and several of his lieutenants will be prosecuted for the attack on the

Iraqi town of Dujail in 1982 — an attack which involved the killing of 150 townspeople, the destruction of their homes and businesses, and the burning of the surrounding date palm groves. Under the headline, "Saddam Expects to Prove Innocence, Lawyer Says," (USA Today, October 13, 2005), Saddam Hussein's lawyer, Khalil al-Dulaimi, is quoted as saying: "Saddam Hussein was on a visit to this village [Dujail], and he was subject to an assassination attempt. Punishing those who carried it out is justifiable all over the world. Any president in the position of Saddam would do the same thing."

Wiping a town out in retaliation for an assassination attempt is certainly not a legitimate defense, but attacking a town to root out terrorists and suppress an insurgency may be another matter.

To prove this line of defense, Dulaimi might call former U.S. President Bill Clinton or other members of his administration to testify in Baghdad or through video link from the United States. After all, in 1993, Clinton ordered the launch of 23 cruise missiles to strike the Iraqi Intelligence Service Headquarters in downtown Baghdad when the U.S. learned that Iraq was behind an attempt to assassinate former President Bush during a visit to Kuwait. Cruise missiles are a blunt instrument when fired into a populous residential area, and numerous civilian casualties were reported. "If Clinton's action was justified in response to an assassination attempt," Dulaimi will ask, "why wouldn't Saddam's be?"

Or Dulaimi might call U.S. General George Casey, who currently commands the U.S. forces in Iraq. Just last week, (October 4, 2005), General Casey ordered the U.S. military to launch a major offensive against three small towns in the Euphrates River valley (Haqlaniyah, Parwana and Haditha), which were reportedly being used by insurgents and members of the al Qaeda terrorist organization as a base of operations in Iraq. The attack, code-named "River Gate," involved air strikes from U.S. warplanes and helicopters, followed by an assault by 2,500 U.S. and Iraqi government soldiers. Most of the buildings in the towns were destroyed, and hundreds of Iraqi casualties were reported, including civilians who were "unavoidable collateral damage." Similar operations have been conducted across Iraq in an effort to "uproot" terrorists and insurgents, and to "suppress" terrorist and insurgent attacks in the months leading to the vote on the Iraqi Constitution. In the context of this aggressive campaign against Iraqi terrorists and insurgents, the Iraqi Department of Health has reported that the U.S. and Iraqi armed forces have been responsible for twice as many civilian casualties than those caused by insurgent and terrorist attacks. "If civilian casualties are acceptable collateral damage for General Casey's troops in their effort to stamp out al Qaeda and suppress insurgency in Iraq in 2005," Dulaimi will ask, "why not for Saddam Hussein's troops facing the same type of threat in 1982?"

This defense strategy would be similar to that successfully employed by counsel for German Grand Admiral Karl Doenitz before the WWII Nuremberg Tribunal. Doenitz was charged with conducting unrestricted submarine warfare in the Atlantic. His lawyer proved (with an affidavit supplied by U.S. Admiral Chester Nimitz) that the American navy did the exact same thing in the Pacific conflict. The Nuremberg Tribunal ruled that Doenitz was not guilty of the charge, since international law could not be said clearly to prohibit unrestricted submarine warfare in light of the fact that all sides were engaging in the practice, believing it to be lawful.

These will be tough questions for the prosecution to respond to, and certainly the line of questioning will raise questions of moral equivalence that may be uncomfortable for the Bush Administration.

For an answer, the Prosecution is likely to turn to the 1969 case of *United States v. Calley*, one of the most important war crimes trials of the Vietnam war era. The Defendant,

Lt. William Calley was charged with commanding troops which executed 102 civilians at the South Vietnamese town of My Lai in 1968. In defense, Calley said that he had received orders by radio to destroy the town, which was being used as a base of operations by the Viet Cong, and to kill all the townspeople since it was impossible to distinguish Viet Cong insurgents from innocent civilians. This was in essence, the same exact argument that Dulaimi is likely to make on behalf of Saddam Hussein and the other defendants in the Dujail case. The Court rejected Calley's obedience to orders defense, finding that an order to kill all of the townspeople, including babies, children, and frail elderly persons, was a manifestly illegal order. The Court reaffirmed that under international law, a person can be held criminally liable for ordering such an atrocity, and that subordinates have a duty to disobey such an illegal order or they too can be held liable for carrying it out.

### Issue: Can the Defendants Raise the "Tu Quoque" Defense?

#### NO: *By Michael Scharf*

"Tu Quoque," Latin for "you also," is a defense in which the defendant argues that since the other side committed the same crimes, it is not legitimate to prosecute the defendants of those crimes. In the case of Saddam Hussein, the defense might be raised in three contexts. First, the defense may seek to argue that since the United States provided financial support and material assistance to aid the Ba'athist Regime's war efforts against Iran, with knowledge of the actions the regime took against Iraqi Kurds and Shi'ites who supported Iran, that it would be unfair for an American-created Tribunal to prosecute the defendants for such actions. Second, the defense may try to argue that since the United States invaded Iraq without Security Council authorization or a legitimate claim to self-defense, it is unfair for an American-created Tribunal to prosecute the defendants for the crime of aggression against Iran or Kuwait. And third, the defense may seek to claim that since the United States has argued that the necessity defense justifies its aggressive actions against towns in Iraq and Afghanistan suspected of being a base of operation for terrorists, that an American-created Tribunal should be estopped from denying the right of the Ba'athist Regime to take actions for the same reason against the northern Kurds and the southern marsh Arabs.

The Tu Quoque defense is a cousin of the equitable "clean hands doctrine," which provides that one who comes to court for help must come with unsoiled hands. The International Criminal Tribunal for the Former Yugoslavia stated in *Prosecutor v. Kupreskic* (2000), that the Tu Quoque defense has been "universally rejected" and that "there is in fact no support either in State practice or in the opinions of publicists for the validity of such a defense." But precedent for applying the doctrine can be found in the case law of the Federal Supreme Court of Germany which held in a 1960 war crimes case that "no State may accuse another State of violations of international law and exercise criminal jurisdiction over the latter's citizens in respect of such violations if it is itself guilty of similar violations against the other State or its allies." See 32 ILR (1966), 564. Based on this precedent, we must ask: Did the U.S. government's involvement in establishing the Iraqi Special Tribunal open the door for the defendants to argue the Tu Quoque defense?

The first answer is that although the United States' CPA initially established the Iraqi Special Tribunal in December 2003, the IST is not a U.S. court. The Tribunal and its judges were approved on August 11, 2005, by the Iraqi National Assembly, and the judges and prosecutor are Iraqi, not American. Moreover, under the IST Statute the judges and prosecutor are independent and are prohibited from taking guidance from any government. Since the Judges and Prosecutors represent the Iraqi people and not the United

States, their hands are not soiled by the actions of the United States, and there is no equitable bar to prosecuting the defendants.

Secondly, Courts that have examined the Tu Quoque defense in the past have held that a guilty State's involvement in creating a Tribunal does not open the door to the Tu Quoque defense where the Tribunal's bench does not include judges from the guilty State. The issue arose in two cases before the post-World War II U.S. Military Tribunal at Nuremberg, where the defense argued that the Tribunal could not legitimately convict the defendants of the crime of aggression when the Soviet Union, which cooperated in the establishment of the Military Tribunal, had also engaged in a war of aggression in complicity with Germany. In the "High Command Case" (*U.S. v. van Leeb*, 1948), the Military Tribunal ruled that "Under general principles of law, an accused does not exculpate himself from a crime by showing that another committed a similar crime, either before or after the alleged commission of the crime by the accused." And in the "Ministries Case" *U.S. v. von Weizsacker*, 1949), the Tribunal stated: "But even if it were true that the London Charter and Control Council Law No. 10 are legislative acts, making that a crime which before was not so recognized, would the defense argument be valid? It has never been suggested that a law duly passed becomes ineffective when it transpires that one of the legislators whose vote enacted it was himself guilty of the same practice."

Thus, the Iraqi Special Tribunal should reject the defendants' attempts to elicit evidence of American actions in an attempt to prove a Tu Quoque defense. There is, however, one argument that the defense can make based on American actions that would be relevant. At Nuremberg, defendant Grand Admiral Carl Doenitz argued that he could not be convicted of waging unrestricted submarine warfare in the Atlantic since American Admiral Chester Nimitz had admitted that the United States had done the same thing in the Pacific. But the defense was not arguing that American violation of international law rendered it unfair to convict the German Admiral for the same acts. Rather, the defense was arguing that the American actions indicated that it was not a violation of international law to conduct unrestricted submarine warfare. Thus, Defense Counsel Kranzbuehler told the Tribunal: "The stand taken by the Prosecution [which had argued against recognition of the Tu Quoque defense] differs entirely from the conception on which my application is based. I in no way wish to prove or even to maintain that the American Admiralty in its U-boat warfare against Japan broke international law. On the contrary, I am of the opinion that it acted strictly in accordance with international law." See 8 Trial of the Major War Criminals before the International Military Tribunal (official version, Nuremberg, 1947), at 549. The Nuremberg Tribunal was persuaded by this argument, and did not convict Doenitz of the charge.

Drawing on the Nuremberg precedent, defense counsel before the Iraqi Special Tribunal may legitimately seek to prove that the international community's mixed reaction and the absence of a General Assembly resolution condemning the 2003 invasion of Iraq, as well as the lack of consensus on a definition of aggression for use by the International Criminal Court, indicate that there does not presently exist sufficient international agreement on the crime of aggression to fairly prosecute the defendants of the charge. Similarly, defense counsel may legitimately seek to prove that the international community's lack of condemnation of American aggressive actions to root out terrorists and insurgents from towns in Iraq and Afghanistan indicates that it was not against international law for Saddam Hussein to take similar action against the town of Dujail in 1982. The prosecution may counter with evidence that the defendants' actions were unnecessary or disproportionate to the threat, but this will ultimately be a question that the Tribunal will have to decide based on the evidence. It is not an argument foreclosed by virtue of the international rejection of the Tu Quoque defense.

**Issue: Has the Iraqi Tribunal learned the lessons of the Milosevic trial?**
by *Michael Scharf*

At the conclusion of the Nuremberg Trial in 1946, Chief Prosecutor Robert Jackson said "Many mistakes have been made and many inadequacies must be confessed. But I am consoled by the fact that in proceedings of this novelty, errors and missteps may also be instructive to the future." Flash forward sixty years. Today (February 12, 2006) is the fourth anniversary of the start of the Slobodan Milosevic Trial at The Hague. As William Schabas and I document in our book "Slobodan Milosevic on Trial" (Continuum Press), the Milosevic proceedings have been subject to frequent disruptions due to difficulties obtaining witnesses, the outlandish behavior and health problems of the defendant, and the death of the presiding judge two years into the trial. During the training sessions for the Saddam Trial judges which I participated in last year, there were many discussions about the lessons from the Milosevic Trial. This essay assesses how well the Saddam Tribunal has learned from the major errors and missteps of the Milosevic proceedings.

**Lesson #1: Keep it short.** The Milosevic trial involves a mega-case. The charges against the former Serb leader span atrocities committed in three conflicts (Croatia, and Bosnia, and Kosovo) over a period of a decade. Hundreds of witnesses have testified and thousands of documents have been admitted into evidence. After four years of proceedings, the end of the Milosevic trial may still be over a year away. Critics maintain that the trial has lost its focus and the world has lost interest as the proceedings in The Hague drag on and on.

In an attempt to avoid this problem, the Iraqi Tribunal decided to conduct a dozen mini-trials rather than one mega-trial for Saddam Hussein. The first case focused on a single atrocity—the retaliatory attack on the town of Dujail and the torture and murder of 143 inhabitants in 1982. This "air tight" case was expected to take no more than thirty court-days, and could be concluded in less than three months. But the Saddam Trial has been subject to a series of postponements to give the defense time to prepare its case, to provide better security to defense counsel and witnesses, to allow for national elections and religious holidays, and to deal with a recurring defense boycott. In over four months, the Tribunal has held only nine days of trial. Unless the pace begins to accelerate, this will be anything but the short trial that was envisioned, and collectively the trials of the Saddam Regime may drag on for years.

**Lesson #2: Keep it fair.** The Milosevic Trial was presided over by Richard May, a judge from the United Kingdom, one of the countries that led the 1999 military intervention against Serbia. For many Serbs, the selection of a Brit to preside over the case was taken as a sign that the Tribunal would not be capable of fairly judging Milosevic, an impression that was magnified by the fact that Judge May sometimes responded to Milosevic's outbursts by shouting at the former Serb leader. Then, when Judge May died of a brain tumor, he was replaced by another British judge, who had not even been present for the first two years of the trial. Unlike Nuremberg, which had four alternate judges who observed the trial, to save money the Yugoslavia Tribunal had not appointed even a single reserve judge. Seen in this light, it should come as no great surprise that opinion polls have indicated that most Serbs view the Milosevic trial as unfair.

In an effort to achieve a greater perception of fairness in the Saddam Trial, the decision was made to select a Kurd to serve as presiding judge for the Dujail case, which involved Shi'ite victims and Sunni perpetrators. The man selected for the task, Rizgar Amin, was known for his calm judicial temperament. This was not a judge who could be provoked into yelling at the defendant. In addition, two reserve judges were appointed. Their job was to watch the proceedings and be ready to step in if any of the five judges had to step down for any reason. Unfortunately, Judge Rizgar resigned after five days of trial in the face of intense media and government criticism of his lenient judging style. He was replaced by Judge al-Hamashi, who in turn immediately resigned in the face of accusations that he had been a member of the Ba'ath party. Judge al-Hamashi was then replaced by Judge Ra'uf Abdul Rhaman, who had not been one of the reserve judges assigned to the Dujail case. And then last week, the media reported that Judge Ra'uf may have been tried in absentia and sentenced to life imprison by the Ba'ath regime for anti-governmental activity in the 1970s—an accusation that the Judge will have to address to avoid the appearance of bias. Within minutes of taking over, Judge Ra'uf was already yelling at the defendants and defense counsel, who he ultimately threw out of the courtroom—a move that has been subject to sharp criticism by human rights groups around the world. The damage all this has done to the credibility of the proceedings may be hard for the Tribunal to overcome, no matter how smoothly things run from here on out. And, with defendants and defense counsel who are committed to disrupting and derailing the trial, things are not likely to run smoothly.

**Lesson #3: Keep it under control.** At the beginning of the Milosevic trial, Judge May ruled that Milosevic had a right to represent himself in the courtroom. Having so ruled, there was little Judge May could do to reign in the defendant as he used self-representation to make disparaging remarks about the Tribunal, to threaten and insult witnesses, and to turn the proceedings into a trial of the U.S./UK military action against Serbia. After judge May died midway through the trial, the Tribunal reversed his earlier ruling, and appointed a lawyer to step in if Milosevic's poor health or disruptive tactics threatened to disrupt the trial. Milosevic's behavior immediately improved, and the pace of the trial sped up considerably.

A year ago, I provided a 60-page memorandum to the Iraqi Tribunal, detailing why Saddam Hussein did not have an international right to self-representation, and explaining the risks of permitting Saddam to act as his own lawyer before the Tribunal. Consistent with my recommendation, in August 2005, the Iraqi National Assembly enacted a revised version of the Tribunal's Statute and Rules, which made clear that Saddam had to act through legal counsel, so that he could not use self-representation to turn the trial into a political stage from which to attack the United States and new Iraqi Government. In keeping with Iraqi legal traditions, however, Judge Rizgar and Judge Ra'uf have both allowed the defendants to pose questions to the witnesses following their cross examination by defense counsel. This has given Saddam an opportunity to make disparaging and offensive remarks about the witnesses, the Tribunal, the Iraqi Government, and the United States during the televised proceedings. Clearly, the proceedings would have run much more smoothly if the judges had taken the position that Saddam had to act through his appointed counsel and could not speak in the courtroom until such time as he took the stand to testify. Given the fact that Saddam has abused the traditional Iraqi privilege to participate in the questioning of witnesses, it is not too late for Judge Ra'uf to make a mid-trial correction ... provided he can first get Saddam to return to the courtroom.

Judge Ra'uf's attempts to restore greater control over the proceedings were met by a walk-out by defense counsel. Judge Ra'uf responded by telling them "you can't walk out, you are fired," and by continuing the trial in their absence with court-appointed public defenders. Saddam and his co-defendants responded by refusing to return to the court. Although the trial sessions have run much more smoothly in the absence of the unruly defendants and their high-powered lawyers, the media and human rights groups have begun to criticize the proceedings as resembling an unfair trial in absentia. To answer this criticism, Judge Ra'uf must do a much better job of explaining his judicial decisions to the public, either by releasing written opinions or by taking a few minutes to do so orally at the beginning of each trial session. In particular, he needs to explain that the defense counsel have (at least temporarily) forfeited their right to continue to represent the defendants through their actions, and that public defenders have been appointed to replace them. He needs to explain that the actions of the defendants constitute a waiver of the right to be present in the courtroom, and that they will watch the proceedings and communicate with their new lawyers from the detention center if they refuse to come to court. And he needs to cite the precedents of the Yugoslavia Tribunal, the Rwanda Tribunal, the Special Court for Sierra Leone, and domestic courts, which indicate that his response to the situation is perfectly consistent with international due process and fair trial standards.

During the training sessions for the Saddam Trial judges last year, one of the judges (it may even have been Judge Ra'uf) asked whether the international trainers thought future war crimes trial judges in other parts of the world would be examining the precedents that were set in the Saddam Trial as we had been looking at the decisions of the Nuremberg and the Yugoslavia Tribunal. For good and bad, the answer is clearly yes.

### A Response *by Professor David M. Crane:*
### The Rule of Law is More Powerful than the Rule of the Gun

Over these past several weeks, tormented and shouting, Saddam Hussein and his henchmen have tried to turn their trial into political theater. To some extent they have. Yet, as we have seen in the past, from Nuremberg, The Hague, Arusha, and Freetown, eventually the calm deliberation of the law, administered by sober and serious judges will generally win the day. It has to or the proceedings will turn into a threat to peace, not a facilitator of peace in Iraq. On the fourth anniversary of another trial, far from Baghdad, in the Milosevic trial, we need to reflect on how we deliver international criminal justice so that the underlying theme of all tribunals, that the rule of law is more powerful than the rule of the gun, will continue to advance.

Professor Michael Scharf's three points are important for our consideration as they are keys to success—they were in Freetown during my tenure as the Chief Prosecutor and they will be in Baghdad. Lengthy court proceedings in this environment, charged with pain, suffering, and political intrigue need to be well planned, with a clear beginning and an anticipated end. Though the law must be seen to be fair, it also must be seen to be efficient and effective. Lengthy proceedings can leave that impression that it is not effective and undermine the respect for the tribunal itself. In my opinion, the longer the trial, the greater the chance for the entire process to unravel around the edges.

The law has to be seen as fair. That was what I told the victims in Sierra Leone at my many town hall meetings with them. Any appearance of bias against the accused on the part of the judges can be fatal. The Iraqi people are going to have to live with the result and if they perceive it as unfair they will not live with the result I can assure you.

I have a concern about an appearance of bias on the part of the new Chief Judge, currently presiding over this stage of the trial of Saddam. An Iraqi Kurd, who lived in a village destroyed by Saddam, a defendant, can give the appearance of just such a bias. This may bring a result that may appear to be unfair to this fledgling democracy. I am surprised that there has not been a stronger move to have the Chief Judge recused.

Despite the perceived bias that could bring the fairness of the proceedings into question, control of the court room is what will allow the proceedings to continue and the victims to come in and to tell the world what took place in their towns and districts. This is a must and must happen very quickly as the proceedings progress. Delay or keep the witnesses from testifying due to control problems and they will be intimidated. Thus another victim may be the truth, further bringing the fairness of the process into question.

All sides have an absolute right to present their case in a way that is fair, open, and efficient. Any one of these ingredients that are missing will show that perhaps in Iraq, the rule of the gun is more powerful than the rule of the law. It is early yet, it remains to be seen.

## 9. Bibliography of Additional Sources

- Aleksandar Fati'c, RECONCILIATION VIA THE WAR CRIMES TRIBUNAL? (2000).

- Arlette El Kaïm-Sartre, SUMMARY OF THE EVIDENCE AND THE JUDGMENTS OF THE INTERNATIONAL WAR CRIMES TRIBUNAL (1968).

- International Tribunal for Rwanda, Legal materials concerning the International Criminal Tribunal for Rwanda, United Nations, International Criminal Tribunal for Rwanda (The Hague: ICTR, 1994).

- John Duffett, INTERNATIONAL WAR CRIMES TRIBUNAL (1968).

- John Pritchard, INTERNATIONAL MILITARY TRIBUNAL FOR THE FAR EAST (1998).

- Virginia Morris and Michael P. Scharf, AN INSIDER'S GUIDE TO THE INTERNATIONAL CRIMINAL TRIBUNAL FOR THE FORMER YUGOSLAVIA (1995).

- Virginia Morris and Michael P. Scharf, THE INTERNATIONAL CRIMINAL TRIBUNAL FOR RWANDA (1998).

- Symposium: Milos evic & Hussein on Trial, 38 CORNELL INT'L L.J. 1 (2005).

# Chapter XXI

# The International Criminal Court

## Introduction

The Security Council-created international criminal tribunals have paved the way for the creation of a permanent International Criminal Court (ICC), whose statute was adopted at a diplomatic conference in Rome in 1998 and ultimately signed by 148 countries. As described in this chapter, at the Rome Diplomatic Conference, the U.S. Delegation unsuccessfully sought special protections to ensure that U.S. officials and personnel could not be subject to the ICC's jurisdiction for military actions abroad. Even though the United States did not succeed in securing all the protections it sought for U.S. official and military personnel, President Clinton nevertheless signed the treaty with the hope that the U.S. could influence the evolution of the court. Despite the numerous safeguards built into the Rome Treaty, the Bush Administration announced its opposition to the ICC, and "unsigned" the treaty and passed legislation aimed at crippling the ICC's effectiveness. However, the U.S. attempt to pressure other states not to ratify or abide by the ICC backfired, as today there are 122 member states to the ICC. This chapter examines whether ratifying the Rome Treaty is in the best interests of the United States and explores the broader issue of U.S. exceptionalism in the context of international organizations.

## Objectives

- To understand the history and background of the establishment of the ICC.
- To debate whether the U.S. should become a Party Member to the Rome Statute.
- To understand the significance and impact of the U.S. "unsigning" the Rome Statute.
- To understand the evolution of the U.S. relationship with the ICC.
- To understand the recent actions of the ICC and the broader implications of ICC actions.
- To examine the recent attempts at including crimes of aggression within ICC jurisdiction.

# Problems

Come to class prepared to debate the issue: "Resolved—the United States should become a party to the International Criminal Court." Members of Group A will argue in favor; members of Groups B and C will argue against.

In preparing for the debate, consider the following questions:

1.  What are the advantages of a permanent international criminal court over the ad hoc approach of Security Council-created tribunals and hybrid courts?

2.  Now that 100 countries have ratified the ICC, will those countries likely block U.S. efforts to create new ad hoc tribunals, making the ICC the only accountability option for the future?

3.  What dangers does the ICC pose for U.S. personnel and U.S. policy? Can the United States avoid those dangers by not ratifying the ICC?

4.  Does membership in the ICC raise Constitutional problems for the United States?

5.  Assuming ratification is unlikely in the near future, should the United States seek to kill the ICC, ignore it, or support it through Security Council referrals?

6.  What are the pros and cons of the independent prosecutor initiating investigations and the Security Council triggering investigations?

# Materials

1.  Lawrence Weschler, Exceptional Cases in Rome: The United States and the Struggle for an ICC, in THE UNITED STATES AND THE INTERNATIONAL CRIMINAL COURT 85–114 (Sarah Sewall and Carl Kasen, eds., 2000)

2.  THE DEBATE OVER THE PERMANENT INTERNATIONAL CRIMINAL COURT, Michael P. Scharf, *The Case for Supporting the International Criminal Court*, Washington University School of Law, Whitney R. Harris Institute for Global Legal Studies, Washington University in St. Louis, International Debate Series, No. 1 (2002). Lee A. Casey, *The Case Against Supporting the International Criminal Court*, Washington University School of Law, Whitney R. Harris Institute for Global Legal Studies, Washington University in St. Louis, International Debate Series, No. 1 (2002).

3.  New York Times, January 1st, 2001, Section: A. "Clinton's Words: 'The Right Action'".

4.  New York Times, May 5, 2005, Section: 1. "U.S. is set to Renounce its Role in Pact for World Tribunal" by Neil A Lewis.

5.  Human Rights Watch, August 3, 2002, "U.S.: Hague Invasion Act Becomes Law" available at http://www.hrw.org/en/news/2002/08/03/us-hague-invasion-act-becomes-law

6.  U.N. Security Council Resolution 1593. S.C. Res. 1593, U.N. Doc. S/RES/1593 (Mar. 31, 2005).

7.  Statement After Voting on United Nations Security Council Resolution 1593 by Anne Woods Patterson, U.S. Ambassador to the United Nations, New York, Mar. 31, 2005.

8.  U.N. Security Council Resolution 1970. S.C. Res. 1970, U.N. Doc. S/RES/1970 (Feb. 26, 2011).

9. Statement After Voting on United Nations Security Council Resolution 1970 by Susan Rice, U.S. Ambassador to the United Nations, New York, Feb. 26, 2011.

10. Letter by Luis Moreno-Ocampo, Chief Prosecutor of the International Criminal Court, The Hague, February 9, 2006.

11. Kevin Jon Heller, "The Sadly Neutered Crime of Aggression", OPINIOJURIS.ORG, (June 13, 2010 9:32 PM) http://opiniojuris.org/2010/06/13/the-sadly-neutered-crime-of-aggression/.

12. John Currie, Joanna Harrington & Valerie Oosterverld, "Ending War Through Justice — In Time: Amendments to ICC Statute would hold leaders personally responsible for 'aggression'", CANADIAN LAWYER MAGAZINE, 14 June 2010 (online).

13. List of States which are Party to ICC at http://www.icc-cpi.int/Menus/ASP/states+parties/.

14. Rome Statute [abridged], see http://untreaty.un.org/cod/icc/statute/romefra.htm.

15. Bibliography of Additional Sources

---

## 1. Lawrence Weschler, Exceptional Cases in Rome: The United States and the Struggle for an ICC

The United States and the International Criminal Court, 2000

### PRELUDE: "THE MOTHER OF ALL MOTHERBOARDS"

"This is easily the most complex international negotiation I have ever been involved in," Philippe Kirsch, the chairman of the International Conference aimed at promulgating an international criminal court (ICC), commented one afternoon during a rare break in the proceedings. The chief legal adviser to the Canadian Foreign Ministry, the youthful-seeming Kirsch could claim an improbably vast experience chairing such convocations (in recent years, he'd spearheaded, among others, conferences on maritime terrorism; the safety and deportment of U.N. workers in the field; refinements of various International Red Cross protocols; and, most recently, nuclear terrorism). As it happened, he wasn't even supposed to be anywhere near this particular process, having been dragooned into his current role, on an emergency basis, when the highly regarded Dutch legal adviser Adriaan Bos, who'd been chairing the painstaking four-year long preparatory committee (PrepCom) process leading up to the Rome meeting, fell gravely ill a mere three weeks before the opening of the final convocation. "We have representatives here from one hundred sixty-two countries," Kirsch continued, "confronting, many of them for the first time, a draft document of over two hundred pages, consisting of one hundred twenty articles, and containing thirteen hundred brackets, that is to say, thirteen hundred issues which the six Preparatory Conferences couldn't resolve, leaving multiple options to be tackled one by one by everybody gathered here — the thirteen hundred hardest issues.

"There's the simple linguistic complexity of the undertaking." (Earlier, the head of the drafting committee had related to me a confounding moment when the Chinese delegate had suddenly started objecting to the eventual Court's seat being in The Hague — although, as it turned out, it wasn't The Hague that was bothering him; rather, "it was the shockingly inappropriate reference to — how shall I put it? — the Court's derriere.") "There's the way we have to interweave all sorts of different legal procedural traditions," Kirsch went on, "for instance, the Napoleonic civil law tradition on the one hand and the Anglo-Saxon common law tradition on the other. The one enshrines an activist investigating judge as the finder of fact; the other favors an adversarial procedure, defense versus prosecution before a studiously impartial judge. The one allows trials in absentia; the other finds such trials utterly abhorrent. And so forth. And that's not even getting into, say, traditions of Islamic law. How does all that get channeled into a single statute?

"And precisely what law is the eventual Court supposed to be enforcing—the Geneva Conventions, the Hague law, the Genocide Treaty, the Crimes against Humanity jurisprudence flowing out of the Nuremberg Tribunal? Not everyone subscribes to all of those standards, and in any case, much of this body of law exists in so called 'customary' form, which is to say the degree to which it is actually observed is subject to evolving customary practice, which is in constant flux. This Statute, on the other hand, has to be precise, every detail spelled out, all the ambiguities clarified. For example, the law of war with regard to international conflict is considerably more developed than that applying to internal conflicts, even though most conflict nowadays comes in the latter form. There are some countries here that don't want the Tribunal having any say over internal conflicts, while others are pushing for a fairly stiff internal conflict regime. Some countries insist on the death penalty, while others insist that they will walk out if the death penalty is included. Some countries want the Tribunal to be as much under the [U.N.] Security Council's control as possible several of the Permanent Five, for example. Others—India, Pakistan—insist on its being completely free of any Security Council role." (There had been a marvelous moment in the Committee of the Whole just that morning when the Indian and the Pakistani delegates had taken to lavishly praising each other for taking precisely that stand. Translation:

They both wanted to be entirely free to enter into savage war, no holds barred, with one another, at any moment, without having to worry about their case getting referred to the Tribunal by any meddlesome Security Council.)

"And it goes on and on," Kirsch continued. "How will the judges be chosen? Who will pay for the entire operation? With everything to be resolved in just five weeks. Some countries want the use or even the threat of using nuclear weapons included as a war crime—India, again, for instance. Others, such as the United States, would storm out of the conference were that to happen. Trinidad and Tobago started this whole recent phase of negotiations back in 1989 by reviving a long dormant proposal for a permanent International Criminal Court—only what they wanted it to address was drug crimes, and they still want that. Others want it to cover the crime of aggression, which nobody at the U.N. has been able to define in fifty years. Others want to include terrorism—but how do you define that?

"Some favor a strong, robust Court; others say they do but clearly don't; while others say they don't and mean it. It often depends on who happens to be in power back home at the moment: a fledgling democracy that a few years ago might have been a dictatorship, or the other way around; a country just coming out of a civil war or just about to go into one. They all look at matters differently, and differently than they might have a few years ago or might a few years from now. It's incredibly dispersed."

"And on top of everything else," Kirsch resumed, "this Conference is transpiring under a truly unprecedented degree of public scrutiny. The NGOs [non-governmental organizations] are here in force, incredibly well disciplined and coordinated. They've got representatives monitoring all the working groups and even inside the Committee of the Whole." (The General Assembly had passed a special measure earlier in the year that allowed NGOs unprecedented access into the Committee of the Whole, at which point the press had been allowed in as well.) "Everything is happening in full view. Nothing happens without everybody knowing about it instantaneously. It's really altogether unique."

"People compare it to the land mines process," Alan Kessel, the acting head of the Canadian delegation, interjected, referring to the international campaign that had culminated the previous year in Ottawa with a comprehensive land mine ban (which the United States, up till then, had pointedly declined to sign onto). "Some of the NGO people sometimes say, 'Well, we can do it like the land mines.' But land mines was ... I mean, by the end, that was a simple on-off switch. Either you were for it or you were against it. This, by contrast, is like a great big motherboard. You touch a switch here and five lights blink off over there. You attend to one of those, and sixteen flash on over here. This conference has to be the Mother of all Motherboards!"

## Double Vision

There were times, sitting on the margins of the Committee of the Whole in Rome, gazing out over the hall and squinting one's eyes in a particular way, that one could momentarily envision the hundreds of delegates and experts gathered there—the blue—black Africans, the turbaned Iranians, the Brits in their Savile Row finery and the Russians in theirs, the Chinese and the Japanese and the Indians, the Americans toting their ever present satchels and briefcases—as a vast convocation of the Family of Man, all gathered together in that one place at last, finally and once and for all, to face down the greatest scandal of the twentieth century, the galling impunity with which millions and indeed hundreds of millions of victims had been hounded to their deaths, and to proclaim, on the cusp of the new millennium, in the firmest possible voice, "Never Again!"—to proclaim it and mean it and make it so: that never again would victims be permitted to sink like that into oblivion, and never again would their tormentors be permitted to harbor such blithe confidence regarding their own indubitable inviability.

It was possible, squinting one's eyes one way, to see it like that. But then, if you squinted them another way or if you cocked your ear such that you were actually listening to some of the speeches, suddenly the same convergence of delegates could transmogrify from standins for the Family of Man to the representatives of 162 separate and distinct states, each one zealously husbanding its own righteous sovereignty, each one all for lavishing such vigilance on the other guy but damned if it was going to subject itself or its compatriots to any such intrusive oversight. In fairness, not all of them felt that way and certainly not all the time; but these were, after all, diplomats first and foremost, whose overriding brief, here as anywhere else (as one of the NGO representatives observed dispiritedly from the margins), was "to protect sovereignty, reduce costs, and dodge obligations."

I mentioned that double vision one afternoon to a young lawyer on an important Southern Hemisphere delegation, a veteran of the PrepCom process and one of the most energetic presences in the working-group trenches; and he noted that many of the delegates experienced themselves in a similarly doubled light. "Especially among some of the younger, middle and lower ranking delegates," he said, "many of whom start out as the representative of Country X to the ICC Diplomatic Conference but slowly find their allegiances shifting, so that they become rather the delegate of the ICC Conference back to their foreign ministry, and presently, even, a sort of secret agent, burrowing toward a successful outcome. 'My minister says this,' they'll tell you, 'but I think if you propose it this other way, he won't notice, and we can still accomplish the same purpose'—that sort of thing."

I was struck by the similarity of that sort of drama to accounts I'd read of the American Constitutional Convention of 1787–88, and indeed I often had the sense of being witness to a parallel sort of historic undertaking. Just as back then, fiercely independent states were being enjoined to surrender part of their precious sovereignty to an as yet inchoate united entity and were doing so at best grudgingly (insisting on the primacy of "state's rights" to the very end—an insistence that could arise out of an honest concern for the more authentic, responsive kind of governance available at the more localized level but that could just as easily arise out of more perverse imperatives, such as the desire to preserve the institution of slavery). So the nation states gathered in Rome seemed driven by a similar amalgam of authentic and then more suspect misgivings.

## THE ROME PROCESS

### Conference Dynamics

For the first three weeks of the Conference, Chairman Kirsch and his multinational associates in the Conference's executive Bureau maintained an almost studied aloofness, allowing the delegates to flounder in the complexities of the evolving document. Although many of the delegates were veterans of the PrepCom process, many more were encountering the Draft Statute for the first time (many of the smaller countries simply hadn't been able to afford to send delegations to the earlier meetings), and there was a cliff steep learning curve. In addition, the Rome meeting had elicited the attendance of higher ranking delegates; and as one of the PrepCom veterans noted wryly, "Such types aren't generally prone to humility. They are incapable, for instance, of saying, 'I don't understand this provision. Could you explain it to me?' Instead they launch into a long flowery statement detailing their own manifest misunderstanding of the matter, all so as to provoke you, at the very end, into responding with the simple clarification they'd been trying to elicit all along. But it can take forever." The various working groups were plowing through the myriad brackets all the while, struggling toward occasional consensus and moving on. But the tough questions—the independence of the Court and its Prosecutor, the oversight role of the U.N. Security Council, the sort of jurisdiction that the Court would be able to extend over precisely what sort of law—remained scarily unresolved, and time seemed to be fast running out.

At the beginning of the fourth week of a five-week Conference, expertly gauging the growing sense of anxiety in the hall, Kirsch launched a series of calibrated interventions—working drafts on major issues in which he attempted to narrow the contours of the sprawling debate, bracketing out extreme positions that weren't any longer likely to elicit consensus, narrowing the options on any given contentious matter to three or four options, floating various compromises, narrowing the options still further. It was remarkable to watch the way he seemed to amass authority—stature he'd doubtless be needing to spend later on—simply by being the one who was at last moving the process demonstrably forward.

By the middle of the fourth week, a range of possible outcomes was beginning to arc into view. One afternoon around that time, I worried out a sort of flow chart with a Latin American delegate. There seemed at that point to be basically three possible outcomes: On the one extreme, the Conference could completely collapse by the end of the next week, the delegates storming home in unbridgeable anger. At the other extreme, they might emerge with a truly robust Court—"Not just a court," in the words of the Canadian Foreign Minister Lloyd Axworthy, "but a court worthy of the name"—a court with powerful jurisdiction over clean, clear law, a strong mandate, and the wherewithal to carry it out. Wasn't going to happen, was the simple verdict of my Latin American friend—no way.

Between the two extremes were middle possibilities: One branch debouched in a sort of crippled court, a Potemkin court, a court in name only; something that would look for all the world like a full-fledged court, but whose tendons—as to jurisdiction, independence, authority—would have been surgically severed from the outset. It would be an excuse court: a court to which the Great Powers could refer intractable problems as if they were actually doing something, confident that nothing would actually get done. The other branch led toward a fledgling court, a baby court, a court whose powers and prospects, at the outset at any rate, would be highly circumscribed but that still had the capacity to grow. "Something like your own Supreme Court in the original Constitution," my Latin American friend volunteered. "I mean, if you look at the Constitution itself, the Supreme Court at the outset really had very little authority, it was very weak. For instance, the Constitution itself doesn't grant it the right of judicial review—the power, that is, to rule on the constitutionality of the acts of other branches or of the sovereign states. That was a power it only grabbed for itself, fifteen years later, with Justice Marshall's ruling in Marbury vs. Madison. And maybe one could imagine a similar development here. A baby court now that gradually gains the confidence of the world community through its baby steps and then, at some moment of crisis in the future, under appropriate leadership … On the other hand, that presupposes that it's given room to grow." This raised the alternatives of a baby in a spacious crib, as it were, or a baby in a tight fitting lead box. "Imagine, for instance," my Latin American friend ventured, "if the U.S. Constitution had specifically forbidden the possibility of judicial review." The baby in the lead box.

"On the other hand," he smiled conspiratorially, "maybe it would be possible to build some hidden trapdoors into that lead box.

### America's Bottom Line

One afternoon, one of the most canny thinkers in the hail, a leading Asian delegate, was parsing some of the 3D game's more intricate strategic considerations for me: "The thing is," he explained, "you want to create a court that the parties that might need it would still be willing to sign on to. I mean, face it, we're not going to need to be investigating Sweden. So, the treaty needs to be 'weak' enough, unthreatening enough, to have its jurisdiction accepted without being so weak and so unthreatening that it would thereafter prove useless. It's one of our many paradoxes."

And yet, paradoxically, those last few weeks, the biggest challenge facing the process no longer seemed to be coming from such neo-renegade states. Rather, it was being presented, with growing insistence, by the United States, whose position was truly paradoxical.

The United States had been one of the principal moving forces behind the Nuremberg Tribunal and more recently was a leading sponsor of the ad hoc tribunals on Rwanda and the former Yugoslavia (dozens of lawyers from the Justice Department, the Pentagon, and other government agencies had been seconded to serve stints in the Prosecutor's office in The Hague, and several of those were now serving on the U.S. delegation in Rome as well). Secretary of State Madeleine Albright herself a childhood witness to the Holocaust in Europe had played a strong role in fostering the ad hoc tribunals during her time as Ambassador to the United Nations. She had made the apprehension and prosecution of accused war criminals one of the rhetorical touchstones of her tenure at State. In addition, on several occasions across the preceding years, President Bill Clinton had issued forceful calls for a permanent war crimes tribunal, most recently in March 1998 when he addressed genocide survivors and government officials in Kigali, Rwanda.

The U.S. delegation—forty strong, and easily the best prepared and most professionally disciplined at the Conference—was spearheaded by David Scheffer, Albright's ambassador-at-large for war crimes issues, who had clearly been consumed by the subject for some time. Over lunch one afternoon, on the rooftop cafeteria atop the Conference proceedings, he became quite emotional, describing a trip he had taken to Rwanda in December 1997, accompanying Secretary Albright: the horrors he had witnessed, the terrible testimonies he had heard. He grew silent for a moment, gazing out toward the Coliseum, before continuing: "I have this recurrent dream in which I walk into a small hut. The place is a bloody mess, terrible carnage, victims barely hanging on, and I stagger out, shouting, 'Get a doctor! Get a doctor!' and I become more and more enraged because no one's reacting fast enough." He went on, passionately invoking the importance of what was going on down below us and insisting on the necessity of its successful outcome.

And yet, as the Conference lumbered toward its climax, the U.S. delegation seemed increasingly gripped by a single overriding concern. Senator Jesse Helms, the Republican head of the Foreign Relations Committee, had already let it be known that any treaty emerging from Rome that left open even the slightest possibility of any Americans ever, under any circumstance, being subjected to judgment or even oversight by the Court would be "dead on arrival" at his committee. The Pentagon was known to be advancing a similarly absolutist line. The State Department, sugarcoating the message only slightly, regularly pointed out how, in Scheffer's words, "The American armed forces have a unique peacekeeping role, posted to hot spots all around the world. Representing the world's sole remaining superpower, American soldiers on such missions stand to be uniquely subject to frivolous, nuisance accusations by parties of all sorts. And we simply cannot be expected to expose our people to those sorts of risks. We are dead serious about this. It is an absolute bottom line with us."

Originally the U.S. team thought it had addressed this concern with a simple provision mandating that the Court only be allowed to take up cases specifically referred to it by the Security Council where the United States has a veto (as do Britain, France, China, and Russia). In effect, the Americans seemed to be favoring a permanent version of the current ad hoc tribunals, the authority of which would all flow from the Security Council but without the cumbersome necessity of having to repeatedly start all over again (statutes, staffing, financing). The rest of the Permanent Five also tended to favor such an approach for obvious reasons of self interest but also out of concern over the Security Council's own paramount mission, enshrined in Chapter VII of the U.N. Charter—the securing and maintenance of world peace.

### The Role of the Security Council

The entire Rome Conference was transpiring under the motto "Peace and Justice," but, as proponents of the Security Council's primacy liked to point out, there would come times when the two might not necessarily coincide, at least not simultaneously. In order to secure peace, the Security Council might need to negotiate with technically indictable war criminals and might even need to extend pledges of full amnesty to them in the context of final peace agreements. At such moments, it couldn't very well have an unguided Prosecutor careering about, upending the most delicate of negotiations. Therefore, if the Security Council was "seized" with an issue—as the term of art has it—it needed to be able to forestall, even if only temporarily, any such Court interference.

Opponents of this line—many of the countries that didn't happen to have such veto power, and the preponderance of the NGO observers—liked to cite a Papal remark to the effect that "If you want peace, seek justice," further pointing out that as often as not, historically, a Security Council "seized" with an issue was a Security Council seized up and paralyzed. The veto encumbered Security Council was the very institution, after all, that for fifty years after Nuremberg had proved incapable of mounting trials in the cases of Idi Amin, Pol Pot, or Saddam Hussein (at the time of his genocidal Anfal campaign against his own Kurdish population). Most of the time over the past fifty years, war criminals have had sheltering patrons among the Permanent Five Pol Pot, for instance, had the Chinese; the Argentine generals had the Americans (just as, more recently, U.S. Ambassador Bill Richardson had actively shielded the Congo's Laurent Kabila from the full force of Security Council oversight into the ghastly massacres involved in the campaign leading up to his installation). In this context, the Yugoslav and the Rwandan ad hoc tribunals had been historic flukes (in both instances, the product, as much as anything else, of Security Council embarrassment over its failure to take any more concerted action to stop the violence itself). "If we're going to have gone to all this trouble," my Latin American friend commented, "only to have ended up with a slightly more streamlined version of the very failed system we gathered here in the first place to overcome, it will hardly have been worth the bother."

As it happened, it was Lionel Ye, a lanky and self effacing, young government attorney out of Singapore, generally regarded as a master of the 3D game, who came up with a possible route out of the impasse through the simple expedient of turning the conundrum on its head. Instead of requiring Permanent Five unanimity to launch a Court investigation, why not require Permanent Five unanimity in order to block one? More specifically, why not establish a regime where a simple majority vote of the Security Council could at any time forestall any further Court action on a given case for a renewable period of up to twelve months (though any single Permanent Five veto could derail the stalling effort). After all, Ye pointed out, if a majority of the Security Council, including all five Permanent Five members, agreed on the peacekeeping necessity of temporarily blocking Court action, there'd likely be something to it.

The Permanent Five were understandably dubious about the so called Singapore Proposal. But in what may have been the single most important development during the PrepCom process, in December 1997, Great Britain, under fresh New Labour auspices (with its highly vaunted new "ethical foreign policy"), swung around behind the Singapore Proposal. In so doing, Britain became the first and only Permanent Five member to join what was becoming known as the "like minded" group a loose coalition of some sixty countries (including, among others, Australia, New Zealand, Canada, most other European countries, except France, and most of the newly democratizing countries in Latin America and sub Saharan Africa) favoring a more robust Court.

### State Referrals and the Independent Prosecutor

To suggest that the Security Council could block certain Court initiatives was likewise to acknowledge that one might want to include other ways, besides Security Council referral, of instigating such cases in the first place. And indeed two further such procedures had been broached during the PrepCom process.

The first would allow so called State referrals, such that any State Party to the Treaty (any State that had both signed and ratified the Treaty) could on its own and by itself refer a complaint to the Court. Some argued that that ought to be enough: if not a single one of the sixty countries that were going to have to ratify the treaty before it went into effect was willing to lodge a complaint—singling out, say, Hussein s Anfal campaign against the Kurds—then how much merit was such a complaint going to be likely to have?

The NGOs were supporting State referral; however, from bitter experience over the past several years, they had come to feel that in fact it would not be enough. As it happened, Human Rights Watch (HRW) had recently spent several years shopping around the very case of Hussein's Anfal campaign, trying to find a country willing to lodge a formal complaint against Iraq with the International Court of Justice (ICJ) in The Hague (the ICJ lacks the authority to hear criminal cases against individuals but is still empowered to adjudicate certain sorts of claims against entire countries). Despite the widespread publicity and documentation regarding Iraq's manifest depredations (including the indiscriminate use of poison gas), HRW was unable to find a single state willing to pursue the matter. (Most fretted over issues of trade—if not now, in the future—or of retaliation, and even some of the Nordic European states in the end backed off, citing domestic political complications.)

For that reason, the "soft coalition" of the NGOs and the like minded group were additionally advocating an independent Prosecutor—a Prosecutor's office, empowered to evaluate complaints from any source (nonparty states, Party States, NGOs, news reports, the petitions of individual victims) and to launch investigations or prosecutions on its own (subject, granted, to majority Security Council postponement). Only an office thus empowered, it was argued, would be able to respond to the worst crimes in real time, as they were happening, efficiently and free of political coercion.

Nonsense, countered that proposal's adamant opponents (the United States chief among them). "For one thing," Scheffer suggested to me, "such a prosecutor would be inundated with complaints from Day One. His fax machine would be permanently jammed up. With no filter between him and the world, and no possible way of responding to all the complaints, his selection process would of necessity take on a political tinge. Why did he choose to pursue one matter and not another? Each time he passed on a given matter, he'd lose that much more of his desperately needed authority."

The proponents of an independent Prosecutor argued that such dilemmas were no different than those faced by any other prosecutor anywhere in the world—all of whom face decisions like that every day.

"But those prosecutors exist in a framework of accountability," Scheffer pointed out, when I rehearsed that argument for him. "States are accountable to their polities; the members of the Security Council are accountable to theirs. There are checks and balances. But who would this independent Prosecutor be accountable to?" Scheffer himself didn't specifically raise the specter, but others did: What would prevent such an independent Prosecutor from ballooning into a sort of global Kenneth Starr—if not worse. This office, after all, stood to become, as it were, the judicial branch of a world government that lacked an effective, functioning, democratically chosen legislative or executive branch to check and oversee it—an untethered international Kenneth Starr, floating free.

The proponents of an independent Prosecutor, for their part, scoffed at the notion. For one thing, the Prosecutor, like every member of the Court, would be answerable to an Assembly of States Parties and removable at any time for cause. Certainly at the outset, his budget would be minuscule and he'd be utterly dependent on the good will and cooperation of states (for instance, he'd have no police or enforcement resources of his own). He'd continually be having to demonstrate his upstanding character and evident fairness because, from the outset, what authority he'd be able to muster would be largely moral. Beyond that, with regard to any specific case, the way the statute was evolving, he'd have to present his evidence and justifications every step of the way before a supervising panel of judges: he wouldn't even be able to launch an investigation without their authorization.

None of this assuaged the U.S. delegation, which remained fixated on the prospect of that lone American marine a peacekeeper stationed, say, in Somalia—getting nabbed on some capricious charge and inexorably dragged into the maw of the machine, his fate at the mercy, as it was sometimes phrased, of some Bangladeshi or Iranian judge.

"What is the United States talking about?" an exasperated like minded diplomat virtually sputtered at me one evening over drinks. "This Prosecutor is going to have a lot more important things to worry about than some poor marine in Mogadishu."

Earlier I'd tried a similar argument on one of those incredibly competent and respected mid level delegates—in this case, a Pentagon lawyer attached to the U.S. delegation: "Surely the Prosecutor is going to have a lot more important things...," I said. "Not necessarily," he countered, recalling some recent proceedings at the International Criminal

Tribunal for the former Yugoslavia (ICTY) where, "At a certain point, word came down from the Prosecutor that they really had to find more Croats to indict. There were too many Serbs getting indicted, it was too unbalanced. The Prosecutor had to be able to project the appearance of fairness.

"And I can almost guarantee you," he continued, "that a similar thing will happen one day up ahead. Say, it's something like the end of Desert Storm, and the Prosecutor has been able to round up and indict dozens of Iraqis. You just watch: the Iraqi government will be lodging all sorts of trumped-up, phony complaints about Americans; and the Prosecutor will come under terrific pressure to indict a few of them as well, just to demonstrate his fairness."

I subsequently related the Pentagon lawyer's scenario to my like minded friend, at which point he immediately shot back, "But that's what complementarily is for!"

## The Principle of Complementarily

Complementarily was perhaps the keystone of the entire Draft Statute, and one would have thought it would have gone a long way toward answering U.S. concerns. For central to the entire enterprise was the notion that national judicial systems would be taking precedence over international ones, and specifically over this Court. That is to say that if a state could show that it was itself already dealing with any given complaint in good faith—investigating and if necessary prosecuting—then those national efforts would automatically trump the ICC's. "In fact," the like minded diplomat continued, "in the best of all possible worlds, one day in the future, the International Court will have no cases whatsoever. Under the pressure of its oversight, all national judicial systems will be dealing in good faith with their own war criminals, at the local level. That would obviously be a better system, and getting to such a point is one of the goals of the entire exercise. In the meantime, democracies like the United States, with highly developed systems of military as well as civilian justice, would invariably be able to shield their own nationals by invoking complementarity." (To further buttress this doctrine of complementarity, the United States had demanded an entire Statute section requiring the Prosecutor to notify any investigative target's home state at the outset of its investigation, so that the home state could apply to the Court on complementarity grounds from the very start.)

As it happened, Conference participants were being afforded a high profile object lesson in the proper workings of a complementarity regime during the very weeks of their deliberations. Earlier that year (1998), a U.S. marine jet flying too low on training maneuvers in the Italian Alps had tragically sheared the cables on a ski lift, an accident that claimed twenty lives. The plane's crew had initially been charged with manslaughter in Italian courts. But from the moment that U.S. military prosecutors filed court martial charges against two of those officers (at the same time clearing two others)—as it happened in the very middle of the fourth week of the Conference—the Italian prosecutor dropped all his charges, exactly as he was required to do in keeping with the complementarity provisions in the bilateral "Status of Forces Agreement" governing the presence of U.S. forces in Italy.

"And on top of that," my like minded drinking companion was continuing, "the Americans have the protection of the chapeau"—the preamble, as it were, of the section defining what sorts of crimes could come under the prosecutor's scrutiny. War crimes were to come under the Court's jurisdiction "in particular when committed as part of a plan or a policy or as part of a large scale commission of such crimes." Crimes against humanity would need to be part of a "widespread or systematic" attack directed against civilians in order for the Court to be able to assert jurisdiction. The Americans would have preferred "widespread and systematic," but still the former wording would likewise have seemed to radically narrow the exposure of any single or group of marine peace keepers who wandered down the wrong alleyway in Mogadishu.

The Americans, however, were not satisfied. As far as they were concerned, there still remained a chance, however slim, that Americans could find themselves exposed on the wrong side of the line. And, as Scheffer insisted to me one afternoon in the halls, almost jabbing his finger into my chest with his intensity, "The exposure of American troops is really serious business, and bland assurances about the unlikelihood of any given outcome simply don't move the mail back where I come from."

### The Requirement of State Consent

Which may be why the American delegation chose to make its stiffest stand on the question of jurisdiction itself.

The legal issue involved went something like this: Suppose the Prosecutor had reason to launch an investigation or a prosecution regarding a particular case, either on her own or because she had had the case referred to her by a State Party or an NGO. What conditions, particularly with regard to states that had not yet chosen to join onto the treaty, would have to be met for the Prosecutor to be able to move forward?

The Germans favored giving the Prosecutor the widest possible latitude in this regard, which is to say universal jurisdiction. They pointed out, for instance, that according to the Geneva Conventions, every signatory (for all intents and purposes, all the countries of the world) not only had the right but also the obligation to pursue war criminals from any countries anywhere and failing anything else, to deliver them up for trial in their own courts. (Granted, in practice, most countries had thus far failed to enact the necessary enabling legislation, but according to their signatures on the Conventions, as well as on the Genocide Treaty, they had acknowledged such universal jurisdiction over war crimes.) All that was being asked here was that states together transfer the rights granted to each one of them separately to the Court they were founding in concert. The Germans did not need to point out that the doctrine of universal jurisdiction had been a cornerstone rationale at the Nuremberg Tribunals — the crimes of which the defendants there had been accused were universal in nature, as hence was the Tribunal's jurisdiction; otherwise all that could have been possible there would have been so called "victor's justice" (which the Americans have always insisted was not what they were perpetrating). If such a principle was good enough for the Germans at Nuremberg, the Germans in Rome seemed to be saying, it ought to be good enough for everybody else now.

This viewpoint, however, so rattled international lawyers affiliated with several of the delegations — not just the Americans — that by the middle of the fourth week, Kirsch's Bureau had already shaved it from its list of four possible remaining options regarding jurisdiction. The broadest of these, the so called Korean Plan, stipulated that in order for the Prosecutor to claim jurisdiction over any given case, at least one of the following four states would have to be a party to the Treaty (or at any rate accept the jurisdiction of the Court in that particular case):

The state where the crime took place

The state of nationality of the accused

The state that had custody of the accused

The state of nationality of the victim

A narrower second option mandated that the state in which the crime took place would have to be a State Party. A yet narrower third option stipulated that both that state and the state having custody would have to be States Parties. Finally, a fourth option would limit the Court's jurisdiction exclusively to accused who were themselves nationals of States Parties. Guess which one the United States was favoring.

**The Soundings Proceed Apace**

Kirsch was inviting all the delegations to stand up and, as briefly as possible, to indicate how they were tending with regard to each of the contentious issues highlighted in his paper, including the issue of jurisdiction. In effect, he was conducting a poll without having to have recourse to any actual vote ("the dreaded v word," as he'd characterized that prospect for me during our conversation), the polarizing consequences of which could have blown the Conference apart at any moment. (He was trying to nudge the process along through a sequence of grudging consensual concessions, culminating only at the very end with a single up or down vote.) So, one by one the delegates were rising to lay out their preferences.

It was vaguely unsettling, once again — this tug of war between the claims of humanity and those of sovereignty, especially if, squinting your eyes, you momentarily chose to visualize the proceedings from the point of view of a victim, or a victim's survivor, who might one day be seeking recourse before this Court. For it is, of course, of the essence of genocide itself that it denies the essential humanity of its victims: they are not humans like the rest of us; they are vermin, swine, sub beings worthy solely of extermination. Granted, here the question wasn't so much one of humanity as one of standing: myriad seemingly arbitrary hoops through which an eventual victim would someday have to jump before being deemed worthy of recognition by this Court (whether his violator was or was not a national of a State Party; whether the war in which the violations took place had or had not been international in scope; and so forth). But in the end it came down to the same thing: victims whose core humanity had already been trampled on in the crime itself facing a good chance of seeing their humanity denied all over again by an abstruse legal process in which, clearly, some stood to be counted as more fully human than others.

Having said that, it was striking how many countries were still coming out in favor of the broadest possible remaining jurisdictional option, and my canny Asian informant's paradox notwithstanding — how many of these included countries only recently, if ever so precariously, emerged from their own totalitarian or genocidal sieges. Many of the Latin American delegates, for example, were lawyers whose own attempts to settle accounts with their countries' earlier military rulers had been stymied by amnesties those militaries had been able to wrest, on leave-taking, from their still timorous civilian successors. The president of Korea, whose country was offering that broadest remaining jurisdictional scheme, had himself been a longtime prisoner of one such regime — as had the president of South Africa been of another. The pattern recurred throughout the hall. The delegate from Sierra Leone, whose country at that very moment was being ravaged by renegade bands of recently dislodged coup plotters, got up and delivered a riveting plea for the most robust possible Court. Afterward, he commented to me, "For many of the delegates here, these pages are just so much text. For me, they are like a mirror of my life. This article here," he said, flipping through the Draft Statute, "this is my uncle; this one here, my late wife; this one here, my niece.

On the other hand, there were others India, Pakistan, most of the Middle Eastern delegations — who were decidedly more suspicious of the Court. ("I had the chief of the

Iranian delegation in here a few minutes ago," the head of the drafting committee told me at one point, "and believe me, he's just as spooked at the prospect of having one of his people dragged before an American judge as the Americans are the other way around.")

Kirsch's sounding continued apace — several delegations going for the Korean option, others going for the second or the third — until eventually David Scheffer got up to deliver the U.S. response. On several issues (the degree of coverage of crimes committed in internal wars, for example), the United States was notably expansive. (Scheffer indicated, for the first time, that under certain conditions the United States might even be willing to entertain something like the Singapore compromise.) But when it came to the question of jurisdiction, Scheffer was adamant: the United States was insisting on the fourth option (that the court be denied jurisdiction over the nationals of any country that had not signed the treaty). Not only, he said, would the United States refuse to sign any treaty that dealt with jurisdiction in any other manner, but it "would have to actively oppose" any resultant Court — whatever that meant. On the other hand, Scheffer concluded, if this and all "the other approaches I have described emerge as an acceptable pack age for the Statute, then the United States delegation could seriously consider favorably recommending to the U.S. government that it sign the ICC Treaty at an appropriate moment in the future." Scheffer's address sent a chill through the auditorium: Defy us and we'll kill the baby; accede to our terms and, well, we're not sure; we'll see.

More startling yet was the seeming ineffectiveness of the American stand: it didn't seem to be changing anybody's mind. A few minutes after Scheffer's presentation, tiny Botswana got up and spoke of "the breathtaking arrogance" of the American position. And, ironically, it was precisely the sort of line represented by Jesse Helms back in Washington that so seemed to be undermining U.S. authority there in Rome (as it had, last year, during the land mines negotiations in Ottawa). "The U.S. struts around like it owns this place," one NGO observer pointed out. "It doesn't own this place: it owes this place." Indeed, the fact that the United States was still well over a billion dollars in arrears in its debt to the United Nations was having a direct impact on the efficient operation of the Conference itself: there was a distinct shortage of interpreters on site; documents had to be sent back to Geneva for overnight translation; inadequate photocopying facilities caused backups.

America's U.N. debt, furthermore, had had a direct impact on many of the countries it was now trying to influence. Samoa's representative commented to me, "The Fijians have peacekeepers scattered all over the world, too, and you don't see them worrying about their boys' exposure before this Court. What they do worry about is how, thanks to the U.S. debt, the U.N. has fallen behind in paying the salaries of those peacekeepers, leaving Fiji itself to have to pick up the tab, which, I assure you, it can afford far less than the U.S." America's implicit threat not to help finance the Court unless it got its way thus tended to get discounted by delegates dubious that it ever would even if it did.

By the same token, many delegates discounted the likelihood of the United States ever ratifying the treaty no matter what. "David Scheffer could draft the entire document, every single word of it," David Matas, a lawyer with the Canadian delegation, commented toward week's end, "and the Senate would never ratify it. It took America forty years to ratify the Genocide Convention. The United States still hasn't even ratified the Convention on the Rights of the Child. There are only two countries in the entire world that have failed to do so — the United States and Somalia — and Somalia, at least, has an excuse: they don't have a government. So, one has to wonder, why even bother trying to meet such demands?"

Beyond that, the logic of the U.S. position seemed all twisted in knots: still obsessed over this question of the status of its own soldiers in the field, the United States was saying that it would only endorse a Treaty that included an explicit provision guaranteeing that the resultant Court would hold no purchase on the nationals of countries that hadn't signed onto the treaty. So, in other words, the United States appeared to be signaling the fact that it had no intention of signing onto the Treaty or, at any rate, of ever ratifying it. (Surely, Helms would be able to shoot down any treaty whose only conceivable, if ever so remote, threat to American soldiers would come if the Senate ratified the plan.) And meanwhile, in the words of KakSoo Shih, the exasperated head of the Korean delegation, "In order to protect against this less than one percent chance of an American peacekeeper's becoming exposed, the U.S. would cut off Court access to well over ninety percent of the cases it would otherwise need to be pursuing. Because what tyrant in his right mind would sign such a treaty? What applies to America also applies to Hussein; and simply by not signing, he could buy himself a pass."

"No, no, NO!" Scheffer insisted, when I brought this argument back to him. "Hussein would still be vulnerable to a Security Council referral under Chapter VII, by virtue of Iraq's being a signatory to the U.N. Charter."

Except, as my like minded drinking companion subsequently pointed out, bringing the argument full circle, that was the very channel that, thanks to the blocking vetoes and with the sole exceptions of Yugoslavia and Rwanda, had failed to work every other time in the past.

Scheffer was unswayed. Furthermore, he pointed out, the U.S. position was grounded both in common sense and in all prior international law, as codified in the Vienna Convention on Treaties, which stipulates that no state can be held to the provisions of a treaty it has not itself ratified. It would be patently unacceptable for Americans to be held to account before a court and under laws they had themselves not democratically endorsed by way of the actions of their legislative representatives.

But that, too, was nonsense, another Canadian lawyer delegate pointed out to me. "Americans are subjected to courts and laws they didn't vote for all the time. You think an American can come to Canada or a Canadian go to the U.S., for that matter—break some local ordinance, and then claim, 'Well, I didn't have any say in passing that ordinance, or voting for this judge, so it doesn't apply to ~ (For that matter, as Michael Posner, the head of the New York—based Lawyers Committee for Human Rights, reminded me, since 1994 the United States has had implementing legislation related to the Torture Convention on its books that allows an American court to go after a visitor from another country for acts of torture he committed in that other country, with penalties ranging from twenty years all the way through death.) "As for American military men on official business," the Canadian lawyer continued, "again, it's a moot point, at least as regards this Court, thanks to the complementarity provisions."

### The Option of Opting Out

For his part, though still unswayed regarding the basic argument, Scheffer, too, hoped the matter might prove moot. As he pointed out, the U.S. delegation was still trying to craft a treaty that the country would one day be able to sign onto, which is where a second jurisdictional issue came into play: the so-called opt out clause. The United States, along with several other important countries (notably including France, which was just as concerned about the status of its Foreign Legionnaires in the field), was supporting language that would make Court jurisdiction automatic for any State ratifying the Treaty as regards the crime of genocide. However, at the time of ratifying, States would have the right to opt out of coverage on war crimes and crimes against humanity, as applied to themselves or to their own nationals. Obviously, the United States had no plans for committing genocide anytime soon, and such a clause would provide yet another way of shielding American forces from the Court's scrutiny.

But the arguments here were virtually identical to those regarding the status of non-state parties. What would prevent Saddam Hussein from opting out as well? For that matter, why would anybody opt in? And to what kind of crazy Swiss-cheese jurisdictional regime would such a scheme lead? William Pace, the head coordinator of the NGO coalition, parsed the matter in terms of numbers: "Having trouble holding the line with a forum in which five countries, including the U.S., could veto Court initiatives, the U.S. now wants in effect to extend veto power to one hundred eighty-five nations, such that in the end the only forum that would really retain the ability to launch Court action would once again be the one with five vetoes."

## THE ENDGAME

### The United States Digs In

"Look," an increasingly grim and embattled Scheffer was almost shouting at me by the end of the fourth week, "The U.S. is not Andorra!" He immediately caught himself up short. "That's off the record!" What, I asked—official State Department policy has it that the U.S. is Andorra? Laughing, he continued, "No" (by which I inferred that the comment was no longer off the record), "but the point is that the world—I mean, people in there, some of the people in there—have yet to grasp that the challenges of the post—Cold War world are so complex that, in some instances, the requirements of those few countries that are still in a position to actually do something by way of accomplishing various humane objectives simply have got to be accommodated. And you can't approach this on the model of the equality of all states. You have to think in terms of the inequality of some states. There have been times, there will come others, when the U.S. as the sole remaining superpower, the indispensable power, has been and will be in a position to confront butchery head on, or anyway to anchor a multilateral intervention along such lines. But in order for that to be able to happen, American interests are going to have to be protected and American soldiers shielded. Otherwise it's going to get that much more difficult, if not impossible, to argue for such humanitarian deployments in the future. Is that really what people here want?"

A few minutes later, Charles Brown, the official spokesman of the U.S. delegation, who'd been listening in on my conversation with Scheffer, pulled me aside. "We're coming to the endgame now," he suggested, "and basically, we're facing three possible outcomes: a Court the U.S. is going to be able to be part of; a Court the U.S. can't yet be part of but could still support—cooperating behind the scenes, assisting in detentions, sharing intelligence, and providing other sorts of background support—and which it might one day still be able to be part of; or a Court the U.S. will find it impossible to work with and may yet have to actively oppose.

"And, frankly, I don't see how this Court is going to be able to flourish without at least the tacit support of the United States." He pointed to my notepad. "Remember that flow chart you were showing me the other day? The baby in the nurturing crib or the baby in the lead box. It seems to me there's a third possibility: a baby alone, unprotected, in the middle of a vast, open field."

### Choosing Sides

"It's as if we're being forced to choose," KakSoo Shih, the Korean delegate, sighed disconsolately late Friday of the fourth week. "A Court crippled by American requirements with regard to state consent, or a Court crippled by lack of American participation."

"The Court could definitely live without U.S. participation," insisted an NGO representative at their news conference that same afternoon. "If all the like minded sign on, that's virtually all of Europe, with the exception of France. That's Canada, Australia, much of Africa and Latin America, all sorts of other countries—there's funding there, support resources, a definite start. And the U.S. in fact would still be pivotally involved through its Security Council referral role. The U.S. claims it wants a weak treaty which could be strengthened later on. But that's being disingenuous: For one thing, the U.S. itself, anxious at the prospect of the process spinning out of control later on, has placed incredibly high thresholds on amending the treaty—in some instances, seven-eighths of States Parties would have to ratify any changes, not just vote for them at the Assembly of States Parties but get their legislatures to ratify them back home. Almost impossible.

"But in any case," he continued, "the main point is a weak treaty won't work. And even more to the point—you've seen the soundings—a majority of those gathered here are calling for a strong treaty. It's a scandal that two of the major democracies—France and America—are the main ones standing against such an outcome.

HansPeter Kaul, the head of the German delegation and one of the most passionate proponents of a strong Court, was meanwhile addressing a news conference of his own: "We desperately, desperately, desperately want the U.S. on board. We are not sure the Court will even be workable without the U.S. We are willing to walk the extra mile, beyond the extra mile, to meet U.S. concerns. So the problem is not on our side, but on the side of the U.S. Will they be willing to move the slightest bit in order to meet us?"

"The trick," Chairman Kirsch explained to me, "is to emerge with a strong Statute with incentives enough that down the line currently reluctant governments may yet want to join on. Because later on it will be far easier to get governments to change their minds than it will be to change the statute itself. And, anyway, no government is going to want to join onto a useless statute."

### Honing the Final Treaty

By Monday of the fifth and final week, Kirsch's Bureau was facing challenges on all sides. The United States was still fuming over state consent. India, dubious about the entire Treaty, was itching to provoke a conference busting vote on the question of the inclusion of nuclear weapons and was lobbying the other members of the Non-Aligned Movement hard in preparation. Mexico was still restive over the Security Council's referral powers. Thailand and others were still trying to dilute coverage of internal wars. Faced with all of these challenges, Kirsch was painstakingly guiding the delegates through a second sounding—narrowing the options—and then a third, steadily aiming toward a Thursday night final vote. Informal meetings were burgeoning off to the side, and the truly hot ticket was the informal informals. Nobody anymore seemed to be pausing for sleep.

The United States, meanwhile, was stepping up the pressure. Albright and Defense Secretary William Cohen were known to be phoning their counterparts all over the world, and President Clinton himself was said to be placing some key calls. (A high American delegate assured me in that last week that Washington was now focused on these negotiations, "at the very highest level" and over "the most specific details.") Some of that pressure was proving remarkably hamfisted. When Defense Secretary Cohen warned his German counterpart that the treaty as it was currently evolving might force the Pentagon to reconsider the advisability of even stationing troops anywhere in Europe, the Germans, far from crumbling in horror, became righteously indignant and leaked word of the demarche back into the auditorium in Rome, provoking a brief firestorm of outrage and embarrassed denials. The Latin Americans, for their part, were still smarting over a March incident in which the Pentagon had convened a meeting of military attaches from throughout the Western Hemisphere, urging them to pressure their home governments to bend to American treaty demands. Several delegates described for me their enduring annoyance over the ploy, how it had only been with the greatest difficulty, over the past decade, that their civilian governments had been succeeding, ever so precariously, in easing their officers back into barracks; and they certainly didn't need any Americans coming around, urging the officers back where they didn't belong.

On Monday night, the Russians hosted an exclusive private dinner, limited to top delegates from the Permanent Five, at which tremendous pressure was brought to bear on renegade Britain. When the NGOs got wind of that meeting the following morning and began worrying over a possible wavering in the British line, they instantaneously swung into a typically impressive lobbying blitz, contacting all their affiliates back in England, who in turn started pulling all the right media and parliamentary levers. New Labour's "ethical foreign policy" had already been taking its share of hits earlier in the month (notably over a scandal involving the sale of arms to the warring parties in Sierra Leone); and faced with such a massive up welling of vigilance, the Brits in Rome appeared to stiffen their position once again.

The Bureau had been aiming to release its final document—the result of hours of front room soundings and back room recalibrations—by midday Thursday; but midday came and nothing emerged. Sierra Leone was brokering a final compromise on the coverage of internal wars. The French were cutting a last minute deal with Kirsch on their main concern: a seven-year opt out clause, inside the treaty itself, limited to war crimes alone. (Since their interventions seldom included carpet aerial bombing campaigns, it was explained to me, they weren't that worried about the Crimes against Humanity provisions.)

Scheffer and Kirsch held several urgent parlays those last few days; both seemed equally desperate to find some way of bringing the United States under the Treaty tent. "And it was amazing," one of Kirsch's top deputies on the Bureau subsequently recounted for me. "Nothing could assuage them. We figured they'd be trying to negotiate, to wrest concessions from us in exchange for concessions on their part. Frankly, as of that Monday morning, we figured the Independent Prosecutor was toast, that we'd have to give him away in the final crunch negotiation. But they never even brought him up. They seemed completely fixated on that Helms/Pentagon imperative—that there be explicit language in the Treaty guaranteeing that no Americans could ever fall under the Court's sway, even if the only way to accomplish that was going to be by the U.S. not joining the treaty. We talked about complementarity, we offered to strengthen complementarity—for instance, a provision requiring the Prosecutor to attain a unanimous vote of a five-judge panel if he was going to challenge the efficacy of any given country's complementarity efforts. In the unlikely event of their ever getting thus challenged, all they would need was one vote out of five. Not enough. In fairness, they seemed on an incredibly short leash. Clearly, they had their instructions from back home—and very little room to maneuver."

Thursday midday dragged into Thursday evening and then past midnight. Still the Bureau's final draft failed to emerge: in fact it only finally came out Friday at two o'clock in the morning. Kirsch was giving delegates less than twenty-four hours to digest the seventy odd page tiny typed document and consult with their capitals. They'd all reconvene for a final Committee of the Whole session that evening at seven.

### The Climactic Session: The Final Vote

"Four words. Four little words," Charles Brown, the spokesman for the U.S. delegation, was almost wailing the next morning. "It's incredible. They're within four words of a draft which, even if we couldn't necessarily join, we would still be able to live with. And they're not going to budge. They're going to stuff them down our throat."

On the question of state consent, the Bureau had ended up splitting the difference, stipulating that the Court could exercise its jurisdiction if "one or more of" the following states were parties to the Statute or had accepted the Court's jurisdiction in a given particular case: (1) the state on the territory of which the crime was alleged to have occurred; (2) the state of which the accused was a national.

The NGOs were none too happy with that compromise, either. "They took the Korean plan, split it in half, and left us with North Korea," the indefatigable and endlessly quotable Richard Dicker of HRS's Rome delegation quipped almost immediately. "By leaving out the state of the victim, and even more crucially the state having custody of the accused, they've spawned a treaty for traveling dictators. Even if France, say, joins the Treaty, the next Mobutu or Baby Doc would still be able to summer blissfully undisturbed on the Riviera and to squirrel away his ill gotten gains in the local banks."

And that, come to think of it, may have been one of the reasons why the French were so avidly pushing for the compromise. My source in the Bureau, on the other hand, told me that several countries besides France had been expressing profound misgivings about the custody clause. In Africa, for instance, former allies are crossing over into each other's countries all the time, and things could get quite messy.

But it was the Americans who, more than anyone else, were denouncing the "state consent" provision, spooking themselves with sordid scenarios. "What if," Scheffer postulated, "the American army finds itself deployed on the territory of Iraq as part of a U.N. force. Now, Hussein and his nationals are not subject to this treaty because he hasn't signed on. But what if suddenly he pulls a fast one, accuses some of our men of war crimes, and, as head of the territory in question, extends the Court permission to go after them on a onetime basis? And one of the really weird anomalies in all this is that, thanks to the French provision, signatories are able to opt out of such exposure for seven years, but non-signatories aren't afforded the same option.

"Well," said HRW's Dicker, when I relayed that observation over to him, "maybe then the U.S. had better sign on. For that matter," he continued, "if I were an American GI, I'd much prefer being held in a cell in The Hague to one in Baghdad."

The United States was going to have one last opportunity to upend the provision at that evening's final meeting of the Committee of the Whole; and all through the day urgent communiqués were coursing from Washington to capitals throughout the world.

Kirsch brought the meeting to order at 7:15 in the evening on Friday, July 17, 1998, and presented the Draft text as a whole, hoping to fend off amendments of any sort. It was generally conceded that if even one provision were called into question, the whole intricately cantilevered structure could start coming apart.

India rose to propose an amendment, reintroducing the use or even the threat to use nuclear weapons as a war crime. Norway immediately moved to table the motion. (The like minded had agreed among themselves that Norway would serve this function with every attempted amendment.) Then, in one of the most significant moments at the Conference, Malawi rose to second Norway's motion. In a brief speech of strikingly understated eloquence, Malawi noted that because the Treaty was a package, everyone had given up something and gained something else, that many of the delegates had sympathy for India's position, but that pursuing the matter any further would no longer advance the process and could threaten to blow everything up. As Malawi sat back down, everyone realized that the Non-Aligneds had fractured and that India was not going to be able to rely on their votes to subvert the Conference. Chile rose to give another second to Norway's motion. A vote was taken on the question of whether to take a vote, and India lost overwhelmingly (114 against, 16 for, and 20 abstentions).

Scheffer now rose. He looked ashen. "I deeply regret, Mr. Chairman," he began, "that we face the end of this Conference and the past four years of work with such profound misgivings and objections as we have today." Going on to note how tragically the Statute was creating "a court that we and others warned of in the opening days—strong on paper but weak in reality," he proceeded to lay out the U.S. position one more time before proposing a simple amendment: that the words "one or more of" be stricken from the non-State Party provision, such that both the territory and the nationality would be required.

After Scheffer was seated, Norway immediately rose up to table the motion. Sweden seconded Norway's motion, and Denmark followed suit. A vote was held, and the United States lost in a similarly lopsided vote (113 against, 17 for, and 25 abstentions).

Kirsch looked over at Mexico and Thailand—both had earlier indicated their intention to file amendments, but both now shook their heads: no, they would pass. There were no other amendments. A mood of heady celebration was rising in the hall. In that case, Kirsch announced, gaveling the meeting to a close, they would all reconvene in half an hour upstairs, in the flag decked ceremonial chamber, for the final plenary session, for speeches and a final vote.

Filing upstairs, several of the longtime NGO activists were discussing Scheffer in remarkably sympathetic terms. Over the years, many had had occasion to work with him, and few doubted the fervency of his commitment and concern. "His instincts were better than his instructions," Dicker surmised. "Would make a good epitaph," someone else observed.

The delegates streamed into the plenary chamber and took their seats amidst the flags. There were broad smiles, fierce hugs, a growing swell of elation. Kirsch handed the gavel to the frail guest by his side—Adriaan Bos, the ailing Dutch legal adviser who had piloted the four-year PrepCom process right up till a few weeks before the opening of the Rome Conference. Bos, beaming, banged the session to order, said a few words, and retired to the side. Kirsch called for a vote. It ended up 120 to 7, with 21 abstentions. Cuba voted for the Statute, as did Russia, Britain, and France. The United States was apparently joined by China, Libya, Iraq, Yemen, Qatar, and Israel in voting against it (at American request, the particulars of the vote itself went officially "non-recorded"). The hall erupted in applause that grew louder and louder, spilling over into rhythmic stomping and hooting that lasted a good ten minutes, the room becoming positively weightless with the mingled senses of exhaustion and achievement.

"This treaty's flawed," Dicker was saying. "It's badly flawed." He cited another nasty little concession, effected at the last minute—the chemical and biological warfare provisions had been deleted so as to undercut India's argument about these being poor men's nuclear weapons, unfairly singled out. He was quiet for a moment, gazing out over the scene. "But it's not fatally flawed."

Theodor Meron, one of the world's most distinguished academic experts on international humanitarian law, who'd been serving as a citizen adviser on the U.S. delegation but who now seemed almost visibly to be doffing that official role so as to revert to his private academic persona, walked over and seemed eerily content. "Oh," he said, "these last few hours have been unpleasant, of course. But flipping through the pages of the final document, there's much here that's very good, very strong. The articulation of war crimes:

completely solid. And the section on crimes against humanity, which heretofore have existed primarily in the form of precedent and custom, here they're codified, in a remarkably robust form, and in particular without any nexus to war. This was a big fight, unclear in the customary law, but here it's clearly articulated that crimes against humanity can even take place in the absence of outright warfare—a major development, as is the section on non-international war, the most frequent and bloody kind today. The section on gender crimes—rape, enforced pregnancy, and the like—all rising out of recent developments at the Yugoslav and the Rwanda tribunals, but codified here for the first time. There's excellent due process language, mens rea, all of this reflecting a strong American influence. The requirement for a clear articulation of elements—what exactly, in clean legal language, constitutes the elements of a crime. Command responsibility, superior orders: American fingerprints are all over this document, and with just a few exceptions, America's concerns were largely accommodated."

"We'll see," my contact in the Bureau was now saying. "It will take three or four years for the Treaty to garner the required number of ratifications and then come into force. Maybe things will change in the U.S.—they'll be able to give it a second look. Or else, once the Court is up and running, sure enough, a few of those nuisance complaints will get lodged against American soldiers, and the U.S. will invoke complementarity, and, BOOM, they'll be popped right out of there—and the U.S. will cease feeling so threatened. Or there will come some great crisis, and suddenly the U.S. will want to make use of the Court. Time will tell. In the meantime, the Court will be able to start growing."

Jerry Fowler, one of the NGO lobbyists affiliated with the Lawyers Committee for Human Rights, was taking an even longer view: "We didn't get Korea, but what we got is still important: the territorial requirement. Because one of these days there's going to come a Baghdad Spring, and one of the first things the reformers there will want to do is to sign onto this treaty as an affirmation of the new order, but also as a protection against backsliding. One by one, countries will go through their Springs, they'll sign on, and the Court's jurisdiction will grow. A hundred years from now who knows?"

A bit later, Fowler's boss, Michael Posner, was gazing back the other way. "Do you realize how long the world has been straining toward this moment—since after World War I, after World War II. It's extraordinary. Who'd have thought it, even ten years ago, that you could get one hundred twenty countries to vote for holding their militaries personally liable before a Prosecutor with even a limited degree of independent initiative? I mean, it's unprecedented, it's absolutely unprecedented. One day it may even be seen to have been the birth of a new epoch."

## CODA: THE FATHER OF ALL EXCEPTIONS

"Today, for the first time in history," Forrest Sawyer, sitting in for Peter Jennings, led off that evening's ABC World News Tonight, just a few hours later, New York time, "a Secret Service agent testified before a grand jury as part of a criminal investigation on a sitting U.S. president." That and adjacent stories regarding Kenneth Starr's ongoing pursuit of the Monica Lewinsky scandal took up the next seven minutes of air time. The developments in Rome never even got mentioned.

Nor were they broached on NBC or CBS. And they received not a single column inch in the following Monday's Time or Newsweek. Monica and Kenneth Starr were everywhere.

It occurred to me how surely the siege by this independent prosecutor must have been coloring President Clinton's responses to the developments in Rome, leaving him especially wary at the very moment the toughest decisions were having to be made.

On the other hand, surely, there was more to it than that. At various times, there in the halls of Rome, various people would invoke the League of Nations.

"If the U.S. walks out on this court," the Syrian delegate assured me, his eyes twinkling with grim satisfaction (he was all for it, he couldn't wait), "it will be like the League of Nations." Perhaps, I remember thinking; but in that case, ought President Clinton be cast in the role of Woodrow Wilson or in that of Henry Cabot Lodge? Of course, the answer, in retrospect, is both. With regard to the Court, Clinton wanted to play both Wilson and Lodge. And not half and half: not a wily Wilson disguising himself as a grimly realistic Lodge, or visa versa. Rather, Whitmanesque, Clinton wanted to contain multitudes. He saw no contradiction in being both Wilson and Lodge, each 100 percent and both simultaneously, which is to say that he was approaching the ICC in much the same way he'd approached just about everything else in his presidency—gays in the military, national health insurance, campaign finance reform, land mines, Bosnia, global warming.

## CONCLUSION

Less than a week later, on Thursday, July 23, 1998, back in Washington, D.C., David Scheffer was called to appear before Jesse Helms's Senate Foreign Relations Committee. He might have been excused a certain feeling of conceptual whiplash.

For if, by the end there in Rome, he was being treated as a sort of pariah or leper, now back in Washington he was being unanimously praised as a kind of returning hero. Positions that had provoked nary a chord of resonance in the Rome Conference hall were almost drowned in a rising chorus of defiant triumphalism on Capitol Hill.

Senators Helms, Rod Grams, Joseph Biden, and Dianne Feinstein each addressed Scheffer in turn, congratulating him on the fortitude of his resolve and pledging their undying contempt for that monstrosity spawned in Rome. Not one of them focused on Bosnia or Rwanda or Pol Pot or Idi Amin or the Holocaust or Nuremberg. (Senator Feinstein did wonder about the possible implications for Israel.) They all seemed utterly and almost uniquely transfixed by the Treaty's exposure implications for American troops, vowing to protect them and fight it. Scheffer indicated that the administration was reviewing its options. For starters, it would be reexamining the more than one hundred bilateral status of forces agreements governing the legal status of American service members just about anywhere they might be posted around the globe, with an eye toward tightening them in such a way as to preclude the possibility of any extradition to the ICC.

At that Senate hearing, it became possible to identify what may have been the true underlying anxiety of the U.S. delegation all along, never broached by any of them back in Rome but veritably palpitating just beneath the surface even there. Helms wasn't afraid to name it outright. The status of individual peacekeepers in some Mogadishu alleyway had never been the real concern. Rather, as Helms picked off the examples defiantly, he was going to be damned if any so called International Court was ever going to be reviewing the legality of the U.S. invasions of Panama or Grenada or of the bombing of Tripoli and to be holding any American presidents, defense secretaries, or generals to account.

"I've been accused by advocates of this Court of engaging in 'eighteenth century thinking,'" Chairman Helms concluded his statement. "Well, I find that to be a compliment. It was the eighteenth century that gave us our Constitution and the fundamental protections of our Bill of Rights. I'll gladly stand with James Madison and the rest of our Founding Fathers over that collection of ne'er do wells in Rome any day."

At some level, of course, Helms was way off the mark in his choice and characterization of antecedents. James Madison, for one thing, was a Federalist with Alexander

Hamilton, the principal author of The Federalist Papers—and as such ranged himself passionately against the nativist states rightsers of his day and in favor of a wider conception of governance.

But at the same time, it seemed to me that Helms was onto something. "We hold these truths to be self-evident, that all men are created equal, that they are endowed by their Creator with certain unalienable rights," Thomas Jefferson strikingly pitched his Declaration of Independence in an assertion of universal human values, an assertion that, cascading down through the ages, from the Rights of Man (1789) through the Universal Declaration of Human Rights (1948), constitutes one of the principal wellsprings of the law feeding into the ICC.

But at the same time, Jefferson cast those assertions in what was, after all, a declaration of independence, of separateness, of American exceptionalism stirring, defiant themes that had been very much in evidence there in Rome as well.

---

## 2. The Debate over the Permanent International Criminal Court

Michael P. Scharf, *The Case for Supporting the International Criminal Court*
Washington University School of Law, Whitney R. Harris Institute for Global Legal Studies, Washington University in St. Louis, International Debate Series, No. 1 (2002)

### Background: The Road to Rome

With the creation of the Yugoslavia and Rwanda Tribunals in the early 1990s, there was hope among U.S. policy makers that Security Council-controlled ad hoc tribunals would be set up for crimes against humanity elsewhere in the world. Even America's most ardent opponents of a permanent international criminal court had come to see the ad hoc tribunals as a useful foreign policy tool. The experience with the former Yugoslavia and Rwanda Tribunals proved that an international indictment and arrest warrant could serve to isolate offending leaders diplomatically, strengthen the hand of domestic rivals, and fortify international political will to impose economic sanctions and take more aggressive actions if necessary. Unlike a permanent international criminal court, there was no perceived risk of American personnel being prosecuted before the ad hoc tribunals since their subject matter, territorial and temporal jurisdiction were determined by the Security Council, which the United States could control with its veto.

But then something known in government circles as "Tribunal Fatigue" set in. The process of reaching agreement on the tribunal's statute; electing judges; selecting a prosecutor; hiring staff; negotiating headquarters agreements and judicial assistance pacts; erecting courtrooms, offices, and prisons; and appropriating funds turned out to be too time consuming and exhausting for the members of the Security Council to undertake on a repeated basis. China and other Permanent Members of the Security Council let it be known that Rwanda would be the last of the Security Council-established ad hoc tribunals.

Consequently, the establishment of a permanent international criminal court began to be seen by many members of the United Nations (as well as some within the U.S. government) as the solution to the impediments preventing a continuation of the ad hoc approach. Having successfully tackled most of the same complex legal and practical issues that U.S. diplomats had earlier identified as obstacles to a permanent international criminal court, the United States Government was left with little basis to justify continued foot-dragging with regard to the ICC. In 1994, the U.N. International Law Commission produced a draft Statute for an ICC which was largely based on the Statutes and Rules of the popular ad hoc tribunals. The International Law Commission's draft was subsequently refined through a series of Preparatory Conferences in which the United States played an active role. During this time, the establishment of a permanent international criminal court began to receive near unanimous support in the United Nations. The only countries that were willing to go on record as opposing the establishment of an ICC were the few states that the United States had labeled "persistent human rights violators" or "terrorist supporting states."

Thus, on the eve of the Rome Diplomatic Conference in the summer of 1998, both the U.S. Congress and the Clinton Administration indicated that they were in favor of an ICC if the right protections were built into its statute. As David Scheffer, then U.S. Ambassador-at-Large for War Crimes Issues, reminded the Senate Foreign Relations Committee on July 23, 1998: "Our experience with the establishment and operation of the International Criminal Tribunals for the former Yugoslavia and Rwanda had convinced us of the merit of creating a permanent court that could be more quickly available for investigations and prosecutions and more cost-efficient in its operation."

### The Politics of Rome

The Rome Diplomatic Conference represented a tension between the United States, which sought a Security Council-controlled Court, and most of the other countries of the world which felt no country's citizens who are accused of serious war crimes or genocide should be exempt from the jurisdiction of a permanent international criminal court. These countries were concerned, moreover, about the possibility that the Security Council would once again slide into the state of paralysis that characterized the Cold War years, rendering a Security-Council controlled court a nullity. The justification for the American position was that, as the world's greatest military and economic power, more than any other country the United States is expected to intervene to halt humanitarian catastrophes around the world. The United States' unique position renders U.S. personnel uniquely vulnerable to the potential jurisdiction of an international criminal court. In sum, the U.S. Administration feared that an independent ICC Prosecutor would turn out to be (in the words of one U.S. official) an "international Ken Starr" who would bedevil U.S. military personnel and officials, and frustrate U.S. foreign policy.

Many of the countries at Rome were in fact sympathetic to the United States' concerns. Thus, what emerged from Rome was a Court with a two-track system of jurisdiction. Track one would constitute situations referred to the Court by the Security Council. This track would create binding obligations on all states to comply with orders for evidence or the surrender of indicted persons under Chapter VII of the U.N. Charter. This track would be enforced by Security Council imposed embargoes, the freezing of assets of leaders and their supporters, and/or by authorizing the use of force. It is this track that the United States favored, and would be likely to utilize in the event of a future Bosnia or Rwanda. The second track would constitute situations referred to the Court by individual countries or the ICC Prosecutor. This track would have no built in process for enforcement, but rather would rely on the good-faith cooperation of the Parties to the Court's statute. Most of the delegates in Rome recognized that the real power was in the first track. But the United States still demanded protection from the second track of the Court's jurisdiction. In order to mollify U.S. concerns, the following protective mechanisms were incorporated into the Court's Statute at the urging of the United States:

First, the Court's jurisdiction under the second track would be based on a concept known as "complementarity" which was defined as meaning the court would be a last resort which comes into play only when domestic authorities are unable or unwilling to prosecute. At the insistence of the United States, the delegates at Rome added teeth to the concept of complementarity by providing in Article 18 of the Court's Statute that the Prosecutor has to notify states with a prosecutive interest in a case of his/her intention to commence an investigation. If, within one month of notification, such a state informs the Court that it is investigating the matter, the Prosecutor must defer to the State's investigation, unless it can convince the Pre-Trial Chamber that the investigation is a sham. The decision of the Pre-Trial Chamber is subject to interlocutory appeal to the Appeals Chamber.

Second, Article 8 of the Court's Statute specifies that the Court would have jurisdiction only over "serious" war crimes that represent a "policy or plan." Thus, random acts of U.S. personnel involved in a foreign peacekeeping operation would not be subject to the Court's jurisdiction. Neither would one-time incidents such as the July 3, 1988 accidental downing of the Iran airbus by the *USS Vincinnes* or the August 20, 1998 U.S. attack on the Al Shiffa suspected chemical weapons facility in Sudan that turned out to be a pharmaceutical plant.

Third, Article 15 of the Court's Statute guards against spurious complaints by the ICC prosecutor by requiring the approval of a three-judge pre-trial chamber before the prosecution can launch an investigation. Further, the decision of the chamber is subject to interlocutory appeal to the Appeals Chamber.

Fourth, Article 16 of the Statute allows the Security Council to affirmatively vote to postpone an investigation or case for up to twelve months, on a renewable basis. While this does not amount to the individual veto the United States had sought, this does give the United States and the other members of the Security Council a collective veto over the Court.

The United States Delegation played hard ball in Rome and got just about everything it wanted, substantially weakening the ICC in the process. As Ambassador Scheffer told the Senate Foreign Relations Committee: "The U.S. delegation certainly reduced exposure to unwarranted prosecutions by the international court through our successful efforts to build into the treaty a range of safeguards that will benefit not only us but also our friends and allies." These protections proved sufficient for other major powers including the United Kingdom, France and Russia, which joined 117 other countries in voting in favor of the Rome Treaty. But without what would amount to an iron-clad veto of jurisdiction over U.S. personnel and officials, the United States felt compelled to join China, Libya, Iraq, Israel, Qatar and Yemen as the only seven countries voting in opposition to the Rome Treaty.

It is an open secret that there was substantial dissension within the U.S. Delegation (especially among Department of State and Department of Justice representatives) about whether to oppose the ICC and that the position of the Secretary of Defense ultimately carried the day. As a former Republican member of Congress, there has been conjecture that Secretary of Defense William Cohen was influenced by Senator Jesse Helms (R-NC), a vocal opponent of the ICC. President Clinton, for his part, had proven to be uniquely vulnerable on issues affecting the military due to his record as a Vietnam "draft dodger" and his unpopular stand on gays in the military. Thus, rather than focus his attention on the negotiations in Rome as they came to a head, Clinton immersed himself in a historic trip to China during the Rome Conference. And in the midst of several breaking White House scandals in the summer of 1998, there was to be no last minute rescue of the Rome Treaty by Vice President Al Gore as had been the case with the Kyoto Climate Accord a year earlier.

## The Question of ICC Jurisdiction over the Nationals of Non-Party States

Once it decided that it would not sign the Court's Statute, the primary goal of the United States government (still bowing to the concerns of the Pentagon) was to prevent the ICC from being able to exercise jurisdiction over U.S. personnel and officials. As Ambassador Scheffer explained to the Senate Foreign Relations Committee: "We sought an amendment to the text that would have required ... the consent of the state of nationality of the perpetrator be obtained before the court could exercise jurisdiction. We asked for a vote on our proposal, but a motion to take no action was overwhelmingly carried by the vote of participating governments in the conference." Had the U.S. amendment been adopted, the United States could have declined to sign the Rome Statute, thereby ensuring its immunity from the second track of the court's jurisdiction, but at the same time permitting the United States to take advantage of the first track of the Court's jurisdiction (Security Council referrals) when it was in America's interest to do so.

Having lost that vote, the U.S. Administration began to argue that international law prohibits an ICC from exercising jurisdiction over the nationals of non-parties. Thus, Ambassador Scheffer told the Senate Foreign Relations Committee that "the treaty purports to establish an arrangement whereby U.S. armed forces operating overseas could be conceivably prosecuted by the international court even if the United States has not agreed to be bound by the treaty.... This is contrary to the most fundamental principles of treaty law" as set forth in the Vienna Convention on the Law of Treaties. Based on the U.S. objection to the ICC's exercise of jurisdiction over nationals of non-party states, Ambassador Scheffer expressed the "hope that on reflection governments that have signed, or are planning to sign, the Rome treaty will begin to recognize the proper limits to Article 12 and how its misuse would do great damage to international law and be very disruptive to the international political system." Senator Helms later quoted this "Vienna Convention" argument in the preamble of his anti-ICC legislation, which is discussed below.

Diplomats and scholars have been quick to point out the flaws in Scheffer's argument. First, it is a distortion to say that the Rome Statute purports to impose obligations on non-party States. Under the terms of the Rome Treaty, the Parties are obligated to provide funding to the ICC, to extradite indicted persons to the ICC, to provide evidence to the ICC, and to provide other forms of cooperation to the Court. Those are the only obligations the Rome Treaty establishes on States, and they apply only to State Parties. Thus, Ambassador Scheffer's objection is not really that the Rome Treaty imposes obligations on the United States as a non-party, but that it affects the sovereignty interests of the United States — an altogether different matter which does not come within the Vienna Convention's proscription. Moreover, although States have a sovereignty interest in their nationals, especially state officials and employees, sovereignty does not provide a basis for exclusive jurisdiction over crimes committed by a State's nationals in a foreign country. Nor does a foreign indictment of a State's nationals for acts committed in the foreign country constitute an impermissible intervention in the State's internal affairs.

Second, the exercise of the ICC's jurisdiction over nationals of non-party states who commit crimes in the territory of a State parties is well grounded in both the universality principle and the territoriality principle of jurisdiction under international law. The core crimes within the ICC's jurisdiction — genocide, crimes against humanity, and war crimes — are crimes of universal jurisdiction. The negotiating record of the Rome Treaty indicates that the consent regime was layered upon the ICC's inherent universal jurisdiction over these crimes, such that with the consent of the State in whose territory the offense was committed, the Court has the authority to issue indictments over the nationals of non-party States. The Nuremberg Tribunal and the ad hoc Tribunal for the former Yugoslavia provide precedent for the collective delegation of universal jurisdiction to an international criminal court without the consent of the State of the nationality of the accused.

In addition, international law recognizes the authority of the state where a crime occurs to delegate its territorial-based jurisdiction to a third State or international Tribunal. Careful analysis of the European Convention on the Transfer of Proceedings indicates that the consent of the State of the nationality of the accused is not a prerequisite for the delegation of territorial jurisdiction under the Convention, and therefore that it provides a precedent for the ICC's jurisdictional regime. There are no compelling policy reasons why territorial jurisdiction cannot be delegated to an international court and the Nuremberg Tribunal provides the precedent for the collective exercise of territorial as well as universal jurisdiction.

Third, Scheffer's argument is inconsistent with past U.S. exercise of universal jurisdiction granted by anti-terrorism, anti-narcotic trafficking, torture, and war crimes treaties over the nationals of states which are not party to these treaties. In light of the past U.S. practice, the claim that a treaty cannot lawfully provide the basis of criminal jurisdiction over the nationals of non-party states, while directed against the ICC, has the potential of negatively effecting existing U.S. law enforcement authority with respect to terrorists, narco-traffickers, torturers, and war criminals.

### An Effort to Modify the Rome Treaty

During hearings before the Senate Foreign Relations Committee on June 23, 1998, Senator Jesse Helms (R-N.C.) urged the Administration to take the following steps in opposition to the establishment of an international criminal court: First, that it announce that it would withdraw U.S. troops from any country that ratified the International Criminal Court Treaty. Second, that it veto any attempt by the Security Council to refer a matter to the Court's jurisdiction. Third, that it block any international organization in which it is a member from providing any funding to the International Criminal Court. Fourth, that it renegotiate its Status of Forces Agreements and Extradition Treaties to prohibit its treaty partners from surrendering U.S. nationals to the International Criminal Court. Finally, that it provide no U.S. soldiers to any regional or international peacekeeping operation where there is any possibility that they will come under the jurisdiction of the International Criminal Court. According to Senator Helms, these measures would ensure that the Rome Treaty will be "dead on arrival."

Ambassador Scheffer was non-committal as to the adoption of Senator Helms' proposals, saying only that "the Administration hopes that in the years ahead other governments will recognize the benefits of potential American participation in the Rome treaty and correct the flawed provisions in the treaty." In the meantime, he added, "more ad hoc judicial mechanisms will need to be considered." Ambassador Scheffer's testimony suggested that the U.S. response to the International Criminal Court might parallel its efforts to reform the 1982 Law of the Sea Convention. The United States refused to sign that treaty until amendments were adopted concerning its seabed mining regime. In 1994, the signatories to the Law of the Sea Convention adopted an Agreement containing the revisions sought by the United States and the United States signed the treaty, which still awaits Senate advice and consent to ratification.

In the following months, the United States tried to secure international backing for a clause to be included in the agreement that was being prepared to govern the relations between the United Nations and the ICC. Without actually amending the ICC Statute, the U.S. proposal would prevent the ICC from taking custody of official personnel of non-party states where the state has acknowledged responsibility for the act in question. This was a major walk back from its earlier position, as this proposal would not prevent the ICC from indicting nationals of non-party states, only prosecuting them. That the Clinton Administration was willing to float this proposal indicated that it was no longer promoting Ambassador Scheffer's questionable reading of the Vienna Convention.

Prior to the Rome Diplomatic Conference, many countries felt that the success of a permanent international criminal court would be in question without U.S. support. But as it became increasingly obvious that the United States was not going to sign the Rome Treaty, the willingness to compromise began to evaporate, culminating in the overwhelming vote against the U.S. amendment requiring the consent of the state of nationality at the Rome Diplomatic Conference. The United States soon discovered that it would have no more luck with the issue through a series of bilateral negotiations than it did in the frenzied atmosphere that characterized the final days of the Rome Conference.

### "If You Can't Beat 'em, Join 'em"

By late 2000, the Clinton Administration had come to realize that the ICC would ultimately enter into force with or without U.S. support. By December 2000, a growing number of countries had ratified the Rome Treaty, and over 120 countries had signed it, indicating their intention to ratify. Sixty ratifications are necessary to bring it into force. The Signatories included every other NATO State except for Turkey, three of the Permanent Members of the Security Council (France, Russia, and the United Kingdom), and both of the United States' closest neighbors (Mexico and Canada). Even Israel, which had been the only Western country to join the United States in voting against the ICC Treaty in Rome in 1998, later changed its position and announced that it would sign the treaty. Israel's change of position was made possible when the ICC Prep Con promulgated definitions of the crimes over which the ICC has jurisdiction, which clarified that the provision in the ICC Statute making altering the demographics of an occupied territory a war crime would be interpreted no more expansively than the existing law contained in the Geneva Conventions.

In the waning days of his presidency, William J. Clinton authorized the U.S. signature of the Rome Treaty, making the United States the 138th country to sign the treaty by the December 31st deadline. According to the ICC Statute, after December 31, 2000, States must accede to the Treaty, which requires full ratification — something that was not likely for the United States in the near term given the current level of Senate opposition to the Treaty. While signature is not the equivalent of ratification, it set the stage for U.S. support of Security Council referrals to the International Criminal Court, as well as other forms of U.S. cooperation with the Court. In addition, it put the United States in a better position to continue to seek additional provisions to protect American personnel from the court's jurisdiction.

### Hostile Outsider or Influential Insider?

Clinton's last minute action drew immediate ire from Senator Jesse Helms, then Chairman of the U.S. Senate Foreign Relations Committee, who has been one of the treaty's greatest opponents. In a Press Release, Helms stated:

> "Today's action is a blatant attempt by a lame-duck President to tie the hands of his successor. Well, I have a message for the outgoing President. This decision will not stand. I will make reversing this decision, and protecting America's fighting

men and women from the jurisdiction of this international kangaroo court, one of my highest priorities in the new Congress."

Helms responded by pushing for passage of the "Service members Protection Act," Senate Bill 2726, which would prohibit any U.S. Government cooperation with the ICC, and cut off U.S. military assistance to any country that has ratified the ICC Treaty (with the exception of major U.S. allies), as long as the United States has not ratified the Rome Treaty. Further, the proposed legislation provides that U.S. military personnel must be immunized from ICC jurisdiction before the U.S. participates in any U.N. peacekeeping operation. The proposed legislation also authorizes the President to use all means necessary to release any U.S. or allied personnel detained on behalf of the Court.

The essence of this debate, then, is whether the national security and foreign policy interests of the United States are better served by playing the role of a hostile outsider (as embodied in Senator Helms' and Lee Casey's "American Service members Protection Act"), or by playing the role of an influential insider (as it has done, for example, with the Yugoslavia Tribunal). In deciding this issue, one must carefully and objectively examine the consequences that would flow from the hostile approach.

First, the hostile approach would transform American exceptionalism into unilateralism and/or isolationism by preventing the United States from participating in U.N. peacekeeping operations and cutting off aid to many countries vital to U.S. national security. This would be especially foolhardy at this moment in history when the United States is working hard to expand and hold together an international coalition against the terrorist organizations and their state supporters that were involved in the terrorist attacks of September 11, 2001.

Further, overt opposition to the ICC would erode the moral legitimacy of the United States, which has historically been as important to achieving U.S. foreign policy goals as military and economic might. A concrete example of this was the recent U.S. loss of its seat in the U.N. Commission of Human Rights, where several western countries cited current U.S. opposition to the ICC as warranting their vote against the United States.

Perversely, the approach embodied in Senator Helms' legislation could even turn the United States into a safe haven for international war criminals, since the U.S. would be prevented from surrendering them directly to the ICC or indirectly to another country which would surrender them to the ICC. And the idea that the President should use all means necessary to release any U.S. or allied personnel detained on behalf of the Court is the height of folly, as reflected in headlines describing the legislation as the "Hague Invasion Act."

Second, under the hostile approach, the United States would be prevented from being able to take advantage of the very real benefits of an ICC. The experience with the Yugoslavia Tribunal has shown that, even absent arrests, an international indictment has the effect of isolating rogue leaders, strengthening domestic opposition, and increasing international support for sanctions and even use of force. The United States has recognized these benefits in pushing for the subsequent creation of the ad hoc tribunals for the Rwanda, Sierra Leone, and Cambodia, as well as proposing the establishment of a tribunal for Iraq. But the establishment of the ICC will signal the end of the era of Security Council-created tribunals, since even our friends and allies at the U.N. will insist that situations involving genocide, crimes against humanity, and war crimes be referred to the existing ICC rather than additional ad hoc tribunals. Thus, when the next Rwanda occurs, the United States will not be able to employ the very useful tool of international criminal justice unless it works through the ICC.

To bring home this point, consider that if the ICC had been in existence on September 11, 2001, the United States and the other members of the Security Council could have referred the case of Osama bin Laden and the other masterminds of the attacks on the World Trade Center and Pentagon to the ICC, rather than creating U.S.-led military tribunals which have been subject to harsh criticism in the United States and abroad. An ICC indictment of these terrorists for their "crimes against humanity" would have strengthened foreign support for the American intervention into Afghanistan and would have deflected bin Laden's attempt to characterize the military action as an American attack against Islam. And if any of the perpetrators fell into any country's custody, an ICC would present a neutral fora for their prosecution that would have enjoyed the support of the Islamic world.

Opponents of the ICC have suggested that without U.S. support, the ICC is destined to be impotent and irrelevant because it will lack the power of the Security Council to enforce its arrest orders. But as the experience of the ad hoc Tribunals for Rwanda, Sierra Leone, and most recently Yugoslavia (with the surrender of Milosevic) has proven, in most cases where an ICC is needed, the perpetrators are no longer in power and are in the custody of a new government or of nearby states which are perfectly willing to hand them over to an international tribunal absent Security Council action. Moreover, the Security Council has been prevented (largely by Russian veto threats) from taking any action to impose sanctions on States that have not cooperated with the Yugoslavia Tribunal despite repeated pleas from the Tribunal's Prosecutor and Judges that it do so. Indeed, in the Yugoslavia context, where the perpetrators were still in power when the Tribunal was established, it was not action by the Security Council, but rather the threatened withholding of foreign aid and IMF loans that have induced Croatia and Serbia to hand over indictees. This indicates that, unlike the League of Nations (which United States officials have frequently referred to in this context), the ICC is likely to be a thriving institution even without United States participation. In other words, the United States may actually need the ICC more than the ICC needs the United States.

Third, the United States achieves no real protection from the ICC by remaining outside the ICC regime. This is because, as explained above, Article 12 of the Rome Statute empowers the ICC to exercise jurisdiction over nationals of non-party States who commit crimes in the territory of State Parties. Further, in its Pollyanna-ish refusal to recognize the legitimacy of the ICC's exercise of jurisdiction over the nationals of non-party states, opponents of the ICC have resorted to a questionable legal interpretation which is not only unlikely to sway the ICC or its founding members, but also has the potential of undermining important U.S. law enforcement interests.

If U.S. officials can be indicted by the ICC whether or not the U.S. is a party to the Rome Treaty, than the United States preserves very little by remaining outside the treaty regime, and could protect itself better by signing the treaty. This has been proven to be the case with the Yugoslavia Tribunal, which the U.S. has supported with contributions exceeding $15 million annually, the loan of top-ranking investigators and lawyers from the federal government, the support of troops to permit the safe exhumation of mass graves, and even the provision of U-2 surveillance photographs to locate the places where Serb authorities had tried to hide the evidence of its wrongdoing. This policy bore fruit when the International Prosecutor opened an investigation into allegations of war crimes committed by NATO during the 1999 Kosovo intervention. Despite the briefs and reports of reputable human rights organizations arguing that NATO had committed breaches of international humanitarian law, on June 8, 2000, the International

Prosecutor issued a report concluding that charges against NATO personnel were not warranted. This is not to suggest that the United States coopted the Yugoslavia Tribunal; but when dealing with close calls regarding application of international humanitarian law it is obviously better to have a sympathetic Prosecutor and Court than a hostile one.

Opponents of the ICC like to raise the specter of politicized indictments against American or Israeli officials drafted by prosecutors and confirmed by judges from countries that oppose our policies. A close examination of the list of the countries that have so far ratified the ICC, however, reveals that the ICC will be dominated not by our diplomatic opponents, but instead by our closest friends and allies. Of these 46 ratifying countries, nineteen are NATO or Western European allies, nine are Latin American and Caribbean countries with which the U.S. enjoys close relations, and four are U.S.-friendly Pacific island countries such as New Zealand and the Marshall Islands. With the possible exception of the Central African Republic, no country on the list would give a U.S. foreign policy-maker any cause for concern. On the other hand, the countries that most frequently oppose the United States in the United Nations (Asian and middle-eastern countries such as China, Cuba, Iraq, Libya, North Korea, Syria, and the Sudan) are the countries least likely to ratify the ICC Statute, so they will not be able to participate in the ICC Assembly of Parties or nominate judges for the ICC's bench or select the Court's Prosecutor. Consequently, even if the U.S. does not ratify the Rome Treaty, the reality is that the ICC is going to be a very U.S.-friendly tribunal, unless, that is, the United States figuratively (and literally) wages war against the institution as suggested in Senator Helms' legislation.

### Rebutting the Constitutional Arguments Against the ICC

Much of argument against the ICC concerns the constitutionality of U.S. participation in the Court. But, as Yale Law School constitutional Law professor Ruth Wedgwood has written, there are three reasons why we must conclude there "is no forbidding constitutional obstacle to U.S. participation in the Rome Treaty."

First, the ICC includes procedural protections negotiated by the U.S. Department of Justice representatives at Rome that closely follow the guarantees and safeguards of the American Bill of Rights. These including a Miranda-type warning, the right to defense counsel, reciprocal discovery, the right to exculpatory evidence, the right to speedy and public trial, the right to confront witnesses, and a prohibition on double jeopardy.

The only significant departures from U.S. law are that the ICC employs a bench trial before three judges rather than a jury, and it permits the Prosecutor to appeal an acquittal (but not to retry a defendant after the appeals have been decided). There were good reasons for these departures: For grave international crimes, qualified judges who issue detailed written opinions should be preferred over lay persons who issue unwritten verdicts. And if the trial judges misinterpret the applicable international law, whether in favor or to the detriment of the accused, an appeal is important to foster uniform interpretation of international criminal law.

Second, the United States has used its treaty power in the past to participate in other international tribunals that have had jurisdiction over U.S. nationals, such as the Yugoslavia Tribunal which was established by the Security Council pursuant to a treaty—the U.N. Charter. Like the ICC, the Yugoslavia Tribunal employs judges rather than a jury, and permits the Prosecutor to appeal acquittals. Moreover, the U.S. Congress has approved legislation authorizing U.S. courts to extradite indicted persons (including those of U.S. nationality) to the Yugoslavia Tribunal where there exists an order for their arrest and surrender. And this legislation has been upheld in a recent federal court case.

Third, the offenses within the ICC's jurisdiction would ordinarily be handled through military courts-martial, which do not permit jury trial, or through extradition of offenders to foreign nations, which often utilize bench trials and do not employ American notions of due process. It should be noted that U.S. federal courts have upheld the extradition of Americans to such foreign jurisdictions for actions that took place on U.S. soil but had an effect abroad.

At the conclusion of the Senate Foreign Relations Committee's hearings on the ICC in July 1998, the Committee submitted several questions about the Constitutionality of U.S. participation in the ICC for the Department of Justice to answer for the record. The answers were prepared by Lee Casey's former colleagues in the Department's Office of Legal Counsel. This part of the Committee's published report should be required reading for anyone who has serious concerns about the Constitutionality of the ICC. The Department of Justice specifically found that U.S. ratification of the Rome Treaty and surrender of persons including U.S. nationals to the ICC would not violate Article III, section 2 of the Constitution nor any of the provisions of the Bill of Rights.

## Conclusion

Opponents of the ICC base their arguments on the assumption that it is not too late for America to prevent the ICC from coming into existence or to marginalize the Court so that it exists as a non-entity. But the spate of ratifications and the numerous powerful countries that are supporting the ICC (including virtually every other member of NATO) indicate that the ICC is a serious international institution that the United States is very soon going to have to learn to live with.

The risks to U.S. service members as well as the potential constitutional problems presented by the ICC have been greatly exaggerated by American opponents of the ICC, while both the practical usefulness of the ICC and the safeguards contained in the ICC Statute have been significantly undervalued. To the extent that American fears of politicized prosecutions are valid, U.S. opposition to the ICC will only increase the likelihood that the ICC will be more hostile than sympathetic to U.S. positions. And, by opposing the Court, the United States may actually engender more international hostility toward U.S. foreign policy than would have resulted from an indictment by the Court. Thus, whether or not the U.S. is able to achieve additional safeguards to prevent the ICC from exercising jurisdiction over U.S. personnel, it will be in the interests of U.S. national security and foreign policy to support, rather than oppose, the ICC.

It is important to recognize that supporting the ICC does not require immediate U.S. ratification of the Rome Treaty. Perhaps it would be prudent for the United States to let the Court prove itself over a period of years before sending the treaty to the Senate. But in the meantime, when the next Rwanda-like situation comes along, the United States will find value in having the option of Security Council referral to the ICC in its arsenal of foreign policy responses—something the United States can do even if it does not ratify the Rome Treaty so long as it does not enact a version of Senator Helms' and Lee Casey's anti-ICC legislation.

**Lee A. Casey,** *The Case Against Supporting the International Criminal Court*
**Washington University School of Law, Whitney R. Harris Institute for Global Legal**
**Studies, Washington University in St. Louis, International Debate Series,**
**No. 1 (2002)**

The United States should not ratify the ICC Treaty. There are two fundamental objections to American participation in the ICC regime. First, U.S. participation would violate our Constitution by subjecting Americans to trial in an international court for offenses otherwise within the judicial power of the United States, and without the guarantees of the Bill of Rights. Second, our ratification of the Rome Treaty would constitute a profound surrender of American sovereignty, undercutting our right of self-government — the first human right, without which all others are simply words on paper, held by grace and favor, and no rights at all.

With respect to the Constitutional objections, by joining the ICC Treaty, the United States would subject American citizens to prosecution and trial in a court that was not established under Article III of the Constitution for criminal offenses otherwise subject to the judicial power of the United States. This, it cannot do. As the Supreme Court explained in the landmark Civil War case of *Ex parte Milligan* (1866), reversing a civilian's conviction by a military tribunal, "[e]very trial involves the exercise of judicial power," and courts not properly established under Article III can exercise "no part of the judicial power of the country."

This rationale is equally, and emphatically, applicable to the ICC, a court where neither the prosecutors nor the judges would have been appointed by the President, by and with the advice and consent of the Senate, and which would not be bound by the fundamental guarantees of the Bill of Rights. In fact, individuals brought before the ICC would only nominally enjoy the rights we in the United States take for granted.

For example, the ICC Treaty guarantees defendants the right "to be tried without undue delay." In the International Criminal Tribunal for the Former Yugoslavia (an institution widely understood to be a model for the permanent ICC), and which also guarantees this "right," defendants often wait more than a year in prison before their trial begins, and many years before a judgment actually is rendered. The Hague prosecutors actually have argued that up to five years would not be too long to wait IN PRISON for a trial, citing case law from the European Court of Human Rights supporting their position.

Such practices, admittedly, have a long pedigree, but they mock the presumption of innocence. Under U.S. law, the federal government must bring a criminal defendant to trial within three months, or let him go.

By the same token, the right of confrontation, guaranteed by the Sixth Amendment, includes the right to know the identity of hostile witnesses, and to exclude most "hearsay" evidence. In the Yugoslavia Tribunal, both anonymous witnesses and virtually unlimited hearsay evidence have been allowed at criminal trials, *large portions of which are conducted in secret*. Again, this is the model for the ICC.

Similarly, under the Constitution's guarantee against double jeopardy a judgment of acquittal cannot be appealed. Under the ICC statute, acquittals are freely appealable by the prosecution, as in the Yugoslav Tribunal, where the Prosecutor has appealed every judgment of acquittal.

In addition, the ICC would not preserve the right to a jury trial. The importance of this right cannot be overstated. Alone among the Constitution's guarantees, the right to a jury trial was stated twice, in Article III (sec. 2) and in the Sixth Amendment. It is not merely a means of determining facts in a judicial proceeding. It is a fundamental check on the abuse of power. As Justice Joseph Story explained: "The great object of a trial by jury in criminal cases is to guard against a spirit of oppression and tyranny on the part of rulers, and against a spirit of violence and vindictiveness on the part of the people." It is "part of that admirable common law, which had fenced round, and interposed barriers on every side against the approaches of arbitrary power." That said, the exclusion of jury trials from the ICC is not surprising, for that Court invites the exercise of arbitrary power by its very design.

The ICC will act as policeman, prosecutor, judge, jury, and jailer—all of these functions will be performed by its personnel, with nothing but bureaucratic divisions of authority, and no division of interest. There would be no appeal from its judgments. If the ICC abuses its power, there will be no recourse. From first to last, the ICC will be the judge in its own case. It will be more absolute than any dictator. As an institution, the ICC is fundamentally inconsistent with the political, philosophical, and legal traditions of the United States.

ICC supporters suggest that U.S. participation in this Court would not violate the Constitution because it would not be "a court of the United States," to which Article III and the Bill of Rights apply. They often point to cases in which the Supreme Court has allowed the extradition of citizens to face charges overseas. There are, however, fundamental differences between United States participation in the ICC Treaty Regime and extradition cases, where American are sought for crimes committed abroad. If the U.S. joined the ICC Treaty, the Court could try Americans who never have left the United States, for actions taken entirely within our borders.

A hypothetical, stripped of the emotional overlay inherent in "war crimes" issues, can best illustrate the constitutional point here: The Bill of Rights undoubtedly impedes efficient enforcement of the drug laws—also a subject of international concern. Could the federal government enter a treaty with Mexico and Canada, establishing an offshore "Special Drug Control Court," which would prosecute and try all drug offenses committed anywhere in North America, without the Bill of Rights guarantees? Could the federal government, through the device of a treaty, establish a special overseas court to try sedition cases—thus circumventing the guarantees of the First Amendment.

Fortunately, the Supreme Court has never faced such a case. However, in the 1998 case of *United States v. Balsys,* the Court suggested that, where a prosecution by a foreign court is, at least in part, undertaken on behalf of the United States, for example, where "the United States and its allies had enacted substantially similar criminal codes aimed at prosecuting offenses of international character ..." then an argument can be made that the Bill of Rights would apply" *simply because that prosecution [would not be] fairly characterized as distinctly 'foreign' The point would be that the prosecution was as much on behalf of the United States as of the prosecuting nation ..."*

This would, of course, be exactly the case with the ICC. If the United States became a "State Party" to the ICC Treaty, any prosecutions undertaken by the Court would be "as much on behalf of the United States as of any other State party. Since the full and undiluted guarantees of the Bill of Rights would not be available in the ICC, the United States cannot, constitutionally, sign and ratify the ICC treaty.

ICC supporters also have argued that the U.S. should sign and ratify the Rome Treaty because the Court would be directed against people like Saddam Hussein and Slobodan Milosevic, and not against the United States. Here, as pretty much everywhere, the past is the best predictor of the future. We already have seen this particular drama staged at the Yugoslav Tribunal. Even though that Tribunal was established to investigate crimes committed during 1991–1995 Yugoslav conflict, and even though NATO's air war against Serbia was fought on entirely humanitarian grounds, and even though it was conducted with the highest level of technical proficiency in history, the Hague prosecutors nevertheless undertook a *politically motivated* investigation—motivated *by international humanitarian rights activists along with Russia and China*—of NATO's actions based upon the civilian deaths that resulted.

At the end of this investigation, the prosecutors gave NATO a pass not because, in their view, there were no violations, but because "[i]n all cases, either the law is not sufficiently clear or investigations are unlikely to result in the acquisition of sufficient evidence to substantiate charges against high level accused or against lower accused for particularly heinous offenses."

Significantly, in their report the prosecutors openly acknowledged the very elastic nature of the legal standards in this area, further highlighting the danger that the United States will be the subject of such politically motivated prosecutions in the future: "[t]he answers to these question [regarding allegedly excessive civilian casualties] are not simple. It may be necessary to resolve them on a case-by-case basis, *and the answers may differ depending on the background and values of the decision-maker.* It is unlikely that a human rights lawyer and an experienced combat commander would assign the same relative values to military advantage and to injury to noncombatants. Further, it is unlikely that military commanders with different doctrinal backgrounds and differing degrees of combat experience or national military histories would always agree in close cases."

These are, in fact, "will-build-to-suit" crimes. Whether prosecutions are brought against American officials will depend entirely upon the motivations and political agenda of the ICC.

In response, ICC supporters claim that we can depend upon the professionalism and good will of the Court's personnel. One of the ICC's strongest advocates, former Yugoslav Tribunal Prosecutor Louise Arbour has argued for a powerful Prosecutor and Court, suggesting that "an institution should not be constructed on the assumption that it will be run by incompetent people, acting in bad faith from improper purposes."

The Framers of our Constitution understood the fallacy of this argument probably better than any other group in history. If there is one particular American contribution to the art of statecraft, it is the principle—incorporated into the very fabric of our Constitution—that *the security of our rights cannot be trusted to the good intentions of our leaders.* By its nature, power is capable of abuse and people are, by nature, flawed. As James Madison wrote "the great difficulty lies in this: you must first enable the government to control the governed; and in the next place *oblige it to control itself.*" The ICC would not be obliged to control itself.

It is also often asserted that the principle of "complementarity," found in Article 17 of the Rome Treaty, will check the Court's ability to undertake prosecution of Americans. This is the principle that prohibits the ICC from taking up a case if the appropriate national authorities investigate and prosecute the matter. In fact, this limit on the ICC's power is, in the case of the United States, entirely illusory.

First, as with all other matters under the Rome Treaty, it will be solely within the discretion of the ICC to interpret and apply this provision.

Second, under Article 17, the Court can pursue a case wherever it determines that the responsible State was "unwilling or unable to carry out the investigation or prosecution." In determining whether a State was "unwilling" the Court will consider whether the national proceedings were conducted "independently or impartially." The United States can never meet that test as an institutional matter. Under the Constitution, the President is both the Chief Executive, i.e., the chief law enforcement officer, and the Commander-in-Chief of the armed forces. In any particular case, both the individuals investigating and prosecuting, and the individuals being investigated and prosecuted, work for the same man. Moreover, under command responsibility theories, the President is always a potential—indeed, a likely, target of any investigation. The ICC will simply note that an individual cannot "impartially" investigate himself, and it will be full steam ahead. As a check on the ICC, complimentarity is meaningless.

Finally, it's important to understand exactly what is at stake here. Today, the officials of the United States are ultimately accountable for their actions to the American electorate. If the United States were to ratify the ICC Treaty this ultimate accountability would be transferred from the American people to the ICC in a very real and immediate way—through the threat of criminal prosecution and punishment. The policies implemented and actions taken by our national leaders, whether at home or abroad, could be scrutinized by the ICC and punished if, *in its opinion,* criminal violations had occurred. As Alexis de Tocqueville wrote, "[h]e who punishes the criminal is ... the real master of society." Ratification of the ICC Treaty would, in short, constitute a profound surrender of American sovereignty—our right of self-government—the first human right. Without self-government, the rest are words on paper, held by grace and favor, and not rights at all.

That surrender would be to an institution that does not share our interests or values. There is no universally recognized and accepted legal system on the international level, particularly in the area of due process, as the Rome Treaty itself recognizes in requiring that, in the selection of judges, "the principal legal systems of the world," should be represented. Moreover, although a number of Western states have signed this treaty, so have states such as Algeria, Iran, Nigeria, Sudan, Syria and Yemen. According to the U.S. State Department, each of these states has been implicated in the use of torture or extra judicial killings, or both. Yet, each of them would have as great a voice as the United States in selecting the ICC's Prosecutor and Judges and in the Assembly of State Parties.

This is especially troubling because, as the ICTY Prosecutor conceded, who is and who is not a war criminal is very much a matter of your point of view. And I'd like to give you a fairly poignant example that I learned of, actually, while practicing before the ICTY.

In this case there was a young officer, 20 or 21 years old, who commanded a detachment of regular soldiers, along with a group of irregulars. Irregulars are, of course, always a problem. I think everyone pretty much agrees that, for example, the worst atrocities in Bosnia were committed by irregulars. At any rate, these irregulars were clearly under the officer's command when they all ran into a body of enemy troops.

There was a short, sharp firefight. A number of the enemy were killed or wounded, and the rest threw down their arms and surrendered. At that point, the officer entirely lost control of the situation. His irregulars began to kill the wounded and then the rest of the prisoners—with knives and axes actually.

After a good deal of confusion, the officer managed to form up his regulars around the remaining prisoners, but about a dozen were killed. Now, under our system of military justice, the perpetrators would be prosecuted, but the officer would very likely not be. He gave no order for the killings, and took some action to stop it.

However, under the command responsibility and "knowing presence" theories now current at the ICTY, the ICC's model, this officer is guilty of a war crime. The fact that he did make some attempt to prevent the killing would certainly be taken into account, but very likely as a matter of mitigation at sentencing.

At any rate, this is a real case. It didn't, however, happen in Central Bosnia, or Kosovo, or Eastern Slavonia, and the individuals involved were not Serbs, Croats, or Muslims. As a matter of fact, it happened in Western Pennsylvania. The soldiers were English subjects, at the time, and the irregulars were Iroquois Indians; their victims were French. The young officer was, as a matter of fact, from the county in which I live — Fairfax, Virginia. And, for those of you who are students here at the University, his name — Washington — will grace each of your diplomas.

War is, inherently, a violent affair and the discretion whether to prosecute any particular case in which Americans are involved should be kept firmly in the hands of our institutions, to be made by individuals who are accountable to us for their actions. The ICC is inconsistent with our Constitution and inimical to our national interests. It is an institution of which we should have no part.

---

## 3. "Clinton's Words: 'The Right Action'"

### *The New York Times*, 2001

[President Clinton's statement on December 31, 2000, authorizing
the United States to sign the Treaty on the International Criminal Court]

The United States is today signing the 1998 Rome Treaty on the International Criminal Court. In taking this action, we join more than 130 other countries that have signed by the December 31, 2000 deadline established in the treaty. We do so to reaffirm our strong support for international accountability and for bringing to justice perpetrators of genocide, war crimes, and crimes against humanity. We do so as well because we wish to remain engaged in making the ICC an instrument of impartial and effective justice in the years to come.

The United States has a long history of commitment to the principle of accountability, from our involvement in the Nuremberg tribunals that brought Nazi war criminals to justice to our leadership in the effort to establish the International Criminal Tribunals for the Former Yugoslavia and Rwanda. Our action today sustains that tradition of moral leadership.

Under the Rome Treaty, the International Criminal Court will come into being with the ratification of 60 governments, and will have jurisdiction over the most heinous abuses that result from international conflict, such as war crimes, crimes against humanity and genocide. The Treaty requires that the ICC not supersede or interfere with functioning national judicial systems; that is, the ICC prosecutor is authorized to take action against a suspect only if the country of nationality is unwilling or unable to investigate allegations of egregious crimes by their national. The U.S. delegation to the Rome conference worked hard to achieve these limitations, which we believer are essential to the international credibility and success of the ICC.

In signing, however, we are not abandoning our concerns about significant flaws in the treaty. In particular, we are concerned that when the court comes into existence, it will not only exercise authority over personnel of states that have ratified the treaty, but also claim jurisdiction over personnel of states that have not. With signature, however, we will be in a position to influence the evolution of the court. Without signature, we will not.

Signature will enhance our ability to further protect U.S. officials from unfounded charges and to achieve the human rights and accountability objectives of the ICC. In fact, in negotiations following the Rome Conference, we have worked effectively to develop procedures that limit the likelihood of politicized prosecutions. For example, U.S. civilian and military negotiators helped to ensure greater precision in the definitions of crimes within the Court's jurisdiction.

But more must be done. Court jurisdictions over U.S. personnel should come only with U.S. ratification of the Treaty. The United States should have the chance to observe and assess the functioning of the Court, over time, before choosing to become subject to its jurisdiction. Given these concerns, I will not, and do not recommend that my successor submit the Treaty to the Senate for advice and consent until our fundamental concerns are satisfied.

Nonetheless, signature is the right action to take at this point. I believe that a properly constituted and structured International Criminal Court would make a profound contribution in deterring egregious human rights abuses worldwide, and that signature increases the chances for productive discussions with other governments to advance these goals in the months and years ahead.

## *Authors' Note*

The following two materials discuss the actions of the United States in "unsigning" from the ICC treaty and the passage of the American Service-Member's Protections Act (ASPA). Technically speaking, the U.S. did not "unsign" the treaty. Rather, the media term "unsigning" refers to the U.S. proclaiming that its signature of the Rome Statute no longer meant it supported the object and purpose of the treaty. The Bush Administration's "unsigning" of the Rome Statute thus legally opened the door for the U.S. to pursue policies that were aimed to hinder the effectiveness of the Rome Statute.

Congress's passage of the ASPA in 2002 was the most prominent measure taken to hinder the effectiveness of the court. ASPA prohibited the U.S. cooperation with an ICC investigation (e.g., handing over intelligence or funds), allowing the U.S. to assist in the extradition of someone to the ICC, and providing troops for U.N. peace operations without immunity from ICC prosecution. The Act even went so far as to prohibit the U.S. from providing military assistance to states that were member of the Court and authorized the President to use military force in order to retrieve an American who was in ICC custody.

## 4. Neil A. Lewis, "U.S. is Set to Renounce Its Role in Pact for World Tribunal"

*The New York Times*, 2005

The Bush administration has decided to renounce formally any involvement in a treaty setting up an international criminal court and is expected to declare that the signing of the document by the Clinton administration is no longer valid, government officials said today.

The "unsigning" of the treaty, which is expected to be announced on Monday, will be a decisive rejection by the Bush White House of the concept of a permanent tribunal designed to prosecute individuals for genocide, crimes against humanity and other war crimes.

The administration has long argued that the court has the potential to create havoc for the United States, exposing American soldiers and officials overseas to capricious and mischievous prosecutions.

"We think it was a mistake to have signed it," an administration official said. "We have said we will not submit it to the Senate for ratification." The renunciation, officials said, also means the United States will not recognize the court's jurisdiction and will not submit to any of its orders.

In addition, other officials said, the United States will simultaneously assert that it will not be bound by the Vienna Convention on the Law of Treaties, a 1969 pact that outlines the obligations of nations to obey other international treaties.

Article 18 of the Vienna Convention requires signatory nations like the United States to refrain from taking steps to undermine treaties they sign, even if they do not ratify them. As with the treaty for the International Criminal Court, the United States signed but did not ratify the Vienna agreement.

A government official said the administration planned to make its decision known on Monday in a speech by Under Secretary of State Marc Grossman in Washington and in a briefing for foreign journalists by Pierre-Richard Prosper, the State Department's ambassador for war crimes issues. Representatives of human rights groups also said they expected the decision, which was first reported by Reuters news service on Friday, to be announced then.

The pointed repudiation of the International Criminal Court, while not unexpected, is certain to add to the friction between the United States and much of the world, notably Europe, where policy makers have grumbled ever more loudly about the Bush administration's inclination to steer away from multinational obligations.

Despite the strong stance by the United States, the International Criminal Court will begin operations next year in The Hague. More than the required number of 60 nations had signed the treaty as of last month, and the court's jurisdiction will cover crimes committed after July 1 of this year.

It will become the first new international judicial body since the International Court of Justice, or World Court, was created in 1945 to adjudicate disputes between states. Until now, individuals were tried in ad hoc or specially created tribunals for war crimes like those now in operation for offenses committed in Rwanda and the countries that formerly made up Yugoslavia, both modeled on the Nuremberg trials of Nazi officials following World War II.

Harold Hongju Koh, a Yale law professor and a former assistant secretary of state in the Clinton administration, said the retraction of the signature on the treaty would be a profound error.

"The result is that the administration is losing a major opportunity to shape the court so it could be useful to the United States," Mr. Koh said. "Now that the court exists, it's important to deal with it. If the administration leaves it unmanaged, it may create difficulties for us and nations like Israel."

He described the opportunity as similar to the United States Supreme Court's 1803 decision in *Marbury v. Madison* that courts could subject the other branches of government to its jurisdiction, decisively defining its role in the new nation.

"This is an international *Marbury versus Madison* moment," he said.

John R. Bolton, the under secretary of state for arms control, who has been a leading voice in opposing American participation in the International Criminal Court, wrote extensively about the subject before he took office, calling it "a product of fuzzy-minded romanticism" and "not just naïve, but dangerous."

Mr. Bolton, in an article in The National Interest in 1999, argued that the court would force the United States to forfeit some of its sovereignty and unique concept of due process to a foreign and possibly unrestrained prosecutor. He said that it was not just American soldiers who would be in the most jeopardy, but "the president, the cabinet officers who comprise the National Security Council, and other senior civilian and military leaders responsible for our defense and foreign policy."

Palitha Kohona, the chief of the treaty section for the United Nations, said it was unheard of for a nation that signed a treaty to withdraw that signature. David J. Scheffer, who was ambassador at large for war crimes and who signed the treaty for the Clinton administration, said that withdrawing the signature exceeded even the actions of the Reagan administration, which in 1987 decided it would not seek ratification of an amendment to the Geneva Conventions that the Carter administration had signed. The action concerned a document known as Protocol 1, which would have extended protections to soldiers of insurgent movements.

"There has never been an attempt to literally remove the document," he said.

Mr. Scheffer said the Bush administration's actions would not only undermine international justice but also damage American interests.

"The perception will be that the United States walked away from international justice and forfeited its leadership role," he said. "It will be a dramatic moment in international legal history."

One official said the Bush White House was prepared to say last September that it would withdraw the signature on the treaty, but the attacks on the World Trade Center and the Pentagon that month delayed an announcement. Officials were not only occupied with the sudden fight against terrorism but also thought that renouncing the treaty would appear unseemly, the official said.

Most democratic nations and all European Union countries have ratified the treaty — except Greece, which is in the process of doing so — along with Canada, New Zealand and a number of African, Eastern European and Central Asian countries. Israel has signed it but not ratified. Egypt, Iran and Syria have signed. India, Pakistan and China have neither signed nor ratified. Russia has signed but not ratified.

---

## 5. U.S.: Hague Invasion Act Becomes Law
### Human Rights Watch, 2002

A new law supposedly protecting U.S. servicemembers from the International Criminal Court shows that the Bush administration will stop at nothing in its campaign against the court.

U.S. President George Bush today signed into law the American Servicemembers Protection Act of 2002, which is intended to intimidate countries that ratify the treaty for the International Criminal Court (ICC). The new law authorizes the use of military force to liberate any American or citizen of a U.S.-allied country being held by the court, which is located in The Hague. This provision, dubbed the "Hague invasion clause," has caused a strong reaction from U.S. allies around the world, particularly in the Netherlands.

In addition, the law provides for the withdrawal of U.S. military assistance from countries ratifying the ICC treaty, and restricts U.S. participation in United Nations peacekeeping unless the United States obtains immunity from prosecution. At the same time, these provisions can be waived by the president on "national interest" grounds.

"The states that have ratified this treaty are trying to strengthen the rule of law," said Richard Dicker, director of the International Justice Program at Human Rights Watch. "The Bush administration is trying to punish them for that."

Dicker pointed out that many of the ICC's biggest supporters are fragile democracies and countries emerging from human rights crises, such as Sierra Leone, Argentina and Fiji.

The law is part of a multi-pronged U.S. effort against the International Criminal Court. On May 6, in an unprecedented move, the Bush administration announced it was "renouncing" U.S. signature on the treaty. In June, the administration vetoed continuation of the U.N. peacekeeping force in Bosnia in an effort to obtain permanent immunity for U.N. peacekeepers. In July, U.S. officials launched a campaign around the world to obtain bilateral agreements that would grant immunity for American from the court's authority. Yesterday, Washington announced that it obtained such an agreement from Romania.

However, another provision of the bill allows the United States to assist international efforts to bring to justice those accused of genocide, war crimes or crimes against humanity—including efforts by the ICC.

"The administration never misses an opportunity to gratuitously antagonize its allies on the ICC," said Dicker. "But it's also true that the new law has more loopholes than a block of Swiss cheese."

Dicker said the law gives the administration discretion to override ASPA's noxious effects on a case-by-case basis. Washington may try to use this to strong-arm additional concessions from the states that support the court, but Dicker urged states supporting the ICC "not to fall into the U.S. trap: the law does not require any punitive measures."

Human Rights Watch believes the International Criminal Court has the potential to be the most important human rights institution created in 50 years, and urged regional groups of states, such as the European Union, to condemn the new law and resist Washington's attempts to obtain bilateral exemption arrangements.

## Authors' Note

### The Situation in Sudan

The ASPA allowed the president the discretion to waive most of the prohibitions imposed. With the exception of the prohibition on military assistance, ASPA is still good law today and so the amount of assistance the U.S. can give to the ICC is limited. However, the U.S. has slowly started to back off the hostility shown in ASPA. The first indicator of a change in the United States' stance towards the ICC occurred in 2005 when the U.S. abstained on the United Nations Security Council Resolution 1593, which referred the situation in Sudan to the ICC. Material 6 provides an excerpt of the text of Security Council 1593. Material 7 provides an explanation of the U.S. interpretation of resolution from Anne Woods Patterson, the U.S. representative at the U.N. Security Council. This statement explains the United States position on the jurisdiction of the ICC over non-State Parties.

## 6. S.C. Resolution 1593

"*The Security Council,*

\* \* \*

"*Determining* that the situation in Sudan continues to constitute a threat to international peace and security,

"*Acting* under Chapter VII of the Charter of the United Nations,

"1. *Decides* to refer the situation in Darfur since 1 July 2002 to the Prosecutor of the International Criminal Court;

"2. *Decides* that the Government of Sudan and all other parties to the conflict in Darfur, shall cooperate fully with and provide any necessary assistance to the Court and the Prosecutor pursuant to this resolution and, while recognizing that States not party to the Rome Statute have no obligation under the Statute, urges all States and concerned regional and other international organizations to cooperate fully;

"3. *Invites* the Court and the African Union to discuss practical arrangements that will facilitate the work of the Prosecutor and of the Court, including the possibility of conducting proceedings in the region, which would contribute to regional efforts in the fight against impunity;

"4. *Also encourages* the Court, as appropriate and in accordance with the Rome Statute, to support international cooperation with domestic efforts to promote the rule of law, protect human rights and combat impunity in Darfur;

"5. *Also emphasizes* the need to promote healing and reconciliation and encourages in this respect the creation of institutions, involving all sectors of Sudanese society, such as truth and/or reconciliation commissions, in order to complement judicial processes and thereby reinforce the efforts to restore long-lasting peace, with African Union and international support as necessary;

"6. *Decides* that nationals, current or former officials or personnel from a contributing State outside Sudan which is not a party to the Rome Statute of the International Criminal Court shall be subject to the exclusive jurisdiction of that contributing State for all alleged acts or omissions arising out of or related to operations in Sudan established or authorized by the Council or the African Union, unless such exclusive jurisdiction has been expressly waived by that contributing State;

"7. *Recognizes* that none of the expenses incurred in connection with the referral including expenses related to investigations or prosecutions in connection with that referral, shall be borne by the United Nations and that such costs shall be borne by the parties to the Rome Statute and those States that wish to contribute voluntarily;

\* \* \*

## 7. Anne Woods Patterson, Statement after Voting on UNSC Res. 1593

### 2005

Protection from the jurisdiction of the Court should not be viewed as unusual. Indeed, under article 124, even parties to the Rome Statue can opt out from the Court's jurisdiction over war crimes for a period of seven full years, and important supporters of the Court have in fact availed themselves of that opportunity to protect their own personnel. If it is appropriate to afford such protection from the jurisdiction of the Court to States that have agreed to the Rome Statute, it cannot be inappropriate to afford protection to those that have never agreed. It is our view that non-party States should be able to opt out of the Court's jurisdiction, as parties to the Statute can, and the Council should be prepared to take action to that effect as appropriate situations arise in the future.

Although we abstained on this Security Council referral to the ICC, we have not dropped, and indeed continue to maintain, our long-standing and firm objections and concerns regarding the ICC. We believe that the Rome Statute is flawed and does not have sufficient protections from the possibility of politicized prosecutions. We reiterate our fundamental objection to the Rome Statute's assertions that the ICC has jurisdiction over the nationals, including government officials, of States that have not become parties to the Rome Statute. Non-parties have no obligations in connection with that treaty unless otherwise decided by the Security Council, upon which Members of this Organization have conferred primary responsibility for the maintenance of international peace and security.

\* \* \*

As is well known, in connection with our concerns about the jurisdiction of the Court and the potential for politicized prosecutions, we have concluded agreements with 99 countries—over half the States Members of this Organization—since the entry into force of the Rome Statute to protect against the possibility of transfer or surrender of United States persons to the Court. We appreciate that the resolution takes note of the existence of those agreements and will continue to pursue additional such agreements with other countries as we move forward.

\* \* \*

That does not mean that there will be immunity for American citizens who act in violation of the law. We will continue to discipline our own people when appropriate.

## Authors' Note

### The Libya Referral

Beginning in early 2011, an unprecedented wave of grassroots protests started in Egypt, Tunisia, Libya, and several other Middle Eastern and Northern African States. In response to these protests, the heads of state in Egypt and Tunisia ultimately stepped down from their positions. In Libya, however, Muammar al-Qaddafi, the head of state of Libya, decided to use military force against his own civilian population in order to quell the protests. Instead of backing down, the protestors decided to militarize and an armed conflict broke out. The U.N. Security Council passed S.C. Resolution 1970 calling for a cessation of the violence in Libya; placing an asset freeze, arms embargo, travel ban, and sanctions on the Libyan political leadership, and referring the situation in Libya to the ICC. Unlike in the Sudan situation, the U.S. voted in favor of the Libya referral to the ICC. Material 8 provides an excerpt of S.C. Resolution 1970. Material 9 provides a statement by Susan Rice, U.S. Ambassador to the U.N., after voting on U.N.S.C. Resolution 1970. The position that the U.S. has taken on the Libya referral indicates the United States has changed its stance politically in regards to the usefulness of the ICC in the international community.

# 8. S.C. Resolution 1970

*The Security Council*

* * *

4. *Decides* to refer the situation in the Libyan Arab Jamahiriya since 15 February 2011 to the Prosecutor of the International Criminal Court;

5. *Decides* that the Libyan authorities shall cooperate fully with and provide any necessary assistance to the Court and the Prosecutor pursuant to this resolution and, while recognizing that States not party to the Rome Statute have no obligation under the Statute, urges all States and concerned regional and other international organizations to cooperate fully with the Court and the Prosecutor;

6. *Decides* that nationals, current or former officials or personnel from a State outside the Libyan Arab Jamahiriya which is not a party to the Rome Statute of the International Criminal Court shall be subject to the exclusive jurisdiction of that State for all alleged acts or omissions arising out of or related to operations in the Libyan Arab Jamahiriya established or authorized by the Council, unless such exclusive jurisdiction has been expressly waived by the State;

7. *Invites* the Prosecutor to address the Security Council within two months of the adoption of this resolution and every six months thereafter on actions taken pursuant to this resolution;

8. *Recognizes* that none of the expenses incurred in connection with the referral, including expenses related to investigations or prosecutions in connection with that referral, shall be borne by the United Nations and that such costs shall be borne by the parties to the Rome Statute and those States that wish to contribute voluntarily;

* * *

# 9. Susan Rice, Statement after Voting on UNSC Res. 1970

## 2011

When atrocities are committed against innocents, the international community must speak with one voice and today, it has. Tonight, acting under Chapter VOO, the Security Council has come together to condemn the violence, pursue accountability and adopt biting sanctions targeting Libya's unrepentant leadership. This is a clear warning to the Libyan Government that it must stop the killing. Those who slaughter civilians will be held accountable. The international community will not tolerate violence of any sort against the Libyan people by their Government or security forces.

Resolution 1970 (2011) is a strong resolution. It includes a travel ban and an assets freeze for key Libyan leaders. It imposes a complete arms embargo on Libya. It takes new steps against the use of mercenaries by the Libyan Government to attack its own people. And, for the first time ever, the Security Council has unanimously referred an egregious human rights situation to the International Criminal Court.

As President Obama said today, when a leader's only means of staying in power is to use mass violence against its own people, he has lost the legitimacy to rule and needs to do what is right for his county, by leaving now.

The protests in Libya are being driven by the people of Libya. This is about people's ability to shape their own future, wherever they may be. It is about human rights and fundamental freedoms. The Security Council has acted today to support the Libyan people's universal rights. These rights are not negotiable. They cannot be denied. Libya's leaders will be held accountable for violating these rights and for failing to meet their most basic responsibilities to their people.

## *Authors' Note*

The following selection provides an example of the ICC Prosecutor's decision concerning the potential initiation of an ICC investigation into events in Iraq. The selection details the Prosecutor's determination of the role of the independent prosecutor and the determination of whether ICC jurisdiction is appropriate.

## 10. Letter by Luis Moreno-Ocampo, Chief Prosecutor of the International Criminal Court
### The Hague, 2006

\* \* \*

[A]s the Prosecutor of the International Criminal Court, I have a very specific role and mandate, as specified in the Rome Statute. My responsibility is to carry out a preliminary phase of gathering and analysing information. I can seek to initiate an investigation only if the available information satisfies the criteria of the Statute. The Rome Statute defines the jurisdiction of the Court and a limited set of international crimes.

### Mandate of the Office

In accordance with Article 15 of the Rome Statute, my duty is to analyse information received on potential crimes, in order to determine whether there is a reasonable basis to proceed with an investigation.

Unlike a national prosecutor, who may initiate an investigation on the basis of very limited information, the Prosecutor of the International Criminal Court is governed by the relevant regime under the Rome Statute. Under this regime, my responsibility is to carry out a preliminary phase of gathering and analyzing information, after which I may seek to initiate an investigation only if the relevant criteria of the Statute are satisfied.

I am required to consider three factors. First, I must consider whether the available information provides a reasonable basis to believe that a crime within the jurisdiction of the Court has been or is being committed. Where this requirement is satisfied, I must then consider admissibility before the Court, in light of the requirements relating to gravity and complementarity with national proceedings. Third, if these factors are positive, I must give consideration to the interests of justice.

\* \* \*

Where the requirements are satisfied, I shall submit to a Pre-Trial Chamber of the Court a request for authorization to initiate an investigation. Where the requirements are not satisfied, I shall inform those who provided the information. This does not preclude me from considering further information regarding the same situation in the light of new facts or evidence.

### The analysis

The analysis of Iraq-related communications was conducted in accordance with Article 15 of the Rome Statute, as no referrals from States have been received.

The Office reviewed all communications, identified those containing substantiated information, and examined the relevant documentation and video-recorded information. In addition, we conducted an exhaustive search of all readily-available open source information, including media, governmental and non-governmental reports. Significant additional material collected from open sources includes, among others, the findings of Amnesty International, Human Rights Watch, Iraq Body Count and Spanish Brigades Against the War in Iraq.

* * *

### Personal and Territorial Jurisdiction

The events in question occurred on the territory of Iraq, which is not a State Party to the Rome Statute and which has not lodged a declaration of acceptance under Article 12(3).

Therefore, in accordance with Article 12, acts on the territory of a non-State Party fall within the jurisdiction of the Court only when the person accused of the crime is a national of a State that has accepted jurisdiction (Article 12(2)(b)). [W]e do not have jurisdiction with respect to actions of non-State Party nationals on the territory of Iraq.

Some communications submitted legal arguments that nationals of States Parties may have been accessories to crimes committed by nationals of non-States Parties. [T]he Office applied the reasonable basis standard for any form of individual criminal responsibility under Article 25.

### Allegations concerning Legality of the Conflict

Many of the communications received related to concerns about the legality of the armed conflict.

While the Rome Statute includes the crime of aggression, it indicates that the Court may not exercise jurisdiction over the crime until a provision has been adopted which defines the crime and sets out the conditions under which the Court may exercise jurisdiction with respect to it (Article 5(2)). This arrangement was established because there was strong support for including the crime of aggression but a lack of agreement as to its definition or the conditions under which the Court could act. States Parties to the Court are currently deliberating on these two issues. In accordance with Article 121 and

123, the first opportunity for an amendment to include such provisions will be at a review conference in 2009. In other words, the International Criminal Court has a mandate to examine the *conduct during the conflict*, but not whether the *decision to engage* in armed conflict was legal.

### Allegations concerning Genocide and Crimes against Humanity

Very few factual allegations were submitted concerning genocide or crimes against humanity. The Office collected information and examined the allegations. The available information provided no reasonable indicia that Coalition forces had "intent to destroy, in whole or in part, a national, ethnical, racial or religious group as such", as required in

---

1. Article 52 of Additional Protocol I to the Geneva Conventions provides a widely-accepted definition of military objective: "In so far as objects are concerned, military objectives are limited to those objects which by their nature, location, purpose or use make an effective contribution to military action and whose total or partial destruction, capture or neutralization, in the circumstances ruling at the time, offers a definite military advantage".

the definition of genocide (Article 6). Similarly, the available information provided no reasonable indicia of the required elements for a crime against humanity, i.e. a widespread or systematic attack directed against any civilian population (Article 7).

**Allegations concerning War Crimes**

1. Allegations concerning the targeting of civilians or clearly excessive attacks

Under international humanitarian law and the Rome Statute, the death of civilians during an armed conflict, no matter how grave and regrettable, does not in itself constitute a war crime.

\* \* \*

A crime occurs if there is an intentional attack directed against civilians (principle of distinction) (Article 8(2)(b)(i)) or an attack is launched on a military objective[1] in the knowledge that the incidental civilian injuries would be clearly excessive in relation to the anticipated military advantage (principle of proportionality) (Article 8(2)(b)(iv).

\* \* \*

Article 8(2)(b)(iv) draws on the principles in Article 51(5)(b) of the 1977 Additional Protocol I to the 1949 Geneva Conventions, but restricts the criminal prohibition to cases that are "*clearly*" excessive.

\* \* \*

Several communications expressed concerns about the use of cluster munitions. The Rome Statute contains a list of weapons whose use is prohibited *per se* (Article 8(2)(b)(xvii)–(xx). Cluster munitions are not included in the list and therefore their use *per se* does not constitute a war crime under the Rome Statute. A war crime could, however, still be established where any weapon is employed in a manner satisfying the elements of other war crimes. Allegations concerning cluster munitions were therefore analyzed in accordance with Article 8(2)(b)(i) and (iv) (targeting of civilians or clearly excessive attacks).

\* \* \*

With respect to Article 8(2)(b)(iv) allegations, the available material with respect to the alleged incidents was characterized by (1) a lack of information indicating clear excessiveness in relation to military advantage and (2) a lack of information indicating the involvement of nationals of States Parties. [For example:]

\* \* \*

[L]ists of potential targets were identified in advance; commanders had legal advice available to them at all times and were aware of the need to comply with international humanitarian law, including the principles of proportionality; detailed computer modeling was used in assessing targets; political, legal and military oversight was established for target approval; and real-time targeting information, including collateral damage assessment, was passed back to headquarters. [ … ] [N]early 85% of weapons released by UK aircraft were precision-guided, a figure which would tend to corroborate effort to minimize casualties.

\* \* \*

After exhausting all measures appropriate during the analysis phase, the Office determined that, while many facts remained undetermined, the available information did not provide a reasonable basis to believe that a crime within the jurisdiction of the Court had been committed.

\* \* \*

## 2. Allegations concerning willful killing or inhuman treatment of civilians

During the course of analysis, allegations came to light in the media concerning incidents of mistreatment of detainees and wilful killing of civilians. General allegations included brutality against persons upon capture and initial custody, causing death or serious injury. In addition, there were incidents in which civilians were killed during policing operations in the occupation phase. The Office collected information with respect to these incidents as well as with respect to the relevant national criminal proceedings undertaken by the governments of States Parties with respect to their nationals. Analysis was conducted in the light of the elements of wilful killing (Article 8(2)(a)(i)) and torture or inhumane treatment (Article 8(2)(a)(ii)).

After analyzing all the available information, it was concluded that there was a reasonable basis to believe that crimes within the jurisdiction of the Court had been committed, namely wilful killing and inhuman treatment. The information available at this time supports a reasonable basis for an estimated 4 to 12 victims of wilful killing and a limited number of victims of inhuman treatment, totaling in all less than 20 persons.

### Admissibility

Even where there is a reasonable basis to believe that a crime has been committed, this is not sufficient for the initiation of an investigation by the International Criminal Court. The Statute then requires consideration of admissibility before the Court, in light of the gravity of the crimes and complementarity with national systems.

While, in a general sense, any crime within the jurisdiction of the Court is "grave", the Statute requires an additional threshold of gravity even where the subject-matter jurisdiction is satisfied.

\* \* \*

For war crimes, a specific gravity threshold is set down in Article 8(1). [ ... ] This threshold is not an element of the crime, and the words "in particular" suggest that this is not a strict requirement. It does, however, provide Statute guidance that the Court is intended to focus on situations meeting these requirements.

According to the available information, it did not appear that any of the criteria of Article 8(1) were satisfied.

Even if one were to assume that Article 8(1) had been satisfied, it would then be necessary to consider the general gravity requirement under Article 53(1)(b). The Office considers various factors in assessing gravity. A key consideration is the number of victims of particularly serious crimes, such as wilful killing or rape. The number of potential victims of crimes within the jurisdiction of the Court in this situation—4 to 12 victims of wilful killing and a limited number of victims of inhuman treatment—was of a different order than the number of victims found in other situations under investigation or analysis by the Office. It is worth bearing in mind that the OTP is currently investigating three situations involving long-running conflicts in Northern Uganda, the Democratic

Republic of Congo and Darfur. Each of the three situations under investigation involves thousands of wilful killings as well as intentional and large-scale sexual violence and abductions. Collectively, they have resulted in the displacement of more than 5 million people. Other situations under analysis also feature hundreds or thousands of such crimes. Taking into account all the considerations, the situation did not appear to meet the required threshold of the Statute.

\* \* \*

## Conclusion

For the above reasons, in accordance with Article 15(6) of the Rome Statute, I wish to inform you of my conclusion that, at this stage, the Statute requirements to seek authorization to initiate an investigation in the situation in Iraq have not been satisfied.

\* \* \*

Bearing in mind the limited jurisdiction of this Court, as well as its complementary nature, effectively functioning national legal systems are in principle the most appropriate and effective forum for addressing allegations of crimes of this nature.

I thank you very much for providing information regarding alleged crimes to the Office of the Prosecutor of the International Criminal Court.

\* \* \*

Yours sincerely,
Luis Moreno-Ocampo
Chief Prosecutor of the International Criminal Court

---

## Authors' Note

One of the shortcomings of the creation of the ICC was the states' inability to agree on the definition of the crime of aggression. The compromise reached in Rome was to agree to have the crime of aggression within the jurisdiction of the Court, but to prevent the exercise of jurisdiction over that crime until the State Parties could agree upon a definition of and the Court's jurisdiction over the crime. A decade later, there was almost no debate over what the definition of the crime of aggression should be, but how the court should exercise jurisdiction over the crime was hotly contested.

The United States became an observer to the ICC (meaning that they could participate in debates over the treaty but had no voting power over amendments to the treaty) largely to prevent the Court from being able to exercise jurisdiction over the crime of aggression unless the Security Council declared an act of aggression. Despite the U.S. attempts to defeat or in the alternative prevent the ICC prosecutor from being able to independently open an investigation into a crime of aggression, the international community finally adopted a definition to the crime of aggression and created two ways to create jurisdiction over the crime. First, if a State Party ratifies the amendment and commits a crime of aggression against another State Party, the Prosecutor can have jurisdiction. Material 13 discusses that this first mechanism is a very narrow grant of jurisdiction for the Prosecutor. The second scenario is through a Security Council referral to the ICC. Material 14 explains the amendments proposed to the Rome Statute concerning crimes of aggression.

---

## 11. Kevin Jon Heller, The Sadly Neutered Crime of Aggression
### Opinio Juris, 2010

I've long supported providing the ICC with jurisdiction over the crime of aggression. Call me old-fashioned, but I believe there is a great deal of truth to the IMT's insistence that "[t]o initiate a war of aggression ... is not only an international crime; it is the supreme international crime differing only from other war crimes in that it contains within itself the accumulated evil of the whole." We cannot collapse the distinction between the jus ad bellum and the jus in bello, but it is no doubt true that war crimes and crimes against humanity are particularly likely to be committed in the context of an illegal war. (See, e.g., Iraq.) Prevent the illegal war, you prevent the subsequent crimes.

The good news: the Review Conference has adopted a definition of aggression. The bad news: the conditions governing the exercise of jurisdiction make it very unlikely that any significant act of aggression will ever be prosecuted. Here is the relevant paragraph, 15 bis, concerning non-Security Council referrals [states]:

> 4. The Court may, in accordance with article 12, exercise jurisdiction over a crime of aggression, arising from an act of aggression committed by a State Party, unless that State Party has previously declared that it does not accept such jurisdiction by lodging a declaration with the Registrar. The withdrawal of such a declaration may be effected at any time and shall be considered by the State Party within three years.

> 5. In respect of a State that is not a party to this Statute, the Court shall not exercise its jurisdiction over the crime of aggression when committed by that State's nationals or on its territory.

This is, to say the least, a very restrictive provision. The following chart explains when the ICC will have jurisdiction over an act of aggression. The two actors refer to the state committing aggression (state of nationality) and the state against whom aggression is committed (territorial state). "OO" refers to a State Party that has opted out of jurisdiction.

- State Party & State Party ——> Jurisdiction
- State Party & State Party OO ——> Jurisdiction
- State Party & Non-State Party ——> No Jurisdiction
- State Party OO & State Party ——> No Jurisdiction
- State Party OO & State Party OO ——> No Jurisdiction
- State Party OO & Non-State Party ——> No Jurisdiction
- Non-State Party & State Party ——> No Jurisdiction
- Non-State Party & State Party OO ——> No Jurisdiction
- Non-State Party & Non-State Party ——> No Jurisdiction

In other words, the ICC will only have jurisdiction over an act of aggression committed by a State Party who has accepted (by omission) that jurisdiction and only when that act is committed against a State Party.

There are a number of problems with this jurisdictional regime, which deviates substantially from the regime that governs the other crimes within the ICC's jurisdiction. First, the Court will have no jurisdiction over a State Party's act of aggression against a non-State Party, even though it would have jurisdiction over war crimes and crimes against humanity committed as a result of that act. That is an unfortunate asymmetry.

Second, it permits States Parties to take an a la carte approach to the ICC's jurisdiction. I could be wrong, but I find it unlikely that any state that routinely uses force against other states (or against non-state actors located in other states) will not opt out of aggression. Why wouldn't they? There may be some reputation cost for a state not to be a part of the ICC, but it is difficult to believe that there will be any such cost for a state that joins the ICC but limits the Court's jurisdiction over it to war crimes, crimes against humanity, and genocide. The ICC's jurisdiction over aggression will thus almost certainly be limited to states that do not have either the motive or the wherewithal to commit the crime in the first place. (To be fair, the opt out provision does eliminate a possible disincentive for a state to join the ICC, which is a good thing.)

Third—and this is a serious problem—it permits States Parties to take a completely hypocritical approach to aggression. As the chart indicates, a State Party that opts out of aggression cannot be prosecuted if it commits an act of aggression against a State Party that has not opted out. But the converse is not true: States Parties that have not opted out could be prosecuted for acts of aggression against an opting-out State Party. An opting-out State Party is thus protected against aggression by other States Parties but is permitted to commit acts of aggression itself, even against States Parties that have not opted out. If anyone can think of a principled rationale for such asymmetry, let me know.

Fourth, and finally, the ICC will not have jurisdiction over a non-State Party that commits an act of aggression against a State Party, even though the Rome Statute specifically provides such territorial jurisdiction for war crimes, crimes against humanity, and genocide. Perhaps that concession was necessary to gain the support of some States Parties, although I don't understand why a State Party (opt in or opt out) would want to deprive the ICC of jurisdiction over an act of aggression committed against itself by a non-State Party. But I do not see any legal rationale for the limitation. Dapo Akande has argued that aggression is different than the other crimes in terms of the territorial state's right under international law to transfer its jurisdiction to an international tribunal. I rarely disagree with Dapo—and I feel great trepidation when I do. But I disagree with him here. It's a complicated argument, one that I hope to discuss in a later post. Suffice it to say for now (perhaps) that I don't believe that applying normal principles of territorial jurisdiction to the crime of aggression would require the Court to adjudicate the "the rights or responsibilities of a non-consenting and absent third State" any more, or any differently, than it already does for a crime against humanity involving a non-Party state agent. After all, just as the crime of aggression requires proof that a state engaged in an act of aggression, a crime against humanity requires proof that the crime took place "pursuant to or in furtherance of a State or organizational policy to commit such attack."

You will hear many voices in the coming weeks praising the Review Conference for breaking the Security Council's stranglehold on determining whether an act of aggression has occurred. There is more than a grain of truth to that; it is indeed important that the ICC will decide that issue for itself in situations within its jurisdiction. But the "within its jurisdiction" qualification is important. As the above discussion indicates, it is an open question how many acts of aggression the ICC will ever have the opportunity to adjudicate.

---

## 12. John Currie, Joanna Harrington & Valerie Oosterveld, Ending War Through Justice—In Time
### *Canadian Lawyer Magazine*, 2010

Over the past two weeks, state parties to the Rome Statute of the International Criminal Court, along with non-state-parties, non-governmental organizations, and academics, have met at a resort on Lake Victoria in Uganda to negotiate amendments to the statute, an international treaty governing the ICC's jurisdiction.

By far the most significant of these amendments would enable the world's first permanent international criminal court to hold state leaders personally responsible for waging illegal war, or the "crime of aggression."

At present, no international judicial forum holds such power. The International Court of Justice in The Hague is designed to address state-to-state disputes and questions of state responsibility. And while the ICC focuses on individual criminal responsibility, to date it has only been empowered to prosecute crimes of genocide, crimes against humanity, and war crimes.

This focused subject-matter jurisdiction was the result of intensive negotiations between states at the Rome Conference in 1998, which led to the ICC's establishment.

Readers may be aware of the court's first case concerning the enforced recruitment of child soldiers in the Democratic Republic of the Congo, its outstanding arrest warrants for leaders of the Lord's Resistance Army on charges of grave atrocities in northern Uganda, and its stated desire to prosecute Sudanese President Omar al-Bashir for mass crimes committed in Darfur.

The crime of aggression is, however, Rome's unfinished business. Following the precedent set by the prosecution at Nuremberg of "crimes against peace," states agreed in 1998 to include the crime of aggression within the nominal jurisdiction of the then-new ICC.

However, they left negotiation of the specifics, including a definition of the crime and the conditions under which the ICC would be able to prosecute it, to a future review conference.

That review conference is what brought states parties and others to Lake Victoria, just outside Kampala, Uganda, from May 31 to June 11. A "special working group on the crime of aggression" had met during the intervening years to draft proposals and lay the groundwork for bringing state parties to consensus at the review conference.

Shortly before the conference, a consensus was reached on the definition of the crime of aggression, although this was not an easy task. For a state to be accused of an act of aggression carries obvious political costs.

Moreover, the international community's previous efforts to define aggression in the 1970s were particularly arduous and in light of that experience, it is not surprising that the 1974 definition of the state act of aggression formed the basis for consensus in Kampala on the definition of the individual crime of aggression.

Some, such as the United States (a non-state-party), argued that this wording is too vague for criminal law purposes and that key issues remain outstanding—such as whether armed force used for humanitarian purposes should be excluded from the definition. However, there was little interest among state parties in reopening this long-standing debate in Kampala.

Instead, the real battle at the review conference focused on the conditions governing the court's exercise of jurisdiction over aggression, on which state delegations were deeply divided.

Some argued there was a need to accommodate a "vetting" role for the United Nations Security Council which, under the U.N. Charter, has authority to determine whether acts of aggression have occurred.

For these states, one could not ignore the post-Second World War system of international relations, which recognizes a primary role for the Security Council—and its five veto-wielding great powers—in the maintenance of international peace and security.

It was thus argued that the ICC's exercise of jurisdiction over the crime of aggression depended critically on Security Council consent.

Others, however, emphasized the Security Council is an inherently political body, dominated by the permanent five (only two of which are parties to the Rome Statute). They argued the ICC, as a judicial body, must be free from interference or fetters by such a highly politicized institution.

There was also an element within the conference that was clearly willing—and perhaps even keen—to dilute the Security Council's near-monopoly on matters of international peace and security.

These divisions were pronounced throughout the conference, notwithstanding proposal after proposal tabled in an effort to accommodate the bottom lines of all delegations.

In the end, and indeed in the very late hours of the warm east African night following a marathon last day of negotiations, it was decided to allow the ICC to exercise jurisdiction over the crime of aggression without the need for prior Security Council authorization. However, this grant of independent jurisdiction is subject to significant caveats. It does not extend to acts of aggression committed on the territory of or by nationals of non-state parties (unless the Security Council refers the matter to the ICC). It is subject to declarations of non-acceptance by state parties.

And, perhaps most significantly, it will not come into effect until 2017 at the earliest, and even then only if state parties positively decide to activate this new aspect of the court's jurisdiction.

Is this a pyrrhic victory in the battle against impunity for the "supreme international crime?"

We do not believe so. Superficially, it may seem self-defeating to define the crime of aggression and agree on the modalities for its prosecution only to defer effective entry into force and allow states to opt out of the regime.

But it is important not to underestimate the significance of two fundamental characteristics of the international legal system: symbolism and incrementalism.

Enforceability has always been international law's Achilles heel, yet international law profoundly influences state behaviour and, increasingly, that of individuals. It largely does so, we believe, through its symbolic power.

The ICC itself is a potent symbol of accountability that has captured the world's imagination. There is every reason to believe the Rome Statute's newly minted (if historically inspired) definition and denunciation of aggression as a "most serious crime of international concern" will play an equally influential symbolic role, whether or not it is actually prosecuted in the short term.

As for incrementalism, it is important to recall—embedded as we are in a culture of instant gratification—that international law, including international criminal law, is a slowly evolving and maturing phenomenon.

From the abortive attempts to prosecute the German kaiser after the First World War for a "supreme offence against international morality," to Nuremberg's successful if limited prosecutions of "crimes against peace," to the long Cold War years that stymied attempts to translate Nuremberg's improvised justice into a system of international criminal law, to the eventual establishment of the ICC in 1998—the road to the Kampala amendments defining aggression and the modalities for its prosecution has been long and tortuous.

In this perspective, the caveats and delays built into those amendments are merely a last few twists on the final approaches to the destination. Those impatient to see the ICC exercise its jurisdiction over the crime of aggression may therefore take comfort that it is now simply a matter of time.

## 13. States Which are Party to the ICC

As of 15 February 2013, 122 countries are States Parties to the Rome Statute of the International Criminal Court. Out of them 34 are African States, 18 are Asia-Pacific States, 18 are from Eastern Europe, 27 are from Latin American and Caribbean States, and 25 are from Western European and other States.

A

Afghanistan, Albania, Andorra, Antigua and Barbuda, Argentina, Australia, and Austria

B

Bangladesh, Barbados, Belgium, Belize, Benin, Bolivia, Bosnia and Herzegovina, Botswana, Brazil, Bulgaria, Burkina Faso, and Burundi

C

Cambodia, Canada, Cape Verde, Central African Republic, Chad, Chile, Colombia, Comoros, Congo, Cook Islands, Costa Rica, Cote d'Ivoire, Croatia, Cyprus, and Czech Republic

D

Democratic Republic of the Congo, Denmark, Djibouti, Dominica, and Dominican Republic

E

Ecuador and Estonia

F

Fiji, Finland, and France

G

Gabon, Gambia, Georgia, Germany, Ghana, Greece, Grenada, Guatemala, Guinea, and Guyana

H

Honduras and Hungary

I

Iceland, Ireland, and Italy

J

Japan and Jordan

K

Kenya

L

Latvia, Lesotho, Liberia, Liechtenstein, Lithuania, and Luxembourg

M

Madagascar, Malawi, Maldives, Mali, Malta, Marshall Islands, Mauritius, Mexico, Mongolia, and Montenegro

N

Namibia, Nauru, Netherlands, New Zealand, Niger, Nigeria, and Norway

P

Panama, Paraguay, Peru, Philippines, Poland, and Portugal

R

Republic of Korea, Republic of Moldova, and Romania

S

Saint Kitts and Nevis, Saint Lucia, Saint Vincent and the Grenadines, Samoa, San Marino Senegal, Serbia, Seychelles, Sierra Leone, Slovakia, Slovenia, South Africa, Spain, Suriname, Sweden, and Switzerland

T

Tajikistan, The Former Yugoslav Republic of Macedonia, Timor-Leste, Trinidad and Tobago, and Tunisia

U

Uganda, United Kingdom, United Republic of Tanzania, and Uruguay

V

Vanuatu and Venezuela

Z

Zambia

---

# 14. Rome Statute of the International Criminal Court [Abridged]

see http://untreaty.un.org/cod/icc/statute/romefra.htm for full copy

### Article 1

### The Court

An International Criminal Court ("the Court") is hereby established. It shall be a permanent institution and shall have the power to exercise its jurisdiction over persons for the most serious crimes of international concern, as referred to in this Statute, and shall be complementary to national criminal jurisdictions. The jurisdiction and functioning of the Court shall be governed by the provisions of this Statute.

\* \* \*

### Article 4

### Legal status and powers of the Court

1. The Court shall have international legal personality. It shall also have such legal capacity as may be necessary for the exercise of its functions and the fulfilment of its purposes.

2. The Court may exercise its functions and powers, as provided in this Statute, on the territory of any State Party and, by special agreement, on the territory of any other State.

### Article 5

### Crimes within the jurisdiction of the Court

1. The jurisdiction of the Court shall be limited to the most serious crimes of concern to the international community as a whole. The Court has jurisdiction in accordance with this Statute with respect to the following crimes:

    (a)  The crime of genocide;

    (b)  Crimes against humanity;

    (c)  War crimes;

    (d)  The crime of aggression.

2.    The Court shall exercise jurisdiction over the crime of aggression [ ... ] Such a provision shall be consistent with the relevant provisions of the Charter of the United Nations.

### Article 6

### Genocide

For the purpose of this Statute, "genocide" means any of the following acts committed with intent to destroy, in whole or in part, a national, ethnical, racial or religious group, as such:

    (a)  Killing members of the group;

    (b)  Causing serious bodily or mental harm to members of the group;

    (c)  Deliberately inflicting on the group conditions of life calculated to bring about its physical destruction in whole or in part;

    (d)  Imposing measures intended to prevent births within the group;

    (e)  Forcibly transferring children of the group to another group.

### Article 7

### Crimes against humanity

1.    For the purpose of this Statute, "crime against humanity" means any of the following acts when committed as part of a widespread or systematic attack directed against any civilian population, with knowledge of the attack:

    (a)  Murder;

    (b)  Extermination;

    (c)  Enslavement;

    (d)  Deportation or forcible transfer of population;

* * *

    (f)  Torture;

    (g)  Rape, sexual slavery, enforced prostitution, forced pregnancy, enforced sterilization, or any other form of sexual violence of comparable gravity;

    (h)  Persecution against any identifiable group or collectivity on political, racial, national, ethnic, cultural, religious, gender [ ... ]

    (i)  Enforced disappearance of persons;

    (j)  The crime of apartheid;

    (k)  Other inhumane acts of a similar character intentionally causing great suffering, or serious injury to body or to mental or physical health.

### Article 8

### War crimes

1.    The Court shall have jurisdiction in respect of war crimes in particular when committed as part of a plan or policy or as part of a large-scale commission of such crimes.

2. For the purpose of this Statute, "war crimes" means:

(a) Grave breaches of the Geneva Conventions of 12 August 1949, namely, any of the following acts against persons or property protected under the provisions of the relevant Geneva Convention:

  (i) Wilful killing;

  (ii) Torture

* * *

(b) Other serious violations of the laws and customs applicable in international armed conflict, within the established framework of international law, namely, any of the following acts:

  (i) Intentionally directing attacks against the civilian population as such or against individual civilians not taking direct part in hostilities;

* * *

  (iv) Intentionally launching an attack in the knowledge that such attack will cause incidental loss of life or injury to civilians or damage to civilian objects or widespread, long-term and severe damage to the natural environment which would be clearly excessive in relation to the concrete and direct overall military advantage anticipated;

* * *

## Article 12

### Preconditions to the exercise of jurisdiction

1. A State which becomes a Party to this Statute thereby accepts the jurisdiction of the Court with respect to the crimes referred to in article 5.

2. In the case of article 13, paragraph (a) or (c), the Court may exercise its jurisdiction if one or more of the following States are Parties to this Statute or have accepted the jurisdiction of the Court in accordance with paragraph 3:

(a) The State on the territory of which the conduct in question occurred or, if the crime was committed on board a vessel or aircraft, the State of registration of that vessel or aircraft;

(b) The State of which the person accused of the crime is a national.

3. If the acceptance of a State which is not a Party to this Statute is required under paragraph 2, that State may, by declaration lodged with the Registrar, accept the exercise of jurisdiction by the Court with respect to the crime in question.

## Article 13

### Exercise of jurisdiction

The Court may exercise its jurisdiction with respect to a crime referred to in article 5 in accordance with the provisions of this Statute if:

(a) A situation in which one or more of such crimes appears to have been committed is referred to the Prosecutor by a State Party in accordance with article 14;

* * *

(c) The Prosecutor has initiated an investigation in respect of such a crime in accordance with article 15.

* * *

## Article 15

### Prosecutor

1. The Prosecutor may initiate investigations proprio motu on the basis of information on crimes within the jurisdiction of the Court.

2. The Prosecutor shall analyse the seriousness of the information received. For this purpose, he or she may seek additional information from States, organs of the United Nations, intergovernmental or non-governmental organizations, or other reliable sources that he or she deems appropriate, and may receive written or oral testimony at the seat of the Court.

3. If the Prosecutor concludes that there is a reasonable basis to proceed with an investigation, he or she shall submit to the Pre-Trial Chamber a request for authorization of an investigation, together with any supporting material collected.

* * *

6. If, after the preliminary examination referred to in paragraphs 1 and 2, the Prosecutor concludes that the information provided does not constitute a reasonable basis for an investigation, he or she shall inform those who provided the information. This shall not preclude the Prosecutor from considering further information submitted to him or her regarding the same situation in the light of new facts or evidence.

* * *

## Article 17

### Issues of admissibility

1. Having regard to paragraph 10 of the Preamble and article 1, the Court shall determine that a case is inadmissible where:

   (a) The case is being investigated or prosecuted by a State which has jurisdiction over it, unless the State is unwilling or unable genuinely to carry out the investigation or prosecution;

   (b) The case has been investigated by a State which has jurisdiction over it and the State has decided not to prosecute the person concerned, unless the decision resulted from the unwillingness or inability of the State genuinely to prosecute.

* * *

## Article 53

### Initiation of an investigation

1. The Prosecutor shall, having evaluated the information made available to him or her, initiate an investigation unless he or she determines that there is no reasonable basis to proceed under this Statute. In deciding whether to initiate an investigation, the Prosecutor shall consider whether:

   (a) The information available to the Prosecutor provides a reasonable basis to believe that a crime within the jurisdiction of the Court has been or is being committed;

   (b) The case is or would be admissible under article 17; and

   (c) Taking into account the gravity of the crime and the interests of victims, there are nonetheless substantial reasons to believe that an investigation would not serve the interests of justice.

# 15. Bibliography of Additional Sources

- Dinah Shelton, INTERNATIONAL CRIMES, PEACE, AND HUMAN RIGHTS: THE ROLE OF THE INTERNATIONAL CRIMINAL COURT (2000).

- Sarah B. Sewall and Carl Kaysen, THE UNITED STATES AND THE INTERNATIONAL CRIMINAL COURT: NATIONAL SECURITY AND INTERNATIONAL LAW (2000).

- Flavia Lattanzi, THE INTERNATIONAL CRIMINAL COURT: COMMENTS ON THE DRAFT STATUTE (1998).

- Roy S. Lee, THE INTERNATIONAL CRIMINAL COURT: THE MAKING OF THE ROME STATUTE (1999).

- Kelly Dawn Askin, WAR CRIMES AGAINST WOMEN: PROSECUTION IN INTERNATIONAL CRIMES TRIBUNALS (1997).

- Gary Jonathan Bass, STAY THE HAND OF VENGEANCE: THE POLITICS OF WAR CRIMES TRIBUNALS (2000).

- M. Cherif Bassiouni, CRIMES AGAINST HUMANITY IN INTERNATIONAL CRIMINAL LAW (1999).

- John R.W.D. Jones, THE PRACTICE OF INTERNATIONAL CRIMINAL TRIBUNALS FOR THE FORMER YUGOSLAVIA AND RWANDA (2000).

- Timothy L.H. McCormack & Gerry J. Simpson (eds.), THE LAW OF WAR CRIMES: NATIONAL AND INTERNATIONAL APPROACHES (1997).

- Virginia Morris and Michael Scharf, AN INSIDER'S GUIDE TO THE INTERNATIONAL CRIMINAL TRIBUNAL FOR THE FORMER YUGOSLAVIA, vol.1 (1995).

- Jordan J. Paust et al., INTERNATIONAL CRIMINAL LAW (1996).

- Steven R. Ratner & Jason S. Abrams, ACCOUNTABILITY FOR HUMAN RIGHTS ATROCITIES IN INTERNATIONAL LAW: BEYOND THE NUREMBERG LEGACY (1997).

- Telford Taylor, THE ANATOMY OF THE NUREMBERG TRIALS (1992).

- Sharon A. Williams ed., INTERNATIONAL CRIMINAL LAW, 8th ed. (1995).

- Sven Alkalaj, Never Again, 23 FORDHAM INT'L L.J. 357 (1999).

- Louise Arbour, The Legal Profession and Human Rights: Progress and Challenges in International Criminal Justice, 21 FORDHAM INT'L L.J. 531 (1997).

- David S. Bloch & Elon Weinstein, Velvet Glove and Iron Fist: A New Paradigm for the Permanent War Crimes Court, 22 HASTINGS INT'L & COMP. L. REV. 1 (1998).

- Carlyn M. Carey, Internal Displacement: Is Prevention Through Accountability Possible? A Kosovo Case Study, 49 AM. U.L. REV. 243 (1999).

- Mark S. Ellis, Achieving Justice Before the International War Crimes Tribunal: Challenges for the Defense, 7 DUKE J. COMP. & INT'L L. 519 (1997).

- The Human Rights Center and the International Human Rights Law Clinic, Justice, Accountability and Social Reconstruction: An Interview Study of Bosnian Judges and Prosecutors, 18 BERK. J. INT'L LAW 102 (2000).

- Matthew Lippman, The Convention on the Prevention and Punishment of the Crime of Genocide: Fifty Years Later, 15 ARIZ. J. INT'L & COMP. LAW 415 (1998).

- Cheryl K. Moralez, Establishing an International Criminal Court: Will it Work? 4 DePaul Int'l L.J. 135 (2000).

- Judge Jon O. Newman, Toward an International Civil War Claims Tribunal, 12 Conn. J. Int'l L. 245 (1997).

- Mary Margaret Penrose, It's Good to Be the King: Prosecuting Heads of State and Former Heads of State Under International Law, 39 Colum. J. Transnat'l L. 193 (2000).

- Mary Margaret Penrose, Lest We Fail: The Importance of Enforcement in International Criminal Law, 15 Am. U. Int'l L. Rev. 321 (2000)

- Peggy E. Rancilio, From Nuremberg to Rome: Establishing an International Criminal Court and the Need for U.S. Participation, 77 U. Det. Mercy L. Rev. 155 (1999)

- Leila Nadya Sadat & S. Richard Carden, The New International Criminal Court: An Uneasy Revolution, 88 Geo. L.J. 381, (2000).
- Ivan Simonovic, The Role of the ICTY in the Development of International Criminal Adjudication, 23 Fordham Int'l L.J. 440 (1999).

- William A. Schabas, Sentencing by International Tribunals: A Human Rights Approach, 7 Duke J. Comp. & Int'l L. 461 (1997).

- Michael P. Scharf, The Tools for Enforcing International Criminal Justice in the New Millennium: Lessons From the Yugoslavia Tribunal, 49 DePaul L. Rev. 925 (2000).

- Michael Scharf & Valerie Epps, The International Trial of the Century? A "Cross-Fire" Exchange on the First Case Before the Yugoslavia War Crimes Tribunal, 29 Cornell Int'l L.J. 635 (1996).

- James L. Taulbee, A Call to Arms Declined: The United States and the International Criminal Court, 14 Emory Int'l L. Rev. 105 (2000).

- Mark R. Von Sternberg, A Comparison of the Yugoslavian and Rwandan War Crimes Tribunals: Universal Jurisdiction and the Elementary Dictates of Humanity, 22 Brooklyn J. Int'l L. 111 (1996).

- Kristijan Zic, The International Criminal Tribunal for the Former Yugoslavia: Applying International Law to War Criminals, 16 B.U. Int'l L.J. 507 (1998).

# Part VI
# Financial Issues and Institutions

# Chapter XXII

# United Nations Financing

## Introduction

This chapter deals with the financial structure of the U.N. and the relationship between the U.N. and the United States vis-à-vis U.N. financing. The chapter begins with an explanation of the U.N.'s basic financing scheme, which provides that U.N. Member States must make financial contributions to the U.N.. While the U.N. Charter establishes a penalty for a Member State's non-payment of its dues, the penalty has never been enforced. Despite this lack of censure for indebted Member States, the negative effects of irregular payment and non-payment of U.N. dues are felt across the spectrum of U.N. initiatives.

The United States is the largest financial contributor to the U.N., but, as of January 2011, it owed the U.N. more than $700 million in arrears. The chapter will explore the political complexities and the desire to reform the U.N., rather than a simple unwillingness to pay, which underlie the accumulation of U.S. arrears.

## Objectives

- To understand the basics of the U.N. financial structure.

- To understand the funding mechanisms for U.N. peacekeeping and development operations, the war crimes tribunals, and the International Criminal Court.

- To understand the impact of non-payment of Member State dues on U.N. agencies and operations.

- To understand the relationship between the U.N. and the United States concerning U.N. financing.

- To understand the complexity of the United States' decision-making concerning its funding of U.N. activities.

# Problems

Students should come to class prepared to discuss the following questions:

1.  What are the various options the framers of the U.N. Charter could have considered for funding the U.N.?

2.  How are the budget of the U.N. and the assessment for each Member State set?

3.  Is the duty of Member States to pay their assessed contributions a moral duty or a legal duty? Is this duty enforceable?

4.  Are there any arguments that can justify unilateral withholdings of assessed contributions?

5.  What are the practical consequences to the U.N. of the U.S. withholdings since the 1980s?

# Case Studies and Negotiation Simulations

Drawing from the materials in this chapter, students should come to class prepared to participate in the following case studies:

**United States:** In 2005, the United States House of Representatives approved the United Nations Reform Act of 2005, which would require the United States to withhold fifty percent of its assessed contributions to the U.N. until the U.N. adopted thirty-two of forty U.S.-proposed reforms. Although the House passed this bill, the Senate did not. For purposes of this study, assume the two houses of Congress have approved the bill by a narrow margin and the President has called a meeting of his advisors to decide whether to veto the legislation or sign it into law. Discuss the following questions from the perspectives of the Secretary of State, the Attorney General, and the National Security Advisor.

On the Regular Budget:

a.  Should the current formula and scale for the payment of assessments be changed. If so, how?

b.  How should payment of assessments be enforced?

c.  Should the United Nations be given the authority to charge interest on late payments?

d.  Should the United Nations impose a special assessment to replenish the reserve fund?

e.  Should the United Nations be prohibited from borrowing funds from the peacekeeping budget to cover regular budget expenditures?

f.  Should the financing of administrative expenses for the voluntary programs be financed as part of the regular budget?

On the Peacekeeping Budget:

a.  Should there be a unified budget to cover the costs of all ongoing missions as well as one or two additional operations?

b.   Should the revolving fund be increased from $150 million?

On Charter Reform:

a.   Should voting on all issues concerning the budget and financing of expenditures require a weighted voting based on contributions. If so, what formula should be used?

b.   Should the United Nations have the power to tax. If so, what should be taxed?

# Materials

1.  U.N. Charter, Articles 17, 19.

2.  Jose E. Alvarez, *Financial Responsibility*, THE UNITED NATIONS AND INTERNATIONAL LAW (Christopher C. Joyner ed., 1995).

3.  U.N. DEPARTMENT OF MANAGEMENT, *Financial Situation*, (June 2011).

4.  Ruben P. Mendez, *Financing the United Nations and the International Public Sector: Problems and Reform*, 3 GLOBAL GOVERNANCE 283, 286–87 (Sept.–Dec. 1997).

5.  UNITED NATIONS PEACEKEEPING, *Financing Peacekeeping*.

6.  Marjorie Ann Browne and Kennon H. Nakamura, CONG. RESEARCH SERV., RL 33611, UNITED NATIONS SYSTEM FUNDING: CONGRESSIONAL ISSUES 32–33 (2011).

7.  1998 Rome Statute of the International Criminal Court [I.C.C.] U.N. Doc. PC-NICC/1999/INF/3.

8.  Cesare Romano & Thordis Ingadottir, PROJECT ON INTERNATIONAL COURTS & TRIBUNALS, THE FINANCING OF THE INTERNATIONAL CRIMINAL COURT: A DISCUSSION PAPER 3–6 (2000).

9.  2008 International Criminal Court [I.C.C.] Doc. ICC-ASP/7/5 (Part II-D).

10.  Michael Scharf and Tamara Shaw, *International Institutions*, 33 THE INTERNATIONAL LAWYER 567–70 (1999).

11.  Sean D. Murphy, *Contemporary Practice of the United States Relating to International Law*, 94 AM. J. INT'L L. 348, 348–54 (2000).

12.  *Statement of U.S. Permanent Representative-Designate Susan E. Rice Before the S. Comm. on Foreign Relations*, 111th Cong. (2009).

13.  Bibliography of Additional Sources

## Authors' Note

Article 17 of the Charter of the United Nations grants the General Assembly the responsibility for determining the budgets of the U.N., as a whole, and specialized U.N. agencies. Article 19 provides that a member state that fails to comply with its financial obligation to the U.N. may be prohibited from voting at the General Assembly, unless it is determined that the state's inability to meet its obligation resulted from a matter outside of its control.

---

## 1. U.N. Charter, Articles 17, 19

### Article 17

1.  The General Assembly shall consider and approve the budget of the Organization.

2.  The expenses of the Organization shall be borne by the Members as apportioned by the General Assembly.

3.  The General Assembly shall consider and approve any financial and budgetary arrangements with specialized agencies referred to in Article 57 and shall examine the administrative budgets of such specialized agencies with a view to making recommendations to the agencies concerned.

### Article 19

A Member of the United Nations which is in arrears in the payment of its financial contributions to the Organization shall have no vote in the General Assembly if the amount of its arrears equals or exceeds the amount of the contributions due from it for the preceding two full years. The General Assembly may, nevertheless, permit such a Member to vote if it is satisfied that the failure to pay is due to conditions beyond the control of the Member.

---

## *Authors' Note*

In the following article, Professor Jose Alvarez discusses the obligation of U.N. Member States to underwrite U.N. system organizations and the various manifestations of this financial obligation. The author also provides an overview of the International Court of Justice (ICJ) 1962 advisory opinion in the Certain Expenses of the United Nations, which concluded that Articles 17 and 19 of the U.N. Charter are legally binding on Member States. Following the Expenses case, many commentators suggested that Member States have no duty to pay for the U.N.'s *ultra vires* activities, but Alvarez seeks to refute these arguments. Alvarez also discusses the inefficacy of Article 19's loss of vote sanction on member states in arrears and the resulting challenges to the U.N. system.

---

## 2. Jose E. Alvarez, Financial Responsibility
### *The United Nations and International Law*, 1995

U.N. system organizations have relied on a variety of methods for financing, not all of which are specified in their constituent instruments. [ … ]

All U.N. system organizations rely on assessed contributions from member states, although the method of apportionment varies. None apportion these assessments in equal shares and most use scales of assessment on which a certain percentage is assessed to each member. The United Nations Charter leaves the formula for determining assessments, as well as the actual level, to be determined by the political will of the U.N.'s plenary organ, the General Assembly, which is charged with the power to approve the budget. The General Assembly, through its Committee on Contributions, has varied the percentage of the regular U.N. budget assessed to individual states over the years but has adhered, at least in principle, to "capacity to pay" as the basis for assessment. It has also adopted both minimum and maximum assessment levels. The U.N. assessment scale has been adopted by many of the other U.N. system organizations, including the ILO, FAQ, WHO, UNESCO, UNJDO, and the IAEA. Other organizations, such as ICAO and the WMO, base their scale of assessments at least in part on the interest individual members have in the work of the organization. Changes in individual members' percentage assessments have varied in response to institutional changes such as the withdrawal of members, as well as to political pressure.

While the U.N. Charter and some of the constituent instruments of other U.N. system organizations say nothing about them, voluntary contributions are the second primary source of funds. Voluntary contributions provide an increasing portion of the total source of funds for U.N. system organizations for a number of reasons. They are a cost-effective way for major donors to achieve influence since these funds, unlike assessed contributions, usually can be earmarked for the donor's favored projects or consist of aid in kind, such as training scholarships, which can also serve to tailor the assistance to a donor's policies. Major donors, such as the United States, can use voluntary contributions to reward some programs or agencies and penalize others. For the U.N., reliance on this seemingly unauthorized source of funds accords with the established practice of several Leagues of Nations-era organizations which had also turned to such contributions from both governmental and nongovernmental sources. The capacity to create separate trust funds for the administration of such funds has been accepted as inherent when not specifically authorized by constitutional provision. Such contributions are, by definition, nonmandatory but have become a customary source of funds. Thus, the IAEA, for example, engages in systematic solicitation of voluntary contributions, in which members are requested to meet specific "targets," to be used to support its "operational programme" (principally technical assistance). "Pledging conferences" at which members announce their voluntary contributions have become common in many U.N. system organizations. The allocation as well as any restrictions on the receipt of such funds, such as with respect to gifts tendered with conditions from both governmental and nongovernmental sources, is sometimes the subject of direct provision in the organization's financial regulations.

Generally speaking, income generated from other sources is not as significant a source of revenue as assessed and voluntary contributions. Nonetheless, certain organizations, such as the IAEA, derive some revenue from equipment, facilities or materials furnished or services rendered to members, individuals, or other organizations. Some, such as the U.N. Postal Administration and UNICEF, sell products directly to the public, while several have raised money from investments or secured commercial or other loans. Since generally U.N. international civil servants pay no national taxes but U.S. nationals in the Secretariat do pay U.S. taxes, many U.N. system organizations attempt to equalize the situation by raising gross salaries for their personnel while imposing a differential salary levy or "staff assessment." For the U.N. this additional source of revenue constitutes approximately 16 percent of all regular income.

Most of the controversy surrounding the financing of U.N. system organizations results from the decision of the drafters of the U.N. Charter to attempt to rectify the "pitfalls which had so hamstrung the financial activities of the League." Thus, Article 17 of the Charter establishes the principle that members of the Organization bear a collective financial responsibility to the Organization. In the words of Article 17(2), the "expenses of the organization shall be borne by the Members as apportioned by the General Assembly." In contradistinction to the original League of Nations Covenant which did not specify which organ was responsible for setting the budget, required unanimity on budgetary matters, and established an inflexible basis of apportionment, the Charter provides that the General Assembly can approve the budget by a two-thirds vote, leaves the level of assessment open to flexible determination, and states that members overdue in their payments for two full years "shall" have no vote in the General Assembly unless the Assembly determines otherwise. The constituent instruments of all U.N. system organizations, with the exception of those financial organizations, such as the IMF, which permit weighted voting, follow a similar approach. The result is that two-thirds of the members of these organizations can impose a budget which is not to the liking of as many as one-third of their members. This potential "tyranny of the majority" is exacerbated by the fact that whereas voting in the plenary or general conference of the organization is typically on the basis of one state, one vote, U.N. system assessments vary from the U.S.'s 25 percent to the minimum of 0.01 percent.

U.N. system organizations have attempted, within the framework of their own constituent instruments and financial regulations, to deal with the potential "tyranny of the majority" problem with varying degrees of success. Some, like the IAEA, turn to two-tier budgets: "administrative" expenses (covering the costs of running the organization, including personnel and buildings) are covered by assessed contributions, while "operational" expenses (costs of projects performed by the organization) are covered by voluntary contributions or on a fee-for-service basis. Since for most U.N. system organizations, administrative expenses constitute by far the largest part of their overall budgets, this approach diffuses the "tyranny of the majority" problem only to a limited extent. The U.N. itself has, particularly since 1962, sometimes turned de facto to a similar approach, despite Article 17 of the Charter which provides only that the Assembly "consider and approve the budget," without limitation to administrative expenses. A variety of operational projects, including some peacekeeping activities, have been funded through voluntary contributions.

Despite these attempts, the U.N., like the League of Nations, is no stranger to financial crises. Withholdings of particular peacekeeping expenses included as part of the regular budget led to the Assembly's nineteenth (1964) session which, rather than confront the question of whether the Article 19 loss of vote sanction should be applied to defaulting states, conducted all business without benefit of vote. In that same year the spiraling budgets of some U.N. specialized agencies led major donors to form an intergovernmental group, the Geneva Group, to press for reduced expenditures and greater financial accountability. In more recent times, concern over the growing dominance of third-world states over UNESCO's budget led the U.S. Congress to withdraw from that organization. In addition, starting in 1978, the United States Congress and/or its Executive enacted a series of specific restrictions on the payment of U.S. assessed contributions to particular U.N. programs, including threats to withhold a progressively higher proportion of U.S. annual assessments unless U.N. system budgets are adopted on the basis of "weighted voting." Such deliberate withholdings by the United States and at one point as many as seventeen other members, delays in making assessed contributions, and threats to withhold either portions of or the entirety of assessments continue to plague the U.N. and many of its specialized agencies. The result, for much of the 1980s, were periodic warnings by the U.N. Secretary-General that the U.N. was in imminent threat of bankruptcy.

"Budgetary reforms" were instituted, including, in 1986, the "gentleman's agreement" contained in GA Res. 41/213 which, while it reaffirmed that the provisions of the Charter on budget-making prevail, opted for decision-making by consensus in budget-making committees. These reforms placated those calling for a change in the "one state/one vote" budget-making scheme without amending the Charter but have not resolved underlying legal and practical difficulties. In the 1990s many member governments, including the

United States, continue to fail to pay their annual assessed contributions to the regular budget within the time period for payment required in the Financial Regulations, thereby causing uncertainty, cash shortages, and increasing resort to alternative, and possibly expensive, sources of funds within affected agencies. As of March 1996, arrearages for member countries were $3.3 billion—$1.6 billion in the regular budget and $1.7 billion for the peacekeeping budget. About one-third of that total is owed by the United States, which is obligated to pay one quarter of both budgets. U.S. pledges to repay its accumulated arrears and future assessed contributions remain contingent, however, on the U.N.'s continued progress in achieving "budgetary restraint" and on the Organization's continued adherence to consensus-based budget-making. Indeed, recent developments have led many to suggest that major contributors to U.N. system organizations are now exercising or threatening to exercise a financial veto never anticipated by the drafters of the U.N. Charter—often in addition to the Security Council veto given permanent members. By 1994 the Organization's finances had come under such severe strain that there was serious discussion of a revision to the scale of assessments.

The ICJ's 1962 Advisory Opinion in Certain Expenses of the United Nations is the necessary starting point to an understanding of the scope of the General Assembly's appropriations power under Article 17. In that instance, France and the Soviet Union challenged the validity of certain peacekeeping expenses. France argued that the General Assembly was not a world legislature or a "super-state" but had only the limited power to impose on members the legal obligation to pay for "administrative" expenses; the costs for peacekeeping were not among the "expenses" included in Article 17. The Soviets contended that such expenses could "be determined only on the basis of special agreements to be concluded by the Security Council and the Member States of the Organization" and that, in any case, since all General Assembly resolutions are hortatory in nature, they "cannot establish legal obligations for the Member States of the Organization." The United States argued by contrast that Article 17 had been intended to state a "general principle ... applicable to all associations, that legally incurred expenses of an association must be borne by all its members in common"; that both the terms of the Charter and subsequent practice confirmed the "exclusive character of the fiscal authority of the General Assembly"; and that the power of the General Assembly to create "legally binding financial obligations" was not limited to "administrative" expenses but extended to peacekeeping. To the U.S., Article 17 was a clear statement that "the United Nations can pay for what it is empowered to do" and "what the United Nations can do, it can pay for."

The ICJ's majority advisory opinion essentially affirmed the legally binding nature of General Assembly budgetary resolutions, rejecting the French and Soviet positions with respect to the specific peacekeeping expenses at issue as well as their more general arguments with respect to the meaning of Article 17. Although the Court refused to define "expenses of the organization" for purposes of Article 17, it stated that "such expenditures must be tested by their relationship to the purposes of the United Nations in the sense that if the expenditure were made for a purpose which is not one of the purposes of the United Nations, it could not be considered an 'expense of the Organization.'" The Court noted that [the Charter] purposes are broad indeed, but neither they nor the powers conferred to effectuate them are unlimited. Save as they have entrusted the Organization with the attainment of these common ends, the Member States retain their freedom of action. But when the Organization takes action which warrants the assertion that it was appropriate for the fulfillment of one of the stated purposes of the United Nations, the presumption is that such action is not ultra vires the Organization.

In response to the contention that General Assembly resolutions are only hortatory under Article 10 of the Charter, Fitzmaurice, in a separate concurring opinion, argued that the rule *generalis specialibus non derogant* applies and "the special obligation to contribute to the expenses incurred in carrying them out prevails, and applies even to Member States voting against." To Fitzmaurice, the duty to contribute to the regular expenses of the organization would have arisen "as a matter of inherent necessity" since even in the absence of Article 17, paragraph 2, a general obligation for Member States collectively to finance the Organization would have to be read into the Charter, on the basis of the same principle as the Court applied in [the Reparations case], namely, "by necessary implication as being essential to the performance of its [i.e., the Organization's] duties." Joining the Organization, in short, means accepting the burden and the obligation of contributing to financing. On this view, a legal duty to pay for at least the administrative expenses of the organization would have arisen, even in the absence of Article 17, based on customary international law.

The General Assembly's subsequent acceptance of this advisory opinion did not lead to any immediate change in either France's or the Soviet Union's position with respect to the questioned expenses. It also did not lead to the application of Article 19 which provides that members in arrears shall have no vote in the General Assembly if the amount of its arrears equals or exceeds the amount of the contributions due from it for the preceding two full years. The General Assembly may, nevertheless, permit such a Member to vote if it is satisfied that the failure to pay is due to conditions beyond the control of the Member.

The United States had urged that this loss of vote sanction was "mandatory and automatic" in the absence of a General Assembly vote to the contrary; the Soviets had argued otherwise. The result was the announcement by U.S. Ambassador Goldberg that, while the U.S. still adhered to its views on the binding nature of Article 17 and the automatic loss of vote sanction of Article 19, the U.S. would not seek to frustrate the consensus of the General Assembly in not applying the sanction in this instance. Instead he indicated that: if any Member State could make an exception to the principle of collective financial responsibility with respect to certain United Nations activities, the United States reserved the same option to make exceptions if, in its view, there were strong and compelling reasons to do so. There could be no double standard among the Members of the Organization.

Despite the enforcement difficulties, the ICJ's advisory opinion had an immediate effect on subsequent Security Council practice. Eventually, the Security Council felt free to assess particular peacekeeping expenses as part of assessed, obligatory contributions. While the legal status of the U.S.'s so-called "Goldberg Reservation" has been repeatedly questioned, more significant ambiguities have emerged in the wake of the Court's acknowledgment that the General Assembly's apportionment power, and presumably members' duties to pay, are limited by the Charter. The opinions rendered in the Expenses case, as well as pleadings in that case, have led most commentators to conclude that members have no legal duty to pay for ultra vires acts, that is, those involving "manifest" violations of the Charter, such as an expense that is not in accord with the substantive purposes of the Charter or has been enacted in violation with the procedural requirements established by the Charter, as, for example, an expense authorized by the wrong organ or by a less than two-thirds vote of the General Assembly. Nonetheless, the consequences that flow from this conclusion are far from clear. In particular, does "manifest" illegality render the Organization's action void ab initio such that a member can unilaterally withhold payment corresponding to such action or is the action merely voidable if the Organization or some third party, such as the World Court, makes a determination that the action is ultra vires?

This question has reemerged in the wake of repeated challenges to U.N. authorized expenses, particularly by the United States. Even at the height of U.S. withholding in the mid-1980s, U.S. officials usually continued to adhere to the U.S. position before the JCJ in 1962 that there is a legally binding duty to pay assessed contributions. To the extent that legalities were raised, U.S. officials characterized many U.S. withholdings as appropriate responses to "ultra vires" acts by the U.N.. U.S. officials condemned expenditures on behalf of the PLO, SWAPO, or the Decade of Racism or GA Resolution 33/79 as violations of the Charter or contrary to international law. Similarly, expenses for the Law of the Sea Preparatory Commission were branded as "illegal" because the Commission was not a "subsidiary organ" answerable to the U.N.. Alleged "kickbacks" by seconded U.N. officials allegedly violated Articles 100–101 of the Charter providing for independent international civil servants.

With the possible exception of U.S. withholdings regarding the Law of the Sea Preparatory Commission, scholars have not found the threadbare U.S. legal justifications for these withholdings convincing. Thus, commentators found at most political, not legal, justifications for those withholdings designed to effect budgetary reforms such as Kassebaum, withholdings for the Ethiopian Conference Center, and other across-the-board cuts. Frederic Kirgis found U.S. threats growing out of the possibility of a change in status of the PLO not justified under treaty law and "disproportionate" as a legitimate reprisal. Further, the factual or legal premises underlying other U.S. withholdings have been or remain questionable. Finally, there are difficulties squaring withholdings with the U.N.'s internal law since nothing in the U.N.'s Financial Regulations authorizes the organization to accept "earmarked" contributions; as the U.S. government repeatedly argued prior to 1980, the Secretary-General is "not authorized to finance some programs in the regular budget and not finance others." Thus, shortfalls in members' contributions to the regular budget, however intended to "target" allegedly ultra vires activities, affect all U.N. programs equally, and not solely the targeted activity. Similar objections have been raised in connection with U.S. withholdings to other U.N. system organizations.

Nonetheless, these withholdings by the U.S. as well as by others, have led to more general arguments concerning the legality of unilateral withholding of assessed contributions to international organizations in response to allegedly ultra vires acts. Three basic approaches have emerged, based on: (a) the law of treaties; (b) doctrines of state responsibility; and (c) international institutional law.

First, the question can be seen as arising out of the interpretation of a multilateral treaty, i.e., from the perspective of the Vienna Convention on the Law of Treaties or the similar Vienna Convention on the Law of Treaties between States and International Organizations or between International Organizations. Unilateral withholding of assessed contributions might be justified under established treaty law if regarded as a "suspension" arising from an unforeseen, fundamental change of circumstances constituting an "essential basis" of the parties' consent to be bound which "radically transform[s] the extent of obligations still to be performed under the treaty."

Problems with this justification abound. First, unless one accepts, for example, the dubious notion that the increase in the number of third-world members, together with the one-state, one-vote budget-making basis of most U.N. organizations, constitutes such a "fundamental change of circumstances," none of the actions by the U.N. which members are apt to challenge present an arguable "radical transformation" of the Organization. Second, even if a particular U.N. activity constitutes such a fundamental change from what members could have anticipated, treaty law does not "contemplate suspension of only a nonseparable part of a party's obligations." The obligation to pay assessed dues would not be separable from the remainder of the constituent instrument. Third, the permissible treaty remedy is only "suspension" which clearly anticipates a "temporary withholding of performance with a view to eventual resumption, if possible." A financial withholding cannot be a "termination clothed as a suspension." Since at least some of the U.S. withholdings purport to be permanent and are not included in any plans by the U.S. to pay arrears, some of them appear to violate this condition. Fourth, there are doubts about the procedural steps a state needs to take under relevant treaty law prior to suspension of its treaty obligations. On one view, applicable treaty law obliges states to notify other treaty parties prior to suspension, indicating the measures "proposed to be taken with respect to the treaty and the reasons therefore." At least one commentator has argued, by contrast, that this does not preclude a state from partially and unilaterally suspending its performance of a treaty obligation by way of reciprocity or reprisal and that procedural preconditions apply only if a state is suspending its performance of the entire treaty, and not merely a part.

Justification under another treaty doctrine, "material breach," permitting suspension of a treaty obligation if there is a "violation of a provision essential to the accomplishment of the object or purpose of the treaty" is also a possibility, albeit a dubious one for this purpose. Whether any of the challenged actions to date rise to the level of violations of essential provisions of the U.N. Charter is questionable. As Kirgis has argued with respect to U.S. threats to withhold on the PLO, "respect for the efficient operation of treaty regimes ... suggests that relatively isolated departures from the strictures of even an essential provision are not material breaches if they do not threaten to defeat the purpose of the treaty." Further, the right to suspend the treaty "in whole or in part" under this doctrine belongs only to states "specially affected by the breach." Neither the U.S. nor any particular U.N. members (with the possible exceptions of Israel and South Africa) usually can claim to be specifically affected by challenged U.N. actions. Further, withholdings cannot be justified on the grounds of reciprocity, i.e., as a permissible response to others' failures to pay, since withholdings do not specifically injure the "responding" member more than others (since its own contribution is not raised as a result) and each member's withholdings affect the organization as a whole and not solely those other states which withhold. In any case, the duty to respond in a proportionate manner, presumptively applicable from the law of state responsibility, presents problems to the extent the withholdings exceed the degree of any prior breach.

A final treaty argument, that unilateral withholdings constitute "reservations" to impermissible action, is even more farfetched. Even assuming what many scholars have denied—that a member upon acceptance of U.N. membership can attach a reservation to its acceptance—reservations must be timely, accepted by the competent organ of the Organization, and compatible with the object and purpose of the constituent instrument. Neither the U.S.'s Goldberg "Reservation" nor any other members' assertion of a similar right to unilaterally withhold fulfills these requirements.

The law of state responsibility, or more specifically, the doctrine of nonforcible reprisals, provides the second potential avenue for legal justification of unilateral withholdings. Commentators and at least one arbitration award support the view that a party may proportionally suspend performance of a treaty for a nonmaterial breach. But apart from the requirement of proportionality (already discussed), non-forcible reprisals are lawful only if (a) directed in good faith at "obtaining redress for the wrong committed" and not at "producing an outcome extraneous to the violation and the situation created by the illegal act"; (b) are previously notified to affected parties; and (c) are not designed to "avoid third party settlement." Such reprisals are illegal when they frustrate the judicial process or are designed to terminate the dispute without regard to judicial settlement. Judged by these standards, withholdings of U.N. financial obligations would only be justified if necessary to prevent irrevocable harm to the member and are accompanied by a good faith effort to seek redress through third-party settlement. Recent withholdings by the U.S. and others would appear to fall far short of these criteria.

The third conceivable approach relies on international institutional law. Some U.S. officials as well as some legal scholars have sought refuge in the idea that "tolerance developed over time" provides a legal justification for the failure to pay. One problem with this approach is that neither the International Court of Justice nor the International Law Commission has ever endorsed the concept that institutional or state practice can modify a clear obligation set forth in the Charter. In fact, under treaty law, subsequent practice may only be "taken into account" when it "establishes the agreement of the parties regarding its interpretation." On at least two occasions the ICJ has distinguished the use of state practice to interpret a vague provision from its use to revise a clear provision. A second problem with this approach is that it is not clear that U.N. system organizations have in fact "tolerated" members' failure to pay assessed contributions by failing to apply constitutionally authorized sanctions. The U.N. Legal Counsel has never opined that the Article 19 loss of vote sanction does not apply to assessed contributions (as opposed to voluntary contributions) or that the duty to pay norm has fallen into desuetude. In fact, the U.N. Legal Counsel has taken the position, consistent with the U.S. position in 1962, that the Article 19 loss of vote sanction applies automatically; for these reasons the names of members with two years' accumulated arrears on assessed contributions are not called out during votes in the General Assembly. Thus, the U.N. General Assembly has not acquiesced in the evisceration of the legal duty to pay since the U.N. has applied the Article 19 sanctions to states in default of their financial obligations. For this reason, Elisabeth Zoller concludes that the so-called "practice" of withholding has not become legally meaningful and has never ceased to be a sequence of departures from the Charter.

Professor Zoller does, however, conclude that international institutional law within the context of the U.N. Charter scheme sanctions unilateral withholdings by U.N. members where, in the views of member states, such withholdings are "compelling" and necessary to protect members from the "tyranny of the majority" since such withholdings are necessitated through the need to keep the organization from turning into "a super-State." While this view has drawn at least general support, a contrary approach, grounded in the "presumptions" of validity found by the Court's majority in the Expenses case and in other advisory opinions rendered by the Court, appears more plausible.

Under this alternative view, international institutional law, viewed from the perspective of the majority and concurring opinions in the Expenses case, licenses in the context of the legally binding duty to pay a reversal of the traditional presumption in the Lotus case that international law will not presume prohibitions on state action. By agreement among its members, the legal order of the Charter imposes certain limitations on unilateral withholding designed to uphold rights of the Organization, including its international legal personality. Implicit in the Court's presumptions of validity in the Expenses case, as well as in the legal preconditions on non-forcible reprisals, are the requirements that at a minimum, prior to withholding, a member state must establish a *prima facie* case for invalidity and seek judicial or third-party resolution of the question. If the majority opinion in the Expenses case is taken seriously, unilateral withholding in response to *ultra vires* action is, at most, an option of last resort, to be taken only after the complaining member has given the organization the opportunity to correct any error.

This conclusion is only strengthened by the seemingly obvious point that an organization has "no alternative but to honor" commitments made to third parties. Were members free to withhold unilaterally, third parties to whom the organization owed debts could be left without a remedy—unless such parties were free to bring claims directly against members of the organization once the organization defaults on payment. Yet the possibility that members of an international organization are concurrently or secondarily liable for the obligations of the organization is in itself dubious.

The next question that naturally arises is how does the organization go about enforcing the duty to pay on members such that it can meet its obligations. Interpretative disputes may arise in connection with those sanctions contained in constituent instruments. Most U.N. system organizations contain a provision similar to Article 19 of the U.N. Charter providing for loss of vote for failure to pay, but some provide for loss of vote in more than one organ and some are more permissive in language than the seemingly "automatic" loss of vote sanction of Article 19. The scope of suspension of voting rights for failure to pay— whether throughout the organization or only in one organ—may give rise to controversy where it is not expressly stated. The triggering event for suspension may be less precise than Article 19's two-year rule, as where the possibility of sanction applies for failure to discharge financial obligations "within a reasonable period." Moreover, Article 19's presumptive distinction between deliberate withholdings and those that occur "due to conditions beyond the control of the Member" may suggest that deliberate withholdings could lead to a greater willingness to apply sanctions where discretion is possible. Perhaps more significant than these questions, however, is whether organizations are limited to enforcement through constitutionally sanctioned remedies such as Article 19, or whether they can, as in a particularly flagrant case, take other action. While it has been suggested that an organization has no power to expel or suspend members in the absence of constitutional provision providing for such possibilities, neither this issue nor the related issue of the possibility of imposition of progressively higher sanctions on defaulting members—loss of vote, suspension, followed by expulsion under provisions such as Articles 19, 5, and 6 of the U.N. Charter—is clearly settled. Repeated and deliberate failure to pay assessments may even constitute a "persistent" violation of the Charter sufficient to trigger expulsion under Article 6 of the U.N. Charter.

If the principle of collective financial responsibility is regarded as imposing a duty on members to make real the financial independence of the organization and there is an inherent right on the part of the organization to enforce such a duty—some of these interpretive issues regarding enforcement of the collective financial principle might be resolved in favor of a more flexible response by U.N. system organizations. The Article 19 loss of vote sanction obviously has not prevented withholdings and untimely payments at the U.N.. As the U.N. Legal Adviser has noted, Article 19 is not an effective weapon; Member States facing the Article 19 sanction may pay the minimum required to bring them just above the line drawn by that Article, without, however, living up to their full commitments. Besides, by the time the Article 19 penalty becomes applicable in respect of the largest contributors, the Organization could no longer survive financially.

Thus, various members of the U.S. Congress argued in 1986 for continuing U.S. withholdings on the premise that since, at the then-current withholding rate, the United States would not lose its General Assembly vote for five to seven years, the United States could continue to keep the Organization "one step ahead of bankruptcy" by paying "as little as we can without losing our standing." But if the loss of vote sanction does not constitute a "self-contained" regime that is "entirely efficacious," the doctrine of necessity or effectiveness would appear to authorize the organization to take other measures, not otherwise contrary to its constituent instrument or international law, required to protect the financial needs of the organization which are therefore part of the inherent powers of the organization. The organization could seek to enforce any procedural preconditions on withholding if these apply, such as the need to make a prima facie case to a third party. It could also attempt to take measures in addition to those specifically authorized by its charter for failure to pay, including charging interest on arrearages, assessing user fees or suspending organizational services, setting off sums which the organization otherwise owes to defaulting members, and most boldly, bringing enforcement actions, if these are possible, in domestic courts to compel payment. The organization might be deemed to have such inherent powers even where no sanction for failure to pay is otherwise specified in the constituent instrument or where the remedy specified is ambiguous either in scope or application, for the same reasons the U.N. was found to have the power to bring claims on behalf of its personnel in the Reparations case: as a necessary attribute of legal personality essential to insuring organizational survival. Institutional practice by U.N. system organizations would appear to support this. Thus, the U.N.'s Financial Regulations, containing rules regarding, for example, the U.N.'s power to undertake revenue-producing activities or internal audits, or stipulating a date certain for payment of assessed contributions, already constitute modest precedents for implied revenue-enhancing (or revenue-protecting) powers. Application of sanctions against defaulting members may not be merely a means to secure payment from particular members but may involve matters of broad principle. If the doctrine of desuetude threatens the principle of collective financial responsibility as some have persistent failure to enforce this principle undermines the legal duty to pay. Should this occur and withholdings or delays become the rule and not the exception, the very survival of the organization may be called into question.

As was evident in the Expenses case, an organization's decision to include a particular expense as part of the "regular" (or "administrative") budget such that a portion of that expense is assessed to every member of the organization has other legal consequences. It constitutes a determination that the particular activity giving rise to the expense is encompassed by the organization's "purposes" as regarded by the membership. Depending on the effect such institutional practice is given in the subsequent interpretation of the organization's charter, such a determination, if made by the proper organ in accord with the proper procedures and particularly if part of a series of similar determinations over a period of time, may serve to estop members or other organs from challenging the legitimacy of that type of activity in the future. Thus, institutional practice, as well as other factors, made it difficult for the U.S. to contend successfully, in 1978, that "technical assistance" was improperly part of the U.N. regular budget.

For similar reasons, absent resort to a doctrine of improper delegation, it may prove difficult for the U.S. today to claim that the expenses of subsidiary bodies in charge of the implementation of a multilateral treaty drafted under U.N. auspices, charged with implementation of activities within broad Charter purposes, such as the Preparatory Commission for the Law of the Sea, cannot generally be included in the U.N.'s regular budget.

The appropriation and collection of assessed contributions may, in turn, have other effects on an organization's internal law and practice. Decisions on remedies for withheld or delayed payments may affect the permissible scope of discretion accorded or the inherent or implied powers of the Secretary-General or the Secretariat. They may also create precedents for the scope of permissible actions by the organization as a whole or by an organ or have an impact on other interpretative disputes. Thus, the General Assembly's decision to adopt a regulation, pursuant to its power to adopt such resolutions within the Headquarters District, to limit its tortious liability and therefore its indemnity insurance premiums, created a modest precedent for what Paul Szasz has called "territorial legislation." A decision to levy assessments for the period of a member's absence from an organization, when that member purports to withdraw from the organization and later seeks to return, may have an impact on whether the organization has accepted in general the possibility of withdrawal in the absence of express Charter provision and may also help determine doubtful issues of representation or succession. Indeed, the process of adopting and executing budgets has generated a body of institutional practice concerning such issues as, for example, the authority of one organ to review decisions taken by another.

At present each U.N. agency experiments with a mix of voluntary contributions, consensus-determined obligatory assessments, and a small stream of self-generated income. In doing so they walk a tightrope between organizational cohesion/fidelity to the principle of collective financial responsibility and a real political need to encourage timely payments. More grandiose "fixes" for the U.N. system's perennial financial problems have been proposed, including such possibilities as a U.N. "tax" on international commodities or services, a more centralized U.N.-budgetary scheme for the U.N. and all specialized agencies, or various forms of weighted voting. Since some of these involve Charter amendment, while others threaten either sovereign rights or the independence of existing organizations, such changes remain (for now) unlikely. In any case, radical reforms may be both unnecessary and unwise. They may be unnecessary because international organizations may already possess, through their inherent powers to enforce collective financial responsibility, basic legal remedies to encourage members to abide by the duty to pay. They may be unwise because they fail to address the basic reason for perennial financial crises: lack of political willingness on the part of organizations and/or their members.

In the face of political constraints, the duty to pay remains an evolving and, like much of international law, an imperfect legal obligation. The U.N. system does not have a perfected power to tax—even though, under Chapter VII, it has exercised, ironically enough, the power to destroy.

## *Authors' Note*

The following article and tables provide an overview of the United Nations financial status, as of mid-2011. In particular, these materials compare several U.N. agencies' May 2010 figures with their May 2011 figures. Although the general forecast has improved since the last quarter of 2010, unpaid assessments of Member States total more than $3 billion.

## Unpaid Assessments by Fund

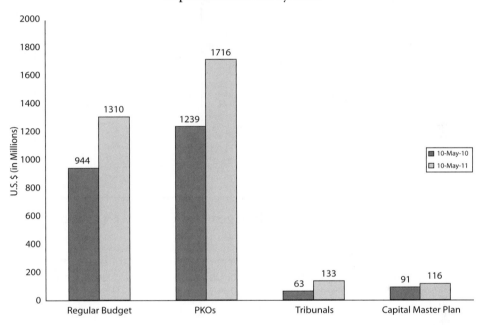

Total Unpaid Assessments at Year-End 2005–2010, May 2011

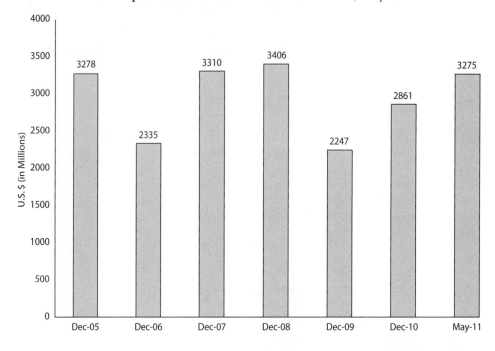

## 3. U.N. Department of Management, Financial Situation
### 2011

The overall financial situation for the first two quarters of 2011 has improved. Although assessments were higher by $3.5 billion, unpaid assessments rose by only $0.6 billion. Cash on hand is up by $0.8 billion mainly in peacekeeping.

The financial position of the regular budget at 10 May 2011 as compared to 10 May 2010 reflects the net result of both higher assessments and lower payments received. Unpaid assessed contributions were $366 million higher on 10 May 2011 than a year earlier. There was an increase of $249 million in the regular budget assessment for 2011, while payments received by 10 May 2011 were $101 million lower than on 10 May 2010.

The total amount outstanding for peacekeeping operations at the end of 2010 was just under $2.5 billion, reflecting an increase of $608 million from the amount of $1.85 billion outstanding at the end of 2009. The financial position of peacekeeping operations at 10 May 2011 shows improvement. New assessments of over $1.6 billion had been issued by that date. Against this, contributions of over $2.4 billion were received, reducing the amount outstanding from over $2.4 billion to about $1.7 billion. The current situation reflects an improvement from one year ago, and from the end 2010 situation.

The financial position of the international tribunals for Rwanda and the former Yugoslavia improved slightly in 2010. Outstanding assessments for the two tribunals decreased from $37 million at the end of 2009 to $27 million at the end of 2010.

* * *

* * *

At the same time, a significant level of outstanding assessments remains, and a few Member States account for the bulk of these amounts.

For peacekeeping, payments for troops and formed police unit costs are current up to February 2011 and payments for contingent-owned equipment are current up to December 2010 for all missions except UNFICYP.

The final outcome for 2011 will depend in large measure on action to be taken by Member States. Some of the outstanding assessment are due to inevitable synchronization issues between Member States' and the U.N.'s accounting cycles.

## Authors' Note

The following excerpt explains that the U.N. creates individual "special accounts" each time it establishes a new peacekeeping operation. Member States are divided into four categories, based on financial capacity, in order to determine the four levels of assessments that are intended to underwrite the peacekeeping special accounts.

## 4. Ruben P. Mendez, Financing the United Nations and the International Public Sector: Problems and Reform
Global Governance, 1997
[footnotes omitted by editors]

\* \* \*

*The Peacekeeping Special Accounts*

The U.N.'s first two peacekeeping operations, the U.N. Truce Supervision Organization (UNTSO) and the U.N. Military Observer Group in India and Pakistan (UNMOGIP), which helped obtain cease-fires between the Arabs and Israel and between India and Pakistan in 1948 and 1949, were charged and continue to be charged to the regular budget. The cost of the U.N. Emergency Force (UNEF 1), which was dispatched to the Suez Canal, Sinai, and Gaza in 1956, was such a strain on the regular budget, however, that a separate "special account" was created. This arrangement has been adopted for most of all subsequent peacekeeping operations.

Peacekeeping costs, like the regular budget, are considered expenses of the organization as defined in Article 17(2) of the charter. This has been the accepted interpretation since July 1962, when the International Court of Justice gave an advisory opinion to this effect. The opinion was in response to a General Assembly request, presented when the Soviet Union refused to pay its share of peacekeeping costs with a claim that they were not expenses of the organization as defined in the U.N. Charter.

Assessments for peacekeeping were originally identical in scale to the regular budget. In 1973, the General Assembly adopted a new formula, under which the permanent members of the Security Council and the richer countries pay a premium and the poorer countries get a discount. Under this formula member states are divided into four groups:

1. Group D—comprising the lowest-income countries, currently fifty seven in number—are assessed at 10 percent of their percentage rates for the regular budget. Thus, the smallest countries are assessed at 0.001 percent (10 percent of 0.01 percent).

2. Group C—roughly the middle-income less-developed countries (about one hundred)—are assessed at 20 percent of their assessment rates for the regular budget.

3. Group B—comprising most of the members of the OECD, one Eastern European state, Ukraine, and South Africa (twenty-five in all)—are assessed at the same rate as their percentage assessments for the regular budget.

4. Group A—the five permanent members of the Security Council—are responsible for the remaining costs. To compensate for the shortfall resulting from the reductions in the assessments of the less-developed countries (Groups D and C), they are assessed at rates about 20 percent higher than their shares of the regular budget.

Each time a peacekeeping operation is authorized by the Security Council, the General Assembly approves a special account. The appropriation usually covers short periods of varying duration, often no more than several months. In 1994, the assembly decided to adopt a 1 July–30 June financial period for each peacekeeping operation, starting in 1996.

Peacekeeping costs have been doubling every two years since the end of the Cold War and averaged more than $3 billion annually from 1993 to 1995. They were drastically reduced to $1.3 billion for the 1996–1997 fiscal year, with the elimination or downsizing of peacekeeping operations in Somalia and the former Yugoslavia. [ ... ] These operations, as can be seen, have taken a number of forms or contributions of forms. These include:

1. "Observer" missions, such as those to monitor and report on peace and conflict in Georgia, Liberia, and Tajikistan, and on observance of demilitarized zone between Kuwait and Iraq

2. A truce-supervision organization, such as what was established following the Arab-Israeli truce of 1948, and which still exists

3. Mediation missions to broker settlements, such as the good-offices mission for Afghanistan and Pakistan from 1988 to 1990

4. De facto "buffers," as in the case of the peacekeeping force separating the Greek- and Turkish-speaking populations in Cyprus and of the interim force in Lebanon

5. Logistical support and protection operations for humanitarian actions for the supply of food, clothing, and medicines, as in the case of Bosnia and Rwanda

6. Missions to conduct and/or monitor democratic elections, as in Haiti, Central America, and Western Sahara

7. Transitional administrations such as the mission in Eastern Slavonia, Baranja, and Western Sirmium in the former Yugoslavia, and the comprehensive operation that conducted elections and provided government services until the formation of a new government in Cambodia in September 1993

*The Social and Development Programs*

[ ... ] The resources of these programs are derived entirely from voluntary contributions, except for UNHCR, UNRWA, and UNEP, which obtain small amounts from the regular budget to cover some administrative expenses. As can be seen, the total contributions to these programs, $6 billion in 1995, exceeded the organization's regular budget and peacekeeping accounts combined. Of the total contributions, more than 87 percent was from governments; the rest, mainly from private sources. In the case of UNICEF, nongovernmental contributions accounted for 21 percent of total receipts in 1995, mainly from its long standing greeting-card operation, which is run together with nongovernmental national committees for UNICEF. The emergency relief programs also receive substantial private contributions—24 percent of total receipts in the case of UNHCR and 24 percent in the case of UNRWA in 1995. This is probably a reflection of the fact that private voluntary aid is most responsive to disasters and emergencies (which are now publicized worldwide by the mass media), but much less to long-term social and development programs.

The budgets of these subsidiary organs and other bodies of the U.N. are approved by governing bodies reporting hierarchically to the Economic and Social Council (ECOSOC) and the General Assembly. This is unlike the case of the specialized agencies, which have their own constitutions and autonomous governing bodies, budgets, and chief executive officers. They do rely substantially, however, on U.N. funding sources, especially UNDP, for much of their assistance programs, which they often carry out as executing or cooperating agencies for UNDP.

*  *  *

## Authors' Note

The following document, published by the United Nations, provides statistics on the financing of the U.N.'s peacekeeping activities. The data below includes the costs of peacekeeping for the 2010–2011 fiscal year, the top financial contributors to the peacekeeping budget, and brief discussions of the budgeting process and remuneration of peacekeeping forces.

## 5. United Nations Peacekeeping, Financing Peacekeeping
### 2011
*  *  *

**How much does peacekeeping cost?**

The budget for U.N. Peacekeeping operations for the fiscal year 1 July 2010–30 June 2011 is about $7.83 billion.

By way of comparison, this is less than half of one per cent of world military expenditures in 2009.

The estimated cost of all U.N. Peacekeeping operations from 1948 to June 2010 amounts to about $69 billion.

The top 10 providers of assessed contributions to United Nations Peacekeeping operations in 2011–2012 are

1. United States (27.14%)
2. Japan (12.53%)
3. United Kingdom (8.15%)
4. Germany (8.02%)
5. France (7.55%)
6. Italy (5.00%)
7. China (3.93%)
8. Canada (3.21%)

9. Spain (3.18%)

10. Republic of Korea (2.26%)

Many countries have also voluntarily made additional resources available to support U.N. Peacekeeping efforts on a non-reimbursable basis in the form of transportation, supplies, personnel and financial contributions above and beyond their assessed share of peacekeeping costs.

Although the payment of peacekeeping assessments is mandatory, as of 28 February 2011, Member States owed approximately $2.41 billion in current and back peacekeeping dues.

**How are resources budgeted?**

Budgets of peacekeeping operations are based on the missions' mandate from the Security Council. As such, they are strategic documents aligning resources to achieve the overall objectives of the operation.

Each peacekeeping operation has its own budget and account which includes operational costs such as transport and logistics and staff costs such as salaries.

\* \* \*

The Secretary-General submits budget proposal to the Advisory Committee on Administrative and Budgetary Questions (ACABQ). The ACABQ reviews the proposal and makes recommendations to the General Assembly's Fifth Committee for its review and approval. Ultimately, the budget is endorsed by the General Assembly as a whole.

\* \* \*

**How are peacekeepers compensated?**

The U.N. has no military forces of its own, and Member States provide, on a voluntary basis, the military and police personnel required for each peacekeeping operation.

Peacekeeping soldiers are paid by their own Governments according to their own national rank and salary scale. Countries volunteering uniformed personnel to peacekeeping operations are reimbursed by the U.N. at a flat rate of a little over $1,028 per soldier per month, as most recently approved by the General Assembly in 2002.

Police and other civilian personnel are paid from the peacekeeping budgets established for each operation.

The U.N. also reimburses Member States for providing equipment, personnel and support services to military or police contingents.

---

## Authors' Note

The following excerpt, from a Congressional Research Service report, describes the United Nations' unique system of financing war crimes tribunals to address transitional justice in Rwanda and the former Yugoslavia. A Member State's assessed contribution to each tribunal is comprised of two parts: one half of the sum is based on the State's assessment rate for the U.N. general budget, and the other half of the sum is based on the State's assessment rate for the U.N. peacekeeping account.

In 2010, U.S. President Barack Obama sought congressional approval for more than $2.7 billion in U.S. monetary contributions to the U.N. system and programs, including $112,802,000 for the International Atomic Energy Agency (IAEA), $109,403,000 for the World Health Organization (WHO), and $75,300,000 for the U.N. Development Program (UNDP). President Obama's request also included $2,182,300,000 for U.N. peacekeeping operations, $37,972,000 of which was to be directed to the U.N. War Crimes Tribunals for Rwanda and Yugoslavia.

While the Obama Administration's approach to the United Nations reflects the U.S.'s renewed commitment to cooperation with supranational organizations, it also reinforces the country's, and Congress's, long-standing concern regarding U.N. reform. The following excerpt discusses the U.S.'s owed assessments to the United Nations, congressional efforts to advance U.N. reform, and resulting measures undertaken by the U.N..

## 6. Marjorie Ann Browne and Kennon H. Nakamura, United Nations System Funding: Congressional Issues
### Congressional Research Service, 2011

* * *

### Arrearages

Under Article 19 of the U.N. Charter, countries with arrears totaling more than the member's assessments for the two preceding years lose their vote in the U.N. General Assembly. As of September 8, 2010, six countries were in that status. On October 8, 2010, however, the U.N. General Assembly decided that the six countries would be permitted to vote in the Assembly until the end of its 65th session, in September 2011.

According to the United Nations, the United States, as of September 22, 2010, owed assessed contributions of $1,231,008,190.87.94 These arrearages broke out in the following way:

$691,301,175.47 for the U.N. regular budget;

$33,541,269.00 for the International Tribunals;

$75,534,800.00 for the Capital Master Plan; and

$430,630,946.40 for peacekeeping assessed accounts.

### Funding the U.N. War Crimes Tribunals

The U.N. Security Council has created two war crimes tribunals to investigate and prosecute those accused of serious crimes against humanity under specified circumstances. The International Criminal Tribunal for the Former Republic of Yugoslavia (ICTY) was set up in 1993 to investigate and prosecute those accused of genocide, crimes against humanity, or violations of international humanitarian law on the territory of the former Yugoslavia since 1991. The International Criminal Tribunal for Rwanda (ICTR) was created in November 1994 to investigate and prosecute persons accused of genocide and other serious violations of international humanitarian law in the territory of Rwanda between January 1 and December 31, 1994, and also Rwandan citizens suspected of such acts or violations in the territory of neighboring states.

The General Assembly decided that each tribunal would be financed through a special assessed account and that U.N. member states would be assessed to contribute to those accounts in a unique way. Half of the annual budget of each would be paid on the basis of the scale of assessments used for contributions to the U.N. regular budget, and half of each account would be funded on the basis of the scale of assessments used for contributions to U.N. peacekeeping operation accounts. For the United States, this means that half of its contribution to each tribunal's account is based on 22%, its regular budget assessment rate, and half is based on its peacekeeping account assessment rate in the current calendar year.

\* \* \*

## Congress and Funding the U.N. System

Congress has, over the years, sought to influence the direction of the United Nations and U.S. policy at the United Nations and in its agencies. A variety of tools have been used, from "sense of Congress" resolutions to restrictions placed in authorization and appropriations legislation. Congressional committees have held hearings to educate and to carry out their oversight functions. U.S. nominees to be ambassadors at the United Nations or its agencies have been queried on various aspects of U.S. policy and U.N. activity. Congress has reduced or increased executive branch funding requests, has withheld funding of the U.S. proportionate share that would finance particular programs or tied release of U.S. contributions to executive branch certifications once certain policy goals had been met.

## U.S. Withholding

Beginning in 1980, Congress prohibited contribution of the U.S. proportionate share for a number of U.N. programs and activities of which Congress did not approve, including the Special Unit on Palestinian Rights, for projects benefitting the Palestine Liberation Organization (PLO), the South West Africa People's Organization (SWAPO), construction of a conference center in Addis Ababa, Ethiopia, the Second Decade to Combat Racism and Racial Discrimination, and for implementation of General Assembly Resolution 3379 (XXX) (Zionism equals racism). In addition, the Administration withheld the U.S. proportionate share of funds for the Preparatory Commission for the Law of the Sea and funds relating to taxes paid by U.S. citizens employed by the United Nations. The only current U.S. legislative-based withholding for the U.N. regular budget is for programs relating to the Palestinians.

\* \* \*

## Kassebaum-Solomon Provisions

Between 1985 and 1988, a number of factors combined to create concern among some in Congress over the use of regular budget funds and the direction of voting in the U.N. General Assembly. Some in Congress viewed many U.N. member states as voting "against" the United States in the Assembly. In 1985, Congress adopted the Kassebaum-Solomon amendment (Section 143, Foreign Relations Authorization Act, FY1986–1987, H.R. 2068, P.L. 99-93, August 17, 1985) that reduced U.S. assessed contributions by 20% unless steps were taken by the United Nations to give the major contributors to the U.N. regular budget an influence on budget questions proportionate to their rates of assessment.

In December 1985, in response to the issues raised by the Kassebaum-Solomon amendment and accompanying congressional debate, the U.N. General Assembly established a Group of High-Level Intergovernmental Experts to "review the efficiency of the administrative and financial functioning" of the United Nations and to offer recommendations for streamlining the organization. This Group of 18 proposed 71 recommendations, most of which were approved by the 1986 Assembly session. In addition, the 1986 Assembly adopted a revised "planning, programming and budgeting process" that sought to ensure an influential role for major contributing countries by, among other changes, using consensus as a basic decision-making mechanism.

On December 22, 1987, Congress recognized that both the U.N. membership and the U.N. Secretary-General had started to respond to its concerns. Title VII of the State Department Authorization Act, FY1988–1989, H.R. 1777, P.L. 100-204, created a new payment schedule that tied full funding of U.S. contributions to the U.N. regular budget to further progress toward reform by providing that:

- 40% of the contribution could be paid on October 1, of each year;
- a second 40% could be paid when the President certified that progress was being made in implementing U.N. reform in three areas:

    (1) consensus decision-making on budget questions,

    (2) reductions in U.N. secretariat staffing, and

    (3) reductions in the number of Soviet U.N. employees on fixed-term contracts.

- the remaining 20% could be paid 30 days after Congress had received the certification, unless Congress passed a joint resolution prohibiting the payment.

Although no deadline was given for submission of the President's certification report, release of up to 60% of the funds appropriated for the U.N. regular budget was dependent on submission of the report and its acceptance by the Congress. This amendment applied to the United Nations and to any specialized agencies for which the United States was assessed more than 20% in regular budget contributions. For specialized agencies, 1987 legislation revising the original provision required a Presidential determination to Congress that each affected agency made substantial progress toward adoption and implementation of reform budget procedures before any contribution over 20% could be paid.

On September 13, 1988, President Reagan certified that progress had been made, and announced release of an initial $44 million in calendar year 1987 regular budget contributions to the United Nations; a later certification resulted in release of $144 million in calendar year 1988 regular budget funds. Reagan also called on the State Department to develop a plan to pay over $500 million in arrears to the entire U.N. system over the next three to five years. It would take several years, however, for the U.S. arrears built up over time to be paid to the United Nations.

### Office of Internal Oversight Services

In 1993, Congress provided that 10% of the U.S. assessed contribution to the U.N. regular budget be available only when the Secretary of State had certified to Congress that "the United Nations has established an independent office with responsibilities and powers substantially similar to offices of Inspectors General authorized by the Inspector General Act of 1978." Many in Congress believed that an independent mechanism was needed to reduce and eliminate instances of "waste, fraud, and abuse" at the United Nations. On November 16, 1993, U.S. Ambassador Madeleine Albright proposed that the United Nations establish such a post. On July 29, 1994, the General Assembly established an Office of Internal Oversight Services (OIOS) headed by an Under-Secretary General appointed by the U.N. Secretary-General with the approval of the General Assembly. Eleven annual reports on the activities of the office through June 30, 2005, have been submitted to the General Assembly, and the office has undertaken an increasing number of monitoring, auditing, and investigative activities.

* * *

## Congress and U.N. Reform: 2005–2006

On June 17, 2005, the House, by a vote of 221 to 184, passed H.R. 2745, the Henry J. Hyde United Nations Reform Act of 2005. The wide-ranging and complex measure would require numerous State Department certifications and reports. The measure would withhold 50% of U.S. assessed dues to the U.N. regular budget beginning with calendar year 2007 (financed from U.S. FY2008 funds), if 32 of 40 changes were not in place, including 15 mandatory reforms. Among the changes sought by the legislation were changing funding for 18 U.N. programs to be totally voluntary; creation of an independent Oversight Board; establishment of a U.N. Office of Ethics; barring membership on human rights bodies to countries under U.N. investigation for human rights abuses; reduction in funding for U.N. General Assembly Affairs and Conference Services as well as for public information; and reform in U.N. peacekeeping and establishment of a Peacebuilding Commission. No new or expanded peacekeeping operations would be allowed until the Secretary of State had certified that U.N. peacekeeping reforms had been achieved.

\* \* \*

A U.N. reform measure was also introduced in the Senate, S. 1383. The Senate measure would allow the President to withhold 50% of U.S. contributions to the United Nations if the President determined that the United Nations was not making sufficient progress on reforms. No Foreign Relations Authorization Act was passed in 2005.

## Reform Initiatives in the United Nations

\* \* \*

As of August 9, 2006, several reform measures have been put into place. These include creation of the Peacebuilding Commission, establishment and operation of a new U.N. Human Rights Council to replace the U.N. Commission on Human Rights, U.N. Democracy Fund, U.N. Ethics Office, strengthened financial disclosure requirements and whistleblower protections, and Central Emergency Response Fund. In addition, the General Assembly has held at least 20 meetings of an Informal Plenary on Mandate Review. This review involves 9,000 mandates that are five years older, with the goal of eliminating or reducing those tasks no longer relevant. No decisions have been taken as a result of this review. No decisions have been taken as a result of this review.

## *Authors' Note*

The following excerpt from the Rome Statute, the document that created the International Criminal Court (ICC), concerns the Court's financing system. This section of the Statute addresses the ICC's financial regulations, various types of funding, and annual audit process.

# 7. Rome Statute of the International Criminal Court
## 1998

\* \* \*

### PART 12. Financing

### Article 113. Financial Regulations

Except as otherwise specifically provided, all financial matters related to the Court and the meetings of the Assembly of States Parties, including its Bureau and subsidiary bodies, shall be governed by this Statute and the Financial Regulations and Rules adopted by the Assembly of States Parties.

### Article 114. Payment of expenses

Expenses of the Court and the Assembly of States Parties, including its Bureau and subsidiary bodies, shall be paid from the funds of the Court.

### Article 115. Funds of the Court and of the Assembly of States Parties

The expenses of the Court and the Assembly of States Parties, including its Bureau and subsidiary bodies, as provided for in the budget decided by the Assembly of States Parties, shall be provided by the following sources:

(a) Assessed contributions made by States Parties;

(b) Funds provided by the United Nations, subject to the approval of the General Assembly, in particular in relation to the expenses incurred due to referrals by the Security Council.

### Article 116. Voluntary contributions

Without prejudice to article 115, the Court may receive and utilize, as additional funds, voluntary contributions from Governments, international organizations, individuals, corporations and other entities, in accordance with relevant criteria adopted by the Assembly of States Parties.

### Article 117. Assessment of contributions

The contributions of States Parties shall be assessed in accordance with an agreed scale of assessment, based on the scale adopted by the United Nations for its regular budget and adjusted in accordance with the principles on which that scale is based.

### Article 118. Annual audit

The records, books and accounts of the Court, including its annual financial statements, shall be audited annually by an independent auditor.

\* \* \*

## *Authors' Note*

The following excerpt from a paper produced by the Project on International Courts and Tribunals elucidates the ICC's financing scheme. The paper, written after the establishment of the Rome Statute, but prior to the adoption of the ICC's Financial Regulations and Rules, also discusses the role of the Financial Regulations in the Court's financial framework and the relationship between the ICC and the United Nations.

---

## 8. Cesare Romano & Thordis Ingadottir, Project on International Courts & Tribunals, The Financing of the International Criminal Court: A Discussion Paper
### 2000
[footnotes omitted by editors]

### 1. Introduction

\* \* \*

Part 12 of the Rome Statute details the basic elements of the financial framework for the International Criminal Court [hereinafter the ICC]. The Financial Regulations and Rules [hereinafter the Financial Regulations] and the budget for the first year, shall be drafted by the Preparatory Commission for the International Criminal Court. The Assembly of States Parties will consider and adopt the committee's recommendations. The remaining task is huge, as this involves highly political as well as technical aspects, which largely remain to be worked out. In addition, the implementation of ICC's unique mandate and structure, which are different from existing international judiciary bodies, requires some inventiveness on part of the Preparatory Commission and the Assembly of States Parties.

One of the most important factors of the ICC's financing is its funding. The Rome Statute stipulates the funds of the Court and the Assembly of State Parties as assessed contributions made by State Parties, and funds provided by the United Nations subject to the approval by the General Assembly. In addition, the Court may receive voluntary contributions, in accordance with relevant criteria adopted by the Assembly of State Parties. The ICC application of these resources must take into consideration various factors, most importantly the preservation of the Court's independence and impartiality.

The unique challenge is to predict the ICC's expenditures. As the Court's future activities are unknown, and as the Court's structure and operation are still being worked out in the Rules of Procedure and Evidence, any estimate will be insufficient. However, some speculation about the Court's start-up costs, including what resources are necessary for the minimum operation of the stand-by years, might be feasible.

The Assembly of State Parties is the sole budgetary authority of the Court, however all budgetary procedures are as yet undecided. The Rome Statute does not stipulate who shall prepare the budget, who shall submit it to the Assembly of States Parties, and how it shall be adopted. The procedures are further complicated as the Statute does not provide the Court with a secretariat. The adopted procedures will inevitably effect the independence of the Chambers and the Office of the Prosecutor, as well as the extent of the Assembly's authority versus the Court.

\* \* \*

### 2. Financial Framework

### 2.1. Basic Elements

The ICC is an independent international organization established by a treaty. As the Court does not function within the wider scope of an international organization, it does not enjoy institutional support. Rather, it will need to establish and operate its own financial and administrative system. Different from most other courts and tribunals, the Court is therefore responsible for its own budget preparation and collection of contributions. Despite the increased responsibilities resulting from the Court's self-sustaining position, the arrangement involves considerable benefits. The Court's financial framework is established and developed solely for the needs of an international judiciary body, which can differ considerably from bigger institutions also engaged in different operations. The Court's own tailored structure and procedures should therefore be well equipped to promote effective and competent organization.

The Rome Statute lays out the basic structure of the Court's financial framework:

- There is a single financial framework for both the Court and its overseeing body, the Assembly of State Parties (art. 113-115).

- The Court and the Assembly are financed from assessed contributions from State Parties, which are based on the scale adopted by the United Nations for its regular budget; and from funds provided by the United Nations, subject to the approval of the General Assembly, in particular in relation to the expenses incurred due to referrals by the Security Council (art. 115).

- Voluntary contributions are allowed, as additional funds, in accordance with relevant criteria adopted by the Assembly of State Parties (art. 116).

- The Assembly of State Parties considers and decides the budget of the Court (art. 112.2(d)).

- The Court has an independent auditor (art. 118).

Various instruments will further develop the Court's financial framework. Most important are the Financial Regulations and the Court's relationship agreement with the U.N.. These instruments must meet Court's objective of being an independent and effective international judicial body.

## 2.2 Financial Rules and Regulations

In addition to technical financial management matters, the Financial Regulations will determine major undecided issues such as who will prepare the budget and what kind of oversight mechanism will be incorporated. Depending on the stipulations of the Assembly, the Financial Regulations could also regulate further delicate issues such as the scale of assessment of State Parties' contributions (e.g., if and how the U.N. minimum and maximum threshold will be used) and the possible U.N. contribution (e.g., guidelines for cases that the Security Council refers to the Court). The Assembly of State Parties' criteria on voluntary contribution could have fundamental bearing on the Court's perceived independence.

* * *

The Financial Regulations shall be adopted by the Assembly of State Parties, and being a decision on a matter of substance, they would need to be approved by a two-thirds majority of those present and voting (art. 112.7(a)).

* * *

## 2.3 Relationship of the Court with the United Nations

According to article 2 of the Rome Statute, the Court shall be brought into relationship with the United Nations through an agreement to be approved by the Assembly of States Parties. The ICC-U.N. relationship agreement might shape the ICC's financial framework in at least three ways. First, the agreement could include U.N. contributions to the Court generally and/or specifically, as in relation to the Court's expenses resulting from Security Council referrals. Second, the agreement will likely oblige the Court to conform as far as possible, to standard U.N. financial practices and forms. Third, the agreement could entail rendering of certain financial and administrative services from the U.N.. This is material, as the Rome Statute does not provide the Court with any secretariat. The Assembly could prefer to use the U.N. Secretariat to carry out certain work such as the preparation of the budget and collection of state contributions. [ ... ]

The ICC-U.N. relationship agreement could also indirectly affect the resources of the Court. Some collaboration between the Court and the U.N. International Criminal Tribunals for the Former Yugoslavia and Rwanda [hereinafter the ICTY and ICTR, respectively] might be feasible in certain circumstances. Such collaboration could be in the form of an exchange of resources, facilities, and equipment.

\* \* \*

## Authors' Note

The following excerpt from the ICC's financial regulations lays out the Court's sources of funding and the organization of Court resources once funds are collected. Funding includes assessed contributions of State Parties, U.N. contributions, voluntary governmental contributions, and other miscellaneous funds. Collected funds are formed into a General Fund, a Working Capital Fund, and a Contingency Fund, according to an annual budget approved by the Assembly of States Parties.

# 9. Financial Regulations and Rules of the International Criminal Court

International Criminal Court, 2008

\* \* \*

**Regulation 5**

**Provision of funds**

5.1 The funds of the Court shall include:

  (a) Assessed contributions made by States Parties in accordance with article 115, subparagraph (a), of the Rome Statute;

  (b) Funds provided by the United Nations in accordance with article 115, subparagraph (b), of the Rome Statute;

  (c) Voluntary contributions by Governments, international organizations, individuals, corporations and other entities, in accordance with article 116 of the Rome Statute;

  (d) Such other funds to which the Court may become entitled or may receive.

5.2 The appropriations, subject to the adjustments effected in accordance with the provisions of regulation 5.4, shall be financed by contributions from States Parties in accordance with an agreed scale of assessment, as provided for in article 117 of the Rome Statute. This scale shall be based on the scale adopted by the United Nations for its regular budget, and adjusted in accordance with the principles on which that scale is based, in order to take into account the differences in membership between the United Nations and the Court. The scale shall be adopted by the Assembly of States Parties. Pending the receipt of such contributions, the appropriations may be financed from the Working Capital Fund.

5.3 The appropriations provided for in regulation 4.2 shall be financed from the assessed contributions from States Parties in accordance with regulation 5.2 up to a limit to be decided upon by the Assembly of States Parties in each budget resolution. Pending the receipt of such contributions, the appropriations may be financed from the Working Capital Fund.

5.4 The contributions of States Parties shall be assessed for a financial period on the basis of the appropriations approved by the Assembly of States Parties for that financial period.

Adjustments to the assessments of States Parties shall be made in respect of:

(a) Any balance of the appropriations surrendered under regulation 4.7;

(b) Contributions resulting from the assessment of new States Parties under the provisions of regulation 5.10;

(c) Miscellaneous income.

5.5 After the Assembly of States Parties has reviewed and adopted the budget and determined the amount of the Working Capital Fund or the Contingency Fund if the Assembly of States Parties has determined in accordance with regulation 6.6 that the Fund shall be financed from assessed contributions, the Registrar shall:

(a) Transmit the relevant documents to the States Parties;

(b) Inform the States Parties of their commitments in respect of annual assessed contributions and advances to the Working Capital Fund or the Contingency Fund;

(c) Request them to remit their contributions and advances.

\* \* \*

## Regulation 6

### Funds

6.1 There shall be established a General Fund for the purpose of accounting for the expenditures of the Court. The contributions referred to in regulation 5.1 by States Parties and miscellaneous income and any advances made from the Working Capital Fund to finance expenditures shall be credited to the General Fund.

6.2 There shall be established a Working Capital Fund to ensure capital for the Court to meet short-term liquidity problems pending receipt of assessed contributions. The amount shall be determined from time to time by the Assembly of States Parties. The Working Capital Fund shall be constituted by advances from States Parties. Advances shall be made in accordance with the agreed scale of assessment pursuant to regulation 5.2. Advances shall be carried to the credit of States Parties which have made such advances.

6.3 Advances made from the Working Capital Fund to finance budgetary appropriations shall be reimbursed to the Fund as soon as and to the extent that income is available for that purpose.

6.4 Income derived from investments of the Working Capital Fund shall be credited to miscellaneous income.

6.5 Trust funds and special accounts funded wholly by voluntary contributions may be established and closed by the Registrar and shall be reported to the Presidency and, through the Committee on Budget and Finance, to the Assembly of States Parties.

Reserve accounts and special accounts funded wholly or in part by assessed contributions may be established by the Assembly of States Parties.

The purposes and limits of each trust fund, reserve and special account shall be clearly defined by the appropriate authority. Unless otherwise decided by the Assembly of States Parties, such funds and accounts shall be administered in accordance with these Regulations.

6.6 There shall be established a Contingency Fund to ensure that the Court can meet:

   (a) Costs associated with an unforeseen situation following a decision by the Prosecutor to open an investigation; or

   (b) Unavoidable expenses for developments in existing situations that could not be foreseen or could not be accurately estimated at the time of adoption of the budget; or

   (c) Costs associated with an unforeseen meeting of the Assembly of States Parties.

The level of the Fund and the means by which it shall be financed (i.e. by assessed contributions and/or cash surpluses in the budget) shall be determined by the Assembly of States Parties.

6.7 If a need to meet unforeseen or unavoidable expenses arises, the Registrar, by his or her own decision or at the request of the Prosecutor, the President or the Assembly of States Parties, is authorized to enter into commitments not exceeding the total level of the Contingency Fund. Before entering into such commitments, the Registrar shall submit a short, supplementary budget notification to the Committee on Budget and Finance through its Chairperson. Two weeks after having notified the Chairperson of the Committee on Budget and Finance, and taking into consideration any financial comments on the funding requirements made by the Committee through its Chairperson, the Registrar may enter into the corresponding commitments. All funding obtained in this way shall relate only to the financial period(s) for which a programme budget has already been approved.

6.8 The Registrar shall report together with the new draft programme budget to the Assembly of States Parties, through the Committee on Budget and Finance, on any exercise of the commitment authority given under regulation 6.7.

6.9 Income derived from Contingency Fund investments shall be classed as miscellaneous income for credit to the General Fund.

\* \* \*

## Authors' Note

The failure of the United States to pay its assessed contributions to the United Nations has caused considerable financial strain the U.N. and, accordingly, has borne a negative impact on the U.N.'s ability to carry out its mandate. The following excerpt describes the United States' debt to the United Nations and the impact of this debt on U.N. budgets.

# 10. Michael Scharf and Tamara Shaw, International Institutions

*The International Lawyer*, 1999
[footnotes omitted by editors]

* * *

## I. The U.N.'s Financial Crisis

### A. Introduction

Eleven years ago, when the United States was just 147 million dollars in arrears to the United Nations, the American Bar Association adopted a resolution that "urges the executive and legislative branches ... to take cooperative action so that payment will be made without delay to the United Nations, including its specialized agencies, of all amounts assessed to the United States." Due to repeated withholdings and nonpayment during the last decade, by the end of 1998, the United States debt to the U.N. had mushroomed to ten times that amount—over 1.3 billion dollars (which constitutes more than sixty percent of the debt of all member states).

As a result of the United States' nonpayment, the United Nations currently faces its most serious financial crisis. According to Joseph E. Connor, U.N. Under-Secretary-General for Administration and Management, the United Nations is "on the financial brink, lacking both stability and liquidity." Connor, an American who previously headed the prestigious Price Waterhouse accounting firm, also revealed that the U.N. will soon be unable to pay its employees or carry out humanitarian operations, and could be driven to bankruptcy. In November of 1998, U.N. Secretary-General Kofi Annan warned that the United Nations was "for all practical purposes, in a state of bankruptcy. Our doors are kept open only because other countries in essence provide interest-free loans to cover largely American-created shortfalls."....

Responding in part to U.S. pressure (and the necessities of getting by with less), in the last few years the United Nations has significantly cut its staff, streamlined its bureaucracy, reduced its programs, established an office of Inspector General, and cut out millions of dollars of redundancy and waste. It has come much closer to becoming the fiscally responsible organization that the United States has demanded. But the U.S. debt has grown so large that it is seriously disrupting the work of the United Nations, instead of moving it toward further reform.

A fiscally healthy United Nations benefits the United States in many ways. The U.N. provides a worldwide forum in which the United States elicits support for its policies, interests, and values, and it establishes worldwide programs that advance those policies, interests, and values. It provides a means for settling disputes peacefully, providing humanitarian relief, furthering human rights, and promoting economic and social development. When dispute settlement requires the use of force, the United Nations provides international legitimacy and support for U.S. actions and sharing of the burden, as has been the case with the Persian Gulf crisis and the conflict in Bosnia. It is ironic that the United States is damaging the United Nations through nonpayment just when the United Nations has been best demonstrating its ability to serve U.S. purposes.

For a typical example of how the financial crisis brought on by the United States effects important U.N. operations, one can look to the experience of the U.N.'s International Criminal Tribunal for the Former Yugoslavia. The tribunal was established by the United Nations in 1993 to investigate atrocities committed during the Balkan conflict and bring those responsible to justice in order to promote reconciliation and lasting peace in the troubled region. In the summer of 1995, with the U.N. literally running out of cash, it was forced to slow the supply of funds to the tribunal to a trickle. As a consequence (and despite voluntary contributions by the United States and others), the office of the prosecutor was prevented from spending money to send investigators into the field to investigate the massacre of 8,000 civilians at the U.N. "safe area" of Srebrenica. The office was also precluded from recruiting lawyers and investigators, or renewing contracts of current personnel, due to restrictions on United Nations agencies imposed by the Secretary-General in the face of the fiscal crisis. Evidence already gathered from refugee interviews began to pile up unsifted and untranslated. Consequently, the work of the tribunal experienced serious delays. In the context of the former Yugoslavia, justice delayed translated into peace denied.

In addition to crippling the important work of the United Nations, the failure of the United States to pay its arrears has undercut a variety of U.S. diplomatic efforts—with our negotiating partners ever more frequently refusing to make concessions to a country which they say has become the world's biggest "deadbeat" nation. According to U.S. Secretary of State Madeleine Albright, "the debt undermines our leadership position in the [United Nations], making it harder for the President or his representatives to bend other members to our will." Albright concluded that the continuing U.S. debt to the U.N. "makes it impossible for us to get what we want at the U.N.." This was a theme that emerged repeatedly at the Rome Diplomatic Conference for a Permanent International Criminal Court in July 1998.

National public opinion polls taken in 1998 demonstrated that the American public recognizes the important role played by the United Nations, with the percent of the public supporting the United Nations (seventy-two percent) at its highest point since 1959. The public also recognizes the importance of the U.S. legal obligation to pay its debt to the organization. By a three-to-one margin, the Americans surveyed favored paying the arrears in full.

* * *

## Authors' Note

During the Clinton Administration, the U.S. Congress developed a plan by which the United States would reduce its debt owed to the U.N. via a series of payments. The plan, the Helms-Biden compromise, made these payments contingent on several reforms to be instituted by the U.N.. The following article discusses the Helms-Biden plan and includes an excerpt of Senator Jesse Helms's 2000 address to the Security Council, which provides insight into one congressional perspective on U.S. funding of the U.N..

## 11. Sean D. Murphy, Contemporary Practice of the United States Relating to International Law

*American Journal of International Law*, 2000
[footnotes omitted by editors]

### States and International Organizations

*Payment of the U.S. Arrears to the United Nations*

Over the course of the 1990s, the United States fell significantly behind in the payment of its assessed contributions to the United Nations. Not only had Congress unilaterally decided not to fund fully the U.N. assessment to the United States for peacekeeping operations, but the cost of those peacekeeping operations, particularly for UNPROFOR in Bosnia, was itself dramatically increasing. Exacerbating the situation and effectively blocking a resolution of the arrearage problem were congressional efforts to link U.S. contributions (or portions thereof) to passage of U.N. reforms and also to other matters unrelated to the United Nations. Because of the resentment by other states over the lack of payments, a U.S. representative was not elected in 1996 to the United States' traditional seat on the U.N. biennial budget committee, known as the Advisory Committee on Administrative and Budgetary Questions. Further, the size of the arrearage raised the possibility that the United States would lose its vote in the General Assembly. As of September 30, 1999, the United Nations estimated that the United States owed the organization and its specialized agencies $1.7 billion, an amount accounting for 65 percent of all unpaid assessments owed by member states. By contrast, the United States acknowledged owing only slightly more than $1 billion.

Although withholding of payments to the United Nations by the United States dates back to 1980, the size of the arrearage dramatically increased in the 1990s after the U.S. Senate and then the U.S. House of Representatives attained Republican Party majorities. In 1997, Senate Foreign Relations Committee Chairman Jesse Helms and the ranking minority committee member, Senator Joseph Biden, proposed the payment of most U.S. arrears and assessments subject to U.N. acceptance of certain reforms. In 1997 and 1998, President Clinton refused to accept the proposal, in part because of the reform conditions and in part because of a provision attached by the House of Representatives that would ban U.S. funding to international family-planning organizations that lobby foreign governments to liberalize their abortion laws. Since such a provision was politically unacceptable to President Clinton, he refused to go along with the legislation in 1997 and again in 1998.

In 1999, President Clinton decided to accept the Helms-Biden compromise, as well as the family planning restrictions, subject to modifications. [ ... ]

On November 29, 1999, President Clinton signed the legislation, thereby allowing $926 million to be paid to the United Nations subject to its acceptance of certain reforms. On November 30 President Clinton exercised the waiver of the family-planning certification. In signing the legislation, President Clinton stated that his administration is "committed to making sure that all of our debts are paid, and, while doing so, pressing for reforms that will make the U.N. more efficient and more effective." [ ... ]

Upon three separate certifications by the secretary of state that the U.N. had met certain conditions, including the implementation of specified reforms, the new legislation authorizes payments to the United Nations in three stages: (1) $100 million in funding, (2) $475 million in funding and a $107 million peacekeeping reimbursement credit, and (3) $244 million in funding. In late December 1999 Secretary of State Albright made the first certification. Combining the $100 million of the first stage with funds available from other appropriations, the United States was able to make a payment totaling $151 million. In combination with earlier payments, the United States thereby exceeded the $255 million required by the end of 1999 in order to prevent the loss of its vote in the General Assembly. Subsequent payments will only occur upon the ability of the secretary of state to certify that further U.N. reforms have been made. Those reforms include: (1) General Assembly reduction of the percentage of the United States' assessment for U.N. regular expenses (from 25 to 22 percent and then to 20 percent) and U.N. peacekeeping expenses (from 31 to 25 percent), (2) creation of inspector general positions at designated U.N. specialized agencies, as well as achievement of zero nominal growth in their budgets, (3) reforms in U.N. personnel management, and (4) U.N. development of criteria for evaluating the relevance and effectiveness of U.N. programs.

*Senator Helms Addresses U.N. Security Council*

In January 2000, the presidency of the Security Council rotated to the United States. The U.S. permanent representative to the United Nations, Ambassador Richard C. Holbrooke, invited Senator Jesse Helms to address an informal session of the Security Council, the first member of the U.S. Congress ever to do so. [ ... ]

In his opening remarks, Senator Helms stated that he hoped that his visit would mark the beginning of a "pattern of understanding and friendship" between U.N. representatives and both U.S. government leaders and the U.S. people. Further, he stated that his remarks were not intended to offend but "to extend to you my hand of friendship and convey the hope that ... we can join in a mutual respect that will enable all of us to work together in an atmosphere of friendship and hope...." Nevertheless, Senator Helms proceeded to criticize the United Nations by objecting to comments made at the United Nations that the United States had become a "deadbeat" nation. He asserted that in 1999 the United States had paid $10.179 billion in support of the United Nations, counting both U.N. assessments and the funding in the U.S. military budget for programs supporting U.N. activities worldwide.

> Now, I grant you, the money we spend on the U.N. is not charity. To the contrary, it is an investment — an investment from which the American people rightly expect a return. They expect a reformed U.N. that works more efficiently, and which respects the sovereignty of the United States.

> That is why in the 1980's Congress began withholding a fraction of our arrears as pressure for reform. And Congressional pressure resulted in some worthwhile reforms, such as the creation of an independent U.N. inspector general and the adoption of consensus budgeting practices. But still, the arrears accumulated as the U.N. resisted more comprehensive reforms.

> When the distinguished Secretary-General, Kofi Annan, was elected, some of us in the Senate decided to try to establish a working relationship. The result is the Helms-Biden law, which President Clinton finally signed into law this past November. The product of three years of arduous negotiations and hard-fought compromises, it was approved by the U.S. Senate by an overwhelming 98–1 margin. You should read that vote as a virtually unanimous mandate for a new relationship with a reformed United Nations.

> Now, I am aware that this law does not sit well with some here at the U.N.. Some do not like to have reforms dictated by the U.S. Congress. Some have even suggested that the U.N. should reject these reforms.

But let me suggest a few things to consider: First, as the figures I have cited clearly demonstrate, the United States is the single largest investor in the United Nations. Under the U.S. Constitution, we in Congress are the sole guardians of the American taxpayers' money. (It is our solemn duty to see that it is wisely invested.) So as the representatives of the U.N.'s largest investors—the American people—we have not only a right, but a responsibility, to insist on specific reforms in exchange for their investment.

Second, I ask you to consider the alternative. The alternative would have been to continue to let the U.S.-U.N. relationship spiral out of control. You would have taken retaliatory measures, such as revoking America's vote in the General Assembly. Congress would likely have responded with retaliatory measures against the U.N.. And the end result, I believe, would have been a breach in U.S.-U.N. relations that would have served the interests of no one.

...

... [A]ll of us want a more effective United Nations. But if the United Nations is to be "effective" it must be an institution that is needed by the great democratic powers of the world.

Most Americans do not regard the United Nations as an end in and of itself— they see it as just one part of America's diplomatic arsenal. To the extent that the U.N. is effective, the American people will support it. To the extent that it becomes ineffective—or worse, a burden—the American people will cast it aside.

The American people want the U.N. to serve the purpose for which it was designed: they want it to help sovereign nations coordinate collective action by "coalitions of the willing," (where the political for such action exists); they want it to provide a forum where diplomats can meet and keep open channels of communication in times of crisis; they want it to provide to the peoples of the world important services, such as peacekeeping, weapons inspections and humanitarian relief.

...

As matters now stand, many Americans sense that the U.N. has greater ambitions than simply being an efficient deliverer of humanitarian aid, a more effective peacekeeper, a better weapons inspector, and a more effective tool of great power diplomacy. They see the U.N. aspiring to establish itself as the central authority of a new international order of global laws and global governance. This is an international order the American people will not countenance.

Senator Helms noted—and said he agreed with—the U.N. secretary-general's statement that the people of the world have "rights beyond borders." Although the sovereignty of nations must be respected, Senator Helms asserted, nations derive their legitimacy from the consent of those they govern, and lose that legitimacy when they oppress their people. In such situations, other nations have a right to intervene to end oppression and promote democracy. Moreover, the United Nations has no power to approve or disapprove such actions. To those who would argue that such actions by the United States violate its obligations under the U.N. Charter, and that Security Council approval is needed, Senator Helms asserted:

Under our system, when international treaties are ratified they simply become domestic U.S. law. As such, they carry no greater or lesser weight than any other domestic U.S. law. Treaty obligations can be superseded by a simple act of Congress. This was the intentional design of our founding fathers, who cautioned against entering into "entangling alliances."

Thus, when the United States joins a treaty organization, it holds no legal authority over us. We abide by our treaty obligations because they are the domestic law of our land, and because our elected leaders have judged that the agreement serves our national interest. But no treaty or law can ever supersede the one document that all Americans hold sacred: The U.S. Constitution.

The American people do not want the United Nations to become an "entangling alliance." That is why Americans look with alarm at U.N. claims to a monopoly on international moral legitimacy. They see this as a threat to the God-given freedoms of the American people, a claim of political authority over America and its elected leaders without their consent.

The effort to establish a United Nations International Criminal Court is a case in point. Consider: the Rome Treaty purports to hold American citizens under its jurisdiction — even when the United States has neither signed nor ratified that treaty. In other words, it claims sovereign authority over American citizens without their consent. How can the nations of the world imagine for one instant that Americans will stand by and allow such a power-grab to take place?

The Court's supporters argue that Americans should be willing to sacrifice some of their sovereignty for the noble cause of international justice. International law did not defeat Hitler, nor did it win the Cold War. What stopped the Nazi march across Europe, and the Communist march across the world, was the principled projection of power by the world's greatest democracies. And that principled projection of force is the only thing that will ensure the peace and the security of the world in the future.

. . .

No U.N. institution — not the Security Council, not the Yugoslav tribunal, not a future ICC — is competent to judge the foreign policy and national security decisions of the United States. [ ... ]

Americans distrust concepts like the International Criminal Court, and claims by the U.N. to be the "sole source of legitimacy" for the use of force, because Americans have a profound distrust of accumulated power. Our founding fathers created a government founded on a system of checks and balances, and dispersal of power.

* * *

Today, while our friends in Europe concede more and more power upwards to supra-national institutions like the European Union, Americans are heading in precisely the opposite direction.

America is in the process of reducing centralized power by taking more and more authority that had been amassed by the Federal government in Washington and referring it to the individual states where it rightly belongs.

This is why Americans reject the idea of a sovereign United Nations that presumes to be the source of legitimacy for the United States Government's policies, foreign or domestic. There is only one source of legitimacy of the American government's policies — and that is the consent of the American people.

...

... A United Nations that focuses on helping sovereign states work together is worth keeping; a United Nations that insists on trying to impose a utopian vision on America and the world will collapse under its own weight.

If the United Nations respects the sovereign rights of the American people, and serves them as an effective tool of diplomacy, it will earn and deserve their respect and support. But a United Nations that seeks to impose its presumed authority on the American people without their consent begs for confrontation and, I want to be candid, eventual U.S. withdrawal.

Most members of the Security Council spoke after Senator Helms, and many were critical of his views. UK Ambassador Sir Jeremy Greenstock stated that there was "nothing more important for the United Nations than its relationship with the United States" and that U.N. reform is needed. He also asserted, however, that the U.S. arrearage problem had hindered reform efforts and that, to the extent the United Nations has performed badly, the United States bears some of the responsibility as a key member state. [ ... ]

Dutch Ambassador van Walsum said that under the U.N. Charter, a member state cannot attach conditions to its willingness to pay its assessed contributions.

\* \* \*

Senator Helms's appearance at the United Nations also raised issues of constitutional significance. Appearing before the Security Council on January 24, Secretary of State Albright noted that "only the President and the Executive Branch can speak for the United States. Today, on behalf of the President, let me say that the Administration, and I believe most Americans, see our role in the world, and our relationship to this organization, quite differently than does Senator Helms."

\* \* \*

## Authors' Note

On January 15, 2009, Ambassador Susan Rice provided a statement to the Senate Foreign Relations Committee during the hearings to confirm her position as the United States permanent representative to the United Nations. In her statement, which is excerpted below, Ambassador Rice discussed the role of the United States in the United Nations, the need for U.N. reform, and the Obama Administration's priorities for engaging the U.N..

## 12. Susan E. Rice, Statement before the Senate Committee on Foreign Relations
### Statement of U.S. Permanent Representative-Designate, 2009

\* \* \*

In the wake of the Cold War, the U.N. was modernized in important ways and did substantial good—from Namibia to Mozambique, from El Salvador to South Africa and Cambodia. At the same time, there were clear failures, witnessed in the unimaginable human tragedies of Somalia, Rwanda and Srebrenica, and the inability to effectively deal with crises in Haiti and Angola. We saw the difficulties and limits of U.N. action when conflicting parties are determined to continue fighting, as well as the imperative of mobilizing broad-based support behind U.N. efforts. We were disappointed when the U.N. occasionally served as a forum for prejudice instead of a force for our shared values. Finally, we learned that mismanagement and corruption can taint the dedicated work of skilled professionals, and that the reprehensible actions of a few can undermine the goodwill of many towards an institution, which most Americans nonetheless continue to support.

\* \* \*

Today, with our security at home affected by instability, violence, disease, or failed states in far corners of the world, the President-elect has affirmed America's commitment to the United Nations as an indispensable, if imperfect, institution for advancing our security and well-being in the 21st century. He has made it clear that we must pursue a national security strategy that builds strong international partnerships to tackle global challenges through the integration of all aspects of American power — military and diplomatic; economic and legal; cultural and moral. The goal of our diplomacy at the United Nations must be to make it a more perfect forum to address the most pressing global challenges: to promote peace, to support democracy, and to strengthen respect for human rights.

There is no country more capable than the United States to exercise leadership in this global institution, and to help frame its programs and shape its actions. My most immediate objective, should I be confirmed, will be to refresh and renew America's leadership in the United Nations and bring to bear the full weight of our influence, voice, resources, values, and diplomacy at the United Nations.

The Obama Administration will work to maximize common interests and build international support to share the burdens of collective action to counter the most pressing threats Americans face, while working to help tackle the poverty, oppression, hunger, disease, fear and war that threaten billions around the world every day.

We will make our case to the U.N., and press for it to become a more effective vehicle of collective action. We will also be prepared to listen and to learn, to seek to understand and respect different perspectives. The task of our diplomacy must be to expand both the will and ability of the international community to respond effectively to the great challenges of our time.

\* \* \*

The choices we face in addressing global challenges can often be difficult: allowing conflict and suffering to spread, mobilizing an American response, or supporting a multinational United Nations effort. The U.N. is not a cure-all; we must be clear-eyed about the problems, challenges and frustrations of the institution. But it is a global institution that can address a tremendous range of critical American and global interests.

\* \* \*

If confirmed, I will work to strengthen the U.N.'s effectiveness to fulfill its many important missions, and working closely with the Secretary of State, I will devote particular attention to four areas:

First, we must make renewed efforts to improve the capacity of the United Nations to undertake complex peace operations effectively. We need to weigh new U.N. mandates more carefully and review existing mandates as they are renewed. Indeed, the gap between number and complexity of the missions the Security Council has committed the U.N. to perform, and its ability to do so, has arguably never been greater. [ ... ] We should work to build global peacekeeping capacity and help streamline the U.N. as well as our own procedures for deploying and supporting U.N. missions. We must also no longer allow host nations to dictate the composition of—and thwart the effective deployment of—Chapter VII U.N. operations.

Second, the Obama Administration will provide strong leadership to address climate change [ ... ]. Under President-elect Obama, the United States will engage vigorously in U.N.-sponsored climate negotiations while we pursue progress in sub-global, regional and bilateral settings. [ ... ]

Third, preventing the spread and use of nuclear weapons is an enormous security challenge that deserves top level attention. [ ... ] There is no more urgent threat to the United States than a terrorist with a nuclear weapon. [ ... ] It is essential to strengthen the global nonproliferation and disarmament regime, dealing with those states in violation of this regime, and upholding our obligations to work constructively and securely toward the goal of a world without nuclear weapons.

\* \* \*

Fourth, President-elect Obama has called for us to "invest in our common humanity." [ ... ] President-elect Obama has long stressed the importance of working with others to promote sustainable economic development, combat poverty, enhance food and economic security, curb conflict and help strengthen democracy and governing institutions.

\* \* \*

Mr. Chairman, the United Nations must be strengthened to meet 21st century challenges. None of us can be fully satisfied with the performance of the U.N., and too often we have been dismayed. The United States must press for high standards and bring to its dealings with the U.N. high expectations for its performance and accountability, and that's what I intend to do. In cooperation with other governments, we must pursue substantial and sustained improvements across the full range of management and performance challenges, including financial accountability, efficiency, transparency, ethics and internal oversight, and program effectiveness. Important work on all of these issues has been undertaken, but we have much further to go. Progress and reform are essential to address flaws in the institutions, to meet the unprecedented demands made on it, and to sustain confidence in and support for the U.N.. I pledge to you to work tirelessly to see that American taxpayer dollars are spent wisely and effectively.

To lead from a position of strength, the United States must consistently act as a responsible, fully-engaged partner in New York. To do so, we must fulfill our financial obligations while insisting on effective accountability. In the past, our failure to pay all of our dues and to pay them on a timely basis has constrained the U.N.'s performance and deprived us of the ability to use our influence most effectively to promote reform. President-elect Obama believes the U.S. should pay our dues to the U.N. in full and on time. I look forward to working with you and other Members of Congress to ensure that we do so, as well as to pay down our newly mounting arrears and to support legislation to permanently lift the cap on U.S. payments to the U.N. peacekeeping budget.

\* \* \*

## 13. Bibliography of Additional Sources

- Jose Alvarez, *Legal Remedies and the United Nations à la carte Problem*, 12 J. MICH. INT'L L. 229 (1991).

- Allan Gerson, THE KIRKPATRICK MISSION, 44–53 (1990).

- Henry J. Hyde United Nations Reform Act, H.R. 2745: of 2005, 109th Cong. (2005).

- Christopher Joyner, THE UNITED NATIONS AND INTERNATIONAL LAW (1997).

- Peter B. Kenen, MANAGING THE WORLD ECONOMY: FIFTY YEARS AFTER BRETTON WOODS (1994).

- Frederic L. Kirgis, *Admission of Palestine as a Member of a Specialized Agency and Withholding the Payment of Assessments in Response*, 84 AM. J. INT'L. L. 218 (1990).

- John Knox, et al., *U.N. Fiscal Crisis Brought on by U.S. Arrears*, 93 AM. SOC'Y INT'L L., 150 (Mar. 24–7, 1999).

- League of Women Voters, *Memorandum to the Members of the U.S. Congress Regarding H.R. 2745* (June 15, 2005).

- Richard W. Nelson, *International Law and U.S. Withholding of Payments to International Organizations*, 80 AM. J. INT'L. L. 973 (1986).

- Shujiro Ogata & Paul Volcker, *Financing an Effective United Nations: A Report of the Independent Advisory Group on U.N. Financing*, FORD FOUNDATION (1993).

- Brett D. Schaefer, *The United Nations Reform Act of 2005: A Powerful Lever to Advance U.N. Reform.*

- U.S. General Accountability Office, *United Nations: Status of U.S. Contributions and Arrears* (1999).

- Peter Willetts, *The Conscience of the World: The Influence of Nongovernmental Organizations in the U.N. System*, BROOKINGS INSTITUTION (1996).

# Chapter XXIII

# The International Monetary Fund: A Mandate to Fight Money Laundering and the Financing of Terrorism

## By Richard Gordon[1]

## Introduction

Since its founding in 1945, the International Monetary Fund's (IMF) mandate has evolved so as better to fit the contemporary needs of its member countries. Some of these adaptations have involved amending the IMF's constitution or charter, known as the Articles of Agreement. However, amending the Articles is a cumbersome and difficult process, and has been used only four times in the IMF's history. In other cases, the IMF's governing bodies have reinterpreted the Articles to address new challenges. This chapter examines the limits to the evolution of the IMF's mandate and the process by which those limits are extended.

## Objectives

- To understand the basic structure and functions of the IMF.
- To understand elements of the U.S. interaction with the IMF.

---

1. In 2005, Richard Gordon joined the Case School of Law law faculty and began teaching courses on international business, corporate governance, and financial sector integrity. Earlier, he practiced law at Dewey Ballantine in Washington, D.C., and taught at Harvard Law School, where he was deputy director of the International Tax Program. He also taught at the School of Oriental and African Studies of the University of London and was Distinguished Visiting Professor at Case in 1999. He has done extensive fieldwork on law and development in both Indonesia and rural India. For nearly 10 years, Prof. Gordon worked with the International Monetary Fund, as both senior counsel and senior financial sector expert working on tax, sovereign debt restructuring, and government corruption. Following the 9/11 attacks, he was appointed to the select IMF Task Force on Terrorism Finance and was a principal author of the report on the role of the IMF and World Bank in countering terrorism finance and money laundering. He is a principal author of the book *Tax Law Design and Drafting* (Kluwer 2000) and the author of numerous reports, articles, and book chapters on law and development, comparative taxation, corporate governance, sovereign debt restructuring, and money laundering.

- To understand the various international issues that the IMF and World Bank are designed to address.

- To understand the problem of money laundering and the efforts of the IMF to combat the issue.

- To understand the IMF and World Bank's emphasis on preventing the international financing of terrorism.

# Problem

On April 17, 2000, Lawrence Summers, who at the time was Secretary of the United States Treasury, wrote a letter to both the IMF and the World Bank laying out a number of concerns that he believed that both institutions should address in the coming months. One issue he raised was abuse of the financial system and, specifically, money laundering.

The Summers Letter set off a debate among staff, management, and members of the IMF Executive Board. The questions debated included: (a) Was money laundering a topic that was relevant to the IMF's purposes as expressed in Article 1 of the Articles of Agreement? (b) If so, should other considerations restrict IMF involvement, such as its relative lack of expertise in the area, high costs (and the money that this would take away from programs more fundamental to the IMF's purposes), and the possible existence of other organizations better suited to the task? (c) If the IMF should be involved, should all aspects of money laundering be included in its mandate — even those that involve law enforcement? (d) If some or all of the aspects of money laundering should be included, should these aspects be part of surveillance, conditionality, or technical assistance? (e) If part of technical assistance, should it be part of program of assessing standards and codes? (f) If so, who was the standard setter and what was the standard, and what parts of that standard should the IMF be involved in assessing?

As can be guessed, different countries had different views with respect to each of these questions. Over the next 5 years, staff and management were asked to consider these questions and report to the Executive Board. This problem looks primarily at four different staff papers, as well as to the response of the Executive Board to the issues discussed in those papers. In reading excerpts from these papers, it is important to consider what effect the various proposals would have on the IMF's main activities, and how this would affect the different countries that constitute the IMF membership.

The problem also includes some introductory material concerning the IMF's structure and activities and an essay on money laundering, and its relationship to the IMF's purposes and activities, written by an IMF staff member.

1. Come to class prepared to discuss the following questions:

    a.   With respect to the IMF staff papers of February 12, 2001 and April 26, 2001:

        i.   Did staff conclude that issues concerning financial sector abuse and money laundering were part of the IMF's mandate as expressed in its Articles of Agreement?

       ii.   What were the main points raised in favor of extending the mandate? How are the IMF's "core competencies" defined, and how are they relevant to the question?

    iii.  In what ways did staff seek to limit the IMF's role in money laundering issues, and what were the arguments they marshaled? Can the issue of money laundering be broken into different areas, some of which were seen as part of the IMF's "core competences" and some of which were not? What is "law enforcement" and how is it relevant to the IMF's purposes?

    iv.  What is the FATF and what are the 40 Recommendations?

    v.  What did staff conclude should be the IMF's new money laundering policy with respect to the three basic areas of IMF activity: surveillance, lending (and conditions), and technical assistance (including endorsement of and assessment of compliance with standards and codes)?

    vi.  What member countries might be relatively less inclined to include money laundering in the IMF's activities, and why?

    vii.  Did Executive Directors agree with the staff positions?

  b.  With respect to the Fund staff paper of November 5, 2001:

    i.  How did the views of staff and of the Executive Board change with respect to the IMF's mandate as a result of the terrorist attacks of September 11, 2001? What were these changed views based on? What is the connection between money laundering and the financing of terrorism? Were staff's recommendations based on a consistent interpretation of the IMF's Articles and "core mandate" based on changed economic circumstances?

    ii.  How did staff seek both to expand and to limit the IMF's involvement? Why the concern over further "mission creep"? What is the "macro-relevance" test? What is an "independent anti-money laundering expert" and why was the participation of such a person proposed by staff? Do the arguments in the paper support staff proposals?

    iii.  What are the consequences of the Fund endorsing a ROSC for money laundering for the IMF's mandate? What practical consequences could this have for surveillance, lending, and technical assistance?

  c.  With respect to the Fund staff paper of March 10, 2004:

    i.  Did the independent anti-money laundering expert work effectively to limit the IMF's involvement in "law enforcement?" What were the problems?

    ii.  What were the main considerations of Executive Directors when they made their choice among the three options in their March 24, 2004 meeting?

2.  Using the key precedents set over the period of February, 2001 and March, 2004 by the IMF's Executive Board with respect to the Fund's role in money laundering, come to class prepared to argue whether adequate implementation of the FATF 40 + 9 Recommendations should be a condition for IMF lending to member countries.

# Materials

1.  Overview of the IMF and its Organization and Activities, by Richard Gordon.

2.  Treasury Secretary Lawrence H. Summers, Statement to the Development Committee of the World Bank and the International Monetary Fund at http://www.imf.org/external/spring/2000/dc/usa.htm.

3. Articles of Agreement of the International Monetary Fund at http://www.imf.org/external/pubs/ft/aa/aa22.htm.

4. Financial Sector Assessment Program (FSAP), Last updated: May 24, 2006 at http://www.imf.org/external/NP/fsap/fsap.asp.

5. IMF; Financial System Abuse, Financial Crime and Money Laundering, Background Paper, February 12, 2001 at http://www.imf.org/external/np/ml/2001/eng/021201.pdf.

6. IMF and World Bank; Enhancing Contributions to Combating Money Laundering: Policy Paper, April 26, 2001 at http://www.imf.org/external/np/ml/2001/eng/042601.pdf.

7. Current Developments in Monetary & Financial Law, International Monetary Fund (1999), Chapter 15: ANTI-MONEY-LAUNDERING POLICIES SELECTED LEGAL, POLITICAL, AND ECONOMIC ISSUES, By Richard K. Gordon.

8. IMF; Intensified Fund Involvement in Anti-Money Laundering Work and Combating the Financing of Terrorism, November 5, 2001 at http://www.imf.org/external/np/mae/aml/2001/eng/110501.pdf.

9. IMF Board Discusses the Fund's Intensified Involvement in Anti-Money Laundering and Combating the Financing of Terrorism, Public Information Notice (PIN) No. 01/120, November 16, 2001, at http://www.imf.org/external/np/sec/pn/2001/pn01120.htm.

10. IMF AND THE WORLD BANK; Twelve-Month Pilot Program of Anti-Money Laundering and Combating the Financing of Terrorism (AML/CFT) Assessments, Joint Report on the Review of the Pilot Program, March 10, 2004, at http://www.imf.org/external/np/aml/eng/2004/031604.pdf.

11. IMF Executive Board Reviews and Enhances Efforts for Anti-Money Laundering and Combating the Financing of Terrorism Public Information, Notice (PIN) No. 04/33, April 2, 2004, at http://www.imf.org/external/np/sec/pn/2004/pn0433.htm.

12. Bibliography of Additional Sources

---

# 1. Richard Gordon, Overview of the IMF and Its Organization and Activities

The IMF's purposes, organization, and activities are spelled out in its founding charter, the IMF's Articles of Agreement. The Articles are interpreted and implemented by its governing bodies and by its management and professional staff.

The IMF membership currently consists of 184 countries, or nearly every nation in the world. Voting rights in the IMF's governing bodies are based on each member country's quota, which is loosely based on the size of the member's economy and participation in world trade. The ultimate governing authority of the IMF is the Board of Governors, which consists of one governor from each country, a position usually held by a finance minister or central bank governor. The Board of Governors usually meets once a year and sets broad policy. The International Monetary and Financial Committee, a subcommittee of the Board, considers key issues at a twice a year meeting, and makes recommendations for action to the full Board. The day-to-day decision-making role is played by the Executive Board, which consists of 24 Directors. The five largest quota holders—the United States (with slightly over 17 percent of total votes), Japan, Germany, France, and the United Kingdom—hold seats, with the rest elected by groups of members. The Executive Board meets three or so times a week to consider IMF policies and specific actions, typically based on recommendations by management and staff of the IMF. A key to this process is the drafting and circulation of staff papers, which normally consist of an analysis of the particular issue or issues at hand and either questions to be addressed by the Executive Board or specific recommendations for action.

The IMF undertakes a number of roles. Perhaps the best known is to make loans to member countries that are experiencing trouble making payments to international creditors. These loans are usually made at close to market rates (that is, market rates for countries with good credit) for relatively short terms. However, the IMF also has programs whereby loans are made to very poor countries at heavily subsidized rates for long terms—for the specific purpose of alleviating poverty and enhancing development. In most cases, IMF loans are made only if the borrowing country agrees to certain conditions. The conditions, however, have to comport with the IMF's purposes as expressed in its Articles and by decisions of the Board of Governors and Executive Board. In general, these conditions relate to improvements in a members economy and balance of payments position, which also help ensure that the loan will be repaid. Conditions may include specific numerical targets, such as agreements by the country to reduce budget deficits by specific amounts, or not to acquire additional debt from non-residents. Conditionality can also include so-called "structural" conditions. These may include commitments by the country to introduce and enforce new laws, for example, banking or bankruptcy laws.

A key role of the IMF is "surveillance" of members' economies and exchange rate policies. Under Article IV of the Articles, the IMF examines each member's economic and financial policies and practices (for most members this happens every year) and makes policy recommendations to the country for improvement. Reports based on such surveillance are often considered when the IMF makes loans to a country, including with respect to how conditions to the loan might best be drafted.

A third key role is to provide technical assistance to the country in tackling problems—often those that are identified in surveillance reports. Such assistance is purely voluntary and is usually provided by staff of the IMF and can be in a broad range of areas where the staff has expertise, including budget policy, taxation, and central banking. Technical assistance may not conflict with IMF's purposes as expressed in its Articles and by decisions of the Board of Governors and Executive Board.

An increasingly important part of the IMF's technical assistance program has been a group of related activities whereby the IMF, in cooperation with the World Bank and other organizations, assesses whether countries are complying with certain international standards and codes that are "useful for the operational work of the IMF and the World Bank." Many of the standards and codes assessed have been created and adopted by other organizations with particular expertise in the subject area. For example, the Basel Core Principles on Banking Supervision were drafted and adopted by the Basel Committee, consisting of a group of (mostly developed country) banking supervisors. Before becoming a standard and code to be assessed by the IMF, the Executive Board had to decide that the standard was "useful for the operational work of the Fund"—in this case, in part because a sound banking system is essential to the implementation of sound economic and financial policies. The Board then had to endorse the Principles as the world standard on banking supervision.

In order to complete an objective assessment of a standard and code, assessors need to use a "methodology document" that outlines in detail what questions need to be answered in order to determine if the particular standard or code is met.

Assessments of standards and codes (which are compiled into Reports on the Observance of Standards and Codes or "ROSCs") include recommendations for improvement.

These are presented to the country as part of technical assistance to that country. They are also discussed by the Executive Board, and are used by management, staff, and the Executive Board for other IMF purposes and, if the country consents, are published on the IMFs website. These assessments are also included in another voluntary IMF technical assistance program that consists of a broad examination of a country's financial sector stability called the Financial Sector Stability Program or (FSAP). ROSCs and FSAPs are also used to inform the IMF's surveillance activities and conditions it attaches to it loan programs.

## Authors' Note

The following material is a statement from the U.S. Treasury Secretary to the Development Committee of the World Bank and IMF. The statement addresses a number of concerns held by the U.S. with respect to the World Bank, IMF, and future international problems. Treasury Secretary Lawrence Summers also suggests a number of solutions to these issues, expressing the gravity and importance of international response to growing anxieties.

## 2. Treasury Secretary Lawrence H. Summers Statement to the Development Committee of the World Bank and the International Monetary Fund

2000
[footnotes omitted by editors]

### Introduction

We welcome the improved prospects for global growth; the most potent weapon for combating poverty ever invented. Supported by sound economic policies, including budget discipline, the United States' economy continues to grow, with strong investment and higher productivity. More dynamic growth is also underway in Europe, and a robust economic recovery continues in the emerging market economies. Global growth this year is expected to return to the pre-crisis rates of the mid-1990s at 4.2 percent.

At the same time, we all recognize that durable and sustainable growth is not inevitable, and will depend crucially on proactive policy. The dramatic impact of innovation and information technology and the spread of market-oriented policies and economic openness provide unprecedented opportunities for economies and peoples. We must all seize these opportunities to establish an environment for strong and sustained growth across all our economies.

A more balanced pattern of growth in the global economy is also in our mutual interests. Additional structural reform will be necessary for European economies to better realize their potential, and similar structural challenges — along with the need for continued supportive macroeconomic policies — are presented on a larger scale in Japan. There must also be no let up in the resolute efforts of emerging market economies to address their severe structural problems, including corporate and financial restructuring.

It is also important to concentrate our collaborative attention and energy on ways to more effectively address the development challenges faced by the world's poorest countries. International development has had major successes — with the incidence of poverty falling in many countries and enormous improvements in human welfare in the successful emerging market economies.

We know that when policies are good, aid can and does have a significant and positive impact. In part for this reason, we also understand better why some assistance works and some doesn't. However, there is no denying that that the overall benefits of aid have been disappointing, particularly in the poorest countries, relative to the efforts and financing expended over the last fifty years. At a time when 1.3 billion people still live on less than a dollar a day, the world is rightly and increasingly demanding that assistance be more effective in raising human development.

This has to be to a crucial priority for the MDBs today. In recent years, the World Bank and its regional counterparts have enacted a wide range of policies to improve project design and the ultimate development impact of their operations. This is to be welcomed. Yet it is also too often the case that there remains a gap between the banks' policies and development aspirations and actual results on the ground. Cases, such as last year's Western China Poverty Reduction Project, serve only to erode credibility and engender public skepticism. And they shortchange development effectiveness.

We can and must build a better record of success and results. The facts overwhelmingly demonstrate the central reality that how fast you grow is by far the most important determinant of how successful you are in raising incomes and reducing poverty and inequality. It is also essential that macroeconomic policies, sound economic management, social development and environmental policies, and poverty reduction be mutually reinforcing. This will lay a secure basis for sustainable growth.

There are other truths that now command broad consensus that should frame our approach to development finance over the years ahead:

- Countries, through their commitment to sound policies, shape their own destiny;
- Market-oriented policies and economic openness work best to combat poverty;
- Public investment in people (basic education and health) and a sustainable environment is crucial to growth;
- Good governance—transparency, accountability, the rule of law, and inclusion— matters enormously; and
- Development assistance must be conditioned to be effective.

These basic truths must increasingly guide the activities of the MDBs.

\* \* \*

*Good Governance*

We very much appreciate the leadership role that President Wolfensohn has played in bringing corruption to the forefront of the development agenda. It is one of the most serious impediments to development and poverty reduction, and is something we must all take very seriously.

But corruption is only one element of the larger, and enormously important, issue of good governance. A key element of good governance is fair revenue collection and government accountability for the use of public funds. This requires: (1) revenue collection that is equitable and based on rule of law; (2) transparent and accountable budgeting; (3) sound public sector management procedures for accounting, financial controls, public reporting, and auditing; (4) appropriate fiscal choices; and (5) purchasing procedures that are transparent and encourage competition. Institutional reforms in these areas should be an operational priority.

In particular, we urge the Bank to integrate the results of its Public Expenditure Reviews, Country Procurement Assessment Reports (CPARs) and Country Financial Accountability Assessments (CFAAs) systematically into all Country Assistance Strategies. Progress in addressing weaknesses in these areas should be a condition for adjustment lending.

The Bank and the Fund have important roles in helping countries establish functioning audit systems to review, verify, and reconcile budgetary expenditures, including full accounting for extra-budgetary and off-budget accounts. As specified in the IDA-12 replenishment agreement, Public Expenditure Reviews should routinely include military expenditures and subsidies and should assess how reallocation of non-productive expenditures such as these could enhance the development impact of public spending. We urge member governments, with the support of the Bank and the Fund, to pursue vigorously optimal transparency in their military budgets. Governments should ensure that all budgetary expenditures, including military spending, are routinely audited, verified, reconciled and reported to the legislature, or another civilian authority. We continue to believe it is incumbent on the IFIs to be fully knowledgeable of the audit and accountability systems in place for military expenditures—like all expenditures—prior to extending financial support.

We also believe the time is right for the international financial institutions to step up further their efforts to help combat money laundering. The increased engagement of the World Bank and the IMF on financial sector issues and assessments provides a good opportunity to expand the operational and analytical scope of their efforts against money laundering. And as a general matter, we urge the international financial institutions to explore mechanisms to encourage and support country efforts to incorporate anti-money laundering measures in their financial sector reform programs.

In the broad scope of anti-corruption efforts, we also strongly support the work of the OECD Bribery Working Group to strengthen and enforce the provisions of the OECD Anti-Bribery Convention. It is essential that the signatories to this "supply-side agreement" against corruption expedite ratification and effective implementation of the Convention. The world's leading exporters and foreign investors must lead by example and take the necessary steps to criminalize bribery of foreign officials by their nationals and companies. And those OECD countries that have not effectively eliminated the tax deductibility of bribes of foreign public officials should do so immediately. To assist in the implementation of the OECD Convention, we also call on non-OECD members to improve the transparency of their procurement of goods and services from abroad and, as appropriate and possible, to share information they may obtain on instances of foreign suppliers and investors offering bribes to secure contracts or licenses.

*Trade and Development*

Another important challenge is to rebuild the momentum for further trade liberalization. Open and competitive markets promote growth, stability, and efficiency, and are essential for our future efforts to promote sustainable development and poverty reduction. In this vein, we welcome the initiation of WTO negotiations in agriculture and services earlier this year and strongly support efforts to build a consensus for the launch of a new round of multilateral trade negotiations.

We urge the World Bank to work with the IMF, WTO, and other relevant institutions as a priority to improve the effectiveness of the Integrated Framework for Trade-Related Technical Assistance for Least Developed Countries. The development of trade-related infrastructure and institutional foundations, as well as assistance in implementing commitments under international agreements, can be critical for a flourishing trade regime. We understand that a review of the Integrated Framework is now underway, and hope that it will lead us to clear recommendations for improvements.

It is also important for the World Bank and IMF more fully to incorporate policies promoting trade integration and trade capacity building in Bank operations and Fund programs. This includes efforts to integrate trade considerations into the Poverty Reduction Strategy Papers process and, on the World Bank side, into country assistance strategies and the Comprehensive Development Framework. Trade liberalization has in the past been an important part of many IMF and Bank structural reform programs as an essential contribution to economic growth and efficiency, and we believe these efforts should continue.

*International Task Force on Commodity Risk Management*

The work of International Task Force on Commodity Risk Management needs to be discussed in much greater detail. We believe that there are many substantive issues that have yet to be addressed and have serious reservations about proposals emerging from the Task Force. We believe greater effort should be made to explore ways to support an enabling environment that would allow developing countries to better access existing commercial risk management instruments that do not introduce potential market distortions. Consideration should also be given to ways developing countries could better manage their macroeconomic and fiscal stability through market-based forms of price risk management or ways to support in-country risk-management mechanisms. The Task Force could also explore alternative, market-based mechanisms, including guarantees for existing risk-management instruments.

*Labor*

We welcome the various initiatives underway to enhance cooperation and collaboration between the World Bank and the International Labor Organization (ILO). We urge both institutions to invest the necessary resources into expanding and operationalizing this cooperation and making the maximum use of the comparative advantage brought to the table by the two organizations.

At the same time, I must express disappointment with the slow pace of implementing the commitments on labor issues agreed to in the IDA-12 replenishment. We urge Management to conduct an effective analysis of core labor standards in its Country Assistance Strategies (CASs), with input, as appropriate, from the ILO, as called for in the agreement. The CAS process provides a good opportunity for the Bank to implement at the country level the improved cooperation with the ILO that has been agreed to at the headquarters level.

While the Bank has moved forward in addressing forced labor, discrimination in employment, and child labor, we would also encourage members to adopt a firm position in support of workers' rights of association and collective bargaining. The exercise of these rights is essential for the effective functioning of democracy and good governance, and can have a positive impact on economic growth and development when implemented together with good industrial relations and pro-growth economic policies.

## V. Conclusion

Global engagement opens unprecedented opportunities for all of us. Securing the benefits of these opportunities also entails major challenges, particularly for the poorest countries. Many of the problems the Committee is discussing today arise not because more countries have integrated themselves with the global economy. It is because so many countries have not.

I believe the challenges of global engagement can be overcome—if we work together and if countries make the sound policies choices available to them—and that greater economic integration, supported by innovative use of advances in technology and communications, can open vast possibilities for improving the human welfare of poor people around the world. It offers the prospect of improvements in health, literacy, and living standards that were unthinkable even two decades ago.

The stakes are high, the risks great, and the outcome uncertain. However, the improved prospects for global growth we are now experiencing provide a firm foundation for deepening the cooperation among all our member countries in support of sound policies and for increasing the effectiveness of domestic and external resources invested for growth and poverty reduction. There is no alternative if the benefits of global integration are to be secured and sustained for the common good.

## 3. Articles of Agreement of the International Monetary Fund

### Article I — Purposes

The purposes of the International Monetary Fund are:

(i)  To promote international monetary cooperation through a permanent institution which provides the machinery for consultation and collaboration on international monetary problems.

(ii)  To facilitate the expansion and balanced growth of international trade, and to contribute thereby to the promotion and maintenance of high levels of employment and real income and to the development of the productive resources of all members as primary objectives of economic policy.

(iii) To promote exchange stability, to maintain orderly exchange arrangements among members, and to avoid competitive exchange depreciation.

(iv) To assist in the establishment of a multilateral system of payments in respect of current transactions between members and in the elimination of foreign exchange restrictions which hamper the growth of world trade.

(v)  To give confidence to members by making the general resources of the Fund temporarily available to them under adequate safeguards, thus providing them with opportunity to correct maladjustments in their balance of payments without resorting to measures destructive of national or international prosperity.

(vi) In accordance with the above, to shorten the duration and lessen the degree of disequilibrium in the international balances of payments of members.

The Fund shall be guided in all its policies and decisions by the purposes set forth in this Article.

* * *

### Article IV — Obligations Regarding Exchange Arrangements

#### Section 1. General obligations of members

Recognizing that the essential purpose of the international monetary system is to provide a framework that facilitates the exchange of goods, services, and capital among countries, and that sustains sound economic growth, and that a principal objective is the continuing development of the orderly underlying conditions that are necessary for financial and economic stability, each member undertakes to collaborate with the Fund and other members to assure orderly exchange arrangements and to promote a stable system of exchange rates. In particular, each member shall:

(i) endeavor to direct its economic and financial policies toward the objective of fostering orderly economic growth with reasonable price stability, with due regard to its circumstances;

(ii) seek to promote stability by fostering orderly underlying economic and financial conditions and a monetary system that does not tend to produce erratic disruptions;

(iii) avoid manipulating exchange rates or the international monetary system in order to prevent effective balance of payments adjustment or to gain an unfair competitive advantage over other members; and

(iv) follow exchange policies compatible with the undertakings under this Section.

\* \* \*

## Section 3. Surveillance over exchange arrangements

(a) The Fund shall oversee the international monetary system in order to ensure its effective operation, and shall oversee the compliance of each member with its obligations under Section 1 of this Article.

(b) In order to fulfill its functions under (a) above, the Fund shall exercise firm surveillance over the exchange rate policies of members, and shall adopt specific principles for the guidance of all members with respect to those policies. Each member shall provide the Fund with the information necessary for such surveillance, and, when requested by the Fund, shall consult with it on the member's exchange rate policies. The principles adopted by the Fund shall be consistent with cooperative arrangements by which members maintain the value of their currencies in relation to the value of the currency or currencies of other members, as well as with other exchange arrangements of a member's choice consistent with the purposes of the Fund and Section 1 of this Article. These principles shall respect the domestic social and political policies of members, and in applying these principles the Fund shall pay due regard to the circumstances of members.

\* \* \*

## Article V — Operations and Transactions of the Fund

\* \* \*

## Section 2. Limitation on the Fund's operations and transactions

\* \* \*

(b) If requested, the Fund may decide to perform financial and technical services, including the administration of resources contributed by members, that are consistent with the purposes of the Fund. Operations involved in the performance of such financial services shall not be on the account of the Fund. Services under this subsection shall not impose any obligation on a member without its consent.

\* \* \*

## Section 3. Conditions governing use of the Fund's general resources

(a) The Fund shall adopt policies on the use of its general resources, including policies on stand-by or similar arrangements, and may adopt special policies for special balance of payments problems, that will assist members to solve their balance of payments problems in a manner consistent with the provisions of this Agreement and that will establish adequate safeguards for the temporary use of the general resources of the Fund.

\* \* \*

## *Authors' Note*

**The Financial Sector Assessment Program (FSAP):**

The following material provides a selection from an FSAP that provides details on Off-shore Financial Centers and the Reports on the Observance of Standards and Codes. The IMF Factsheet provides details concerning the issuance of the FSAP:[2]

> **The recent global crisis has shown that the health of a country's financial sector has far reaching implications for its economy as well as for other economies. The Financial Sector Assessment Program (FSAP), established in 1999, is a comprehensive and in-depth analysis of a country's financial sector. FSAP assessments are the joint responsibility of the IMF and World Bank in developing and emerging market countries and of the Fund alone in advanced economies, and include two major components: a financial stability assessment, which is the responsibility of the Fund and, in developing and emerging market countries, a financial development assessment, the responsibility of the World Bank. To date, more than three-quarters of the member countries have undergone assessments.**

Assess financial stability and development

The focus of FSAP assessments is twofold: to gauge the stability of the financial sector and to assess its potential contribution to growth and development.

- To assess the stability of the financial sector, FSAP teams examine the soundness of the banking and other financial sectors; conduct stress tests; rate the quality of bank, insurance, and financial market supervision against accepted international standards; and evaluate the ability of supervisors, policymakers, and financial safety nets to respond effectively in case of systemic stress. While FSAPs do not evaluate the health of individual financial institutions and cannot predict or prevent financial crises, they identify the main vulnerabilities that could trigger one.

- To assess the development aspects of the financial sector, FSAPs examine the quality of the legal framework and of financial infrastructure, such as the payments and settlements system; identify obstacles to the competitiveness and efficiency of the sector; and examine its contribution to economic growth and development. Issues related to access to banking services and the development of domestic capital markets are particularly important in low-income countries.

## 4. Financial Sector Assessment Program (FSAP)

Resilient, well-regulated financial systems are essential for macroeconomic and financial stability in a world of increased capital flows. The FSAP, a joint IMF and World Bank effort introduced in May 1999, aims to increase the effectiveness of efforts to promote the soundness of financial systems in member countries. Supported by experts from a range of national agencies and standard-setting bodies, work under the program seeks to identify the strengths and vulnerabilities of a country's financial system; to determine how key sources of risk are being managed; to ascertain the sector's developmental and

---

2. International Monetary Fund, Factsheet: The Financial Sector Assessment Program, available at http://www.imf.org/external/np/exr/facts/fsap.htm, last viewed August 24, 2012.

technical assistance needs; and to help prioritize policy responses. Detailed assessments of observance of relevant financial sector standards and codes, which give rise to Reports on Observance of Standards and Codes (ROSCs) as a by-product, are a key component of the FSAP. The FSAP also forms the basis of Financial System Stability Assessments (FSSAs), in which IMF staff address issues of relevance to IMF surveillance, including risks to macroeconomic stability stemming from the financial sector and the capacity of the sector to absorb macroeconomic shocks.

**Offshore Financial Centers (OFCs)**
**IMF Staff Assessments**
**Last Update: February 22, 2006**
**http://www.imf.org/external/np/ofca/ofca.asp**

In recent years, there has been increased recognition of the need to improve understanding of the activities of offshore financial centers. Some OFCs have captured a significant part of global financial flows, and their linkages with other financial centers creates the potential for their activities to affect financial stability in many countries. In July 2000, the IMF's Executive Board asked staff to extend financial sector work to include OFCs through a voluntary program of assessments and technical assistance. The aim is to help strengthen financial supervision of OFCs, so that international rules and arrangements apply to OFCs to promote greater cooperation among supervisors. To this end, IMF staff undertake detailed assessments of the extent to which OFCs meet the standards advocated by the international standard-setters, and of any further action required to meet these standards.

**Reports on the Observance of Standards and Codes (ROSCs)**
**http://www.imf.org/external/np/rosc/rosc.asp**

ROSCs summarize the extent to which countries observe certain internationally recognized standards and codes. The IMF has recognized 12 areas and associated standards as useful for the operational work of the Fund and the World Bank. These comprise accounting; auditing; anti-money laundering and countering the financing of terrorism (AML/CFT); banking supervision; corporate governance; data dissemination; fiscal transparency; insolvency and creditor rights; insurance supervision; monetary and financial policy transparency; payments systems; and securities regulation; AML/CFT was added in November 2002. Reports summarizing countries' observance of these standards are prepared and published at the request of the member country. They are used to help sharpen the institutions' policy discussions with national authorities, and in the private sector (including by rating agencies) for risk assessment. Short updates are produced regularly and new reports are produced every few years.

---

## Authors' Note

The remaining materials in this chapter address the prevalent issues that plague the international financial system as well as the efforts of the IMF and World Bank to combat these issues. Materials 5, 6, and 7 discuss the role of IMF and World Bank in addressing financial crimes, especially the pervasive international crime of money laundering. Material 5, a background paper from the IMF, provides an overview of financial crimes and introduces the international financial issues that the IMF was designed to combat. Material 6, a policy paper from the IMF and World Bank, illustrates the policy initiates undertaken to address money-laundering. The selection demonstrates the role of each international financial institution in the joint effort to prevent money-laundering. In Material 7, an article by Richard Gordon, the policies under-taken by the IMF and World Bank to combat money-laundering and financial crimes are analyzed. The material poses questions concerning the efficacy of the process and possible ways to remedy deficiencies.

The last four materials represent a significant shift in IMF and World Bank policy prioritizations when addressing the financing of international terrorism after September 11, 2001. Material 8, a selection from an IMF publication, describes the extension of IMF efforts to specifically address the international financing of terrorism. Material 9 is a Public Information Notice from the IMF that presents the discussion of the IMF Board to intensify the organization's involvement in combating money-laundering and the financing of terrorism. The IMF established a pilot program on anti-money laundering and preventing the financing terrorism. Material 10 provides the required assessment of the pilot program, which provides a number of recommendations. Material 11, a public information notice, provides the background of the efforts to combat money-laundering and financing terrorism as well as a discussion of the IMF Executive Board's response to the recommendations proposed in the assessment of the pilot program.

---

# 5. Financial System Abuse, Financial Crime and Money Laundering Background Paper

International Monetary Fund, 2001

## I. INTRODUCTION

1. At its September, 2000, meeting the International Monetary and Financial Committee (IMFC), requested that the Fund prepare a joint paper with the World Bank on their respective roles in combating money laundering and financial crime, and in protecting the international financial system. Moreover, the Fund was specifically asked "to explore incorporating work on financial system abuse, particularly with respect to international efforts to fight against money laundering into its various activities, as relevant and appropriate." (See Annex I). The purpose of this paper is to present background information prior to the forthcoming consideration of this requested joint paper with the World Bank.

\* \* \*

### Financial crime

9. No internationally accepted definition of financial crime exists. Rather, the term expresses different concepts depending on the jurisdiction and on the context. This paper interprets financial crime in a broad sense, as any non-violent crime resulting in a financial loss. When a financial institution is involved, the term financial sector crime is used. This difference among jurisdictions is reflected in the Organization for Economic Cooperation and Development (OECD) Convention on Combating Bribery of Officials in International Business Transactions ("OECD Anti-Bribery Convention"), which in requiring signatories to make the bribery of foreign public officials a crime excludes facilitation payments. See Article 1, OECD Anti-Bribery Convention (entered into force February 15, 1999); Article 1, Commentaries on the OECD Anti-Bribery Convention (adopted by the Negotiating Conference on November 21, 1997).

10. Financial institutions can be involved in financial crime in three ways: as victim, as perpetrator, or as an instrumentality. Under the first category, financial institutions can be subject to the different types of fraud including, e.g., misrepresentation of financial information, embezzlement, check and credit card fraud, securities fraud, insurance fraud,

and pension fraud. Under the second (less common) category, financial institutions can commit different types of fraud on others, including, e.g., the sale of fraudulent financial products, self dealing, and misappropriation of client funds. In the third category are instances where financial institutions are used to keep or transfer funds, either wittingly or unwittingly, that are themselves the profits or proceeds of a crime, regardless of whether the crime is itself financial in nature. One of the most important examples of this third category is money laundering.

11. Financial institutions can be used as an instrumentality to keep or transfer the proceeds of a crime. In addition, whenever a financial institution is an instrumentality of crime, the underlying, or predicate, crime is itself often a financial crime. There is a growing perception in many key jurisdictions that the most rapidly growing category of predicate crimes are financial, although illegal drug trafficking remains a major predicate crime. Although the circumstances vary from country to country, the preeminence of financial crimes as predicate offenses is found mainly: (i) in major financial centers, and (ii) in the location of a financial institution (e.g., where the criminal profits are laundered) which may be a different location from where the predicate crime was committed.

**Money laundering**

12. As noted above, money laundering is frequently referred to as a financial crime. It is generally defined as "transferring illegally obtained money or investments through an outside party to conceal the true source." This activity may prevent law enforcement from uncovering or confiscating the proceeds of crime, or using the proceeds as evidence in a criminal prosecution. Such processing may involve disguising the beneficial owner of either the actual criminal proceeds or of other property that might be subject to confiscation. Money laundering can be done with or without the knowledge of the financial institution or counterparty to financial transactions, although to be guilty of the crime of money laundering, actual or implied knowledge is required.

13. The number and variety of transactions used to launder money has become increasingly complex, often involving numerous financial institutions from many jurisdictions, and increasingly using non-bank financial institutions (e.g., bureau de change, check cashing services, insurers, brokers, traders). In addition, because predicate crimes are often financial crimes, laundered proceeds may not be cash but other financial instruments. Also, the use of non-financial businesses and markets for laundering appears to be increasing, including not only illegitimate institutions such as shell companies created as laundering instrumentalities, but legitimate companies where illicit funds are intermingled with legitimate funds. Money laundering methods are diverse and are constantly evolving. They range from trade-related operations to on-line banking. Money launderers may also operate outside financial systems, for example, through alternative remittance systems.

14. Other financial crimes can be associated with, or exist in parallel with, money laundering, for example, corruption, fraud, or the control of a financial institution by organized crime. Upon the receipt of criminal proceeds, criminals may seek to launder them through the financial system. This, in turn, may also require a series of fraudulent activities such as counterfeiting invoices and the corrupting of bank employees. Thus, a whole chain of criminal or illegal activities may culminate in the flow of criminal money through the financial system. Tax evasion, a form of financial crime, is facilitated by the existence of jurisdictions that have low tax rates, maintain relatively lax financial regulations and

practices and that do not share information on client accounts with the tax authorities of relevant jurisdictions.

## III. THE ECONOMIC EFFECTS OF FINANCIAL ABUSE, FINANCIAL CRIME, AND MONEY LAUNDERING

15. Financial system abuse has potentially negative consequences for a country's macroeconomic performance, may impose welfare losses, and may also have negative crossborder negative externalities. Globalization and financial market integration in particular facilitates financial abuse. This section briefly reviews the very limited empirical and indirect evidence on the magnitude of financial system abuse, financial crime, and money laundering.

16. Trust underpins the existence and development of financial markets. The effective functioning of financial markets relies heavily on the expectation that high professional, legal, and ethical standards are observed and enforced. A reputation for integrity—soundness, honesty, adherence to standards and codes—is one of the most valued assets by investors, financial institutions, and jurisdictions. Various forms of financial system abuse may compromise financial institutions' and jurisdictions' reputation, undermine investors' trust in them, and therefore weaken the financial system. The important link between financial market integrity and financial stability is underscored in the Basel Core Principles for Effective Supervision and in the Code of Good Practices on Transparency in Monetary and Financial Policies, particularly those principles and codes that most directly address the prevention, uncovering, and reporting of financial system abuse, including financial crime, and money laundering.

17. Financial system abuse may have other negative macroeconomic consequences. For example, it could compromise bank soundness with potentially large fiscal liabilities, lessen the ability to attract foreign investment, and increase the volatility of international capital flows and exchange rates. In the era of very high capital mobility, abuse of the global financial system makes national tax collection and law enforcement more difficult. Financial system abuse, financial crime, and money laundering may also distort the allocation of resources and the distribution of wealth and can be costly to detect and eradicate. A common theme in research is that "if crime, underground activity and the associated money laundering take place on a sufficiently large scale, then macroeconomic policymakers must take them into account."

18. Economic damage can arise not only directly from financial system abuse, but also from allegations that affect the reputation of a country, or from one country's actions against perceived financial system abuse in another economy. Such allegations or actions can through reputational effects affect the willingness of economic agents, particularly those outside the country, to conduct business in a given country (e.g., inward investment, banking correspondent relationships) with adverse consequences.

* * *

23. The costs associated with other elements of financial system abuse, including the damage caused by abuse of poor regulatory frameworks which may contribute to financial crises or undermine confidence in financial system, are even more difficult to identify. The fiscal and output losses from financial crises have been extensively documented. These losses relate to the total costs of the crises—usually caused by a combination of macroeconomic shocks and a fragile financial system—and it is not possible to disentangle the cost of abusing weak regulations on its own. Similarly, difficulties are encountered in estimating the macroeconomic effects of tax evasion and harmful tax competition, and corruption.

24. In sum, the empirical evidence on the magnitude of financial system abuse, financial crime or money laundering is limited but significant impact on individual countries cannot be ruled out. Measurements based on reported crimes underestimate the actual magnitude of financial system abuse, while estimates based on the underground economy clearly exaggerate it.

* * *

**Annex VI**

INTERNATIONAL ORGANIZATIONS INVOLVED IN COUNTERING FINANCIAL SYSTEM ABUSE, FINANCIAL CRIME, AND MONEY LAUNDERING

International efforts to combat financial system abuse, financial crime, and money laundering intensified in the late 1980s, sparked by the growing concerns about drug trafficking and the recognition that the internationalization of trade and finance and advancements in communication technology may facilitate money laundering. Since then, countering financial crime, and money laundering became an integral part of the agenda of many multilateral organizations. The interagency response is led primarily by the Financial Action Task Force (FATF) and the affiliated regional organizations. Other international organizations, including those with a general mandate (such as the United Nations) and those with a specialized focus (particularly, the Financial Stability Forum and international standard-setting bodies of financial sector supervisors) also contribute. The nature and activities of the principal multilateral organizations currently involved in countering financial system abuse, financial crime, and money laundering is summarized in this Annex.

**The Financial Action Task Force on Money Laundering and the Affiliated Multilateral Organizations**

**1. FATF**

The FATF was established by the G-7 in 1989 with a mandate to examine measures to combat money laundering, largely in recognition of the enormous proportions of the drug problem. The FATF now includes 29 member countries and two regional organizations from the Americas, Europe, and Asia, as well as 18 observers (including the Fund and the World Bank). Although located at the OECD, where it maintains a small secretariat, the FATF is independent of the OECD. The FATF is the principal anti-money laundering multilateral organization.

Since the FATF is a voluntary task force and not a treaty organization, its *Forty Recommendations* do not constitute a binding international convention. However, each FATF member undertakes a firm political commitment to combat money laundering by implementing the recommendations. Besides self-assessment exercises and mutual evaluations, the FATF, in close collaboration with its members and other organizations, conducts regular *typology exercises* to uncover new money laundering techniques and to develop strategies for countering them.

The FATF's anti-money laundering efforts summarized in the Forty Recommendations relate to the enforcement of criminal laws and to complementary measures in the financial sector, and international cooperation. The recommendations that apply to law enforcement can be grouped according to those for: (i) the criminalization of money laundering, (ii) the seizure and confiscation of money laundering proceeds, (iii) suspicious transaction reporting, and (iv) international cooperation in the investigation, prosecution and extradition of crime suspects. Recommendations dealing with financial sector regulations relate primarily to customer identification and record keeping requirements, which together are commonly referred to as "know-your-customer" standards.

FATF members are reviewed for their compliance with the FATF *Forty Recommendations*(issued in 1990 and modified in 1996) through mutual evaluation by their peers, where assessors from member countries carry out on-site assessments on implementation and prepare a detailed report on compliance. To date, most members have undergone two rounds of mutual evaluations, which are supported by annual self-assessments to track progress by individual countries in correcting deficiencies. Results from the mutual evaluations and the annual self-assessments are summarized in FATF publications. Although *infra*ctions are identified, the extent of noncompliance is not, and seldom has the FATF found it necessary to recommended punitive actions against its members.

\* \* \*

### 5. International Standard-Setting Bodies in the Area of Financial Sector

### Regulation and Supervision and Accounting

### Basel Committee on Banking Supervision

In the area of countering financial system abuse, financial crime, and money laundering, the Basel Committee has been active on several fronts. With regard to anti-money laundering guidance, the Basel Committee has issued a total of four papers, the last of which remains in draft. The papers give special emphasis to the need for an adequate "know your customer" (KYC) program.

The first paper, the *Statement on Prevention of Criminal Use of the Banking System for the Purpose of Money-Laundering*, highlighted key principles which seek to ensure that banks are not used to hide or launder the profits of crime: (i) customer identification; (ii) compliance with laws; (iii) cooperation with law enforcement authorities, and (iv) policies, procedures and training. The Statement noted in this context that "public confidence in banks, and hence their stability, can be undermined by adverse publicity as a result of inadvertent association by banks with criminals. In addition, banks may lay themselves open to direct losses from fraud, either through negligence in screening undesirable customers or where the integrity of the loan officers has been undermined through association with criminals."

\* \* \*

### International Organization of Securities Commissions (IOSCO)

As with other financial sector standard-setting bodies, IOSCO guidelines seek to prevent the use of securities intermediaries for purposes of financial crime. In October 1992, the President's Committee of IOSCO passed the *Resolution on Money Laundering*, which, *inter alia*, stated that each member should consider: (i) the extent to which customer identifying-information is gathered and recorded by financial institutions under its supervision; (ii) the extent and adequacy of record keeping requirements; (iii) the system of reporting suspicious transactions; (iv) procedures in place to prevent criminals from obtaining control of securities and futures businesses; (v) the means to ensure that securities and futures firms maintain appropriate monitoring and compliance procedures; (vi) the most appropriate means to share information.53

\* \* \*

## THE FINANCIAL ACTION TASK FORCE—FORTY RECOMMENDATIONS AND THE FUND

This Annex provides an overview of how the work of FATF *Forty Recommendations* are partially incorporated in Fund work. As indicated in Annex XVI, the FATF *Forty Recommendations* cover law enforcement, regulation of the financial system and international cooperation. The recommendations for the regulation of financial systems significantly overlap with Basel Core Principles for Banking Supervision, and in line with the Fund Executive Board guidance, staff undertakes assessment of members' compliance with Basel Core Principles (BCP). Also consistently with Board guidance, however, the law enforcement aspects of the FATF recommendations are considered as not appropriate for the Fund to assess.

The FATF recommendations pertaining to the broad areas of law enforcement by general category relate to (i) the criminalization of money laundering (FATF 1, 4, 5 and 6); (ii) the seizure and confiscation of money laundering proceeds (FATF 7, 35 and 38); and (iii) the international cooperation in the investigation, prosecution and extradition of crime suspects (FATF 3, 31, 33, 34, 36, 37, 38, 39 and 40). The Basel Committee's anti-money laundering guidance can be found in the Core Principles for Effective Banking Supervision, specifically Core Principle 15, which states that: "Banking supervisors must determine that banks have adequate policies, practices and procedures in place, including strict "know-your-customer" rules, that promote high ethical and professional standards in the financial sector and prevent the bank being used, intentionally or unintentionally, by criminal elements." The BCP methodology used by assessors to review compliance with essential and additional criteria embodies the FATF recommendations that are relevant to the financial sector.

\* \* \*

### Essential criteria applicable to Core Principle 15

1. The supervisor determines that banks have in place adequate policies, practices and procedures that promote high ethical and professional standards and prevent the bank from being used, intentionally or unintentionally, by criminal elements. This includes the prevention and detection of criminal activity or fraud, and reporting of such suspected activities to the appropriate authorities.

2. The supervisor determines that banks have documented and enforced policies for identification of customers and those acting on their behalf as part of their anti money laundering program. There are clear rules on what records must be kept on customer identification and individual transactions and the retention period. (FATF 10, 11 and 12)

3. The supervisor determines that banks have formal procedures to recognize potentially suspicious transactions. These might include additional authorization for large cash (or similar) deposits or withdrawals and special procedures for unusual transactions. (FATF 14)

4. The supervisor determines that banks appoint a senior officer with explicit responsibility for ensuring that the bank's policies and procedures are, at a minimum, in accordance with local statutory and regulatory anti-money laundering requirements. (FATF 19)

5. The supervisor determines that banks have clear procedures, communicated to all personnel, for staff to report suspicious transactions to the dedicated senior officer responsible for anti-money laundering compliance. (FATF 15)

6. The supervisor determines that banks have established lines of communication both to management and to an internal security (guardian) function for reporting problems. (**FATF 15**)

7. In addition to reporting to the appropriate criminal authorities, banks report to the supervisor suspicious activities and incidents of fraud material to the safety, soundness or reputation of the bank. (**FATF 14**)

8. Laws, regulations and/or banks' policies ensure that a member of staff who reports suspicious transactions in good faith to the dedicated senior officer, internal security function, or directly to the relevant authority cannot be held liable. (**FATF 16**)

9. The supervisor periodically checks that banks' money laundering controls and their systems for preventing, identifying and reporting fraud are sufficient. The supervisor has adequate enforcement powers (regulatory and/or criminal prosecution) to take action against a bank that does not comply with its anti-money laundering obligations. (**FATF 26**)

10. The supervisor is able, directly or indirectly, to share with domestic and foreign financial sector supervisory authorities information related to suspected or actual criminal activities. (**FATF 23 and 32**)

11. The supervisor determines that banks have a policy statement on ethics and professional behavior that is clearly communicated to all staff.

**Additional criteria**

1. The laws and/or regulations embody international sound practices, such as compliance with the relevant forty Financial Action Task Force Recommendations issued in 1990 (revised 1996). (**FATF 10-29**)

2. The supervisor determines that bank staff is adequately trained in money laundering detection and prevention.

3. The supervisor has the legal obligation to inform the relevant criminal authorities of any suspicious transactions.

4. The supervisor is able, directly or indirectly, to share with relevant judicial authorities information related to suspected or actual criminal activities. (**FATF 23**)

5. If not performed by another agency, the supervisor has in-house resources with specialist expertise on financial fraud and anti-money laundering obligations.

# 6. Enhancing Contributions to Combating Money Laundering: Policy Paper
International Monetary Fund and World Bank, 2001
[footnotes omitted by editors]

## I. INTRODUCTION

1. The International Monetary and Financial Committee (IMFC), at its September 2000, meeting, requested "the Fund to prepare a joint paper with the Bank on their respective roles in combating money laundering and financial crime, and in protecting the international financial system." Moreover, the two institutions were asked to explore incorporating work on financial system abuse, particularly with respect to international efforts to fight against money laundering into its various activities, as relevant and appropriate.

2. An informal question and answer session with the Fund Board was held in February 2001 on the basis of the staff paper *Financial System Abuse, Financial Crime and Money Laundering Background Paper* (SM/01/46); in September 2000, Bank staff prepared an information note for the Bank Board on *The Role of the World Bank Group in Promoting the Integrity of Financial Markets* (September 21, 2000). These documents provide relevant background material for this paper. A joint Fund/Bank workshop on financial abuse, with seven outside speakers (including the current President of the Financial Action Task Force (FATF)), was held at the Fund on February 27, 2001.

3. Although no formal conclusions were drawn from these meetings, the following propositions seemed to gain some acceptance:

(i) while financial abuse covers a variety of activities, it would be productive at the present time to concentrate on the role of the Fund and Bank in efforts to combat money laundering;

(ii) the Fund and the Bank are already helping countries strengthen their financial supervision and regulation, as well as legal and governance structures, contributing to the prevention of financial sector crime and money laundering;

(iii) substantial efforts relevant to countering money laundering are undertaken by other bodies and closer international cooperation would benefit all; and

(iv) the Fund's and the Bank's work on strengthening financial supervision through the application of financial standards, including the preparation of relevant Report on the Observance of Standards and Codes (ROSC), overlaps with the financial/supervisory aspects of the Financial Action Task Force 40 Recommendations (FATF 40).

4. This paper proposes that the Fund and the Bank strengthen their role in the global fight against financial sector abuse, and money laundering specifically, by (i) publicizing, through official statements and other forms of outreach, both the need to put in place the necessary economic, financial, and legal systems designed to protect against money laundering and the role that the Bank and the Fund are playing in helping to meet this need; (ii) recognizing the FATF 40 as a standard for anti-money laundering useful for Fund/Bank operational work, (iii) when undertaking Financial Sector Assessment Program (FSAP), ROSCs and Offshore Financial Center (OFC) assessments, intensifying the focus on anti-money laundering elements in the assessment of supervisory standards Basel Committee Principles (BCPs), International Organization of Securities Commissions' Objectives and Principles for Securities Regulation (IOSCO Principles), and the International Association of Insurance Supervisors Insurance Supervisory Principles (IAIS Principles) and producing a detailed assessment which, with the concerned country's permission, could be published or shared with the FATF and/or the appropriate regional anti-money laundering task forces; (iv) working more closely with the major international anti-money laundering groups; and (v) increasing the provision of technical assistance (TA) from the Bank and Fund in this area.

5. Section II discusses work currently undertaken by the Fund and Bank that is relevant to countering financial abuse, especially with respect to helping national authorities improve their systems of financial regulation and supervision so as to create the environment within financial institutions to deter financial crime and money laundering. The paper then reports in Section III on the wider international efforts, including the work of the FATF and regional anti-money laundering task forces, in combating money laundering. Steps to enhance the Fund and Bank contributions to anti-money laundering efforts are proposed in Section IV. Section V discusses the resource implications. The key questions

before Executive Directors (Section VI) are (a) whether the FATF 40 should be recognized as a standard for Fund and Bank operational work; and (b) how to enhance work on money laundering issues in Fund and Bank activities, in particular in technical assistance, including with respect to FSAP, ROSCs and OFC assessments, as well as in the context of technical assistance.

## II. THE FUND'S AND THE BANK'S ACTIVITIES RELEVANT TO THE COUNTERING OF FINANCIAL SYSTEM ABUSE

6. Money laundering is a problem of global concern, requiring concerted and cooperative action on the part of a broad range of institutions. The Fund and the Bank's principal contributions to the fight against money laundering have been in their work to promote stronger financial, economic, and legal systems in general. Strengthened supervisory systems and robust legal and institutional framework for financial institutions help prevent a broad range of financial sector abuses, including money laundering. This section first discusses the activities special to each institution, then turns to those pursed jointly.

### A. Fund Activities

7. Financial sector issues are central to the Fund's mandate as they are rooted in its purpose to promote macroeconomic stability and growth. Anti-money laundering issues related to financial supervision and regulation (primarily those included in BCPs, IOSCO or IAIS Principles) are germane to the Fund's core responsibilities, while other anti-money laundering issues associated with criminal law enforcement (primarily those not included in BCPs, IOSCO or IAIS Principles) are beyond the Fund's core areas. Under existing Fund policies, anti-money laundering issues other than those relating to financial sector regulation and supervision are covered under surveillance and conditionality, as with other governance matters, only if they pass the macro-relevance test. The Fund could raise the issue of cross-border implications of money laundering, e.g., during the Article IV consultation, for a given member when this is macro-relevant for other members or important for stability of the international financial system (under Article XII, Section 8).

8. The Fund in its broad operational activities surveillance, conditionality and technical assistance promotes stronger financial systems, including through FSAPs, OFC assessments, and ROSC exercises. The Fund's work helps national authorities strengthen their supervisory and regulatory systems, which in turn, helps both to promote the safety and soundness of the financial sector and to create an environment that prevents financial system abuse. In particular, assessments of observance of international standards, codes, and best practices in the areas of financial supervision, prudential regulation, transparency of fiscal and monetary policies, and data provision and dissemination have the potential to play a major role in fostering financial market integrity. In this context, the Fund staff has followed the guidance given in *Concluding Remarks Following the Executive Board Discussion of the Fund's Role in OFC Assessments(Offshore Financial Centers — The Role of the Fund* (BUFF/00/98), July 14, 2000). Directors stressed that effective anti-money laundering measures were important for the integrity of the financial system as well as for fighting financial crime, and that such measures were part of the core supervisory principles covering all financial sectors. Directors also noted, however, that anti-money laundering measures promoted by FATF included law enforcement measures, which would not be appropriate for the Fund to assess.

### Surveillance and conditionality

9. The emphasis on financial sector soundness in Article IV surveillance has increased in recent years. In an earlier review **of the coverage of financial sector issues in Article IV**

surveillance, staff found that assessments of banking systems and prudential and supervisory frameworks were discussed in almost every report reviewed. As a follow-up and in order to provide a snapshot of the treatment of financial system abuse issues, a sample of staff reports in the context of Article IV consultations and use of Fund resources was reviewed for references to financial system abuse issues. Taking into account that explicit operational guidance to staff on the Fund's role in addressing anti-money laundering issues is both limited and recent, the sample focused on staff reports for members hosting major financial centers and those members included in the lists published by the Financial Stability Forum (FSF), FATF, and OECD.6 Accordingly, the staff survey covered 48 staff reports issued during January 1999–December 2007. Staff reports were examined for the coverage of money laundering, other financial crime (e.g., pyramid schemes, fraudulent sale of financial instruments), tax evasion, and corruption related to the financial sector. The reports were also reviewed for coverage of banking secrecy, which may contribute to financial abuse, as well as of the offshore financial activities that may be subject to less stringent regulation and supervision and thus potentially susceptible to financial system abuse.

10. **More than half of the staff reports reviewed included references to financial system abuse-related issues.** Specifically, 19 reports covered money laundering, six referred to financial crime generally, eight to banking secrecy, 12 to tax avoidance (or tax havens),and six to corruption. Six staff reports included specific references to the authorities' reaction to their countries being placed on one of the lists promulgated by the FSF, FATF or OECD alleging substandard compliance with their particular criteria.

**Technical assistance**

11. Staff has provided **technical assistance on the design of prudential regulation and banking supervision schemes of many Fund members.** The most extensive TA in this area has been provided in the context of OFCs, FSAP, and ROSC modules. **The OFC assessment program** has involved missions to 17 jurisdictions between October 2000 and March 2001. A progress report on the program was provided to the Fund Board on February9, 2001. Anti-money laundering legislation, regulations and practices are being put in place by a number of jurisdictions, some with the support of Fund TA. Many of these OFC jurisdictions intend to request a Fund assisted assessment of financial sector standards and codes or an FSAP-type comprehensive assessment of their financial systems. FSAPs and ROSCs involve both the Fund and the Bank, and are discussed below.

* * *

## C. Fund/Bank Joint Work

21. The Fund and the Bank have been contributing jointly to the countering of financial system abuse in the context of FSAP and ROSC program.

22. **The Financial Sector Assessment Program**, introduced in 1999, aims to identify other financial vulnerabilities and development needs. At the most general level, joint Fund/Bank FSAP work reduces the opportunities for financial crime through improving financial supervision and the preconditions (legal, governance, administrative, etc.) for effective regulation and supervision. More specifically, FSAPs assess, by examining supervisory core principles, the susceptibility of the financial system to financial crime and money laundering, for example, because of excessive bank secrecy laws. All FSAPs include an assessment of BCPs (in particular CP15, which relates directly to money laundering); most contain assessments of the equivalent IOSCO and IAIS principles. The

principle findings from the FSAPs are communicated to the Fund's and Bank's Executive Boards in the form of a Financial Sector Stability Assessment report (FSSA) and a Financial Sector Assessment report. As of end March 2001, 14 FSSAs and nine FSAs have been issued to Executive Directors.

23. In the area of anti-money laundering, advice and recommendations arising from FSAPs include (i) introduction of legislation to do away with anonymous banking accounts; (ii) improvements to "know-your-customer" procedures in the context of the assessment of BCP 15; (iii) modifications to secrecy legislation to verify implementation of know your customer requirements; and (iv) implementation of new anti-money laundering laws.

24. The IMF and the Bank have also been collaborating closely in assessing progress in implementing selected international standards through the program on Reports on Observance of Standards and Codes. The international community has emphasized the development and implementation of standards as one of the key elements in strengthening the architecture of the international financial system by promoting the sound functioning of members' economic and financial systems. The assessment and disclosure of observance of standards can highlight potential vulnerabilities, help national authorities in their efforts to strengthen domestic economic and financial sector policy frameworks, and promote transparency and market discipline. Largely in the context of the FSAP, the Bank and the Fund conduct assessments of relevant financial sector standards (the Basel Core Principles, the IOSCO Principles and the IAIS Principles) that lead to the preparation of ROSCs. As of end March, 2001, 38 ROSC modules in these three areas have been completed for 23 countries, of which 21 have been published.

* * *

## IV. ENHANCING CONTRIBUTIONS TO COMBATING MONEY LAUNDERING: ISSUES FOR THE FUND AND THE BANK

31. The breadth and cross-cutting nature of the global agenda to curb money laundering calls for a cooperative approach among many different international institutions.

International efforts against money laundering are led by the relevant specialized institutions, notably the FATF, the regional anti-money laundering groups and the UNDCP. The Bank and Fund's work in financial sector areas has complemented anti-money laundering efforts, while remaining within their respective mandates and areas of expertise.

32. The Fund and the Bank can increase their participation in the global fight against financial abuse and money laundering by (i) publicizing both the need to put in place the necessary economic, financial, and legal systems designed to protect against money laundering and the role that the Bank and the Fund are playing in helping meet this need; (ii) recognizing the FATF 40 as a standard for anti-money laundering useful for Fund/ Bank operational work, (iii) intensifying the focus on anti-money laundering elements in relevant supervisory principles, (iv) working more closely with the major international anti-money laundering groups, and (v) increasing the provision of technical assistance in this area. These proposals are discussed below and summarized in Box 1.

### Publicize the importance of countries acting to protect against financial abuse and money laundering

33. The Fund and the Bank can publicize in general terms both the need to put in place the necessary economic, financial, and legal systems designed to protect against financial abuse and money laundering and the role that the Fund and the Bank are playing in helping meet this need. The IMFC and DC, as well as the Boards of the Fund and the Bank could make appropriate public statements; the Fund and the Bank could better publicize

their respective activities; and both institutions could undertake additional studies, engaging in workshops, focusing on the macroeconomic and development affects of money laundering.

**Box 1. Steps to Enhance the Fund's and Bank's Contribution to International Efforts Countering Money Laundering**

*   *Publicize importance of countries acting to protect against financial abuse and money laundering.* The IMFC and DC, as well as the Boards of the Fund and the Bank, to make appropriate public statements; the Fund and the Bank to publicize relevant information on their activities; and both to undertake additional studies, engage in workshops etc. with respect to the macroeconomic and development affects of money laundering.

*   *Recognize the FATF 40 as a standard for anti-money laundering useful for Fund/Bank operational work.* The FATF (and possibly regional groups) could be invited to prepare a ROSC module provided that the underlying ROSC process is observed, i.e., that there is uniformity of treatment, the FATF 40 is used for all assessments (including FATF nonmembers) and the approach to assessments is cooperative and voluntary. At this time the conditions for the ROSC process are not met and therefore the staffs do not recommend that FATF (or other groups) be invited to prepare ROSC modules.

*   *Intensify focus on anti-money laundering elements in relevant supervisory principles.* The Fund and the Bank to develop a methodology document for determining compliance with key anti-money laundering elements in the relevant BCP, IOSCO and IAIS principles (see Annex II). The methodology document would draw from guidance material available from relevant organizations/entities, including Basel Committee, IOSCO, IAIS and the FATF. (About half of the FATF 40, which pertain to financial/supervisory matters, would be relevant in crafting the methodology document.) Detailed assessments could be published or shared with the FATF and other regional anti-money laundering task forces.

*   *Work more closely with major international anti-money laundering groups.* The Fund and the Bank would work more closely with other international anti-money laundering groups, including participating in more meetings and joint workshops, and exchanging information, particularly on compliance with financial standards. To avoid confusing different purposes and methods, the Fund and the Bank would not undertake joint missions with the FATF or regional task forces.

*   *Increase the provision of technical assistance.* The delivery of TA by the Bank and the Fund when combined with other bilateral and multilateral TA providers would achieve greater efficiency and effectiveness.

34. The Boards of the Fund and the Bank could seek a statement by IMFC and the DC that would (i) recognize that money laundering is a global concern requiring concerted and cooperative action on the part of a range of institutions, with the lead taken by the FATF and the UNDCP that effective anti-money laundering measures are important to all Fund and Bank members (though especially to those with large financial markets) and that implementing such measures is a primary responsibility of national authorities; and (ii) encourage the Fund and the Bank to enhance their current contributions to counter money laundering by helping countries strengthen their economic, financial and legal systems broadly.

35. Next, the Fund and the Bank could communicate to the public more effectively their various contributions to preventing financial abuse and money laundering. They could do this by emphasizing in their public outreach activities the role that the institutions play,

through support of economic programs and technical assistance in helping countries to develop and reform their financial systems and assisting them towards putting in place a proper regulatory and supervisory environment. In particular, the activities with respect to financial sector standards and codes assessed by the Fund and the Bank could be stressed. Methods for improving outreach could include speeches, articles, and seminars.

36. The Fund and the Bank could undertake additional research into the macroeconomic and development effects of financial crime and money laundering. Because the scale and consequence of financial sector abuse in general, and of money laundering in particular, are not well understood (for the obvious reason that illegal activities are difficult to measure) such additional research would be difficult. At a minimum, however, the research would review effects of financial crime on the macro economy and would aim at providing an indication of the significance with which crime impacts industrial and developing country markets. The output of such research could be brought together in 2002 in a paper for both the Fund and Bank Boards.

**Recognize the FATF 40 as an international anti-money laundering standard**

37. The Fund and the Bank could recognize the FATF 40 as the internationally accepted standard for anti-money laundering policies useful for Bank and Fund operational work, which would increase the number of recognized standards to 12. The FSF already includes the FATF 40 among its 12 key standards for sound financial systems. In deciding to recognize the FATF 40, Directors could consider the relevance of the FATF 40 to macroeconomic stability and financial soundness. Directors may also wish to consider whether the FATF 40 are broadly recognized as an international standard, and if they are appropriate for developing as well as developed countries. In this context it should be noted that the FATF recommendations have become dated and that, as a result, the FATF is revising its existing 40 recommendations to reflect the evolution of money-laundering activities and to address inconsistencies in the treatment within the FATF membership and vis-a-vis non-members. The process of revising the FATF 40 Recommendations is likely to extend beyond 2001. The FATF 40 is not, however, the only standard undergoing revision.

38. With respect to assessment, neither the Fund nor the Bank could be expected to assess compliance with those aspects of the FATF 40 that relate to legal/criminal enforcement matters. One possibility would be for the Fund and the Bank to assess only those aspects of the FATF 40 relating to financial/supervisory matters. However, an expert from the UNDCP stated most recently at the February workshop that the FATF 40, while covering many areas that are primarily financial/supervisory in nature, were designed to be assessed as a unified whole. Separating out those principles that concerned legal/criminal enforcement matters from financial regulation and supervision would be problematic in his view.

39. One possibility would be to invite the FATF (perhaps in cooperation with regional task forces and other anti-money laundering organizations) to assess compliance with the FATF 40. FATF would prepare a ROSC module on anti-money laundering provided that established Bank-Fund guidance for incorporating standards as ROSCs were observed. The FATF and the regional groups are already carrying out assessments of compliance with the FATF 40 Recommendations. However, the FATF has applied the FATF 40 when conducting mutual evaluations of its members, but the FATF has used the FATF 25 Criteria, to assess jurisdictions that are not FATF members. Evaluations by the FATF of nonmembers are involuntary and involve a "name and shame" approach to induce compliance. The FATF is also considering the possibility of recommending that sanctions be imposed on non-

complying jurisdictions in some circumstances. For ROSCs, a single international standard such as the FATF 40 should be applied in a uniform fashion and on a voluntary basis.

40. Because the FATF process lacks conformity with the principles of the Bank-Fund ROSC initiative, the two staffs recommend that FATF would not be invited at this time to prepare a ROSC module on the FATF 40. Instead, the two staffs could contribute to the ongoing revision of the FATF 40 and discuss with the FATF the principles behind the ROSC procedures, and come back to the Board with a report and recommendations.

### Intensify focus by the Fund and the Bank on relevant anti-money laundering principles

41. Independent of a decision to recognize the FATF 40 as a standard for operational work, the Fund and the Bank could deepen the emphasis on anti-money laundering elements of the BCP, IOSCO and IAIS Principles, which are already assessed under the FSAP. Observance of these and other principles helps ensure that financial institutions have in place needed management and risk control systems, which are crucial in helping to prevent financial crimes, including money laundering. The Fund and the Bank could deepen their assessment of compliance with the anti-money laundering elements of BCPs and the IOSCO and IAIS principles drawing on a new methodology document (to be developed) that sets out criteria for assessment and procedures for preparation of the report. Such a methodology document, while not directly using the FATF 40 as a standard, would cover the essence of the FATF 40 relating to financial/supervision matters (about half of the FATF 40). Using the methodology document, a focused assessment of relevant anti-money laundering elements will be included as part of the detailed assessments of compliance with BCPs, IOSCO and IAIS Principles.

42. The release of detailed assessments, including the focused assessment of relevant anti-money laundering elements, would follow the policy established for technical assistance reports. In addition, the country concerned could share the reports with the FATF and other regional anti-money laundering task forces. Because of the Fund and Bank's comparative advantage in the financial sector, the detailed assessments could reduce the burden on the FATF and other anti-money laundering groups by limiting duplication of efforts.

43. As more FSAPs are undertaken, the coverage of anti-money laundering issues in financial sector work will deepen. In line with the Fund and Bank Executive Boards' guidance, the schedule for FSAPs should give the highest priority to systemically important countries. The Fund and the Bank would send a clear signal of the importance of effective anti-money laundering measures for national financial systems and the international financial system. It would also emphasize that both the Fund and the Bank are giving heightened attention to governance as an important factor influencing economic performance.

### Work more closely with major international anti-money laundering groups

44. The Fund and the Bank could work more closely with other international anti-money laundering groups and task forces. The most important of these are the FATF and the regional anti-money laundering task forces. Fund and Bank staff attend the main FATF meetings and now also some of the regional groupings. Staff could work more closely with FATF by playing a role in the current substantial revisions to the FATF 40 and exchanging information, particularly on compliance with financial standards. On the sharing of information, FATF has already agreed to share results from their exercises with Fund and Bank staff conducting financial assessments, for example in the context of FSAPs. In addition, Bank and Fund members that have undergone assessments could voluntarily share information on the observance of relevant principles with FATF. Such exchanges would eliminate some duplication between FATF and Bank and Fund assess-

ments, and improve the quality and timeliness of assessments by both institutions. The staffs do not propose to undertake joint missions with the FATF or regional task forces.

**Increase the provision of technical assistance**

45. The Bank and the Fund could help countries improve their anti-money laundering laws and practices through the provision of technical assistance. At present, TA for anti-money laundering is provided bilaterally (especially from FATF members), by the UNDCP, Egmont Group, INTERPOL, and to a more limited extent through the capacity building of the Bank, the Fund and other multilateral agencies. Bank and Fund staff should co-ordinate more closely with these other TA providers, sharing knowledge and experience (within the confines of confidentiality protocols) wherever possible.

46. In the context of their regular activities, the Fund and the Bank already solicit infor-mation on TA and training needs to enhance countries' capacity to strengthen adherence to international standards, including in some areas directly pertinent to countering finan-cial sector abuse and specifically money laundering. To assess comprehensively the scale of needed resources (human and financial), however, would require an evaluation of institutional and legal infrastructure. The G7 has offered to provide TA to jurisdictions that commit to make improvements in their regimes to counter money laundering. The Fund and the Bank have been asked to play a role in coordinating this effort. Such an assessment of TA needs, coordination of TA delivery, and direct provision of TA would represent a significant re-source commitment for the Fund and the Bank that would take both institutions into areas outside their expertise and mandates. The Boards need to consider whether they want the Fund and the Bank to (i) increase TA in relevant prevention areas; (ii) identify TA needs for addressing money laundering issues; or (iii) coordinate all TA on money laundering, i.e., also in law enforcement areas. A preferred option would be to increase TA in relevant prevention areas, with the extra work by the Fund and the Bank focusing on adherence to relevant standards (outside law enforcement). More general TA and coordination of all money laundering TA would probably be best left to the FATF, the U.N. and others.

---

## 7. Richard K. Gordon, Current Developments in Monetary & Financial Law, International Monetary Fund

Chapter 15: Anti-Money-Laundering Policies Selected Legal, Political, and Economic Issues, 1999
[footnotes omitted by editors]

Efforts by governments to control cross-border money laundering have intensified in recent years. Over the past decade, a broad political consensus appears to have arisen in favor of the implementation of effective anti-money-launderers, policies, at least in most developing countries. However, the question has also arisen of whether, in some instances, the war against money laundering may be going too far. For example, a 1998 *Wall Street Journal* article entitled "How Money Laundering Hit a Wealthy Family" related the story of how $54 million, virtually the entire financial assets of a Chilean extended family, were effectively frozen by the U.S. Government under U.S. anti-money-laundering and civil for-feiture legislation. The family, formerly prized Citibank customers who held their wealth legitimately, lost control over their U.S. based assets because the federal government as-serted that they had helped to launder money for a Mexican drug lord.

According to the article, the money-laundering transaction occurred when a bank owned by the Chilean family cashed $400,000 in travelers checks. At first blush this would seem to be a huge amount of money that naturally would arouse the suspicions of the bank.

Indeed, the size of the cash transactions did trigger some questions. The customer insisted that he needed the cash to buy a house, which turned out to be true, and what was at least a cursory inquiry into her identity raised no red flags. It turned out, however, that the customer was a suspected drug lord operating under an alias. In ordering the seizure of $54 million in assets, U.S. investigators had not proven that the Chilean bank had not exercised reasonable effort to ascertain the valid needs of their Mexican customer. However, because the costs to the bank of even a temporary seizure of its American assets were so substantial, they agreed to settle the case by paying over the entire value of the traveler's check transaction to the United States.

A number of relevant facts should be noted. There were no allegations that the traveler's checks themselves were stolen from U.S. citizens, or in some other way represented a fraud upon a U.S. citizen, only that they may have been purchased using the proceeds (profits) of a criminal activity. That criminal activity was solely the production and sale of illegal narcotics. Much of the profits came from the voluntary purchase of such narcotics by U.S. residents, activity that the U.S. government, including law enforcement agents, was unable to prevent. There were no serious allegations that the bank was knowingly participating or somehow conspiring with the Mexican drug lord in furthering his criminal enterprise, at least as such terms are normally understood. Therefore, one way to interpret what had happened was that the U.S. government was forcing a Chilean bank to take responsibility to enforce U.S. narcotics laws when the United States could not, or would not, do so itself.

The attorney who represented the Chilean family called U.S. money laundering law "draconian." However, U.S. laws are less draconian than many. Could it be that the pursuit of ever more effective anti-money-laundering was may be going too far? If this is the case, why? And, more specifically, should anti-money-laundering policies be a matter that international financial institutions, especially the IMF, should make central to their operations?

This paper seeks to raise some questions about the way in which the international community has advanced the anti-money-laundering crusade. It starts by looking at the history of anti-money-laundering efforts and the laws that may have gone too far. Finally, given this analysis, it raises some questions, over the role of international financial institutions, particularly the IMF, in the fight against money laundering.

### The Origins of Anti-Money-Laundering Policies

Sustained interest in what has come to be known as money laundering began in the early 1980s, primarily within the context of concern over the growing problem of drug abuse, and particularly of international drug trafficking by organized crime. Existing efforts to reduce the availability of drugs, including the arrest of both users and producers, the destruction of drug manufacturing facilities, and the interception of drugs at the border, appeared insufficient to national leaders. Although their scope was to expand beyond narcodollars, anti-money-laundering policies began largely as an additional weapon in the armory against the international drug trade.

Over the past 25 years, international drug trafficking has become an enormous business, generating huge domestic and international cash flows. However, criminal sanctions against narcotics trafficking could include long prison sentences and the seizure of both the receipts and working capital of the enterprise. In order to protect both their property from forfeiture and themselves from prison, narcotics traffickers needed to disguise the illegal origins of what came to be known generically as narcodollars. This process of disguising what was known as "money laundering," was created because it "washes away" the "stain" of illegality. The first anti-money-laundering laws were drafted primarily as a way of attacking this process. Also, the net profits from narcotics vastly exceeded the amount necessary for additional investment in drug trafficking, and new investment opportunities were needed. Therefore, in addition to hiding money for personal consumption and for reinvestment in the drug trade, money laundering was designed to free up cash to invest in legitimate business.

By and large, the drug trade was based in a number of Latin American and East and Central Asian countries, where most of the poppies, cocoa, and cannabis were grown arid processed into narcotics, primarily but not exclusively for export to industrial countries. Narcodollars from this trade, realized in both the countries of production and the countries of consumption, were laundered through a number of financial centers, often those with strong bank secrecy laws. The laundered Bonds were then invested throughout the world, in both developed and emerging markets.

### International Agreements

The United States became one of the first countries to enact effective anti-money-laundering laws. However, not every important money laundering center implemented effective anti-money-laundering policies. Countries like the United States took the lead in pressing for what became the United Nations Convention Against Illicit Traffic in Narcotic Drugs and Psycho Tropic Substances (Vienna Convention). This was the first major international agreement to encourage all nations to reduce the international narcotics trade by enacting uniform anti-money-laundering laws. The Vienna Convention requires every member nation to enact legislation providing for a identification and confiscation of laundered drug money. It also set out procedures for mutual legal assistance in countering drug-trafficking and money laundering, including both criminal process and informal sharing. In July 1989, as anti-drug rhetoric continued. to increase, mo particularly in the developed world, the Group of Seven set up the financial Action Task Force on Money Laundering (FATF). The declaration setting up the FATF stressed the importance of developing more effective ways of tackling the financial aspects of drug trafficking.

A key to the Vienna Convention and the FATF Recommendations is that they are intended to reduce not only crimes that occur domestically but that occur abroad as well. The fact that money-laundering often takes place outside the jurisdiction where drugs are grown, processed, or sold, resulted in the international effort to enact anti-money-laundering legislation.

While the impetus for most early anti-money-laundering legislation, and for the adoption of the Vienna Convention and the FATF's first set of 40 recommendations, came as part of a road anti-narcotics strategy, the scope of at least some national, anti-money-laundering legislation was not always limited to drug trafficking per se. During the late 1980s, while attention was still largely focused on the problem of narcotics, both national and international anti-crime organizations noted that international organized crime was involved not only in narcotics, but in other forms of illegal activities, including gambling, extortion, prostitution, counterfeiting and arms trafficking. They also noted that other forms of illegal activities such as industrial espionage and intellectual property theft, though not typically carried out by traditional organized crime, were also producing considerable sums of money in need of laundering. It was argued that anti-money-laundering legislation did not need to be limited to narcodollars.

Although the Vienna Convention was concerned only with drug trafficking, the 1990 Council of the European Convention on the Laundering, Search, Seizure, and Confiscation of the Proceeds of Crime (European Convention) accepted the fact that anti-money-laundering laws need not be restricted to narcotics proceeds. The Preamble of the European Convention states that it is directed against "serious crime," while the definition of what crimes are discovered is left to the enacting state. The FATF's 1990 Report (EATF Report) stressed that while most laundered money came from drug profits, each country should consider "extending the offense of drug money laundering to other crimes for which there is a link to narcotics; an alternative approach is to criminalize money laundering based on all serious offenses...." The European Convention Directive stated that "since money laundering occurs not only in relation to the proceeds of drug-related offenses but also in relation to the proceeds of other criminal activities (such as organized crime terrorism), the Member States should, within the meaning of their legislation, extend the effects of the Directive to include the proceeds of such actions...."

The purpose of anti-money-laundering laws and treaties is to suppress certain criminal behavior, most importantly, though certainly not always, narcotics trafficking. This behavior is often, though again not always, undertaken in various jurisdictions. At least, this is the general purpose for which anti-money-laundering treaties, and the FATF's recommendations, were concluded. Anti-money-laundering rules work by reducing the profitability of criminal enterprises, by either making it harder to consume or invest profits, and by making it easier to prosecute the criminals.

The focus of anti-money-laundering policies has grown from narcotics trafficking to other serious crimes, the most important of which are financial crimes. The FATF's 1997–98 Report on Money Laundering Typologies noted that several members cited increased cigarette and alcohol smuggling as the main origin of capital for laundering. Others cited usury, investment and VAT fraud, and false invoicing.

* * *

## Money Laundering and the International Financial System

While the prevention of the underlying or predicate crimes was the goal of anti-money-laundering legislation, recent commentators have suggested other purposes. Each attempts to attribute to laundered money adverse macroeconomic effects. Those adverse effects include inaccuracies in macroeconomic data, which can result in less effective fiscal policy;

- investment decisions based on ease of money laundering rather than rate of return, which can result in an international misallocation of capital;
- erosion of confidence in financial markets, which can result in unpredictable international capital movements and which can weaken financial institutions;
- tax evasion, which can cause national budget deficits; and
- increase in underlying criminal activities (predicate offenses resulting in dirty money), which can result in the promotion of private economic over social welfare.

An implicit, although not expressly stated, ancillary argument appears to be that these macroeconomic effects justify the involvement of international financial institutions in promoting anti-money-laundering policies among its members. This is because such institutions do not include in their mandates Interpol-like mandates against crime in general. However, such institutions have recently given increased attention to the issue of money laundering, and their staff have attended meetings of the anti-money-laundering Financial Action Task Force.

Questions have been raised as to whether these arguments suggesting adverse macroeconomic effects of money laundering are in fact convincing. These questions are not surprising, given that anti-money-laundering policies are fundamentally the tools of crime prevention, while the motivation behind such policies is one of morality, not of macro-economics. No domestic legislation or international treaty apparently suggests otherwise. Some of the issues are the following.

**1. Inaccuracies in macroeconomic data may result in less effective fiscal policy.**

The argument that the secrecy involved in money laundering results in inaccurate macroeconomic data is based less on the effects of money laundering than it is on the effects of crime in general. To the extent that anti-money-laundering policies reduce predicate crimes, one can argue that there would be less "black" money in the economy. This would make anti-money-laundering policies no more of a macroeconomic tool than any other anti-crime policy, including interdiction, drug education, methadone maintenance therapy, policing, incarceration, probation supervision, and a host of other activities recommended by criminologists to reduce the incidence of crime, most especially drug abuse.

With regard to money laundering itself, the case is far less strongly made. The purpose of money laundering is to disguise the ownership or illegal origins of property, and to invest the profits of illegal activities in legitimate business. It is not generally to hide the existence of profits or property. In fact, it is the operation of money laundering that brings "black" money into the formal economy, and that makes it subject to macroeconomic reporting. Probably most money laundering activities are undertaken through formal financial institutions, often by using unnamed bank accounts and bearer instruments. Although the illegal origins or actual ownership of such property may be disguised, the act of money laundering makes the existence of the property known to the formal economy. One might even argue that anti-money-laundering policies, by forcing criminals to launder their proceeds outside of the formal economy, make macroeconomic data even less accurate.

**2. Investment decisions based on ease of money laundering and not rates of return may result in an international misallocation of capital.**

The argument is not very convincing that criminal proceeds in the form of investment capital are directed not by the highest rate of return but by the ease with which money can be laundered. It would be difficult to argue with a conclusion that criminal proceeds are directed for laundering to financial centers with relatively lax anti-money-laundering measures. However, this by no means suggests that laundered proceeds are then invested in those jurisdictions. Capital that is properly laundered can be invested in a legitimate (or, for that matter, illegitimate) enterprise anywhere. This is, after all, the principal reason for engaging in laundering in the first place. In fact, it can be argued more easily that money laundering facilitates the reinvestment of criminal proceeds into legitimate business, thereby allowing such proceeds to seek the highest rate of return.

As with (1) above, one could argue that money laundering facilitates underlying crimes and that underlying crimes misallocate capital. However, also as with (1), this would make anti-money-laundering activities no more of a macroeconomic tool than any other anti-crime policy.

**3. Erosion of confidence in financial markets may result in unpredictable international capital movements and a weakness in financial institutions.**

The argument that money laundering erodes confidence in financial markets is based on two suppositions: first, markets handling the proceeds of crime are somehow generally suspect by investors and, second, specific financial institutions engaging in laundering are less sound. The first supposition maintains that criminal proceeds are invested on a more short-term basis than are other types of capital, and are therefore more susceptible to faster, more unpredictable movements. However, to my knowledge there is no empirical evidence to this effect, nor is there a convincing theoretical argument that this might be so. Effectively laundered money should be no more or less short term than any other type of capital. It can be used for short-term indirect or long-term direct investment.

The second supposition is that markets and institutions engaged in money laundering are less sound because the funds might be subject to seizure or the institutions to sanctions under anti-money-laundering policies. This argument states in essence that the anti-money-laundering policies have negative macroeconomic implications, not the money laundering itself. A corollary would be that an absence of anti-money-laundering policies protects the integrity of markets and financial institutions that handle large sums of illegal proceeds.

It also might reasonably be argued that not all jurisdictions have adopted or are likely to adopt truly effective anti-money-laundering policies. Established markets in jurisdictions with effective investor protection and prudential regulation are most likely to be subject to anti-money-laundering policies. As a result, it is more likely that illegal proceeds will be increasingly shifted to relatively unestablished markets with little investor protection or prudential regulation. Therefore, the spread of anti-money-laundering policies is likely to subject ever greater amounts of capital to the risks of untried and unregulated markets and financial institutions.

### 4. Tax evasion.

The purpose of money laundering is to conceal the ownership or origins of the proceeds of crime. In many jurisdictions, evaded taxes have come to be included as criminal proceeds. So, to the extent that anti-money-laundering policies make it easier to collect these taxes, one can reasonably argue that they would have a positive effect on budgets, and therefore on macroeconomics. However, it should be noted that anti-money-laundering policies may have a counterbalancing effect as well. By making it more difficult to launder criminal proceeds, anti-money-laundering policies would make it more difficult to invest criminal profits in legitimate, taxpaying business. Also, any jurisdiction that loses business to nonresident financial institutions as a result of its anti-money-laundering policies would also lose tax revenues on that financial business.

### 5. Increase in underlying criminal activities can result in promotion of private economic over social welfare.

The argument that less crime is good, for the economy, and that anti-money-laundering policies reduce crime, is the most straightforward of all those presented. However, this conclusion may not always hold true. As discussed above, anti-money-laundering policies are directed not only to predicate crimes committed domestically but to predicate crimes committed abroad. In fact, this latter effect is the main focus of international anti-money-laundering policies. Two jurisdictions, however, may not necessarily bear equally the costs of a crime committed only within one. For example, a country that grows and processes narcotics may not consume them in significant quantities, but may instead sell them abroad, promoting its own economic welfare and an improved balance of payments. Only the importing countries may suffer a decline in social welfare. In such an instance, it would be counterproductive, at least from a macroeconomic perspective, for the producing country to pursue anti-money-laundering policies. It would also be counterproductive, again from a macroeconomic perspective, for the producing countries if the importing countries were to pursue such policies.

Another problem arises from there being no international congruency as to what constitutes a serious crime. As a result, the anti-laundering policies of some countries could actually infringe upon both the economic and social welfare of others. While trafficking in the strongest narcotics is a serious crime in most if not all jurisdictions, this is not the case with the weaker narcotics. For example, in some jurisdictions enforcing strict Islamic law the manufacture, sale, or ingestion of alcohol is often a very serious crime. Under an anti-money-laundering statute similar to those found in many developed country jurisdictions, the production and sale of alcoholic beverages would give rise to criminal proceeds. However, in many other countries the manufacture of alcoholic beverages is not only legal, but constitutes a major industry contributing substantially to employment. In fact, in some countries, such as Britain, France, Canada, and the United States, the export of alcoholic beverages has played a material role in improving balance of payments. As a result, any anti-money-laundering law that helped an Islamic country could have at least some adverse economic and social consequences for a country where the manufacture and sale of alcohol is permitted.

The point of this discussion is not to suggest that some jurisdictions have either more stringent or more lax social standards, or that some behavior is more or less benign. Jurisdictions with different social, religious, and moral traditions view behavior differently. However, even in those instances where one can categorically agree that the predicate crime damages social welfare, anti-money-laundering activities would be no more of a macroeconomic tool than would any other anti-crime policy. This point is significant when one considers anti-money-laundering polices arid the mandates of international financial institutions.

## The Severity of Money-Laundering Laws

It can be reasonably argued that anti-money-laundering rules are not designed to protect the international financial system, but to reduce the incidence of the predicate crime. In effect, anti-money-laundering rules are designed to accomplish what the laws prohibiting the predicate crime themselves cannot alone accomplish. They are, in effect, an attempt to plug a hole. If one cannot, for example, prevent drug abuse directly, the theory goes, one must do it indirectly, through anti-money-laundering rules. If one cannot stop the drugs from crossing borders, one can try and stop the cash.

Such a strategy itself may be flawed. Certainly, there is no reason not to augment a partially successful strategy with new techniques. However, relying too heavily on anti-money-laundering rules to play this role in the control of international crimes may not be wise. To begin with, it may, as suggested above, involve a country "exporting" its problems overseas. If, for example, the government of an illegal drug-consuming country is incapable of convincing its own people to stop using illegal drugs, or is unable to protect its own borders, or—more likely—refuses to spend the necessary public funds to accomplish either of these goals, it may wish to turn the problem into a money-laundering issue. It then becomes the duty of private parties at home and abroad to stop the flow of drugs by stopping the flow of profits.

One of the problems with this approach may be an incentive, and perhaps even a tendency, for countries to create ever more draconian anti-money-laundering laws. It may be less expensive (and can, thanks to civil forfeiture, actually even be profitable) to use these laws. As suggested by the incident reported in the Wall Street Journal, anti-money-laundering laws can turn out to be exceptionally harsh, although they need not be. The basic elements of anti-money-laundering legislation are organized around three basic themes. First, the act of money laundering is made illegal, criminal and civil penalties are provide, and laundered money, as well as profits generated by such money, is made forfeitable to the government. Second, designated legal and physical persons who are likely to be used to launder money are required to exercise a high degree of vigilance in the lookout for laundering and are required to report serious suspicions to an anti-money-laundering authority. This is often referred to as the "know your customer" requirement. Third, provisions for cooperation with foreign jurisdictions are outlined.

However, these general "themes" can be implemented in different ways, some of which can be extremely onerous. One example defines money laundering as "engaging, directly or indirectly, in a transaction that involves property that is proceeds of crime...." It should be noted that in this definition there is no requirement that there be any act or attempted actually launder criminal proceeds, i.e., to hide the ownership of proceeds or make proceeds appear to be legitimate.

### Money Laundering and International Financial Institutions

Given that anti-money-laundering rules are primarily tools to help governments prevent underlying crimes and are not typically concerned with macroeconomic or financial matters, and given that such rules can be quite draconian in nature, some questions should naturally be raised as to the proper role of international financial institutions in money-laundering issues. Perhaps such institutions should concentrate on anti-money-laundering policies only to the extent that the underlying crime gives rise to problems with which they are otherwise concerned. Even then, perhaps they should only do so with great care so as to ensure that in the zeal to prevent money laundering, broadly accepted international principles of civil and political rights are not abridged. In the case of the IMF, for example, what crimes might these be?

Narcotics consumption has not appeared regularly as a concern in Article IV16 staff reports or in documents relating to IMF-supported programs, at least not in those that are publicly available. However, the presence of narco-terrorists in certain producing countries can have serious adverse economic effects in those countries. Therefore, one could argue that consumption of narcotics contributes to such ill effects, and that therefore anti-narcotics policies should be of concern to the IMF. Of course, others will argue that narco-terrorism is a result not of narcotics consumption, but of pressure brought by governments of consuming countries to stop production and sale by using any means. Some might suggest that such efforts, including enforcing anti-money-laundering rules, would better be spent on anti-drug education or to treat addicts in the consuming country. If macroeconomics is the issue, these questions probably should be addressed. In fact, much the same can be said for prostitution; as well as other crimes.

Financial crime, one might think, would be of greater importance to a country's macroeconomic health than would drug abuse. Again, however, a perusal of Article IV staff reports and other documents publicly available suggests that general, private-sector financial crime has not always been a central concern of IMF economists. However, one type of financial crime, the theft of state resources by corrupt government officials, has been cited by IMF staff as being of concern, as has most recently the financial crimes known as "crony capitalism." Working to prevent the laundering of proceeds from these crimes would logically flow from the IMF's concern with the crimes themselves.

How are the proceeds of government corruption and crony capitalism "laundered"? In some cases, it means sending the money abroad into secret bank accounts, or purchasing foreign real estate by shell corporations. But often, the "proceeds" are "laundered" simply by acquiring interests in legitimate domestic businesses. While it might be difficult for the IMF to address this type of "laundering," particularly in the context of IMF conditionality, it might not be impossible.

For example, assume that a government official, or a member of his family, bequeaths certain government benefits to a domestic business enterprise, in exchange for which he acquires an interest in that business. The country then experiences a foreign exchange crisis, in part because of the corrupt nature of business dealings between this government official and business, in other words, because of crony capitalism. In fact, one could say that the government official has "laundered" the proceeds of crime (the profits of crony capitalism) by using them to purchase interests in legitimate business. The IMF could then agree to support a program in that country based on the implementation of certain conditions, including that laws be changed to reduce or eliminate such crony capitalism. The IMF could also require as a condition for access to IMF resources that the government official or his family give back what they got as a result of corruption. As a result, the IMF, through the provision of financial support, allows the country's economy to recover, while requiring the officials to make restitution. In fact, if the IMF did not, could someone argue that the IMF had helped to "legitimate" the "proceeds of crime?" Would that be money laundering?

To pose another question, should the IMF exercise a certain diligence ("know its customer") with respect to the source of its members' financial transactions with it?

Of course, the IMF is neither a policeman nor a private bank, and must consider many different issues, including the health of the international financial system in general. But these examples may serve as a warning as to a number of matters, ranging from the definition of what constitutes money laundering (including such questions as "intent" and "the proceeds of crime"), to what issues with which the IMF should concern itself.

### Some Conclusions

It is not the intent of this paper to argue that governments should give up using anti-money-laundering legislation to fight underlying crimes, nor to suggest that international cooperation cannot assist in this process. In fact, it would appear that international financial institutions like the IMF may have a relevant role to play in this process. However, this paper does intend to raise a number of questions about this process, and suggest that the issues may not be as obvious as some may think. Careful consideration of these questions is required before adequate answers can be given.

---

## 8. Intensified Fund Involvement in Anti-Money Laundering Work and Combating the Financing of Terrorism

International Monetary Fund, 2001
[footnotes omitted by editors]

### I. INTRODUCTION

1. **Money laundering and the financing of terrorism are issues that affect countries at every stage of development, and involve both onshore and offshore financial centers.** Recent events have demonstrated all too clearly that terrorism can not only imperil the peace of nations, but also have far-reaching negative consequences for global economic growth and financial stability. These events and their aftermath have therefore prompted a reexamination at national and international levels of mechanisms for the promotion and enforcement of laws against both money laundering and the financing of terrorism. In these circumstances the Fund too needs to reconsider its contribution to these international efforts. The primary responsibility for combating money laundering and the financing of terrorism rests with the supervisory authorities and other relevant institutions of individual countries. However, the Fund can play a facilitating role within its mandate and expertise, which imply that its involvement must concentrate on those areas that relate to the

integrity and stability of the international financial system. The Fund's contribution should also be complementary to the new undertakings of the Financial Action Task Force on Money Laundering (FATF), which remains in the lead on these issues, and should be closely coordinated with other standard-setters and with the World Bank.

* * *

## II. THE BOARD DECISIONS OF APRIL 2001 AND FOLLOW-UP

A. The Board Decision on Enhancing Contributions to Combating Money Laundering

3. **The Executive Board met on April 13, 2001 to discuss an enhanced role for the Fund in the area of anti-money laundering,** and agreed that the Fund should enhance its contribution to international efforts to counter money laundering within its core mandate, confirming that it would not be appropriate for the Fund to become involved in law enforcement activities. In particular, it was agreed to:

- Intensify its focus on AML elements in all relevant supervisory principles;
- work more closely with major international AML groups;
- increase the provision of technical assistance;
- include AML concerns in Fund surveillance and other operational activities when macroeconomic relevant; and
- undertake additional studies and publicize the importance of countries acting to protect themselves against money laundering.

4. **Directors generally agreed that the FATF 40 Recommendations (FATF 40) should be recognized as the appropriate standard for combating money laundering, and that work should go forward to help adapt the standard assessment process with the view to preparing** *Reports on Observance of Standards and Codes*(ROSC). Following the development of an appropriate methodology and an assessment procedure for the FATF Standard that would be uniform, cooperative, and voluntary, FATF could be invited to participate in the preparation of a ROSC module on money laundering. The Board invited staff to discuss these principles with FATF, as well as to contribute to the ongoing revision of the FATF 40 Recommendations. Most Directors felt at that time that the Fund should cover only those issues in the FATF 40 Recommendations that deal with financial regulation and supervision, and that responsibility for assessing legal/crime enforcement should be left to others.

## III. CONSIDERATIONS IN DETERMINING MEASURES FOR INTENSIFIED INVOLVEMENT

5. **The events of September 11 have brought to the fore the questions of whether and how the Fund could extend its activities to prevent the use of financial systems for terrorist financing.** At a general level, one approach would be to extend the Fund's current AML efforts, focused on financial supervisory principles, to incorporate areas germane to countering terrorist financing. An alternative would be to expand the Fund's role to include also the legal and institutional issues and, when relevant, the unsupervised financial sector that impact on the effectiveness of financial sector policies, including financial supervision, and that are germane to AML and anti-terrorist financing issues. (Law enforcement issues would always be left to others, in line with the April Board decision.) The second approach would respond to the great importance that the international community now attaches to the problems of money laundering and terrorist financing. However, complex questions arise concerning consistency with the Fund's mandate and possible "mission creep," as well as the division of labor amongst international bodies, particu-

larly FATF. Questions also arise as to where to draw the line between activities related to financial supervision and legal and institutional aspects of supervision and financial sector policy generally, and law enforcement. These issues need to be reviewed in formulating effective and suitable measures for the Fund's enhanced involvement.

6. **Like money laundering, the financing of terrorism can involve both domestic and international financial systems. Both crimes are varieties of financial abuse that can compromise the integrity of the national and international financial system.** As such they must be of concern to the Fund. However, in substance terrorist financing is an issue distinct from money laundering because it involves the processing of funds, often from legitimate origins, to be used for future crimes, rather than the processing of criminal proceeds to disguise their illegitimate origin (see Annex I). Nonetheless, many of the measures to combat each are closely related. Effective coverage and implementation of these measures raises a host of issues relating to information exchange among supervisory and other authorities, the scope of financial policies including supervisory principles, the role of both supervised and unsupervised institutions, and the related legal and institutional framework.

## A. Information Exchange and International Cooperation

7. **To be effective, financial supervisors and enforcement agencies need access to a broad range of information with respect to financial activities and transactions.** Without such information, neither money laundering nor terrorist financing can be effectively identified nor appropriate countermeasures be applied. However, critical information gaps occur both at the national level (financial intermediaries do not convey information to authorities, authorities do not share information among themselves), and at the international level (authorities do not share information across borders). Because money laundering and terrorism often involve many jurisdictions, the failure to share information creates significant negative cross-border externalities that compromise the fight against predicate crime and terrorism.

8. The costliness of information gaps has two important implications. First, a concerted effort is needed to combat money laundering and terrorist financing. No country can resolve this issue alone. Second, the information gaps that lead to the negative externality need to be tackled through institution building at the national levels and through cooperative arrangements to foster the exchange of information at all appropriate levels.

9. Money laundering and financing for terrorism are complex phenomena, which cut across several quite separate dimensions (e.g., law enforcement, financial supervision, corporate vehicles, etc.). This complexity implies that no single agency can be expected to resolve the problem independently; multiple actors at the national and international levels must contribute.

10. **All of this calls for a disciplined and collaborative approach.** In this strategic vision, every partner engaged in the global fight against money laundering and the financing of terrorism must concentrate on a set of actions which respect the expertise, scope, and mandate of the other involved institutions. This approach makes best use of the limited resources at hand.

## B. Financial Policies, Supervisory Principles, and Measures to Combat Terrorist Financing

11. **Because the April Board meeting took place before the events of September 11, there was no discussion of financing of terrorism.** As noted above, most Directors felt that the Fund's contribution to AML efforts should cover financial regulation and supervision. There were at that time no financial supervisory principles specifically directed to preventing the use of the regulated financial sector for financing terrorism. However, since Septem-

ber 11 there have been two major relevant multilateral developments.

12. **On September 28, the U.N. Security Council adopted Resolution 1373, which requires that all member states of the U.N. prevent and suppress the financing of terrorism, including confiscating terrorist assets.** A U.N. Security Council Committee has been appointed, chaired by the United Kingdom, to report within 90 days on compliance with the Resolution.

13. **On October 29 and 30 FATF, meeting in an extraordinary plenary, adopted eight new recommendations on terrorist financing**, a number of which have relevance for financial supervision. Briefly, these new recommendations include:

1. take steps to ratify and implement relevant United Nations instruments,

2. criminalize the financing of terrorism and terrorist organizations,

3. freeze and confiscate terrorist assets,

4. report suspicious transactions linked to terrorism,

5. provide assistance to other countries' terrorist financing investigations,

6. impose anti-money laundering requirements on alternative remittance systems,

7. strengthen customer identification measures for wire transfers, and

8. ensure that entities, in particular nonprofit organizations, cannot be misused to finance terrorism.

14. **FATF will develop additional guidance for financial institutions** on the techniques and mechanisms used by terrorists to receive and launder their funds. FATF has requested that all countries undertake an immediate self-assessment against the new recommendations, which information could be used to assist the Security Council in evaluating compliance with Resolution 1373.

\* \* \*

C. National and International Systems for Information Sharing

20. **The scope of national and international cooperation and information sharing on financial transactions has two distinct dimensions:** the first deals with cooperation and information exchange arrangements for supervisory or regulatory purposes; the second is information exchange to uncover and prosecute criminal abuse of the financial system (e.g., money laundering crime).

21. **In implementing supervision, domestic and international cooperation is essential to cover all material risk areas of a regulated financial institution.** The cooperation is particularly important to provide effective supervision and oversight of (i) a financial conglomerate engaged in banking, insurance, securities, and/or other financial activities; The Fund's assessments of OFCs normally include, in addition to a review of the licensing and regulation of a variety of financial sector services, the regulation and supervision of company and trust service providers, and the licensing of companies. (ii) a financial institution that operates in more than one jurisdiction; or (iii) a financial institution whose size or activities are systemically relevant in relation to the financial system.

\* \* \*

24. **The overall effectiveness of fighting money laundering crime (and now terrorist financing), which often involves financial transactions in more than one country, depends on the sharing of information and intelligence among several jurisdictions.**

This sharing of information frequently involves interaction between FIUs, law enforcement agencies and supervisory agencies. Through the sharing of information, money-laundering crime, and now the financing of terrorists, can be discovered and appropriate law enforcement be brought to bear. While there have been some advances in cooperation among FIUs (in particular there is a trend towards greater regional cooperation in the European Union, the Caribbean, and the Pacific Islands region), there is currently no formal global multilateral framework in place. However, international cooperation is encouraged through the informal association within the Egmont Group.

25. **While the primary responsibility for strengthening information sharing and avoiding critical information gaps lies with supervisors and other national authorities, the Fund can play a facilitating role in its assessments and technical assistance.** For example, compliance with supervisory standards in information exchange is assessed in FSAP and OFC work. Also, the Fund-Bank Methodology Document expressly considers the legal and regulatory requirements whereby financial institutions must report suspicious activity to the FIU or other proper authority. Also, the methodology document inquires about the mechanism in place for sharing suspicious activity reporting information with foreign authorities.

## IV. THE FUND'S COMPARATIVE ADVANTAGES AND COORDINATION WITH OTHER GROUPS

### A. The Fund's Mandate and Expertise

26. **A range of activities is available to allow the Fund to intensify its involvement in anti-money laundering policies and extend its activities to support systems to combat the financing of terrorism. The Fund should pursue those activities that exploit the Fund's core competencies and capacities, recognizing its unique global coverage and its expertise in certain financial sector issues.** The Fund is a collaborative institution with near universal membership, which lends the Fund legitimacy and acceptance, and makes it a natural forum for sharing information and developing common approaches to issues. These strengths also make the Fund a vehicle for actively promoting desirable policies and standards in member countries.

27. **The Fund has broad experience in conducting assessments and providing technical assistance in the financial sector.** FSAPs, conducted jointly by the Bank and Fund, are the preferred vehicles to identify gaps and vulnerabilities in financial sectors, and ROSCs and FSAPs allow compliance with agreed international standards to be assessed. The FSSAs derived from FSAPs and Article IV consultation discussions, and the financial sector ROSC modules contained in the FSSAs are explicitly integrated in the Article IV consultation discussions and reports to the Board. They thus inform the Fund's surveillance activities. At the same time, technical assistance in strengthening financial systems is increasingly being targeted to support follow-up on FSAP and ROSC assessments.

28. **In addition, the Fund has long experience in exercising surveillance over members' exchange systems** in the context of Article IV missions, and providing technical assistance to reform such systems as part of its core mandate to assist in the development of a multilateral system of payments for current international transactions. In this context the Fund has often had to address issues relating to exchange and currency transactions in parallel exchange markets outside of official supervision, which can provide channels for money laundering and the financing of terrorism. Fund surveillance, advice, and technical assistance in this area has sought, inter alia, to eliminate distortions and restrictions in the exchange system, and to rectify deficiencies in the foreign exchange market organization and infrastructure, and thus to reduce the importance of the parallel exchange markets.

29. **Yet, the Fund has a limited mandate and must respect the sovereignty of its members and the division of labor and responsibilities with other international organizations.** In April 2001, the Board stressed that money laundering issues should continue to be addressed in Fund surveillance when they have macroeconomic effects, including effects arising from financial instability and reputational damage. A number of Directors considered that the cross-border implications of money laundering should be raised during Article IV consultations, even if it is not macroeconomic relevant for that member but when it had significant externalities for other countries. With regard to conditionality, many Directors were of the view that the "macro-relevance" test should continue to be applied, but a few Directors were opposed to applying conditionality to anti-money laundering measures. In July 2001, Directors agreed that those measures that are critical to achieving a program's macroeconomic objectives should continue to be included in Fund conditionality, with a number of Directors stressing the need for strong justification when including measures outside the Fund's core areas of responsibility and expertise. Some Directors cautioned against applying this criterion too narrowly, noting that in some cases criticality might be difficult to define ex ante, and that there is a risk that important areas of reform would not be properly covered.

30. **Under the Board's existing policies and guidance in the area of anti-money laundering policies, attention has focused on the Fund's capacities in the areas of technical assistance and the assessment of financial systems.** The April Board decision emphasized the Fund's efforts in assessing compliance with financial supervisory principles and providing corresponding technical assistance. However, implementation of financial supervisory principles is not readily separable from the legal framework in which they are applied, and depends on other institutional structures. This distinction is made more complicated as the objective is extended to encompass the combating of terrorist financing. The staff has already been involved in advising countries on AML legislation, and, in a limited number of cases, the registration of nonfinancial intermediaries and the creation of FIUs. The August report containing the draft AML Methodology Document makes reference to communication and cooperation between supervisors and relevant enforcement bodies. The Fund is not able or mandated to become involved in law enforcement, but greater attention to issues of immediate relevance to the effectiveness of financial sector policies, and especially financial supervisory principles is feasible and worthwhile.

## B. Coordination with FATF

31. **There was broad agreement at the Fund Board in April that the FATF 40 Recommendations be recognized as the appropriate standard for combating money laundering, and that work should go forward to determine how the Recommendations could be adapted and made operational in the Fund's work.** While FATF (like a number of other standard-setters) has a limited membership, the worldwide acceptability of its AML standards, the processes by which they are assessed, and how the results are used are crucial to an invitation to participate in the ROSC process.

\* \* \*

## V. MEASURES FOR INTENSIFYING THE FUND'S INVOLVEMENT

37. The considerations presented above suggest the direction in which the Fund's involvement in AML might be intensified and extended to combating the finance of terrorism. **The specific elements have been selected on the basis of their expected contribution to (i) achieving results, including the strengthening of the international financial system; (ii) maintaining consistency with the policies in place; (iii) exploiting Fund expertise and limiting the resource demands; and (iv) achieving "ownership" by member countries.**

38. **The approach goes substantially and visibly beyond that envisaged in the April Board decision, yet does not go outside the Fund's mandate or area of expertise.** The elements presented are those that seem essential to achieve a qualitative and quantitative intensification of the Fund's involvement in AML and combating the financing of terrorism. Furthermore, the suggested measures seem appropriate and feasible at this time; the Board could revisit the issue and consider additional measures after the effectiveness of this approach has been assessed, taking account also of the need for flexibility in the light of rapidly changing events and initiatives. The measures proposed below indicate the direction for future work, and additional technical refinement of the proposals is needed before implementation can be initiated. The approach would not create the need for any special procedure not used elsewhere in the Fund's work.

- **The Fund-Bank AML Methodology Document would be amplified and expanded by including: (i) relevant parts of the anti-terrorist financing recommendations of FATF** (see Annex I and Annex II). The recommendations relating to the reporting of suspicious transactions and remittance and wire-transfer systems have implications for a range of financial sector standards, including standards on payments system design and oversight. (ii) **legal and institutional issues related to the effectiveness of financial sector policies in this area** (see Annex II). Added to the prudential supervisory aspects of AML would be relevant legal and institutional issues such as the extension of KYC and other **anti-terrorist financing** AML/principles to the unsupervised sector, the existence of a suitable legal framework including criminal and civil statutes, institutions for effective implementation (including FIUs), resources and training needs of supervisors, and bilateral or multilateral arrangements for the exchange of information. Many of these topics can be addressed only by considering the relationship between the financial supervisor, financial institutions, and such organizations as the national and foreign FIUs. Once drafted, the expanded Methodology Document would be circulated to the Board to update the earlier document circulated in August 2001.

- **The expanded AML Methodology Document would be applied in all FSAP and OFC assessments.** The AML assessment would be presented in detail as part of FSAP reports to the authorities, and would be included as a substantive chapter in the related FSSA reports, which, as now, would be made available to the Board. In addition, countries would be encouraged to approve the distribution of the detailed assessments in this area (either as separate documents or as part of larger technical assistance reports) to the Board and relevant bodies, such as FATF. Thus, the range of countries to which the AML Methodology Document would apply would be expanded, and the results could be made more widely available.

- **The number of OFC assessments to be concluded would increase from a target of 10 to a target of 20 per year.** At the accelerated pace, the Fund OFC program would have conducted assessments of some two-thirds of all the 42 OFCs in the Financial Stability Forum list by the end of 2002, and OFC assessments would be completed in about two years rather than four, as currently envisaged. Most of the OFC assessments would be of supervisory standards (Module 2), and would include in 2002 many of the larger, systemically more important OFCs.

- **Where an FSAP or OFC assessment had been undertaken, the Article IV consultation mission would be expected to follow up** on the authorities' reaction to the relevant AML report, and on the implementation of recommendations in the area of AML and combating the financing of terrorism. The results of the discussions would be mentioned in the staff report.

* * *

## VII. SUMMARY

43. **Money laundering and the financing of terrorism are global problems that affect not only security, but also potentially harm economic prosperity and the state of the international financial system.** The Fund's mandate and core areas of expertise entail that it can and should help its member countries strengthen their defenses against these pernicious activities. The Board decided in April 2001 to enhance the Fund's activates in AML, notably through the development and application of a detailed methodology to assess compliance with relevant financial supervisory principles, and closer cooperation with FATF, which is the recognized standard-setter in this area. Work has already begun in implementing this Board decision. For example, the current AML methodology is being applied in pilot cases, and Fund staff have contributed to the recent actions by FATF to prepare an AML ROSC module.

44. **Recent events make the Fund's contribution more urgent, and prompt a reexamination of what additional areas should be addressed in the Fund's work.** It has become clearer that protecting against abuses such as money laundering and the financing of terrorism requires effective supervision, national coordination and cooperation in the collection and processing of relevant information, and fluid cross-border exchange of information in both offshore and onshore financial centers. Combating the financing of terrorism is distinct from AML efforts, but they share some common elements, and international standards addressed directly at the former are now being developed. Relevant components of these standards can be added to the Fund's assessment of supervisory principles, and promoted through associated technical assistance. At the same time, the Fund must recognize in its assessments and technical assistance that effective preventative measures depend not only on adherence to financial supervisory principles, but also upon the legal and institutional framework in which those principles can be applied, and coordination with measures covering the unsupervised financial sector.

45. **On this basis the Fund could adopt a number of measures to intensify its involvement in AML and combating the financing of terrorism.** First, the scope of FSAPs and OFC assessments could be expanded to include a more detailed evaluation of financial policies and in particular supervisory principles and the legal and institutional framework related to both AML and combating the financing of terrorism. Second, the provision of related technical assistance and OFC assessments could be accelerated. Third, these issues could receive more attention in Article IV consultation discussions, for example, in following up recommendations contained in FSAPs. Finally, the Fund would cooperate closely with FATF so that FATF can move ahead rapidly with an appropriate AML ROSC procedure. These measures would go beyond the April 2001 Board decision by addressing anti-terrorist financing, and broadening the scope of the staff's work to cover the legal and institutional framework in which financial sector policies and financial supervisory principles are applied to deter money laundering and the financing of terrorism.

46. These additional measures, taken together, would add substantively to the Fund's output in this area, and to the international effort to counter money laundering and **terrorist financing. The Fund would provide significant reinforcement to national authorities, and especially supervisors, in developing the architecture of preventative systems in the financial sector, which form one essential component of this effort. Yet, the Fund's contribution will be limited.** The Fund is not and will not be in a position to identify or help others identify individual instances of money laundering or terrorist financing. Nor will it normally be possible for regulated institutions to identify small amounts of money from legitimate sources—which may often be the way in which terrorism is financed.

\* \* \*

## FINANCING OF TERRORISM

### Conceptual and Legal Issues

1. In general, money laundering involves the processing of the proceeds of crimes already committed so as to disguise their illegal origin, while the financing of terrorism involves the processing of funds (often legitimately acquired) to be used in future crimes. As a result, many of the measures to deter money laundering, especially those that involve identifying criminal proceeds, are not effective in deterring terrorism. However, while what constitutes "laundering" and "financing" are understood and broadly accepted, what constitutes a predicate crime to money laundering and what constitutes the crime of terrorism are not. Terrorism involves certain actions, such as kidnapping, extortion, assault, murder, or the destruction of property, that are themselves already serious crimes. The concept of terrorism as a separate crime relates to the reason or purpose for which these already serious crimes are carried out.

2. The 1999 International Convention for the Suppression of the Financing of Terrorism, which was adopted by the U.N. General Assembly but is not yet in force (ratified by only four countries), contains extensive provisions on international cooperation against financing for terrorism. The Convention's definition of terrorism is based on two alternative criteria: terrorism is either an offense within the scope of one of the treaties listed in the annex to the Convention (e.g., hijacking of aircraft, bombings, taking of hostages) or "any other act intended to cause death or serious bodily injury to a civilian, or to any other person not taking an active part in the hostilities in a situation of armed conflict, when the purpose of such act, by its nature or context, is to intimidate a population, or to compel a government or an international organization to do or to abstain from doing any act."

3. International law has generally recognized that governments need not cooperate in criminal matters when the act was also political in nature; this is because governments may differ as to whether a violent act might be acceptable due to a compelling political justification. The Convention would exclude this political exception.

4. The Convention also establishes a duty to investigate persons suspected of financing terrorism, to avoid the risk of flight by an offender (or alleged offender), to make terrorism an extraditable offense, and to refer for domestic prosecution those offenders who are not extradited. Prosecutorial discretion is maintained. The Convention provides no sanctions for countries if they fail to cooperate.

5. The Security Council's Resolution No. 1373 (2001) of September 28, 2001 requires the adoption by all States of certain measures against terrorism, and creates a Committee, chaired by the United Kingdom, to report within 90 days on compliance with the Resolution. The Resolution includes no definition of terrorism.

6. With respect to the financing of terrorism, paragraph 1 of the resolution requires each state to prevent and suppress the financing of terrorist acts, criminalize the willful financing of terrorism, freeze the assets of terrorists and related entities, and prohibit payments to terrorists and related entities. Moreover, the resolution imposes an obligation on all States to "bring to justice" terrorists or persons assisting or funding terrorist activities; although the concept of "bringing to justice" is not defined by the resolution, it would seem that this obligation may be performed either by extraditing the offender or prosecuting the offender in local courts. The same resolution calls upon—but does not

require—all states to become parties to the U.N. Convention for the Suppression of the Financing of Terrorism of December 9, 1999.

## FATF Special Recommendations on Terrorist Financing

The following statement was issued following the FATF extraordinary plenary meeting:

7. Recognizing the vital importance of taking action to combat the financing of terrorism, FATF has agreed these Recommendations, which, when combined with the FATF 40 Recommendations on money laundering, set out the basic framework to detect, prevent, and suppress the financing of terrorism and terrorist acts.

### *Ratification and implementation of U.N. instruments*

8. Each country should take immediate steps to ratify and to implement fully the 1999 United Nations International Convention for the Suppression of the Financing of Terrorism. Countries should also immediately implement the United Nations resolutions relating to the prevention and suppression of the financing of terrorist acts, particularly United Nations Security Council Resolution 1373.

### *Criminalizing the financing of terrorism and associated money laundering*

9. Each country should criminalize the financing of terrorism, terrorist acts and terrorist organizations. Countries should ensure that such offenses are designated as money laundering predicate offences.

### *Freezing and confiscating terrorist assets*

10. Each country should implement measures to freeze without delay funds or other assets of terrorists, those who finance terrorism, and terrorist organizations in accordance with the United Nations resolutions relating to the prevention and suppression of the financing of terrorist acts.

11. Each country should also adopt and implement measures, including legislative ones, which would enable the competent authorities to seize and confiscate property that is the proceeds of, or used in, or intended or allocated for use in, the financing of terrorism, terrorist acts or terrorist organizations.

### *Reporting suspicious transactions related to terrorism*

12. If financial institutions, or other businesses or entities subject to anti-money laundering obligations, suspect or have reasonable grounds to suspect that funds are linked or related to, or are to be used for terrorism, terrorist acts or by terrorist organizations, they should be required to report promptly their suspicions to the competent authorities.

### *International cooperation*

13. Each country should afford another country, on the basis of a treaty, arrangement or other mechanism for mutual legal assistance or information exchange, the greatest possible measure of assistance in connection with criminal, civil enforcement, and administrative investigations, inquiries and proceedings relating to the financing of terrorism, terrorist acts and terrorist organizations.

14. Countries should also take all possible measures to ensure that they do not provide safe havens for individuals charged with the financing of terrorism, terrorist acts or terrorist organizations, and should have procedures in place to extradite, where possible, such individuals.

### Alternative remittance

15. Each country should take measures to ensure that persons or legal entities, including agents, that provide a service for the transmission of money or value, including transmission through an informal money or value transfer system or network, should be licensed or registered and subject to all the FATF Recommendations that apply to banks and nonbank financial institutions. Each country should ensure that persons or legal entities that carry out this service illegally are subject to administrative, civil, or criminal sanctions.

### Wire transfers

16. Countries should take measures to require financial institutions, including money remitters, to include accurate and meaningful originator information (name, address, and account number) on funds transfers and related messages that are sent, and the information should remain with the transfer or related message through the payment chain. Countries should take measures to ensure that financial institutions, including money remitters, conduct enhanced scrutiny of and monitor for suspicious activity funds transfers, which do not contain complete originator information (name, address, and account number).

### Nonprofit organizations

17. Countries should review the adequacy of laws and regulations that relate to entities that can be abused for the financing of terrorism. Nonprofit organizations are particularly vulnerable, and countries should ensure that they cannot be misused: (i) by terrorist organizations posing as legitimate entities; (ii) to exploit legitimate entities as conduits for terrorist financing, including for the purpose of escaping asset freezing measures; and (iii) to conceal or obscure the clandestine diversion of funds intended for legitimate purposes to terrorist organizations.

## AML ELEMENTS IN SUPERVISORY PRINCIPLES, AND POSSIBLE SCOPE FOR AN EXPANDED METHODOLOGY

### Supervisory Principles Related to AML, and the Supporting Legal and Institutional Framework

1. The Basel Committee, IOSCO, and IAIS each have included due diligence reviews on those who control or use regulated financial intermediaries, which includes both fitness tests for owners/managers and know-your-customer rules (KYC). KYC procedures with respect to customers (as amended to include the prevention of terrorist financing) involve (i) identifying if the potential or actual customer (or beneficiary), or the maker or recipient of assets transfers, is a criminal or terrorist; (ii) reporting transactions that suggest criminal activity to the appropriate authorities; and (iii) cooperating with supervisors and law enforcement agencies; and (iv) putting in place anti-money laundering policies, procedures and training.

2. These procedures are designed primarily to control three types of risk, the first two of which relate to the use of institutions for laundering money or financing crime. These are reputational risk (the public's confidence in the integrity of the institution can be damaged if it is used as a vehicle for advancing serious crime) and operational and legal risk (failure to control money laundering or the financing of terrorism can result in the seizing of tainted assets held by the institution, as well as the imposition of fines or penalties on the institution itself). If risk is controlled for individual institutions, risk to the financial system is also controlled.

3. To be effective, principles of financial supervision must be implemented, which requires that supervisors have (i) the authority to require adherence to the supervisory principles and (ii) the means to administer them. Both require that there be adequate sanctions

(which can involve regulatory, civil, and even criminal sanctions) to deter noncompliance. This includes having in place both the appropriate statutory authority and effective administrative and adjudicatory institutions (including for civil and criminal prosecution), including procedures for sharing of information relevant to supervision with other domestic and foreign supervisory agencies.

**The Current Methodology Document**

4. The Fund-Bank AML Methodology Document, which is still in draft form, guides assessment teams in the review of AML elements in Fund and Bank financial sector assessment activities related to the financial sector assessment program (FSAP) and the offshore financial center (OFC) initiative. The methodology document is intended to ensure both comprehensiveness and uniformity in the assessments of the AML elements in financial sector supervisory standards. It is now being used, with agreement of the authorities, in FSAPs in Luxembourg, Switzerland, Sweden, and the Philippines.

5. The starting point for the Fund-Bank Methodology Document was the existing principles of prudential supervision, in the areas of banking, securities, and insurance, determined by the standard-setting bodies. Of particular importance is Basel Core Principle 15 on preventing banks being used by criminal elements; IAIS Core Principles 1–5, 10 and 16; and IOSCPO principles 5, 10–13, 17, 21 and 23. These basic principles are augmented by the criteria developed in the standard-setters' own methodology papers, additional and later papers by the supervisory standard-setters relevant to AML work, and on the FATF 40 Recommendations.

6. The Fund-Bank Methodology Document assesses the AML elements present within the financial sector supervisory and regulatory framework to ensure that adequate controls and procedures are in place to prevent abuse of the financial system by criminals. Areas covered by the document include requirements for due diligence reviews on those who control or use regulated financial intermediaries (which includes both fitness tests for owners/managers and KYC rules) as a key part of these controls. In all financial institutions, there are four basic anti-money laundering principles that should be adhered to:

- comply with anti-money laundering laws, including suspicious transaction reporting, to an administrative body or Financial Intelligence Unit (FIU);
- customer identification (KYC rules) and suspicious transaction monitoring;
- cooperation with supervisors and law enforcement agencies; and
- have in place anti-money laundering policies, procedures and training.

7. These principles are detailed and made concrete in the Methodology Document, which contains numerous specific criteria which should be met by an effective system to discourage and detect money laundering. These criteria include some related to such issues as the ability of the supervisor to share with domestic and foreign financial supervisory authorities information on suspected or actual criminal activities; the obligation of the supervisor to inform the relevant criminal and judicial authorities of suspected transactions; and the incorporation into laws and regulations international sound practices in this area. However, these legal and institutional issues are not covered in detail, and law enforcement issues are not emphasized as they are in the FATF 40 Recommendations. Issues relating to civil and criminal sanctions, including adjudicatory mechanisms, are not now included; nor are those matters that have only a secondary application to supervision, e.g., financial intelligence units. Nonetheless, 19 of the FATF 40 Recommendations have some counterpart in the supervisory principles elaborated in the current draft methodology document.

### Possible Expanded Methodology

8. The purpose of the full 40 Recommendations (as amended to include the prevention of terrorist financing) is extensive: to prevent the financial system (as broadly defined) from being used to further crime. To be effective, this requires a host of additional measures that extend beyond financial supervision, but each of which has an analogue in the legal and institutional framework for application of financial supervisory principles. These would include the extension of customer due diligence beyond the supervised sector, the criminalization of money laundering and the financing of terrorism, and the related administrative and adjudicatory institutions.

9. Expanding the Methodology Document to address the legal and institutional framework in which relevant financial policies and supervisory principles are applied would involve, first, elaborating further on some of the issues mentioned briefly in the current document, such as the criterion that the laws and/or regulations embody international sound practices. Second, criteria would be added that correspond to some aspects of several additional FATF 40 Recommendations, notably but not exhaustively recommendations 1–3 on the general framework for the Recommendations (including ratification and implementation of the U.N. Convention against Illicit Traffic in Narcotic Drugs and Psychotropic Substances); Recommendations 4–6 on criminalizing money laundering; Recommendation 7 on the legal authority to confiscate laundered property; Recommendation 30 on collecting information on international flows of cash and providing it to the Fund to facilitate international studies; and Recommendations 34 and 35 on establishing a network of bilateral and multilateral agreements, and ratification and implementation of relevant international conventions on money laundering. The expanded Methodology Document could thus cover to some degree about 29 of the FATF 40 Recommendations.

10. The expanded Methodology Document would in addition include criteria related to the FATF Special Recommendations on Terrorism Financing (see Annex I). The criteria in the Methodology Document would be based on the institutional aspects of those recommendations (such as the enactment of legislation to permit the seizure of property that is connected to terrorist financing), rather than those aspects that relate to enforcement (such as the actual freezing of assets).

11. Development of the Fund-Bank Methodology Document is running parallel to work by FATF to develop an assessment methodology for the entire FATF 40 Recommendations. The substantive difference between these two efforts is that the FATF 40 assessment methodology will be used to assess all FATF 40 Recommendations, including criminal and civil law enforcement recommendations. Because of the overlaps between the two efforts, the Fund and Bank are participants in the FATF working group that is developing the FATF 40 assessment methodology. At the October 31, 2001 meeting the FATF working group agreed to incorporate into its assessment methodology the detailed criteria from the Fund-Bank AML Methodology Document dealing with supervisory and regulatory AML principles.

### FATF, THE FATF 40 RECOMMENDATIONS, AND THE ROSC PROCESS

### Organization of FATF

1. The Financial Action Task Force on Money Laundering (FATF) was created by the G-7 in 1989 to develop and promote global anti-money laundering efforts. Today, FATF has 29 members, whose delegations include representatives of finance and justice ministries, as well as law enforcement, legal, and financial sector regulatory experts. The formal work of FATF (policy development, planning, and assessments) is carried out

largely through the plenary sessions, which meet normally three times a year. Topical policy development work is prepared by working groups formed from FATF member delegations, meeting in the context of the plenary. Administrative and support functions are performed by a small secretariat based at the OECD. FATF has two principal roles: that of a standard-setter and that of an assessor of compliance with the AML standard.

### FATF's Role as a Standard-setter

2. In 1989, FATF developed an international AML standard—The FATF 40 Recommendations (revised in 1996)—which cover the criminal justice system, law enforcement, international cooperation, and financial system regulation. In 2000, FATF adopted the 25 criteria for assessing compliance of nonmembers with AML principles. These criteria have been used to identify the Noncooperative Countries and Territories (NCCT). Since September 2000, work is underway to revise and update the FATF 40 Recommendations and reconcile them with the NCCT assessment criteria (see below), with the objective of creating a uniform anti-money laundering standard. Following the September 11 events, the revisions also encompass the anti-terrorist financing measures.

### FATF's Role as Assessor of Compliance with AML Standard

3. FATF carries out three types of assessments—self assessments, mutual evaluations, which are reserved for FATF members, and NCCT assessments, which are nonvoluntary and applied only to non-FATF members. Though these assessments have a similar AML objective, the NCCT process is based on the 25 criteria that do not coincide fully with the FATF 40 Recommendations. Under the mutual evaluations for FATF members, non-complying countries face scrutiny and requests for improvement from fellow members. In contrast, the NCCT assessments include the possibility of countermeasures, if necessary, for countries judged by FATF to be noncooperating. Currently there are 19 jurisdictions listed as noncooperative, although some cases are expected to be reviewed shortly.

4. The FATF assessments—both mutual evaluation and NCCT—are carried out by experts drawn from FATF member countries and include lawyers, regulators and law enforcement personnel with experience in criminal justice systems, law enforcement and financial sector regulation. The conclusions of these assessments are discussed in the plenary sessions.

### Development of a ROSC for the FATF 40 Recommendations

5. In April 2001, the Fund's (and Bank) Board agreed that the FATF 40 Recommendations be recognized as the appropriate standard for combating money laundering, and the work should go forward to determine how the Recommendations could be adapted and made operational in the Fund's work. However, at that point most Directors felt that the Fund should only cover those issues in the FATF 40 Recommendations that deal with financial regulation and supervision, and that the responsibility for law enforcement related activities should be left to others. The Fund Board stressed that FATF could be invited to participate in the preparation of a ROSC module on money laundering provided that the FATF AML standard and the assessment process are consistent with the ROSC process—that is, the standard needs to be applied uniformly, cooperatively, and on a voluntary basis.

6. A FATF working group (with Fund and Bank participation) is working on the revisions of the FATF 40 Recommendations and their reconciliation with the 25 NCCT cri-

teria and is preparing an assessment methodology for the FATF 40 Recommendations that could be used to prepare AML ROSC modules. A preliminary draft has been reviewed and discussed at the end October 2001, FATF plenary meeting and in the working group meeting. The next draft will be presented for the next FATF plenary meeting scheduled. It is envisaged that the drafting of the AML standard and of the assessment methodology will be completed by FATF by February 2002.

## STANDARDS ASSESSMENTS AND ROSCS

1. The Fund (and Bank) Executive Board endorsed 11 areas and associated standards as useful for their operational work and for which *Reports on the Observance of Standards and Codes* (ROSCs) could be produced. The Executive Board also agreed on a formal procedure for adding new standards to the agreed list, whereby the list should only be reviewed and modified by the Fund Executive Board, in consultation with the Bank when appropriate. It also left open the possibility of inviting other institutions to undertake assessments in their areas of competency.

### Key Attributes of ROSCs

- The adoption and assessment of internationally recognized standards should remain voluntary.

- Assessments need to be independently conducted and consistently applied across countries.

- ROSCs should allow for the different stages of country economic development, range of administrative capacities, and the different cultural and legal traditions across the membership.

- ROSCs should provide the context for the assessment, including the progress made by the country in implementing standards, and the authorities' plans for further implementation. In this regard, caution should be exercised to ensure that Fund assessments do not resemble ratings for countries, and are not presented as pass-fail judgments.

- Members are to be assessed only against those standards, and those parts of standards, that are relevant to their situation. Accordingly, standards increasingly set out benchmarks for countries at different stages of development.

- Financial system standards are assessed generally in the context of FSAPs, and the summary assessments are then presented as part of FSSAs to serve as inputs into overall stability assessments that feed into surveillance, and are also issued as financial sector modules of ROSCs. Other standards, such as fiscal transparency, SDDS, corporate governance, etc., are typically assessed on a stand-alone basis.

---

## 9. IMF Board Discusses the Fund's Intensified Involvement in Anti-Money Laundering and Combating the Financing of Terrorism

### Public Information Notice (PIN), 2001

Public Information Notices (PINs) form part of the IMF's efforts to promote transparency of the IMF's views and analysis of economic developments and policies. With the consent of the country (or countries) concerned, PINs are issued after Executive Board discussions of Article IV consultations with member countries, of its surveillance of developments at the regional level, of post-program monitoring, and of ex post assessments of member countries with longer-term program engagements. PINs are also issued after Executive Board discussions of general policy matters, unless otherwise decided by the Executive Board in a particular case.

On November 12, 2001, the Executive Board of the International Monetary Fund (IMF) discussed how the Fund should intensify its involvement in anti-money laundering (AML) efforts and combating the financing of terrorism.

### Background

Money laundering and the financing of terrorism are issues that concern countries at every stage of development, and involve both onshore and offshore financial centers. These are global problems that not only affect security, but also potentially harm economic prosperity and the international financial system.

On April 13, 2001, the Executive Board agreed to enhance the Fund's contributions to the global efforts to counter money laundering by

- intensifying its focus on anti-money laundering elements in all relevant financial supervisory principles, in particular by developing a methodology that would enhance the assessment of financial standards relevant for countering money laundering,

- working more closely with major international anti-money laundering groups,

- increasing the provision of technical assistance in this area,

- including anti-money laundering concerns in its surveillance and other operational activities when macroeconomic relevant, and

- undertaking additional studies and publicizing the importance of countries acting to protect themselves against money laundering.

Directors generally agreed that the 40 Recommendations on AML made by the Financial Action Task Force on Money Laundering (FATF) should be recognized as the appropriate standard for combating money laundering. Directors also agreed that work should go forward to determine how the Recommendations could be adapted and made operational to the Fund's work with a view eventually to preparing related Reports on Standards and Codes (ROSC). Further information on the April 13 Executive Board discussion of these issues is available in Public Information Notice 01/41 of April 29, 2001.

* * *

In considering how the Fund could extend its activities to limit the use of financial systems for terrorism financing, and to make its anti-money laundering work more effective, Directors stressed that the Fund's involvement in these areas should be consistent with its mandate and core areas of expertise. Recognizing that no single agency can resolve the problems independently, they emphasized that the Fund should adopt a disciplined and collaborative approach that respects the expertise, scope, and mandate of other relevant institutions, and that the roles of the various institutions involved should be clarified. Directors reaffirmed that the Fund's primary efforts should be in assessing compliance with financial supervisory principles and providing corresponding technical assistance. They confirmed, in particular, that it would be inappropriate for the Fund to become involved in law enforcement issues.

Directors generally agreed that the set of measures in the staff paper were an appropriate response by the Fund to the challenges facing the institution, in a way that is consistent with the Fund's mandate and existing practices. In particular, Directors supported:

- expanding the Fund's involvement beyond anti-money laundering to efforts aimed at countering terrorism financing;

- expanding the joint Fund/World Bank AML Methodology Document and Fund technical assistance to include aspects relating to anti-terrorism financing. In addition, Directors noted that effective implementation of financial supervisory principles depends on a sound legal framework and on other institutional structures. Thus, most Directors considered it appropriate to expand coverage to legal and institutional issues in the AML methodology. Some Directors considered that the methodology document should eventually cover all the FATF Recommendations, both the original 40 (as revised) and the additional 8 on anti-terrorist financing. However, several Directors supported an evolutionary approach whereby the staff would work on expanding coverage of the assessment methodology to these issues while experience in the implementation of the present Methodology Document accumulates. The revised Fund/World Bank AML Methodology Document will be circulated to the Board as soon as it is ready.

---

## 10. Twelve-Month Pilot Program of Anti-Money Laundering and Combating the Financing of Terrorism (AML/CFT) Assessments
### Joint Report on the Review of the Pilot Program
International Monetary Fund and the World Bank, 2004

### EXECUTIVE SUMMARY

In July and August 2002, respectively, the IMF and World Bank Boards endorsed a 12-month pilot program of *anti-money laundering and combating the financing of terrorism* (AML/CFT) assessments using the methodology adopted by the Financial Action Task Force (FATF) and endorsed by the Fund/Bank Boards. They requested a comprehensive review at the end of the pilot program.

* * *

### II. THE AML/CFT PILOT PROGRAM AND TECHNICAL ASSISTANCE

#### A. Key Elements of the Pilot Program of Assessments

4. As endorsed by the Fund and Bank Boards, there are two approaches to assessments using the common methodology and leading to the preparation of ROSCs:

- Fund/Bank staff-led assessments. Fund/Bank staff (and experts under staff supervision) assess compliance with all criteria except those relating to the implementation of criminal justice measures and to sectors that, while vulnerable to money laundering or financing of terrorism, are not macroeconomically relevant. One or more independent AML/CFT experts (IAEs) assess the remaining criteria. The substantive work of the IAE is not supervised by Fund/Bank staff, and their participation is not financed by the Fund/Bank.

- FATF/FSRB assessments. Representatives from FATF/FSRB member jurisdictions and staff from the FATF/FSRB Secretariats conduct the entire assessment according to the common methodology without Fund/Bank staff participation.

5. Current policy for Fund/Bank-led assessments establishes a clear line between work done by the IAE and work done by Fund/Bank staff. Consistent with Board guidance that staff would not be involved in assessing implementation of criminal laws and the activities of those parts of the non-prudentially-regulated financial sector that are not macro-relevant, the staffs have relied on IAEs to assess (i) the implementation of criminal laws; and (ii) the implementation of preventive measures for non-prudentially regulated financial sectors that are not macroeconomically relevant.

6. In order to implement the procedures for Fund/Bank led assessments, national authorities that are members of the FATF and some FSRBs agreed to provide and finance the IAEs for the Fund/Bank-led missions, and also to provide reviewers for the work of the IAEs. A roster of IAEs was created to include the names of experts nominated by participating countries, and IAEs were identified for individual missions either through contact with national authorities or through the secretariats of the FATF and FSRBs. A protocol was agreed with the FATF/FSRBs for the IAE's involvement in Fund/Bank led missions, for the sharing of reports with the IAE reviewers, and for the review of the IAE's work.

\* \* \*

## D. AML/CFT Technical Assistance

18. Fund/Bank technical assistance has increased substantially in the last two years as staff intensified assistance to countries and regional organizations to strengthen their AML/CFT regimes. AML/CFT technical assistance provided by Fund and Bank staff has focused on drafting of laws and regulations, implementation of preventive measures in the financial system, and training of evaluators. Staff have also advised on the establishment of FIUs and the implementation of AML/CFT measures in the financial system.

\* \* \*

## III. LESSONS LEARNED

25. The 12-month pilot program has provided a practical vehicle to learn lessons about the assessment methodology, the two assessment approaches, and more generally about the Fund/Bank's role in AML/CFT. This section discusses the lessons learned from the pilot program with a focus on those elements that worked well and those elements which could be improved.

### A. What has Worked Well

26. First, the adoption of AML/CFT as one of the standards for which ROSCs are prepared, and the inclusion of assessments as part of FSAPs and OFC assessments, has significantly deepened the international attention to the standard. This attention has been reflected, for example, in the increasing demand for technical assistance focused on AML/CFT as discussed in Section II. The assessments conducted during the pilot have proved to be a useful diagnostic tool for determining strengths and weaknesses in country AML/CFT regimes, and technical assistance needs. Most countries have initiated actions to implement the recommendations that were made as part of the assessments.

\* \* \*

### Supervision and integration of AML/CFT work

34. Coordination and integration of AML/CFT work has been a challenge in view of the multidisciplinary composition of the missions. AML/CFT assessments (and technical assistance) require teams made up of legal, financial sector, and law enforcement professionals.

35. The Fund/Bank AML/CFT assessments are also unique in that they used independent outside experts (IAEs) not under the supervision of staff, which has led to a mixed

experience under the pilot. In a number of cases, their work dovetailed smoothly with that of the other parts of the assessment. Problems encountered in other cases included (i) difficulties in recruiting IAEs for some assessments (especially for the assessment of low income countries); (ii) variable quality of the work produced by IAEs; and (iii) lack of integration and consistency of the IAE's work.

\* \* \*

## IV. GOING FORWARD

39. Based on the generally successful experience with the pilot program, the staff recommends that AML/CFT work continues to be a regular part of the work of the Fund/Bank. Nevertheless, in taking forward this work, there are a number of policy, budget, and procedural issues that need to be addressed. This section sets out the issues and possible approaches going forward.

\* \* \*

## B. Scope of Fund/Bank Involvement in AML/CFT Assessments

43. The revision to the FATF Recommendations and methodology will increase the assessment workload, in particular with regard to the work undertaken by the IAE under the current policy. The ability to conduct comprehensive assessments at a sustained pace will depend on the availability of greater resources to cover the assessment of (i) the implementation of criminal laws; and (ii) the implementation of preventive measures for nonmacroeconomically relevant activities.

\* \* \*

46. Three options could be considered to improve the availability of adequate IAE resources and the integration of their work in AML/CFT assessments (the different options are summarized below):

- The first option would maintain the current policy limiting Fund/Bank involvement. It envisages the possibility that an outside body would establish an external financing mechanism and outside review panels that would enhance the overall quality of the work done by the IAEs, and to a certain extent, their integration into the Fund/Bank work product. Its feasibility depends on the continued willingness and ability of FATF/FSRB members to provide IAEs, and to finance and manage their activities. This would require additional discussion with FATF and FSRBs.

- The second and third option would require a change to the Fund/Bank's policy to make the staffs accountable for the assessment of implementation of the criminal justice systems and AML/CFT preventive measures in the nonmacroeconomically relevant sectors. Under these options, the Fund/Bank would employ and supervise experts and be fully accountable for the assessment of the complete AML/CFT standard and ensure the preparation of integrated and consistent reports. The Fund and Bank would need to recruit additional expertise, and there would be a cost to the Fund/Bank budgets to supervise/undertake this work.

\* \* \*

47. Under the second and third options, the Fund/Bank would become accountable for the assessment of a much expanded range of activities, leading to both quantitative and qualitative changes in Fund/Bank work. Options 2 and 3 would extend the Fund and Bank's operations into two new areas, previously the sole responsibility of the IAEs:

- Assessing the Implementation of Criminal Laws. Staff would become accountable for the assessment of the implementation of AML/CFT-related criminal laws (and potentially the provision of related technical assistance). This work would include, inter alia: (i) review of the adequacy of an authority's capacity to implement the legal framework by financial intelligence units and law enforcement agencies (police), including the existence of structures with adequate resources and means; (ii) assessment of the existence and — in some cases — the implication of the statistics relating to prosecution, investigations, and FIUs; (iii) assessment of the existence of arrangements to improve cooperation with foreign countries, including the existence of mutual legal assistance mechanisms.

- Nonmacroeconomically relevant sectors. The Fund and the Bank would become accountable for assessing AML/CFT procedures in place in a wide range of financial sector and non financial business and professional activities that may not be macroeconomically relevant in a number of cases. The new methodology includes specific AML/CFT requirements for lawyers, casinos, real estate brokers, precious metal dealers, dealers in precious stones, accountants, charities, money remittance systems, trust and company service providers, and all entities covered under the FATF definition of financial institutions, which goes extensively beyond banks, insurance companies and security firms.

48. Taking on these new areas would constitute a significant expansion in the involvement of the Fund and the Bank in the AML/CFT area, and it would be advisable to acknowledge the exceptional character of this extension and seek ways to demarcate it from other Fund and Bank's activities. Delineation to a particular area of work may be difficult to maintain in practice, because of the dynamic nature of ML/TF activities.

\* \* \*

49. Recognition of the exceptional character, as well as the need for demarcation of the Fund and Bank involvement in AML/CFT under either the second or third option, could be provided for through organizational changes. Organizational changes could help achieve a number of objectives:

- improve the efficiency and accountability in the delivery of AML/CFT assessments and technical assistance by better integrating the expertise and supervision on AML/CFT that is now spread across four departments (MFD and LEG in the Fund and the Financial Sector Vice-presidency and Legal Department in the Bank). The need to consider AML/CFT issues comprehensively require substantial time in coordinating the work of different units;

- increase the flexibility to recruit and develop the necessary expertise outside the existing Fund/Bank career streams; and

- more clearly delineate the resources that the Fund/Bank would commit to AML/CFT work, so as to avoid open ended commitments, while providing a framework for garnering external financing for AML/CFT, for example through the establishment of a dedicated trust fund for AML/CFT technical assistance.

50. There would be a number of possible ways to organize AML/CFT work of the Fund and the Bank that could help to achieve the above objectives. Different reporting mechanism, funding arrangements and human resource management practices could be considered drawing on past experience with alternative organizational structures in the Bank and the Fund. Capacity to maintain the "value added" of explicit Fund/Bank engagement would be critical. An evolutionary approach to organizational changes might be desirable as experience is gained with the implementation of the full AML/CFT standard.

## 11. IMF Executive Board Reviews and Enhances Efforts for Anti-Money Laundering and Combating the Financing of Terrorism

Public Information Notice (PIN), 2004

*Public Information Notices (PINs)* are issued, (i) at the request of a member country, following the conclusion of the **Article IV** consultation for countries seeking to make known the views of the IMF to the public. This action is intended to strengthen IMF surveillance over the economic policies of member countries by increasing the transparency of the IMF's assessment of these policies; and (ii) following policy discussions in the Executive Board at the decision of the Board.

On March 24, 2004 the Executive Board of the International Monetary Fund (IMF) reviewed the **Twelve-Month Pilot Program of Anti-Money Laundering and Combating the Financing of Terrorism (AML/CFT) Assessments** jointly undertaken by the IMF and World Bank, and adopted proposals to make such assessments a regular part of Fund work. As part of the review, the Executive Board endorsed the revised 40 Recommendations of the Financial Action Task Force (FATF) as the new standard for AML/CFT Reports on the Observance of Standards and Codes (ROSCs) that will be prepared, as well as the revised methodology to assess that standard. Drawing on the positive experience under the 12-month pilot program (see **Press Release No. 02/52**), the Executive Board decided to expand the Fund's AML/CFT assessment and technical assistance work to cover the full scope of the expanded FATF recommendations.

### Background

The 40 Recommendations on Anti-Money Laundering and the 8 Special Recommendations on Combating the Financing of Terrorism, developed by FATF (the so-called FATF 40 +8 Recommendations), were endorsed by the IMF and the World Bank in 2002 to be used as the international standard for the AML/CFT work that the Fund and Bank are jointly undertaking. During the 12-month period that ended in October 2003, the IMF and the World Bank, in collaboration with FATF and FATF-style regional bodies (FSRBs), undertook a pilot program of AML/CFT assessments of 41 jurisdictions. The assessments employed a common methodology based on the FATF 40 + 8 Recommendations. The Fund conducted 20 of the assessments, the World Bank conducted six assessments, and seven assessments were conducted jointly by the Fund and the Bank. FATF and the FSRBs conducted the remaining eight assessments. ROSCs, which summarize the findings of assessments of compliance with standards and codes of best practices, have been or will be completed for all of the pilot assessments, and, with the consent of national authorities, the ROSCs are being posted to the IMF website for public information. In parallel with the AML/CFT pilot program, the delivery of technical assistance for AML/CFT has been greatly increased. During the last two years there have been 85 country-specific technical assistance projects benefiting 63 countries, and 32 regional projects reaching more than 130 countries.

Experience with the 12-month pilot program shows that the enhanced work of the IMF and World Bank is having a positive impact on international awareness of the importance of strong AML/CFT regimes. Most jurisdictions have developed and are implementing action plans to correct shortcomings identified during the assessments.

### The findings of the pilot also show that:

- Many countries show a high level of compliance with the original FATF 40 Recommendations but compliance with the newer (2001) 8 Special Recommendations on Terrorist Financing is weaker, frequently because necessary legislation had not yet been adopted.

- Wealthier jurisdictions generally have well developed regimes but require additional action on CFT. Middle-income jurisdictions generally have well developed legal and institutional frameworks but frequently have gaps in implementation of the regime. Many lower-income countries have put in place the essential legal elements of an AML/CFT regime but implementation remains a challenge due to insufficient resources and training.

- Implementation weaknesses identified include: poor coordination among government agencies, ineffective law enforcement, weak supervision, inadequate systems and controls among financial firms, and shortcomings in international cooperation.

Experience under the pilot with both assessments and with technical assistance considerably deepened collaboration between the Fund/Bank and the FATF and the FSRBs, and with other international bodies involved in AML/CFT work, such as the U.N. Counterterrorism Committee, the U.N. Office on Drugs and Crime, and various donor aid organizations. Review of the pilot pointed to several areas where further operational improvements could be made and where policy evolution should be considered. These included the need for close coordination with FATF and FSRBs on the timing of assessments, more equitable sharing of the assessment burden among agencies, and broadening the responsibilities of Fund and Bank staff for the supervision and integration of assessment missions to insure comprehensive and high quality assessments. The scope of both assessments and of technical assistance will be expanded as a result of adoption of the revised FATF 40 recommendations, which call for a wider range of financial and non-financial business and professions to come under AML/CFT obligations

**Executive Board Assessment**

Executive Directors welcomed the opportunity to review the experience of the joint Fund/Bank program for assessments and technical assistance for Anti-Money Laundering and Combating the Financing of Terrorism (AML/CFT). They commended the Fund/Bank staffs on the overall success of the pilot program, noting that AML/CFT assessments and technical assistance have now become an important component of the Fund and the Bank's work to strengthen the integrity of financial systems and deter financial abuse.

Directors welcomed the participation by the Financial Action Task Force (FATF) and FATF-style regional bodies (FSRBs) in the pilot program. Although a full review of the quality and consistency of their reports will take place at a later date, Directors were encouraged by the initial finding that the FATF/FSRBs' assessments were prepared in accordance with the principles of the Reports on the Observance of Standards and Codes (ROSCs) and were linked to the Financial Sector Assessment Program (FSAP), and that the reports received to date were generally of good quality. They underlined the importance of coordinating the Fund/Bank's work with that of the FATF and the FSRBs to avoid duplication of assessments. Directors looked forward to receiving the full review of the quality of the FATF/FSRBs' assessments and their consistency with the ROSC principles, as well as the effectiveness of coordination efforts, in about 18 months' time.

Directors noted that the pilot program had achieved the initial objectives agreed to by the Executive Board and, in particular, that it had led to a considerable deepening of international attention to AML/CFT issues and to the provision of substantial technical assistance in this area. They were encouraged that most jurisdictions have responded positively to assessments. Directors commended the generally high level of compliance with the FATF recommendations in higher- and middle-income countries, while noting that many lower-income countries face a challenge in implementing the FATF standard owing in part to shortages of resources to devote to this purpose. While observing that there are more general weaknesses regarding compliance with the eight special recommendations on terrorist financing, Directors welcomed the increased awareness among jurisdictions of the need for strong legislative and institutional frameworks in this area.

Directors emphasized that a key element of raising global compliance with the FATF standard is the delivery of technical assistance. In this regard, they welcomed the significant and increased contribution by the Fund in the delivery of technical assistance on AML/CFT in legislative drafting, support to supervisory bodies, establishment of financial intelligence units, and training. At the same time, Directors recognized that the Fund is only one of many technical assistance providers, and emphasized the Fund's need to work closely with bilateral and other multilateral donors, while respecting their different mandates and expertise. They agreed that the delivery of technical assistance to strengthen the capacity of FSRBs to conduct assessments was a cost-effective way of strengthening the global efforts on AML/CFT.

Directors noted that the Fund/Bank had conducted the great majority of assessments during the pilot program, reflecting the late start of the FATF/FSRBs in conducting assessments during the pilot program. Further, they observed that the Fund had conducted a greater share of the assessments, in part reflecting the intensified work on Offshore Financial Centers (OFCs), in which the Bank is not involved. Looking ahead, Directors welcomed the commitment by the FATF President to ensure that the FATF takes on a more equitable sharing of the burden. They noted that the FATF and the FSRBs combined are expected to conduct assessments of 15 to 20 countries per year. They requested the staff to ensure close collaboration and coordination with the FATF/FSRBs on assessment schedules. Directors also welcomed the commitment by the Bank to share the assessment burden equally with the Fund during the transition period and later.

In view of the success of the pilot program and the importance attached to AML/CFT work, Directors agreed that it should be a regular part of the Fund's work, and that AML/CFT assessments, whether prepared by the Fund/Bank or the FATF/FSRBs, should continue to be included in all FSAP and OFC assessments. Going forward, the Executive Board endorsed the revised FATF standard that expands the scope of activities, and the revised assessment methodology for the Fund's operational work, in view of the international acceptance that the revised FATF 40+8 is the relevant standard for the preparation of the AML/CFT ROSCs. Directors, moreover, agreed on the importance of continuing collaboration with the FATF in light of its indication that it has no plans at present to conduct a further round of the Non-Cooperative Countries and Territories (NCCT) exercise. In addition, in this regard, some Directors expressed concern that the FATF had left open the possibility of further rounds of the NCCT exercise, and noted that if the FATF were to resume the NCCT exercise, the Fund would need to reconsider collaboration with the FATF, as the exercise is at odds with the uniform, voluntary, and cooperative nature of the ROSC exercise. They indicated that the suspension of the exercise should continue to be a condition for the Fund's joint work.

Directors acknowledged that some areas of the assessment process could be improved, particularly with regard to the integration of the work now carried out by the independent AML/CFT experts (IAEs) into the overall assessment process. They stressed that the need to ensure effective integration and quality control of the IAEs' work would become more pressing with the adoption of the new FATF recommendations, and therefore supported the adoption of measures to strengthen the contribution of IAEs in Fund assessments, within resource constraints.

In considering the options for advancing the Fund's work on AML/CFT, many Directors expressed a preference for continuing the status quo, as outlined under Option 1 in the staff paper, which they thought is working well and limits the staff's involvement in the assessments to those areas that they felt were within the core mandate and expertise of the Fund. They considered that extending the Fund's involvement to law enforcement issues would risk jeopardizing the cooperative nature of the Fund's relations with its members and the support of the membership for AML/CFT. These Directors also felt that the identified need to improve the work of the independent AML/CFT experts (IAEs) could be accommodated without expanding the areas of involvement of the Fund and the Bank in AML/CFT. However, the majority of the Executive Board agreed to support the Fund becoming fully accountable, together with the Bank, for AML/CFT assessments and for providing technical assistance, including in the sectors covered by IAEs, as outlined under Option 3 in the staff paper. These Directors agreed that assessing whether countries have the capacity to implement AML/CFT laws effectively is part of the core mandate of the Fund and does not contravene the prohibition of the Fund to exercise law enforcement powers. They supported a more comprehensive and integrated approach to conducting AML/CFT assessments in order to enhance the efficiency and quality of the process.

In considering Option 3, which calls for the costs of assessments to be borne by the Fund/Bank, Directors noted that there is uncertainty about the eventual cost of taking on the additional assessment and technical assistance work. In particular, they noted that developing more precise cost estimates for assessments will require practical experience with implementation of the new standard in the transition period in fiscal year 2005. Directors also noted that actual experience will help refine estimates of the resource costs. Some Directors indicated that without better estimates of the costs, it was difficult for them to assess fully the merits of the different options, and thought it appropriate to introduce a cap in the fiscal year 2005 budget for the assessments. Directors emphasized, however, that the extension of this work should not crowd out other essential activities, including ongoing technical assistance. They noted that specific redeployment and allocation of the additional resources and staff positions to undertake the expanded assessment and technical assistance work in the next year will be taken up as part of the fiscal year 2005 budget discussion. In this regard, Directors urged bilateral and multilateral donors of financing and of expert resources to support this initiative generously.

Directors indicated their interest in receiving reports on (i) the review of the quality and consistency of the FATF/FSRBs' assessments and coordination in about 18 months' time; and (ii) a comprehensive review of the overall effectiveness of the Fund/Bank program in about three years' time.

## 12. Bibliography of Additional Sources

- U.S. Sanctions Programs and Country Summaries at http://www.treas.gov/offices/enforcement/ofac/sanctions/.

- FinCEN Financial Crimes Advisory at http://www.fincen.gov/pub_main.html.

- Protecting Charitable Organizations (Dates with U.S. and U.N. Designations) at http://www.treas.gov/offices/enforcement/keyissues/protecting/charities_execorder_13224-a.shtml.

- Consolidated List of Financial Sanction Targets in the UK at http://www.bankofengland.co.uk/publications/financialsanctions/regimes/terrorism.htm.

- EU-Persons and Entities Subject to Financial Sanctions at http://www. europa.eu.int/comm/external_relations/cfsp/sanctions/list/version4/global/e_ctlview.html.

- U.N.-Individuals and Entities associated with Al-Qaida at http://www.un.org/Docs/sc/committees/1267/pdflist.pdf.

- U.S. Treasury-Office of Foreign Asset Control-Specially Designated Blocked Persons and Nationals at http://www.treas.gov/offices/enforcement/ofac/sdn/t11sdn.pdf.

- Designated Charities and Potential Fundraising Front Organizations for FTOs at http://www.treas.gov/offices/enforcement/key-issues/protecting/fto.shtml.

- State Department Listing of Foreign Terrorist Organizations (FTOs) at http://www.state.gov/s/ct/rls/fs/37191.htm.

- www.faft-gafi.org Website of the Financial Action Task Force.

- www.unodc.org/unodc/en/money_laundering.htm Website of the UNODC Global Programme Against Money Laundering.

- www.bis.org/bcbs Website of the Basel Committee on Banking Supervision.

- www.imf.org/external/np/exr/facts/aml.htm The IMF's anti-money laundering and terrorism finance website.

- THE CONSEQUENCES OF MONEY LAUNDERING AND FINANCIAL CRIME, Economic Perspectives, United States Department of State, Volume 6, Number 2, May 2001.

# Annex

# Researching International Organizations on the Internet

## U.N. Sites

**U.N. Homepage**
http://www.un.org
**U.N. Documentation Center**
http://www.un.org/documents/index.html
**International Court of Justice**
http://www.icj-cij.org/icjwww/icj002.htm
**International Criminal Tribunals**
http://www.un.org/icty
http://www.un.org/ictr
**U.N. GA Resolutions**
http://www.un.org/ga/55/lista55.htm
**Security Council Resolutions**
http://www.un.org/documents/scres.htm
**Reportoire of the Practice of the Security Council**
http://www.un.org/Depts/dpa/repertoire/index.html
**U.N. Voting Records**
http://unbisnet.un.org/webpac-bin/wgbroker?new+access+top.vote
Gen. Assembly 1983–Present
Security Council 1946–Present
*After searching click "view record" to view Nation by Nation vote.
**Index to Speeches**
Gen. Assembly 1983–Present
Security Council 1983–Present
http://unbisnet.un.org/webpac-bin/wgbroker?new+access+top.speech
**Hypertext Chart of U.N. System**
http://www.un.org/aboutun/chart.html

# International Courts and Tribunals

European Court of Justice (http://europa.eu.int/cj/en/index.htm)
International Court of Justice (http://www.icj-cij.org/)
ICJ Research Guide (http://www.lawschool.cornell.edu/library/Finding the_Law/Guides_by_Topic/icj.htm)
International Criminal Court (http://www.un.org/law/icc/index.html), see also (http://www.igc.apc.org/icc)
Nuremberg Tribunals (http://www.yale.edu/lawweb/avalon/imt/imt.htm)
Permanent Court of Arbitration (http://www.pca-cpa.org/) Project on International Courts and Tribunals (http://www.pict-pcti.org/news/archive.html)

# Other International Organizations

EUROPA (http://europa.eu.int/index-en.htm) and Eur-Lex (http://europa.eu.int/eur-lex/en/index.html)
Best European Union Law Websites (http://www.eurunion.org/infores/BestLawSites.HTM)
Food and Agriculture Organization (http://www.fao.org)
International Atomic Energy Agency (http://www.iaea.or.at)
International Chamber of Commerce (http://www.iccwbo.org)
Organisation for Economic Co-operation & Development (http://www.oecd.org)
Organization of American States (http://www.oas.org)
United Nations Commission on International Trade Law (http://www.uncitral.org)
International Institute for the Unification of Law (http://www.unidroit.org)
World Health Organization (http://www.who.int/home-page)
World Trade Organization (http://www.wto.org/)

# International Organizations Collections

International Organizations (http://www.library.nwu.edu/govpub/resource/internat/igo.html)
International Agencies and Information on the Web (http://www.lib.umich.edu/libhome/Documents.center/intl.html)
Official Web Site Locator for the United Nations Systems Organizations (http://www.un-system.org)
International Organization Web Sites: Index Page (http://www.uia.org/website.htm)

# General International Law Sites

ASIL Guide to Electronic Resources for International Law (http://www.asil.org/resource/home.htm)
Foreign and International Law Web (http://www.washlaw.edu/forint/forintmain.html)
Guide to Foreign and International Legal Databases (http://www.law.nyu.edu/library/foreignjntl/)
International and Foreign Law Resource Center (http://www.llrx.com/resources4.htm)

International Law in Brief (http://www.asil.org/ilibindx.htm)
Keeping Current with International Law Developments via the Web by Jill Watson at the
American Society of International Law (http://www.llrx.com/features/keeping.htm).
Legal Research on International Law Issues Using the Internet (http://www.asil.org/re-
source/home.htm)
Max Planck Institute for Comparative Public Law and International Law, Compilation
of Relevant Links (http://www.virtual-institute.de/en/link/eeinf.cfm)
Public International Law (http://www.law.ecel.uwa.edu.au/intlaw/)
Researching International Economic Law on the Internet (http://www.ll.georgetown.edu/
intl/iiel/home.htm)
What's Online In International Law (http://www.asil.org/wonindx.htm)
WWW Virtual Library, Foreign and International Law (http://www.law.indiana.edu/v-lib)

# Multilateral Treaties

Avalon Project (http://www.yale.edu/lawweb/avalon/avalon.htm)
Council of Europe Treaties (http://conventions.coe.int/)
European Union Treaties (http://www-nt.who.int/idhllen/ConsultIDHL.cfm)
Hague Conventions on Private International Law (http://www.hcch.net/e/conventions/
index.html)
Multilaterals Project (http://fletcher.tufts.edu/)
Organization of American States Treaties (http://www.oas.org/EN/PROG/JURIDICO/
english/treaties.html)
Project DIAL Treaties and International Agreements (http://www.austlii.edu.au/links/
World/International/Treaties_and_InternationalAgreements/)
United Nations Treaty Collection (fee-based) (http://untreaty.un.org)

# U.S. Treaties & Agreements

Treaties in Force (http://www.state.gov/www/global/legal.affairs/tifindex.html)
Treaty Actions (http://www.state.gov/www/global/legalaffairs/treatyactions_2000.html)
Legislative Activities (http://www.senate.gov/legislative/legisact_treaties.html)
Senate, House & Treaty Documents (http://www.access.gpo.gov/congress/cong006.html)
Private International Law Database (http://www.state.gov/www/global/legaLatiairs/pri-
vate_intl_law.html)
Trade and Related Agreements (http://www.mac.doc.gov/tcc/data/index.html)
Oceana Online, TIARA Database (fee-based service) (http://www.oceanalaw.com)

# Some Topical Sources

Institute of International Commercial Law (http://cisgw3.law.pace.edu)
ECOLEX (http://www.ecolex.org)
Foreign Trade Information System (http://www.sice.oas.org)
Human Rights Library (http://www.umn.edu/humanrts)

Human Rights Instruments (List of Ratifications) (http://www.unesco.org/ human_rights/ index.htm)
International Humanitarian Law (http://www.icrc.org/eng/ihl)
International Labour Organization (http://www.ilo.org)
Juris International (http://www.jurisint.org/pub/page00_en.htm)
Trade/Commercial Law (http://www.jus.uio.no/lm/index.html)
World Intellectual Property Organization (http://www.wipo.int/treaties/index.html)

# Foreign Law

## General Foreign Law Sites

Foreign Governments (http://www.library.nwu.edu/govpub/resource/internat/foreign.html)
Foreign Primary Law on the Web (http://www.law.uh.edu/librarians/tmulligan/foreign-law.html)
Guide to Law Online: Nations of the World (http://lcweb2.loc.gov/glin/x-nation.html)
Global Legal Information Network (http://lcweb2.loc.gov/law/GLINv1/GLIN.html)
Governments on WWW (http://www.gksoft.com/govt/en/world.html)
Legal Materials Around the Globe (http://www.law.cornell.edu/world/)
NYU's Guide to foreign databases — collections (http://www.law.nyu.edu/library/for-eign_intl/foreign.html) and foreign databases by jurisdiction (http://www.law.nyu.edu/ library/foreign_intl/country.html)
Social Science Information Gateway (http://www.sosig.ac.uk/law/)
Virtuelle Rechtsvergleicher (http://viadrina.euv-frankfurt-o.de/%7EdvrlWelcome.html)
Web Sites of National Parliaments (http://www.ipu.org/english/parlweb.htm)
The World Law Guide (http://www.lexadin.nl/wlg/legis/nofr/legis.htm)
World Law Index (http://www.austlii.edu.au/links/World/)

## Foreign Laws by Jurisdiction

American Law Sources Online (http://www.lawsource.com/also/)
Australasian Legal Information Institute (http://www.austlii.edu.au/)
British & Irish Legal Information Institute (http://www.bailii.org/)
Department of Justice, Canada (http://canada.justice.gc.ca/Loireg/index_en.html)
Chinese Laws in English (http://www.qis.net/chinalaw/lawtran.htm)
ELSweb (http://www.unimaas.nl/elsweb/)
HMSO (http://www.hmso.gov.uk/)
International and Foreign Law Resource Center (http://www.llrx.com/resources4.htm)
Latin American Government Documents Project — National Legislative Documents (http://lib1.library.cornell.edu/colldev/lalegisdocs.html)
Law-Related Internet Project, University of Saarland, German Law (http://www.jura.uni-sb.de/english/glsindex.html)
South African Acts Online (http://www.acts.co.za/)

## Foreign Laws by Topic

Annual Review of Population Law (http://www.law.harvard.edu/programs/annualreview/index.html)
Collection of Laws for Electronic Access (http://clea.wipo.int/)
Doing Business in ... Guides (http://www.hg.org/guides.html)
FAOLEX (http://www.fao.org/Legal/default.htm)
Foreign Penal Codes (http://wings.buffalo.edu/law/belc/resource.htm)
Global Banking Law Database (http://www.gbld.org/)
Global E-Commerce (http://www.bmck.com/ecommerce/intlegis.htm)
International Digest of Health Legislation (http://www-nt.who.int/idhl/en/ConsultIDHL.cfm)
Intellectual Property Rights (http://www.sice.oas.org/intprop/ipnale.asp)
International Constitutional Law (http://www.uni-wuerzburg.de:80/law/home.html)
National Legislation on Authors Rights and Neighboring Rights (http://www.unesco.org/culture/copy/index.html)
NATLEX (http://natlex.ilo.org/)

## Foreign Case Law

Foreign Supreme Court Decisions (http://www.mossbyrett.of.no/info/links.html)
Court Net (http://www.sigov.silus/courtnet.html)
GLAW Project (http://www.uni-wuerzburg.de/glaw/info.html)
Governments on the WWW:Courts (http://www.gksoft.com/govt/en/courts.html)
Constitutional Courts and Equivalent Bodies (http://www.coe.fr/venice/links-e.htm)
Japan Supreme Court (http://www.courts.go.jp/english/ehome.htm)
Germany's Federal Constitutional Court, Report Abstracts in English (http://www.jura.uni-sb.de/Entscheidungen/abstracts/entsch-e.html)

# Periodicals

Harvard Jean Monnet Table of Contents Service (http://www.law.harvard.edu/ programs/JeanMonnet/TOC/index.html)
Hieros Gamos, Legal and Law Related Journals (http://www.hg.org/journals.html)
RAVE (http://www.jura.uni-duesseldorf.de/rave/e/englhome.htm)
Max Planck's Online Documentation of Articles (http://www.virtual-institute.de/en/VI/eaufsystematik_vr.cfm)

# Resources for Teachers

International and Comparative Law Course Pages (http://jurist.law.pitt.edu/sg_il.htm#Courses)
Lessons from the Web (http://jurist.law.pitt.edu/lessons.htm)
LEXIS Publishing Virtual Classroom, Course Web Sites (http://www.wcbcourses.com/wcb/)
Michael Geist Web Lecture Series (http://lawschool.lexis.com/weblec/index.html)

World Lecture Hall—, Law (http://www.utexas.edu/world/lecture/law/)
Research Guides: Georgetown Law Library (http://www.11.georgetown.edu/intl/index.htm),
Harvard Law School

# Search Engines

For a good comparison of the major search engines, see Update to Search Engines Compared (http://www.llrx.com/features/engine3.htm).
AltaVista (http://www.altavista.com/) See also BabelFish (http://babelfish.altavista.com/translate.dyn).
FINDLAW (http://www.findlaw.com/)
HotBot (http://hotbot.lycos.com/)
Google (http://www.google.com/)
LawCrawler (http://lawcrawler.lp.findlaw.com/)
Metacrawler (http://www.metacrawler.com/)
Northern Light (http://www.northernlight.com/)
Yahoo (http://dir.yahoo.com/government/law/)
Direct Search (http://gwis2.circ.gwu.edu/%7Egprice/direct.htm)
The Invisible Web (http://www.invisibleweb.com)
Mining Deeper into the Invisible Web (http://www.llrx.com/features/mining.htm)

# Index